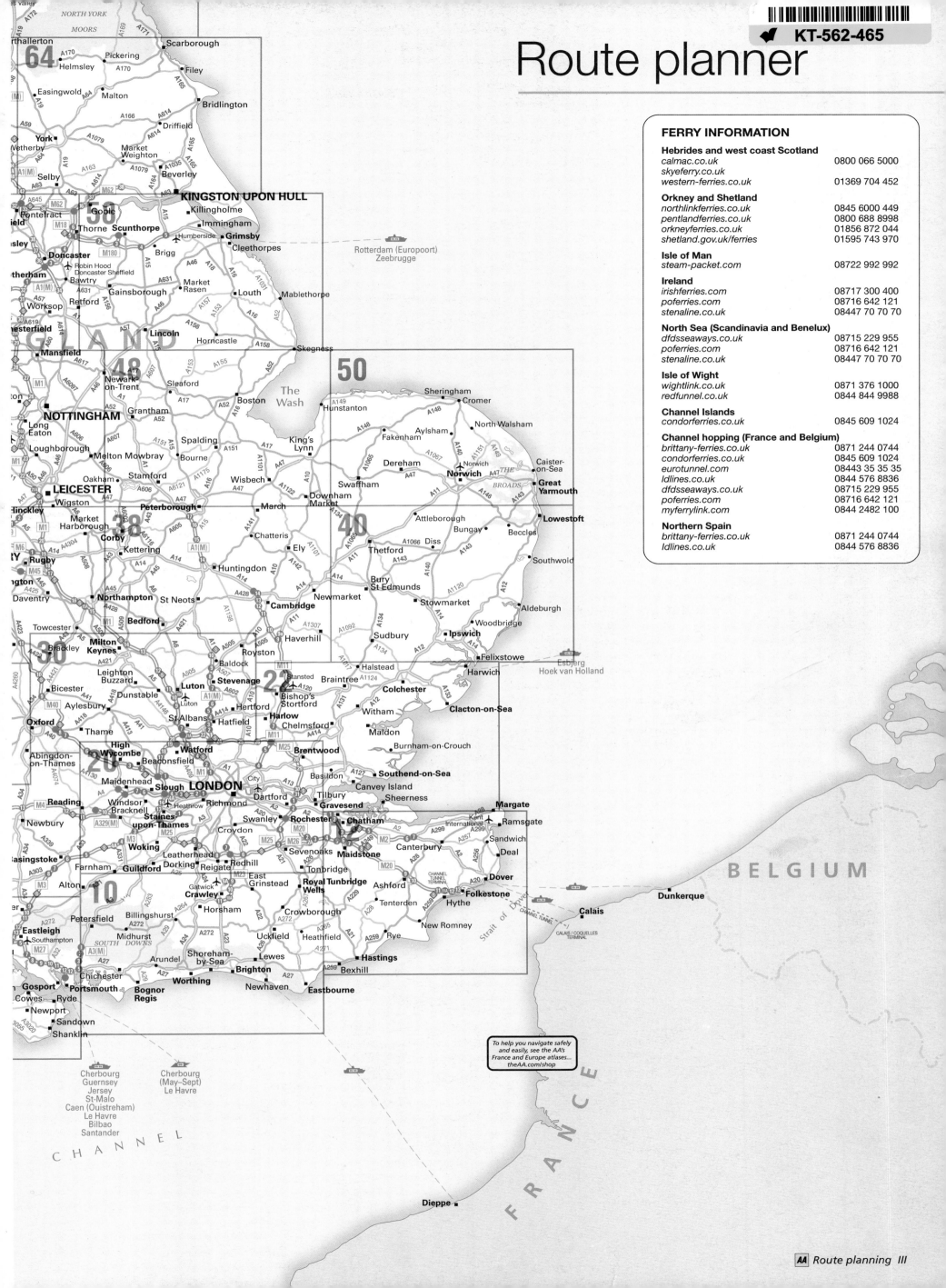

KT-562-465

FERRY INFORMATION

Hebrides and west coast Scotland
calmac.co.uk — 0800 066 5000
skyeferry.co.uk
western-ferries.co.uk — 01369 704 452

Orkney and Shetland
northlinkferries.co.uk — 0845 6000 449
pentlandferries.co.uk — 0800 688 8998
orkneyferries.co.uk — 01856 872 044
shetland.gov.uk/ferries — 01595 743 970

Isle of Man
steam-packet.com — 08722 992 992

Ireland
irishferries.com — 08717 300 400
poferries.com — 08716 642 121
stenaline.co.uk — 08447 70 70 70

North Sea (Scandinavia and Benelux)
dfdsseaways.co.uk — 08715 229 955
poferries.com — 08716 642 121
stenaline.co.uk — 08447 70 70 70

Isle of Wight
wightlink.co.uk — 0871 376 1000
redfunnel.co.uk — 0844 844 9988

Channel Islands
condorferries.co.uk — 0845 609 1024

Channel hopping (France and Belgium)
brittany-ferries.co.uk — 0871 244 0744
condorferries.co.uk — 0845 609 1024
eurotunnel.com — 08443 35 35 35
ldlines.co.uk — 0844 576 8836
dfdsseaways.co.uk — 08715 229 955
poferries.com — 08716 642 121
myferrylink.com — 0844 2482 100

Northern Spain
brittany-ferries.co.uk — 0871 244 0744
ldlines.co.uk — 0844 576 8836

To help you navigate safely and easily, see the AA's France and Europe atlases...
theAA.com/shop

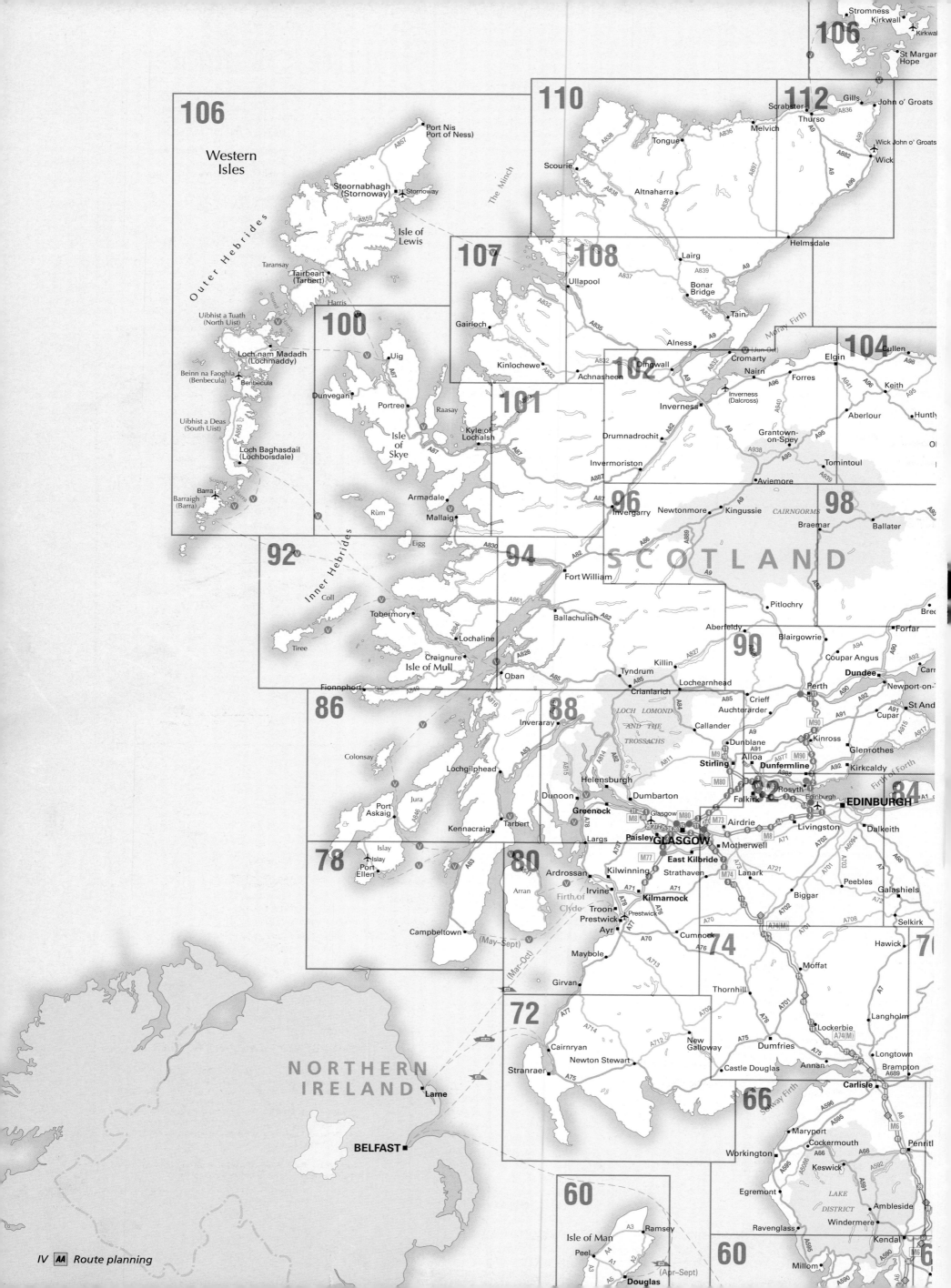

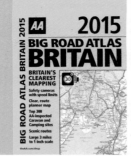

Atlas contents

Scale 1:190,000 or 3 miles to 1 inch

Map pages	inside front cover

Route planning	**II–XVI**
Route planner	II–V
London district	VI–VII
Distances and journey times	VIII
Tourist sites with satnav friendly postcodes	IX
Caravan and camping sites in Britain	X–XI
Traffic signs and road markings	XII–XIII
Channel hopping	XIV–XV
Ferries to Ireland and the Isle of Man	XVI

Atlas symbols	**1**

Road maps 1:190,000 scale	**2–112**
Channel Islands 1:135,000 scale	6–7
Isle of Man 1:190,000 scale	60
Skye & The Small Isles 1:340,000 scale	100
Western Isles 1:703,000 scale	106
Orkney and Shetland Islands 1:709,000 scale	106

Ferry ports

Aberdeen Harbour	99	Heysham Harbour	XVI	Poole, Port of	XIV
Calais	XV	Holyhead Harbour	XVI	Port of Tyne	77
Channel Tunnel	13	Liverpool Docks	XVI	Portsmouth Harbour	XV
Dover, Port of	XV	Newhaven Harbour	XV	Weymouth Harbour	XIV
Fishguard Harbour	XVI	Pembroke Dock	XVI		
Harwich Int. Port	23	Plymouth, Port of	XIV		

Restricted junctions	**113**

Ireland road maps 1:1 million scale	**114–115**

Town plans

Aberdeen	99	Great Yarmouth	51	Nottingham	120
Aberystwyth	32	Harrogate	118	Oxford	120
Bath	116	Inverness	118	Peterborough	121
Birmingham	116	Ipswich	119	Plymouth	121
Blackpool	116	Kingston upon Hull	119	Portsmouth	121
Bradford	116	Leeds	119	Salisbury	121
Bristol	116	Leicester	119	Sheffield	121
Cambridge	116	Lincoln	119	Southampton	121
Canterbury	117	Liverpool	54	Southend-on-Sea	23
Cardiff	117	Llandudno	53	Stratford-	
Chester	117	LONDON	119	upon-Avon	122
Coventry	117	Manchester	120	Sunderland	71
Derby	117	Middlesbrough	71	Swansea	122
Dundee	117	Milton Keynes	120	Swindon	122
Durham	118	Newcastle		Wolverhampton	122
Edinburgh	118	upon Tyne	120	Worcester	122
Exeter	118	Newquay	3	York	122
Glasgow	118	Norwich	120		

Index to place names	**123–144**
County, administrative area map	123

Distances and journey times	inside back cover

24th edition June 2014

© AA Media Limited 2014

Original edition printed 1991.

Cartography:
All cartography in this atlas edited, designed and produced by the Mapping Services Department of AA Publishing (A05182).

This atlas contains Ordnance Survey data © Crown copyright and database right 2014 and Royal Mail data © Royal Mail copyright and database right 2014.

This atlas is based upon Crown Copyright and is reproduced with the permission of Land & Property Services under delegated authority from the Controller of Her Majesty's Stationery Office, © Crown copyright and database right 2014. PMLPA No. 100497.

© Ordnance Survey Ireland/Government of Ireland. Copyright Permit No. MP0000314.

Publisher's Notes:
Published by AA Publishing (a trading name of AA Media Limited, whose registered office is Fanum House, Basing View, Basingstoke, Hampshire RG21 4EA, UK. Registered number 06112600).

All rights reserved. No part of this publication may be reproduced, stored in a retrieval system, or transmitted in any form or by any means – electronic, mechanical, photocopying, recording or otherwise – unless the permission of the publisher has been given beforehand.

ISBN: 978 0 7495 7605 9 (spiral bound)
ISBN: 978 0 7495 7604 2 (paperback)

A CIP catalogue record for this book is available from The British Library.

Disclaimer:
The contents of this atlas are believed to be correct at the time of the latest revision, it will not contain any subsequent amended, new or temporary information including diversions and traffic control or enforcement systems. The publishers cannot be held responsible or liable for any loss or damage occasioned to any person acting or refraining from action as a result of any use of or reliance upon the contents of this atlas, whether such loss or damage results from negligence, breach of contract or otherwise.

The publishers would welcome information to correct any errors or omissions and to keep this atlas up to date. Please write to the Atlas Editor, AA Publishing, The Automobile Association, Fanum House, Basing View, Basingstoke, Hampshire RG21 4EA, UK.
E-mail: roadatlasfeedback@theaa.com

Acknowledgements:
AA Publishing would like to thank the following for their assistance in producing this atlas:

RoadPilot® Information on fixed speed camera locations provided by and © 2014 RoadPilot® Driving Technology. Crematoria data provided by the Cremation Society of Great Britain. Cadw, English Heritage, Forestry Commission, Historic Scotland, Johnsons, National Trust and National Trust for Scotland, RSPB, The Wildlife Trust, Scottish Natural Heritage, Natural England, The Countryside Council for Wales (road maps).

Road signs are © Crown Copyright 2014. Reproduced under the terms of the Open Government Licence.

Printer:
Printed in Italy by Canale & C. S.p.A.

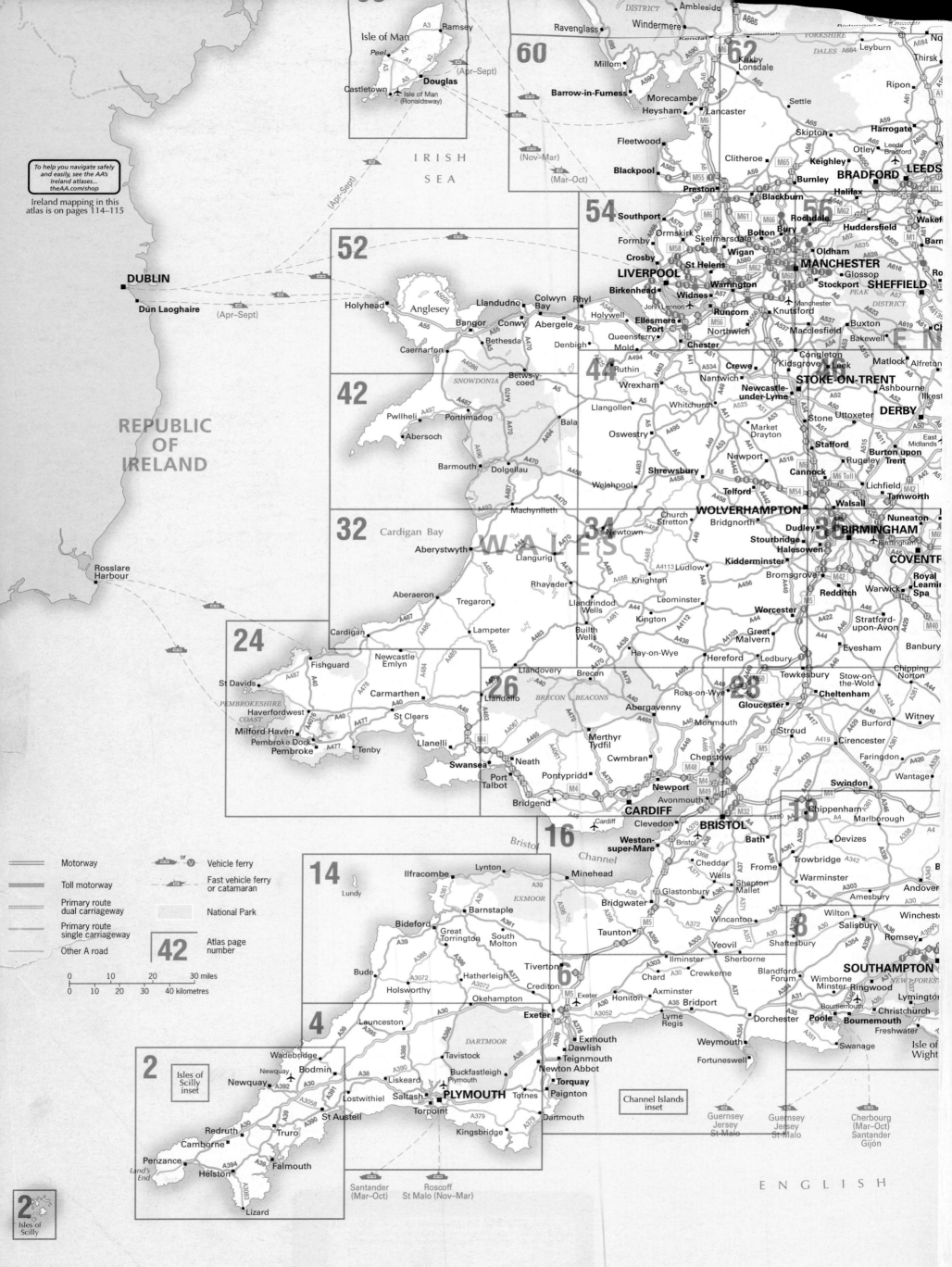

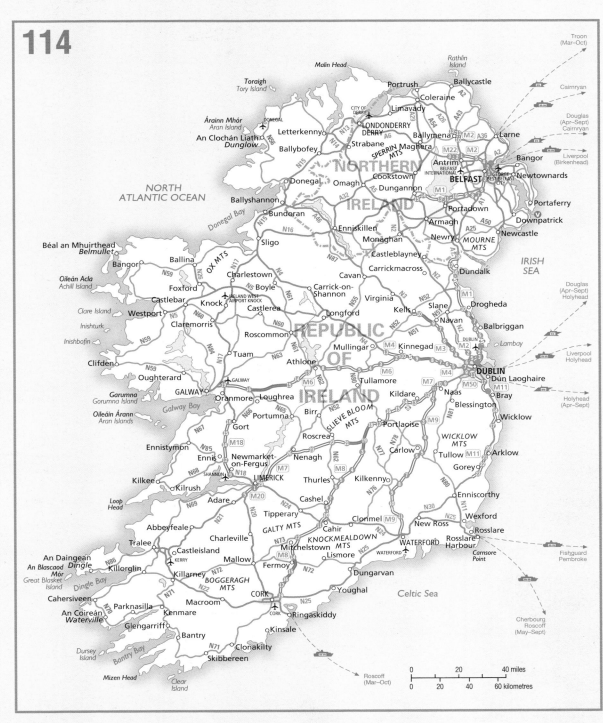

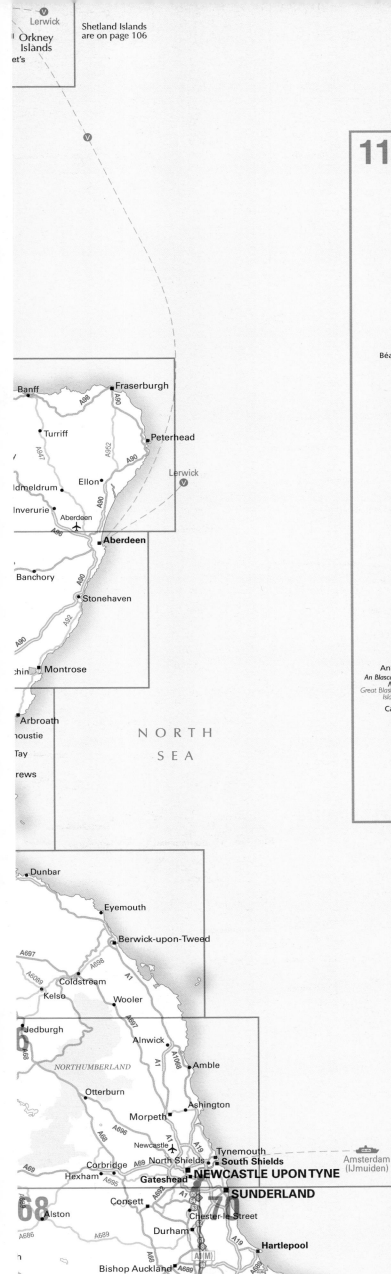

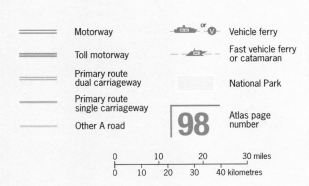

Motorway

Toll motorway

Primary route
dual carriageway

Primary route
single carriageway

Other A road

Vehicle ferry

Fast vehicle ferry
or catamaran

National Park

98 Atlas page
number

EMERGENCY DIVERSION ROUTES

In an emergency it may be necessary to close a section
of motorway or other main road to traffic, so a
temporary sign may advise drivers to follow a diversion
route. To help drivers navigate the route, black symbols
on yellow patches may be permanently displayed on
existing direction signs, including motorway signs.
Symbols may also be used on separate signs with
yellow backgrounds.

For further information see www.highways.gov.uk,
trafficscotland.org and traffic-wales.com

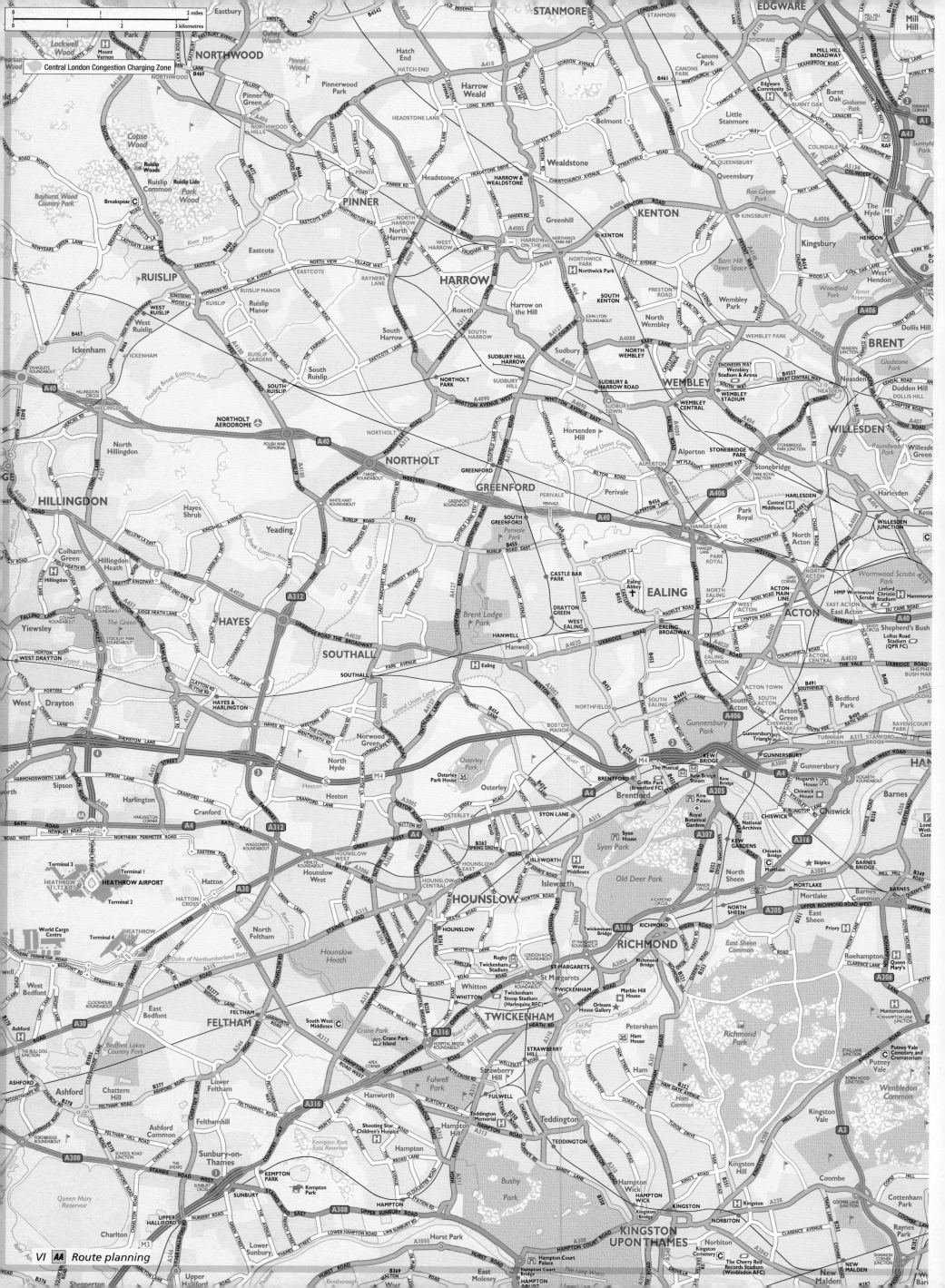

Distances and journey times

The mileage chart shows distances in miles between two towns along AA-recommended routes. Using motorways and other main roads this is normally the fastest route, though not necessarily the shortest.

The journey times, shown in hours and minutes, are average off-peak driving times along AA-recommended routes. These times should be used as a guide only and do not allow for unforeseen traffic delays, rest breaks or fuel stops.

For example, the 378 miles (608 km) journey between Glasgow and Norwich should take approximately 7 hours 28 minutes.

Journey times

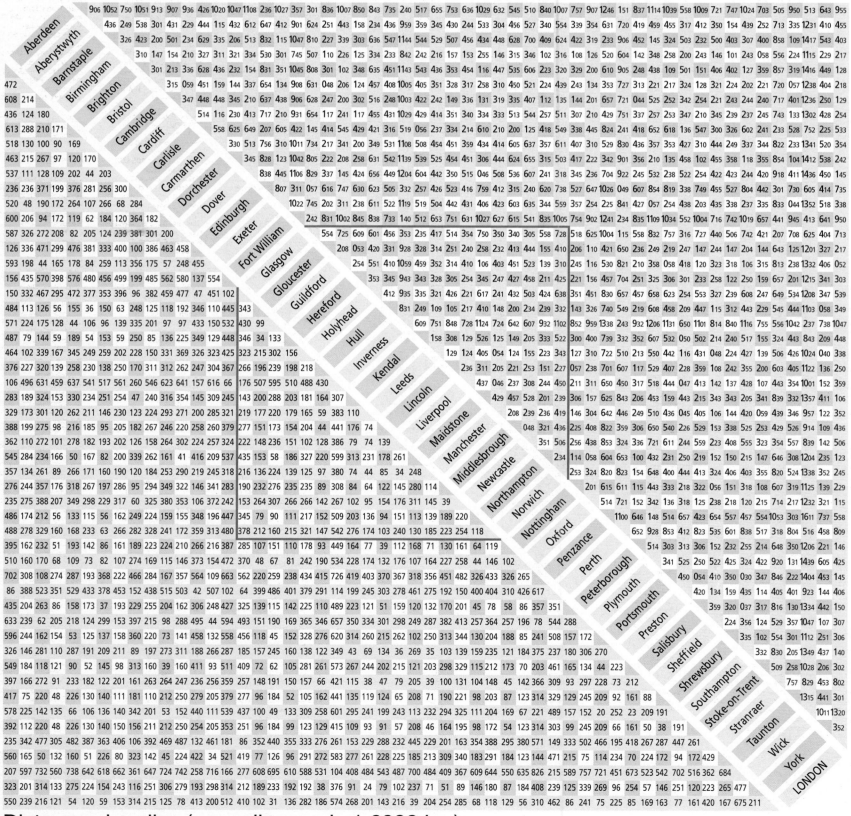

Distances in miles (one mile equals 1.6093 km)

Tourist sites with satnav friendly postcodes

ENGLAND

- Acorn Bank Garden CA10 1SP Cumb 68 D7
- Aldborough Roman Site YO51 9ES N York 63 U6
- Alfriston Clergy House BN26 5TL E Susx 11 S10
- Alton Towers ST10 4DB Staffs 46 E5
- Anglesey Abbey CB25 9EJ Cambs 39 R8
- Anne Hathaway's Cottage CV37 9HH Warwks 36 G10
- Antony House PL11 2QA Cnwll 5 L9
- Appuldurcombe House PO38 3EW IoW 9 Q13
- Apsley House W1J 7NT Gt Lon 21 N7
- Arlington Court EX31 4LP Devon 15 P4
- Ascott LU7 0PS Bucks 30 J8
- Ashby-de-la-Zouch Castle LE65 1BR Leics 47 L10
- Athelhampton House & Gardens DT2 7LG Dorset 7 U6
- Attingham Park SY4 4TP Shrops 45 M11
- Audley End House & Gardens CB11 4JF Essex 39 R13
- Avebury Manor & Garden SN8 1RF Wilts 18 G6
- Baconsthorpe Castle NR25 6LN Norfk 50 K6
- Baddesley Clinton Hall B93 0DQ Warwks 36 H6
- Bamburgh Castle NE69 7DF Nthumb 85 T11
- Barnard Castle DL12 8PR Dur 69 M9
- Barrington Court TA19 0NQ Somset 17 L13
- Basildon Park RG8 9NR W Berk 19 T5
- Bateman's TN19 7DS E Susx 12 C11
- Battle of Britain Memorial Flight Visitor Centre LN4 4SY Lincs 48 K2
- Beamish Living Museum of the North DH9 0RG Dur 69 R2
- Beatrix Potter Gallery LA22 0NS Cumb 67 N13
- Beaulieu SO42 7ZN Hants 9 M8
- Belton House NG32 2LS Lincs 48 D6
- Belvoir Castle NG32 1PE Leics 48 B7
- Bembridge Windmill PO35 5SQ IoW 9 S11
- Beningbrough Hall & Gardens YO30 1DD N York 64 C8
- Benthall Hall TF12 5RX Shrops 45 Q13
- Berkeley Castle GL13 9PJ Gloucs 28 C8
- Berrington Hall HR6 0DW Herefs 35 M8
- Berry Pomeroy Castle TQ9 6LJ Devon 5 U8
- Beth Chatto Gardens CO7 7DB Essex 23 Q3
- Biddulph Grange Garden ST8 7SD Staffs 45 U2
- Bishop's Waltham Palace SO32 1DH Hants 9 Q5
- Blackpool Zoo FY3 8PP Bpool 61 Q12
- Blenheim Palace OX20 1PX Oxon 29 T4
- Blickling Estate NR11 6NF Norfk 51 L8
- Blue John Cavern S33 8WA Derbys 56 H10
- Bodiam Castle TN32 5UA E Susx 12 E10
- Bolsover Castle S44 6PR Derbys 57 Q12
- Boscobel House ST19 9AR Staffs 45 T12
- Bovington Tank Museum BH20 6JG Dorset 8 A11
- Bowes Castle DL12 9LD Dur 69 L10
- Bradford Industrial Museum BD2 3HP W Yorks 63 P13
- Bradley Manor TQ12 6BN Devon 5 U6
- Bramber Castle BN44 3WW W Susx 10 K8
- Brinkburn Priory NE65 8AR Nthumb 77 N6
- Bristol Zoo Gardens BS8 3HA Bristl 27 V13
- British Library NW1 2DB Gt Lon 21 N6
- British Museum WC1B 3DG Gt Lon 21 N6
- Brockhampton Estate WR6 5TB Herefs 35 Q9
- Brough Castle CA17 4EJ Cumb 68 G10
- Buckfast Abbey TQ11 0EE Devon 5 S7
- Buckingham Palace SW1A 1AA Gt Lon 21 N7
- Buckland Abbey PL20 6EY Devon 5 M7
- Buscot Park SN7 8BU Oxon 29 P8
- Byland Abbey YO61 4BD N York 64 C4
- Calke Abbey DE73 7LE Derbys 47 L9
- Canons Ashby House NN11 3SD Nhants 37 Q10
- Canterbury Cathedral CT1 2EH Kent 13 N4
- Carisbrooke Castle PO30 1XY IoW 9 P11
- Carlyle's House SW3 5HL Gt Lon 21 N7
- Castle Drogo EX6 6PB Devon 5 S2
- Castle Howard YO60 7DA N York 64 G5
- Castle Rising Castle PE31 6AH Norfk 49 U9
- Charlecote Park CV35 9ER Warwks 36 J9
- Chartwell TN16 1PS Kent 21 S12
- Chastleton House GL56 0SU Oxon 29 P2
- Chatsworth DE45 1PP Derbys 57 L12
- Chedworth Roman Villa GL54 3LJ Gloucs 29 L5
- Chessington World of Adventures KT9 2NE Gt Lon 21 L10
- Chester Cathedral CH1 2HU Ches W 54 K13
- Chester Zoo CH2 1EU Ches W 54 K12
- Chesters Roman Fort NE46 4EU Nthumb 76 J11
- Chiswick House W4 2RP Gt Lon 21 M7
- Chysauster Ancient Village TR20 8XA Cnwll 2 D10
- Claremont Landscape Garden KT10 9JG Surrey 20 K10
- Claydon House MK18 2EY Bucks 30 F7
- Cleeve Abbey TA23 0PS Somset 16 D8
- Clevedon Court BS21 6QU N Som 17 M2
- Cliveden SL6 0JA Bucks 20 F5
- Clouds Hill BH20 7NQ Dorset 7 V6
- Clumber Park S80 3AZ Notts 57 T12
- Colchester Zoo CO3 0SL Essex 23 N3
- Coleridge Cottage TA5 1NQ Somset 16 G9
- Coleton Fishacre TQ6 0EQ Devon 6 B14
- Compton Castle TQ3 1TA Devon 5 V8
- Conisbrough Castle DN12 3BU Donc 57 R7
- Corbridge Roman Town NE45 5NT Nthumb 76 K13
- Corfe Castle BH20 5EZ Dorset 8 D12
- Corsham Court SN13 0BZ Wilts 18 C6
- Cotehele PL12 6TA Cnwll 5 L7
- Coughton Court B49 5JA Warwks 36 E8
- Courts Garden BA14 6RR Wilts 18 C8
- Cragside NE65 7PX Nthumb 77 M5
- Crealy Great Adventure Park EX5 1DR Devon 6 D6
- Crich Tramway Village DE4 5DP Derbys 46 K2
- Croft Castle HR6 9PW Herefs 34 K7
- Croome Park WR8 9JS Worcs 35 U12
- Deddington Castle OX15 0TE Oxon 29 U1
- Didcot Railway Centre OX11 7NJ Oxon 19 R2
- Dover Castle CT16 1HU Kent 13 R7
- Drayton Manor Theme Park B78 3SA Staffs 46 G13
- Dudmaston Estate WV15 6QN Shrops 35 R3
- Dunham Massey WA14 4SJ Traffd 55 R9
- Dunstanburgh Castle NE66 3TT Nthumb 77 R1
- Dunster Castle TA24 6SL Somset 16 C8
- Durham Cathedral DH1 3EH Dur 69 S4
- Dyrham Park SN14 8HY S Glos 28 D12
- East Riddlesden Hall BD20 5EL Brad 63 M11
- Eden Project PL24 2SG Cnwll 3 R6
- Eltham Palace & Gardens SE9 5QE Gt Lon 21 R8
- Emmetts Garden TN14 6BA Kent 21 S12
- Exmoor Zoo EX31 4SG Devon 15 Q4
- Farleigh Hungerford Castle BA2 7RS Somset 18 B9
- Farnborough Hall OX17 1DU Warwks 37 M11
- Felbrigg Hall NR11 8PR Norfk 51 L6
- Fenton House & Garden NW3 6SP Gt Lon 21 N5
- Finch Foundry EX20 2NW Devon 5 Q2
- Finchale Priory DH1 5SH Dur 69 S3
- Fishbourne Roman Palace PO19 3QR W Susx 10 C9
- Flamingo Land YO17 6UX N York 64 H4
- Forde Abbey TA20 4LU Somset 7 L3
- Fountains Abbey & Studley Royal HG4 3DY N York 63 R6
- Gawthorpe Hall BB12 8UA Lancs 62 G13
- Gisborough Priory TS14 6HG R & Cl 70 K9
- Glendurgan Garden TR11 5JZ Cnwll 2 K11
- Goodrich Castle HR9 6HY Herefs 28 A4
- Great Chalfield Manor & Garden SN12 8NH Wilts 18 C8
- Great Coxwell Barn SN7 7LZ Oxon 29 Q9
- Greenway TQ5 0ES Devon 5 V10
- Haddon Hall DE45 1LA Derbys 56 K13
- Hailes Abbey GL54 5PB Gloucs 28 L1
- Ham House & Garden TW10 7RS Gt Lon 21 L8
- Hampton Court Palace KT8 9AU Gt Lon 21 L9
- Hanbury Hall WR9 7EA Worcs 36 B8
- Hardwick Hall S44 5QJ Derbys 57 Q14
- Hardy's Cottage DT2 8QJ Dorset 7 T6
- Hare Hill SK10 4PY Ches E 56 C11
- Hatchlands Park GU4 7RT Surrey 20 J12
- Heale Gardens SP4 6NU Wilts 18 H13
- Helmsley Castle YO62 5AB N York 64 E3
- Hereford Cathedral HR1 2NG Herefs 35 M13
- Hergest Croft Gardens HR5 3EG Herefs 34 G9
- Hever Castle & Gardens TN8 7NG Kent 21 S13
- Hidcote Manor Garden GL55 6LR Gloucs 36 G12
- Hill Top LA22 0LF Cumb 67 N13
- Hinton Ampner SO24 0LA Hants 9 R3
- Holkham Hall NR23 1AB Norfk 50 E5
- Housesteads Roman Fort NE47 6NN Nthumb 76 F12
- Howletts Wild Animal Park CT4 5EL Kent 13 N4
- Hughenden Manor HP14 4LA Bucks 20 E3
- Hurst Castle SO41 0TP Hants 9 L11
- Ickworth IP29 5QE Suffk 40 D8
- Ightham Mote TN15 0NT Kent 21 U12
- Ironbridge Gorge Museums TF8 7DQ Wrekin 45 Q13
- Keddleston Hall DE22 5JH Derbys 46 K5
- Kenilworth Castle & Elizabethan Garden CV8 1NE Warwks 36 J6
- Kenwood House NW3 7JR Gt Lon 21 N5
- Killerton EX5 3LE Devon 6 C4
- King John's Hunting Lodge BS26 2AP Somset 17 M6
- Kingston Lacy BH21 4EA Dorset 8 D8
- Kirby Hall NN17 3EN Nhants 38 D2
- Knightshayes Court EX16 7RQ Devon 16 C13
- Knole House TN13 1HU Kent 21 T12
- Knowsley Safari Park L34 4AN Knows 55 L8
- Lacock Abbey SN15 2LG Wilts 18 D7
- Lamb House TN31 7ES E Susx 12 H11
- Lanhydrock House PL30 5AD Cnwll 3 R4
- Launceston Castle PL15 7DR Cnwll 4 J4
- Leeds Castle ME17 1PB Kent 12 F5
- Legoland SL4 4AY W&M 20 F8
- Lindisfarne Castle TD15 2SH Nthumb 85 S10
- Lindisfarne Priory TD15 2RX Nthumb 85 S10
- Little Moreton Hall CW12 4SD Ches E 45 T2
- Liverpool Cathedral L1 7AZ Lpool 54 J9
- Longleat BA12 7NW Wilts 18 B12
- Losely Park GU3 1HS Surrey 20 G13
- Lost Gardens of Heligan PL26 6EN Cnwll 3 P7
- Ludgershall Castle SP11 9QR Wilts 19 L10
- Lydford Castle EX20 4BH Devon 5 N4
- Lyme Park, House & Garden SK12 2NX Ches E 56 E10
- Lytes Cary Manor TA11 7HU Somset 17 P11
- Lyveden New Bield PE8 5AT Nhants 38 E3
- Maiden Castle DT2 9PP Dorset 7 S7
- Mapledurham RG4 7TR Oxon 19 U5
- Marble Hill House TW1 2NL Gt Lon 21 L8
- Marwell Wildlife SO21 1JH Hants 9 Q4
- Melford Hall CO10 9AA Suffk 40 E11
- Merseyside Maritime Museum L3 4AQ Lpool 54 H9
- Minster Lovell Hall OX29 0RR Oxon 29 R5
- Mompesson House SP1 2EL Wilts 8 G3
- Monk Bretton Priory S71 5QD Barns 57 N5
- Montacute House TA15 6XP Somset 17 N13
- Morwellham Quay PL19 8JL Devon 5 L7
- Moseley Old Hall WV10 7HY Staffs 46 B13
- Mottisfont SO51 0LP Hants 9 L3
- Mottistone Manor Garden PO30 4ED IoW 9 N12
- Mount Grace Priory DL6 3JG N York 70 F13
- National Gallery WC2N 5DN Gt Lon 21 N6
- National Maritime Museum SE10 9NF Gt Lon 21 Q7
- National Motorcycle Museum B92 0ED Solhll 36 H4
- National Portrait Gallery WC2H 0HE Gt Lon 21 N6
- National Railway Museum YO26 4XJ York 64 D9
- National Space Centre LE4 5NS C Leic 47 Q12
- Natural History Museum SW7 5BD Gt Lon 21 N7
- Needles Old Battery PO39 0JH IoW 8 K12
- Nene Valley Railway PE8 6LR Cambs 38 H1
- Netley Abbey SO31 5FB Hants 9 P7
- Newark Air Museum NG24 2NY Notts 48 B2
- Newtown Old Town Hall PO30 4PA IoW 9 N10
- North Leigh Roman Villa OX29 6QB Oxon 29 S4
- Norwich Cathedral NR1 4DH Norfk 51 M12
- Nostell Priory WF4 1QE Wakefd 57 P3
- Nunnington Hall YO62 5UY N York 64 F4
- Nymans RH17 6EB W Susx 11 M5
- Old Royal Naval College SE10 9NN Gt Lon 21 Q7
- Old Sarum SP1 3SD Wilts 8 G2
- Old Wardour Castle SP3 6RR Wilts 8 C3
- Oliver Cromwell's House CB7 4HF Cambs 39 R4
- Orford Castle IP12 2ND Suffk 41 R10
- Ormesby Hall TS3 0SR R & Cl 70 H9
- Osborne House PO32 6JX IoW 9 Q9
- Osterley Park & House TW7 4RB Gt Lon 20 K7
- Overbeck's TQ8 8LW Devon 5 S13
- Oxburgh Hall PE33 9PS Norfk 50 B13
- Packwood House B94 6AT Warwks 36 G6
- Paignton Zoo TQ4 7EU Torbay 6 A13
- Paycocke's CO6 1NS Essex 22 K3
- Peckover House & Garden PE13 1JR Cambs 49 Q12
- Pendennis Castle TR11 4LP Cnwll 3 L10
- Petworth House & Park GU28 0AE W Susx 10 F6
- Pevensey Castle BN24 5LE E Susx 11 U10
- Peveril Castle S33 8WQ Derbys 56 J10
- Polesden Lacey RH5 6BD Surrey 20 K12
- Portland Castle DT5 1AZ Dorset 7 S10
- Portsmouth Historic Dockyard PO1 3LJ C Port 9 S8
- Powderham Castle EX6 8JQ Devon 6 C8
- Prior Park Landscape Garden BA2 5AH BaNES 17 U4
- Prudhoe Castle NE42 6NA Nthumb 77 M13
- Quarry Bank Mill SK9 4LA Ches E 55 T10
- Quebec House TN16 1TD Kent 21 R12
- Ramsey Abbey Gatehouse PE17 1DH Cambs 39 L3
- Reculver Towers & Roman Fort CT6 6SU Kent 13 P2
- Red House DA6 8JF Gt Lon 21 S7
- Restormel Castle PL22 0EE Cnwll 4 E8
- Richborough Roman Fort CT13 9JW Kent 13 R3
- Richmond Castle DL10 4QW N York 69 Q12
- Roche Abbey S66 8NW Rothm 57 R9
- Rochester Castle ME1 1SW Medway 12 D2
- Rockbourne Roman Villa SP6 3PG Hants 8 G5
- Roman Baths & Pump Room BA1 1LZ BaNES 17 U4
- Royal Botanic Gardens, Kew TW9 3AB Gt Lon 21 L7
- Royal Observatory Greenwich SE10 8XJ Gt Lon 21 Q7
- Rufford Old Hall L40 1SG Lancs 55 L3
- Runnymede SL4 2JJ W & M 20 G8
- Rushton Triangular Lodge NN14 1RP Nhants 38 B4
- Rycote Chapel OX9 2PA Oxon 30 E12
- St Leonard's Tower ME19 6PE Kent 12 C4
- St Michael's Mount TR17 0HT Cnwll 2 E11
- St Paul's Cathedral EC4M 8AD Gt Lon 21 P6
- Salisbury Cathedral SP1 2EJ Wilts 8 G3
- Saltram PL7 1UH C Plym 5 N9
- Sandham Memorial Chapel RG20 9JT Hants 19 Q8
- Sandringham House & Grounds PE35 6EH Norfk 49 U8
- Saxtead Green Post Mill IP13 9QQ Suffk 41 N8
- Scarborough Castle YO11 1HY N York 65 P2
- Science Museum SW7 2DD Gt Lon 21 N7
- Scotney Castle TN3 8JN Kent 12 C8
- Shaw's Corner AL6 9BX Herts 31 Q9
- Sheffield Park & Garden TN22 3QX E Susx 11 Q6
- Sherborne Old Castle DT9 3SA Dorset 17 R13
- Sissinghurst Castle Garden TN17 2AB Kent 12 F8
- Sizergh Castle & Garden LA8 8AE Cumb 61 T2
- Smallhythe Place TN30 7NG Kent 12 G10
- Snowshill Manor & Garden WR12 7JU Gloucs 36 E14
- Souter Lighthouse SR6 7NH S Tyne 77 U13
- Speke Hall, Garden & Estate L24 1XD Lpool 54 K10
- Spinnaker Tower PO1 3TT C Port 9 S9
- Stokesay Castle SY7 9AH Shrops 34 K4
- Stonehenge SP4 7DE Wilts 18 H12
- Stourhead BA12 6QD Wilts 17 U10
- Stowe Landscape Gardens MK18 5EQ Bucks 30 E5
- Sudbury Hall DE6 5HT Derbys 46 G7
- Sulgrave Manor OX17 2SD Nhants 37 Q11
- Sunnycroft TF1 2DR Wrekin 45 Q11
- Sutton Hoo IP12 3DJ Suffk 41 N11
- Sutton House E9 6JQ Gt Lon 21 Q5
- Tate Britain SW1P 4RG Gt Lon 21 N7
- Tate Liverpool L3 4BB Lpool 54 H9
- Tate Modern SE1 9TG Gt Lon 21 P6
- Tattershall Castle LN4 4LR Lincs 48 K2
- Tatton Park WA16 6QN Ches E 55 R10
- The Lowry M50 3AZ Salfd 55 T7
- The Vyne RG24 9HL Hants 19 T9
- The Weir HR4 7QF Herefs 34 K12
- Thornton Abbey & Gatehouse DN39 6TU N Linc 58 K3
- Thorpe Park KT16 8PN Surrey 20 H9
- Tilbury Fort RM18 7NR Thurr 22 G12
- Tintagel Castle PL34 0HE Cnwll 4 C3
- Tintinhull Garden BA22 8PZ Somset 17 P13
- Totnes Castle TQ9 5NU Devon 5 U8
- Tower of London EC3N 4AB Gt Lon 21 P6
- Townend LA23 1LB Cumb 67 P12
- Treasurer's House YO1 7JL York 64 E9
- Trelissick Garden TR3 6QL Cnwll 3 L9
- Trengwainton Garden TR20 8RZ Cnwll 2 C10
- Trerice TR8 4PG Cnwll 3 L5
- Twycross Zoo CV9 3PX Leics 46 K12
- Upnor Castle ME2 4XG Medway 22 J13
- Uppark House & Garden GU31 5QR W Susx 10 B7
- Upton House & Garden OX15 6HT Warwks 37 L11
- Victoria & Albert Museum SW7 2RL Gt Lon 21 N7
- Waddesdon Manor HP18 0JH Bucks 30 F9
- Wakehurst Place RH17 6TN W Susx 11 N4
- Wall Roman Site WS14 0AW Staffs 46 E12
- Wallington NE61 4AR Nthumb 77 L9
- Walmer Castle & Gardens CT14 7LJ Kent 13 S6
- Warkworth Castle & Hermitage NE65 0UJ Nthumb 77 Q4
- Warner Bros Studio Tour WD25 7LS Herts 31 N12
- Warwick Castle CV34 4QU Warwks 36 J8
- Washington Old Hall NE38 7LE Sundld 70 D1
- Waterperry Gardens OX33 1LG Oxon 30 D11
- Weeting Castle IP27 0RQ Norfk 40 C3
- Wenlock Priory TF13 6HS Shrops 45 P13
- West Midland Safari Park DY12 1LF Worcs 35 T5
- West Wycombe Park HP14 3AJ Bucks 20 D4
- Westbury Court Garden GL14 1PD Gloucs 28 D5
- Westminster Abbey SW1P 3PA Gt Lon 21 N7
- Westonbirt Arboretum GL8 8QS Gloucs 28 G9
- Westwood Manor BA15 2AF Wilts 18 B9
- Whitby Abbey YO22 4JT N York 71 R10
- Wightwick Manor & Gardens WV6 8EE Wolves 45 U14
- Wimpole Estate SG8 0BW Cambs 39 M10
- Winchester Cathedral SO23 9LS Hants 9 P3
- Winchester City Mill SO23 0EJ Hants 9 P3
- Windsor Castle SL4 1NJ W & M 20 G7
- Winkworth Arboretum GU8 4AD Surrey 10 F2
- Wisley RHS Garden GU23 6QB Surrey 20 J11
- Woburn Safari Park MK17 9QN Beds C 31 L6
- Wookey Hole Caves BA5 1BA Somset 17 P7
- Woolsthorpe Manor NG33 5PD Lincs 48 D9
- Wordsworth House CA13 9RX Cumb 66 H6
- Wrest Park MK45 4HR Beds C 31 N5
- Wroxeter Roman City SY5 6PR Shrops 45 N12
- WWT Arundel Wetland Centre BN18 9PB W Susx 10 G9
- Yarmouth Castle PO41 0PB IoW 9 M11
- York Minster YO1 7HH York 64 E9
- ZSL London Zoo NW1 4RY Gt Lon 21 N6
- ZSL Whipsnade Zoo LU6 2LF Beds C 31 M9

SCOTLAND

- Aberdour Castle KY3 0SL Fife 83 N1
- Alloa Tower FK10 1PP Clacks 90 C13
- Angus Folk Museum DD8 1RT Angus 91 N2
- Arbroath Abbey DD11 1EG Angus 91 T3
- Arduaine Garden PA34 4XQ Ag & B 87 P3
- Bachelors' Club KA5 5RB S Ayrs 81 N7
- Balmoral Castle Grounds AB35 5TB Abers 98 D5
- Balvenie Castle AB55 4DH Moray 104 C7
- Bannockburn Heritage Centre FK7 0LJ Stirlg 89 S7
- Blackness Castle EH49 7NH Falk 83 L2
- Blair Castle PH18 5TL P & K 97 P10
- Bothwell Castle G71 8BL S Lans 82 C7
- Branklyn Garden PH2 7BB P & K 90 H7
- Brodick Castle, Garden & Country Park KA27 8HY N Ayrs 80 E5
- Brodie Castle IV36 2TE Moray 103 Q4
- Broughton House & Garden DG6 4JX D & G 73 R9
- Burleigh Castle KY13 9GG P & K 90 H11
- Burrell Collection G43 1AT C Glas 89 N13
- Caerlaverock Castle DG1 4RU D & G 74 K12
- Cardoness Castle DG7 2EH D & G 73 P8
- Carnassarie Castle PA31 8RQ Ag & B 87 Q5
- Castle Campbell & Garden FK14 7PP Clacks 90 E12
- Castle Fraser, Garden & Estate AB51 7LD Abers 105 L13
- Castle Kennedy & Gardens DG9 8BX D & G 72 E7
- Castle Menzies PH15 2JD P & K 90 B2
- Corgarff Castle AB36 8YP Abers 98 D2
- Craigievar Castle AB33 8JF Abers 98 K2
- Craigmillar Castle EH16 4SY C Edin 83 Q4
- Crarae Garden PA32 8YA Ag & B 87 T6
- Crathes Castle & Garden AB31 5QJ Abers 99 N4
- Crichton Castle EH37 5XA Mdloth 83 S6
- Crossraguel Abbey KA19 8HQ S Ayrs 80 K11
- Culloden Battlefield IV2 5EU Highld 102 K6
- Culross Palace KY12 8JH Fife 82 J1
- Culzean Castle & Country Park KA19 8LE S Ayrs 80 J10
- Dallas Dhu Distillery IV36 2RR Moray 103 R4
- David Livingstone Centre G72 9BY S Lans 82 C7
- Dirleton Castle & Garden EH39 5ER E Loth 84 E2
- Doune Castle FK16 6EA Stirlg 89 R5
- Drum Castle, Garden & Estate AB31 5EY Abers 99 P3
- Dryburgh Abbey TD6 0RQ Border 84 F12
- Duff House AB45 3SX Abers 104 K3
- Dumbarton Castle G82 1JJ W Duns 88 J11
- Dundrennan Abbey DG6 4QH D & G 73 S10
- Dunnottar Castle AB39 2TL Abers 99 R7
- Dunstaffnage Castle PA37 1PZ Ag & B 94 B12
- Edinburgh Castle EH1 2NG C Edin 83 Q4
- Edinburgh Zoo EH12 6TS C Edin 83 P4
- Edzell Castle & Garden DD9 7UE Angus 98 K10
- Elgin Cathedral IV30 1HU Moray 103 V3
- Falkirk Wheel FK1 4RS Falk 82 G2
- Falkland Palace & Garden KY15 7BU Fife 91 L10
- Fort George IV2 7TE Highld 103 L4
- Fyvie Castle AB53 8JS Abers 105 M8
- Georgian House EH2 4DR C Edin 83 P4
- Gladstone's Land EH1 2NT C Edin 83 Q4
- Glamis Castle DD8 1RJ Angus 91 N2
- Glasgow Botanic Gardens G12 0UE C Glas 89 N12
- Glasgow Cathedral G4 0QZ C Glas 89 P12
- Glasgow Science Centre G51 1EA C Glas 89 N12
- Glen Grant Distillery AB38 7BS Moray 104 B6
- Glenluce Abbey DG8 0AF D & G 72 F8
- Greenbank Garden G76 8RB E Rens 81 R1
- Haddo House AB41 7EQ Abers 105 P9
- Harmony Garden TD6 9LJ Border 84 E12
- Hermitage Castle TD9 0LU Border 75 U6
- Highland Wildlife Park PH21 1NL Highld 97 N3
- Hill House G84 9AJ Ag & B 88 G9
- Hill of Tarvit Mansionhouse & Garden KY15 5PB Fife 91 N9
- Holmwood G44 3YG C Glas 89 N14
- House of Dun DD10 9LQ Angus 99 M12
- House of the Binns EH49 7NA W Loth 83 L3
- Hunterian Museum G12 8QQ C Glas 89 N12
- Huntingtower Castle PH1 3JL P & K 90 G7
- Huntly Castle AB54 4SH Abers 104 G7
- Hutchesons' Hall G1 1EJ C Glas 89 N12
- Inchmahome Priory FK8 3RA Stirlg 89 N5
- Inveresk Lodge Garden EH21 7TE E Loth 83 R4
- Inverewe Garden & Estate IV22 2LG Highld 107 Q8
- Inverlochy Castle PH33 6SN Highld 94 G3
- Kellie Castle & Garden KY10 2RF Fife 91 R10
- Kildrummy Castle AB33 8RA Abers 104 F12
- Killiecrankie Visitor Centre PH16 5LG P & K 97 Q11
- Leith Hall Garden & Estate AB54 4NQ Abers 104 G10
- Linlithgow Palace EH49 7AL W Loth 82 K3
- Lochleven Castle KY13 8UF P & K 90 H11
- Logan Botanic Garden DG9 9ND D & G 72 D11
- Malleny Garden EH14 7AF C Edin 83 N5
- Melrose Abbey TD6 9LG Border 84 E12
- National Museum of Scotland EH1 1JF C Edin 83 Q4
- Newark Castle PA14 5NH Inver 88 H11
- Palace of Holyroodhouse EH8 8DX C Edin 83 Q4
- Pitmedden Garden AB41 7PD Abers 105 P10
- Preston Mill EH40 3DS E Loth 84 F3
- Priorwood Garden TD6 9PX Border 84 E12
- Robert Smail's Printing Works EH44 6HA Border 83 R11
- Rothesay Castle PA20 0DA Ag & B 88 C13
- Royal Botanic Garden Edinburgh EH3 5LR C Edin 83 P3
- Royal Yacht Britannia EH6 6JJ C Edin 83 Q3
- St Andrews Aquarium KY16 9AS Fife 91 R8
- Scone Palace PH2 6BD P & K 90 H6
- Smailholm Tower TD5 7PG Border 84 G12
- Souter Johnnie's Cottage KA19 8HY S Ayrs 80 J11
- Stirling Castle FK8 1EJ Stirlg 89 S7
- Sweetheart Abbey DG2 8BU D & G 74 J12
- Tantallon Castle EH39 5PN E Loth 84 F1
- Tenement House G3 6QN C Glas 89 N12
- Threave Castle DG7 1TJ D & G 74 D13
- Threave Garden DG7 1RX D & G 74 E13
- Tolquhon Castle AB41 7LP Abers 105 P10
- Traquair House EH44 6PW Border 83 R11
- Urquhart Castle IV63 6XJ Highld 102 F10
- Weaver's Cottage PA10 2JG Rens 88 K13
- Whithorn Priory & Museum DG8 8PY D & G 73 L11

WALES

- Aberconwy House LL32 8AY Conwy 53 N7
- Aberdulais Tin Works & Waterfall SA10 8EU Neath 26 D8
- Beaumaris Castle LL58 8AP IoA 52 K7
- Big Pit: National Coal Museum NP4 9XP Torfn 27 N6
- Bodnant Garden LL28 5RE Conwy 53 P8
- Caerleon Roman Fortress & Baths NP18 1AE Newpt 27 Q9
- Caernarfon Castle LL55 2AY Gwynd 52 G10
- Caldicot Castle & Country Park NP26 4HU Mons 27 T10
- Cardiff Castle CF10 3RB Cardif 27 M12
- Castell Coch CF15 7JS Cardif 27 L11
- Chirk Castle LL14 5AF Wrexhm 44 G6
- Colby Woodland Garden SA67 8PP Pembks 25 L9
- Conwy Castle LL32 8AY Conwy 53 N7
- Criccieth Castle LL52 0DP Gwynd 42 K6
- Dinefwr Park & Castle SA19 6RT Carmth 25 V6
- Dolaucothi Gold Mines SA19 8US Carmth 33 N12
- Erddig LL13 0YT Wrexhm 44 H4
- Ffestiniog Railway LL49 9NF Gwynd 43 N5
- Harlech Castle LL46 2YH Gwynd 43 L7
- Llanerchaeron SA48 8DG Cerdgn 32 J8
- National Showcaves Centre for Wales SA9 1GJ Powys 26 E4
- Penrhyn Castle LL57 4HT Gwynd 52 K8
- Plas Newydd LL61 6DQ IoA 52 H9
- Plas yn Rhiw LL53 8AB Gwynd 42 D8
- Portmeirion LL48 6ER Gwynd 43 L6
- Powis Castle & Garden SY21 8RF Powys 44 F12
- Raglan Castle NP15 2BT Mons 27 S6
- Sygun Copper Mine LL55 4NE Gwynd 43 M4
- Tintern Abbey NP16 6SE Mons 27 U7
- Tudor Merchant's House SA70 7BX Pembks 24 K10
- Tŷ Mawr Wybrnant LL25 0HJ Conwy 43 Q3
- Valle Crucis Abbey LL20 8DD Denbgs 44 F5

Caravan and camping sites in Britain

These pages list the top 300 AA-inspected Caravan and Camping (C & C) sites in the Pennant rating scheme. **Five Pennant Premier sites are shown in green, Four Pennant sites are shown in blue.**

Listings include addresses, telephone numbers and websites together with page and grid references to locate the sites in the atlas. The total number of touring pitches is also included for each site, together with the type of pitch available. The following abbreviations are used: **C = Caravan CV = Campervan T = Tent**

To find out more about the AA's Pennant rating scheme and other rated caravan and camping sites not included on these pages please visit ***theAA.com***

ENGLAND

Alders Caravan Park
Home Farm, Alne, York
YO61 1RY
Tel: 01347 838722 **64 C6**
alderscaravanpark.co.uk
Total Pitches: 87 (C, CV & T)

Andrewshayes Holiday Park
Dalwood, Axminster
EX13 7DY
Tel: 01404 831225 **6 H5**
andrewshayes.co.uk
Total Pitches: 150 (C, CV & T)

Apple Tree Park C & C Site
A38, Claypits, Stonehouse
GL10 3AL
Tel: 01452 742362 **75 T13**
appletreepark.co.uk
Total Pitches: 65 (C, CV & T)

Appuldurcombe Gardens Holiday Park
Appuldurcombe Road, Wroxall, Isle of Wight
PO38 3EP
Tel: 01983 852597 **9 Q12**
appuldurcombegardens.co.uk
Total Pitches: 130 (C, CV & T)

Atlantic Bays Holiday Park
St Merryn, Padstow
PL28 8PY
Tel: 01841 520855 **3 M2**
atlanticbaysholidaypark.co.uk
Total Pitches: 70 (C, CV & T)

Ayr Holiday Park
St Ives, Cornwall
TR26 1EJ
Tel: 01736 795855 **2 E8**
ayrholidaypark.co.uk
Total Pitches: 40 (C, CV & T)

Back of Beyond Touring Park
234 Ringwood Rd, St Leonards, Dorset
BH24 2SB
Tel: 01202 876968 **8 F8**
backofbeyondtouringpark.co.uk
Total Pitches: 80 (C, CV & T)

Bagwell Farm Touring Park
Knights in the Bottom, Chickerell, Weymouth
DT3 4EA
Tel: 01305 782575 **7 R8**
bagwellfarm.co.uk
Total Pitches: 320 (C, CV & T)

Bardsea Leisure Park
Priory Road, Ulverston
LA12 9QE
Tel: 01229 584712 **61 P4**
bardsealeisure.co.uk
Total Pitches: 83 (C & CV)

Barn Farm Campsite
Barn Farm, Birchover, Matlock
DE4 2BL
Tel: 01629 650245 **46 H1**
barnfarmcamping.com
Total Pitches: 50 (C, CV & T)

Barnstones C & C Site
Great Bourton, Banbury
OX17 1QU
Tel: 01295 750289 **37 N12**
Total Pitches: 49 (C, CV & T)

Bath Chew Valley Caravan Park
Ham Lane, Bishop Sutton
BS39 5TZ
Tel: 01275 332127 **17 Q5**
bathchewvalley.co.uk
Total Pitches: 45 (C, CV & T)

Bay View Holiday Park
Bolton le Sands, Carnforth
LA5 9TN
Tel: 01524 701508 **61 T6**
holgates.co.uk
Total Pitches: 100 (C, CV & T)

Beaconsfield Farm Caravan Park
Battlefield, Shrewsbury
SY4 4AA
Tel: 01939 210370 **45 M10**
beaconsfield-farm.co.uk
Total Pitches: 60 (C & CV)

Beech Croft Farm
Beech Croft, Blackwell in the Peak, Buxton
SK17 9TQ
Tel: 01298 85330 **56 H12**
beechcroftfarm.co.uk
Total Pitches: 30 (C, CV & T)

Bellingham C & C Club Site
Brown Rigg, Bellingham
NE48 2JY
Tel: 01434 220175 **76 G9**
campingandcaravanningclub.co.uk/bellingham
Total Pitches: 64 (C, CV & T)

Beverley Parks Caravan & Camping Park
Goodrington Road, Paignton
TQ14 7JE
Tel: 01803 661979 **6 A13**
beverley-holidays.co.uk
Total Pitches: 172 (C, CV & T)

Bingham Grange Touring & Camping Park
Melplash, Bridport
DT6 3TT
Tel: 01308 488234 **7 N5**
binghamgrange.co.uk
Total Pitches: 150 (C, CV & T)

Blue Rose Caravan Country Park
Star Carr Lane, Brandesburton
YO25 8RU
Tel: 01964 543366 **65 Q10**
bluerosepark.com
Total Pitches: 58 (C & CV)

Bo Peep Farm Caravan Park
Bo Peep Farm, Aynho Road, Adderbury, Banbury
OX17 3NP
Tel: 01295 810605 **37 N14**
bo-peep.co.uk
Total Pitches: 104 (C, CV & T)

Broadhembury C & C Park
Steeds Lane, Kingsnorth, Ashford
TN26 1NQ
Tel: 01233 620859 **12 K8**
broadhembury.co.uk
Total Pitches: 110 (C, CV & T)

Brokerswood Country Park
Brokerswood, Westbury
BA13 4EH
Tel: 01373 822238 **18 B10**
brokerswoodcountrypark.co.uk
Total Pitches: 69 (C, CV & T)

Budemeadows Touring Park
Widemouth Bay, Bude
EX23 0NA
Tel: 01288 361646 **14 F12**
budemeadows.com
Total Pitches: 145 (C, CV & T)

Burrowhayes Farm C & C Site & Riding Stables
West Luccombe, Porlock, Minehead
TA24 8HT
Tel: 01643 862463 **16 B7**
burrowhayes.co.uk
Total Pitches: 120 (C, CV & T)

Burton Constable Holiday Park & Arboretum
Old Lodges, Sproatley, Hull
HU11 4LJ
Tel: 01964 562508 **65 R12**
burtonconstable.co.uk
Total Pitches: 140 (C, CV & T)

Calloose C & C Park
Leedstown, Hayle
TR27 5ET
Tel: 01736 850431 **2 F10**
calloose.co.uk
Total Pitches: 109 (C, CV & T)

Camping Caradon Touring Park
Trelawne, Looe
PL13 2NA
Tel: 01503 272388 **4 G10**
campingcaradon.co.uk
Total Pitches: 75 (C, CV & T)

Capesthorne Hall
Congleton Road, Siddington, Macclesfield
SK11 9JY
Tel: 01625 861221 **55 T112**
capesthorne.com
Total Pitches: 50 (C & CV)

Carlton Meres Country Park
Rendham Road, Carlton, Saxmundham
IP17 2QP
Tel: 01728 603344 **41 Q7**
carlton-meres.co.uk
Total Pitches: 96 (C, CV & T)

Carlyon Bay C & C Park
Bethesda, Cypress Avenue, Carlyon Bay
PL25 3RE
Tel: 01726 812735 **3 R6**
carlyonbay.net
Total Pitches: 180 (C, CV & T)

Carnevas Holiday Park & Farm Cottages
Carnevas Farm, St Merryn
PL28 8PN
Tel: 01841 520230 **3 M2**
carnevasholidaypark.co.uk
Total Pitches: 195 (C, CV & T)

Carnon Downs C & C Park
Carnon Downs, Truro
TR3 6JJ
Tel: 01872 862283 **3 L8**
carnon-downs-caravanpark.co.uk
Total Pitches: 150 (C, CV & T)

Carvynick Country Club
Summercourt, Newquay
TR8 5AF
Tel: 01872 510716 **3 M5**
carvynick.co.uk
Total Pitches: 47 (C & CV)

Castlerigg Hall C & C Park
Castlerigg Hall, Keswick
CA12 4TE
Tel: 017687 74499 **67 L8**
castlerigg.co.uk
Total Pitches: 48 (C, CV & T)

Cayton Village Caravan Park
Mill Lane, Cayton Bay, Scarborough
YO11 3NN
Tel: 01723 583171 **65 P3**
caytontouring.co.uk
Total Pitches: 310 (C, CV & T)

Cheddar Bridge Touring Park
Draycott Rd, Cheddar
BS27 3RJ
Tel: 01934 743048 **17 N6**
cheddarbridge.co.uk
Total Pitches: 45 (C, CV & T)

Cheddar Mendip Heights C & C Club Site
Townsend, Priddy, Wells
BA5 3BP
Tel: 01749 870241 **17 P6**
campingandcaravanningclub.co.uk/cheddar
Total Pitches: 90 (C, CV & T)

Chiverton Park
East Hill, Blackwater
TR4 8HS
Tel: 01872 560667 **2 J7**
chivertonpark.co.uk
Total Pitches: 12 (C, CV & T)

Church Farm C & C Park
The Bungalow, Church Farm, High Street, Sixpenny Handley, Salisbury
SP5 5ND
Tel: 01725 552563 **8 D5**
churchfarmcandcpark.co.uk
Total Pitches: 35 (C, CV & T)

Chy Carne Holiday Park
Kuggar, Ruan Minor, Helston
TR12 7LX
Tel: 01326 290200 **2 J13**
chycarne.co.uk
Total Pitches: 30 (C, CV & T)

Claylands Caravan Park
Cabus, Garstang
PR3 1AJ
Tel: 01524 791242 **61 T10**
claylands.com
Total Pitches: 30 (C, CV & T)

Clippesby Hall
Hall Lane, Clippesby, Great Yarmouth
NR29 3BL
Tel: 01493 367800 **51 R11**
clippesby.com
Total Pitches: 120 (C, CV & T)

Cofton Country Holidays
Starcross, Dawlish
EX6 8RP
Tel: 01626 890111 **6 C8**
coftonholidays.co.uk
Total Pitches: 450 (C, CV & T)

Coombe Touring Park
Race Plain, Netherhampton, Salisbury
SP2 8PN
Tel: 01722 328451 **8 F3**
coombecaravanpark.co.uk
Total Pitches: 50 (C, CV & T)

Corfe Castle C & C Club Site
Bucknowle, Wareham
BH20 5PQ
Tel: 01929 480280 **8 C12**
campingandcaravanningclub.co.uk/corfecastle
Total Pitches: 80 (C, CV & T)

Cornish Farm Touring Park
Shoreditch, Taunton
TA3 7BS
Tel: 01823 327746 **16 H12**
cornishfarm.com
Total Pitches: 50 (C, CV & T)

Cosawes Park
Perranarworthal, Truro
TR3 7QS
Tel: 01872 863724 **2 K9**
cosawestouringandcamping.co.uk
Total Pitches: 59 (C, CV & T)

Cote Ghyll C & C Park
Osmotherley, Northallerton
DL6 3AH
Tel: 01609 883425 **70 G13**
coteghyll.com
Total Pitches: 77 (C, CV & T)

Cotswold View Touring Park
Enstone Road, Charlbury
OX7 3JH
Tel: 01608 810314 **29 S3**
cotswoldview.co.uk
Total Pitches: 125 (C, CV & T)

Country View Holiday Park
Sand Road, Sand Bay, Weston-super-Mare
BS22 9UJ
Tel: 01934 627595 **16 K4**
cvhp.co.uk
Total Pitches: 190 (C, CV & T)

Cove C & C Park
Ullswater, Watermillock
CA11 0LS
Tel: 017684 86549 **67 P8**
cove-park.co.uk
Total Pitches: 50 (C, CV & T)

Crealy Meadows C & C Park
Sidmouth Road, Clyst St Mary, Exeter
EX5 1DR
Tel: 01395 234888 **6 D6**
Total Pitches: 120 (C, CV & T)

Crows Nest Caravan Park
Gristhorpe, Filey
YO14 9PS
Tel: 01723 582206 **65 P3**
crowsnestcaravanpark.com
Total Pitches: 49 (C, CV & T)

Dell Touring Park
Beyton Road, Thurston, Bury St Edmunds
IP31 3RB
Tel: 01359 270121 **40 F8**
thedellcaravanpark.co.uk
Total Pitches: 50 (C, CV & T)

Diamond Farm C & C Park
Islip Road, Bletchingdon
OX5 3DR
Tel: 01869 350909 **30 B9**
diamondpark.co.uk
Total Pitches: 37 (C, CV & T)

Dibles Park
Dibles Road, Warsash, Southampton
SO31 9SA
Tel: 01489 575232 **9 Q7**
diblespark.co.uk
Total Pitches: 14 (C, CV & T)

Dolbeare Park C & C
St Ive Road, Landrake, Saltash
PL12 5AF
Tel: 01752 851332 **4 K8**
dolbeare.co.uk
Total Pitches: 60 (C, CV & T)

Dornafield
Dornafield Farm, Two Mile Oak, Newton Abbot
TQ12 6DD
Tel: 01803 812732 **5 U7**
dornafield.com
Total Pitches: 135 (C, CV & T)

East Fleet Farm Touring Park
Chickerell, Weymouth
DT3 4DW
Tel: 01305 785768 **7 R9**
eastfleet.co.uk
Total Pitches: 400 (C, CV & T)

Eden Valley Holiday Park
Lanlivery, Nr Lostwithiel
PL30 5BU
Tel: 01208 872277 **3 R5**
edenvalleyholidaypark.co.uk
Total Pitches: 56 (C, CV & T)

Eskdale C & C Club Site
Boot, Holmrook
CA19 1TH
Tel: 019467 23253 **66 J12**
campingandcaravanningclub.co.uk/eskdale
Total Pitches: 100 (CV & T)

Exe Valley Caravan Site
Mill House, Bridgetown, Dulverton
TA22 9JR
Tel: 01643 851432 **16 B10**
exevalleycamping.co.uk
Total Pitches: 50 (C, CV & T)

Fallbarrow Park
Rayrigg Road, Windermere
LA23 3DL
Tel: 015395 69835 **67 P13**
slholidays.co.uk
Total Pitches: 32 (C & CV)

Fernwood Caravan Park
Lyneal, Ellesmere
SY12 0QF
Tel: 01948 710221 **45 L7**
fernwoodpark.co.uk
Total Pitches: 60 (C & CV)

Fields End Water Caravan Park & Fishery
Benwick Road, Doddington, March
PE15 0TY
Tel: 01354 740199 **39 N2**
fieldsendcaravans.co.uk
Total Pitches: 52 (C, CV & T)

Fishpool Farm Caravan Park
Fishpool Road, Delamere, Northwich
CW8 2HP
Tel: 01606 883970 **55 N13**
fishpoolfarmcaravanpark.co.uk
Total Pitches: 50 (C, CV & T)

Flusco Wood
Flusco, Penrith
CA11 0JB
Tel: 017684 80020 **67 Q7**
fluscowood.co.uk
Total Pitches: 46 (C & CV)

Forest Park
Northrepps Road, Cromer
NR27 0JR
Tel: 01263 513290 **51 M5**
forest-park.co.uk
Total Pitches: 262 (C, CV & T)

Globe Vale Holiday Park
Radnor, Redruth
TR16 4BH
Tel: 01209 891183 **2 J8**
globevale.co.uk
Total Pitches: 138 (C, CV & T)

Glororum Caravan Park
Glororum Farm, Bamburgh
NE69 7AW
Tel: 01670 860256 **85 T12**
northumbrianleisure.co.uk
Total Pitches: 43 (C & CV)

Golden Cap Holiday Park
Seatown, Chideock, Bridport
DT6 6JX
Tel: 01308 422139 **7 M6**
wdlh.co.uk
Total Pitches: 108 (C, CV & T)

Golden Square Touring Caravan Park
Oswaldkirk, Helmsley
YO62 5YQ
Tel: 01439 788269 **64 E4**
goldensquarecaravanpark.com
Total Pitches: 129 (C, CV & T)

Golden Valley C & C Park
Coach Road, Ripley
DE55 4ES
Tel: 01773 513881 **47 M3**
goldenvalleycaravanpark.co.uk
Total Pitches: 45 (C, CV & T)

Goosewood Caravan Park
Sutton-on-the-Forest, York
YO61 1ET
Tel: 01347 810829 **64 D7**
flowerofmay.com
Total Pitches: 100 (C & CV)

Green Acres Caravan Park
High Knells, Houghton, Carlisle
CA6 4JW
Tel: 01228 675418 **75 T13**
caravanpark-cumbria.com
Total Pitches: 30 (C, CV & T)

Greenacres Touring Park
Haywards Lane, Chelston, Wellington
TA21 9PH
Tel: 01823 652844 **16 G12**
greenacres-wellington.co.uk
Total Pitches: 40 (C & CV)

Greenhill Farm C & C Park
Greenhill Farm, New Road, Landford, Salisbury
SP5 2AZ
Tel: 01794 324117 **8 K5**
greenhillholidays.co.uk
Total Pitches: 160 (C, CV & T)

Greenhill Leisure Park
Greenhill Farm, Station Road, Bletchingdon, Oxford
OX5 3BQ
Tel: 01869 351600 **29 U4**
greenhill-leisure-park.co.uk
Total Pitches: 92 (C, CV & T)

Grouse Hill Caravan Park
Flask Bungalow Farm, Fylingdales, Robin Hood's Bay
YO22 4QH
Tel: 01947 880543 **71 R12**
grousehill.co.uk
Total Pitches: 175 (C, CV & T)

Gunvenna Caravan Park
St Minver, Wadebridge
PL27 6QN
Tel: 01208 862405 **4 B5**
gunvenna.co.uk
Total Pitches: 75 (C, CV & T)

Gwithian Farm Campsite
Gwithian Farm, Gwithian, Hayle
TR27 5BX
Tel: 01736 753127 **2 F8**
gwithianfarm.co.uk
Total Pitches: 87 (C, CV & T)

Harbury Fields
Harbury Fields Farm, Harbury, Nr Leamington Spa
CV33 9JN
Tel: 01926 612457 **37 L8**
harburyfields.co.uk
Total Pitches: 32 (C & CV)

Heathfield Farm Camping
Heathfield Road, Freshwater, Isle of Wight
PO40 9SH
Tel: 01983 407822 **9 L11**
heathfieldcamping.co.uk
Total Pitches: 60 (C, CV & T)

Heathland Beach Caravan Park
London Road, Kessingland
NR33 7PJ
Tel: 01502 740337 **41 T3**
heathlandbeach.co.uk
Total Pitches: 63 (C, CV & T)

Hele Valley Holiday Park
Hele Bay, Ilfracombe, North Devon
EX34 9RD
Tel: 01271 862460 **15 M3**
helevalley.co.uk
Total Pitches: 50 (C, CV & T)

Hendra Holiday Park
Newquay
TR8 4NY
Tel: 01637 875778 **3 L4**
hendra-holidays.com
Total Pitches: 548 (C, CV & T)

Hidden Valley Park
West Down, Braunton, Ilfracombe
EX34 8NU
Tel: 01271 813837 **15 M4**
hiddenvalleypark.com
Total Pitches: 100 (C, CV & T)

Highfield Farm Touring Park
Long Road, Comberton, Cambridge
CB23 7DG
Tel: 01223 262308 **39 N9**
highfieldfarmtouringpark.co.uk
Total Pitches: 120 (C, CV & T)

Highlands End Holiday Park
Eype, Bridport, Dorset
DT6 6AR
Tel: 01308 422139 **7 N6**
wdlh.co.uk
Total Pitches: 195 (C, CV & T)

Hill Cottage Farm C & C Park
Sandleheath Road, Alderholt, Fordingbridge
SP6 3EG
Tel: 01425 650513 **8 G6**
hillcottagefarmcampingandcaravanpark.co.uk
Total Pitches: 75 (C, CV & T)

Hill Farm Caravan Park
Branches Lane, Sherfield English, Romsey
SO51 6FH
Tel: 01794 340402 **8 K4**
hillfarmpark.com
Total Pitches: 70 (C, CV & T)

Hill of Oaks & Blakeholme
Windermere
LA12 8NR
Tel: 015395 31578 **61 R2**
hillofoaks.co.uk
Total Pitches: 43 (C & CV)

Hillside Caravan Park
Canvas Farm, Moor Road, Thirsk
YO7 4BR
Tel: 01845 537349 **63 U2**
hillsidecaravanpark.co.uk
Total Pitches: 35 (C & CV)

Hollins Farm C & C
Far Arnside, Carnforth
LA5 0SL
Tel: 01524 701508 **61 S4**
holgates.co.uk
Total Pitches: 12 (C, CV & T)

Homing Park
Church Lane, Seasalter, Whitstable
CT5 4BU
Tel: 01227 771777 **13 L3**
homingpark.co.uk
Total Pitches: 43 (C, CV & T)

Honeybridge Park
Honeybridge Lane, Dial Post, Horsham
RH13 8NX
Tel: 01403 710923 **10 K7**
honeybridgepark.co.uk
Total Pitches: 130 (C, CV & T)

Hurley Riverside Park
Park Office, Hurley, Nr Maidenhead
SL6 5NE
Tel: 01628 824493 **20 D6**
hurleyriversidepark.co.uk
Total Pitches: 200 (C, CV & T)

Hylton Caravan Park
Eden Street, Silloth
CA7 4AY
Tel: 016973 31707 **66 H2**
stanwix.com
Total Pitches: 90 (C, CV & T)

Jacobs Mount Caravan Park
Jacobs Mount, Stepney Road, Scarborough
YO12 5NL
Tel: 01723 361178 **65 N2**
jacobsmount.com
Total Pitches: 156 (C, CV & T)

Jasmine Caravan Park
Cross Lane, Snainton, Scarborough
YO13 9BE
Tel: 01723 859240 **65 L3**
jasminepark.co.uk
Total Pitches: 68 (C, CV & T)

Juliot's Well Holiday Park
Camelford, Cornwall
PL32 9RF
Tel: 01840 213302 **4 D4**
juliotswell.com
Total Pitches: 39 (C, CV & T)

Kenneggy Cove Holiday Park
Higher Kenneggy, Rosudgeon, Penzance
TR20 9AU
Tel: 01736 763453 **2 F11**
kenneggycove.co.uk
Total Pitches: 45 (C, CV & T)

King's Lynn C & C Park
New Road, North Runcton, King's Lynn
PE33 0RA
Tel: 01553 840004 **49 T10**
kl-cc.co.uk
Total Pitches: 150 (C, CV & T)

Kloofs Caravan Park
Sandhurst Lane, Bexhill
TN39 4RG
Tel: 01424 842839 **12 D14**
kloofs.com
Total Pitches: 50 (C, CV & T)

Kneps Farm Holiday Park
River Road, Stanah, Thornton-Cleveleys, Blackpool
FY5 5LR
Tel: 01253 823632 **61 R11**
knepsfarm.co.uk
Total Pitches: 40 (C & CV)

Ladycross Plantation Caravan Park
Egton, Whitby
YO21 1UA
Tel: 01947 895502 **71 P11**
ladycrossplantation.co.uk
Total Pitches: 130 (C, CV & T)

Lamb Cottage Caravan Park
Dalefords Lane, Whitegate, Northwich
CW8 2BN
Tel: 01606 882302 **55 P13**
lambcottage.co.uk
Total Pitches: 45 (C & CV)

Langstone Manor C & C Park
Moortown, Tavistock
PL19 9JZ
Tel: 01822 613371 **5 N6**
langstone-manor.co.uk
Total Pitches: 40 (C, CV & T)

Lebberston Touring Park
Filey Road, Lebberston, Scarborough
YO11 3PE
Tel: 01723 585723 **65 P3**
lebberstontouring.co.uk
Total Pitches: 125 (C & CV)

Lee Valley C & C Park
Meridian Way, Edmonton, London
N9 0AR
Tel: 020 8803 6900 **21 Q4**
visitleevalley.org.uk
Total Pitches: 100 (C, CV & T)

Lee Valley Campsite
Sewardstone Road, Chingford, London
E4 7RA
Tel: 020 8529 5689 **21 Q3**
visitleevalley.org.uk
Total Pitches: 81 (C, CV & T)

Lickpenny Caravan Site
Lickpenny Lane, Tansley, Matlock
DE4 5GF
Tel: 01629 583040 **46 K2**
lickpennycaravanpark.co.uk
Total Pitches: 80 (C & CV)

Lime Tree Park
Dukes Drive, Buxton
SK17 9RP
Tel: 01298 22988 **56 G12**
limetreeparkbuxton.co.uk
Total Pitches: 106 (C, CV & T)

Lincoln Farm Park Oxfordshire
High Street, Standlake
OX29 7RH
Tel: 01865 300239 **29 S7**
lincolnfarmpark.co.uk
Total Pitches: 90 (C, CV & T)

Little Cotton Caravan Park
Little Cotton, Dartmouth
TQ6 0LB
Tel: 01803 832558 **5 V10**
littlecotton.co.uk
Total Pitches: 95 (C, CV & T)

Little Lakeland Caravan Park
Wortwell, Harleston
IP20 0EL
Tel: 01986 788646 **41 N3**
littlelakeland.co.uk
Total Pitches: 38 (C, CV & T)

Long Acres Touring Park
Station Road, Old Leake, Boston
PE22 9RF
Tel: 01205 871555 **49 N3**
longacres-caravanpark.co.uk
Total Pitches: 40 (C, CV & T)

Long Hazel Park
High Street, Sparkford, Yeovil
BA22 7JH
Tel: 01963 440002 **17 R11**
longhazelpark.co.uk
Total Pitches: 50 (C, CV & T)

Longnor Wood Holiday Park
Newtown, Longnor, Nr Buxton
SK17 0NG
Tel: 01298 83648 **56 G14**
longnorwood.co.uk
Total Pitches: 47 (C, CV & T)

Lower Polladras Touring Park
Carleen, Breage, Helston
TR13 9NX
Tel: 01736 762220 **2 G10**
lower-polladras.co.uk
Total Pitches: 39 (C, CV & T)

Lowther Holiday Park
Eamont Bridge, Penrith
CA10 2JB
Tel: 01768 863631 **67 R7**
lowther-holidaypark.co.uk
Total Pitches: 180 (C, CV & T)

Lytton Lawn Touring Park
Lymore Lane, Milford on Sea
SO41 0TX
Tel: 01590 648331 **8 K10**
shorefield.co.uk
Total Pitches: 136 (C, CV & T)

Manor Wood Country Caravan Park
Manor Wood, Coddington, Chester
CH3 9EN
Tel: 01829 782990 **45 L2**
cheshire-caravan-sites.co.uk
Total Pitches: 45 (C, CV & T)

Meadow Lakes
Hewas Water, St Austell
PL26 7JG
Tel: 01726 882540 **3 P7**
meadow-lakes.co.uk
Total Pitches: 190 (C, CV & T)

Meadowbank Holidays
Stour Way, Christchurch
BH23 2PQ
Tel: 01202 483597 **8 G10**
meadowbank-holidays.co.uk
Total Pitches: 41 (C & CV)

Merley Court
Merley, Wimborne Minster
BH21 3AA
Tel: 01590 648331 **8 E9**
shorefield.co.uk
Total Pitches: 160 (C, CV & T)

Middlewood Farm Holiday Park
Middlewood Lane, Fylingthorpe, Robin Hood's Bay, Whitby
YO22 4UF
Tel: 01947 880414 **71 R12**
middlewoodfarm.com
Total Pitches: 100 (C, CV & T)

Minnows Touring Park
Holbrook Lane, Sampford Peverell
EX16 7EN
Tel: 01884 821770 **16 D13**
ukparks.co.uk/minnows
Total Pitches: 59 (C, CV & T)

Moon & Sixpence
Newbourn Road, Waldringfield, Woodbridge
IP12 4PP
Tel: 01473 736650 **41 N11**
moonandsixpence.eu
Total Pitches: 65 (C & CV)

Moss Wood Caravan Park
Crimbles Lane, Cockerham
LA2 0ES
Tel: 01524 791041 **61 T10**
mosswood.co.uk
Total Pitches: 25 (C, CV & T)

Newberry Valley Park
Woodlands, Combe Martin
EX34 0AT
Tel: 01271 882334 **15 N3**
newberryvalleypark.co.uk
Total Pitches: 120 (C, CV & T)

Newhaven Caravan & Camping Park
Newhaven, Nr Buxton
SK17 0DT
Tel: 01298 84300 **46 G2**
newhavencaravanpark.co.uk
Total Pitches: 125 (C, CV & T)

Newlands C & C Park
Charmouth, Bridport
DT6 6RB
Tel: 01297 560259 **7 L6**
newlandsholidays.co.uk
Total Pitches: 240 (C, CV & T)

Newperran Holiday Park
Rejerrah, Newquay
TR8 5QJ
Tel: 01872 572407 **2 K6**
newperran.co.uk
Total Pitches: 357 (C, CV & T)

Newton Mill Holiday Park
Newton Road, Bath
BA2 9JF
Tel: 0844 272 9503 **17 T4**
newtonmillpark.co.uk
Total Pitches: 106 (C, CV & T)

Ninham Country Holidays
Ninham, Shanklin, Isle of Wight
PO37 7PL
Tel: 01983 864243 **9 R12**
ninham-holidays.co.uk
Total Pitches: 150 (C, CV & T)

North Morte Farm C & C Park
North Morte Road, Mortehoe, Woolacombe, N Devon
EX34 7EG
Tel: 01271 870381 **15 L3**
northmortefarm.co.uk
Total Pitches: 180 (C, CV & T)

Northam Farm Caravan & Touring Park
Brean, Burnham-on-Sea
TA8 2SE
Tel: 01278 751244 **16 K5**
northamfarm.co.uk
Total Pitches: 350 (C, CV & T)

Oakdown Country Holiday Park
Gatedown Lane, Sidmouth
EX10 0PT
Tel: 01297 680387 **6 G6**
oakdown.co.uk
Total Pitches: 150 (C, CV & T)

Oathill Farm Touring and Camping Site
Oathill, Crewkerne
TA18 8PZ
Tel: 01460 30234 **7 M3**
oathillfarmleisure.co.uk
Total Pitches: 13 (C, CV & T)

Old Hall Caravan Park
Capernwray, Carnforth
LA6 1AD
Tel: 01524 733276 **61 U5**
oldhallcaravanpark.co.uk
Total Pitches: 38 (C & CV)

Ord House Country Park
East Ord, Berwick-upon-Tweed
TD15 2NS
Tel: 01289 305288 **85 P8**
ordhouse.co.uk
Total Pitches: 79 (C, CV & T)

Oxon Hall Touring Park
Welshpool Road, Shrewsbury
SY3 5FB
Tel: 01743 340868 **45 L11**
morris-leisure.co.uk
Total Pitches: 105 (C, CV & T)

Padstow Touring Park
Padstow
PL28 8LE
Tel: 01841 532061 **3 N2**
padstowtouringpark.co.uk
Total Pitches: 150 (C, CV & T)

Park Cliffe Camping & Caravan Estate
Birks Road, Tower Wood, Windermere
LA23 3PG
Tel: 01539 531344 — 61 R1
parkcliffe.co.uk
Total Pitches: 60 (C, CV & T)

Parkers Farm Holiday Park
Higher Mead Farm, Ashburton, Devon
TQ13 7LJ
Tel: 01364 654869 — 5 T6
parkersfarmholidays.co.uk
Total Pitches: 100 (C, CV & T)

Parkland C & C Site
Sorley Green Cross, Kingsbridge
TQ7 4AF
Tel: 01364 654869 — 5 S11
parkersfarmholidays.co.uk
Total Pitches: 100 (C, CV & T)

Pear Tree Holiday Park
Organford Road, Holton Heath, Organford, Poole
BH16 6LA
Tel: 01202 622434 — 8 C10
peartreepark.co.uk
Total Pitches: 154 (C, CV & T)

Penderleath C & C Park
Towednack, St Ives
TR26 3AF
Tel: 01736 798403 — 2 D9
penderleath.co.uk
Total Pitches: 75 (C, CV & T)

Penrose Holiday Park
Goonhavern, Truro
TR4 9QF
Tel: 01872 573185 — 2 K6
penroseholidaypark.com
Total Pitches: 110 (C, CV & T)

Pentire Haven Holiday Park
Stibb Road, Kilkhampton, Bude
EX23 9QY
Tel: 01288 321601 — 14 F10
pentirehaven.co.uk
Total Pitches: 120 (C, CV & T)

Piccadilly Caravan Park
Folly Lane West, Lacock
SN15 2LP
Tel: 01249 730260 — 18 D7
piccadillylacock.co.uk
Total Pitches: 41 (C, CV & T)

Pilgrims Way C & C Park
Church Green Road, Fishtoft, Boston
PE21 0QY
Tel: 01205 366646 — 49 N5
pilgrimsway-caravanandcamping.com
Total Pitches: 22 (C, CV & T)

Polborder House C & C Park
Bucklawren Road, St Martin, Looe
PL13 1NZ
Tel: 01503 240265 — 4 H9
polborderhouse.co.uk
Total Pitches: 31 (C, CV & T)

Polmanter Touring Park
Halsetown, St Ives
TR26 3LX
Tel: 01736 795640 — 2 E9
polmanter.com
Total Pitches: 270 (C, CV & T)

Porlock Caravan Park
Porlock, Minehead
TA24 8ND
Tel: 01643 862269 — 15 U3
porlockcaravanpark.co.uk
Total Pitches: 40 (C, CV & T)

Porthtowan Tourist Park
Mile Hill, Porthtowan, Truro
TR4 8TY
Tel: 01209 890256 — 2 H7
porthtowantouristpark.co.uk
Total Pitches: 80 (C, CV & T)

Quantock Orchard Caravan Park
Flaxpool, Crowcombe, Taunton
TA4 4AW
Tel: 01984 618618 — 16 F9
quantock-orchard.co.uk
Total Pitches: 69 (C, CV & T)

Ranch Caravan Park
Station Road, Honeybourne, Evesham
WR11 7PR
Tel: 01386 830744 — 36 F12
ranch.co.uk
Total Pitches: 120 (C & CV)

Ripley Caravan Park
Knaresborough Road, Ripley, Harrogate
HG3 3AU
Tel: 01423 770050 — 63 R7
ripleycaravanpark.com
Total Pitches: 100 (C, CV & T)

River Dart Country Park
Holne Park, Ashburton
TQ13 7NP
Tel: 01364 652511 — 5 S7
riverdart.co.uk
Total Pitches: 170 (C, CV & T)

River Valley Holiday Park
London Apprentice, St Austell
PL26 7AP
Tel: 01726 73533 — 3 Q6
rivervalleyholidaypark.co.uk
Total Pitches: 45 (C, CV & T)

Riverside C & C Park
Marsh Lane, North Molton Road, South Molton
EX36 3HQ
Tel: 01769 579269 — 15 R7
exmoorriverside.co.uk
Total Pitches: 42 (C, CV & T)

Riverside Caravan Park
High Bentham, Lancaster
LA2 7FJ
Tel: 015242 61272 — 5 N9
riversidecaravanpark.co.uk
Total Pitches: 61 (C & CV)

Riverside Caravan Park
Leigham Manor Drive, Marsh Mills, Plymouth
PL6 8LL
Tel: 01752 344122 — 62 D6
riversidecaravanpark.com
Total Pitches: 259 (C, CV & T)

Riverside Meadows Country Caravan Park
Ure Bank Top, Ripon
HG4 1JD
Tel: 01765 602964 — 63 S5
flowerofmay.com
Total Pitches: 80 (C, CV & T)

Rose Farm Touring & Camping Park
Stepshort, Belton, Nr Great Yarmouth
NR31 9JS
Tel: 01493 780896 — 51 S13
rosefarmtouringpark.co.uk
Total Pitches: 145 (C, CV & T)

Ross Park
Park Hill Farm, Ipplepen, Newton Abbot
TQ12 5TT
Tel: 01803 812983 — 5 U7
rossparkcaravanpark.co.uk
Total Pitches: 110 (C, CV & T)

Rudding Holiday Park
Follifoot, Harrogate
HG3 1JH
Tel: 01423 870439 — 63 S9
ruddingholidaypark.co.uk
Total Pitches: 141 (C, CV & T)

Run Cottage Touring Park
Alderton Road, Hollesley, Woodbridge
IP12 3RQ
Tel: 01394 411309 — 41 Q12
run-cottage.co.uk
Total Pitches: 45 (C, CV & T)

Rutland C & C
Park Lane, Greetham, Oakham
LE15 7FN
Tel: 01572 813520 — 48 D11
rutlandcaravanandcamping.co.uk
Total Pitches: 130 (C, CV & T)

St Helens Caravan Park
Wykeham, Scarborough
YO13 9QD
Tel: 01723 862771 — 65 M3
sthelenscaravanpark.co.uk
Total Pitches: 250 (C, CV & T)

St Mabyn Holiday Park
Longstone Road, St Mabyn, Wadebridge
PL30 3BY
Tel: 01208 841677 — 3 R2
stmabynholidaypark.co.uk
Total Pitches: 120 (C, CV & T)

Sandy Balls Holiday Village
Sandy Balls Estate Ltd, Godshill, Fordingbridge
SP6 2JZ
Tel: 0844 693 1336 — 8 H6
sandyballs.co.uk
Total Pitches: 225 (C, CV & T)

Seaview International Holiday Park
Boswinger, Mevagissey
PL26 6LL
Tel: 01726 843425 — 3 P8
seaviewinternational.com
Total Pitches: 201 (C, CV & T)

Severn Gorge Park
Bridgnorth Road, Tweedale, Telford
TF7 4JB
Tel: 01952 684789 — 45 R12
severngorgepark.co.uk
Total Pitches: 10 (C & CV)

Shamba Holidays
230 Ringwood Road, St Leonards, Ringwood
BH24 2SB
Tel: 01202 873302 — 8 G8
shambaholidays.co.uk
Total Pitches: 150 (C, CV & T)

Shaw Hall Holiday Park
Smithy Lane, Scarisbrick, Ormskirk
L40 8HJ
Tel: 01704 840298 — 54 J4
shawhall.co.uk
Total Pitches: 37 (C, CV & T)

Shrubbery Touring Park
Rousdon, Lyme Regis
DT7 3XW
Tel: 01297 442227 — 6 J6
shrubberypark.co.uk
Total Pitches: 120 (C, CV & T)

Silverbow Park
Perranwell, Goonhaven
TR4 9NX
Tel: 01872 572347 — 2 K6
chycor.co.uk/parks/silverbow
Total Pitches: 100 (C, CV & T)

Silverdale Caravan Park
Middlebarrow Plain, Cove Road, Silverdale, Nr Carnforth
LA5 0SH
Tel: 01524 701508 — 61 T4
holgates.co.uk
Total Pitches: 80 (C, CV & T)

Skelwith Fold Caravan Park
Ambleside, Cumbria
LA22 0HX
Tel: 015394 32277 — 67 N12
skelwith.com
Total Pitches: 150 (C & CV)

Somers Wood Caravan Park
Somers Road, Meriden
CV7 7PL
Tel: 01676 522978 — 36 H4
somerswood.co.uk
Total Pitches: 48 (C & CV)

South Lytchett Manor C & C Park
Dorchester Road, Lytchett Minster, Poole
BH16 6JB
Tel: 01202 622577 — 8 D10
southlytchettmanor.co.uk
Total Pitches: 150 (C, CV & T)

South Meadows Caravan Park
South Road, Belford
NE70 7DP
Tel: 01668 213326 — 85 S12
southmeadows.co.uk
Total Pitches: 120 (C, CV & T)

Southfork Caravan Park
Parrett Works, Martock
TA12 6AE
Tel: 01935 825661 — 17 M13
southforkcaravans.co.uk
Total Pitches: 27 (C, CV & T)

Springfield Holiday Park
Tedburn St Mary, Exeter
EX6 6EW
Tel: 01647 24242 — 5 U2
springfieldholidaypark.co.uk
Total Pitches: 48 (C, CV & T)

Stanmore Hall Touring Park
Stourbridge Road, Bridgnorth
WV15 6DT
Tel: 01746 761761 — 35 R2
morris-leisure.co.uk
Total Pitches: 131 (C, CV & T)

Stowford Farm Meadows
Berry Down, Combe Martin
EX34 0PW
Tel: 01271 882476 — 15 N4
stowford.co.uk
Total Pitches: 700 (C, CV & T)

Stroud Hill Park
Fen Road, Pidley
PE28 3DE
Tel: 01487 741333 — 39 M5
stroudhillpark.co.uk
Total Pitches: 60 (C, CV & T)

Sumners Ponds Fishery & Campsite
Chapel Road, Barns Green, Horsham
RH13 0PR
Tel: 01403 732539 — 10 J5
sumnersponds.co.uk
Total Pitches: 85 (C, CV & T)

Sun Valley Holiday Park
Pentewan Road, St Austell
PL26 6DJ
Tel: 01726 843266 — 3 Q7
sunvalleyholidays.co.uk
Total Pitches: 29 (C, CV & T)

Swiss Farm Touring & Camping
Marlow Road, Henley-on-Thames
RG9 2HY
Tel: 01491 573419 — 20 C6
swissfarmcamping.co.uk
Total Pitches: 140 (C, CV & T)

Tanner Farm Touring C & C Park
Tanner Farm, Goudhurst Road, Marden
TN12 9ND
Tel: 01622 832399 — 12 D7
tannerfarmpark.co.uk
Total Pitches: 100 (C, CV & T)

Tattershall Lakes Country Park
Sleaford Road, Tattershall
LN4 4LR
Tel: 01526 348800 — 48 K2
tattershall-lakes.com
Total Pitches: 186 (C, CV & T)

Tehidy Holiday Park
Harris Mill, Illogan, Portreath
TR16 4JQ
Tel: 01209 216489 — 2 H8
tehidy.co.uk
Total Pitches: 18 (C, CV & T)

Teversal C & C Club Site
Silverhill Lane, Teversal
NG17 3JJ
Tel: 01623 551838 — 47 N1
campingandcaravanningclub.co.uk/teversal
Total Pitches: 126 (C, CV & T)

The Laurels Holiday Park
Padstow Road, Whitecross, Wadebridge
PL27 7JQ
Tel: 01209 313474 — 3 P2
thelaurelsholidaypark.co.uk
Total Pitches: 30 (C, CV & T)

The Old Brick Kilns
Little Barney Lane, Barney, Fakenham
NR21 0NL
Tel: 01328 878305 — 50 H7
old-brick-kilns.co.uk
Total Pitches: 65 (C, CV & T)

The Old Oaks Touring Park
Wick Farm, Wick, Glastonbury
BA6 8JS
Tel: 01458 831437 — 17 P9
theoldoaks.co.uk
Total Pitches: 100 (C, CV & T)

The Orchards Holiday Caravan Park
Main Road, Newbridge, Yarmouth, Isle of Wight
PO41 0TS
Tel: 01983 531331 — 9 N11
orchards-holiday-park.co.uk
Total Pitches: 171 (C, CV & T)

The Quiet Site
Ullswater, Watermillock
CA11 0LS
Tel: 07768 727016 — 67 P8
thequietsite.co.uk
Total Pitches: 100 (C, CV & T)

Tollgate Farm C & C Park
Budnick Hill, Perranporth
TR6 0AD
Tel: 01872 572130 — 2 K6
tollgatefarm.co.uk
Total Pitches: 102 (C, CV & T)

Townsend Touring Park
Townsend Farm, Pembridge, Leominster
HR6 9HB
Tel: 01544 388527 — 34 J9
townsendfarm.co.uk
Total Pitches: 60 (C, CV & T)

Treago Farm Caravan Site
Crantock, Newquay
TR8 5QS
Tel: 01637 830277 — 2 K4
treagofarm.co.uk
Total Pitches: 90 (C, CV & T)

Trencreek Holiday Park
Hillcrest, Higher Trencreek, Newquay
TR8 4NS
Tel: 01637 874210 — 3 L4
trencreekholidaypark.co.uk
Total Pitches: 194 (C, CV & T)

Trethem Mill Touring Park
St Just-in-Roseland, Nr St Mawes, Truro
TR2 5JF
Tel: 01872 580504 — 3 M9
trethem.com
Total Pitches: 84 (C, CV & T)

Trevarth Holiday Park
Blackwater, Truro
TR4 8HR
Tel: 01872 560266 — 2 J7
trevarth.co.uk
Total Pitches: 30 (C, CV & T)

Trevella Tourist Park
Crantock, Newquay
TR8 5EW
Tel: 01637 830308 — 3 L5
trevella.co.uk
Total Pitches: 313 (C, CV & T)

Troutbeck C & C Club Site
Hutton Moor End, Troutbeck, Penrith
CA11 0SX
Tel: 017687 79149 — 67 N7
campingandcaravanningclub.co.uk/troutbeck
Total Pitches: 54 (C, CV & T)

Truro C & C Park
Truro
TR4 8QN
Tel: 01872 560274 — 2 K7
trurocaravanandcampingpark.co.uk
Total Pitches: 51 (C, CV & T)

Tudor C & C
Shepherds Patch, Slimbridge, Gloucester
GL2 7BP
Tel: 01453 890483 — 28 D7
tudorcaravanpark.com
Total Pitches: 75 (C, CV & T)

Two Mills Touring Park
Yarmouth Road, North Walsham
NR28 9NA
Tel: 01692 405829 — 51 N8
twomills.co.uk
Total Pitches: 81 (C, CV & T)

Ullswater Caravan, Camping & Marine Park
High Longthwaite, Watermillock, Penrith
CA11 0LR
Tel: 017684 86666 — 67 P8
ullswatercaravanpark.co.uk
Total Pitches: 160 (C, CV & T)

Ulwell Cottage Caravan Park
Ulwell Cottage, Ulwell, Swanage
BH19 3DG
Tel: 01929 422823 — 8 E12
ulwellcottagepark.co.uk
Total Pitches: 77 (C, CV & T)

Vale of Pickering Caravan Park
Carr House Farm, Allerston, Pickering
YO18 7PQ
Tel: 01723 859280 — 64 K3
valeofpickering.co.uk
Total Pitches: 120 (C, CV & T)

Wagtail Country Park
Cliff Lane, Marston, Grantham
NG32 2HU
Tel: 01400 251955 — 48 C5
wagtailcountrypark.co.uk
Total Pitches: 49 (C & CV)

Warcombe Farm C & C Park
Station Road, Mortehoe
EX34 7EJ
Tel: 01271 870690 — 15 L3
warcombefarm.co.uk
Total Pitches: 250 (C, CV & T)

Wareham Forest Tourist Park
North Trigon, Wareham
BH20 7NZ
Tel: 01929 551393 — 8 B10
warehamforest.co.uk
Total Pitches: 200 (C, CV & T)

Watergate Bay Touring Park
Watergate Bay, Tregurrian
TR8 4AD
Tel: 01637 860387 — 3 L4
watergatebaytouringpark.co.uk
Total Pitches: 171 (C, CV & T)

Waterrow Touring Park
Wiveliscombe, Taunton
TA4 2AZ
Tel: 01984 623464 — 16 E11
waterrowpark.co.uk
Total Pitches: 45 (C, CV & T)

Waters Edge Caravan Park
Crooklands, Nr Kendal
LA7 7NN
Tel: 015395 67708 — 61 U3
watersedgecaravanpark.co.uk
Total Pitches: 26 (C, CV & T)

Wayfarers C & C Park
Relubbus Lane, St Hilary, Penzance
TR20 9EF
Tel: 01736 763326 — 2 F10
wayfarerspark.co.uk
Total Pitches: 39 (C, CV & T)

Wells Holiday Park
Haybridge, Wells
BA5 1AJ
Tel: 01749 676869 — 17 P7
wellsholidaypark.co.uk
Total Pitches: 72 (C, CV & T)

Westwood Caravan Park
Old Felixstowe Road, Bucklesham, Ipswich
IP10 0BN
Tel: 01473 659637 — 41 N12
westwoodcaravanpark.co.uk
Total Pitches: 100 (C, CV & T)

Wheathill Touring Park
Wheathill, Bridgnorth
WV16 6QT
Tel: 01584 823456 — 35 P4
wheathillpark.co.uk
Total Pitches: 25 (C, CV & T)

Whitefield Forest Touring Park
Brading Road, Ryde, Isle of Wight
PO33 1QL
Tel: 01983 617069 — 9 S11
whitefieldforest.co.uk
Total Pitches: 80 (C, CV & T)

Widdicombe Farm Touring Park
Marldon, Paignton
TQ3 1ST
Tel: 01803 558325 — 5 V8
widdicombefarm.co.uk
Total Pitches: 180 (C, CV & T)

Widemouth Fields C & C Park
Park Farm, Poundstock, Bude
EX23 0NA
Tel: 01288 361351 — 14 F12
widemouthbaytouring.co.uk
Total Pitches: 156 (C, CV & T)

Wild Rose Park
Ormside, Appleby-in-Westmorland
CA16 6EJ
Tel: 017683 51077 — 68 E9
wildrose.co.uk
Total Pitches: 226 (C, CV & T)

Wilksworth Farm Caravan Park
Cranborne Road, Wimborne Minster
BH21 4HW
Tel: 01202 885467 — 8 E8
wilksworthfarmcaravanpark.co.uk
Total Pitches: 85 (C, CV & T)

Wood Farm C & C Park
Axminster Road, Charmouth
DT6 6BT
Tel: 01297 560697 — 7 L6
woodfarm.co.uk
Total Pitches: 175 (C, CV & T)

Wooda Farm Holiday Park
Poughill, Bude
EX23 9HJ
Tel: 01288 352069 — 14 F11
wooda.co.uk
Total Pitches: 200 (C, CV & T)

Woodclose Caravan Park
High Casterton, Kirkby Lonsdale
LA6 2SE
Tel: 01524 271597 — 62 C4
woodclosepark.com
Total Pitches: 29 (C, CV & T)

Woodhall Country Park
Stixwold Road, Woodhall Spa
LN10 6UJ
Tel: 01526 353710 — 59 L14
woodhallcountrypark.co.uk
Total Pitches: 80 (C, CV & T)

Woodland Springs Adult Touring Park
Venton, Drewsteignton
EX6 6PG
Tel: 01647 231695 — 5 R2
woodlandsprings.co.uk
Total Pitches: 81 (C, CV & T)

Woodlands Grove C & C Park
Blackawton, Dartmouth
TQ9 7DQ
Tel: 01803 712598 — 5 U10
woodlands-caravanpark.com
Total Pitches: 350 (C, CV & T)

Woodovis Park
Gulworthy, Tavistock
PL19 8NY
Tel: 01822 832968 — 5 L6
woodovis.com
Total Pitches: 50 (C, CV & T)

Yeatheridge Farm Caravan Park
East Worlington, Crediton
EX17 4TN
Tel: 01884 860330 — 15 S10
yeatheridge.co.uk
Total Pitches: 85 (C, CV & T)

Zeacombe House Caravan Park
Blackerton Cross, East Anstey, Tiverton
EX16 9JU
Tel: 01398 341279 — 15 U8
zeacombeadultretreat.co.uk
Total Pitches: 50 (C, CV & T)

SCOTLAND

Beecraigs C & C Site
Beecraigs Country Park, The Visitor Centre, Linlithgow
EH49 6PL
Tel: 01506 844516 — 82 K4
beecraigs.com
Total Pitches: 36 (C, CV & T)

Blair Castle Caravan Park
Blair Atholl, Pitlochry
PH18 5SR
Tel: 01796 481263 — 97 P10
blaircastlecaravanpark.co.uk
Total Pitches: 241 (C, CV & T)

Brighouse Bay Holiday Park
Brighouse Bay, Borgue, Kirkcudbright
DG6 4TS
Tel: 01557 870267 — 73 Q10
gillespie-leisure.co.uk
Total Pitches: 190 (C, CV & T)

Cairnsmill Holiday Park
Largo Road, St Andrews
KY16 8NN
Tel: 01334 473604 — 91 Q9
Total Pitches: 62 (C, CV & T)

Castle Cary Holiday Park
Creetown, Newton Stewart
DG8 7DQ
Tel: 01671 820264 — 73 M8
castlecary-caravans.com
Total Pitches: 50 (C, CV & T)

Craigtoun Meadows Holiday Park
Mount Melville, St Andrews
KY16 8PQ
Tel: 01334 475959 — 91 Q8
craigtounmeadows.co.uk
Total Pitches: 57 (C, CV & T)

Drum Mohr Caravan Park
Levenhall, Musselburgh
EH21 8JS
Tel: 0131 665 6867 — 83 S4
drummohr.org
Total Pitches: 120 (C, CV & T)

Faskally Caravan Park
Pitlochry
PH16 5LA
Tel: 01796 472007 — 97 Q11
faskally.co.uk
Total Pitches: 300 (C, CV & T)

Gart Caravan Park
The Gart, Callander
FK17 8LE
Tel: 01877 330002 — 89 P4
theholidaypark.co.uk
Total Pitches: 128 (C & CV)

Glen Nevis C & C Park
Glen Nevis, Fort William
PH33 6SX
Tel: 01397 702191 — 94 G4
glen-nevis.co.uk
Total Pitches: 380 (C, CV & T)

Hoddom Castle Caravan Park
Hoddom, Lockerbie
DG11 1AS
Tel: 01576 300251 — 75 N11
hoddomcastle.co.uk
Total Pitches: 200 (C, CV & T)

Huntly Castle Caravan Park
The Meadow, Huntly
AB54 4UJ
Tel: 01466 794999 — 104 G7
huntlycastle.co.uk
Total Pitches: 90 (C, CV & T)

Invercoe C & C Park
Glencoe, Ballachulish
PH49 4HP
Tel: 01855 811210 — 94 F7
invercoe.co.uk
Total Pitches: 60 (C, CV & T)

Linnhe Lochside Holidays
Corpach, Fort William
PH33 7NL
Tel: 01397 772376 — 94 F3
linnhe-lochside-holidays.co.uk
Total Pitches: 85 (C, CV & T)

Linwater Caravan Park
West Clifton, East Calder
EH53 0HT
Tel: 0131 333 3326 — 83 M5
linwater.co.uk
Total Pitches: 60 (C, CV & T)

Loch Ken Holiday Park
Parton, Castle Douglas
DG7 3NE
Tel: 01644 470282 — 73 R5
lochkenholidaypark.co.uk
Total Pitches: 40 (C, CV & T)

Lomond Woods Holiday Park
Old Luss Road, Balloch, Loch Lomond
G83 8QP
Tel: 01389 755000 — 88 J9
holiday-parks.co.uk
Total Pitches: 100 (C & CV)

Milton of Fonab Caravan Park
Bridge Road, Pitlochry
PH16 5NA
Tel: 01796 472882 — 97 Q12
fonab.co.uk
Total Pitches: 154 (C, CV & T)

River Tilt Caravan Park
Blair Atholl, Pitlochry
PH18 5TE
Tel: 01796 481467 — 97 P10
rivertilt.co.uk
Total Pitches: 30 (C, CV & T)

Seaward Caravan Park
Dhoon Bay, Kirkudbright
DG6 4TJ
Tel: 01557 870267 — 73 R10
gillespie-leisure.co.uk
Total Pitches: 26 (C, CV & T)

Shieling Holidays
Craignure, Isle of Mull
PA65 6AY
Tel: 01680 812496 — 93 S11
shielingholidays.co.uk
Total Pitches: 90 (C, CV & T)

Skye C & C Club Site
Loch Greshornish, Borve, Arnisort, Edinbane, Isle of Skye
IV51 9PS
Tel: 01470 582230 — 100 c4
campingandcaravanningclub.co.uk/skye
Total Pitches: 105 (C, CV & T)

Thurston Manor Leisure Park
Innerwick, Dunbar
EH42 1SA
Tel: 01368 840643 — 84 J4
thurstonmanor.co.uk
Total Pitches: 120 (C, CV & T)

Trossachs Holiday Park
Aberfoyle
FK8 3SA
Tel: 01877 382614 — 89 M6
trossachsholidays.co.uk
Total Pitches: 66 (C, CV & T)

Witches Craig C & C Park
Blairlogie, Stirling
FK9 5PX
Tel: 01786 474947 — 89 T6
witchescraig.co.uk
Total Pitches: 60 (C, CV & T)

WALES

Argoed Meadow C & C Site
Argoed Farm, Cenarth, Newcastle Emlyn
SA38 9JL
Tel: 01239 710690 — 32 E12
cenarthcampsite.co.uk
Total Pitches: 30 (C, CV & T)

Barcdy Touring C & C Park
Talsarnau
LL47 6YG
Tel: 01766 770736 — 43 M6
barcdy.co.uk
Total Pitches: 80 (C, CV & T)

Bodnant Caravan Park
Nebo Road, Llanrwst, Conwy Valley
LL26 0SD
Tel: 01492 640248 — 53 P10
bodnant-caravan-park.co.uk
Total Pitches: 54 (C, CV & T)

Bron Derw Touring Caravan Park
Llanrwst
LL26 0YT
Tel: 01492 640494 — 53 N10
bronderw-wales.co.uk
Total Pitches: 48 (C & CV)

Bron-Y-Wendon Caravan Park
Wern Road, Llanddulas, Colwyn Bay
LL22 8HG
Tel: 01492 512903 — 53 R7
northwales-holidays.co.uk
Total Pitches: 130 (C & CV)

Caerfai Bay Caravan & Tent Park
Caerfai Bay, St Davids, Haverfordwest
SA62 6QT
Tel: 01437 720274 — 24 C6
caerfaibay.co.uk
Total Pitches: 106 (C, CV & T)

Cenarth Falls Holiday Park
Cenarth, Newcastle Emlyn
SA38 9JS
Tel: 01239 710345 — 32 E12
cenarth-holipark.co.uk
Total Pitches: 30 (C, CV & T)

Daisy Bank Caravan Park
Snead, Churchstoke
SY15 6EB
Tel: 01588 620471 — 34 H2
daisy-bank.co.uk
Total Pitches: 80 (C, CV & T)

Dinlle Caravan Park
Dinas Dinlle, Caernarfon
LL54 5TW
Tel: 01286 830324 — 52 F11
thornleyleisure.co.uk
Total Pitches: 175 (C, CV & T)

Disserth C & C Park
Disserth, Howey, Llandrindod Wells
LD1 6NL
Tel: 01597 860277 — 34 B9
disserth.biz
Total Pitches: 30 (C, CV & T)

Eisteddfa
Eisteddfa Lodge, Pentrefelin, Criccieth
LL52 0PT
Tel: 01766 522696 — 42 K6
eisteddfapark.co.uk
Total Pitches: 100 (C, CV & T)

Erwlon C & C Park
Brecon Road, Llandovery
SA20 0RD
Tel: 01550 721021 — 33 Q14
erwlon.co.uk
Total Pitches: 75 (C, CV & T)

Fforest Fields C & C Park
Hundred House, Builth Wells
LD1 5RT
Tel: 01982 570406 — 34 D10
fforestfields.co.uk
Total Pitches: 60 (C, CV & T)

Hendre Mynach Touring C & C Park
Llanaber Road, Barmouth
LL42 1YR
Tel: 01341 280262 — 43 M10
hendremynach.co.uk
Total Pitches: 240 (C, CV & T)

Home Farm Caravan Park
Marian-Glas, Isle of Anglesey
LL73 8PH
Tel: 01248 410614 — 52 G6
homefarm-anglesey.co.uk
Total Pitches: 102 (C, CV & T)

Hunters Hamlet Caravan Park
Sirior Goch Farm, Betws-yn-Rhos, Abergele
LL22 8PL
Tel: 01745 832237 — 53 R8
huntershamlet.co.uk
Total Pitches: 30 (C & CV)

Islawrffordd Caravan Park
Tal-y-bont, Barmouth
LL43 2AQ
Tel: 01341 247269 — 43 L9
islawrffordd.co.uk
Total Pitches: 105 (C, CV & T)

Kingsbridge Caravan Park
Camp Road, Llanfaes, Beaumaris, Isle of Anglesey
LL58 8LR
Tel: 01248 490636 — 52 K7
kingsbridgecaravanpark.co.uk
Total Pitches: 90 (C, CV & T)

Llys Derwen C & C Site
Ffordd Bryngwyn, Llanrug, Caernarfon
LL55 4RD
Tel: 01286 673322 — 52 H10
llysderwen.co.uk
Total Pitches: 20 (C, CV & T)

Pencelli Castle C & C Park
Pencelli, Brecon
LD3 7LX
Tel: 01874 665451 — 26 K3
pencelli-castle.com
Total Pitches: 80 (C, CV & T)

Penisar Mynydd Caravan Park
Caerwys Road, Rhuallt, St Asaph
LL17 0TY
Tel: 01745 582227 — 54 C11
penisarmynydd.co.uk
Total Pitches: 75 (C, CV & T)

Plas Farm Caravan Park
Betws-yn-Rhos, Abergele
LL22 8AU
Tel: 01492 680254 — 53 Q8
plasfarmcaravanpark.co.uk
Total Pitches: 54 (C, CV & T)

Pont Kemys C & C Park
Chainbridge, Abergavenny
NP7 9DS
Tel: 01873 880688 — 27 Q6
pontkemys.com
Total Pitches: 65 (C, CV & T)

River View Touring Park
The Dingle, Llanedi, Pontarddulais
SA4 0FH
Tel: 01269 844876 — 25 U9
riverviewtouringpark.com
Total Pitches: 60 (C, CV & T)

Riverside Camping
Seiont Nurseries, Pont Rug, Caernarfon
LL55 2BB
Tel: 01286 678781 — 52 H10
riversidecamping.co.uk
Total Pitches: 73 (C, CV & T)

St David's Park
Red Wharf Bay, Pentraeth, Isle of Anglesey
LL75 8RJ
Tel: 01248 852341 — 52 H6
stdavidspark.com
Total Pitches: 45 (C, CV & T)

The Plassey Leisure Park
The Plassey, Eyton, Wrexham
LL13 0SP
Tel: 01978 780277 — 44 J4
plassey.com
Total Pitches: 90 (C, CV & T)

Trawsdir Touring C & C Park
Llanaber, Barmouth
LL42 1RR
Tel: 01341 280999 — 43 L10
barmouthholidays.co.uk
Total Pitches: 70 (C, CV & T)

Trefalun Park
Devonshire Drive, St Florence, Tenby
SA70 8RD
Tel: 01646 651514 — 24 J10
trefalunpark.co.uk
Total Pitches: 90 (C, CV & T)

Tyddyn Isaf Caravan Park
Lligwy Bay, Dulas, Isle of Anglesey
LL70 9PQ
Tel: 01248 410203 — 52 G5
tyddynisaf.co.uk
Total Pitches: 30 (C, CV & T)

Well Park C & C Site
Tenby
SA70 8TL
Tel: 01834 842179 — 24 K10
wellparkcaravans.co.uk
Total Pitches: 100 (C, CV & T)

Wernddu Caravan Park
Old Ross Road, Abergavenny
NP7 8NG
Tel: 01873 856223 — 27 Q4
wernddu-golf-club.co.uk
Total Pitches: 70 (C, CV & T)

CHANNEL ISLANDS

Beuvelande Camp Site
Beuvelande, St Martin, Jersey
JE3 6EZ
Tel: 01534 853575 — 7 e2
campingjersey.com
Total Pitches: 150 (C, CV & T)

Fauxquets Valley Campsite
Castel, Guernsey
GY5 7QL
Tel: 01481 255460 — 6 d3
fauxquets.co.uk
Total Pitches: 120 (C, CV & T)

Rozel Camping Park
Summerville Farm, St Martin, Jersey
JE3 6AX
Tel: 01534 855200 — 7 f2
rozelcamping.co.uk
Total Pitches: 100 (C, CV & T)

Traffic signs and road markings

Traffic signs

Signs giving orders

Signs with red circles are mostly prohibitive.
Plates below signs qualify their message.

 20 ZONE — Entry to 20mph zone

 30 Zone ENDS — End of 20mph zone

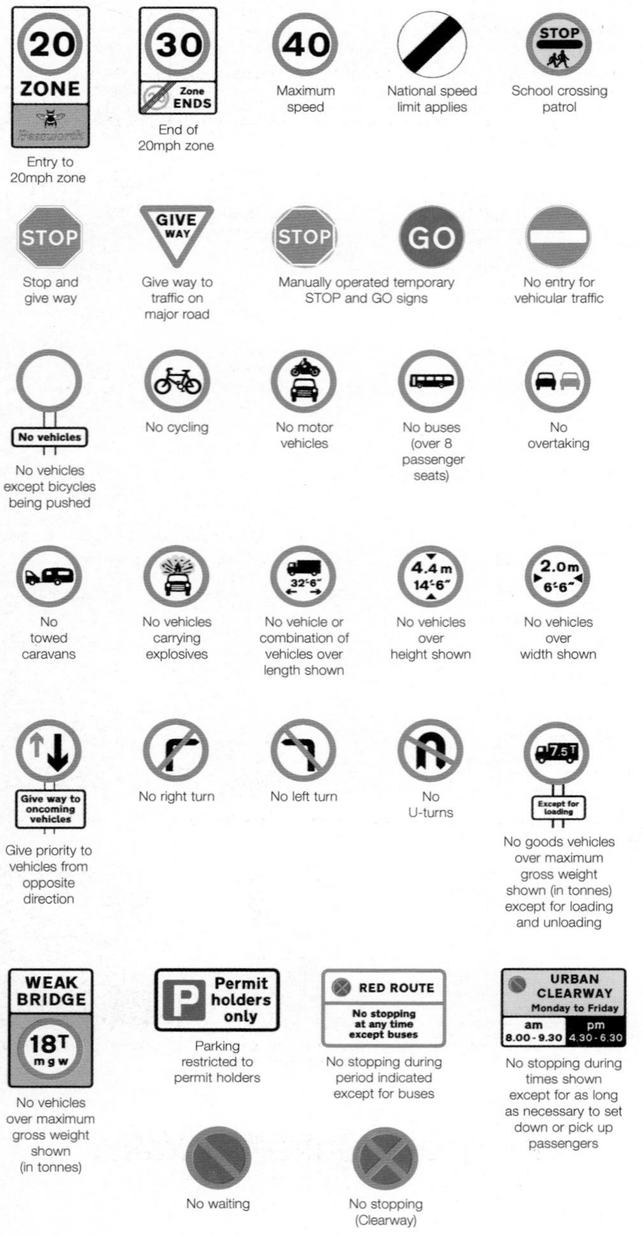

40 — Maximum speed

National speed limit applies

 **STOP** — School crossing patrol

STOP — Stop and give way

GIVE WAY — Give way to traffic on major road

STOP — Manually operated temporary STOP and GO signs

GO

No entry for vehicular traffic

 No vehicles — No vehicles except bicycles being pushed

No cycling

No motor vehicles

No buses (over 8 passenger seats)

No overtaking

No towed caravans

No vehicles carrying explosives

32'-6" No vehicle or combination of vehicles over length shown

4.4m 14'-6" No vehicles over height shown

2.0m 6'-6" No vehicles over width shown

 Give way to oncoming vehicles — Give priority to vehicles from opposite direction

No right turn

No left turn

No U-turns

 7.5T Except for loading — No goods vehicles over maximum gross weight shown (in tonnes) except for loading and unloading

WEAK BRIDGE 18T m.g.w. — No vehicles over maximum gross weight shown (in tonnes)

P Permit holders only — Parking restricted to permit holders

RED ROUTE No stopping at any time except buses — No stopping during period indicated except for buses

URBAN CLEARWAY Monday to Friday am 8.00 - 9.30 pm 4.30 - 6.30 — No stopping during times shown except for as long as necessary to set down or pick up passengers

 No waiting

No stopping (Clearway)

Signs with blue circles but no red border mostly give positive instruction.

Ahead only

Turn left ahead (right if symbol reversed)

Turn left (right if symbol reversed)

Keep left (right if symbol reversed)

Vehicles may pass either side to reach same destination

Mini-roundabout (roundabout circulation - give way to vehicles from the immediate right)

Route to be used by pedal cycles only

Segregated pedal cycle and pedestrian route

30 Minimum speed

30 End of minimum speed

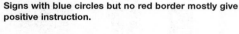 **Only** — Buses and cycles only

Only — Trams only

TRAMWAY LOOK BOTH WAYS — Pedestrian crossing point over tramway

One-way traffic (note: compare circular 'Ahead only' sign)

With-flow bus and cycle lane

Contraflow bus lane

With-flow pedal cycle lane

 **THE HIGHWAY CODE** **KNOW YOUR ROAD SIGNS**

Note: The signs shown in this road atlas are those most commonly in use and are not all drawn to the same scale. In Scotland and Wales bilingual versions of some signs are used, showing both English and Gaelic or Welsh spellings. Some older designs of signs may still be seen on the roads. A comprehensive explanation of the signing system illustrating the vast majority of road signs can be found in the AA's handbook *Know Your Road Signs*. Where there is a reference to a rule number, this refers to *The Highway Code*, which is detailed in the AA's guide. Both of these publications are on sale at theaa.com/shop and booksellers.

Warning signs

Mostly triangular

 STOP 100 yds — Distance to 'STOP' line ahead

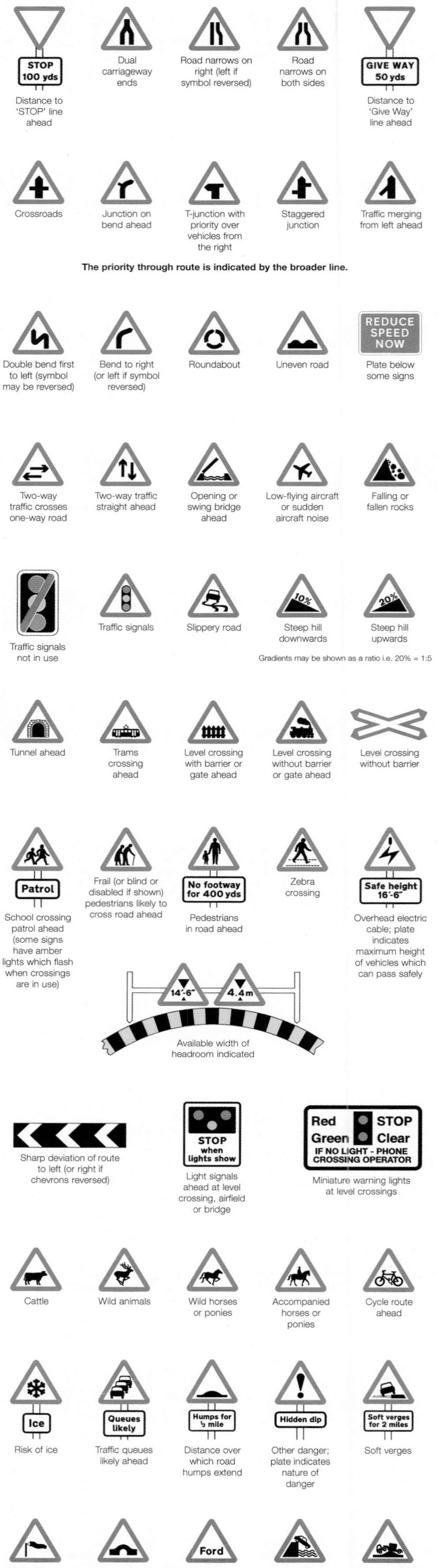

Dual carriageway ends

Road narrows on right (left if symbol reversed)

Road narrows on both sides

GIVE WAY 50 yds — Distance to 'Give Way' line ahead

Crossroads

Junction on bend ahead

T-junction with priority over vehicles from the right

Staggered junction

Traffic merging from left ahead

The priority through route is indicated by the broader line.

Double bend first to left (symbol may be reversed)

Bend to right (or left if symbol reversed)

Roundabout

Uneven road

REDUCE SPEED NOW — Plate below some signs

Two-way traffic crosses one-way road

Two-way traffic straight ahead

Opening or swing bridge ahead

Low-flying aircraft or sudden aircraft noise

Falling or fallen rocks

Traffic signals not in use

Traffic signals

Slippery road

10% Steep hill downwards

20% Steep hill upwards

Gradients may be shown as a ratio i.e. 20% = 1:5

Tunnel ahead

Trams crossing ahead

Level crossing with barrier or gate ahead

Level crossing without barrier or gate ahead

Level crossing without barrier

 Patrol — School crossing patrol ahead (some signs have amber lights which flash when crossings are in use)

Frail (or blind or disabled if shown) pedestrians likely to cross road ahead

No footway for 400 yds — Pedestrians in road ahead

Zebra crossing

Safe height 16'-6" — Overhead electric cable; plate indicates maximum height of vehicles which can pass safely

14'-6" **4.4m** — Available width of headroom indicated

Sharp deviation of route to left (or right if chevrons reversed)

STOP when lights show — Light signals ahead at level crossing, airfield or bridge

Red STOP Green Clear IF NO LIGHT - PHONE CROSSING OPERATOR — Miniature warning lights at level crossings

Cattle

Wild animals

Wild horses or ponies

Accompanied horses or ponies

Cycle route ahead

 Ice — Risk of ice

Queues likely — Traffic queues likely ahead

Humps for ½ mile — Distance over which road humps extend

Hidden dip — Other danger; plate indicates nature of danger

Soft verges for 2 miles — Soft verges

Side winds

Hump bridge

Ford — Worded warning sign

Quayside or river bank

Risk of grounding

Direction signs

Mostly rectangular

Signs on motorways – blue backgrounds

 Nottingham 23 M1 — At a junction leading directly into a motorway (junction number may be shown on a black background)

 **Nottingham A 52 25 ½ m** — On approaches to junctions (junction number on black background)

 M1 The NORTH Sheffield 32 Leeds 59 — Route confirmatory sign after junction

 **A 404 Marlow — Birmingham, Oxford M 40**
Downward pointing arrows mean 'Get in lane'
The left-hand lane leads to a different destination from the other lanes.

 A 46 (M 69) Leicester, Coventry (E) — The NORTH WEST, Birmingham, Coventry (N) M 6
The panel with the inclined arrow indicates the destinations which can be reached by leaving the motorway at the next junction

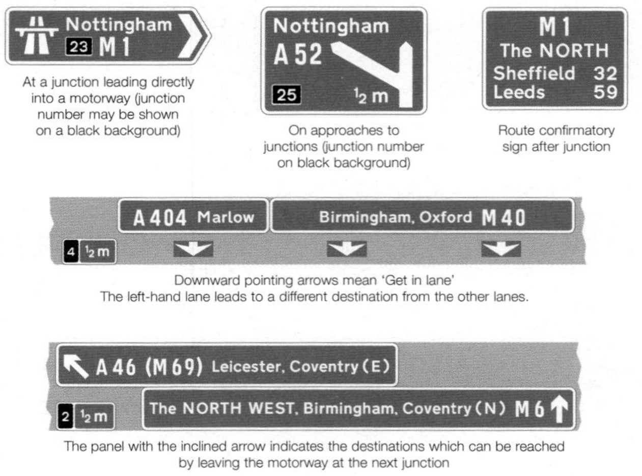

Signs on primary routes - green backgrounds

 **PARK STREET ROUNDABOUT Birmingham Bourne M 15 (M1) (M 14) Penderton A 105 Walsham A 1183 Nutfield A 1183** — On approaches to junctions

 Lampton Axtley A 11 14'-6" 1 mile — At the junction

 **TURPIN'S CROSSROADS Biggleswick A 11 Lampton (M 11) Dorfield A 123 Axtley B 1991 Steam railway** — On approaches to junctions

 **A 46 The SOUTH Nottingham 17 Leicester 32 (M 1 South) 35** — Route confirmatory sign after junction

 Swansea Abertawe A 483 — On approach to a junction in Wales (bilingual)

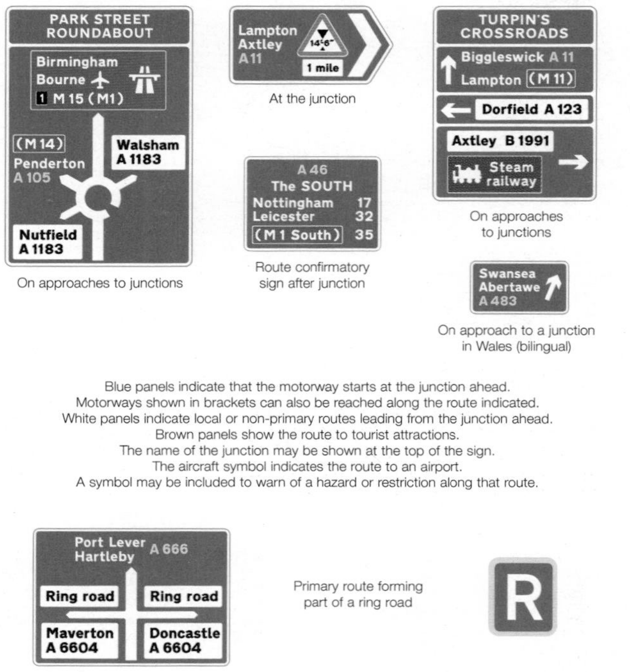

Blue panels indicate that the motorway starts at the junction ahead.
Motorways shown in brackets can also be reached along the route indicated.
White panels indicate local or non-primary routes leading from the junction ahead.
Brown panels show the route to tourist attractions.
The name of the junction may be shown at the top of the sign.
The aircraft symbol indicates the route to an airport.
A symbol may be included to warn of a hazard or restriction along that route.

 **Port Lever Hartleby A 666 Ring road Ring road Maverton A 6604 Doncastle A 6604** — Primary route forming part of a ring road

 R

Signs on non-primary and local routes - black borders

 HANGMAN'S CROSSROADS Axtley B 1234 (M 11) Lampton A 11 Townley A 11 — On approaches to junctions

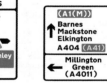 **(A1(M)) 8 Barnes 10 Mackstone 2½ Elkington 1 A 404 (A41) Millington Green 3 (A4011)**

 Market Walborough B 486 7 — At the junction

 **WC** — Direction to toilets with access for the disabled

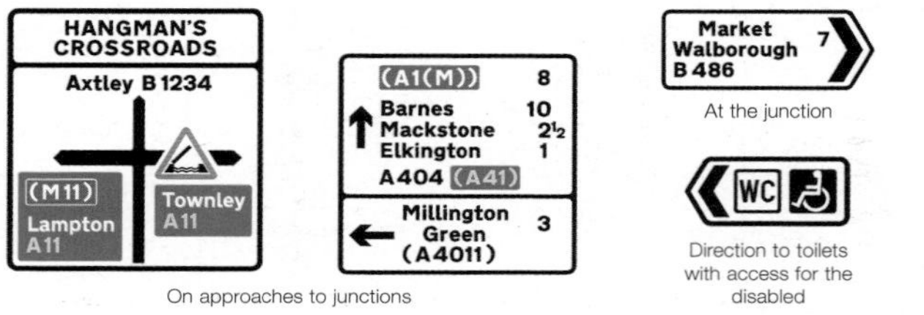

Green panels indicate that the primary route starts at the junction ahead.
Route numbers on a blue background show the direction to a motorway.
Route numbers on a green background show the direction to a primary route.

Other direction signs

 **150 yds** — Picnic site

 Wrest Park — Ancient monument in the care of English Heritage

 **P Saturday only** — Direction to a car park

 **Zoo** — Tourist attraction

 **300 yds** — Direction to camping and caravan site

 **(A33) (M1)** — Advisory route for lorries

 **4** — Route for pedal cycles forming part of a network

 **Marton 3** — Recommended route for pedal cycles to place shown

 **Public library Council offices** — Route for pedestrians

Emergency diversion routes

    — Symbols showing emergency diversion route for motorway and other main road traffic

 Northtown — Diversion route

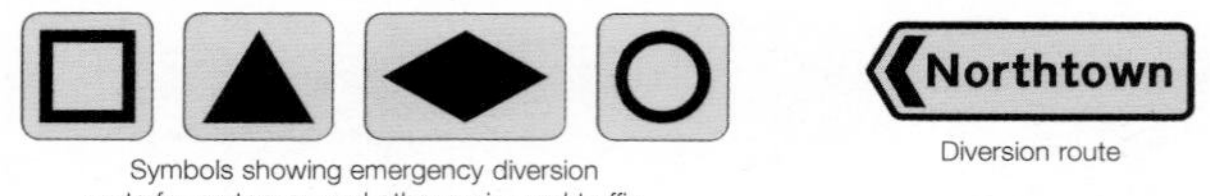

In an emergency it may be necessary to close a section of motorway or other main road to traffic, so a temporary sign may advise drivers to follow a diversion route. To help drivers navigate the route, black symbols on yellow patches may be permanently displayed on existing direction signs, including motorway signs. Symbols may also be used on separate signs with yellow backgrounds.

For further information see highways.gov.uk, trafficscotland.org and traffic-wales.com

Road markings

Information signs

All rectangular

Entrance to controlled parking zone

Entrance to congestion charging zone

Greater London Low Emission Zone (LEZ)

Advance warning of restriction or prohibition ahead

Parking place for solo motorcycles

With-flow bus lane ahead which pedal cycles and taxis may also use

Lane designated for use by high occupancy vehicles (HOV) - see rule 142

Vehicles permitted to use an HOV lane ahead

End of motorway

Start of motorway and point from which motorway regulations apply

Appropriate traffic lanes at junction ahead

Traffic on the main carriageway coming from right has priority over joining traffic

Additional traffic joining from left ahead. Traffic on main carriageway has priority over joining traffic from right hand of slip road

Traffic in right hand lane of slip road joining the main carriageway has priority over left hand lane

'Countdown' markers at exit from motorway (each bar represents 100 yards to the exit). Green-backed markers may be used on primary routes and white-backed markers with black bars on other routes. At approaches to concealed level crossings white-backed markers with red bars may be used. Although these will be erected at equal distances the bars do not represent 100 yard intervals.

GOOD FOOD
Puddleworth services
Motorway service area sign showing the operator's name

Traffic has priority over oncoming vehicles

Hospital ahead with Accident and Emergency facilities

Tourist information point

No through road for vehicles

Recommended route for pedal cycles

Home Zone Entry*

Area in which cameras are used to enforce traffic regulations

Bus lane on road at junction ahead

*Home Zone Entry – You are entering an area where people could be using the whole street for a range of activities. You should drive slowly and carefully and be prepared to stop to allow people time to move out of the way.

Roadworks signs

Road works

Loose chippings

SLOW WET TAR
Temporary hazard at roadworks

800 yards
Temporary lane closure (the number and position of arrows and red bars may be varied according to lanes open and closed)

Slow-moving or stationary works vehicle blocking a traffic lane. Pass in the direction shown by the arrow.

50 ¾ mile ahead
Mandatory speed limit ahead

Delays possible until Sept
Roadworks 1 mile ahead

Sorry for any delay
End of roadworks and any temporary restrictions including speed limits

800 yds
Signs used on the back of slow-moving or stationary works warning of a lane closed ahead by a works vehicle. There are no cones on the road.

450 yds

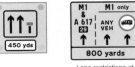
Lane restrictions at roadworks ahead

STAY IN LANE
Max speed 30
One lane crossover at contraflow roadworks

Across the carriageway

Stop line at signals or police control

Stop line at 'Stop' sign

Stop line for pedestrians at a level crossing

Give way to traffic on major road (can also be used at mini roundabouts)

Give way to traffic from the right at a roundabout

Give way to traffic from the right at a mini-roundabout

Along the carriageway

Edge line

Centre line See Rule 127

Hazard warning line See Rule 127

Double white lines See Rules 128 and 129

See Rule 130

Lane line See Rule 131

Along the edge of the carriageway

Waiting restrictions

Waiting restrictions indicated by yellow lines apply to the carriageway, pavement and verge. You may stop to load or unload (unless there are also loading restrictions as described below) or while passengers board or alight. Double yellow lines mean no waiting at any time, unless there are signs that specifically indicate seasonal restrictions. The times at which the restrictions apply for other road markings are shown on nearby plates or on entry signs to controlled parking zones. If no days are shown on the signs, the restrictions are in force every day including Sundays and Bank Holidays. White bay markings and upright signs (see below) indicate where parking is allowed.

No waiting at any time

8 am - 6 pm
No waiting during times shown on sign

P Mon - Sat 8 am - 7 pm 20 mins No return within 40 mins
Waiting is limited to the duration specified during the days and times shown

Red Route stopping controls

Red lines are used on some roads instead of yellow lines. In London the double and single red lines used on Red Routes indicate that stopping to park, load/unload or to board and alight from a vehicle (except for a licensed taxi or if you hold a Blue Badge) is prohibited. The red lines apply to the carriageway, pavement and verge. The times at which the red line prohibitions apply are shown on nearby signs, but the double red line ALWAYS means no stopping at any time. On Red Routes you may stop to park, load/unload in specially marked boxes and adjacent signs specify the times and purposes and duration allowed. A box MARKED IN RED indicates that it may only be available for the purpose specified for part of the day (e.g. between busy peak periods). A box MARKED IN WHITE means that it is available throughout the day.

RED AND SINGLE YELLOW LINES CAN ONLY GIVE A GUIDE TO THE RESTRICTIONS AND CONTROLS IN FORCE AND SIGNS, NEARBY OR AT A ZONE ENTRY, MUST BE CONSULTED.

RED ROUTE No stopping at any time

No stopping at any time

RED ROUTE No stopping Mon - Sat 7am - 7pm

No stopping during times shown on sign

RED ROUTE P Mon - Sat 7am - 7pm No return within 2 hours

Parking is limited to the duration specified during the days and times shown

RED ROUTE No stopping Mon - Sat 7am - 7pm Except 10 am - 4 pm loading max 20 mins

Only loading may take place at the times shown for up to a maximum duration of 20 mins

On the kerb or at the edge of the carriageway

Loading restrictions on roads other than Red Routes

Yellow marks on the kerb or at the edge of the carriageway indicate that loading or unloading is prohibited at the times shown on the nearby black and white plates. You may stop while passengers board or alight. If no days are indicated on the signs the restrictions are in force every day including Sundays and Bank Holidays.

ALWAYS CHECK THE TIMES SHOWN ON THE PLATES.

Lengths of road reserved for vehicles loading and unloading are indicated by a white 'bay' marking with the words 'Loading Only' and a sign with the white on blue 'trolley' symbol. This sign also shows whether loading and unloading is restricted to goods vehicles and the times at which the bay can be used. If no times or days are shown it may be used at any time. Vehicles may not park here if they are not loading or unloading.

No loading at any time
No loading or unloading at any time

No loading Mon - Sat 8.30 am - 6.30 pm
No loading or unloading at the times shown

Loading only
Loading bay

Other road markings

— SCHOOL — KEEP — CLEAR —
Keep entrance clear of stationary vehicles, even if picking up or setting down children

Warning of 'Give Way' just ahead

DOCTOR
Parking space reserved for vehicles named

BUS STOP
See Rule 243

BUS LANE
See Rule 141

Box junction - See Rule 174

KEEP CLEAR
Do not block that part of the carriageway indicated

CITY A3 YORK ST
Indication of traffic lanes

Light signals controlling traffic

Traffic Light Signals

RED means 'Stop'. Wait behind the stop line on the carriageway

RED AND AMBER also means 'Stop'. Do not pass through or start until GREEN shows

GREEN means you may go on if the way is clear. Take special care if you intend to turn left or right and give way to pedestrians who are crossing

AMBER means 'Stop' at the stop line. You may go on only if the AMBER appears after you have crossed the stop line or are so close to it that to pull up might cause an accident

A GREEN ARROW may be provided in addition to the full green signal if movement in a certain direction is allowed before or after the full green phase. If the way is clear you may go but only in the direction shown by the arrow. You may do this whatever other lights may be showing. White light signals may be provided for trams

Flashing red lights

Alternately flashing red lights mean YOU MUST STOP

At level crossings, lifting bridges, airfields, fire stations, etc.

Motorway signals

You MUST NOT proceed further in this lane

Change lane

Fog
Reduced visibility ahead

Lane ahead closed

ACCIDENT AHEAD 30
Temporary maximum speed advised and information message

Leave motorway at next exit

50
Temporary maximum speed advised

End
End of restriction

Lane control signals

Green arrow – lane available to traffic facing the sign
Red crosses – lane closed to traffic facing the sign
White diagonal arrow – change lanes in direction shown

Channel Hopping

For business or pleasure, hopping on a ferry across to France, Belgium or the Channel Islands has never been easier.

The vehicle ferry routes shown on this map give you all the options, together with detailed port plans to help you navigate to and from the ferry terminals. Simply choose your preferred route, not forgetting the fast sailings; then check the colour-coded table for ferry operators, crossing times and contact details.

Bon voyage!

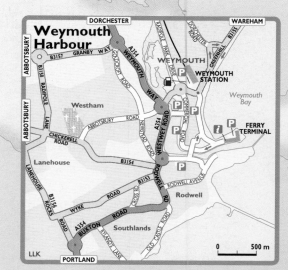

Weymouth Harbour

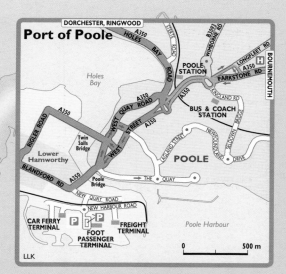

Port of Poole

Port of Plymouth

Plymouth

Weymouth

Poole

Isle of Wight

ENGLISH

Alderney

St Peter Port
Herm
Guernsey
Sark

Channel Islands

Jersey

St Helier

Cherbourg

Roscoff

St-Malo

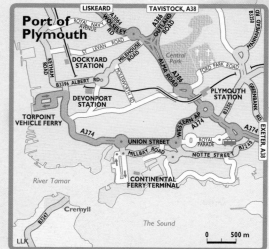 Fast ferry

Conventional ferry

ENGLISH CHANNEL FERRY CROSSINGS AND OPERATORS

From	To	Journey Time	Operator	Telephone	Website
Dover	Calais	1 hr 30 mins	DFDS Seaways	0871 522 9955	dfdsseaways.co.uk
Dover	Calais	1 hr 30 mins	LD Lines/DFDS	0844 576 8836	ldlines.co.uk
Dover	Calais	1 hr 30 mins	My Ferry Link	0844 248 2100	myferrylink.com
Dover	Calais	1 hr 30 mins	P&O Ferries	0871 664 2121	poferries.com
Dover	Dunkerque	2 hrs	DFDS Seaways	0871 522 9955	dfdsseaways.co.uk
Folkestone	Calais (Coquelles)	35 mins	Eurotunnel	0844 335 3535	eurotunnel.com
Newhaven	Dieppe	4 hrs	DFDS Seaways	0871 522 9955	dfdsseaways.co.uk
Plymouth	Roscoff	6–8 hrs	Brittany Ferries	0871 244 0744	brittany-ferries.co.uk
Plymouth	St-Malo	10 hrs 15 mins (Nov–Mar)	Brittany Ferries	0871 244 0744	brittany-ferries.co.uk
Poole	Cherbourg	4 hrs 15 mins (Mar–Oct)	Brittany Ferries	0871 244 0744	brittany-ferries.co.uk
Poole	Guernsey	3 hrs	Condor Ferries	0845 609 1024	condorferries.co.uk
Poole	Jersey	4 hrs 30 mins	Condor Ferries	0845 609 1024	condorferries.co.uk
Poole	St-Malo	7–12 hrs (via Channel Is.)	Condor Ferries	0845 609 1024	condorferries.co.uk
Portsmouth	Caen (Ouistreham)	6–7 hrs	Brittany Ferries	0871 244 0744	brittany-ferries.co.uk
Portsmouth	Cherbourg	3 hrs (May–Sept)	Brittany Ferries	0871 244 0744	brittany-ferries.co.uk
Portsmouth	Cherbourg	6 hrs 30 mins (May–Sept, Sun only)	Condor Ferries	0845 609 1024	condorferries.co.uk
Portsmouth	Guernsey	7 hrs	Condor Ferries	0845 609 1024	condorferries.co.uk
Portsmouth	Jersey	8–11 hrs	Condor Ferries	0845 609 1024	condorferries.co.uk
Portsmouth	Le Havre	3 hrs 45 mins	Brittany Ferries	0871 244 0744	brittany-ferries.co.uk
Portsmouth	Le Havre	5–8 hrs	DFDS Seaways	0871 522 9955	dfdsseaways.co.uk
Portsmouth	St-Malo	9–11 hrs	Brittany Ferries	0871 244 0744	brittany-ferries.co.uk
Weymouth	Guernsey	2 hrs 30 mins	Condor Ferries	0845 609 1024	condorferries.co.uk
Weymouth	Jersey	4 hrs	Condor Ferries	0845 609 1024	condorferries.co.uk
Weymouth	St-Malo	7 hrs 30 mins (via Channel Is.)	Condor Ferries	0845 609 1024	condorferries.co.uk

Ferry services listed are provided as a guide only and are liable to change at short notice.

Please check sailings before planning your journey.

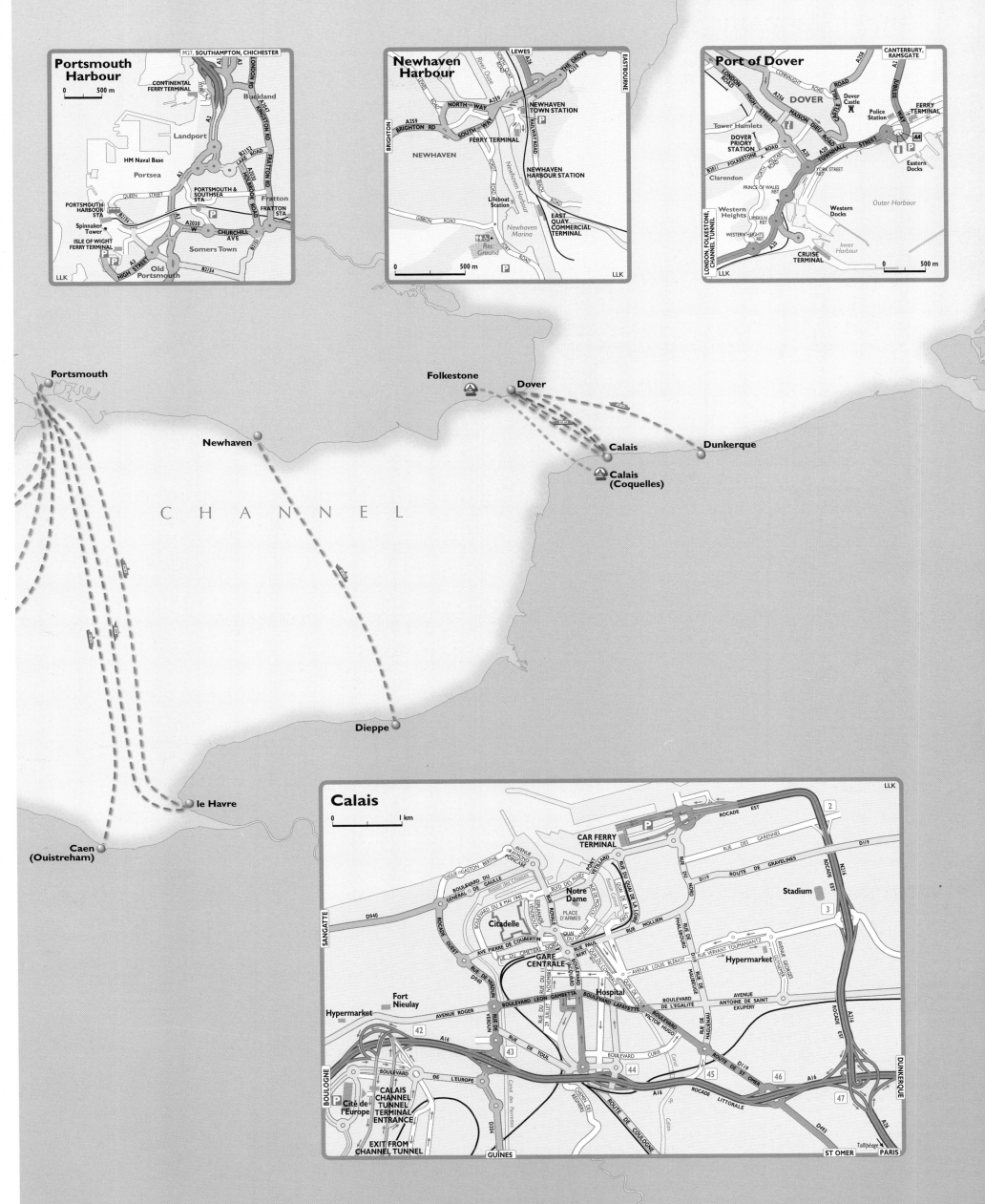

Portsmouth Harbour

M27, SOUTHAMPTON, CHICHESTER
CONTINENTAL FERRY TERMINAL
LONDON RD
KINGSTON RD
Buckland
Landport
A3
HM Naval Base
Portsea
A2030 COPNOR ROAD
FRATTON RD
QUEEN STREET
PORTSMOUTH & SOUTHSEA STA
Fratton
FRATTON STA
PORTSMOUTH HARBOUR STA
Spinnaker Tower
A2030
CHURCHILL AVE
ISLE OF WIGHT FERRY TERMINAL
A3
HIGH STREET
Old Portsmouth
B2154
Somers Town
LLK
0   500 m

Newhaven Harbour

LEWES
River Ouse
A26
THE GROVE
A259
EASTBOURNE
NORTH WAY
A259 BRIGHTON RD
SOUTH WAY
NEWHAVEN TOWN STATION
BRIGHTON
FERRY TERMINAL
RAILWAY ROAD
NEWHAVEN
NEWHAVEN HARBOUR STATION
Newhaven Harbour
Lifeboat Station
EAST QUAY COMMERCIAL TERMINAL
GIBBON ROAD
Newhaven Marina
Rec Ground
0   500 m
LLK

Port of Dover

CANTERBURY, RAMSGATE
A256
CONNAUGHT ROAD
A258 HIGH STREET
CASTLE HILL ROAD
MAISON DIEU ROAD
JUBILEE WAY
DOVER
Dover Castle
FERRY TERMINAL
Police Station
LONDON ROAD
Tower Hamlets
DOVER PRIORY STATION
TOWNHALL STREET
A20
AA
P
Eastern Docks
B3011 FOLKESTONE ROAD
Clarendon
YORK STREET RBT
PRINCE OF WALES RBT
Outer Harbour
LONDON, FOLKESTONE, CHANNEL TUNNEL
Western Heights
LIMEKILN RBT
Western Docks
WESTERN HEIGHTS RBT
A39
CRUISE TERMINAL
Inner Harbour
LLK
0   500 m

Portsmouth

Newhaven

Folkestone   Dover

Calais   Dunkerque

Calais (Coquelles)

C H A N N E L

Dieppe

le Havre

Caen (Ouistreham)

Calais

0   1 km

ROCADE EST
2
CAR FERRY TERMINAL
RUE DES GARENNES
D119
ROUTE DE GRAVELINES
N116
BOULEVARD DU GÉNÉRAL DE GAULLE
AVENUE RAYMOND POINCARÉ
Bassin des Chasses
BLVD DES ALLIÉS
RUE DU QUAI DE LA LOIRE
RUE DU NORD
ROCADE EST
3
Stadium
Notre Dame
RUE ROYALE
Quai de la Loire
D940
SANGATTE
ROCADE OUEST
Citadelle
PLACE D'ARMES
RUE MOLLIEN
RUE VERVANT TOURNANANTZ
AVENUE GEORGES
Hypermarket
AVE PIERRE DE COUBERTIN
RUE PAUL
GARE CENTRALE
BOULEVARD JACQUARD
AVENUE LOUIS BLÉRIOT
RUE DE MARBURG
AVENUE ANTOINE DE SAINT EXUPÉRY
Fort Nieulay
Hospital
BOULEVARD LÉON GAMBETTA
BOULEVARD LAFAYETTE
BOULEVARD DE L'ÉGALITÉ
Hypermarket
AVENUE ROGER
BOULEVARD DE VERDUN
RUE DU 11 NOVEMBRE
RUE DU 29 JUILLET
VICTOR HUGO
RUE DE HAGUENAU
ROCADE EST
A116
42
A16
43
RUE DE TOUL
44
BOULEVARD CURIE
Canal
D119
ROUTE DE ST OMER
45
46
A16
BOULEVARD DE L'EUROPE
47
DUNKERQUE
BOULOGNE
P
Cité de l'Europe
CALAIS CHANNEL TUNNEL TERMINAL ENTRANCE
Canal des Pierrettes
D304
A16
Colon
ROCADE LITTORALE
D491
Toll/péage
EXIT FROM CHANNEL TUNNEL
GUÎNES
ROUTE DE COULOGNE
ST OMER
PARIS
LLK

Ferries to Ireland and the Isle of Man

With so many sea crossings to Ireland and the Isle of Man this map will help you make the right choice.

The vehicle ferry routes shown on this map give you all the options, together with detailed port plans to help you navigate to and from the ferry terminals. Simply choose your preferred route, not forgetting the fast sailings; then check the colour-coded table for ferry operators, crossing times and contact details.

🚢 Fast ferry   🚢 Conventional ferry

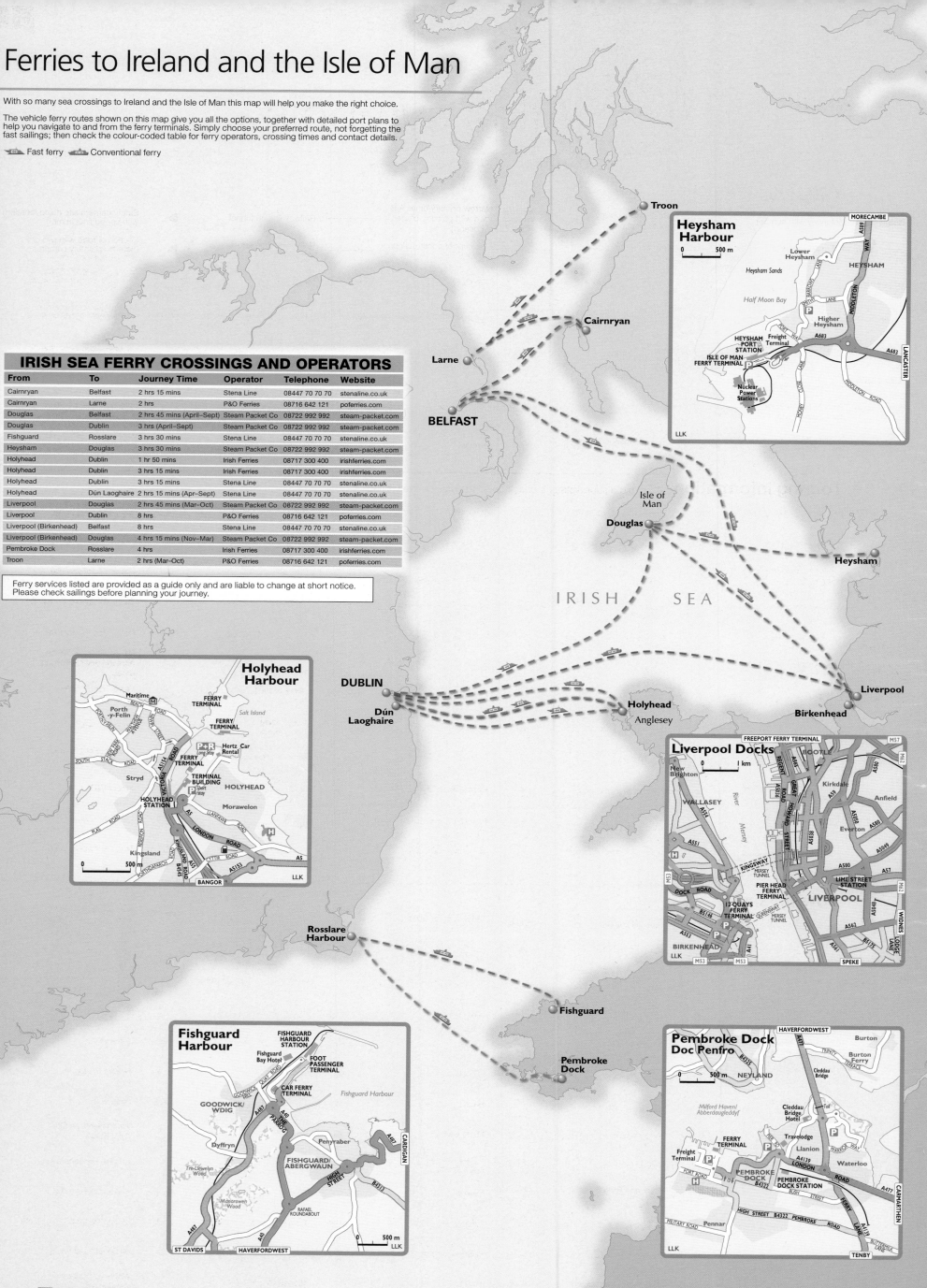

IRISH SEA FERRY CROSSINGS AND OPERATORS

From	To	Journey Time	Operator	Telephone	Website
Cairnryan	Belfast	2 hrs 15 mins	Stena Line	08447 70 70 70	stenaline.co.uk
Cairnryan	Larne	2 hrs	P&O Ferries	08716 642 121	poferries.com
Douglas	Belfast	2 hrs 45 mins (April–Sept)	Steam Packet Co	08722 992 992	steam-packet.com
Douglas	Dublin	3 hrs (April–Sept)	Steam Packet Co	08722 992 992	steam-packet.com
Fishguard	Rosslare	3 hrs 30 mins	Stena Line	08447 70 70 70	stenaline.co.uk
Heysham	Douglas	3 hrs 30 mins	Steam Packet Co	08722 992 992	steam-packet.com
Holyhead	Dublin	1 hr 50 mins	Irish Ferries	08717 300 400	irishferries.com
Holyhead	Dublin	3 hrs 15 mins	Irish Ferries	08717 300 400	irishferries.com
Holyhead	Dublin	3 hrs 15 mins	Stena Line	08447 70 70 70	stenaline.co.uk
Holyhead	Dún Laoghaire	2 hrs 15 mins (Apr–Sept)	Stena Line	08447 70 70 70	stenaline.co.uk
Liverpool	Douglas	2 hrs 45 mins (Mar–Oct)	Steam Packet Co	08722 992 992	steam-packet.com
Liverpool	Dublin	8 hrs	P&O Ferries	08716 642 121	poferries.com
Liverpool (Birkenhead)	Belfast	8 hrs	Stena Line	08447 70 70 70	stenaline.co.uk
Liverpool (Birkenhead)	Douglas	4 hrs 15 mins (Nov–Mar)	Steam Packet Co	08722 992 992	steam-packet.com
Pembroke Dock	Rosslare	4 hrs	Irish Ferries	08717 300 400	irishferries.com
Troon	Larne	2 hrs (Mar–Oct)	P&O Ferries	08716 642 121	poferries.com

Ferry services listed are provided as a guide only and are liable to change at short notice.
Please check sailings before planning your journey.

Atlas symbols

Motoring information

M4	Motorway with number	3	Restricted primary route junctions
Toll T4	Toll motorway with toll station	S	Primary route service area
6	Motorway junction with and without number	BATH	Primary route destination
5	Restricted motorway junctions	A1123	Other A road single/dual carriageway
Fleet S	Motorway service area	B2070	B road single/dual carriageway
	Motorway and junction under construction		Minor road more than 4 metres wide, less than 4 metres wide
A3	Primary route single/dual carriageway		Roundabout
1	Primary route junction with and without number		Interchange/junction

	Narrow primary/other A/B road with passing places (Scotland)		Railway line, in tunnel
	Road under construction/approved	X	Railway station and level crossing
	Road tunnel	+++	Tourist railway
Toll	Road toll, steep gradient (arrows point downhill)		City, town, village or other built-up area
5	Distance in miles between symbols	✈ H	Airport, heliport
or V	Vehicle ferry	H	24-hour Accident & Emergency hospital
	Fast vehicle ferry or catamaran	C	Crematorium
F	International freight terminal		Sandy beach

30	Safety camera site (fixed location) with speed limit in mph
50	Section of road with two or more fixed safety cameras, with speed limit in mph
40 40	Average speed (SPECS™) camera system with speed limit in mph
V	Fixed safety camera site with variable speed limit
P•R	Park and Ride (at least 6 days per week)
628 ▲	637 Lecht Summit — Height in metres, mountain pass
	National boundary
	County, administrative boundary

Touring information
To avoid disappointment, check opening times before visiting

	Scenic Route		Museum or art gallery		Aquarium
i	Tourist Information Centre		Industrial interest	RSPB	RSPB site
i	Tourist Information Centre (seasonal)		Aqueduct or viaduct		National Nature Reserve (England, Scotland, Wales)
V	Visitor or heritage centre	✳	Garden		Wildlife Trust reserve
⚲	Picnic site		Arboretum		Local nature reserve
	Caravan site (AA inspected)		Vineyard		Forest drive
▲	Camping site (AA inspected)		Country park		National trail
▲	Caravan & camping site (AA inspected)		Agricultural showground	☀	Viewpoint
	Abbey, cathedral or priory		Theme park		Hill-fort
	Ruined abbey, cathedral or priory		Farm or animal centre		Roman antiquity
✗	Castle		Zoological or wildlife collection		Prehistoric monument
	Historic house or building		Bird collection	✗ 1066	Battle site with year

	Steam railway centre		National Trust for Scotland property
	Cave		English Heritage site
⚔	Windmill, monument		Historic Scotland site
⚑	Golf course (AA listed)		Cadw (Welsh heritage) site
	County cricket ground	★	Other place of interest
	Rugby Union national stadium		Boxed symbols indicate attractions within urban areas
	International athletics stadium	◉	World Heritage Site (UNESCO)
	Horse racing, show jumping		National Park
	Motor-racing circuit		National Scenic Area (Scotland)
	Air show venue		Forest Park
	Ski slope (natural, artificial)		Heritage coast
	National Trust property		Major shopping centre

Town plans

2	Motorway and junction		Railway station		Toilet, with facilities for the less able
	Primary road single/dual carriageway		Tramway		Building of interest
	A road single/dual carriageway		London Underground station		Ruined building
	B road single/dual carriageway		London Overground station		City wall
	Local road single/dual carriageway		Rail interchange		Cliff lift
	Other road single/dual carriageway, minor road		Docklands Light Railway (DLR) station		Cliff escarpment
	One-way, gated/closed road	○	Light rapid transit system station		River/canal, lake
	Restricted access	✈ H	Airport, heliport		Lock, weir
	Pedestrian area	R	Railair terminal		Park/sports ground/open space
	Footpath	P+	Park and Ride (at least 6 days per week)		Cemetery
	Road under construction	P	Car park		Woodland
	Road tunnel		Bus/coach station		Built-up area
	Level crossing	H H	24-hour Accident & Emergency hospital, other hospital		Beach

i	Tourist Information Centre	†	Abbey, chapel, church
V	Visitor or heritage centre	✡	Synagogue
✉	Post Office	☾	Mosque
	Public library	⚑	Golf course
	Shopping centre		Racecourse
	Shopmobility		Nature reserve
	Theatre or performing arts centre		Aquarium
	Cinema	◉	World Heritage Site (UNESCO)
M	Museum		English Heritage site
✗	Castle		Historic Scotland site
	Castle mound		Cadw (Welsh heritage) site
•	Monument, statue		National Trust site
	Viewpoint		National Trust for Scotland site

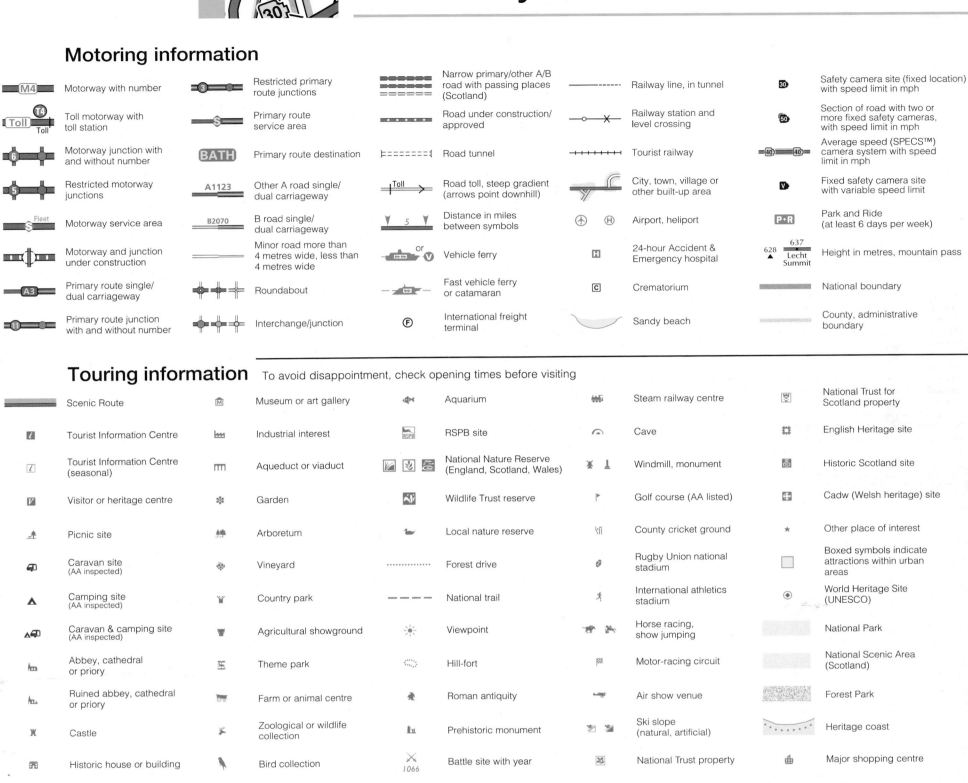

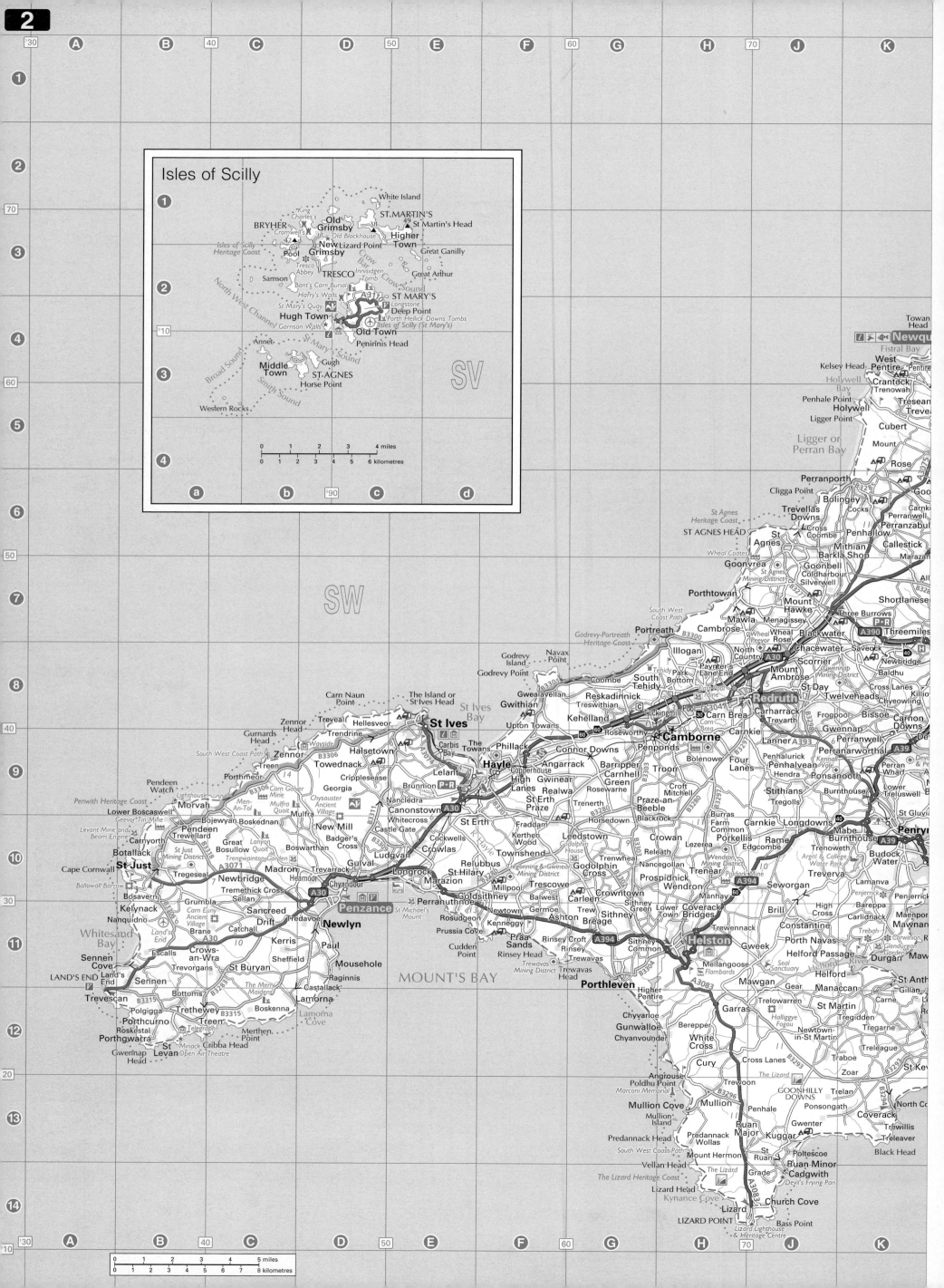

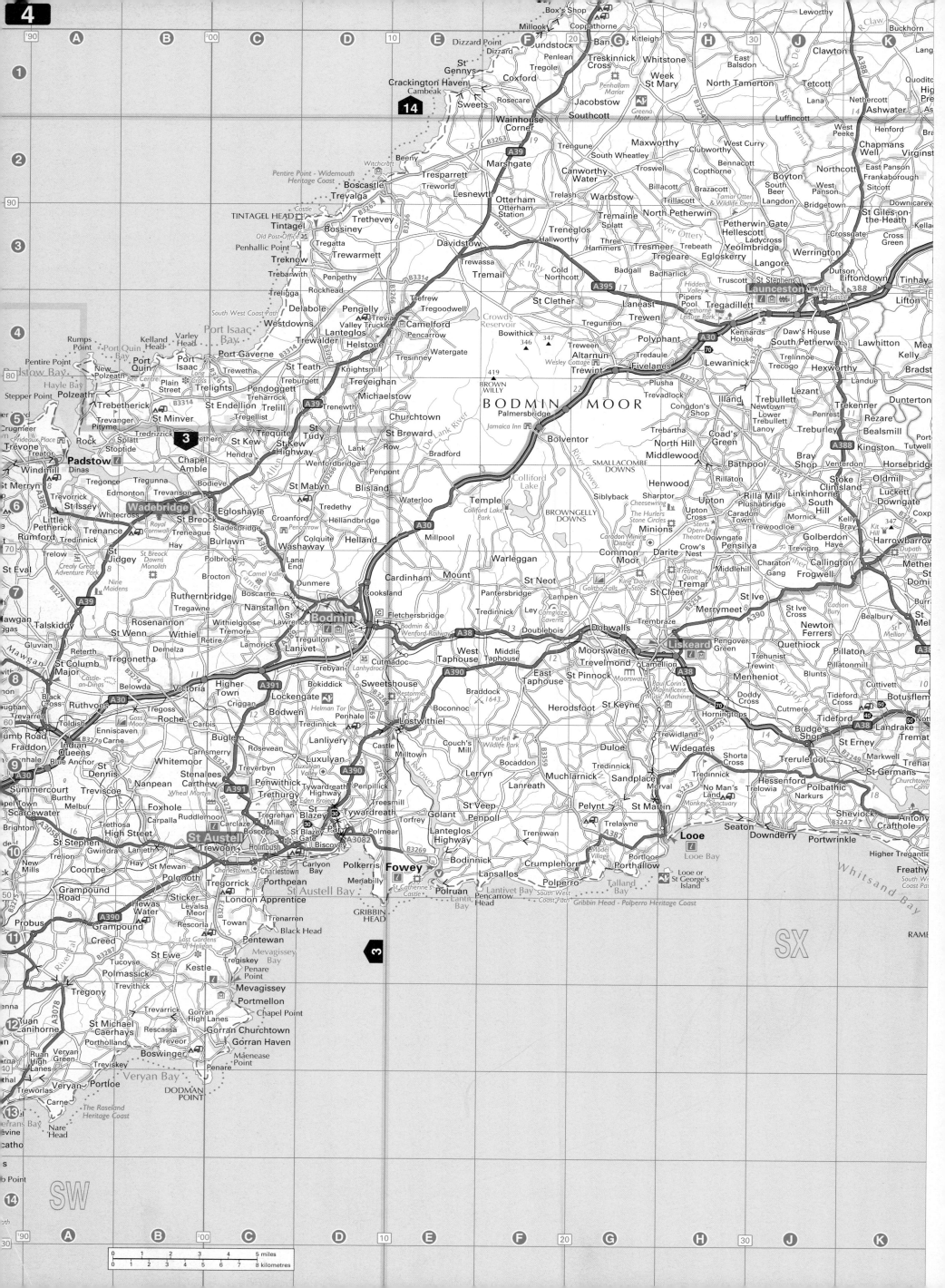

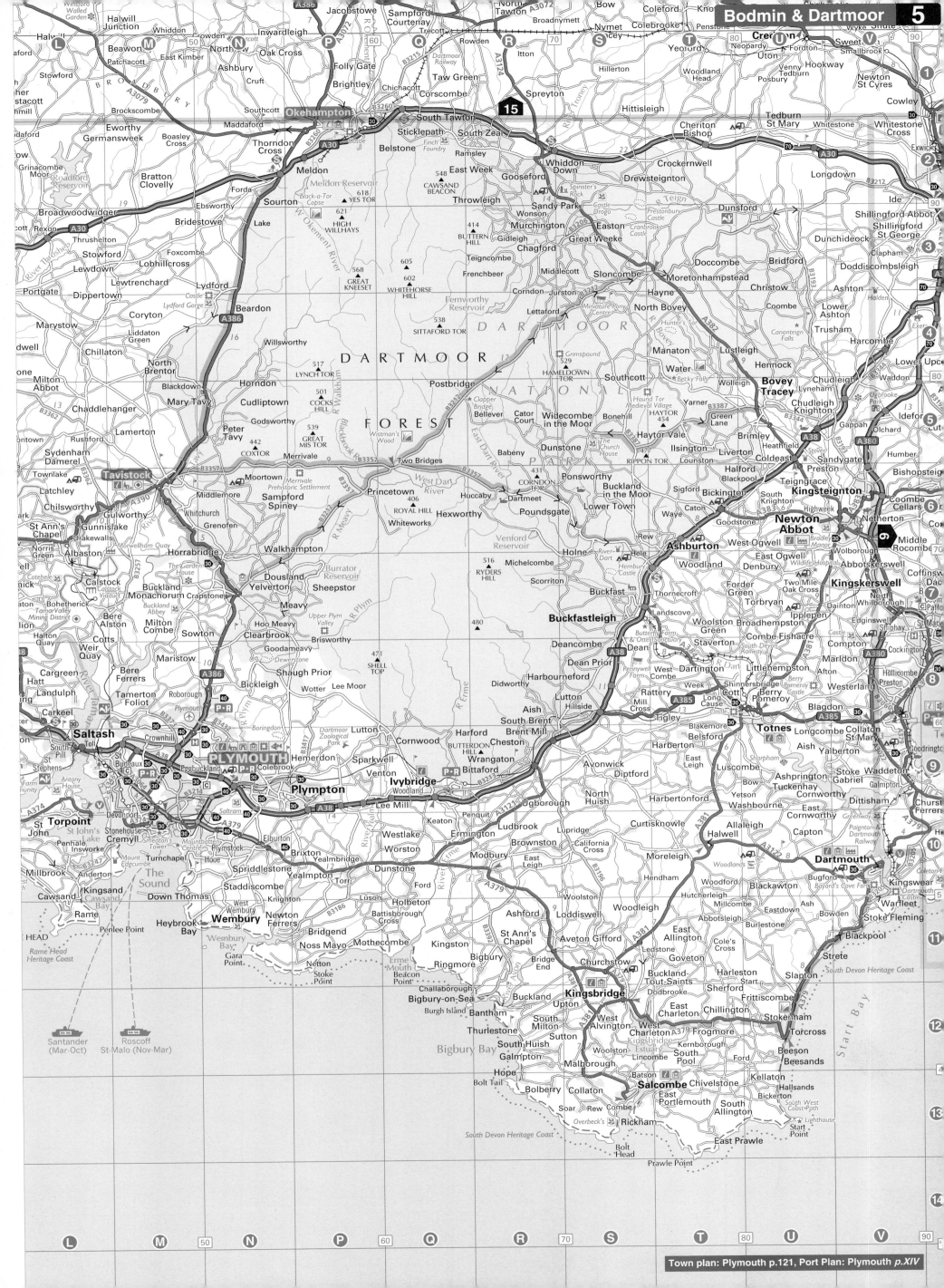

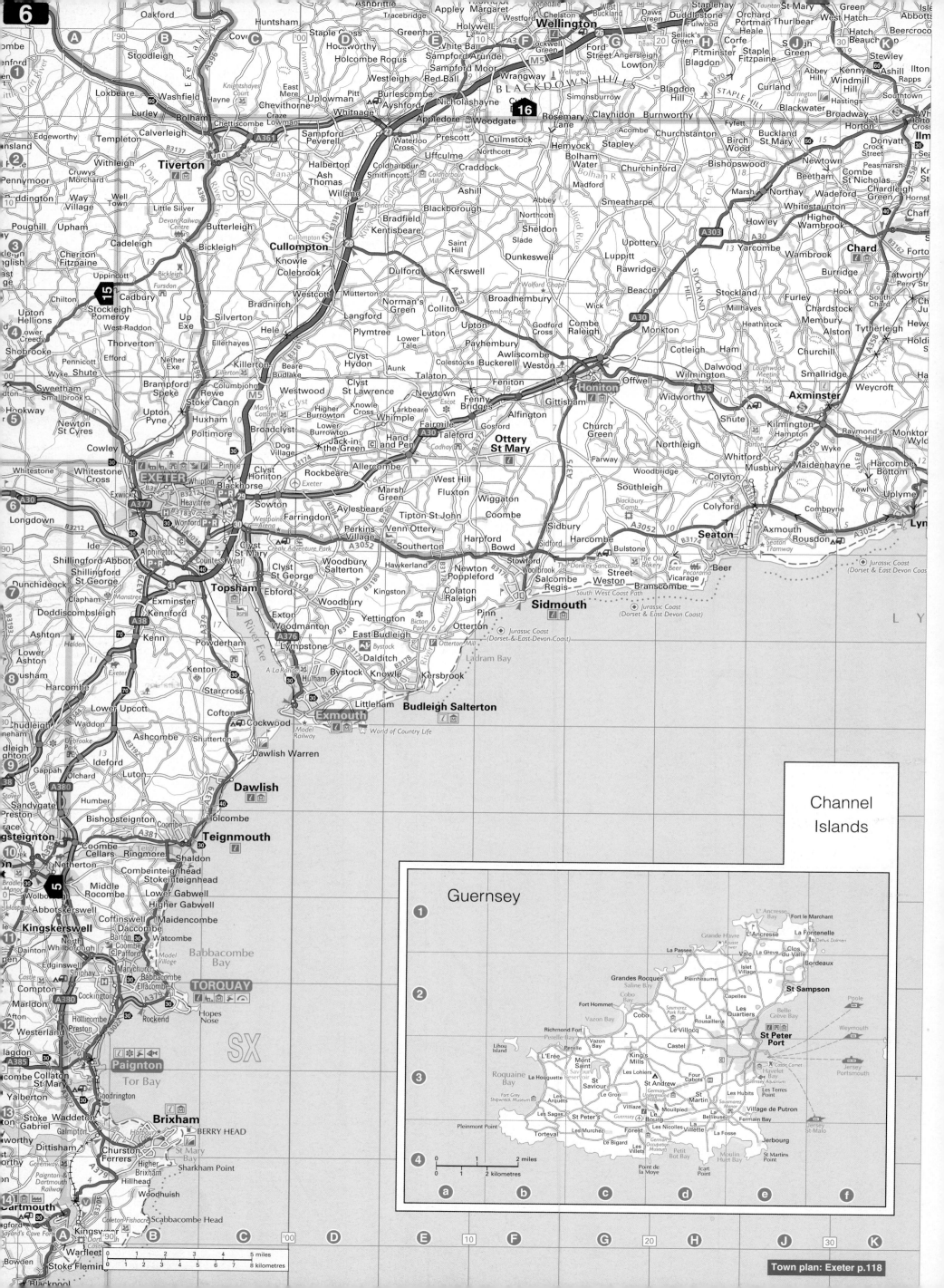

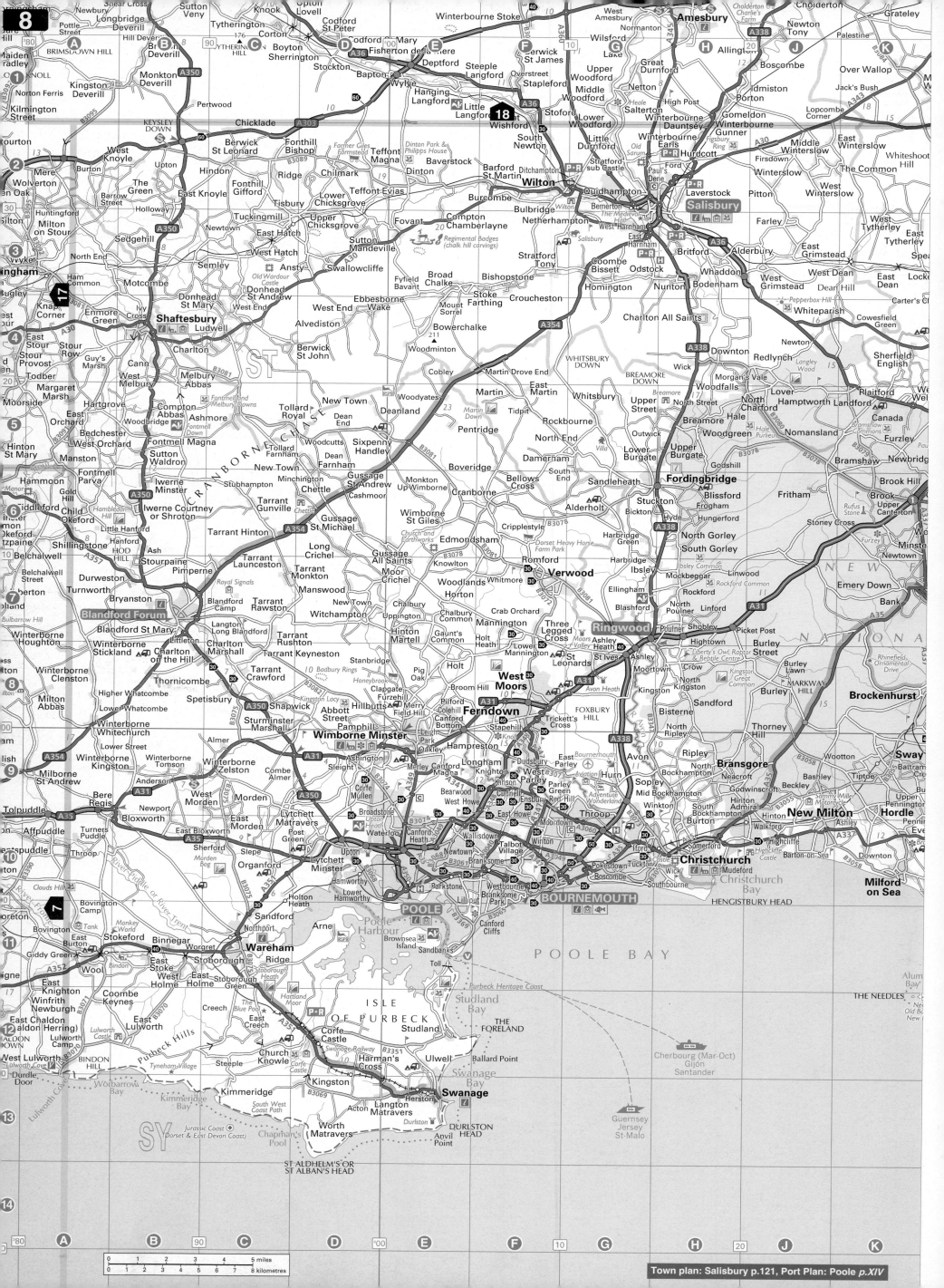

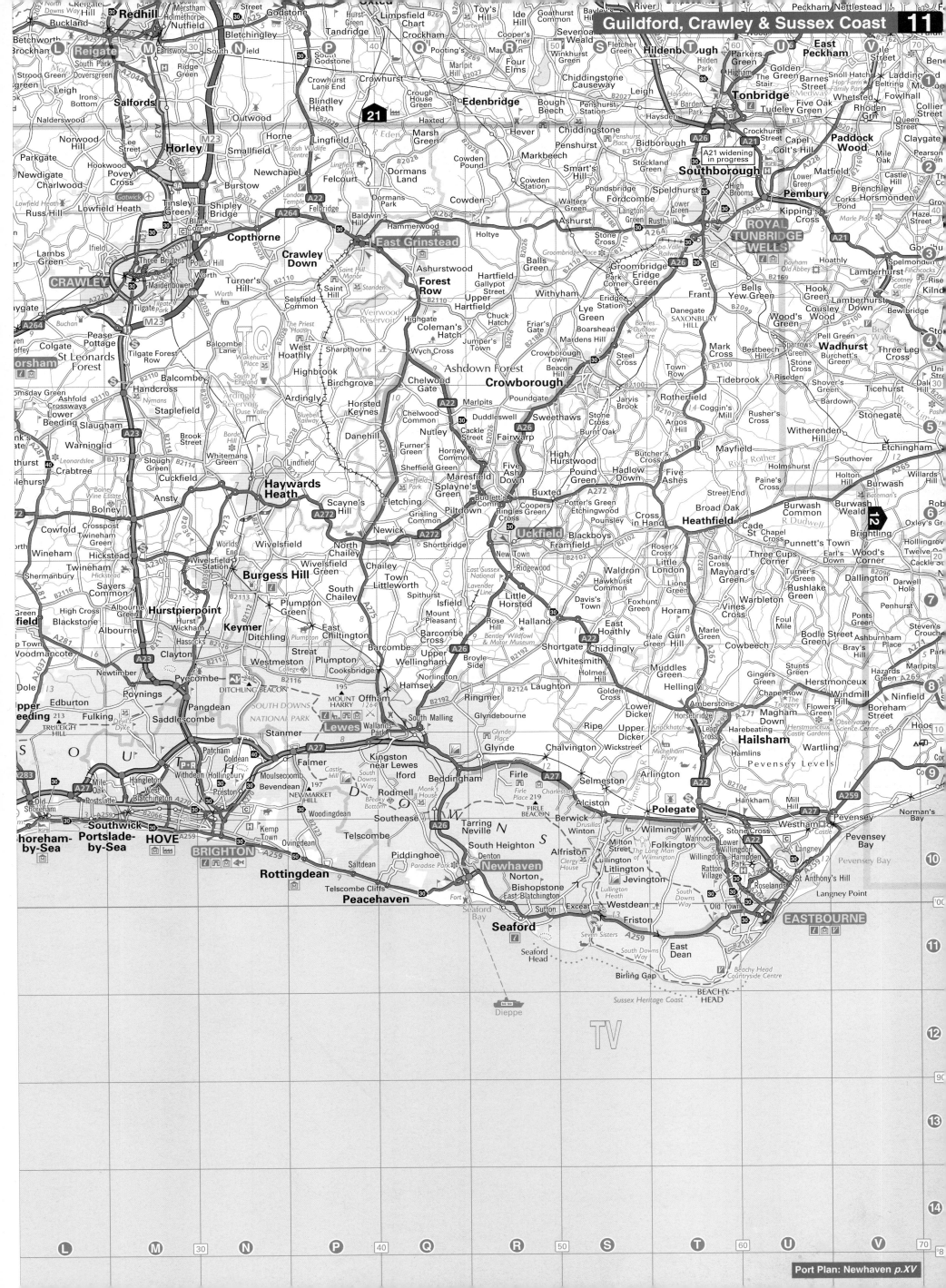

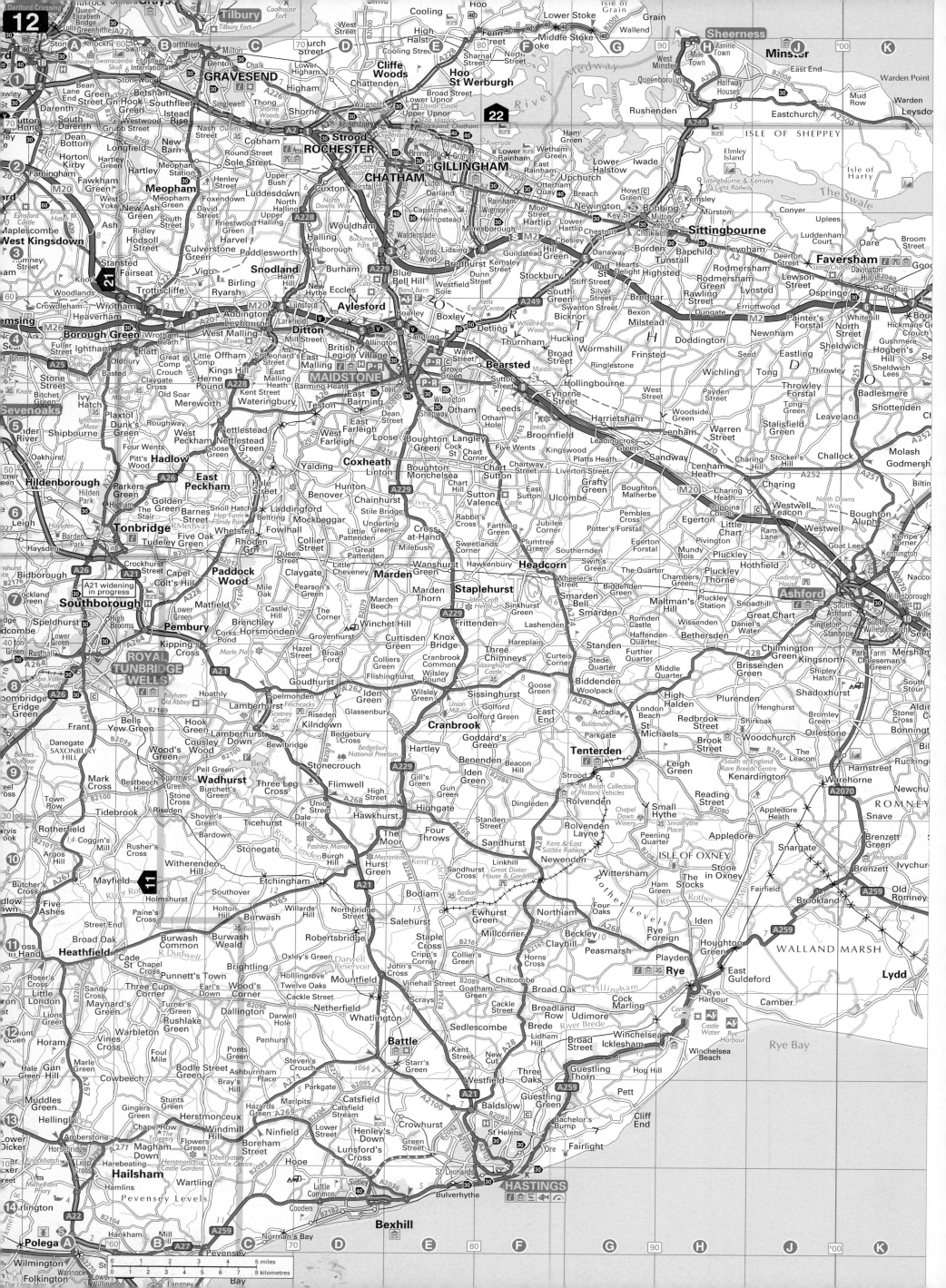

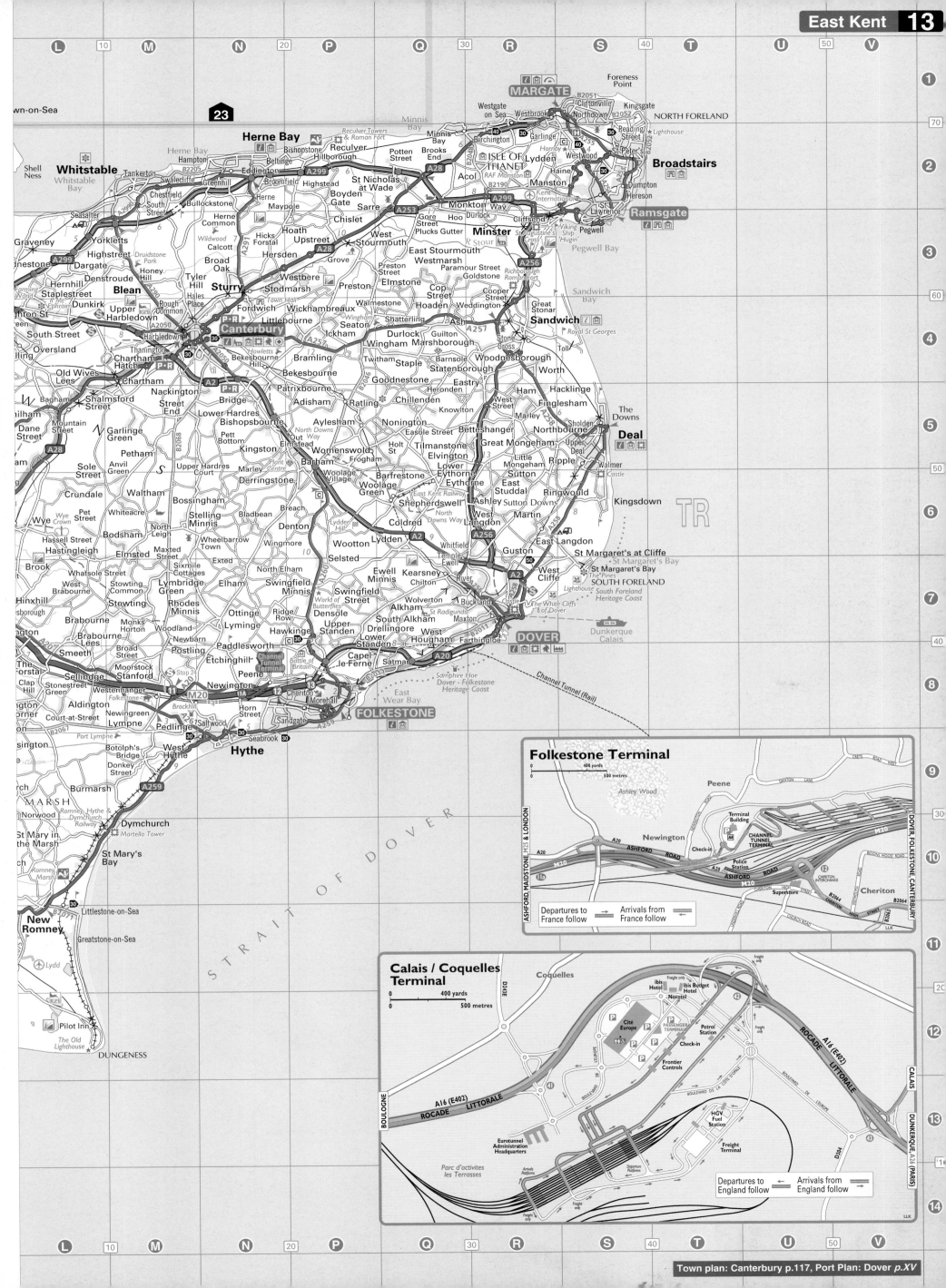

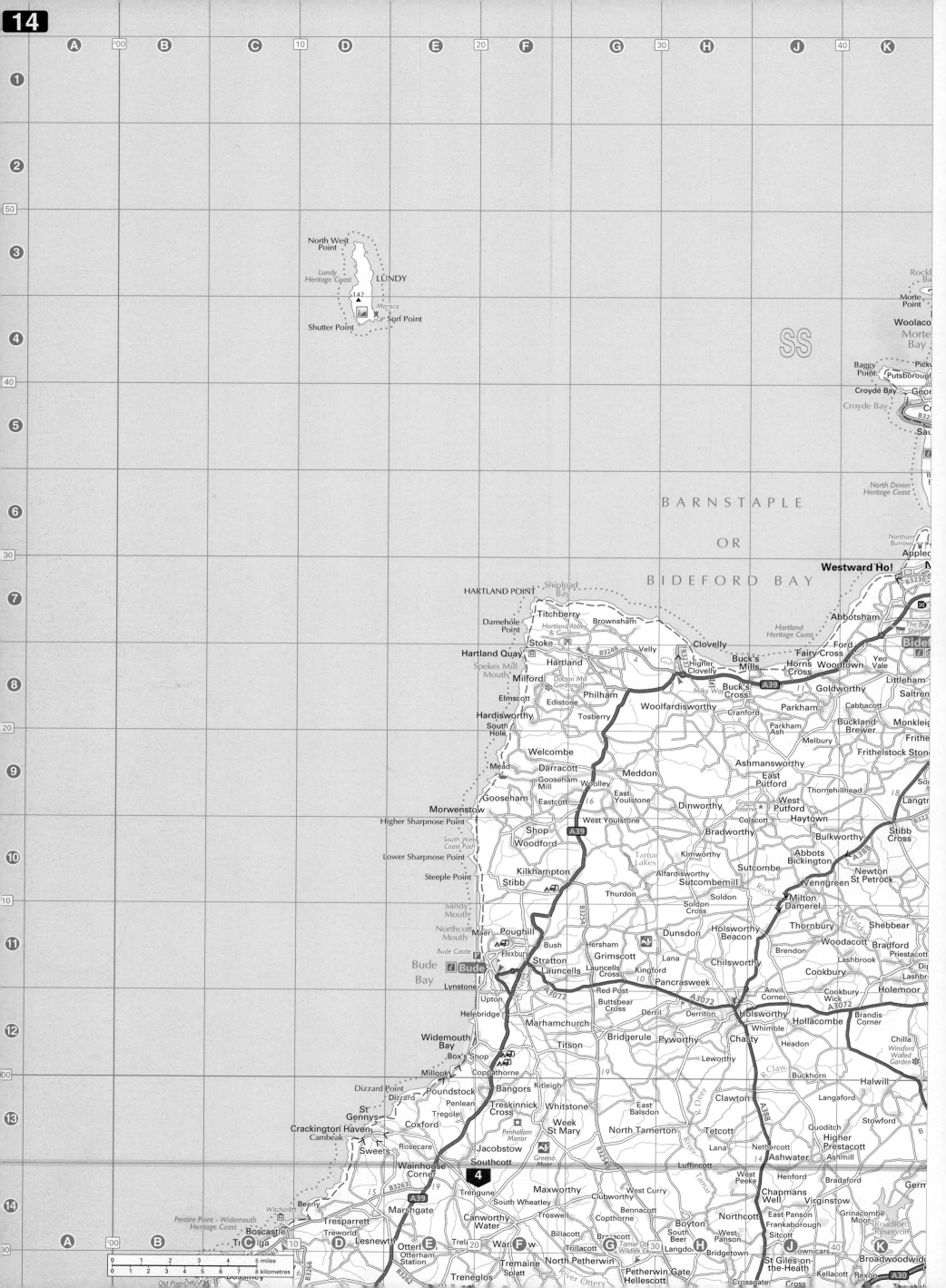

North West
Point

*Lundy
Heritage Coast* LUNDY

▲142 *Marisco*

Shutter Point Surf Point

SS

BARNSTAPLE

OR

BIDEFORD BAY

Rockl
Ba

Morte
Point

Woolaco
Morte
Bay

Baggy
Point Putsborough
Croydé Bay Geor
Croyde Bay Cr
Sau

*North Devon
Heritage Coast*

Northam
Burrows

Apple

Westward Ho! N

HARTLAND POINT *Shipload
Bay* B3236

Damehole
Point Titchberry Brownsham
Stoke *Hartland Abbey
& Gardens* Velly Clovelly *Hartland
Heritage Coast* Abbotsham The Big
Shee
Ford Bide
Hartland Quay B324B Buck's
Clovelly Fairy Cross
*Spekes Mill
Mouth* Hartland 4 Higher
Clovelly Buck's
Mills Horns Woodtown Yeo
Vale
Milford *Docton Mill
Gardens* A39 Buck's
Cross Goldworthy Littleham Saltren

Elmscott Edistone Philham Woolfardisworthy Cranford Parkham Cabbacott Monkleig
Tosberry Parkham
Ash Buckland
Brewer Frithe

Hardisworthy Melbury Frithelstock Ston
South
Hole Ashmansworthy Thornehillhead

Welcombe Meddon East
Putford West
Putford Langtr
B323
Mead Darracott Woolley *Gnome
Reserv* ★ Haytown Sou
Gooseham
Mill East
Youlstone Dinworthy 18
Eastcott 16

Morwenstow Gooseham West Youlstone Bradworthy Bulkworthy Stibb
Cross
Higher Sharpnose Point Colscott

*South West
Coast Path* Shop
Woodford A39 Kimworthy Sutcombe Abbots
Bickington Newton
St Petrock
Lower Sharpnose Point *Tamar
Lakes* Alfardisworthy Sutcombemill A388

Steeple Point Kilkhampton Venngreen Milton
Damerel
Stibb Thurdon Soldon River Shebbear
*Sandy
Mouth* ▲ Soldon
Cross Thornbury Woodacott Bradford
*Northcott
Mouth* Maer Poughill Dunsdon Holsworthy
Beacon Brendon Lashbrook Priestacott
Bush Hersham Lana Chilsworthy Dip
Flexbury Grimscott Cookbury Lashb
Bude Castle Stratton Anvil
Corner Cookbury
Wick Holemoor
Bude Launcells Launcells
Cross Kingford Pancrasweek A3072
Bay Lynstone Red Post Holsworthy
Upton Buttsbear
Cross Derril Derriton Whimble Hollacombe Brandis
Corner
Helebridge A3072 Chilla
Marhamchurch Bridgerule Pyworthy Chasty Headon *Winsford
Walled
Garden*
Widemouth
Bay Titson Leworthy Buckhorn Halwill
Box's Shop R Claw 19
Millook Coppathorne Clawton Langaford
Dizzard Point Bangors Kitleigh East
Balsdon A388
Dizzard Poundstock Whitstone North Tamerton Tetcott Quoditch Stowford
St
Gennys Penlean Treskinnick
Cross Nethercott Higher
Prestacott
Crackington Haven Coxford Tregole *Penhallam
Manor* Week
St Mary Lana Ashwater Ashmill
Cambeak Rosecare Jacobstow *Greena
Moor* 14 Luffincott Henford Bradaford Germ
Sweets Southcott B3254 West
Peeke Chapmans
Well Virginstow
Wainhouse
Corner Maxworthy West Curry Clubworthy Boyton Northcott East Panson
Beeny 15 A39 Trengune South Wheatley Troswell Copthorne Bennacott South
Beer Frankaborough Grinacombe
Moor
Witchcroft Marshgate Canworthy
Water Bracott West
Panson Sitcott Roadford
Reservoir
*Pentire Point - Widemouth
Heritage Coast* Billacott Trillacott Langdon Bridgetown Cross
Tresparrett Treworld Tremaine Otterl Trel War w *Tamar Ot
Wildlife* Petherwin
Gate St Giles-on-
the-Heath nicare
Boscastle Tr lga Lesnewth Otterham
Station North Petherwin Hellescott Langdon Kellacott Rexon A30
Broadwoodwi

Old Post Office B3263 Splatt B3266 Tremaine River Ottery Crossgate
Treneglos

4

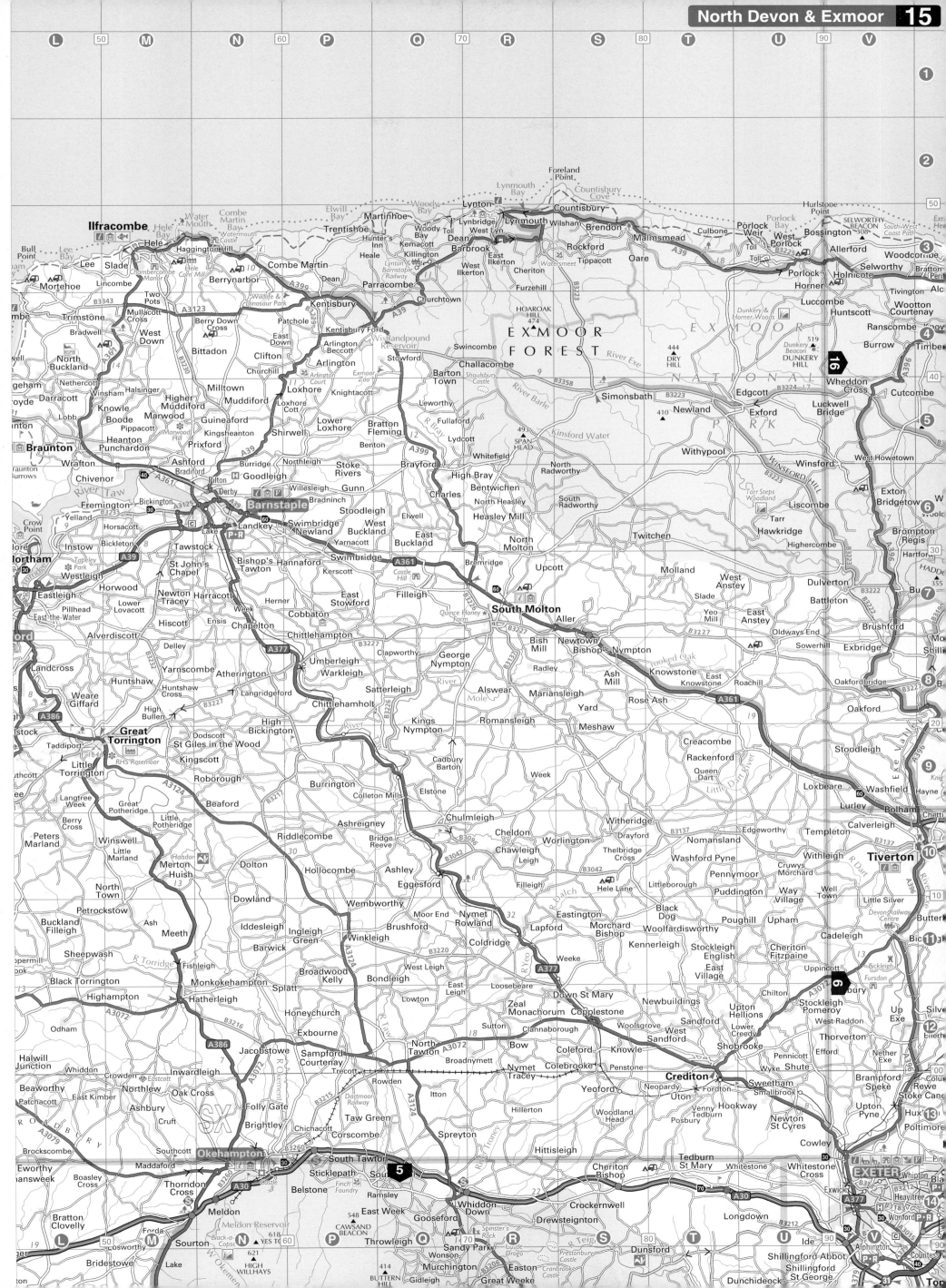

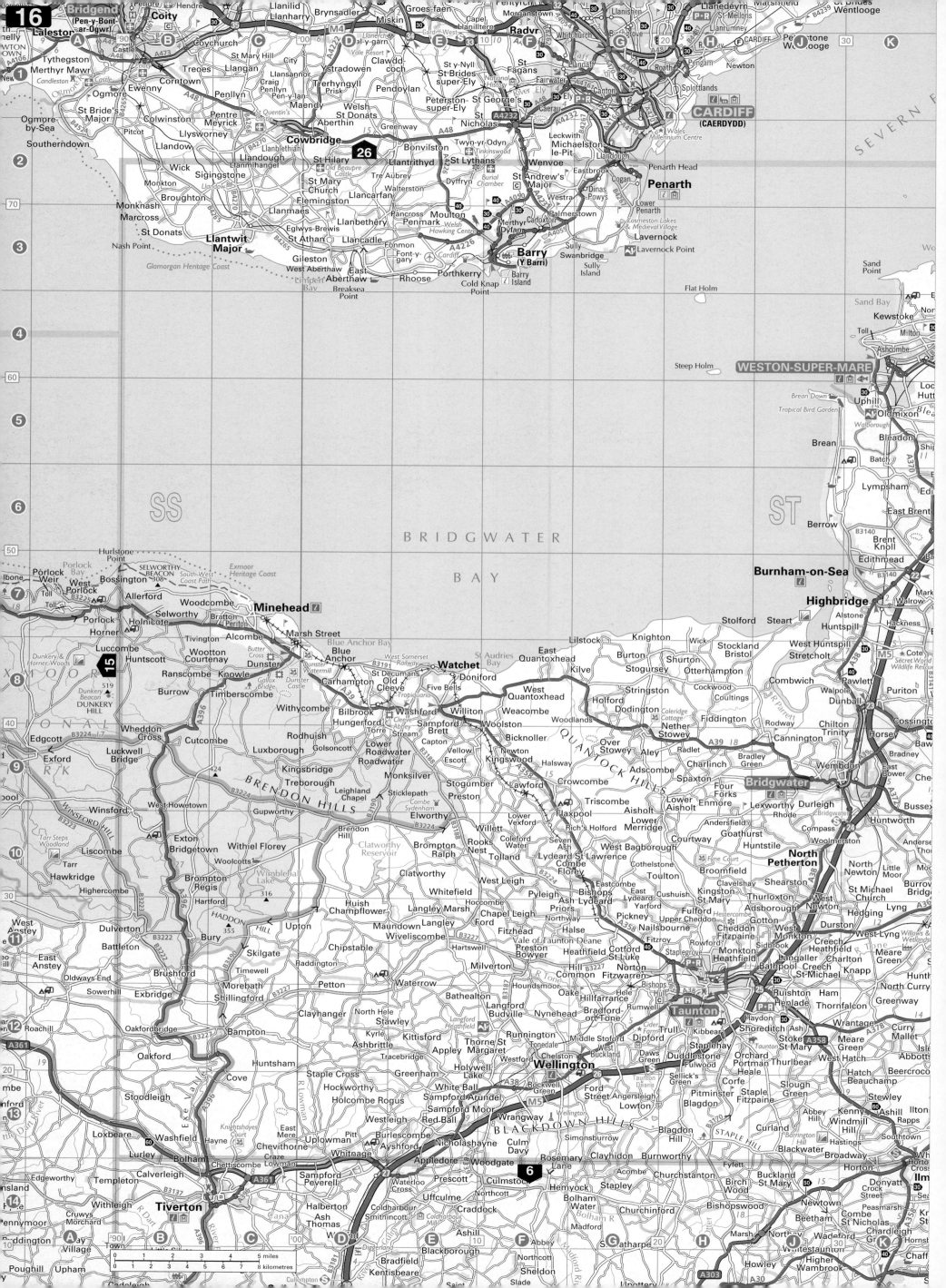

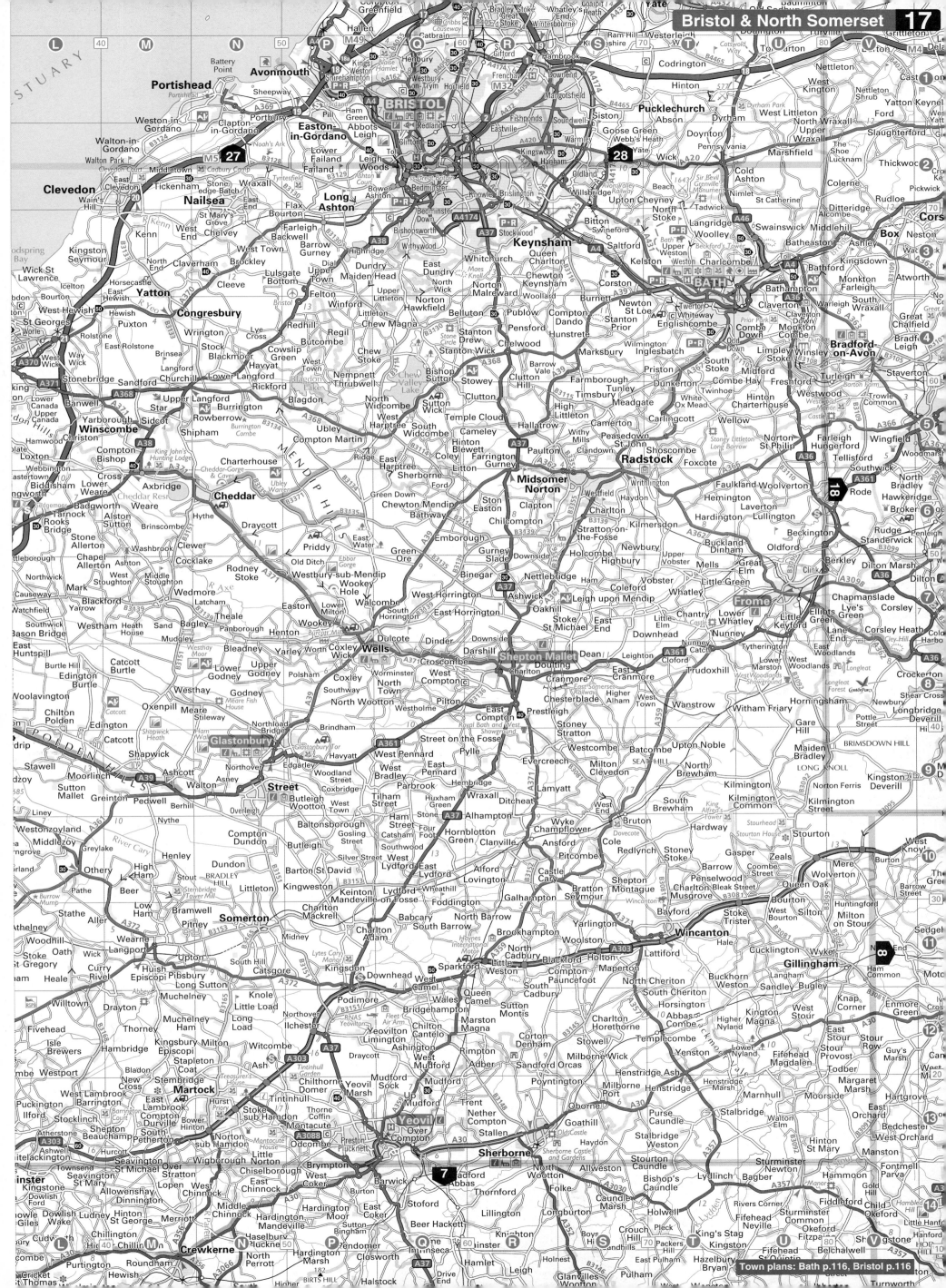

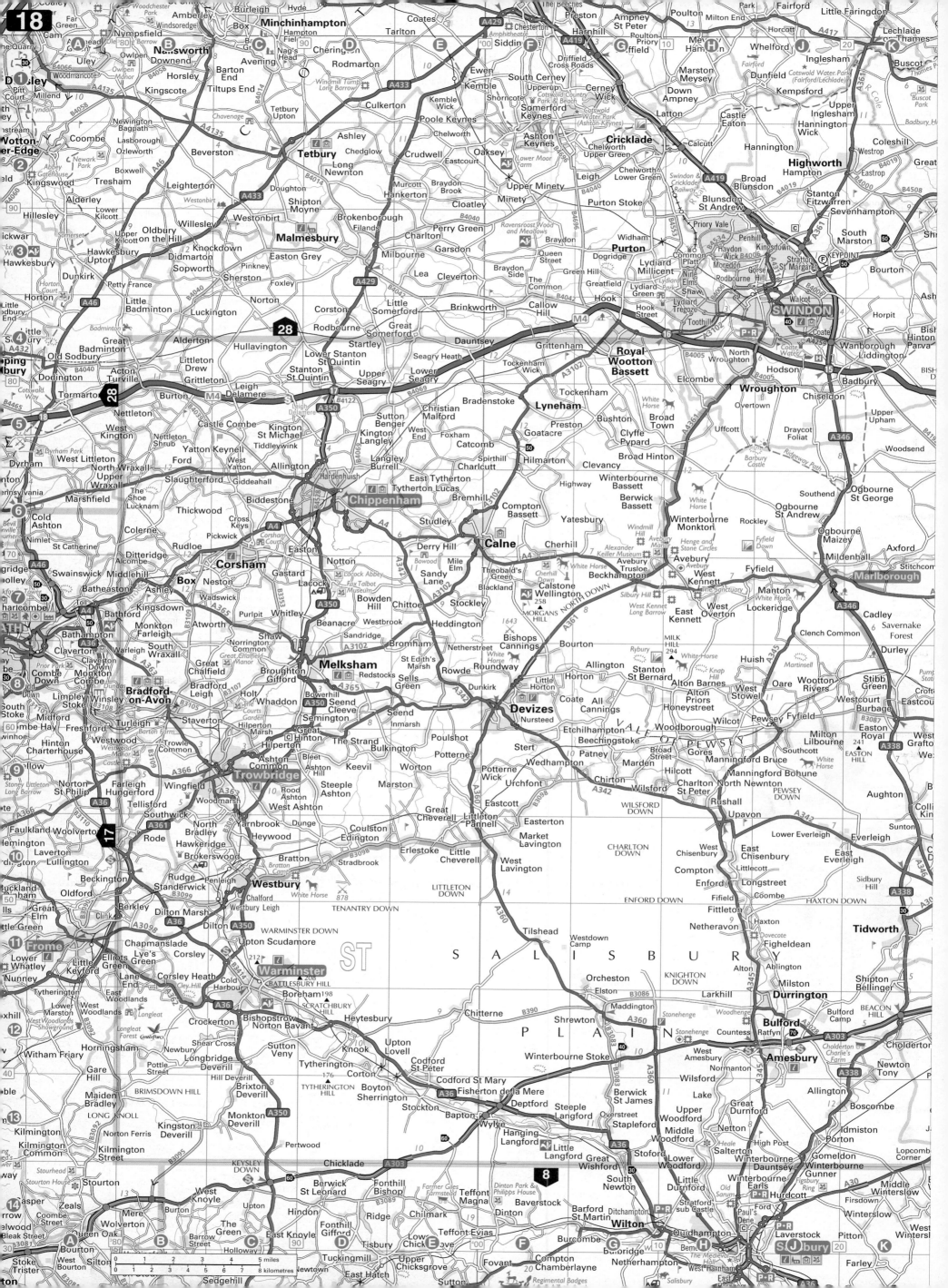

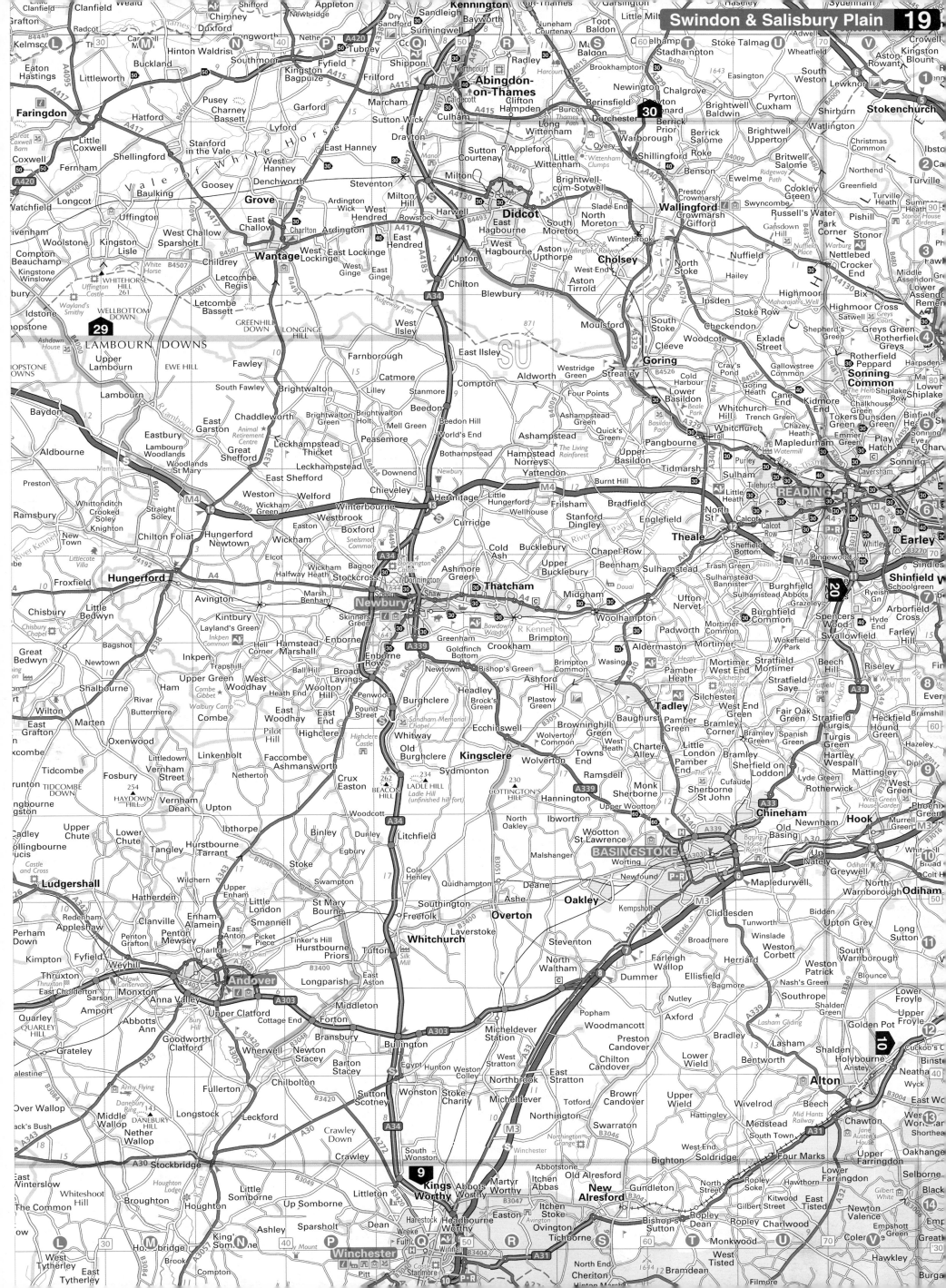

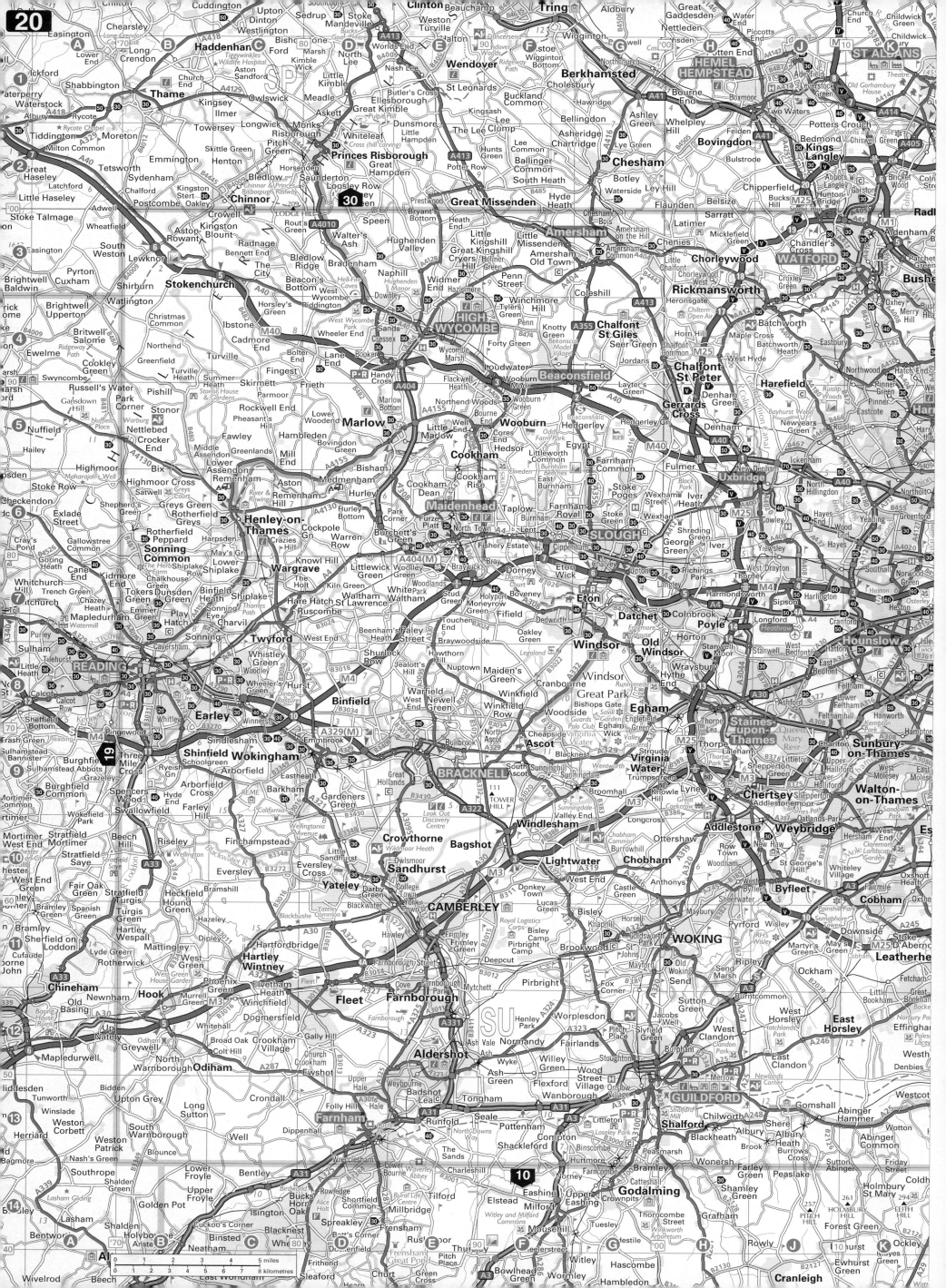

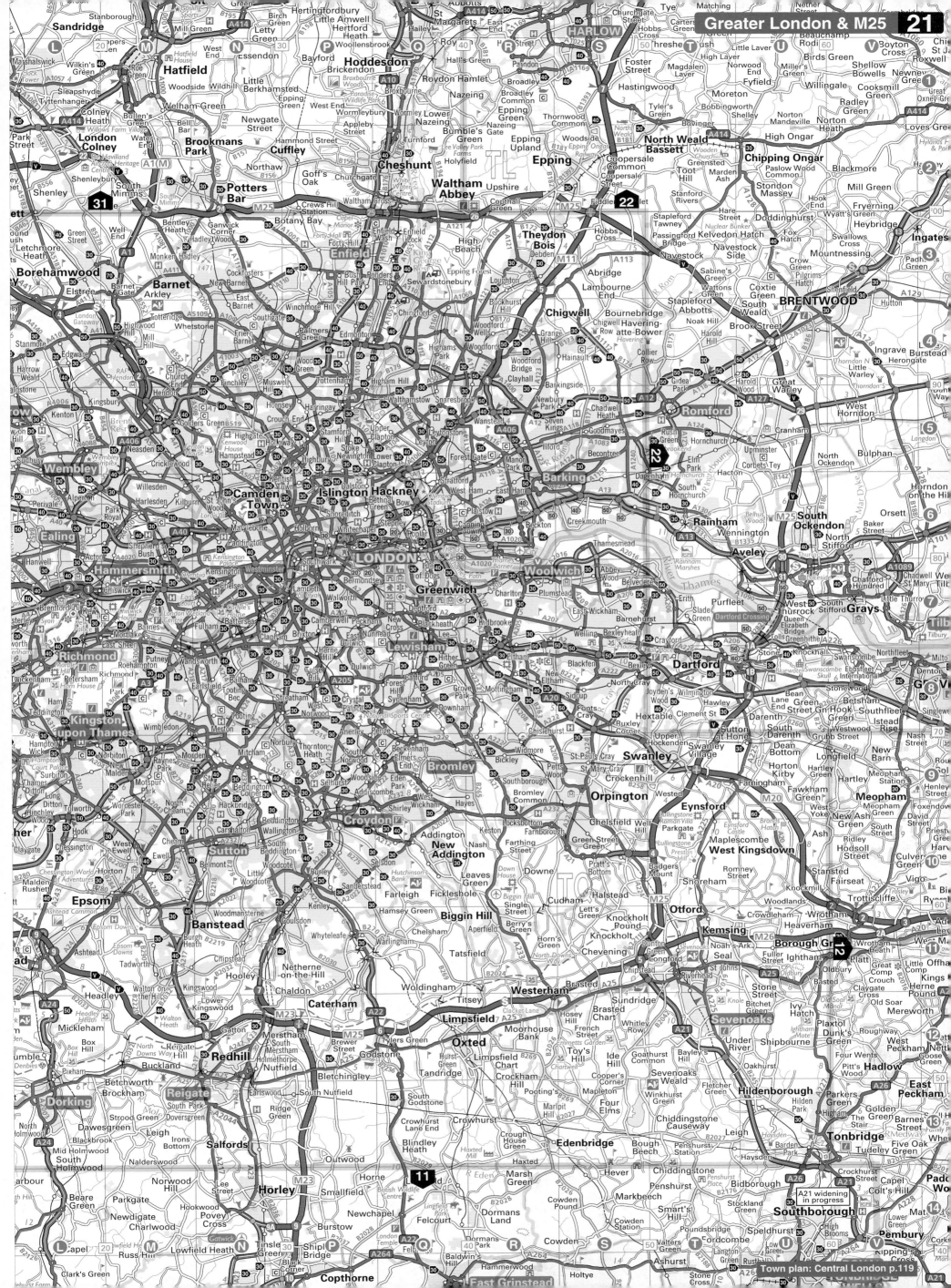

Harwich International Port

0 400 m

PASSENGER & CRUISE TERMINAL
HARWICH INTERNATIONAL STATION
CAR FERRY TERMINAL
CONTAINER TERMINAL
Parkeston
Harwich Industrial Estate
Superstore
PARKESTON ROUNDABOUT
ST NICHOLAS ROUNDABOUT
Dovercourt
IPSWICH COLCHESTER
A120
Upper Dovercourt
HARWICH
A120
LLK

Southend-on-Sea

LONDON, BASILDON

0 200 m

HM Customs & Excise
Museum & Planetarium
SOUTHEND VICTORIA STATION
Surgery COLEMAN
All Saints
Superstore
The Victoria
QUEENSWAY
SOUTHCHURCH ROAD
Kingdom Hall
Sacred Heart Sch
Surgery
South Essex College
Porters Civic House
Porters Grange School
Travelodge
WARRIOR SQ NTH
WARRIOR SQUARE
Leisure Centre
University of Essex
South Essex College
SOUTHEND CENTRAL STATION
County Court
Uni of Essex
Salvation Army
The Royals
CHANCELLOR RD
QUEENSWAY
SOUTHCHURCH AVENUE
Naval, News & Military Club
Royal Hotel
St John's
Kursaal Entertainment Centre
Victoria Statue
Palace Hotel
WESTERN ESPLANADE
MARINE PARADE
EASTERN ESPLANADE
Adventure Island
Adventure Island
SeaLife Adventure
SHOEBURY
Pier
LLK

SOUTHEND-ON-SEA

ESTUARY

TQ

TR

TM

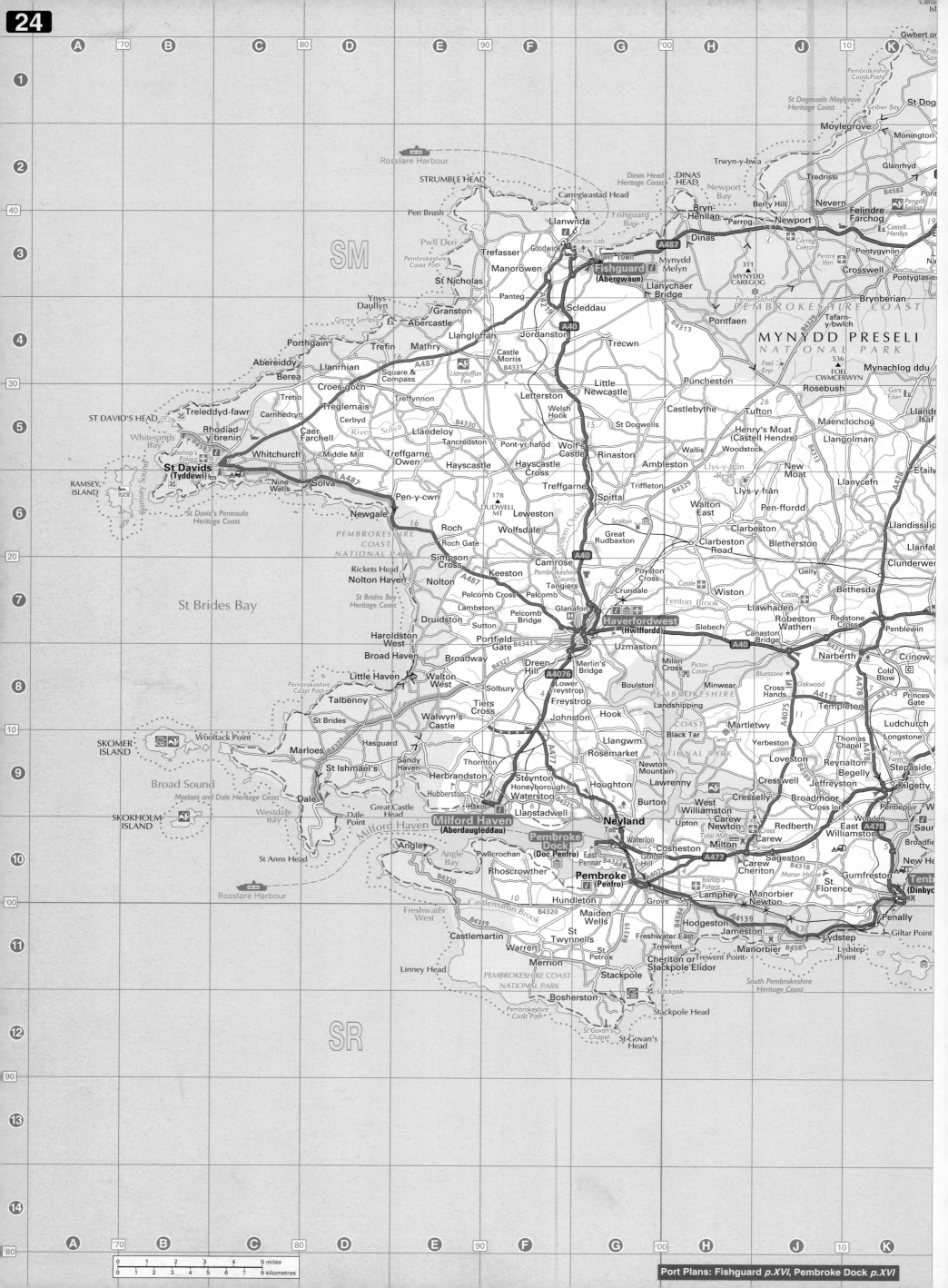

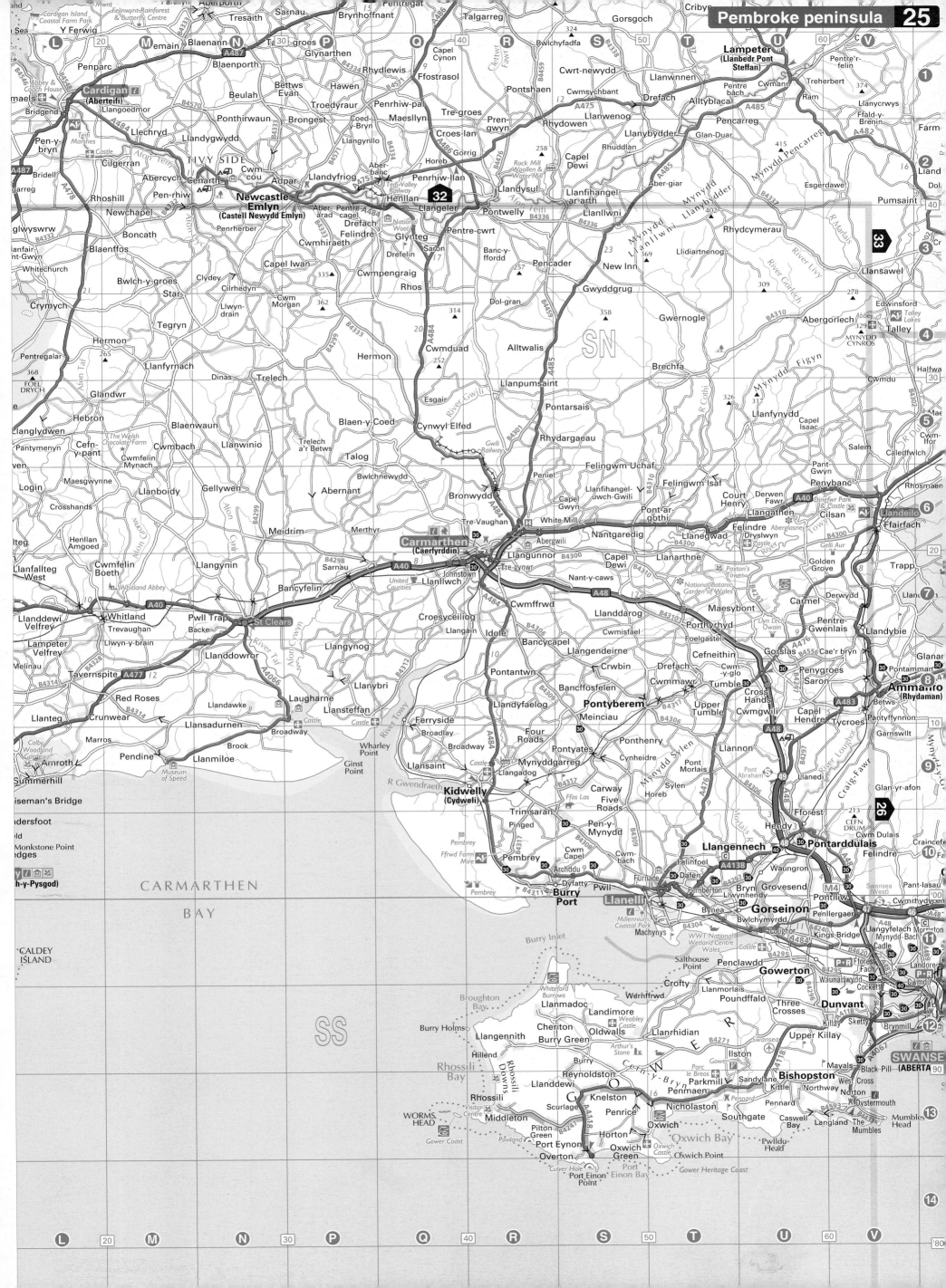

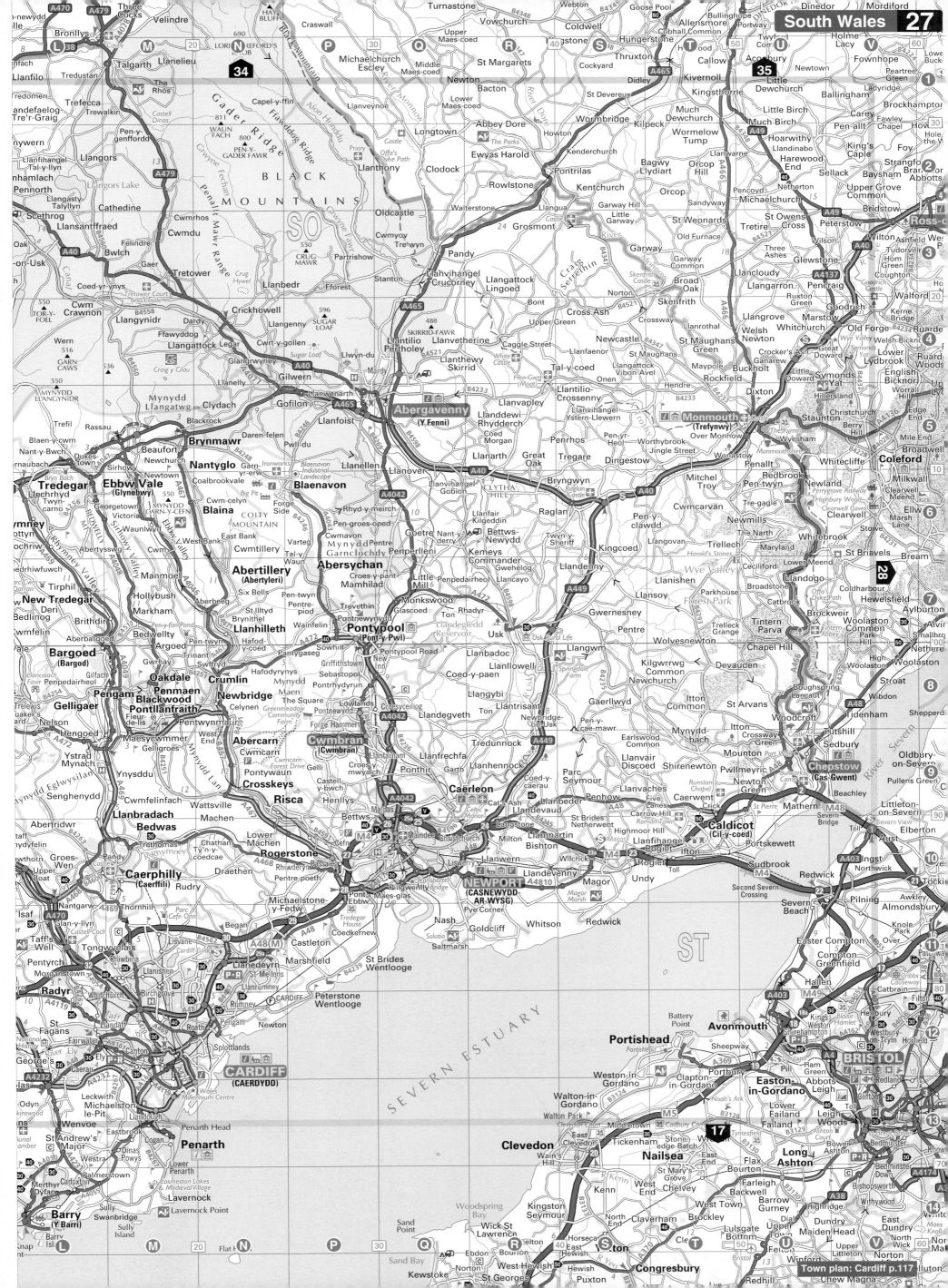

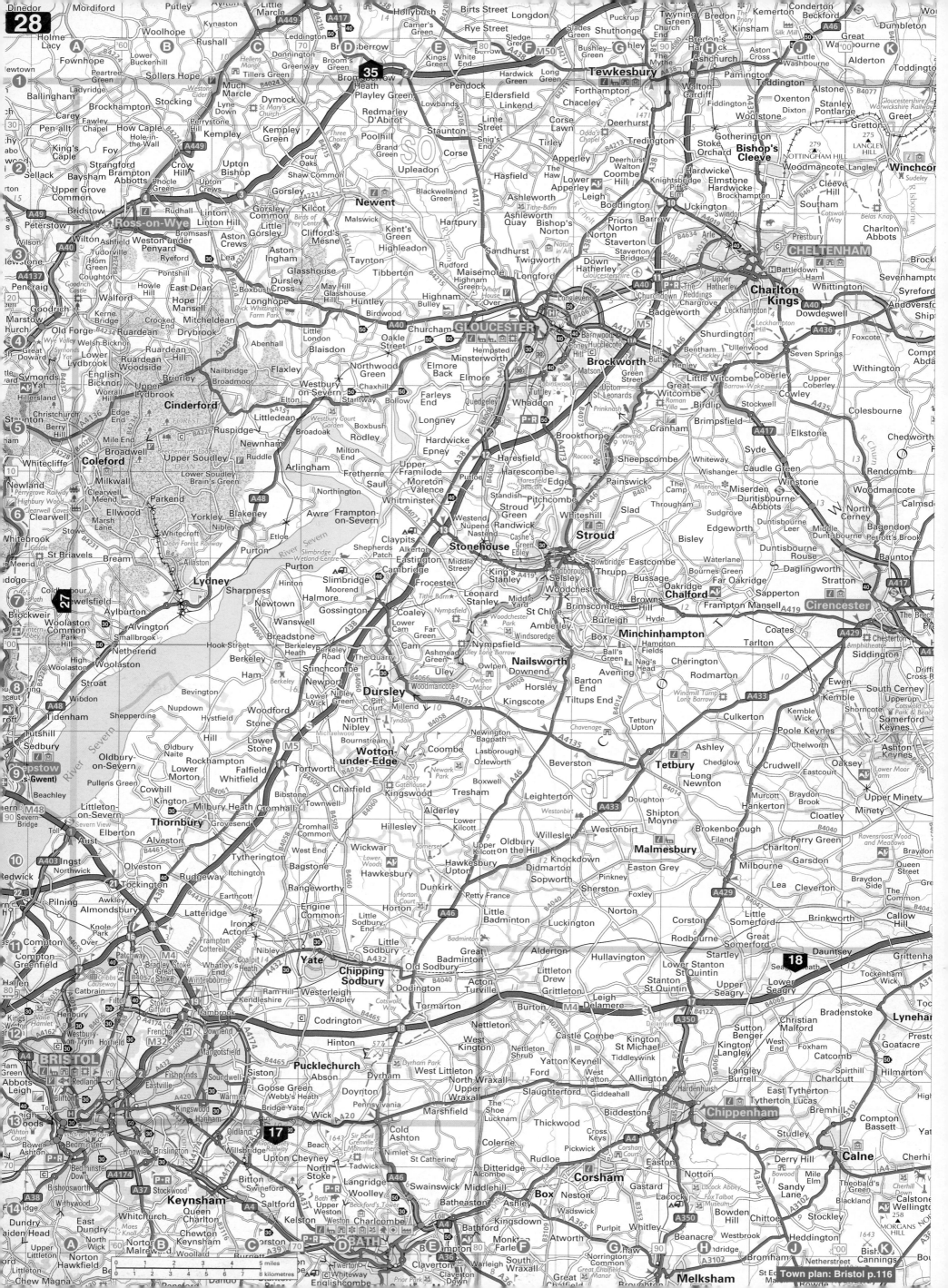

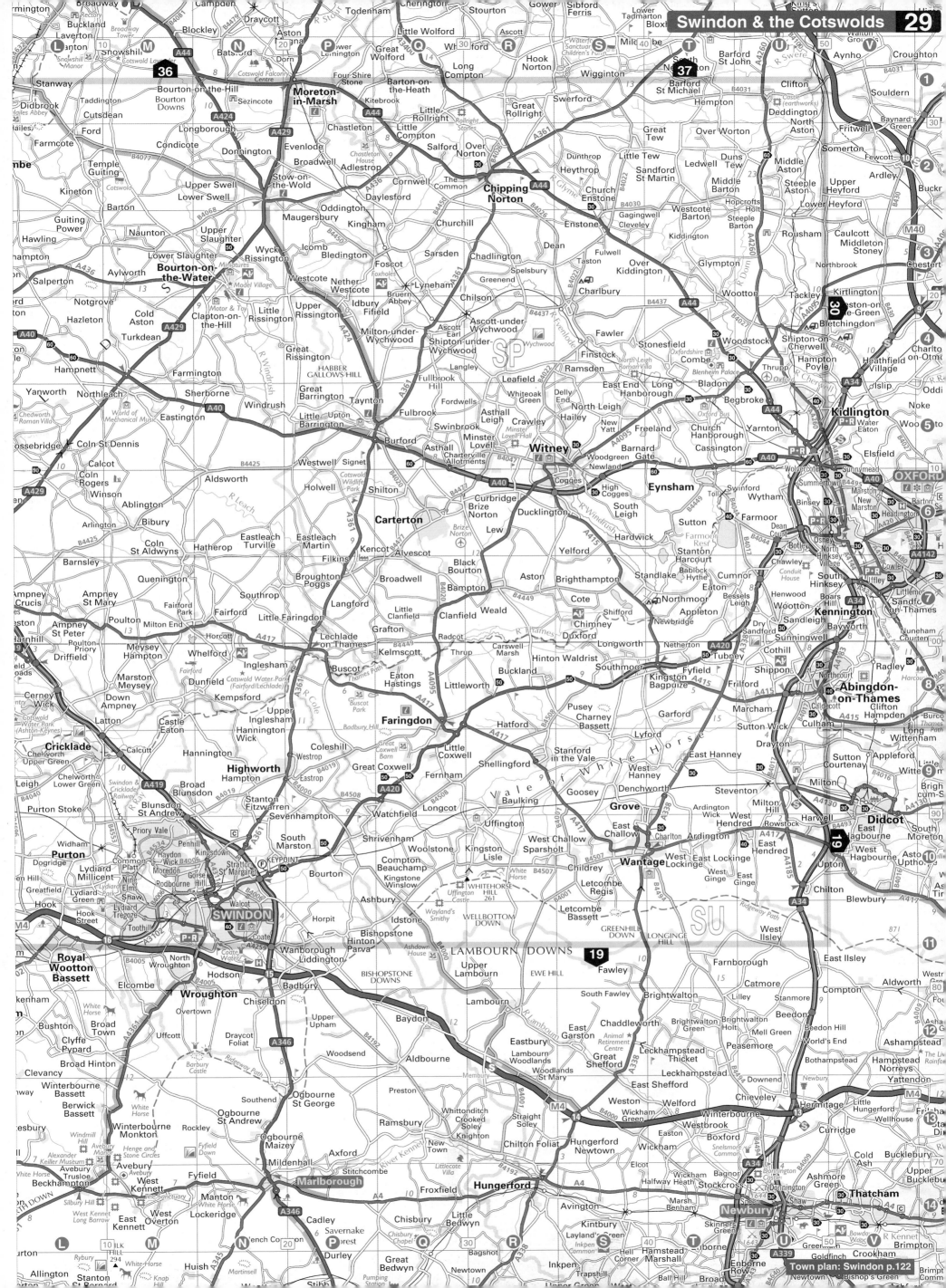

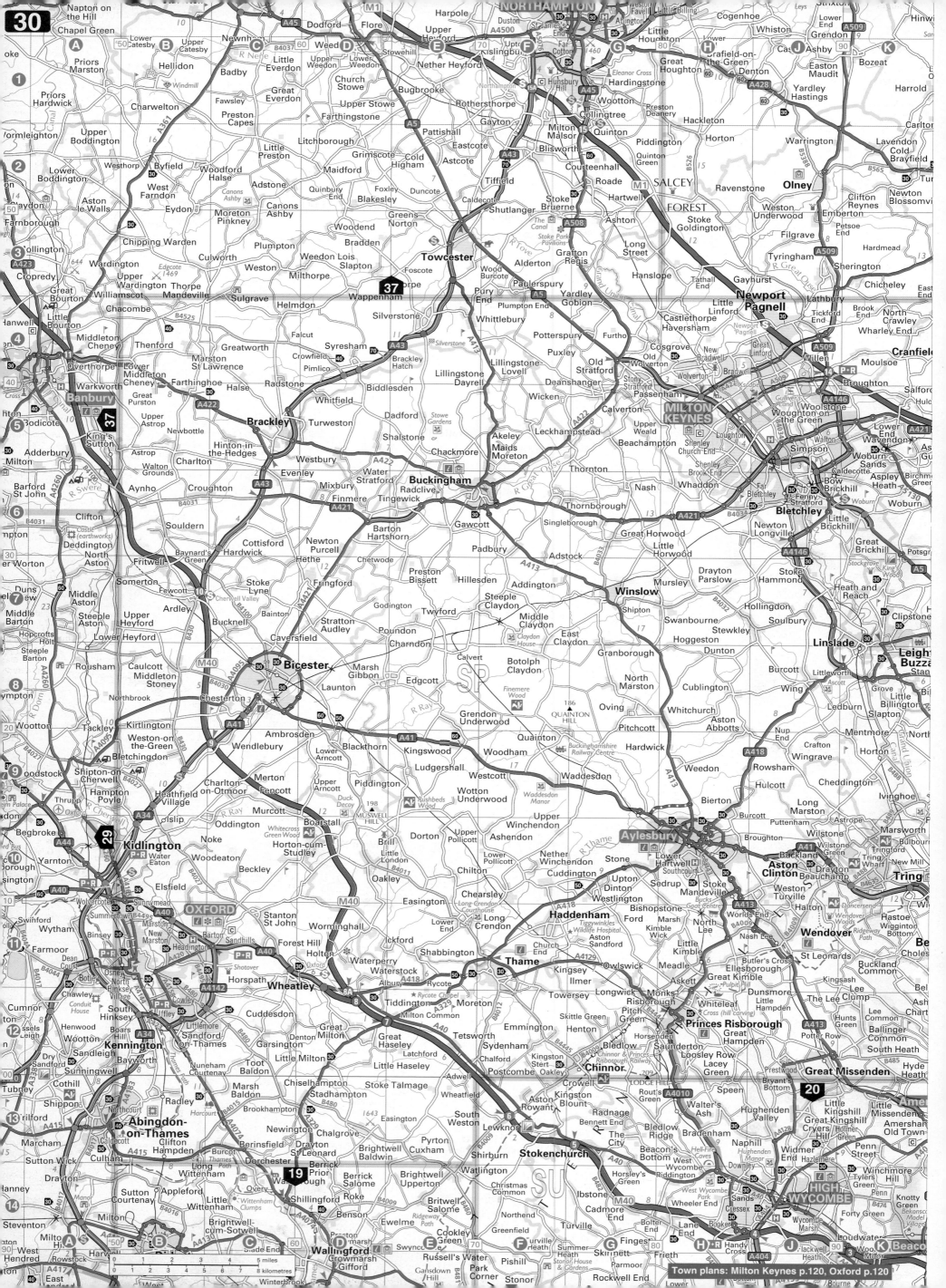

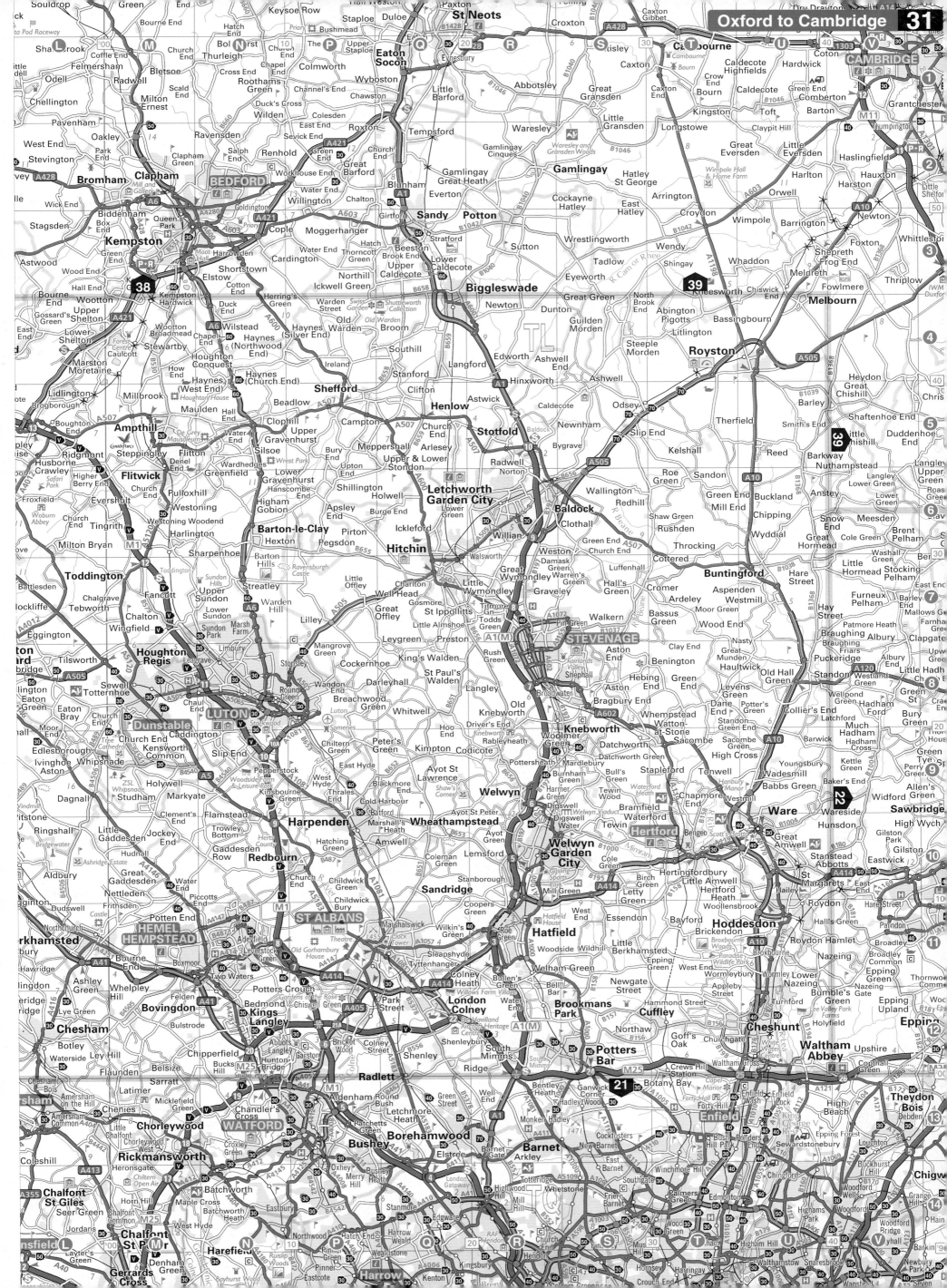

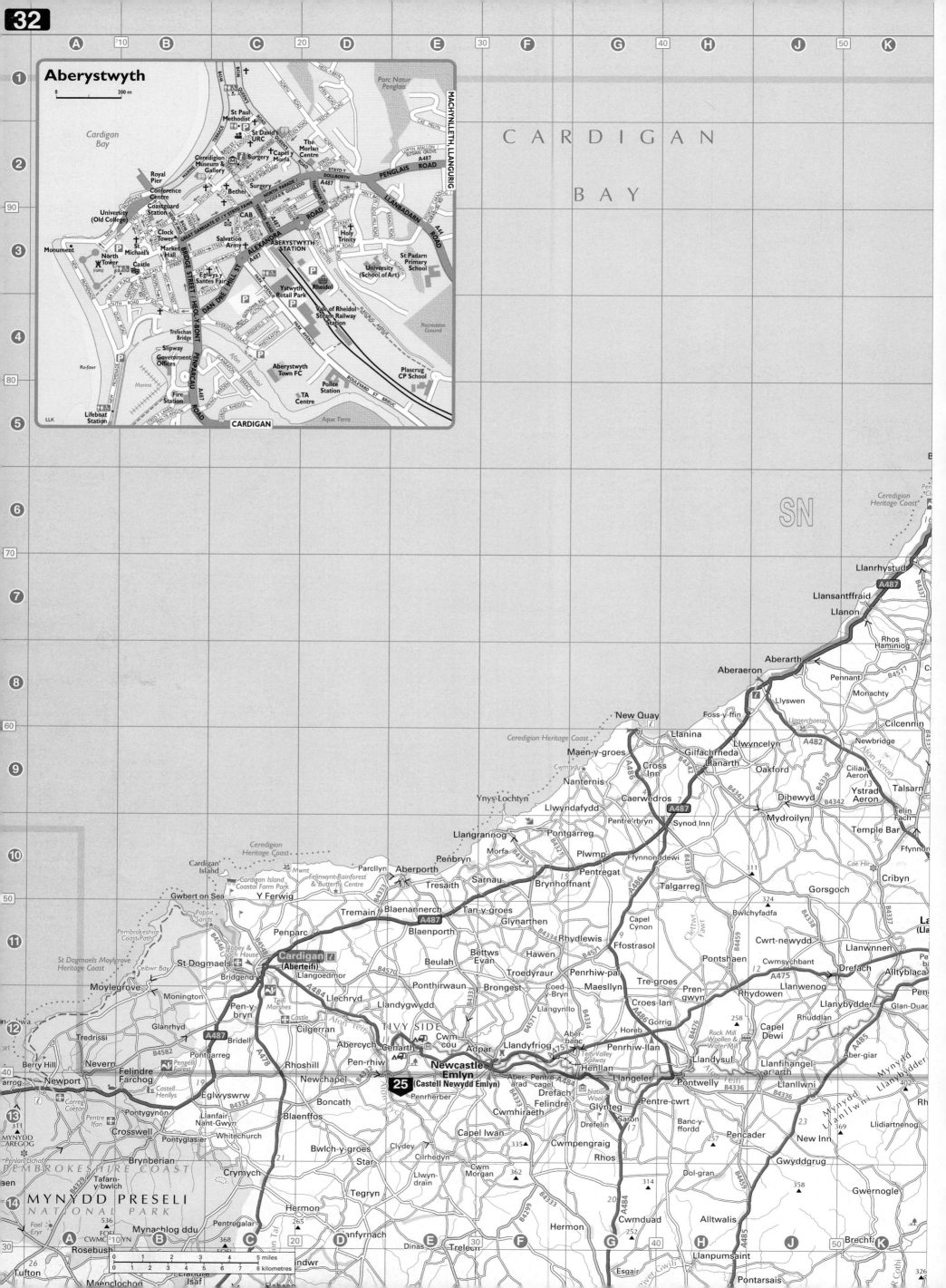

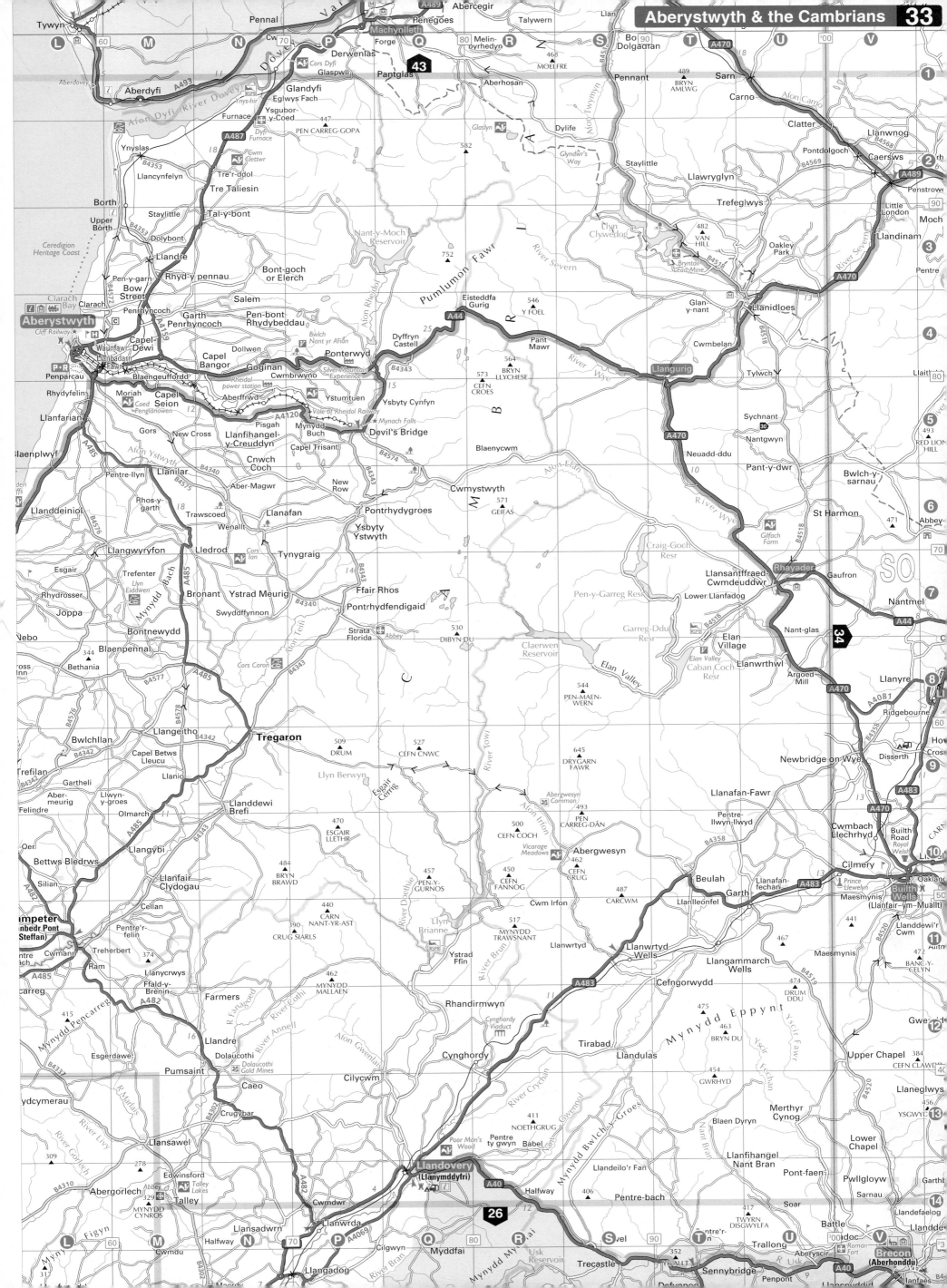

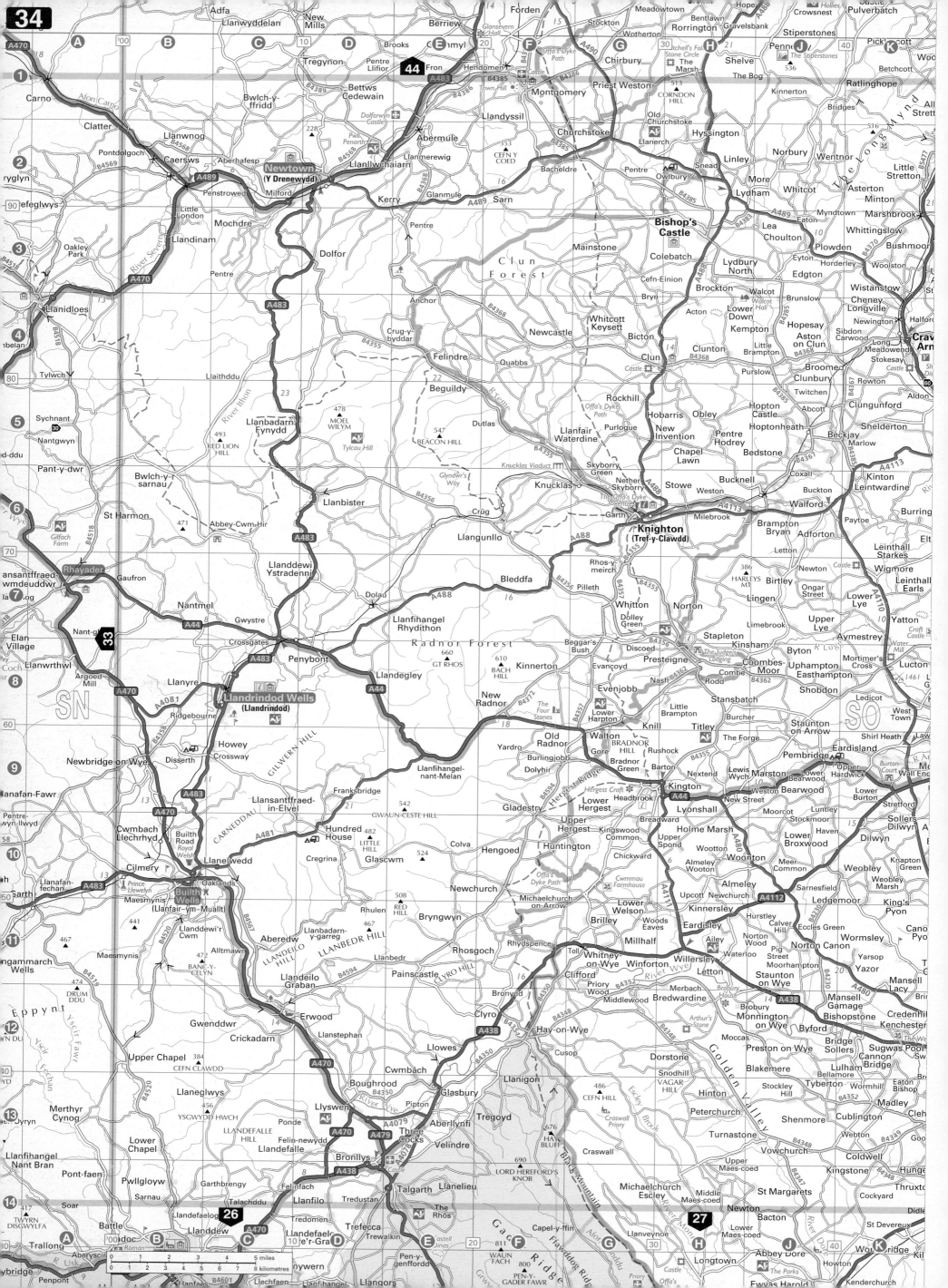

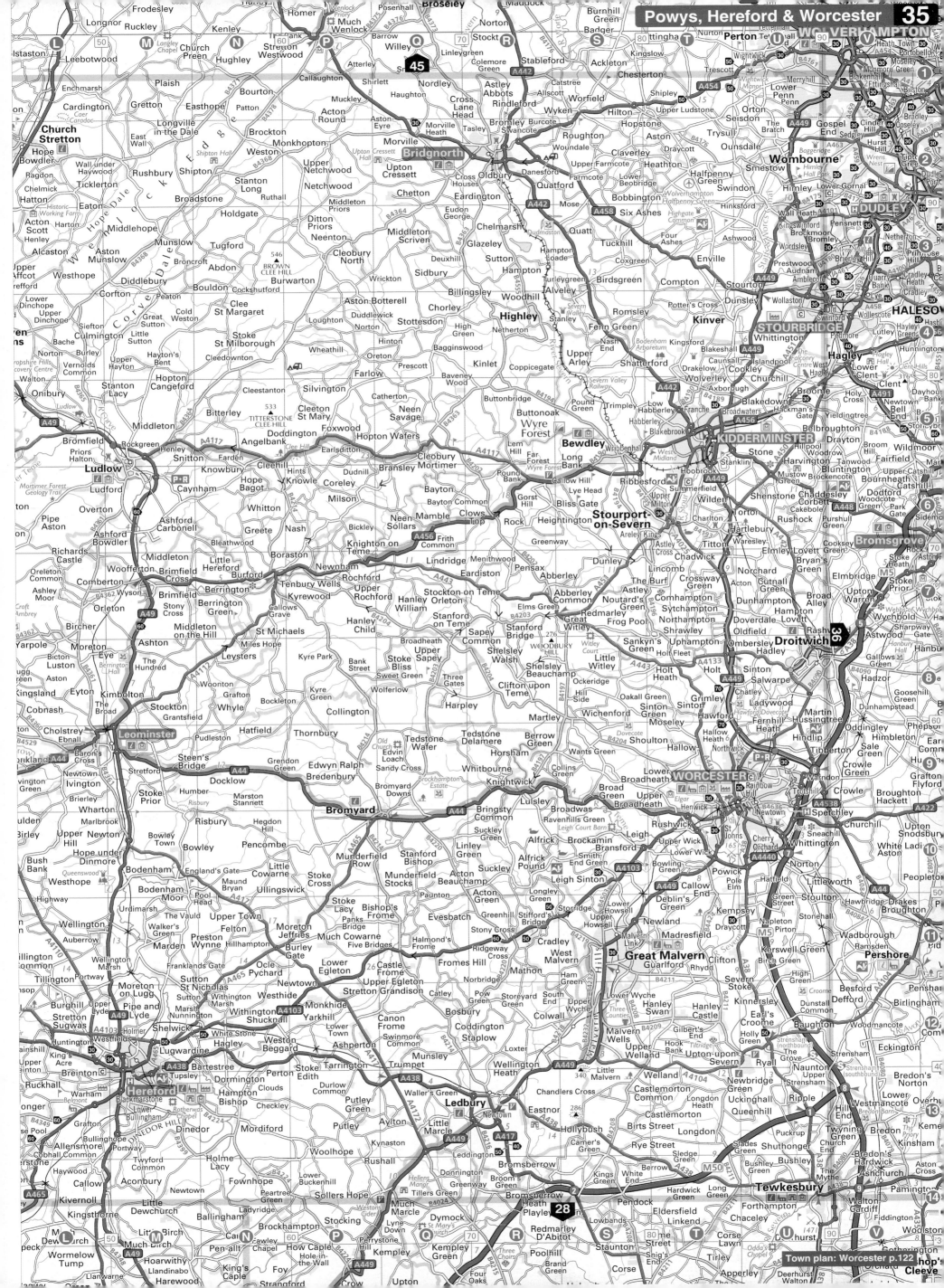

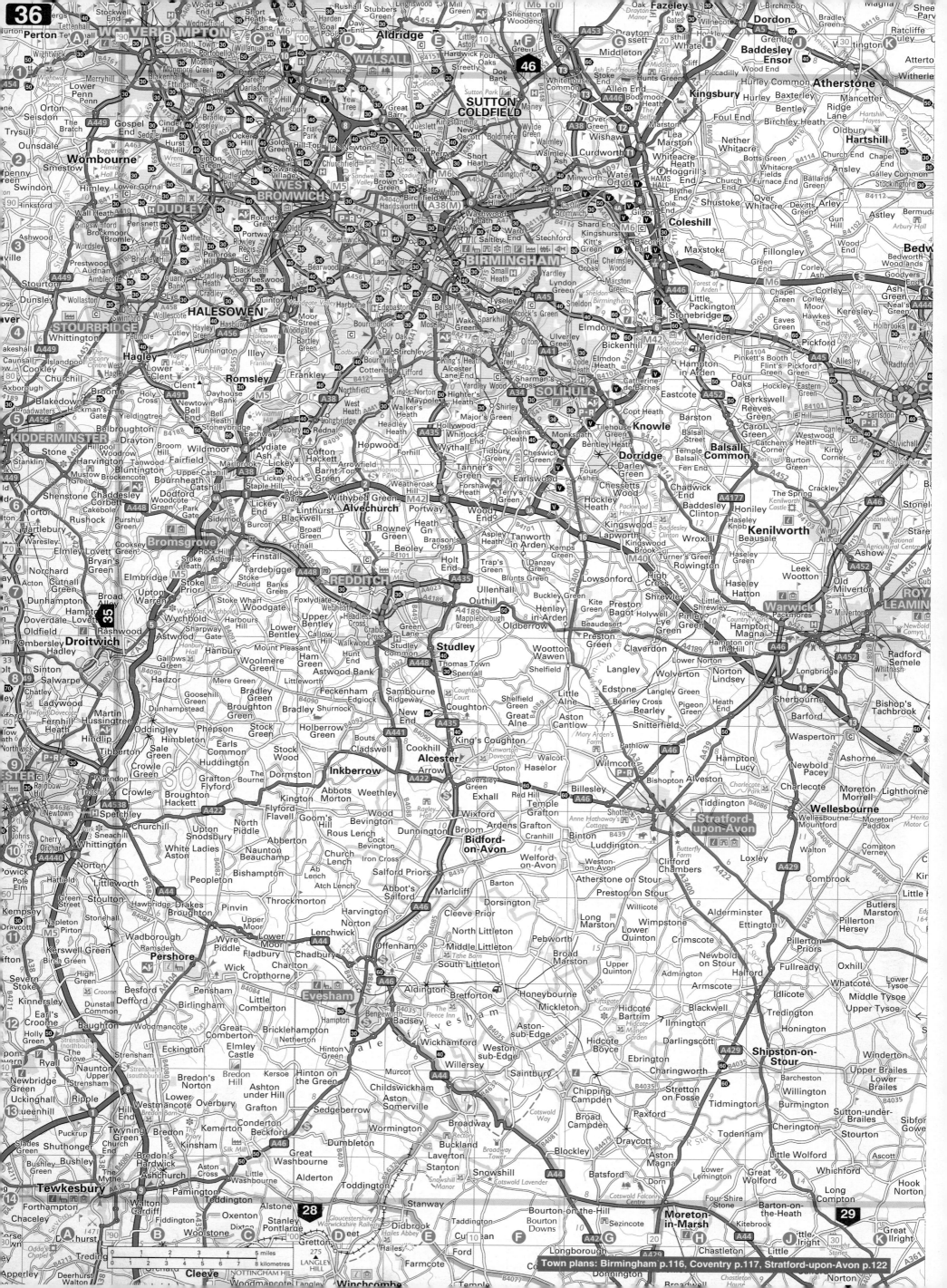

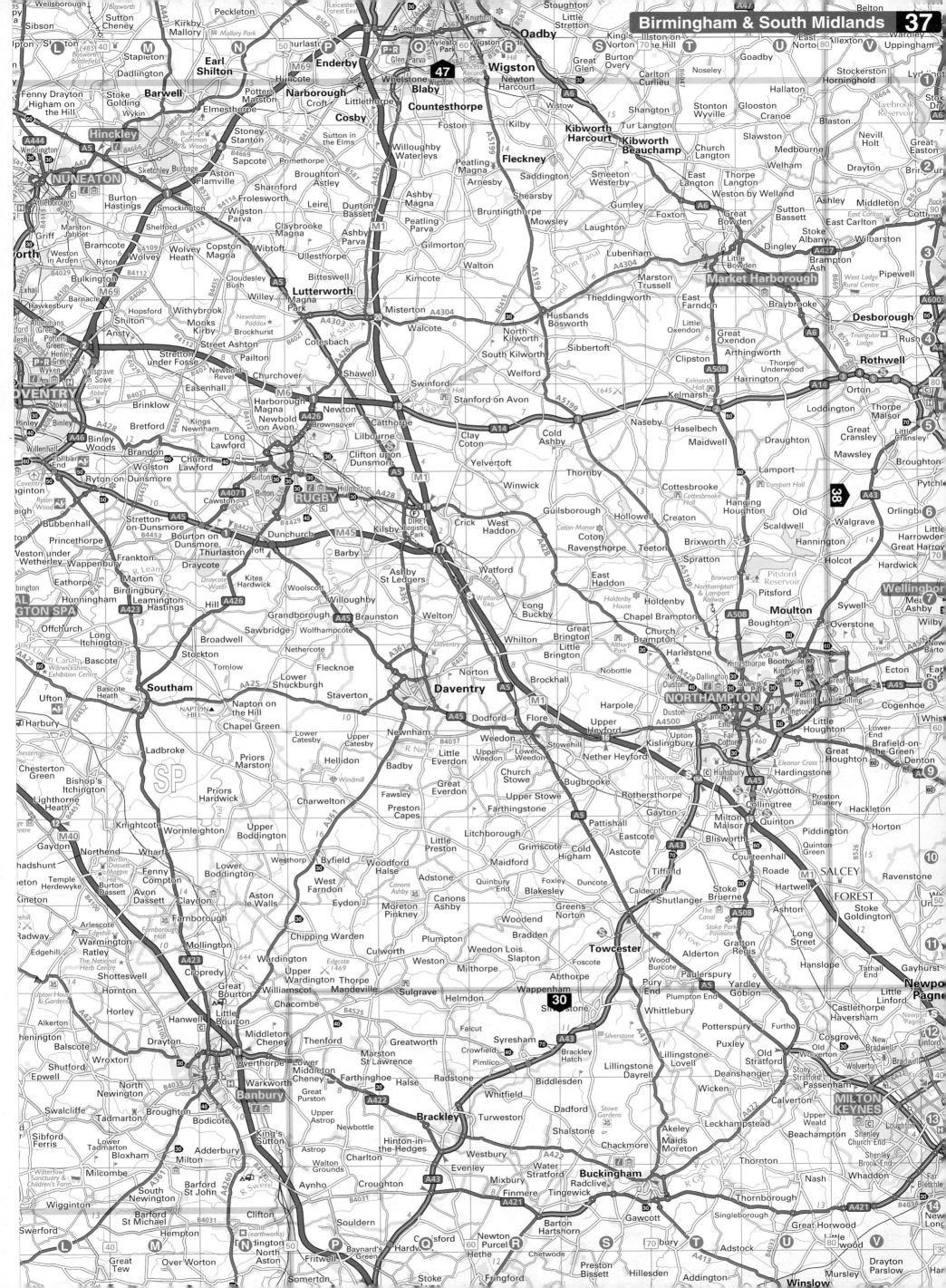

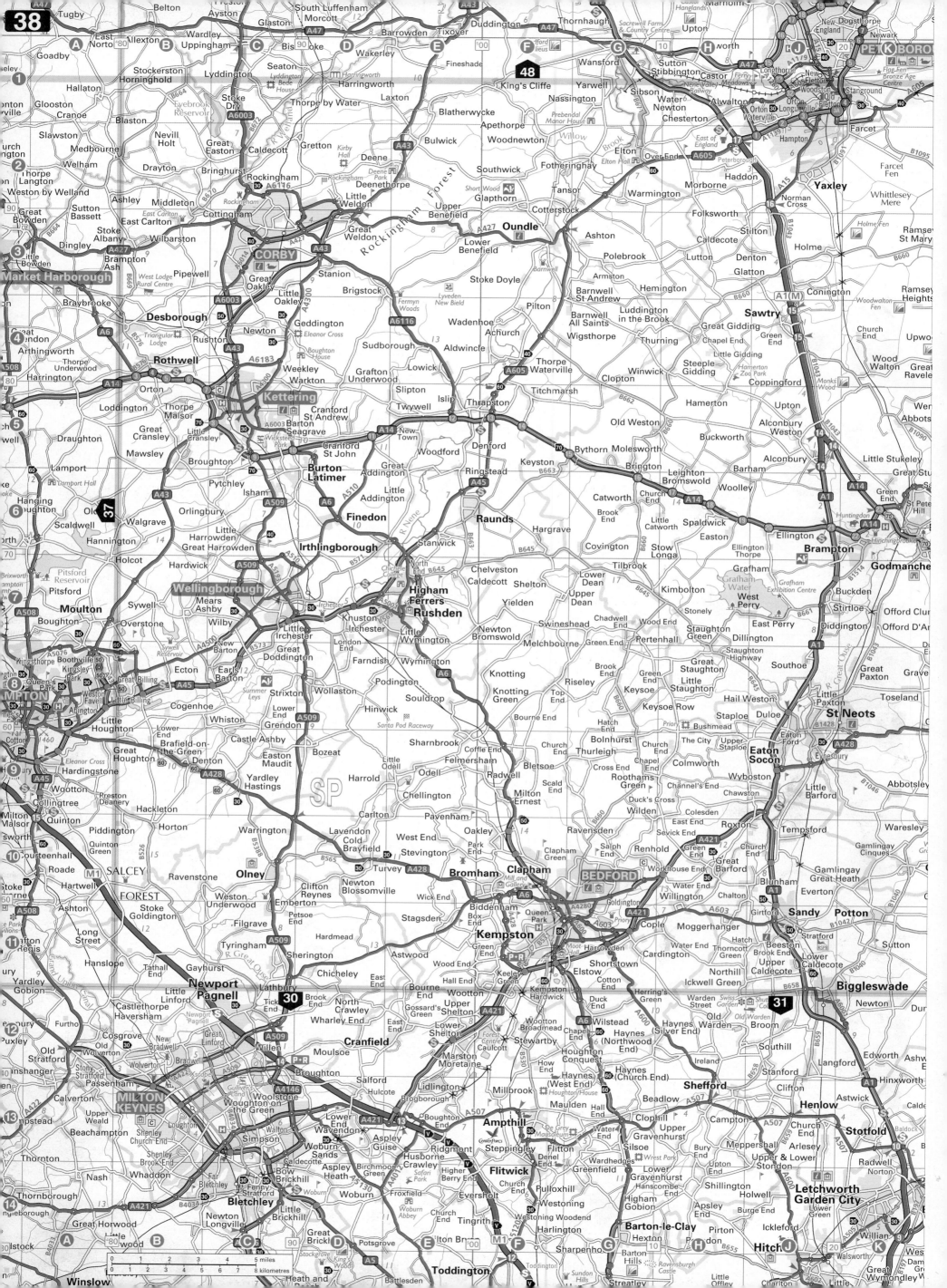

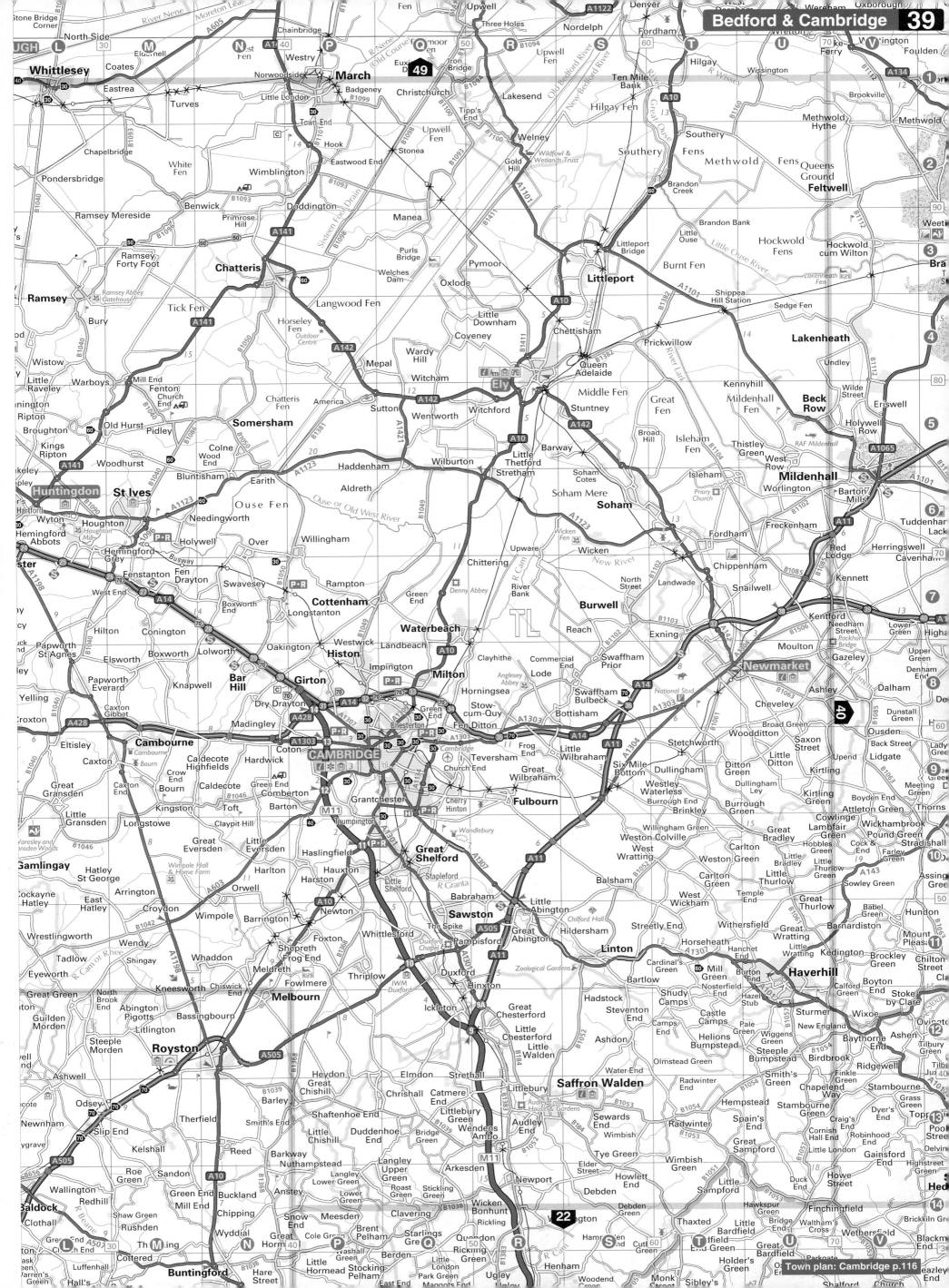

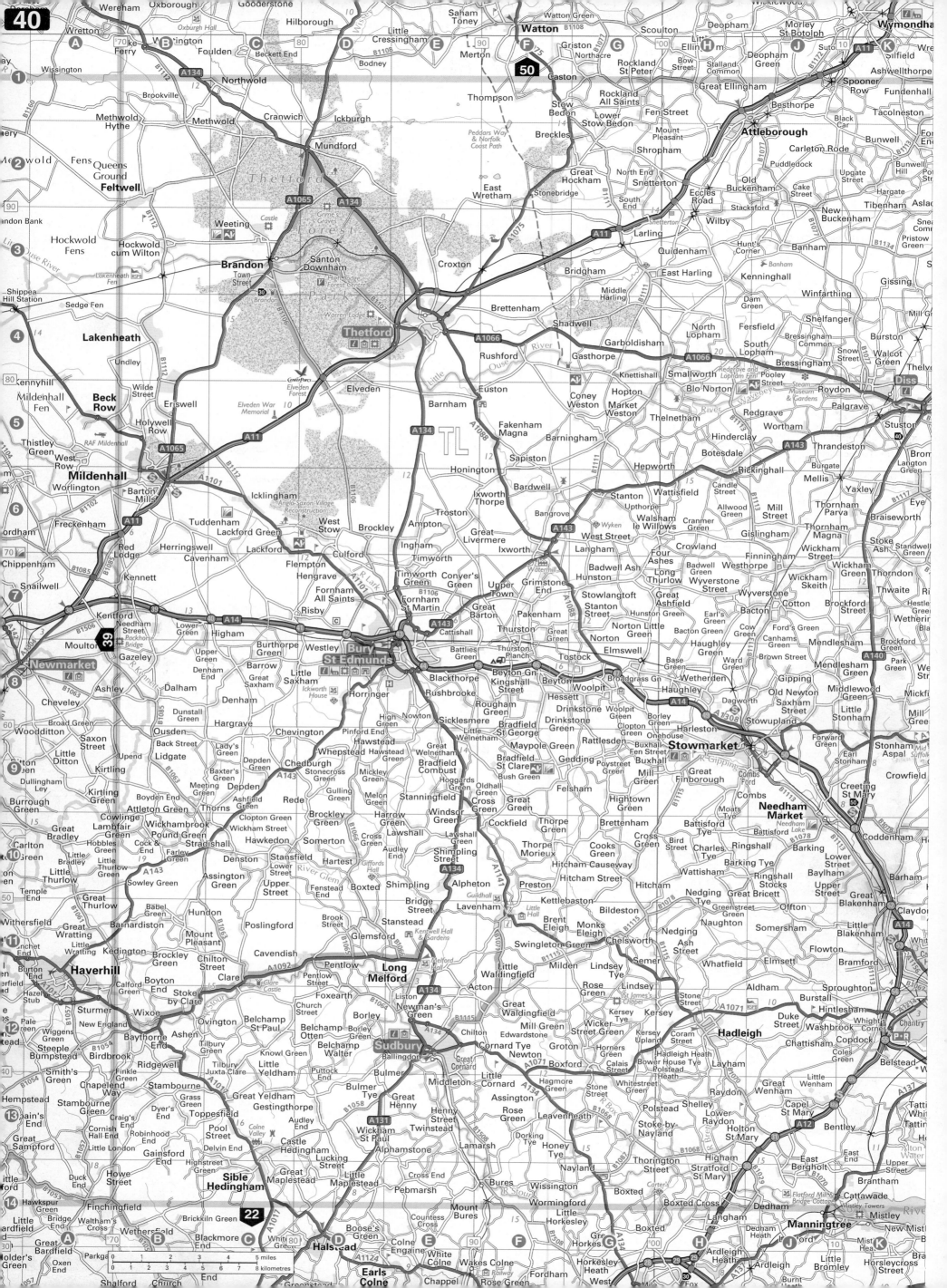

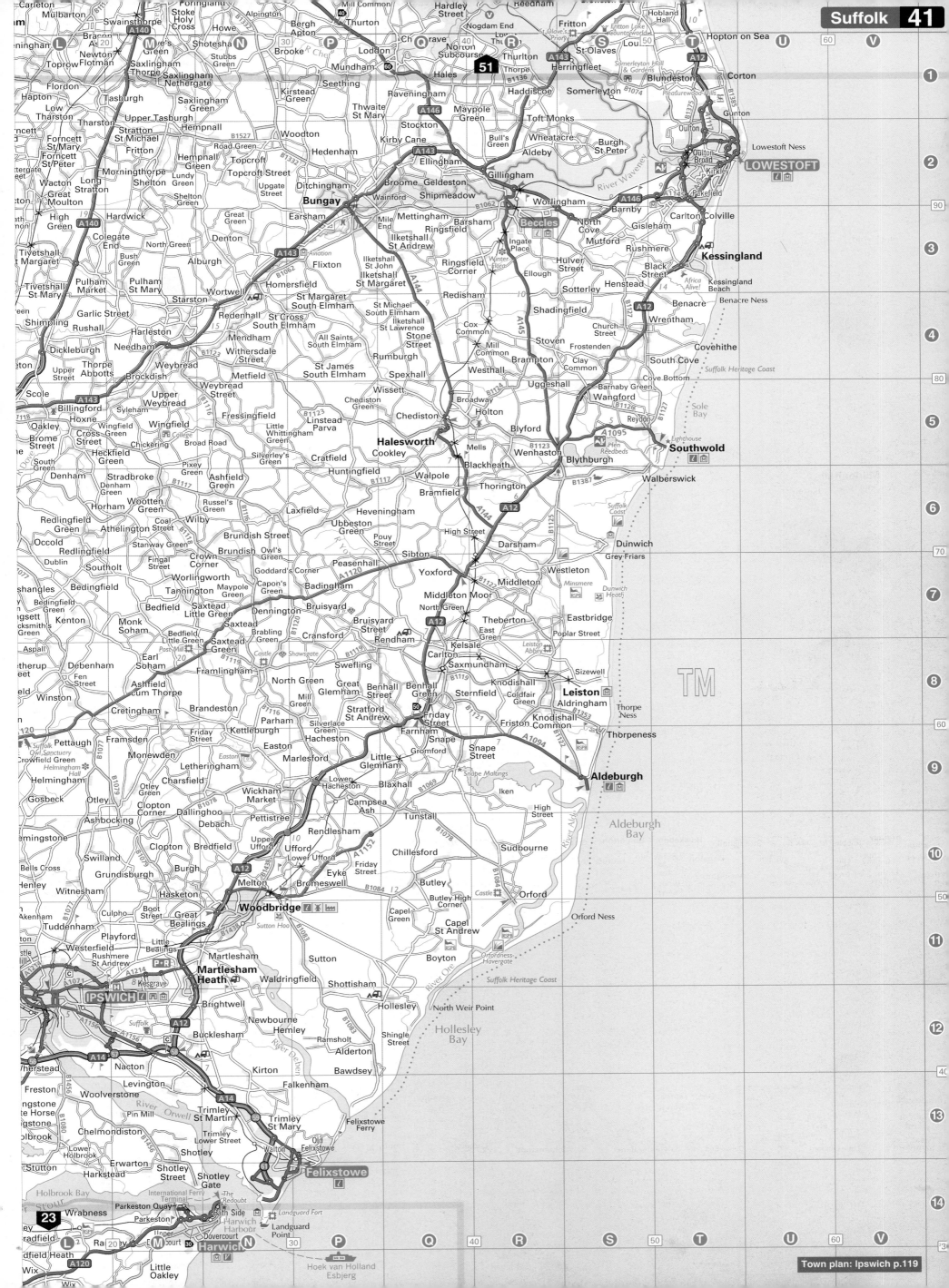

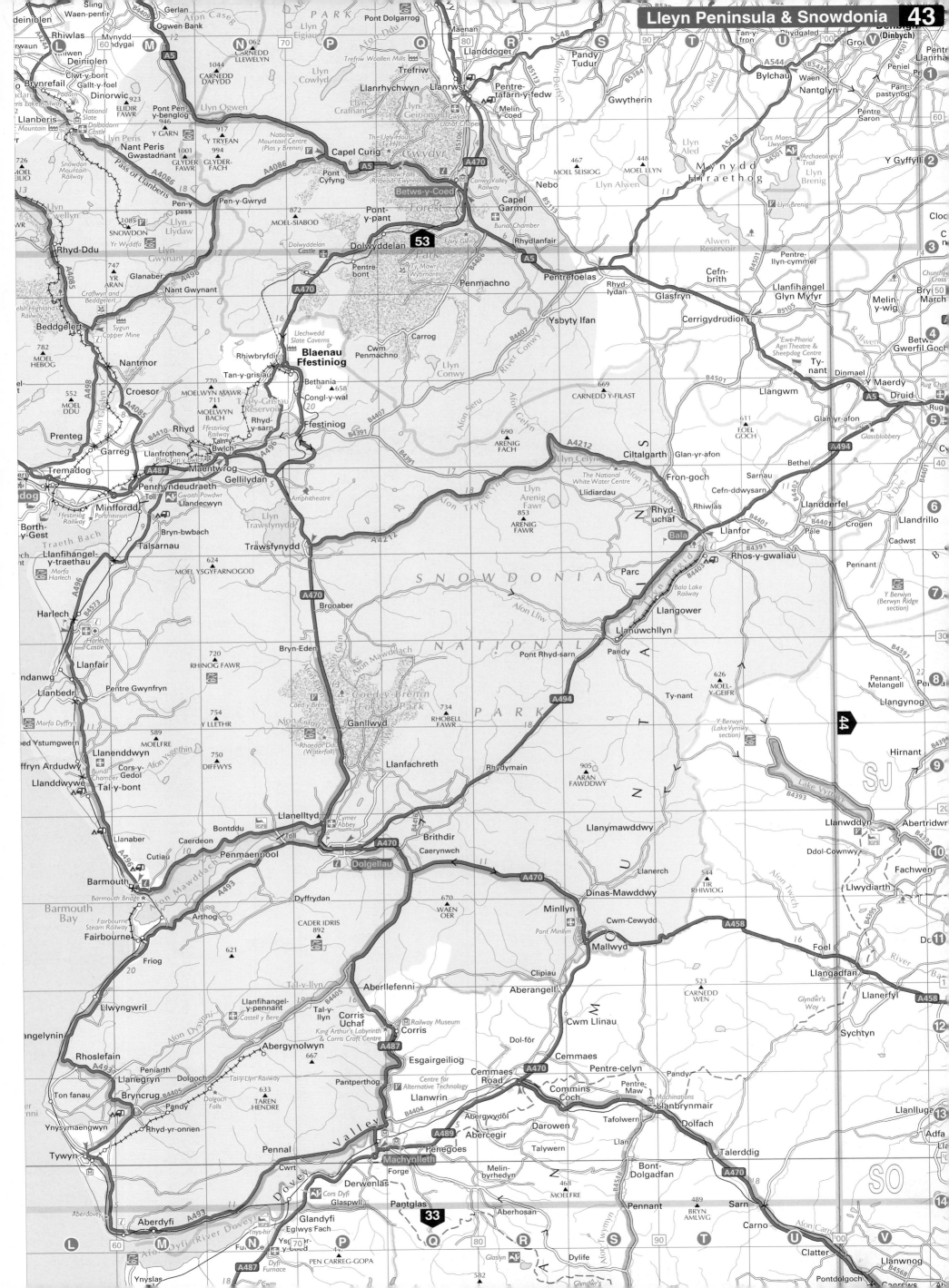

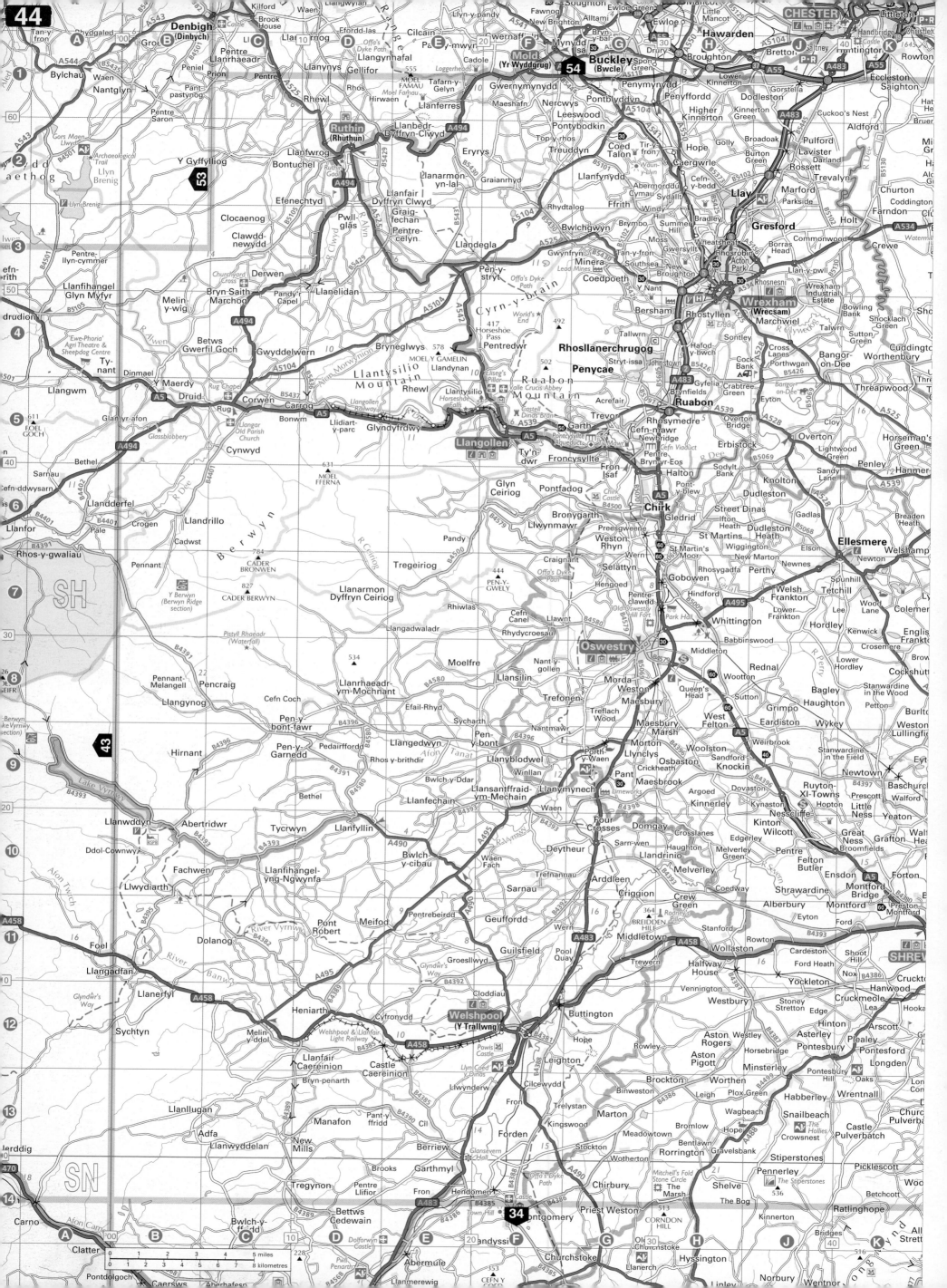

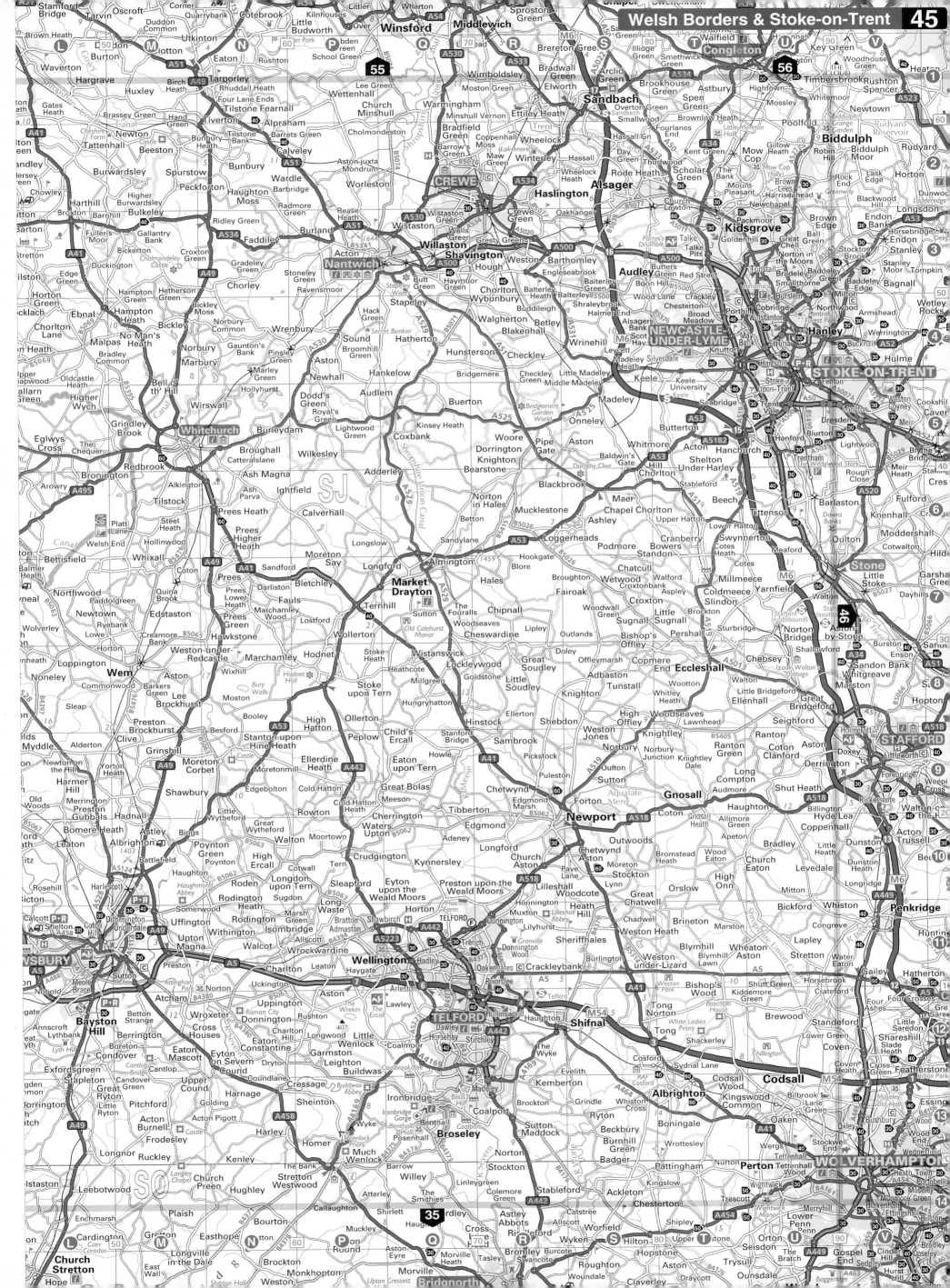

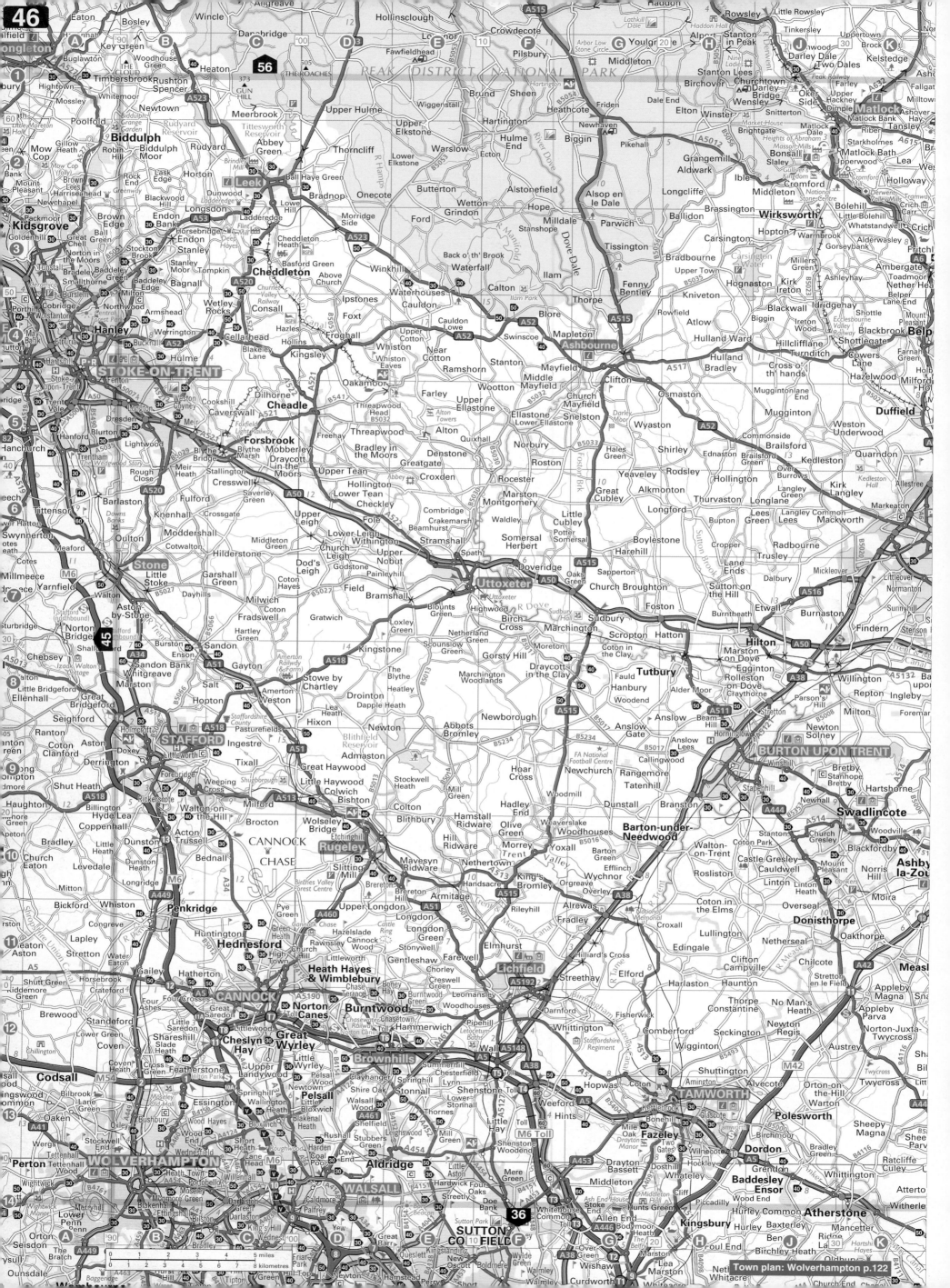

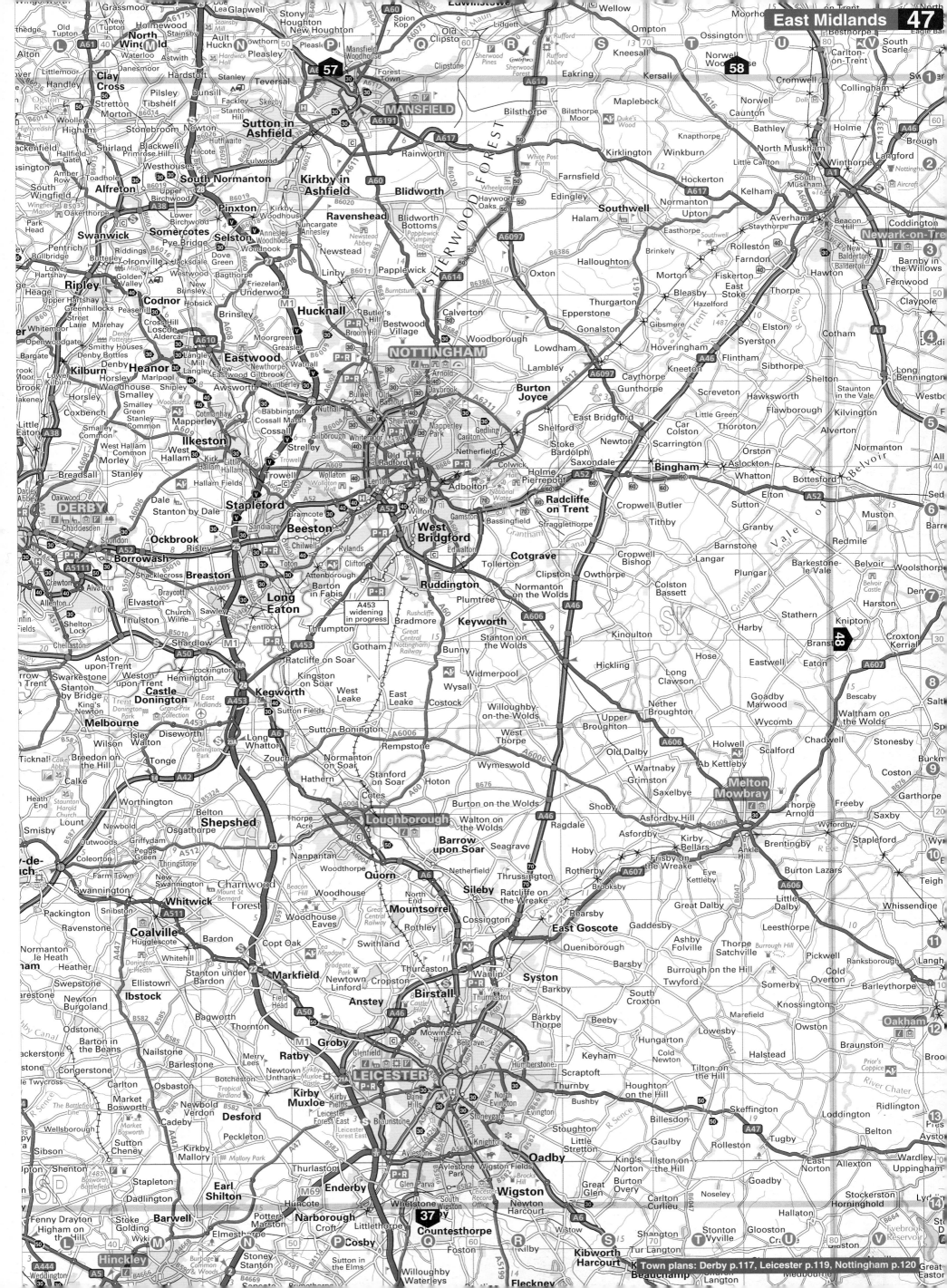

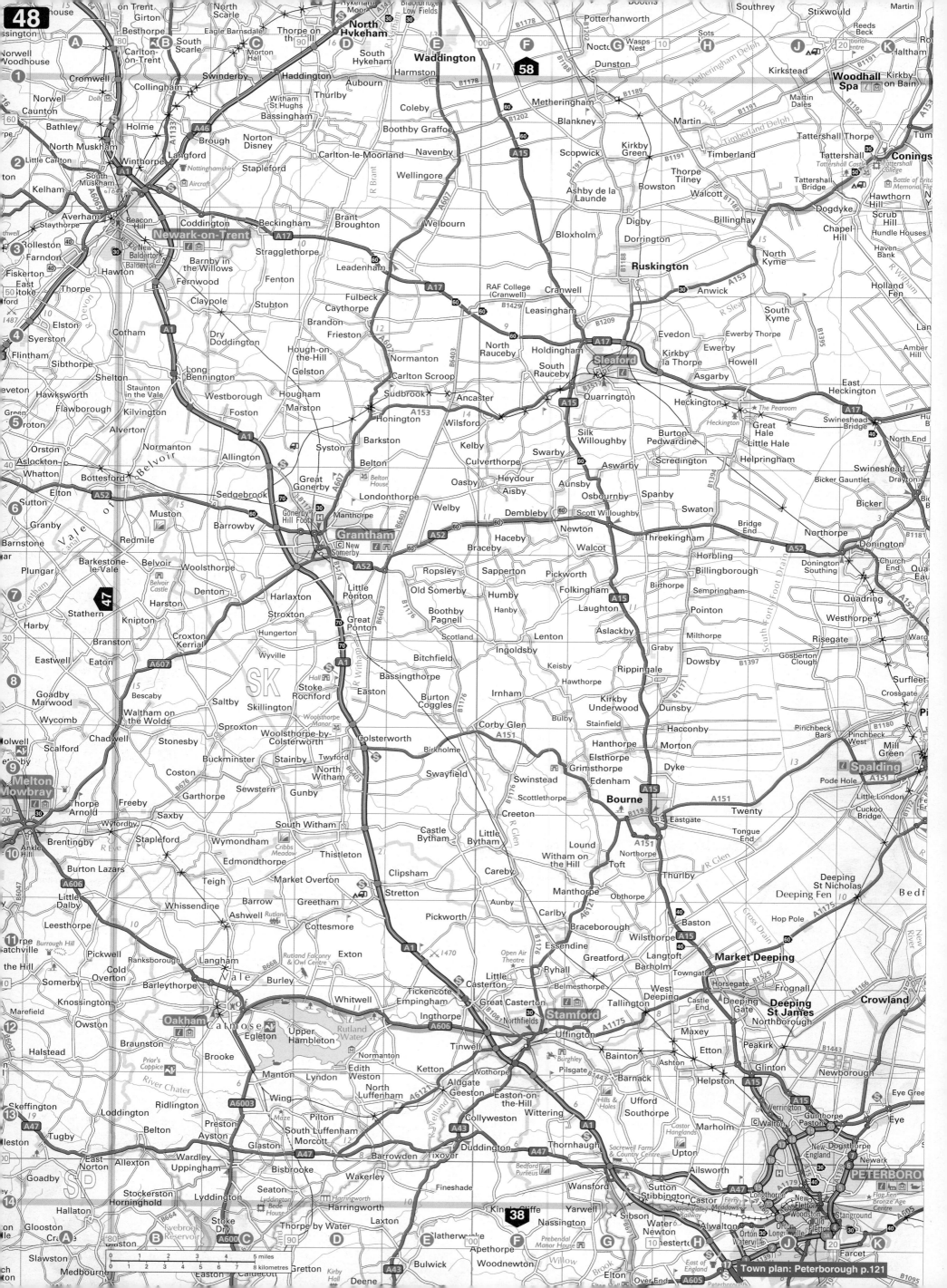

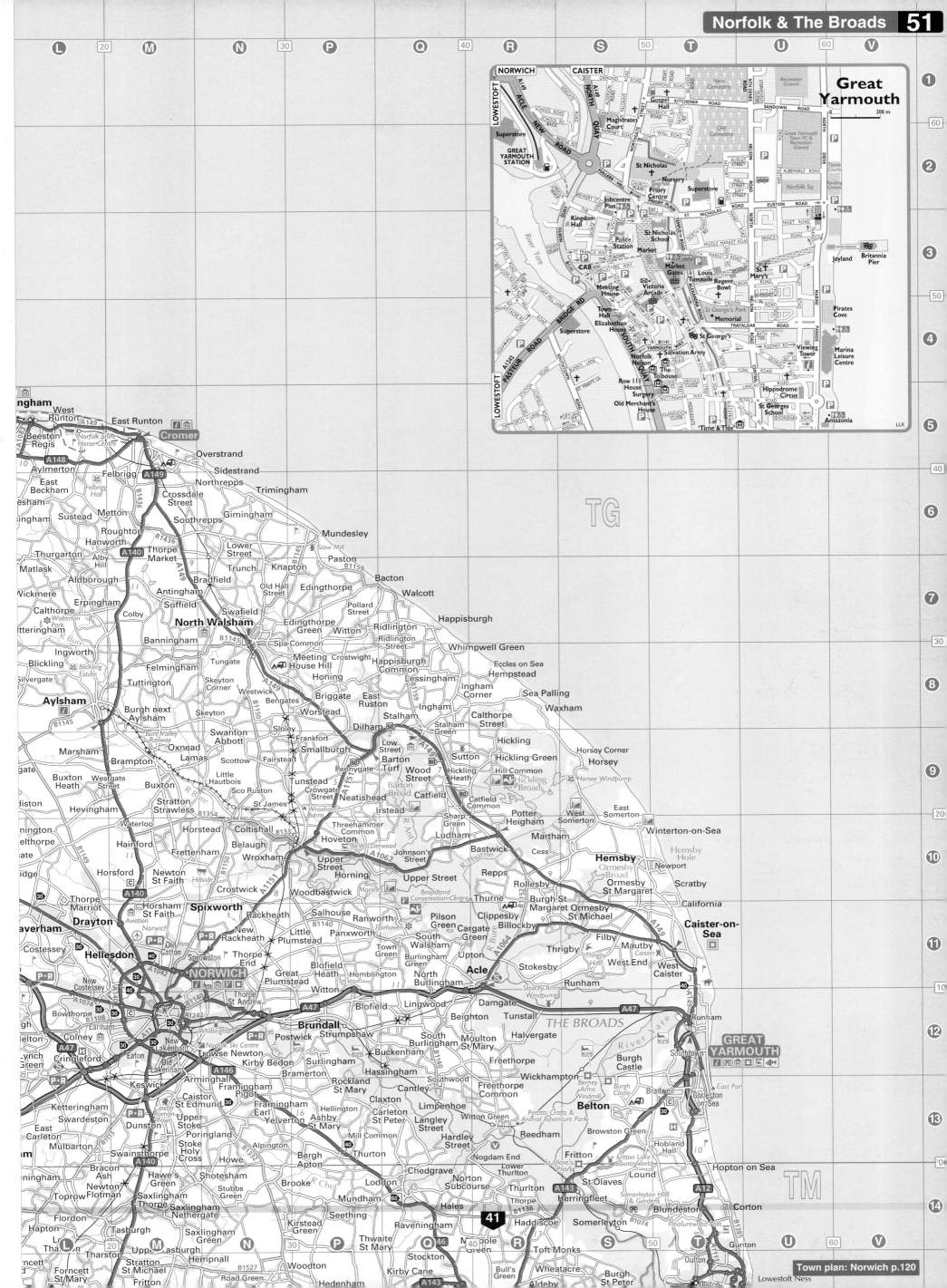

Great Yarmouth

Town plan: Norwich p.120

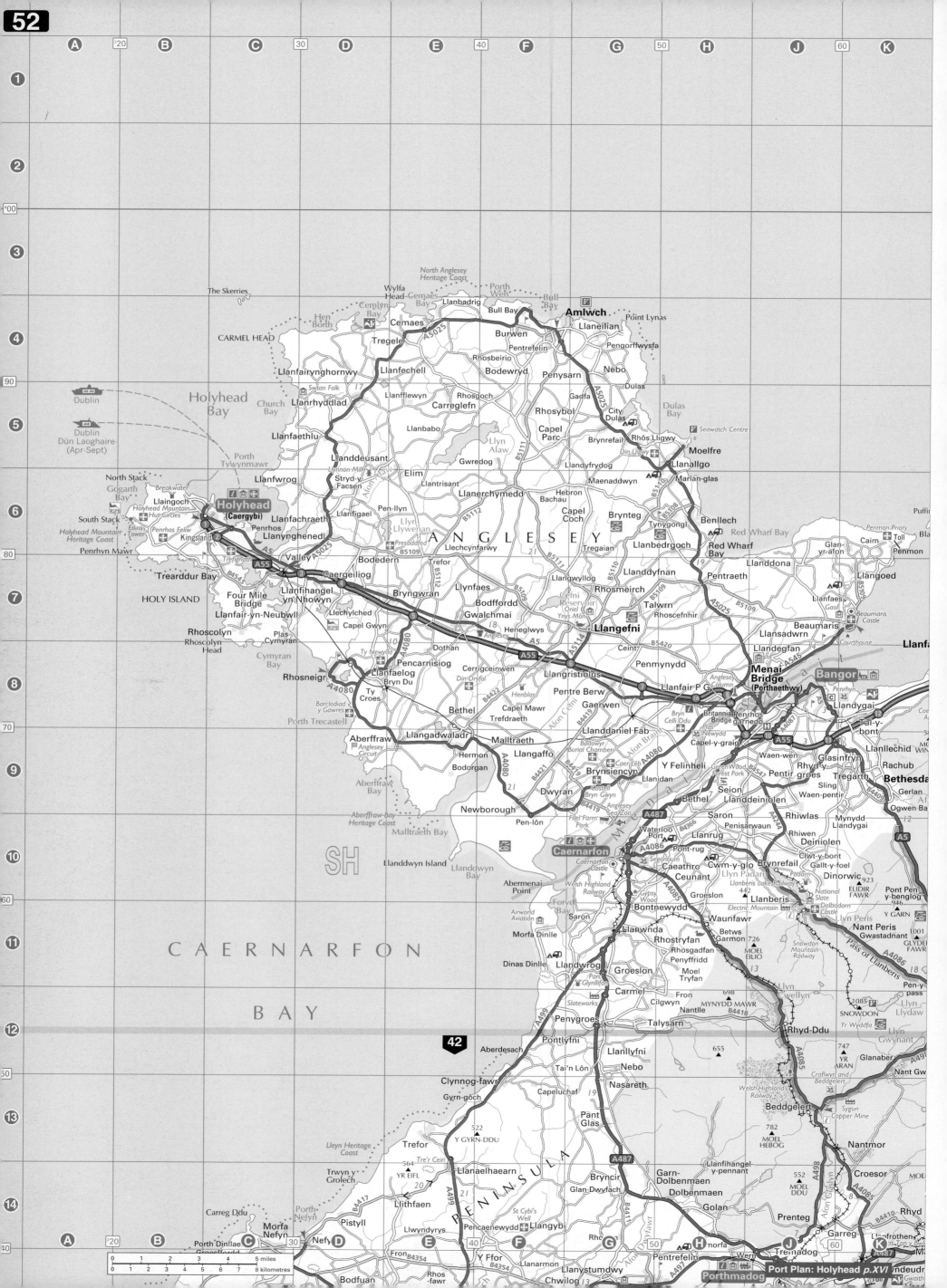

Port Plan: Holyhead p.XVI

Llandudno

Great Orme Tramway
Old Mill Road
TABOR HILL
Great Orme
Tramway
HILL TERRACE
The Grand Hotel
Victoria Station
PLAS ROAD
CLEMENT AVENUE
The Old Bank Gallery
GLODDAETH AVENUE
War Memorial
SOUTH PARADE
NORTH STREET
VAUGHAN ST
LLOYD ST
MADOC STREET
A546
The Promenade
Llandudno Bay
St John's
Town Hall
Our Lady Star of the Sea
Holy Trinity
THE PARADE
MOSTYN BROADWAY
Medical Centre
Conwy Archive Service
TRINITY AVENUE
CONWY ROAD
CYLCH TUDUR
Mostyn Gallery
LLANDUDNO STATION
Venue Cymru
Swimming Pool
St Paul's
MOSTYN AVE
B5115
Police Station
Magistrates' Court
Parc Llandudno Retail Park
Mostyn Champneys Retail Park
Ysgol Tudno
Fire & Ambulance Station
Bowling Alley
CLARENCE CRESCENT
CLYD
CAE FERN
Superstore
Ysgol Craig Y Don
CLARENCE DRIVE
Ysgol Ffordd Dyffryn
Ysgol Morfa Rhianedd
Llandudno FC
Ysgol John Bright
A470
DEGANWY
CONWAY ROAD
BETWS-Y-COED
0   200 m

54

SJ

Point of Ayr
RSPB
Talacre
GREAT ORMES HEAD
Great Orme Heritage Coast
Little Ormes Head
Penrhyn Bay
Rhôs-on-Sea
Colwyn Bay (Bae Colwyn)
Prestatyn
Gronant
Llanasa
Gwespyr
Ffynnongroyw
Rhyl
Meliden
Gwaenysgor
Picton
Rhewl-fawr
Rhewl Mostyn
Conwy Bay
Llandudno
Deganwy
Penrhynside
Llandrillo
Pydew
Esgyryn
Mochdre
Old Colwyn
Llanddulas
Kinmel Bay
Abergele Roads
Kinmel Bay
Towyn
Pensarn
Meliden
Axton
Trelogan
Walwen
Tre-Mostyn
Berthengam
Whitford
Penmaenmawr
Dwygyfylchi
Conwy
Capelulo
Penmaenan
Henryd
Llandudno Junction
Llansanffraid Glan Conwy
Bryn-y-Maen
Llanelian-yn-Rhôs
Llysfaen
Rhyd-y-foel
Dolwen
Betws-yn-Rhos
Abergele
St George
Bodelwyddan
Pengwern
Bodelwyddan Castle
Glascoed
Rhuddlan
Rhuallt
St Asaph
Tremeirchion
Pen-y-cefn
Cwm
Dyserth
Lloc
Caerwys
Babell
Mynd
Ysceifiog
Afon-wen
Pen-y-felin
Clwydian Range
Sodom
Bodfari
Fairfechan
Garizim
Nant-y-pandy
Abergwyngregyn
Gorddinog
SNOWDONIA
TAL-Y-FAN
610
Rowen
Ty'n-y-Groes
Caerhun
Castell
Graig
Eglwysbach
Dawn
Trofarth
Pentre Isaf
Llanfair Talhaiarn
Pentre'r Felin
Groesffordd Marli
Llannefydd
Trefnant
Graig
Denbigh Friary
Kilford
Llandyrnog
Llangwyfan
Llanynys
Gellifor
Y DROSGL
757
FOEL-FRAS
942
NATIONAL
PARK
Llanbedr-y-Cennin
Tal-y-Bont
Dolgarrog
Pont Dolgarrog
Maenan
Llanddoget
Hafodunos
Llangernyw
Llansannan
Tan-y-fron
Groes
Bylchau
Waen
Nantglyn
Pentre Saron
Prion
Peniel
Pant pastynog
Denbigh (Dinbych)
Llwyn
Pentre Llanrhaeadr
Brook House
Rhewl
Llangynhafal
Offa's Dyke Path
CARNEDD LLEWELYN
1062
CARNEDD DAFYDD
1044
917
Y TRYFAN
994
GLYDER-FACH
Llyn Ogwen
Llyn Eigiau
Llyn Cowlyd
Trefriw Woollen Mills
Trefriw
Llanrwst
Pentre-tafarn-y-fedw
Melin-y-coed
Gwytherin
Llyn Aled
Cefn Berain
Rhydgaled
Llyn Alwen
MOEL SEISIOG
448
MOEL LLYN
Llyn Alwen
Gors Maen Llwyd
Archaeological Trail
Llyn Brenig
 Y Gyffylliog
Pentre
Rhos
Moel Famau
Hiraethog
Ruthin (Rhuthun)
Llanfwrog
Bontuchel
Efenechtyd
Clocaenog
Clawdd-newydd
Derwen
Churchyard Cross
Llanelidan
Bryn Saith Marchog
Pandy'r Capel
Llantysilio Mountain
A5
A494
Betws Gwerfil Goch
Gwyddelwern
Bryneglwys
Llangollen Old Parish Church
Glyndyfrdwy
Llangwm
Maerdy
Druid
Dinmael
Ty-nant
Rug
Corwen
Carrog
Bonwm
Llidiart-y-parc
Glyndy
Blaenau Ffestiniog
Rhiwbryfdir
Llechwedd Slate Caverns
Tan-y-grisiau
Bethania
Congl-y-wal
Cwm Penmachno
Carrog
Penmachno
Pentre-bont
Dolwyddelan
Capel Garmon
Rhydlanfair
Pentrefoelas
Ysbyty Ifan
Glasfryn
Cerrigydrudion
Cefn-brith
Llanfihangel Glyn Myfyr
Melin-y-wig
'Ewe-Phoria' Agri Theatre & Sheepdog Centre
Glan-yr-afon
Glassblobbery
MOEL-SIABOD
872
Capel Curig
National Mountain Centre (Plas y Brenin)
Pen-y-Gwryd
Pont Cyfyng
Swallow Falls (Rhaeadr Ewynnol)
Betws-y-Coed
The Ugly House (Ty Hyll)
Uchaf Chapel
Gwydyr Forest
Conwy Valley Railway
Fairy Glen
Burial Chamber
Pont-y-pant
Dolwyddelan Castle
Ty Mawr Wybrnant
43
A5
Nebo
Rhyd-lydan
Y TRYFAN
FOEL GOCH
611
CARNEDD Y FILAST
669
ARENIG FACH
690
Llyn Conwy
Llyn Celyn
Cynwyd
MOEL FFERNA
631
Ffestiniog
Rhyd-y-sarn
Bwlch
Ffestiniog Railway
Gellilydan
The National White Water Centre
Llangwm
Sarnau
Cefn-ddwysarn
Llidiardau
Llandderfel

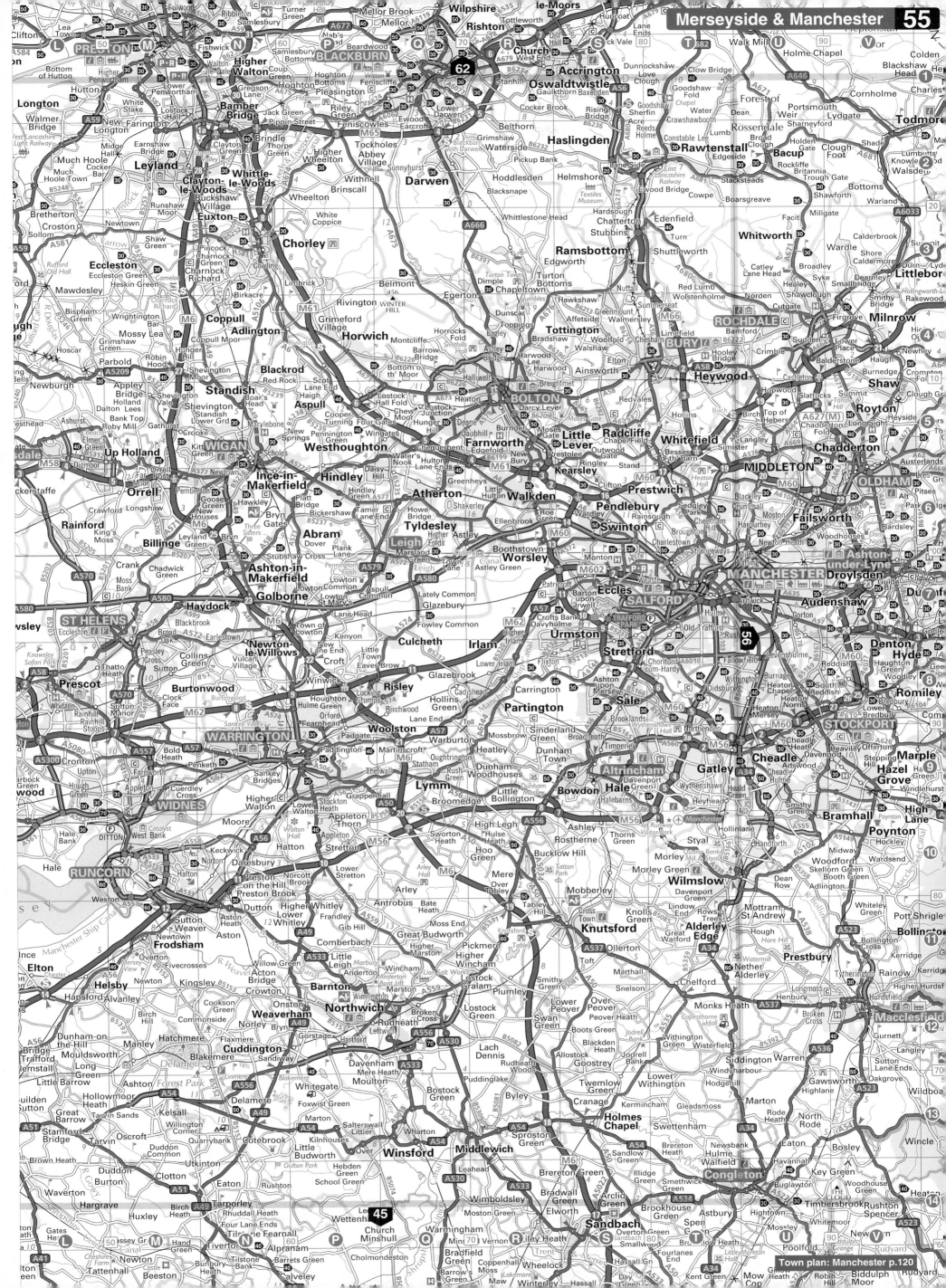

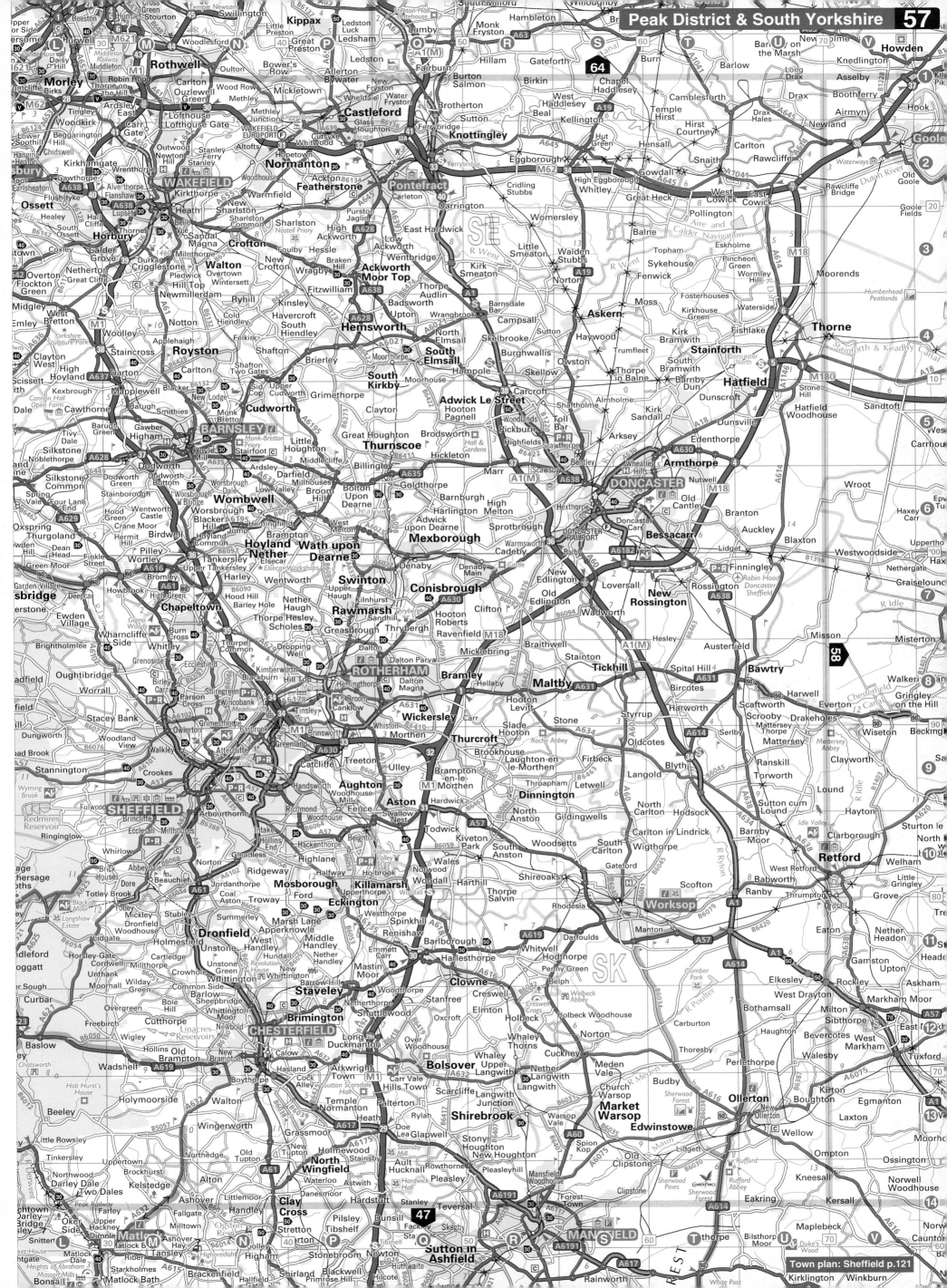

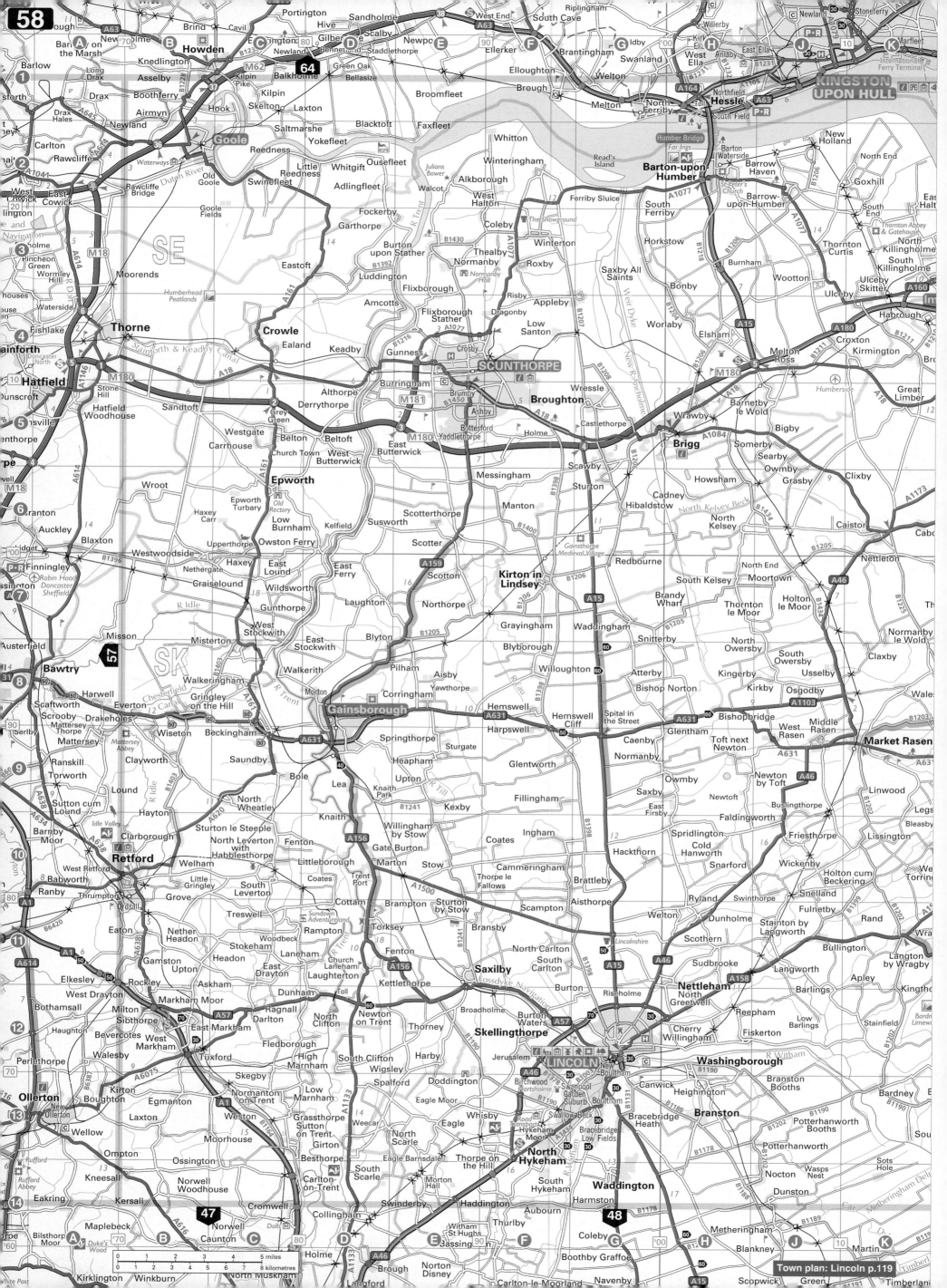

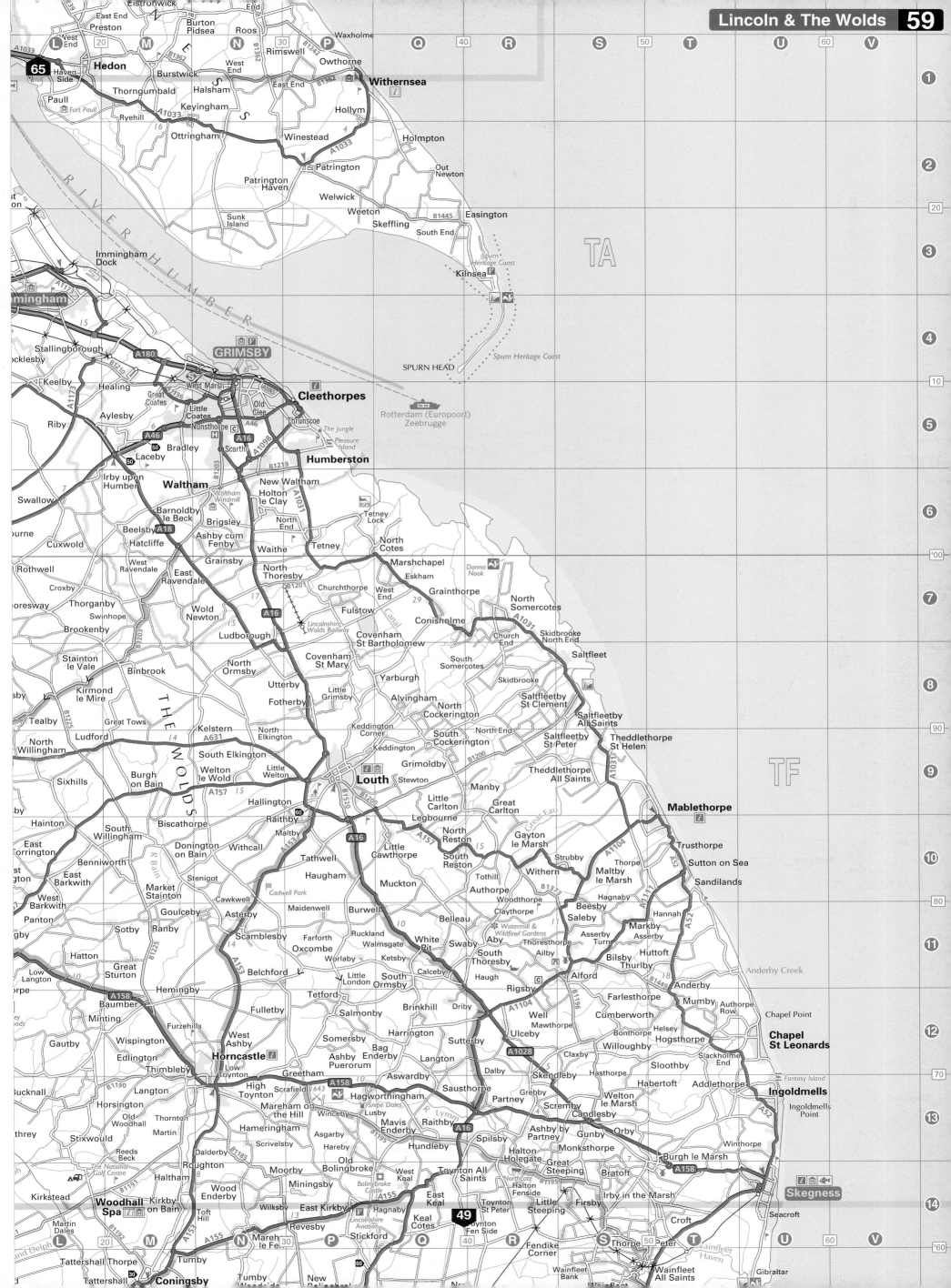

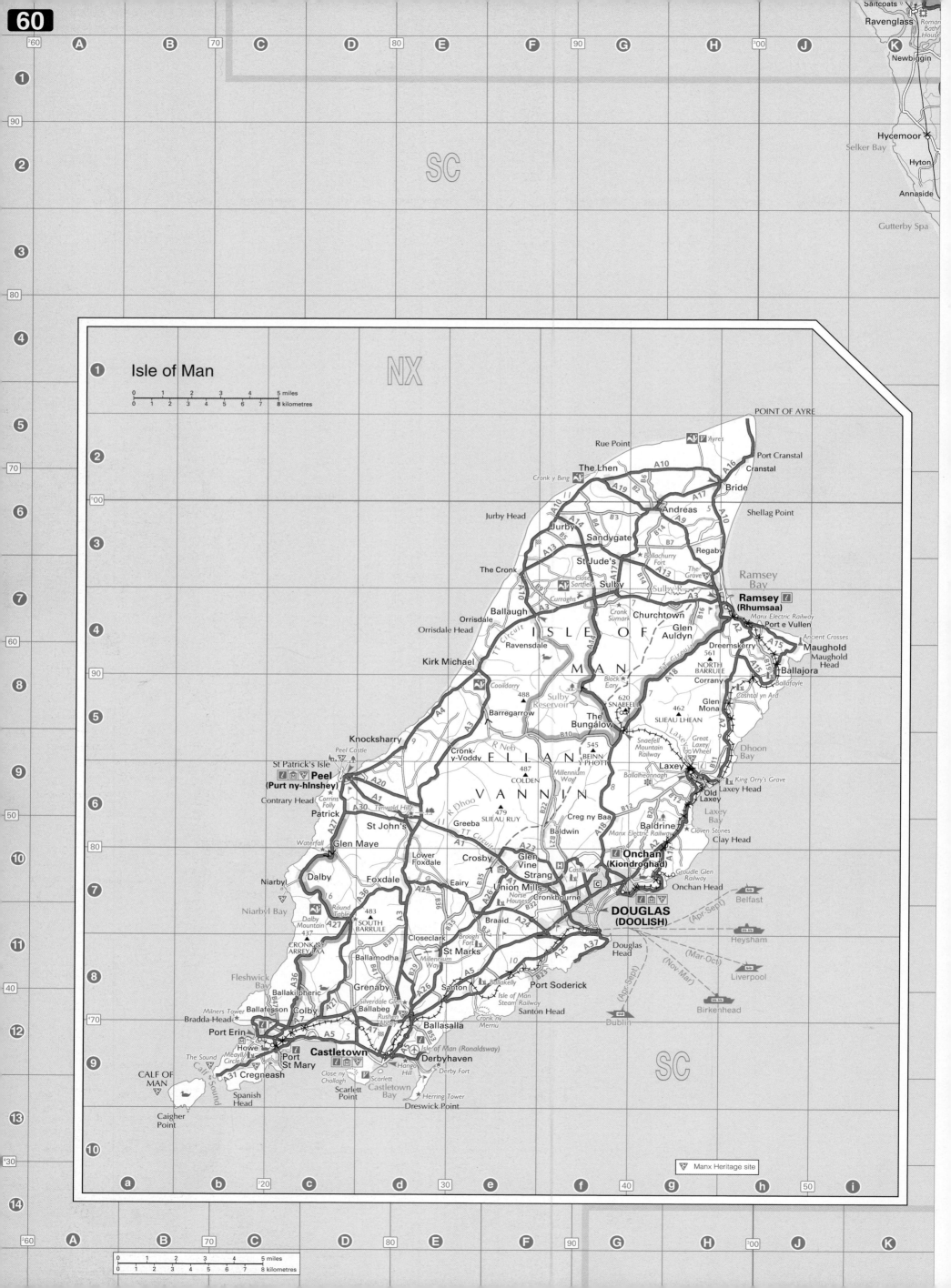

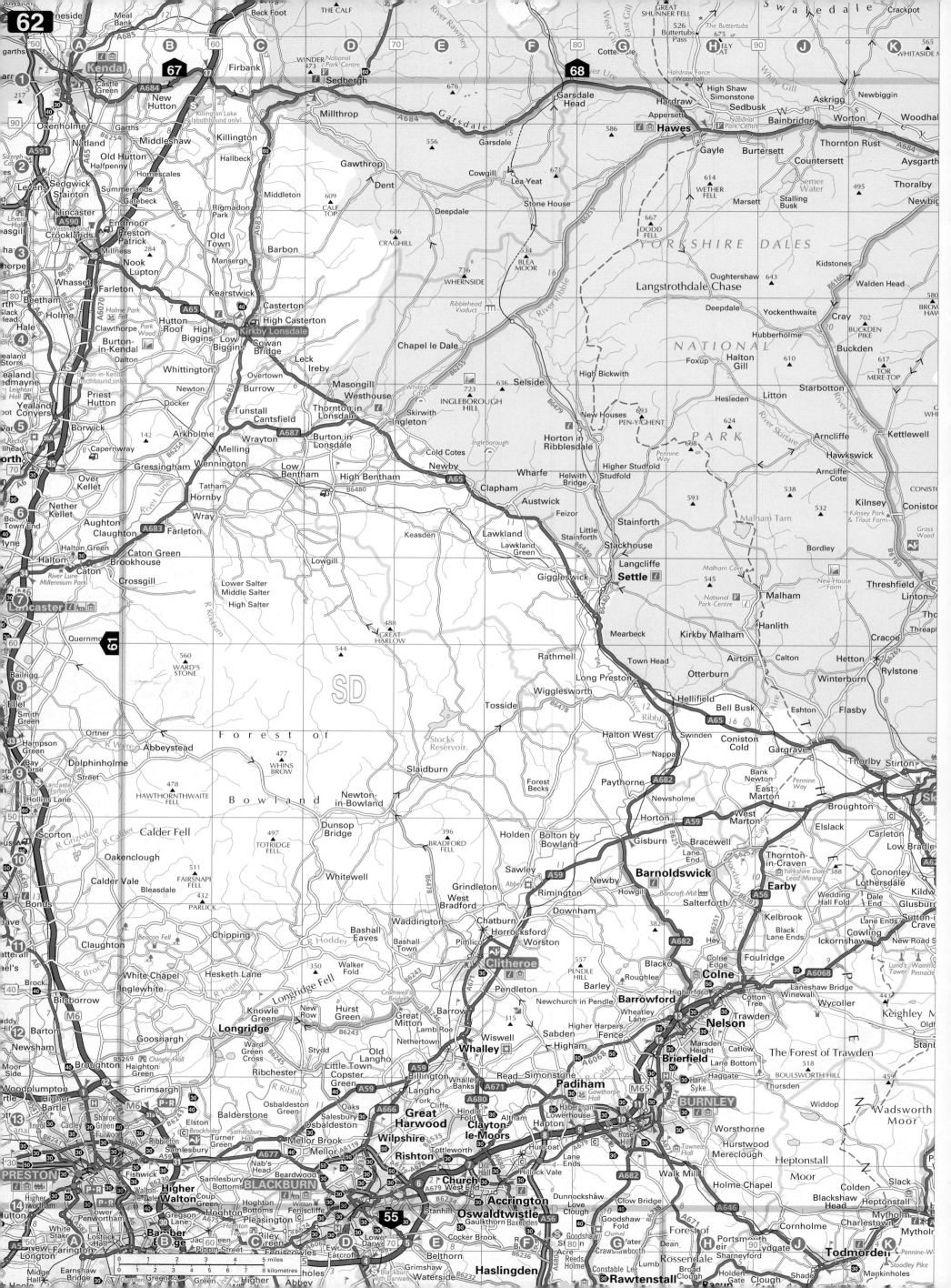

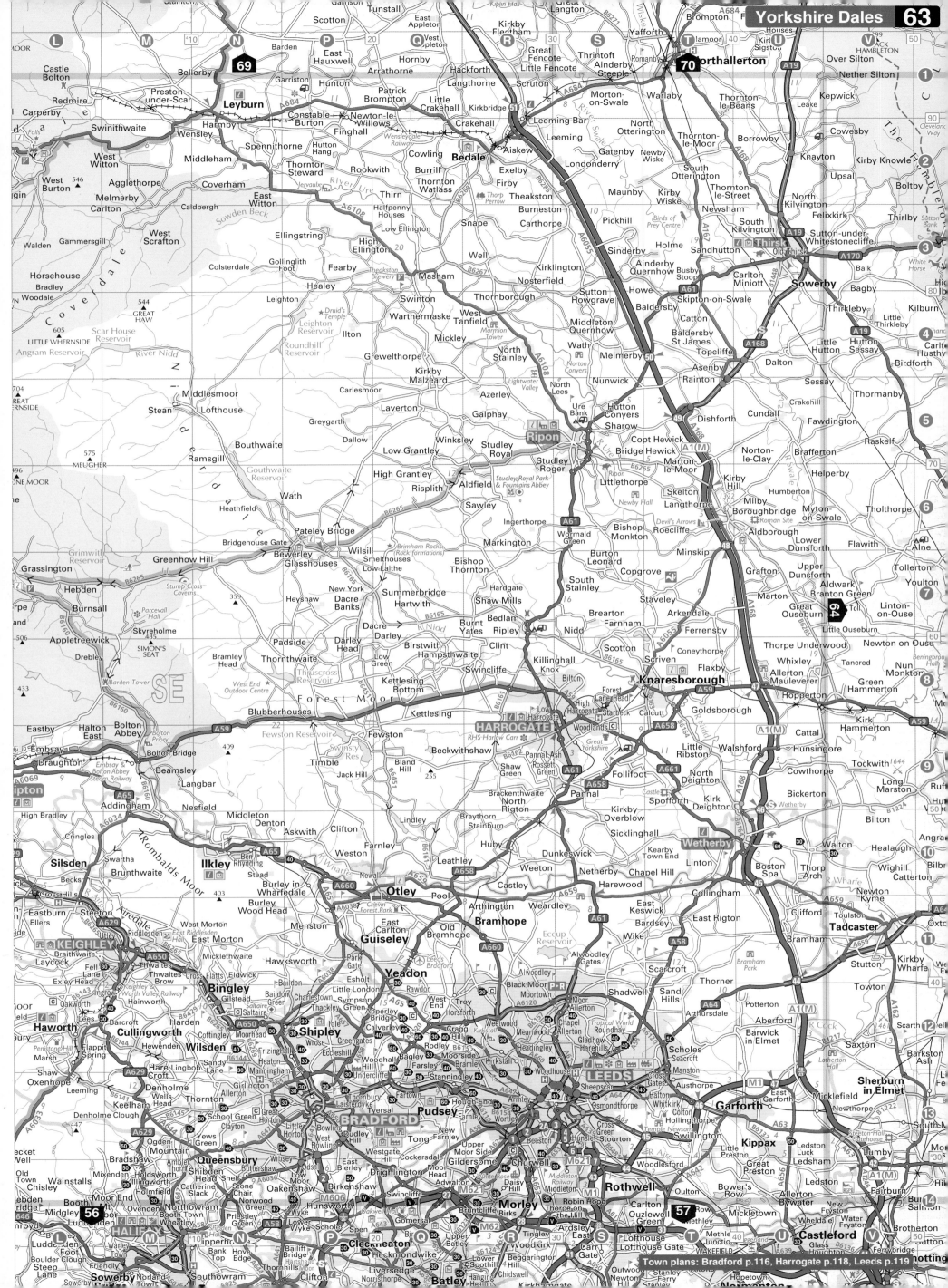

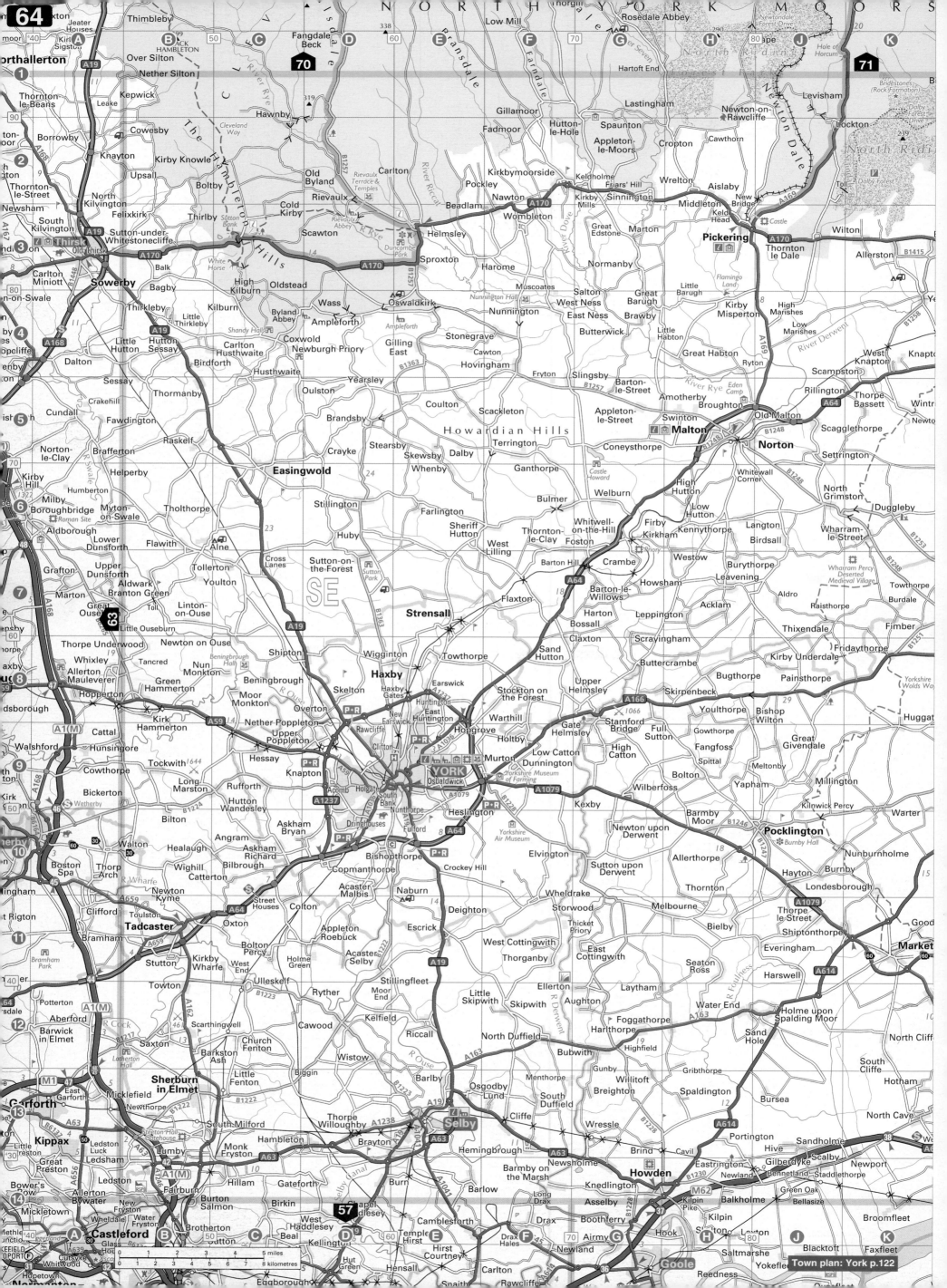

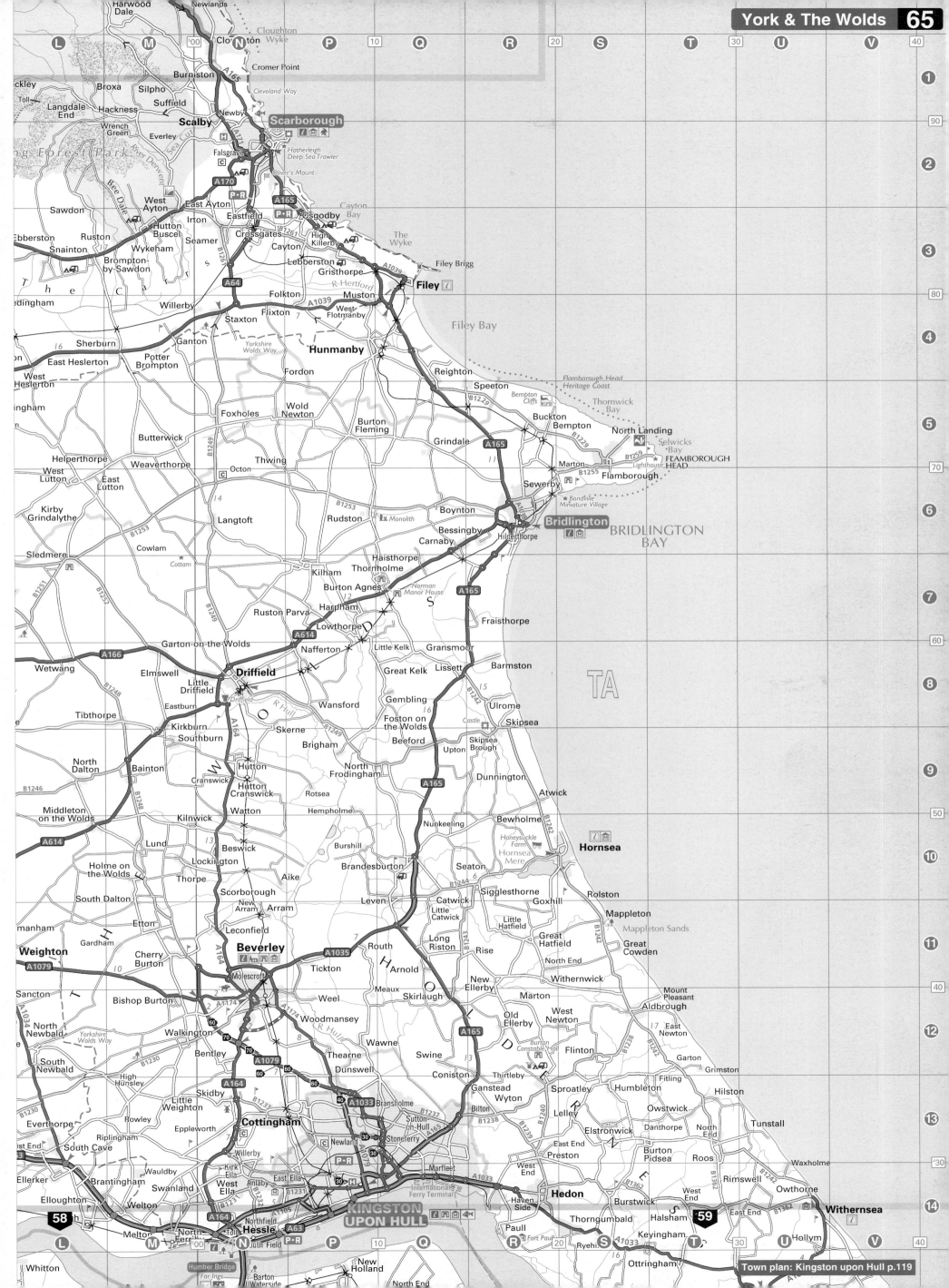

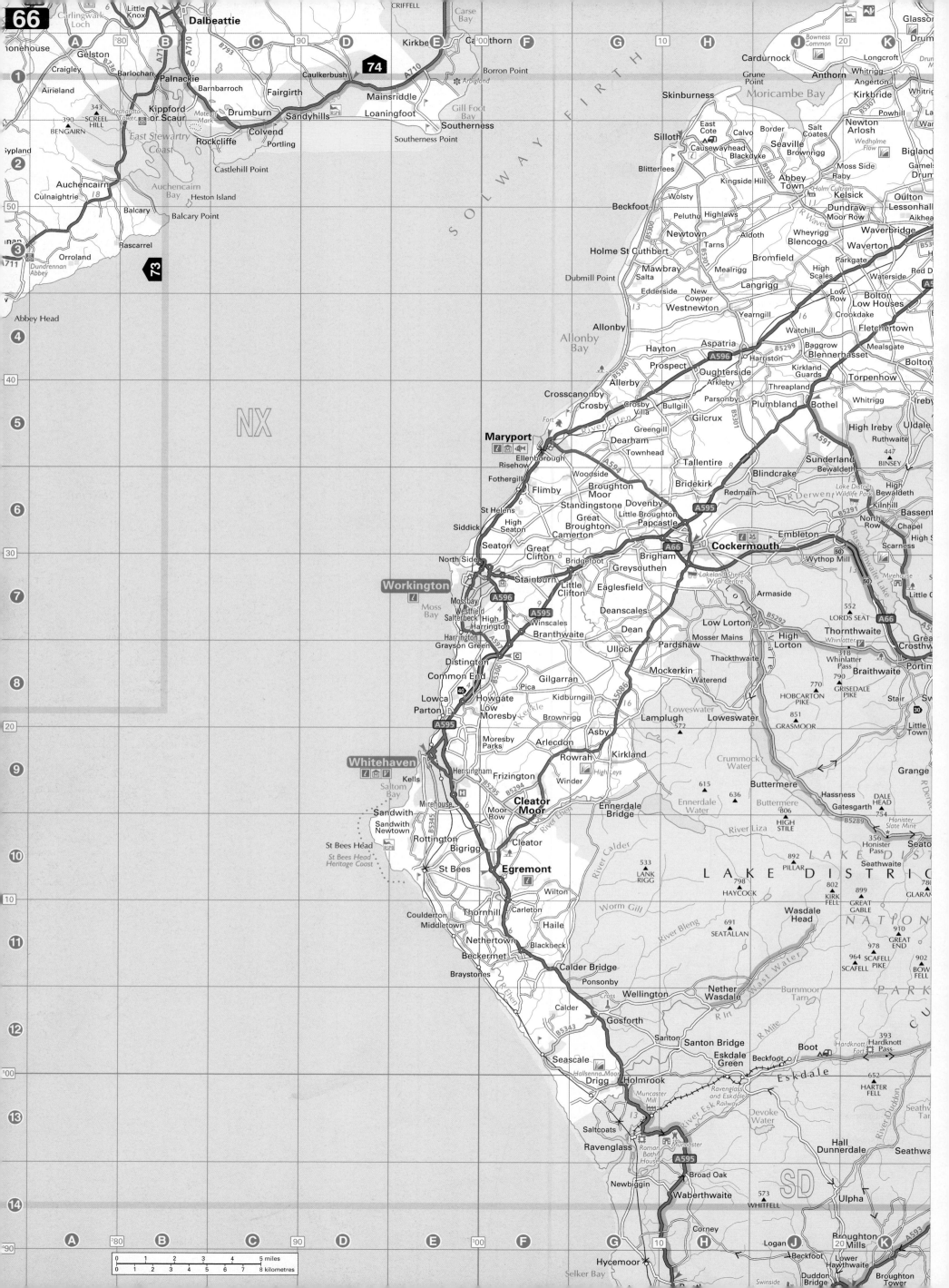

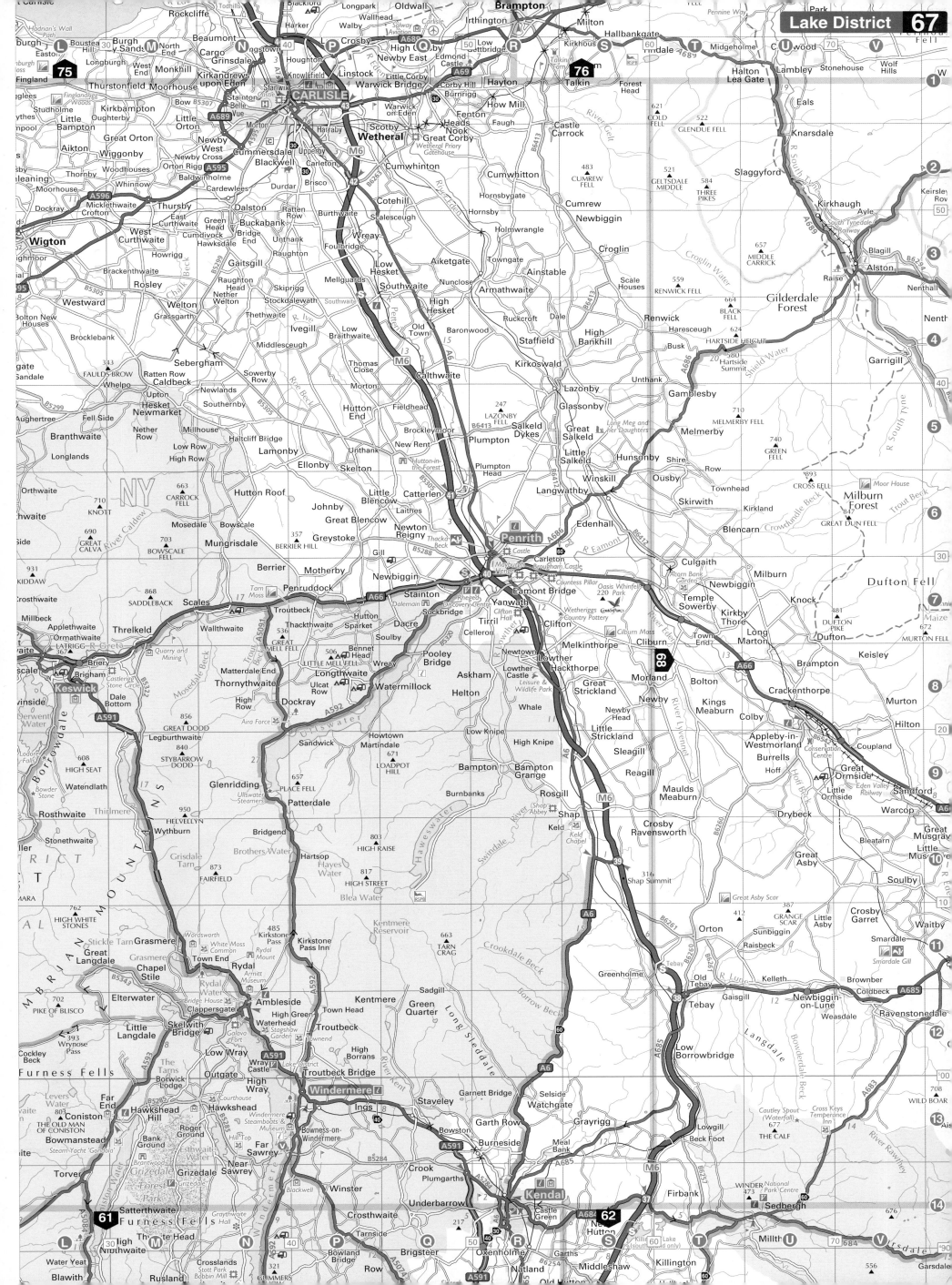

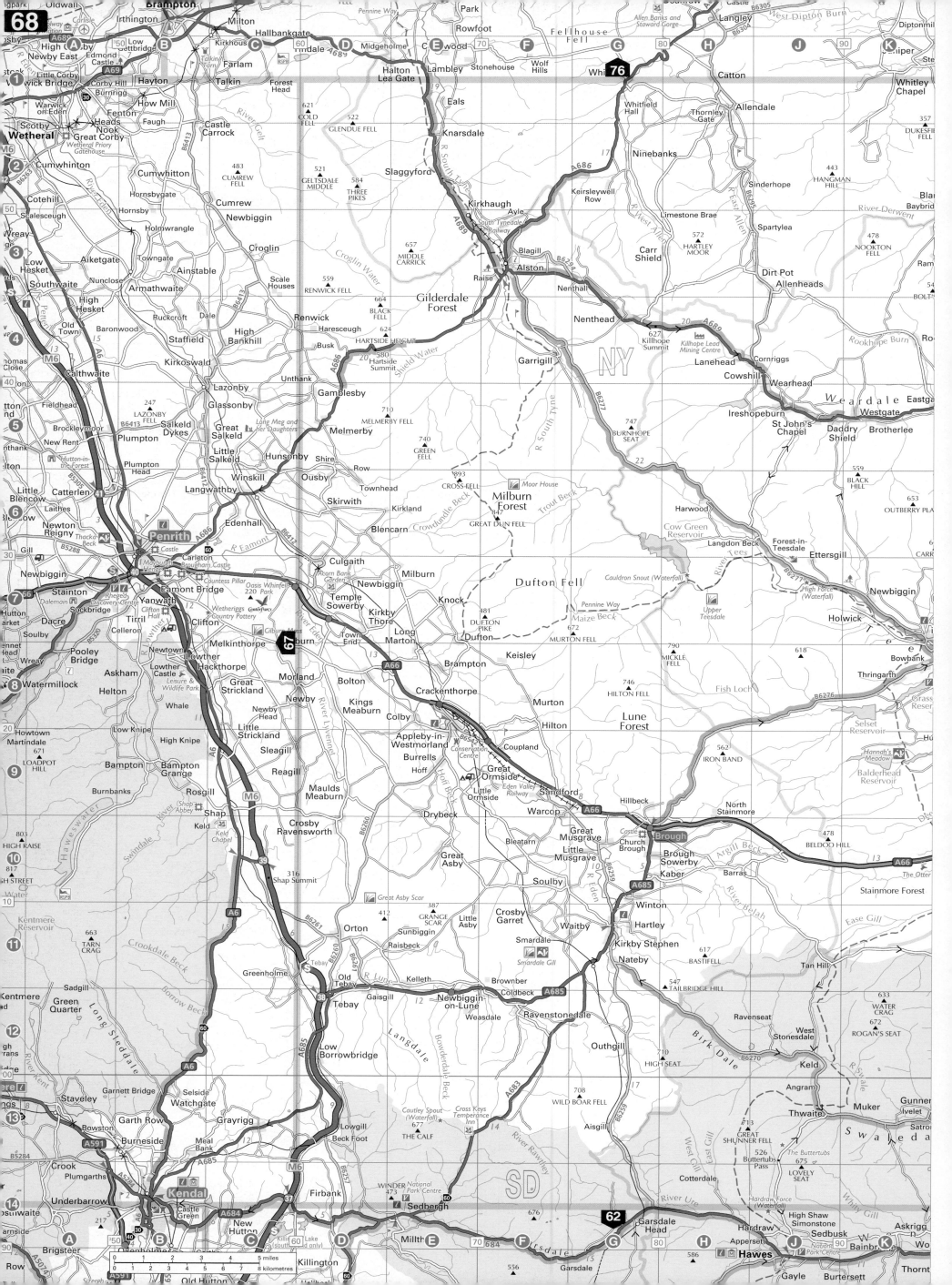

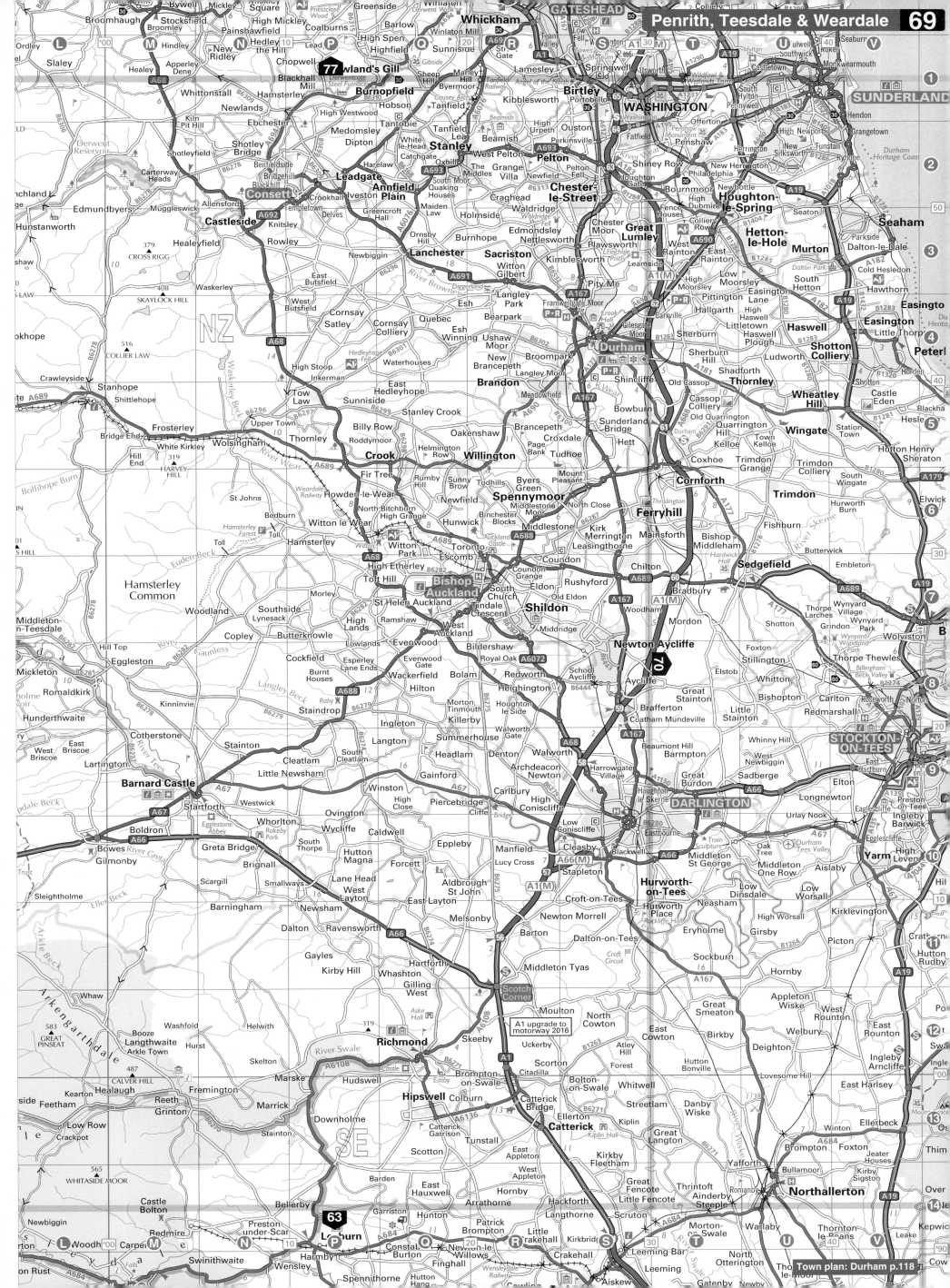

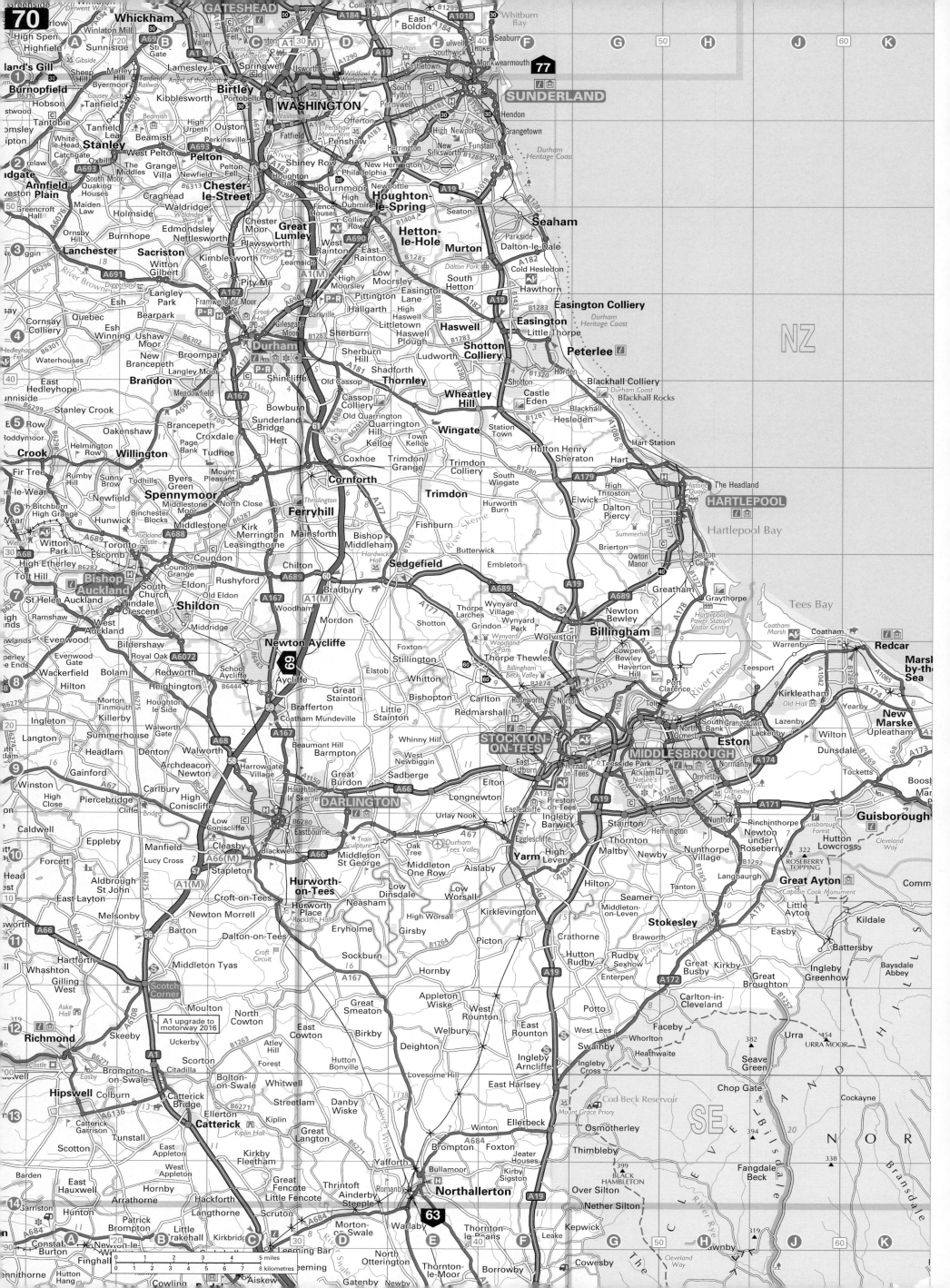

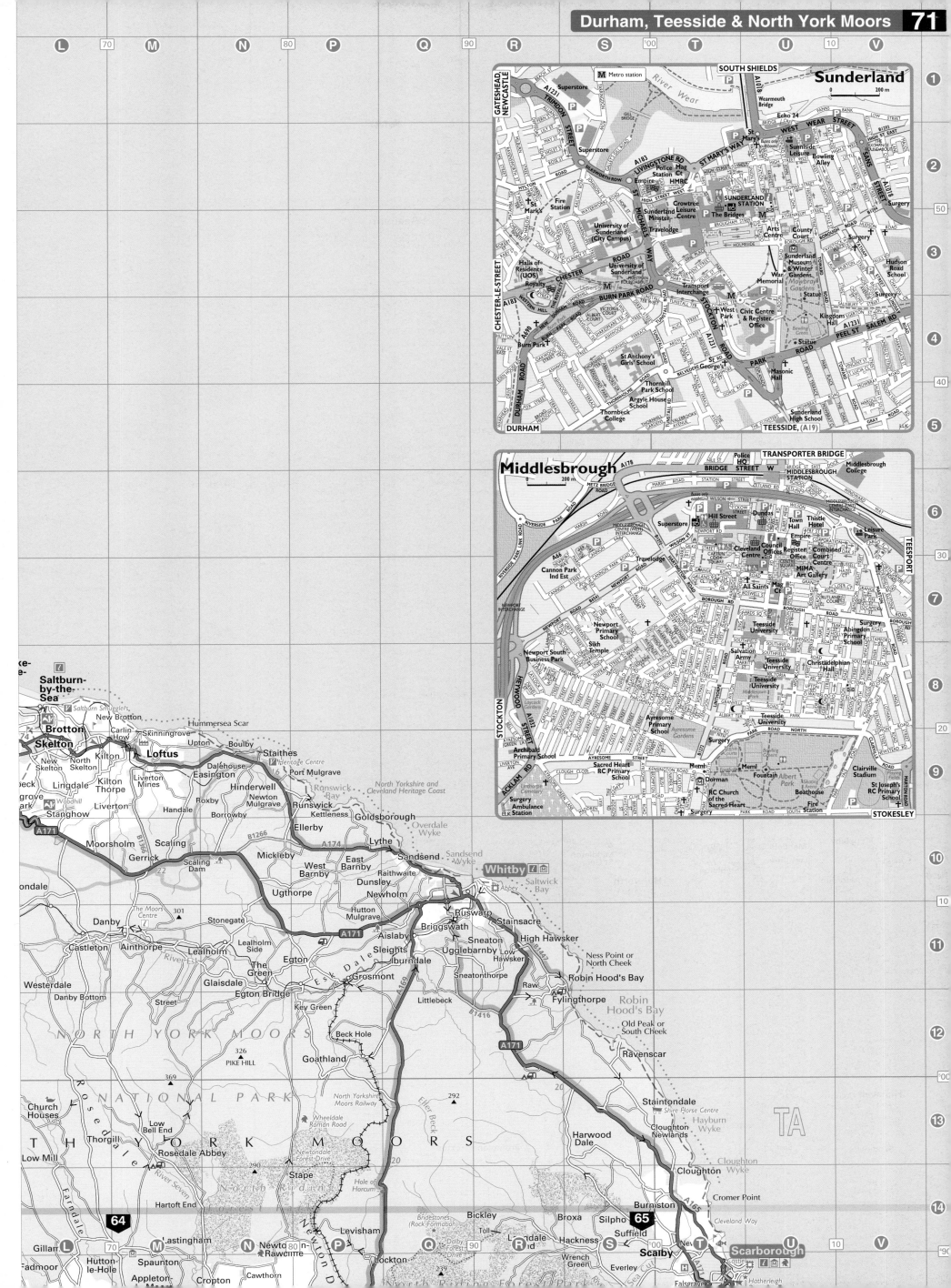

Sunderland

SOUTH SHIELDS

GATESHEAD, NEWCASTLE

River Wear

Metro station

Superstore
Superstore
Superstore

Wearmouth Bridge
Echo 24
WEST WEAR STREET

St Mary's
Police Station
Empire
HMRC
St Mark's
Fire Station
University of Sunderland (City Campus)
Travelodge
Sunderland Minster
Crowtree Leisure Centre
The Bridges
SUNDERLAND STATION
Sunnside Leisure
Bowling Alley
Surgery
Arts Centre
County Court
Hudson Road School
Surgery
Sunderland Museum & Winter Gardens
Mowbray Gardens
Halls of Residence (UOS)
Royalty
University of Sunderland
War Memorial
Transport Interchange
West Park
Civic Centre & Register Office
West Hall
Kingdom Hall
Burn Park
St Anthony's Girl's School
St George's
Masonic Hall
PEEL ST
SALEM RD
Thornhill Park School
Argyle House School
Thornbeck College
Sunderland High School

DURHAM
TEESSIDE, (A19)

Middlesbrough

TRANSPORTER BRIDGE
Police HQ
STREET
BRIDGE STREET
MIDDLESBROUGH STATION
Middlesbrough College
TEESPORT

Riverside Park
Superstore
Town Hall
Dundas
Thistle Hotel
Leisure Park
Cleveland Centre
Empire
Council Offices
Register Office
Combined Court Centre
Travelodge
MIMA Art Gallery
Cannon Park Ind Est
All Saints
Newport Interchange
Newport Primary School
Teesside University
Surgery
Abingdon Primary School
Newport South Business Park
Sikh Temple
Salvation Army
Teesside University
Christadelphian Hall
Teesside University
Ayresome Primary School
Teesside University
Surgery
Archibald Primary School
Sacred Heart RC Primary School
Meml
Meml
Fountain
Albert Park
Clairville Stadium
Dorman
Linthorpe Cemetery
Surgery
Ambulance Station
RC Church of the Sacred Heart
Surgery
Boathouse
Fire Station
St Joseph's RC Primary School
STOKESLEY

Saltburn-by-the-Sea
Saltburn Smugglers
New Brotton
Hummersea Scar
Brotton
Skinningrove
Upton
Boulby
Skelton
Carlin How
Staithes
Kilton
North Skelton
Loftus
Dalehouse
Port Mulgrave
New Skelton
Kilton Thorpe
Easington
Hinderwell
Newton Mulgrave
Runswick
North Yorkshire and Cleveland Heritage Coast
Lingdale
Liverton Mines
Roxby
Kettleness
Stanghow
Liverton
Handale
Borrowby
Runswick Bay
Goldsborough
Woodhill
Moorsholm
Scaling
Mickleby
Ellerby
Lythe
Overdale Wyke
Sandsend Wyke
Gerrick
Scaling Dam
West Barnby
East Barnby
Raithwaite
Sandsend
Whitby
Saltwick Bay
Danby
Stonegate
Ugthorpe
Dunsley
Newholm
Hutton Mulgrave
Ruswarp
Stainsacre
Abbey
The Moors Centre
Aislaby
Briggswath
High Hawsker
Castleton
Ainthorpe
Lealholm
Lealholm Side
Egton
Sleights
Sneaton
Low Hawsker
Westerdale
Glaisdale
Iburndale
Ugglebarnby
Ness Point or North Cheek
The Green
Grosmont
Sneatonthorpe
Robin Hood's Bay
Danby Bottom
Egton Bridge
Raw
Fylingthorpe
Street
Key Green
Littlebeck
Robin Hood's Bay
NORTH YORK MOORS
Beck Hole
Old Peak or South Cheek
PIKE HILL
Goathland
Ravenscar
NATIONAL PARK
North Yorkshire Moors Railway
Staintondale
Shire Horse Centre
Church Houses
Low Bell End
Harwood Dale
Cloughton Newlands
Hayburn Wyke
Thorgill
Wheeldale Roman Road
Low Mill
Rosedale Abbey
Newtondale Forest Drive
Hole of Horcum
Stape
Cloughton
THE YORK MOORS
North Riding
Cloughton Wyke
Hartoft End
Bridestones (Rock Formation)
Bickley
Broxa
Silpho
Cromer Point
Burniston
Cleveland Way
Gillar
Lastingham
Levisham
Toll
Suffield
Scalby
Scarborough
Hutton-le-Hole
Spaunton
Newton Rawcliffe
Lockton
Dalby Forest Drive
Wrench Green
Everley
Hackness
Appleton
Cropton
Cawthorn
North Riding Forest Park
Falsgrave

64
65
TA

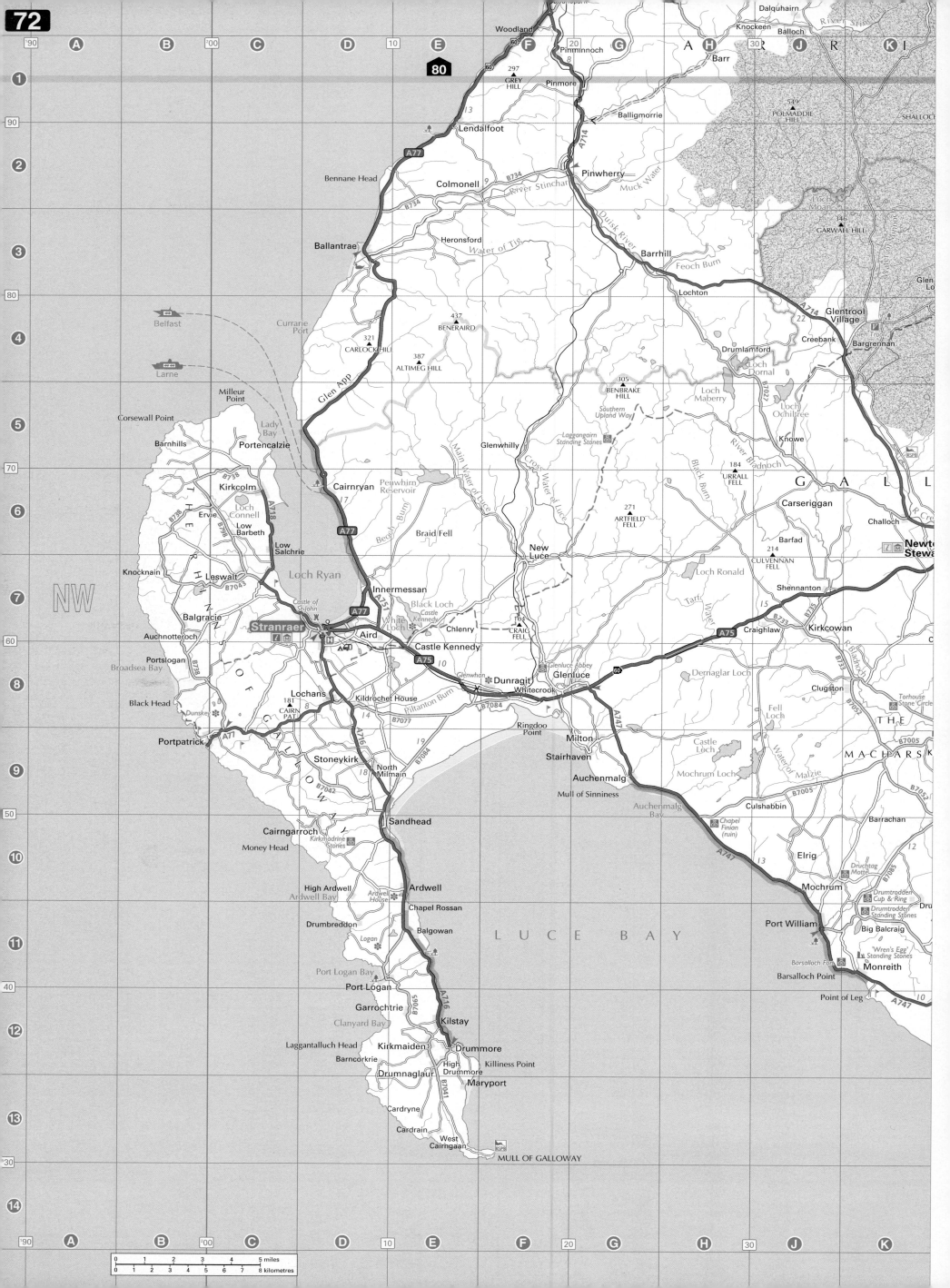

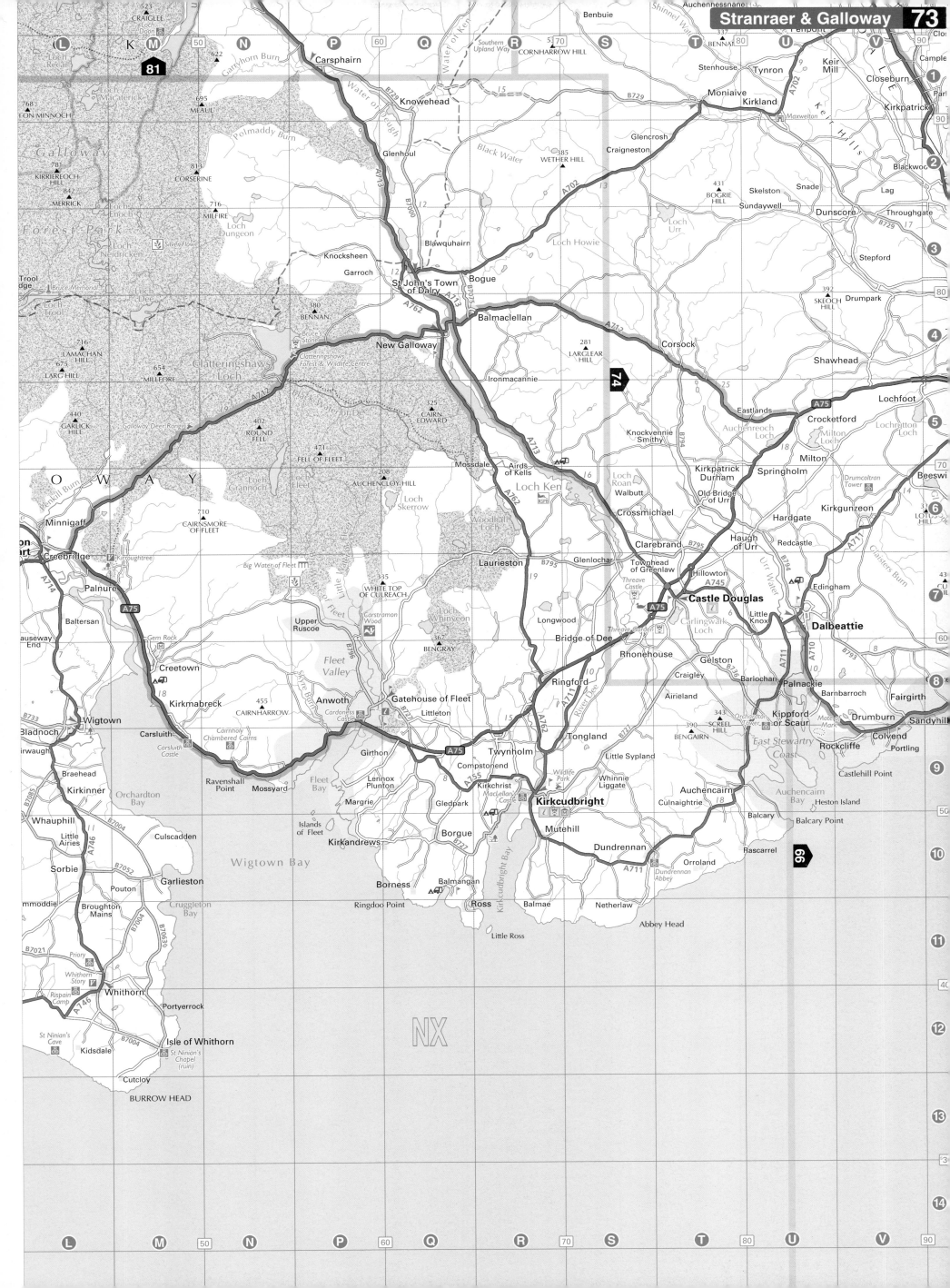

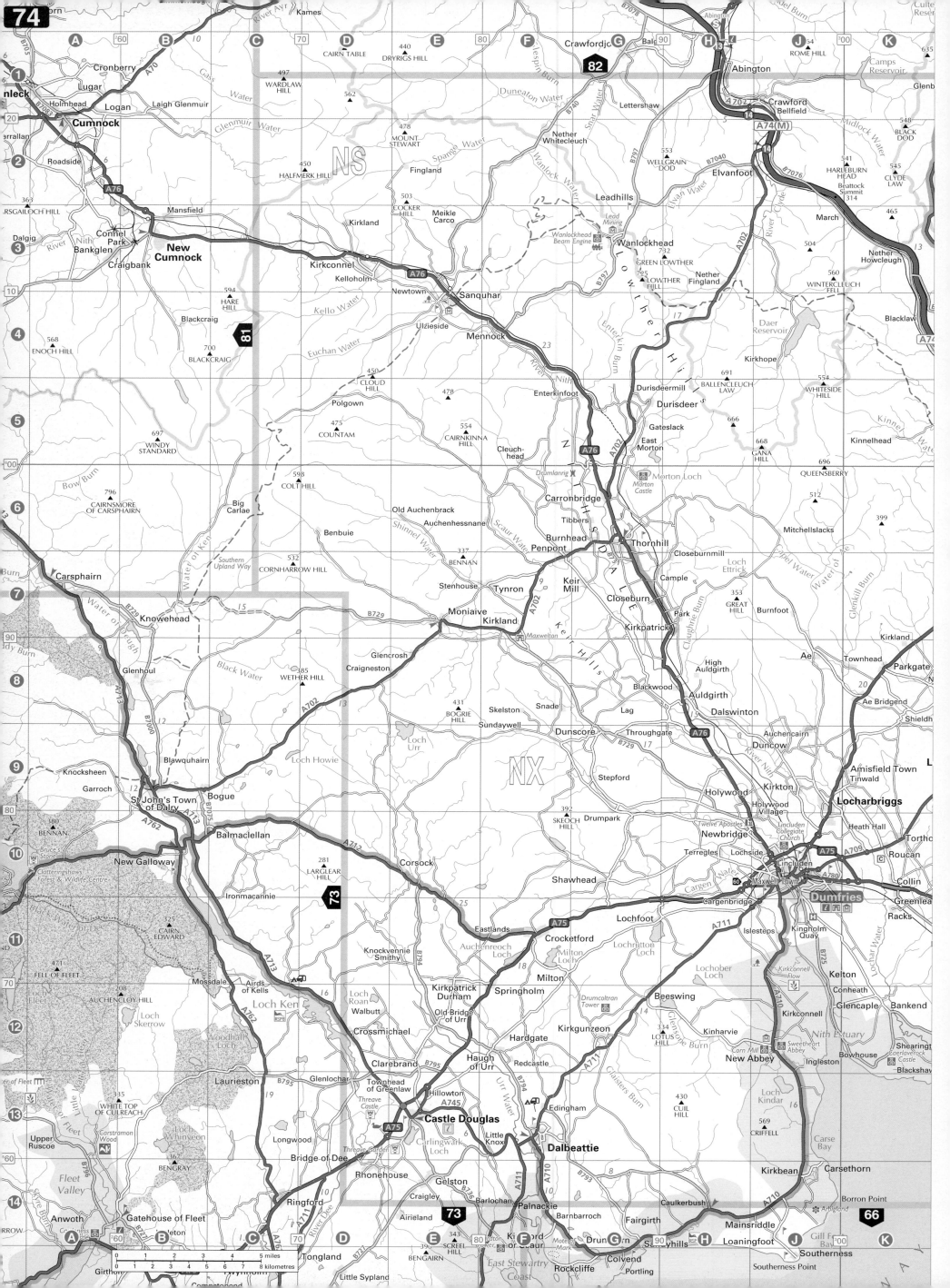

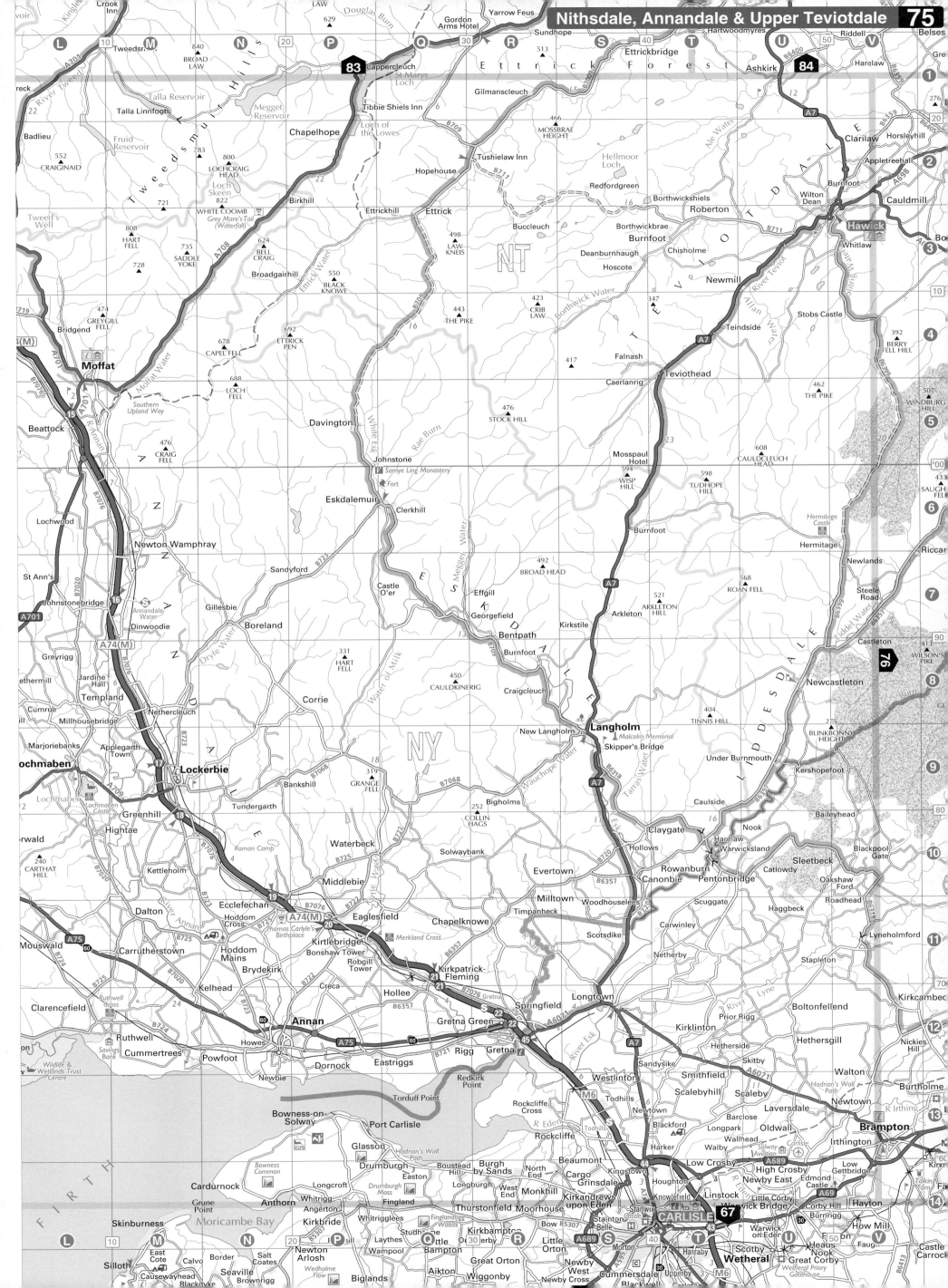

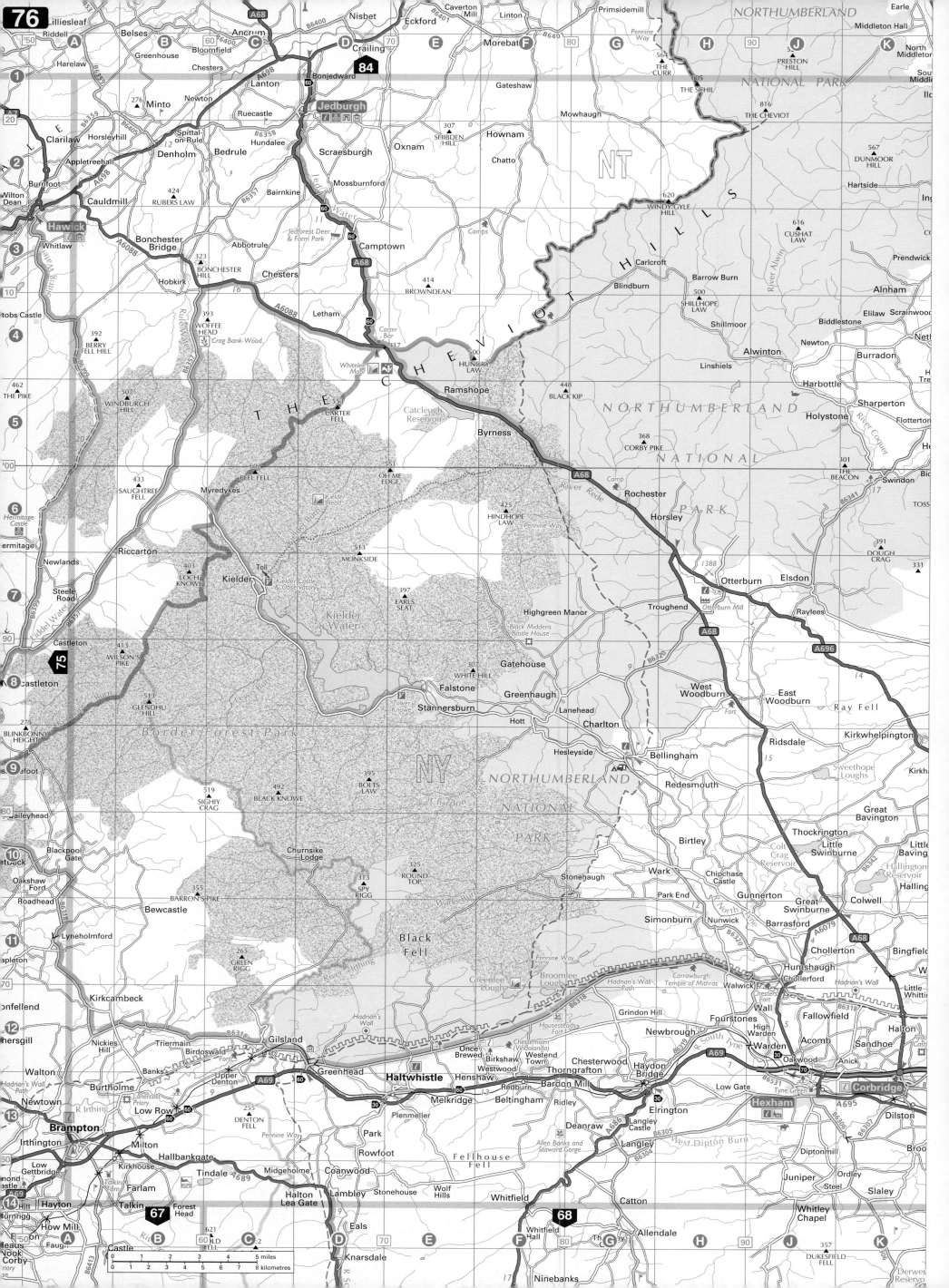

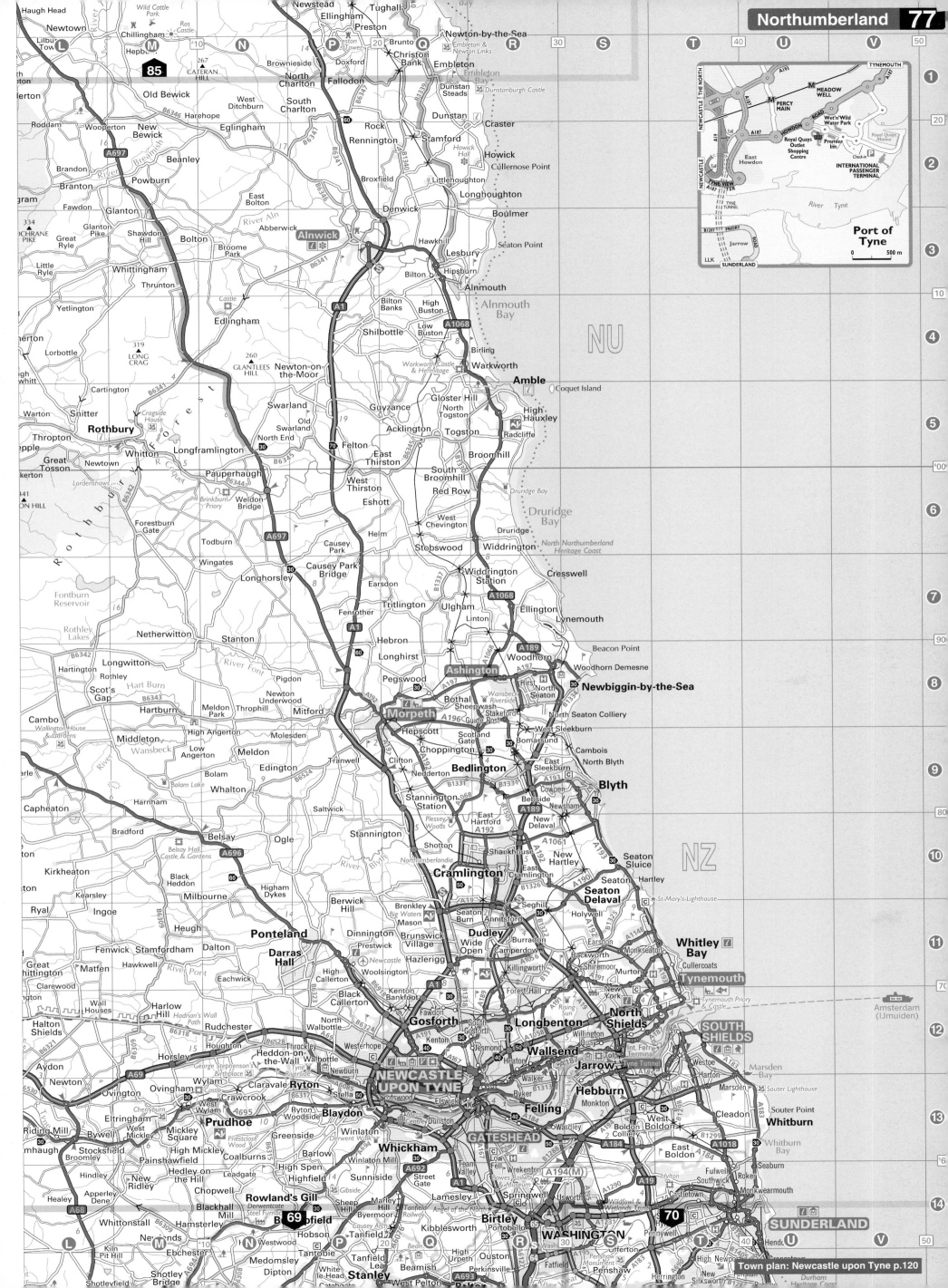

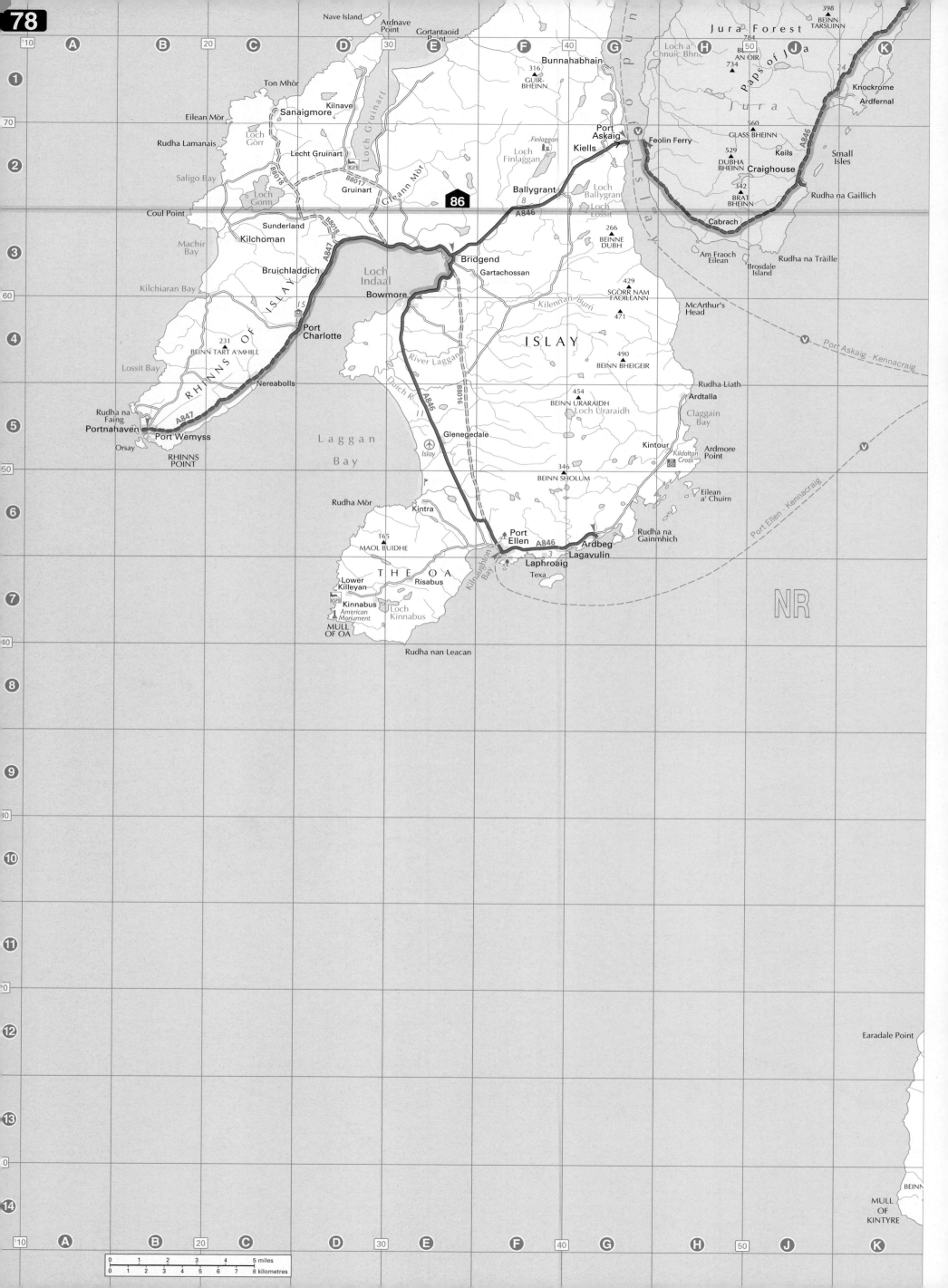

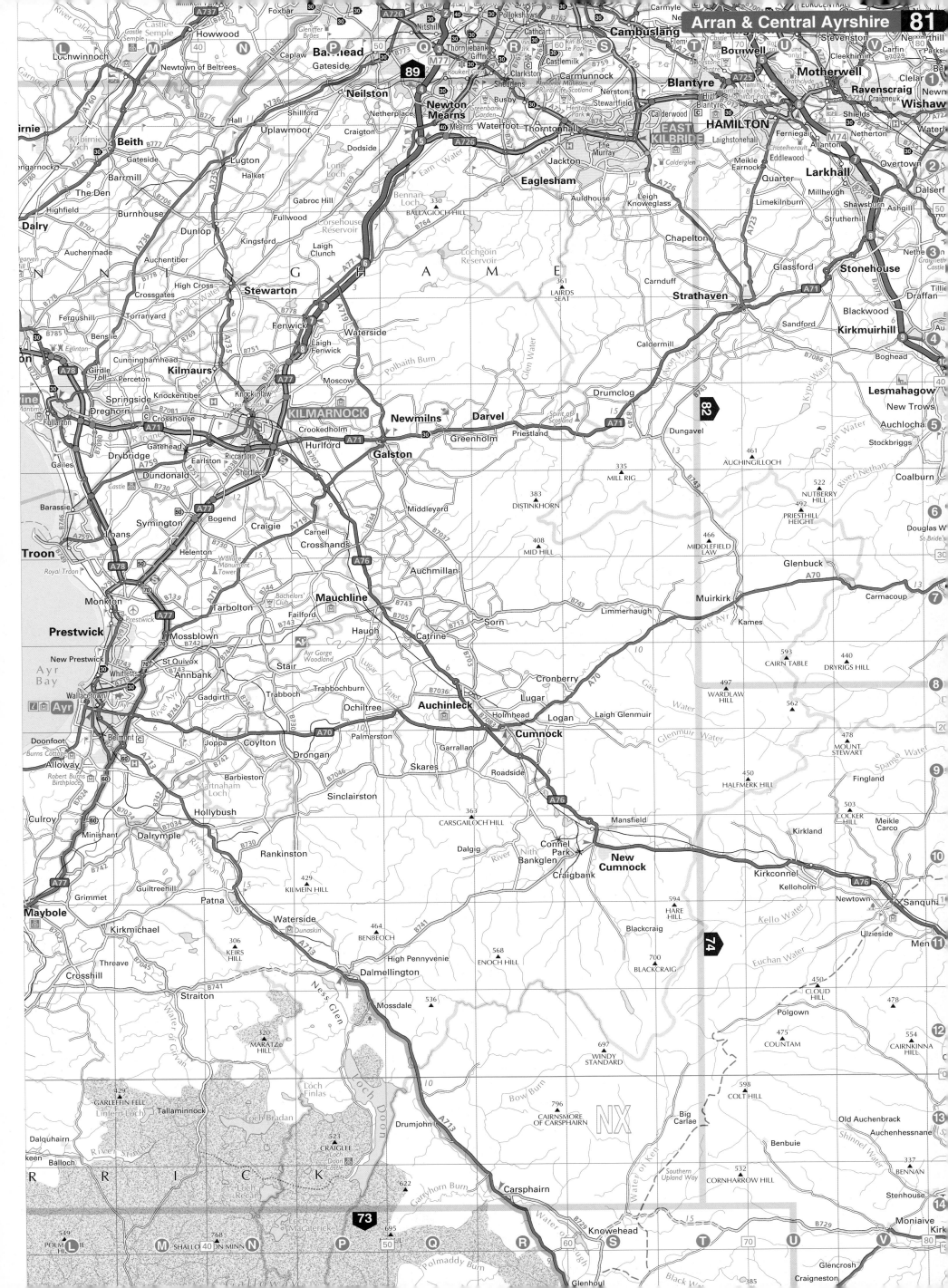

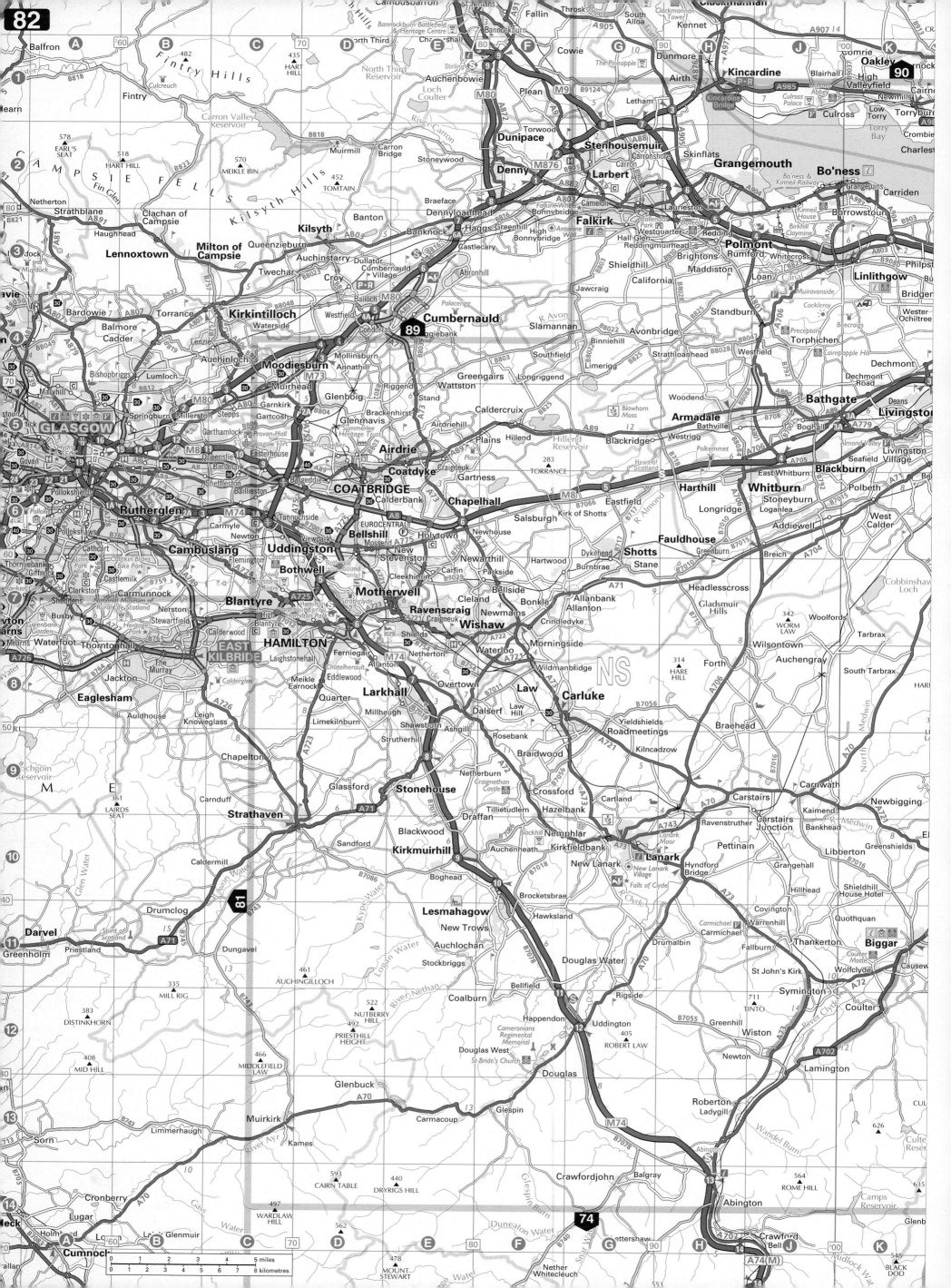

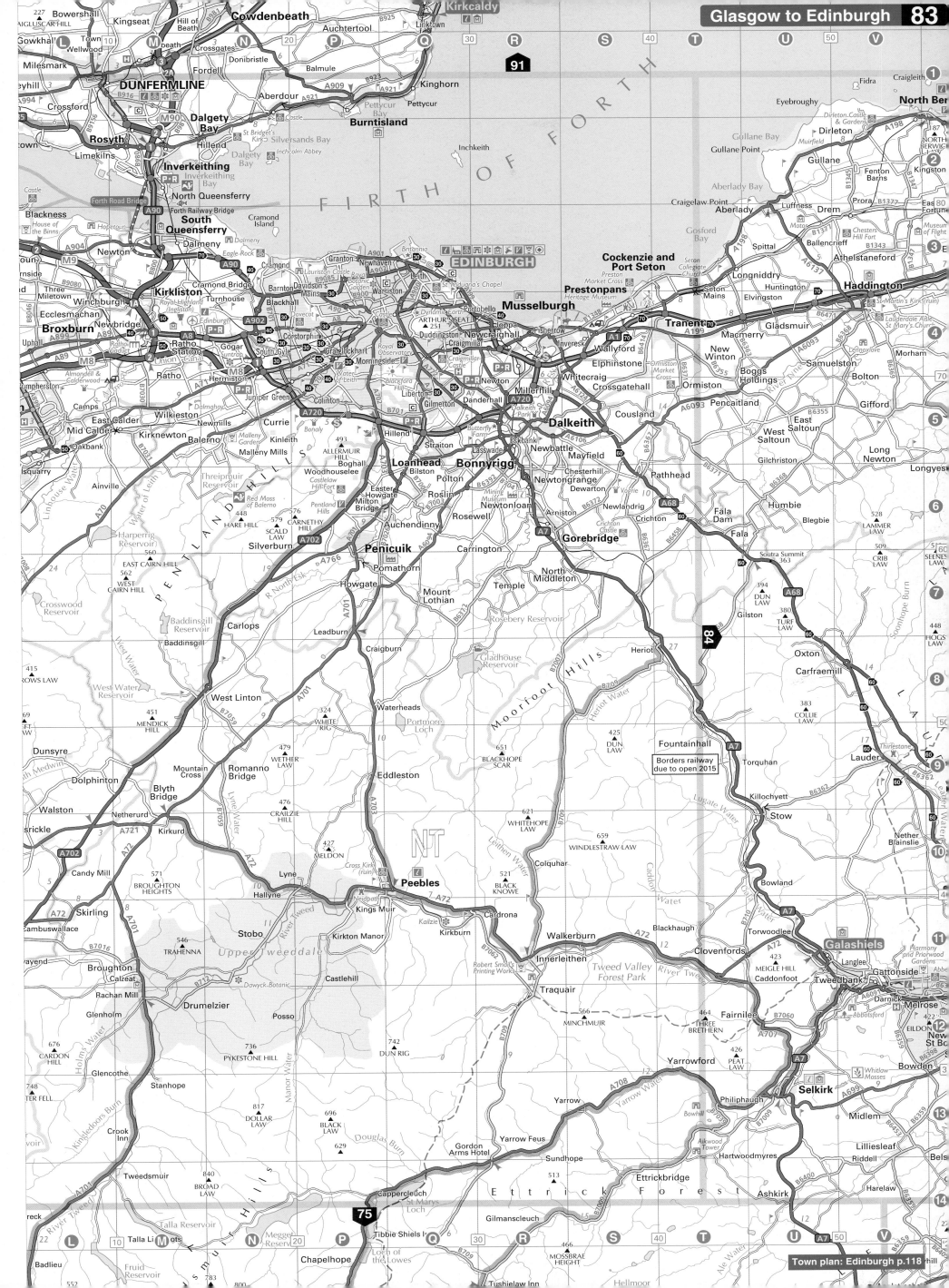

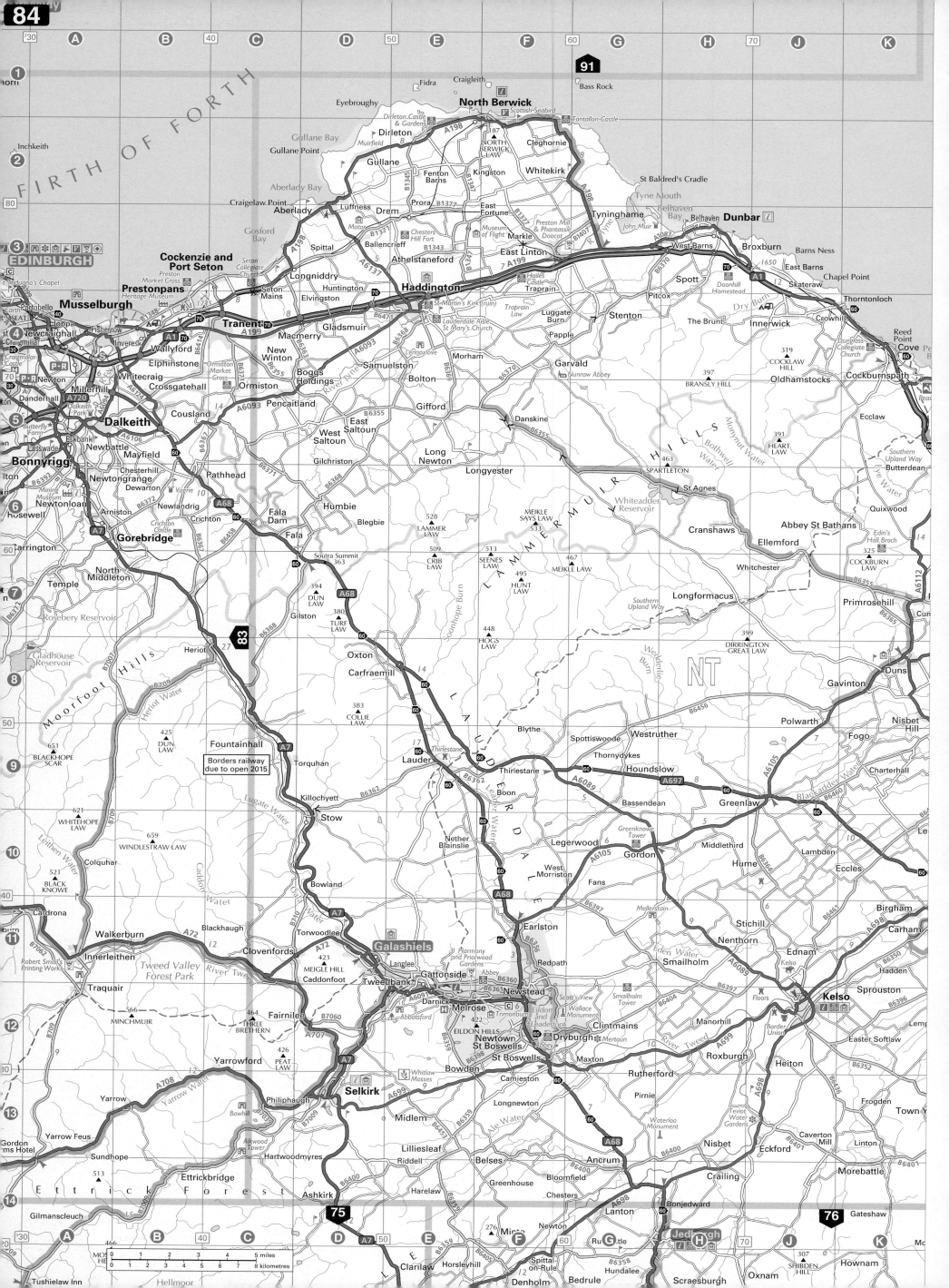

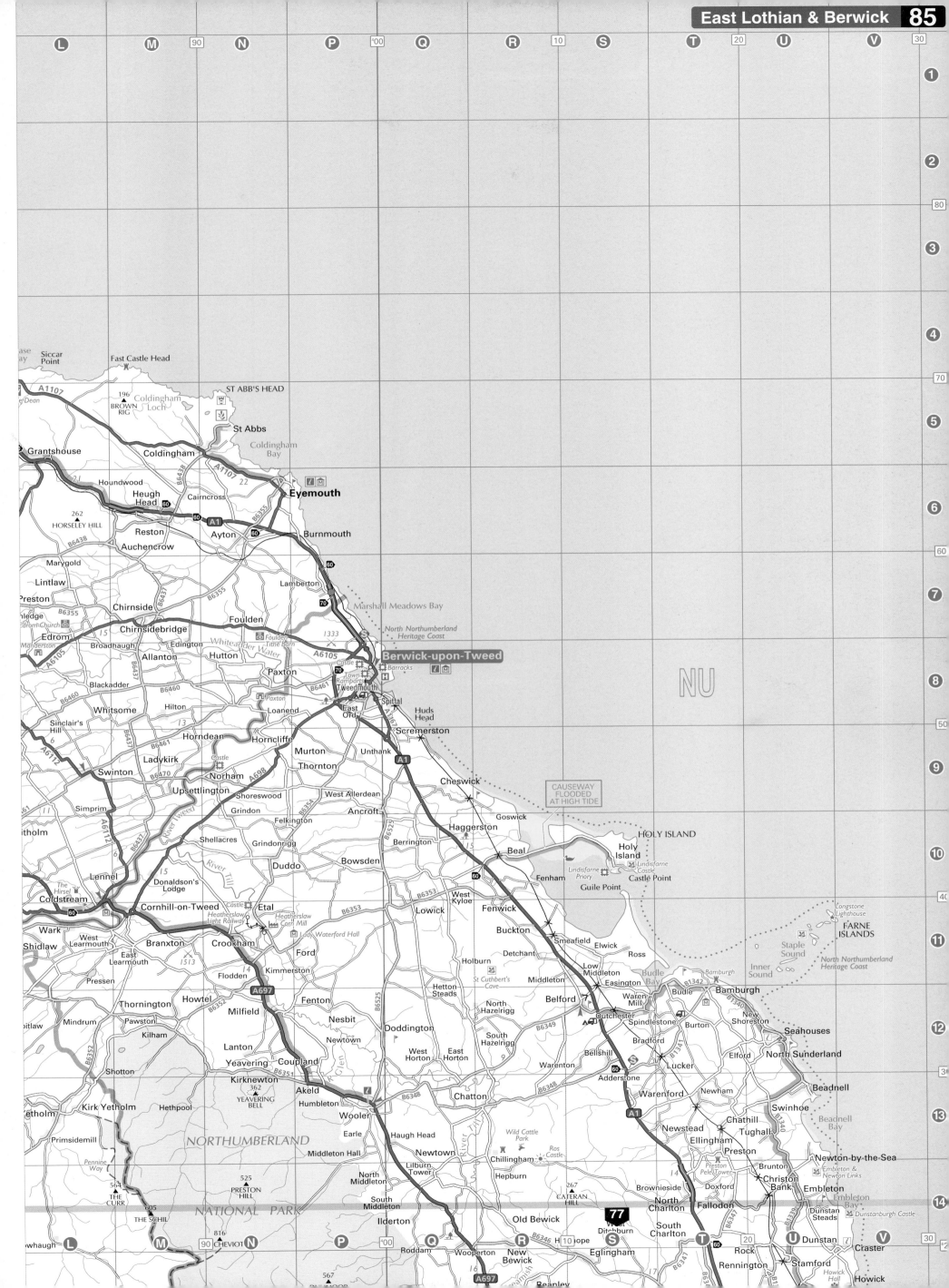

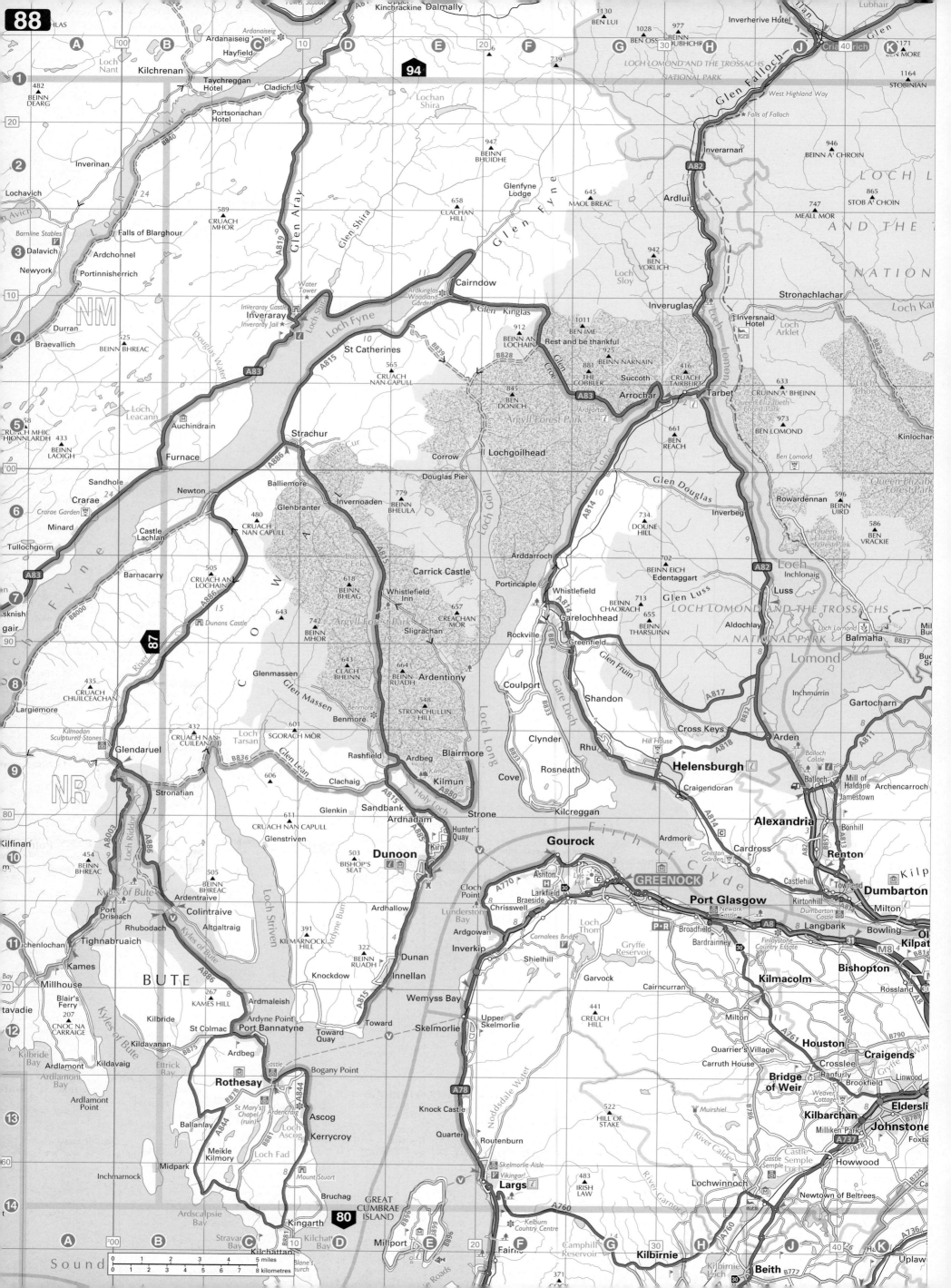

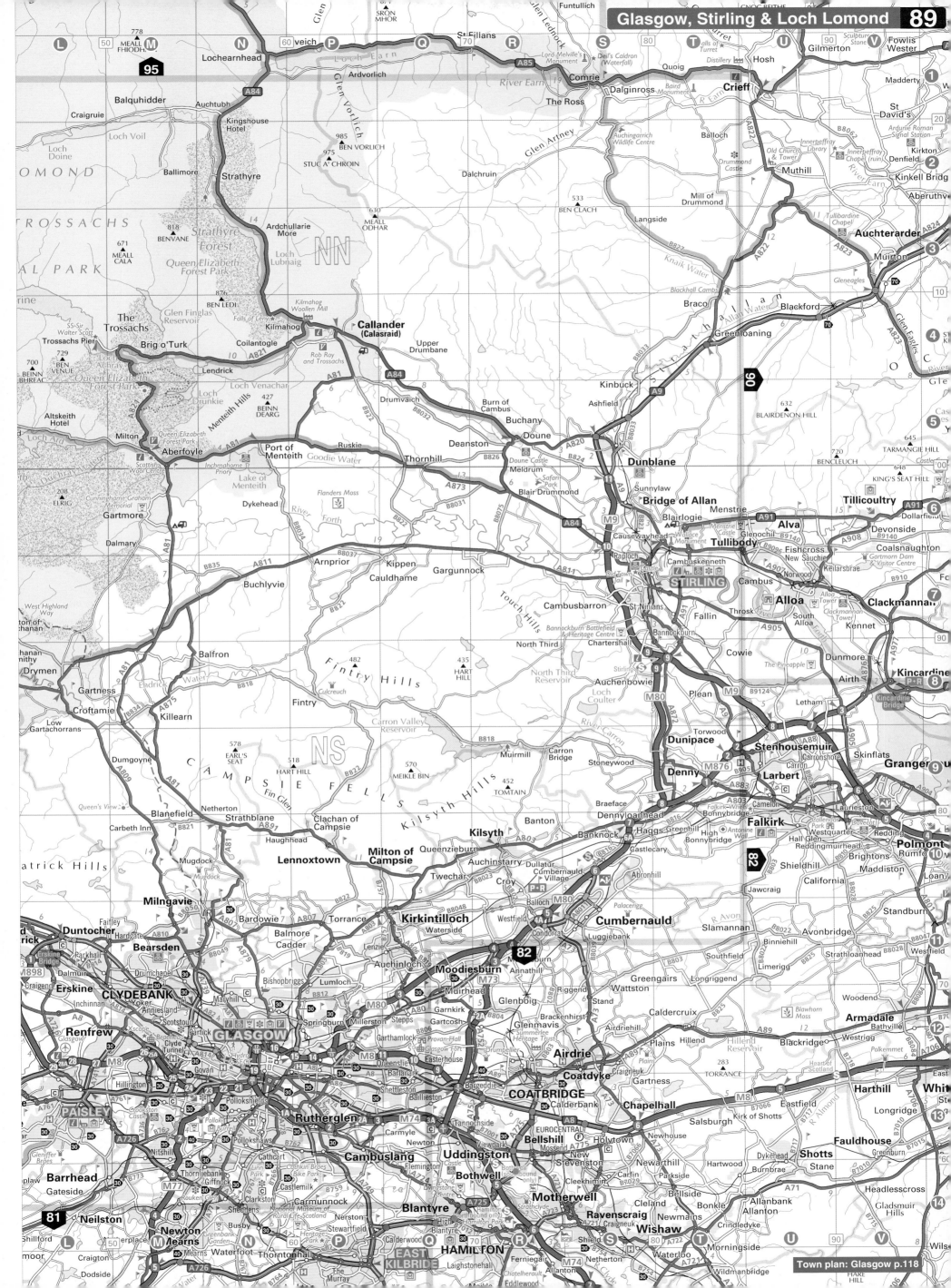

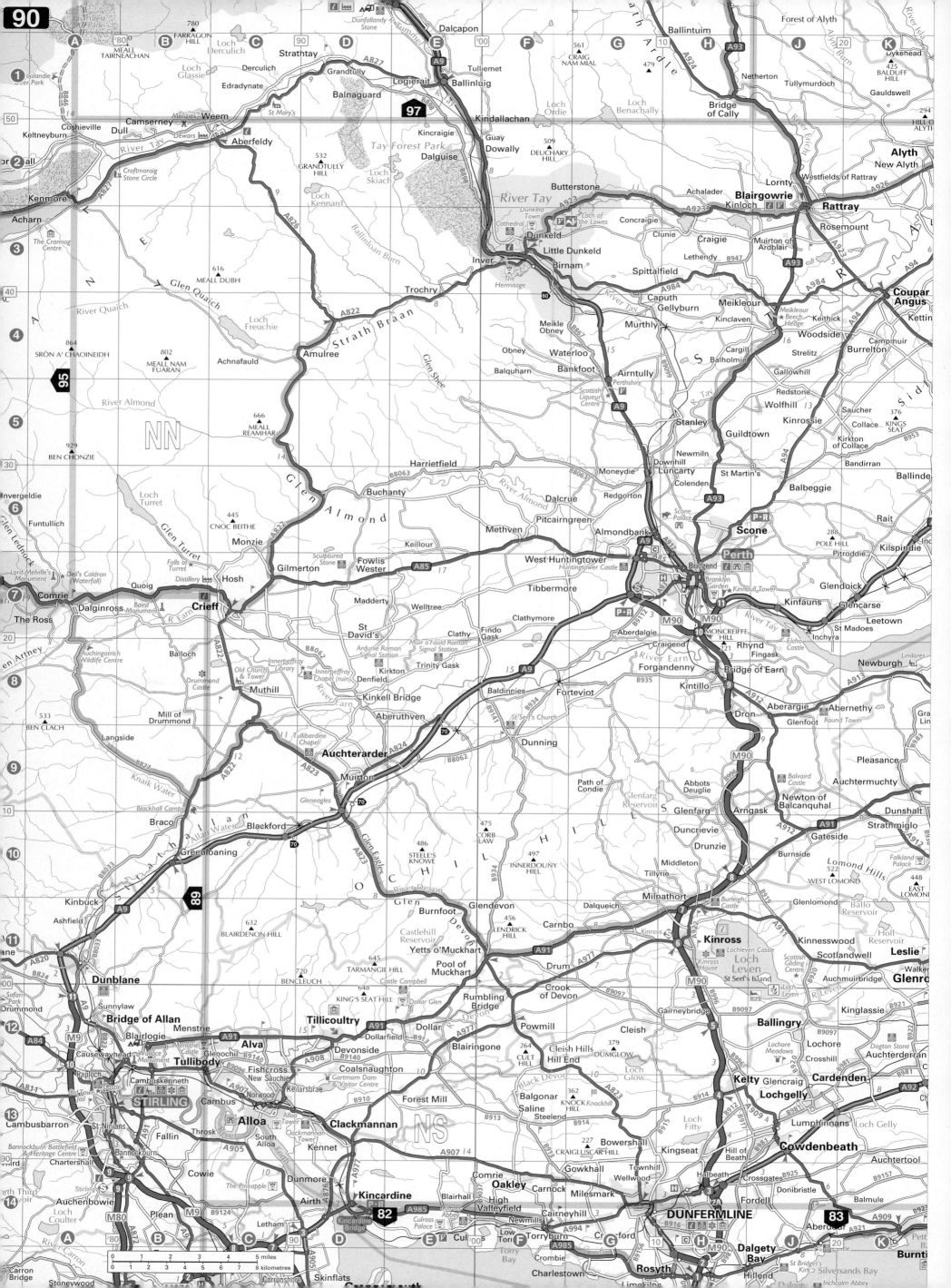

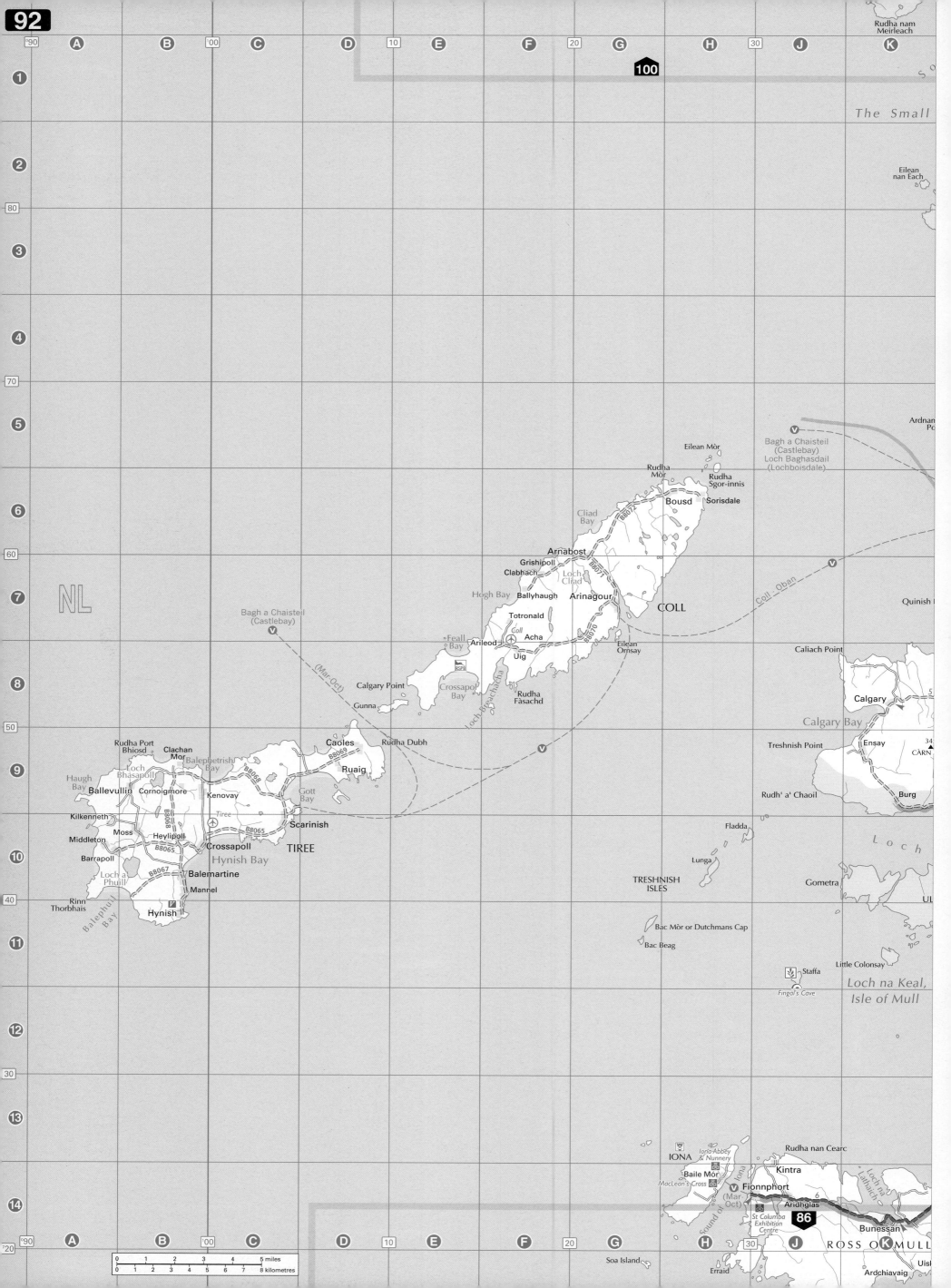

Rudha nam
Meirleach

The Small

Eilean
nan Each

100

NL

Ardnan
Po

Bagh a Chaisteil
(Castlebay)
Loch Baghasdail
(Lochboisdale)

Eilean Mòr

Rudha
Mòr
Rudha
Sgor-innis
Bousd   Sorisdale

Cliad
Bay

Arnabost

Grishipoll
Clabhach
Loch
Cliad
Arinagour
COLL
Coll - Oban

Hogh Bay   Ballyhaugh
Quinish

Bagh a Chaisteil
(Castlebay)
Totronald
Coll
Arileod   Acha
Feall
Bay   Uig
Eilean
Ornsay
Caliach Point

(Mar-Oct)
Calgary Point   Crossapol
Bay
Rudha
Fàsachd   Calgary

Gunna   Loch Breachacha   Calgary Bay

Rudha Dubh   Treshnish Point   Ensay
CÀRN

Rudha Port
Bhiosd   Clachan
Mòr
Balephetrish
Bay   Caoles
B8069   Ruaig   Fladda
Rudh' a' Chaoil   Burg

Haugh
Bay   Loch
Bhasapoll   B8068   Gott
Bay
Kilkenneth   Ballevullin   Cornoigmore   Kenovay   Tiree   Lunga
Moss   Heylipoll   Scarinish   TRESHNISH
ISLES   Gometra   UL
Middleton   B8065   Crossapoll
Barrapoll   B8065   TIREE
Balemartine   Bac Mòr or Dutchmans Cap
Rinn
Thorbhais   Loch
a'
Phuill   B8067   Mannel   Hynish Bay   Bac Beag
Balephuil
Bay   Hynish   Little Colonsay
Staffa   Loch na Keal,
Isle of Mull
Fingal's Cave

Iona Abbey
& Nunnery   Rudha nan Cearc
IONA
Baile Mòr   Kintra
MacLean's Cross   Fionnphort
(Mar-
Oct)   Aridhglas   Loch na
Lathaich
St Columba
Exhibition
Centre   **86**   Bunessan
Soa Island   ROSS O MULL
Erraid   Ardchiavaig   Uisl

0   1   2   3   4   5 miles
0   1   2   3   4   5   6   7   8 kilometres

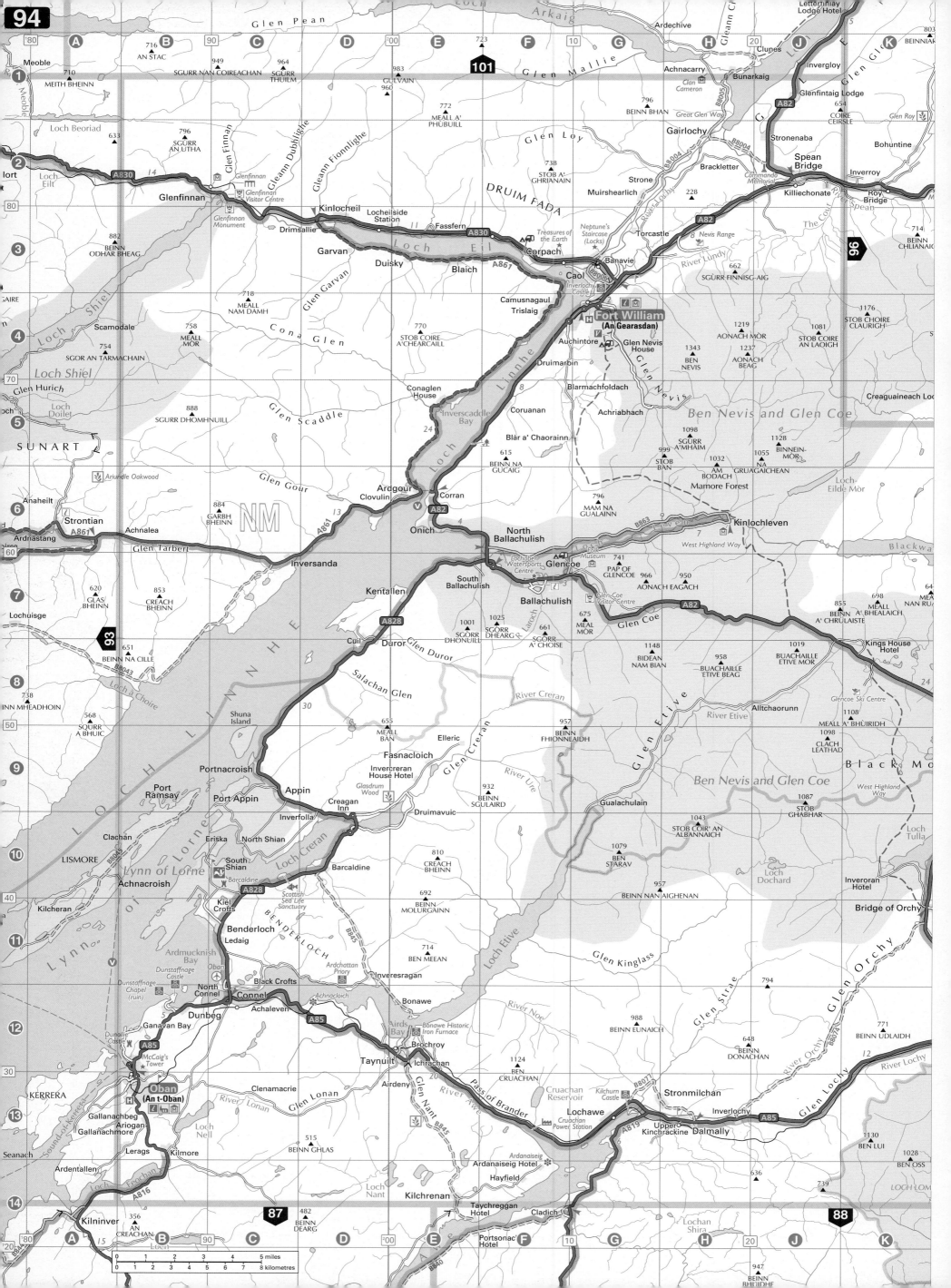

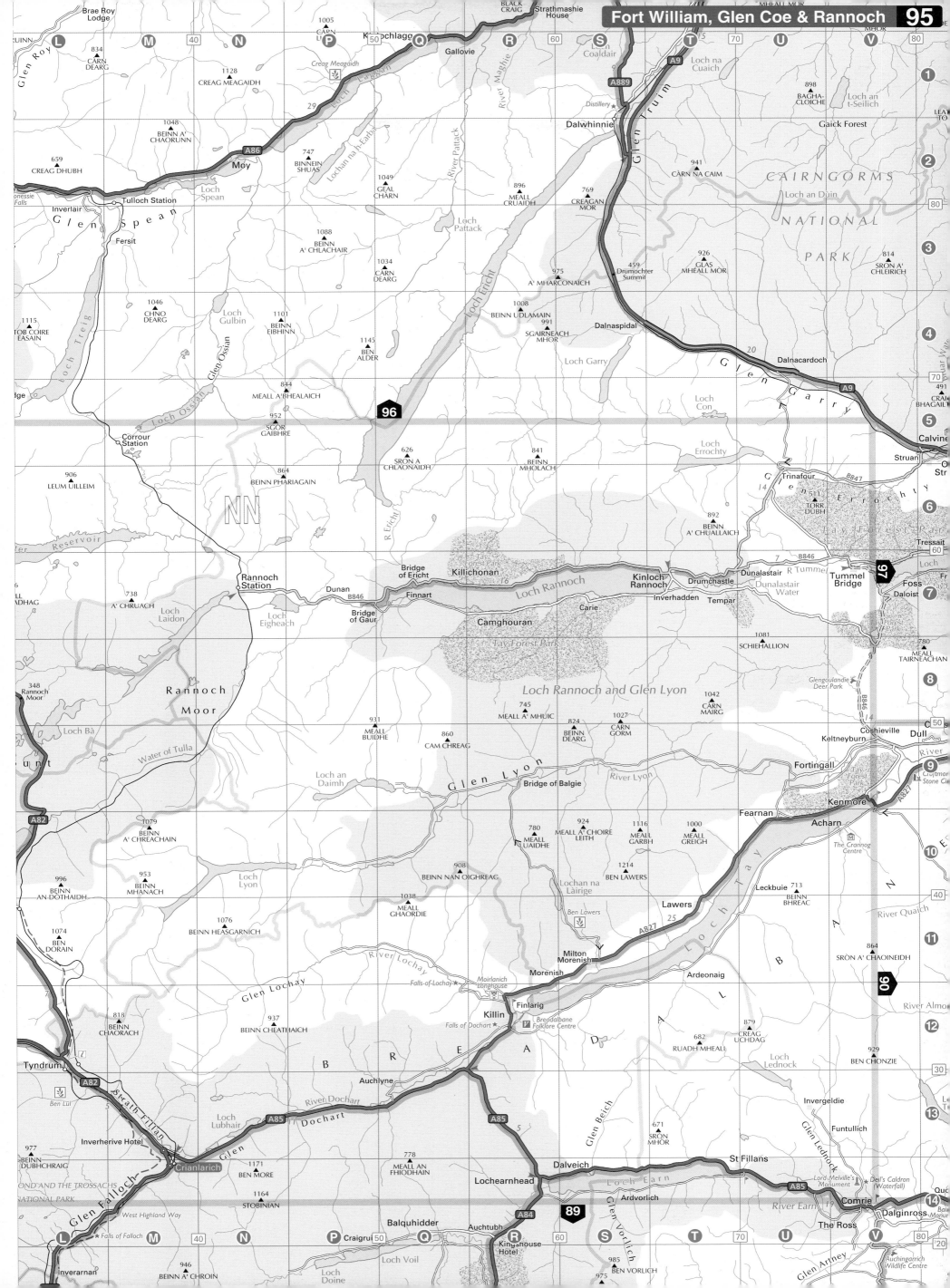

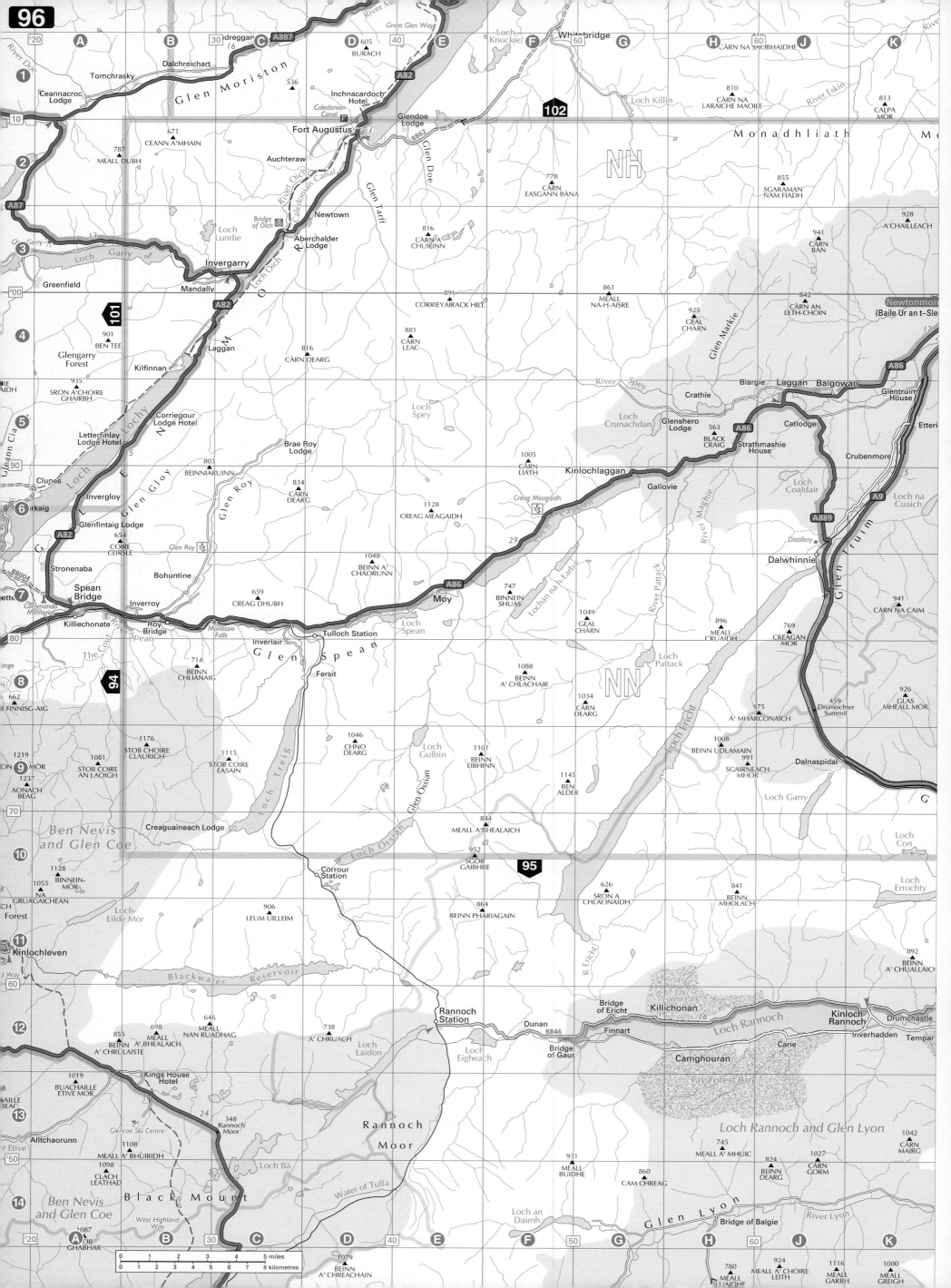

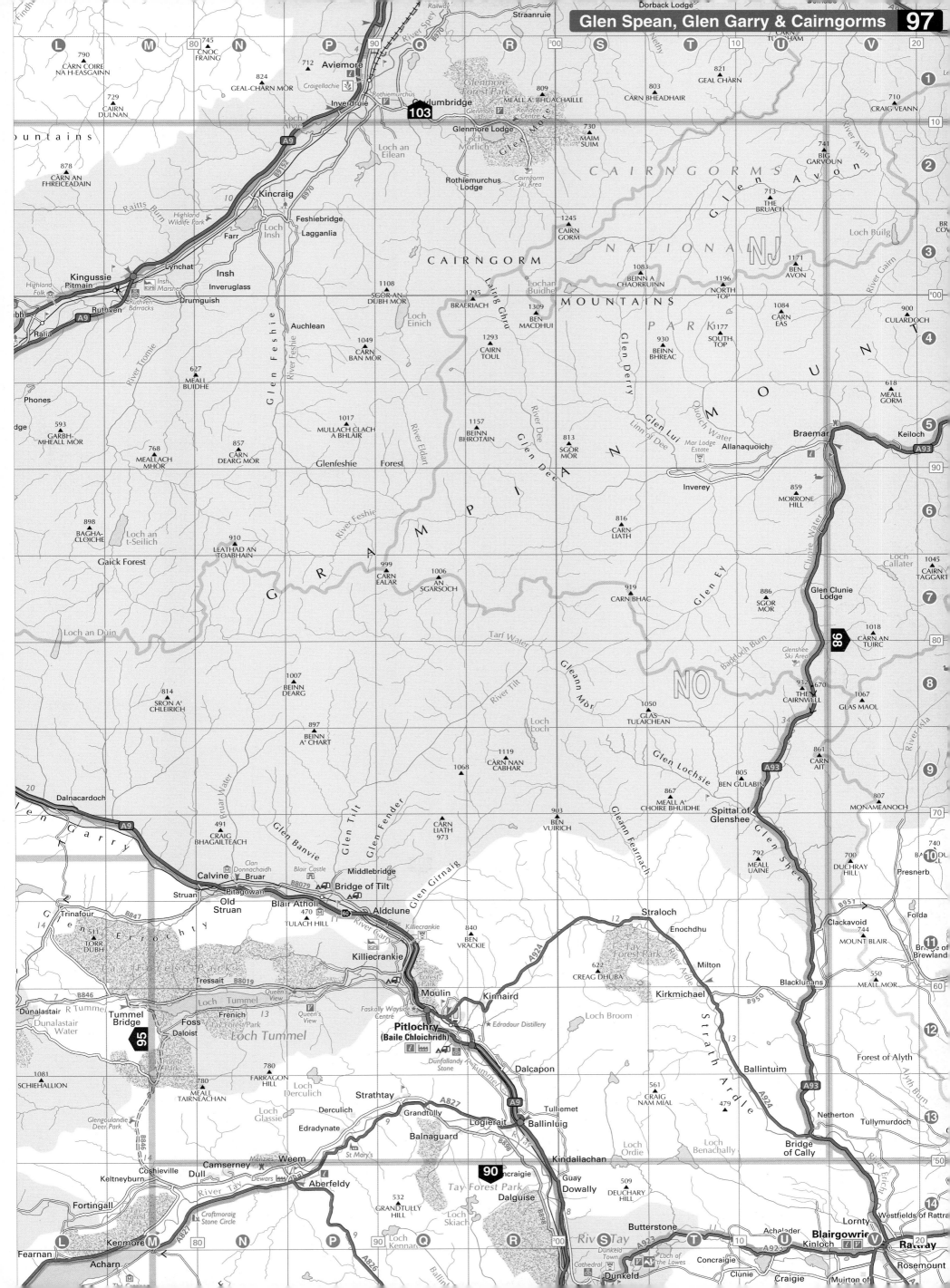

L   M   80 745   N   P   Q   00   R   S   T   10   U   V   20

Dorback Lodge
Straanruie
River Spey
Railway

790
CÀRN COIRE
NA H-EASGAINN
CNOC
FRAING
712
Aviemore
821
GEAL CHÀRN
710
CRAIG VEANN

824
GEAL-CHÀRN MÓR
Craigellachie
Rothiemurchus
Coylumbridge
Glenmore
Forest Park
Meall a' Bhuachaille
809
803
CÀRN BHEADHAIR

729
CAIRN
DULNAN
Inverdruie
103
Glenmore Lodge
Glen More
Reindeer
Centre
730
MAIM
SUIM
741
BIG
GARVOUN
River Avon

878
CÀRN AN
FHREICEADAIN
A9
Loch an
Eilean
Loch
Morlich
713
THE
BRUACH
Glen Avon
Loch Builg

Kincraig
Rothiemurchus
Lodge
Cairngorm
Ski Area
1245
CAIRN
GORM
CAIRNGORMS
NATIONAL
NJ
1171
BEN
AVON

Feshiebridge
Lagganlia
CAIRNGORM
1083
BEINN A
CHAORRUINN
1196
NORTH
TOP
1084
CÀRN
EÀS
900
CULARDOCH

Farr
Loch Insh
1108
SGÒR AN
DUBH MÓR
1295
BRAERIACH
Lairig Ghru
1309
BEN
MACDHUI
MOUNTAINS
PARK
K
1177
SOUTH
TOP

Kingussie
Pitmain
Lynchat
Insh
Inveruglass
Drumguish
Loch
Einich
1293
CAIRN
TOUL
930
BEINN
BHREAC
618
MEALL
GORM

Ruthven
Ruthven
Barracks
Insh
Marshes
Auchlean
1049
CÀRN
BAN MÓR
Lochan
Buidhe
Glen Derry
Glen Lui
Quoich Water

Ralia
627
MEALL
BUIDHE
Glen Feshie
River Feshie
1017
MULLACH CLACH
A BHLÀIR
1157
BEINN
BHROTAIN
813
SGÒR
MÓR
Linn of Dee
Mar Lodge
Estate
Allanaquoich
Braemar
Keiloch
A93

Phones
593
GARBH-
MHEALL MÓR
768
MEALLACH
MHÓR
857
CÀRN
DEARG MÓR
Glenfeshie   Forest
River Eildart
Glen Dee
Inverey
859
MORRONE
HILL

898
BAGHA-
CLOICHE
Loch an
t-Seilich
910
LEATHAD AN
TAOBHAIN
River Feshie
816
CÀRN
LIATH

Gaick Forest
999
CÀRN
EALAR
1006
AN
SGARSOCH
919
CÀRN BHAC
886
SGÒR
MÓR
Glen Clunie
Lodge
1045
CAIRN
TAGGART
Loch
Callater

Loch an Duin
Tarf Water
Glen Ey
Clunie Water
86
1018
CÀRN AN
TUIRC
80

1007
BEINN
DEARG
Glenshee
Ski Area
932
THE
CAIRNWELL
1670
1067
GLAS MAOL

814
SRON A'
CHLEIRICH
897
BEINN
A' CHART
River Tilt
Gleann Mòr
1050
GLAS
TULAICHEAN
NO
A93
Glen Lochsie
861
CÀRN
AIT

Dalnacardoch
491
CRAIG
BHAGAILTEACH
1068
1119
CÀRN NAN
CABHAR
Loch
Loch
867
MEALL A'
CHOIRE BHUIDHE
805
BEN GULABIN
Spittal of
Glenshee
807
MONAMEANOCH
70

Glen Garry
A9
Glen Banvie
Glen Tilt
Glen Fender
CÀRN
LIATH
973
903
BEN
VUIRICH
Gleann Feàrnach
Glen Shee
792
MEALL
UAINE
700
DUCHRAY
HILL
740
BA
DU
10
Presnerb

Calvine
Bruar
Clan
Donnachaidh
Blair Castle
Middlebridge
Straloch
B957

Trinafour
Pitagowan
Old
Struan
Blair Atholl
Aldclune
Glen Girnaig
Enochdhu
Clackavoid
744
MOUNT BLAIR
Bridge of
Brewland

Struan
470
TULACH HILL
60
Killiecrankie
840
BEN
VRACKIE
Tay
Forest
Park
Milton
Kirkmichael
550
MEALL MÓR
11

TORR
DUBH
511
Tay Forest Park
River Garry
Killiecrankie
Blacklunans
B950

Tressait
B8019
Queen's
View
Moulin
Kinnaird
622
CREAG DHUBA
561
CRAIG
NAM MIAL
Ballintuim
Forest of Alyth

Dunalastair
R Tummel
Frenich
Queen's
View
Faskally Wayside
Centre
Loch Broom
479
Strath Ardle
12

Tummel
Bridge
95
Foss
Daloist
Loch Tummel
Pitlochry
(Baile Chloichridh)
Edradour Distillery
Dalcapon
Kirkmichael
A924
A93
Bridge
of Cally

Schiehallion
1081
780
MEALL
TAIRNEACHAN
FARRAGON
HILL
Dunfallandy
Stone
Strathtay
Grandtully
Logierait
Dalguise
Netherton
Tullymurdoch
13

Glengoulandie
Deer Park
Loch
Glassie
Derculich
Edradynate
A827
Balnaguard
Ballinluig
509
DUCHARY
HILL
Bridge
of Cally

Fortingall
Camserney
Weem
Dull
St Mary's
Menzies
Kindallachan
Guay
Dowally
Tay Forest Park
Butterstone
Lornty
14

Keltneyburn
Coshieville
Aberfeldy
532
GRANDTULLY
HILL
Guay
Dalguise
Achalader
Blairgowrie
Westfields of Rattr

L   M   80   N   P   90   Q   00   R   S   T   U   V   20
Kenmore
Acharn
Fearnan
River Tay
Dewars
Loch
Kennan
Loch
Skiach
Dunkeld
River Tay
Blairgowrie
Kinloch
Rattray
Rosemount

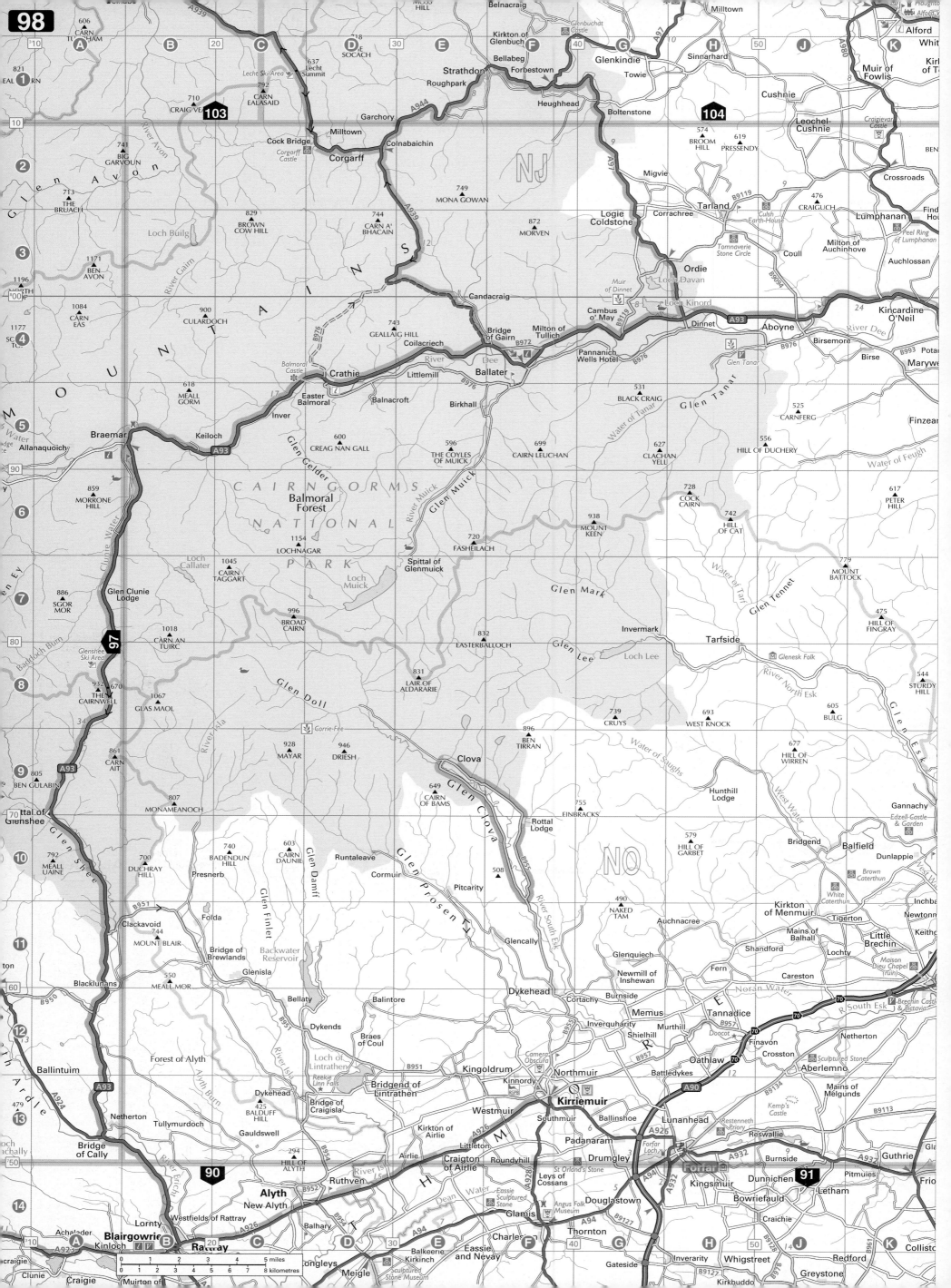

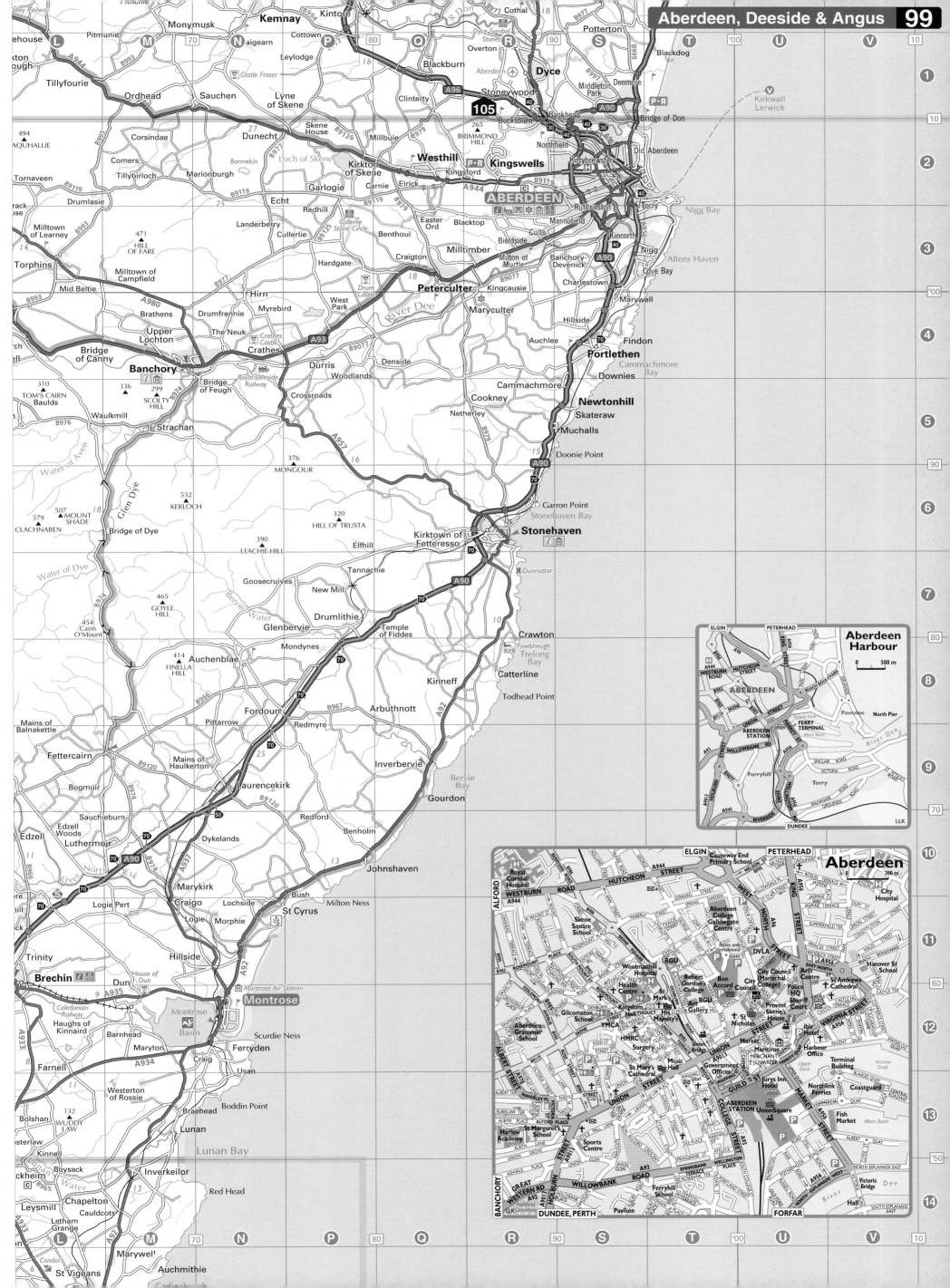

Aberdeen Harbour

Aberdeen

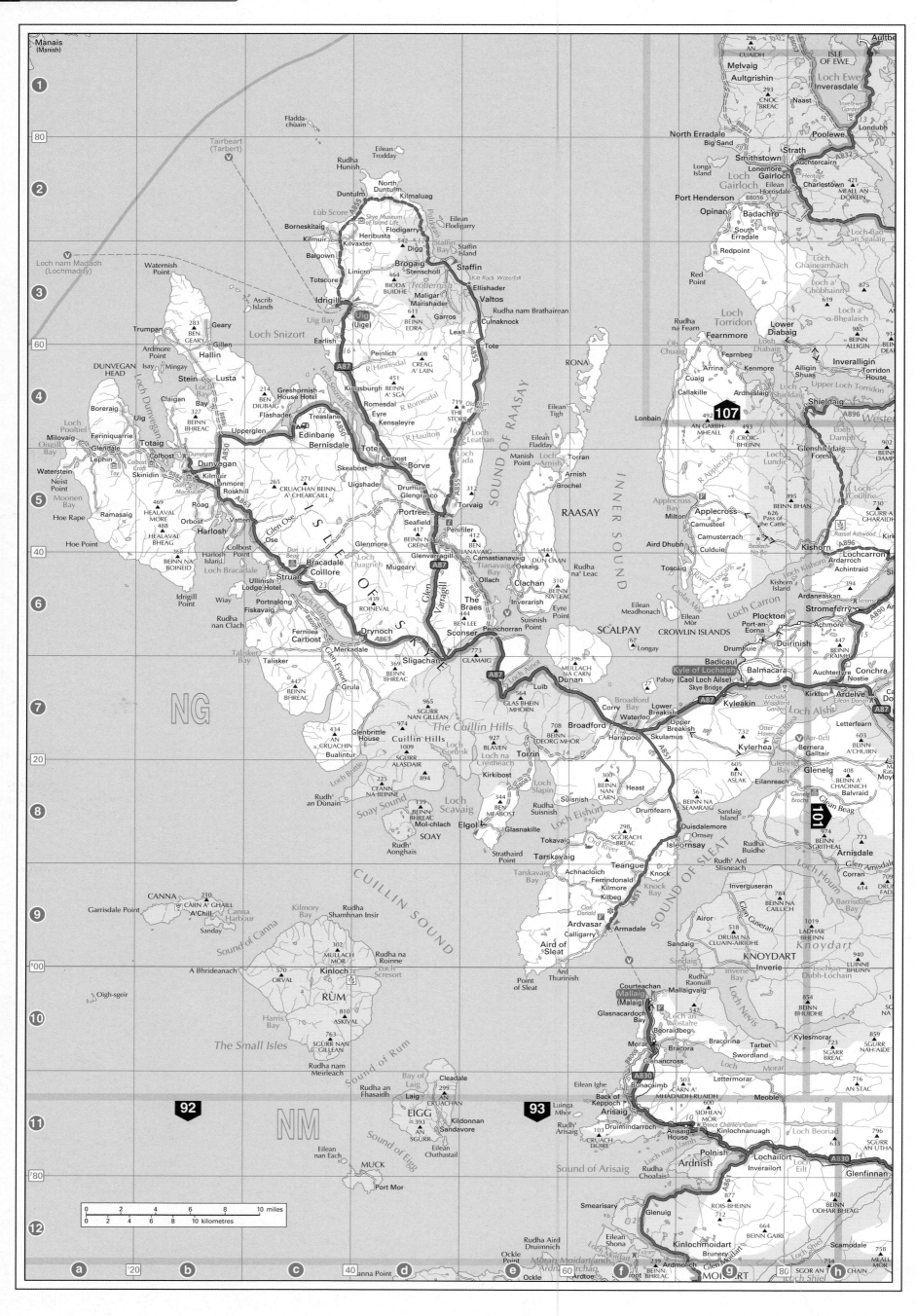

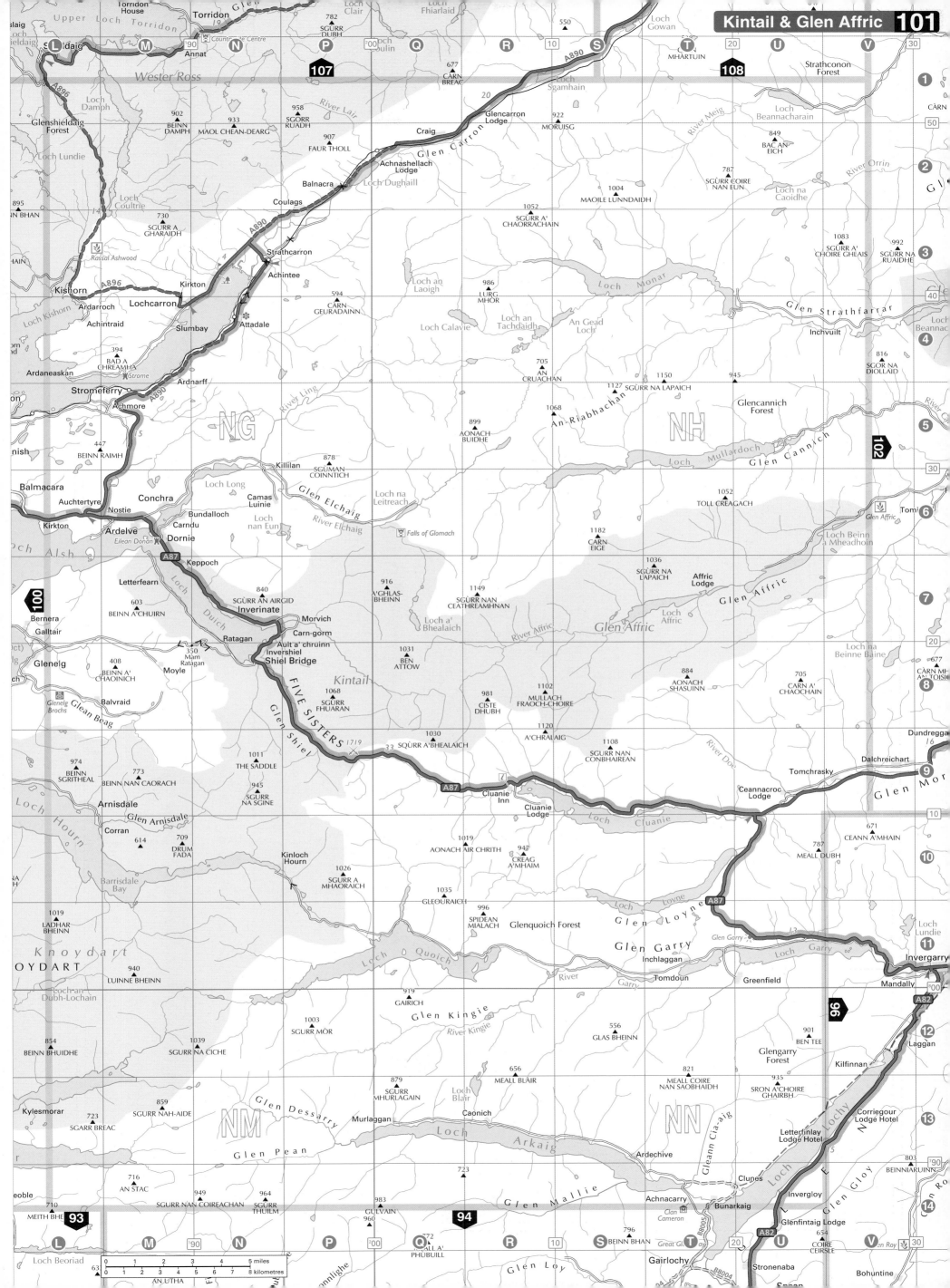

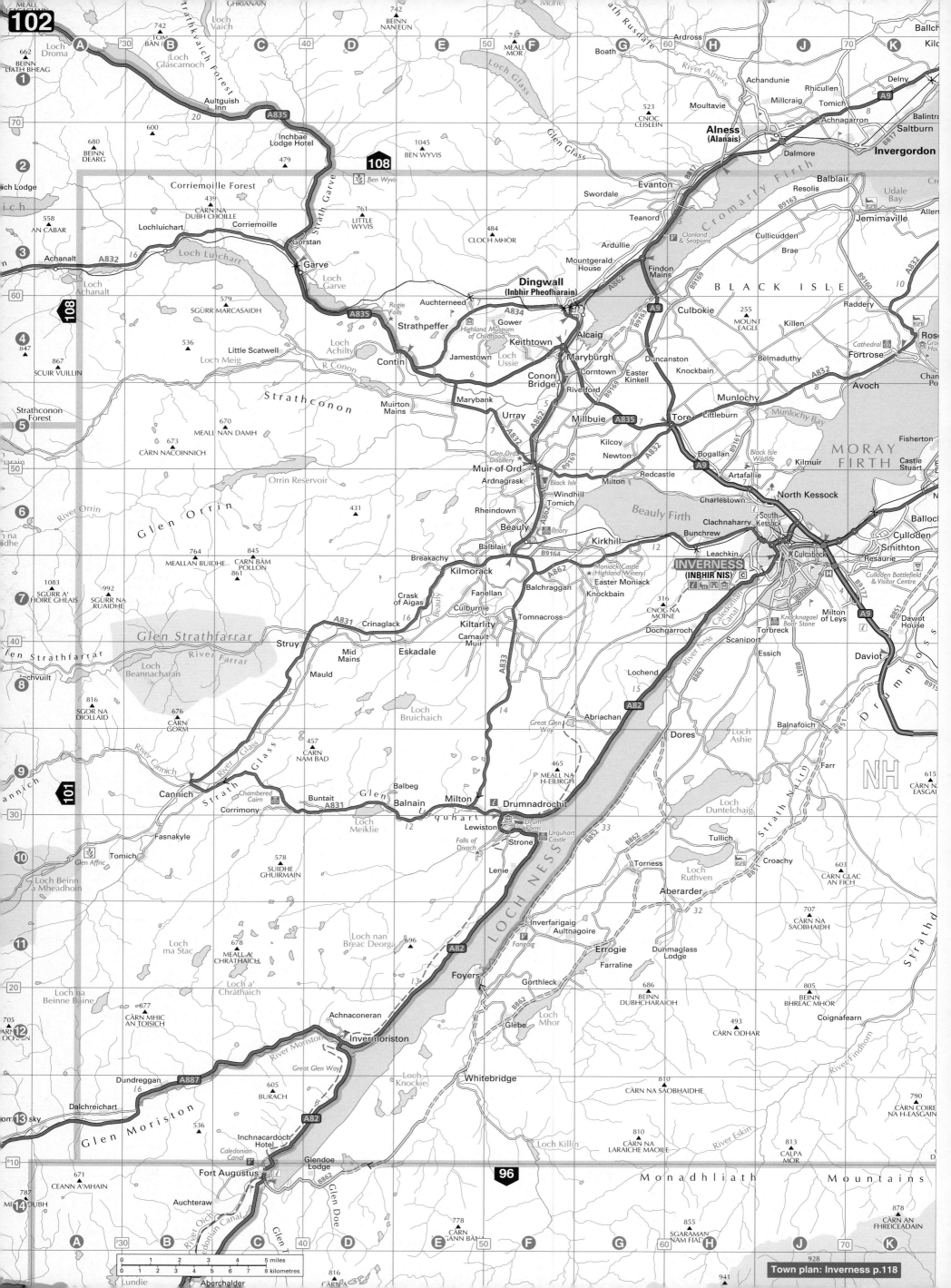

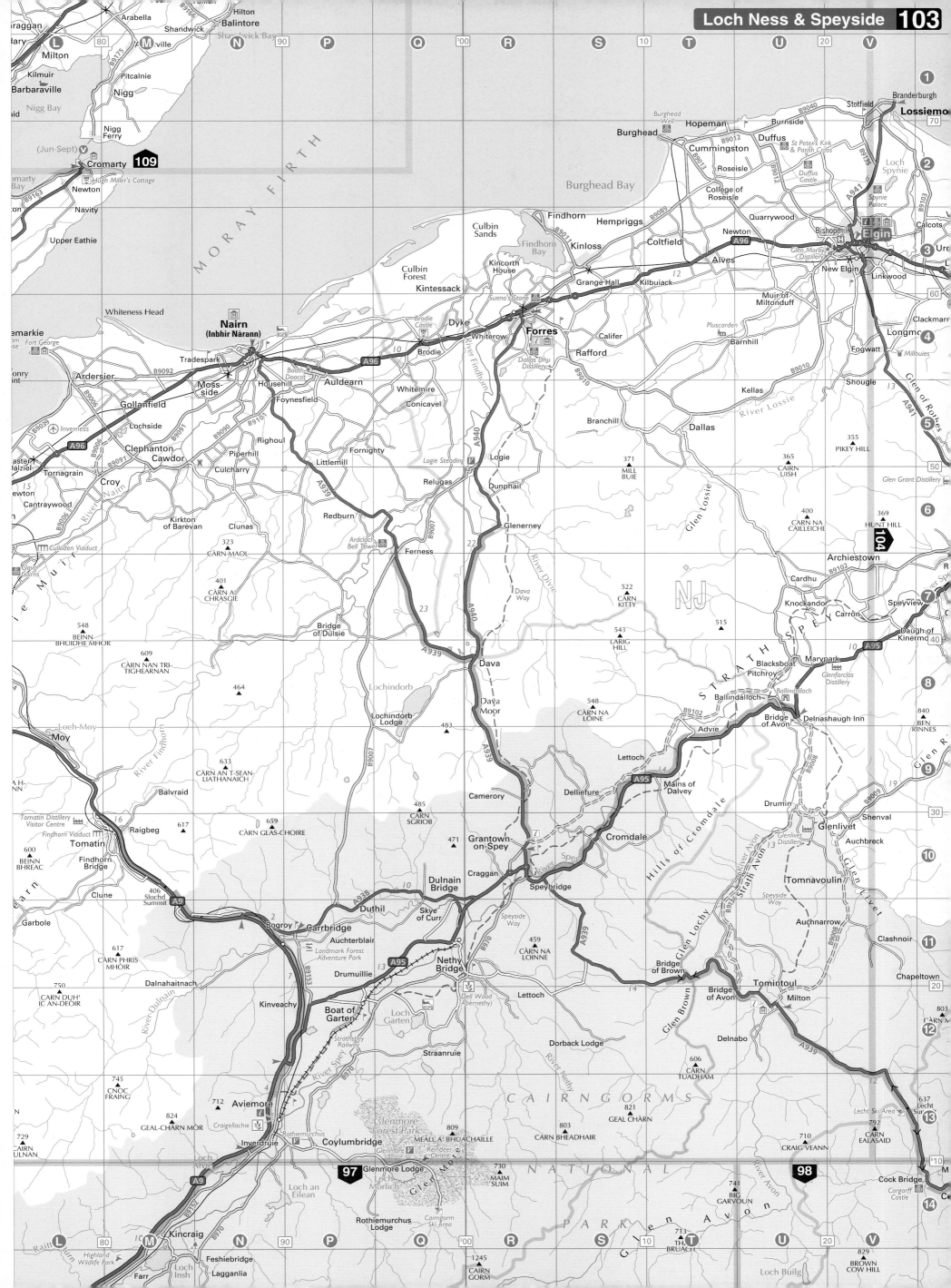

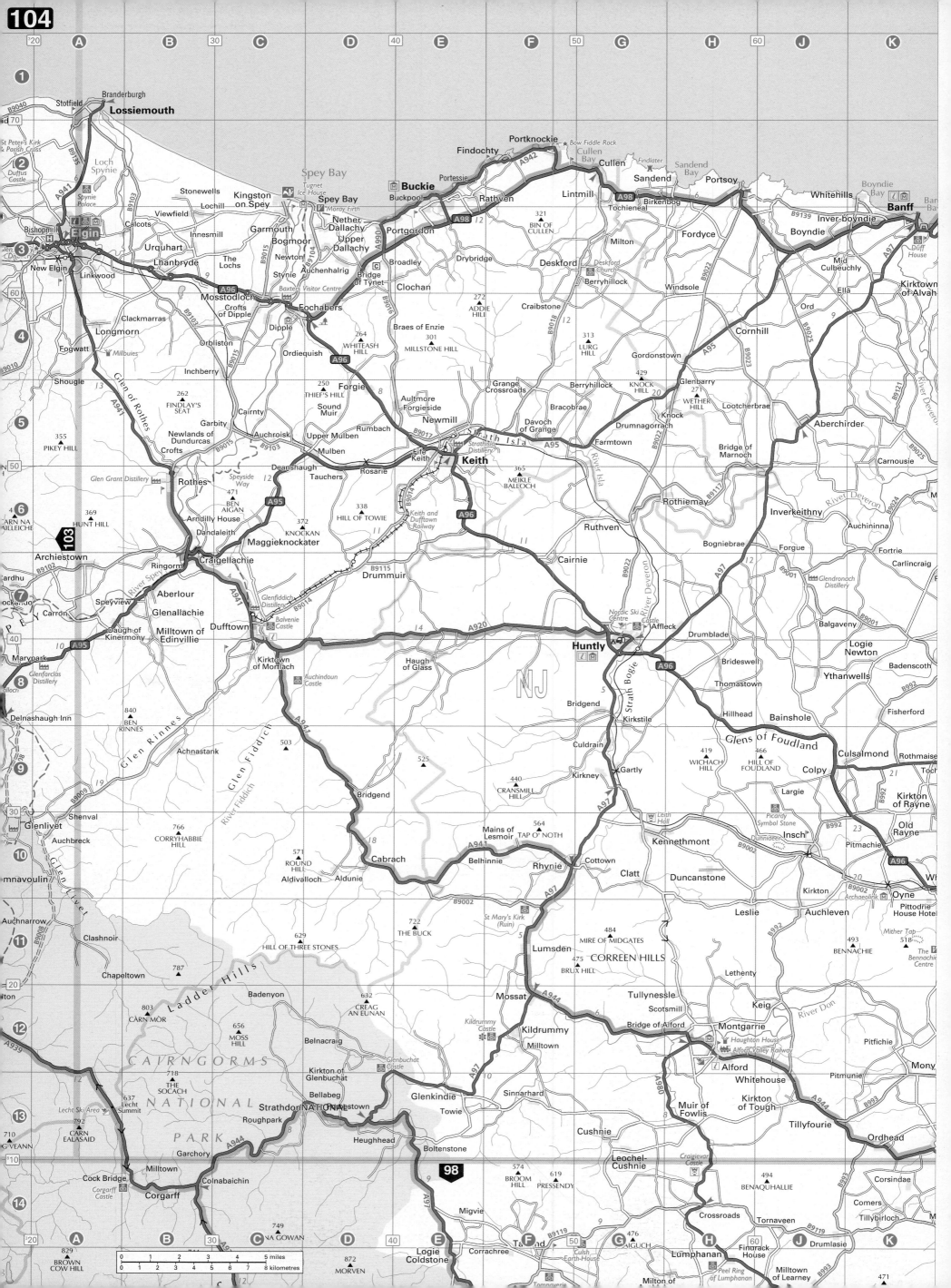

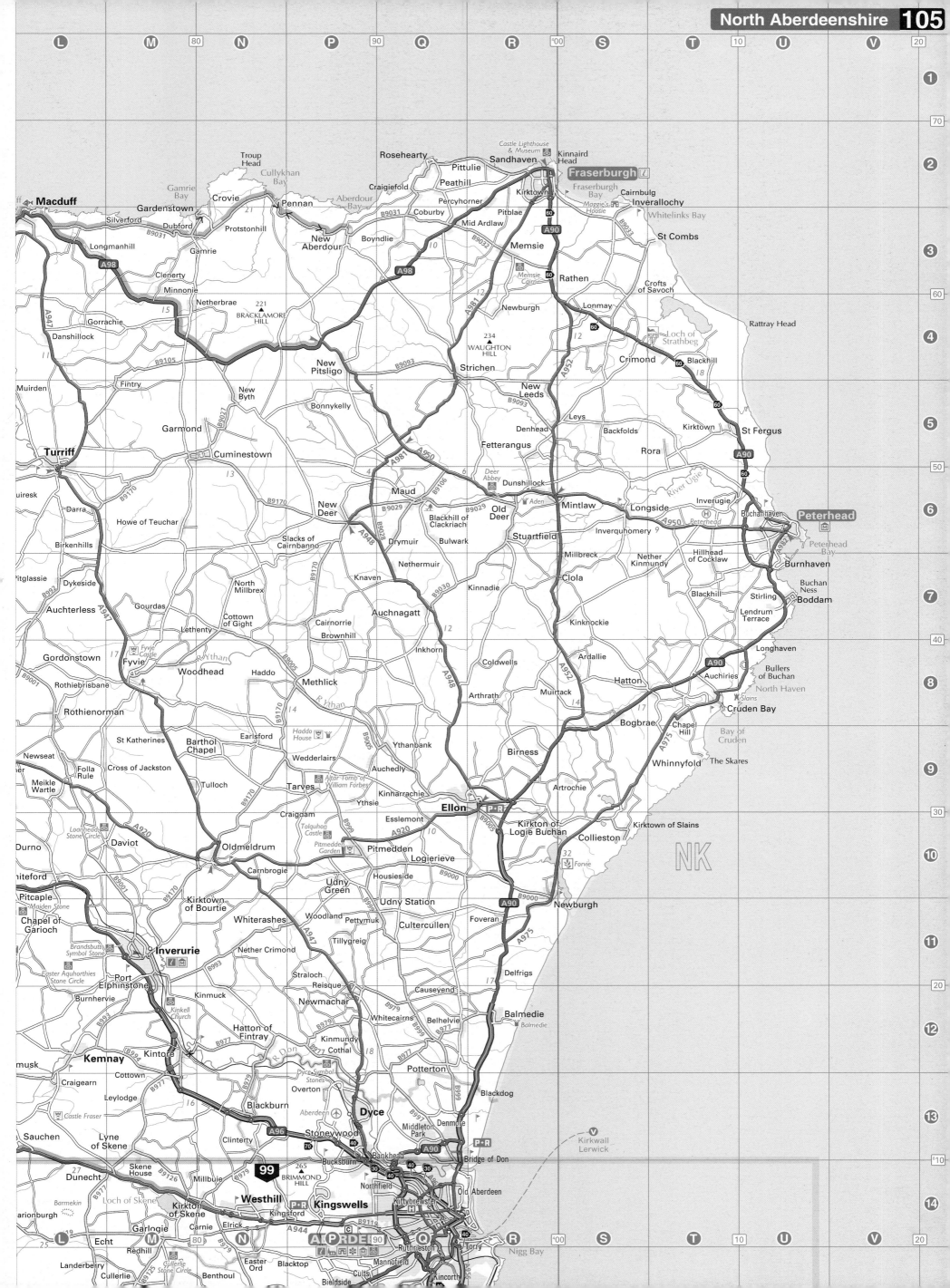

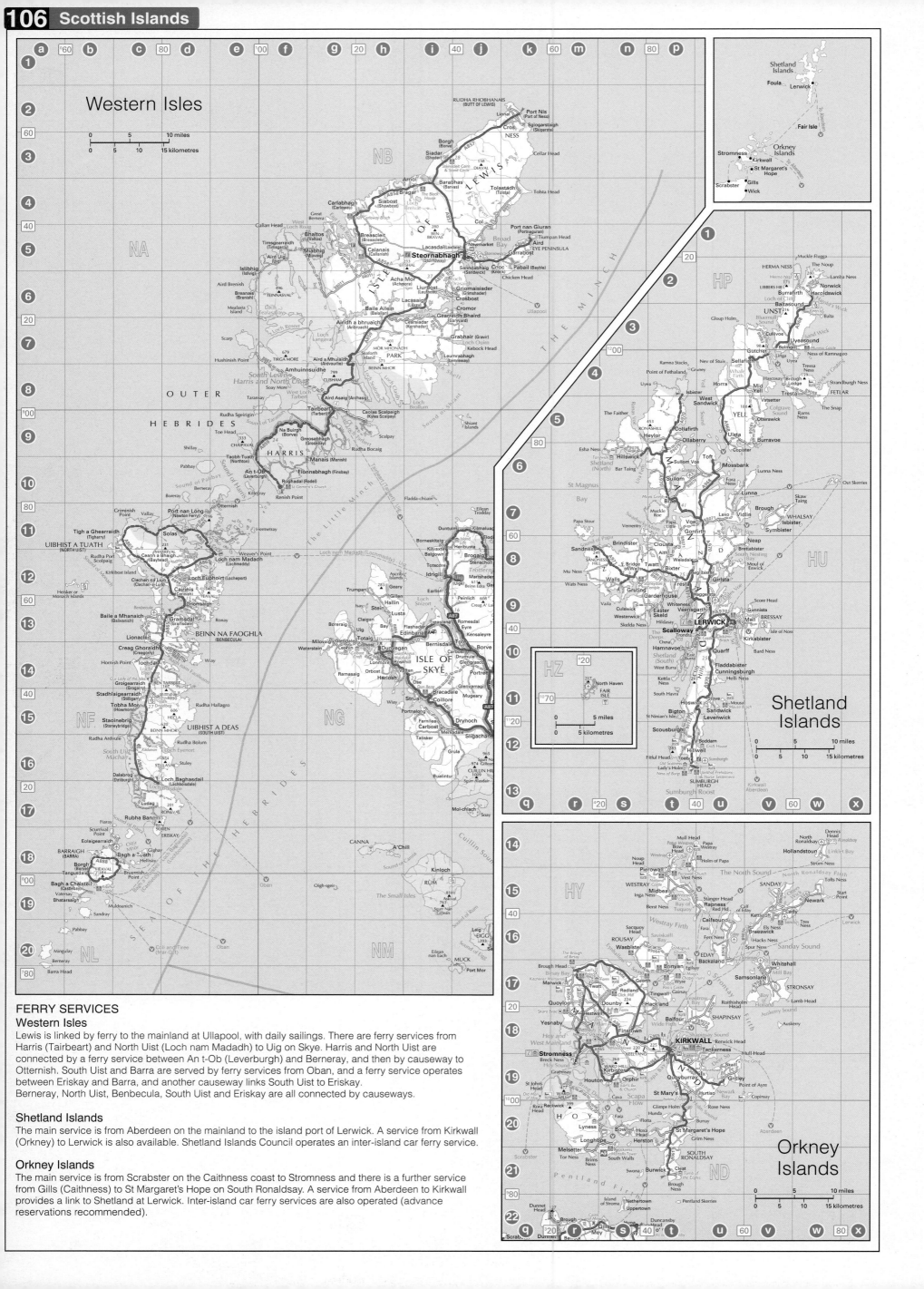

Western Isles

Shetland Islands

Orkney Islands

FERRY SERVICES

Western Isles
Lewis is linked by ferry to the mainland at Ullapool, with daily sailings. There are ferry services from Harris (Tairbeart) and North Uist (Loch nam Madadh) to Uig on Skye. Harris and North Uist are connected by a ferry service between An t-Ob (Leverburgh) and Berneray, and then by causeway to Otternish. South Uist and Barra are served by ferry services from Oban, and a ferry service operates between Eriskay and Barra, and another causeway links South Uist to Eriskay.
Berneray, North Uist, Benbecula, South Uist and Eriskay are all connected by causeways.

Shetland Islands
The main service is from Aberdeen on the mainland to the island port of Lerwick. A service from Kirkwall (Orkney) to Lerwick is also available. Shetland Islands Council operates an inter-island car ferry service.

Orkney Islands
The main service is from Scrabster on the Caithness coast to Stromness and there is a further service from Gills (Caithness) to St Margaret's Hope on South Ronaldsay. A service from Aberdeen to Kirkwall provides a link to Shetland at Lerwick. Inter-island car ferry services are also operated (advance reservations recommended).

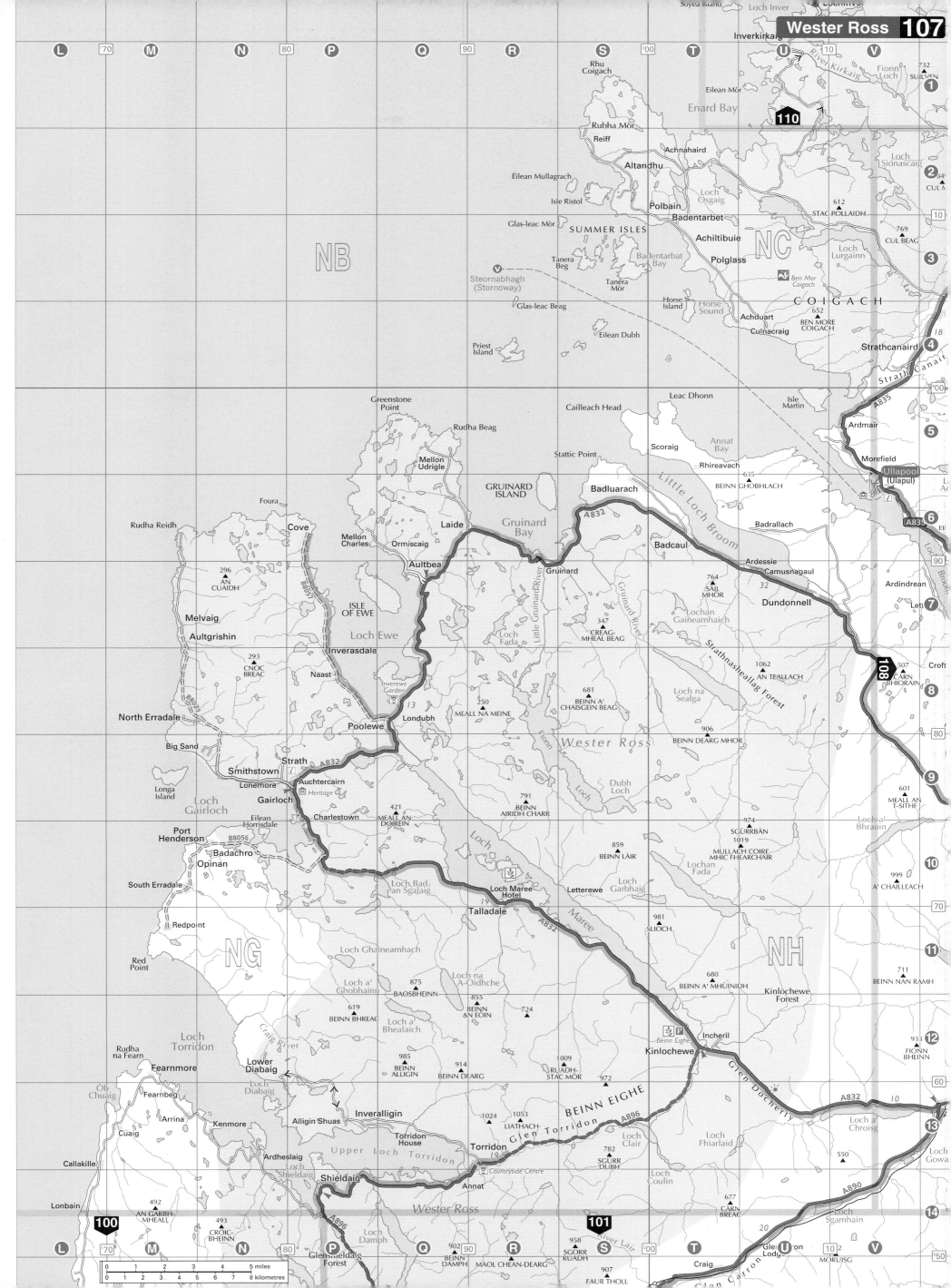

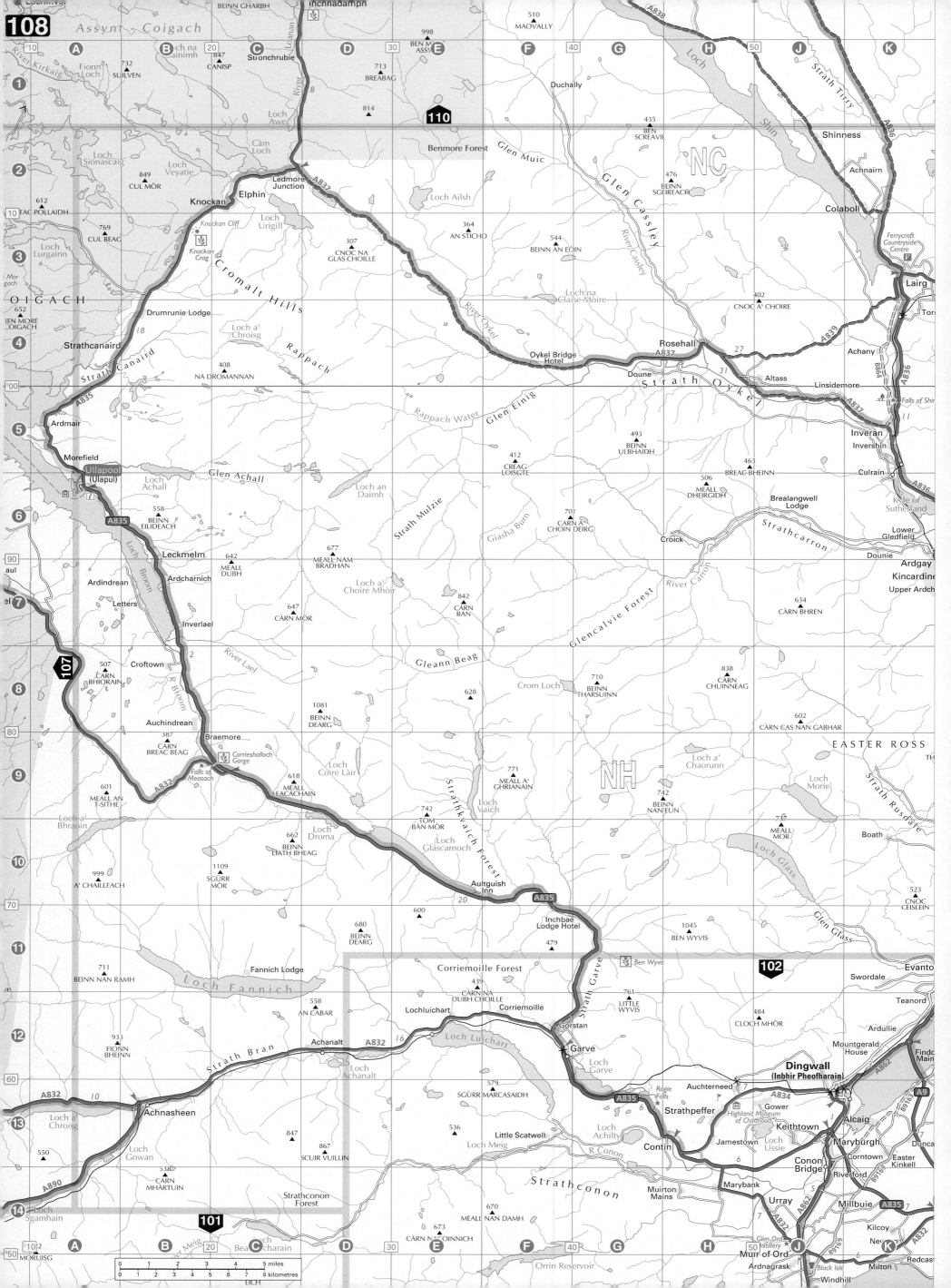

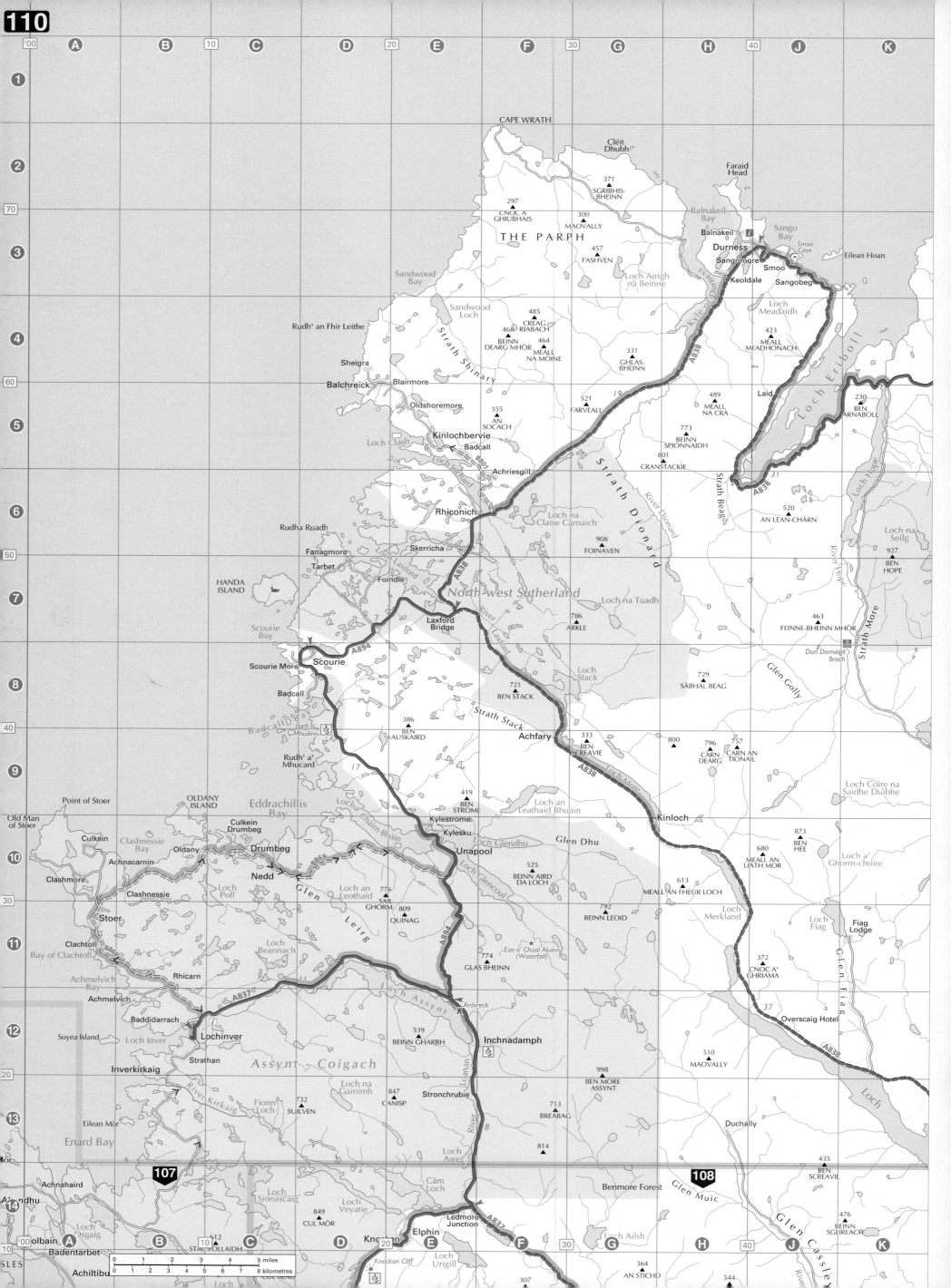

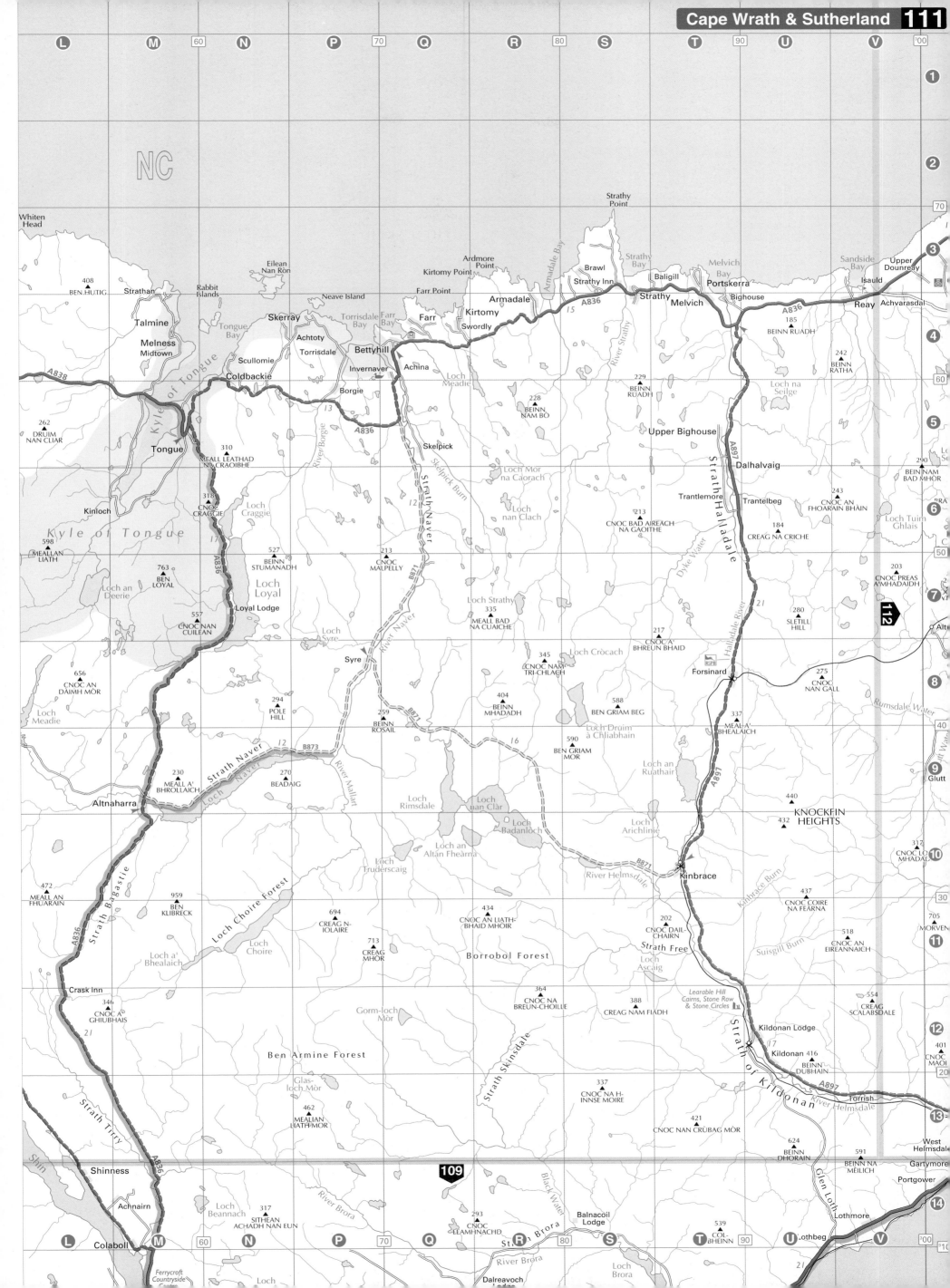

NC

Whiten Head

408 BEN HUTIG
Strathan
Rabbit Islands
Eilean Nan Ròn
Neave Island
Ardmore Point
Kirtomy Point
Farr Point
Strathy Point
Strathy Bay
Brawl
Strathy Inn
Baligill
Melvich Bay
Portskerra
Sandside Bay
Upper Dounreay
Isauld

Talmine
Melness
Midtown
Skerray
Achtoty
Torrisdale Bay
Farr Bay
Farr
Armadale
Kirtomy
Swordly
A836
Strathy
Melvich
Bighouse
A836
Reay
Achvarasdal

A838
Coldbackie
Scullomie
Torrisdale
Bettyhill
Invernaver
Achina
15
185 BEINN RUADH
242 BEINN RATHA

262 DRUIM NAN CLIAR
Borgie
A836
13
229 BEINN RUADH
Loch na Seilge

Tongue
310 MEALL LEATHAD NA CRAOIBHE
River Borgie
Skelpick
Loch Meadie
228 BEINN NAM BO
Upper Bighouse
290 BEINN NAM BAD MHOR

Kinloch
318 CNOC CRAGGIE
Loch Craggie
Skelpick Burn
12
Loch Mòr na Caorach
Dalhalvaig
243 CNOC AN FHOARAIN BHÀIN
Loch Tuim Ghlais

Kyle of Tongue
17
527 BEINN STUMANADH
213 CNOC MALPELLY
Loch nan Clach
213 CNOC BAD AIREACH NA GAOITHE
Trantlemore
Trantelbeg
184 CREAG NA CRICHE

598 MEALLAN LIATH
Loch Loyal
763 BEN LOYAL
B871
Strath Naver
Loch Strathy
335 MEALL BAD NA CUAICHE
203 CNOC PREAS A'MHADAIDH

Loch an Deerie
557 CNOC NAN CUILEAN
Loyal Lodge
Loch A' Syre
River Naver
217 CNOC A' BHREUN BHAID
280 SLETILL HILL
21

656 CNOC NA DAIMH MÒR
Syre
345 CNOC NAM TRI-CHLACH
Loch Cròcach
Forsinard
275 CNOC NAN GALL

Loch Meadie
294 POLE HILL
259 BEINN ROSAIL
404 BEINN MHADADH
588 BEN GRIAM BEG
Loch Druim à Chliabhain
337 MEALL A' BHEALAICH
Rumsdale Water

Altnaharra
230 MEALL A' BHROLLAICH
Strath Naver
12
B873
270 BEADAIG
River Mallart
590 BEN GRIAM MÒR
Loch an Ruathair
440
432
KNOCKFIN HEIGHTS
Glutt
317 CNOC LO MHADAD

472 MEALL AN FHUARAIN
Strath Bagastie
959 BEN KLIBRECK
Loch Choire Forest
16
Loch Rimsdale
Loch nan Clàr
Loch Badanlòch
Loch Arichlinie
B871
River Helmsdale
Kinbrace
437 CNOC COIRE NA FEARNA

A836
Strath Tirry
Loch a' Bhealaich
Loch Choire
694 CREAG N-IOLAIRE
Loch Truderscaig
Loch an Altán Fheàrna
434 CNOC AN LIATH-BHAID MHÒR
202 CNOC DAIL-CHAIRN
Strath Free
705 MORVEN
518 CNOC AN EIREANNAICH

Crask Inn
346 CNOC A' GHIUBHAIS
713 CREAG MHÒR
Borrobol Forest
Loch Ascaig
Learable Hill Cairns, Stone Row & Stone Circles
Kildonan Lodge
554 CREAG SCALABSDALE

21
Ben Armine Forest
Gorm-loch Mòr
364 CNOC NA BREUN-CHOILLE
388 CREAG NAM FIADH
Strath of Kildonan
17
Kildonan
416 BEINN DUBHAIN
401 CNOC MAOI

Glas-loch Mòr
337 CNOC NA H-INNSE MOIRE
Strath Skinsdale
River Helmsdale
Torrish
West Helmsdale

462 MEALLAN LIATH MÒR
421 CNOC NAN CRÙBAG MÒR
624 BEINN DHORAIN
591 BEINN NA MÈILICH
Gartymore
Portgower

Shin
Shinness
River Brora
293 CNOC LEAMHNACHD
Balnacoil Lodge
Black Water
539 COL-BHEINN
Glen Loth
Lothmore

Achnairn
Colaboll
Loch Beannach
317 SITHEAN ACHADH NAN EUN
River Brora
Strath Brora
Loch Brora
Lothbeg

Ferrycroft Countryside
Dalreavoch Lodge

109

112

A897
Strath Halladale
Halldale River
Dyke Water
A897
River Brora
A897

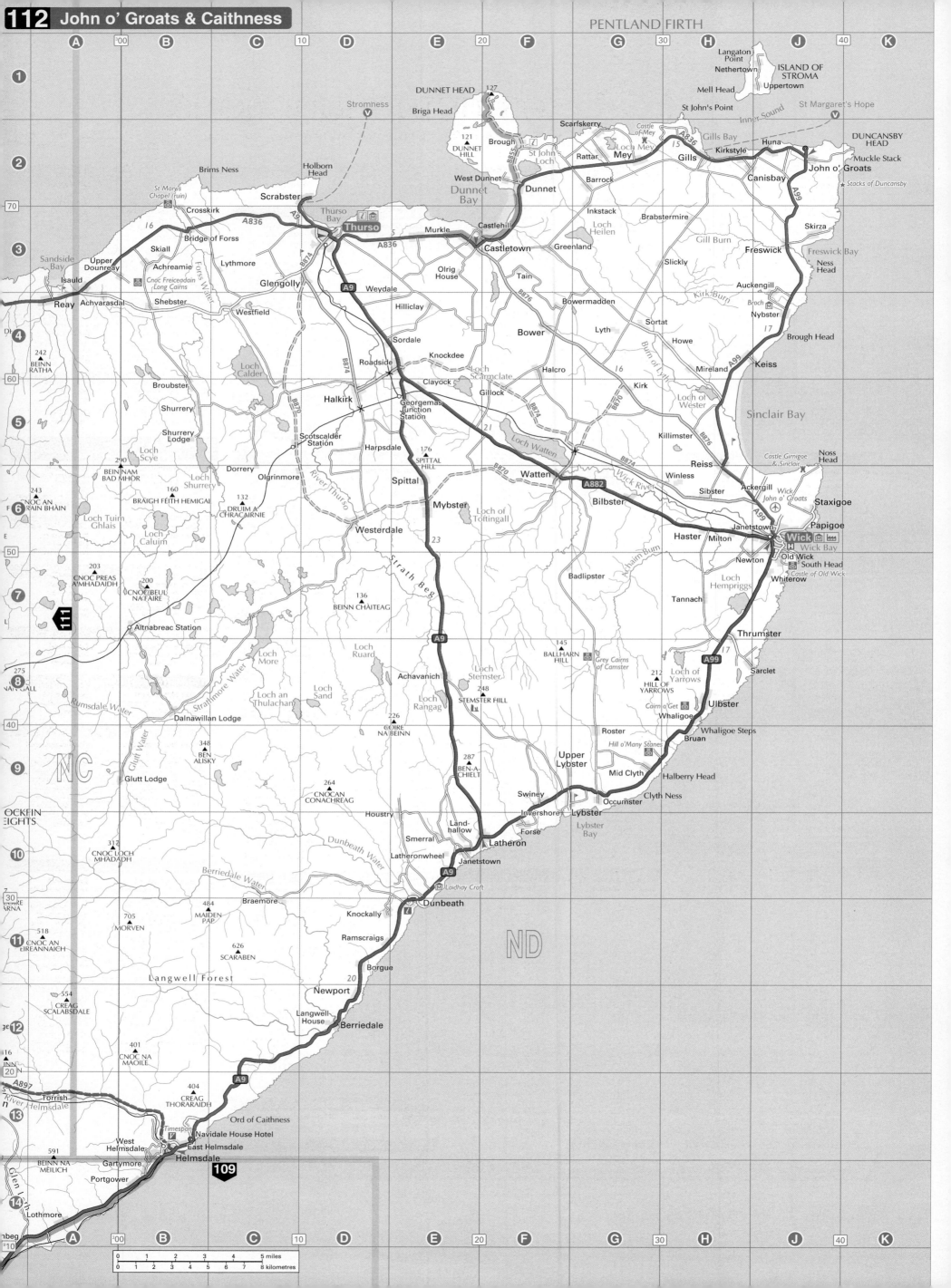

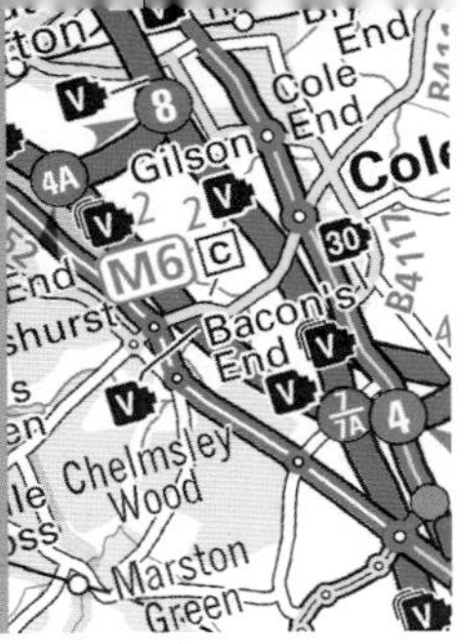

Restricted junctions

Motorway and Primary Route junctions which have access or exit restrictions are shown on the map pages thus:

M1 London - Leeds

Junction	Northbound	Southbound
2	Access only from A1 (northbound)	Exit only to A1 (southbound)
4	Access only from A41 (northbound)	Exit only to A41 (southbound)
6A	Access only from M25 (no link from A405)	Exit only to M25 (no link from A405)
7	Access only from A414	Exit only to A414
17	Exit only to M45	Access only from M45
19	Exit only to M6 (northbound)	Access only from M6
21A	Exit only, no access	Access only, no exit
23A	Access only from A42	No restriction
24A	Access only, no exit	Exit only, no access
35A	Exit only, no access	Access only, no exit
43	Exit only to M621	Access only from M621
48	Exit only to A1(M) (northbound)	Access only from A1(M) (southbound)

M2 Rochester - Faversham

Junction	Westbound	Eastbound
1	No exit to A2 (eastbound)	No access from A2 (westbound)

M3 Sunbury - Southampton

Junction	Northeastbound	Southwestbound
8	Access only from A303, no exit	Exit only to A303, no access
10	Exit only, no access	Access only, no exit
14	Access from M27 only, no exit	No access to M27 (westbound)

M4 London - South Wales

Junction	Westbound	Eastbound
1	Access only from A4 (westbound)	Exit only to A4 (eastbound)
21	Exit only to M48	Access only from M48
23	Access only from M48	Exit only to M48
25	Exit only, no access	Access only, no exit
25A	Exit only, no access	Access only, no exit
29	Exit only to A48(M)	Access only from A48(M)
38	Exit only, no access	No restriction
39	Access only, no exit	No access or exit

M5 Birmingham - Exeter

Junction	Northeastbound	Southwestbound
10	Access only, no exit	Exit only, no access
11A	Access only from A417 (westbound)	Exit only to A417 (eastbound)
18A	Exit only to M49	Access only from M49
18	Exit only, no access	Access only, no exit
29	No restriction	Access only from A30 (westbound)

M6 Toll Motorway

Junction	Northwestbound	Southeastbound
T1	Access only, no exit	No access or exit
T2	No access or exit	Exit only, no access
T3	Staggered junction, follow signs - access only from A38 (northbound)	Staggered junction, follow signs - access only from A38 (southbound)
T5	Access only, no exit	Exit only to A5148 (northbound), no access
T7	Exit only, no access	Access only, no exit
T8	Exit only, no access	Access only, no exit

M6 Rugby - Carlisle

Junction	Northbound	Southbound
3A	Exit only to M6 Toll	Access only from M6 Toll
4A	Access only from M42 (southbound)	Exit only to M42
5	Exit only, no access	Access only, no exit
10A	Exit only to M54	Access only from M54
11A	Access only from M6 Toll	Exit only to M6 Toll
with M56 (jct 20A)	No restriction	Access only from M56 (eastbound)
20	Access only, no exit	No restriction
24	Access only, no exit	Exit only, no access
25	Exit only, no access	Access only, no exit
29	No direct access, use adjacent slip road to jct 29A	No direct exit, use adjacent slip road from jct 29A
29A	Access only, no exit	Exit only, no access
30	Access only from M61	Exit only to M61
31A	Exit only, no access	Access only, no exit
45	Exit only, no access	Access only, no exit

M8 Edinburgh - Bishopton

Junction	Westbound	Eastbound
8	No access from M73 (southbound) or from A8 (eastbound) & A89	No exit to M73 (northbound) or to A8 (westbound) & A89
9	Access only, no exit	Exit only, no access
13	Access only from M80 (southbound)	Exit only to M80 (northbound)
14	Access only, no exit	Exit only, no access
16	Exit only to A804	Access only from A879
17	Exit only to A82	No restriction
18	Access only from A82 (eastbound)	Exit only to A814
19	No access from A814 (westbound)	Exit only to A814 (westbound)
20	Exit only, no access	Access only, no exit
21	Access only, no exit	Exit only to A8
22	Exit only to M77 (southbound)	Access only from M77 (northbound)
23	Exit only to B768	Access only from B768
25	No access or exit from or to A8	No access or exit from or to A8
25A	Exit only, no access	Access only, no exit
28	Exit only, no access	Access only, no exit
28A	Exit only to A737	Access only from A737

M9 Edinburgh - Dunblane

Junction	Northwestbound	Southeastbound
1A	Exit only to M9 spur	Access only from M9 spur
2	Access only, no exit	Exit only, no access
3	Exit only, no access	Access only, no exit
6	Access only, no exit	Exit only to A905
8	Exit only to M876 (southwestbound)	Access only from M876 (northeastbound)

M11 London - Cambridge

Junction	Northbound	Southbound
4	Access only from A406 (eastbound)	Exit only to A406
5	Exit only, no access	Access only, no exit
9	Exit only to A11	Access only from A11
13	Exit only, no access	Access only, no exit
14	Exit only, no access	Access only, no exit

M20 Swanley - Folkestone

Junction	Northwestbound	Southeastbound
2	Staggered junction; follow signs - access only	Staggered junction; follow signs - exit only
3	Exit only to M26 (westbound)	Access only from M26 (eastbound)
5	Access only from A20	For access follow signs - exit only to A20
6	No restriction	For exit follow signs
11A	Access only, no exit	Exit only, no access

M23 Hooley - Crawley

Junction	Northbound	Southbound
7	Exit only to A23 (northbound)	Access only from A23 (southbound)
10A	Access only, no exit	Exit only, no access

M25 London Orbital Motorway

Junction	Clockwise	Anticlockwise
1B	No direct access, use slip road to Jct 2. Exit only	Access only, no exit
5	No exit to M26 (eastbound)	No access from M26
19	Exit only, no access	Access only, no exit
21	Access only from M1 (southbound). Exit only to M1 (northbound)	Access only from M1 (southbound). Exit only to M1 (northbound)
31	No exit (use slip road via jct 30), access only	No access (use slip road via jct 30), exit only

M26 Sevenoaks - Wrotham

Junction	Westbound	Eastbound
with M25 (jct 5)	Exit only to clockwise M25 (westbound)	Access only from anticlockwise M25 (eastbound)
with M20 (jct 3)	Access only from M20 (northwestbound)	Exit only to M20 (southeastbound)

M27 Cadnam - Portsmouth

Junction	Westbound	Eastbound
4	Staggered junction; follow signs - access only from M3 (southbound). Exit only to M3 (northbound)	Staggered junction; follow signs - access only from M3 (southbound). Exit only to M3 (northbound)
10	Exit only, no access	Access only, no exit
12	Staggered junction; follow signs - exit only to M275 (southbound)	Staggered junction; follow signs - access only from M275 (northbound)

M40 London - Birmingham

Junction	Northwestbound	Southeastbound
3	Exit only, no access	Access only, no exit
7	Exit only, no access	Access only, no exit
8	Exit only to M40/A40	Access only from M40/A40
13	Exit only, no access	Access only, no exit
14	Access only, no exit	Exit only, no access
16	Access only, no exit	Exit only, no access

M42 Bromsgrove - Measham

Junction	Northeastbound	Southwestbound
1	Access only, no exit	Exit only, no access
7	Exit only to M6 (northwestbound)	Access only from M6 (northwestbound)
7A	Exit only to M6 (southeastbound)	No access or exit
8	Access only from M6 (southeastbound)	Exit only to M6 (northwestbound)

M45 Coventry - M1

Junction	Westbound	Eastbound
Dunchurch (unnumbered)	Access only from A45	Exit only, no access
with M1 (jct 17)	Access only from M1 (northbound)	Exit only to M1 (southbound)

M53 Mersey Tunnel - Chester

Junction	Northbound	Southbound
11	Access only from M56 (westbound). Exit only to M56 (eastbound)	Access only from M56 (westbound). Exit only to M56 (eastbound)

M54 Telford

Junction	Westbound	Eastbound
with M6 (jct 10A)	Access only from M6 (northbound)	Exit only to M6 (southbound)

M56 North Cheshire

Junction	Westbound	Eastbound
1	Access only from M60 (westbound)	Exit only to M60 (eastbound) & A34 (northbound)
2	Exit only, no access	Access only, no exit
3	Access only, no exit	Exit only, no access
4	Exit only, no access	Access only, no exit
7	Exit only, no access	No restriction
8	Access only, no exit	No access or exit
15	Exit only to M53	Access only from M53
16	No access or exit	No restriction

M57 Liverpool Outer Ring Road

Junction	Northwestbound	Southeastbound
3	Access only, no exit	Exit only, no access
5	Access only from A580 (westbound)	Exit only, no access

M58 Liverpool - Wigan

Junction	Westbound	Eastbound
1	Exit only, no access	Access only, no exit

M60 Manchester Orbital

Junction	Clockwise	Anticlockwise
2	Access only, no exit	Exit only, no access
3	No access from M56	Access only from A34 (northbound)
4	Access only from A34 (northbound). Exit only to M56	Access only from M56 (eastbound). Exit only to A34 (southbound)
5	Access and exit only from and to A5103 (northbound)	Access and exit only from and to A5103 (southbound)
7	No direct access, use slip road to jct 8. Exit only to A56	Access only from A56. No exit - use jct 8
14	Access from A580 (eastbound)	Exit only to A580 (westbound)
16	Access only, no exit	Exit only, no access
20	Exit only, no access	Access only, no exit
22	No restriction	Exit only, no access
25	Exit only, no access	No restriction
26	No restriction	Exit only, no access
27	Access only, no exit	Exit only, no access

M61 Manchester - Preston

Junction	Northwestbound	Southeastbound
3	No access or exit	Exit only, no access
with M6 (jct 30)	Exit only to M6 (northbound)	Access only from M6 (southbound)

M62 Liverpool - Kingston upon Hull

Junction	Westbound	Eastbound
23	Access only, no exit	Exit only, no access
32A	No access to A1(M) (southbound)	No restriction

M65 Preston - Colne

Junction	Northeastbound	Southwestbound
9	Exit only, no access	Access only, no exit
11	Access only, no exit	Exit only, no access

M66 Bury

Junction	Northbound	Southbound
with A56	Exit only to A56 (northbound)	Access only from A56 (southbound)
1	Exit only, no access	Access only, no exit

M67 Hyde Bypass

Junction	Westbound	Eastbound
1	Access only, no exit	Exit only, no access
2	Exit only, no access	Access only, no exit
3	Exit only, no access	No restriction

M69 Coventry - Leicester

Junction	Northbound	Southbound
2	Access only, no exit	Exit only, no access

M73 East of Glasgow

Junction	Northbound	Southbound
2	No access from or exit to A89. No access from M8 (eastbound)	No access from or exit to A89. No exit to M8 (westbound)

M74 and A74(M) Glasgow - Gretna

Junction	Northbound	Southbound
3	Exit only, no access	Access only, no exit
3A	Access only, no exit	Exit only, no access
7	Access only, no exit	Exit only, no access
9	No access or exit	Exit only, no access
10	No restrictions	Access only, no exit
11	Access only, no exit	Exit only, no access
12	Exit only, no access	Access only, no exit
18	Exit only, no access	Access only, no exit

M77 South of Glasgow

Junction	Northbound	Southbound
with M8 (jct 22)	No exit to M8 (westbound)	No access from M8 (eastbound)
4	Access only, no exit	Exit only, no access
6	Access only, no exit	Exit only, no access
7	Access only, no exit	No restriction

M80 Glasgow - Stirling

Junction	Northbound	Southbound
4A	Exit only, no access	Access only, no exit
6A	Access only, no exit	Exit only, no access
8	Exit only to M876 (northeastbound)	Access only from M876 (southwestbound)

M90 Forth Road Bridge - Perth

Junction	Northbound	Southbound
2A	Exit only to A92 (eastbound)	Access only from A92 (westbound)
7	Access only, no exit	Exit only, no access
8	Exit only, no access	Access only, no exit
10	No access from A912. No exit to A912 (southbound)	No access from A912 (northbound). No exit to A912

M180 Doncaster - Grimsby

Junction	Westbound	Eastbound
1	Access only, no exit	Exit only, no access

M606 Bradford Spur

Junction	Northbound	Southbound
2	Exit only, no access	No restriction

M621 Leeds - M1

Junction	Clockwise	Anticlockwise
2A	Access only, no exit	Exit only, no access
4	No exit or access	No restriction
5	Access only, no exit	Exit only, no access
6	Exit only, no access	Access only, no exit
with M1 (jct 43)	Exit only to M1 (southbound)	Access only from M1 (northbound)

M876 Bonnybridge - Kincardine Bridge

Junction	Northeastbound	Southwestbound
with M80 (jct 5)	Access only from M80 (northbound)	Exit only to M80 (southbound)
with M9 (jct 8)	Exit only to M9 (eastbound)	Access only from M9 (westbound)

A1(M) South Mimms - Baldock

Junction	Northbound	Southbound
2	Exit only, no access	Access only, no exit
3	No restriction	Exit only, no access
5	Access only, no exit	No access or exit

A1(M) Pontefract - Bedale

Junction	Northbound	Southbound
41	No access to M62 (eastbound)	No restriction
43	Access only from M1 (northbound)	Exit only to M1 (southbound)

A1(M) Scotch Corner - Newcastle upon Tyne

Junction	Northbound	Southbound
57	Exit only to A66(M) (eastbound)	Access only from A66(M) (westbound)
65	No access Exit only to A194(M) & A1 (northbound)	No exit Access only from A194(M) & A1 (southbound)

A3(M) Horndean - Havant

Junction	Northbound	Southbound
1	Access only from A3	Exit only to A3
4	Exit only, no access	Access only, no exit

A48(M) Cardiff Spur

Junction	Westbound	Eastbound
29	Access only from M4 (westbound)	Exit only to M4 (eastbound)
29A	Exit only to A48 (westbound)	Access only from A48 (eastbound)

A66(M) Darlington Spur

Junction	Westbound	Eastbound
with A1(M) (jct 57)	Exit only to A1(M) (southbound)	Access only from A1(M) (northbound)

A194(M) Newcastle upon Tyne

Junction	Northbound	Southbound
with A1(M) (jct 65)	Access only from A1(M) (northbound)	Exit only to A1(M) (southbound)

A12 M25 - Ipswich

Junction	Northeastbound	Southwestbound
13	Access only, no exit	No restriction
14	Exit only, no access	Access only, no exit
20A	Exit only, no access	Access only, no exit
20B	Access only, no exit	Exit only, no access
21	No restriction	Access only, no exit
23	Exit only, no access	Access only, no exit
24	Access only, no exit	Exit only, no access
27	Exit only, no access	Access only, no exit
Dedham & Stratford St Mary (unnumbered)	Exit only	Access only

A14 M1 - Felixstowe

Junction	Westbound	Eastbound
with M1/M6 (jct19)	Exit only to M6 and M1 (northbound)	Access only from M6 and M1 (southbound)
4	Exit only, no access	Access only, no exit
31	Access only from A1307	Exit only, to A1307
34	Access only, no exit	Exit only, no access
36	Exit only to A11 Access only from A1303	Access only from A11
38	Access only from A11	Exit only to A11
39	Exit only, no access	Access only, no exit
61	Access only, no exit	Exit only, no access

A55 Holyhead - Chester

Junction	Westbound	Eastbound
8a	Exit only, no access	Access only, no exit
23A	Access only, no exit	Exit only, no access
24A	Exit only, no access	No access or exit
33A	Exit only, no access	No access or exit
33B	Exit only, no access	Access only, no exit
37	Exit only to A5104	Access only from A5104

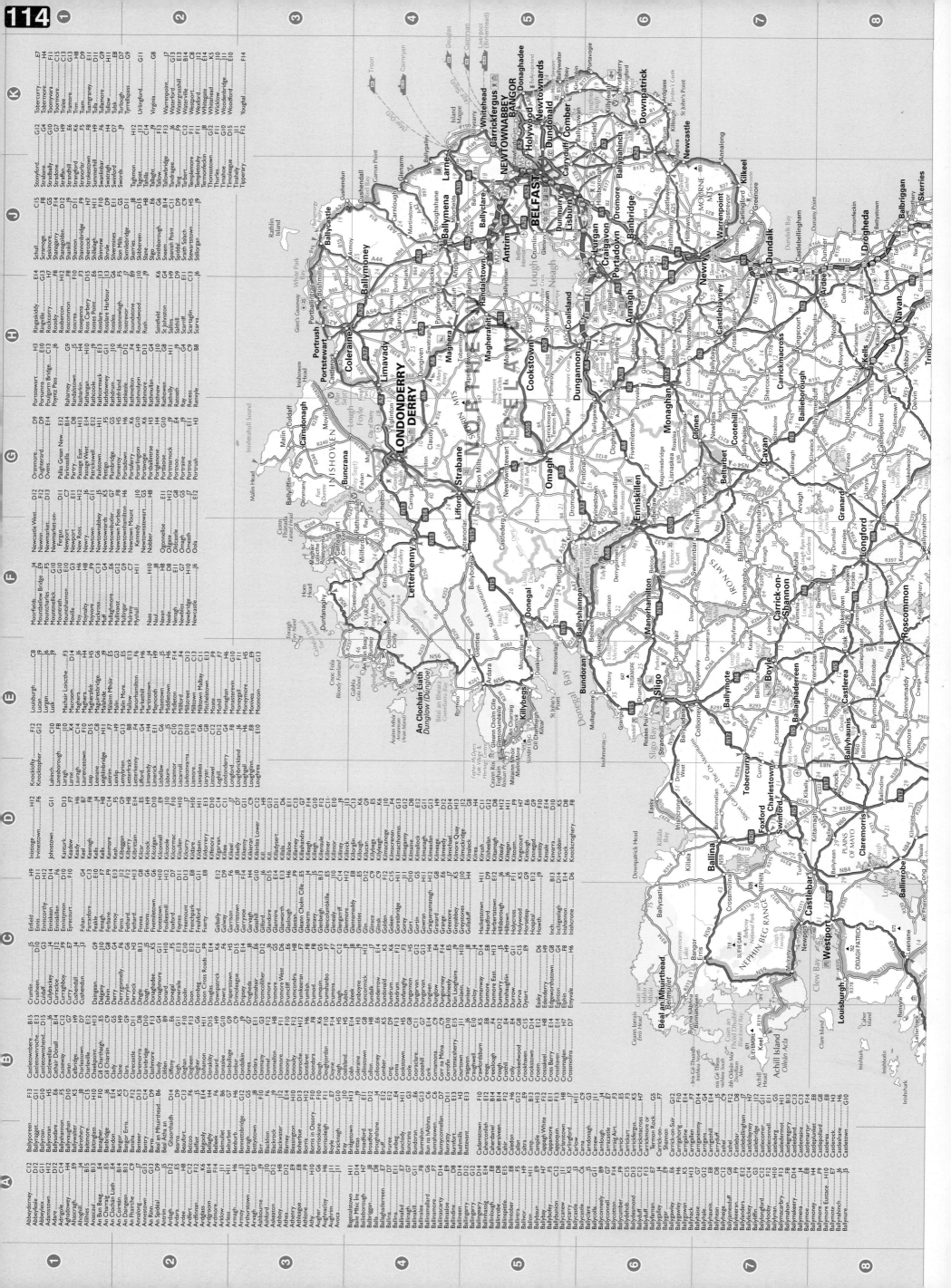

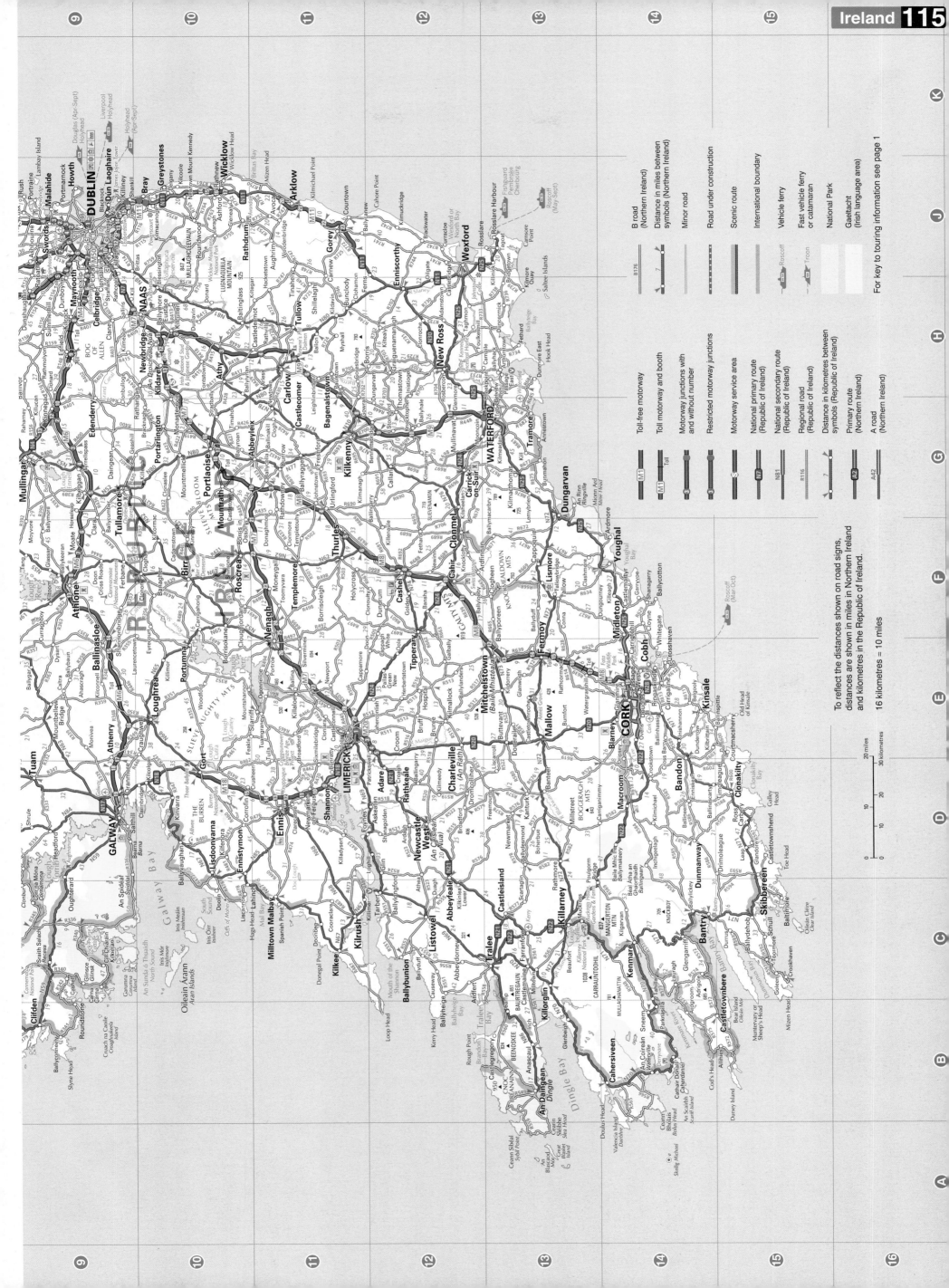

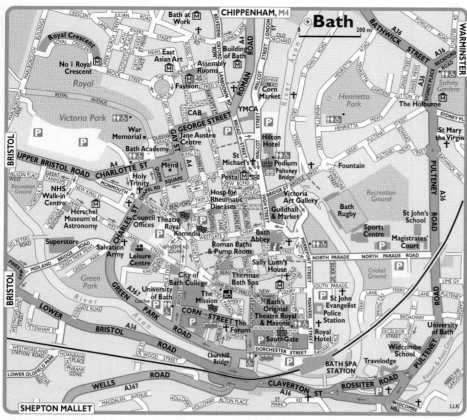

Bath

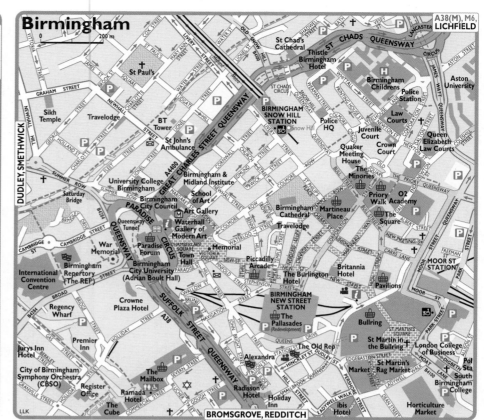

Birmingham

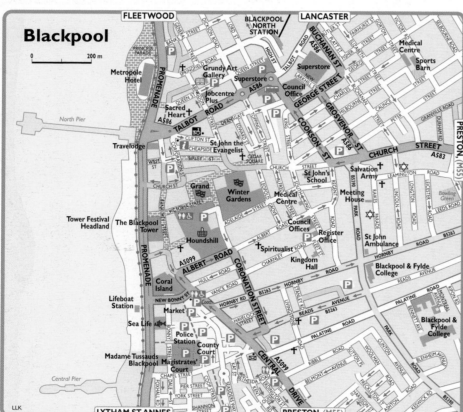

Blackpool

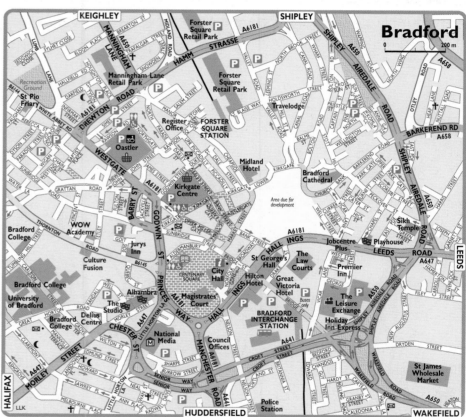

Bradford

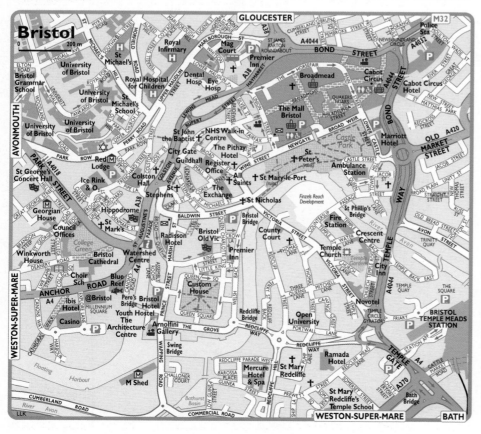

Bristol

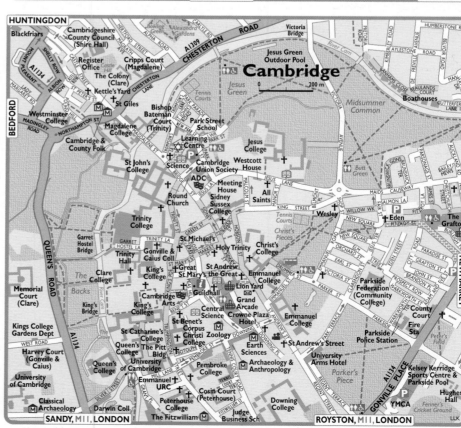

Cambridge

Canterbury
Cardiff

Chester
Coventry

Derby
Dundee

117

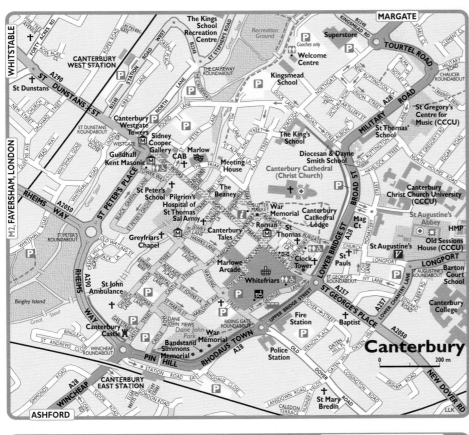

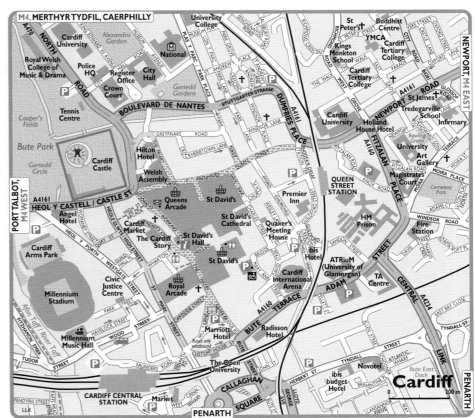

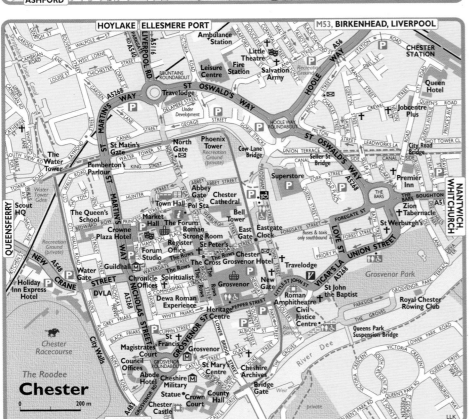

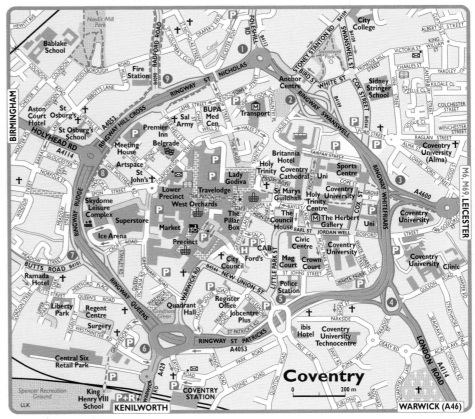

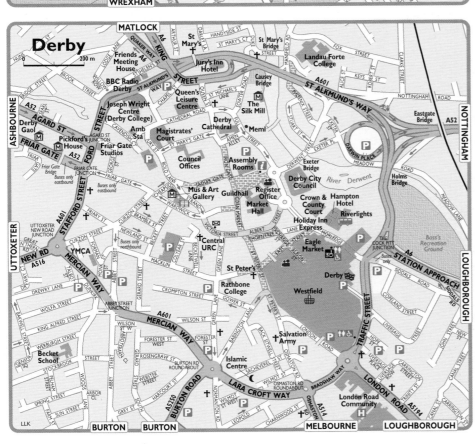

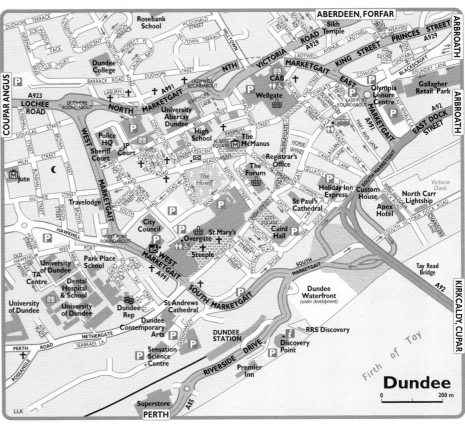

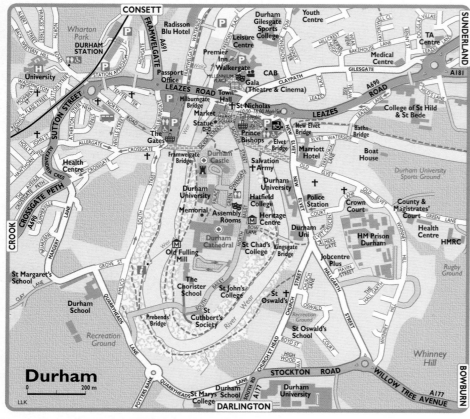

Durham

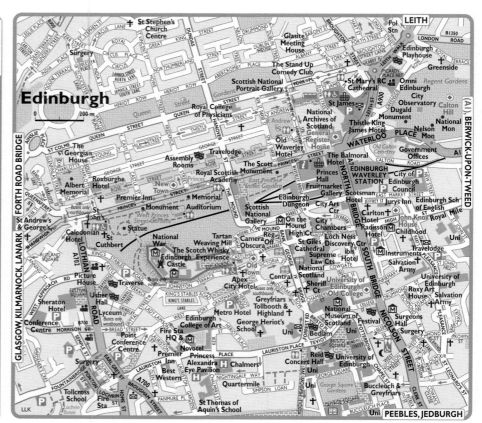

Edinburgh

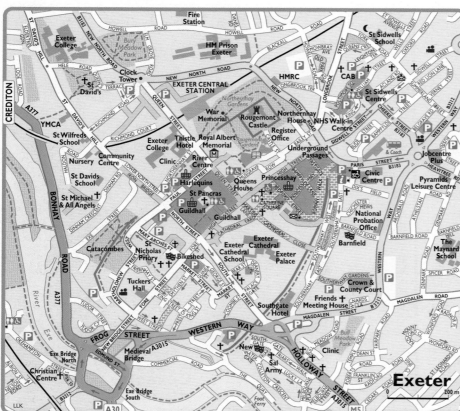

Exeter

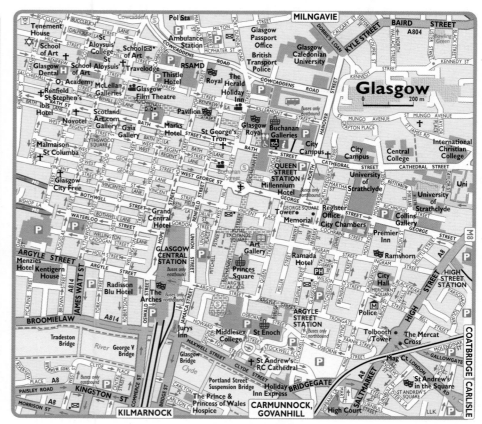

Glasgow

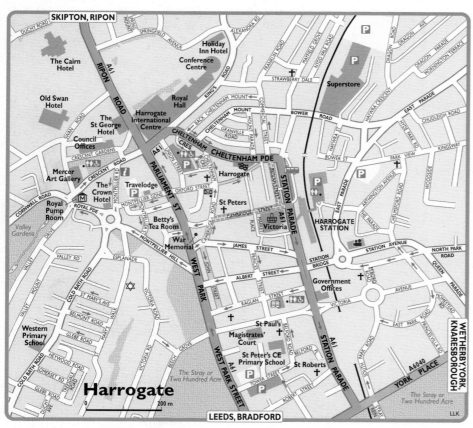

Harrogate

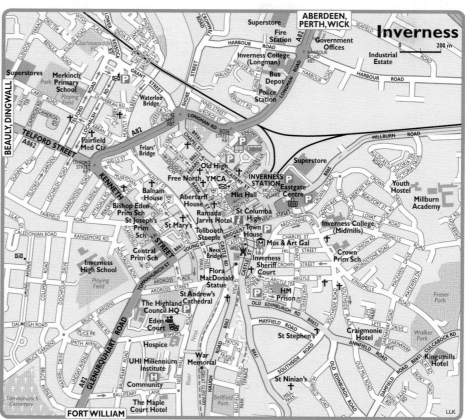

Inverness

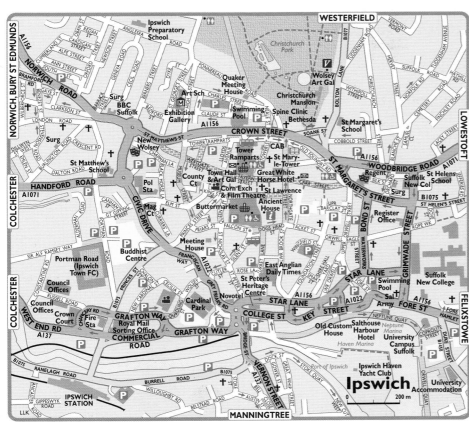

Ipswich

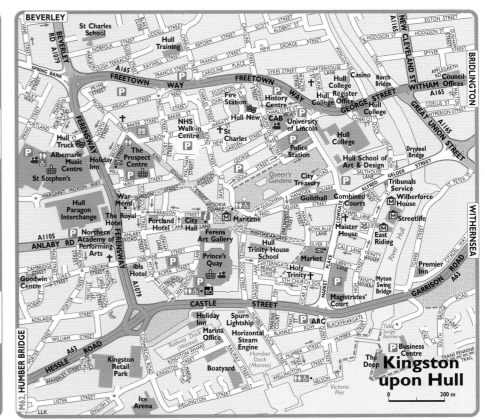

Kingston upon Hull

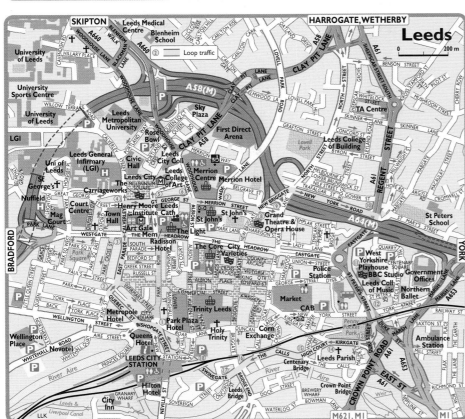

Leeds

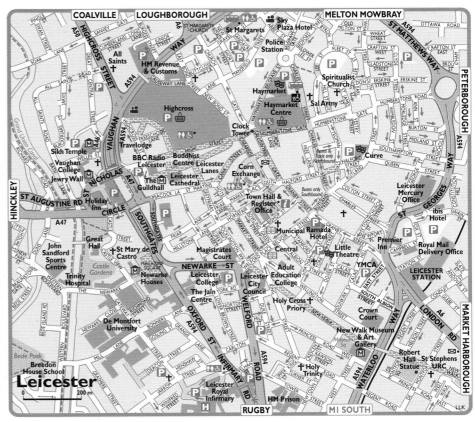

Leicester

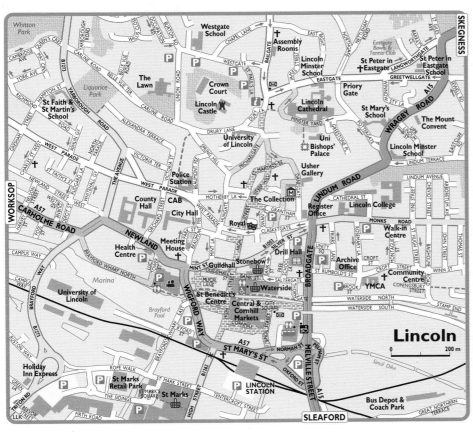

Lincoln

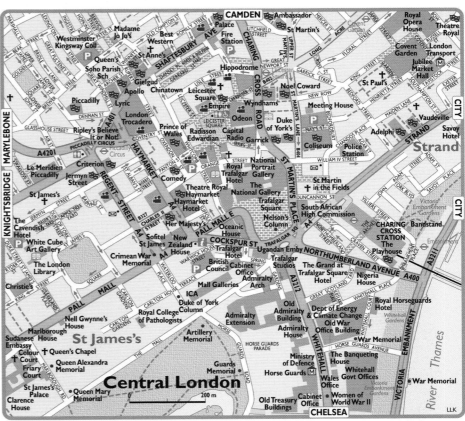

Central London

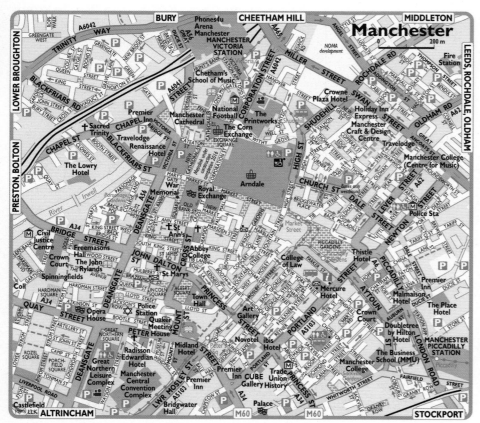

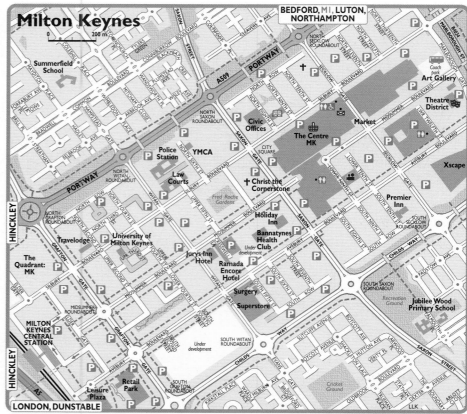

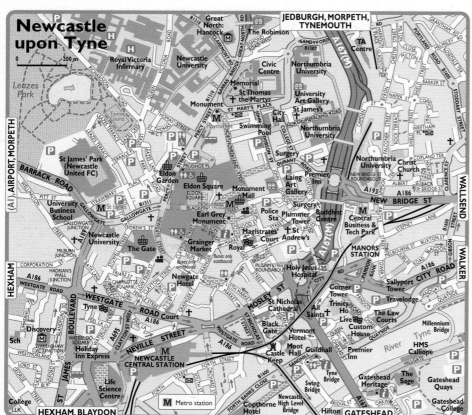

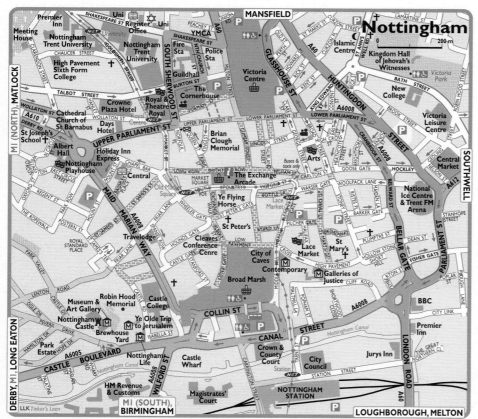

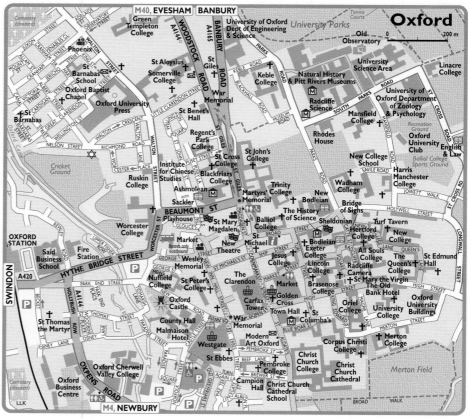

Peterborough
Plymouth

Portsmouth
Salisbury

Sheffield
Southampton

121

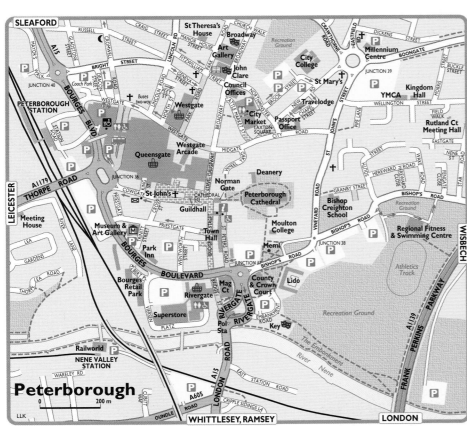

Peterborough

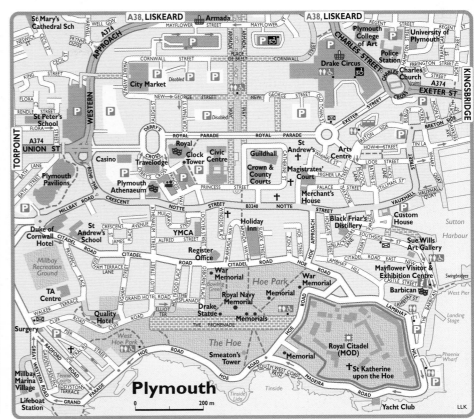

Plymouth

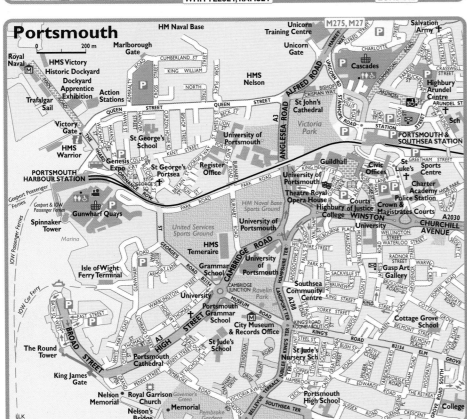

Portsmouth

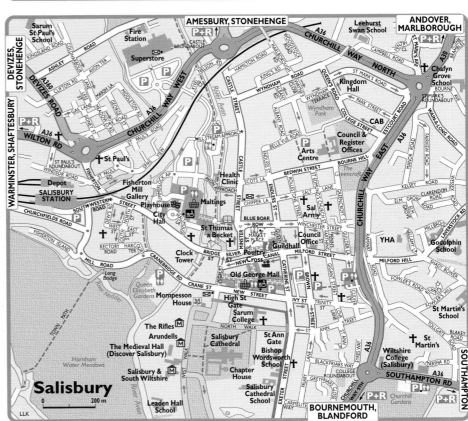

Salisbury

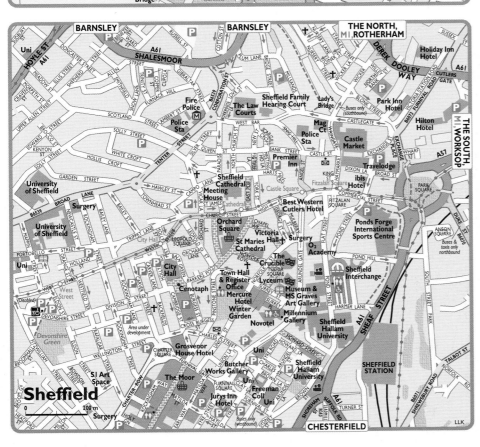

Sheffield

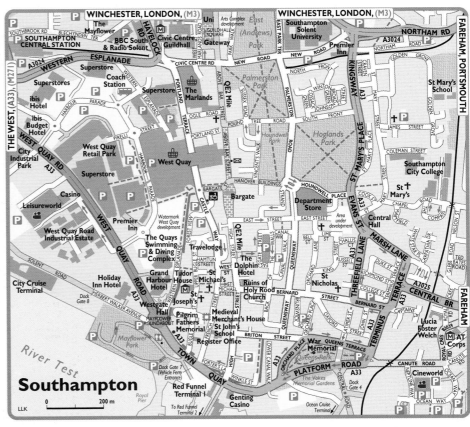

Southampton

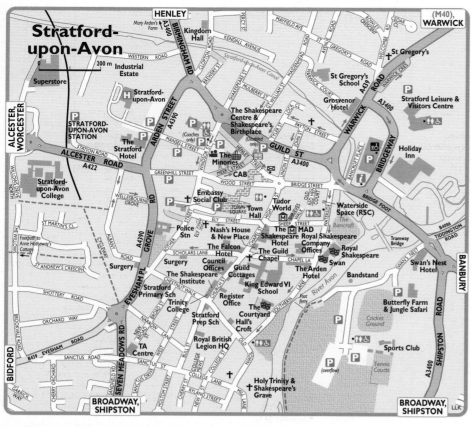

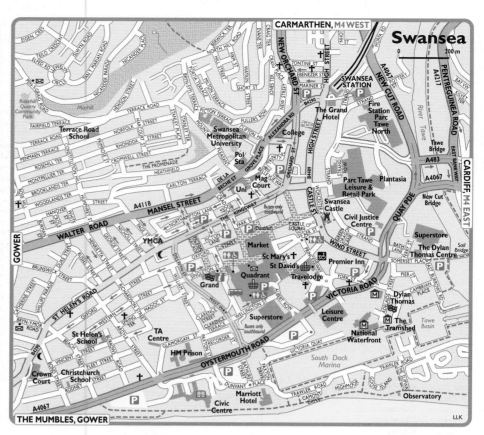

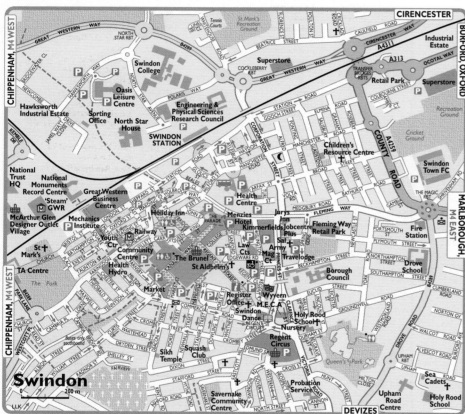

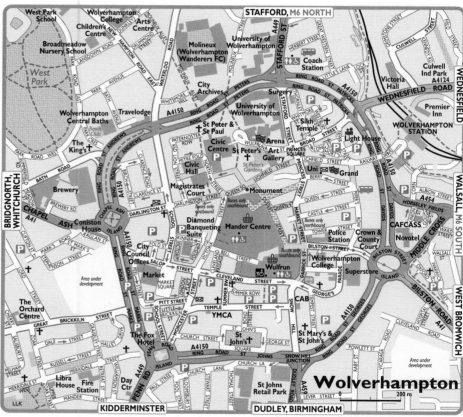

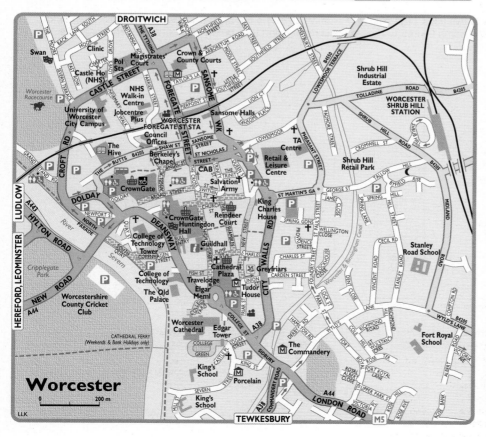

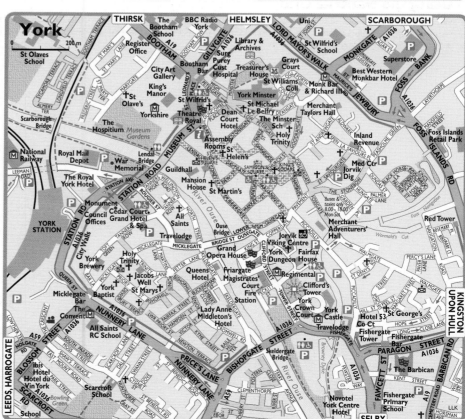

Index to place names

This index lists places appearing in the main-map section of the atlas in alphabetical order. The reference following each name gives the atlas page number and grid reference of the square in which the place appears. The map shows counties, unitary authorities and administrative areas, together with a list of the abbreviated name forms used in the index. The top 100 places of tourist interest are indexed in **red**, World Heritage sites in **green**, motorway service areas in **blue**, airports in blue *italic* and National Park names in green *italic*.

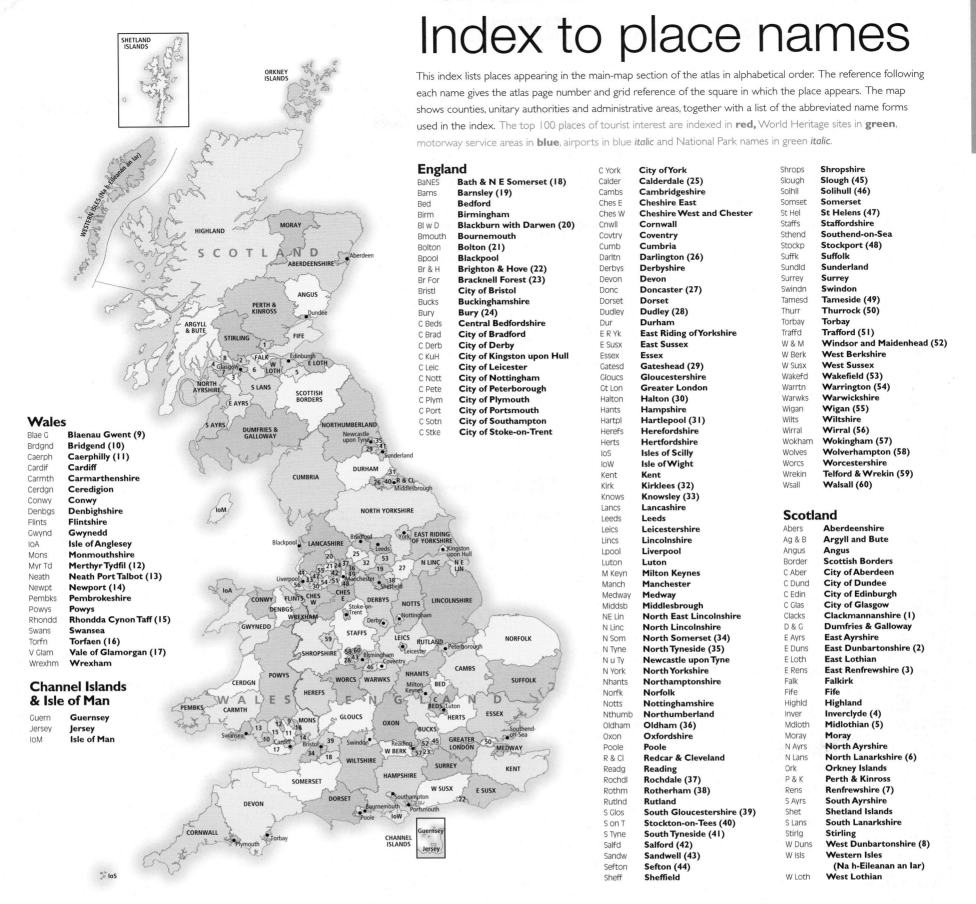

Wales

Blae G	**Blaenau Gwent (9)**
Brdgnd	**Bridgend (10)**
Caerph	**Caerphilly (11)**
Cardif	**Cardiff**
Carmth	**Carmarthenshire**
Cerdgn	**Ceredigion**
Conwy	**Conwy**
Denbgs	**Denbighshire**
Flints	**Flintshire**
Gwynd	**Gwynedd**
IoA	**Isle of Anglesey**
Mons	**Monmouthshire**
Myr Td	**Merthyr Tydfil (12)**
Neath	**Neath Port Talbot (13)**
Newpt	**Newport (14)**
Pembks	**Pembrokeshire**
Powys	**Powys**
Rhondd	**Rhondda Cynon Taff (15)**
Swans	**Swansea**
Torfn	**Torfaen (16)**
V Glam	**Vale of Glamorgan (17)**
Wrexhm	**Wrexham**

Channel Islands & Isle of Man

Guern	**Guernsey**
Jersey	**Jersey**
IoM	**Isle of Man**

England

BaNES	**Bath & N E Somerset (18)**
Barns	**Barnsley (19)**
Bed	**Bedford**
Birm	**Birmingham**
Bl w D	**Blackburn with Darwen (20)**
Bmouth	**Bournemouth**
Bolton	**Bolton (21)**
Bpool	**Blackpool**
Br & H	**Brighton & Hove (22)**
Br For	**Bracknell Forest (23)**
Bristl	**City of Bristol**
Bucks	**Buckinghamshire**
Bury	**Bury (24)**
C Beds	**Central Bedfordshire**
C Brad	**City of Bradford**
C Derb	**City of Derby**
C KuH	**City of Kingston upon Hull**
C Leic	**City of Leicester**
C Nott	**City of Nottingham**
C Pete	**City of Peterborough**
C Plym	**City of Plymouth**
C Port	**City of Portsmouth**
C Sotn	**City of Southampton**
C Stke	**City of Stoke-on-Trent**
C York	**City of York**
Calder	**Calderdale (25)**
Cambs	**Cambridgeshire**
Ches E	**Cheshire East**
Ches W	**Cheshire West and Chester**
Cnwll	**Cornwall**
Covtry	**Coventry**
Cumb	**Cumbria**
Darltn	**Darlington (26)**
Derbys	**Derbyshire**
Devon	**Devon**
Donc	**Doncaster (27)**
Dorset	**Dorset**
Dudley	**Dudley (28)**
Dur	**Durham**
E R Yk	**East Riding of Yorkshire**
E Susx	**East Sussex**
Essex	**Essex**
Gatesd	**Gateshead (29)**
Gloucs	**Gloucestershire**
Gt Lon	**Greater London**
Halton	**Halton (30)**
Hants	**Hampshire**
Hartpl	**Hartlepool (31)**
Herefs	**Herefordshire**
Herts	**Hertfordshire**
IoS	**Isles of Scilly**
IoW	**Isle of Wight**
Kent	**Kent**
Kirk	**Kirklees (32)**
Knows	**Knowsley (33)**
Lancs	**Lancashire**
Leeds	**Leeds**
Leics	**Leicestershire**
Lincs	**Lincolnshire**
Lpool	**Liverpool**
Luton	**Luton**
M Keyn	**Milton Keynes**
Manch	**Manchester**
Medway	**Medway**
Middsb	**Middlesbrough**
NE Lin	**North East Lincolnshire**
N Linc	**North Lincolnshire**
N Som	**North Somerset (34)**
N Tyne	**North Tyneside (35)**
N u Ty	**Newcastle upon Tyne**
N York	**North Yorkshire**
Nhants	**Northamptonshire**
Norfk	**Norfolk**
Notts	**Nottinghamshire**
Nthumb	**Northumberland**
Oldham	**Oldham (36)**
Oxon	**Oxfordshire**
Poole	**Poole**
R & Cl	**Redcar & Cleveland**
Readg	**Reading**
Rochdl	**Rochdale (37)**
Rothm	**Rotherham (38)**
Rutlnd	**Rutland**
S Glos	**South Gloucestershire (39)**
S on T	**Stockton-on-Tees (40)**
S Tyne	**South Tyneside (41)**
Salfd	**Salford (42)**
Sandw	**Sandwell (43)**
Sefton	**Sefton (44)**
Sheff	**Sheffield**
Shrops	**Shropshire**
Slough	**Slough (45)**
Solhll	**Solihull (46)**
Somset	**Somerset**
St Hel	**St Helens (47)**
Staffs	**Staffordshire**
Sthend	**Southend-on-Sea**
Stockp	**Stockport (48)**
Suffk	**Suffolk**
Sundld	**Sunderland**
Surrey	**Surrey**
Swindn	**Swindon**
Tamesd	**Tameside (49)**
Thurr	**Thurrock (50)**
Torbay	**Torbay**
Traffd	**Trafford (51)**
W & M	**Windsor and Maidenhead (52)**
W Berk	**West Berkshire**
W Susx	**West Sussex**
Wakefd	**Wakefield (53)**
Warrtn	**Warrington (54)**
Warwks	**Warwickshire**
Wigan	**Wigan (55)**
Wilts	**Wiltshire**
Wirral	**Wirral (56)**
Wokham	**Wokingham (57)**
Wolves	**Wolverhampton (58)**
Worcs	**Worcestershire**
Wrekin	**Telford & Wrekin (59)**
Wsall	**Walsall (60)**

Scotland

Abers	**Aberdeenshire**
Ag & B	**Argyll and Bute**
Angus	**Angus**
Border	**Scottish Borders**
C Aber	**City of Aberdeen**
C Dund	**City of Dundee**
C Edin	**City of Edinburgh**
C Glas	**City of Glasgow**
Clacks	**Clackmannanshire (1)**
D & G	**Dumfries & Galloway**
E Ayrs	**East Ayrshire**
E Duns	**East Dunbartonshire (2)**
E Loth	**East Lothian**
E Rens	**East Renfrewshire (3)**
Falk	**Falkirk**
Fife	**Fife**
Highld	**Highland**
Inver	**Inverclyde (4)**
Mdloth	**Midlothian (5)**
Moray	**Moray**
N Ayrs	**North Ayrshire**
N Lans	**North Lanarkshire (6)**
Ork	**Orkney Islands**
P & K	**Perth & Kinross**
Rens	**Renfrewshire (7)**
S Ayrs	**South Ayrshire**
Shet	**Shetland Islands**
S Lans	**South Lanarkshire**
Stirlg	**Stirling**
W Duns	**West Dunbartonshire (8)**
W Isls	**Western Isles (Na h-Eileanan an Iar)**
W Loth	**West Lothian**

Using the National Grid

With an Ordnance Survey National Grid reference you can pinpoint anywhere in the country in this atlas. The blue grid lines which divide the main-map pages into 5km squares for ease of indexing also match the National Grid. A National Grid reference gives two letters and some figures. An example is how to find the summit of mount Snowdon using its 4-figure grid reference of **SH6154**.

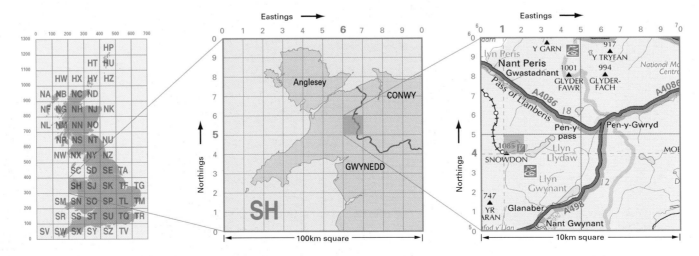

The letters **SH** indicate the 100km square of the National Grid in which Snowdon is located.

In a 4-figure grid reference the first two figures (eastings) are read along the map from left to right, the second two (northings) up the map. The figures **6** and **5**, the first and third figures of the Snowdon reference, indicate the 10km square within the **SH** square, lying above (north) and right (east) of the intersection of the vertical (easting) line **6** and horizontal (northing) line **5**.

The summit is finally pinpointed by figures **1** and **4** which locate a 1km square within the 10km square. At road atlas scales these grid lines are normally estimated by eye.

A

Abbas Combe Somset 17 T12
Abberley Worcs 35 S7
Abberley Common
  Worcs 35 S7
Abberton Essex 23 P4
Abberton Worcs 36 C10
Abberwick Nthumb 77 N3
Abbess Roding Essex 22 K5
Abbey Devon 6 F2
Abbey-Cwm-Hir Powys 34 C5
Abbeydale Sheff 57 M10
Abbey Dore Herefs 27 Q1
Abbeygreen S Lans 86 C2
Abbey Hill Somset 16 K13
Abbey St Bathans
  Border 84 K6
Abbeystead Lancs 62 B9
Abbey Town Cumb 66 J2
Abbey Village Lancs 55 P2
Abbeywood Gt Lon 21 S7
Abbotrule Border 76 C3
Abbots Bickington
  Devon 14 J10
Abbots Bromley Staffs 46 E9
Abbot's Chair Derbys 56 F8
Abbotsbury Dorset 7 Q7
Abbotsham Devon 14 J7
Abbotskerswell Devon 5 V7
Abbots Langley Herts 31 N12
Abbotsleigh S Lans 5 U11
Abbotsley Cambs 38 K9
Abbots Morton Worcs 36 D9
Abbots Ripton Cambs 38 K5
Abbot's Salford Warwks 36 E10
Abbotstone Hants 9 R2
Abbots Worthy Hants 9 M4
Abbots Ann Hants 19 M12
Abbott Street Dorset 8 D8
Abdon Shrops 35 N4
Abdon N York 35 N5
Abenhall Gloucs 28 C4
Aberaeron Cerdgn 32 J8
Aberaman Rhondd 26 J7
Aberangell Gwynd 43 R11
Aber-arad Carmth 32 F12
Aberarder Highld 102 H10
Aberargie P & K 90 J8
Aberarth Cerdgn 32 J8
Aberavon Neath 26 C12
Aber-banc Cerdgn 32 G12
Aberbeeg Blae G 27 N7
Abercanaid Myr Td 26 K7
Abercarn Caerph 27 N8
Abercastle Pembks 24 E4
Abercegir Powys 43 R13
Aberchalder Lodge
  Highld 96 C3
Aberchirder Abers 104 H5
Aber Clydach Powys 27 L3
Abercraf Powys 26 E5
Abercregan Neath 26 E8
Abercrombie Fife 91 R10
Abercwmboi Rhondd 26 J7
Abercych Pembks 32 D12
Abercynon Rhondd 26 K8
Aberdalgie P & K 90 G7
Aberdare Rhondd 26 J7
Aberdaron Gwynd 42 C8
Aberdeen C Aber 99 S2
Aberdeen Airport C Aber 105 P13
Aberdeen Crematorium
  C Aber 99 R2
Aberdesach Gwynd 42 H3
Aberdour Fife 83 N1
Aberdulais Neath 26 D8
Aberdyfi Gwynd 33 M3
Aberedw Powys 34 C11
Abereiddy Pembks 24 D4
Abererch Gwynd 42 G5
Aberfan Myr Td 26 K7
Aberfeldy P & K 90 C2
Aberffraw IoA 52 E8
Aberffrwd Cerdgn 33 N5
Aberford Leeds 63 U12
Aberfoyle Stirlg 89 N5
Abergarw Brdgnd 26 G11
Abergarwed Neath 26 E7
Abergavenny Mons 27 P5
Abergele Conwy 53 P7
Aber-giar Carmth 32 J11
Abergorlech Carmth 25 U3
Abergwesyn Powys 33 S10
Abergwili Carmth 25 S6
Abergwydol Powys 43 Q13
Abergwynfi Neath 26 E8
Abergwyngregyn
  Gwynd 53 L8
Abergynolwyn Gwynd 43 N12
Aberhafesp Powys 34 C1
Aberhosan Powys 33 Q2
Aberkenfig Brdgnd 26 F11
Aberlady E Loth 84 D3
Aberlemno Angus 98 J12
Aberllefenni Gwynd 43 P12
Aberllynfi Powys 34 E13
Abermagwr Cerdgn 33 N6
Aber-meurig Cerdgn 33 L9
Abermorddu Flints 44 H2
Abermule Powys 34 D2
Abernant Carmth 25 P6
Aber-nant Rhondd 26 J7
Abernethy P & K 90 J8
Abernyte P & K 91 L5
Aberporth Cerdgn 32 E10
Abersoch Gwynd 42 F8
Abersychan Torfn 27 P7
Aberthin V Glam 16 D2
Abertillery Blae G 27 N7
Abertridwr Caerph 27 L10
Abertridwr Powys 44 B10
Aberuthven P & K 90 E8
Aberyscir Powys 26 H2
Aberystwyth Cerdgn 33 L4
Aberystwyth
  Crematorium Cerdgn 33 M4
Abingdon-on-Thames
  Oxon 29 U8
Abinger Common Surrey 20 K13
Abinger Hammer Surrey 20 J13
Abington Nhants 37 U8
Abington S Lans 82 H14
Abington Pigotts Cambs 31 N4
Abingworth W Susx 10 J7
Ab Kettleby Leics 47 T9
Ab Lench Worcs 36 D10
Ablington Gloucs 29 M6
Ablington Wilts 18 J10
Abney Derbys 56 J10
Above Church Staffs 46 E3
Aboyne Abers 98 J4
Abram Wigan 55 P6
Abriachan Highld 102 F8
Abridge Essex 21 S3
Abronhill N Lans 89 S10
Abson S Glos 28 D13
Abthorpe Nhants 37 R11
Aby Lincs 59 R11
Acaster Malbis C York 64 D10
Acaster Selby N York 64 D11
Accrington Lancs 62 F14
Accrington
  Crematorium Lancs 62 F14
Acha Ag & B 92 F8
Achahoish Ag & B 87 P10
Achalader P & K 90 H2
Achaleven Ag & B 94 C12
Acha Mor W Isls 106 i6
Achanalt Highld 108 D12
Achandunie Highld 109 L10
Achany Highld 108 J5
Acharacle Highld 93 S5
Acharn Highld 93 S8
Acharn P & K 90 B2
Achavanich Highld 112 E8
Achduart Highld 107 T3
Achfary Highld 110 F9
A'Chill Highld 100 b9
Achiltibuie Highld 107 T3
Achina Highld 111 Q4
Achinhoan Ag & B 79 P12
Achintee Highld 101 M4
Achintraid Highld 101 M5
Achlyness Highld 110 F5
Achmelvich Highld 110 B12
Achmore Highld 101 M5
Achmore W Isls 106 i6
Achnacarnin Highld 110 B10
Achnacarry Highld 101 R14
Achnacloich Ag & B 94 B10
Achnaconeran Highld 102 E9
Achnacroish Ag & B 94 B10
Achnadrish House
  Ag & B 93 N8
Achnafauld P & K 90 D4
Achnagarron Highld 109 M10
Achnaha Highld 93 N5
Achnahaird Highld 107 S3
Achnahannet Highld 103 R10
Achnairn Highld 108 J4
Achnamara Ag & B 87 P8
Achnasheen Highld 108 D13
Achnashellach Lodge
  Highld 101 Q2
Achnastank Moray 104 B8
Achosnich Highld 93 L5
Achranich Highld 93 S9

Achreamie Highld 112 B3
Achriabhach Highld 94 G5
Achriesgill Highld 110 F6
Achurch Nhants 38 F4
Achvaich Highld 109 N6
Achvarasdal Highld 112 A3
Ackergill Highld 112 J6
Acklam Middsb 70 G9
Acklam N York 64 H7
Ackleton Shrops 45 S14
Acklington Nthumb 77 Q5
Ackworth Moor Top
  Wakefd 57 P3
Acle Norfk 51 R11
Acock's Green Birm 36 F4
Acol Kent 13 R2
Acomb C York 64 D9
Acomb Nthumb 76 J12
Aconbury Herefs 35 M14
Acre Lancs 55 S1
Acrefair Wrexhm 44 G5
Acton Ches E 45 P3
Acton Gt Lon 21 M6
Acton Shrops 34 J4
Acton Staffs 45 T5
Acton Suffk 40 E11
Acton Worcs 35 Q10
Acton Beauchamp
  Herefs 35 Q10
Acton Bridge Ches W 55 N11
Acton Burnell Shrops 45 M13
Acton Green Herefs 35 Q10
Acton Pigott Shrops 45 M13
Acton Round Shrops 35 Q1
Acton Scott Shrops 35 L3
Acton Trussell Staffs 46 B10
Acton Turville S Glos 28 F11
Adbaston Staffs 45 S8
Adber Dorset 17 Q12
Adbolton Notts 47 R6
Adderbury Oxon 37 N13
Adderley Shrops 45 Q6
Adderstone Nthumb 85 S12
Addiewell W Loth 82 J6
Addingham C Brad 63 M10
Addington Bucks 30 F7
Addington Gt Lon 21 Q10
Addington Kent 12 C4
Addiscombe Gt Lon 21 P9
Addlestone Surrey 20 J10
Addlestonemoor Surrey 20 J9
Addlethorpe Lincs 59 T13
Adeney Wrekin 45 S10
Adeyfield Herts 31 N11
Adfa Powys 44 C13
Adforton Herefs 34 K6
Adisham Kent 13 P5
Adlestrop Gloucs 29 P2
Adlingfleet E R Yk 58 D2
Adlington Ches E 56 D10
Adlington Lancs 55 P4
Admaston Staffs 46 D9
Admaston Wrekin 45 P11
Admington Warwks 36 H12
Adpar Cerdgn 32 G12
Adsborough Somset 16 J11
Adscombe Somset 16 G9
Adstock Bucks 30 F7
Adstone Nhants 37 Q10
Adswood Stockp 56 C9
Adversane W Susx 10 H6
Advie Highld 103 T9
Adwalton Leeds 63 Q14
Adwell Oxon 30 E13
Adwick le Street Donc 57 R5
Adwick upon Dearne
  Donc 57 Q6
Ae D & G 75 L9
Ae Bridgend D & G 74 K8
Afan Forest Park Neath 26 E8
Affetside Bury 55 R4
Affleck Abers 104 H7
Affpuddle Dorset 7 V6
Affric Lodge Highld 101 T7
Afon-wen Flints 54 D12
Afton IoW 9 L11
Agecroft Crematorium
  Salfd 55 T6
Agglethorpe N York 63 M2
Aigburth Lpool 54 H9
Aike E R Yk 65 N10
Aiketgate Cumb 67 Q3
Aikton Cumb 67 L2
Ailby Lincs 59 R11
Ailey Herefs 34 H11
Ailsworth C Pete 48 H14
Ainderby Quernhow
  N York 63 S3
Ainderby Steeple N York 63 S1
Aingers Green Essex 23 R3
Ainsdale Sefton 54 H4
Ainsdale-on-Sea Sefton 54 G4
Ainstable Cumb 67 R3
Ainsworth Bury 55 S5
Ainthorpe N York 71 M11
Aintree Sefton 54 J7
Ainville W Loth 83 M6
Aird Ag & B 87 N3
Aird D & G 72 D7
Aird W Isls 106 k5
Aird a Mhulaidh W Isls 106 h7
Aird Asaig W Isls 106 g8
Aird Dhubh Highld 100 g5
Airdeny Ag & B 94 C12
Aird of Kinloch Ag & B 93 P13
Aird of Sleat Highld 100 d9
Airdrie N Lans 82 E5
Airdriehill N Lans 82 F5
Aird Uig W Isls 106 f5
Airds of Kells D & G 73 R5
Airidh a bhruaich W Isls 106 h7
Airieland D & G 73 S8
Airlie Angus 98 F13
Airmyn E R Yk 58 B2
Airntully P & K 90 G4
Airor Highld 100 g9
Airth Falk 82 H1
Airton N York 62 J8
Aisby Lincs 48 F6
Aisby Lincs 58 D8
Aisgill Cumb 68 G13
Aish Devon 5 Q8
Aish Devon 5 U8
Aisholt Somset 16 H9
Aiskew N York 63 R2
Aislaby N York 64 H2
Aislaby N York 71 P11
Aislaby S on T 70 D10
Aisthorpe Lincs 58 F10
Aith Shet 106 t8
Akeld Nthumb 85 P13
Akeley Bucks 30 F6
Akenham Suffk 40 K11
Albaston Cnwll 5 L6
Alberbury Shrops 44 J11
Albourne W Susx 11 M7
Albourne Green W Susx 11 M7
Albrighton Shrops 45 T12
Albrighton Shrops 45 L10
Alburgh Norfk 41 N3
Albury Herts 31 R10
Albury Oxon 30 E11
Albury Surrey 20 J13
Albury End Herts 22 B3
Albury Heath Surrey 20 J13
Alby Hill Norfk 51 L7
Alcaig Highld 102 G4
Alcaston Shrops 35 L3
Alcester Warwks 36 E9
Alcester Lane End Birm 36 E4
Alciston E Susx 11 R9
Alcombe Somset 16 B7
Alcombe Wilts 18 B7
Alconbury Cambs 38 J5
Alconbury Weston
  Cambs 38 J5
Aldborough Norfk 51 L7
Aldborough N York 63 U7
Aldbourne Wilts 18 K6
Aldbrough E R Yk 65 S12

Aldgate Rutlnd 48 E13
Aldham Essex 23 M2
Aldham Suffk 40 J11
Aldingbourne W Susx 10 E9
Aldingham Cumb 61 P5
Aldington Kent 13 L8
Aldington Worcs 36 E12
Aldington Corner Kent 13 L8
Aldivalloch Moray 104 B11
Aldochlay Ag & B 88 J7
Aldon Shrops 34 K5
Aldoth Cumb 66 H3
Aldreth Cambs 39 Q5
Aldridge Wsall 46 E13
Aldringham Suffk 41 S8
Aldro N York 64 J7
Aldsworth Gloucs 29 N5
Aldsworth W Berk 19 N6
Aldunie Moray 104 D10
Aldwark Derbys 46 J1
Aldwark N York 64 C7
Aldwick W Susx 10 E11
Aldwincle Nhants 38 F4
Aldworth W Berk 19 R5
Alexandria W Duns 88 J10
Aley Somset 16 G9
Alfardisworthy Devon 14 G10
Alfington Devon 6 F5
Alfold Surrey 10 G4
Alfold Bars W Susx 10 G4
Alfold Crossways Surrey 10 G3
Alford Abers 104 H12
Alford Lincs 59 S11
Alford Somset 17 R10
Alford Crematorium
  Lincs 59 R11
Alfreton Derbys 47 M2
Alfrick Worcs 35 S10
Alfrick Pound Worcs 35 R10
Alfriston E Susx 11 S10
Algarkirk Lincs 49 L6
Alhampton Somset 17 R10
Alkborough N Linc 58 E2
Alkerton Gloucs 28 E7
Alkerton Oxon 37 M12
Alkham Kent 13 Q7
Alkington Shrops 45 M6
Alkmonton Derbys 46 G6
Allaleigh Devon 5 U10
Allanaquoich Abers 97 U5
Allanbank N Lans 82 F7
Allanton Border 85 M8
Allanton N Lans 82 F7
Allanton S Lans 82 D7
Allaston Gloucs 28 B7
Allbrook Hants 9 P4
All Cannings Wilts 18 G8
Allendale Nthumb 68 H2
Allen End Warwks 36 G1
Allenheads Nthumb 68 J3
Allensford Dur 69 N2
Allen's Green Herts 22 C4
Allensmore Herefs 35 L13
Allenton C Derb 47 L7
Aller Devon 5 V6
Aller Somset 17 M11
Allerby Cumb 66 G5
Allercombe Devon 6 D6
Allerford Somset 16 B7
Allerston N York 64 K3
Allerthorpe E R Yk 64 H10
Allerton C Brad 63 N13
Allerton Highld 109 L2
Allerton Lpool 54 J9
Allerton Bywater Leeds 57 N1
Allerton Mauleverer
  N York 63 U8
Allesley Covtry 36 J4
Allestree C Derb 46 K6
Allet Common Cnwll 2 K7
Allexton Leics 48 B13
Allgreave Ches E 56 E13
Allhallows Medway 22 K12
Allhallows-on-Sea
  Medway 22 K12
Alligin Shuas Highld 107 P13
Allimore Green Staffs 45 U10
Allington Dorset 7 M6
Allington Kent 12 E4
Allington Lincs 48 B5
Allington Wilts 18 K12
Allington Wilts 18 G8
Allington Wilts 18 K13
Allithwaite Cumb 61 R4
Alloa Clacks 90 C13
Allonby Cumb 66 G4
Allostock Ches W 55 R12
Alloway S Ayrs 81 L9
Allowenshay Somset 7 L2
All Saints South Elmham
  Suffk 41 P4
Allscott Shrops 35 R1
Allscott Wrekin 45 P11
All Stretton Shrops 35 L1
Alltami Flints 54 G13
Alltchaorunn Highld 94 H8
Alltmawr Powys 34 C12
Alltwalis Carmth 25 R4
Alltwen Neath 26 C7
Alltyblaca Cerdgn 32 K11
Allweston Dorset 7 S2
Allwood Green Suffk 40 J6
Almeley Herefs 34 H10
Almeley Wooton Herefs 34 H10
Almer Dorset 8 C8
Almholme Donc 57 S5
Almington Staffs 45 S7
Alminstone Cross Devon 14 G8
Almodington W Susx 10 C11
Almondbank P & K 90 G6
Almondbury Kirk 56 J3
Almondsbury S Glos 28 B11
Almondvale W Loth 83 L5
Alne N York 64 C7
Alness Highld 109 M10
Alnham Nthumb 76 K2
Alnmouth Nthumb 77 Q3
Alnwick Nthumb 77 P3
Alperton Gt Lon 21 L5
Alphamstone Essex 40 E13
Alpheton Suffk 40 E10
Alphington Devon 6 B6
Alpington Norfk 51 N13
Alport Derbys 46 J1
Alpraham Ches E 45 N2
Alresford Essex 23 Q3
Alrewas Staffs 46 F10
Alsager Ches E 45 T2
Alsagers Bank Staffs 45 T4
Alsop en le Dale Derbys 46 G3
Alston Cumb 68 F3
Alston Devon 6 K4
Alstone Gloucs 36 C14
Alstone Somset 16 K7
Alstonefield Staffs 46 F2
Alston Sutton Somset 17 M6
Alswear Devon 15 R8
Alt Oldham 56 D6
Altandhu Highld 107 S3
Altarnun Cnwll 4 G4
Altass Highld 108 J4
Altcreich Ag & B 93 R11
Altgaltraig Ag & B 88 C11
Altham Lancs 62 F13
Althorne Essex 23 M8
Althorpe N Linc 58 D5
Alticane N Ayrs 81 V3
Alticry D & G 72 H8
Altnabreac Station
  Highld 112 B8
Altnaharra Highld 111 M8
Altofts Wakefd 57 N2
Alton Derbys 57 L14
Alton Hants 9 U2
Alton Staffs 46 E5
Alton Barnes Wilts 18 H8
Alton Pancras Dorset 7 T4
Alton Priors Wilts 18 H8
Alton Towers Staffs 46 E5
Altrincham Traffd 55 R9
Altrincham
  Crematorium Traffd 55 R9
Altskeith Hotel Stirlg 89 L5
Alva Clacks 90 C12
Alvanley Ches W 55 L11
Alvaston C Derb 47 L7
Alvechurch Worcs 36 E6
Alvecote Warwks 46 J12
Alvediston Wilts 8 D4
Alveley Shrops 35 S4
Alverdiscott Devon 15 M7
Alverstoke Hants 9 S9
Alverstone IoW 9 R12
Alverthorpe Wakefd 57 M2
Alverton Notts 47 U5
Alves Moray 103 T3
Alvescot Oxon 29 Q7
Alveston S Glos 28 B10
Alveston Warwks 36 H9
Alvingham Lincs 59 Q8
Alvington Gloucs 28 B7
Alwalton C Pete 48 H14
Alweston Dorset 7 S2
Alwington Devon 14 J8
Alwinton Nthumb 76 J4
Alwoodley Leeds 63 S11
Alwoodley Gates Leeds 63 S11
Alyth P & K 90 K2
Ambergate Derbys 47 L3
Amber Hill Lincs 48 K4
Amberley Gloucs 28 F7
Amberley W Susx 10 H7
Amber Row Derbys 47 L2
Amberstone E Susx 11 T8
Amble Nthumb 77 R5
Amblecote Dudley 35 U4
Ambler Thorn C Brad 63 M14
Ambleside Cumb 67 N12
Ambleston Pembks 24 H5
Ambrosden Oxon 30 D9
Amcotts N Linc 58 E4

America Cambs 39 P5
America Bucks 20 G3
Amersham Bucks 20 G3
Amersham Common
  Bucks 20 G3
Amersham Old Town
  Bucks 20 G3
Amersham on the Hill
  Bucks 20 G3
Amerton Staffs 46 C8
Amerton Railway &
  Farm Staffs 46 C8
Amesbury Wilts 18 J12
Amhuinnsuidhe W Isls 106 f8
Amington Staffs 46 H12
Amisfield Town D & G 74 K9
Amlwch IoA 52 G4
Ammanford Carmth 25 U7
Amotherby N York 64 G5
Ampfield Hants 9 M4
Ampleforth N York 64 D4
Ampney Crucis Gloucs 28 K7
Ampney St Mary Gloucs 29 L7
Ampney St Peter Gloucs 29 L7
Amport Hants 19 L11
Ampthill C Beds 31 N5
Ampton Suffk 40 E6
Amroth Pembks 25 L9
Amulree P & K 90 D4
Amwell Herts 31 Q10
Anaheilt Highld 93 U5
Ancaster Lincs 48 E4
Anchor Shrops 34 E3
Anchorsholme Bpool 61 Q12
Ancroft Nthumb 85 P9
Ancrum Border 84 G14
Ancton W Susx 10 F10
Anderby Lincs 59 T11
Anderby Creek Lincs 59 T11
Andersea Somset 16 K10
Andersfield Somset 16 J10
Anderson Dorset 8 B9
Anderton Ches W 55 P11
Anderton Cnwll 5 M10
Andover Hants 19 M11
Andoversford Gloucs 28 K4
Andreas IoM 60 g3
Anelog Gwynd 42 C8
Anerley Gt Lon 21 Q9
Anfield Lpool 54 J8
Anfield Crematorium
  Lpool 54 J8
Angarrack Cnwll 2 F9
Angarrick Cnwll 2 K10
Angelbank Shrops 35 N5
Angersleigh Somset 16 G13
Angerton Cumb 66 K2
Anglesey IoA 52 F6
Anglesey Abbey Cambs 39 R8
Angmering W Susx 10 H9
Angram N York 64 C10
Angram N York 68 J1
Angrouse Cnwll 2 H12
Anick Nthumb 76 J12
Ankerville Highld 109 Q9
Anlaby E R Yk 65 N14
Anmer Norfk 50 B9
Anmore Hants 9 T6
Anna Valley Hants 19 M11
Annan D & G 75 P12
Annat Highld 107 P13
Annathill N Lans 82 D4
Anna Valley Hants 19 M11
Annbank S Ayrs 81 N8
Annesley Notts 47 P3
Annesley Woodhouse
  Notts 47 N3
Annfield Plain Dur 69 Q2
Anniesland C Glas 89 M12
Annitsford N Tyne 77 R11
Annscroft Shrops 45 L12
Ansdell Lancs 61 Q14
Ansford Somset 17 R10
Ansley Warwks 36 J2
Anslow Staffs 46 H8
Anslow Gate Staffs 46 G8
Anslow Lees Staffs 46 H8
Ansteadbrook Surrey 10 E3
Anstey Herts 22 C2
Anstey Leics 47 Q12
Anstruther Fife 91 S10
Ansty Warwks 37 M4
Ansty W Susx 11 M6
Ansty Wilts 8 D3
Ansty Cross Dorset 7 U4
Anthill Common Hants 9 S6
Anthonys Surrey 20 H10
Anthorn Cumb 66 J1
Antingham Norfk 51 N7
Anton's Gowt Lincs 49 M4
Antony Cnwll 5 L10
Antrobus Ches W 55 P11
Anvil Corner Devon 14 J11
Anvil Green Kent 13 M6
Anwick Lincs 48 H3
Anwoth D & G 73 P8
Aperfield Gt Lon 21 S11
Apes Dale Worcs 36 D6
Apethorpe Nhants 38 F1
Apeton Staffs 45 U10
Apley Lincs 58 J11
Apperknowle Derbys 57 N11
Apperley Gloucs 28 F3
Apperley Bridge C Brad 63 P12
Apperley Dene Nthumb 77 L14
Appersett N York 62 H1
Appin Ag & B 94 C9
Appleby N Linc 58 F4
Appleby-in-
  Westmorland Cumb 68 E8
Appleby Magna Leics 46 K12
Appleby Parva Leics 46 K12
Appleby Street Herts 31 T11
Applecross Highld 100 g5
Appledore Devon 6 F2
Appledore Devon 15 L5
Appledore Kent 12 J9
Appledore Heath Kent 12 J8
Appleford Oxon 19 R2
Applegarth Town D & G 75 M9
Applehaigh Wakefd 57 N4
Appleshaw Hants 19 M11
Applethwaite Cumb 67 L7
Appleton Halton 55 M9
Appleton Oxon 29 T7
Appleton Warrtn 55 N10
Appleton-le-Moors
  N York 64 F2
Appleton-le-Street
  N York 64 G5
Appleton Roebuck
  N York 64 D11
Appleton Thorn Warrtn 55 P10
Appleton Wiske N York 70 D11
Appletreehall Border 75 U3
Appletreewick N York 63 L7
Appley Somset 16 E12
Appley Bridge Lancs 55 L5
Apse Heath IoW 9 R12
Apsley End C Beds 31 P6
Apuldram W Susx 10 C10
Arabella Highld 109 Q9
Arbirlot Angus 91 S3
Arborfield Wokham 20 C9
Arborfield Cross
  Wokham 20 C9
Arborfield Green
  Wokham 20 C9
Arbourthorne Sheff 57 N9
Arbroath Angus 91 T3
Arbuthnott Abers 99 P8
Archddu Carmth 25 R8
Archdeacon Newton
  Darltn 69 S9
Archencarroch W Duns 88 K9
Archiestown Moray 104 A7
Archirondel Jersey 7 e2
Arclid Green Ches E 45 T1
Ardachu Highld 109 L4
Ardalanish Ag & B 92 K14
Ardaneaskan Highld 101 L5
Ardanaiseig Hotel Ag & B 94 F14
Ardarroch Highld 101 L4
Ardbeg Ag & B 78 G6
Ardbeg Ag & B 88 C9
Ardbeg Ag & B 88 C11
Ardcharnich Highld 108 A6
Ardchiavaig Ag & B 92 K14
Ardchonnel Ag & B 87 T2
Ardchullarie More Stirlg 89 N4
Ardchyle Stirlg 89 M3
Arddarroch Ag & B 88 F6
Arddleen Powys 44 F11
Ard Dorch Highld 100 e6
Ardeley Herts 31 T8
Ardelve Highld 101 M6
Arden Ag & B 88 J9
Ardens Grafton Warwks 36 G9
Ardentallen Ag & B 93 U13
Ardentinny Ag & B 88 E7
Ardentraive Ag & B 88 C11
Ardeonaig Stirlg 89 S2
Ardersier Highld 103 L5
Ardersier Highld 103 L5
Ardessie Highld 107 U6
Ardfern Ag & B 87 Q3
Ardfernal Ag & B 86 J11
Ardgay Highld 108 K6
Ardgour Highld 94 E4
Ardgowan Inver 88 F11
Ardhasig W Isls 106 g8
Ardheslaig Highld 107 M13
Ardindrean Highld 108 B7
Ardingly W Susx 11 N5
Ardington Oxon 29 T10
Ardington Wick Oxon 29 T10
Ardlamont Ag & B 87 T12
Ardleigh Essex 23 Q2
Ardleigh Heath Essex 23 Q1
Ardler P & K 91 L3
Ardley Oxon 30 B7
Ardley End Essex 22 D5
Ardlui Ag & B 88 J3
Ardlussa Ag & B 87 L7
Ardmaddy Ag & B 94 G13
Ardmair Highld 107 U5
Ardmaleish Ag & B 88 C12
Ardminish Ag & B 79 L6
Ardmolich Highld 93 T4
Ardmore Ag & B 88 H11
Ardmore Highld 109 N7
Ardnadam Ag & B 88 E9
Ardnagrask Highld 102 F6
Ardnarff Highld 101 M5
Ardnastang Highld 93 U5
Ardpatrick Ag & B 79 N3
Ardrishaig Ag & B 87 R8
Ardross Highld 109 L9
Ardrossan N Ayrs 80 J4
Ardshealach Highld 93 R5
Ardslignish Highld 93 P5
Ardtalla Ag & B 78 H6
Ardtalnaig P & K 90 B3
Ardtoe Highld 93 R4
Arduaine Ag & B 87 P3
Ardullie Highld 102 G3
Ardvasar Highld 100 f8
Ardvorlich P & K 89 R3
Ardvourlie W Isls 106 h7
Ardwell D & G 72 E10
Ardwick Manch 56 C8
Areley Kings Worcs 35 S6
Arevegaig Highld 93 R5
Arford Hants 10 C3
Argoed Caerph 27 M8
Argoed Powys 33 U9
Argoed Mill Powys 33 U8
Argos Hill E Susx 11 T5
Argyll Forest Park
  Ag & B 88 F5
Aribruach W Isls 106 h7
Aridhglas Ag & B 92 J13
Arileod Ag & B 92 F8
Arinagour Ag & B 92 G7
Ariogan Ag & B 94 B13
Arisaig Highld 93 R1
Arisaig House Highld 93 R2
Arkendale N York 63 T7
Arkesden Essex 39 Q14
Arkholme Lancs 62 B5
Arkleby Cumb 66 H4
Arkleton D & G 75 R6
Arkle Town N York 69 N12
Arkley Gt Lon 21 M3
Arksey Donc 57 S5
Arkwright Town Derbys 57 P12
Arle Gloucs 28 H3
Arlecdon Cumb 66 F9
Arlescote Warwks 37 M11
Arlesey C Beds 31 Q5
Arleston Wrekin 45 P11
Arley Ches E 55 P10
Arlingham Gloucs 28 D5
Arlington Devon 15 P4
Arlington E Susx 11 S9
Arlington Gloucs 29 L6
Arlington Beccott Devon 15 P4
Armadale Highld 93 P2
Armadale Highld 111 R3
Armadale W Loth 82 H5
Armaside Cumb 66 J8
Armathwaite Cumb 67 R3
Arminghall Norfk 51 N12
Armitage Staffs 46 E10
Armitage Bridge Kirk 56 H4
Armley Leeds 63 R13
Armscote Warwks 36 H12
Armshead Staffs 46 B4
Armston Nhants 38 F3
Armthorpe Donc 57 T5
Arnabost Ag & B 92 G7
Arnaby Cumb 61 L3
Arncliffe N York 62 J4
Arncliffe Cote N York 62 J4
Arncroach Fife 91 R10
Arndilly House Moray 104 B6
Arne Dorset 8 D11
Arnesby Leics 37 R2
Arngask P & K 90 H9
Arnisdale Highld 100 h8
Arnish Highld 100 e5
Arniston Mdloth 83 R6
Arnol W Isls 106 i4
Arnold E R Yk 65 Q11
Arnold Notts 47 Q5
Arnprior Stirlg 89 P6
Arnside Cumb 61 T4
Aros Ag & B 93 P9
Arowry Wrexhm 45 L5
Arrad Foot Cumb 61 Q3
Arram E R Yk 65 N11
Arrathorne N York 69 Q14
Arreton IoW 9 Q12
Arrina Highld 107 L13
Arrington Cambs 39 M10
Arrochar Ag & B 88 H5
Arrow Warwks 36 E9
Arscott Shrops 44 K12
Artafallie Highld 102 H6
Arthington Leeds 63 R11
Arthingworth Nhants 37 U4
Arthog Gwynd 43 M11
Arthrath Abers 105 R8
Arthursdale Leeds 63 T12
Artrochie Abers 105 S9
Aruadh Ag & B 86 D12
Arundel W Susx 10 G9
Asby Cumb 66 G8
Ascog Ag & B 88 D13
Ascot W & M 20 G9
Ascott Warwks 36 K13
Ascott Earl Oxon 29 Q4
Ascott-under-
  Wychwood Oxon 29 R4
Asenby N York 63 T4
Asfordby Leics 47 T10
Asfordby Hill Leics 47 T10
Asgarby Lincs 48 H4
Asgarby Lincs 59 L14
Ash Devon 5 U11
Ash Dorset 8 B5
Ash Kent 12 A3
Ash Kent 13 Q4
Ash Somset 7 L2
Ash Somset 17 M11
Ash Surrey 20 F12
Ashampstead W Berk 19 S5
Ashampstead Green
  W Berk 19 S5
Ashbocking Suffk 41 L10
Ashbourne Derbys 46 G4
Ashbrittle Somset 16 E12
Ash Bullayne Devon 15 S11
Ashburnham Place
  E Susx 12 C13
Ashburton Devon 5 S6
Ashbury Devon 15 L13
Ashbury Oxon 29 P10
Ashby N Linc 58 E5
Ashby by Partney Lincs 59 R13
Ashby cum Fenby NE Lin 59 N6
Ashby de la Launde
  Lincs 48 G2
Ashby-de-la-Zouch Leics 47 L10
Ashby Folville Leics 47 T11
Ashby Magna Leics 37 Q2
Ashby Parva Leics 37 P3
Ashby Puerorum Lincs 59 P12
Ashby St Ledgers Nhants 37 P7
Ashby St Mary Norfk 51 P13
Ashchurch Gloucs 28 H1
Ashcombe Devon 6 B9
Ashcombe N Som 17 L4
Ashcott Somset 17 M9
Ashdon Essex 39 S12
Ashe Hants 19 S11
Asheldham Essex 23 N7
Ashen Essex 40 B12
Ashendon Bucks 30 E10
Asheridge Bucks 30 K12
Ashfield Hants 9 L5
Ashfield Herefs 27 V3
Ashfield Stirlg 89 R6
Ashfield Suffk 41 M7
Ashfield cum Thorpe
  Suffk 41 M7
Ashfield Green Suffk 41 N6
Ashfold Crossways
  W Susx 11 L5
Ashford Devon 5 R11
Ashford Devon 15 N6
Ashford Kent 13 L7
Ashford Surrey 20 J8
Ashford Bowdler Shrops 35 M6
Ashford Carbonell
  Shrops 35 M6
Ashford Hill Hants 19 R8
Ashford in the Water
  Derbys 56 J13
Ashgill S Lans 82 D9
Ash Green Surrey 20 F13
Ash Green Warwks 36 K4

Ashill Devon 6 E2
Ashill Norfk 50 E13
Ashill Somset 16 K13
Ashingdon Essex 23 L8
Ashington Nthumb 77 R9
Ashington Poole 8 D9
Ashington Somset 17 Q12
Ashington W Susx 10 J7
Ashkirk Border 75 U1
Ashlett Hants 9 P8
Ashleworth Gloucs 28 F3
Ashleworth Quay Gloucs 28 F2
Ashley Cambs 39 U8
Ashley Ches E 55 R10
Ashley Devon 15 Q9
Ashley Dorset 8 H7
Ashley Gloucs 28 H8
Ashley Hants 9 L9
Ashley Hants 9 M3
Ashley Kent 13 R6
Ashley Nhants 37 U3
Ashley Staffs 45 S7
Ashley Wilts 18 B7
Ashley Green Bucks 31 L11
Ashley Heath Dorset 8 G7
Ashley Moor Herefs 35 L7
Ash Magna Shrops 45 M5
Ashmansworth Hants 19 P9
Ashmansworthy Devon 14 H9
Ashmead Green Gloucs 28 E8
Ashmill Devon 14 J13
Ash Mill Devon 15 R8
Ashmore Dorset 8 C4
Ashmore Green W Berk 19 R7
Ashorne Warwks 36 K9
Ashover Derbys 46 K1
Ashover Hay Derbys 46 K1
Ashow Warwks 36 K6
Ashperton Herefs 35 Q12
Ashprington Devon 5 U9
Ash Priors Somset 16 G11
Ashreigney Devon 15 P10
Ash Street Suffk 40 H11
Ashtead Surrey 21 L11
Ash Thomas Devon 6 E2
Ashton C Pete 48 H12
Ashton Cnwll 2 G11
Ashton Herefs 35 M8
Ashton Inver 88 F10
Ashton Nhants 38 G11
Ashton Nhants 37 U11
Ashton Somset 17 N12
Ashton Common Wilts 18 C9
Ashton-in-Makerfield
  Wigan 55 N7
Ashton Keynes Wilts 28 K8
Ashton under Hill Worcs 36 C13
Ashton-under-Lyne
  Tamesd 56 D7
Ashton upon Mersey
  Traffd 55 S8
Ashurst Hants 9 L6
Ashurst Kent 11 S3
Ashurst Lancs 55 L5
Ashurst W Susx 10 K7
Ashurst Wood W Susx 11 R3
Ash Vale Surrey 20 E12
Ashwater Devon 14 J13
Ashwell Herts 31 S5
Ashwell Rutlnd 48 C11
Ashwellthorpe Norfk 51 L14
Ashwick Somset 17 R7
Ashwicken Norfk 50 B10
Ashwood Staffs 35 U3
Askam in Furness Cumb 61 N4
Askern Donc 57 S4
Askerswell Dorset 7 P6
Askett Bucks 30 H11
Askham Cumb 67 R8
Askham Notts 58 C12
Askham Bryan C York 64 D10
Askham Richard C York 64 C10
Asknish Ag & B 87 S6
Askrigg N York 62 J1
Askwith N York 63 P10
Aslackby Lincs 48 G7
Aslacton Norfk 41 L2
Aslockton Notts 47 U5
Asney Somset 17 N9
Aspall Suffk 40 K7
Aspatria Cumb 66 H4
Aspenden Herts 31 U7
Asperton Lincs 49 L5
Aspley Staffs 45 T7
Aspley Guise C Beds 30 K5
Aspley Heath C Beds 30 K5
Aspley Heath Warwks 36 F6
Aspull Wigan 55 P5
Asselby E R Yk 64 G14
Asserby Lincs 59 S11
Asserby Turn Lincs 59 S11
Assington Suffk 40 F13
Assington Green Suffk 40 C10
Astbury Ches E 45 T1
Astcote Nhants 37 R10
Asterby Lincs 59 N11
Asterley Shrops 44 J12
Asterton Shrops 34 J2
Asthall Oxon 29 Q5
Asthall Leigh Oxon 29 R5
Astle Highld 109 N5
Astley Shrops 45 M10
Astley Warwks 36 K3
Astley Wigan 55 R7
Astley Worcs 35 S7
Astley Abbots Shrops 35 R1
Astley Bridge Bolton 55 R4
Astley Cross Worcs 35 T7
Astley Green Wigan 55 R7
Aston Ches E 45 Q4
Aston Ches W 55 N11
Aston Derbys 56 H10
Aston Flints 54 G13
Aston Herefs 34 K7
Aston Herefs 35 M8
Aston Herts 31 S9
Aston Oxon 29 R7
Aston Rothm 57 P9
Aston Shrops 45 N9
Aston Shrops 45 R12
Aston Staffs 45 S5
Aston Staffs 45 T4
Aston Wokham 20 C7
Aston Wrekin 45 Q12
Aston Abbotts Bucks 30 H8
Aston Botterell Shrops 35 P4
Aston-by-Stone Staffs 46 B7
Aston Cantlow Warwks 36 F9
Aston Clinton Bucks 30 J10
Aston Crews Herefs 28 C3
Aston Cross Gloucs 28 H1
Aston End Herts 31 S9
Aston Fields Worcs 36 C7
Aston Flamville Leics 37 N2
Aston Heath Ches W 55 N11
Aston Ingham Herefs 28 C3
Aston juxta Mondrum
  Ches E 45 P2
Aston le Walls Nhants 37 N10
Aston Magna Gloucs 36 G13
Aston Munslow Shrops 35 M3
Aston on Carrant Gloucs 28 H1
Aston on Clun Shrops 34 J4
Aston Pigott Shrops 44 H12
Aston Rogers Shrops 44 H12
Aston Rowant Oxon 20 C3
Aston Sandford Bucks 30 F11
Aston Somerville Worcs 36 D13
Aston-sub-Edge Gloucs 36 F12
Aston Tirrold Oxon 19 R3
Aston-upon-Trent
  Derbys 47 M8
Aston Upthorpe Oxon 19 R3
Astrop Nhants 37 N13
Astwick C Beds 31 R5
Astwood M Keyn 38 D11
Astwood Worcs 36 C8
Astwood Bank Worcs 36 D8
Aswarby Lincs 48 G5
Aswardby Lincs 59 Q12
Atcham Shrops 45 M12
Atch Lench Worcs 36 D10
Athelhampton Dorset 7 U5
Athelington Suffk 41 M6
Athelney Somset 16 K11
Athelstaneford E Loth 84 E3
Atherfield Green IoW 9 P13
Atherington Devon 15 N8
Atherington W Susx 10 H9
Atherstone Somset 17 L12
Atherstone Warwks 36 K1
Atherstone on Stour
  Warwks 36 H10
Atherton Wigan 55 Q6
Atley Hill N York 69 S12
Atlow Derbys 46 H4
Attadale Highld 101 N5
Attenborough Notts 47 P6
Atterby Lincs 58 F8
Attercliffe Sheff 57 N9
Atterley Shrops 45 P14

Atterton Leics 47 L14
Attingham Park Shrops 45 M12
Attleborough Norfk 40 J1
Attleborough Warwks 37 L2
Attlebridge Norfk 50 K10
Attleton Green Suffk 40 B9
Atwick E R Yk 65 R9
Atworth Wilts 18 C7
Auberrow Herefs 35 L11
Aubourn Lincs 58 F14
Auchbreck Moray 103 V10
Auchedly Abers 105 Q9
Auchenbardie Abers 99 N8
Auchenblae Abers 99 N8
Auchenbowie Stirlg 89 S8
Auchencairn D & G 73 T9
Auchencairn D & G 74 J9
Auchencairn N Ayrs 80 E7
Auchencrow Border 85 M7
Auchendinny Mdloth 83 Q6
Auchengray S Lans 82 J7
Auchenhalrig Moray 104 D3
Auchenheath S Lans 82 F10
Auchenhessnane
  D & G 74 E6
Auchenlochan Ag & B 87 T11
Auchenmade N Ayrs 81 M4
Auchenmalg D & G 72 H8
Auchentiber N Ayrs 81 M4
Auchindrain Ag & B 87 T5
Auchindrean Highld 108 A7
Auchininna Abers 104 K6
Auchinleck E Ayrs 81 R8
Auchinloch N Lans 89 Q11
Auchinstarry N Lans 89 R10
Auchintore Highld 94 F3
Auchiries Abers 105 T8
Auchlean Highld 97 M5
Auchlee Abers 99 R4
Auchleven Abers 104 J11
Auchlochan S Lans 82 F11
Auchlossan Abers 98 K3
Auchlunies Abers 99 R4
Auchlyne Stirlg 89 P2
Auchmacoy Abers 105 S9
Auchmillan E Ayrs 81 Q7
Auchmithie Angus 91 U3
Auchmuirbridge Fife 90 K11
Auchnacree Angus 98 H11
Auchnagatt Abers 105 Q7
Auchnarrow Moray 104 A10
Auchnotteroch D & G 72 C7
Auchroisk Moray 104 D6
Auchterarder P & K 90 D8
Auchteraw Highld 96 C3
Auchterblair Highld 103 R9
Auchtercairn Highld 107 N9
Auchterderran Fife 91 L12
Auchterhouse Angus 91 M4
Auchterless Abers 105 L7
Auchtermuchty Fife 91 L9
Auchterneed Highld 102 F3
Auchtertool Fife 91 L13
Auchtertyre Highld 101 M6
Auchtubh Stirlg 89 P3
Auckengill Highld 112 J4
Auckley Donc 57 T6
Audenshaw Tamesd 56 D7
Audlem Ches E 45 Q5
Audley Staffs 45 T3
Audley End Essex 39 Q13
Audley End Essex 40 D13
Audley End Suffk 40 E10
Audley End House &
  Gardens Essex 39 R13
Audmore Staffs 45 T9
Audnam Dudley 35 U4
Aughertree Cumb 67 L5
Aughton E R Yk 64 G12
Aughton Lancs 54 J5
Aughton Lancs 62 B6
Aughton Rothm 57 P9
Aughton Wilts 18 K9
Aughton Park Lancs 54 K5
Auldearn Highld 103 P5
Aulden Herefs 35 L9
Auldgirth D & G 74 J8
Auldhouse S Lans 81 S1
Ault a' chruinn Highld 101 P7
Aultbea Highld 107 P6
Aultgrishan Highld 107 M7
Aultguish Inn Highld 108 G10
Ault Hucknall Derbys 57 P13
Aultmore Moray 104 E5
Aultnagoire Highld 102 F10
Aultnamain Inn Highld 109 M8
Aunby Lincs 48 F11
Aunk Devon 6 D4
Aunsby Lincs 48 F6
Auquhorthies Abers 105 N10
Aust S Glos 28 A10
Austendike Lincs 49 L9
Austerfield Donc 57 U7
Austerlands Oldham 56 E6
Austhorpe Leeds 63 U13
Austonley Kirk 56 H5
Austrey Warwks 46 J13
Austwick N York 62 F6
Authorpe Lincs 59 R10
Authorpe Row Lincs 59 T12
Avebury Wilts 18 G7
Avebury Trusloe Wilts 18 F7
Aveley Thurr 22 E11
Avening Gloucs 28 G8
Averham Notts 47 U3
Aveton Gifford Devon 5 R11
Aviemore Highld 97 N3
Avington W Berk 19 P7
Avoch Highld 102 J5
Avon Hants 8 H9
Avonbridge Falk 82 H4
Avon Dassett Warwks 37 M10
Avonmouth Bristl 27 U12
Avonwick Devon 5 S9
Awbridge Hants 9 L3
Awhirk D & G 72 D7
Awkley S Glos 28 A10
Awliscombe Devon 6 F4
Awre Gloucs 28 C6
Awsworth Notts 47 N5
Axborough Worcs 35 T5
Axbridge Somset 17 L5
Axford Hants 19 T11
Axford Wilts 18 K6
Axminster Devon 6 K5
Axmouth Devon 6 K6
Axton Flints 54 C10
Aycliffe Dur 69 S7
Aydon Nthumb 77 L13
Aylburton Gloucs 28 B7
Ayle Nthumb 68 F3
Aylesbeare Devon 6 D6
Aylesbury Bucks 30 H10
Aylesby NE Lin 59 M5
Aylesford Kent 12 D4
Aylesham Kent 13 P5
Aylestone C Leic 47 Q13
Aylestone Park C Leic 47 Q13
Aylmerton Norfk 51 L6
Aylsham Norfk 51 L8
Aylton Herefs 35 Q13
Aylworth Gloucs 29 M3
Aymestrey Herefs 34 K8
Aynho Nhants 37 N13
Ayot Green Herts 31 R10
Ayot St Lawrence Herts 31 Q9
Ayot St Peter Herts 31 R9
Ayr S Ayrs 81 L8
Aysgarth N York 69 M14
Ayshford Devon 16 D13
Ayside Cumb 61 R3
Ayston Rutlnd 48 C13
Aythorpe Roding Essex 22 E4
Ayton Border 85 N6
Azerley N York 63 R5

B

Babbacombe Torbay 6 B11
Babbington Notts 47 N5
Babbinswood Shrops 44 H7
Babbs Green Herts 31 U10
Babcary Somset 17 Q11
Babel Carmth 33 Q14
Babell Flints 54 D12
Babeny Devon 5 Q5
Babraham Cambs 39 R10
Babworth Notts 57 U11
Bachau IoA 52 G6
Bache Shrops 35 L4
Back of Keppoch Highld 100 e13
Back o' th' Brook Staffs 46 E3
Back Street Suffk 40 B9
Backaland Ork 106 u16
Backbarrow Cumb 61 R2
Backe Carmth 25 N7
Backfolds Abers 105 S5
Backford Ches W 54 J12
Backies Highld 109 P4
Backlass Highld 112 F6
Back o' th' Brook Staffs 46 E3
Backwell N Som 17 N3
Backworth N Tyne 77 S11
Bacon's End Solhll 36 G3
Baconsthorpe Norfk 50 K6
Bacton Herefs 34 J13
Bacton Norfk 51 P7
Bacton Suffk 40 J7
Bacton Green Suffk 40 J7
Bacup Lancs 56 C2
Badachro Highld 107 M9
Badanloch Highld 111 P7
Badbury Swindn 18 J4
Badby Nhants 37 Q9
Badcall Highld 110 E6
Badcall Highld 110 E5

Badcall Highld 110 E5
Badcaul Highld 107 T6
Baddeley Edge C Stke 46 B3
Baddeley Green C Stke 46 B3
Baddesley Ensor Warwks 36 J2
Baddesley Clinton
  Warwks 36 H6
Baddidarroch Highld 110 B13
Baddinsgill Border 83 M8
Badenscoth Abers 104 K8
Badentarbet Highld 107 S3
Badenyon Abers 104 C12
Badgall Cnwll 4 G3
Badgeney Cambs 49 P13
Badger Shrops 35 R1
Badgers Cross Cnwll 2 D10
Badgers Mount Kent 21 S10
Badgeworth Gloucs 28 H4
Badgworth Somset 17 L6
Badharlick Cnwll 4 H3
Badicaul Highld 100 g7
Badingham Suffk 41 P7
Badlesmere Kent 12 K5
Badlieu Border 75 L2
Badluarach Highld 107 S5
Badnaban Highld 110 B13
Badninish Highld 109 P5
Badrallach Highld 107 U5
Badsey Worcs 36 E12
Badshot Lea Surrey 20 E13
Badsworth Wakefd 57 Q4
Badwell Ash Suffk 40 G7
Bag Enderby Lincs 59 Q12
Bagby N York 64 B3
Bag Enderby Lincs 59 Q12
Bagginswood Shrops 35 Q4
Baggrow Cumb 66 J4
Bagh a Chaisteil W Isls 106 b19
Bagh a' Tuath W Isls 106 b18
Bagillt Flints 54 F11
Baginton Warwks 36 K6
Baglan Neath 26 C9
Bagley Shrops 44 K8
Bagley Somset 17 M7
Bagmore Hants 19 U12
Bagnall Staffs 46 B3
Bagnor W Berk 19 P7
Bagshot Surrey 20 F10
Bagshot Wilts 19 L7
Bagstone S Glos 28 C10
Bagthorpe Norfk 50 C7
Bagthorpe Notts 47 N3
Bagworth Leics 47 N12
Bagwy Llydiart Herefs 27 T2
Baildon C Brad 63 P12
Baildon Green C Brad 63 P12
Baile Ailein W Isls 106 h6
Baile a Mhanaich W Isls 106 c14
Baile Mor Ag & B 92 H14
Bailey Green Hants 9 T3
Baileyhead Cumb 75 U8
Bailiff Bridge Calder 56 H1
Baillieston C Glas 89 Q13
Bailrigg Lancs 61 T8
Bainbridge N York 62 J1
Bainshole Abers 104 K8
Bainton C Pete 48 G12
Bainton E R Yk 65 L9
Bainton Oxon 30 B7
Baintown Fife 91 N10
Bairnkine Border 76 D3
Baker's Bridge E Susx 12 C13
Baker Street Thurr 22 F12
Bakewell Derbys 56 K13
Balallan W Isls 106 h6
Balbeg Highld 102 E8
Balbeggie P & K 90 J6
Balblair Highld 102 H5
Balblair Highld 109 M7
Balby Donc 57 S6
Balcary D & G 73 T9
Balchraggan Highld 102 F7
Balchreick Highld 110 D4
Balcombe W Susx 11 N4
Balcombe Lane W Susx 11 N4
Balcomie Links Fife 91 T9
Baldersby N York 63 T4
Baldersby St James
  N York 63 T4
Balderstone Lancs 62 C13
Balderstone Rochdl 56 D4
Balderton Ches W 54 H13
Balderton Notts 48 B2
Baldhu Cnwll 2 K8
Baldinnie Fife 91 P8
Baldock Herts 31 R6
Baldock Services Herts 31 R6
Baldovie C Dund 91 P5
Baldrine IoM 60 g6
Baldslow E Susx 12 E13
Baldwin IoM 60 f6
Baldwinholme Cumb 67 M2
Baldwin's Gate Staffs 45 S5
Baldwin's Hill W Susx 11 R3
Bale Norfk 50 H6
Baledgarno P & K 91 L5
Balemartine Ag & B 92 B10
Balerno C Edin 83 N5
Balevullin Ag & B 92 B9
Balfarg Fife 91 L10
Balfield Angus 98 J11
Balfour Ork 106 t18
Balfron Stirlg 89 M8
Balgaveny Abers 104 K7
Balgonar Fife 90 E13
Balgowan D & G 72 E10
Balgowan Highld 96 K5
Balgown Highld 100 c3
Balgracie D & G 72 B7
Balgray S Lans 82 K11
Balgy Highld 107 N13
Balhaldie Stirlg 89 S5
Balhalgardy Abers 105 L10
Balham Gt Lon 21 N8
Balhary P & K 90 K2
Baligill Highld 111 S3
Balintore Angus 98 D12
Balintore Highld 109 R9
Balintraid Highld 109 N9
Balivanich W Isls 106 c14
Balk N York 64 B3
Balkeerie Angus 91 M3
Balkholme E R Yk 64 H14
Ball Shrops 44 H8
Ballabeg IoM 60 c8
Ballacannell IoM 60 g5
Ballafesson IoM 60 b8
Ballajora IoM 60 h4
Ballakilpheric IoM 60 c8
Ballamodha IoM 60 c8
Ballanlay Ag & B 88 C13
Ballantrae S Ayrs 72 C3
Ballards Gore Essex 23 M8
Ballards Green Warwks 36 J2
Ballasalla IoM 60 d4
Ballasalla IoM 60 c8
Ballater Abers 98 D4
Ballaugh IoM 60 e4
Ballchraggan Highld 109 N9
Ballencrieff E Loth 84 D3
Ballevullin Ag & B 92 B9
Ball Green C Stke 46 B3
Ball Haye Green Staffs 46 C2
Ball Hill Hants 19 P8
Ballidon Derbys 46 H3
Balliekine N Ayrs 79 R7
Balliemore Ag & B 87 U6
Balligmorrie S Ayrs 80 J13
Ballimore Stirlg 89 N4
Ballindalloch Moray 103 V9
Ballindean P & K 91 L6
Ballingdon Suffk 40 E12
Ballinger Common
  Bucks 30 K12
Ballingham Herefs 35 N13
Ballingry Fife 90 K12
Ballinluig P & K 97 R13
Ballinshoe Angus 91 M2
Ballintuim P & K 97 U13
Balloch Highld 103 L6
Balloch N Lans 89 R11
Balloch P & K 90 C7
Balloch S Ayrs 80 K13
Balloch W Duns 88 K9
Ballochan Abers 98 H4
Ballochgair Ag & B 79 P10
Ballochmyle E Ayrs 81 R8
Ballochroy Ag & B 79 M5
Ballogie Abers 98 J4
Balls Cross W Susx 10 F5
Balls Green E Susx 11 R3
Ball's Green Gloucs 28 G8
Ballygown Ag & B 93 M9
Ballygrant Ag & B 86 F12
Ballyhaugh Ag & B 92 F7
Ballymenoch Ag & B 88 H8
Ballymichael N Ayrs 79 S8
Balmacara Highld 101 M7
Balmaclellan D & G 73 R4
Balmade D & G 72 K9
Balmadies Angus 91 S2
Balmalcolm Fife 91 M10
Balmartin W Isls 106 c12
Balmedie Abers 105 Q12
Balmer Heath Shrops 44 K6
Balmerino Fife 91 M6
Balmerlawn Hants 9 L8
Balmichael N Ayrs 79 S8
Balmore E Duns 89 P11
Balmuchy Highld 109 R8
Balmule Fife 91 L14
Balmullo Fife 91 P7
Balnacoil Highld 109 N1
Balnacra Highld 101 N3
Balnacroft Abers 98 C5
Balnafoich Highld 102 H8
Balnaguard P & K 97 R13
Balnaguisich Highld 109 L9
Balnahard Ag & B 86 H7
Balnain Highld 102 E8
Balnakeil Highld 110 J3
Balnapaling Highld 109 P10
Balne N York 57 T3
Balquharn P & K 90 G5
Balquharn Highld 102 J3

Balquhidder Stirlg...89 M1
Balsall Common Solhll...36 H5
Balsall Heath Birm...36 E4
Balsall Street Solhll...36 H5
Balscote Oxon...37 L12
Balsham Cambs...39 S10
Baltasound Shet...106 w3
Balterley Staffs...45 S3
Balterley Green Staffs...45 S3
Baltersan D & G...73 L7
Baltonsborough Somset...17 R10
Balvicar Ag & B...92 B2
Balvraid Highld...101 L8
Balvraid Highld...97 M9
Bamber Bridge Lancs...55 N1
Bamburgh Nthumb...85 T12
Bamburgh Castle Nthumb...85 T11
Bamford Derbys...56 K10
Bamford Rochdl...56 C4
Bampton Cumb...67 R9
Bampton Devon...16 C12
Bampton Oxon...29 R7
Bampton Grange Cumb...67 R9
Banavie Highld...94 G3
Banbury Oxon...37 N12
Banbury Crematorium Oxon...37 N12
Bancffosfelen Carmth...25 S8
Banchory Abers...99 M4
Banchory-Devenick Abers...99 S3
Bancycapel Carmth...25 R8
Bancyfelin Carmth...25 P7
Banc-y-ffordd Carmth...25 Q3
Bandirran P & K...90 K5
Bandrake Head Cumb...61 Q2
Banff Abers...104 K3
Bangor Gwynd...52 J8
Bangor Crematorium Gwynd...52 J8
Bangor-on-Dee Wrexhm...44 J4
Bangors Cnwll...14 F13
Bangor's Green Lancs...54 J5
Bangrove Suffk...40 F6
Banham Norfk...40 J3
Bank Hants...8 K7
Bankend D & G...74 K12
Bankfoot P & K...90 G4
Bankglen E Ayrs...81 R10
Bank Ground Cumb...67 M13
Bankhead C Aber...99 S2
Bankhead S Lans...82 J10
Bankhead N York...69 J9
Banknock Falk...89 S10
Banks Cumb...76 B13
Banks Lancs...54 J2
Banks Green Worcs...36 C7
Bankshill D & G...75 N9
Bank Street Worcs...35 P8
Bank Top Lancs...55 M5
Bank Top Calder...56 H2
Banningham Norfk...51 M8
Bannister Green Essex...22 G3
Bannockburn Stirlg...89 T7
Banstead Surrey...21 N11
Bantham Devon...5 R12
Banton N Lans...89 R10
Banwell N Som...17 L5
Bapchild Kent...12 H3
Bapton Wilts...18 E13
Barabhas W Isls...106 i4
Barassie S Ayrs...81 L5
Barbaraville Highld...109 N11
Barber Booth Derbys...56 H10
Barber Green Cumb...61 R3
Barbieston S Ayrs...81 N9
Barbon Cumb...62 C3
Barbridge Ches E...45 P2
Barbrook Devon...15 R3
Barby Nhants...37 P6
Barcaldine Ag & B...94 D10
Barcheston Warwks...36 J13
Barclose Cumb...75 T13
Barcombe E Susx...11 Q8
Barcombe Cross E Susx...11 Q7
Barcroft C Brad...63 L12
Barden N York...69 P1
Barden Park Kent...21 U13
Bardfield End Green Essex...22 F1
Bardfield Saling Essex...22 G2
Bardney Lincs...58 K13
Bardon Leics...47 M11
Bardon Mill Nthumb...76 E13
Bardowie E Duns...89 N11
Bardown E Susx...12 C10
Bardrainney Inver...88 H11
Bardsea Cumb...61 Q5
Bardsey Leeds...63 T11
Bardsey Island Gwynd...42 B9
Bardsley Oldham...56 D6
Bardwell Suffk...40 F6
Bare Lancs...61 T7
Bareppa Cnwll...2 K11
Barewood Herefs...34 J10
Barford Norfk...50 K12
Barford Warwks...36 J8
Barford St John Oxon...37 M14
Barford St Martin Wilts...8 F2
Barford St Michael Oxon...37 M14
Barfrestone Kent...13 Q5
Bargate Derbys...47 L4
Bargeddie N Lans...82 C6
Bargoed Caerph...27 M8
Bargrennan D & G...72 K4
Barham Cambs...38 J5
Barham Kent...13 N5
Barham Suffk...40 K10
Barham Crematorium Kent...13 N5
Bar Hill Cambs...39 N8
Barholm Lincs...48 G11
Barkby Leics...47 R12
Barkby Thorpe Leics...47 R12
Barkers Green Shrops...45 M8
Barkestone-le-Vale Leics...47 U7
Barkham Wokham...20 C9
Barking Gt Lon...21 R6
Barking Suffk...40 J10
Barkingside Gt Lon...21 R5
Barking Tye Suffk...40 J10
Barkisland Calder...56 G3
Barkla Shop Cnwll...2 J7
Barkston Lincs...48 D5
Barkston Ash N York...63 U11
Barkway Herts...39 N13
Barlanark C Glas...89 Q13
Barlavington W Susx...10 F7
Barlborough Derbys...57 Q11
Barlby N York...64 E13
Barlestone Leics...47 N13
Barley Herts...39 N13
Barley Lancs...62 G11
Barleycroft End Herts...22 B2
Barley Hole Rothm...57 N7
Barleythorpe Rutlnd...48 B12
Barling Essex...23 M10
Barlings Lincs...58 J12
Barlochan D & G...73 S9
Barlow Derbys...57 M12
Barlow Gatesd...77 P13
Barlow N York...64 E14
Barmby Moor E R Yk...64 H10
Barmby on the Marsh E R Yk...64 F14
Barmer Norfk...50 D7
Barming Heath Kent...12 D4
Barmollack Ag & B...79 Q7
Barmouth Gwynd...43 M10
Barmpton Darltn...70 D9
Barmston E R Yk...65 R8
Barnaby Green Suffk...41 S4
Barnacarry Ag & B...87 T5
Barnack C Pete...48 G12
Barnacle Warwks...37 L4
Barnard Castle Dur...69 N9
Barnard Gate Oxon...29 S5
Barnardiston Suffk...40 B11
Barnbarroch D & G...66 B11
Barnburgh Donc...57 Q6
Barnby Suffk...41 R3
Barnby Dun Donc...57 T5
Barnby in the Willows Notts...48 C3
Barnby Moor Notts...57 U10
Barncorkrie D & G...72 D12
Barnehurst Gt Lon...21 S7
Barnes Gt Lon...21 L7
Barnes Street Kent...12 B6
Barnet Gt Lon...21 M3
Barnet Gate Gt Lon...21 L4
Barnetby le Wold N Linc...58 H5
Barney Norfk...50 G7
Barnham Suffk...40 E5
Barnham W Susx...10 F10
Barnham Broom Norfk...50 J12
Barnhead Angus...99 M13
Barnhill C Dund...91 Q5
Barnhill Ches W...45 L3
Barnhill Moray...103 T4
Barnhills D & G...72 B6
Barningham Dur...69 N10
Barningham Suffk...40 G6
Barnoldby le Beck NE Lin...59 M6
Barnoldswick Lancs...62 H10
Barnsdale Bar Donc...57 R4
Barns Green W Susx...10 J5
Barnsley Barns...57 M5
Barnsley Gloucs...29 L7

Barnsley Crematorium Barns...57 N5
Barnsole Kent...13 Q4
Barnstaple Devon...15 N5
Barnston Essex...22 F4
Barnston Wirral...54 G10
Barnstone Notts...47 T6
Barnt Green Worcs...36 D6
Barnton C Edin...83 N3
Barnton Ches W...55 P12
Barnwell All Saints Nhants...38 F4
Barnwell St Andrew Nhants...38 G4
Barnwood Gloucs...28 G4
Baron's Cross Herefs...35 L9
Baronwood Cumb...67 R4
Barr S Ayrs...80 K14
Barra W Isls...106 b18
Barrachan D & G...72 K10
Barra Airport W Isls...106 c18
Barraglom W Isls...106 g5
Barrapoll Ag & B...92 B10
Barras Cumb...68 G10
Barrasford Nthumb...76 J11
Barrets Green Ches E...45 N2
Barrhead E Rens...89 L14
Barrhill S Ayrs...72 H3
Barri V Glam...16 F3
Barrington Cambs...39 N11
Barrington Somset...17 L13
Barripper Cnwll...2 G9
Barrmill N Ayrs...81 M2
Barrock Highld...112 G2
Barrow Gloucs...28 G3
Barrow Lancs...62 E12
Barrow Rutlnd...48 C10
Barrow Shrops...45 Q13
Barrow Somset...17 T10
Barrow Burn Nthumb...76 H3
Barroway Drove Norfk...49 Q13
Barrow Bridge Bolton...55 Q4
Barrowby Lincs...48 C6
Barrowden Rutlnd...48 D13
Barrowford Lancs...62 H12
Barrow Gurney N Som...17 P3
Barrow Haven N Linc...58 J2
Barrow Hill Derbys...57 P11
Barrow-in-Furness Cumb...61 N6
Barrow Island Cumb...61 M6
Barrow Nook Lancs...54 K6
Barrow's Green Ches E...45 Q3
Barrow Street Wilts...8 B2
Barrow-upon-Humber N Linc...58 J2
Barrow upon Soar Leics...47 Q10
Barrow upon Trent Derbys...47 L8
Barry Angus...91 R4
Barry V Glam...16 F3
Barry Island V Glam...16 F3
Barsby Leics...47 S11
Barsham Suffk...41 Q3
Barston Solhll...36 H5
Bartestree Herefs...35 N12
Barthol Chapel Abers...105 N9
Bartholomew Green Essex...22 H4
Barthomley Ches E...45 S3
Bartley Hants...9 L6
Bartley Green Birm...36 D4
Bartlow Cambs...39 R12
Barton Cambs...39 N9
Barton Ches W...44 K3
Barton Gloucs...28 K2
Barton Herefs...34 J11
Barton Lancs...54 J5
Barton Lancs...61 U13
Barton N York...69 R11
Barton Oxon...30 B11
Barton Torbay...6 B11
Barton Warwks...36 F10
Barton Bendish Norfk...50 B13
Barton End Gloucs...28 F8
Barton Green Staffs...46 G10
Barton Hartshorn Bucks...30 D6
Barton Hill N York...64 G7
Barton in Fabis Notts...47 P7
Barton in the Beans Leics...47 L12
Barton-le-Clay C Beds...31 N6
Barton-le-Street N York...64 G5
Barton-le-Willows N York...64 F7
Barton Mills Suffk...40 B6
Barton-on-Sea Hants...8 K10
Barton-on-the-Heath Warwks...36 J14
Barton St David Somset...17 P10
Barton Seagrave Nhants...38 C5
Barton Stacey Hants...19 P12
Barton Town Devon...15 Q4
Barton Turf Norfk...51 Q8
Barton-under-Needwood Staffs...46 G10
Barton-upon-Humber N Linc...58 H2
Barton Waterside N Linc...58 H2
Barugh Barns...57 M5
Barugh Green Barns...57 M5
Barvas W Isls...106 i4
Barway Cambs...39 S5
Barwell Leics...47 M1
Barwick Devon...15 N10
Barwick Herts...31 U9
Barwick Somset...17 P13
Barwick in Elmet Leeds...63 U12
Baschurch Shrops...44 K9
Bascote Warwks...37 M8
Bascote Heath Warwks...37 M8
Base Green Suffk...40 J8
Basford Green Staffs...46 C3
Bashall Eaves Lancs...62 E11
Bashall Town Lancs...62 F11
Bashley Hants...8 K9
Basildon Essex...22 H10
Basildon & District Crematorium Essex...22 H10
Basingstoke Hants...19 T10
Basingstoke Crematorium Hants...19 S10
Baslow Derbys...57 L12
Bason Bridge Somset...16 K7
Bassaleg Newpt...27 P10
Bassendean Border...84 F9
Bassenthwaite Cumb...66 K6
Bassett C Sotn...9 N5
Bassingbourn Cambs...39 N11
Bassingfield Notts...47 R6
Bassingham Lincs...58 E14
Bassingthorpe Lincs...48 D9
Bassus Green Herts...31 T7
Basted Kent...21 U11
Baston Lincs...48 H11
Bastwick Norfk...51 R10
Batch Somset...16 K5
Batchworth Herts...20 J3
Batchworth Heath Herts...20 J3
Batcombe Dorset...7 R3
Batcombe Somset...17 S9
Bate Heath Ches E...55 Q11
Batford Herts...31 Q9
Bath BaNES...17 T4
Bath, City of BaNES...17 T4
Bathampton BaNES...17 U4
Bathealton Somset...16 E12
Batheaston BaNES...17 U3
Bathford BaNES...17 U3
Bathgate W Loth...82 J5
Bathley Notts...47 U2
Bathpool Cnwll...4 H6
Bathpool Somset...16 J11
Bath Side Essex...23 T1
Bathville W Loth...82 H5
Bathway Somset...17 Q6
Batley Kirk...57 L1
Batsford Gloucs...36 G14
Batson Devon...5 S13
Battersby N York...70 J11
Battersea Gt Lon...21 N7
Battisborough Cross Devon...5 P11
Battisford Suffk...40 J10
Battisford Tye Suffk...40 J10
Battle E Susx...12 D12
Battle Powys...26 J1
Battledown Gloucs...28 H3
Battledykes Angus...98 H12
Battlesbridge Essex...22 J9
Battlesden C Beds...31 L6
Battleton Somset...16 C11
Battramsley Hants...9 L9
Batt's Corner Hants...10 C2
Baughton Worcs...35 U12
Baughurst Hants...19 R8
Baulds Abers...99 L5
Baulking Oxon...29 R9
Baumber Lincs...59 L12
Baunton Gloucs...28 K7
Baveney Wood Shrops...35 Q5
Baverstock Wilts...8 F2
Bawburgh Norfk...50 K12
Bawdeswell Norfk...50 H9
Bawdrip Somset...16 K9
Bawdsey Suffk...41 P12
Bawsey Norfk...49 T10
Bawtry Donc...57 U8
Baxenden Lancs...55 S2
Baxterley Warwks...36 J1
Baxter's Green Suffk...40 C9

Bay Highld...100 b4
Baybridge Nthumb...69 M2
Baycliff Cumb...61 P5
Baydon Wilts...19 L5
Bayford Herts...31 T11
Bayford Somset...17 T11
Bayley's Hill Kent...21 T12
Bayham Suffk...40 K10
Baynard's Green Oxon...30 B7
Bayston Hill Shrops...45 L12
Bayton Worcs...35 R6
Bayton Common Worcs...35 R6
Bayworth Oxon...29 U7
Beachampton Bucks...30 G5
Beachamwell Norfk...50 C12
Beachley Gloucs...27 U9
Beachy Head E Susx...11 U11
Beacon Devon...6 G4
Beacon End Essex...23 N3
Beacon Hill Kent...11 T12
Beacon Hill Notts...48 B3
Beacon's Bottom Bucks...20 C4
Beaconsfield Bucks...20 F4
Beaconsfield Services Bucks...20 G5
Beadlam N York...64 F3
Beadlow C Beds...31 P5
Beadnell Nthumb...85 U13
Beaford Devon...15 N10
Beal Nthumb...85 R10
Beal N York...57 R1
Bealbury Cnwll...4 K7
Bealsmill Cnwll...4 K5
Beam Hill Staffs...46 H8
Beamhurst Staffs...46 E6
Beaminster Dorset...7 N4
Beamish Dur...69 R2
Beamish Museum Dur...69 R2
Beamsley N York...63 M9
Bean Kent...22 E13
Beanacre Wilts...18 D7
Beanley Nthumb...77 M2
Beardon Devon...5 N4
Beardwood Bl w D...55 Q1
Beare Devon...6 C4
Beare Green Surrey...10 K2
Bearley Warwks...36 G8
Bearley Cross Warwks...36 G8
Bearpark Dur...69 R4
Bearsden E Duns...89 M11
Bearsted Kent...12 E4
Bearstone Shrops...45 R6
Bearwood Herefs...34 J9
Bearwood Poole...8 E9
Beattock D & G...75 L5
Beauchamp Roding Essex...22 E6
Beauchief Sheff...57 M10
Beaudesert Warwks...36 G8
Beaufort Blae G...27 M5
Beaulieu Hants...9 M8
Beaulieu Road Station Hants...9 L7
Beauly Highld...102 F7
Beaumaris IoA...52 K7
Beaumaris Castle IoA...52 K7
Beaumont Cumb...75 R14
Beaumont Essex...23 R3
Beaumont Jersey...7 c3
Beaumont Hill Darltn...69 S9
Beausale Warwks...36 J6
Beauworth Hants...9 R3
Beaworthy Devon...15 L13
Beazley End Essex...22 H2
Bebington Wirral...54 H10
Bebside Nthumb...77 R9
Beccles Suffk...41 R3
Becconsall Lancs...55 L2
Beckbury Shrops...45 S13
Beckenham Gt Lon...21 Q9
Beckenham Crematorium Gt Lon...21 Q9
Beckermet Cumb...66 F11
Beckett End Norfk...50 C14
Beckfoot Cumb...66 F12
Beckfoot Cumb...66 H2
Beckfoot Cumb...66 J12
Beck Foot Cumb...68 D13
Beckford Worcs...36 C13
Beckhampton Wilts...18 G7
Beck Hole N York...71 P12
Beckingham Lincs...48 B2
Beckingham Notts...58 C8
Beckington Somset...18 B10
Beckjay Shrops...34 J5
Beckley E Susx...12 G11
Beckley Hants...8 J10
Beckley Oxon...30 C10
Beck Row Suffk...39 U5
Beck Side Cumb...61 Q2
Beck Side Cumb...61 R3
Beckton Gt Lon...21 R6
Beckwithshaw N York...63 R9
Becontree Gt Lon...21 R5
Becquet Vincent Jersey...7 e2
Bedale N York...63 R1
Bedburn Dur...69 P5
Bedchester Dorset...8 B5
Beddgelert Gwynd...43 L3
Beddingham E Susx...11 Q9
Beddington Gt Lon...21 N9
Beddington Corner Gt Lon...21 N9
Bedfield Suffk...41 M7
Bedford Bed...38 G10
Bedford Crematorium Bed...38 G10
Bedgebury Cross Kent...12 D9
Bedham W Susx...10 G6
Bedhampton Hants...9 U7
Bedingfield Suffk...41 L7
Bedingham Green Norfk...41 N2
Bedlam N York...63 R7
Bedlington Nthumb...77 Q9
Bedlinog Myr Td...26 K6
Bedminster Bristl...17 Q3
Bedminster Down Bristl...17 Q3
Bedmond Herts...31 N12
Bednall Staffs...46 B10
Bedrule Border...76 B2
Bedstone Shrops...34 J5
Bedwas Caerph...27 M9
Bedwellty Caerph...27 M6
Bedworth Warwks...37 L3
Bedworth Woodlands Warwks...37 K3
Beeby Leics...47 S12
Beech Hants...9 U2
Beech Staffs...45 U6
Beech Hill W Berk...20 B9
Beechingstoke Wilts...18 G8
Beedon W Berk...19 R5
Beedon Hill W Berk...19 R5
Beeford E R Yk...65 Q9
Beeley Derbys...57 L13
Beelsby NE Lin...59 M6
Beenham W Berk...19 S7
Beeny Cnwll...14 D13
Beer Devon...6 J7
Beercrocombe Somset...16 K12
Beer Hackett Dorset...7 R2
Beesands Devon...5 U12
Beesby Lincs...59 S10
Beeson Devon...5 U12
Beeston C Beds...38 J11
Beeston Ches W...45 M2
Beeston Leeds...63 R14
Beeston Norfk...50 F11
Beeston Notts...47 P6
Beeston Regis Norfk...51 L5
Beeswing D & G...74 G11
Beetham Cumb...61 T4
Beetham Somset...6 K2
Beetley Norfk...50 G10
Begbroke Oxon...29 U5
Begdale Cambs...49 Q12
Begelly Pembks...24 K8
Beggarington Hill Leeds...57 L1
Beggar's Bush Powys...34 H8
Beguildy Powys...34 E5
Beighton Norfk...51 Q12
Beighton Sheff...57 P9
Beighton Hill Derbys...46 J3
Beinn Na Faoghla W Isls...106 d13
Beith N Ayrs...81 M1
Bekesbourne Kent...13 N4
Bekesbourne Hill Kent...13 N4
Belaugh Norfk...51 N10
Belbroughton Worcs...36 B5
Belchalwell Dorset...7 U3
Belchalwell Street Dorset...7 U3
Belchamp Otten Essex...40 D12
Belchamp St Paul Essex...40 C12
Belchamp Walter Essex...40 D12
Belchford Lincs...59 L11

Belford Nthumb...85 S12
Belgrave C Leic...47 Q12
Belhaven E Loth...84 H3
Belhelvie Abers...105 Q12
Belhinnie Abers...104 G9
Bellabeg Abers...104 D13
Bellamore Herefs...34 J12
Bellanoch Ag & B...87 P7
Bellasize E R Yk...64 J14
Bellaty Angus...98 C12
Bell Busk N York...62 J9
Belleau Lincs...59 R11
Bell End Worcs...36 B5
Bellerby N York...69 P13
Bellever Devon...5 R4
Belle Vue Cumb...67 N1
Belle Vue Wakefd...57 M3
Bellfield S Lans...74 J1
Bellfield S Lans...82 F11
Bell Heath Worcs...36 B5
Bell Hill Hants...9 U3
Bellingdon Bucks...30 K12
Bellingham Nthumb...76 G9
Belloch Ag & B...79 M7
Bellochantuy Ag & B...79 M7
Bell o' th' Hill Ches W...45 M4
Bellows Cross Dorset...8 F6
Bells Cross Suffk...40 K10
Bellshill N Lans...82 D6
Bellshill Nthumb...85 S11
Bellside N Lans...82 F7
Bellsquarry W Loth...82 K6
Bells Yew Green E Susx...11 U3
Belluton BaNES...17 R4
Belmaduthie Highld...102 H4
Belmesthorpe Rutlnd...48 F11
Belmont Bl w D...55 Q3
Belmont C Bed...31 P5
Belmont Gt Lon...21 N10
Belmont S Ayrs...81 L9
Belmont Shet...106 v3
Belnacraig Abers...104 D12
Belowda Cnwll...3 P4
Belper Derbys...47 L4
Belper Lane End Derbys...46 K3
Belph Derbys...57 R11
Belsay Nthumb...77 M10
Belses Border...84 F13
Belsford Devon...5 S9
Belsize Herts...31 M11
Belstead Suffk...40 K12
Belston Devon...5 Q2
Belstone Devon...5 Q2
Belstone Corner Devon...5 S13
Belthorn Bl w D...55 S2
Beltingham Nthumb...76 F13
Beltoft N Linc...58 D5
Belton Leics...47 N9
Belton Lincs...48 D5
Belton N Linc...58 C5
Belton Norfk...51 S13
Belton Rutlnd...48 C13
Belton House Lincs...48 D6
Beltring Kent...12 C6
Belvedere Gt Lon...21 S7
Belvoir Leics...48 B7
Bembridge IoW...9 S11
Bemerton Wilts...8 G2
Bempton E R Yk...65 R5
Benacre Suffk...41 T4
Benbecula W Isls...106 d13
Benbuie D & G...74 D9
Benderloch Ag & B...94 C11
Benenden Kent...12 G8
Benfieldside Dur...69 N2
Bengates Norfk...51 P8
Bengeworth Worcs...36 D12
Benhall Green Suffk...41 Q8
Benhall Street Suffk...41 Q8
Benholm Abers...99 Q10
Beningbrough N York...64 C8
Benington Herts...31 T8
Benington Lincs...49 N4
Benington Sea End Lincs...49 P4
Benllech IoA...52 H6
Benmore Ag & B...88 C8
Bennacott Cnwll...4 H2
Bennan N Ayrs...79 S11
Bennet Head Cumb...67 P8
Bennett End Bucks...20 C4
Benniworth Lincs...59 M11
Benover Kent...12 D6
Ben Rhydding C Brad...63 N10
Benson Oxon...19 U2
Benston Jersey...7 e3
Benthall Shrops...45 Q13
Bentham Gloucs...28 H4
Benthoul C Aber...99 R3
Bentlawnt Shrops...44 H13
Bentley Donc...57 S5
Bentley E R Yk...65 N12
Bentley Hants...10 B2
Bentley Suffk...40 K13
Bentley Warwks...36 J2
Bentley Crematorium Essex...22 E8
Bentley Heath Herts...21 N3
Bentley Heath Solhll...36 G5
Benton Devon...15 Q5
Benton Square N Tyne...77 S12
Bentpath D & G...75 R7
Bentwichen Devon...15 R6
Bentworth Hants...19 U13
Benvie Angus...91 M5
Benville Dorset...7 P3
Benwick Cambs...39 M2
Beoley Worcs...36 E7
Beoraidbeg Highld...100 e10
Bepton W Susx...10 D7
Berden Essex...22 C2
Bere Alston Devon...5 L7
Berea Pembks...24 C4
Bere Ferrers Devon...5 L8
Berepper Cnwll...2 H12
Bere Regis Dorset...8 A9
Bergh Apton Norfk...51 P13
Berinsfield Oxon...30 B13
Berkeley Gloucs...28 C7
Berkeley Heath Gloucs...28 C8
Berkeley Road Gloucs...28 D7
Berkhamsted Herts...31 L11
Berkley Somset...18 B11
Berkswell Solhll...36 J5
Bermondsey Gt Lon...21 P7
Bermuda Warwks...37 L3
Bernera Highld...100 h7
Bernisdale Highld...100 d4
Berrick Prior Oxon...19 U2
Berrick Salome Oxon...19 U2
Berriedale Highld...112 D12
Berrier Cumb...67 N7
Berriew Powys...44 E13
Berrington Nthumb...85 Q10
Berrington Shrops...45 M12
Berrington Worcs...35 M7
Berrington Green Worcs...35 M7
Berrow Somset...16 J6
Berrow Worcs...35 S14
Berrow Green Worcs...35 S9
Berry Brow Kirk...56 J4
Berry Cross Devon...15 L10
Berry Down Cross Devon...15 N4
Berry Hill Gloucs...27 V5
Berry Hill Pembks...24 J3
Berryhillock Moray...104 G4
Berrynarbor Devon...15 N3
Berry Pomeroy Devon...5 U8
Berry's Green Gt Lon...21 R11
Bersham Wrexhm...44 H3
Berthengam Flints...54 D11
Berwick E Susx...11 S9
Berwick Bassett Wilts...18 H6
Berwick Hill Nthumb...77 N10
Berwick St James Wilts...18 G13
Berwick St John Wilts...8 C4
Berwick St Leonard Wilts...8 C2
Berwick-upon-Tweed Nthumb...85 Q8
Bescaby Leics...48 B8
Bescar Lancs...54 J4
Besford Shrops...45 M9
Besford Worcs...36 B11
Bessacarr Donc...57 T6
Bessels Leigh Oxon...29 U7
Besses o' th' Barn Bury...55 T5
Bessingby E R Yk...65 Q6
Bessingham Norfk...50 K6
Best Beech Hill E Susx...12 B9
Besthorpe Norfk...40 J1
Besthorpe Notts...58 D13
Bestwood Village Notts...47 Q4
Beswick E R Yk...65 N10
Beswick Manch...55 T7
Betchcott Shrops...45 L13
Betchworth Surrey...21 M12
Bethania Cerdgn...32 K8
Bethania Gwynd...43 N4
Bethel Gwynd...52 H9
Bethel IoA...52 E7
Bethel Powys...44 C8
Bethersden Kent...12 H7
Bethesda Gwynd...52 J9
Bethesda Pembks...24 J7
Bethlehem Carmth...26 C2
Bethnal Green Gt Lon...21 P6
Betley Staffs...45 S4
Betsham Kent...22 F13
Betteshanger Kent...13 R5
Bettiscombe Dorset...7 L5
Bettisfield Wrexhm...45 L6

Betton Shrops...45 Q6
Betton Strange Shrops...45 M12
Bettws Newpt...27 P9
Bettws Bledrws Cerdgn...33 L10
Bettws Cedewain Powys...34 D1
Bettws Evan Cerdgn...32 F11
Bettws-Newydd Mons...27 R6
Bettyhill Highld...111 R4
Betws Carmth...26 A5
Betws Gwerfil Goch Denbgs...44 B4
Betws-y-Coed Conwy...53 N11
Betws-yn-Rhos Conwy...53 P8
Beulah Cerdgn...32 E11
Beulah Powys...33 T10
Bevendean Br & H...11 N9
Bevercotes Notts...57 U12
Beverley E R Yk...65 N12
Beverston Gloucs...28 G8
Bevington Gloucs...28 C8
Bewaldeth Cumb...66 K6
Bewcastle Cumb...76 B11
Bewdley Worcs...35 S5
Bewerley N York...63 P6
Bewholme E R Yk...65 R9
Bewlie Border...84 E13
Bexhill E Susx...12 D14
Bexley Gt Lon...21 S7
Bexleyheath Gt Lon...21 S7
Bexleyhill W Susx...10 E6
Bexon Kent...12 F4
Bexwell Norfk...49 T13
Beyton Suffk...40 F8
Beyton Green Suffk...40 F8
Bhaltos W Isls...106 f5
Bhatarsaigh W Isls...106 b19
Bibury Gloucs...29 M6
Bicester Oxon...30 B8
Bickenhill Solhll...36 G4
Bicker Lincs...48 K6
Bicker Bar Lincs...48 K6
Bicker Gauntlet Lincs...48 K5
Bickershaw Wigan...55 P6
Bickerstaffe Lancs...54 K6
Bickerton Ches E...45 M3
Bickerton Devon...5 T13
Bickerton N York...64 B9
Bickerton Nthumb...76 K5
Bickford Staffs...45 U11
Bickington Devon...5 U6
Bickington Devon...15 M6
Bickleigh Devon...5 N8
Bickleigh Devon...15 U12
Bickleton Devon...15 M6
Bickley Ches W...45 M3
Bickley N York...71 Q13
Bickley Worcs...35 Q5
Bickley Moss Ches W...45 M3
Bickmarsh Warwks...36 F11
Bicknacre Essex...22 J7
Bicknoller Somset...16 F9
Bicknor Kent...12 F4
Bickton Hants...8 G5
Bicton Herefs...35 L8
Bicton Shrops...44 G11
Bicton Shrops...45 L11
Bidborough Kent...11 T2
Bidden Hants...20 B12
Biddenden Kent...12 G7
Biddenden Green Kent...12 G6
Biddenham Bed...38 G10
Biddestone Wilts...18 C6
Biddisham Somset...17 L6
Biddlesden Bucks...30 E5
Biddlestone Nthumb...76 K5
Biddulph Staffs...45 U2
Biddulph Moor Staffs...46 B2
Bideford Devon...15 L8
Bidford-on-Avon Warwks...36 F10
Bidston Wirral...54 G8
Bielby E R Yk...64 H11
Bieldside C Aber...99 R3
Bierley IoW...9 Q13
Bierton Bucks...30 H9
Big Balcraig D & G...72 K11
Bigbury Devon...5 R11
Bigbury-on-Sea Devon...5 R12
Big Carlae D & G...81 T13
Biggar Cumb...61 M6
Biggar S Lans...82 K11
Biggin Derbys...46 G2
Biggin Derbys...46 H4
Biggin N York...64 D12
Biggin Hill Gt Lon...21 R11
Biggleswade C Beds...31 Q3
Bighouse Highld...111 U4
Bighton Hants...19 T13
Biglands Cumb...67 L1
Bignor W Susx...10 F8
Bigrigg Cumb...66 F10
Big Sand Highld...107 M9
Bigton Shet...106 t11
Bilbrook Somset...16 E8
Bilbrook Staffs...45 U12
Bilbrough N York...64 C10
Bilbster Highld...112 H6
Bildershaw Dur...69 R8
Bildeston Suffk...40 G11
Billacott Cnwll...4 H2
Billericay Essex...22 G8
Billesdon Leics...47 T13
Billesley Warwks...36 F9
Billingborough Lincs...48 H6
Billinge St Hel...54 M6
Billingford Norfk...40 K6
Billingford Norfk...50 J9
Billingham S on T...70 G8
Billinghay Lincs...48 J2
Billingley Barns...57 P5
Billingshurst W Susx...10 H5
Billingsley Shrops...35 Q3
Billington C Beds...31 L8
Billington Lancs...62 E13
Billington Staffs...45 U9
Billockby Norfk...51 R11
Billy Row Dur...69 Q5
Bilsborrow Lancs...61 U12
Bilsby Lincs...59 R12
Bilsham W Susx...10 F10
Bilsington Kent...13 L8
Bilson Green Gloucs...28 B5
Bilsthorpe Notts...47 S1
Bilsthorpe Moor Notts...47 T2
Bilston Mdloth...83 P5
Bilston Wolves...46 B14
Bilstone Leics...47 L13
Bilting Kent...13 L6
Bilton E R Yk...65 R13
Bilton N York...63 S9
Bilton Nthumb...77 Q2
Bilton Warwks...37 N6
Bilton-in-Ainsty N York...64 B9
Binbrook Lincs...59 M8
Bincombe Dorset...7 S8
Binegar Somset...17 R7
Bines Green W Susx...10 K7
Binfield Br For...20 D8
Binfield Heath Oxon...20 B7
Bingfield Nthumb...76 K12
Bingham Notts...47 T6
Bingham's Melcombe Dorset...7 U4
Bingley C Brad...63 M12
Bings Shrops...45 N10
Binham Norfk...50 G6
Binley Covtry...37 L4
Binley Hants...19 P9
Binley Woods Warwks...37 L5
Binnegar Dorset...8 B11
Binniehill Falk...82 G4
Binscombe Surrey...10 F2
Binsey Oxon...29 U6
Binsted Hants...10 B2
Binsted W Susx...10 F9
Binton Warwks...36 F10
Bintree Norfk...50 H9
Binweston Shrops...44 H13
Birch Essex...23 M4
Birch Rochdl...56 C5
Bircham Newton Norfk...50 C7
Bircham Tofts Norfk...50 C7
Birchanger Green Essex...22 D3
Birch Cross Staffs...46 F7
Bircher Herefs...35 L7
Birchencliffe Kirk...56 H3
Birchfield Birm...36 E2
Birch Green Essex...23 N4
Birch Green Herts...31 S10
Birch Green Worcs...35 U11
Birchgrove Cardif...27 M11
Birchgrove Swans...26 B8
Birch Heath Ches W...45 M1
Birch Hill Ches W...55 M12
Birchington Kent...13 Q2
Birchley Heath Warwks...36 J2
Birchmoor Warwks...46 J13
Birchmoor Green C Beds...31 L5
Birchover Derbys...56 K14
Birch Services Rochdl...56 C5
Birch Vale Derbys...56 F9
Birchwood Lincs...58 F13
Birchwood Somset...6 H2
Birchwood Warrtn...55 P8
Bircotes Notts...57 T8
Birdbrook Essex...40 B12
Birdforth N York...64 B4
Birdham W Susx...10 C10
Birdingbury Warwks...37 M7
Birdlip Gloucs...28 H5
Birdoswald Cumb...76 C12
Birds Edge Kirk...56 K5
Birds Green Essex...22 E6
Birdsgreen Shrops...35 S3
Birdsmoorgate Dorset...7 L4
Birdston E Duns...89 P10
Birdwell Barns...57 M6
Birdwood Gloucs...28 D4
Birgham Border...84 K11
Birichin Highld...109 P6
Birkacre Lancs...55 N3
Birkby N York...70 D12
Birkdale Sefton...54 H4
Birkenbog Abers...104 H3
Birkenhead Wirral...54 H9
Birkenhills Abers...105 L6
Birkenshaw N York...63 Q14
Birkhall Abers...98 D5
Birkhill Angus...91 M5
Birkhill D & G...75 P3
Birkholme Lincs...48 D9
Birkin N York...64 D13
Birley Herefs...35 L10
Birley Carr Sheff...57 M7
Birling Kent...22 E13
Birling Nthumb...77 Q5
Birling Gap E Susx...11 T11
Birlingham Worcs...36 B12
Birmingham Birm...36 E3
Birmingham Airport Solhll...36 G4
Birnam P & K...90 F3
Birness Abers...105 Q8
Birse Abers...98 K4
Birsemore Abers...98 K4
Birstall Leics...47 Q12
Birstall Kirk...63 Q14
Birstwith N York...63 R8
Birthorpe Lincs...48 H6
Birtley Herefs...34 J7
Birtley Nthumb...76 H10
Birtley Gatesd...77 R14
Birtley Crematorium Gatesd...69 S1
Birts Street Worcs...35 S13
Bisbrooke Rutlnd...48 C13
Biscathorpe Lincs...59 M10
Bish Mill Devon...15 R7
Bisham W & M...20 D6
Bishampton Worcs...36 C10
Bishop Auckland Dur...69 R7
Bishopbridge Lincs...58 H8
Bishopbriggs E Duns...89 P12
Bishop Burton E R Yk...65 M12
Bishop Middleham Dur...70 D5
Bishopmill Moray...103 V3
Bishop Monkton N York...63 S6
Bishop Norton Lincs...58 G8
Bishopsbourne Kent...13 N5
Bishops Cannings Wilts...18 G7
Bishop's Castle Shrops...34 H3
Bishop's Caundle Dorset...7 S2
Bishop's Cleeve Gloucs...28 H2
Bishops Frome Herefs...35 Q11
Bishops Gate Surrey...20 G8
Bishop's Green Essex...22 G4
Bishop's Green Hants...19 R8
Bishop's Hull Somset...16 H12
Bishop's Itchington Warwks...37 M9
Bishops Lydeard Somset...16 G11
Bishop's Norton Gloucs...28 F3
Bishop's Nympton Devon...15 S8
Bishop's Offley Staffs...45 S8
Bishop's Stortford Herts...22 C3
Bishop's Sutton Hants...19 T13
Bishop's Tachbrook Warwks...37 L8
Bishop's Tawton Devon...15 N6
Bishopsteignton Devon...6 B9
Bishopstoke Hants...9 P5
Bishopston Swans...25 U13
Bishopstone Bucks...30 H10
Bishopstone E Susx...11 Q10
Bishopstone Herefs...34 K12
Bishopstone Swindn...19 L4
Bishopstone Wilts...8 F3
Bishopstrow Wilts...18 C12
Bishop Sutton BaNES...17 Q5
Bishops Waltham Hants...9 Q5
Bishopswood Somset...6 J2
Bishop's Wood Staffs...45 T12
Bishopsworth Bristl...17 Q3
Bishop Thornton N York...63 R7
Bishopthorpe C York...64 D10
Bishopton Darltn...70 E7
Bishopton Rens...88 K11
Bishopton Warwks...36 G9
Bishop Wilton E R Yk...64 G8
Bishton Newpt...27 R11
Bishton Staffs...46 C9
Bisley Gloucs...28 H6
Bisley Surrey...20 F11
Bisley Camp Surrey...20 F11
Bispham Bpool...61 Q11
Bispham Green Lancs...54 K4
Bissoe Cnwll...2 K8
Bisterne Hants...8 H8
Bisterne Close Hants...8 K8
Bitchet Green Kent...21 U11
Bitchfield Lincs...48 E9
Bittadon Devon...15 M4
Bittaford Devon...5 R9
Bittering Norfk...50 F10
Bitterley Shrops...35 N5
Bitterne C Sotn...9 P6
Bitteswell Leics...37 Q3
Bitton S Glos...17 S3
Bix Oxon...20 B6
Bixter Shet...106 t8
Blaby Leics...47 Q13
Blackadder Border...85 L8
Blackawton Devon...5 U10
Blackborough Devon...6 E3
Blackborough End Norfk...49 T11
Blackboys E Susx...11 S6
Blackbrook Derbys...47 L4
Blackbrook St Hel...55 M7
Blackbrook Staffs...45 S6
Blackbrook Surrey...21 L13
Blackburn Abers...105 N13
Blackburn Bl w D...55 Q1
Blackburn Rothm...57 N8
Blackburn W Loth...82 J6
Blackburn with Darwen Services Bl w D...55 R2
Black Callerton N u Ty...77 P12
Black Car Norfk...40 J1
Black Corner W Susx...11 M3
Blackcraig E Ayrs...81 R9
Black Crofts Ag & B...94 C12
Black Cross Cnwll...3 N4
Blackden Heath Ches E...55 R12
Blackdog Abers...105 Q13
Black Dog Devon...15 T10
Blackdown Dorset...7 L3
Blackdyke Cumb...66 H2
Blacker Hill Barns...57 M6
Blackfield Hants...9 N8
Blackford Cumb...75 S13
Blackford P & K...90 C10
Blackford Somset...17 L7
Blackford Somset...17 T10
Blackfordby Leics...46 K10
Blackgang IoW...9 N13
Blackhall C Edin...83 P4
Blackhall Colliery Dur...70 F5
Blackhall Mill Gatesd...69 P2
Blackhall Rocks Dur...70 G5
Blackhaugh Border...83 R12
Blackheath Essex...23 P3
Blackheath Gt Lon...21 Q7
Blackheath Sandw...36 C4
Blackheath Suffk...41 S6
Blackheath Surrey...10 G2
Black Heddon Nthumb...77 M10
Blackhill Abers...105 T6
Blackhill Abers...105 T5
Blackhill Dur...69 N2
Blackhill of Clackriach Abers...105 R5
Blackhorse Devon...6 C5
Blackjack Lincs...49 L5
Blackland Wilts...18 F7
Black Lane Ends Lancs...62 J11
Blackley Manch...55 T6
Blackley Crematorium Manch...55 T6
Blacklunans P & K...98 C12
Blackmarstone Herefs...35 M13
Blackmill Brdgnd...26 G10
Blackmoor Hants...10 B4
Blackmoor N Som...17 M4
Blackmoorfoot Kirk...56 H4
Blackmoor Gate Devon...15 P3
Blackmore Essex...22 F7
Blackmore End Essex...22 J1
Blackmore End Herts...31 Q10
Black Mount Ag & B...94 H9
Blackness Falk...83 L3
Blacknest Hants...10 B2
Black Notley Essex...22 H3
Blacko Lancs...62 H11
Black Pill Swans...25 V12
Blackpool Bpool...61 Q12
Blackpool Devon...5 U11
Blackpool Airport Lancs...61 Q13
Blackpool Gate Cumb...76 A11
Blackridge W Loth...82 G5
Blackrock Cnwll...2 H10
Blackrock Mons...27 N5
Blackrod Bolton...55 P4
Blackshaw D & G...74 K12
Blackshaw Head Calder...62 K14
Blacksmith's Green Suffk...40 K7
Blacksnape Bl w D...55 R2
Blackstone W Susx...10 K7
Black Street Suffk...41 T3
Black Tar Pembks...24 G8
Blackthorn Oxon...30 C9
Blackthorpe Suffk...40 F8
Blacktoft E R Yk...64 J14
Blacktop C Aber...99 R3
Black Torrington Devon...14 K11
Blackwall Derbys...46 H4
Blackwater Cnwll...2 J7
Blackwater Hants...20 D10
Blackwater IoW...9 Q11
Blackwater Somset...6 H2
Blackwaterfoot N Ayrs...79 S10
Blackwell Cumb...67 P2
Blackwell Darltn...70 D10
Blackwell Derbys...56 H12
Blackwell Derbys...47 M2
Blackwell Warwks...36 J11
Blackwell Worcs...36 C6
Blackwellsend Green Gloucs...28 E2
Blackwood Caerph...27 M8
Blackwood D & G...74 H8
Blackwood S Lans...82 E9
Blackwood Hill Staffs...46 B2
Blacon Ches W...54 J13
Bladbean Kent...13 N6
Bladnoch D & G...73 L9
Bladon Oxon...29 T5
Blaenannerch Cerdgn...32 E11
Blaenau Ffestiniog Gwynd...43 N3
Blaenavon Torfn...27 N6
Blaenawey Mons...27 P4
Blaen Dyryn Powys...33 T13
Blaenffos Pembks...25 L3
Blaengarw Brdgnd...26 G9
Blaengeuffordd Cerdgn...33 M4
Blaengwrach Neath...26 F6
Blaengwynfi Neath...26 F8
Blaenllechau Rhondd...26 J8
Blaenpennal Cerdgn...33 M8
Blaenplwyf Cerdgn...33 L5
Blaenporth Cerdgn...32 E11
Blaenrhondda Rhondd...26 G7
Blaenwaun Carmth...25 L5
Blaen-y-coed Carmth...25 N5
Blaen-y-cwm Blae G...27 M5
Blaen-y-cwm Rhondd...26 G7
Blaen-y-cwm Gwynd...43 T7
Blaenycwm Cerdgn...33 R5
Blagdon N Som...17 N5
Blagdon Somset...6 H13
Blagdon Torbay...6 A12
Blagdon Hill Somset...16 H13
Blagill Cumb...68 F3
Blaguegate Lancs...54 K5
Blaich Highld...94 F3
Blain Highld...93 R5
Blaina Blae G...27 M6
Blair Atholl P & K...97 P10
Blair Drummond Stirlg...89 R6
Blairgowrie P & K...90 H2
Blairhall Fife...82 K2
Blairingone P & K...90 E12
Blairlogie Stirlg...89 T6
Blairmore Ag & B...88 E9
Blairmore Highld...110 E5
Blair's Ferry Ag & B...87 T11
Blaisdon Gloucs...28 D5
Blakebrook Worcs...35 T5
Blakedown Worcs...35 U5
Blake End Essex...22 H3
Blakemere Ches W...55 M12
Blakemere Herefs...34 J12
Blakemore Devon...5 U9
Blakenall Heath Wsall...46 D14
Blakeney Gloucs...28 C6
Blakeney Norfk...50 H5
Blakenhall Ches E...45 S4
Blakenhall Wolves...46 B14
Blakeshall Worcs...35 T4
Blakesley Nhants...37 R10
Blanchland Nthumb...69 L2
Blandford Camp Dorset...8 C7
Blandford Forum Dorset...8 B7
Blandford St Mary Dorset...8 B7
Bland Hill N York...63 R9
Blanefield Stirlg...89 M10
Blankney Lincs...58 H14
Blantyre S Lans...82 C7
Blar a' Chaorainn Highld...94 G4
Blargie Highld...96 G6
Blarmachfoldach Highld...94 F4
Blashford Hants...8 H7
Blaston Leics...48 C14
Blatherwycke Nhants...48 E14
Blawith Cumb...61 Q2
Blawquhairn D & G...74 E9
Blaxhall Suffk...41 Q9
Blaxton Donc...57 U6
Blaydon Gatesd...77 P13
Bleadney Somset...17 N7
Bleadon N Som...16 K5
Bleak Street Somset...17 U10
Bleasby Lincs...58 K10
Bleasby Notts...47 T4
Bleasby Moor Lincs...58 K10
Bleatarn Cumb...68 F10
Bleathwood Herefs...35 M7
Blebocraigs Fife...91 P8
Bleddfa Powys...34 F7
Bledington Gloucs...29 P3
Bledlow Bucks...30 G12
Bledlow Ridge Bucks...30 F13
Bleet Wilts...18 C9
Blegbie E Loth...84 C6
Blencarn Cumb...68 D6
Blencogo Cumb...66 J3
Blendworth Hants...9 U6
Blenheim Palace Oxon...29 T5
Blennerhasset Cumb...66 J4
Bletchingdon Oxon...29 U5
Bletchingley Surrey...21 P12
Bletchley M Keyn...30 J6
Bletchley Shrops...45 P7
Bletherston Pembks...24 J6
Bletsoe Bed...38 F9
Blewbury Oxon...19 S3
Blickling Norfk...50 K8
Blidworth Notts...47 Q2
Blidworth Bottoms Notts...47 Q2
Blindburn Nthumb...76 H4
Blindcrake Cumb...66 J5
Blindley Heath Surrey...21 P13
Blisland Cnwll...4 F6
Bliss Gate Worcs...35 R6
Blissford Hants...8 H6
Blisworth Nhants...37 T10
Blithbury Staffs...46 E9
Blitterlees Cumb...66 H2
Blockley Gloucs...36 G14
Blofield Norfk...51 P12
Blofield Heath Norfk...51 P11
Blo Norton Norfk...40 H5
Bloomfield Border...84 E14
Blore Staffs...46 F4
Blounce Hants...19 U12
Blount's Green Staffs...46 E7
Bloxham Oxon...37 M14
Bloxholm Lincs...48 G2
Bloxwich Wsall...46 D13
Bloxworth Dorset...8 B10
Blubberhouses N York...63 Q8
Blue Anchor Cnwll...3 N4
Blue Anchor Somset...16 E8
Blue Bell Hill Kent...12 D3
Blue John Cavern Derbys...56 H10
Blundellsands Sefton...54 H7
Blundeston Suffk...41 T2
Blunham C Beds...38 H10
Blunsdon St Andrew Swindn...29 M10
Bluntington Worcs...35 U6
Bluntisham Cambs...39 M5
Blunts Cnwll...4 J8
Blunts Green Warwks...36 F7
Blurton C Stke...45 U5
Blyborough Lincs...58 F8
Blyford Suffk...41 R5
Blymhill Staffs...45 T11
Blymhill Lawn Staffs...45 T11
Blyth Notts...57 T9
Blyth Nthumb...77 S10
Blyth Border...83 R9
Blyth Bridge Border...83 N9
Blythburgh Suffk...41 S6
Blyth Crematorium Nthumb...77 S10

Column 8

Blythe Border...84 F9
Blythe Bridge Staffs...46 B5
Blythe Marsh Staffs...46 B5
Blyton Lincs...58 E8
Boarhills Fife...91 R8
Boarhunt Hants...9 R7
Boarley Kent...12 D4
Boars Head Wigan...55 N5
Boarsgreave Lancs...55 S1
Boarshead E Susx...11 S4
Boars Hill Oxon...29 U7
Boarstall Bucks...30 D10
Boasley Cross Devon...5 N2
Boath Highld...108 K10
Boat of Garten Highld...103 P12
Bobbing Kent...12 G3
Bobbington Staffs...35 T2
Bobbingworth Essex...22 D6
Bocaddon Cnwll...4 F9
Bocking Essex...22 J3
Bocking Churchstreet Essex...22 J2
Bockleton Worcs...35 N8
Boconnoc Cnwll...4 F8
Boddam Abers...105 U6
Boddam Shet...106 t12
Boddington Gloucs...28 G3
Bodedern IoA...52 D6
Bodelwyddan Denbgs...53 T7
Bodenham Herefs...35 M10
Bodenham Wilts...8 G3
Bodenham Moor Herefs...35 M10
Bodewryd IoA...52 E3
Bodfari Denbgs...54 C12
Bodffordd IoA...52 F7
Bodfuan Gwynd...42 F5
Bodham Norfk...50 K5
Bodiam E Susx...12 E10
Bodicote Oxon...37 N13
Bodieve Cnwll...3 P2
Bodinnick Cnwll...4 E10
Bodle Street Green E Susx...11 V8
Bodmin Cnwll...3 R3
Bodmin Moor Cnwll...4 F6
Bodnant Conwy...53 P8
Bodney Norfk...50 D14
Bodorgan IoA...52 E8
Bodsham Kent...13 M6
Bodwen Cnwll...3 Q4
Bodymoor Heath Warwks...36 G2
Bogallan Highld...102 H5
Bogbrae Abers...105 S8
Bogend S Ayrs...81 N5
Boggs Holdings E Loth...83 T4
Boghall Mdloth...83 P5
Boghall W Loth...82 H5
Boghead S Lans...82 E10
Bogmoor Moray...104 C3
Bogmuir Abers...99 M9
Bogniebrae Abers...104 H6
Bognor Regis W Susx...10 E11
Bogroy Highld...103 P11
Bogue D & G...74 D9
Bohetherick Cnwll...5 L7
Bohortha Cnwll...3 L9
Bohuntine Highld...96 D7
Bojewyan Cnwll...2 B9
Bokiddick Cnwll...3 R4
Bolam Dur...69 R8
Bolam Nthumb...77 M9
Bolberry Devon...5 R13
Bold Heath St Hel...55 M8
Boldmere Birm...36 F2
Boldon Colliery S Tyne...77 T13
Boldre Hants...9 L9
Boldron Dur...69 N10
Bole Notts...58 C9
Bolehill Derbys...46 J2
Bolenowe Cnwll...2 H9
Bolham Devon...16 C13
Bolham Water Devon...6 G2
Bolingey Cnwll...2 K6
Bollington Ches E...56 D11
Bollington Cross Ches E...56 D11
Bollow Gloucs...28 D5
Bolney W Susx...11 M6
Bolnhurst Bed...38 G9
Bolshan Angus...99 M13
Bolsover Derbys...57 Q12
Bolster Moor Kirk...56 G4
Bolsterstone Sheff...57 L7
Bolstone Herefs...35 M13
Boltby N York...64 B2
Bolter End Bucks...20 C4
Bolton Bolton...55 R5
Bolton Cumb...68 D7
Bolton E Loth...84 D4
Bolton E R Yk...64 G9
Bolton Nthumb...77 P4
Bolton by Bowland Lancs...62 F10
Boltonfellend Cumb...75 U12
Boltongate Cumb...66 K4
Bolton-le-Sands Lancs...61 T6
Bolton Low Houses Cumb...66 K4
Bolton New Houses Cumb...66 K4
Bolton-on-Swale N York...69 S13
Bolton Percy N York...64 C11
Bolton Town End Lancs...61 T6
Bolton upon Dearne Barns...57 Q5
Bolventor Cnwll...4 F5
Bomarsund Nthumb...77 R9
Bomere Heath Shrops...45 L10
Bonar Bridge Highld...108 K5
Bonawe Ag & B...94 E12
Bonby N Linc...58 H4
Boncath Pembks...25 L3
Bonchester Bridge Border...76 B2
Bonchurch IoW...9 R13
Bondleigh Devon...15 Q11
Bonds Lancs...61 T11
Bonehill Devon...5 S5
Bonehill Staffs...46 G13
Boney Hay Staffs...46 E12
Bonhill W Duns...88 J10
Boningale Shrops...45 T13
Bonjedward Border...84 G14
Bonkle N Lans...82 F7
Bonnington Angus...91 P4
Bonnington Kent...13 L8
Bonnybank Fife...91 N11
Bonnybridge Falk...82 F2
Bonnykelly Abers...105 P4
Bonnyrigg Mdloth...83 R5
Bonnyton Angus...91 M5
Bonsall Derbys...46 J2
Bont Mons...27 Q4
Bontddu Gwynd...43 M10
Bont-Dolgadfan Powys...43 R12
Bont-goch or Elerch Cerdgn...33 N3
Bonthorpe Lincs...59 S12
Bontnewydd Cerdgn...33 M8
Bontnewydd Gwynd...52 G10
Bontuchel Denbgs...44 C2
Bonvilston V Glam...16 E2
Bon-y-maen Swans...26 B8
Booker Bucks...20 D4
Booley Shrops...45 N8
Boon Border...84 E9
Boorley Green Hants...9 Q6
Boosbeck R & Cl...71 L9
Boose's Green Essex...22 K1
Boot Cumb...66 K12
Booth Calder...56 G1
Boothby Graffoe Lincs...58 F14
Boothby Pagnell Lincs...48 E7
Boothferry E R Yk...64 G14
Boothgate Derbys...47 L3
Booth Green Ches E...56 D10
Boothstown Salfd...55 R6
Booth Town Calder...56 G1
Boothville Nhants...37 U8
Bootle Cumb...61 L2
Bootle Sefton...54 H7
Booton Norfk...50 K9
Boots Green Ches E...55 R12
Boot Street Suffk...41 M11
Booze N York...69 M12
Boraston Shrops...35 P6
Bordeaux Guern...6 e2
Borden Kent...12 G3
Borden W Susx...10 C5
Border Cumb...66 H2
Bordley N York...62 J7
Bordon Hants...10 B3
Boreham Essex...22 H6
Boreham Wilts...18 C12
Boreham Street E Susx...11 V8
Borehamwood Herts...21 L3
Boreland D & G...75 N8
Boreraig Highld...100 a4
Borgh W Isls...106 b18
Borgh W Isls...106 j4
Borgie Highld...111 Q5
Borgue D & G...73 P10
Borgue Highld...112 C12
Borley Essex...40 D12
Borley Green Essex...40 D12
Borley Green Suffk...40 G8

Borley Green Essex....40 D12
Borley Green Suffk....40 C8
Borneskitaig Highld....100 C2
Borness D & G....73 Q10
Boroughbridge N York....63 T6
Borough Green Kent....12 B4
Borras Head Wrexhm....44 J3
Borrowash Derbys....47 M7
Borrowby N York....63 U2
Borrowby N York....71 N9
Borrowstoun Falk....82 J2
Borstal Medway....12 D2
Borth Cerdgn....33 M2
Borthwickbrae Border....75 T3
Borthwickshiels Border....75 T2
Borth-y-Gest Gwynd....43 L6
Borve Highld....100 d5
Borve W Isls....106 f9
Borve W Isls....106 j5
Borve W Isls....106 j3
Borwick Lodge Cumb....67 M13
Borwick Rails Cumb....61 M4
Bosavern Cnwll....2 B10
Boscarne Cnwll....3 Q2
Boscastle Cnwll....4 D2
Boscombe Bmouth....8 G10
Boscombe Wilts....18 K13
Boscoppa Cnwll....3 Q6
Bosham W Susx....10 C10
Bosham Hoe W Susx....10 C10
Bosherston Pembks....24 G11
Boskednan Cnwll....2 C10
Boskenna Cnwll....2 C12
Bosley Ches E....56 D13
Bosoughan Cnwll....3 M4
Bossall N York....64 G7
Bossiney Cnwll....4 D3
Bossingham Kent....13 N6
Bossington Somset....15 U3
Bostock Green Ches W....55 Q13
Boston Lincs....49 M5
Boston Crematorium Lincs....49 M4
Boston Spa Leeds....63 U10
Boswarthan Cnwll....2 C10
Boswinger Cnwll....3 P8
Botallack Cnwll....2 B10
Botany Bay Gt Lon....21 N3
Botcheston Leics....47 N13
Botesdale Suffk....40 H5
Bothal Nthumb....77 Q8
Bothampstead W Berk....19 R5
Bothamsall Notts....57 U12
Bothel Cumb....66 J5
Bothenhampton Dorset....7 N6
Bothwell S Lans....82 D7
Bothwell Services S Lans....82 D7
Botley Bucks....31 L12
Botley Hants....9 Q6
Botley Oxon....29 U6
Botolph Claydon Bucks....30 F8
Botolphs W Susx....10 K9
Botolph's Bridge Kent....13 M9
Bottesford Leics....48 B6
Bottesford N Linc....58 E5
Bottisham Cambs....39 R8
Bottom o' th' Moor Bolton....55 Q4
Bottoms Calder....56 E2
Bottoms Cnwll....2 B12
Botts Green Warwks....36 H2
Botusfleming Cnwll....5 L8
Botwnnog Gwynd....42 E7
Bough Beech Kent....21 S13
Boughrood Powys....34 D13
Boughspring Gloucs....28 A9
Boughton Nhants....37 U7
Boughton Norfk....50 B13
Boughton Notts....57 U13
Boughton Aluph Kent....12 K6
Boughton End C Beds....31 L5
Boughton Green Kent....12 E5
Boughton Malherbe Kent....12 G6
Boughton Monchelsea Kent....12 E5
Boughton Street Kent....13 L4
Boulby R & Cl....71 N9
Boulder Clough Calder....56 G2
Bouldnor IoW....9 M11
Bouldon Shrops....35 M3
Boulmer Nthumb....77 R3
Boulston Pembks....24 G8
Boultham Lincs....58 G13
Bourn Cambs....39 M9
Bournbrook Birm....36 D4
Bourne Lincs....48 G9
Bournebridge Essex....22 D9
Bournebrook Birm....36 D4
Bourne End Bed....38 E8
Bourne End Bucks....20 E6
Bourne End C Beds....31 L4
Bourne End Herts....31 M11
Bournemouth Bmouth....8 F10
Bournemouth Airport Dorset....8 G9
Bournemouth Crematorium Bmouth....8 G10
Bournes Green Gloucs....28 H7
Bournes Green Sthend....23 M10
Bournheath Worcs....36 C6
Bournmoor Dur....70 D2
Bournstream Gloucs....28 D9
Bournville Birm....36 D4
Bourton Dorset....17 U10
Bourton N Som....16 L4
Bourton Oxon....29 P10
Bourton Shrops....35 N1
Bourton Wilts....18 G8
Bourton on Dunsmore Warwks....37 M6
Bourton-on-the-Hill Gloucs....29 N1
Bourton-on-the-Water Gloucs....29 N3
Bousd Ag & B....92 H6
Boustead Hill Cumb....67 Q14
Bouth Cumb....61 Q2
Bouthwaite N York....63 N5
Bouts Worcs....36 D9
Boveney Bucks....20 F7
Boveridge Dorset....8 F6
Boverton V Glam....16 B3
Bovey Tracey Devon....5 U5
Bovingdon Herts....31 M12
Bovingdon Green Bucks....20 D6
Bovinger Essex....22 D6
Bovington Dorset....8 A11
Bovington Camp Dorset....8 A11
Bow Cumb....67 M1
Bow Devon....5 S2
Bow Gt Lon....21 Q7
Bow Ork....106 s20
Bowbank Dur....68 K8
Bow Brickhill M Keyn....30 K6
Bowbridge Gloucs....28 G6
Bowburn Dur....70 D5
Bowcombe IoW....9 N11
Bowd Devon....6 F6
Bowden Border....84 F12
Bowden Hill Wilts....18 D7
Bowdon Traffd....55 S9
Bower Highld....112 H4
Bower Ashton Bristl....17 Q2
Bowerchalke Wilts....8 E4
Bowerhill Wilts....18 D8
Bower Hinton Somset....17 N13
Bower House Tye Suffk....40 G12
Bowermadden Highld....112 F4
Bowers Staffs....45 T6
Bowers Gifford Essex....22 J10
Bowershall Fife....90 F13
Bower's Row Leeds....57 P1
Bowes Dur....69 L10
Bowgreave Lancs....61 T11
Bowhouse D & G....74 K12
Bowithick Cnwll....4 F4
Bowker's Green Lancs....54 K5
Bowland Border....84 D10
Bowley Herefs....35 M10
Bowley Town Herefs....35 M10
Bowlhead Green Surrey....10 E3
Bowling W Duns....88 K11
Bowling Wrexhm....44 J4
Bowling Bank Wrexhm....44 J4
Bowling Green Worcs....35 T10
Bowmanstead Cumb....67 M13
Bowmore Ag & B....78 E4
Bowness-on-Solway Cumb....75 P14
Bowness-on-Windermere Cumb....67 P13
Bow of Fife Fife....91 M9
Bowriefauld Angus....91 R2
Bowscale Cumb....67 N6
Bowsden Nthumb....85 P10
Bowston Cumb....67 Q12
Bow Street Cerdgn....33 M3
Bow Street Norfk....50 H14
Bowthorpe Norfk....51 L12
Box Gloucs....28 F7
Box Wilts....18 B7
Boxbush Gloucs....28 D4
Boxbush Gloucs....28 C3
Box End Bed....38 F11
Boxford Suffk....40 G12
Boxford W Berk....19 P6
Boxgrove W Susx....10 E9

Boxley Kent....12 E4
Box's Shop Cnwll....14 F12
Boxted Essex....23 P1
Boxted Suffk....40 D10
Boxted Cross Essex....23 P1
Boxwell Gloucs....28 F9
Boxworth Cambs....39 M8
Boxworth End Cambs....39 M7
Boyden End Suffk....40 B9
Boyden Gate Kent....13 Q3
Boylestone Derbys....46 G6
Boyndie Abers....104 J3
Boyndlie Abers....105 Q3
Boynton E R Yk....65 Q7
Boys Hall Kent....12 K7
Boysack Angus....91 T2
Boythorpe Derbys....57 N13
Boyton Cnwll....4 J2
Boyton Suffk....41 Q11
Boyton Wilts....18 E13
Boyton Cross Essex....22 F6
Boyton End Suffk....40 B12
Bozeat Nhants....38 D8
Braaid IoM....60 e7
Brabling Green Suffk....41 N8
Brabourne Kent....13 L7
Brabourne Lees Kent....13 L7
Brabstermire Highld....112 H3
Bracadale Highld....100 c6
Braceborough Lincs....48 G11
Bracebridge Heath Lincs....58 G13
Bracebridge Low Fields Lincs....58 G13
Braceby Lincs....48 F6
Bracewell Lancs....62 H11
Brackenfield Derbys....47 L2
Brackenhirst N Lans....82 E6
Brackenthwaite Cumb....67 L8
Brackenthwaite N York....63 Q9
Brackla Brdgnd....26 G12
Bracklesham W Susx....10 C11
Brackletter Highld....94 H2
Brackley Nhants....30 C5
Brackley Hatch Nhants....30 D4
Bracknell Br For....20 E9
Braco P & K....89 R5
Bracobrae Moray....104 G5
Bracora Highld....100 g9
Bracorina Highld....100 g9
Bradaford Devon....4 K2
Bradbourne Derbys....46 H3
Bradbury Dur....70 D7
Bradda IoM....60 b7
Braddock Cnwll....4 F8
Bradeley C Stke....45 U3
Bradenham Bucks....20 D3
Bradenstoke Wilts....18 G5
Bradfield Devon....6 E4
Bradfield Essex....23 R1
Bradfield Norfk....51 N7
Bradfield Sheff....57 L8
Bradfield W Berk....19 T6
Bradfield Combust Suffk....40 E9
Bradfield Green Ches E....45 Q2
Bradfield Heath Essex....23 R2
Bradfield St Clare Suffk....40 E9
Bradfield St George Suffk....40 E9
Bradford C Brad....63 P13
Bradford Cnwll....4 F6
Bradford Devon....14 K11
Bradford Nthumb....77 M10
Bradford Nthumb....85 T12
Bradford Abbas Dorset....7 R2
Bradford Leigh Wilts....18 B8
Bradford-on-Avon Wilts....18 B8
Bradford-on-Tone Somset....16 G12
Bradford Peverell Dorset....7 S6
Bradley Derbys....46 H4
Bradley Hants....19 S11
Bradley IoW....9 S14
Bradley Kirk....56 J2
Bradley NE Lin....59 M5
Bradley Staffs....45 U10
Bradley Wolves....46 C1
Bradley Wrexhm....44 J4
Bradley Common Ches W....45 M4
Bradley Green Somset....16 J9
Bradley Green Warwks....46 J13
Bradley Green Worcs....36 C8
Bradley in the Moors Staffs....46 E5
Bradley Stoke S Glos....28 B11
Bradmore Notts....47 Q7
Bradney Somset....16 K9
Bradninch Devon....6 D3
Bradnop Staffs....46 D2
Bradpole Dorset....7 N6
Bradshaw Bolton....55 R4
Bradshaw Calder....56 G2
Bradstone Devon....4 K5
Bradwall Green Ches E....45 S1
Bradwell Derbys....56 J10
Bradwell Devon....15 M4
Bradwell Essex....23 L3
Bradwell M Keyn....30 H4
Bradwell Norfk....51 T13
Bradwell Crematorium Staffs....45 U4
Bradwell-on-Sea Essex....23 N6
Bradwell Waterside Essex....23 N6
Bradworthy Devon....14 H10
Brae Highld....102 H3
Brae Shet....106 t7
Braefield Highld....102 E7
Braehead Angus....91 T2
Braehead D & G....73 L9
Braehead S Lans....82 H9
Braemar Abers....98 B5
Braemore Highld....102 B7
Braemore Highld....112 C11
Brae Roy Lodge Highld....96 C5
Braeside Inver....88 F11
Braes of Coul Angus....98 D12
Braes of Enzie Moray....104 D4
Braevallich Ag & B....87 T4
Brafferton Darltn....70 C8
Brafferton N York....63 U5
Brafield-on-the-Green Nhants....38 B9
Bragar W Isls....106 h4
Bragbury End Herts....31 S9
Braidwood S Lans....82 G9
Brailsford Derbys....46 H5
Brailsford Green Derbys....46 H5
Brain's Green Gloucs....28 C6
Braintree Essex....22 J3
Braiseworth Suffk....41 L6
Braishfield Hants....9 M3
Braithwaite C Brad....63 M11
Braithwaite Cumb....67 L8
Braithwaite Wakefd....57 R3
Braithwell Donc....57 R8
Bramber W Susx....10 K8
Brambridge Hants....9 P4
Bramcote Notts....47 P6
Bramcote Warwks....37 M3
Bramcote Crematorium Notts....47 P6
Bramdean Hants....9 S3
Bramerton Norfk....51 N13
Bramfield Herts....31 S9
Bramfield Suffk....41 R6
Bramford Suffk....40 K11
Bramhall Stockp....56 C9
Bramham Leeds....63 U11
Bramhope Leeds....63 R11
Bramley Hants....19 U9
Bramley Leeds....63 Q12
Bramley Rothm....57 Q8
Bramley Surrey....10 G2
Bramley Corner Hants....19 T9
Bramley Head N York....63 N8
Bramling Kent....13 P4
Brampford Speke Devon....6 B5
Brampton Cambs....38 K6
Brampton Cumb....67 S2
Brampton Cumb....68 B14
Brampton Lincs....58 E12
Brampton Norfk....51 M9
Brampton Rothm....57 P6
Brampton Suffk....41 R4
Brampton Abbotts Herefs....28 B2
Brampton Ash Nhants....37 U3
Brampton Bryan Herefs....34 J6
Brampton-en-le-Morthen Rothm....57 Q9
Bramshall Staffs....46 E7
Bramshaw Hants....8 K5
Bramshill Hants....20 B10
Bramshott Hants....10 C4
Bramwell Somset....17 M11
Branault Highld....93 P5
Brancaster Norfk....50 C5
Brancaster Staithe Norfk....50 C5
Brancepeth Dur....69 R5
Branchill Moray....103 R5
Brand End Lincs....49 N4
Branderburgh Moray....104 A1
Brandesburton E R Yk....65 Q10
Brandeston Suffk....41 M8
Brand Green Gloucs....28 D2
Brandis Corner Devon....14 K12
Brandiston Norfk....50 K9
Brandon Dur....69 R5
Brandon Lincs....48 D4
Brandon Nthumb....77 L2
Brandon Suffk....40 B3
Brandon Warwks....37 M5
Brandon Bank Norfk....39 T3
Brandon Creek Norfk....39 T2
Brandon Parva Norfk....50 J12
Brandsby N York....64 E5
Brandy Wharf Lincs....58 H7
Brane Cnwll....2 C11
Bran End Essex....22 G2
Branksome Poole....8 E10
Branksome Park Poole....8 F10
Bransbury Hants....19 P12
Bransby Lincs....58 E11
Branscombe Devon....6 G7
Bransford Worcs....35 S10
Bransgore Hants....8 H9
Bransholme C KuH....65 R13
Branson's Cross Worcs....36 E6
Branston Leics....48 B8
Branston Lincs....58 H13
Branston Staffs....46 H9
Branston Booths Lincs....58 J13
Branstone IoW....9 R12
Brant Broughton Lincs....48 D2
Brantham Suffk....40 K14
Branthwaite Cumb....66 G8
Branthwaite Cumb....67 L7
Branton Donc....57 T6
Branton Nthumb....77 L2
Branton Green N York....63 U7
Branxton Nthumb....85 M11
Brassey Green Ches W....45 M1
Brassington Derbys....46 H2
Brasted Kent....21 S11
Brasted Chart Kent....21 S12
Brathens Abers....99 M4
Bratoft Lincs....59 S14
Brattleby Lincs....58 F10
Bratton Somset....16 B7
Bratton Wrekin....45 P11
Bratton Clovelly Devon....5 M2
Bratton Fleming Devon....15 P5
Bratton Seymour Somset....17 S11
Braughing Herts....22 B3
Braughing Friars Herts....22 B3
Braunston Nhants....37 P7
Braunston Rutlnd....48 B12
Braunstone Leics....47 Q13
Braunton Devon....15 L5
Brawby N York....64 G4
Brawl Highld....111 V3
Braworth N York....70 H10
Bray W & M....20 F7
Braybrooke Nhants....37 U4
Braydon Brook Wilts....28 J9
Braydon Side Wilts....28 K10
Bray's Hill E Susx....12 C13
Bray Shop Cnwll....4 J6
Braystones Cumb....66 F11
Braythorn N York....63 Q10
Brayton N York....64 E13
Braywick W & M....20 E7
Braywoodside W & M....20 E7
Brazacott Cnwll....4 H2
Breach Kent....12 F2
Breachwood Green Herts....31 Q8
Breaden Heath Shrops....44 K6
Breadsall Derbys....47 L6
Breadstone Gloucs....28 D7
Breadward Herefs....34 G10
Breage Cnwll....2 G11
Breakachy Highld....102 E7
Breakspear Crematorium Gt Lon....20 J5
Brealangwell Lodge Highld....108 J6
Bream Gloucs....28 B6
Breamore Hants....8 H5
Brean Somset....16 J5
Breanais W Isls....106 e6
Brearley Calder....56 H2
Brearton N York....63 S7
Breascleit W Isls....106 h5
Breaston Derbys....47 N7
Brechfa Carmth....25 V2
Brechin Angus....99 L12
Breckles Norfk....40 G2
Brecon Powys....26 K2
Brecon Beacons National Park....26 J3
Bredbury Stockp....56 D8
Brede E Susx....12 F12
Bredenbury Herefs....35 N9
Bredfield Suffk....41 N10
Bredgar Kent....12 G3
Bredhurst Kent....12 E3
Bredon Worcs....36 B13
Bredon's Hardwick Worcs....36 B13
Bredon's Norton Worcs....36 B13
Bredwardine Herefs....34 J12
Breedon on the Hill Leics....47 M9
Breich W Loth....82 H6
Breightmet Bolton....55 R5
Breighton E R Yk....64 G13
Breinton Herefs....35 L13
Breinton Common Herefs....35 L12
Bremhill Wilts....18 E6
Bremridge Devon....15 Q7
Brenchley Kent....12 C7
Brendon Devon....15 R3
Brendon Devon....14 J11
Brenfield Ag & B....87 Q9
Brenish W Isls....106 e6
Brenkley N u Ty....77 R11
Brent Eleigh Suffk....40 F11
Brentford Gt Lon....21 L7
Brentingby Leics....47 U10
Brent Knoll Somset....16 K6
Brent Mill Devon....5 R9
Brent Pelham Herts....22 C1
Brentwood Essex....22 E9
Brenzett Kent....12 K10
Brenzett Green Kent....12 K10
Brereton Staffs....46 D10
Brereton Green Ches E....55 S14
Brereton Heath Ches E....55 T14
Brereton Hill Staffs....46 D10
Bressay Shet....106 v9
Bressingham Norfk....40 J4
Bressingham Common Norfk....40 J3
Bretby Derbys....46 J9
Bretby Crematorium Derbys....46 J9
Bretford Warwks....37 M5
Bretforton Worcs....36 E12
Bretherdale Head Cumb....67 S12
Bretherton Lancs....55 L2
Brettabister Shet....106 u8
Brettenham Norfk....40 F4
Brettenham Suffk....40 G10
Bretton Flints....44 J1
Bretton Derbys....56 J11
Brewers End Essex....22 D4
Brewer Street Surrey....21 P12
Brewood Staffs....45 U12
Briantspuddle Dorset....7 V5
Brick End Essex....22 E2
Brickendon Herts....31 T11
Bricket Wood Herts....31 P11
Brick Houses Sheff....57 M10
Bricklehampton Worcs....36 C12
Bride IoM....60 g2
Bridekirk Cumb....66 H6
Bridell Pembks....32 C12
Brideswell Abers....104 H8
Bridford Devon....5 U3
Bridge Kent....13 N5
Bridge End Bed....38 G10
Bridge End Cumb....67 L4
Bridge End Cumb....67 P4
Bridge End Devon....5 R11
Bridge End Essex....22 G1
Bridge End Lincs....48 H6
Bridge End Nthumb....76 J12
Bridge End Surrey....20 H10
Bridgefoot Angus....91 N4
Bridgefoot Cumb....66 G7
Bridge Green Essex....39 Q14
Bridgehampton Somset....17 Q12
Bridgehill Dur....69 N2
Bridgehouse Gate N York....63 N6
Bridgemary Hants....9 R8
Bridgemere Ches E....45 R4
Bridgend Abers....104 H8
Bridgend Ag & B....78 F3
Bridgend Ag & B....87 Q9
Bridgend Angus....98 K11
Bridgend Brdgnd....26 G11
Bridgend Cerdgn....32 D11
Bridgend Cumb....67 P9
Bridgend D & G....74 H7
Bridgend Devon....5 Q10
Bridgend Fife....91 L9
Bridgend Moray....104 D7
Bridgend P & K....90 H7
Bridgend W Loth....82 K3

Bridgend of Lintrathen Angus....98 D13
Bridge of Alford Abers....104 H12
Bridge of Allan Stirlg....89 S6
Bridge of Avon Moray....103 U11
Bridge of Avon Moray....103 R9
Bridge of Balgie P & K....95 R9
Bridge of Brewlands Angus....98 D13
Bridge of Brown Highld....103 T11
Bridge of Cally P & K....97 V13
Bridge of Canny Abers....99 M4
Bridge of Craigisla Angus....98 D13
Bridge of Dee D & G....74 F14
Bridge of Don C Aber....99 S2
Bridge of Dulsie Highld....103 Q8
Bridge of Dye Abers....99 L6
Bridge of Earn P & K....90 H8
Bridge of Ericht P & K....95 R6
Bridge of Feugh Abers....99 N5
Bridge of Forss Highld....112 B3
Bridge of Gairn Abers....98 E5
Bridge of Gaur P & K....95 Q7
Bridge of Marnoch Abers....104 H5
Bridge of Orchy Ag & B....94 K11
Bridge of Tilt P & K....97 S10
Bridge of Tynet Moray....104 D3
Bridge of Walls Shet....106 s8
Bridge of Weir Rens....88 J12
Bridge Reeve Devon....15 Q10
Bridgerule Devon....14 G12
Bridges Shrops....34 J1
Bridge Sollers Herefs....34 K12
Bridge Street Suffk....40 E11
Bridgetown Cnwll....4 J4
Bridgetown Somset....16 B10
Bridge Trafford Ches W....55 L12
Bridge Yate S Glos....28 C13
Bridgham Norfk....40 G3
Bridgnorth Shrops....35 R2
Bridgwater Somset....16 J9
Bridgwater Services Somset....16 J10
Bridlington E R Yk....65 R6
Bridport Dorset....7 N6
Bridstow Herefs....28 A3
Brierfield Lancs....62 G12
Brierley Barns....57 P4
Brierley Gloucs....28 B4
Brierley Herefs....35 L9
Brierley Hill Dudley....36 B3
Brierton Hartpl....70 G6
Briery Cumb....67 L8
Brig W Isls....106 g9
Briggate Norfk....51 P8
Briggswath N York....71 Q11
Brigham Cumb....66 G6
Brigham Cumb....67 L7
Brigham E R Yk....65 P9
Brighouse Calder....56 H2
Brighstone IoW....9 N12
Brightgate Derbys....46 H2
Brighthampton Oxon....29 S7
Brightholmlee Sheff....57 L7
Brightley Devon....15 P13
Brightling E Susx....12 C11
Brightlingsea Essex....23 Q4
Brighton Br & H....11 N10
Brighton Cnwll....3 N6
Brighton City Airport W Susx....10 K10
Brighton le Sands Sefton....54 H7
Brightons Falk....82 H3
Brightwalton W Berk....19 P5
Brightwalton Green W Berk....19 P5
Brightwalton Holt W Berk....19 P5
Brightwell Suffk....41 N12
Brightwell Baldwin Oxon....30 E13
Brightwell-cum-Sotwell Oxon....19 U2
Brightwell Upperton Oxon....19 U2
Brignall Dur....69 N10
Brig o'Turk Stirlg....89 M4
Brigsley NE Lin....59 N6
Brigsteer Cumb....61 T2
Brigstock Nhants....38 D3
Brill Bucks....30 E10
Brill Cnwll....2 J11
Brilley Herefs....34 G11
Brimfield Herefs....35 M7
Brimfield Cross Herefs....35 M7
Brimington Derbys....57 P12
Brimley Devon....5 U5
Brimpsfield Gloucs....28 H4
Brimpton W Berk....19 S8
Brimpton Common W Berk....19 S8
Brimscombe Gloucs....28 G7
Brimstage Wirral....54 H10
Brincliffe Sheff....57 M9
Brind E R Yk....64 G13
Brindham Somset....17 P8
Brindister Shet....106 s9
Brindle Lancs....55 P2
Brineton Staffs....45 T11
Bringhurst Leics....37 U2
Bringsty Common Herefs....35 Q9
Brington Cambs....38 G5
Briningham Norfk....50 H6
Brinkhill Lincs....59 Q12
Brinkley Cambs....39 T10
Brinklow Warwks....37 M5
Brinkworth Wilts....28 K10
Brinscall Lancs....55 P2
Brinscombe Somset....17 M6
Brinsea N Som....17 M4
Brinsley Notts....47 N4
Brinsop Herefs....34 K12
Brinsworth Rothm....57 P8
Brinton Norfk....50 H6
Brisco Cumb....67 P2
Brisley Norfk....50 G9
Brislington Bristl....17 R3
Brissenden Green Kent....12 J8
Bristol Bristl....27 V13
Bristol Airport N Som....17 P4
Bristol Zoo Gardens Bristl....27 V13
Briston Norfk....50 J7
Brisworthy Devon....5 N8
Britannia Lancs....56 D2
Britford Wilts....8 G3
Brithdir Caerph....27 L7
Brithdir Gwynd....43 Q10
British Legion Village Kent....12 D4
Briton Ferry Neath....26 D9
Britwell Salome Oxon....19 U2
Brixham Torbay....6 B13
Brixton Devon....5 P10
Brixton Gt Lon....21 P7
Brixton Deverill Wilts....18 B13
Brixworth Nhants....37 U6
Brize Norton Oxon....29 Q6
Brize Norton Airport Oxon....29 Q6
Broad Alley Worcs....35 U7
Broad Blunsdon Swindn....29 M9
Broadbottom Tamesd....56 E8
Broadbridge W Susx....10 C9
Broadbridge Heath W Susx....10 J4
Broad Campden Gloucs....36 F13
Broad Carr Calder....56 G3
Broad Chalke Wilts....8 E3
Broad Clough Lancs....56 C2
Broadclyst Devon....6 C5
Broadfield Inver....88 H11
Broadfield Pembks....24 K9
Broadford Highld....100 f7
Broadford Bridge W Susx....10 H6
Broad Green Cambs....39 U9
Broad Green Essex....23 L3
Broad Green Essex....22 H7
Broad Green Worcs....35 S10
Broad Haven Pembks....24 E8
Broadhaugh Border....85 M10
Broadheath Traffd....55 S9
Broadheath Worcs....35 Q8
Broadhembury Devon....6 F4
Broadhempston Devon....5 U7
Broad Hill Cambs....39 S6
Broad Hinton Wilts....18 H5
Broadholme Lincs....58 E12
Broadland Row E Susx....12 F12
Broadlay Carmth....25 Q9
Broad Laying Hants....19 P8
Broadley Lancs....56 C4
Broadley Moray....104 D4
Broadley Common Essex....22 B6
Broad Marston Worcs....36 F11
Broadmayne Dorset....7 U6
Broad Meadow Staffs....45 S4
Broadmere Hants....19 S11
Broadmoor Pembks....24 J9
Broadmoor Gloucs....28 B5
Broadnymett Devon....15 R12
Broadoak Dorset....7 M4
Broad Oak Carmth....25 U7
Broadoak Gloucs....28 C5
Broad Oak Cumb....66 K13
Broad Oak E Susx....12 D11
Broad Oak E Susx....12 F11
Broad Oak Hants....20 C12

Broad Oak Herefs....27 T3
Broad Oak Kent....13 N3
Broad Oak St Hel....55 M7
Broadoak Wrexhm....44 J4
Broad Road Suffk....41 N5
Broad's Green Essex....22 G5
Broadstairs Kent....13 S2
Broadstone Mons....27 S5
Broadstone Poole....8 E9
Broad Street E Susx....12 G12
Broad Street Kent....12 G4
Broad Street Kent....22 E14
Broad Street Medway....13 L2
Broad Street Wilts....18 H8
Broad Street Green Essex....23 L5
Broad Town Wilts....18 H5
Broadwas Worcs....35 S10
Broadwater Herts....31 S8
Broadwater W Susx....10 K10
Broadwaters Worcs....35 U6
Broadway Carmth....25 N8
Broadway Carmth....25 Q9
Broadway Pembks....24 E8
Broadway Somset....16 K13
Broadway Suffk....41 Q6
Broadway Worcs....36 E13
Broadwell Gloucs....29 P3
Broadwell Gloucs....28 A5
Broadwell Oxon....29 P7
Broadwell Warwks....37 N7
Broadwey Dorset....7 S8
Broadwindsor Dorset....7 M4
Broadwood Kelly Devon....15 P11
Broadwoodwidger Devon....4 L3
Brobury Herefs....34 J12
Brochel Highld....100 e5
Brochroy Ag & B....94 E12
Brock Lancs....61 U11
Brockamin Worcs....35 S10
Brockbridge Hants....9 S5
Brockdish Norfk....41 M5
Brockencote Worcs....35 U6
Brockenhurst Hants....9 L8
Brocketsbrae S Lans....82 F11
Brockford Street Suffk....40 K7
Brockhall Nhants....37 R8
Brockhampton Gloucs....28 K3
Brockhampton Hants....9 U8
Brockhampton Herefs....28 A1
Brockhampton Green Dorset....7 T4
Brockhill Border....75 Q2
Brockholes Kirk....56 J4
Brockhurst Derbys....57 M14
Brockhurst Warwks....37 L4
Brocklebank Cumb....67 M4
Brocklesby Lincs....59 L4
Brockley N Som....17 N3
Brockley Suffk....40 D8
Brockley Green Suffk....40 C11
Brockleymoor Cumb....67 Q6
Brockmoor Dudley....35 U3
Brockscombe Devon....15 L13
Brock's Green Hants....19 Q8
Brockton Shrops....35 N2
Brockton Shrops....45 L13
Brockton Shrops....35 P1
Brockton Shrops....44 J14
Brockton Staffs....45 T7
Brockweir Gloucs....27 U7
Brockwood Park Hants....9 S4
Brockworth Gloucs....28 G4
Brocton Cnwll....4 G6
Brocton Staffs....46 B10
Brodick N Ayrs....80 E5
Brodie Moray....103 Q4
Brodsworth Donc....57 R5
Brogaig Highld....100 d3
Brogborough C Beds....31 L5
Broken Cross Ches E....56 C12
Broken Cross Ches W....55 Q12
Brokenborough Wilts....28 H10
Brokerswood Wilts....18 B10
Bromborough Wirral....54 J10
Brome Suffk....40 K5
Brome Street Suffk....40 K5
Bromeswell Suffk....41 P10
Bromfield Cumb....66 J4
Bromfield Shrops....35 L5
Bromford Birm....36 F2
Bromham Bed....38 F10
Bromham Wilts....18 E7
Bromley Dudley....36 B3
Bromley Gt Lon....21 R8
Bromley Shrops....35 R1
Bromley Common Gt Lon....21 R9
Bromley Cross Bolton....55 R4
Bromley Green Kent....12 J8
Brompton Medway....12 E2
Brompton N York....70 E13
Brompton N York....65 L3
Brompton-by-Sawdon N York....65 L3
Brompton-on-Swale N York....69 R13
Brompton Ralph Somset....16 E10
Brompton Regis Somset....16 C10
Bromsash Herefs....28 B3
Bromsberrow Gloucs....35 R14
Bromsberrow Heath Gloucs....35 R14
Bromsgrove Worcs....36 C6
Bromstead Heath Staffs....45 S10
Bromyard Herefs....35 Q9
Bromyard Downs Herefs....35 Q9
Bronaber Gwynd....43 Q7
Bronant Cerdgn....33 M7
Broncroft Shrops....35 M3
Brongest Cerdgn....32 F11
Bronington Wrexhm....45 L5
Bronllys Powys....34 E14
Bronnant Cerdgn....33 M7
Bronwydd Carmth....25 R5
Bronydd Powys....34 F11
Bronygarth Shrops....44 G6
Brook Carmth....25 N9
Brook Hants....8 K5
Brook Hants....9 M4
Brook IoW....9 M12
Brook Kent....13 L6
Brook Surrey....10 F2
Brook Surrey....10 G2
Brooke Norfk....51 P14
Brooke Rutlnd....48 B12
Brookenby Lincs....59 L7
Brook End Bed....38 F7
Brook End C Beds....38 H8
Brook End Cambs....38 H6
Brook End M Keyn....38 C9
Brookfield Rens....88 K12
Brookhampton Oxon....30 B12
Brook Hill Hants....8 K5
Brookhouse Lancs....61 U7
Brookhouse Rothm....57 R9
Brookhouse Green Ches E....45 T1
Brookhouses Derbys....56 F9
Brookland Kent....12 J10
Brooklands Traffd....55 S8
Brookmans Park Herts....31 S11
Brooks Powys....44 D14
Brooksby Leics....47 S10
Brooks End Kent....13 Q2
Brooks Green W Susx....10 J5
Brook Street Essex....22 E9
Brook Street Kent....12 J8
Brook Street Suffk....40 D11
Brook Street W Susx....11 N5
Brookthorpe Gloucs....28 F5
Brookville Norfk....50 B14
Brookwood Surrey....20 G11
Broom Bed....38 J11
Broom C Beds....31 Q4
Broom Rothm....57 P7
Broom Warwks....36 E10
Broome Norfk....41 Q2
Broome Shrops....34 K4
Broome Worcs....35 U4
Broomedge Warrtn....55 R10
Broome Park Nthumb....77 N3
Broomer's Corner W Susx....10 J6
Broomershill W Susx....10 H6
Broomfield Essex....22 H5
Broomfield Kent....12 F4
Broomfield Kent....13 N3
Broomfield Somset....16 H10
Broomfields Shrops....44 J10
Broomfleet E R Yk....58 E1
Broomhall W & M....20 G9
Broomhaugh Nthumb....77 M13
Broom Hill Barns....57 N5
Broom Hill Dorset....8 F8
Broomhill Nthumb....77 Q5
Broom Hill Worcs....35 U5
Broomhill Green Ches E....45 N4
Broom's Green Gloucs....35 R14
Brora Highld....109 S4
Broseley Shrops....45 Q13

Brotherlee Dur....68 K5
Brotherton N York....57 R1
Brotton R & Cl....71 L9
Broubster Highld....112 B5
Brough Cumb....68 G10
Brough Derbys....56 J10
Brough E R Yk....58 F1
Brough Highld....112 G2
Brough Notts....58 C14
Brough Shet....106 v7
Brough Shet....106 v5
Broughall Shrops....45 N5
Brough Lodge Shet....106 v4
Brough Sowerby Cumb....68 G10
Broughton Border....83 M11
Broughton Bucks....30 H10
Broughton Cambs....39 L5
Broughton Flints....44 J1
Broughton Hants....9 L2
Broughton Lancs....61 U13
Broughton M Keyn....30 J4
Broughton N Linc....58 F5
Broughton N York....62 J9
Broughton N York....64 H4
Broughton Nhants....37 U5
Broughton Oxon....37 M13
Broughton Salfd....55 T6
Broughton Staffs....45 S7
Broughton V Glam....26 G12
Broughton Astley Leics....37 P2
Broughton Beck Cumb....61 N2
Broughton Gifford Wilts....18 C8
Broughton Green Worcs....36 C8
Broughton Hackett Worcs....36 B10
Broughton-in-Furness Cumb....61 N2
Broughton Mains D & G....73 L9
Broughton Mills Cumb....61 M1
Broughton Moor Cumb....66 G6
Broughton Poggs Oxon....29 P7
Broughty Ferry C Dund....91 P5
Bround Devon....6 F5
Browland Shet....106 s8
Brown Candover Hants....19 S13
Brown Edge Lancs....54 J4
Brown Edge Staffs....46 B3
Brown Heath Ches W....55 L13
Brownhill Abers....105 N6
Brownhills Fife....91 R8
Brownhills Wsall....46 E13
Brownieside Nthumb....85 T14
Browninghill Green Hants....19 S9
Brown Lees Staffs....45 U2
Brownlow Heath Ches E....45 U1
Brownrigg Cumb....66 F7
Brownrigg Cumb....66 J2
Brownsea Island Dorset....8 E11
Brown's Green Birm....36 D2
Brownsham Devon....14 G7
Brownshill Gloucs....28 G7
Brownsover Warwks....37 P5
Brownston Devon....5 Q10
Brown Street Suffk....40 J8
Brow-of-the-Hill Norfk....49 U10
Browston Green Norfk....51 S13
Broxa N York....65 L1
Broxbourne Herts....31 U11
Broxburn E Loth....84 G3
Broxburn W Loth....82 K4
Broxfield Nthumb....77 Q2
Broxted Essex....22 E2
Broxton Ches W....45 L3
Broxwood Herefs....34 K10
Broyle Side E Susx....11 Q8
Bruan Highld....112 H9
Bruar P & K....97 R10
Brucefield Highld....109 N7
Bruchag Ag & B....88 C14
Bruera Ches W....45 L1
Bruern Abbey Oxon....29 Q3
Bruichladdich Ag & B....78 D4
Bruisyard Suffk....41 P8
Bruisyard Street Suffk....41 P8
Brumby N Linc....58 E5
Brund Staffs....56 G14
Brundall Norfk....51 P12
Brundish Suffk....41 N7
Brundish Street Suffk....41 N6
Brunery Highld....93 S4
Brunnion Cnwll....2 F9
Brunslow Shrops....34 J3
Brunswick Village N u Ty....77 R11
Bruntcliffe Leeds....57 L1
Brunthwaite C Brad....63 L10
Bruntingthorpe Leics....37 R3
Brunton Fife....91 L7
Brunton Nthumb....85 U14
Brunton Wilts....19 L9
Brushford Devon....15 R11
Brushford Somset....16 B11
Bruton Somset....17 S9
Bryan's Green Worcs....35 U7
Bryanston Dorset....8 B8
Bryant's Bottom Bucks....20 D3
Brydekirk D & G....75 N11
Bryher IoS....2 b2
Brymbo Wrexhm....44 H3
Brympton Somset....17 N13
Bryn Carmth....25 T9
Bryn Ches W....55 P12
Bryn Neath....26 E8
Bryn Shrops....34 G3
Bryn Wigan....55 N6
Brynamman Carmth....26 B6
Brynberian Pembks....24 K3
Brynbryddan Neath....26 D9
Bryn-bwbach Gwynd....43 M6
Bryncae Rhondd....26 H11
Bryncethin Brdgnd....26 G11
Bryncir Gwynd....42 J4
Bryn-coch Neath....26 D8
Bryncroes Gwynd....42 E7
Bryncrug Gwynd....43 M12
Bryn Du IoA....52 D7
Bryn-Eden Gwynd....43 P8
Bryneglwys Denbgs....44 E4
Brynfields Wrexhm....44 H4
Brynford Flints....54 E12
Bryn Gates Wigan....55 N6
Bryn Golau Rhondd....26 H10
Bryngwran IoA....52 D7
Bryngwyn Mons....27 R6
Bryngwyn Powys....34 E11
Bryn-Henllan Pembks....24 H3
Brynhoffnant Cerdgn....32 F10
Bryning Lancs....61 S13
Brynithel Blae G....27 N6
Brynmawr Blae G....27 M5
Bryn-mawr Gwynd....42 E7
Brynmenyn Brdgnd....26 G11
Brynmill Swans....25 V12
Brynna Rhondd....26 H11
Bryn-penarth Powys....44 D13
Brynrefail Gwynd....52 H9
Brynrefail IoA....52 G5
Bryn Saith Marchog Denbgs....44 C3
Brynsadler Rhondd....26 J11
Brynsiencyn IoA....52 G9
Brynteg IoA....52 G6
Bryn-y-bal Flints....54 G14
Bryn-y-Maen Conwy....53 P7
Bryn-yr-Eos Wrexhm....44 G5
Buaichaig Highld....100 D9
Bualintur Highld....100 d7
Buarth-draw Flints....54 E11
Bubbenhall Warwks....37 L5
Bubwith E R Yk....64 G12
Buccleuch Border....75 Q2
Buchanan Smithy Stirlg....88 K8
Buchanhaven Abers....105 U5
Buchanty P & K....90 E6
Buchany Stirlg....89 R5
Buchlyvie Stirlg....89 M6
Buckabank Cumb....67 N3
Buckden Cambs....38 J7
Buckden N York....62 K4
Buckenham Norfk....51 Q13
Buckerell Devon....6 F4
Buckfast Devon....5 S7
Buckfastleigh Devon....5 S7
Buckhaven Fife....91 M13
Buckholt Mons....27 U4
Buckhorn Devon....14 J13
Buckhorn Weston Dorset....17 U12
Buckhurst Hill Essex....21 U4
Buckie Moray....104 E2
Buckingham Bucks....30 F6
Buckland Bucks....30 J10
Buckland Devon....5 R11
Buckland Gloucs....36 E13
Buckland Hants....9 L9
Buckland Herts....31 U5
Buckland Kent....13 R6
Buckland Oxon....29 R8
Buckland Surrey....21 M12
Buckland Brewer Devon....14 K8
Buckland Common Bucks....30 K11
Buckland Dinham Somset....17 U6
Buckland Filleigh Devon....15 L11
Buckland in the Moor Devon....5 S6
Buckland Monachorum Devon....5 M7
Buckland Newton Dorset....7 S3
Buckland Ripers Dorset....7 S8
Buckland St Mary Somset....6 J2

Buckland-Tout-Saints Devon....5 T11
Bucklebury W Berk....19 S6
Bucklers Hard Hants....9 N9
Bucklesham Suffk....41 M12
Buckley Flints....54 G14
Buckley Green Warwks....36 F7
Buckley Hill Sefton....54 H6
Buckminster Leics....48 C9
Bucknall C Stke....46 B4
Bucknall Lincs....58 K13
Bucknell Oxon....30 C7
Bucknell Shrops....34 J6
Buckpool Moray....104 E2
Bucksburn C Aber....99 R2
Buck's Cross Devon....14 H8
Buckshaw Village Lancs....55 N2
Bucks Green W Susx....10 H4
Buckshill Herts....31 N12
Bucks Horn Oak Hants....10 C2
Buck's Mills Devon....14 H8
Buckton E R Yk....65 Q5
Buckton Herefs....34 J6
Buckton Nthumb....85 R11
Buckworth Cambs....38 H5
Budby Notts....57 S13
Budd's Titson Cnwll....14 F11
Bude Cnwll....14 F11
Budge's Shop Cnwll....4 J9
Budlake Devon....6 C5
Budle Nthumb....85 T11
Budleigh Salterton Devon....6 E8
Budlett's Common E Susx....11 R6
Budock Water Cnwll....2 K10
Buerton Ches E....45 Q5
Bugbrooke Nhants....37 S9
Buglawton Ches E....56 C14
Bugle Cnwll....3 Q5
Bugley Dorset....17 U12
Bugthorpe E R Yk....64 H8
Buildwas Shrops....45 P13
Builth Road Powys....34 B10
Builth Wells Powys....34 B10
Bulbourne Herts....30 K10
Bulby Lincs....48 G8
Bulcote Notts....47 R5
Buldoo Highld....112 A3
Bulford Wilts....18 J12
Bulford Camp Wilts....18 J12
Bulkeley Ches E....45 M3
Bulkington Warwks....37 L3
Bulkington Wilts....18 D9
Bulkworthy Devon....14 J10
Bullamoor N York....70 E13
Bullbridge Derbys....47 L3
Bullbrook Br For....20 E9
Bullen's Green Herts....31 R11
Bulley Gloucs....28 E4
Bullgill Cumb....66 G5
Bullinghope Herefs....35 L13
Bullington Hants....19 Q12
Bullington Lincs....58 J11
Bull's Green Herts....31 S9
Bull's Green Norfk....41 R2
Bulmer Essex....40 D12
Bulmer N York....64 F6
Bulmer Tye Essex....40 D13
Bulphan Thurr....22 F10
Bulstone Devon....6 G7
Bulverhythe E Susx....12 E14
Bulwark Abers....105 P5
Bulwell C Nott....47 Q5
Bulwick Nhants....38 E2
Bumble's Green Essex....22 B6
Bunacaimb Highld....93 R2
Bunarkaig Highld....101 T14
Bunbury Ches E....45 N3
Bunbury Heath Ches E....45 N3
Bunchrew Highld....102 J6
Buncton W Susx....10 J7
Bundalloch Highld....101 M6
Bunessan Ag & B....86 H2
Bungay Suffk....41 Q3
Bunker's Hill Lincs....49 L2
Bunnahabhain Ag & B....78 F2
Bunny Notts....47 Q8
Buntait Highld....102 D8
Buntingford Herts....31 U6
Bunwell Norfk....40 K1
Bunwell Hill Norfk....40 K1
Bupton Derbys....46 G5
Burbage Derbys....56 F12
Burbage Leics....37 N2
Burbage Wilts....18 K8
Burcher Herefs....34 J9
Burchett's Green E Susx....11 U4
Burchett's Green W & M....20 D6
Burcombe Wilts....8 F2
Burcot Oxon....19 S2
Burcot Worcs....36 C6
Burcote Shrops....35 S2
Burcott Bucks....30 H8
Burcott Bucks....30 J9
Burdale N York....64 J7
Bures Essex....40 F13
Burford Oxon....29 Q5
Burford Shrops....35 M7
Burg Ag & B....92 J10
Burgate Hants....8 H5
Burgate Suffk....40 J6
Burgates Hants....10 B5
Burgess Hill W Susx....11 M6
Burgh Suffk....41 M10
Burgh by Sands Cumb....67 N1
Burgh Castle Norfk....51 S13
Burghclere Hants....19 Q8
Burghead Moray....103 T2
Burghfield W Berk....19 U7
Burghfield Common W Berk....19 U7
Burgh Heath Surrey....21 M11
Burghill Herefs....34 K11
Burgh Hill E Susx....12 D10
Burgh le Marsh Lincs....59 T13
Burgh next Aylsham Norfk....51 M8
Burgh on Bain Lincs....59 M9
Burgh St Margaret Norfk....51 S11
Burgh St Peter Norfk....41 S2
Burghwallis Donc....57 R4
Burham Kent....12 D3
Buriton Hants....9 U4
Burland Ches E....45 P3
Burlawn Cnwll....3 P2
Burleigh Gloucs....28 G7
Burlescombe Devon....16 E13
Burleston Dorset....7 U5
Burlestone Devon....5 U11
Burley Hants....8 J8
Burley Rutlnd....48 B11
Burley Shrops....35 L5
Burleydam Ches E....45 P5
Burley Gate Herefs....35 N11
Burley in Wharfedale C Brad....63 P10
Burley Lawn Hants....8 J8
Burley Street Hants....8 J8
Burley Wood Head C Brad....63 P10
Burlingjobb Powys....34 G10
Burlington Shrops....45 S11
Burlton Shrops....45 L8
Burmarsh Kent....13 M9
Burmington Warwks....36 J13
Burn N York....57 S1
Burnage Manch....56 C8
Burnaston Derbys....46 J7
Burnbanks Cumb....67 R9
Burnbrae N Lans....82 G6
Burn Cross Sheff....57 M7
Burndell W Susx....10 F9
Burnden Bolton....55 R5
Burnedge Rochdl....56 D4
Burneside Cumb....67 R13
Burness Ork....106 v15
Burneston N York....63 S2
Burnett BaNES....17 S3
Burnfoot Border....75 S4
Burnfoot Border....75 U2
Burnfoot D & G....74 J8
Burnfoot D & G....74 K7
Burnfoot D & G....75 N7
Burnfoot P & K....90 D9
Burnham Bucks....20 F6
Burnham N Linc....58 J4
Burnham Deepdale Norfk....50 D5
Burnham Green Herts....31 S9
Burnham Market Norfk....50 D5
Burnham Norton Norfk....50 D5
Burnham-on-Crouch Essex....23 M7
Burnham-on-Sea Somset....16 K7
Burnham Overy Norfk....50 D5
Burnham Overy Staithe Norfk....50 D5
Burnham Thorpe Norfk....50 E5
Burnhaven Abers....105 U6
Burnhead D & G....74 F6
Burnhervie Abers....105 L12
Burnhill Green Staffs....45 S13
Burnhope Dur....69 Q3
Burnhouse N Ayrs....81 L3
Burniston N York....65 N1
Burnley Lancs....62 G13
Burnley Crematorium Lancs....62 G13
Burnmouth Border....85 P6
Burn Naze Lancs....61 Q11
Burn of Cambus Stirlg....89 R5
Burnopfield Dur....69 Q1
Burnsall N York....63 L7
Burnside Angus....98 G12
Burnside Angus....98 J13
Burnside Fife....90 J11
Burnside Moray....103 U3
Burnside W Loth....82 K3
Burnside of Duntrune Angus....91 P5
Burntcommon Surrey....20 H12
Burnt Heath Essex....23 Q2
Burnthouse Cnwll....2 K10
Burnt Hill W Berk....19 S6
Burnt Houses Dur....69 Q8
Burntisland Fife....83 N1
Burnt Oak E Susx....11 S5
Burntwood Staffs....46 E12
Burntwood Green Staffs....46 E12
Burnt Yates N York....63 R7
Burnworthy Somset....16 G13
Burpham Surrey....20 H12
Burpham W Susx....10 G9
Burradon Nthumb....76 K4
Burradon N Tyne....77 R11
Burrafirth Shet....106 w2
Burras Cnwll....2 H10
Burraton Cnwll....5 L8
Burravoe Shet....106 v6
Burrells Cumb....68 E10
Burrelton P & K....90 J5
Burridge Devon....15 Q6
Burridge Hants....9 Q6
Burrill N York....63 Q2
Burringham N Linc....58 D5
Burrington Devon....15 Q9
Burrington Herefs....34 K6
Burrington N Som....17 N5
Burrough End Cambs....39 U9
Burrough Green Cambs....39 U9
Burrough on the Hill Leics....47 U11
Burrow Lancs....62 C4
Burrow Somset....16 B8
Burrow Bridge Somset....16 K10
Burrowhill Surrey....20 G10
Burrow Cross Surrey....20 G10
Burry Swans....25 R10
Burry Green Swans....25 R11
Burry Port Carmth....25 R10
Burscough Lancs....54 K4
Burscough Bridge Lancs....54 K4
Bursea E R Yk....64 H13
Burshill E R Yk....65 P10
Bursledon Hants....9 P7
Burslem C Stke....45 U4
Burstall Suffk....40 J12
Burstock Dorset....7 M3
Burston Norfk....40 K4
Burston Staffs....46 B7
Burstow Surrey....11 N3
Burstwick E R Yk....65 T14
Burtersett N York....62 J2
Burthorpe Green Suffk....40 C8
Burthwaite Cumb....67 P3
Burtle Somset....17 L8
Burtoft Lincs....49 L6
Burton BCP....8 H9
Burton Ches W....54 H12
Burton Ches W....45 M2
Burton Dorset....7 U7
Burton Nthumb....85 T11
Burton Pembks....24 G9
Burton Somset....16 G8
Burton Wilts....18 B5
Burton Wilts....17 V10
Burton Agnes E R Yk....65 Q8
Burton Bradstock Dorset....7 N7
Burton Coggles Lincs....48 E9
Burton Dassett Warwks....37 L10
Burton End Essex....22 D3
Burton End Suffk....39 U11
Burton Fleming E R Yk....65 Q5
Burton Green Warwks....36 H5
Burton Green Wrexhm....44 H2
Burton Hastings Warwks....37 M3
Burton-in-Kendal Cumb....61 U4
Burton-in-Lonsdale N York....62 C5
Burton Joyce Notts....47 R5
Burton Latimer Nhants....38 C6
Burton Lazars Leics....47 U10
Burton Leonard N York....63 S7
Burton on the Wolds Leics....47 R9
Burton Overy Leics....47 S14
Burton Pedwardine Lincs....48 H5
Burton Pidsea E R Yk....65 S13
Burton Salmon N York....57 R1
Burton's Green Essex....22 K3
Burton upon Stather N Linc....58 E3
Burton upon Trent Staffs....46 H9
Burtonwood Warrtn....55 N8
Burtonwood Services Warrtn....55 N8
Burwardsley Ches W....45 M2
Burwarton Shrops....35 P4
Burwash E Susx....12 C11
Burwash Common E Susx....11 V6
Burwash Weald E Susx....11 V6
Burwell Cambs....39 S8
Burwell Lincs....59 Q11
Burwen IoA....52 F3
Burwick Ork....106 t21
Bury Bury....55 S4
Bury Cambs....39 L4
Bury Somset....16 C11
Bury W Susx....10 G7
Bury End Bucks....30 K5
Bury Green Herts....22 B3
Bury St Edmunds Suffk....40 D7
Burythorpe N York....64 H7
Busby E Rens....81 R2
Busby P & K....90 F6
Buscot Oxon....29 P8
Bush Abers....99 N8
Bush Cnwll....14 F11
Bush Bank Herefs....35 L10
Bushbury Wolves....46 B13
Bushby Leics....47 S13
Bushey Herts....31 N12
Bushey Heath Herts....31 N12
Bush Green Norfk....41 L3
Bush Hill Park Gt Lon....21 Q4
Bushley Worcs....35 U13
Bushley Green Worcs....35 U13
Bushmead Bed....38 H8
Bushmoor Shrops....34 K3
Bushton Wilts....18 G5
Bushy Common Norfk....50 G11
Busk Cumb....68 D4
Buslingthorpe Lincs....58 H9
Bussage Gloucs....28 G7
Bussex Somset....16 K9
Busta Shet....106 s7
Butcher Haugh Highld....108 K5
Butcher's Cross E Susx....11 T5
Butcher's Pasture Essex....22 F3
Butcombe N Som....17 P4
Bute Town Caerph....27 L6
Butleigh Somset....17 P10
Butleigh Wootton Somset....17 P9
Butlers Marston Warwks....36 K11
Butley Suffk....41 Q11
Butley High Corner Suffk....41 Q12
Butlocks Heath Hants....9 P7
Butterbank Staffs....45 U9
Buttercrambe N York....64 G8
Butterknowle Dur....69 Q8
Butterleigh Devon....6 C3
Buttermere Cumb....66 K9
Buttermere Wilts....19 M8
Buttershaw C Brad....63 N14
Butterstone P & K....90 F3
Butterton Staffs....46 C2
Butterton Staffs....45 U4
Butterwick Dur....70 E6
Butterwick Lincs....49 N4
Butterwick N York....64 J4
Butterwick N York....65 L5
Butt Green Ches E....45 Q3
Buttington Powys....44 F12
Buttonoak Shrops....35 S5
Buttonbridge Shrops....35 S5
Buttsash Hants....9 N7
Butt's Green Essex....22 H6
Buttsole Kent....13 Q5
Buxhall Suffk....40 H9
Buxhall Fen Street Suffk....40 H9
Buxted E Susx....11 R6
Buxton Derbys....56 F12
Buxton Norfk....51 M9
Buxton Heath Norfk....50 K9
Bwlch Powys....27 L3
Bwlch-derwin Gwynd....42 J4
Bwlchgwyn Wrexhm....44 G3
Bwlchllan Cerdgn....33 L9

Bwlchnewydd Carmth 25 Q6
Bwlchtocyn Gwynd 42 F8
Bwlch-y-cibau Powys 44 E10
Bwlch-y-Ddar Powys 44 E9
Bwlchyfadfa Cerdgn 32 H11
Bwlch-y-ffridd Powys 34 C1
Bwlch-y-groes Pembks 25 M3
Bwlchymyrdd Swans 25 U11
Bwlch-y-sarnau Powys 34 B6
Byermoor Gatesd 69 Q1
Byers Green Dur 69 R6
Byfield Nhants 37 P10
Byfleet Surrey 20 J10
Byford Herefs 34 J12
Bygrave Herts 31 S5
Byker N u Ty 77 R13
Byland Abbey N York 64 C4
Bylchau Conwy 53 S10
Byley Ches W 55 R13
Bynea Carmth 25 T11
Byrness Nthumb 76 F5
Bystock Devon 6 D8
Bythorn Cambs 38 G5
Byton Herefs 34 J8
Bywell Nthumb 77 L13
Byworth W Susx 10 F6

C

Cabbacott Devon 14 K8
Cabourne Lincs 58 K6
Cabrach Ag & B 78 H3
Cabrach Moray 104 D10
Cabus Lancs 61 T10
Cackle Street E Susx 11 R5
Cackle Street E Susx 12 C12
Cackle Street E Susx 12 F12
Cadbury Devon 6 B3
Cadbury Barton Devon 15 Q9
Cadbury World Birm 36 D4
Cadder E Duns 89 P11
Caddington C Beds 31 N9
Caddonfoot Border 84 D11
Cadeby Donc 57 R6
Cadeby Leics 47 M13
Cadeleigh Devon 6 B3
Cade Street E Susx 11 U6
Cadgwith Cnwll 2 J14
Cadham Fife 91 L11
Cadishead Salfd 55 R8
Cadle Swans 25 V11
Cadley Lancs 61 U13
Cadley Wilts 18 K10
Cadley Wilts 18 K7
Cadmore End Bucks 20 C4
Cadnam Hants 9 L6
Cadney N Linc 58 H6
Cadole Flints 54 F14
Cadoxton V Glam 16 F3
Cadoxton Juxta-Neath Neath 26 D8
Cadwst Denbgs 44 B6
Caeathro Gwynd 52 H10
Caehopkin Powys 26 E5
Caenby Lincs 58 G9
Caeo Carmth 33 N12
Caerau Brdgnd 26 F9
Caerau Cardif 27 L12
Cae'r-bont Powys 26 E5
Cae'r bryn Carmth 25 U8
Caerdeon Gwynd 43 N10
Caer Farchell Pembks 24 C5
Caergeiliog IoA 52 D7
Caergwrle Flints 44 H2
Caerhun Conwy 53 N8
Caerlanrig Border 75 S5
Caerleon Newpt 27 Q9
Caernarfon Gwynd 52 G10
Caernarfon Castle Gwynd 52 G10
Caerphilly Caerph 27 M10
Caersws Powys 34 B2
Caerwedros Cerdgn 32 G9
Caerwent Mons 27 T9
Caerwys Flints 54 D12
Caerynwch Gwynd 43 Q10
Caggle Street Mons 27 R4
Caim IoA 52 K6
Cairinis W Isls 106 d12
Cairnbaan Ag & B 87 Q7
Cairnbulg Abers 105 S2
Cairncross Border 85 M6
Cairncurran Inver 88 H11
Cairndow Ag & B 88 E3
Cairneyhill Fife 82 K1
Cairngarroch D & G 72 D10
Cairngorms National Park 97 T3
Cairnie Abers 104 F7
Cairnorrie Abers 105 P7
Cairnryan D & G 72 D6
Cairnty Moray 104 C5
Caister-on-Sea Norfk 51 T11
Caistor Lincs 58 K6
Caistor St Edmund Norfk 51 M13
Cakebole Worcs 35 U6
Cake Street Norfk 40 J2
Calais Street Suffk 40 G13
Calanais W Isls 106 h5
Calbourne IoW 9 N11
Calceby Lincs 59 Q11
Calcot Flints 54 E12
Calcot Gloucs 29 L5
Calcot W Berk 19 U6
Calcot Row W Berk 19 U6
Calcots Moray 104 B3
Calcott Kent 13 N3
Calcott Shrops 44 K11
Calcutt N York 63 S8
Calcutt Wilts 29 M9
Caldbeck Cumb 67 M4
Caldbergh N York 63 M2
Caldecote Cambs 38 H3
Caldecote Cambs 39 M9
Caldecote Herts 31 R5
Caldecote Nhants 37 S10
Caldecote Highfields Cambs 39 N9
Caldecott Nhants 38 E7
Caldecott Oxon 29 U8
Caldecott Rutlnd 38 C2
Caldecotte M Keyn 30 J5
Calder Cumb 66 F12
Calderbank N Lans 82 E6
Calder Bridge Cumb 66 F11
Calderbrook Rochdl 56 D3
Caldercruix N Lans 82 F5
Calder Grove Wakefd 57 M3
Caldermill S Lans 81 T4
Caldermore Rochdl 56 D3
Calder Vale Lancs 61 U10
Calderwood S Lans 81 T1
Caldey Island Pembks 24 K11
Caldicot Mons 27 T10
Caldmore Wsall 46 D14
Caldwell N York 69 Q10
Caldy Wirral 54 F9
Caledfwlch Carmth 26 B2
Calenick Cnwll 3 L8
Calf of Man IoM 60 b9
Calford Green Suffk 40 B11
Calfsound Ork 106 u16
Calgary Ag & B 92 K8
Califer Moray 103 S4
California Falk 82 H3
California Norfk 51 T10
California Cross Devon 5 S10
Calke Derbys 47 L9
Calke Abbey Derbys 47 L9
Callakille Highld 107 L13
Callander Stirlg 89 P4
Callanish W Isls 106 h5
Callaughton Shrops 45 P14
Callestick Cnwll 2 K6
Calligarry Highld 100 f9
Callington Cnwll 4 K7
Callingwood Staffs 46 G9
Callow Herefs 35 L14
Callow End Worcs 35 T10
Callow Hill Wilts 28 K11
Callow Hill Worcs 35 R6
Callow Hill Worcs 36 D8
Callows Grave Worcs 35 N7
Calmore Hants 9 L6
Calmsden Gloucs 28 K6
Calne Wilts 18 E6
Calow Derbys 57 P12
Calshot Hants 9 P8
Calstock Cnwll 5 L7
Calstone Wellington Wilts 18 F7
Calthorpe Norfk 51 L7
Calthorpe Street Norfk 51 R8
Calthwaite Cumb 67 Q4
Calton N York 62 J8
Calton Staffs 46 F4
Calveley Ches E 45 N2
Calver Derbys 56 K12
Calverhall Shrops 45 P6
Calver Hill Herefs 34 J11
Calverleigh Devon 6 B2
Calverley Leeds 63 Q12
Calver Sough Derbys 56 K12
Calvert Bucks 30 E8
Calverton M Keyn 30 G5
Calverton Notts 47 R4
Calvine P & K 97 N10
Calvo Cumb 66 H2
Calzeat Border 83 M11
Cam Gloucs 28 E8
Camasachoirce Highld 93 T6
Camasine Highld 93 T6
Camas Luinie Highld 101 N6
Camastianavaig Highld 100 e6
Camault Muir Highld 102 F7
Camber E Susx 12 J12
Camberley Surrey 20 E10
Camberwell Gt Lon 21 P7
Camblesforth N York 57 T1
Cambo Nthumb 77 L8
Cambois Nthumb 77 S9
Camborne Cnwll 2 G8
Camborne and Redruth Mining District Cnwll 2 G8
Cambourne Cambs 39 M9
Cambridge Cambs 39 Q9
Cambridge Gloucs 28 D7
Cambridge Airport Cambs 39 Q9
Cambridge City Crematorium Cambs 39 N8
Cambrose Cnwll 2 H7
Cambus Clacks 90 C13
Cambusavie Platform Highld 109 P5
Cambusbarron Stirlg 89 S7
Cambuskenneth Stirlg 89 T7
Cambuslang S Lans 89 P13
Cambus o' May Abers 98 G4
Cambuswallace S Lans 82 K11
Camden Town Gt Lon 21 N6
Cameley BaNES 17 R5
Camelford Cnwll 4 E4
Camelon Falk 82 G2
Camerory Highld 103 R9
Camer's Green Worcs 35 S13
Camerton BaNES 17 S5
Camerton Cumb 66 F6
Camghouran P & K 95 R7
Camieston Border 84 F12
Cammachmore Abers 99 S4
Cammeringham Lincs 58 F10
Camore Highld 109 P7
Campbeltown Ag & B 79 N11
Campbeltown Airport Ag & B 79 M11
Camperdown N Tyne 77 R11
Cample D & G 74 G7
Campmuir P & K 90 K4
Camps W Loth 83 L5
Campsall Donc 57 R4
Campsea Ash Suffk 41 P9
Camps End Cambs 39 T12
Campton C Beds 31 P5
Camptown Border 76 D3
Camrose Pembks 24 F6
Camserney P & K 90 B2
Camusnagaul Highld 94 F4
Camusnagaul Highld 107 U7
Camusteel Highld 100 g5
Camusterrach Highld 100 g5
Canada Hants 8 K5
Canal Foot Cumb 61 Q4
Canaston Bridge Pembks 24 J7
Candacraig Abers 98 E4
Candlesby Lincs 59 S13
Candle Street Suffk 40 H6
Candover Green Shrops 45 M12
Candy Mill Border 83 L10
Cane End Oxon 19 U5
Canewdon Essex 23 M9
Canford Bottom Dorset 8 E8
Canford Cliffs Poole 8 F11
Canford Crematorium Bristl 27 V12
Canford Heath Poole 8 E10
Canford Magna Poole 8 E9
Canhams Green Suffk 40 J7
Canisbay Highld 112 H2
Canklow Rothm 57 P8
Canley Covtry 36 K5
Canley Crematorium Covtry 36 K5
Cann Dorset 8 B4
Canna Highld 100 b9
Cannich Highld 102 B9
Cannington Somset 16 J9
Canning Town Gt Lon 21 R6
Cannock Staffs 46 C11
Cannock Chase Staffs 46 C10
Cannock Wood Staffs 46 D11
Cannon Bridge Herefs 34 K12
Canonbie D & G 75 S10
Canon Frome Herefs 35 P12
Canon Pyon Herefs 35 L11
Canons Ashby Nhants 37 Q10
Canonstown Cnwll 2 E9
Canterbury Kent 13 M4
Canterbury Cathedral Kent 13 N4
Cantley Norfk 51 Q13
Cantlop Shrops 45 M12
Canton Cardif 27 M12
Cantraywood Highld 103 L6
Cantsfield Lancs 62 C5
Canvey Island Essex 22 J11
Canwick Lincs 58 G13
Canworthy Water Cnwll 4 G2
Caol Highld 94 G3
Caolas Scalpaigh W Isls 106 h9
Caoles Ag & B 92 D9
Caonich Highld 101 R13
Capel Kent 12 B7
Capel Surrey 10 K2
Capel Bangor Cerdgn 33 N4
Capel Betws Lleucu Cerdgn 33 M9
Capel Coch IoA 52 G6
Capel Curig Conwy 53 M11
Capel Cynon Cerdgn 32 G11
Capel Dewi Carmth 25 S6
Capel Dewi Cerdgn 32 J12
Capel-Dewi Cerdgn 33 M4
Capel Garmon Conwy 53 P11
Capel Green Suffk 41 Q11
Capel Gwyn Carmth 25 S6
Capel Gwyn IoA 52 D7
Capel Gwynfe Carmth 26 C3
Capel Hendre Carmth 25 U8
Capel Isaac Carmth 25 U5
Capel Iwan Carmth 25 N3
Capel le Ferne Kent 13 Q8
Capelles Guern 6 d2
Capel Llanilltern Cardif 26 K12
Capel Mawr IoA 52 F8
Capel Parc IoA 52 F5
Capel St Andrew Suffk 41 Q11
Capel St Mary Suffk 40 J13
Capel Seion Cerdgn 33 M5
Capel Trisant Cerdgn 33 P5
Capeluchaf Gwynd 42 H4
Capelulo Conwy 53 M7
Capel-y-ffin Powys 27 P1
Capel-y-graig Gwynd 52 H9
Capenhurst Ches W 54 J12
Capernwray Lancs 61 U5
Capheaton Nthumb 77 L9
Caplaw E Rens 88 K14
Capon's Green Suffk 41 N7
Cappercleuch Border 83 P14
Capstone Medway 12 E2
Capton Devon 5 U10
Capton Somset 16 E9
Caputh P & K 90 G3
Caradon Mining District Cnwll 4 G6
Caradon Town Cnwll 4 H6
Carbeth Inn Stirlg 89 M10
Carbis Cnwll 3 Q5
Carbis Bay Cnwll 2 E9
Carbost Highld 100 c6
Carbost Highld 100 d5
Carbrook Sheff 57 N9
Carbrooke Norfk 50 F13
Carburton Notts 57 T12
Carclaze Cnwll 3 Q6
Car Colston Notts 47 T5
Carcroft Donc 57 R5
Cardenden Fife 90 K12
Cardeston Shrops 44 J11
Cardewlees Cumb 67 N2
Cardhu Moray 103 U7
Cardiff Cardif 27 M12
Cardiff Airport V Glam 16 E3
Cardiff Gate Services Cardif 27 N11
Cardiff West Services Cardif 26 K12
Cardigan Cerdgn 32 C11
Cardinal's Green Cambs 39 T11
Cardington Bed 38 G11
Cardington Shrops 35 M1
Cardinham Cnwll 4 E7
Cardrain D & G 72 E13
Cardrona Border 83 R11
Cardross Ag & B 88 H10
Cardross Crematorium Ag & B 88 H10
Cardryne D & G 72 E13
Cardurnock Cumb 75 N14
Careby Lincs 48 F10
Careston Angus 98 J11
Carew Pembks 24 H10
Carew Cheriton Pembks 24 H10
Carew Newton Pembks 24 H10
Carey Herefs 27 V1
Carfin N Lans 82 E7
Carfraemill Border 84 E8
Cargate Green Norfk 51 Q11
Cargenbridge D & G 74 J10
Cargill P & K 90 J4
Cargo Cumb 75 S14
Cargreen Cnwll 5 L8
Cargurrel Cnwll 3 M9
Carham Nthumb 84 K11
Carhampton Somset 16 D8
Carharrack Cnwll 2 J8
Carie P & K 95 S7
Carinish W Isls 106 d12
Carisbrooke IoW 9 P11
Cark Cumb 61 R4
Carkeel Cnwll 5 L8
Carlabhagh W Isls 106 h4
Carland Cross Cnwll 3 M6
Carlbury Darltn 69 R9
Carlby Lincs 48 F11
Carlcroft Nthumb 76 G3
Carlecotes Barns 56 J6
Carleen Cnwll 2 G10
Carlesmoor N York 63 Q5
Carleton Cumb 66 F11
Carleton Cumb 67 P2
Carleton Cumb 67 R7
Carleton Lancs 61 Q12
Carleton N York 62 K10
Carleton Wakefd 57 Q2
Carleton Crematorium Bpool 61 Q12
Carleton Forehoe Norfk 50 J12
Carleton Rode Norfk 40 K2
Carleton St Peter Norfk 51 P13
Carlidnack Cnwll 2 K11
Carlincraig Abers 104 K7
Carlingcott BaNES 17 S5
Carlin How R & Cl 71 M9
Carlisle Cumb 67 N1
Carlisle Airport Cumb 75 U13
Carlisle Crematorium Cumb 67 N2
Carloggas Cnwll 3 M3
Carlops Border 83 N7
Carloway W Isls 106 h4
Carlton Barns 57 N4
Carlton Bed 38 E9
Carlton Cambs 39 T10
Carlton Leeds 57 M1
Carlton Leics 47 L13
Carlton N York 57 T2
Carlton N York 63 M3
Carlton N York 64 E2
Carlton Notts 47 R5
Carlton S on T 70 E8
Carlton Suffk 41 Q8
Carlton Colville Suffk 41 T3
Carlton Curlieu Leics 37 S1
Carlton Green Cambs 39 T10
Carlton Husthwaite N York 64 B4
Carlton-in-Cleveland N York 70 H12
Carlton in Lindrick Notts 57 S10
Carlton-le-Moorland Lincs 48 D2
Carlton Miniott N York 63 T3
Carlton-on-Trent Notts 58 C14
Carlton Scroop Lincs 48 D4
Carluke S Lans 82 F8
Carlyon Bay Cnwll 3 R6
Carmacoup S Lans 82 E13
Carmarthen Carmth 25 R6
Carmel Carmth 25 U7
Carmel Flints 54 E11
Carmel Gwynd 52 G12
Carmichael S Lans 82 H11
Carmountside Crematorium C Stke 46 B4
Carmunnock C Glas 89 N14
Carmyle C Glas 89 P13
Carmyllie Angus 91 R3
Carnaby E R Yk 65 Q6
Carnbee Fife 91 R10
Carnbo P & K 90 G11
Carn Brea Cnwll 2 H8
Carnbrogie Abers 105 P10
Carndu Highld 101 M6
Carnduff S Lans 81 T3
Carne Cnwll 2 K12
Carne Cnwll 3 N9
Carne Cnwll 3 P5
Carnell E Ayrs 81 P6
Carnewas Cnwll 3 M3
Carnforth Lancs 61 T5
Carn-gorm Highld 101 P7
Carnhedryn Pembks 24 D5
Carnhell Green Cnwll 2 G9
Carnie Abers 99 Q2
Carnkie Cnwll 2 H8
Carnkie Cnwll 2 J10
Carnkiet Cnwll 2 K6
Carno Powys 33 U1
Carnock Fife 90 F14
Carnon Downs Cnwll 2 K8
Carnousie Abers 104 K5
Carnoustie Angus 91 S5
Carnsmerry Cnwll 3 Q5
Carnwath S Lans 82 J9
Carnyorth Cnwll 2 B10
Carol Green Solhll 36 J5
Carpalla Cnwll 3 P6
Carperby N York 63 L2
Carr Rothm 57 R8
Carradale Ag & B 79 Q8
Carrbridge Highld 103 P11
Carrbrook Tamesd 56 E6
Carrefour Jersey 7 c2
Carreglefn IoA 52 E5
Carr Gate Wakefd 57 M2
Carrhouse N Linc 58 C5
Carrick Ag & B 87 S8
Carrick Castle Ag & B 88 E7
Carriden Falk 82 K2
Carrington Lincs 49 M2
Carrington Mdloth 83 R6
Carrington Traffd 55 R8
Carrog Conwy 43 Q4
Carrog Denbgs 44 D5
Carron Falk 82 G2
Carron Moray 103 V7
Carronbridge D & G 74 G6
Carron Bridge Stirlg 89 R9
Carronshore Falk 82 G2
Carrow Hill Mons 27 S9
Carr Shield Nthumb 68 H3
Carrutherstown D & G 75 M11
Carruth House Inver 88 J12
Carr Vale Derbys 57 Q13
Carrville Dur 70 D4
Carsaig Ag & B 86 J1
Carseriggan D & G 72 J6
Carsethorn D & G 74 J14
Carshalton Gt Lon 21 N10
Carsington Derbys 46 J3
Carskey Ag & B 79 M14
Carsluith D & G 73 M9
Carsphairn D & G 81 R14
Carstairs S Lans 82 H9
Carstairs Junction S Lans 82 J9
Carswell Marsh Oxon 29 R8
Carter's Clay Hants 9 L4
Carters Green Essex 22 D5
Carterton Oxon 29 Q6
Carterway Heads Nthumb 69 M2
Carthew Cnwll 3 Q5
Carthorpe N York 63 S3
Cartington Nthumb 77 L5
Cartland S Lans 82 G9
Cartledge Derbys 57 M11
Cartmel Cumb 61 R4
Cartmel Fell Cumb 61 S2
Carway Carmth 25 S9
Carwinley Cumb 75 T11
Cashe's Green Gloucs 28 F6
Cashmoor Dorset 8 D6
Cassington Oxon 29 U5
Cassop Colliery Dur 70 D5
Castallack Cnwll 2 D11
Castel Guern 6 d3
Castell Conwy 53 N9
Castell-y-bwch Torfn 27 P9
Casterton Cumb 62 C4
Castle Cnwll 3 R5
Castle Acre Norfk 50 D10
Castle Ashby Nhants 38 C9
Castlebay W Isls 106 b19
Castle Bolton N York 63 L1
Castle Bromwich Solhll 36 F3
Castle Bytham Lincs 48 E10
Castlebythe Pembks 24 H5
Castle Caereinion Powys 44 E12
Castle Camps Cambs 39 T12
Castle Carrock Cumb 67 R1
Castlecary Falk 89 S10
Castle Cary Somset 17 R10
Castle Combe Wilts 18 B5
Castle Donington Leics 47 M8
Castle Douglas D & G 74 E13
Castle Eaton Swindn 29 M8
Castle Eden Dur 70 F5
Castle End C Pete 48 H12
Castleford Wakefd 57 P1
Castle Frome Herefs 35 Q11
Castle Gate Cnwll 2 D10
Castle Green Cumb 61 U1
Castle Green Surrey 20 G10
Castle Gresley Derbys 46 J10
Castle Hedingham Essex 40 C13
Castlehill Border 83 P11
Castlehill Highld 112 E3
Castle Hill Kent 12 C7
Castle Hill Suffk 40 K11
Castlehill W Duns 88 J10
Castle Howard N York 64 G5
Castle Kennedy D & G 72 E8
Castle Lachlan Ag & B 87 U6
Castlemartin Pembks 24 F11
Castlemilk C Glas 89 N14
Castle Morris Pembks 24 F4
Castlemorton Worcs 35 S13
Castlemorton Common Worcs 35 S13
Castle O'er D & G 75 P7
Castle Pulverbatch Shrops 44 K13
Castle Rising Norfk 49 U9
Castleside Dur 69 N3
Castle Stuart Highld 102 K6
Castlethorpe M Keyn 30 H4
Castlethorpe N Linc 58 G5
Castleton Border 75 V8
Castleton Derbys 56 J10
Castleton N York 71 L11
Castleton Newpt 27 P11
Castleton Rochdl 56 C4
Castletown Dorset 7 S10
Castletown Highld 112 E3
Castletown IoM 60 d9
Castletown Sundld 77 T14
Castley N York 63 R10
Caston Norfk 50 G14
Castor C Pete 48 H14
Caswell Bay Swans 25 U13
Catacol N Ayrs 79 S6
Cat and Fiddle Derbys 56 F12
Catbrain S Glos 27 V11
Catbrook Mons 27 U7
Catch Flints 54 F12
Catchall Cnwll 2 C11
Catchem's Corner Solhll 36 J5
Catchgate Dur 69 Q2
Catcliffe Rothm 57 P9
Catcomb Wilts 18 F5
Catcott Somset 17 L9
Catcott Burtle Somset 17 M8
Caterham Surrey 21 P11
Catfield Norfk 51 Q9
Catfield Common Norfk 51 R9
Catford Gt Lon 21 Q8
Catforth Lancs 61 T12
Cathcart C Glas 89 N13
Cathedine Powys 27 L2
Catherine-de-Barnes Solhll 36 G4
Catherine Slack C Brad 63 M14
Catherington Hants 9 T6
Catherston Leweston Dorset 7 L6
Catherton Shrops 35 Q5
Catisfield Hants 9 R7
Catley Herefs 35 Q12
Catley Lane Head Rochdl 56 C3
Catlodge Highld 96 J5
Catlow Lancs 62 H12
Catlowdy Cumb 75 U10
Catmere End Essex 39 Q13
Catmore W Berk 19 Q4
Caton Devon 5 T6
Caton Lancs 61 U7
Caton Green Lancs 62 B6
Cator Court Devon 5 R5
Catrine E Ayrs 81 Q7
Cat's Ash Newpt 27 R9
Catsfield E Susx 12 D13
Catsfield Stream E Susx 12 D13
Catsgore Somset 17 P11
Catsham Somset 17 Q10
Catshill Worcs 36 C6
Catstree Shrops 35 R1
Cattadale Ag & B 79 M13
Cattal N York 63 U9
Cattawade Suffk 40 K14
Catterall Lancs 61 T11
Catteralslane Shrops 45 N5
Catterick N York 69 R13
Catterick Bridge N York 69 R13
Catterick Garrison N York 69 Q13
Catterlen Cumb 67 Q6
Catterline Abers 99 R8
Catterton N York 64 C10
Catteshall Surrey 10 F2
Catthorpe Leics 37 Q5
Cattishall Suffk 40 E7
Cattistock Dorset 7 Q5
Catton N York 63 T4
Catton Nthumb 76 G14
Catwick E R Yk 65 Q10
Catworth Cambs 38 G6
Caudle Green Gloucs 28 H5
Caulcott C Beds 31 M4
Caulcott Oxon 30 B8
Cauldcots Angus 91 U2
Cauldhame Stirlg 89 P7
Cauldmill Border 76 A2
Cauldon Staffs 46 E4
Cauldon Lowe Staffs 46 E4
Cauldwell Derbys 46 J10
Caulkerbush D & G 66 D1
Caulside D & G 75 T9
Caundle Marsh Dorset 7 S2
Caunsall Worcs 35 U4
Caunton Notts 47 T1
Causeway Hants 9 U4
Causeway End Cumb 61 T2
Causeway End D & G 73 L8
Causeway End Essex 22 G4
Causewayend S Lans 82 K11
Causewayhead Cumb 66 H2
Causewayhead Stirlg 89 T6
Causeyend Abers 105 Q12
Causey Park Nthumb 77 P7
Causey Park Bridge Nthumb 77 P7
Cavendish Suffk 40 D11
Cavenham Suffk 40 C6
Caversfield Oxon 30 C7
Caversham Readg 20 B8
Caverswall Staffs 46 C5
Caverton Mill Border 84 J13
Cavil E R Yk 64 H13
Cawdor Highld 103 M5
Cawkwell Lincs 59 N11
Cawood N York 64 D12
Cawsand Cnwll 5 L10
Cawston Norfk 50 K9
Cawston Warwks 37 N6
Cawthorn N York 64 H2
Cawthorne Barns 57 L5
Cawton N York 64 E4
Caxton Cambs 39 M9
Caxton End Cambs 39 M9
Caxton Gibbet Cambs 39 L8
Caynham Shrops 35 N6
Caythorpe Lincs 48 D4
Caythorpe Notts 47 S4
Cayton N York 65 P3
Ceann a Bhaigh W Isls 106 c12
Ceannacroc Lodge Highld 101 U9
Cearsiadar W Isls 106 i6
Ceciliford Mons 27 U7
Cefn Newpt 27 P10
Cefn Berain Conwy 53 S9
Cefn-brith Conwy 43 T3
Cefn-bryn-brain Carmth 26 C5
Cefn Byrle Powys 26 E5
Cefn Canel Powys 44 F7
Cefn Coch Powys 44 D8
Cefn-coed-y-cymmer Myr Td 26 J6
Cefn Cribwr Brdgnd 26 F11
Cefn Cross Brdgnd 26 F11
Cefn-ddwysarn Gwynd 43 U6
Cefn-Einion Shrops 34 G3
Cefneithin Carmth 25 U8
Cefngorwydd Powys 33 T11
Cefn-mawr Wrexhm 44 G5
Cefnpennar Rhondd 26 J7
Cefn-y-bedd Flints 44 H2
Cefn-y-pant Carmth 25 L5
Ceint IoA 52 G7
Cellan Cerdgn 33 M11
Cellardyke Fife 91 S11
Cellarhead Staffs 46 C4
Celleron Cumb 67 Q7
Celynen Caerph 27 N8
Cemaes IoA 52 E4
Cemmaes Powys 43 R12
Cemmaes Road Powys 43 R13
Cenarth Cerdgn 32 E12
Cerbyd Pembks 24 D5
Ceres Fife 91 P9
Cerne Abbas Dorset 7 S4
Cerney Wick Gloucs 29 L8
Cerrigceinwen IoA 52 F8
Cerrigydrudion Conwy 43 U4
Cess Norfk 51 R10
Ceunant Gwynd 52 H10
Chaceley Gloucs 28 G1
Chacewater Cnwll 2 K8
Chackmore Bucks 30 E5
Chacombe Nhants 37 N12
Chadbury Worcs 36 D11
Chadderton Oldham 56 D5
Chadderton Fold Oldham 56 D5
Chaddesden C Derb 47 L6
Chaddesley Corbett Worcs 35 U6
Chaddlehanger Devon 5 M5
Chaddleworth W Berk 19 P5
Chadlington Oxon 29 R3
Chadshunt Warwks 36 K10
Chadwell Leics 47 U9
Chadwell Shrops 45 S11
Chadwell End Bed 38 G7
Chadwell Heath Gt Lon 21 S5
Chadwell St Mary Thurr 22 F12
Chadwick Worcs 35 T7
Chadwick End Solhll 36 H6
Chadwick Green St Hel 55 M7
Chaffcombe Somset 7 L2
Chafford Hundred Thurr 22 F12
Chagford Devon 5 S3
Chailey E Susx 11 P7
Chainbridge Cambs 49 P13
Chainhurst Kent 12 D6
Chalbury Dorset 8 E7
Chalbury Common Dorset 8 E7
Chaldon Surrey 21 P11
Chale IoW 9 P13
Chale Green IoW 9 P13
Chalfont Common Bucks 20 H4
Chalfont St Giles Bucks 20 G4
Chalfont St Peter Bucks 20 H4
Chalford Gloucs 28 G7
Chalford Oxon 30 F12
Chalford Wilts 18 C10
Chalgrave C Beds 31 M7
Chalgrove Oxon 30 D13
Chalk Kent 22 G13
Chalk End Essex 22 F5
Chalkhouse Green Oxon 20 B7
Chalkway Somset 7 L3
Chalkwell Kent 12 G3
Challaborough Devon 5 R12
Challacombe Devon 15 Q4
Challoch D & G 72 K6
Challock Kent 12 K5
Chalmington Dorset 7 Q4
Chalton C Beds 31 M7
Chalton C Beds 38 H10
Chalton Hants 9 U5
Chalvey Slough 20 G7
Chalvington E Susx 11 S9
Chambers Green Kent 12 H7
Chandler's Cross Herts 20 J3
Chandlers Cross Worcs 35 S13
Chandler's Ford Hants 9 N5
Channel's End Bed 38 H9
Chanterlands Crematorium C KuH 65 P13
Chantry Somset 17 T7
Chantry Suffk 40 K12
Chapel Cumb 66 K6
Chapel Fife 91 L13
Chapel Allerton Leeds 63 S12
Chapel Allerton Somset 17 M6
Chapel Amble Cnwll 3 P1
Chapel Brampton Nhants 37 T7
Chapelbridge Cambs 39 L2
Chapel Chorlton Staffs 45 T6
Chapel Cross E Susx 11 U6
Chapel End Bed 38 H9
Chapel End C Beds 31 N4
Chapel End Cambs 38 H4
Chapel End Warwks 36 K2
Chapelend Way Essex 40 B13
Chapel-en-le-Frith Derbys 56 G10
Chapel Field Bury 55 S5
Chapelgate Lincs 49 P9
Chapel Green Warwks 36 J3
Chapel Green Warwks 37 N8
Chapel Haddlesey N York 57 S1
Chapelhall N Lans 82 E6
Chapel Hill Abers 105 T8
Chapel Hill Lincs 48 K3
Chapel Hill Mons 27 U8
Chapel Hill N York 63 S10
Chapelhope Border 75 P2
Chapelknowe D & G 75 R11
Chapel Lawn Shrops 34 H5
Chapel le Dale N York 62 E4
Chapel Leigh Somset 16 F11
Chapel Milton Derbys 56 G10
Chapel of Garioch Abers 105 L11
Chapel Rossan D & G 72 E11
Chapel Row E Susx 11 U8
Chapel Row Essex 22 J7
Chapel Row W Berk 19 S7
Chapels Cumb 61 N3
Chapel St Leonards Lincs 59 U12
Chapel Stile Cumb 67 M11
Chapelton Angus 91 T2
Chapelton Devon 15 N7
Chapelton S Lans 82 C9
Chapeltown Bl w D 55 R3
Chapel Town Cnwll 3 M5
Chapeltown Moray 104 A11
Chapeltown Sheff 57 N7
Chapmanslade Wilts 18 B11
Chapmans Well Devon 4 K2
Chapmore End Herts 31 T9
Chappel Essex 23 L2
Charaton Cnwll 4 J7
Chard Somset 6 K3
Chard Junction Somset 6 K4
Chardleigh Green Somset 6 K2
Chardstock Devon 6 K4
Charfield S Glos 28 D9
Chargrove Gloucs 28 H4
Charing Kent 12 J6
Charing Crematorium Kent 12 J6
Charing Heath Kent 12 H6
Charing Hill Kent 12 J5
Charingworth Gloucs 36 G13
Charlbury Oxon 29 S4
Charlcombe BaNES 17 T3
Charlcutt Wilts 18 E5
Charlecote Warwks 36 J9
Charlemont Sandw 36 D2
Charles Devon 15 Q6
Charleshill Surrey 10 D2
Charleston Angus 91 N2
Charlestown C Aber 99 S3
Charlestown C Brad 63 P12
Charlestown Calder 56 E1
Charlestown Cnwll 3 Q6
Charlestown Cnwll 3 Q6
Charlestown Derbys 56 F8
Charlestown Dorset 7 S9
Charlestown Fife 83 L2
Charlestown Highld 102 H6
Charlestown Highld 107 P10
Charlestown Salfd 55 T6
Charles Tye Suffk 40 H10
Charlesworth Derbys 56 F8
Charlinch Somset 16 H9
Charlottetown Fife 91 L9
Charlton Gt Lon 21 R7
Charlton Hants 19 N11
Charlton Herts 31 Q7
Charlton Nhants 30 B5
Charlton Nthumb 76 G9
Charlton Oxon 29 T10
Charlton Somset 16 J11
Charlton Somset 17 R8
Charlton Somset 17 S6
Charlton Surrey 20 J9
Charlton W Susx 10 D8
Charlton Wilts 8 C4
Charlton Wilts 28 J10
Charlton Worcs 35 T6
Charlton Worcs 36 D11
Charlton Wrekin 45 N11
Charlton Abbots Gloucs 28 K3
Charlton Adam Somset 17 P11
Charlton All Saints Wilts 8 H4
Charlton Down Dorset 7 S5
Charlton Hill Shrops 45 N12
Charlton Horethorne Somset 17 S12
Charlton Kings Gloucs 28 J3
Charlton Mackrell Somset 17 P11
Charlton Marshall Dorset 8 C8
Charlton Musgrove Somset 17 T11
Charlton-on-Otmoor Oxon 30 C9
Charlton on the Hill Dorset 8 B8
Charlton St Peter Wilts 18 H9
Charlwood Hants 9 T2
Charlwood Surrey 11 L2
Charminster Dorset 7 S6
Charmouth Dorset 7 L6
Charndon Bucks 30 E8
Charney Bassett Oxon 29 S9
Charnock Green Lancs 55 N3
Charnock Richard Lancs 55 N3
Charnock Richard Crematorium Lancs 55 N3
Charnock Richard Services Lancs 55 M3
Charsfield Suffk 41 N9
Chart Corner Kent 12 E5
Charter Alley Hants 19 S9
Charterhall Border 84 K9
Charterhouse Somset 17 N5
Chartershall Stirlg 89 S7
Charterville Allotments Oxon 29 R5
Chartham Kent 13 M5
Chartham Hatch Kent 13 M4
Chart Hill Kent 12 E6
Chartridge Bucks 30 K12
Chart Sutton Kent 12 F6
Chartway Street Kent 12 F5
Charvil Wokham 20 C7
Charwelton Nhants 37 P9
Chase Terrace Staffs 46 D12
Chasetown Staffs 46 D12
Chastleton Oxon 29 P2
Chasty Devon 14 H12
Chatburn Lancs 62 F11
Chatcull Staffs 45 S7
Chatham Caerph 27 N10
Chatham Medway 12 E2
Chatham Green Essex 22 H4
Chathill Nthumb 85 T13
Chatley Worcs 35 U8
Chatsworth House Derbys 57 L12
Chattenden Medway 22 J13
Chatter End Essex 22 C2
Chatteris Cambs 39 N3
Chatterton Lancs 55 S3
Chattisham Suffk 40 J12
Chatto Border 76 F2
Chatton Nthumb 85 R13
Chaul End C Beds 31 N8
Chawleigh Devon 15 R10
Chawley Oxon 29 U7
Chawston Bed 38 J9
Chawton Hants 19 V13
Chaxhill Gloucs 28 D5
Chazey Heath Oxon 19 U5
Cheadle Staffs 46 D5
Cheadle Stockp 56 C9
Cheadle Heath Stockp 56 C9
Cheadle Hulme Stockp 56 C9
Cheam Gt Lon 21 M10
Cheapside W & M 20 F9
Chearsley Bucks 30 F10
Chebsey Staffs 45 U8
Checkendon Oxon 19 U4
Checkley Ches E 45 R4
Checkley Herefs 35 N13
Checkley Staffs 46 D6
Checkley Green Ches E 45 R4
Chedburgh Suffk 40 C9
Cheddar Somset 17 N6
Cheddington Bucks 30 K9
Cheddleton Staffs 46 C3
Cheddleton Heath Staffs 46 C3
Cheddon Fitzpaine Somset 16 H11
Chedglow Wilts 28 H9
Chedgrave Norfk 51 Q14
Chedington Dorset 7 N3
Chediston Suffk 41 Q5
Chediston Green Suffk 41 Q5
Chedworth Gloucs 29 L5
Chedzoy Somset 16 K9
Cheeseman's Green Kent 12 K8
Cheetham Hill Manch 55 T6
Cheldon Devon 15 R10
Chelford Ches E 55 T12
Chellaston C Derb 47 L7
Chellington Bed 38 E9
Chelmarsh Shrops 35 R3
Chelmick Shrops 35 L2
Chelmondiston Suffk 41 M13
Chelmorton Derbys 56 H13
Chelmsford Essex 22 H6
Chelmsford Crematorium Essex 22 G6
Chelmsley Wood Solhll 36 G3
Chelsea Gt Lon 21 N7
Chelsfield Gt Lon 21 S10
Chelsham Surrey 21 Q11
Chelston Somset 16 G12
Chelsworth Suffk 40 G11
Cheltenham Gloucs 28 H3
Cheltenham Crematorium Gloucs 28 J3
Chelveston Nhants 38 E7
Chelvey N Som 17 N3
Chelwood BaNES 17 R4
Chelwood Common E Susx 11 Q5
Chelwood Gate E Susx 11 Q4
Chelworth Wilts 28 J9
Chelworth Lower Green Wilts 29 L9
Chelworth Upper Green Wilts 29 L9
Cheney Longville Shrops 34 K4
Chenies Bucks 20 H3
Chepstow Mons 27 U9
Chequerbent Bolton 55 Q5
Chequers Corner Norfk 49 Q12
Cherhill Wilts 18 F6
Cherington Gloucs 28 H8
Cherington Warwks 36 J13
Cheriton Devon 15 R3
Cheriton Hants 9 R3
Cheriton Kent 13 P8
Cheriton Swans 25 S12
Cheriton Bishop Devon 5 T2
Cheriton Fitzpaine Devon 15 U11
Cheriton or Stackpole Elidor Pembks 24 G11
Cherrington Wrekin 45 Q10
Cherry Burton E R Yk 65 M11
Cherry Hinton Cambs 39 Q9
Cherry Orchard Worcs 35 U10
Cherry Willingham Lincs 58 H12
Chertsey Surrey 20 H9
Cherwell Valley Services Oxon 30 B7
Cheselbourne Dorset 7 U5
Chesham Bucks 31 L12
Chesham Bury 55 T4
Chesham Bois Bucks 20 G3
Cheshire Farm Ice Cream Ches W 45 M2
Cheshunt Herts 31 U12
Chesil Beach Dorset 7 R9
Chesley Kent 12 G3
Cheslyn Hay Staffs 46 C12
Chessetts Wood Warwks 36 G6
Chessington Gt Lon 21 L10
Chessington World of Adventures Gt Lon 21 L10
Chester Ches W 54 K13
Chesterblade Somset 17 S8
Chester Crematorium Ches W 54 J13
Chesterfield Derbys 57 N12
Chesterfield Staffs 46 E12
Chesterfield Crematorium Derbys 57 N12
Chesterhill Mdloth 83 S6
Chester-le-Street Dur 69 S2
Chester Moor Dur 69 S3
Chesters Border 76 C3
Chesters Border 84 G14
Chester Services Ches W 55 L12
Chesterton Cambs 38 H1
Chesterton Cambs 39 Q8
Chesterton Gloucs 28 K7
Chesterton Oxon 30 C8
Chesterton Shrops 35 S1
Chesterton Staffs 45 T4
Chesterton Green Warwks 37 L9
Chesterwood Nthumb 76 G12
Chester Zoo Ches W 54 K12
Chestfield Kent 13 M2
Chestnut Street Kent 12 G3
Cheston Devon 5 R9
Cheswardine Shrops 45 R7
Cheswick Nthumb 85 Q9
Cheswick Green Solhll 36 F5
Chetnole Dorset 7 R3
Chettiscombe Devon 6 C2
Chettisham Cambs 39 R4
Chettle Dorset 8 D6
Chetton Shrops 35 Q2
Chetwode Bucks 30 D7
Chetwynd Wrekin 45 R9
Chetwynd Aston Wrekin 45 S10
Cheveley Cambs 39 U8
Chevening Kent 21 S11
Cheverton IoW 9 P12
Chevington Suffk 40 C9
Cheviot Hills 76 F4
Chevithorne Devon 16 C13
Chew Magna BaNES 17 Q4
Chew Moor Bolton 55 Q5
Chew Stoke BaNES 17 Q4
Chewton Keynsham BaNES 17 S3
Chewton Mendip Somset 17 Q6
Chichacott Devon 15 P13
Chicheley M Keyn 38 D11
Chichester W Susx 10 D10
Chichester Crematorium W Susx 10 D9
Chickerell Dorset 7 R8
Chickering Suffk 41 M5
Chicklade Wilts 8 C2
Chickward Herefs 34 G10
Chidden Hants 9 T5
Chiddingfold Surrey 10 F3
Chiddingly E Susx 11 S8
Chiddingstone Kent 21 T14
Chiddingstone Causeway Kent 21 T13
Chideock Dorset 7 M6
Chidham W Susx 10 B10
Chidswell Kirk 57 L2
Chieveley W Berk 19 Q6
Chignall St James Essex 22 G5
Chignall Smealy Essex 22 G5
Chigwell Essex 21 R4
Chigwell Row Essex 21 S4
Chilbolton Hants 19 N12
Chilcomb Hants 9 Q3
Chilcombe Dorset 7 P6
Chilcompton Somset 17 R6
Chilcote Leics 46 J11
Childer Thornton Ches W 54 J11
Child Okeford Dorset 8 A6
Childrey Oxon 29 S10
Child's Ercall Shrops 45 Q8
Childswickham Worcs 36 E13
Childwall Lpool 54 K9
Childwick Bury Herts 31 P10
Childwick Green Herts 31 P10
Chilfrome Dorset 7 Q5
Chilgrove W Susx 10 C8
Chilham Kent 13 L5
Chilla Devon 14 K12
Chillaton Devon 5 L4
Chillenden Kent 13 Q5
Chillerton IoW 9 P12
Chillesford Suffk 41 Q10
Chillingham Nthumb 85 R13
Chillington Devon 5 T12
Chillington Somset 7 L2
Chilmark Wilts 8 D2
Chilmington Green Kent 12 J7
Chilson Oxon 29 R4
Chilsworthy Cnwll 5 L6
Chilsworthy Devon 14 H11
Chiltern Green C Beds 31 P9
Chiltern Hills 20 C3
Chilterns Crematorium Bucks 20 F3
Chilthorne Domer Somset 17 P13
Chilton Bucks 30 E10
Chilton Devon 15 U12
Chilton Dur 69 S7
Chilton Kent 13 Q7
Chilton Oxon 29 U10
Chilton Suffk 40 E12
Chilton Candover Hants 19 S12
Chilton Cantelo Somset 17 Q12
Chilton Foliat Wilts 19 M6
Chilton Polden Somset 17 L8
Chilton Street Suffk 40 C11
Chilton Trinity Somset 16 J9
Chilwell Notts 47 P6
Chilworth Hants 9 N5
Chilworth Surrey 20 H13
Chimney Oxon 29 S7
Chineham Hants 19 U9
Chingford Gt Lon 21 Q4
Chinley Derbys 56 F10
Chinnor Oxon 30 G12
Chipchase Castle Nthumb 76 H10
Chipnall Shrops 45 R7
Chippenham Cambs 39 U7
Chippenham Wilts 18 D6
Chipperfield Herts 31 M12
Chipping Herts 31 U6
Chipping Lancs 62 C11
Chipping Campden Gloucs 36 G13
Chipping Hill Essex 22 K4
Chipping Norton Oxon 29 R2
Chipping Ongar Essex 22 E7
Chipping Sodbury S Glos 28 D11
Chipping Warden Nhants 37 N11
Chipstable Somset 16 D11
Chipstead Kent 21 T11
Chipstead Surrey 21 N11
Chirbury Shrops 44 G14
Chirk Wrexhm 44 G6
Chirnside Border 85 M7
Chirnsidebridge Border 85 M7
Chirton Wilts 18 G9
Chisbury Wilts 19 L7
Chiselborough Somset 7 N2
Chiseldon Swindn 18 J4
Chiselhampton Oxon 30 C13
Chisholme Border 75 T3
Chislehurst Gt Lon 21 R8
Chislet Kent 13 P3
Chisley Calder 63 L14
Chiswell Green Herts 31 P12
Chiswick Gt Lon 21 M7
Chiswick End Cambs 39 N11
Chisworth Derbys 56 E8
Chitcombe E Susx 12 F11
Chithurst W Susx 10 C6
Chittering Cambs 39 Q7
Chitterne Wilts 18 E12
Chittlehamholt Devon 15 Q8
Chittlehampton Devon 15 P7
Chittoe Wilts 18 E7
Chivelstone Devon 5 T13
Chivenor Devon 15 M6
Chlenry D & G 72 E7
Chobham Surrey 20 G10
Cholderton Wilts 18 K12
Cholesbury Bucks 30 K11
Chollerford Nthumb 76 J11
Chollerton Nthumb 76 J11
Cholmondeston Ches E 45 P2
Cholsey Oxon 19 S3
Cholstrey Herefs 35 L9
Chop Gate N York 70 J13
Choppington Nthumb 77 R9
Chopwell Gatesd 77 N14
Chorley Ches E 45 N3
Chorley Lancs 55 N3
Chorley Shrops 35 Q4
Chorley Staffs 46 E11
Chorleywood Herts 20 H3
Chorleywood West Herts 20 H3
Chorlton Ches E 45 R3
Chorlton-cum-Hardy Manch 55 T8
Chorlton Lane Ches W 45 L4
Choulton Shrops 34 J3
Chowley Ches W 45 L2
Chrishall Essex 39 P13
Chrisswell Inver 88 F11
Christchurch Cambs 39 Q1
Christchurch Dorset 8 H10
Christchurch Gloucs 27 V5
Christchurch Newpt 27 Q10
Christian Malford Wilts 18 E5
Christleton Ches W 54 K13
Christmas Common Oxon 20 B4
Christon N Som 17 L5
Christon Bank Nthumb 85 U14
Christow Devon 5 U3
Christ's Hospital W Susx 10 J5
Chuck Hatch E Susx 11 R4
Chudleigh Devon 5 V5
Chudleigh Knighton Devon 5 U5
Chulmleigh Devon 15 Q10
Chunal Derbys 56 F8
Church Lancs 62 E14
Churcham Gloucs 28 E4
Church Aston Wrekin 45 R10
Church Brampton Nhants 37 T7
Church Brough Cumb 68 G10
Church Broughton Derbys 46 H7
Church Cove Cnwll 2 J14
Church Crookham Hants 20 D12
Churchdown Gloucs 28 G4
Church Eaton Staffs 45 T10
Church End Bed 38 G9
Church End Bed 38 H9
Church End Bucks 30 F11
Church End C Beds 31 L6
Church End C Beds 31 L8
Church End C Beds 31 M6
Church End C Beds 31 M9
Church End C Beds 31 Q5
Church End C Beds 38 J10
Church End Cambs 38 G6
Church End Cambs 38 K4
Church End Cambs 39 M5
Church End Cambs 39 Q9
Church End Essex 22 F3
Church End Essex 22 H2
Church End Essex 22 H4
Churchend Essex 23 P9
Church End Gloucs 35 U13
Church End Gt Lon 21 M4
Church End Herts 22 B3
Church End Herts 31 P10
Church End Herts 31 S6
Church End Lincs 48 K7
Church End Lincs 59 R7
Church End Warwks 36 H2
Church End Warwks 36 J2
Church Enstone Oxon 29 S2
Church Fenton N York 64 C12
Churchfield Sandw 36 D2
Churchgate Herts 31 T12
Churchgate Street Essex 22 C5
Church Green Devon 6 G5
Church Gresley Derbys 46 J10
Church Hanborough Oxon 29 T5
Church Hill Staffs 46 D11
Church Houses N York 71 L13
Churchill Devon 6 J4
Churchill Devon 15 N4
Churchill N Som 17 M5
Churchill Oxon 29 Q3
Churchill Worcs 35 U5
Churchill Worcs 36 B10
Churchinford Somset 6 H2
Church Knowle Dorset 8 C12
Church Laneham Notts 58 D11
Church Langton Leics 37 T2
Church Lawford Warwks 37 N5
Church Lawton Ches E 45 T2
Church Leigh Staffs 46 D6
Church Lench Worcs 36 D10
Church Mayfield Staffs 46 G5
Church Minshull Ches E 45 Q1
Church Norton W Susx 10 D11
Churchover Warwks 37 P4
Church Preen Shrops 45 M14
Church Pulverbatch Shrops 44 K13
Churchstanton Somset 6 G2
Churchstoke Powys 34 G2
Churchstow Devon 5 S11
Church Stowe Nhants 37 R9
Church Street Essex 40 C12
Church Street Kent 22 H13
Church Street Suffk 41 S4
Church Stretton Shrops 35 L2
Churchthorpe Lincs 59 P7
Churchtown Bpool 61 Q11
Churchtown Cnwll 4 D5
Churchtown Derbys 57 L14
Churchtown Devon 15 Q4
Churchtown IoM 60 g4
Churchtown Lancs 61 T11
Church Town N Linc 58 C5
Churchtown Sefton 54 J3
Church Village Rhondd 26 K10
Church Warsop Notts 57 S13
Church Wilne Derbys 47 M7
Churnsike Lodge Nthumb 76 D10
Churston Ferrers Torbay 6 B13
Churt Surrey 10 D3
Churton Ches W 44 K2
Churwell Leeds 63 R14
Chwilog Gwynd 42 H6
Chyandour Cnwll 2 D10
Chyanvounder Cnwll 2 H12
Chyeowling Cnwll 2 K8
Chyvarloe Cnwll 2 H12
Cil Powys 44 E13
Cilcain Flints 54 E13
Cilcennin Cerdgn 32 K8
Cilcewydd Powys 44 F13
Cilfrew Neath 26 D7
Cilfynydd Rhondd 26 K9
Cilgerran Pembks 32 C12
Cilgwyn Carmth 26 C2
Cilgwyn Gwynd 52 G12
Ciliau-Aeron Cerdgn 32 K9
Cilmaengwyn Neath 26 C6
Cilmery Powys 34 B10
Cilrhedyn Pembks 25 N4
Cilsan Carmth 25 U6
Ciltalgarth Gwynd 43 S5
Cilycwm Carmth 33 Q13
Cimla Neath 26 D8
Cinderford Gloucs 28 C5
Cinder Hill Wolves 36 B2
Cippenham Slough 20 G6
Cirencester Gloucs 28 K7
Citadilla N York 69 R13
City Gt Lon 21 P6
City V Glam 26 H12
City Airport Gt Lon 21 R6
City Dulas IoA 52 G5
City of London Crematorium Gt Lon 21 R5
Clabhach Ag & B 92 F7
Clachaig Ag & B 88 D9
Clachan Ag & B 79 P4
Clachan Ag & B 87 P2
Clachan Ag & B 94 B10
Clachan Highld 100 e6
Clachan-a-Luib W Isls 106 d12
Clachan Mor Ag & B 92 B9
Clachan na Luib W Isls 106 d12
Clachan of Campsie E Duns 89 P10
Clachan-Seil Ag & B 87 P2
Clachnaharry Highld 102 H6
Clachtoll Highld 110 A11
Clackavoid P & K 97 U11
Clacket Lane Services Surrey 21 R12
Clackmannan Clacks 90 D13
Clackmarras Moray 104 A4
Clacton-on-Sea Essex 23 S4
Cladich Ag & B 88 C1
Cladswell Worcs 36 E9
Claggan Highld 93 S9
Claigan Highld 100 b4
Clandown BaNES 17 S5
Clanfield Hants 9 T5
Clanfield Oxon 29 Q7
Clannaborough Devon 15 R12
Clanville Hants 19 M11
Clanville Somset 17 R10
Claonaig Ag & B 79 R4
Clapgate Dorset 8 E8
Clapgate Herts 22 B3
Clapham Bed 38 F10
Clapham Devon 6 A7
Clapham Gt Lon 21 N7
Clapham N York 62 E6
Clapham W Susx 10 H9
Clapham Green Bed 38 F10
Clap Hill Kent 13 L8
Clappersgate Cumb 67 N12
Clapton Somset 7 M3
Clapton Somset 17 R6
Clapton-in-Gordano N Som 27 T13
Clapton-on-the-Hill Gloucs 29 N4
Clapworthy Devon 15 Q8
Clarach Cerdgn 33 M4
Claravale Gatesd 77 N13
Clarbeston Pembks 24 J6
Clarbeston Road Pembks 24 H6
Clarborough Notts 58 B10
Clare Suffk 40 C11
Clarebrand D & G 74 E12
Clarencefield D & G 75 L12
Clarewood Nthumb 77 L12
Clarilaw Border 76 A2
Clark's Green Surrey 10 K3
Clarkston E Rens 89 N14
Clashmore Highld 109 N7
Clashmore Highld 110 A10
Clashnessie Highld 110 B10
Clashnoir Moray 104 A11
Clathy P & K 90 E7
Clathymore P & K 90 F7
Clatt Abers 104 G10
Clatter Powys 33 U2
Clatterford End Essex 22 F5
Clatworthy Somset 16 E10
Claughton Lancs 61 U11
Claughton Lancs 62 B6
Claughton Wirral 54 H9
Clavelshay Somset 16 J10
Claverdon Warwks 36 G7
Claverham N Som 17 N3
Clavering Essex 22 C1
Claverley Shrops 35 S2
Claverton BaNES 17 U4
Claverton Down BaNES 17 U4
Clawdd-coch V Glam 26 K12
Clawdd-newydd Denbgs 44 C3
Clawthorpe Cumb 61 U4
Clawton Devon 14 J13
Claxby Lincs 58 K8
Claxby Lincs 59 S12
Claxton N York 64 F8
Claxton Norfk 51 P13
Claybrooke Magna Leics 37 N3
Clay Common Suffk 41 S4
Clay Coton Nhants 37 Q5
Clay Cross Derbys 57 N14
Claydon Oxon 37 N11
Claydon Suffk 40 K11
Clay End Herts 31 T8
Claygate D & G 75 S10
Claygate Kent 12 D7
Claygate Surrey 21 L10
Claygate Cross Kent 12 B4
Clayhall Gt Lon 21 R4
Clayhanger Devon 16 D12
Clayhanger Wsall 46 D13
Clayhidon Devon 16 G13
Clayhill E Susx 12 F11
Clayhill Hants 9 L7
Clayhithe Cambs 39 R8
Clayock Highld 112 E5
Claypit Hill Cambs 39 N10
Claypits Gloucs 28 E6
Claypole Lincs 48 B4
Claythorpe Lincs 59 R11
Clayton C Brad 63 N13
Clayton Donc 57 Q5
Clayton W Susx 11 M8
Clayton Green Lancs 55 N2
Clayton-le-Moors Lancs 62 F13
Clayton-le-Woods Lancs 55 N2
Clayton West Kirk 57 L4
Clayworth Notts 58 B9
Cleadale Highld 100 d11
Cleadon S Tyne 77 T13
Clearbrook Devon 5 N7
Clearwell Gloucs 27 V6
Clearwell Meend Gloucs 28 A6
Cleasby N York 69 S10
Cleat Ork 106 t21
Cleatlam Dur 69 P9
Cleator Cumb 66 F10
Cleator Moor Cumb 66 F9
Cleckheaton Kirk 56 J1
Cleedownton Shrops 35 N4
Cleehill Shrops 35 N5
Cleekhimin N Lans 82 E7
Clee St Margaret Shrops 35 N4
Cleestanton Shrops 35 N5
Cleethorpes NE Lin 59 P5
Cleeton St Mary Shrops 35 P5
Cleeve N Som 17 N3
Cleeve Oxon 19 T4
Cleeve Hill Gloucs 28 J2
Cleeve Prior Worcs 36 E11
Cleghornie E Loth 84 F2
Clehonger Herefs 34 K13
Cleish P & K 90 G12
Cleland N Lans 82 E7
Clement's End C Beds 31 M10
Clement Street Kent 22 D13
Clenamacrie Ag & B 94 C13
Clench Common Wilts 18 J7
Clenchwarton Norfk 49 S9
Clenerty Abers 105 M3
Clent Worcs 36 B5

Cleobury Mortimer Shrops ... 35 Q5
Cleobury North Shrops ... 35 P3
Cleongart Ag & B ... 79 M9
Clephanton Highld ... 103 M5
Clerkhill D & G ... 75 Q4
Cleuch-head D & G ... 74 F5
Clevancy Wilts ... 18 G5
Clevedon N Som ... 17 M2
Cleveley Oxon ... 29 S3
Cleveleys Lancs ... 61 Q11
Cleverton Wilts ... 28 J10
Clewer Somset ... 17 M6
Cley next the Sea Norfk ... 50 H3
Cliburn Cumb ... 67 S8
Cliddesden Hants ... 19 T11
Cliff Warwks ... 36 J1
Cliffe Lancs ... 62 E13
Cliffe Medway ... 22 H12
Cliffe N York ... 69 R9
Cliff End E Susx ... 12 G13
Cliffe Woods Medway ... 22 H13
Clifford Herefs ... 34 F11
Clifford Leeds ... 63 U11
Clifford Chambers Warwks ... 36 G10
Clifford's Mesne Gloucs ... 28 D3
Cliffsend Kent ... 13 R3
Clifton Bristl ... 27 V13
Clifton C Beds ... 31 Q5
Clifton C Nott ... 47 P7
Clifton Calder ... 56 J2
Clifton Cumb ... 67 S7
Clifton Derbys ... 46 G4
Clifton Devon ... 15 P4
Clifton Donc ... 57 R7
Clifton Lancs ... 61 T13
Clifton N York ... 63 P10
Clifton Nthumb ... 77 Q9
Clifton Oxon ... 29 U1
Clifton Salfd ... 55 T11
Clifton Campville Staffs ... 46 J11
Clifton Hampden Oxon ... 30 B13
Clifton Reynes M Keyn ... 38 D10
Clifton upon Dunsmore Warwks ... 37 P5
Clifton upon Teme Worcs ... 35 R8
Cliftonville Kent ... 13 S1
Climping W Susx ... 10 F10
Clink Somset ... 17 T8
Clint N York ... 63 R8
Clinterty C Aber ... 105 N13
Clint Green Norfk ... 50 H11
Clintmains Border ... 84 F11
Clipiau Gwynd ... 43 R11
Clippesby Norfk ... 51 R11
Clipsham Rutlnd ... 48 E10
Clipston Nhants ... 37 T4
Clipston Notts ... 47 S7
Clipstone C Beds ... 30 K7
Clipstone Notts ... 57 S14
Clitheroe Lancs ... 62 E11
Clive Shrops ... 45 M9
Cliveden Bucks ... 20 F5
Clixby Lincs ... 58 K5
Cloatley Wilts ... 28 J9
Clocaenog Denbgs ... 44 C3
Clochan Moray ... 104 E3
Clock Face St Hel ... 55 M8
Cloddiau Powys ... 44 E12
Clodock Herefs ... 27 Q3
Cloford Somset ... 17 T8
Clola Abers ... 105 S7
Clophill C Beds ... 31 N5
Clopton Nhants ... 38 G4
Clopton Suffk ... 41 M10
Clopton Corner Suffk ... 41 M10
Clopton Green Suffk ... 40 C9
Clos du Valle Guern ... 6 e1
Closeburn D & G ... 74 H7
Closeburnmill D & G ... 74 H6
Closeclark IoM ... 60 d7
Closworth Somset ... 7 Q2
Clothall Herts ... 31 S6
Clotton Ches W ... 55 M14
Cloudesley Bush Warwks ... 37 N3
Clouds Herefs ... 35 N13
Clough Calder ... 56 D5
Clough Foot Calder ... 56 D2
Clough Head Calder ... 56 G3
Cloughton N York ... 71 T13
Cloughton Newlands N York ... 71 T13
Clousta Shet ... 106 t8
Clova Angus ... 98 E9
Clovelly Devon ... 14 H8
Clovenfords Border ... 84 D11
Clovullin Highld ... 94 E6
Clow Bridge Lancs ... 62 G14
Clowne Derbys ... 57 Q11
Clows Top Worcs ... 35 R6
Cloy Wrexhm ... 44 J5
Cluanie Inn Highld ... 101 Q8
Cluanie Lodge Highld ... 101 M9
Clubworthy Cnwll ... 4 J2
Clugston D & G ... 72 K8
Clun Shrops ... 34 J4
Clunas Highld ... 103 N6
Clunbury Shrops ... 34 J4
Clunderwen Carmth ... 24 J7
Clune Highld ... 103 L10
Clungunford Shrops ... 34 J5
Clunie P & K ... 90 H3
Clunton Shrops ... 34 J4
Cluny Fife ... 90 K12
Clutton BaNES ... 17 R5
Clutton Ches W ... 45 L3
Clutton Hill BaNES ... 17 R5
Clwt-y-bont Gwynd ... 52 J10
Clydach Mons ... 27 N5
Clydach Swans ... 26 B7
Clydach Vale Rhondd ... 26 H9
Clydebank W Duns
Clydebank Crematorium W Duns ... 89 L11
Clydey Pembks ... 25 M3
Clyffe Pypard Wilts ... 18 H5
Clynder Ag & B ... 88 E9
Clyne Neath ... 26 E7
Clynnog-fawr Gwynd ... 42 H4
Clyro Powys ... 34 F12
Clyst Honiton Devon ... 6 C6
Clyst St George Devon ... 6 C7
Clyst St Lawrence Devon ... 6 D4
Clyst St Mary Devon ... 6 C6
Cnoc Highld ... 106 j5
Cnwch Coch Cerdgn ... 33 N5
Coad's Green Cnwll ... 4 H5
Coal Aston Derbys ... 57 N11
Coalbrookvale Blae G ... 27 M6
Coalburn S Lans ... 82 F12
Coalburns Gatesd ... 77 N13
Coaley Gloucs ... 28 E7
Coalhill Essex ... 22 J8
Coalmoor Wrekin ... 45 Q12
Coalpit Heath S Glos ... 28 C11
Coal Pool Wsall ... 46 D14
Coalport Wrekin ... 45 Q13
Coalsnaughton Clacks ... 90 D13
Coal Street Suffk ... 41 M6
Coaltown of Balgonie Fife
Coaltown of Wemyss Fife ... 91 M12
Coalville Leics ... 47 M11
Coanwood Nthumb ... 76 D14
Coat Somset ... 17 M11
Coatbridge N Lans ... 82 D5
Coatdyke N Lans ... 82 D5
Coate Swindn ... 18 H4
Coate Wilts ... 18 E8
Coates Cambs ... 39 M14
Coates Gloucs ... 28 H7
Coates Lincs ... 58 F10
Coates Notts ... 58 D10
Coates W Susx ... 10 F7
Coatham R & Cl ... 70 J7
Coatham Mundeville Darltn
Cobbaton Devon ... 15 P7
Coberley Gloucs ... 28 H4
Cobhall Common Herefs ... 35 L13
Cobham Kent ... 12 C2
Cobham Surrey ... 20 K10
Cobham Services Surrey ... 20 K11
Coblers Green Essex ... 22 G4
Cobley Dorset ... 8 E4
Cobnash Herefs ... 35 L8
Cobo Guern ... 6 c2
Cobridge C Stke ... 45 U4
Cock Alley Derbys ... 57 P12
Cockayne N York ... 71 L13
Cockayne Hatley C Beds ... 31 R11
Cock Bank Wrexhm ... 44 J4
Cock Bevington Warwks ... 36 E10
Cockburnspath Border ... 84 K4
Cock Clarks Essex ... 23 L7
Cock & End Suffk
Cockenzie and Port Seton E Loth ... 83 T8
Cocker Bar Lancs ... 55 M2
Cocker Brook Lancs
Cockerham Lancs ... 61 T10
Cockermouth Cumb ... 66 H6
Cockernhoe Herts ... 31 P8

Cockersdale Leeds ... 63 Q14
Cockett Swans ... 26 A9
Cockfield Dur ... 69 P8
Cockfield Suffk ... 40 F10
Cockfosters Gt Lon ... 21 N3
Cock Green Essex ... 22 G4
Cocking W Susx ... 10 D7
Cocking Causeway W Susx ... 10 D7
Cockington Torbay ... 6 A12
Cocklake Somset ... 17 M7
Cockley Beck Cumb ... 66 K12
Cockley Cley Norfk ... 50 C13
Cock Marling E Susx ... 12 F13
Cockpole Green Wokham ... 20 C6
Cocks Cnwll ... 2 K6
Cockshutford Shrops ... 35 N3
Cockshutt Shrops ... 44 K8
Cock Street Kent ... 12 E5
Cockthorpe Norfk ... 50 G5
Cockwells Cnwll ... 2 E10
Cockwood Devon ... 6 C8
Cockyard Derbys ... 56 F11
Cockyard Herefs ... 34 K14
Coddenham Suffk ... 40 K10
Coddenham Green Suffk ... 40 K10
Coddington Herefs ... 35 Q12
Coddington Notts ... 48 B2
Codford St Mary Wilts ... 18 E13
Codford St Peter Wilts ... 18 E13
Codicote Herts ... 31 R9
Codmore Hill W Susx ... 10 H6
Codnor Derbys ... 47 M4
Codrington S Glos ... 28 D12
Codsall Staffs ... 45 U13
Codsall Wood Staffs ... 45 T13
Coedely Rhondd ... 26 J10
Coedkernew Newpt ... 27 P11
Coed Morgan Mons ... 27 R5
Coedpoeth Wrexhm ... 44 G3
Coed Talon Flints ... 44 G2
Coedway Powys ... 44 H11
Coed-y-Bryn Cerdgn ... 32 G11
Coed-y-caerau Newpt ... 27 Q9
Coed-y-paen Mons ... 27 Q8
Coed-yr-ynys Powys ... 27 M3
Coed Ystumgwern Gwynd ... 43 L9
Coelbren Powys ... 26 F5
Coffinswell Devon ... 6 A11
Coffle End Bed ... 38 F9
Cofton Devon ... 6 C8
Cofton Hackett Worcs ... 36 D5
Cogan V Glam ... 16 G2
Cogenhoe Nhants ... 38 B8
Cogges Oxon ... 29 S6
Coggeshall Essex ... 23 L3
Coggeshall Hamlet Essex ... 23 L3
Coignafearn Highld ... 102 K12
Coilacriech Abers ... 98 E4
Coilantogle Stirlg ... 89 M4
Coillore Highld ... 100 c6
Coity Brdgnd ... 26 G11
Col W Isls ... 106 j5
Colaboll Highld ... 108 J1
Colan Cnwll ... 3 M4
Colaton Raleigh Devon ... 6 E7
Colbost Highld ... 100 b5
Colburn N York ... 69 Q13
Colby Cumb ... 68 E8
Colby IoM ... 60 d8
Colby Norfk ... 51 M7
Colchester Essex ... 23 N2
Colchester Crematorium Essex ... 23 N3
Colchester Zoo Essex ... 23 N3
Cold Ash W Berk ... 19 R6
Cold Ashby Nhants ... 37 S5
Cold Ashton S Glos ... 28 E13
Cold Aston Gloucs ... 29 M4
Coldbackie Highld ... 111 N4
Coldbeck Cumb ... 68 F12
Cold Blow Pembks ... 24 K8
Cold Brayfield M Keyn ... 38 D10
Cold Cotes N York ... 62 E5
Coldean Br & H ... 11 N9
Coldeast Devon ... 5 U5
Colden Calder ... 62 K14
Colden Common Hants ... 9 P4
Coldfair Green Suffk ... 41 R8
Coldham Cambs ... 49 P13
Cold Hanworth Lincs ... 58 H10
Coldharbour Cnwll ... 2 J8
Coldharbour Devon ... 6 E2
Cold Harbour Herts ... 31 P10
Coldharbour Gloucs ... 27 V7
Coldharbour Surrey ... 10 K2
Cold Hatton Wrekin ... 45 P9
Cold Hatton Heath Wrekin ... 45 P9
Cold Hesledon Dur ... 70 F3
Cold Hiendley Wakefd ... 57 N4
Cold Higham Nhants ... 37 S10
Coldingham Border ... 85 N5
Cold Kirby N York ... 64 C3
Coldmeece Staffs ... 45 U7
Cold Newton Leics ... 47 T12
Cold Northcott Cnwll ... 4 G3
Cold Norton Essex ... 23 L7
Cold Overton Leics ... 48 B11
Coldred Kent ... 13 P6
Coldridge Devon ... 15 R11
Coldstream Border ... 85 L11
Coldwaltham W Susx ... 10 G7
Coldwell Herefs ... 34 K13
Coldwells Abers ... 105 T8
Cold Weston Shrops ... 35 N4
Cole Somset ... 17 R10
Colebatch Shrops ... 34 H3
Colebrook Devon ... 6 D3
Colebrook C Plym ... 5 N9
Colebrooke Devon ... 15 S13
Coleby Lincs ... 48 F1
Coleby N Linc ... 58 F3
Coleford Devon ... 15 T12
Coleford Gloucs ... 27 V6
Coleford Somset ... 17 S7
Coleford Water Somset ... 16 F10
Colegate End Norfk ... 41 L3
Cole Green Herts ... 31 S10
Cole Green Herts ... 31 S10
Cole Henley Hants ... 19 R10
Colehill Dorset ... 8 E8
Coleman Green Herts ... 31 Q10
Coleman's Hatch E Susx ... 11 R4
Colemere Shrops ... 44 K7
Colemore Hants ... 9 U3
Colemore Green Shrops ... 45 R14
Coleorton Leics ... 47 M10
Colerne Wilts ... 18 B6
Colesbourne Gloucs ... 28 J5
Coles Cross Dorset ... 7 L3
Coles Green Suffk ... 40 K12
Colesden Bed ... 38 H9
Coleshill Bucks ... 20 G3
Coleshill Oxon ... 29 P9
Coleshill Warwks ... 36 H3
Colestocks Devon ... 6 E4
Colgate W Susx ... 11 L4
Colgrain Ag & B ... 88 H9
Colinsburgh Fife ... 91 Q11
Colinton C Edin ... 83 P5
Colintraive Ag & B ... 88 B11
Colkirk Norfk ... 50 F8
Coll Ag & B ... 92 C7
Collace P & K ... 90 K5
Collafirth Shet ... 106 u5
Collaton Devon ... 5 P12
Collaton St Mary Torbay ... 5 V8
College of Roseisle Moray ... 103 T2
College Town Br For ... 20 E10
Collessie Fife ... 91 L9
Colleton Mills Devon ... 15 Q9
Collier Row Gt Lon ... 21 T5
Collier's End Herts ... 31 U8
Colliers Green Kent ... 12 E8
Collier Street Kent ... 12 D6
Colliery Row Sundld ... 70 D2
Collieston Abers ... 105 T11
Collin D & G ... 74 K10
Collingbourne Ducis Wilts ... 18 K9
Collingbourne Kingston Wilts ... 18 K9
Collingham Leeds ... 63 S10
Collingham Notts ... 58 B14
Collington Herefs ... 35 P8
Collingtree Nhants ... 37 U9
Collins Green Warrtn ... 55 M8
Collins Green Worcs ... 35 S9
Colliston Angus ... 91 T2
Colliton Devon ... 6 E4
Collyweston Nhants ... 48 F13
Colmonell S Ayrs ... 72 E2
Colmworth Bed ... 38 G9
Colnbrook Slough ... 20 H7
Colne Cambs ... 39 M6
Colne Lancs ... 62 H11
Colne Bridge Kirk ... 56 J3
Colne Edge Lancs ... 62 H11
Colne Engaine Essex ... 23 L1
Colney Norfk ... 51 L12
Colney Heath Herts ... 31 Q11
Colney Street Herts ... 31 Q12
Coln Rogers Gloucs ... 29 L6

Coln St Aldwyns Gloucs ... 29 M6
Coln St Dennis Gloucs ... 29 L5
Colonsay Ag & B ... 86 F6
Colonsay Airport Ag & B ... 86 F7
Colpy Abers ... 104 J9
Colquite Cnwll ... 3 R2
Colscott Devon ... 14 J10
Colsterdale N York ... 63 N2
Colsterworth Lincs ... 48 D9
Colston Bassett Notts ... 47 T7
Coltfield Moray ... 103 T3
Colt Hill Hants ... 20 C12
Coltishall Norfk ... 51 N10
Colton Cumb ... 61 Q2
Colton Leeds ... 63 T13
Colton N York ... 64 B10
Colton Norfk ... 50 K12
Colton Staffs ... 46 D9
Colt's Hill Kent ... 12 C7
Columbjohn Devon ... 6 B5
Colva Powys ... 34 F10
Colvend D & G ... 66 C1
Colwall Herefs ... 35 S12
Colwell Nthumb ... 76 K10
Colwich Staffs ... 46 C9
Colwick Notts ... 47 R5
Colwinston V Glam ... 26 G12
Colworth W Susx ... 10 E10
Colwyn Bay Conwy ... 53 Q7
Colyford Devon ... 6 J6
Colyton Devon ... 6 J6
Combe Devon ... 5 S13
Combe Herefs ... 34 J8
Combe Oxon ... 29 T4
Combe W Berk ... 19 N8
Combe Almer Dorset ... 8 D9
Combe Common Surrey ... 10 E3
Combe Down BaNES ... 17 T4
Combe Fishacre Devon ... 5 U7
Combe Florey Somset ... 16 G10
Combe Hay BaNES ... 17 T5
Combeinteignhead Devon ... 6 B10
Combe Martin Devon ... 15 N3
Combe Raleigh Devon ... 6 G4
Comberbach Ches W ... 55 P11
Comberford Staffs ... 46 G12
Comberton Cambs ... 39 N9
Comberton Herefs ... 35 L7
Combe St Nicholas Somset ... 6 K2
Combpyne Devon ... 6 J6
Combridge Staffs ... 46 E6
Combrook Warwks ... 36 K10
Combs Derbys ... 56 F11
Combs Suffk ... 40 H9
Combs Ford Suffk ... 40 H10
Combwich Somset ... 16 J8
Comers Abers ... 99 M2
Comhampton Worcs ... 35 T7
Commercial End Cambs ... 39 S8
Commins Coch Powys ... 43 R13
Commondale N York ... 71 L10
Common Edge Bpool ... 61 Q13
Common End Cumb ... 66 F8
Common Moor Cnwll ... 4 G7
Common Platt Wilts ... 29 M10
Common Side Derbys ... 57 M11
Commonwood Shrops ... 45 L6
Commonwood Wrexhm ... 44 J3
Compass Somset ... 16 J10
Compstall Stockp ... 56 E8
Compstonend D & G ... 73 R9
Compton Devon ... 5 V8
Compton Hants ... 9 N3
Compton Hants ... 9 P3
Compton Staffs ... 35 T4
Compton Surrey ... 20 G13
Compton W Berk ... 19 R5
Compton W Susx ... 9 U6
Compton Wilts ... 18 J11
Compton Abbas Dorset ... 8 B5
Compton Abdale Gloucs ... 29 L4
Compton Bassett Wilts ... 18 F6
Compton Beauchamp Oxon ... 29 P9
Compton Bishop Somset ... 17 L5
Compton Chamberlayne Wilts ... 8 E3
Compton Dando BaNES ... 17 R4
Compton Dundon Somset ... 17 N10
Compton Durville Somset ... 17 M13
Compton Greenfield S Glos ... 27 V11
Compton Martin BaNES ... 17 P5
Compton Pauncefoot Somset ... 17 R11
Compton Valence Dorset ... 7 Q6
Compton Verney Warwks ... 36 K9
Comrie Fife ... 90 F14
Comrie P & K ... 89 T4
Conaglen House Highld ... 94 E5
Conchra Highld ... 101 M6
Concraigie P & K ... 90 H3
Conder Green Lancs ... 61 T8
Conderton Worcs ... 36 C13
Condicote Gloucs ... 29 N2
Condorrat N Lans ... 89 S11
Condover Shrops ... 45 L12
Coney Hill Gloucs ... 28 G4
Coneyhurst Common W Susx ... 10 J6
Coneysthorpe N York ... 64 G5
Coneythorpe N York ... 63 T8
Coney Weston Suffk ... 40 G5
Conford Hants ... 10 C3
Congdon's Shop Cnwll ... 4 H5
Congerstone Leics ... 47 L12
Congham Norfk ... 50 B9
Congleton Ches E ... 56 C14
Congl-y-wal Gwynd ... 43 P5
Congresbury N Som ... 17 M4
Congreve Staffs ... 46 B11
Conham Bristl ... 27 U2
Conicavel Moray ... 103 Q5
Coningsby Lincs ... 48 K2
Conington Cambs ... 39 L7
Conington Cambs ... 38 K4
Conisbrough Donc ... 57 R7
Conisby Ag & B ... 86 C13
Conisholme Lincs ... 59 S7
Coniston Cumb ... 67 M13
Coniston E R Yk ... 65 R12
Coniston Cold N York ... 62 J9
Conistone N York ... 62 K6
Connah's Quay Flints ... 54 G13
Connel Ag & B ... 94 C12
Connel Park E Ayrs ... 81 R10
Conner Downs Cnwll ... 2 F10
Connor Bridge Highld ... 102 H4
Cononley N York ... 62 K10
Cononsyth Angus ... 91 T2
Consall Staffs ... 46 C4
Consett Dur ... 69 N2
Constable Burton N York ... 69 N13
Constable Lee Lancs ... 55 T2
Constantine Cnwll ... 2 J11
Constantine Bay Cnwll ... 3 M2
Contin Highld ... 102 E4
Conwy Conwy ... 53 N7
Conwy Castle Conwy ... 53 N7
Conyer Kent ... 12 K3
Conyer's Green Suffk ... 40 E7
Cooden E Susx ... 12 D14
Cooil IoM ... 60 d7
Cookbury Devon ... 14 K11
Cookbury Wick Devon ... 14 J11
Cookham W & M ... 20 E6
Cookham Dean W & M ... 20 E5
Cookham Rise W & M ... 20 E6
Cookhill Worcs ... 36 E9
Cookley Suffk ... 41 Q6
Cookley Worcs ... 35 T4
Cookley Green Oxon ... 19 U2
Cookney Abers ... 99 R5
Cooksbridge E Susx ... 11 Q8
Cooksey Green Worcs ... 36 B7
Cook's Green Essex ... 23 S3
Cooks Green Suffk ... 40 G10
Cookshill Staffs ... 46 B5
Cooksmill Green Essex ... 22 F6
Coolham W Susx ... 10 J6
Cooling Medway ... 22 H13
Cooling Street Medway ... 22 H13
Coombe Cnwll ... 2 K8
Coombe Cnwll ... 3 N6
Coombe Cnwll ... 14 F10
Coombe Devon ... 6 C6
Coombe Devon ... 6 E6
Coombe Devon ... 6 G6
Coombe Gloucs ... 28 D8
Coombe Hants ... 9 S4
Coombe Wilts ... 18 H10
Coombe Abbey Warwks ... 37 L5
Coombe Bissett Wilts ... 8 G3
Coombe Cellars Devon ... 6 B10
Coombe Hill Gloucs ... 28 G3
Coombe Keynes Dorset ... 8 A12
Coombe Pafford Torbay ... 6 B11
Coombes W Susx ... 10 K9
Coombeswood Dudley ... 36 C3
Coopersale Common Essex ... 21 S7
Coopersale Street Essex ... 22 C7
Cooper's Corner Kent ... 21 S13
Cooper's Green E Susx ... 11 R5
Coopers Green Herts ... 31 Q11

Cooper Street Kent ... 13 R3
Cooper Turning Bolton ... 55 P5
Cootham W Susx ... 10 H8
Copdock Suffk ... 40 K12
Copford Green Essex ... 23 M3
Copgrove N York ... 63 S7
Copister Shet ... 106 u6
Cople Bed ... 38 H11
Copley Calder ... 56 G2
Copley Dur ... 69 N7
Copley Tamesd ... 56 E7
Coplow Dale Derbys ... 56 H11
Copmanthorpe C York ... 64 D10
Copmere End Staffs ... 45 S8
Copp Lancs ... 61 S12
Coppathorne Cnwll ... 14 F12
Coppenhall Staffs ... 46 B10
Coppenhall Moss Ches E ... 45 R2
Copperhouse Cnwll ... 2 F10
Coppicegate Shrops ... 35 R4
Coppingford Cambs ... 38 J4
Coppins Corner Kent ... 12 H6
Copplestone Devon ... 15 S12
Coppull Lancs ... 55 N4
Coppull Moor Lancs ... 55 N4
Copsale W Susx ... 10 K6
Copster Green Lancs ... 62 D13
Copston Magna Warwks ... 37 N3
Cop Street Kent ... 13 R4
Copt Heath Solhll ... 36 G5
Copt Hewick N York ... 63 S5
Copthorne Cnwll ... 4 H4
Copthorne W Susx ... 11 M3
Copt Oak Leics ... 47 N11
Copy's Green Norfk ... 50 F6
Copythorne Hants ... 9 L6
Coram Street Suffk ... 40 H12
Corbets Tey Gt Lon ... 22 D10
Corbiere Jersey ... 7 a3
Corbridge Nthumb ... 76 K13
Corby Nhants ... 38 C3
Corby Glen Lincs ... 48 E8
Corby Hill Cumb ... 75 U14
Cordon N Ayrs ... 80 E6
Cordwell Derbys ... 57 M11
Coreley Shrops ... 35 P6
Cores End Bucks ... 20 F5
Corfe Somset ... 16 H13
Corfe Castle Dorset ... 8 D12
Corfe Mullen Dorset ... 8 D10
Corfton Shrops ... 35 L3
Corgarff Abers ... 98 D2
Corhampton Hants ... 9 S4
Corlae D & G ... 74 D10
Corley Warwks ... 36 K3
Corley Ash Warwks ... 36 J3
Corley Moor Warwks ... 36 J4
Corley Services Warwks ... 36 K3
Cornaa IoM ... 60 g4
Cornard Tye Suffk ... 40 F12
Corndon Devon ... 5 S3
Corner Row Lancs ... 61 S13
Corney Cumb ... 61 L1
Cornforth Dur ... 70 D6
Cornhill Abers ... 104 H4
Cornhill-on-Tweed Nthumb ... 85 M11
Cornholme Calder ... 56 D1
Cornish Hall End Essex ... 39 U13
Cornoigmore Ag & B ... 92 B9
Cornriggs Dur ... 68 H4
Cornsay Dur ... 69 P4
Cornsay Colliery Dur ... 69 P4
Corntown Highld ... 102 G4
Corntown V Glam ... 26 G12
Cornwell Oxon ... 29 Q2
Cornwood Devon ... 5 Q9
Cornworthy Devon ... 5 U9
Corpach Highld ... 94 F3
Corpusty Norfk ... 50 K7
Corrachree Abers ... 98 H3
Corran Highld ... 94 E6
Corran Highld ... 101 L10
Corranbuie Ag & B ... 79 Q4
Corrany IoM ... 60 g5
Corribeg Highld ... 94 D3
Corrie D & G ... 75 N7
Corrie N Ayrs ... 80 E4
Corriecravie N Ayrs ... 79 S11
Corriegills N Ayrs ... 80 E5
Corriegour Lodge Hotel Highld ... 102 C13
Corriemoille Highld ... 102 C3
Corrimony Highld ... 102 D8
Corringham Lincs ... 58 E8
Corringham Thurr ... 22 H11
Corris Gwynd ... 43 P12
Corris Uchaf Gwynd ... 43 P12
Corrow Ag & B ... 88 E5
Corry Highld ... 100 f7
Corry of Ardnagrask Highld ... 102 F6
Corscombe Devon ... 15 P13
Corscombe Dorset ... 7 P3
Corse Gloucs ... 28 E2
Corse Lawn Gloucs ... 28 F2
Corsindae Abers ... 99 M2
Corsley Wilts ... 18 B12
Corsley Heath Wilts ... 18 B12
Corsock D & G ... 74 E10
Corston BaNES ... 17 S3
Corston Wilts ... 28 H10
Corstorphine C Edin ... 83 N4
Cortachy Angus ... 98 F12
Corton Suffk ... 41 T1
Corton Wilts ... 18 D12
Corton Denham Somset ... 17 R12
Coruanan Highld ... 94 F5
Corwen Denbgs ... 44 C5
Coryates Dorset ... 7 R7
Coryton Devon ... 5 M4
Coryton Thurr ... 22 J11
Cosby Leics ... 37 P1
Coseley Dudley ... 36 B2
Cosford Shrops ... 45 S12
Cosgrove Nhants ... 30 G4
Cosham C Port ... 9 S7
Cosheston Pembks ... 24 H9
Coshieville P & K ... 90 A2
Cossall Notts ... 47 N5
Cossall Marsh Notts ... 47 N5
Cossington Leics ... 47 R11
Cossington Somset ... 17 L8
Costessey Norfk ... 51 L11
Costock Notts ... 47 Q8
Coston Leics ... 48 B10
Coston Norfk ... 50 J12
Cote Oxon ... 29 R7
Cotebrook Ches W ... 55 N13
Cotehill Cumb ... 67 Q2
Cotes Cumb ... 61 S3
Cotes Leics ... 47 Q9
Cotes Staffs ... 45 T7
Cotesbach Leics ... 37 Q4
Cotes Heath Staffs ... 45 T7
Cotford St Luke Somset ... 16 G11
Cotgrave Notts ... 47 R6
Cotham Notts ... 47 U3
Cothelstone Somset ... 16 G10
Cotheridge Worcs ... 35 S10
Cotherstone Dur ... 69 L8
Cothill Oxon ... 29 U8
Cotleigh Devon ... 6 H4
Cotmanhay Derbys ... 47 M5
Coton Cambs ... 39 N9
Coton Nhants ... 37 S6
Coton Shrops ... 45 L7
Coton Staffs ... 45 U8
Coton Staffs ... 46 H9
Coton Clanford Staffs ... 45 U9
Coton Hayes Staffs ... 45 U9
Coton Hill Shrops ... 45 L11
Coton in the Clay Staffs ... 46 G8
Coton in the Elms Derbys ... 46 J10
Cott Devon ... 5 T8
Cottage End Hants ... 19 P12
Cottam E R Yk ... 65 M7
Cottam Lancs ... 61 U13
Cottam Notts ... 58 D11
Cottenham Cambs ... 39 P7
Cotterdale N York ... 68 H14
Cottered Herts ... 31 T7
Cotteridge Birm ... 36 D4
Cotterstock Nhants ... 38 F2
Cottesbrooke Nhants ... 37 T6
Cottesmore Rutlnd ... 48 D11
Cotteylands Devon ... 16 C13
Cottingham E R Yk ... 65 N13
Cottingham Nhants ... 38 B2
Cottingley C Brad ... 63 N12
Cottingley Hall Crematorium Leeds ... 63 R13
Cottisford Oxon ... 30 B6
Cotton Suffk ... 40 J7
Cotton End Bed ... 38 G11
Cotton Tree Lancs ... 62 H11
Cottown Abers ... 104 K9
Cottown of Gight Abers ... 105 M8
Cotts Devon ... 5 M7
Cotwall Wrekin ... 45 P10
Cotwalton Staffs ... 46 B7
Couch's Mill Cnwll ... 4 F9
Coughton Herefs ... 27 U3
Coughton Warwks ... 36 E8
Coulaghailtro Ag & B ... 79 P5
Coulags Highld ... 101 N4
Coulderton Cumb ... 66 E11
Coull Abers ... 98 K3
Coulport Ag & B ... 88 F8
Coulsdon Gt Lon ... 21 N11

Coulston Wilts ... 18 E10
Coulter S Lans ... 82 K12
Coultershaw Bridge W Susx ... 10 E7
Coultings Somset ... 16 H8
Coulton N York ... 64 F5
Coultra Fife ... 91 N7
Cound Shrops ... 45 N12
Coundlane Shrops ... 45 N12
Coundon Dur ... 69 R7
Coundon Grange Dur ... 69 R7
Countersett N York ... 62 J1
Countess Wilts ... 18 J12
Countess Cross Essex ... 23 L1
Countesthorpe Leics ... 37 Q2
Countess Wear Devon ... 6 C7
Countisbury Devon ... 15 R3
Coupar Angus P & K ... 90 K3
Coup Green Lancs ... 55 N1
Coupland Cumb ... 68 F9
Coupland Nthumb ... 85 N12
Cour Ag & B ... 79 R7
Courance D & G ... 74 K7
Court-at-Street Kent ... 13 L8
Courteenhall Nhants ... 37 U10
Court Henry Carmth ... 25 U6
Courtsend Essex ... 23 N8
Courtway Somset ... 16 H10
Cousland Mdloth ... 83 S5
Cousley Wood E Susx ... 12 B9
Cove Ag & B ... 88 F8
Cove Border ... 84 K4
Cove Devon ... 16 C13
Cove Hants ... 20 E11
Cove Highld ... 107 P6
Covehithe Suffk ... 41 T4
Coven Staffs ... 46 B12
Coveney Cambs ... 39 Q4
Covenham St Bartholomew Lincs ... 59 P8
Covenham St Mary Lincs ... 59 P8
Coven Heath Staffs ... 46 B12
Coventry Covtry ... 36 K5
Coventry Airport Warwks ... 37 L6
Coverack Cnwll ... 2 K13
Coverack Bridges Cnwll ... 2 H11
Coverham N York ... 63 M1
Covington Cambs ... 38 G6
Covington S Lans ... 82 J11
Cowan Bridge Lancs ... 62 C5
Cowbeech E Susx ... 11 U8
Cowbit Lincs ... 49 L10
Cowbridge V Glam ... 16 C2
Cowdale Derbys ... 56 G12
Cowden Kent ... 11 R2
Cowdenbeath Fife ... 90 K13
Cowden Pound Kent ... 11 R2
Cowden Station Kent ... 11 S2
Cowers Lane Derbys ... 46 K4
Cowes IoW ... 9 P10
Cowesby N York ... 64 B2
Cowesfield Green Wilts ... 8 K3
Cowfold W Susx ... 11 L6
Cowgill Cumb ... 62 F2
Cow Green Suffk ... 40 J7
Cowhill S Glos ... 28 B9
Cowie Abers ... 99 R7
Cowie Stirlg ... 89 T8
Cowlam E R Yk ... 65 M6
Cowley Devon ... 6 B6
Cowley Gloucs ... 28 J5
Cowley Gt Lon ... 20 J6
Cowley Oxon ... 30 B12
Cowling Lancs ... 55 N3
Cowling N York ... 62 J11
Cowling N York ... 63 Q1
Cowlinge Suffk ... 40 B10
Cowmes Kirk ... 56 J4
Cowpe Lancs ... 55 T2
Cowpen Nthumb ... 77 R9
Cowpen Bewley S on T ... 70 G7
Cowplain Hants ... 9 T6
Cowshill Dur ... 68 H4
Cowslip Green N Som ... 17 N4
Cowthorpe N York ... 63 U9
Coxall Herefs ... 34 J6
Coxbank Ches E ... 45 Q5
Coxbench Derbys ... 47 L5
Coxbridge Somset ... 17 P9
Cox Common Suffk ... 41 R4
Coxford Norfk ... 50 D8
Coxgreen Staffs ... 35 T3
Coxheath Kent ... 12 D5
Coxhoe Dur ... 70 D5
Coxley Somset ... 17 P8
Coxley Wick Wakefd ... 57 M3
Coxpark Cnwll ... 5 L6
Coxtie Green Essex ... 22 D9
Coxwold N York ... 64 C4
Coychurch Brdgnd ... 26 G11
Coychurch Crematorium Brdgnd ... 26 G11
Coylton S Ayrs ... 81 N9
Coylumbridge Highld ... 103 P13
Coytrahen Brdgnd ... 26 F10
Crabbs Cross Worcs ... 36 D7
Crab Orchard Dorset ... 8 F8
Crabtree W Susx ... 11 L5
Crabtree Green Wrexhm ... 44 H5
Crackenthorpe Cumb ... 68 E8
Crackington Haven Cnwll ... 14 D13
Crackley Staffs ... 45 T3
Crackley Warwks ... 36 J6
Crackleybank Shrops ... 45 S11
Crackpot N York ... 68 K13
Cracoe N York ... 62 K7
Craddock Devon ... 6 F2
Cradle End Herts ... 22 B3
Cradley Dudley ... 36 B3
Cradley Herefs ... 35 R11
Cradley Heath Sandw ... 36 B3
Cradoc Powys ... 26 J2
Crafthole Cnwll ... 4 K10
Cragabus Ag & B ... 78 E6
Crag Foot Lancs ... 61 T6
Craggan Highld ... 103 R10
Cragg Hill Leeds ... 63 Q12
Craghead Dur ... 69 R2
Crai Powys ... 26 F3
Craibstone Moray ... 104 F5
Craichie Angus ... 91 S2
Craig Angus ... 99 L13
Craig D & G ... 73 R7
Craig Highld ... 101 Q3
Craiganour Lodge P & K ... 95 S6
Craigbank E Ayrs ... 81 R10
Craigburn Border ... 83 N7
Craigcefnparc Swans ... 26 A6
Craigcleuch D & G ... 75 R6
Craigdallie P & K ... 90 K6
Craigdam Abers ... 105 N9
Craigdarroch D & G ... 74 D6
Craigdhu Ag & B ... 87 N9
Craigearn Abers ... 105 L13
Craigellachie Moray ... 104 B7
Craigend P & K ... 90 H7
Craigend Rens ... 89 L12
Craigendoran Ag & B ... 88 H9
Craigends Rens ... 89 L13
Craighat Stirlg ... 89 L9
Craighlaw D & G ... 72 K7
Craighouse Ag & B ... 78 K4
Craigie P & K ... 90 H5
Craigie S Ayrs ... 81 M6
Craigiefold Abers ... 105 Q3
Craigley D & G ... 74 E13
Craig Llangiwg Neath ... 26 C6
Craiglockhart C Edin ... 83 P4
Craigmillar C Edin ... 83 Q4
Craignant Shrops ... 44 G6
Craigneuk N Lans ... 82 D7
Craigneuk N Lans ... 82 E6
Craignure Ag & B ... 93 S11
Craigo Angus ... 99 L13
Craigrothie Fife ... 91 N9
Craigruie Stirlg ... 95 L14
Craig's End Essex ... 40 B13
Craigton Angus ... 91 T4
Craigton C Aber ... 99 R3
Craigton E Rens ... 89 M14
Craigton of Airlie Angus ... 98 E13
Craig-y-Duke Neath ... 26 C7
Craig-y-nos Powys ... 26 F4
Crail Fife ... 91 T10
Crailing Border ... 84 F13
Crailinghall Border ... 84 G13
Craiselound N Linc ... 58 C6
Crakehall N York ... 69 R14
Crakemarsh Staffs ... 46 E6
Crambe N York ... 64 G7
Crambeck N York ... 64 G6
Cramlington Nthumb ... 77 R11
Cramond C Edin ... 83 N3
Cramond Bridge C Edin ... 83 N3
Crampmoor Hants ... 9 M4
Cranage Ches E ... 55 S13
Cranberry Staffs ... 45 T6
Cranborne Dorset ... 8 F6
Cranbourne Br For ... 20 G8
Cranbrook Devon ... 6 D6
Cranbrook Kent ... 12 E8
Cranbrook Common Kent ... 12 E7
Crane Moor Barns ... 57 M6
Crane's Corner Norfk ... 50 F11
Cranfield C Beds ... 38 D11
Cranford Devon ... 14 H8
Cranford Gt Lon ... 20 K7
Cranford St Andrew Nhants ... 38 D5
Cranford St John Nhants ... 38 D5

Cranham Gloucs ... 28 G5
Cranham Gt Lon ... 22 E10
Cranhill Warwks ... 36 F10
Crank St Hel ... 55 M7
Cranleigh Surrey ... 10 H3
Cranmer Green Suffk ... 40 H6
Cranmore IoW ... 9 M10
Cranmore Somset ... 17 S8
Cranna Abers ... 104 K5
Crannich Ag & B ... 93 P9
Crannoch Moray ... 104 F5
Cransford Suffk ... 41 P8
Cranshaws Border ... 84 J5
Cranstal IoM ... 60 g2
Cranswick E R Yk ... 65 N9
Crantock Cnwll ... 3 L4
Cranwell Lincs ... 48 F4
Cranwich Norfk ... 40 B2
Cranworth Norfk ... 50 G12
Craobh Haven Ag & B ... 87 N2
Crapstone Devon ... 5 N7
Crarae Ag & B ... 87 T6
Crask Inn Highld ... 111 L10
Crask of Aigas Highld ... 102 E7
Craster Nthumb ... 77 R2
Craswall Herefs ... 34 F13
Cratfield Suffk ... 41 P6
Crathes Abers ... 99 N4
Crathie Abers ... 98 D4
Crathie Highld ... 96 H5
Crathorne N York ... 70 G11
Craven Arms Shrops ... 34 K4
Crawcrook Gatesd ... 77 N13
Crawford Lancs ... 55 L6
Crawford S Lans ... 74 J1
Crawfordjohn S Lans ... 82 G14
Crawley Hants ... 19 N13
Crawley Oxon ... 29 R5
Crawley W Susx ... 11 L3
Crawley Down W Susx ... 11 N3
Crawleyside Dur ... 69 L4
Crawshawbooth Lancs ... 55 T1
Crawton Abers ... 99 R8
Craxe's Green Essex ... 23 M4
Cray N York ... 62 J5
Crayford Gt Lon ... 22 D12
Crayke N York ... 64 D5
Craymere Beck Norfk ... 50 J7
Crays Hill Essex ... 22 H9
Cray's Pond Oxon ... 19 U4
Crazies Hill Wokham ... 20 C6
Creacombe Devon ... 15 U9
Creagan Inn Ag & B ... 94 D10
Creag Ghoraidh W Isls ... 106 c14
Creagorry W Isls ... 106 c14
Creaguaineach Lodge Highld ... 96 C6
Creamore Bank Shrops ... 45 M7
Creaton Nhants ... 37 T6
Creca D & G ... 75 P11
Credenhill Herefs ... 34 K12
Crediton Devon ... 15 T13
Creebridge D & G ... 73 L6
Creech Dorset ... 8 C12
Creech Heathfield Somset ... 16 J11
Creech St Michael Somset ... 16 J11
Creed Cnwll ... 3 N7
Creegbrawse Cnwll ... 2 J7
Creekmouth Gt Lon ... 21 S6
Creeksea Essex ... 23 M8
Creeting St Mary Suffk ... 40 J9
Creeton Lincs ... 48 F8
Creetown D & G ... 73 M8
Cregneash IoM ... 60 b9
Creg ny Baa IoM ... 60 f6
Cregrina Powys ... 34 E10
Creich Fife ... 91 M7
Creigiau Cardif ... 26 K11
Crelly Cnwll ... 2 H10
Cremyll Cnwll ... 5 M10
Cressage Shrops ... 45 N13
Cressbrook Derbys ... 56 J12
Cresselly Pembks ... 24 J9
Cressex Bucks ... 20 D4
Cressing Essex ... 22 K3
Cresswell Nthumb ... 77 S8
Cresswell Pembks ... 24 J9
Cresswell Staffs ... 46 C6
Creswell Derbys ... 57 R12
Creswell Green Staffs ... 46 E11
Cretingham Suffk ... 41 M8
Cretshengan Ag & B ... 79 P4
Crewe Ches E ... 45 R2
Crewe-by-Farndon Ches E ... 44 K3
Crewe Crematorium Ches E ... 45 R3
Crewe Green Ches E ... 45 R2
Crew Green Powys ... 44 H10
Crewkerne Somset ... 7 M3
Crews Hill Station Gt Lon ... 31 T12
Crewton C Derb ... 47 L7
Crianlarich Stirlg ... 95 L12
Cribyn Cerdgn ... 33 L10
Criccieth Gwynd ... 42 K6
Crich Derbys ... 46 K3
Crich Carr Derbys ... 46 K3
Crichton Mdloth ... 83 S6
Crick Mons ... 27 T9
Crick Nhants ... 37 Q6
Crickadarn Powys ... 34 C12
Cricket St Thomas Somset ... 7 L3
Crickheath Shrops ... 44 G9
Crickhowell Powys ... 27 M4
Cricklade Wilts ... 29 L9
Cricklewood Gt Lon ... 21 M5
Cridling Stubbs N York ... 57 R2
Crieff P & K ... 90 C7
Criggan Cnwll ... 3 Q4
Criggion Powys ... 44 G10
Crigglestone Wakefd ... 57 M3
Crimble Rochdl ... 56 C4
Crimond Abers ... 105 T4
Crimonmogate Abers ... 105 T4
Crimplesham Norfk ... 49 T13
Crimscote Warwks ... 36 H12
Crinaglack Highld ... 102 E7
Crinan Ag & B ... 87 N7
Crindledyke N Lans ... 82 F7
Cringleford Norfk ... 51 L12
Cringles C Brad ... 63 L10
Crinow Pembks ... 24 K7
Cripplesease Cnwll ... 2 E10
Cripplestyle Dorset ... 8 F6
Cripp's Corner E Susx ... 12 E11
Croanford Cnwll ... 3 Q2
Crockenhill Kent ... 21 T9
Crocker End Oxon ... 20 B5
Crockerhill W Susx ... 10 E9
Crockernwell Devon ... 5 S2
Crocker's Ash Herefs ... 27 U5
Crockerton Wilts ... 18 C12
Crocketford D & G ... 74 F11
Crockey Hill C York ... 64 E10
Crockham Hill Kent ... 21 R12
Crockhurst Street Kent ... 12 B7
Crockleford Heath Essex ... 23 P2
Croesau Bach Shrops ... 44 G8
Croeserw Neath ... 26 F8
Croes-goch Pembks ... 24 D4
Croes-lan Cerdgn ... 32 G11
Croesor Gwynd ... 43 M4
Croesyceiliog Carmth ... 25 R7
Croesyceiliog Torfn ... 27 Q8
Croes-y-mwyalch Torfn ... 27 Q9
Croes-y-pant Mons ... 27 Q7
Croft Devon ... 15 L11
Croft Leics ... 37 P1
Croft Lincs ... 59 S14
Croft Warrtn ... 55 P8
Croftamie Stirlg ... 89 L9
Croft Mitchell Cnwll ... 2 H10
Crofton Cumb ... 67 M2
Crofton Wakefd ... 57 N4
Crofton Wilts ... 18 K8
Croft-on-Tees N York ... 69 S11
Crofts Moray ... 104 B6
Crofts Bank Traffd ... 55 S7
Crofts of Dipple Moray ... 104 C5
Crofts of Savoch Abers ... 105 S4
Crofty Swans ... 25 T11
Crogen Gwynd ... 44 C6
Croggan Ag & B ... 93 S13
Croglin Cumb ... 67 S3
Croick Highld ... 108 G6
Cromarty Highld ... 103 L3
Crombie Fife ... 90 G14
Cromblet Abers ... 105 L8
Cromdale Highld ... 103 R10
Cromer Herts ... 31 S7
Cromer Norfk ... 51 M5
Cromford Derbys ... 46 J2
Cromhall S Glos ... 28 C9
Cromhall Common S Glos ... 28 C10
Cromor W Isls ... 106 j6
Crompton Fold Oldham ... 56 D5
Cromwell Notts ... 58 B14
Cronberry E Ayrs ... 81 R8
Crondall Hants ... 20 C13
Cronk-y-Voddy IoM ... 60 e4
Cronton Knows ... 55 L9
Crook Cumb ... 67 Q13
Crook Dur ... 69 Q5
Crookdake Cumb ... 66 K4
Crooked End Gloucs ... 28 B4
Crooked Holme Cumb ... 76 B14
Crooked Soley Wilts ... 19 M6
Crookes Sheff ... 57 M9
Crookgate Bank Gatesd ... 69 Q1
Crookhall Dur ... 69 P2
Crookham Nthumb ... 85 N11
Crookham W Berk ... 19 R8
Crookham Village Hants ... 20 C12
Crook Inn Border ... 83 M13
Crooklands Cumb ... 61 U3
Crook of Devon P & K ... 90 F11
Cropper Derbys ... 46 H7
Cropredy Oxon ... 37 M11
Cropston Leics ... 47 Q11
Cropthorne Worcs ... 36 C11
Cropton N York ... 64 H2
Cropwell Bishop Notts ... 47 S6
Cropwell Butler Notts ... 47 S6
Cros W Isls ... 106 k3
Crosbost W Isls ... 106 i6
Crosby Cumb ... 66 G6
Crosby IoM ... 60 e6
Crosby N Linc ... 58 E4
Crosby Sefton ... 54 H7
Crosby Garret Cumb ... 68 F12
Crosby-on-Eden Cumb ... 67 P1
Crosby Ravensworth Cumb ... 68 D9
Crosby Villa Cumb ... 66 G5
Croscombe Somset ... 17 Q8
Crosemere Shrops ... 44 K8
Crosland Edge Kirk ... 56 H4
Crosland Hill Kirk ... 56 H4
Cross Somset ... 17 M6
Crossaig Ag & B ... 79 R5
Crossapol Ag & B ... 92 B10
Cross Ash Mons ... 27 S4
Cross-at-Hand Kent ... 12 E6
Crossbush W Susx ... 10 G9
Crosscanonby Cumb ... 66 G5
Crosscoombe Cnwll ... 2 J7
Crossdale Street Norfk ... 51 M6
Cross End Bed ... 38 G9
Cross End Essex ... 40 E14
Crossens Sefton ... 54 J3
Cross Flatts C Brad ... 63 N11
Crossford Fife ... 90 H14
Crossford S Lans ... 82 F10
Crossgate Cnwll ... 4 H4
Crossgate Lincs ... 48 K8
Crossgate Staffs ... 46 B6
Crossgatehall E Loth ... 83 S5
Crossgates E Ayrs ... 81 M4
Crossgates Fife ... 90 J14
Cross Gates Leeds ... 63 T13
Crossgates N York ... 65 N2
Crossgates Powys ... 34 C8
Crossgill Lancs ... 61 U6
Cross Green Devon ... 4 K3
Cross Green Leeds ... 63 S13
Cross Green Suffk ... 40 D10
Cross Green Suffk ... 40 E10
Cross Green Suffk ... 40 G9
Crosshands Carmth ... 25 Q6
Cross Hands Carmth ... 25 U8
Cross Hands Pembks ... 24 J6
Crosshill E Ayrs ... 81 M10
Crosshill Fife ... 90 J12
Cross Hill Derbys ... 47 M4
Crosshill S Ayrs ... 81 L12
Crosshouse E Ayrs ... 81 M5
Cross Houses Shrops ... 45 M12
Cross in Hand E Susx ... 11 S5
Cross Inn Cerdgn ... 32 J8
Cross Inn Cerdgn ... 33 L7
Cross Inn Rhondd ... 26 K10
Cross Keys Ag & B ... 88 H7
Crosskeys Caerph ... 27 N8
Cross Keys Wilts ... 18 B6
Crosskirk Highld ... 112 C3
Crosslands Cumb ... 61 Q2
Cross Lane Head Shrops ... 35 R1
Cross Lanes Cnwll ... 2 H11
Cross Lanes Cnwll ... 3 L8
Cross Lanes N York ... 64 C7
Cross Lanes Wrexhm ... 44 J4
Crosslee Rens ... 88 K13
Crossmichael D & G ... 74 E13
Cross Oak Powys ... 27 L3
Cross o' th' hands Derbys ... 46 J4
Crosspost W Susx ... 11 L6
Crossroads Abers ... 99 M4
Crossroads Abers ... 99 P4
Cross Street Suffk ... 41 L5
Crosston Angus ... 98 H13
Cross Town Ches E ... 55 S11
Crossway Mons ... 27 S4
Crossway Powys ... 34 C9
Crossway Green Mons ... 27 T8
Crossway Green Worcs ... 35 T7
Crosswell Pembks ... 24 K3
Crosswood Cerdgn ... 33 M6
Crosthwaite Cumb ... 67 P13
Croston Lancs ... 55 L3
Crostwick Norfk ... 51 N11
Crostwight Norfk ... 51 P8
Crothair W Isls ... 106 g5
Crouch Kent ... 21 U12
Croucheston Wilts ... 8 F3
Crouch End Gt Lon ... 21 N5
Crouch Hill Dorset ... 7 S2
Crouch House Green Kent ... 21 R13
Croughton Nhants ... 30 B5
Crovie Abers ... 105 N2
Crow Hants ... 8 H8
Crowan Cnwll ... 2 G10
Crowborough E Susx ... 11 S4
Crowborough Town E Susx ... 11 S4
Crowcombe Somset ... 16 G9
Crowdecote Derbys ... 56 H13
Crowden Derbys ... 56 G6
Crowden Devon ... 15 N12
Crow Edge Barns ... 56 J6
Crowell Oxon ... 20 C3
Crowfield Nhants ... 37 R12
Crowfield Suffk ... 40 K9
Crow Green Essex ... 22 E8
Crowhill E Loth ... 84 J4
Crow Hill Herefs ... 28 B3
Crowhole Derbys ... 57 M11
Crowhurst E Susx ... 12 D13
Crowhurst Surrey ... 21 P13
Crowhurst Lane End Surrey ... 21 P13
Crowland Lincs ... 48 K11
Crowland Suffk ... 40 H6
Crowlas Cnwll ... 2 E10
Crowle N Linc ... 58 C4
Crowle Worcs ... 36 B9
Crowle Green Worcs ... 36 B9
Crowmarsh Gifford Oxon ... 19 T3
Crown Corner Suffk ... 41 M6
Crownhill C Plym ... 5 M9
Crownpits Surrey ... 20 G13
Crownthorpe Norfk ... 50 J13
Crowntown Cnwll ... 2 G10
Crows-an-Wra Cnwll ... 2 B11
Crow's Green Essex ... 22 G2
Crowshill Norfk ... 50 G12
Crow's Nest Cnwll ... 4 G7
Crowsnest Shrops ... 44 J13
Crowthorne Wokham ... 20 D10
Crowton Ches W ... 55 N12
Croxall Staffs ... 46 H11
Croxby Lincs ... 58 K7
Croxdale Dur ... 69 S5
Croxden Staffs ... 46 E6
Croxley Green Herts ... 20 J3
Croxteth Lpool ... 54 K7
Croxton Cambs ... 38 K8
Croxton N Linc ... 58 J3
Croxton Norfk ... 40 E4
Croxton Norfk ... 50 D6
Croxton Staffs ... 45 S7
Croxton Green Ches E ... 45 N2
Croxton Kerrial Leics ... 48 B8
Croxtonbank Staffs ... 45 S7
Croy Highld ... 103 M6
Croy N Lans ... 89 S10
Croyde Devon ... 14 K5
Croyde Bay Devon ... 14 K5
Croydon Cambs ... 39 M11
Croydon Gt Lon ... 21 P10
Croydon Crematorium Gt Lon ... 21 N9
Crubenmore Highld ... 96 K5
Cruckmeole Shrops ... 44 K12
Cruckton Shrops ... 44 K11
Cruden Bay Abers ... 105 T8
Crudgington Wrekin ... 45 P10
Crudwell Wilts ... 28 J8
Cruft Devon ... 15 M13
Crug Powys ... 34 D6
Crug-y-byddar Powys ... 34 E4
Crumlin Caerph ... 27 N7
Crumpsall Manch ... 56 C6
Crumplehorn Cnwll ... 4 F10
Crundale Kent ... 13 L6
Crundale Pembks ... 24 G7
Crunwere Carmth ... 25 L8
Cruwys Morchard Devon ... 15 U10
Crux Easton Hants ... 19 Q9

Column 7

Cruxton Dorset ... 7 R5
Crwbin Carmth ... 25 S8
Cryers Hill Bucks ... 20 E3
Crymych Pembks ... 24 K4
Crynant Neath ... 26 D7
Crystal Palace Gt Lon ... 21 P8
Cuaig Highld ... 100 g3
Cubbington Warwks ... 36 K7
Cubert Cnwll ... 2 K5
Cubley Barns ... 57 L6
Cubley Common Derbys ... 46 G7
Cublington Bucks ... 30 H8
Cublington Herefs ... 34 K13
Cuckfield W Susx ... 11 M5
Cucklington Somset ... 17 T11
Cuckney Notts ... 57 S12
Cuckoo Bridge Lincs ... 48 K9
Cuckoo's Corner Hants ... 20 A13
Cuckoo's Nest Ches W ... 44 J1
Cuddesdon Oxon ... 30 C12
Cuddington Bucks ... 30 F10
Cuddington Ches W ... 55 N12
Cuddington Heath Ches W ... 45 L4
Cuddy Hill Lancs ... 61 T12
Cudham Gt Lon ... 21 R11
Cudliptown Devon ... 5 N5
Cudnell Bmouth ... 8 F9
Cudworth Barns ... 57 N5
Cudworth Somset ... 7 L2
Cuerdley Cross Warrtn ... 55 M9
Cufaude Hants ... 19 U9
Cuffley Herts ... 31 T12
Cuil Highld ... 94 E8
Culbokie Highld ... 102 H4
Culbone Somset ... 15 U3
Culburnie Highld ... 102 E7
Culcabock Highld ... 102 J7
Culcharry Highld ... 103 M5
Culcheth Warrtn ... 55 Q8
Culdrain Abers ... 104 H8
Culduie Highld ... 100 g6
Culford Suffk ... 40 D6
Culgaith Cumb ... 68 D7
Culham Oxon ... 30 B13
Culkein Highld ... 110 A10
Culkein Drumbeg Highld ... 110 C10
Culkerton Gloucs ... 28 H8
Cullen Moray ... 104 G2
Cullercoats N Tyne ... 77 T11
Cullerlie Abers ... 99 N3
Cullicudden Highld ... 102 K3
Cullingworth C Brad ... 63 M12
Cuillin Hills Highld ... 100 d7
Cullipool Ag & B ... 87 N3
Cullivoe Shet ... 106 v3
Culloden Highld ... 103 L6
Cullompton Devon ... 6 D3
Cullompton Services Devon ... 6 D3
Culm Davy Devon ... 16 F13
Culmington Shrops ... 35 L4
Culmstock Devon ... 6 F2
Culnacraig Highld ... 107 T2
Culnaightrie D & G ... 73 T9
Culnaknock Highld ... 100 e3
Culpho Suffk ... 41 M11
Culrain Highld ... 108 K6
Culross Fife ... 82 J1
Culroy S Ayrs ... 81 L10
Culsh Abers ... 98 H4
Culswick Shet ... 106 s9
Cults C Aber ... 99 R3
Culverstone Green Kent ... 12 B3
Culverthorpe Lincs ... 48 F5
Culworth Nhants ... 37 P11
Culzean Castle & Country Park S Ayrs ... 80 J10
Cumberhead S Lans ... 82 F12
Cumbernauld N Lans ... 89 S10
Cumbernauld Village N Lans ... 89 S10
Cumberworth Lincs ... 59 T12
Cumdivock Cumb ... 67 M3
Cuminestown Abers ... 105 M5
Cumledge Border ... 84 K7
Cummersdale Cumb ... 67 M2
Cummertrees D & G ... 75 M12
Cummingstown Moray ... 103 U2
Cumnock E Ayrs ... 81 R8
Cumnor Oxon ... 29 U7
Cumrew Cumb ... 67 R3
Cumrue D & G ... 75 L8
Cumwhinton Cumb ... 67 P2
Cumwhitton Cumb ... 67 R3
Cundall N York ... 63 U5
Cunninghamhead N Ayrs ... 81 M4
Cunningsburgh Shet ... 106 u11
Cupar Fife ... 91 N9
Cupar Muir Fife ... 91 N9
Cupernham Hants ... 9 M4
Curbar Derbys ... 56 K12
Curbridge Hants ... 9 Q6
Curbridge Oxon ... 29 R6
Curdridge Hants ... 9 Q6
Curdworth Warwks ... 36 G2
Curland Somset ... 16 J13
Curland Common Somset ... 16 J13
Curridge W Berk ... 19 Q6
Currie C Edin ... 83 N5
Curry Mallet Somset ... 16 K12
Curry Rivel Somset ... 17 L12
Curteis' Corner Kent ... 12 G8
Curtisden Green Kent ... 12 D7
Curtisknowle Devon ... 5 S10
Cury Cnwll ... 2 H12
Cusgarne Cnwll ... 2 J8
Cushuish Somset ... 16 G10
Cusop Herefs ... 34 F12
Cutcloy D & G ... 73 M13
Cutcombe Somset ... 16 B9
Cutgate Rochdl ... 56 C4
Cuthill Highld ... 109 P6
Cutiau Gwynd ... 43 M10
Cutler's Green Essex ... 22 E1
Cutmadoc Cnwll ... 3 R3
Cutmere Cnwll ... 4 J8
Cutnall Green Worcs ... 35 U7
Cutsdean Gloucs ... 29 L1
Cutthorpe Derbys ... 57 M12
Cuttivett Cnwll ... 4 J8
Cuxham Oxon ... 19 U2
Cuxton Medway ... 12 D2
Cuxwold Lincs ... 59 L6
Cwm Blae G ... 27 M6
Cwm Denbgs ... 54 C12
Cwmafan Neath ... 26 D9
Cwmaman Rhondd ... 26 J7
Cwmann Carmth ... 33 L11
Cwmavon Torfn ... 27 N6
Cwmbach Carmth ... 25 L5
Cwm-bach Carmth ... 25 R8
Cwmbach Powys ... 34 E13
Cwmbach Rhondd ... 26 J6
Cwmbach Llechrhyd Powys ... 34 B10
Cwmbelan Powys ... 33 T4
Cwmbran Torfn ... 27 P8
Cwmbrwyno Cerdgn ... 33 P4
Cwm Capel Carmth ... 25 R9
Cwmcarn Caerph ... 27 N8
Cwmcarvan Mons ... 27 T6
Cwm-celyn Blae G ... 27 N6
Cwm-Cewydd Gwynd ... 43 S10
Cwm-cou Cerdgn ... 32 E12
Cwmcrawnon Powys ... 27 L4
Cwmdare Rhondd ... 26 H7
Cwmdu Carmth ... 25 U3
Cwmdu Powys ... 27 L3
Cwmdu Swans ... 26 A9
Cwmduad Carmth ... 25 P4
Cwm Dulais Swans ... 25 V10
Cwmdwr Carmth ... 26 D3
Cwmfelin Brdgnd ... 26 F9
Cwmfelin Myr Td ... 26 K7
Cwmfelin Boeth Carmth ... 25 L7
Cwm-felin-fach Caerph ... 27 M8
Cwmfelinfach Myr Td
Cwmffrwd Carmth ... 25 R7
Cwmgiedd Powys ... 26 C5
Cwmgorse Carmth ... 26 B6
Cwmgwili Carmth ... 25 U8
Cwmgwrach Neath ... 26 E7
Cwm-Ifor Carmth ... 26 A3
Cwm Irfon Powys ... 33 T11
Cwmisfael Carmth ... 25 S7
Cwm-Llinau Powys ... 43 R12
Cwmllynfell Neath ... 26 B5
Cwmmawr Carmth ... 25 U8
Cwm Morgan Carmth ... 25 N4
Cwm-Parc Rhondd ... 26 G8
Cwm Penmachno Conwy ... 43 Q4
Cwmpengraig Carmth ... 25 P3
Cwmpennar Rhondd ... 26 K6
Cwmrhos Powys ... 27 L3
Cwmrhydyceirw Swans ... 26 A8
Cwmsychbant Cerdgn ... 32 K11
Cwmsyfiog Caerph ... 27 M6
Cwmtillery Blae G ... 27 N6
Cwm-twrch Isaf Powys ... 26 C6
Cwm-twrch Uchaf Powys ... 26 C5
Cwm-y-glo Carmth ... 25 U8
Cwm-y-glo Gwynd ... 52 J10
Cwmyoy Mons ... 27 Q3
Cwmystwyth Cerdgn ... 33 Q6
Cwrt Gwynd ... 43 N13
Cwrt-newydd Cerdgn ... 32 K10
Cwrt-y-gollen Powys ... 27 N4
Cyfarthfa Castle Museum Myr Td ... 26 K6
Cyffylliog Denbgs ... 44 C2
Cymau Flints ... 44 G2
Cymmer Neath ... 26 F8
Cymmer Rhondd ... 26 J9
Cyncoed Cardif ... 27 M11
Cynghordy Carmth ... 26 D1
Cynheidre Carmth ... 25 S9
Cynonville Neath ... 26 F8
Cynwyd Denbgs ... 44 C5
Cynwyl Elfed Carmth ... 25 P5
Cyfronydd Powys ... 44 D12

Cylibebyll Neath 26 C7
Cymau Flints 44 G2
Cymer Neath 26 K8
Cymmer Rhondd 26 J9
Cyncoed Cardiff 19 R12
Cynghordy Carmth 25 S9
Cynheidre Carmth 25 S9
Cynonville Neath 26 K8
Cynwyd Denbgs 44 C5
Cynwyl Elfed Carmth 25 Q5

D

Daccombe Devon 6 B11
Dacre Cumb 67 Q7
Dacre N York 63 P7
Dacre Banks N York 63 P7
Daddry Shield Dur 68 J5
Dadford Bucks 30 E5
Dadlington Leics 47 M14
Dafen Carmth 26 C6
Daffy Green Norfk 50 G12
Dagenham Gt Lon 22 D11
Daglingworth Gloucs 28 J6
Dagnall Bucks 31 L9
Dagworth Suffk 40 H8
Dailly S Ayrs 80 K12
Dainton Devon 5 V7
Dairsie Fife 91 P8
Daisy Hill Bolton 56 Q6
Daisy Hill Leeds 63 H14
Dalabrog W Is 106 C16
Dalavich Ag & B 83 T3
Dalbeattie D & G 74 F13
Dalbury Derbys 46 J7
Dalby IoM 60 d7
Dalby Lincs 59 R13
Dalby N York 64 E5
Dalcapon P & K 90 E2
Dalchalm Highld 109 S3
Dalchreichart Highld 102 A13
Dalchruin P & K 89 R2
Dalcrue P & K 90 F6
Dalderby Lincs 59 N13
Dalditch Devon 6 E5

Daldowie Crematorium C Glas 82 C6
Dale Cumb 67 R4
Dale Derbys 47 M6
Dale Bottom Cumb 67 L8
Dale End N York 62 J11
Dale End Derbys 56 J1
Dalehouse N York 71 N9
Dalelia Highld 93 S5
Dalgarven N Ayrs 80 K3
Dalgety Bay Fife 83 N2
Dalgig E Ayrs 81 R10
Dalginross P & K 89 S1
Dalguise P & K 90 E2
Dalhalvaig Highld 111 R6
Dalham Suffk 40 B8
Dalinlongart Ag & B 88 B8
Daloist P & K 97 M12
Dalqueich P & K 90 G11
Dalreavoch Highld 109 P3
Dalry N Ayrs 80 K3
Dalrymple E Ayrs 81 M8
Dalserf S Lans 82 E8
Dalsmeran Ag & B 79 L13
Dalston Cumb 67 N2
Dalston Gt Lon 21 P6
Dalswinton D & G 74 H8
Dalton Cumb 61 Q4
Dalton Dur 69 Q13
Dalton Lancs 55 L5
Dalton N York 63 U4
Dalton N York 69 S10
Dalton Nthumb 77 N11
Dalton Rothm 57 Q8
Dalton-in-Furness Cumb 61 N5
Dalton-le-Dale Dur 70 F3
Dalton Magna Rothm 57 Q8
Dalton-on-Tees N York 69 S11
Dalton Piercy Hartpl 70 G6
Dalveich Stirlg 95 R14
Dalwhinnie Highld 96 J7
Dalwood Devon 6 J4
Damask Green Herts 31 S7
Damerham Hants 8 G5
Damgate Norfk 51 R12
Dam Green Norfk 40 J3
Danaway Kent 12 G3
Danbury Essex 22 J6
Danby N York 71 M11
Danby Bottom N York 71 P11
Danby Wiske N York 69 T13
Dandaleith Moray 104 B6
Danderhall Mdloth 83 R5
Dane End Herts 31 T8
Danebridge Ches E 56 E13
Dane Hills C Leic 47 Q13
Danemoor Green Norfk 50 J13
Danesford Shrops 35 R2
Danesmoor Derbys 57 P14
Dane Street Kent 13 L5
Daniel's Water Kent 12 J7
Danshillock Abers 105 L4
Danskine E Loth 84 F5
Danthorpe E R Yk 65 T13
Danzey Green Warwks 36 F7
Dapple Heath Staffs 46 D8
Darby Green Hants 20 D10
Darby Lever Bolton 55 R5
Dardy Powys 27 N4
Daren-felen Mons 27 N5
Darenth Kent 22 E13
Daresbury Halton 55 N10
Darfield Barns 57 P6
Darfoulds Notts 57 S12
Dargate Kent 13 L3
Darite Cnwll 4 H7
Darland Medway 12 E2
Darland Wrexhm 44 H2
Darlaston Wsall 36 C1
Darlaston Green Wsall 36 C1
Darley N York 63 P8
Darley Abbey C Derb 47 L6
Darley Bridge Derbys 46 J1
Darley Dale Derbys 46 J1
Darley Green Solhll 36 G6
Darleyhall Herts 31 P8
Darley Head N York 63 P8
Darlingscott Warwks 36 H12
Darlington Crematorium Darltn 69 S10
Darliston Shrops 45 N7
Darlton Notts 58 C12
Darnford Staffs 46 F12
Darnick Border 84 E12
Darowen Powys 43 R13
Darra Abers 105 L6
Darracott Devon 14 J9
Darracott Devon 16 L5
Darras Hall Nthumb 77 P11
Darrington Wakefd 57 P2
Darsham Suffk 41 R7
Darshill Somset 17 R8
Dartford Kent 22 E13
Dartford Crematorium Kent 22 E13
Dartington Devon 5 T8
Dartmeet Devon 5 R6
Dartmoor National Park Devon 5 R5
Dartmouth Devon 6 V10
Darton Barns 57 M4
Darvel E Ayrs 81 R5
Darwell Hole E Susx 12 C12
Darwen Bl w D 55 Q2
Datchet W & M 20 G7
Datchworth Herts 31 S9
Datchworth Green Herts 31 S9
Daugh of Kinnermony Moray 104 A7
Dauntsey Highld 18 E4
Dauntsey Wilts 18 E4
Davenham Ches W 55 Q12
Davenport Stockp 56 C10
Davenport Green Ches E 55 T11
Davenport Green Traffd 55 T9
Daventry Nhants 37 Q8
Daventry Services Nhants ...
Davidson's Mains C Edin 83 P3
Davidstow Cnwll 4 F4
David Street Kent 12 B3
Davington D & G 75 T7
Davington Kent 13 L3
Daviot Abers 105 L10
Daviot Highld 102 K8

Daviot House Highld 102 K7
Davis's Town E Susx 11 S7
Davoch of Grange Moray 104 F5
Dawesgreen Surrey 21 M13
Dawley Wrekin 45 Q12
Dawlish Devon 6 B9
Dawlish Warren Devon 6 C9
Daws Green Somset 16 G12
Daws Heath Essex 23 L10
Daw's House Cnwll 4 J4
Dawsmere Lincs 49 P7
Daybrook Notts 47 Q4
Day Green Ches E 45 T2
Dayhills Staffs 46 C7
Dayhouse Bank Worcs 36 C5
Daylesford Gloucs 29 P3
Ddol Flints 54 D11
Ddol-Cownwy Powys 44 B10
Deal Kent 13 S5
Dean Cumb 66 G7
Dean Devon 15 P3
Dean Devon 15 R4
Dean Devon 5 U6
Dean Dorset 8 C6
Dean Hants 9 Q4
Dean Hants 9 S3
Dean Lancs 62 H14
Dean Oxon 29 S3
Dean Somset 17 S8
Dean Bottom Kent 21 R9
Deanburnhaugh Border 75 S3
Deancombe Devon 5 S7
Dean Court Oxon 29 U6
Dean End Dorset 8 C6
Deane Bolton 55 Q5
Deane Hants 19 R10
Dean Head Barns 56 L6
Deanhead Kirk 56 F3
Deanland Dorset 8 D5
Deanlane End W Susx 9 U6
Dean Prior Devon 5 S7
Dean Raw Nthumb 76 G13
Dean Row Ches E 56 C10
Deans W Loth 82 K5
Deanscales Cumb 66 G8
Deanshanger Nhants 30 F5
Deanshaugh Moray 104 D5
Deanston Stirlg 89 R5
Dean Street Kent 12 D5
Dearham Cumb 66 G5
Dearnley Rochdl 56 D4
Debach Suffk 41 M10
Debden Essex 39 R14
Debden Green Essex 22 E1
Debenham Suffk 41 L8
Deblin's Green Worcs 35 T11
Dechmont W Loth 82 K4
Dechmont Road W Loth 82 K5
Deddington Oxon 29 U1
Dedham Essex 40 J14
Dedham Heath Essex 23 P1
Dedworth W & M 20 F7
Deene Nhants 38 E2
Deenethorpe Nhants 38 E2
Deepcar Sheff 57 L7
Deepcut Surrey 20 F11
Deepdale Cumb 62 E2
Deepdale N York 62 H5
Deeping Gate C Pete 48 H12
Deeping St James Lincs 48 J12
Deeping St Nicholas Lincs 48 K10
Deerhurst Gloucs 28 G2
Deerhurst Walton Gloucs 28 G2
Deerton Street Kent 12 J3
Defford Worcs 36 B12
Defynnog Powys 26 G2
Deganwy Conwy 53 N7
Deighton N York 63 S2
Deighton N York 69 T12
Deighton York 64 F11
Deiniolen Gwynd 52 J10
Delabole Cnwll 4 D4
Delamere Ches W 55 N13
Delfrigs Abers 105 R11
Dell Quay W Susx 10 C10
Delley Devon 15 N6
Delliefure Highld 103 S9
Delly End Oxon 29 S5
Delnabo Moray 103 U12
Delnashaugh Inn Moray 103 U8
Delny Highld 109 N10
Delph Oldham 56 E5
Delves Dur 69 P3
Delvin End Essex 40 C14
Dembleby Lincs 48 F6
Demelza Cnwll 3 N4
Denaby Donc 57 Q7
Denaby Main Donc 57 Q7
Denbies Surrey 20 K12
Denbigh Denbgs 53 S10
Denbrae Fife 91 N8
Denbury Devon 5 U7
Denby Derbys 47 L4
Denby Bottles Derbys 47 L4
Denby Dale Kirk 56 K5
Denchworth Oxon 29 S9
Dendron Cumb 61 N5
Denel End C Beds 31 N5
Denfield P & K 90 D7
Denford Nhants 38 E6
Dengie Essex 23 N6
Denham Bucks 20 H5
Denham Suffk 40 B8
Denham Suffk 40 J6
Denham End Suffk 40 B8
Denham Green Suffk 40 J6
Denhead Abers 105 R5
Denhead Fife 91 Q9
Denhead of Gray C Dund 91 M6
Denholm Border 76 B2
Denholme C Brad 63 M13
Denholme Clough C Brad 63 M13
Denio Gwynd 42 F6
Denmead Hants 9 T6
Denmore C Aber 105 R12
Denne Park W Susx 10 K5
Dennington Suffk 41 N8
Denny Falk 89 S9
Dennyloanhead Falk 89 S9
Den of Lindores Fife 91 L8
Denshaw Oldham 56 E4
Densole Kent 13 N7
Denston Suffk 40 B10
Denstone Staffs 46 F5
Denstroude Kent 13 L3
Dent Cumb 62 G2
Denton Cambs 38 J4
Denton Darltn 69 R9
Denton E Susx 11 Q10
Denton Kent 13 P6
Denton Kent 22 G13
Denton Lincs 48 C6
Denton N York 63 P10
Denton Nhants 38 B9
Denton Norfk 41 N3
Denton Oxon 30 B12
Denton Tamesd 56 D8
Denver Norfk 49 U13
Denwick Nthumb 77 Q3
Deopham Norfk 50 J13
Deopham Green Norfk 50 H14
Depden Suffk 40 B9
Depden Green Suffk 40 B9
Deptford Gt Lon 21 Q7
Deptford Wilts 18 F13
Derby C Derb 47 L6
Derby Crematorium Derbys 47 L6
Derbyhaven IoM 60 d8
Derculich P & K 97 P13
Dereham Norfk 50 G11
Deri Caerph 27 L6
Derril Devon 14 J12
Derringstone Kent 13 P6
Derrington Shrops 45 L14
Derrington Staffs 45 U9
Derriton Devon 14 J11
Derry Hill Wilts 18 E6
Derrythorpe N Linc 58 D5
Dersingham Norfk 49 U8
Dervaig Ag & B 93 L7
Derwen Denbgs 44 C3
Derwen Fawr Carmth 25 Q5
Derwenlas Powys 43 Q14
Derwent Valley Mills Derbys 46 K2
Derwent Water Cumb 67 L8
Derwydd Carmth 26 A3
Desborough Nhants 38 B4
Desford Leics 47 N12
Detchant Nthumb 85 R11
Detling Kent 12 E4
Deuddwr Powys 44 G11
Deunant Conwy 53 R10
Deuxhill Shrops 35 Q3
Devauden Mons 27 T8
Devil's Bridge Cerdgn 33 P5
Devitts Green Warwks 36 J2
Devizes Wilts 18 F8
Devonport C Plym 4 J9
Devonside Clacks 90 D12
Devoran Cnwll 2 K9
Devoran & Perran Cnwll 2 K9
Dewarton Mdloth 83 S6
Dewlish Dorset 7 U5
Dewsbury Kirk 56 K2
Dewsbury Moor Kirk 56 K2
Dewsbury Moor Crematorium Kirk 56 K2
Deytheur Powys 44 F10

Dial N Som 17 P3
Dial Green W Susx 10 E5
Dial Post W Susx 10 K7
Dibberford Dorset 7 N4
Dibden Hants 9 N7
Dibden Purlieu Hants 9 N7
Dickens Heath Solhll 36 F5
Dickleburgh Norfk 41 L4
Didbrook Gloucs 28 K1
Didcot Oxon 19 R2
Diddington Cambs 38 J8
Diddlebury Shrops 35 M3
Didley Herefs 27 T1
Didling W Susx 10 C7
Didmarton Gloucs 28 F9
Didsbury Manch 55 T8
Didworthy Devon 5 R7
Digby Lincs 48 G3
Digg Highld 100 d3
Diggle Oldham 56 F5
Digmoor Lancs 55 L5
Digswell Herts 31 R9
Digswell Water Herts 31 S9
Dihewyd Cerdgn 32 K9
Dilham Norfk 51 P8
Dilhorne Staffs 46 C5
Dillarburn S Lans 82 G9
Dilston Nthumb 76 K13
Dilton Wilts 18 C11
Dilton Marsh Wilts 18 B11
Dilwyn Herefs 34 K10
Dimple Bolton 55 R3
Dimple Derbys 46 J1
Dinas Carmth 25 M4
Dinas Gwynd 42 E6
Dinas Pembks 24 H3
Dinas-Mawddwy Gwynd 43 R10
Dinas Powys V Glam 16 G2
Dinder Somset 17 Q8
Dinedor Herefs 35 M13
Dingestow Mons 27 T5
Dingle Lpool 54 J9
Dingleden Kent 12 F9
Dingley Nhants 37 U3
Dingwall Highld 102 G5
Dinmael Conwy 44 B4
Dinnet Abers 98 H4
Dinnington N u Ty 77 R11
Dinnington Rothm 57 R9
Dinnington Somset 7 M2
Dinorwic Gwynd 52 J10
Dinton Bucks 30 F10
Dinton Wilts 8 E2
Dinwoodie D & G 75 N6
Dinworthy Devon 14 H9
Dipley Hants 20 B11
Dippen Ag & B 79 Q8
Dippenhall Surrey 20 D13
Dippermill Devon 14 K11
Dippertown Devon 4 K4
Dipple Moray 104 D4
Dipple S Ayrs 80 J12
Diptford Devon 5 S9
Dipton Dur 69 Q2
Diptonmill Nthumb 76 J13
Dirleton E Loth 84 E2
Dirt Pot Nthumb 68 J3
Discoed Powys 34 G8
Diseworth Leics 47 N9
Dishforth N York 63 U5
Disley Ches E 56 D9
Diss Norfk 40 K5
Disserth Powys 34 B9
Distington Cumb 66 F8
Distington Hall Crematorium Cumb 66 F8
Ditcham Hants 9 U4
Ditchampton Wilts 8 F2
Ditcheat Somset 17 R9
Ditchingham Norfk 41 Q2
Ditchling E Susx 11 N7
Ditherington Shrops 45 M11
Ditteridge Wilts 18 B7
Dittisham Devon 5 V9
Ditton Kent 12 D4
Ditton Green Cambs 39 T9
Ditton Priors Shrops 35 P3
Dixton Gloucs 28 J1
Dixton Mons 27 U5
Dizzard Cnwll 14 E13
Dobcross Oldham 56 E6
Dobwalls Cnwll 4 G8
Doccombe Devon 5 T3
Dochgarroch Highld 102 H7
Dockenfield Surrey 10 C2
Docker Lancs 61 U5
Docking Norfk 50 B6
Docklow Herefs 35 N9
Dockray Cumb 67 N8
Dodbrooke Devon 5 S12
Doddinghurst Essex 22 E8
Doddington Cambs 39 P2
Doddington Kent 12 J4
Doddington Lincs 58 E12
Doddington Nthumb 85 P12
Doddington Shrops 35 P5
Doddiscombsleigh Devon 5 V3
Dodd's Green Ches E 45 P4
Doddshill Norfk 49 U6
Doddy Cross Cnwll 4 J8
Dodford Nhants 37 R8
Dodford Worcs 36 B6
Dodington S Glos 28 E11
Dodington Somset 16 G8
Dodleston Ches W 54 J1
Dodscott Devon 15 N9
Dodside E Rens 81 Q1
Dod's Leigh Staffs 46 D6
Dodworth Barns 57 M5
Dodworth Bottom Barns 57 M5
Doe Bank Birm 46 F14
Doe Lea Derbys 57 Q13
Dogdyke Lincs 48 K2
Dogley Lane Kirk 56 J4
Dogmersfield Hants 20 C12
Dogridge Wilts 29 L10
Dogsthorpe C Pete 48 J13
Dog Village Devon 6 C5
Dolanog Powys 44 C11
Dolau Powys 34 D8
Dolaucothi Carmth 33 N11
Dolbenmaen Gwynd 42 K5
Doley Staffs 45 S8
Dol-for Powys 43 R13
Dolfach Powys 43 T13
Dolgarrog Conwy 53 N9
Dolgellau Gwynd 43 P10
Dolgoch Gwynd 43 N13
Dol-gran Carmth 25 R4
Doll Highld 109 P4
Dollar Clacks 90 E12
Dollarfield Clacks 90 E12
Dolley Green Powys 34 G7
Dollwen Cerdgn 33 N4
Dolphin Flints 54 E12
Dolphinholme Lancs 61 U10
Dolphinton S Lans 83 M9
Dolton Devon 15 M10
Dolwen Conwy 53 Q7
Dolwyddelan Conwy 53 M11
Dolybont Cerdgn 33 M3
Dolyhir Powys 34 G9
Dolywern Wrexhm 44 F6
Domgay Powys 44 G10
Donaldson's Lodge Nthumb 85 M10
Doncaster Donc 57 S6
Doncaster Carr Donc 57 S6
Doncaster North Services Donc 57 U4

Dorn Gloucs 36 H14
Dorney Bucks 20 F7
Dornie Highld 101 M6
Dornoch Highld 109 P7
Dornock D & G 75 P12
Dorrery Highld 112 C6
Dorridge Solhll 36 G6
Dorrington Lincs 48 G3
Dorrington Shrops 45 R5
Dorrington Shrops 45 Q14
Dorsington Warwks 36 F11
Dorstone Herefs 34 H12
Dorton Bucks 30 E10
Dosthill Staffs 46 H14
Dothan IoA 52 E8
Dottery Dorset 7 N5
Doublebois Cnwll 4 F8
Doughton Gloucs 28 G8
Douglas IoM 60 f7
Douglas and Angus C Dund ...
Douglas Pier Ag & B 88 G6
Douglas Borough Crematorium IoM 60 f7
Douglastown Angus 91 P2
Douglas Water S Lans 82 G11
Douglas West S Lans 82 F11
Doulting Somset 17 R8
Dounby Ork 106 r18
Doune Highld 108 A7
Doune Stirlg 89 R5
Dounepark S Ayrs 80 H13
Dounie Highld 108 J5
Dounreay Highld 111 R3
Dousland Devon 5 N6
Dovaston Shrops 44 H9
Dove Green Notts 47 N3
Dove Holes Derbys 56 G11
Dovenby Cumb 66 G6
Dover Kent 13 R7
Dover Castle Kent 13 R7
Dovercourt Essex 23 T1
Doverdale Worcs 35 U7
Doveridge Derbys 46 G6
Doversgreen Surrey 21 M13
Dowally P & K 90 E2
Dowbridge Lancs 61 S13
Dowdeswell Gloucs 28 K4
Dowlais Myr Td 26 K6
Dowland Devon 15 N10
Dowlish Ford Somset 7 L2
Dowlish Wake Somset 7 L2
Down Ampney Gloucs 29 L8
Downderry Cnwll 4 J10
Downe Gt Lon 21 R10
Downend Gloucs 28 F8
Downend IoW 9 Q11
Downend S Glos 28 C12
Downend W Berk 19 Q5
Downfield C Dund 91 M6
Downgate Cnwll 4 H6
Downgate Cnwll 4 J5
Downham Essex 22 H8
Downham Gt Lon 21 Q8
Downham Lancs 62 F11
Downham Market Norfk 49 U13
Down Hatherley Gloucs 28 G3
Downhead Somset 17 P11
Downhead Somset 17 S8
Downhill P & K 90 F6
Downholland Cross Lancs 54 J5
Downholme N York 69 P13
Downicarey Devon 4 K3
Downies Abers 99 S5
Downing Flints 54 E11
Downley Bucks 20 D3
Down St Mary Devon 15 R11
Downside Somset 17 R6
Downside Somset 17 S8
Downside Surrey 20 K11
Down Thomas Devon 5 N10
Downton Hants 8 K10
Downton Wilts 8 H4
Dowsby Lincs 48 H8
Dowsdale Lincs 49 L11
Doxey Staffs 45 U9
Doxford Nthumb 85 T14
Doynton S Glos 28 D13
Draethen Caerph 27 M10
Draffan S Lans 82 E9
Dragonby N Linc 58 G4
Dragons Green W Susx 10 J6
Drakeholes Notts 58 B8
Drakelow Worcs 35 T3
Drakemyre N Ayrs 80 K2
Drakes Broughton Worcs 36 B11
Drakewalls Cnwll 5 L7
Draughton N York 63 L9
Draughton Nhants 37 U5
Drax N York 57 U1
Drax Hales N York 57 U1
Draycot Swindn 18 J5
Draycote Warwks 37 N6
Draycot Foliat Swindn 18 J6
Draycott Derbys 47 M7
Draycott Gloucs 36 G13
Draycott Shrops 35 T2
Draycott Somset 17 M6
Draycott Somset 17 Q12
Draycott Worcs 35 U11
Draycott in the Clay Staffs 46 G8
Draycott in the Moors Staffs 46 C5
Drayford Devon 15 S10
Drayton C Port 9 T7
Drayton Leics 38 B2
Drayton Lincs 49 L6
Drayton Norfk 51 L11
Drayton Oxon 19 S8
Drayton Oxon 37 M12
Drayton Somset 17 M12
Drayton Worcs 36 B6
Drayton Bassett Staffs 46 G14
Drayton Beauchamp Bucks 30 K10
Drayton Manor Park Staffs 46 G13
Drayton Parslow Bucks 30 H7
Drayton St Leonard Oxon 19 T2
Drebley N York 63 L8
Dreemskerry IoM 60 h4
Dreen Hill Pembks 24 F7
Drefach Carmth 25 M4
Drefach Carmth 25 Q3
Drefelin Carmth 25 Q3
Dreghorn N Ayrs 81 M5
Drellingore Kent 13 P7
Drem E Loth 84 E3
Dresden C Stke 46 B5
Drewsteignton Devon 5 S2
Driby Lincs 59 Q12
Driffield E R Yk 65 N8
Driffield Gloucs 29 L8
Driffield Cross Roads Gloucs 29 L8
Drift Cnwll 2 C11
Drigg Cumb 66 G13
Drighlington Leeds 63 Q14
Drimnin Highld 93 P8
Drimpton Dorset 7 M3
Drimsallie Highld 94 F3
Dringhouses York 64 D9
Drinkstone Suffk 40 F8
Drinkstone Green Suffk 40 F8
Drive End Dorset 7 R3
Driver's End Herts 31 R9
Droitwich Worcs 35 U8
Droman Highld 110 D5
Dron P & K 90 H8
Dronfield Derbys 57 N11
Dronfield Woodhouse Derbys 57 M11
Drongan E Ayrs 81 N9
Dronley Angus 91 L5
Droop Dorset 7 U3
Dropping Well Rothm 57 N8
Droxford Hants 9 S5
Droylsden Tamesd 56 C7
Druid Denbgs 44 B5
Druidston Pembks 24 E7
Druimarbin Highld 94 G3
Druimavuic Ag & B 94 G10
Druimdrishaig Ag & B 87 P9
Druimindarroch Highld 93 R2
Drum Ag & B 87 U9
Drum P & K 90 G10
Drumalbin S Lans 82 H11
Drumbeg Highld 110 D9
Drumblade Abers 104 H7
Drumblair Abers 104 K6
Drumbuie D & G 74 C5
Drumbuie Highld 100 H5
Drumburgh Cumb 75 N14
Drumburn D & G 66 C1
Drumchapel C Glas 89 M11
Drumchastle P & K 95 U7
Drumclog S Lans 81 S7
Drumeldrie Fife 91 Q11
Drumelzier Border 83 M12
Drumfearn Highld 100 f8
Drumfrennie Abers 99 M4
Drumgley Angus 91 N1
Drumguish Highld 96 K4
Drumin Moray 103 U9
Drumjohn D & G 81 M13
Drumlamford S Ayrs 72 H3
Drumlasie Abers 99 L3
Drumleaning Cumb 67 M2

Drumlemble Ag & B 79 M12
Drumlithie Abers 99 P7
Drummoddie D & G 72 K10
Drummond Highld 109 L10
Drummore D & G 72 D12
Drummuir Moray 104 E6
Drumnadrochit Highld 102 F9
Drumnagorrach Moray 104 G5
Drumpark D & G 74 G10
Drumrunie Lodge Highld 108 B4
Drumshang S Ayrs 80 K10
Drumuie Highld 100 d5
Drumuillie Highld 103 P11
Drumvaich Stirlg 89 Q5
Drunzie P & K 90 H9
Druridge Nthumb 77 R7
Drury Flints 54 G14
Drybeck Cumb 68 E9
Drybridge Moray 104 E3
Drybridge N Ayrs 81 M5
Drybrook Gloucs 28 B4
Dryburgh Border 84 F12
Dry Doddington Lincs 48 C4
Dry Drayton Cambs 39 N8
Drym Cnwll 2 G9
Drymen Stirlg 89 L8
Drymuir Abers 105 Q6
Drynoch Highld 100 d6
Dry Sandford Oxon 29 U7
Dryslwyn Carmth 25 U6
Dryton Shrops 45 N12
Dubford Abers 105 M3
Dublin Suffk 41 L7
Duchally Highld 108 J2
Duck End Bed 38 H10
Duck End Cambs 38 K6
Duck End Essex 22 F2
Duck End Essex 22 G2
Duckend Green Essex 22 H3
Duckington Ches W 45 L3
Ducklington Oxon 29 R6
Duck's Cross Bed 38 J10
Duddenhoe End Essex 39 Q13
Duddingston C Edin 83 Q4
Duddington Nhants 48 E13
Duddlestone Somset 16 H12
Duddleswell E Susx 11 R5
Duddlewick Shrops 35 Q4
Duddo Nthumb 85 N10
Duddon Ches W 55 M13
Duddon Bridge Cumb 61 M2
Duddon Common Ches W 55 M13
Dudleston Shrops 44 H6
Dudleston Heath Shrops 44 H6
Dudley Dudley 36 B2
Dudley N Tyne 77 R11
Dudley Hill C Brad 63 P13
Dudley Port Sandw 36 C2
Duffield Derbys 47 L5
Duffryn Neath 26 F8
Duffryn Myr Td 26 K7
Dufftown Moray 104 D7
Duffus Moray 103 U2
Dufton Cumb 68 E7
Duggleby N York 64 K6
Duirinish Highld 100 H5
Duisdalemore Highld 100 g8
Duisky Highld 94 F3
Dukestown Blae G 27 L5
Duke Street Suffk 40 J12
Dukinfield Tamesd 56 D7
Dukinfield Crematorium Tamesd 56 D7
Dulas IoA 52 G5
Dulcote Somset 17 Q8
Dulford Devon 6 E3
Dull P & K 97 N13
Dullatur N Lans 89 R10
Dullingham Cambs 39 T9
Dullingham Ley Cambs 39 T10
Dulnain Bridge Highld 103 Q11
Duloe Bed 38 J8
Duloe Cnwll 4 G9
Dulverton Somset 16 B11
Dulwich Gt Lon 21 P7
Dumbarton W Duns 88 K11
Dumbleton Gloucs 36 D13
Dumfries D & G 74 J10
Dumgoyne Stirlg 89 M9
Dummer Hants 19 R11
Dumpton Kent 13 S2
Dun Angus 99 M12
Dunalastair P & K 95 U7
Dunan Ag & B 88 D10
Dunan Highld 100 f7
Dunball Somset 16 K8
Dunbar E Loth 84 J3
Dunbeath Highld 112 E11
Dunbeg Ag & B 94 B12
Dunblane Stirlg 89 S5
Dunbog Fife 91 L8
Dunbridge Hants 9 L3
Duncanston Highld 102 G4
Duncanstone Abers 104 H10
Dunchideock Devon 6 A7
Dunchurch Warwks 37 N6
Duncote Nhants 37 R10
Duncow D & G 74 J9
Duncrievie P & K 90 H9
Duncton W Susx 10 F7
Dundee C Dund 91 N5
Dundee Airport C Dund 91 N6
Dundee Crematorium C Dund 91 N5
Dundon Somset 17 N10
Dundonald S Ayrs 81 M6
Dundonnell Highld 107 R7
Dundraw Cumb 67 L3
Dundreggan Highld 102 A10
Dundrennan D & G 73 U11
Dundry N Som 17 Q3
Dunecht Abers 99 N2
Dunfermline Fife 90 H14
Dunfermline Crematorium Fife 83 M1
Dunfield Gloucs 29 L8
Dunford Bridge Barns 56 J6
Dungate Kent 12 H4
Dunge Wilts 18 D9
Dungeness Kent 13 M12
Dungworth Sheff 57 L9
Dunham-on-the-Hill Ches W 55 L12
Dunhampstead Worcs 36 B8
Dunhampton Worcs 35 U7
Dunham Town Traffd 55 R9
Dunham Woodhouses Traffd 55 R9
Dunholme Lincs 58 H11
Dunino Fife 91 R9
Dunipace Falk 89 S9
Dunkeld P & K 90 F3
Dunkerton BaNES 17 T5
Dunkeswell Devon 6 F3
Dunkeswick N York 63 S10
Dunkirk Ches W 54 J11
Dunkirk Kent 13 L4
Dunkirk S Glos 28 E10
Dunkirk Wilts 18 E8
Dunk's Green Kent 21 U12
Dunlappie Angus 99 L11
Dunley Hants 19 Q9
Dunley Worcs 35 S7
Dunlop E Ayrs 81 N2
Dunmaglass Highld 102 G10
Dunmere Cnwll 3 Q3
Dunmore Ag & B 87 P10
Dunmore Falk 89 T9
Dunnet Highld 112 F2
Dunnichen Angus 91 Q1
Dunnington E R Yk 65 Q10
Dunnington N York 64 F9
Dunnington Warwks 36 E9
Dunnockshaw Lancs 62 G14
Dunn Street Kent 12 E3
Dunoon Ag & B 88 D11
Dunphail Moray 103 R6
Dunragit D & G 72 E8
Dunrod Inver 88 F11
Dunsa Derbys 56 K12
Dunsby Lincs 48 H8

Dunscar Bolton 55 R4
Dunscore D & G 74 G9
Dunscroft Donc 57 U5
Dunsdale R & Cl 70 J9
Dunsden Green Oxon 20 B6
Dunsdon Devon 14 H11
Dunsfold Surrey 10 G3
Dunsford Devon 5 U3
Dunshalt Fife 91 L9
Dunshillock Abers 105 R6
Dunsill Notts 47 N1
Dunsley N York 71 Q9
Dunsley Staffs 35 T4
Dunsmore Bucks 30 J11
Dunstable C Beds 31 M8
Dunstall Staffs 46 G9
Dunstall Common Worcs 35 U12
Dunstall Green Suffk 40 B8
Dunstan Nthumb 77 Q2
Dunster Somset 16 C8
Duns Tew Oxon 29 U2
Dunston Gatesd 77 Q13
Dunston Lincs 58 H13
Dunston Norfk 51 L13
Dunston Staffs 46 B10
Dunston Heath Staffs 46 B10
Dunstone Devon 5 N10
Dunstone Devon 5 S5
Dunsville Donc 57 U5
Dunswell E R Yk 65 Q13
Dunsyre S Lans 83 L9
Dunterton Devon 4 K5
Duntisbourne Abbots Gloucs 28 J6
Duntisbourne Leer Gloucs 28 J6
Duntisbourne Rouse Gloucs 28 J6
Duntish Dorset 7 R4
Duntocher W Duns 88 K11
Dunton Bucks 30 H8
Dunton C Beds 31 R4
Dunton Norfk 50 E7
Dunton Bassett Leics 37 P3
Dunton Green Kent 21 T11
Dunton Wayletts Essex 22 F9
Duntulm Highld 100 c2
Dunure S Ayrs 80 K9
Dunvant Swans 25 U12
Dunvegan Highld 100 b5
Dunwich Suffk 41 S6
Dunwood Staffs 46 B2
Durdar Cumb 67 P2
Durdale Devon 5 T12
Durgan Cnwll 2 K11
Durgates E Susx 12 B9
Durham Dur 69 S4
Durham Cathedral Dur 69 S4
Durham Services Dur 70 D5
Durham Tees Valley Airport S on T 70 E10
Durisdeer D & G 74 G3
Durisdeermill D & G 74 F3
Durkar Wakefd 57 M3
Durleigh Somset 16 H9
Durley Hants 9 Q5
Durley Wilts 18 K8
Durley Street Hants 9 Q5
Durlock Kent 13 Q3
Durlow Common Herefs 35 N13
Durn Rochdl 56 D3
Durness Highld 110 J3
Durno Abers 105 L10
Durran Ag & B 87 R4
Durrington Wilts 18 J12
Durrington W Susx 10 J10
Durris Abers 99 P4
Dursley Gloucs 28 D8
Dursley Cross Gloucs 28 C4
Durston Somset 16 J11
Durweston Dorset 8 B7
Duston Nhants 37 T8
Duthil Highld 103 P10
Dutlas Powys 34 F5
Dutson Cnwll 4 J3
Dutton Ches W 55 N11
Duxford Cambs 39 Q11
Duxford Oxon 29 R8
Duxford IWM Cambs 39 Q11
Dwygyfylchi Conwy 53 N7
Dwyran IoA 52 F9
Dyce C Aber 105 P12
Dyer's End Essex 40 B13
Dyfatty Carmth 25 S10
Dyffryn Brdgnd 26 G9
Dyffryn Carmth 25 Q4
Dyffryn Myr Td 26 K7
Dyffryn V Glam 16 E2
Dyffryn Ardudwy Gwynd 43 L9
Dyffryn Castell Cerdgn 33 P4
Dyffryn Cellwen Neath 26 F5
Dyke Lincs 48 H8
Dyke Moray 103 Q4
Dykehead Angus 98 F12
Dykehead Angus 98 K13
Dykehead N Lans 82 G7
Dykehead Stirlg 89 N6
Dykelands Abers 99 N10
Dykends Angus 98 D13
Dykeside Abers 105 L6
Dylife Powys 33 S2
Dymchurch Kent 13 M10
Dymock Gloucs 35 R13
Dyrham S Glos 28 D12
Dysart Fife 91 M12
Dyserth Denbgs 54 C11

E

Eachway Worcs 36 C5
Eachwick Nthumb 77 N11
Eagland Hill Lancs 61 S11
Eagle Lincs 58 E13
Eagle Barnsdale Lincs 58 E13
Eagle Moor Lincs 58 E13
Eaglescliffe S on T 70 G9
Eaglesfield Cumb 66 G7
Eaglesfield D & G 75 P11
Eaglesham E Rens 81 R2
Eaglethorpe Nhants 48 G14
Eairy IoM 60 d7
Eakley Lanes M Keyn 38 B10
Eakring Notts 47 T1
Ealand N Linc 58 C4
Ealing Gt Lon 21 L6
Eals Nthumb 68 G2
Eamont Bridge Cumb 67 R7
Earby Lancs 62 J11
Earcroft Bl w D 55 Q2
Eardington Shrops 35 R2
Eardisland Herefs 34 K9
Eardisley Herefs 34 H11
Eardiston Shrops 44 J8
Eardiston Worcs 35 Q7
Earith Cambs 39 N6
Earlestown St Hel 55 N7
Earley Wokham 20 C8
Earlham Norfk 51 L12
Earlish Highld 100 c3
Earls Barton Nhants 38 C8
Earls Colne Essex 23 L2
Earls Common Worcs 36 B9
Earl's Croome Worcs 35 U12
Earlsditton Shrops 35 P5
Earlsdon Covtry 37 L5
Earl's Down E Susx 11 U7
Earl's Green Suffk 40 H7
Earlsferry Fife 91 R11
Earlsfield Lincs 48 E6
Earlsford Abers 105 N8
Earl's Green Suffk 40 H7
Earl Shilton Leics 37 N2
Earl Soham Suffk 41 M8
Earl Sterndale Derbys 56 G12
Earlston Border 84 F11
Earlston E Ayrs 81 N4
Earl Stonham Suffk 40 K10
Earlswood Surrey 21 M13
Earlswood Warwks 36 F6
Earlswood Common Mons 27 T9
Earnley W Susx 10 B11
Earsairidh W Is 106 b19
Earsdon Nthumb 77 S11
Earsham Norfk 41 Q3
Earswick York 64 E8
Eartham W Susx 10 E9
Earthcott S Glos 28 B10
Easby N York 70 H11
Easdale Ag & B 87 N2
Easebourne W Susx 10 D6
Easenhall Warwks 37 N5
Eashing Surrey 20 F13
Easington Bucks 30 D10
Easington Dur 70 E4
Easington E R Yk 59 R1
Easington Nthumb 85 T11
Easington Oxon 19 U2
Easington R & Cl 71 L9
Easington Colliery Dur 70 E4
Easington Lane Sundld 70 D3
Easingwold N York 64 C6
Eassie and Nevay Angus 91 L3
East Aberthaw V Glam 16 E3
East Allington Devon 5 T11
East Anstey Devon 15 U7
East Appleton N York 69 R13
East Ashey IoW 9 R11
East Ashling W Susx 10 C9
East Aston Hants 19 Q11
East Ayton N York 65 M3
East Balsdon Cnwll 14 H13
East Bank Blae G 27 M6
East Barkwith Lincs 58 K10
East Barming Kent 12 D4
East Barnby N York 71 P9
East Barnet Gt Lon 21 N4
East Barns E Loth 84 K3
East Barsham Norfk 50 F7
East Beckham Norfk 51 L6
East Bedfont Gt Lon 20 J8
East Bergholt Suffk 40 J13
East Bierley Kirk 63 P14
East Bilney Norfk 50 G10
East Blatchington E Susx 11 Q10
East Bloxworth Dorset 8 B10
East Boldon S Tyne 77 T13
East Boldre Hants 9 M8
East Bolton Nthumb 77 P3
Eastbourne Darltn 70 D10
Eastbourne E Susx 11 U11
East Briscoe Dur 69 L9
East Brent Somset 17 L6
Eastbrook V Glam 16 G2
East Buckland Devon 15 Q6
East Budleigh Devon 6 E8
Eastburn E R Yk 65 L9
Eastburn C Brad 63 L11
East Burnham Bucks 20 G6
Eastbury Herts 20 J4
Eastbury W Berk 19 M5
East Butsfield Dur 69 P3
East Butterwick N Linc 58 D5
Eastby N York 63 L9
East Calder W Loth 83 L5
East Carleton Norfk 51 L13
East Carlton Leeds 63 Q11
East Carlton Nhants 38 B3
Eastchurch Kent 23 N13
East Chaldon (Chaldon Herring) Dorset 7 U8
East Challow Oxon 29 S10
East Chelborough Dorset 7 Q3
East Chiltington E Susx 11 P7
East Chinnock Somset 7 N2
East Chisenbury Wilts 18 H10
East Cholderton Hants 19 L11
East Clandon Surrey 20 J12
East Claydon Bucks 30 F7
East Coker Somset 7 P2
Eastcombe Gloucs 28 G6
East Compton Somset 17 R8
East Cornworthy Devon 5 U9
Eastcote Gt Lon 20 K5
Eastcote Nhants 37 R10
Eastcote Solhll 36 G5
East Cottingwith E R Yk 64 G11
Eastcott Cnwll 14 F9
Eastcott Wilts 18 F9
East Cowes IoW 9 Q10
East Cowick E R Yk 57 U2
East Cowton N York 69 S12
East Cramlington Nthumb 77 R10
East Cranmore Somset 17 S8
East Creech Dorset 8 C11
East Curthwaite Cumb 67 M3
East Dean E Susx 11 S11
East Dean Gloucs 28 B4
East Dean Hants 8 K3
East Dean W Susx 10 E7
East Devon Crematorium Devon 6 E5
East Down Devon 15 P4
East Drayton Notts 58 C11
East Dulwich Gt Lon 21 P7
East Dundry N Som 17 Q3
East Ella C KuH 65 P14
East End Bed 38 H9
East End C Beds 31 L4
East End E R Yk 65 S14
East End Essex 23 M5
East End Hants 9 L9
East End Hants 19 N7
East End Herts 22 C3
East End Kent 12 F9
East End Kent 23 L13
East End M Keyn 30 K4
East End N Som 17 N2
East End Oxon 29 S5
East End Somset 17 S7
East End Suffk 40 K13
East Farleigh Kent 12 D5
East Farndon Nhants 37 T4
East Ferry Lincs 58 C7
Eastfield N Lans 82 G6
Eastfield N York 65 N3
Eastfield Hall Nthumb 77 Q5
East Firsby Lincs 58 G9
East Fortune E Loth 84 F3
East Garforth Leeds 63 U13
East Garston W Berk 19 M5
Eastgate Dur 69 L5
Eastgate Lincs 48 H11
Eastgate Norfk 50 K9
East Ginge Oxon 19 R3
East Goscote Leics 47 R11
East Grafton Wilts 18 K8
East Green Suffk 41 R8
East Grimstead Wilts 8 J3
East Grinstead W Susx 11 P3
East Guldeford E Susx 12 H10
East Haddon Nhants 37 S8
East Hagbourne Oxon 19 S3
East Halton N Linc 59 L2
East Ham Gt Lon 21 R6
Eastham Wirral 54 J10
Eastham Ferry Wirral 54 J10
Easthampstead Br For 20 E9
Easthampton Herefs 34 K8
East Hanney Oxon 29 S9
East Hanningfield Essex 22 H7
East Hardwick Wakefd 57 Q3
East Harling Norfk 40 G3
East Harlsey N York 70 F13
East Harnham Wilts 8 G3
East Harptree BaNES 17 Q5
East Hartburn S on T 70 F9
East Hartford Nthumb 77 R10
East Harting W Susx 9 U5
East Hatch Wilts 8 D3
East Hatley Cambs 39 N10
East Hauxwell N York 69 Q13
East Haven Angus 91 S5
Eastheath Wokham 20 D9
East Heckington Lincs 48 J4
East Hedleyhope Dur 69 Q4
East Helmsdale Highld 112 D14
East Hendred Oxon 19 R3
East Heslerton N York 65 L4
East Hewish N Som 17 M4
East Hoathly E Susx 11 S7
East Holme Dorset 8 B11
Easthope Shrops 35 N2
Easthorpe Essex 23 M3
Easthorpe Leics 48 B6
Easthorpe Notts 47 U2
East Horrington Somset 17 Q7
East Horsley Surrey 20 K12
East Horton Nthumb 85 R12
East Howe Bmouth 8 F9
East Huntington C York 64 F8
East Huntspill Somset 17 L8
East Hyde C Beds 31 P9
East Ilsley W Berk 19 Q4
Eastington Devon 15 S11
Eastington Gloucs 28 E6
Eastington Gloucs 28 K5
East Keal Lincs 59 P14
East Kennett Wilts 18 H7
East Keswick Leeds 63 T10
East Kilbride S Lans 81 R2
East Kimber Devon 14 K13
East Kirkby Lincs 59 P14
East Knapton N York 64 K5
East Knighton Dorset 7 V7
East Knowstone Devon 15 U9
East Knoyle Wilts 8 B2
East Kyloe Nthumb 85 R11
East Lambrook Somset 17 M12
East Langdon Kent 13 R6
East Langton Leics 37 U2
East Langwell Highld 109 N4
East Lavant W Susx 10 D9
East Lavington W Susx 10 F7
East Layton N York 69 Q11
Eastleach Martin Gloucs 29 N6
Eastleach Turville Gloucs 29 N6
East Leake Notts 47 Q8
East Learmouth Nthumb 85 M11
Eastleigh Devon 15 L7
Eastleigh Hants 9 P5
East Leigh Devon 5 S9
East Leigh Devon 15 R11
Eastleigh Crematorium Hants 9 P5
East Lexham Norfk 50 E11
East Lilburn Nthumb 85 Q14
Eastling Kent 12 J4
East Linton E Loth 84 F3
East Liss Hants 10 B5
East Lockinge Oxon 29 T10
East London Crematorium Gt Lon 21 Q6
East Lound N Linc 58 C7
East Lulworth Dorset 8 B12
East Lutton N York 65 L6
East Lydeard Somset 16 G11
East Lydford Somset 17 Q10
East Mains Abers 99 M4
East Malling Kent 12 D4
East Malling Heath Kent 12 C4
East Marden W Susx 10 C8
East Markham Notts 58 B12
East Martin Hants 8 F5
East Marton N York 62 J9
East Meon Hants 9 T4
East Mere Devon 16 C12
East Mersea Essex 23 P5
East Midlands Airport 47 N8
East Molesey Surrey 21 L9
Eastmoor Norfk 50 B13
East Morden Dorset 8 C10
East Morton C Brad 63 M11
East Morton D & G 74 F5
East Ness N York 64 F4
East Newton E R Yk 65 U12
Eastney C Port 9 S9
Eastnor Herefs 35 R13
East Norton Leics 47 U13
Eastoft N Linc 58 D3
Eastoke Hants 9 U10
Easton Cambs 38 H6
Easton Cumb 67 N1
Easton Cumb 75 R14
Easton Devon 5 S3
Easton Dorset 7 S10
Easton Hants 9 R2
Easton Lincs 48 D8
Easton Norfk 50 K11
Easton Somset 17 P7
Easton Suffk 41 N9
Easton W Berk 19 P6
Easton Wilts 18 C6
Easton-in-Gordano N Som 17 U12
Easton Grey Wilts 28 G10
Easton Maudit Nhants 38 C9
Easton-on-the-Hill Nhants 48 F13
Easton Royal Wilts 18 K8
East Orchard Dorset 8 B4
East Ord Nthumb 85 P8
East Panson Devon 4 J2
East Parley Dorset 8 G9
East Peckham Kent 12 C6
East Pennard Somset 17 Q9
East Perry Cambs 38 J7
East Portlemouth Devon 5 T13
East Prawle Devon 5 T13
East Preston W Susx 10 H10
East Pulham Dorset 7 T3
East Putford Devon 14 J9
East Quantoxhead Somset 16 F8
East Rainham Medway 12 F2
East Rainton Sundld 70 D3
East Ravendale NE Lin 59 M7
East Raynham Norfk 50 E8
Eastrea Cambs 39 L1
East Riding Crematorium E R Yk 65 N6
Eastrington E R Yk 64 H13
Eastrip Wilts 18 B6
East Rolstone N Som 17 L4
Eastrop Swindn 29 N10
East Rounton N York 70 F12
East Rudham Norfk 50 D8
East Runton Norfk 51 L5
East Ruston Norfk 51 Q7
Eastry Kent 13 R5
East Saltoun E Loth 84 E5
East Sheen Gt Lon 21 M7
East Shefford W Berk 19 N6
East Sleekburn Nthumb 77 R9
East Somerton Norfk 51 S10
East Stockwith Lincs 58 B8
East Stoke Dorset 8 B11
East Stoke Notts 47 U3
East Stour Dorset 17 U12
East Stourmouth Kent 13 Q3
East Stowford Devon 15 Q7
East Stratton Hants 19 R13
East Studdal Kent 13 R6
East Sutton Kent 12 F6
East Taphouse Cnwll 4 F8
East Thirston Nthumb 77 P6
East-the-Water Devon 15 L7
East Tilbury Thurr 22 G12
East Tisted Hants 9 U2
East Torrington Lincs 58 K9
East Tuddenham Norfk 50 J11
East Tytherley Hants 8 K3
East Tytherton Wilts 18 E6
East Village Devon 15 T12
East Wall Shrops 35 M2
East Walton Norfk 50 B10
East Week Devon 5 R2
East Wellow Hants 9 L4
East Wemyss Fife 91 M12
East Whitburn W Loth 82 J5
East Wickham Gt Lon 21 S7
East Williamston Pembks 24 J9
East Winch Norfk 49 U10
East Winterslow Wilts 8 J2
East Wittering W Susx 10 B10
East Witton N York 63 P2
Eastwood Notts 47 N4
Eastwood Sthend 23 L10
East Woodburn Nthumb 76 K8
Eastwood End Cambs 39 Q1
East Woodhay Hants 19 P8
East Woodlands Somset 17 U8
East Worldham Hants 9 U2
East Wretham Norfk 50 F14
East Youlstone Devon 14 G9
Eathorpe Warwks 37 L7
Eaton Ches E 56 C13
Eaton Ches W 55 N14
Eaton Leics 47 U9
Eaton Norfk 51 M12
Eaton Notts 58 B11
Eaton Oxon 29 T7
Eaton Shrops 34 K4
Eaton Shrops 35 M3
Eaton Bishop Herefs 34 K13
Eaton Bray C Beds 31 L8
Eaton Constantine Shrops 45 N12
Eaton Ford Bed 38 J9
Eaton Green C Beds 31 L8
Eaton Hastings Oxon 29 P8
Eaton Mascott Shrops 45 M12
Eaton Socon Cambs 38 J9
Eaton upon Tern Shrops 45 Q9
Eaves Brow Warrtn 55 Q8
Eaves Green Solhll 36 J4
Ebberston N York 64 K3
Ebbesborne Wake Wilts 8 D4
Ebblake Dorset 8 G8
Ebbw Vale Blae G 27 M6
Ebchester Dur 69 P2
Ebdon N Som 17 L4
Ebernoe W Susx 10 F6
Ebford Devon 6 D7
Ebley Gloucs 28 F6
Ebnal Ches W 45 L4
Ebnall Herefs 35 L9
Ebrington Gloucs 36 G12
Ecchinswell Hants 19 Q9
Ecclaw Border 84 K5
Ecclefechan D & G 75 N10
Eccles Border 84 K10
Eccles Kent 12 D3
Eccles Salfd 55 S7
Eccles Crematorium Bury 55 S5
Ecclesall Sheff 57 M9
Ecclesfield Sheff 57 N8
Eccleshall Staffs 45 T8
Eccleshill C Brad 63 P13
Eccles Road Norfk 40 H3
Ecclesmachan W Loth 82 K4
Eccleston Ches W 54 K13
Eccleston Lancs 55 M3
Eccleston St Hel 55 L7
Eccleston Green Lancs 55 M3
Echt Abers 99 N2
Eckford Border 84 H13
Eckington Derbys 57 Q11
Eckington Worcs 36 B12
Ecton Nhants 38 B8
Ecton Staffs 46 F2
Edale Derbys 56 H10
Edburton W Susx 11 L8
Edderside Cumb 66 H3
Edderton Highld 109 N8
Eddington Kent 13 N2
Eddleston Border 83 P9
Eddlewood S Lans 82 D8
Edenbridge Kent 21 S13
Edenfield Lancs 55 S3
Edenhall Cumb 68 D7
Edenham Lincs 48 G8
Eden Mount Cumb 61 S4

Eden Park Gt Lon 21 Q9
Eden Project Cnwll 3 Q6
Edensor Derbys 56 K13
Edentaggart Ag & B 88 H7
Edenthorpe Donc 57 T5
Edern Gwynd 42 E6
Edgarley Somset 17 P9
Edgbaston Birm 36 E3
Edgcombe Cnwll 2 J10
Edgcott Bucks 30 E8
Edgcott Somset 15 T5
Edge Gloucs 28 F6
Edge Shrops 44 J12
Edgebolton Shrops 45 N9
Edge End Gloucs 28 A5
Edgefield Norfk 50 J7
Edgefield Green Norfk 50 J7
Edgefold Bolton 55 R5
Edge Green Ches W 45 L3
Edgehill Warwks 37 L11
Edgerley Shrops 44 J10
Edgerton Kirk 56 H3
Edgeside Lancs 55 T2
Edgeworth Gloucs 28 H6
Edgeworthy Devon 15 T10
Edginswell Torbay 5 V7
Edgiock Worcs 36 D8
Edgmond Wrekin 45 R9
Edgmond Marsh Wrekin 45 R9
Edgton Shrops 34 J3
Edgware Gt Lon 21 L4
Edgworth Bl w D 55 R3
Edinbane Highld 100 c4
Edinburgh Castle C Edin 83 Q4
Edinburgh Airport C Edin 83 M4
Edinburgh Old & New Town C Edin 83 Q4
Edinburgh Royal Botanic Gardens C Edin 83 P3
Edinburgh Zoo C Edin 83 N4
Edingale Staffs 46 H11
Edingham D & G 8 J1
Edingley Notts 47 S2
Edingthorpe Norfk 51 P7
Edingthorpe Green Norfk 51 P7
Edington Border 85 M7
Edington Nthumb 77 P9
Edington Somset 17 L8
Edington Burtle Somset 17 L8
Edingworth Somset 17 L6
Edithmead Somset 16 K7
Edlesborough Bucks 31 L9
Edlingham Nthumb 77 N4
Edlington Lincs 59 M12
Edmond Castle Cumb 75 U14
Edmondsham Dorset 8 F6
Edmondsley Dur 69 S4
Edmondthorpe Leics 48 C10
Edmonton Cnwll 3 N2
Edmonton Gt Lon 21 P4
Edmundbyers Dur 69 M2
Ednam Border 84 J11
Ednaston Derbys 46 J5
Edradynate P & K 90 D13 — 97 R13
Edrom Border 85 L7
Edstaston Shrops 45 M7
Edstone Warwks 36 G8
Edvin Loach Herefs 35 Q9
Edwalton Notts 47 Q6
Edwardstone Suffk 40 F12
Edwardsville Myr Td 26 K8
Edwinsford Carmth 33 M14
Edwinstowe Notts 57 T13
Edworth C Beds 31 R4
Edwyn Ralph Herefs 35 P9
Edzell Angus 99 L10
Edzell Woods Abers 99 L10
Efail-fach Neath 26 D8
Efail Isaf Rhondd 26 K11
Efailnewydd Gwynd 42 F6
Efail-Rhyd Powys 44 E8
Efailwen Carmth 24 K5
Efenechtyd Denbgs 44 D2
Effgill D & G 75 R7
Effingham Surrey 20 K11
Effirth Shet 106 s8
Efford Crematorium C Plym 5 N9
Egbury Hants 19 P10
Egdean W Susx 10 F6
Egerton Bolton 55 R4
Egerton Kent 12 H6
Egerton Forstal Kent 12 G6
Eggborough N York 57 T2
Eggbuckland C Plym 5 N9
Eggesford Devon 15 Q10
Eggington C Beds 31 L7
Egginton Derbys 46 J8
Egglescliffe S on T 70 F10
Eggleston Dur 69 M8
Egham Surrey 20 H8
Egham Wick Surrey 20 G8
Egleton Rutlnd 48 C12
Eglingham Nthumb 77 N2
Egloshayle Cnwll 3 Q2
Egloskerry Cnwll 4 H3
Eglwys-Brewis V Glam 16 D3
Eglwys Cross Wrexhm 44 K5
Eglwys Fach Cerdgn 33 N3
Eglwyswrw Pembks 24 K3
Egmanton Notts 58 B13
Egremont Cumb 66 F10
Egremont Wirral 54 H8
Egton N York 71 P11
Egton Bridge N York 71 P12
Egypt Bucks 20 F5
Egypt Hants 19 Q12
Eight Ash Green Essex 23 N3
Eilanreach Highld 100 h8
Eilean Donan Castle Highld 101 M6
Eisteddfa Gurig Cerdgn 33 Q5
Elan Valley Powys 33 S8
Elan Village Powys 33 S8
Elberton S Glos 28 B10
Elbridge W Susx 10 E10
Elburton C Plym 5 N10
Elcot W Berk 19 P6
Eldernell Cambs 49 M14
Eldersfield Worcs 35 T14
Elderslie Rens 89 L13
Elder Street Essex 39 S14
Eldon Dur 69 S7
Eldwick C Brad 63 N11
Elfhill Abers 99 Q6
Elford Nthumb 85 T12
Elford Staffs 46 G11
Elgin Moray 103 V3
Elgol Highld 100 f8
Elham Kent 13 N7
Elie Fife 91 R11
Elilaw Nthumb 76 K4
Elim IoA 52 E6
Eling Hants 9 M6
Elkesley Notts 57 U11
Elkstone Gloucs 28 H5
Ellacombe Torbay 5 B12
Elland Calder 56 G2
Elland Lower Edge Calder 56 H2
Ellary Ag & B 87 N10
Ellastone Staffs 46 F5
Ellel Lancs 61 T8
Ellemford Border 84 K6
Ellenborough Cumb 66 G6
Ellenbrook Salfd 55 R6
Ellenhall Staffs 45 T8
Ellen's Green Surrey 10 H3
Ellerbeck N York 70 G13
Ellerby N York 71 N10
Ellerdine Heath Wrekin 45 P9
Ellerhayes Devon 6 C4
Elleric Ag & B 94 F9
Ellerker E R Yk 58 H1
Ellers N York 63 L11
Ellerton E R Yk 64 F11
Ellerton Shrops 45 R8
Ellesborough Bucks 30 H11
Ellesmere Shrops 44 K6
Ellesmere Port Ches W 54 K11
Ellingham Hants 8 H8
Ellingham Norfk 41 Q2
Ellingham Nthumb 85 T13
Ellingstring N York 63 P3
Ellington Cambs 38 J6
Ellington Nthumb 77 R8
Ellington Thorpe Cambs 38 J6
Elliots Green Somset 17 U8
Ellisfield Hants 19 U12
Ellishader Highld 100 e3
Ellistown Leics 47 M11
Ellon Abers 105 R9
Ellonby Cumb 67 P5
Ellough Suffk 41 R3
Elloughton E R Yk 58 H1
Ellwood Gloucs 28 A6
Elm Cambs 49 P12
Elmbridge Worcs 35 U8
Elmdon Essex 39 Q13
Elmdon Solhll 36 G4
Elmdon Heath Solhll 36 G4
Elmer W Susx 10 F10

Elmers End Gt Lon 21 Q9
Elmesthorpe Leics 37 N1
Elm Green Essex 22 J7
Elmhurst Staffs 46 F11
Elmley Castle Worcs 36 C12
Elmley Lovett Worcs 35 T7
Elmore Gloucs 28 E4
Elmore Back Gloucs 28 E4
Elm Park Gt Lon 22 D10
Elmscott Devon 14 F8
Elmsett Suffk 40 J11
Elmstead Heath Essex 23 Q3
Elmstead Market Essex 23 Q3
Elmstead Row Essex 23 Q3
Elmsted Kent 13 M7
Elmstone Kent 13 Q3
Elmstone Hardwicke Gloucs 28 H3
Elmswell E R Yk 65 M8
Elmswell Suffk 40 G8
Elmton Derbys 57 R12
Elphin Highld 108 C12
Elphinstone E Loth 83 S4
Elrick Abers 99 Q2
Elrig D & G 72 J10
Elrington Nthumb 76 H13
Elsdon Nthumb 76 K7
Elsecar Barns 57 N7
Elsenham Essex 22 D2
Elsfield Oxon 30 B10
Elsham N Linc 58 H4
Elsing Norfk 50 J10
Elslack N York 62 J10
Elson Hants 9 S8
Elson Shrops 44 J6
Elsrickle S Lans 83 L10
Elstead Surrey 10 E2
Elsted W Susx 10 C7
Elsthorpe Lincs 48 G9
Elstob Dur 70 D8
Elston Lancs 62 B13
Elston Notts 47 U4
Elston Wilts 18 G12
Elstone Devon 15 Q9
Elstow Bed 38 G11
Elstree Herts 21 L3
Elstronwick E R Yk 65 S13
Elswick Lancs 61 S12
Elswick N u Ty 77 Q13
Elsworth Cambs 39 M8
Elterwater Cumb 67 L12
Eltham Gt Lon 21 R8
Eltham Crematorium Gt Lon 21 R8
Eltisley Cambs 39 L9
Elton Bury 55 S4
Elton Cambs 38 G1
Elton Ches W 55 L11
Elton Derbys 56 K14
Elton Gloucs 28 D5
Elton Herefs 34 K6
Elton Notts 47 U6
Elton S on T 70 F9
Elton Green Ches W 55 L12
Eltringham Nthumb 77 M13
Elvanfoot S Lans 74 J2
Elvaston Derbys 47 M7
Elveden Suffk 40 D5
Elvetham Heath Hants 20 D11
Elvingston E Loth 84 D4
Elvington C York 64 G10
Elvington Kent 13 Q5
Elwell Devon 15 S5
Elwick Hartpl 70 G6
Elwick Nthumb 85 S11
Elworth Ches E 45 T1
Elworthy Somset 16 E9
Ely Cambs 39 R5
Ely Cardif 27 L12
Emberton M Keyn 38 C11
Embleton Cumb 66 J6
Embleton Dur 70 F7
Embleton Nthumb 85 U14
Embo Highld 109 Q5
Emborough Somset 17 R6
Embo Street Highld 109 Q6
Embsay N York 63 L9
Emery Down Hants 9 L7
Emley Kirk 56 K4
Emley Moor Kirk 56 K4
Emmbrook Wokham 20 D9
Emmer Green Readg 20 B7
Emmett Carr Derbys 57 Q11
Emmington Oxon 30 F12
Emneth Norfk 49 Q12
Emneth Hungate Norfk 49 R12
Empingham Rutlnd 48 D12
Empshott Hants 10 B3
Empshott Green Hants 10 B3
Emstrey Crematorium Shrops 45 M11
Emsworth Hants 9 U8
Enborne W Berk 19 P8
Enborne Row W Berk 19 P8
Enchmarsh Shrops 35 M1
Enderby Leics 37 P14
Endmoor Cumb 61 U3
Endon Staffs 46 B3
Endon Bank Staffs 46 B3
Enfield Gt Lon 21 P3
Enfield Crematorium Gt Lon 21 P3
Enfield Lock Gt Lon 21 Q3
Enfield Wash Gt Lon 21 Q3
Enford Wilts 18 H10
Engine Common S Glos 28 C10
England's Gate Herefs 35 N10
Englefield W Berk 19 T6
Englefield Green Surrey 20 G8
Engleseabrook Ches E 45 S3
English Bicknor Gloucs 28 A4
Englishcombe BaNES 17 T4
English Frankton Shrops 45 L8
Engollan Cnwll 3 M2
Enham-Alamein Hants 19 N11
Enmore Somset 16 H9
Enmore Green Dorset 8 B4
Ennerdale Bridge Cumb 66 G11
Enniscaven Cnwll 3 P5
Enochdhu P & K 97 T11
Ensay Ag & B 92 K9
Ensbury Brmouth 8 F9
Ensdon Shrops 44 K10
Ensis Devon 15 N7
Enstone Oxon 29 S3
Enterkinfoot D & G 74 G5
Enterpen N York 70 G11
Enville Staffs 35 T3
Eolaigearraidh W Isls 106 c18
Epney Gloucs 28 E5
Epperstone Notts 47 S4
Epping Essex 22 C7
Epping Green Essex 22 C6
Epping Green Herts 31 S11
Epping Upland Essex 22 C6
Eppleby N York 69 Q10
Eppleworth E R Yk 65 N13
Epsom Surrey 21 M10
Epwell Oxon 37 L12
Epworth N Linc 58 C5
Epworth Turbary N Linc 58 C5
Erbistock Wrexhm 44 J5
Erdington Birm 36 F2
Eridge Green E Susx 11 S3
Eridge Station E Susx 11 S4
Erines Ag & B 87 R9
Eriska Ag & B 94 B9
Eriskay W Isls 106 c18
Eriswell Suffk 40 B5
Erith Gt Lon 22 D12
Erlestoke Wilts 18 E10
Ermington Devon 5 Q10
Ernesettle C Plym 5 L8
Erpingham Norfk 51 L7
Erriottwood Kent 12 H3
Errogie Highld 102 G11
Errol P & K 90 K7
Erskine Rens 89 L11
Ervie D & G 72 C7
Erwarton Suffk 41 M14
Erwood Powys 34 C11
Eryholme N York 70 D11
Eryrys Denbgs 44 F2
Escalls Cnwll 2 B11
Escomb Dur 69 Q7
Escott Somset 16 E9
Escrick N York 64 F11
Esgair Carmth 25 Q5
Esgairdawe Carmth 33 M12
Esgerdawe Carmth 33 M12
Esgyryn Conwy 53 P7
Esh Dur 69 Q4
Esher Surrey 21 L9
Esholt C Brad 63 P11
Eshott Nthumb 77 Q7
Eshton N York 62 J8
Esh Winning Dur 69 Q4
Eskadale Highld 102 E8
Eskbank Mdloth 83 R5
Eskdale Green Cumb 66 H12
Eskdalemuir D & G 75 P6
Eskham Lincs 59 Q7
Eskholme Donc 57 T4
Esperley Lane Ends Dur 69 P8
Esprick Lancs 61 S12
Essendine Rutlnd 48 F11
Essendon Herts 31 S11
Essich Highld 102 H8
Essington Staffs 46 C13
Esslemont Abers 105 Q9
Eston R & Cl 70 H9
Etal Nthumb 85 N11

Etchilhampton Wilts 18 F8
Etchingham E Susx 12 D10
Etchinghill Kent 13 N8
Etchinghill Staffs 46 D10
Etchingwood E Susx 11 S6
Etling Green Norfk 50 H11
Etloe Gloucs 28 C6
Eton W & M 20 G7
Eton Wick W & M 20 F7
Etruria C Stke 45 U4
Etteridge Highld 96 H11
Ettersgill Dur 68 J8
Ettiley Heath Ches E 45 R1
Ettingshall Wolves 36 B1
Ettington Warwks 36 J11
Etton C Pete 48 H12
Etton E R Yk 65 M11
Ettrick Border 75 Q1
Ettrickbridge Border 83 S14
Ettrickhill Border 75 Q1
Etwall Derbys 46 J7
Eudon George Shrops 35 Q3
Euston Suffk 40 E5
Euximoor Drove Cambs 49 Q14
Euxton Lancs 55 N2
Evancoyd Powys 34 G9
Evanton Highld 102 H2
Evedon Lincs 48 F4
Evelix Highld 109 P6
Evenjobb Powys 34 G8
Evenley Nhants 30 C6
Evenlode Gloucs 29 P3
Evenwood Dur 69 Q8
Evenwood Gate Dur 69 Q8
Evercreech Somset 17 R9
Everdon Nhants 37 Q9
Everingham E R Yk 64 J11
Everleigh Wilts 18 K10
Everley N York 65 M2
Eversholt C Beds 31 L6
Evershot Dorset 7 Q4
Eversley Hants 20 C10
Eversley Cross Hants 20 C10
Everthorpe E R Yk 65 L13
Everton C Beds 38 J10
Everton Hants 9 L9
Everton Lpool 54 H8
Everton Notts 57 U9
Evertown D & G 75 S11
Evesbatch Herefs 35 Q11
Evesham Worcs 36 D12
Evington C Leic 47 R13
Ewart Newtown Nthumb 85 N13
Ewden Village Sheff 57 L7
Ewell Surrey 21 M10
Ewell Minnis Kent 13 Q7
Ewelme Oxon 19 T2
Ewen Gloucs 28 K8
Ewenny V Glam 26 G12
Ewerby Lincs 48 H4
Ewerby Thorpe Lincs 48 H4
Ewhurst Surrey 10 H2
Ewhurst Green E Susx 12 E11
Ewhurst Green Surrey 10 H3
Ewloe Flints 54 G13
Ewloe Green Flints 54 G13
Eworthy Devon 14 K13
Ewshot Hants 20 D12
Ewyas Harold Herefs 27 R2
Exbourne Devon 15 P12
Exbridge Somset 16 C11
Exbury Hants 9 N8
Exceat E Susx 11 S11
Exebridge Somset 16 C12
Exelby N York 63 R2
Exeter Devon 6 B6
Exeter Airport Devon 6 D6
Exeter & Devon Crematorium Devon 6 B6
Exeter Services Devon 6 D6
Exford Somset 16 B9
Exfordsgreen Shrops 45 L12
Exhall Warwks 36 F9
Exhall Warwks 37 L3
Exlade Street Oxon 19 U5
Exley Head C Brad 63 L11
Exminster Devon 6 B7
Exmoor National Park 16 A7
Exmouth Devon 6 D8
Exning Suffk 39 T7
Exted Kent 13 N7
Exton Devon 6 C7
Exton Hants 9 S4
Exton Rutlnd 48 C11
Exton Somset 16 B10
Exwick Devon 6 B6
Eyam Derbys 56 K12
Eydon Nhants 37 Q10
Eye C Pete 48 K12
Eye Herefs 35 L7
Eye Suffk 40 K6
Eye Green C Pete 48 K12
Eye Kettleby Leics 47 T10
Eyemouth Border 85 N6
Eyeworth C Beds 38 J11
Eyhorne Street Kent 12 F5
Eyke Suffk 41 P10
Eynesbury Cambs 38 J9
Eynsford Kent 21 T9
Eynsham Oxon 29 T6
Eype Dorset 7 M6
Eyre Highld 100 d4
Eythorne Kent 13 Q6
Eyton Herefs 35 L8
Eyton Shrops 44 J7
Eyton Shrops 45 L13
Eyton Wrexhm 44 J4
Eyton on Severn Shrops 45 N12
Eyton upon the Weald Moors Wrekin 45 Q11

F

Faccombe Hants 19 N9
Faceby N York 70 G12
Fachwen Powys 44 E11
Facit Lancs 56 C3
Fackley Notts 47 N1
Faddiley Ches E 45 N3
Fadmoor N York 64 F2
Faerdre Swans 26 B7
Fagwyr Swans 26 B7
Failand N Som 17 P2
Failford S Ayrs 81 P7
Failsworth Oldham 56 C6
Fairbourne Gwynd 43 M11
Fairburn N York 64 B14
Fairfield Derbys 56 G12
Fairfield Worcs 36 B6
Fairford Gloucs 29 N7
Fairford Park Gloucs 29 N7
Fairgirth D & G 66 C1
Fair Green Norfk 49 U10
Fairhaven Lancs 61 Q14
Fair Isle Shet 106 t11
Fairlands Surrey 20 G12
Fairlie N Ayrs 80 J2
Fairlight E Susx 12 G13
Fairmile Devon 6 E5
Fairmile Surrey 20 K10
Fairmilehead C Edin 83 P5
Fairnilee Border 84 E12
Fair Oak Hants 9 P5
Fairoak Staffs 45 S7
Fair Oak Green Hants 19 U8
Fairseat Kent 12 B3
Fairstead Essex 22 J4
Fairstead Norfk 49 U10
Fairwarp E Susx 11 R5
Fairwater Cardif 27 L12
Fairy Cross Devon 14 K8
Fakenham Norfk 50 F8
Fakenham Magna Suffk 40 F5
Fala Mdloth 84 C6
Fala Dam Mdloth 84 C6
Falcut Nhants 30 C4
Faldingworth Lincs 58 H10
Faldouet Jersey 7 e2
Falfield S Glos 28 C9
Falkenham Suffk 41 N13
Falkirk Falk 82 G3
Falkirk Crematorium Falk 82 G2
Falkirk Wheel Falk 82 G2
Falkland Fife 91 L10
Fallgate Derbys 47 L1
Fallin Stirlg 89 T7
Fallodon Nthumb 85 T14
Fallowfield Manch 56 B7
Fallowfield Nthumb 76 J12
Falls of Blarghour Ag & B 87 T4
Falmer E Susx 11 N9
Falmouth Cnwll 3 L10
Falnash Border 75 R5
Falsgrave N York 65 N2
Falstone Nthumb 76 E8
Fanagmore Highld 110 D7
Fancott C Beds 31 N7
Fanellan Highld 102 E7
Fangdale Beck N York 70 H14
Fangfoss E R Yk 64 H9
Fankerton Falk 89 S8
Fanmore Ag & B 93 N9
Fannich Lodge Highld 108 F14
Fans Border 84 F10
Far Bletchley M Keyn 30 H6
Far Cotton Nhants 37 U9

Farden Shrops 35 N5
Fareham Hants 9 R7
Farewell Staffs 46 E11
Far Forest Worcs 35 R5
Farforth Lincs 59 P11
Far Green Gloucs 28 E7
Faringdon Oxon 29 Q8
Farington Lancs 55 N1
Farlam Cumb 76 B14
Farleigh N Som 17 N3
Farleigh Surrey 21 Q10
Farleigh Hungerford Somset 18 B9
Farleigh Wallop Hants 19 T11
Farlesthorpe Lincs 59 S12
Farleton Cumb 61 U3
Farleton Lancs 62 B6
Farley Derbys 46 J1
Farley Staffs 46 E5
Farley Wilts 8 J3
Farley Green Suffk 40 B10
Farley Green Surrey 20 J13
Farley Hill Wokham 20 B10
Farleys End Gloucs 28 E5
Farlington C Port 9 T7
Farlington N York 64 F6
Farlow Shrops 35 P4
Farmborough BaNES 17 S4
Farmbridge End Essex 22 F5
Farmcote Gloucs 29 L2
Farmcote Shrops 35 S2
Farmers Carmth 33 N11
Farmington Gloucs 29 N5
Far Moor Wigan 55 M5
Farmoor Oxon 29 T6
Farms Common Cnwll 2 H10
Farmtown Moray 104 G5
Farnah Green Derbys 46 K4
Farnborough Gt Lon 21 R10
Farnborough Hants 20 E11
Farnborough W Berk 19 Q4
Farnborough Warwks 37 N11
Farnborough Park Hants 20 E11
Farnborough Street Hants 20 E11
Farncombe Surrey 10 F2
Farndish Bed 38 D8
Farndon Ches W 44 K3
Farndon Notts 47 U3
Farne Islands Nthumb 85 V11
Farnell Angus 99 M13
Farnham Dorset 8 D6
Farnham Essex 22 C2
Farnham N York 63 S7
Farnham Suffk 41 R8
Farnham Surrey 20 D13
Farnham Common Bucks 20 G6
Farnham Green Essex 22 C2
Farnham Royal Bucks 20 G6
Farnhill N York 63 L10
Farningham Kent 22 D10
Farnley Leeds 63 R13
Farnley N York 63 Q10
Farnley Tyas Kirk 56 H4
Farnsfield Notts 47 S2
Farnworth Bolton 55 R5
Farnworth Halton 55 M9
Far Oakridge Gloucs 28 H7
Farr Highld 96 G4
Farr Highld 102 J8
Farr Highld 111 Q4
Farraline Highld 102 G10
Farringdon Devon 6 D6
Farrington Gurney Somset 17 R5
Far Sawrey Cumb 67 N13
Farsley Leeds 63 Q12
Farther Howegreen Essex 22 K7
Farthing Green Kent 12 F6
Farthinghoe Nhants 30 B5
Farthingloe Kent 13 Q7
Farthingstone Nhants 37 R9
Farthing Street Gt Lon 21 R10
Fartown Kirk 56 J3
Fartown Leeds 63 Q13
Farway Devon 6 G5
Fasnacloich Ag & B 94 D9
Fasnakyle Highld 102 D10
Fassfern Highld 94 F3
Fatfield Sundld 70 D2
Faugh Cumb 67 Q2
Fauld Staffs 46 G8
Fauldhouse W Loth 82 H6
Faulkbourne Essex 22 J4
Faulkland Somset 17 T6
Fauls Shrops 45 N7
Faversham Kent 12 K3
Fawdington N York 63 U5
Fawdon N u Ty 77 Q12
Fawdon Nthumb 77 L2
Fawfieldhead Staffs 46 E1
Fawkham Green Kent 21 U9
Fawler Oxon 29 S5
Fawley Bucks 20 C5
Fawley Hants 9 N8
Fawley W Berk 19 Q4
Fawley Chapel Herefs 28 A2
Fawsley Nhants 37 Q9
Faxfleet E R Yk 58 F1
Faygate W Susx 11 L4
Fazakerley Lpool 54 J7
Fazeley Staffs 46 H13
Fearby N York 63 P3
Fearn Highld 109 R11
Fearnan P & K 95 S11
Fearnbeg Highld 107 M13
Fearnhead Warrtn 55 P8
Fearnmore Highld 107 M12
Feering Essex 23 L4
Feetham N York 69 L13
Feizor N York 62 F7
Felbridge Surrey 11 P3
Felbrigg Norfk 51 M6
Felcourt Surrey 11 P2
Felden Herts 31 N12
Felin Fach Cerdgn 32 K9
Felin-fach Powys 34 C14
Felindre Carmth 25 Q7
Felindre Carmth 25 U9
Felindre Carmth 26 A3
Felindre Cerdgn 33 M9
Felindre Powys 34 D3
Felindre Powys 33 U3
Felindre Swans 26 B7
Felindre Farchog Pembks 24 K3
Felinfach Cerdgn 32 K9
Felinfoel Carmth 25 T9
Felingwmisaf Carmth 25 U7
Felingwmuchaf Carmth 25 U7
Felin-newydd Powys 34 D14
Felixkirk N York 64 B3
Felixstowe Suffk 41 P14
Felixstowe Ferry Suffk 41 Q14
Felkington Nthumb 85 N10
Felkirk Wakefd 57 N4
Fell End Cumb 68 F13
Felldownhead Devon 5 L4
Fell Foot Cumb 61 Q1
Felling Gatesd 77 R13
Fell Lane C Brad 63 L11
Fell Side Cumb 67 M5
Felmersham Bed 38 E9
Felmingham Norfk 51 N8
Felpham W Susx 10 F11
Felsham Suffk 40 F9
Felsted Essex 22 G3
Feltham Gt Lon 20 K8
Felthamhill Surrey 20 K9
Felthorpe Norfk 51 L10
Felton Herefs 35 N11
Felton N Som 17 P3
Felton Nthumb 77 Q6
Felton Butler Shrops 44 J10
Feltwell Norfk 40 B2
Fenay Bridge Kirk 56 J4
Fence Lancs 62 G12
Fence Rothm 57 Q9
Fence Houses Sundld 70 D2
Fencott Oxon 30 C9
Fen Ditton Cambs 39 Q8
Fen Drayton Cambs 39 M7
Fen End Lincs 49 L9
Fen End Solhll 36 H5
Fengate Norfk 50 K10
Feniscowles Bl w D 55 P1
Feniton Devon 6 E5
Fenland Crematorium Cambs 49 M14
Fenn Green Shrops 35 R4
Fenn Street Medway 22 J13
Fenny Bentley Derbys 46 G3
Fenny Bridges Devon 6 F5
Fenny Compton Warwks 37 M10
Fenny Drayton Leics 37 L2
Fenny Stratford M Keyn 30 J6
Fenrother Nthumb 77 P8
Fenstanton Cambs 39 M7
Fenstead End Suffk 40 D11
Fen Street Norfk 40 H3
Fen Street Suffk 40 K6
Fenton C Stke 45 U5
Fenton Cambs 39 M5
Fenton Cumb 76 B14
Fenton Lincs 58 D13
Fenton Lincs 58 C2
Fenton Notts 58 B10
Fenton Nthumb 85 N12
Fenton Barns E Loth 84 E2
Fenwick Donc 57 S3
Fenwick E Ayrs 81 P4
Fenwick Nthumb 77 M11
Fenwick Nthumb 85 R10
Feock Cnwll 3 L9
Feolin Ferry Ag & B 86 G12
Fergushill N Ayrs 81 L4
Feriniquarrie Highld 100 a4
Fermain Bay Guern 6 d3
Fern Angus 98 H11
Ferndale Rhondd 26 J8
Ferndown Dorset 8 F8
Ferness Highld 103 Q8
Fernham Oxon 29 Q9
Fernhill Heath Worcs 35 U9
Fernhurst W Susx 10 D5
Fernie Fife 91 M9
Ferniegair S Lans 82 D7
Fernilea Highld 100 c6
Fernilee Derbys 56 F11
Fernwood Notts 48 B3
Ferrensby N York 63 T7
Ferrindonald Highld 100 f9
Ferring W Susx 10 J10
Ferrybridge Wakefd 57 Q2
Ferrybridge Services Wakefd 57 Q2
Ferryden Angus 99 N12
Ferryhill Dur 69 S6
Ferry Point Highld 109 P7
Ferryside Carmth 25 Q8
Ferrytown Highld 109 P7
Fersfield Norfk 40 K4
Fersit Highld 95 U4
Feshiebridge Highld 97 N4
Fetcham Surrey 20 K11
Fetlar Shet 106 w3
Fetterangus Abers 105 R5
Fettercairn Abers 99 M9
Fewcott Oxon 30 B7
Fewston N York 63 P9
Ffairfach Carmth 33 N14
Ffair Rhos Cerdgn 33 P7
Ffald-y-Brenin Carmth 33 M12
Ffawyddog Powys 27 N4
Ffestiniog Gwynd 43 P5
Ffestiniog Railway Gwynd 43 N5
Fforld-las Denbgs 54 D14
Fforest Carmth 25 U10
Fforest Mons 27 T5
Fforest Fach Swans 26 B8
Fforest Goch Neath 26 D7
Ffostrasol Cerdgn 32 G11
Ffrith Flints 44 F2
Ffrwdgrech Powys 26 K2
Ffynnonddewi Cerdgn 32 G11
Ffynnongroyw Flints 54 D10
Ffynnon-Oer Cerdgn 32 K9
Fiag Lodge Highld 110 H10
Fickleshole Surrey 21 Q10
Fiddington Gloucs 28 H1
Fiddington Somset 16 H8
Fiddleford Dorset 8 B6
Fiddlers Green Cnwll 3 L5
Fiddlers Hamlet Essex 22 C7
Field Staffs 46 D6
Field Broughton Cumb 61 R2
Field Dalling Norfk 50 H6
Fieldhead Cumb 67 Q6
Field Head Leics 47 N12
Fifehead Magdalen Dorset 17 U12
Fifehead Neville Dorset 8 A6
Fifehead St Quintin Dorset 7 U3
Fife Keith Moray 104 E5
Fifield Oxon 29 P5
Fifield W & M 20 F7
Fifield Wilts 18 H10
Fifield Bavant Wilts 8 E3
Figheldean Wilts 18 J11
Filands Wilts 28 J10
Filby Norfk 51 S11
Filey N York 65 R3
Filgrave M Keyn 38 C11
Filkins Oxon 29 P7
Filleigh Devon 15 P7
Filleigh Devon 15 T10
Fillingham Lincs 58 F10
Fillongley Warwks 36 J3
Filmore Hill Hants 9 T3
Filton S Glos 28 B12
Fimber E R Yk 64 K7
Finavon Angus 98 H12
Fincham Norfk 49 U12
Finchampstead Wokham 20 C9
Fincharn Ag & B 87 S4
Finchdean Hants 9 U6
Finchingfield Essex 22 G1
Finchley Gt Lon 21 N4
Findern Derbys 46 K7
Findhorn Moray 103 R3
Findhorn Bridge Highld 103 N10
Findo Gask P & K 90 F7
Findon Abers 99 S4
Findon W Susx 10 J9
Findon Mains Highld 102 H3
Findrack House Abers 99 L3
Finedon Nhants 38 D6
Fingal Street Suffk 41 M7
Fingask P & K 90 K6
Fingerpost Worcs 35 R5
Fingest Bucks 20 C4
Finghall N York 63 P2
Fingland Cumb 75 M14
Fingland D & G 74 E4
Fingringhoe Essex 23 P4
Finkle Green Essex 40 B12
Finkle Street Barns 57 M7
Finlarig Stirlg 95 N11
Finmere Oxon 30 D6
Finnart P & K 95 P9
Finningham Suffk 40 J7
Finningley Donc 57 U7
Finnygaud Abers 104 J4
Finsbay W Isls 106 f10
Finstall Worcs 36 C7
Finsthwaite Cumb 61 R1
Finstock Oxon 29 S5
Finstown Ork 106 s18
Fintry Abers 105 L5
Fintry Stirlg 89 Q7
Finzean Abers 98 K4
Fionnphort Ag & B 92 K13
Fionnsbhagh W Isls 106 f10
Firbank Cumb 68 D13
Firbeck Rothm 57 S9
Firby N York 64 G6
Firby N York 63 R2
Firgrove Rochdl 56 D4
Firle E Susx 11 Q9
Firsby Lincs 59 S14
Firsdown Wilts 8 J2
First Coast Highld 107 S7
Fir Tree Dur 69 Q6
Fishbourne IoW 9 R10
Fishbourne W Susx 10 C9
Fishburn Dur 70 E6
Fishcross Clacks 90 C12
Fisher W Susx 10 D8
Fisherford Abers 104 K8
Fisher's Pond Hants 9 P4
Fisher's Row Lancs 61 S11
Fisherstreet W Susx 10 F4
Fisherton Highld 102 K5
Fisherton S Ayrs 80 J9
Fisherton de la Mere Wilts 18 F13
Fisherwick Staffs 46 G12
Fishery Estate W & M 20 F7
Fishguard Pembks 24 G3
Fishlake Donc 57 T3
Fishleigh Devon 15 N11
Fishmere End Lincs 49 L5
Fishnish Pier Ag & B 93 R10
Fishpond Bottom Dorset 7 L5
Fishponds Bristl 28 B13
Fishpool Gloucs 28 C3
Fishtoft Lincs 49 N4
Fishtoft Drove Lincs 49 M3
Fishwick Lancs 62 B14
Fiskavaig Highld 100 c6
Fiskerton Lincs 58 H12
Fiskerton Notts 47 U3
Fittleton Wilts 18 H11
Fittleworth W Susx 10 G7
Fitton End Cambs 49 P11
Fitton Hill Oldham 56 D6
Fitz Shrops 44 K10
Fitzhead Somset 16 F11
Fitzwilliam Wakefd 57 P4
Five Acres Gloucs 28 A5
Five Ash Down E Susx 11 R5
Five Ashes E Susx 11 T5
Five Bells Somset 16 E8
Five Bridges Herefs 35 Q11
Fivecrosses Ches W 55 M11
Fivehead Somset 16 K11
Fivelanes Cnwll 4 G4
Five Lanes Mons 27 T9
Five Oak Green Kent 12 C6
Five Oaks Jersey 7 e3
Five Oaks W Susx 10 H5
Five Roads Carmth 25 S9
Five Wents Kent 12 F5
Flack's Green Essex 22 J5
Flackwell Heath Bucks 20 E4
Fladbury Worcs 36 C11
Fladdabister Shet 106 u10
Flagg Derbys 56 J13
Flamborough E R Yk 65 S5
Flamborough Head E R Yk 65 T5
Flamingo Land Theme Park N York 64 H4

Flamstead Herts 31 N10
Flansham W Susx 10 F10
Flanshaw Wakefd 57 M2
Flapit Spring C Brad 63 M12
Flasby N York 62 J8
Flash Staffs 56 F13
Flashader Highld 100 c4
Flask Inn N York 71 R12
Flaunden Herts 31 N12
Flawborough Notts 47 U5
Flawith N York 64 B6
Flaxby N York 63 U8
Flaxholme Derbys 46 K5
Flaxley Gloucs 28 C4
Flaxmere Ches W 55 M12
Flaxpool Somset 16 F9
Flaxton N York 64 F6
Flecknoe Warwks 37 P8
Fledborough Notts 58 C12
Fleet Hants 9 S8
Fleet Hants 20 D11
Fleet Lincs 49 M8
Fleet Hargate Lincs 49 M9
Fleetend Hants 9 Q7
Fleet Services Hants 20 D11
Fleetwood Lancs 61 Q10
Fleggburgh Norfk 51 S11
Fleisirin W Isls 106 k5
Flemingston V Glam 16 D2
Flemington S Lans 89 Q14
Flempton Suffk 40 D7
Fleoideabhagh W Isls 106 f10
Fletcher's Green Kent 21 S13
Fletchersbridge Cnwll 4 F7
Fletchertown Cumb 66 K4
Fletching E Susx 11 Q5
Fleur-de-lis Caerph 27 L8
Flexbury Cnwll 14 F11
Flexford Surrey 20 F12
Flimby Cumb 66 F6
Flimwell E Susx 12 D9
Flint Flints 54 F11
Flintham Notts 47 U4
Flint Mountain Flints 54 F11
Flinton E R Yk 65 S13
Flishinghurst Kent 12 E8
Flitcham Norfk 50 B9
Flitton C Beds 31 N5
Flitwick C Beds 31 N5
Flixborough N Linc 58 E3
Flixborough Stather N Linc 58 E4
Flixton Gt Man 55 R7
Flixton N York 65 N4
Flixton Suffk 41 Q3
Flixton Traffd 55 R7
Flockton Kirk 56 K4
Flockton Green Kirk 56 K4
Flodden Nthumb 85 N12
Flodigarry Highld 100 d2
Flookburgh Cumb 61 R4
Flordon Norfk 41 L1
Flore Nhants 37 R8
Flotterton Nthumb 76 K5
Flowers Green E Susx 11 U8
Flowton Suffk 40 J11
Flushdyke Wakefd 57 L2
Flushing Cnwll 2 K10
Flushing Cnwll 3 L10
Fluxton Devon 6 E6
Flyford Flavell Worcs 36 C10
Fobbing Thurr 22 H11
Fochabers Moray 104 C4
Fochriw Caerph 27 L6
Fockerby N Linc 58 E3
Fodderletter Moray 103 T10
Foddington Somset 17 Q11
Foel Powys 43 U11
Foelgastell Carmth 25 T8
Foggathorpe E R Yk 64 G12
Fogo Border 84 K9
Fogwatt Moray 104 B4
Foindle Highld 110 D7
Folda Angus 98 D11
Fole Staffs 46 D6
Foleshill Covtry 37 L4
Folke Dorset 17 S13
Folkestone Kent 13 P8
Folkingham Lincs 48 G6
Folkington E Susx 11 T10
Folksworth Cambs 38 J3
Folkton N York 65 N4
Folla Rule Abers 105 L8
Follifoot N York 63 S9
Folly Dorset 8 B8
Folly Gate Devon 15 N13
Fonmon V Glam 16 E3
Fonthill Bishop Wilts 8 C2
Fonthill Gifford Wilts 8 C2
Fontmell Magna Dorset 8 B5
Fontmell Parva Dorset 8 B6
Fontwell W Susx 10 F9
Font-y-gary V Glam 16 E3
Foolow Derbys 56 J12
Footbridge Gloucs 28 K1
Foots Cray Gt Lon 21 S8
Forbestown Abers 104 D13
Force Forge Cumb 67 N14
Force Mills Cumb 67 N14
Forcett N York 69 R10
Ford Ag & B 87 R5
Ford Bucks 30 F11
Ford Derbys 57 Q11
Ford Devon 5 Q10
Ford Devon 14 J8
Ford Devon 5 T12
Ford Gloucs 29 L2
Ford Nthumb 85 N12
Ford Shrops 44 K11
Ford Somset 16 E11
Ford Somset 17 Q8
Ford Staffs 46 D2
Ford W Susx 10 G9
Ford Wilts 18 B6
Ford Wilts 18 K5
Forda Devon 15 N13
Ford Street Somset 16 F13
Fordcombe Kent 11 S2
Fordell Fife 90 K14
Forden Powys 44 F13
Ford End Essex 22 G4
Forder Green Devon 5 T6
Fordgate Somset 16 K9
Fordham Cambs 39 T6
Fordham Essex 23 N3
Fordham Norfk 49 T13
Fordham Heath Essex 23 N3
Ford Heath Shrops 44 K11
Fordingbridge Hants 8 G6
Fordon E R Yk 65 N4
Fordoun Abers 99 M7
Ford's Green Suffk 40 J7
Fordstreet Essex 23 M3
Fordton Devon 15 T13
Fordwells Oxon 29 R5
Fordwich Kent 13 N4
Fordyce Abers 104 H3
Forebridge Staffs 46 B9
Foremark Derbys 47 L8
Forest Guern 6 c4
Forest N York 70 D11
Forest Becks Lancs 62 E9
Forestburn Gate Nthumb 77 N6
Forest Chapel Ches E 56 E12
Forest Coal Pit Mons 27 P4
Forest Gate Gt Lon 21 R6
Forest Green Gloucs 28 F7
Forest Green Surrey 10 J2
Forest Hall Cumb 67 S11
Forest Hall N Tyne 77 R12
Forest Head Cumb 76 B14
Forest Hill Gt Lon 21 Q8
Forest Hill Oxon 30 C11
Forest-in-Teesdale Dur 68 J7
Forest Lane Head N York 63 S8
Forest Mill Clacks 90 D13
Forest Row E Susx 11 Q3
Forest Side IoW 9 P11
Forestside W Susx 10 B7
Forest Town Notts 57 R13
Forfar Angus 98 H13
Forgandenny P & K 90 G8
Forge Powys 33 Q3
Forge Hammer Torfn 27 Q7
Forge Side Torfn 27 N6
Forgie Moray 104 D5
Forgieside Moray 104 E5
Forgue Abers 104 K6
Forhill Worcs 36 E5
Formby Sefton 54 H6
Forncett End Norfk 41 L2
Forncett St Mary Norfk 41 L2
Forncett St Peter Norfk 41 L2
Fornham All Saints Suffk 40 E7
Fornham St Martin Suffk 40 E7
Fornside Cumb 67 M8
Forres Moray 103 R4
Forsbrook Staffs 46 C5
Forse Highld 112 G9
Forshaw Heath Warwks 36 F6
Forsinard Highld 112 B7
Fort Augustus Highld 96 E3
Forteviot P & K 90 F8
Fort George Highld 102 K4
Forth S Lans 82 J8
Forthampton Gloucs 35 T14
Forthay Gloucs 28 D8
Fortingall P & K 95 S10
Forton Hants 19 P11
Forton Lancs 61 T9
Forton Shrops 44 K10
Forton Somset 7 L3
Forton Staffs 45 S9
Fortrie Abers 104 K6
Fortrose Highld 102 K4
Fortuneswell Dorset 7 R10
Fort William Highld 94 G3
Forty Green Bucks 20 F3
Forty Hill Gt Lon 21 P3

Frith Bank Lincs 49 M3
Frith Common Worcs 35 Q7
Frithelstock Devon 15 L9
Frithelstock Stone Devon 15 L9
Frithsden Herts 31 M11
Frithville Lincs 49 M2
Frittenden Kent 12 F7
Frittiscombe Devon 5 U12
Fritton Norfk 41 M2
Fritton Norfk 51 S13
Fritwell Oxon 30 B7
Frizinghall C Brad 63 N13
Frizington Cumb 66 F10
Frocester Gloucs 28 E7
Frodesley Shrops 45 M13
Frodsham Ches W 55 M11
Frog End Cambs 39 Q9
Frog End Cambs 39 R9
Froggatt Derbys 56 K12
Froghall Staffs 46 D4
Frogham Hants 8 H6
Frogham Kent 13 Q5
Frogmore Devon 5 S12
Frognall Lincs 48 H11
Frogpool Cnwll 3 L8
Frog Pool Worcs 35 S7
Frolesworth Leics 37 P2
Frome Somset 17 U7
Frome St Quintin Dorset 7 Q4
Fromes Hill Herefs 35 Q11
Fron Gwynd 42 H4
Fron Gwynd 52 F11
Fron Powys 34 E1
Fron Powys 44 E12
Froncysyllte Denbgs 44 F5
Fron-goch Gwynd 43 T6
Fron Isaf Wrexhm 44 G5
Frostenden Suffk 41 S4
Frosterley Dur 69 N5
Froxfield C Beds 31 L5
Froxfield Wilts 19 L7
Froxfield Green Hants 9 U4
Fryern Hill Hants 9 N4
Fryerning Essex 22 F7
Fryton N York 64 F5
Fuinary Highld 93 R9
Fulbeck Lincs 48 D3
Fulbourn Cambs 39 R9
Fulbrook Oxon 29 Q5
Fulflood Hants 9 P3
Fulford C York 64 F10
Fulford Somset 16 H11
Fulford Staffs 46 B6
Fulham Gt Lon 21 N7
Fulking W Susx 11 L8
Fullabrook Devon 15 M4
Fullaford Devon 15 Q6
Fuller's End Essex 22 D2
Fuller's Moor Ches W 45 L3
Fuller Street Essex 22 H4
Fuller Street Kent 21 U11
Fullerton Hants 19 N13
Fulletby Lincs 59 N12
Fullready Warwks 36 J11
Full Sutton E R Yk 64 G8
Fullwood E Ayrs 81 N2
Fulmer Bucks 20 G6
Fulmodeston Norfk 50 G7
Fulnetby Lincs 58 J11
Fulney Lincs 49 L8
Fulstone Kirk 56 J5
Fulstow Lincs 59 Q7
Fulwell Oxon 29 S3
Fulwood Lancs 61 U13
Fulwood Notts 47 N2
Fulwood Sheff 57 M9
Fulwood Somset 16 H12
Fundenhall Norfk 41 L1
Funtington W Susx 10 C9
Funtley Hants 9 R7
Funtullich P & K 95 S13
Furley Devon 6 J4
Furnace Ag & B 87 T6
Furnace Carmth 25 T10
Furnace Cerdgn 33 N3
Furnace End Warwks 36 H2
Furner's Green E Susx 11 Q5
Furness Vale Derbys 56 F10
Further Quarter Kent 12 G8
Furtho Nhants 30 G4
Furzehill Devon 15 R3
Furzehills Lincs 59 N12
Furzeley Corner Hants 9 S6
Furze Platt W & M 20 E6
Furzley Hants 8 K5
Fyfett Somset 6 H2
Fyfield Essex 22 E6
Fyfield Hants 19 L11
Fyfield Oxon 29 T8
Fyfield Wilts 18 H7
Fyfield Wilts 18 J7
Fyfield Bavant Wilts 8 E3
Fylingthorpe N York 71 R12
Fyning W Susx 10 C6
Fyvie Abers 105 L8

G

Gabroc Hill E Ayrs 81 P2
Gaddesby Leics 47 S11
Gaddesden Row Herts 31 N10
Gadfa IoA 52 G5
Gadgirth S Ayrs 81 N8
Gadlas Shrops 44 J6
Gaer Powys 27 M3
Gaer-llwyd Mons 27 S8
Gaerwen IoA 52 G8
Gagingwell Oxon 29 T3
Gailes N Ayrs 81 L5
Gailey Staffs 46 B11
Gainford Dur 69 Q9
Gainsborough Lincs 58 D9
Gainsford End Essex 40 B13
Gairloch Highld 107 N9
Gairlochy Highld 94 H2
Gairneybridge P & K 90 H11
Gaisgill Cumb 68 D10
Gaitsgill Cumb 67 N3
Galashiels Border 84 D12
Galgate Lancs 61 T8
Gallanach Ag & B 93 T13
Gallantry Bank Ches E 45 L3
Gallatown Fife 91 L12
Galley Common Warwks 36 K2
Galleywood Essex 22 H7
Gallovie Highld 96 J6
Galloway Forest Park 73 N4
Gallowfauld Angus 91 N2
Gallowhill P & K 90 H5
Gallows Green Essex 23 M3
Gallows Green Worcs 35 U8
Gallowstree Common Oxon 19 U5
Galltair Highld 100 h7
Gally Hill Hants 20 D12
Gallt-y-foel Gwynd 52 J10
Gallypot Street E Susx 11 R3
Galmington Somset 16 H12
Galmisdale Highld 93 L1
Galmpton Devon 5 R12
Galmpton Torbay 5 V9
Galphay N York 63 R5
Galston E Ayrs 81 Q5
Gamballs Green Staffs 56 F13
Gambles Green Essex 22 J5
Gamblesby Cumb 68 C5
Gamelsby Cumb 67 L2
Gamesley Derbys 56 F8
Gamlingay Cambs 38 K10
Gamlingay Cinques Cambs 38 K10
Gamlingay Great Heath Cambs 38 K10
Gammersgill N York 63 L3
Gamrie Abers 105 L3
Gamston Notts 47 R6
Gamston Notts 58 B11
Ganarew Herefs 27 U4
Ganavan Ag & B 93 U13
Gang Cnwll 4 J7
Ganllwyd Gwynd 43 P8
Gannachy Angus 98 K9
Ganstead E R Yk 65 R13
Ganthorpe N York 64 F5
Ganton N York 65 M4
Gants Hill Gt Lon 21 R5
Ganwick Corner Herts 21 N3
Gappah Devon 5 V5
Garbity Moray 104 C5
Garboldisham Norfk 40 H4
Garchory Abers 104 C13
Garden City Flints 54 H13
Gardeners Green Wokham 20 D9
Gardenstown Abers 105 L2
Garden Village Sheff 57 M7
Garderhouse Shet 106 s8
Gardham E R Yk 65 M11
Gare Hill Somset 17 U8
Garelochhead Ag & B 88 E7
Garford Oxon 29 T8
Garforth Leeds 63 U13
Gargrave N York 62 J8
Gargunnock Stirlg 89 R7

Garizim Conwy 53 L7
Garlic Street Norfk 41 M4
Garlieston D & G 73 M10
Garlinge Kent 13 R2
Garlinge Green Kent 13 M5
Garlogie Abers 99 P2
Garmond Abers 105 N5
Garmouth Moray 104 C3
Garmston Shrops 45 P12
Garnant Carmth 26 B5
Garn-Dolbenmaen Gwynd 42 J5
Garnett Bridge Cumb 67 R13
Garnfadryn Gwynd 42 E7
Garnkirk N Lans 82 C5
Garnswllt Swans 26 A6
Garn-yr-erw Torfn 27 N6
Garrabost W Isls 106 k5
Garrallan E Ayrs 81 Q9
Garras Cnwll 2 J12
Garreg Gwynd 43 M5
Garrigill Cumb 68 F4
Garriston N York 69 Q14
Garroch D & G 73 P3
Garrochtrie D & G 72 E12
Garrochty Ag & B 80 F2
Garros Highld 100 d3
Garsdale Cumb 62 E2
Garsdale Head Cumb 62 F1
Garsdon Wilts 28 J10
Garshall Green Staffs 46 C7
Garsington Oxon 30 C12
Garstang Lancs 61 T10
Garston Herts 31 P12
Garston Lpool 54 K10
Gartachossan Ag & B 78 E3
Gartcosh N Lans 82 C5
Garth Brdgnd 26 F9
Garth Mons 27 Q9
Garth Powys 33 U11
Garth Powys 34 G6
Garth Wrexhm 44 G5
Garthamlock C Glas 89 Q12
Garthbrengy Powys 34 B14
Gartheli Cerdgn 33 L9
Garthmyl Powys 44 E14
Garthorpe Leics 48 B9
Garthorpe N Linc 58 D3
Garth Penrhyncoch Cerdgn 33 M4
Garth Row Cumb 67 R13
Garths Cumb 61 U2
Gartly Abers 104 G9
Gartmore Stirlg 89 M6
Gartness N Lans 82 E6
Gartness Stirlg 89 M8
Gartocharn W Duns 88 K8
Garton E R Yk 65 T12
Garton-on-the-Wolds E R Yk 65 M8
Gartymore Highld 109 U2
Garvald E Loth 84 F4
Garvan Highld 94 D3
Garvard Ag & B 86 F7
Garve Highld 102 C3
Garvellachs Ag & B 87 M3
Garvestone Norfk 50 H12
Garvock Inver 88 G11
Garway Herefs 27 T3
Garway Common Herefs 27 T3
Garway Hill Herefs 27 S2
Garyvard W Isls 106 i7
Gasper Wilts 17 U10
Gastard Wilts 18 C7
Gasthorpe Norfk 40 G4
Gaston Green Essex 22 C4
Gatcombe IoW 9 P11
Gatebeck Cumb 61 U2
Gate Burton Lincs 58 D10
Gateford Notts 57 S10
Gateforth N York 64 D14
Gatehead E Ayrs 81 M5
Gate Helmsley N York 64 F8
Gatehouse Nthumb 76 F8
Gatehouse of Fleet D & G 73 P8
Gateley Norfk 50 G9
Gatenby N York 63 S2
Gatesgarth Cumb 66 J9
Gateshaw Border 76 F1
Gateshead Gatesd 77 R13
Gates Heath Ches W 45 L1
Gateside Angus 91 P3
Gateside E Rens 89 L14
Gateside Fife 90 J10
Gateside N Ayrs 81 M2
Gateslack D & G 74 G5
Gathurst Wigan 55 M5
Gatley Stockp 55 T9
Gatton Surrey 21 N12
Gattonside Border 84 E11
Gatwick Airport W Susx 11 M2
Gaufron Powys 33 U7
Gaulby Leics 47 S13
Gauldry Fife 91 N7
Gauldswell P & K 98 C13
Gaulkthorn Lancs 55 S1
Gaultree Norfk 49 Q12
Gaunton's Bank Ches E 45 N4
Gaunt's Common Dorset 8 E7
Gaunt's End Essex 22 E2
Gautby Lincs 59 L12
Gavinton Border 84 K8
Gawber Barns 57 M5
Gawcott Bucks 30 E6
Gawsworth Ches E 56 C13
Gawthorpe Wakefd 57 L2
Gawthrop Cumb 62 D2
Gawthwaite Cumb 61 P3
Gay Bowers Essex 22 J7
Gaydon Warwks 37 L10
Gayhurst M Keyn 38 B11
Gayle N York 62 H2
Gayles N York 69 P11
Gay Street W Susx 10 H6
Gayton Nhants 37 T10
Gayton Norfk 50 B10
Gayton Staffs 46 C8
Gayton Wirral 54 G10
Gayton le Marsh Lincs 59 R10
Gayton Thorpe Norfk 50 B10
Gaywood Norfk 49 T9
Gazeley Suffk 40 B8
Gear Cnwll 2 J12
Gearraidh Bhaird W Isls 106 i7
Geary Highld 100 b3
Gedding Suffk 40 F9
Geddington Nhants 38 C4
Gedling Notts 47 R5
Gedney Lincs 49 P9
Gedney Broadgate Lincs 49 P9
Gedney Drove End Lincs 49 Q8
Gedney Dyke Lincs 49 P8
Gedney Hill Lincs 49 M11
Gee Cross Tamesd 56 E8
Geeston Rutlnd 48 E13
Geldeston Norfk 41 Q2
Gelli Rhondd 26 H9
Gelli Torfn 27 P9
Gellifor Denbgs 44 D1
Gelligaer Caerph 27 L8
Gelligroes Caerph 27 M9
Gelligron Neath 26 C7
Gellilydan Gwynd 43 N6
Gellinudd Neath 26 C7
Gelly Pembks 24 J7
Gellyburn P & K 90 G4
Gellywen Carmth 25 N6
Gelston D & G 74 E14
Gelston Lincs 48 D4
Gembling E R Yk 65 Q8
Gentleshaw Staffs 46 E11
Georgefield D & G 75 Q7
George Green Bucks 20 G6
Georgeham Devon 15 L5
Georgemas Junction Station Highld 112 E5
George Nympton Devon 15 R8
Georgetown Blae G 27 M6
Georgia Cnwll 2 D9
Georth Ork 106 s17
Gerlan Gwynd 52 K9
Germansweek Devon 5 L2
Germoe Cnwll 2 F11
Gerrans Cnwll 3 M9
Gerrards Cross Bucks 20 H5
Gerrick R & Cl 71 M10
Gestingthorpe Essex 40 D13
Geuffordd Powys 44 F11
Gib Hill Ches W 55 P11
Gibraltar Lincs 49 S2
Gibsmere Notts 47 T4
Giddeahall Wilts 18 C6
Giddy Green Dorset 8 A11
Gidea Park Gt Lon 22 D9
Gidleigh Devon 5 R3
Giffnock E Rens 89 N14
Gifford E Loth 84 E5
Giffordtown Fife 91 L9
Giggleswick N York 62 G7
Gigha Ag & B 79 L6
Gilberdyke E R Yk 64 J14
Gilbert's End Worcs 35 T12
Gilbert Street Hants 9 S2
Gilchriston E Loth 84 D5
Gilcrux Cumb 66 H5
Gildersome Leeds 63 Q14
Gildingwells Rothm 57 S9
Gilesgate Moor Dur 69 S4
Gileston V Glam 16 D3
Gilfach Caerph 27 M8
Gilfach Goch Brdgnd 26 H9
Gilfachrheda Cerdgn 32 H9
Gilgarran Cumb 66 F8
Gill Cumb 67 P7
Gillamoor N York 64 F2
Gillan Cnwll 2 K11
Gillen Highld 100 b4
Gillesbie D & G 75 N7
Gilling East N York 64 E4
Gillingham Dorset 17 V11
Gillingham Medway 12 E2
Gillingham Norfk 41 R2
Gilling West N York 69 Q11
Gillock Highld 112 F5
Gillow Heath Staffs 45 U2
Gills Highld 112 H2
Gill's Green Kent 12 E9
Gilmanscleuch Border 75 R1
Gilmerton C Edin 83 Q5
Gilmerton P & K 90 C7
Gilmonby Dur 69 L10
Gilmorton Leics 37 Q3
Gilroes Crematorium C Leic 47 Q12
Gilsland Nthumb 76 C12
Gilson Warwks 36 G3
Gilstead C Brad 63 N12
Gilston Border 84 C7
Gilston Herts 22 B5
Gilston Park Herts 22 B5
Giltbrook Notts 47 N4
Gilwern Mons 27 N5
Gimingham Norfk 51 N6
Ginclough Ches E 56 E11
Gingers Green E Susx 11 U8
Gipping Suffk 40 J8
Gipsey Bridge Lincs 49 L4
Girdle Toll N Ayrs 81 L4
Girlington C Brad 63 N13
Girlsta Shet 106 u8
Girsby N York 70 E11
Girtford C Beds 38 J11
Girthon D & G 73 Q9
Girton Cambs 39 P8
Girton Notts 58 D13
Girvan S Ayrs 80 H13
Gisburn Lancs 62 G10
Gisleham Suffk 41 T3
Gislingham Suffk 40 J6
Gissing Norfk 40 K3
Gittisham Devon 6 F5
Gladestry Powys 34 F9
Gladsmuir E Loth 84 D4
Glais Swans 26 C7
Glaisdale N York 71 N11
Glamis Angus 91 N2
Glanaber Gwynd 43 M3
Glanafon Pembks 24 G7
Glanaman Carmth 26 B5
Glandford Norfk 50 H5
Glan-Duar Carmth 32 K12
Glandwr Pembks 25 L5
Glan-Dwyfach Gwynd 42 J5
Glandyfi Cerdgn 33 N1
Glangrwyney Powys 27 N4
Glanllynfi Brdgnd 26 F9
Glanmule Powys 34 E2
Glanrhyd Pembks 32 B12
Glan-rhyd Powys 26 D6
Glanton Nthumb 77 M3
Glanton Pike Nthumb 77 M3
Glanvilles Wootton Dorset 7 S3
Glan-y-don Flints 54 E11
Glan-y-llyn Rhondd 27 L11
Glan-y-nant Powys 33 T4
Glan-yr-afon Gwynd 43 T5
Glan-yr-afon Gwynd 44 B5
Glan-yr-afon IoA 52 K6
Glan-yr-afon Swans 26 A6
Glapthorn Nhants 38 F2
Glapwell Derbys 57 Q13
Glasbury Powys 34 E13
Glascoed Denbgs 53 S8
Glascoed Mons 27 Q7
Glascote Staffs 46 H13
Glascwm Powys 34 E10
Glasfryn Conwy 43 T3
Glasgow C Glas 89 N12
Glasgow Airport Rens 89 L12
Glasgow Science Centre C Glas 89 N12
Glasinfryn Gwynd 52 J9
Glasnacardoch Bay Highld 100 f10
Glasnakille Highld 100 e8
Glaspwll Powys 43 P14
Glassenbury Kent 12 E8
Glassford S Lans 82 D9
Glass Houghton Wakefd 57 P2
Glasshouse Gloucs 28 D3
Glasshouse Hill Gloucs 28 D3
Glasshouses N York 63 P7
Glasson Cumb 75 Q13
Glasson Lancs 61 S8
Glassonby Cumb 67 S5
Glasterlaw Angus 98 K13
Glaston Rutlnd 48 C13
Glastonbury Somset 17 P9
Glatton Cambs 38 J3
Glazebrook Warrtn 55 Q8
Glazebury Warrtn 55 Q7
Glazeley Shrops 35 R3
Gleadless Sheff 57 N10
Gleadsmoss Ches E 55 T13
Gleaston Cumb 61 P5
Glebe Highld 102 F12
Gledhow Leeds 63 S12
Gledpark D & G 73 Q9
Gledrid Shrops 44 H6
Glemsford Suffk 40 D11
Glenallachie Moray 104 B7
Glenancross Highld 100 f10
Glenaros House Ag & B 93 P10
Glen Auldyn IoM 60 g4
Glenbarr Ag & B 79 M8
Glenbarry Abers 104 H5
Glenbeg Highld 93 P6
Glenbervie Abers 99 P7
Glenboig N Lans 82 D5
Glenborrodale Highld 93 Q6
Glenbranter Ag & B 88 D6
Glenbreck Border 75 L1
Glenbrittle House Highld 100 d7
Glenbuck E Ayrs 82 D13
Glencally Angus 98 F11
Glencaple D & G 74 J12
Glencarron Lodge Highld 101 R1
Glencarse P & K 90 J7
Glen Clunie Lodge Abers 97 U7
Glencoe Highld 94 G7
Glencothe Border 83 L13
Glencraig Fife 90 J13
Glencrosh D & G 74 E8
Glendale Highld 100 a5
Glendaruel Ag & B 87 T9
Glendevon P & K 90 E11
Glendoe Lodge Highld 96 E2
Glendoick P & K 90 K7
Glenduckie Fife 91 L8
Glenegedale Ag & B 78 E5
Glenelg Highld 100 h8
Glenerney Moray 103 R6
Glenfarg P & K 90 H9
Glenfield Leics 47 P12
Glenfinnan Highld 94 C2
Glenfintaig Lodge Highld 94 J1
Glenfoot P & K 90 J8
Glenfyne Lodge Ag & B 88 F2
Glengarnock N Ayrs 81 L2
Glengolly Highld 112 D3
Glengorm Castle Ag & B 93 L7
Glengrasco Highld 100 d5
Glenholm Border 83 M12
Glenhoul D & G 73 Q2
Glenisla Angus 98 C11
Glenkin Ag & B 88 D9
Glenkindie Abers 104 E13
Glenlivet Moray 103 U10
Glenlochar D & G 74 D13
Glenlomond P & K 90 J11
Glenluce D & G 72 F8
Glenmassen Ag & B 88 D8
Glenmavis N Lans 82 E5
Glen Maye IoM 60 c7
Glen Mona IoM 60 h5
Glenmore Highld 100 d5
Glenmore Lodge Highld 97 R2
Glen Nevis House Highld 94 G4
Glenochil Clacks 90 C12
Glen Parva Leics 47 Q14
Glenquiech Angus 98 G11
Glenralloch Ag & B 87 R12
Glenridding Cumb 67 N9
Glenrothes Fife 91 L11
Glenshero Lodge Highld 96 H5
Glenstriven Ag & B 88 C10
Glentham Lincs 58 H8
Glen Trool Lodge D & G 73 L3
Glentrool Village D & G 72 K4
Glentruim House Highld 96 K5
Glentworth Lincs 58 F9
Glenuig Highld 93 R3
Glenvarragill Highld 100 d6
Glen Vine IoM 60 e7
Glenwhilly D & G 72 F5
Glespin S Lans 82 F13
Glewstone Herefs 27 V3
Glinton C Pete 48 J12
Glooston Leics 37 U1
Glossop Derbys 56 F8
Gloster Hill Nthumb 77 R5
Gloucester Gloucs 28 F4
Gloucester Crematorium Gloucs 28 G4
Gloucestershire Airport Gloucs 28 G3
Glusburn N York 63 L10
Glutt Lodge Highld 112 B9
Gluvian Cnwll 3 N4
Glympton Oxon 29 T3
Glynarthen Cerdgn 32 F11
Glyn Ceiriog Wrexhm 44 F6
Glyncorrwg Neath 26 F8
Glynde E Susx 11 R9
Glyndebourne E Susx 11 R8
Glyndyfrdwy Denbgs 44 D5
Glynneath Neath 26 F6
Glynn Valley Crematorium Cnwll 3 R3
Glyntaff Rhondd 26 K10
Glyntaff Crematorium Rhondd 26 K10
Glyntawe Powys 26 E4
Glynteg Carmth 25 Q3
Gnosall Staffs 45 T9
Gnosall Heath Staffs 45 T9
Goadby Leics 47 U14
Goadby Marwood Leics 47 U8
Goatacre Wilts 18 F5
Goatham Green E Susx 12 F11
Goathill Dorset 17 S13
Goathland N York 71 P12
Goathurst Somset 16 J10
Goathurst Common Kent 21 S12
Goat Lees Kent 12 K6
Gobowen Shrops 44 H7
Godalming Surrey 10 F2
Goddard's Corner Suffk 41 N7
Goddard's Green Kent 12 F9
Godford Cross Devon 6 F4
Godington Oxon 30 D7
Godley Tamesd 56 E7
Godmanchester Cambs 38 K6
Godmanstone Dorset 7 S5
Godmersham Kent 13 L5
Godney Somset 17 N8
Godolphin Cross Cnwll 2 G10
Godre'r-graig Neath 26 D6
Godshill Hants 8 H5
Godshill IoW 9 Q12
Godstone Staffs 46 D7
Godstone Surrey 21 Q12
Godsworthy Devon 5 N5
Godwinscroft Hants 8 H9
Goetre Mons 27 Q6
Goff's Oak Herts 31 T12
Gofilon Mons 27 P5
Gogar C Edin 83 N4
Goginan Cerdgn 33 N4
Golan Gwynd 42 K5
Golant Cnwll 4 E10
Golberdon Cnwll 4 J6
Golborne Wigan 55 P7
Golcar Kirk 56 G3
Goldcliff Newpt 27 R11
Golden Cross E Susx 11 S8
Golden Green Kent 12 B6
Golden Grove Carmth 25 U7
Goldenhill C Stke 45 U3
Golden Hill Pembks 24 G10
Golden Pot Hants 19 V12
Golden Valley Derbys 47 M3
Golders Green Gt Lon 21 M5
Golders Green Crematorium Gt Lon 21 N5
Goldfinch Bottom W Berk 19 R8
Goldhanger Essex 23 M6
Gold Hill Cambs 39 R2
Gold Hill Dorset 8 A6
Golding Shrops 45 M13
Goldington Bed 38 G10
Goldsborough N York 63 T8
Goldsborough N York 71 P10
Golds Green Sandw 36 C2
Goldsithney Cnwll 2 E10
Goldstone Kent 13 Q3
Goldstone Shrops 45 R8
Goldsworth Park Surrey 20 G11
Goldthorpe Barns 57 Q6
Goldworthy Devon 14 J8
Golford Kent 12 E8
Golford Green Kent 12 E8
Gollanfield Highld 103 M5
Gollinglith Foot N York 63 N3
Golly Wrexhm 44 H2
Golsoncott Somset 16 D9
Golspie Highld 109 Q4
Gomeldon Wilts 18 J13
Gomersal Kirk 56 K1
Gomshall Surrey 20 J13
Gonalston Notts 47 S4
Gonerby Hill Foot Lincs 48 D6
Gonfirth Shet 106 t7
Goodameavy Devon 5 N8
Good Easter Essex 22 F5
Gooderstone Norfk 50 C13
Goodleigh Devon 15 P6
Goodmanham E R Yk 64 K11
Goodmayes Gt Lon 21 S5
Goodnestone Kent 12 K3
Goodnestone Kent 13 Q5
Goodrich Herefs 27 V4
Goodrich Castle Herefs 28 A4
Goodrington Torbay 6 A13
Goodshaw Lancs 55 T1
Goodshaw Fold Lancs 55 T1
Goodstone Devon 5 T6
Goodwick Pembks 24 F3
Goodworth Clatford Hants 19 N12
Goodyers End Warwks 36 K3
Goole E R Yk 58 B2
Goole Fields E R Yk 58 C2
Goom's Hill Worcs 36 D10
Goonbell Cnwll 2 J7
Goonhavern Cnwll 2 K6
Goonvrea Cnwll 2 J7
Goosecruives Abers 99 P7
Gooseford Devon 5 R2
Goose Green Essex 23 R2
Goose Green Kent 12 B5
Goose Green Kent 12 F8
Goose Green S Glos 28 C13
Goose Green W Susx 10 J7
Goose Green Wigan 55 N6
Gooseham Cnwll 14 F9
Gooseham Mill Cnwll 14 F9
Goosehill Green Worcs 36 B8
Goose Pool Herefs 35 L13
Goosey Oxon 29 S9
Goosnargh Lancs 62 B12
Goostrey Ches E 55 S12
Gordano Services N Som 27 U12
Gorddinog Conwy 53 L8
Gordon Border 84 G10
Gordon Arms Hotel Border 83 R13
Gordonstown Abers 104 H4
Gordonstown Abers 105 L8
Gore Powys 34 G9
Gorebridge Mdloth 83 R6
Gorefield Cambs 49 P11
Gore Pit Essex 23 L4
Gores Wilts 18 H9
Gore Street Kent 13 Q2
Gorey Jersey 7 f3
Goring Oxon 19 T4
Goring-by-Sea W Susx 10 J10
Goring Heath Oxon 19 U5
Gorleston on Sea Norfk 51 T13
Gornal Wood Crematorium Dudley 36 B2
Gorrachie Abers 105 L4
Gorran Churchtown Cnwll 3 P8
Gorran Haven Cnwll 3 Q8
Gorran High Lanes Cnwll 3 P8
Gorrig Cerdgn 32 H12
Gors Cerdgn 33 M5
Gorsedd Flints 54 E11
Gorse Hill Swindn 29 N10
Gorseinon Swans 25 U11
Gorseybank Derbys 46 J3
Gorsgoch Cerdgn 32 J10
Gorslas Carmth 25 U8
Gorsley Gloucs 28 C2
Gorsley Common Herefs 28 C2
Gorstage Ches W 55 P12
Gorstan Highld 102 C3
Gorstella Ches W 44 J1
Gorst Hill Worcs 35 R6
Gorsty Hill Staffs 46 F8
Gorten Ag & B 93 S12
Gorthleck Highld 102 F11
Gorton Manch 56 C7
Gosbeck Suffk 41 L9
Gosberton Lincs 48 K7
Gosberton Clough Lincs 48 J8
Gosfield Essex 22 J2
Gosford Devon 6 F5
Gosforth Cumb 66 G12
Gosforth N u Ty 77 Q12
Gosling Street Somset 17 P10
Gosmore Herts 31 Q7
Gospel End Staffs 35 U2
Gospel Green W Susx 10 E4
Gosport Hants 9 S9
Gossard's Green C Beds 31 L4
Gossington Gloucs 28 D7
Goswick Nthumb 85 R10
Gotham Notts 47 P7
Gotherington Gloucs 28 J2
Gotton Somset 16 H11
Goudhurst Kent 12 D8
Goulceby Lincs 59 N11
Gourdas Abers 105 M7
Gourdie C Dund 91 N5
Gourdon Abers 99 Q9
Gourock Inver 88 F10
Govan C Glas 89 M12
Goveton Devon 5 T11
Gowdall E R Yk 57 T2
Gower Highld 102 F4
Gower Swans 25 T12
Gowerton Swans 25 U11
Gowkhall Fife 90 G14
Gowthorpe E R Yk 64 H9
Goxhill E R Yk 65 R11
Goxhill N Linc 58 K2
Grabhair W Isls 106 i7
Graby Lincs 48 G8
Grade Cnwll 2 J14
Gradeley Green Ches E 45 N3
Graffham W Susx 10 E7
Grafham Cambs 38 J7
Grafham Surrey 10 G2
Grafton Herefs 35 L13
Grafton N York 63 U7
Grafton Oxon 29 Q7
Grafton Shrops 44 K10
Grafton Worcs 35 N8
Grafton Worcs 36 C13
Grafton Flyford Worcs 36 C9
Grafton Regis Nhants 37 U11
Grafton Underwood Nhants 38 D4
Grafty Green Kent 12 G6
Graianrhyd Denbgs 44 F2
Graig Conwy 53 P8
Graig Denbgs 54 C12
Graig-fechan Denbgs 44 D3
Grain Medway 23 L12
Grains Bar Oldham 56 E5
Grainsby Lincs 59 N7
Grainthorpe Lincs 59 Q7
Grampound Cnwll 3 N7
Grampound Road Cnwll 3 N6
Gramsdal W Isls 106 d13
Gramsdale W Isls 106 d13
Granborough Bucks 30 G7
Granby Notts 47 U6
Grandborough Warwks 37 N7
Grand Chemins Jersey 7 e3
Grandes Rocques Guern 6 d2
Grandtully P & K 97 Q13
Grange Cumb 67 L9
Grange Medway 12 E2
Grange P & K 91 L6
Grange Wirral 54 F9
Grange Crossroads Moray 104 F5
Grange Hall Moray 103 S3
Grangehall S Lans 82 J10
Grange Hill Essex 21 R4
Grangemill Derbys 46 H2
Grange Moor Kirk 56 K3
Grangemouth Falk 82 H2
Grange of Lindores Fife 91 L8
Grange-over-Sands Cumb 61 S4
Grangepans Falk 82 K2
Grangetown R & Cl 70 H8
Grangetown Sundld 70 F2
Grange Villa Dur 69 R2
Gransmoor E R Yk 65 Q8
Gransmore Green Essex 22 G3
Granston Pembks 24 E4
Grantchester Cambs 39 P9
Grantham Lincs 48 D6
Grantham Crematorium Lincs 48 D6
Granton C Edin 83 P3
Grantown-on-Spey Highld 103 R10
Grantsfield Herefs 35 M8
Grantshouse Border 85 L5
Grappenhall Warrtn 55 P9
Grasby Lincs 58 J6
Grasmere Cumb 67 M11
Grasscroft Oldham 56 E6
Grassendale Lpool 54 J9
Grassgarth Cumb 67 M4
Grass Green Essex 40 B13
Grassington N York 63 L7
Grassmoor Derbys 57 P13
Grassthorpe Notts 58 C13
Grateley Hants 19 L12
Gratwich Staffs 46 D7
Graveley Cambs 39 L8
Graveley Herts 31 R7
Gravelly Hill Birm 36 F2
Gravelsbank Shrops 44 H13
Graveney Kent 13 L3
Gravesend Kent 22 G13
Gravir W Isls 106 i7
Grayingham Lincs 58 F7
Grayrigg Cumb 67 S13
Grays Thurr 22 F12
Grayshott Hants 10 D3
Grayson Green Cumb 66 E7
Grayswood Surrey 10 E4
Graythorpe Hartpl 70 H7
Grazeley Wokham 19 U7
Greasbrough Rothm 57 P7
Greasby Wirral 54 G9
Greasley Notts 47 N4
Great Abington Cambs 39 R11
Great Addington Nhants 38 E5
Great Alne Warwks 36 F9
Great Altcar Lancs 54 H5
Great Amwell Herts 31 U10
Great Asby Cumb 68 E10
Great Ashfield Suffk 40 G7
Great Ayton N York 70 J10
Great Baddow Essex 22 H7
Great Badminton S Glos 28 F11
Great Bardfield Essex 22 G1
Great Barford Bed 38 H10
Great Barr Sandw 36 D1
Great Barrington Gloucs 29 P5
Great Barrow Ches W 55 L13
Great Barton Suffk 40 E7
Great Barugh N York 64 G4
Great Bavington Nthumb 76 K9
Great Bealings Suffk 41 M11
Great Bedwyn Wilts 19 L8
Great Bentley Essex 23 R3
Great Billing Nhants 38 B8
Great Bircham Norfk 50 C7
Great Blakenham Suffk 40 K10
Great Blencow Cumb 67 Q6
Great Bolas Wrekin 45 P9
Great Bookham Surrey 20 K12
Great Bosullow Cnwll 2 C10
Great Bourton Oxon 37 N11
Great Bowden Leics 37 T3
Great Bradley Suffk 39 U10
Great Braxted Essex 23 L5
Great Bricett Suffk 40 H10
Great Brickhill Bucks 30 K6
Great Bridgeford Staffs 45 U8
Great Brington Nhants 37 S7
Great Bromley Essex 23 Q2
Great Broughton Cumb 66 G6
Great Broughton N York 70 H11
Great Budworth Ches W 55 Q11
Great Burdon Darltn 70 D9
Great Burstead Essex 22 G9
Great Busby N York 70 H11
Great Canfield Essex 22 E4
Great Carlton Lincs 59 R9
Great Casterton Rutlnd 48 F12
Great Chalfield Wilts 18 C8
Great Chart Kent 12 J7
Great Chatwell Staffs 45 S11
Great Chell C Stke 45 U3
Great Chesterford Essex 39 R12
Great Cheverell Wilts 18 E10
Great Chishill Cambs 39 P13
Great Clacton Essex 23 S4
Great Cliffe Wakefd 57 M3
Great Clifton Cumb 66 F7
Great Coates NE Lin 59 M5
Great Comberton Worcs 36 C12
Great Comp Kent 12 B4
Great Corby Cumb 67 Q2
Great Cornard Suffk 40 E12
Great Cowden E R Yk 65 S11
Great Coxwell Oxon 29 Q9
Great Cransley Nhants 38 B5
Great Cressingham Norfk 50 E13
Great Crosthwaite Cumb 67 L8
Great Cubley Derbys 46 G6
Great Cumbrae Island N Ayrs 80 H1
Great Dalby Leics 47 T11
Great Doddington Nhants 38 C8
Great Doward Herefs 27 U4
Great Dunham Norfk 50 E11
Great Dunmow Essex 22 F3
Great Durnford Wilts 18 H13
Great Easton Essex 22 F2
Great Easton Leics 38 B2
Great Eccleston Lancs 61 S11
Great Edstone N York 64 G3
Great Ellingham Norfk 40 H1
Great Elm Somset 17 T7
Great Everdon Nhants 37 Q9
Great Eversden Cambs 39 N10
Great Fencote N York 69 S14
Greatfield Wilts 29 L10
Great Finborough Suffk 40 H9
Greatford Lincs 48 G11
Great Fransham Norfk 50 E11
Great Gaddesden Herts 31 M10
Greatgate Staffs 46 E6
Great Gidding Cambs 38 H4
Great Givendale E R Yk 64 J9
Great Glemham Suffk 41 P8
Great Glen Leics 47 S14
Great Gonerby Lincs 48 C6
Great Gransden Cambs 39 L9
Great Green Cambs 31 S4
Great Green Norfk 41 N3
Great Green Suffk 40 F7
Great Green Suffk 40 F9
Great Habton N York 64 H4
Great Hale Lincs 48 H5
Great Hallingbury Essex 22 D4
Greatham Hants 10 B4
Greatham Hartpl 70 G7
Greatham W Susx 10 G7
Great Hampden Bucks 30 H12
Great Harrowden Nhants 38 C6
Great Harwood Lancs 62 E13
Great Haseley Oxon 30 D12
Great Hatfield E R Yk 65 R11
Great Haywood Staffs 46 C9
Great Heck N York 57 S2
Great Henny Essex 40 E13
Great Hinton Wilts 18 D9
Great Hockham Norfk 40 G2
Great Holland Essex 23 T4
Great Hollands Br For 20 E9
Great Horkesley Essex 23 N1
Great Hormead Herts 22 B2
Great Horton C Brad 63 N13
Great Horwood Bucks 30 G6
Great Houghton Barns 57 P5
Great Houghton Nhants 37 U9
Great Hucklow Derbys 56 J11
Great Kelk E R Yk 65 Q8
Great Kimble Bucks 30 H11
Great Kingshill Bucks 20 E3
Great Langdale Cumb 67 L11
Great Langton N York 69 S13
Great Leighs Essex 22 H4
Great Limber Lincs 58 K5
Great Linford M Keyn 30 J4
Great Livermere Suffk 40 E6
Great Longstone Derbys 56 K12
Great Lumley Dur 69 S3
Great Lyth Shrops 45 L12
Great Malvern Worcs 35 S11
Great Maplestead Essex 40 D14
Great Marton Bpool 61 Q12
Great Massingham Norfk 50 C9
Great Melton Norfk 50 K12
Great Meols Wirral 54 F8
Great Milton Oxon 30 D12
Great Missenden Bucks 30 J12
Great Mitton Lancs 62 E12
Great Mongeham Kent 13 S5
Great Moulton Norfk 41 L2
Great Munden Herts 31 U8
Great Musgrave Cumb 68 G10
Great Ness Shrops 44 J10
Great Notley Essex 22 H3
Great Oak Mons 27 R5
Great Oakley Essex 23 S2
Great Oakley Nhants 38 C3
Great Offley Herts 31 P7
Great Ormside Cumb 68 F9
Great Orton Cumb 67 M2
Great Ouseburn N York 63 U7
Great Oxendon Nhants 37 T4
Great Oxney Green Essex 22 G6
Great Palgrave Norfk 50 D11
Great Pattenden Kent 12 D7
Great Paxton Cambs 38 K8
Great Plumpton Lancs 61 R13
Great Plumstead Norfk 51 P11
Great Ponton Lincs 48 D7
Great Potheridge Devon 15 M10
Great Preston Leeds 63 U14
Great Purston Nhants 30 B5
Great Raveley Cambs 39 L4
Great Rissington Gloucs 29 N4
Great Rollright Oxon 29 R1
Great Rudbaxton Pembks 24 G6
Great Ryburgh Norfk 50 G8
Great Ryle Nthumb 77 L3
Great Ryton Shrops 45 L13
Great Saling Essex 22 G2
Great Salkeld Cumb 67 S5
Great Sampford Essex 39 T13
Great Saredon Staffs 46 C12
Great Saughall Ches W 54 J13
Great Saxham Suffk 40 C8
Great Shefford W Berk 19 N5
Great Shelford Cambs 39 Q10
Great Smeaton N York 70 D12
Great Snoring Norfk 50 F7
Great Somerford Wilts 28 J11
Great Soudley Shrops 45 R8
Great Stainton Darltn 70 D8
Great Stambridge Essex 23 L9
Great Staughton Cambs 38 H8
Great Steeping Lincs 59 R14
Great Stoke S Glos 28 B11
Great Stonar Kent 13 R4
Greatstone-on-Sea Kent 13 L11
Great Strickland Cumb 67 S8
Great Stukeley Cambs 38 K6
Great Sturton Lincs 59 M11
Great Sutton Ches W 54 J11
Great Sutton Shrops 35 M4
Great Swinburne Nthumb 76 J10
Great Tew Oxon 29 T2
Great Tey Essex 23 L2
Great Thurlow Suffk 39 U10
Great Torrington Devon 15 L9
Great Tosson Nthumb 77 L5
Great Totham Essex 23 L5
Great Totham Essex 23 L5
Great Tows Lincs 59 M8
Great Urswick Cumb 61 P5
Great Wakering Essex 23 M10
Great Waldingfield Suffk 40 F12
Great Walsingham Norfk 50 F6
Great Waltham Essex 22 G5
Great Warford Ches E 55 T11
Great Warley Essex 22 E9
Great Washbourne Gloucs 36 C14
Great Weeke Devon 5 S3
Great Weldon Nhants 38 D3
Great Welnetham Suffk 40 E9
Great Wenham Suffk 40 J13
Great Whittington Nthumb 77 L11
Great Wigborough Essex 23 N4
Great Wilbraham Cambs 39 S9
Great Wishford Wilts 18 G13
Great Witchingham Norfk 50 K9
Great Witcombe Gloucs 28 H5
Great Witley Worcs 35 S7
Great Wolford Warwks 36 J14
Greatworth Nhants 30 C4
Great Wratting Suffk 39 U11
Great Wymondley Herts 31 R7
Great Wyrley Staffs 46 C12
Great Wytheford Shrops 45 N10
Great Yarmouth Norfk 51 T12
Great Yarmouth Crematorium Norfk 51 T13
Great Yeldham Essex 40 C13
Grebby Lincs 59 R13
Greeba IoM 60 e6
Green Denbgs 54 C13
Green Bank Cumb 61 R3
Greenburn W Loth 82 H6
Greencroft Hall Dur 69 Q3
Green Cross Surrey 10 D3
Green Down Somset 17 Q6
Green End Bed 38 F11
Green End Bed 38 G8
Green End Bed 38 H10
Green End Bed 38 H8
Green End Cambs 38 J4
Green End Cambs 38 K6
Green End Cambs 39 N9
Green End Cambs 39 Q7
Green End Cambs 39 Q8
Green End Herts 31 S6
Green End Herts 31 T6
Green End Herts 31 T8
Greenend Oxon 29 R3
Green End Warwks 36 J3
Greenfield Ag & B 88 F7
Greenfield C Beds 31 N6
Greenfield Flints 54 E11
Greenfield Highld 101 U11
Greenfield Oldham 56 E6
Greenfield Oxon 20 B4
Greenford Gt Lon 20 K6
Greengairs N Lans 82 E4
Greengates C Brad 63 P12
Greengill Cumb 66 H5
Greenhalgh Lancs 61 S12
Greenham Somset 16 E12
Greenham W Berk 19 Q7
Green Hammerton N York 64 B8
Greenhaugh Nthumb 76 F8
Green Head Cumb 67 N3
Greenhead Nthumb 76 D12
Green Heath Staffs 46 C11
Greenheys Salfd 55 R6
Greenhill D & G 75 M10
Greenhill Falk 89 T10
Greenhill Herefs 35 R11
Greenhill Kent 13 N2
Greenhill S Lans 82 H12
Green Hill Wilts 29 L10
Greenhillocks Derbys 47 M4
Greenhithe Kent 22 E12
Greenholm E Ayrs 81 Q5
Greenholme Cumb 67 S11
Greenhouse Border 84 F14
Greenhow Hill N York 63 N7
Greenland Highld 112 F3
Greenland Sheff 57 N9
Greenlands Bucks 20 C5
Green Lane Devon 5 T5
Green Lane Worcs 36 E8
Greenlaw Border 84 J9
Greenlea D & G 74 K10
Greenloaning P & K 89 T4
Green Moor Barns 57 L7
Greenmount Bury 55 S4
Green Oak E R Yk 64 J14
Greenock Inver 88 G10
Greenock Crematorium Inver 88 G10
Greenodd Cumb 61 Q3
Green Ore Somset 17 Q6
Green Quarter Cumb 67 Q12
Greensgate Norfk 50 K10
Greenshields S Lans 82 K10
Greenside Gatesd 77 N13
Greenside Kirk 56 J3
Greens Norton Nhants 37 S11
Greenstead Green Essex 22 K2
Greensted Essex 22 D7
Green Street E Susx 12 E13
Green Street Gloucs 28 G4
Green Street Herts 21 L3
Green Street Herts 22 C3
Green Street Worcs 35 U11
Green Street Green Gt Lon 21 S10
Green Street Green Kent 22 E13
Greenstreet Green Suffk 40 H11
Green Tye Herts 22 B4
Greenway Gloucs 35 R14
Greenway Somset 16 K12
Greenway V Glam 26 K13
Greenway Worcs 35 R6
Greenwich Gt Lon 21 Q7
Greenwich Maritime Gt Lon 21 Q7
Greet Gloucs 28 K1
Greete Shrops 35 N6
Greetham Lincs 59 P12
Greetham Rutlnd 48 D11
Greetland Calder 56 G2
Gregson Lane Lancs 55 N1
Greinton Somset 17 M9
Grenaby IoM 60 d8
Grendon Nhants 38 C8
Grendon Warwks 46 J14
Grendon Green Herefs 35 N9
Grendon Underwood Bucks 30 E8
Grenofen Devon 5 M6
Grenoside Sheff 57 M8
Grenoside Crematorium Sheff 57 M8
Greosabhagh W Isls 106 g9
Gresford Wrexhm 44 H3
Gresham Norfk 51 L6
Greshornish House Hotel Highld 100 c4
Gressenhall Norfk 50 G10
Gressenhall Green Norfk 50 G10
Gressingham Lancs 62 B6
Gresty Green Ches E 45 R3
Greta Bridge Dur 69 N10
Gretna D & G 75 R12
Gretna Green D & G 75 R12
Gretna Services D & G 75 R12
Gretton Gloucs 28 K1
Gretton Nhants 38 C2
Gretton Shrops 35 M1
Grewelthorpe N York 63 Q4
Grey Friars Suffk 41 S6
Greygarth N York 63 P5
Grey Green N Linc 58 C5
Greylake Somset 17 L10
Greyrigg D & G 75 L8
Greys Green Oxon 20 B6
Greysouthen Cumb 66 G7
Greystoke Cumb 67 P6
Greystone Angus 91 R3
Greywell Hants 20 B12
Gribb Dorset 7 L4
Gribthorpe E R Yk 64 H12
Griff Warwks 37 L3
Griffithstown Torfn 27 P8
Griffydam Leics 47 M10
Griggs Green Hants 10 C4
Grimeford Village Lancs 55 P4
Grimesthorpe Sheff 57 N9
Grimethorpe Barns 57 P5
Grimley Worcs 35 T8
Grimmet S Ayrs 81 L10
Grimoldby Lincs 59 Q9
Grimpo Shrops 44 J8
Grimsargh Lancs 62 B13
Grimsby NE Lin 59 N4
Grimsby Crematorium NE Lin 59 N5
Grimscote Nhants 37 S10
Grimscott Cnwll 14 G11
Grimshader W Isls 106 j6
Grimshaw Bl w D 55 R2
Grimshaw Green Lancs 55 L4
Grimsthorpe Lincs 48 F9
Grimston E R Yk 65 T12
Grimston Leics 47 S9
Grimston Norfk 50 B9
Grimstone Dorset 7 R6
Grimstone End Suffk 40 F7
Grinacombe Moor Devon 5 L2
Grindale E R Yk 65 Q5
Grindle Shrops 45 S13
Grindleford Derbys 56 K11
Grindleton Lancs 62 F10
Grindley Brook Shrops 45 M5
Grindlow Derbys 56 J11
Grindon Nthumb 85 N10
Grindon S on T 70 E7
Grindon Staffs 46 E3
Grindon Hill Nthumb 76 G12
Grindonrigg Nthumb 85 N10
Gringley on the Hill Notts 58 B8
Grinsdale Cumb 75 S14
Grinshill Shrops 45 M9
Grinton N York 69 M13
Griomaisiader W Isls 106 j6
Griomsaigh W Isls 106 d13
Grishipoll Ag & B 92 F7
Grisling Common E Susx 11 Q6
Gristhorpe N York 65 P3
Griston Norfk 50 F14
Gritley Ork 106 u19
Grittenham Wilts 28 K11
Grittleton Wilts 18 C4
Grizebeck Cumb 61 N3
Grizedale Cumb 67 M14
Groby Leics 47 P12
Groes Conwy 53 T10
Groes-faen Rhondd 26 K11
Groesffordd Gwynd 42 E6
Groesffordd Marli Denbgs 53 T8
Groesllwyd Powys 44 F11
Groeslon Gwynd 52 G11
Groeslon Gwynd 52 H10
Groes-Wen Caerph 27 L10
Grogarry W Isls 106 c15
Grogport Ag & B 79 Q7
Groigearraidh W Isls 106 c15
Gromford Suffk 41 Q9
Gronant Flints 54 C10
Groombridge E Susx 11 S3
Grosebay W Isls 106 g9
Grosmont Mons 27 S3
Grosmont N York 71 P11
Groton Suffk 40 G12
Grotton Oldham 56 E6
Grouville Jersey 7 e3
Grove Bucks 30 K8
Grove Dorset 7 S10
Grove Kent 13 P3
Grove Notts 58 B11
Grove Oxon 29 T9
Grove Pembks 24 G10
Grove Green Kent 12 E4
Grovenhurst Kent 12 D7
Grove Park Gt Lon 21 R8
Grovesend S Glos 28 C10
Grovesend Swans 25 U10
Grubb Street Kent 21 U9
Gruinard Highld 107 R7
Gruinart Ag & B 86 D12
Grula Highld 100 c7
Gruline Ag & B 93 N10
Grumbla Cnwll 2 C11
Grundisburgh Suffk 41 M10
Gruting Shet 106 s9
Gualachulain Highld 94 G9
Guanockgate Lincs 49 N11
Guardbridge Fife 91 Q8
Guarlford Worcs 35 T11
Guay P & K 90 F2
Guernsey Guern 6 d3
Guernsey Airport Guern 6 c3
Guestling Green E Susx 12 G13
Guestling Thorn E Susx 12 G12
Guestwick Norfk 50 J8
Guide Bridge Tamesd 56 D7
Guide Post Nthumb 77 R8
Guilden Morden Cambs 31 S4
Guilden Sutton Ches W 54 K13
Guildford Surrey 20 G13
Guildford Crematorium Surrey 20 G13
Guildstead Kent 12 F3
Guildtown P & K 90 H5
Guilsborough Nhants 37 S6
Guilsfield Powys 44 F11
Guilton Kent 13 Q4
Guiltreehill S Ayrs 81 M10
Guineaford Devon 15 N5
Guisborough R & Cl 70 K9
Guiseley Leeds 63 P11
Guist Norfk 50 H8
Guiting Power Gloucs 29 L3
Gullane E Loth 84 D2
Gulling Green Suffk 40 D9
Gulval Cnwll 2 D10
Gulworthy Devon 5 M6
Gumfreston Pembks 24 K10
Gumley Leics 37 S3
Gummow's Shop Cnwll 3 M5
Gunby E R Yk 64 G12
Gunby Lincs 48 D9
Gunby Lincs 59 S13
Gundleton Hants 9 S2
Gun Green Kent 12 E9
Gun Hill E Susx 11 T8
Gun Hill Warwks 36 J3
Gunn Devon 15 P6
Gunnerside N York 69 L13
Gunnerton Nthumb 76 J11
Gunness N Linc 58 D4
Gunnislake Cnwll 5 L6
Gunnista Shet 106 v9
Gunthorpe C Pete 48 J13
Gunthorpe N Linc 58 D7
Gunthorpe Norfk 50 H7
Gunthorpe Notts 47 S5
Gunton Suffk 41 T1
Gunwalloe Cnwll 2 H12
Gupworthy Somset 16 C10
Gurnard IoW 9 P9
Gurnett Ches E 56 D12
Gurney Slade Somset 17 R7
Gurnos Powys 26 D6
Gushmere Kent 12 K4
Gussage All Saints Dorset 8 E6
Gussage St Andrew Dorset 8 D6
Gussage St Michael Dorset 8 D6
Guston Kent 13 R7
Gutcher Shet 106 v4
Guthrie Angus 98 K13
Guyhirn Cambs 49 P13
Guyhirn Gull Cambs 49 N13
Guy's Marsh Dorset 8 A4
Guyzance Nthumb 77 Q5
Gwaenysgor Flints 54 C10
Gwalchmai IoA 52 E7
Gwastadnant Gwynd 52 K11
Gwaun-Cae-Gurwen Carmth 26 B5
Gwbert on Sea Cerdgn 32 C10
Gwealavellan Cnwll 2 G8
Gweek Cnwll 2 J11
Gwehelog Mons 27 R7
Gwenddwr Powys 34 C12
Gwennap Cnwll 2 J8
Gwennap Mining District Cnwll 2 K8
Gwent Crematorium Mons 27 Q8
Gwenter Cnwll 2 J13
Gwernaffield Flints 54 F13
Gwernesney Mons 27 S7
Gwernogle Carmth 25 T4
Gwernymynydd Flints 44 F1
Gwersyllt Wrexhm 44 H3
Gwespyr Flints 54 D10
Gwindra Cnwll 3 P6
Gwinear Cnwll 2 F9
Gwithian Cnwll 2 F8
Gwredog IoA 52 F5
Gwrhay Caerph 27 M8
Gwyddelwern Denbgs 44 C4
Gwyddgrug Carmth 25 S3
Gwynfryn Wrexhm 44 G3
Gwystre Powys 34 C7
Gwytherin Conwy 53 Q10
Gyfelia Wrexhm 44 H4
Gyrn-goch Gwynd 42 H4

H

Habberley Shrops 44 J13
Habberley Worcs 35 T5
Habergham Lancs 62 G13
Habertoft Lincs 59 T13
Habin W Susx 10 C6
Habrough NE Lin 58 K4
Hacconby Lincs 48 H8
Haceby Lincs 48 F6
Hacheston Suffk 41 P9
Hackbridge Gt Lon 21 N9
Hackenthorpe Sheff 57 P10
Hackford Norfk 50 J13
Hackforth N York 69 R14
Hack Green Ches E 45 P4
Hackland Ork 106 s17
Hackleton Nhants 38 B9
Hacklinge Kent 13 R5
Hackman's Gate Worcs 35 U5
Hackness N York 65 M1
Hackness Somset 16 K7
Hackney Gt Lon 21 P6
Hackthorn Lincs 58 G10
Hackthorpe Cumb 67 R8
Hacton Gt Lon 22 E10
Hadden Border 84 K11
Haddenham Bucks 30 F11
Haddenham Cambs 39 Q5
Haddington E Loth 84 E4
Haddington Lincs 58 F14
Haddiscoe Norfk 41 R1
Haddo Abers 105 N8
Haddon Cambs 38 H2
Hade Edge Kirk 56 H6
Hadfield Derbys 56 F7
Hadham Cross Herts 22 B4
Hadham Ford Herts 22 B3
Hadleigh Essex 22 K10
Hadleigh Suffk 40 H12
Hadleigh Heath Suffk 40 G12
Hadley Worcs 35 U8
Hadley Wrekin 45 Q11
Hadley End Staffs 46 F9
Hadley Wood Gt Lon 21 N3
Hadlow Kent 12 B5
Hadlow Down E Susx 11 S6
Hadnall Shrops 45 M9
Hadrian's Wall 76 K12
Hadstock Essex 39 S12
Hadzor Worcs 36 B8
Haffenden Quarter Kent 12 G7
Hafodunos Conwy 53 Q9
Hafod-y-bwch Wrexhm 44 H4
Hafod-y-coed Blae G 27 N7
Hafodyrynys Caerph 27 N8
Haggate Lancs 62 H12
Haggbeck Cumb 75 U11
Haggersta Shet 106 t9
Haggerston Nthumb 85 Q10
Haggington Hill Devon 15 N3
Haggs Falk 89 S10
Hagley Herefs 35 N12
Hagley Worcs 36 B4
Hagmore Green Suffk 40 G13
Hagnaby Lincs 59 P14
Hagnaby Lincs 59 S11
Hagworthingham Lincs 59 P13
Haigh Wigan 55 P5
Haighton Green Lancs 62 B13
Haile Cumb 66 F11
Hailes Gloucs 28 K1
Hailey Herts 31 U10
Hailey Oxon 19 T3
Hailey Oxon 29 S5
Hailsham E Susx 11 T9
Hail Weston Cambs 38 J8
Hainault Gt Lon 21 S4
Haine Kent 13 S2
Hainford Norfk 51 M10
Hainton Lincs 59 L10
Hainworth C Brad 63 M12
Haisthorpe E R Yk 65 Q7
Hakin Pembks 24 E9
Halam Notts 47 S3
Halbeath Fife 90 H14
Halberton Devon 6 D2
Halcro Highld 112 F4
Hale Cumb 61 U4
Hale Halton 55 L10
Hale Hants 8 H5
Hale Somset 17 T11
Hale Surrey 20 D13
Hale Traffd 55 S9
Hale Bank Halton 55 L10
Halebarns Traffd 55 S9
Hale Green E Susx 11 T8
Hale Nook Lancs 61 R11
Hales Norfk 41 Q1
Hales Staffs 45 R7
Halesgate Lincs 49 M8
Hales Green Derbys 46 G5
Halesowen Dudley 36 C4
Hales Place Kent 13 M4
Hale Street Kent 12 C6
Halesville Essex 23 M9
Halesworth Suffk 41 Q5
Halewood Knows 55 L9
Halford Devon 5 U6
Halford Shrops 34 K4
Halford Warwks 36 J11
Halfpenny Cumb 61 U2
Halfpenny Green Staffs 35 T2
Halfpenny Houses N York 63 Q3
Halfway Carmth 26 A1
Halfway Carmth 33 R14
Halfway Sheff 57 P10
Halfway W Berk 19 P7
Halfway Bridge W Susx 10 E6
Halfway House Shrops 44 H11
Halfway Houses Kent 23 M13
Halifax Calder 56 G1
Halket E Ayrs 81 N2
Halkirk Highld 112 D5
Halkyn Flints 54 F12
Hall E Rens 81 N2
Hallam Fields Derbys 47 N6
Halland E Susx 11 R7
Hallaton Leics 37 U1
Hallatrow BaNES 17 R5
Hallbankgate Cumb 76 B14
Hallbeck Cumb 62 C2
Hall Cliffe Wakefd 57 L3
Hall Cross Lancs 61 S13
Hall Dunnerdale Cumb 66 K13
Hallen S Glos 27 V11
Hall End Bed 38 F11
Hall End C Beds 31 N5
Hallfield Gate Derbys 47 L2
Hallgarth Dur 70 D4
Hall Glen Falk 82 G3
Hall Green Birm 36 F4
Hallin Highld 100 b4
Halling Medway 12 D3
Hallington Lincs 59 P9
Hallington Nthumb 76 K10
Halliwell Bolton 55 Q4
Halloughton Notts 47 S3
Hallow Worcs 35 T9
Hallow Heath Worcs 35 T9
Hallsands Devon 5 U13
Hall's Green Essex 22 B6
Hall's Green Herts 31 S7
Hallthwaites Cumb 61 M2
Hallworthy Cnwll 4 F3
Hallyne Border 83 N10
Halmer End Staffs 45 S4
Halmond's Frome Herefs 35 Q11
Halmore Gloucs 28 D7
Halnaker W Susx 10 E9
Halsall Lancs 54 J4
Halse Nhants 30 C4
Halse Somset 16 F11
Halsetown Cnwll 2 E9
Halsham E R Yk 59 N1
Halsinger Devon 15 M5
Halstead Essex 22 K1
Halstead Kent 21 S10
Halstead Leics 47 U12
Halstock Dorset 7 P3
Halsway Somset 16 F9
Haltcliff Bridge Cumb 67 N5
Haltemprice Crematorium E R Yk 65 N13
Haltham Lincs 59 M14
Haltoft End Lincs 49 N4
Halton Bucks 30 J11
Halton Halton 55 M10
Halton Lancs 61 U7
Halton Leeds 63 T13
Halton Nthumb 76 K12
Halton Wrexhm 44 H6
Halton East N York 63 L9
Halton Fenside Lincs 59 R14
Halton Gill N York 62 H4
Halton Green Lancs 61 U6
Halton Holegate Lincs 59 R13
Halton Lea Gate Nthumb 76 C14
Halton Quay Cnwll 5 L7
Halton Shields Nthumb 77 L12
Halton West N York 62 G9
Haltwhistle Nthumb 76 E13
Halvergate Norfk 51 R12
Halwell Devon 5 T10
Halwill Devon 14 K13
Halwill Junction Devon 14 K12
Ham Devon 6 H4
Ham Gloucs 28 C8
Ham Gloucs 28 J3
Ham Gt Lon 21 L8
Ham Kent 13 R5
Ham Somset 16 J11
Ham Somset 17 S7
Ham Wilts 19 M8
Hambleden Bucks 20 C5
Hambledon Hants 9 S6
Hambledon Surrey 10 F3
Hamble-le-Rice Hants 9 P7
Hambleton Lancs 61 R11
Hambleton N York 64 D13
Hambleton Moss Side Lancs 61 R11
Hambridge Somset 17 L12
Hambrook S Glos 28 B12
Hambrook W Susx 10 B9
Ham Common Dorset 17 V11
Hameringham Lincs 59 P13
Hamerton Cambs 38 H5
Ham Green Herefs 35 S12
Ham Green Kent 12 F2
Ham Green Kent 12 G10
Ham Green N Som 27 U12
Ham Green Worcs 36 D8
Ham Hill Kent 12 C3
Hamilton S Lans 82 D7
Hamilton Services S Lans 82 D7
Hamlet Dorset 7 Q3
Hamlins E Susx 11 T9
Hammerpot W Susx 10 H9
Hammersmith Gt Lon 21 M7
Hammerwich Staffs 46 E12
Hammerwood E Susx 11 Q3
Hammond Street Herts 31 T12
Hammoon Dorset 7 V2
Hamnavoe Shet 106 t10
Hampden Park E Susx 11 U10
Hamperden End Essex 22 E1
Hampnett Gloucs 29 L4
Hampole Donc 57 R4
Hampreston Dorset 8 F9
Hampsfield Cumb 61 S3
Hampson Green Lancs 61 T9
Hampstead Gt Lon 21 N5
Hampstead Norreys W Berk 19 R5
Hampsthwaite N York 63 R8
Hampton C Pete 38 J2
Hampton Devon 6 J5
Hampton Gt Lon 20 K9
Hampton Kent 13 N2
Hampton Shrops 35 R3
Hampton Swindn 29 N9
Hampton Worcs 36 D12
Hampton Bishop Herefs 35 N13
Hampton Court Palace Gt Lon 21 L9
Hampton Fields Gloucs 28 G8
Hampton Green Ches W 45 M4
Hampton Heath Ches W 45 M4
Hampton in Arden Solhll 36 H4
Hampton Loade Shrops 35 R3
Hampton Lovett Worcs 35 U7
Hampton Lucy Warwks 36 J9
Hampton Magna Warwks 36 J7
Hampton on the Hill Warwks 36 J8
Hampton Poyle Oxon 30 B9
Hampton Wick Gt Lon 21 L9
Hamptworth Wilts 8 J5
Hamrow Norfk 50 F9
Hamsey E Susx 11 Q8
Hamsey Green Surrey 21 Q11
Hamstall Ridware Staffs 46 F10
Hamstead Birm 36 E2
Hamstead IoW 9 N10
Hamstead Marshall W Berk 19 P7
Hamsterley Dur 69 P1
Hamsterley Dur 69 P6
Hamstreet Kent 12 K9
Ham Street Somset 17 Q10
Hamwood N Som 17 L5
Hamworthy Poole 8 D10
Hanbury Staffs 46 G8
Hanbury Worcs 36 C8
Hanby Lincs 48 F7
Hanchet End Suffk 39 T11
Hanchurch Staffs 45 T5
Handa Island Highld 110 C7
Handale R & Cl 71 M9
Hand and Pen Devon 6 D5
Handbridge Ches W 54 K13
Handcross W Susx 11 M5
Handforth Ches E 56 C10
Hand Green Ches W 45 M1
Handley Ches W 45 L2
Handley Derbys 47 L1
Handley Green Essex 22 G7
Handsacre Staffs 46 E10
Handsworth Birm 36 D3
Handsworth Sheff 57 P9
Handy Cross Bucks 20 E4
Hanford C Stke 45 U5
Hanford Dorset 8 A6
Hanging Heaton Kirk 57 L2
Hanging Houghton Nhants 37 U6
Hanging Langford Wilts 18 F13
Hangleton Br & H 11 M9
Hangleton W Susx 10 H10
Hanham S Glos 17 R2
Hankelow Ches E 45 Q4
Hankerton Wilts 28 J9
Hankham E Susx 11 U9
Hanley C Stke 45 U4
Hanley Castle Worcs 35 T12
Hanley Child Worcs 35 Q7
Hanley Swan Worcs 35 T12
Hanley William Worcs 35 Q7
Hanlith N York 62 H7

Hannaford Devon 15 P7
Hannah Lincs 59 S11
Hannington Hants 19 R9
Hannington Nhants 38 B6
Hannington Swindn 29 N9
Hannington Wick Swindn 29 N8
Hanscombe End C Beds 31 P6
Hanslope M Keyn 38 B11
Hanthorpe Lincs 48 G9
Hanwell Gt Lon 21 L7
Hanwood Shrops 44 K12
Hanwood Green Shrops 44 K12
Hanworth Gt Lon 20 K8
Hanworth Norfk 51 L6
Happendon S Lans 82 C12
Happisburgh Norfk 51 Q7
Happisburgh Common Norfk 51 Q8
Hapsford Ches W 55 L12
Hapton Lancs 62 F13
Hapton Norfk 45 L1
Harberton Devon 5 T9
Harbertonford Devon 5 T9
Harbledown Kent 13 M4
Harborne Birm 36 D4
Harborough Magna Warwks 37 N5
Harbottle Nthumb 76 J5
Harbourneford Devon 5 S8
Harbours Hill Worcs 36 C7
Harbridge Hants 8 G6
Harbridge Green Hants 8 G6
Harbury Warwks 37 K8
Harby Leics 47 T7
Harby Notts 58 E12
Harcombe Devon 6 A6
Harcombe Devon 6 G8
Harcombe Bottom Devon 6 K5
Harden C Brad 63 M12
Harden Wsall 46 D13
Hardenhuish Wilts 18 D6
Hardgate Abers 99 P3
Hardgate D & G 74 F12
Hardgate N York 63 R7
Hardgate W Duns 89 M11
Hardham W Susx 10 G7
Hardhorn Lancs 61 R12
Hardingham Norfk 50 H13
Hardingstone Nhants 37 U9
Hardington Somset 17 T6
Hardington Mandeville Somset 7 P2
Hardington Marsh Somset 7 P3
Hardington Moor Somset 7 P2
Hardisworthy Devon 14 F8
Hardley Hants 9 N8
Hardley Street Norfk 51 Q13
Hardmead M Keyn 38 D11
Hardraw N York 62 H1
Hardsough Lancs 55 S3
Hardstoft Derbys 57 P14
Hardway Hants 9 S8
Hardway Somset 17 T10
Hardwick Bucks 30 H9
Hardwick Cambs 39 N9
Hardwick Nhants 38 B7
Hardwick Norfk 45 M1
Hardwick Oxon 29 S6
Hardwick Oxon 30 C7
Hardwick Rothm 57 Q9
Hardwick Wsall 46 D13
Hardwicke Gloucs 28 E5
Hardwicke Gloucs 28 H2
Hardwick Hall Derbys 70 D7
Hardy's Green Essex 23 M3
Harebeating E Susx 11 T8
Hareby Lincs 59 P13
Hare Croft C Brad 63 M12
Hareden Lancs 62 C10
Harefield Gt Lon 20 J4
Hare Green Essex 23 R2
Hare Hatch Wokham 20 D7
Harehills Leeds 63 S13
Harehope Nthumb 77 M1
Harelaw Border 77 H12
Harelaw D & G 75 T10
Harelaw Dur 69 Q2
Hareplain Kent 12 F8
Haresceugh Cumb 68 D4
Harescombe Gloucs 28 F5
Haresfield Gloucs 28 F5
Harestock Hants 9 P2
Hare Street Essex 22 C4
Hare Street Essex 22 C3
Hare Street Herts 31 U7
Harewood Leeds 63 S10
Harewood End Herefs 27 U3
Harford Devon 5 Q8
Hargate Norfk 45 L2
Hargatewall Derbys 56 H11
Hargrave Ches W 45 L1
Hargrave Nhants 38 F6
Hargrave Suffk 40 C9
Harker Cumb 75 S13
Harkstead Suffk 23 Q5
Harlaston Staffs 46 H11
Harlaxton Lincs 48 C7
Harlech Gwynd 43 L7
Harlescott Shrops 45 L10
Harlesden Gt Lon 21 L6
Harleston Devon 5 S11
Harleston Norfk 41 M4
Harleston Suffk 40 H9
Harlestone Nhants 37 S8
Harle Syke Lancs 62 H12
Harley Rothm 57 N7
Harley Shrops 45 N13
Harlington C Beds 31 N6
Harlington Donc 57 Q6
Harlington Gt Lon 20 J7
Harlosh Highld 100 C5
Harlow Essex 22 C6
Harlow Carr RHS N York 63 R9
Harlow Hill Nthumb 77 M12
Harlthorpe E R Yk 64 G12
Harlton Cambs 39 N10
Harlyn Cnwll 3 M2
Harman's Cross Dorset 8 D12
Harmby N York 63 N1
Harmer Green Herts 31 S10
Harmer Hill Shrops 45 L9
Harmondsworth Gt Lon 20 J7
Harmston Lincs 48 E1
Harnage Shrops 45 N13
Harnham Nthumb 77 M9
Harnhill Gloucs 29 L7
Harold Hill Gt Lon 22 D9
Haroldston West Pembks 24 E7
Harold Wood Gt Lon 22 D9
Harome N York 64 E3
Harpenden Herts 31 P10
Harpford Devon 6 E6
Harpham E R Yk 65 P7
Harpley Norfk 50 B8
Harpley Worcs 35 Q8
Harpole Nhants 37 S8
Harpsdale Highld 112 D5
Harpsden Oxon 20 B6
Harpswell Lincs 58 F9
Harpurhey Manch 56 C6
Harpur Hill Derbys 56 G12
Harraby Cumb 67 P2
Harracott Devon 15 N7
Harrapool Highld 100 F7
Harrietfield P & K 90 E6
Harrietsham Kent 12 F5
Harringay Gt Lon 21 N5
Harrington Cumb 66 F8
Harrington Lincs 59 Q12
Harrington Nhants 37 U4
Harringworth Nhants 48 D13
Harris W Isls 106 f9
Harriseahead Staffs 45 T2
Harrogate N York 63 S9
Harrogate Crematorium N York 63 S9
Harrold Bed 38 D9
Harrop Dale Oldham 56 F5
Harrow Gt Lon 21 L5
Harrowbarrow Cnwll 4 K7
Harrowden Bed 38 G11
Harrowgate Village Darltn 70 D9
Harrow Green Suffk 40 E10
Harrow on the Hill Gt Lon 21 L5
Harrow Weald Gt Lon 21 L4
Hart Hartpl 70 G6
Hartburn Nthumb 77 M9
Hartburn S on T 70 F9
Hartest Suffk 40 D10
Hartfield E Susx 11 R3
Hartford Cambs 39 L6
Hartford Ches W 55 P12
Hartford Somset 16 C11
Hartford End Essex 22 G5
Hartfordbridge Hants 20 C11
Hartforth N York 69 Q11
Hartgrove Dorset 8 A5
Harthill Ches W 45 M2
Harthill N Lans 82 H6
Harthill Rothm 57 Q10
Hartington Derbys 56 G1
Hartland Devon 14 E8

Hartington Nthumb 77 L8
Hartland Devon 14 G8
Hartland Quay Devon 14 E8
Hartlebury Worcs 35 T6
Hartlepool Hartpl 70 H6
Hartlepool Crematorium Hartpl 70 H6
Hartley Cumb 68 G11
Hartley Kent 12 B8
Hartley Kent 12 E9
Hartley Nthumb 77 S11
Hartley Green Kent 12 B2
Hartley Green Staffs 46 C8
Hartley Wespall Hants 19 U9
Hartley Wintney Hants 20 C11
Hartlip Kent 12 F3
Hartoft End N York 71 M14
Harton N York 64 G7
Harton S Tyne 77 T12
Harton Shrops 35 L3
Hartpury Gloucs 28 E3
Hartshead Calder 56 J2
Hartshead Moor Services Calder 56 J2
Hartshill C Stke 45 U4
Hartshill Warwks 36 K2
Hartshorne Derbys 46 K9
Hartside Nthumb 76 K2
Hartsop Cumb 67 P10
Hart Station Hartpl 70 H5
Hartswell Somset 16 E11
Hartwell Nhants 37 U10
Hartwith N York 63 Q7
Hartwood N Lans 82 F7
Hartwoodmyres Border 84 F12
Harvel Kent 12 C3
Harvington Worcs 36 D11
Harvington Worcs 36 K6
Harwell Notts 57 U8
Harwell Oxon 29 U10
Harwich Essex 23 U1
Harwood Bolton 55 R4
Harwood Dur 68 H6
Harwood Dale N York 71 R14
Harwood Lee Bolton 55 R4
Harwood Park Crematorium Herts 31 R8
Harworth Notts 57 T8
Hasbury Dudley 36 C4
Hascombe Surrey 10 G2
Haselbech Nhants 37 T5
Haselbury Plucknett Somset 7 N2
Haseley Warwks 36 H7
Haseley Green Warwks 36 H7
Haseley Knob Warwks 36 H6
Haselor Warwks 36 G9
Hasfield Gloucs 28 F2
Hasguard Pembks 24 E9
Haskayne Lancs 54 J5
Hasketon Suffk 41 M10
Hasland Derbys 57 N13
Haslemere Surrey 10 E3
Haslingden Lancs 55 S2
Haslingfield Cambs 39 N10
Haslington Ches E 45 R2
Hassall Ches E 45 R2
Hassall Green Ches E 45 R2
Hassell Street Kent 13 L6
Hassingham Norfk 51 Q12
Hassness Cumb 66 J9
Hassocks W Susx 11 M7
Hassop Derbys 56 K12
Haste Hill Surrey 10 E3
Hasthorpe Lincs 59 S13
Haswell Dur 70 D3
Haswell Plough Dur 70 D3
Hatch Beauchamp Somset 16 K12
Hatch End Bed 38 G8
Hatch End Gt Lon 21 L4
Hatchet Gate Hants 9 L8
Hatching Green Herts 31 P10
Hatchmere Ches W 55 N12
Hatcliffe NE Lin 59 M6
Hatfield Donc 57 U5
Hatfield Herefs 35 N9
Hatfield Herts 31 R11
Hatfield Broad Oak Essex 22 D4
Hatfield Heath Essex 22 D5
Hatfield Peverel Essex 22 J5
Hatfield Woodhouse Donc 57 U5
Hatford Oxon 29 R9
Hatherden Hants 19 M10
Hatherleigh Devon 15 M12
Hathern Leics 47 N9
Hatherop Gloucs 29 N6
Hathersage Derbys 56 K10
Hathersage Booths Derbys 56 K10
Hatherton Ches E 45 R4
Hatherton Staffs 46 C11
Hatley St George Cambs 39 L10
Hatt Cnwll 4 J8
Hattersley Tamesd 56 E8
Hattingley Hants 19 T13
Hatton Abers 105 T8
Hatton Angus 91 Q3
Hatton Derbys 46 H7
Hatton Gt Lon 20 K7
Hatton Lincs 59 L11
Hatton Shrops 35 L2
Hatton Warrtn 55 N10
Hatton Warwks 36 H7
Hatton Heath Ches W 45 L1
Hatton of Fintray Abers 105 P13
Haugh E Ayrs 81 P8
Haugh Rochdl 56 D4
Haugham Lincs 59 P10
Haughhead E Duns 89 P10
Haugh Head Nthumb 85 Q3
Haughley Suffk 40 H8
Haughley Green Suffk 40 H8
Haugh of Glass Moray 104 F8
Haugh of Urr D & G 74 F12
Haughs of Kinnaird Angus 91 R1
Haughton Notts 57 U12
Haughton Powys 44 H10
Haughton Shrops 35 Q3
Haughton Shrops 44 J8
Haughton Shrops 44 K10
Haughton Shrops 45 R12
Haughton Shrops 45 S11
Haughton Staffs 45 U9
Haughton Green Tamesd 56 D7
Haughton le Skerne Darltn 70 D9
Haultwick Herts 31 T8
Haunton Staffs 46 H11
Hautes Croix Jersey 7 d1
Hauxton Cambs 39 P10
Havannah Ches E 56 C14
Havant Hants 9 U8
Havant Crematorium Hants 9 U7
Haven Herefs 34 K10
Haven Bank Lincs 48 K3
Haven Side E R Yk 65 R14
Havenstreet IoW 9 R10
Havercroft Wakefd 57 N4
Haverfordwest Pembks 24 G7
Haverhill Suffk 39 U11
Haverigg Cumb 61 M4
Havering-atte-Bower Gt Lon 22 D9
Haversham M Keyn 30 H4
Haverthwaite Cumb 61 R3
Havyatt N Som 17 N7
Hawarden Flints 54 H13
Hawbush Green Essex 22 J4
Hawcoat Cumb 61 N5
Hawen Cerdgn 32 F11
Hawes N York 62 H2
Hawford Worcs 35 T8
Hawick Border 75 V3
Hawkchurch Devon 6 K4
Hawkedon Suffk 40 C10
Hawkenbury Kent 12 D7
Hawkeridge Wilts 18 C10
Hawkerland Devon 6 E7
Hawkesbury Gloucs 28 F10
Hawkesbury Warwks 37 L3
Hawkesbury Upton S Glos 28 F10
Hawkes End Covtry 36 J4
Hawk Green Stockp 56 E9
Hawkhill Nthumb 77 Q3
Hawkhurst Kent 12 E9
Hawkhurst Common E Susx 11 S6
Hawkinge Kent 13 N7
Hawkinge Crematorium Kent 13 N7
Hawkley Hants 9 V2
Hawkridge Somset 15 U6
Hawksdale Cumb 67 N3

Hawkshaw Bury 55 S3
Hawkshead Cumb 67 N13
Hawkshead Hill Cumb 67 M13
Hawksland S Lans 82 F11
Hawkspur Green Essex 22 G1
Hawkstone Shrops 45 N7
Hawkswick N York 62 K5
Hawksworth Leeds 63 P11
Hawksworth Notts 47 U4
Hawkwell Essex 23 L9
Hawkwell Nthumb 77 M11
Hawley Hants 20 E11
Hawley Kent 22 E13
Hawling Gloucs 29 L3
Hawnby N York 64 C2
Haworth C Brad 63 L12
Hawstead Suffk 40 E9
Hawthorn Dur 70 E3
Hawthorn Hants 9 U2
Hawthorn Rhondd 27 L9
Hawthorn Hill Br For 20 E8
Hawthorn Hill Lincs 48 K2
Hawthorpe Lincs 48 F8
Hawton Notts 47 U3
Haxby C York 64 E8
Haxey N Linc 58 C7
Haxey Carr N Linc 58 C6
Haxted Surrey 21 R14
Haxton Wilts 18 H11
Hay Cnwll 3 P6
Hay Cnwll 3 Q4
Haycombe Crematorium BaNES 17 T4
Haydock St Hel 55 N7
Haydon BaNES 17 S6
Haydon Dorset 17 S13
Haydon Somset 16 J12
Haydon Bridge Nthumb 76 F13
Haydon Wick Swindn 29 M10
Haye Cnwll 4 J7
Hayes Gt Lon 20 J6
Hayes Gt Lon 21 R9
Hayes End Gt Lon 20 J6
Hayfield Ag & B 94 F14
Hayfield Derbys 56 F9
Haygate Wrekin 45 P11
Hay Green Norfk 49 R11
Hayhillock Angus 91 R3
Hayle Cnwll 2 F9
Hayle Port Cnwll 2 F9
Hayley Green Dudley 36 B4
Hayling Island Hants 9 U9
Haymoor Green Ches E 45 Q3
Hayne Devon 5 V2
Hayne Devon 16 C13
Haynes (Church End) C Beds 31 N4
Haynes (Northwood End) C Beds 31 N4
Haynes (Silver End) C Beds 31 N4
Haynes (West End) C Beds 31 N4
Hay-on-Wye Powys 34 F12
Hayscastle Pembks 24 F5
Hayscastle Cross Pembks 24 F5
Haysden Kent 21 U13
Hay Street Herts 31 U7
Hayton Cumb 66 H2
Hayton Cumb 75 U14
Hayton E R Yk 64 J10
Hayton Notts 58 B10
Hayton's Bent Shrops 35 M4
Haytor Vale Devon 5 T5
Haytown Devon 14 J10
Haywards Heath W Susx 11 N6
Haywood Donc 57 S4
Haywood Oaks Notts 47 R2
Hazards Green E Susx 12 C13
Hazelbank S Lans 82 F9
Hazelbury Bryan Dorset 7 T3
Hazeleigh Essex 23 L7
Hazeley Hants 20 B10
Hazelford Notts 47 T4
Hazel Grove Stockp 56 D9
Hazelhurst Tamesd 56 D11
Hazelslade Staffs 46 D11
Hazel Street Kent 12 C8
Hazel Stub Suffk 39 U12
Hazelton Walls Fife 91 M7
Hazelwood Derbys 46 K4
Hazlemere Bucks 20 E3
Hazlerigg N u Ty 77 R11
Hazles Staffs 46 D4
Hazleton Gloucs 29 L4
Heacham Norfk 49 U6
Headbourne Worthy Hants 9 P2
Headbrook Herefs 34 H10
Headcorn Kent 12 F7
Headingley Leeds 63 R12
Headington Oxon 30 B11
Headlam Dur 69 R9
Headless Cross Worcs 36 D7
Headley Hants 10 C3
Headley Hants 19 U8
Headley Surrey 21 L12
Headley Down Hants 10 C3
Headley Heath Worcs 36 E6
Headon Devon 14 J12
Headon Notts 58 B11
Heads Nook Cumb 67 R2
Heage Derbys 47 L3
Healaugh N York 64 C10
Healaugh N York 69 L13
Heald Green Stockp 56 C9
Heale Devon 15 P3
Heale Somset 16 K11
Heale Somset 17 U11
Healey N York 63 N2
Healey Nthumb 77 L14
Healey Rochdl 56 C3
Healeyfield Dur 69 N3
Healing NE Lin 59 M4
Heamoor Cnwll 2 D10
Heanor Derbys 47 M4
Heanton Punchardon Devon 15 M5
Heapham Lincs 58 E9
Hearn Hants 10 D3
Heart of England Crematorium Warwks 36 H2
Heart of Scotland Services N Lans 82 H6
Hearts Delight Kent 12 G3
Heasley Mill Devon 15 R6
Heast Highld 100 f8
Heath Derbys 57 Q13
Heath Wakefd 57 N3
Heath and Reach C Beds 30 K7
Heath Common W Susx 10 H7
Heathcote Derbys 56 G14
Heath End Bucks 20 E3
Heath End Hants 19 R8
Heath End Surrey 20 E13
Heath End Warwks 36 H8
Heather Leics 47 L11
Heathfield Devon 5 U5
Heathfield E Susx 11 T5
Heathfield N York 63 N6
Heathfield Somset 16 G11
Heathfield Village Oxon 30 B8
Heath Green Worcs 36 E6
Heath Hall D & G 74 J10
Heath Hayes & Wimblebury Staffs 46 D11
Heath Hill Shrops 45 S11
Heath House Somset 17 M8
Heathrow Airport Gt Lon 20 J7
Heathstock Devon 6 H4
Heathton Shrops 35 T2
Heath Town Wolves 46 B14
Heatley Warrtn 55 R9
Heatley Staffs 46 E8
Heaton Bolton 55 R5
Heaton C Brad 63 N12
Heaton N u Ty 77 R12
Heaton Staffs 56 D14
Heaton Chapel Stockp 56 C8
Heaton Mersey Stockp 56 C8
Heaton Norris Stockp 56 C8
Heaton's Bridge Lancs 54 K4
Heaverham Kent 21 U11
Heavitree Devon 6 B6
Hebburn S Tyne 77 S13
Hebden N York 63 L7
Hebden Bridge Calder 63 L14
Hebden Green Ches W 55 P14
Hebing End Herts 31 T8
Hebron Carmth 25 L5
Hebron Nthumb 77 P8
Heck D & G 75 L10
Heckfield Hants 20 B10
Heckfield Green Suffk 41 L5
Heckfordbridge Essex 23 N3
Heckington Lincs 48 H4
Heckmondwike Kirk 57 L2
Heddington Wilts 18 E7
Heddon-on-the-Wall Nthumb 77 N12
Hedenham Norfk 41 P2
Hedge End Hants 9 P6
Hedgerley Bucks 20 G5

Hedgerley Green Bucks 20 G5
Hedging Somset 16 K11
Hedley on the Hill Nthumb 77 M14
Hednesford Staffs 46 C11
Hedon E R Yk 65 R14
Hedsor Bucks 20 F5
Hegdon Hill Herefs 35 N10
Heglibister Shet 106 t8
Heighington Darltn 69 S8
Heighington Lincs 58 H13
Heightington Worcs 35 S6
Heiton Border 84 J12
Hele Devon 5 S4
Hele Devon 6 C4
Hele Devon 15 M3
Hele Somset 16 F12
Hele Torbay 5 V7
Helebridge Cnwll 14 F12
Hele Lane Devon 15 T11
Helensburgh Ag & B 88 G9
Helenton S Ayrs 81 M6
Helford Cnwll 2 K11
Helford Passage Cnwll 2 K11
Helhoughton Norfk 50 E8
Hellaby Rothm 57 R8
Helland Cnwll 3 R2
Helland Somset 16 K12
Hellandbridge Cnwll 3 R2
Hell Corner W Berk 19 M8
Hellescott Cnwll 14 K3
Hellesveor Cnwll 2 E8
Hellidon Nhants 37 P9
Hellifield N York 62 H8
Hellingly E Susx 11 T8
Hellington Norfk 51 P13
Helm N u Ty 77 P6
Helmdon Nhants 30 C4
Helme Kirk 56 G4
Helmingham Suffk 41 L9
Helmington Row Dur 69 Q5
Helmsdale Highld 112 A3
Helmshore Lancs 55 S2
Helmsley N York 64 E3
Helperby N York 63 U6
Helperthorpe N York 65 M4
Helpringham Lincs 48 H5
Helpston C Pete 48 H13
Helsby Ches W 55 M11
Helsey Lincs 59 T12
Helston Cnwll 2 H11
Helstone Cnwll 4 D4
Helton Cumb 67 R8
Helwith Bridge N York 62 G6
Hemblington Norfk 51 P11
Hembridge Somset 17 Q8
Hemel Hempstead Herts 31 N11
Hemerdon Devon 5 N9
Hemingbrough N York 64 F13
Hemingby Lincs 59 L12
Hemingfield Barns 57 N5
Hemingford Abbots Cambs 39 L6
Hemingford Grey Cambs 39 L6
Hemingstone Suffk 40 K10
Hemington Leics 47 M8
Hemington Nhants 38 G3
Hemington Somset 17 T6
Hemley Suffk 41 N12
Hemlington Middsb 70 H10
Hempholme E R Yk 65 P9
Hempnall Norfk 41 M2
Hempnall Green Norfk 41 M2
Hempriggs Moray 103 T3
Hempstead Essex 39 T13
Hempstead Medway 12 E3
Hempstead Norfk 50 K6
Hempstead Norfk 51 R8
Hempsted Gloucs 28 F4
Hempton Norfk 50 F8
Hempton Oxon 29 U1
Hemsby Norfk 51 S10
Hemswell Lincs 58 F8
Hemswell Cliff Lincs 58 F9
Hemsworth Wakefd 57 P4
Hemyock Devon 6 F2
Henbury Bristl 27 V12
Henbury Ches E 56 C12
Hendham Devon 5 S10
Hendomen Powys 44 E14
Hendon Gt Lon 21 M5
Hendon Sundld 70 F1
Hendra Cnwll 3 M4
Hendra Cnwll 3 J9
Hendre D & G 74 H8
Hendre Brdgnd 26 G11
Hendre Flints 54 E13
Hendrerwydd Denbgs 44 C2
Hendy Carmth 25 U10
Heneglwys IoA 52 G7
Henfield S Glos 28 C11
Henfield W Susx 11 K7
Henford Devon 14 K2
Henghurst Kent 12 J8
Hengoed Caerph 27 M9
Hengoed Powys 34 G10
Hengoed Shrops 44 G7
Hengrave Suffk 40 D7
Henham Essex 22 D2
Heniarth Powys 44 D12
Henlade Somset 16 H11
Henley Dorset 7 S3
Henley Shrops 35 L5
Henley Shrops 35 M6
Henley Somset 17 M10
Henley Suffk 41 L10
Henley W Susx 10 D5
Henley Green Covtry 37 L4
Henley-in-Arden Warwks 36 G7
Henley-on-Thames Oxon 20 C6
Henley Park Surrey 20 F12
Henley's Down E Susx 12 D13
Henley Street Kent 12 C2
Henllan Cerdgn 32 G11
Henllan Denbgs 53 T9
Henllan Amgoed Carmth 25 L6
Henllys Torfn 27 P9
Henlow C Beds 31 Q5
Hennock Devon 5 U4
Henny Street Essex 40 E13
Henryd Conwy 53 N8
Henry's Moat (Castell Hendre) Pembks 24 H5
Hensall N York 57 T2
Henshaw Nthumb 76 E13
Hensingham Cumb 66 E9
Henstead Suffk 41 S3
Hensting Hants 9 P4
Henstridge Somset 17 T12
Henstridge Ash Somset 17 T12
Henstridge Marsh Somset 17 T12
Henton Oxon 30 F12
Henton Somset 17 N7
Henwick Worcs 35 T10
Henwood Cnwll 4 H6
Heol-las Swans 26 B8
Heol Senni Powys 26 G3
Heol-y-Cyw Brdgnd 26 G11
Hepburn Nthumb 85 P14
Hepple Nthumb 76 K5
Hepscott Nthumb 77 R8
Heptonstall Calder 63 L14
Hepworth Suffk 40 G6
Hepworth Kirk 56 J5
Herbrandston Pembks 24 E9
Hereford Herefs 35 M13
Hereford Crematorium Herefs 35 L12
Hereson Kent 13 R3
Heribusta Highld 100 d2
Heriot Border 83 T8
Hermiston C Edin 83 M4
Hermitage Border 75 U6
Hermitage Dorset 7 R3
Hermitage W Berk 19 R5
Hermitage Worcs 35 L12
Hermit Hill Barns 57 M6
Hermon Carmth 25 Q3
Hermon IoA 52 E8
Hermon Pembks 25 M3
Herne Kent 13 N2
Herne Bay Kent 13 N2
Herne Common Kent 13 N3
Herne Hill Gt Lon 21 N7
Herne Pound Kent 12 C5
Herner Devon 15 N7
Hernhill Kent 13 L3
Herodsfoot Cnwll 4 G8
Heronden Kent 13 Q5
Herongate Essex 22 F9
Heronsford S Ayrs 72 E2
Heronsgate Herts 20 H3
Heron's Ghyll E Susx 11 R5
Herriard Hants 19 U11
Herringfleet Suffk 41 S2
Herring's Green Bed 31 N4
Herringswell Suffk 40 B6
Herrington Sundld 70 D2
Hersden Kent 13 N3
Hersham Cnwll 14 F11
Hersham Surrey 20 K9
Herstmonceux E Susx 11 U8
Herston Dorset 8 D13
Herston Ork 106 t20
Hertford Herts 31 T10
Hertford Heath Herts 31 U10
Hertingfordbury Herts 31 T10
Hesketh Bank Lancs 54 K2
Hesketh Lane Lancs 62 C11

Hesket Newmarket Cumb 67 M5
Heskin Green Lancs 55 M3
Hesleden Dur 70 F5
Hesleden N York 62 H5
Hesledon Donc 57 T8
Hesleyside Nthumb 76 G9
Heslington C York 64 E9
Hessay C York 64 C9
Hessenford Cnwll 4 J9
Hessett Suffk 40 F8
Hessle E R Yk 58 H1
Hessle Wakefd 57 N4
Hest Bank Lancs 61 T6
Hestley Green Suffk 41 L7
Heston Gt Lon 20 K7
Heston Services Gt Lon 20 K7
Hestwall Ork 106 r18
Heswall Wirral 54 G10
Hethe Oxon 30 C7
Hethersett Norfk 51 L13
Hethersgill Cumb 75 U12
Hetherside Cumb 75 T12
Hetherson Green Ches W 45 M3
Hethpool Nthumb 85 L13
Hett Dur 69 S5
Hetton N York 62 K8
Hetton-le-Hole Sundld 70 D3
Hetton Steads Nthumb 85 Q11
Heugh Nthumb 77 M11
Heughhead Abers 104 D13
Heveningham Suffk 41 P6
Hever Kent 21 S13
Heversham Cumb 61 T3
Hevingham Norfk 51 L9
Hewas Water Cnwll 3 P7
Hewelsfield Gloucs 27 V7
Hewenden C Brad 63 M12
Hewish N Som 17 L4
Hewish Somset 7 M3
Hewood Dorset 7 L4
Heworth C York 64 E9
Hexham Nthumb 76 K13
Hextable Kent 22 D13
Hexton Herts 31 P6
Hexworthy Cnwll 4 K5
Hexworthy Devon 5 R5
Hey Lancs 62 H11
Heybridge Essex 22 F9
Heybridge Essex 23 L6
Heybridge Basin Essex 23 L6
Heybrook Bay Devon 5 M11
Heydon Cambs 39 P12
Heydon Norfk 50 K8
Heydour Lincs 48 F6
Heylipol Ag & B 92 B10
Heylor Shet 106 s5
Heyrod Tamesd 56 E7
Heysham Lancs 61 S7
Heyshott W Susx 10 D6
Heyside Oldham 56 D5
Heytesbury Wilts 18 D12
Heythrop Oxon 29 S3
Heywood Rochdl 56 C4
Heywood Wilts 18 C10
Hibaldstow N Linc 58 G6
Hickleton Donc 57 Q5
Hickling Norfk 51 R8
Hickling Notts 47 S8
Hickling Green Norfk 51 R8
Hickling Heath Norfk 51 R8
Hickmans Green Kent 13 L4
Hicks Forstal Kent 13 M3
Hickstead W Susx 11 L6
Hidcote Bartrim Gloucs 36 G12
Hidcote Boyce Gloucs 36 G12
High Ackworth Wakefd 57 P4
Higham Barns 57 M5
Higham Derbys 47 L2
Higham Kent 12 D2
Higham Lancs 62 G12
Higham Suffk 40 C7
Higham Suffk 40 H14
Higham Dykes Nthumb 77 P10
Higham Ferrers Nhants 38 D7
Higham Gobion C Beds 31 P5
Higham Hill Gt Lon 21 P5
Higham on the Hill Leics 37 L1
Highampton Devon 15 L12
Higham Wood Kent 12 C6
High Angerton Nthumb 77 M9
High Ardwell D & G 72 C10
High Auldgirth D & G 74 J8
High Bankhill Cumb 68 B3
High Beach Essex 21 R3
High Bentham N York 62 C6
High Bickington Devon 15 N8
High Biggins Cumb 62 B4
High Birkwith N York 62 F5
High Blantyre S Lans 82 C7
High Bonnybridge Falk 89 T10
High Borrans Cumb 67 P12
High Bradley N York 63 L10
High Bray Devon 15 Q6
Highbridge Hants 9 P4
Highbridge Somset 16 K7
Highbrook W Susx 11 N4
High Brooms Kent 11 T2
High Bullen Devon 15 N8
Highburton Kirk 56 J4
Highbury Gt Lon 21 N6
Highbury Somset 17 S7
High Buston Nthumb 77 Q4
High Callerton Nthumb 77 P11
High Casterton Cumb 62 C4
High Catton E R Yk 64 G9
Highclere Hants 19 P8
Highcliffe Dorset 8 J10
High Close Dur 69 Q8
High Cogges Oxon 29 S6
High Common Norfk 50 G12
High Coniscliffe Darltn 69 R9
High Crosby Cumb 75 T13
High Cross E Ayrs 81 M3
High Cross Hants 9 V3
High Cross Herts 31 U9
High Cross Warwks 36 H7
Highcross Lancs 61 S12
High Cross W Susx 11 L7
High Dubmire Sundld 70 D2
High Easter Essex 22 F5
High Eggborough N York 57 T2
High Ellington N York 63 P3
Higher Alham Somset 17 S8
Higher Ansty Dorset 7 U4
Higher Bartle Lancs 61 U13
Higher Berry End C Beds 31 L5
Higher Bockhampton Dorset 7 T6
Higher Brixham Torbay 5 B14
Higher Burrowton Devon 6 D5
Higher Burwardsley Ches W 45 M1
Higher Chillington Somset 7 L2
Higher Clovelly Devon 14 H8
Higher Combe Somset 16 B10
Higher Coombe Dorset 7 P6
Higher Disley Ches E 56 E10
Higher Folds Wigan 55 Q7
Higherford Lancs 62 H11
Higher Gabwell Devon 5 B13
Higher Halstock Leigh Dorset 7 P3
Higher Harpers Lancs 62 F12
Higher Heysham Lancs 61 S7
Higher Hurdsfield Ches E 56 D12
Higher Irlam Salfd 55 R7
Higher Kingcombe Dorset 7 P5
Higher Kinnerton Flints 44 H1
Higher Marston Ches W 55 P12
Higher Muddiford Devon 15 N5
Higher Nyland Dorset 17 T12
Higher Ogden Rochdl 56 E4
Higher Penwortham Lancs 61 U14
Higher Prestacott Devon 14 J13
Higher Studfold N York 62 G6
Higher Town Cnwll 2 C1
Higher Town Cnwll 3 N3
Higher Town IoS 2 c1
Higher Tregantle Cnwll 4 J10
Higher Walton Lancs 62 C14
Higher Walton Warrtn 55 N9
Higher Wambrook Somset 6 J3
Higher Waterston Dorset 7 T5
Higher Whatcombe Dorset 8 A8
Higher Wheelton Lancs 55 P2
Higher Whitley Ches W 55 P10
Higher Wincham Ches W 55 Q12
Higher Wraxall Dorset 7 Q4
Higher Wych Ches W 45 L4
Highfield E R Yk 64 G12
Highfield Gatesd 77 N14
Highfield N Ayrs 81 M2
Highfields Donc 57 S5
Highfields Caldecote Cambs 39 N9
High Ferry Lincs 49 L4
Highgate Gt Lon 21 N5
High Flats Kirk 56 K5

High Garrett Essex 22 J2
High Grantley N York 63 Q5
High Green Cumb 67 P12
High Green Norfk 51 L13
High Green Sheff 57 M7
High Green Shrops 35 U5
High Green Suffk 40 E8
High Green Worcs 35 U11
High Halden Kent 12 H8
High Halstow Medway 22 J13
High Ham Somset 17 M10
High Harrington Cumb 66 F8
High Haswell Dur 70 E4
High Hatton Shrops 45 P9
High Hauxley Nthumb 77 R6
High Hawsker N York 71 R11
High Hesket Cumb 67 R3
High Hoyland Barns 57 L4
High Hunsley E R Yk 65 M12
High Hurstwood E Susx 11 R5
High Hutton N York 64 H6
High Ireby Cumb 66 K5
High Kelling Norfk 50 K5
High Kilburn N York 64 B4
High Killerby N York 65 N3
High Knipe Cumb 67 R9
Highlane Ches E 56 C13
Highlane Derbys 57 P10
High Lands Dur 69 P7
High Lane Stockp 56 E9
High Lanes Cnwll 2 F9
High Laver Essex 22 D6
Highlaws Cumb 66 H3
Highleadon Gloucs 28 E3
High Legh Ches E 55 R10
Highleigh W Susx 10 C11
High Leven S on T 70 G10
Highley Shrops 35 R4
High Littleton BaNES 17 R5
High Lorton Cumb 66 H7
High Marishes N York 64 J4
High Marnham Notts 58 D12
High Melton Donc 57 R6
High Mickley Nthumb 77 M13
Highmoor Cumb 66 K3
Highmoor Oxon 20 B6
Highmoor Cross Oxon 20 B6
Highmoor Hill Mons 27 T10
High Moorsley Sundld 70 D3
Highnam Gloucs 28 E4
High Newport Sundld 70 E2
High Newton Cumb 61 R3
High Newton-by-the-Sea Nthumb 85 U14
Highnam Green Gloucs 28 E3
High Nibthwaite Cumb 61 Q2
High Offley Staffs 45 S9
High Ongar Essex 22 E7
High Onn Staffs 45 T10
High Park Corner Essex 23 P3
High Pennyvenie E Ayrs 81 P11
High Post Wilts 18 H13
Highridge N Som 17 P4
High Roding Essex 22 F5
High Row Cumb 67 L7
High Row Cumb 67 N5
High Salter Lancs 62 B6
High Salvington W Susx 10 J10
High Scales Cumb 66 J3
High Seaton Cumb 66 F6
High Shaw N York 62 J1
High Side Cumb 66 K6
High Spen Gatesd 77 N14
Highstead Kent 13 N2
Highsted Kent 12 H3
Highstreet Kent 13 L3
High Street Cnwll 3 P5
High Street Kent 11 U3
High Street Suffk 41 R7
High Street Suffk 41 S5
Highstreet Green Essex 40 C14
Highstreet Green Surrey 10 F3
Hightae D & G 75 L10
High Throston Hartpl 70 G5
Hightown Ches E 56 C13
Hightown Hants 8 H7
Hightown Sefton 54 H6
Hightown Green Suffk 40 G10
High Toynton Lincs 59 N13
High Trewhitt Nthumb 77 M5
High Urpeth Dur 69 R2
High Valleyfield Fife 82 K1
High Warden Nthumb 76 J12
Highway Cnwll 2 J8
Highway Herefs 35 L11
Highway Wilts 18 F6
Highweek Devon 5 U6
High Westwood Dur 69 P2
Highwood Essex 22 F7
Highwood Staffs 46 E7
High Woolaston Gloucs 27 V8
High Worsall N York 70 F11
Highworth Swindn 29 P10
High Wray Cumb 67 N13
High Wych Herts 22 C5
High Wycombe Bucks 20 E4
Hilborough Norfk 50 D13
Hilcote Derbys 47 M1
Hilcott Wilts 18 H9
Hildenborough Kent 21 U13
Hilden Park Kent 21 U13
Hildersham Cambs 39 R11
Hilderstone Staffs 46 C7
Hilderthorpe E R Yk 65 R6
Hilfield Dorset 7 R3
Hilgay Norfk 49 R14
Hill S Glos 28 B9
Hill Warwks 37 N7
Hillam N York 64 C14
Hillbeck Cumb 68 G10
Hillborough Kent 13 N2
Hillbutts Dorset 8 D8
Hill Chorlton Staffs 45 S6
Hillclifflane Derbys 46 J4
Hill Common Norfk 51 R9
Hill Deverill Wilts 18 C12
Hilldyke Lincs 49 L4
Hill End Dur 69 N5
Hill End Fife 90 F12
Hill End Gloucs 36 B13
Hillend Fife 82 K1
Hillend Mdloth 83 P5
Hillend N Lans 82 E6
Hillend Swans 25 S12
Hillersland Gloucs 27 V5
Hillerton Devon 15 S12
Hillesden Bucks 30 E7
Hillesley Gloucs 28 E10
Hillfarrance Somset 16 G12
Hill Gate Herefs 27 T3
Hillgrove W Susx 10 E5
Hillhampton Herefs 35 N10
Hillhead Abers 104 J8
Hillhead Devon 5 B14
Hillhead S Lans 82 J10
Hillhead of Cocklaw Abers 105 T6
Hilliard's Cross Staffs 46 G11
Hilliclay Highld 112 D4
Hillingdon Gt Lon 20 J6
Hillington C Glas 89 N12
Hillington Norfk 50 B9
Hillis Corner IoW 9 P10
Hillmorton Warwks 37 P6
Hill of Beath Fife 90 J13
Hill of Fearn Highld 109 R9
Hill Ridware Staffs 46 E10
Hillside Abers 99 S4
Hillside Angus 99 N12
Hillside Devon 5 S12
Hillside Hants 8 K7
Hillside Worcs 35 R7
Hill Side Worcs 35 T8
Hills Town Derbys 57 Q13
Hillstreet Hants 9 L5
Hillswick Shet 106 s6
Hill Top Dur 69 L7
Hill Top Hants 9 N8
Hill Top Kirk 56 J3
Hill Top Rothm 57 P7
Hill Top Sandw 36 C2
Hill Top Wakefd 57 L3
Hilltown Hants 9 L5
Hillway IoW 9 S11
Hillwell Shet 106 t12
Hilmarton Wilts 18 F5
Hilperton Wilts 18 C9
Hilperton Marsh Wilts 18 C9
Hilsea C Port 9 T8
Hilston E R Yk 65 U13
Hilton Border 85 L8
Hilton Cambs 39 L7
Hilton Cumb 68 F9
Hilton Derbys 46 H7
Hilton Dorset 7 U4
Hilton Dur 69 Q8
Hilton Highld 109 Q8
Hilton S on T 70 G10
Hilton Shrops 35 S1
Hilton Park Services Staffs 46 C13

Himbleton Worcs 36 B9
Himley Staffs 35 U2
Hincaster Cumb 61 U3
Hinchley Wood Surrey 21 L9
Hinckley Leics 37 M2
Hinderclay Suffk 40 H5
Hinderwell N York 71 M9
Hindford Shrops 44 H7
Hindhead Surrey 10 D3
Hindley Nthumb 77 L14
Hindley Wigan 55 P6
Hindley Green Wigan 55 P6
Hindlip Worcs 35 U9
Hindolveston Norfk 50 H8
Hindon Wilts 8 C2
Hindringham Norfk 50 G6
Hingham Norfk 50 H13
Hinksford Staffs 35 U3
Hinstock Shrops 45 Q8
Hintlesham Suffk 40 H12
Hinton Gloucs 28 D7
Hinton Hants 8 J9
Hinton Herefs 34 H13
Hinton S Glos 28 E12
Hinton Shrops 44 K12
Hinton Admiral Hants 8 J9
Hinton Ampner Hants 9 R3
Hinton Blewett BaNES 17 Q5
Hinton Charterhouse BaNES 17 U5
Hinton-in-the-Hedges Nhants 30 B5
Hinton Marsh Hants 9 R3
Hinton Martell Dorset 8 E8
Hinton on the Green Worcs 36 D12
Hinton Parva Swindn 29 P11
Hinton St George Somset 7 M2
Hinton St Mary Dorset 17 U13
Hinton Waldrist Oxon 29 S7
Hints Shrops 35 P6
Hints Staffs 46 G13
Hinwick Bed 38 D8
Hinxhill Kent 13 L7
Hinxton Cambs 39 Q11
Hinxworth Herts 31 R4
Hipperholme Calder 56 H1
Hipsburn Nthumb 77 Q4
Hipswell N York 69 Q13
Hirn Abers 99 P3
Hirnant Powys 44 B9
Hirst Nthumb 77 R8
Hirst Courtney N York 57 T2
Hirwaingurff Neath 26 G7
Hirwaun Rhondd 26 H6
Hiscott Devon 15 N7
Histon Cambs 39 P8
Hitcham Suffk 40 G10
Hitcham Causeway Suffk 40 G10
Hitcham Street Suffk 40 G10
Hither Green Gt Lon 21 Q7
Hittisleigh Devon 15 S13
Hittisleigh Barton Devon 15 S13
Hive E R Yk 64 J13
Hixon Staffs 46 D8
Hoaden Kent 13 P4
Hoar Cross Staffs 46 F9
Hoarwithy Herefs 27 U2
Hoath Kent 13 P3
Hoathly Kent 12 D7
Hobarris Shrops 34 G5
Hobbles Green Suffk 40 B10
Hobbs Cross Essex 22 C7
Hobbs Cross Essex 22 C8
Hobkirk Border 76 B3
Hobland Hall Norfk 51 T13
Hobsick Notts 47 N4
Hobson Dur 69 Q1
Hoby Leics 47 S10
Hoccombe Somset 16 E11
Hockering Norfk 50 J11
Hockering Heath Norfk 50 J11
Hockerton Notts 47 T2
Hockley Ches E 56 D10
Hockley Covtry 37 L4
Hockley Essex 23 L8
Hockley Staffs 46 H13
Hockley Heath Solhll 36 G5
Hockliffe C Beds 31 L7
Hockwold cum Wilton Norfk 39 U3
Hockworthy Devon 16 D13
Hoddesdon Herts 31 U11
Hoddlesden Bl w D 55 R2
Hoddom Cross D & G 75 N11
Hoddom Mains D & G 75 M11
Hodgehill Ches E 55 T13
Hodgeston Pembks 24 H11
Hodnet Shrops 45 P8
Hodnetheath Shrops 45 P8
Hodsock Notts 57 T9
Hodsoll Street Kent 12 B3
Hodson Swindn 29 N11
Hodthorpe Derbys 57 R12
Hoe Hants 9 R5
Hoe Norfk 50 G10
Hoe Gate Hants 9 S6
Hoff Cumb 68 E9
Hoggards Green Suffk 40 E10
Hoggeston Bucks 30 G8
Hoggrill's End Warwks 36 H2
Hog Hill E Susx 12 G12
Hoghton Lancs 55 P1
Hoghton Bottoms Lancs 55 P1
Hognaston Derbys 46 H3
Hogsthorpe Lincs 59 T11
Holbeach Lincs 49 N8
Holbeach Bank Lincs 49 N7
Holbeach Clough Lincs 49 M7
Holbeach Drove Lincs 49 M11
Holbeach Hurn Lincs 49 N7
Holbeach St Johns Lincs 49 M9
Holbeach St Marks Lincs 49 N6
Holbeach St Matthew Lincs 49 N6
Holbeck Notts 57 R12
Holbeck Woodhouse Notts 57 R12
Holberrow Green Worcs 36 D9
Holbeton Devon 5 P10
Holborn Gt Lon 21 N6
Holbrook Derbys 47 L4
Holbrook S York 57 P9
Holbrook Suffk 41 L13
Holbrook Moor Derbys 47 L4
Holburn Nthumb 85 Q11
Holbury Hants 9 N8
Holcombe Devon 6 B8
Holcombe Somset 17 S7
Holcombe Rogus Devon 16 E13
Holcot Nhants 37 U7
Holden Lancs 62 F11
Holdenby Nhants 37 S7
Holdenhurst Bmouth 8 G9
Holder's Green Essex 22 F2
Holdgate Shrops 35 N3
Holdingham Lincs 48 G4
Holditch Dorset 6 K4
Holemoor Devon 14 K11
Hole-in-the-Wall Herefs 28 B2
Holehouse Derbys 56 F9
Holford Somset 16 G8
Holgate C York 64 D9
Holker Cumb 61 R4
Holkham Norfk 50 E5
Hollacombe Devon 14 J12
Holland Fen Lincs 48 K4
Holland Lees Lancs 55 L5
Holland-on-Sea Essex 23 S4
Hollandstoun Ork 106 w14
Hollee D & G 75 P13
Hollesley Suffk 41 P12
Hollicombe Torbay 5 V8
Hollin Green Ches E 45 N3
Hollingbourne Kent 12 F4
Hollingbury Br & H 11 N8
Hollingdon Bucks 30 H7
Hollingrove E Susx 12 C11
Hollington Derbys 46 H6
Hollington Staffs 46 E6
Hollingworth Tamesd 56 F7
Hollins Bury 55 T5
Hollins Derbys 57 M12
Hollinsclough Staffs 56 F13
Hollins End Sheff 57 N9
Hollins Green Warrtn 55 Q8
Hollins Lane Lancs 61 T10
Hollinswood Wrekin 45 Q12
Hollinwood Shrops 45 M6
Hollinwood Oldham 56 D6
Hollocombe Devon 15 P10
Holloway Derbys 46 K2
Holloway Gt Lon 21 N6
Holloway Wilts 8 C3
Hollowell Nhants 37 S6
Hollow Meadows Sheff 56 K9
Hollows D & G 75 R11
Hollybush Caerph 27 M7
Hollybush E Ayrs 81 M9
Hollybush Herefs 35 S13
Hollybush Worcs 35 U12
Holly End Norfk 49 Q12
Holly Green Worcs 35 U12

Hollyhurst Ches E 45 N5
Hollym E R Yk 59 P1
Hollywood Worcs 36 E5
Holmbridge Kirk 56 H5
Holmbury St Mary Surrey 10 J2
Holmbush Cnwll 3 Q6
Holmcroft Staffs 46 B9
Holme Cambs 38 J3
Holme Cumb 61 U4
Holme N Linc 58 F5
Holme N York 63 T2
Holme Notts 48 B3
Holme W Isls
Holme Chapel Lancs 62 H14
Holme Green N York 64 D11
Holme Hale Norfk 50 E12
Holme Lacy Herefs 35 N13
Holme Marsh Herefs 34 H10
Holme next the Sea Norfk 50 B5
Holme on the Wolds E R Yk 65 M10
Holme Pierrepont Notts 47 R6
Holmer Herefs 35 M12
Holmer Green Bucks 20 F3
Holme St Cuthbert Cumb 66 H3
Holmes Chapel Ches E 55 S13
Holmescales Cumb 61 U2
Holmesfield Derbys 57 M11
Holmeswood Lancs 54 K3
Holmethorpe Surrey 21 N12
Holme upon Spalding Moor E R Yk 64 J12
Holmewood Derbys 57 P13
Holmfield Calder 63 M14
Holmfirth Kirk 56 H5
Holmgate Derbys 57 N14
Holmhead E Ayrs 81 R8
Holmpton E R Yk 59 R1
Holmrook Cumb 66 G13
Holmsford Bridge Crematorium N Ayrs 81 M5
Holmshurst E Susx 11 U5
Holmside Dur 69 R3
Holmwrangle Cumb 67 R3
Holne Devon 5 S7
Holnest Dorset 7 S3
Holnicote Somset 16 B7
Holsworthy Devon 14 H12
Holsworthy Beacon Devon 14 J11
Holt Dorset 8 E8
Holt Norfk 50 J6
Holt Wilts 18 B8
Holt Worcs 35 T8
Holt Wrexhm 44 K3
Holt End Hants 9 U1
Holt End Worcs 36 E7
Holt Fleet Worcs 35 T8
Holt Green Lancs 54 J5
Holt Heath Worcs 35 T8
Holt Heath Dorset 8 E8
Holton Oxon 30 D11
Holton Somset 17 R11
Holton Suffk 41 R5
Holton cum Beckering Lincs 58 J10
Holton Heath Dorset 8 C10
Holton le Clay Lincs 59 N6
Holton le Moor Lincs 58 J7
Holton St Mary Suffk 40 J13
Holt Street Kent 13 P5
Holtye E Susx 11 R3
Holwell Dorset 7 S2
Holwell Herts 31 Q6
Holwell Leics 47 T9
Holwell Oxon 29 P6
Holwell Somset 17 T7
Holwick Dur 68 K7
Holworth Dorset 7 U8
Holybourne Hants 10 A2
Holy Cross Worcs 35 U5
Holyhead IoA 52 C6
Holy Island IoA 52 C6
Holy Island Nthumb 85 S10
Holyport Wndsr 20 E7
Holystone Nthumb 76 K5
Holytown N Lans 82 E6
Holytown Crematorium N Lans 82 E6
Holywell C Beds 31 M9
Holywell Cambs 39 M6
Holywell Cnwll 3 L5
Holywell Dorset 7 P4
Holywell Flints 54 E11
Holywell Green Calder 56 H3
Holywell Lake Somset 16 F12
Holywell Row Suffk 40 B5
Holywood D & G 74 J9
Holywood Village D & G 74 J9
Homer Shrops 45 P13
Homer Green Sefton 54 J6
Homersfield Suffk 41 N4
Hom Green Herefs 27 V3
Honeyborough Pembks 24 G9
Honeybourne Worcs 36 F12
Honeychurch Devon 15 P12
Honey Hill Kent 13 M3
Honey Street Wilts 18 H8
Honey Tye Suffk 40 F13
Honeywick C Beds 31 M8
Honing Norfk 51 Q8
Honingham Norfk 50 K11
Honington Lincs 48 D4
Honington Suffk 40 F6
Honington Warwks 36 J12
Honiton Devon 6 G4
Honley Kirk 56 H4
Honnington Wrekin 45 S10
Honor Oak Crematorium Gt Lon 21 Q8
Hoo Kent 13 L3
Hoobrook Worcs 35 T6
Hood Green Barns 57 M6
Hood Hill Rothm 57 N7
Hooe C Port 9 T8
Hooe E Susx 12 C13
Hoo End Herts 31 R9
Hoo Green Ches E 55 R10
Hoohill Bpool 61 Q12
Hook Cambs 49 P14
Hook Devon 6 K5
Hook E R Yk 58 C1
Hook Gt Lon 21 L9
Hook Hants 9 T10
Hook Hants 20 B11
Hook Pembks 24 G8
Hook Wilts 29 L11
Hook-a-Gate Shrops 45 L12
Hook Bank Worcs 35 U12
Hooke Dorset 7 P4
Hookgate Staffs 45 R6
Hook Green Kent 12 B3
Hook Green Kent 12 C7
Hook Norton Oxon 29 S2
Hook Street Gloucs 28 C8
Hook Street Wilts 29 L11
Hookway Devon 15 T13
Hookwood Surrey 11 L2
Hoole Ches W 54 K13
Hooley Surrey 21 M12
Hooley Bridge Rochdl 56 C4
Hoo Meavy Devon 5 N7
Hoo St Werburgh Medway 22 K13
Hooton Ches W 54 J11
Hooton Levitt Rothm 57 R8
Hooton Pagnell Donc 57 Q5
Hooton Roberts Rothm 57 Q7
Hopcrofts Holt Oxon 29 U3
Hope Derbys 56 J10
Hope Devon 5 R12
Hope Flints 44 H2
Hope Powys 44 F12
Hope Shrops 44 H12
Hope Staffs 46 F3
Hope Bagot Shrops 35 N6
Hope Bowdler Shrops 35 L2
Hope End Green Essex 22 E3
Hope Mansell Herefs 28 B4
Hopesay Shrops 34 J4
Hope under Dinmore Herefs 35 M10
Hopgrove C York 64 E9
Hop Pole Lincs 48 J11
Hopsford Warwks 37 M4
Hopstone Shrops 35 S2
Hopton Derbys 46 J2
Hopton Shrops 45 N6
Hopton Staffs 46 B9
Hopton Suffk 40 G5
Hopton Cangeford Shrops 35 M4
Hopton Castle Shrops 34 J5
Hoptonheath Shrops 34 J5
Hopton on Sea Norfk 51 T14
Hopton Wafers Shrops 35 P5
Hopwas Staffs 46 G13
Hopwood Worcs 36 D5
Hopwood Park Services Worcs 36 D5
Horam E Susx 11 T7

Column 1

Horbling Lincs	48	H6
Horbury Wakefd	57	L3
Horcott Gloucs	29	N7
Horden Dur	70	F4
Horderley Shrops	34	K3
Hordle Hants	9	K5
Hordley Shrops	44	H9
Horeb Cerdgn	25	S9
Horeb Carmth	25	S9
Horfield Bristl	28	A12
Horham Suffk	41	M6
Horkesley Heath Essex	23	G3
Horkstow N Linc	58	G3
Horley Oxon	37	M12
Horley Surrey	11	M2
Hornblotton Green Somset	17	Q10
Hornby Lancs	62	B6
Hornby N York	69	R14
Hornby N York	70	E13
Horncastle Lincs	59	N13
Hornchurch Gt Lon	22	D10
Horncliffe Nthumb	85	N9
Horndean Border	85	M9
Horndean Hants	9	U6
Horndon Devon	5	N4
Horndon on the Hill Essex	22	G11
Horne Surrey	11	N2
Horner Somset	16	B7
Horne Row Essex	22	J7
Horners Green Suffk	40	G12
Horn Hill Bucks	20	H4
Horning Norfk	51	P10
Horninghold Leics	38	B1
Horninglow Staffs	46	H8
Horningsea Cambs	39	Q8
Horningsham Wilts	18	B12
Horningtoft Norfk	50	F9
Horningtops Cnwll	4	H8
Hornsbury Somset	6	K2
Hornsby Cumb	67	R2
Hornsbygate Cumb	67	R2
Horns Cross Devon	14	H8
Horns Cross E Susx	12	F11
Hornsea E R Yk	65	R10
Hornsey Gt Lon	21	P5
Horn's Green Gt Lon	21	S11
Hornton Oxon	37	L11
Horpit Swindn	29	P11
Horra Shet	106	u4
Horrabridge Devon	5	N7
Horringer Suffk	40	D8
Horringford IoW	9	Q11
Horrocks Fold Bolton	55	R4
Horrocksford Lancs	62	E11
Horsacott Devon	15	M6
Horsebridge Devon	5	L5
Horsebridge Hants	9	L2
Horsebridge Shrops	44	J12
Horsebridge Staffs	45	T3
Horsebrook Staffs	45	U11
Horsecastle N Som	17	M3
Horsedown Cnwll	2	J10
Horsehay Wrekin	45	Q12
Horseheath Cambs	39	T11
Horsehouse N York	63	L3
Horsell Surrey	20	G11
Horseman's Green Wrexhm	44	K5
Horsenden Bucks	30	G12
Horsey Norfk	51	S9
Horsey Somset	16	K9
Horsey Corner Norfk	51	S9
Horsford Norfk	51	L10
Horsforth Leeds	63	Q12
Horsham W Susx	10	K4
Horsham Worcs	35	R9
Horsham St Faith Norfk	51	M10
Horsington Lincs	59	L13
Horsington Somset	17	T11
Horsley Derbys	47	L5
Horsley Gloucs	28	F8
Horsley Nthumb	76	H11
Horsley Nthumb	77	M12
Horsley Cross Essex	23	R2
Horsleycross Street Essex	23	R2
Horsleyhill Border	76	B2
Horsley's Green Bucks	20	C4
Horsley Woodhouse Derbys	47	L5
Horsmonden Kent	12	D7
Horspath Oxon	30	B11
Horstead Norfk	51	N10
Horsted Keynes W Susx	11	P5
Horton Bucks	30	K9
Horton Dorset	8	F7
Horton Lancs	62	H9
Horton Nhants	38	B10
Horton S Glos	28	E11
Horton Shrops	44	L9
Horton Somset	6	K2
Horton Staffs	46	B2
Horton Surrey	21	L10
Horton Swans	25	S13
Horton W & M	20	H7
Horton Wilts	18	H8
Horton Green Ches W	45	L3
Horton Heath Hants	9	P5
Horton Cross Somset	16	K13
Horton-cum-Studley Oxon	30	C10
Horton Green Ches W	45	L4
Horton Heath Hants	9	P5
Horton in Ribblesdale N York	62	G5
Horton Kirby Kent	21	U9
Horwich Bolton	55	P4
Horwich End Derbys	56	F10
Horwood Devon	15	L8
Hoscar Lancs	54	K4
Hoscote Border	75	S3
Hose Leics	47	T8
Hosey Hill Kent	21	S12
Hosh P & K	90	C7
Hoswick Shet	106	u11
Hotham E R Yk	64	J12
Hothfield Kent	12	J7
Hoton Leics	47	Q9
Hott Nthumb	76	F8
Hough Ches E	45	R3
Hough Ches E	56	C11
Hougham Lincs	48	C5
Hough End Leeds	63	Q13
Hough Green Halton	55	L9
Hough-on-the-Hill Lincs	48	D3
Houghton Cambs	39	L6
Houghton Cumb	75	T14
Houghton Hants	9	L2
Houghton Nthumb	77	N12
Houghton Pembks	24	G9
Houghton W Susx	10	G8
Houghton Conquest C Beds	31	M4
Houghton Gate Dur	70	D2
Houghton Green E Susx	12	H11
Houghton Green Warrtn	55	P8
Houghton le Side Darltn	69	Q8
Houghton-le-Spring Sundld	70	D3
Houghton on the Hill Leics	47	S13
Houghton Regis C Beds	31	M8
Houghton St Giles Norfk	50	F6
Houndslow Border	84	G9
Houndsmoor Somset	16	F11
Houndwood Border	85	L6
Hounslow Gt Lon	20	K7
Househill Highld	103	N4
Houses Hill Kirk	56	J3
Housieside Abers	105	P10
Houston Rens	88	K12
Houstry Highld	112	E9
Houton Ork	106	s19
Hove Br & H	11	M10
Hove Edge Calder	56	H2
Hoveringham Notts	47	S4
Hoveton Norfk	51	P10
Hovingham N York	64	F4
Howbrook Barns	57	M7
How Caple Herefs	28	B1
Howden E R Yk	64	H13
Howden-le-Wear Dur	69	Q6
Howe Highld	112	H4
Howe IoM	60	b9
Howe N York	63	S3
Howe Norfk	51	N14
Howe Bridge Wigan	55	Q6
Howe Green Essex	22	H7
Howegreen Essex	22	H7
Howell Lincs	48	H4
How End C Beds	31	M4
Howe of Teuchar Abers	105	M6
Howes D & G	75	N12
Howe Street Essex	22	G4
Howe Street Essex	39	U14
Howey Powys	34	B8
Howgate Cumb	66	F9
Howgate Mdloth	83	P6
Howgill Lancs	62	H11
Howick Nthumb	77	R3
Howle Dur	69	M8
Howle Wrekin	45	Q9
Howle Hill Herefs	28	B3
Howlett End Essex	39	S13
Howley Somset	6	K3
Howmore W Isls	106	c15

Column 2

Hownam Border	76	F2
Howrigg Cumb	67	M3
Howsham N Linc	58	H5
Howsham N York	64	G7
Howtel Nthumb	85	M12
Howt Green Kent	12	G2
Howton Herefs	27	S2
Howton Cumb	67	P9
Howwood Rens	88	J13
Hoxne Suffk	41	L5
Hoy Ork	106	r20
Hoylake Wirral	54	F9
Hoyland Barns	57	N5
Hoylandswaine Barns	57	M6
Hoyle W Susx	10	E7
Hoyle Mill Barns	57	N5
Hubberholme N York	62	J4
Hubberston Pembks	24	E9
Hubbert's Bridge Lincs	49	L5
Huby N York	63	S8
Huby N York	64	D6
Huccaby Devon	5	R6
Hucclecote Gloucs	28	G4
Hucking Kent	12	F4
Hucknall Notts	47	P3
Huddersfield Kirk	56	H3
Huddington Worcs	36	B9
Hudnall Herts	31	M10
Hudswell N York	69	P12
Huggate E R Yk	64	K8
Hugglescote Leics	47	M11
Hughenden Valley Bucks	20	E3
Hughley Shrops	45	N14
Hugh Town IoS	2	C2
Huish Devon	15	M10
Huish Wilts	18	H8
Huish Champflower Somset	16	E11
Huish Episcopi Somset	17	M11
Hulcote C Beds	30	K5
Hulcott Bucks	30	J9
Hulham Devon	6	D8
Hulland Derbys	46	H4
Hulland Ward Derbys	46	J4
Hullavington Wilts	28	G10
Hullbridge Essex	22	K8
Hull, Kingston upon C Ku H	65	Q14
Hulme Manch	55	T7
Hulme Staffs	45	U4
Hulme Warrtn	55	P8
Hulme End Staffs	46	F2
Hulme Walfield Ches E	55	T1
Hulse Heath Ches E	55	R10
Hulton Lane Ends Bolton	55	Q5
Hulverstone IoW	9	M12
Hulver Street Norfk	51	T14
Humber Devon	5	V8
Humber Herefs	35	M9
Humberside Airport N Lin	58	J4
Humberston NE Lin	59	P5
Humberston N York	69	R12
Humberton N York	63	U6
Humbie E Loth	84	D6
Humbleton E R Yk	65	S13
Humbleton Nthumb	85	P13
Humby Lincs	48	F7
Hume Border	84	J11
Humshaugh Nthumb	76	J11
Huna Highld	112	J2
Huncoat Lancs	62	F14
Huncote Leics	47	P14
Hundalee Border	76	C2
Hundall Derbys	57	N11
Hunderthwaite Dur	69	L8
Hundle Houses Lincs	48	K3
Hundleton Pembks	24	G10
Hundon Suffk	40	B11
Hundred End Lancs	54	K2
Hundred House Powys	34	D10
Hungarton Leics	47	S12
Hungerford Hants	8	H6
Hungerford Somset	16	E8
Hungerford W Berk	19	M7
Hungerford Newtown W Berk	19	N6
Hunger Hill Bolton	55	M4
Hunger Hill Lancs	55	M4
Hungerstone Herefs	34	K13
Hungerton Lincs	48	C8
Hungryhatton Shrops	45	Q8
Hunmanby N York	65	N4
Hunningham Warwks	37	L7
Hunnington Worcs	36	B4
Hunsbury Hill Nhants	37	T9
Hunsdon Herts	22	B5
Hunsingore N York	63	U9
Hunslet Leeds	63	S13
Hunsonby Cumb	67	S6
Hunspow Highld	112	G2
Hunstanton Norfk	49	U5
Hunstanworth Dur	69	L3
Hunston Suffk	40	G7
Hunston W Susx	10	D10
Hunston Green Suffk	40	G7
Hunstrete BaNES	17	R4
Hunsworth Kirk	56	H1
Hunt End Worcs	36	D8
Hunter's Inn Devon	15	P3
Hunter's Quay Ag & B	88	D11
Huntham Somset	16	K11
Hunthill Lodge Angus	98	H9
Huntingdon Cambs	38	K6
Huntingfield Suffk	41	Q6
Huntingford Dorset	17	U11
Huntington Ches W	54	K14
Huntington E Loth	84	D4
Huntington Herefs	34	G10
Huntington Herefs	35	L11
Huntington Staffs	46	C11
Huntington York	64	E8
Huntley Gloucs	28	D4
Huntly Abers	104	G8
Hunton Hants	19	Q13
Hunton Kent	12	D6
Hunton N York	63	P1
Hunton Bridge Herts	31	N12
Hunt's Corner Norfk	40	H3
Hunt's Cross Lpool	54	K9
Hunts Green Bucks	30	K12
Hunts Green Warwks	36	H1
Huntsham Devon	16	D12
Huntshaw Devon	15	M8
Huntshaw Cross Devon	15	M8
Huntspill Somset	16	K7
Huntworth Somset	16	K10
Hunwick Dur	69	Q6
Hunworth Norfk	50	J6
Hurcott Somset	17	N13
Hurdcott Wilts	8	H2
Hurdsfield Ches E	56	D12
Hurley W & M	20	D6
Hurley Warwks	36	J1
Hurley Bottom W & M	20	D6
Hurley Common Warwks	36	H1
Hurlford E Ayrs	81	P5
Hurliness Ork	106	r21
Hurlston Green Lancs	54	J4
Hurn Dorset	8	G9
Hursey Dorset	7	M4
Hurst Dorset	7	Q6
Hurst N York	69	M12
Hurst Somset	17	M13
Hurst Wokham	20	C8
Hurstbourne Priors Hants	19	P11
Hurstbourne Tarrant Hants	19	N10
Hurst Green E Susx	12	E11
Hurst Green Essex	23	Q4
Hurst Green Lancs	62	D12
Hurst Green Surrey	21	Q12
Hurst Hill Dudley	36	B2
Hurstley Herefs	34	J11
Hurstpierpoint W Susx	11	M7
Hurst Wickham W Susx	11	M7
Hurstwood Lancs	62	H13
Hurtiso Ork	106	t20
Hurworth Burn Dur	70	F7
Hurworth-on-Tees Darltn	70	D11
Hurworth Place Darltn	69	S11
Husbands Bosworth Leics	37	R4
Husborne Crawley C Beds	31	L5
Husthwaite N York	64	C5
Hutcherleigh Devon	5	T10
Hut Green N York	57	T2
Huthwaite N York	56	J15
Huthwaite Notts	47	N2
Huttoft Lincs	59	T11
Hutton Border	85	N8
Hutton Cumb	67	P7
Hutton E R Yk	65	M8
Hutton Essex	22	F9
Hutton Lancs	55	L1
Hutton N Som	16	K5
Hutton Bonville N York	70	D12
Hutton Buscel N York	65	M3
Hutton Conyers N York	63	S4
Hutton Cranswick E R Yk	65	N9
Hutton End Cumb	67	N5
Hutton Hang N York	63	P2

Column 3

Hutton Henry Dur	70	F5
Hutton-le-Hole N York	64	H2
Hutton Lowcross R & C	70	J10
Hutton Magna Dur	69	P10
Hutton Mulgrave N York	71	P11
Hutton Roof Cumb	62	C4
Hutton Roof Cumb	67	N6
Hutton Rudby N York	70	G11
Hutton Sessay N York	64	B4
Hutton Wandesley N York	64	C9
Huxham Devon	6	C5
Huxham Green Somset	17	Q9
Huxley Ches W	45	M1
Huyton Knows	54	K8
Hycemoor Cnwll	61	K1
Hyde Gloucs	28	G7
Hyde Hants	8	G7
Hyde Tamesd	56	D8
Hyde End Wokham	20	B9
Hyde Heath Bucks	30	K12
Hyde Lea Staffs	46	B10
Hydestile Surrey	10	F2
Hykeham Moor Lincs	58	F13
Hylands House & Park Essex	22	G7
Hyndford Bridge S Lans	82	H10
Hynish Ag & B	92	B11
Hyssington Powys	34	H2
Hystfield Gloucs	28	C8
Hythe Hants	9	N7
Hythe Somset	17	L5
Hythe Kent	13	N9
Hythe End W & M	20	H8
Hyton Cumb	61	K2

I

Ibberton Dorset	7	U3
Ible Derbys	46	H2
Ibsley Hants	8	H7
Ibstock Leics	47	M11
Ibstone Bucks	20	C4
Ibthorpe Hants	19	N10
Iburndale N York	71	Q11
Ibworth Hants	19	S10
Iceldon N York	71	L8
Ichrachan Ag & B	94	E12
Ickburgh Norfk	50	D14
Ickenham Gt Lon	20	J5
Ickford Bucks	30	D11
Ickham Kent	13	P4
Ickleford Herts	31	Q6
Icklesham E Susx	12	G12
Ickleton Cambs	39	Q11
Icklingham Suffk	40	C6
Ickornshaw N York	63	L11
Ickwell Green C Beds	38	H11
Icomb Gloucs	29	P3
Idbury Oxon	29	P4
Iddesleigh Devon	15	N11
Ide Devon	6	A6
Ideford Devon	6	A9
Ide Hill Kent	21	S12
Iden E Susx	12	H11
Iden Green Kent	12	E9
Iden Green Kent	12	F9
Idle C Brad	63	P12
Idless Cnwll	3	L7
Idlicote Warwks	36	J12
Idmiston Wilts	8	H2
Idole Carmth	25	R7
Idridgehay Derbys	46	J4
Idrigill Highld	100	b4
Idstone Oxon	29	P10
Iffley Oxon	30	B12
Ifield W Susx	11	L3
Ifold W Susx	10	G4
Ifton Mons	27	T10
Ifton Heath Shrops	44	H6
Ightfield Shrops	45	N6
Ightham Kent	21	U12
Iken Suffk	41	R9
Ilam Staffs	46	F3
Ilchester Somset	17	P12
Ilderton Nthumb	77	L1
Ilford Gt Lon	21	R5
Ilford Somset	16	K13
Ilfracombe Devon	15	M3
Ilkeston Derbys	47	N5
Ilketshall St Andrew Suffk	41	Q3
Ilketshall St John Suffk	41	Q3
Ilketshall St Lawrence Suffk	41	Q4
Ilketshall St Margaret Suffk	41	Q4
Ilkley C Brad	63	N10
Illand Cnwll	4	H5
Illey Dudley	36	C4
Illidge Green Ches E	55	S14
Illingworth Calder	63	L14
Illogan Cnwll	2	H8
Illston on the Hill Leics	47	T14
Ilmer Bucks	30	F11
Ilmington Warwks	36	H12
Ilminster Somset	16	K13
Ilsington Devon	5	U6
Ilsington Dorset	7	U6
Ilston Swans	25	U12
Ilton N York	63	P4
Ilton Somset	7	L1
Imachar Ag & B	79	R7
Immervoulin Stirlg	95	M15
Immingham NE Lin	59	L3
Immingham Dock NE Lin	59	L3
Impington Cambs	39	P8
Ince Ches W	55	L11
Ince Blundell Sefton	54	H6
Ince-in-Makerfield Wigan	55	N6
Inchbae Lodge Hotel Highld	108	G11
Inchbare Angus	99	L11
Inchberry Moray	104	C4
Incheril Highld	107	T12
Inchinnan Rens	88	K12
Inchlaggan Highld	101	Q11
Inchmichael P & K	91	K6
Inchnacardoch Hotel Highld	102	C13
Inchnadamph Highld	111	B11
Inchture P & K	91	K6
Inchvuilt Highld	101	U1
Inchyra P & K	91	J7
Indian Queens Cnwll	3	N5
Ingate Place Suffk	41	T3
Ingatestone Essex	22	F8
Ingbirchworth Barns	56	K5
Ingerthorpe N York	63	R6
Ingestre Staffs	46	C9
Ingham Lincs	58	F10
Ingham Norfk	51	Q9
Ingham Suffk	40	D6
Ingham Corner Norfk	51	Q9
Ingleborough Norfk	49	Q10
Ingleby Derbys	46	K8
Ingleby Arncliffe N York	70	F12
Ingleby Barwick S on T	70	G10
Ingleby Cross N York	70	G12
Ingleby Greenhow N York	70	J11
Inglesbatch BaNES	17	T4
Inglesham Swindn	29	P8
Ingleton D & G	73	L7
Ingleton N York	62	D5
Inglewhite Lancs	61	U12
Ingliston C Edin	83	M4
Ingmire Hall Cumb	62	C2
Ingoe Nthumb	77	L11
Ingol Lancs	61	U13
Ingoldisthorpe Norfk	49	U7
Ingoldmells Lincs	59	U13
Ingoldsby Lincs	48	F7
Ingram Nthumb	77	L2
Ingrave Essex	22	F9
Ingrow C Brad	63	M12
Ings Cumb	67	P13
Ingst S Glos	28	A10
Ingthorpe Rutlnd	48	E12
Ingworth Norfk	51	L8
Inkberrow Worcs	36	D9
Inkerman Dur	69	P6
Inkhorn Abers	105	P8
Inkpen W Berk	19	N8
Inkstack Highld	112	G2
Inmarsh Wilts	18	E8
Innellan Ag & B	88	E11
Innerleithen Border	83	R12
Innerleven Fife	91	M11
Innermessan D & G	72	D7
Innerwick E Loth	84	K4
Innerwick P & K	95	R9
Innsworth Gloucs	28	G3
Insch Abers	104	J10
Insh Highld	102	K5
Inshes Highld	102	K6
Inskip Lancs	61	T12
Inskip Moss Side Lancs	61	T12
Instow Devon	15	L6
Insworke Cnwll	5	L9
Intake Sheff	57	N9
Inver Abers	98	C5
Inver Highld	109	R9
Inver P & K	90	G2
Inverailort Highld	93	R3
Inveralligin Highld	107	P13
Inverallochy Abers	105	T2
Inveran Highld	108	K5
Inveraray Ag & B	87	T5

Column 4

Inverarnan Stirlg	88	H2
Inverasdale Highld	107	P8
Inverbeg Ag & B	88	H7
Inverbervie Abers	99	Q9
Inver-boyndie Abers	104	K3
Invercreran House Hotel Ag & B	94	E9
Inverdruie Highld	103	N13
Inveresk E Loth	83	S4
Inveresragan Ag & B	94	D11
Inverey Abers	97	T6
Inverfarigaig Highld	102	G10
Inverfolla Ag & B	94	C10
Invergarry Highld	96	C3
Invergeldie P & K	95	R13
Invergloy Highld	101	V14
Invergordon Highld	109	N11
Invergowrie P & K	91	N5
Inverguseran Highld	100	g9
Inverhadden P & K	95	U7
Inverherive Hotel Stirlg	95	M13
Inverie Highld	100	g10
Inverinan Ag & B	87	R3
Inverinate Highld	101	N7
Inverkeilor Angus	91	U2
Inverkeithing Fife	83	N1
Inverkeithny Abers	104	K7
Inverkip Inver	88	F11
Inverkirkaig Highld	110	B13
Inverlael Highld	108	B7
Inverlauren Ag & B	88	H8
Inverliever Lodge Ag & B	87	R4
Inverlochy Ag & B	94	H13
Invermark Angus	98	H7
Invermoriston Highld	102	F11
Invernaver Highld	111	Q4
Inverneill Ag & B	87	P9
Inverness Highld	102	J6
Inverness Airport Highld	103	L5
Inverness Crematorium Highld	102	H7
Invernoaden Ag & B	88	D6
Inveroran Hotel Ag & B	94	J10
Inverquharity Angus	98	G12
Inverquhomery Abers	105	S6
Inverroy Highld	96	B2
Inversanda Highld	94	C6
Invershiel Highld	101	N8
Invershin Highld	108	K5
Invershore Highld	112	H9
Inversnaid Hotel Stirlg	88	H4
Inverugie Abers	105	T6
Inveruglas Ag & B	88	H4
Inveruglass Highld	97	N3
Inverurie Abers	105	M13
Inwardleigh Devon	15	N13
Inworth Essex	23	L4
Iochdar W Isls	106	c14
Iping W Susx	10	D5
Ipplepen Devon	5	U7
Ipsden Oxon	19	U3
Ipstones Staffs	46	D3
Ipswich Suffk	41	L12
Ipswich Crematorium Suffk	41	L12
Irby Wirral	54	G10
Irby in the Marsh Lincs	59	R14
Irby upon Humber NE Lin	59	L6
Irchester Nhants	38	D7
Ireby Cumb	66	K5
Ireby Lancs	62	D4
Ireland C Beds	31	P4
Ireland S Shet	106	t12
Ireleth Cumb	61	N4
Ireshopeburn Dur	68	J5
Ireton Wood Derbys	46	J4
Irlam Salfd	55	R8
Irnham Lincs	48	F8
Iron Acton S Glos	28	C11
Iron Bridge Cambs	39	Q14
Ironbridge Wrekin	45	Q13
Iron Cross Warwks	36	E9
Ironmacannie D & G	73	R4
Irons Bottom Surrey	11	M2
Ironville Derbys	47	M3
Irstead Norfk	51	Q9
Irthington Cumb	75	U13
Irthlingborough Nhants	38	D6
Irton N York	65	N3
Irvine N Ayrs	81	L5
Isauld Highld	112	A3
Isbister Shet	106	s4
Isbister Shet	106	v7
Isfield E Susx	11	Q7
Isham Nhants	38	C6
Island Hill Worcs	35	U5
Islandpool Worcs	35	U3
Islay Ag & B	78	E5
Islay Airport Ag & B	78	E5
Isle Abbotts Somset	17	L12
Isle Brewers Somset	17	L12
Isleham Cambs	39	T6
Isle of Dogs Gt Lon	21	Q7
Isle of Grain Medway	23	L13
Isle of Lewis W Isls	106	j5
Isle of Man IoM	60	f5
Isle of Man Ronaldsway Airport IoM	60	d9
Isle of Mull Ag & B	93	N9
Isle of Purbeck Dorset	8	E12
Isle of Sheppey Kent	12	J2
Isle of Skye Highld	100	d6
Isle of Thanet Kent	13	S2
Isle of Walney Cumb	61	M6
Isle of Whithorn D & G	73	L11
Isle of Wight Wilts	9	Q11
Isles of Scilly Crematorium IoS	2	C2
Isleornsay Highld	100	g8
Isles of Scilly St Mary's Airport IoS	2	c2
Islesteps D & G	74	J11
Islet Village Guern	6	e2
Isleworth Gt Lon	21	L7
Isley Walton Leics	47	M9
Islibhig W Isls	106	e6
Islington Gt Lon	21	P6
Islington Crematorium Gt Lon	21	N4
Islip Nhants	38	E5
Islip Oxon	30	B10
Islivig W Isls	106	e6
Isombridge Wrekin	45	P11
Istead Rise Kent	22	F13
Itchen Abbas Hants	9	R2
Itchen Stoke Hants	9	R2
Itchingfield W Susx	10	J5
Itchington S Glos	28	C10
Itteringham Norfk	50	K7
Itton Devon	5	R2
Itton Mons	27	T8
Itton Common Mons	27	T8
Ivegill Cumb	67	N4
Ivelet N York	68	K13
Iver Bucks	20	H6
Iver Heath Bucks	20	H5
Iveston Dur	69	Q2
Ivinghoe Bucks	30	K9
Ivinghoe Aston Bucks	30	K9
Ivington Herefs	34	K9
Ivington Green Herefs	34	K9
Ivybridge Devon	5	Q9
Ivychurch Kent	12	K10
Ivy Cross Dorset	8	B3
Ivy Hatch Kent	21	U12
Ivy Todd Norfk	50	E12
Iwade Kent	12	H2
Iwerne Courtney or Shroton Dorset	8	B6
Iwerne Minster Dorset	8	B5
Ixworth Suffk	40	F6
Ixworth Thorpe Suffk	40	F6

J

Jack Green Lancs	55	N1
Jack Hill N York	63	P9
Jack-in-the-Green Devon	6	D5
Jackson Bridge Kirk	56	J5
Jacksdale Notts	47	M3
Jackton S Lans	81	R1
Jacobstow Cnwll	14	E13
Jacobstowe Devon	15	M12
Jacobs Well Surrey	20	G12
Jameston Pembks	24	H11
Jamestown Highld	108	E4
Jamestown W Duns	88	J9
Janetstown Highld	112	E10
Janetstown Highld	112	H4
Jardine Hall D & G	75	M10
Jarrow S Tyne	77	S13
Jarvis Brook E Susx	11	S5
Jasper's Green Essex	22	H2
Jaywick Essex	23	S4
Jealott's Hill Br For	20	E8
Jeater Houses N York	70	F13
Jedburgh Border	76	C2
Jeffreyston Pembks	24	J9
Jemimaville Highld	109	N11
Jerbourg Guern	6	e4
Jersey Jersey	7	b2
Jersey Airport Jersey	7	a2
Jersey Crematorium Jersey	7	b2
Jersey Marine Neath	26	C9
Jerusalem Lincs	58	F12
Jesmond N u Ty	77	R12
Jevington E Susx	11	T10
Jingle Street Mons	27	T5

Column 5

Jockey End Herts	31	M10
Jodrell Bank Ches E	55	S12
Johnby Cumb	67	P6
John Lennon Airport Lpool	54	K10
John o' Groats Highld	112	J2
John's Cross E Susx	12	D11
Johnshaven Abers	99	P10
Johnson Street Norfk	51	Q10
Johnston Pembks	24	F8
Johnstone D & G	75	P5
Johnstone Rens	88	K13
Johnstonebridge D & G	75	M8
Johnstown Carmth	25	Q7
Johnstown Wrexhm	44	H4
Joppa C Edin	83	R4
Joppa Cerdgn	33	L6
Joppa S Ayrs	81	N9
Jordans Bucks	20	G4
Jordanston Pembks	24	F4
Jordanthorpe Sheff	57	N10
Joyden's Wood Kent	22	D13
Jubilee Corner Kent	12	F6
Jump Barns	57	N6
Jumper's Town E Susx	11	R4
Juniper Nthumb	76	J14
Juniper Green C Edin	83	N5
Jura Ag & B	86	K7
Jurassic Coast	7	N8
Jurby IoM	60	f3
Jurston Devon	5	S3

K

Kaber Cumb	68	G10
Kaimend S Lans	82	J10
Kames Ag & B	87	T11
Kames E Ayrs	82	C13
Kea Cnwll	3	L8
Keadby N Linc	58	D4
Keal Cotes Lincs	49	N1
Kearby Town End N York	63	S10
Kearsley Bolton	55	S6
Kearsney Kent	13	P6
Kearstwick Cumb	62	C4
Kearton N York	69	L13
Keasden N York	62	E6
Keaton Devon	5	Q10
Keckwick Halton	55	N10
Keddington Lincs	59	P9
Keddington Corner Lincs	59	P9
Kedington Suffk	40	B11
Kedleston Derbys	46	K5
Keelby Lincs	59	L4
Keele Staffs	45	T4
Keele Services Staffs	45	T5
Keele University Staffs	45	T4
Keeley Green Bed	38	F11
Keelham C Brad	63	M13
Keevil Wilts	18	E9
Kegworth Leics	47	N8
Kehelland Cnwll	2	G8
Keig Abers	104	K13
Keighley C Brad	63	M11
Keighley Crematorium C Brad	63	L12
Keilarsbrae Clacks	90	C13
Keillour P & K	90	E6
Keiloch Abers	98	B5
Keills Ag & B	86	E12
Keinton Mandeville Somset	17	P10
Keir Mill D & G	74	G7
Keirsleywell Row Nthumb	68	G2
Keisby Lincs	48	F8
Keisley Cumb	68	F8
Keiss Highld	112	H4
Keith Moray	104	E5
Keithick P & K	90	K4
Keithock Angus	99	L11
Keithtown Highld	102	G4
Kelbrook Lancs	62	J11
Kelby Lincs	48	F4
Keld Cumb	67	S10
Keld N York	68	J12
Keld Head N York	64	H3
Keldholme N York	64	G2
Kelfield N Linc	58	D5
Kelfield N York	64	D11
Kelham Notts	47	U2
Kelhead D & G	75	M12
Kellacott Devon	5	L3
Kellamergh Lancs	61	S14
Kellas Angus	91	P4
Kellas Moray	103	U5
Kellaton Devon	5	U13
Kelleth Cumb	68	D11
Kelling Norfk	50	J5
Kellington N York	57	T2
Kelloe Dur	70	E5
Kelloholm D & G	74	D3
Kells Cumb	66	F10
Kelly Bray Cnwll	4	K6
Kelmarsh Nhants	37	U5
Kelmscott Oxon	29	P8
Kelsale Suffk	41	Q7
Kelsall Ches W	55	M13
Kelshall Herts	31	T5
Kelsick Cumb	66	K1
Kelso Border	84	K12
Kelstedge Derbys	57	M14
Kelstern Lincs	59	N7
Kelsterton Flints	54	G12
Kelston BaNES	17	T3
Keltneyburn P & K	95	U9
Kelton D & G	74	J11
Kelty Fife	90	H13
Kelvedon Essex	23	L4
Kelvedon Hatch Essex	22	E8
Kelynack Cnwll	2	B11
Kemacott Devon	15	P3
Kemback Fife	91	P8
Kemberton Shrops	45	R13
Kemble Gloucs	28	J8
Kemble Wick Gloucs	28	J8
Kemerton Worcs	36	C13
Kemeys Commander Mons	27	R7
Kemnay Abers	105	M13
Kempe's Corner Kent	13	L6
Kempley Gloucs	28	D2
Kempley Green Gloucs	28	D2
Kempsey Worcs	35	T11
Kempsford Gloucs	29	N8
Kemps Green Warwks	36	G6
Kempshott Hants	19	T10
Kempston Bed	38	F11
Kempston Hardwick Bed	38	F12
Kempton Shrops	34	J3
Kemp Town Br & H	11	N10
Kemsing Kent	21	U11
Kemsley Kent	12	H2
Kemsley Street Kent	12	F3
Kenardington Kent	12	J8
Kenchester Herefs	34	K12
Kencot Oxon	29	Q7
Kendal Cumb	67	R13
Kenderchurch Herefs	27	S2
Kenfig Brdgnd	26	E11
Kenfig Hill Brdgnd	26	E11
Kenilworth Warwks	36	J6
Kenley Gt Lon	21	P11
Kenley Shrops	45	N13
Kenmore Highld	107	M13
Kenmore P & K	95	V9
Kenn Devon	6	B7
Kenn N Som	17	M3
Kennacraig Ag & B	79	Q3
Kennall Vale Cnwll	2	K10
Kennards House Cnwll	4	H4
Kennavay W Isls	106	h8
Kenneggy Cnwll	2	E11
Kennerleigh Devon	15	T11
Kennessee Green Sefton	54	H6
Kennet Clacks	90	D13
Kennethmont Abers	104	H10
Kennett Cambs	39	U7
Kennford Devon	6	B7
Kenninghall Norfk	40	H3
Kennington Kent	12	K6
Kennington Oxon	30	B12
Kennoway Fife	91	M11
Kenny Somset	16	K13
Kennyhill Suffk	39	T5
Kennythorpe N York	64	H6
Kenovay Ag & B	92	B10
Kensaleyre Highld	100	d4
Kensington Gt Lon	21	N7
Kensington Palace Gt Lon	21	N6
Kensworth C Beds	31	M10
Kensworth Common C Beds	31	M10
Kentallen Highld	94	E6
Kent and East Sussex Railway Kent	12	F9
Kentchurch Herefs	27	S2
Kentford Suffk	40	B7
Kentisbeare Devon	6	E3
Kentisbury Devon	15	P3
Kentisbury Ford Devon	15	P3
Kentish Town Gt Lon	21	N6
Kentmere Cumb	67	Q12
Kenton Devon	6	C8
Kenton Gt Lon	21	L5
Kenton Suffk	41	L7

Column 6

Kenton N u Ty	77	Q12
Kenton Suffk	41	L7
Kenton Bankfoot N u Ty	77	Q12
Kentra Highld	93	R6
Kents Bank Cumb	61	R5
Kent's Green Gloucs	28	D3
Kent's Oak Hants	9	L4
Kenwick Shrops	44	K7
Kenwick Street Suffk	41	L7
Kenwyn Cnwll	3	L7
Kenyon Warrtn	55	P7
Keoldale Highld	110	H3
Keppoch Highld	101	M7
Kepwick N York	64	B2
Keresley Covtry	36	K4
Kermincham Ches E	55	T13
Kernborough Devon	5	T12
Kerne Bridge Herefs	28	A4
Kerridge Ches E	56	D11
Kerridge-end Ches E	56	D11
Kerris Cnwll	2	C11
Kerry Powys	34	D2
Kerrycroy Ag & B	88	D13
Kersall Notts	47	T1
Kersbrook Devon	6	E8
Kerscott Devon	15	P7
Kersey Suffk	40	H12
Kersey Tye Suffk	40	H12
Kersey Upland Suffk	40	H12
Kershader W Isls	106	i6
Kersoe Worcs	36	C12
Kerswell Devon	6	E4
Kerswell Green Worcs	35	U11
Kerthen Wood Cnwll	2	F10
Kesgrave Suffk	41	M11
Kessingland Suffk	41	T3
Kessingland Beach Suffk	41	T3
Kestle Cnwll	3	P7
Kestle Mill Cnwll	3	M5
Keston Gt Lon	21	R10
Keswick Cumb	67	L8
Keswick Norfk	51	L13
Keswick Norfk	51	Q7
Ketsby Lincs	59	Q11
Kettering Nhants	38	C5
Kettering Crematorium Nhants	38	C5
Ketteringham Norfk	51	L13
Kettins P & K	91	L4
Kettlebaston Suffk	40	G10
Kettlebridge Fife	91	L10
Kettlebrook Staffs	46	H13
Kettleburgh Suffk	41	M8
Kettle Green Herts	22	B4
Kettleholm D & G	75	M11
Kettleness N York	71	Q10
Kettleshulme Ches E	56	E11
Kettlesing N York	63	Q8
Kettlesing Bottom N York	63	R8
Kettlestone Norfk	50	G7
Kettlethorpe Lincs	58	E11
Kettletoft Ork	106	v16
Kettlewell N York	62	K5
Ketton Rutlnd	48	E13
Kew Gt Lon	21	M7
Kew Royal Botanic Gardens Gt Lon	21	L7
Kewstoke N Som	16	K4
Kexbrough Barns	57	M5
Kexby Lincs	58	E10
Kexby York	64	G9
Key Green Ches E	56	C14
Key Green N York	71	P11
Keyham Leics	47	S12
Keyhaven Hants	9	L10
Keyingham E R Yk	65	S14
Keymer W Susx	11	N7
Keynsham BaNES	17	S3
Keysoe Bed	38	G8
Keysoe Row Bed	38	G8
Key Street Kent	12	G3
Keyston Cambs	38	F6
Keyworth Notts	47	R7
Kibbear Somset	16	H12
Kibblesworth Gatesd	69	R1
Kibworth Beauchamp Leics	37	S2
Kibworth Harcourt Leics	37	S2
Kidbrooke Gt Lon	21	R7
Kiddemore Green Staffs	45	U12
Kidderminster Worcs	35	U5
Kiddington Oxon	29	T3
Kidd's Moor Norfk	50	K13
Kidmore End Oxon	19	U5
Kidsdale D & G	73	L12
Kidsgrove Staffs	45	T3
Kidstones N York	62	K3
Kidwelly Carmth	25	R9
Kiel Crofts Ag & B	94	C11
Kielder Nthumb	76	C7
Kiells Ag & B	86	G12
Kilbarchan Rens	88	K13
Kilbeg Highld	100	f9
Kilberry Ag & B	79	N3
Kilbirnie N Ayrs	88	J14
Kilbride Ag & B	79	N3
Kilbride Ag & B	94	B13
Kilbridemore Ag & B	87	U6
Kilburn Derbys	47	L4
Kilburn Gt Lon	21	N6
Kilburn N York	64	C4
Kilby Leics	37	R1
Kilchamaig Ag & B	79	Q4
Kilchattan Ag & B	86	J2
Kilchattan Ag & B	88	D14
Kilcheran Ag & B	93	T11
Kilchoan Highld	93	N6
Kilchoman Ag & B	78	C4
Kilchrenan Ag & B	94	F13
Kilconquhar Fife	91	Q11
Kilcot Gloucs	28	C3
Kilcoy Highld	102	G4
Kilcreggan Ag & B	88	F9
Kildale N York	70	K11
Kildalloig Ag & B	79	P12
Kildary Highld	109	P10
Kildavanan Ag & B	88	B12
Kildonan Highld	112	B12
Kildonan N Ayrs	79	S10
Kildonan Lodge Highld	112	A11
Kildonnan Highld	93	M3
Kildrochet House D & G	72	C8
Kildrummy Abers	104	F13
Kildwick N York	63	L11
Kilfinan Ag & B	87	T11
Kilfinnan Highld	96	C2
Kilford Denbgs	53	T11
Kilgetty Pembks	24	K9
Kilgrammie S Ayrs	80	J11
Kilgwrrwg Common Mons	27	T8
Kilham E R Yk	65	N6
Kilham Nthumb	85	N12
Kilkenneth Ag & B	92	B10
Kilkenzie Ag & B	79	M13
Kilkerran Ag & B	79	P13
Kilkhampton Cnwll	14	F10
Killamarsh Derbys	57	Q10
Killay Swans	25	V12
Killean Ag & B	79	M6
Killearn Stirlg	89	M8
Killellan Ag & B	79	M14
Killen Highld	102	J4
Killerby Darltn	69	Q9
Killerton Devon	6	C4
Killichonan P & K	95	S7
Killiechronan Ag & B	93	N8
Killiecrankie P & K	97	P11
Killilan Highld	101	N5
Killin Stirlg	95	R11
Killinallan Ag & B	78	E3
Killinghall N York	63	R8
Killington Cumb	62	C2
Killington Devon	15	Q3
Killington Lake Services Cumb	62	B1
Killingworth N Tyne	77	R11
Killiow Cnwll	3	L8
Killochyett Border	84	D10
Killocraw Ag & B	79	L9
Kilmacolm Inver	88	J11
Kilmaha Ag & B	87	S4
Kilmahog Stirlg	89	N4
Kilmahumaig Ag & B	87	N7
Kilmalieu Highld	94	C5
Kilmaluag Highld	100	d2
Kilmany Fife	91	N7
Kilmarie Highld	100	e8
Kilmarnock E Ayrs	81	N5
Kilmartin Ag & B	87	P6
Kilmaurs E Ayrs	81	N4
Kilmelford Ag & B	87	Q3
Kilmersdon Somset	17	S6
Kilmeston Hants	9	R3
Kilmichael Ag & B	79	N12
Kilmichael Glassary Ag & B	87	P7
Kilmichael of Inverlussa Ag & B	87	N9
Kilmington Devon	6	J5
Kilmington Wilts	17	U10
Kilmington Common Wilts	17	U10
Kilmington Street Wilts	17	U10
Kilmorack Highld	102	F6
Kilmore Ag & B	94	B13
Kilmore Highld	100	f8
Kilmory Ag & B	87	N10
Kilmory Highld	93	P4
Kilmory N Ayrs	79	S10
Kilmuir Highld	100	c3
Kilmuir Highld	100	d6
Kilmuir Highld	102	K6
Kilmuir Highld	109	P10

Column 7 (Kingswood... – Kirksanton)

Kingswood Brook Warwks	36	G6
Kingswood Common Herefs	34	G10
Kingswood Common Staffs	45	T13
Kings Worthy Hants	9	P2
Kington Herefs	34	G9
Kington S Glos	28	C9
Kington Worcs	36	C9
Kington Langley Wilts	18	D5
Kington Magna Dorset	17	U12
Kington St Michael Wilts	18	D5
Kingussie Highld	102	K6
Kingweston Somset	17	P10
Kinharrachie Abers	105	Q9
Kinharvie D & G	74	J12
Kinkell Bridge P & K	90	D7
Kinknockie Abers	105	S7
Kinleith C Edin	83	N5
Kinlet Shrops	35	R4
Kinloch Highld	93	Q4
Kinloch Highld	100	f10
Kinloch Highld	110	K6
Kinloch Highld	111	M6
Kinloch P & K	90	J3
Kinloch Stirlg	89	L5
Kinlochard Stirlg	89	L4
Kinlochbervie Highld	110	F5
Kinlocheil Highld	94	D4
Kinlochewe Highld	107	T12
Kinloch Hourn Highld	101	M10
Kinlochlaggan Highld	96	H6
Kinlochleven Highld	94	H6
Kinlochmoidart Highld	93	R4
Kinlochnanuagh Highld	93	S2
Kinloch Rannoch P & K	95	T7
Kinloss Moray	103	Q3
Kinmel Bay Conwy	53	S6
Kinmuck Abers	105	N12
Kinmundy Abers	105	P12
Kinnabus Ag & B	78	D6
Kinnadie Abers	105	Q7
Kinnaird P & K	90	K5
Kinneff Abers	99	Q8
Kinnelhead D & G	75	L5
Kinnell Angus	99	M13
Kinnerley Shrops	44	H9
Kinnersley Herefs	34	H11
Kinnersley Worcs	35	U12
Kinnerton Powys	34	G8
Kinnerton Shrops	34	J1
Kinnerton Green Flints	44	H1
Kinnesswood P & K	90	K10
Kinninvie Dur	69	N8
Kinnordy Angus	98	F12
Kinoulton Notts	47	S7
Kinross P & K	90	H11
Kinross Services P & K	90	H11
Kinrossie P & K	90	J5
Kinsbourne Green Herts	31	P9
Kinsey Heath Ches E	45	P4
Kinsham Herefs	34	H8
Kinsham Worcs	36	B13
Kinsley Wakefd	57	P4
Kinson Bmouth	8	F9
Kintail Highld	101	P8
Kintbury W Berk	19	N7
Kintessack Moray	103	Q3
Kintillo P & K	90	H8
Kinton Herefs	34	J6
Kinton Shrops	44	H10
Kintore Abers	105	M13
Kintour Ag & B	78	H5
Kintra Ag & B	78	E6
Kintra Ag & B	92	J13
Kintraw Ag & B	87	P4
Kintyre Ag & B	79	N8
Kinveachy Highld	103	N12
Kinver Staffs	35	T4
Kippax Leeds	63	U13
Kippen Stirlg	89	P6
Kippford or Scaur D & G	66	C2
Kipping's Cross Kent	12	B7
Kirbister Ork	106	s19
Kirbuster Ork	106	r17
Kirby Bedon Norfk	51	N12
Kirby Bellars Leics	47	T10
Kirby Cane Norfk	41	Q2
Kirby Corner Covtry	36	J5
Kirby Cross Essex	23	T3
Kirby Fields Leics	47	P13
Kirby Grindalythe N York	65	M6
Kirby Hill N York	63	T7
Kirby Hill N York	69	Q11
Kirby Knowle N York	64	B3
Kirby-le-Soken Essex	23	T3
Kirby Misperton N York	64	G4
Kirby Muxloe Leics	47	P13
Kirby Sigston N York	70	E14
Kirby Underdale E R Yk	64	J8
Kirby Wiske N York	63	T2
Kirdford W Susx	10	G5
Kirk Highld	112	G6
Kirkabister Shet	106	u10
Kirkandrews D & G	73	P9
Kirkandrews upon Eden Cumb	75	S14
Kirkbampton Cumb	75	S14
Kirkbean D & G	66	E1
Kirk Bramwith Donc	57	T4
Kirkbride Cumb	66	K1
Kirkbridge N York	63	R1
Kirkbuddo Angus	91	R3
Kirkburn Border	83	Q11
Kirkburn E R Yk	65	M9
Kirkburton Kirk	56	J4
Kirkby Knows	54	K7
Kirkby Lincs	58	H7
Kirkby N York	70	H11
Kirkby Fleetham N York	63	R1
Kirkby Green Lincs	48	G2
Kirkby in Ashfield Notts	47	N2
Kirkby-in-Furness Cumb	61	N3
Kirkby la Thorpe Lincs	48	G4
Kirkby Lonsdale Cumb	62	C4
Kirkby Malham N York	62	H7
Kirkby Mallory Leics	47	N13
Kirkby Malzeard N York	63	Q5
Kirkby Mills N York	64	G3
Kirkbymoorside N York	64	G3
Kirkby on Bain Lincs	59	L14
Kirkby Overblow N York	63	S11
Kirkby Stephen Cumb	68	F11
Kirkby Thore Cumb	68	D8
Kirkby Underwood Lincs	48	G8
Kirkby Wharfe N York	64	C11
Kirkby Woodhouse Notts	47	N3
Kirkcaldy Fife	91	L13
Kirkcaldy Crematorium Fife	91	L13
Kirkcambeck Cumb	76	A12
Kirkcolm D & G	72	C6
Kirkconnel D & G	74	D2
Kirkconnell D & G	74	J12
Kirkcowan D & G	72	K7
Kirkcudbright D & G	73	R9
Kirkdale Lpool	54	H8
Kirk Deighton N York	63	T9
Kirk Ella E R Yk	65	N14
Kirkfieldbank S Lans	82	G10
Kirkgunzeon D & G	66	C1
Kirk Hallam Derbys	47	N5
Kirkham Lancs	61	T13
Kirkham N York	64	G7
Kirkhamgate Wakefd	57	L2
Kirk Hammerton N York	63	U9
Kirkharle Nthumb	77	L9
Kirkhaugh Nthumb	68	E3
Kirkheaton Kirk	56	J3
Kirkheaton Nthumb	77	L10
Kirkhill Highld	102	G6
Kirkhope S Lans	82	F14
Kirkhouse Cumb	76	B14
Kirkhouse Green Donc	57	U4
Kirkibost Highld	100	e8
Kirkinch P & K	91	L2
Kirkinner D & G	73	L8
Kirkintilloch E Duns	89	P11
Kirk Ireton Derbys	46	J4
Kirkland Cumb	66	G9
Kirkland Cumb	67	S5
Kirkland D & G	74	D2
Kirkland D & G	74	F5
Kirkland D & G	74	H6
Kirkland Guards Cumb	66	K4
Kirk Langley Derbys	46	J6
Kirkleatham R & C	70	J8
Kirklevington S on T	70	F11
Kirkley Suffk	41	T2
Kirklington N York	63	S3
Kirklington Notts	47	S2
Kirklinton Cumb	75	T12
Kirkliston C Edin	83	M4
Kirkmabreck D & G	73	N8
Kirkmaiden D & G	72	D12
Kirk Merrington Dur	69	S5
Kirk Michael IoM	60	e4
Kirkmichael P & K	97	R12
Kirkmichael S Ayrs	81	L11
Kirkmuirhill S Lans	82	E9
Kirknewton Nthumb	85	M12
Kirknewton W Loth	83	M5
Kirkney Abers	104	G9
Kirk of Shotts N Lans	82	G5
Kirkoswald Cumb	67	R4
Kirkoswald S Ayrs	80	J10
Kirkpatrick D & G	74	H6
Kirkpatrick Durham D & G	74	F12
Kirkpatrick-Fleming D & G	75	Q11
Kirk Sandall Donc	57	T5
Kirksanton Cumb	61	L3

Kirk Smeaton N York 57 R3
Kirkstall Leeds 63 R12
Kirkstead Lincs 48 J1
Kirkstile Abers 104 G8
Kirkstile D & G 75 S7
Kirkstone Pass Inn
Cumb 67 N10
Kirkstyle Highld 112 H2
Kirkthorpe Wakefd 57 N2
Kirkton Abers 104 J10
Kirkton D & G 74 J9
Kirkton Fife 91 N6
Kirkton Highld 101 N5
Kirkton Highld 101 N5
Kirkton P & K 90 E8
Kirkton Manor Border 83 P11
Kirkton of Airlie Angus 91 N5
Kirkton of
Auchterhouse Angus 91 M4
Kirkton of Barevan
Abers 105 D12
Kirkton of Collace P & K 90 J5
Kirkton of Glenbuchat
Abers 104 C8
Kirkton of Logie Buchan
Abers 105 N10
Kirkton of Menmuir
Angus 98 J11
Kirkton of Monikie
Angus 91 R4
Kirkton of Rayne Abers 104 K9
Kirkton of Skene Abers 99 Q2
Kirkton of
Strathmartine Angus 91 N4
Kirkton of Tealing Angus 91 P4
Kirkton of Tough Abers 105 R2
Kirktown Abers 105 R2
Kirktown of Alvah Abers 104 K3
Kirktown of Bourtie
Abers 105 N10
Kirktown of Fetteresso
Abers 99 R6
Kirktown of Mortlach
Moray 104 C8
Kirkwall Ork 106 t18
Kirkwall Airport Ork 106 t19
Kirkwhelpington
Nthumb 76 K9
Kirk Yetholm Border 85 L13
Kirmington N Linc 59 L8
Kirmond le Mire Lincs 59 L8
Kirn Ag & B 88 E10
Kirriemuir Angus 98 F13
Kirstead Green Norfk 41 M5
Kirtlebridge D & G 75 P11
Kirtling Cambs 39 U9
Kirtling Green Cambs 39 U9
Kirtlington Oxon 29 B4
Kirtomy Highld 111 Q4
Kirton Lincs 49 M6
Kirton Notts 57 U13
Kirton Suffk 41 N12
Kirton End Lincs 49 L5
Kirtonhill W Duns 88 J10
Kirton Holme Lincs 49 L4
Kirton in Lindsey N Linc 58 F7
Kirwaugh D & G 73 L9
Kishorn Highld 101 L4
Kislingbury Nhants 37 S9
Kitebrook Warwks 29 H1
Kite Green Warwks 36 G7
Kite's Hardwick Warwks 37 N7
Kitleigh Cnwll 14 F13
Kitt Green Wigan 55 M5
Kittisford Somset 16 E12
Kittle Swans 25 U13
Kitt's Green Birm 36 G3
Kittybrewster C Aber 99 S2
Kitwood Hants 9 S2
Kivernoll Herefs 27 T1
Kiveton Park Rothm 57 Q10
Knaith Lincs 58 D10
Knaith Park Lincs 58 D9
Knaphill Surrey 20 G11
Knapp Somset 16 K11
Knapp Hill Hants 9 N4
Knapthorpe Notts 47 T2
Knapton C York 64 D9
Knapton N York 64 K4
Knapton Norfk 51 N6
Knapton Green Herefs 34 K10
Knapwell Cambs 39 M8
Knaresborough N York 63 S8
Knarsdale Nthumb 68 F2
Knaven Abers 105 P7
Knayton N York 63 U2
Knebworth Herts 31 S8
Knedlington E R Yk 64 H14
Kneesall Notts 58 B14
Kneesworth Cambs 31 T4
Kneeton Notts 47 T4
Knelston Swans 25 S13
Knenhall Staffs 46 B6
Knettishall Suffk 40 G4
Knightacott Devon 15 Q5
Knightcote Warwks 37 M10
Knightley Staffs 45 T8
Knightley Dale Staffs 45 T9
Knighton C Leic 47 R13
Knighton Devon 5 N11
Knighton Dorset 7 R2
Knighton Poole 8 F9
Knighton Powys 34 G6
Knighton Somset 16 G8
Knighton Staffs 45 R5
Knighton Staffs 45 S8
Knighton on Teme
Worcs 35 P7
Knightsbridge Gloucs 28 G2
Knightsmill Cnwll 4 D4
Knightwick Worcs 35 R9
Knill Herefs 34 G8
Knipton Leics 48 B7
Knitsley Dur 69 P3
Kniveton Derbys 46 H3
Knock Cumb 68 E7
Knock Highld 100 f9
Knock Moray 104 H5
Knock W Isls 106 j5
Knockally Highld 112 D11
Knockan Highld 108 C3
Knockando Moray 103 U7
Knockbain Highld 102 H4
Knock Castle N Ayrs 88 E13
Knockdee Highld 112 E4
Knockdow Ag & B 88 F10
Knockdown Wilts 28 F10
Knockeen S Ayrs 81 L13
Knockenkelly N Ayrs 80 E7
Knockentiber E Ayrs 81 N5
Knockhall Kent 21 S11
Knockholt Kent 21 S11
Knockholt Pound Kent 21 S11
Knockin Shrops 44 H9
Knockinlaw E Ayrs 81 N5
Knockmill Kent 21 U10
Knocknain D & G 72 B7
Knockrome Ag & B 86 K11
Knocksharry IoM 60 d5
Knocksheen D & G 73 Q5
Knockvennie Smithy
D & G 74 E11
Knodishall Suffk 41 R8
Knodishall Common
Suffk 41 R8
Knole Somset 17 N11
Knole Park S Glos 28 A11
Knolls Green Ches E 55 T11
Knolton Wrexhm 44 J6
Knook Wilts 18 D12
Knossington Leics 48 B12
Knott End-on-Sea Lancs 61 R10
Knotting Bed 38 F8
Knotting Green Bed 38 F8
Knottingley Wakefd 57 R2
Knotty Ash Lpool 54 K8
Knotty Green Bucks 20 F4
Knowbury Shrops 35 N5
Knowe D & G 72 K6
Knowehead D & G 73 R5
Knowesgate Nthumb 76 K9
Knoweside S Ayrs 80 K10
Knowe Bristl 17 R3
Knowe Devon 5 P10
Knowe Devon 15 R5
Knowe Devon 15 S12
Knowe Shrops 35 N6
Knowe Solhll 36 G5
Knowe Cross Devon 6 D5
Knowefield Cumb 67 P1
Knowe Green Lancs 62 C12
Knowe Hill Surrey 20 H9
Knowe St Giles Somset 6 K2
Knowe Village Hants 9 R6
Knowe Wood Calder 56 E2
Knowl Green Essex 40 C12
Knowl Hill W & M 20 D7
Knowlton
Knowl 55 L8
Knowstone Devon 15 U8
Knox N York 63 R8
Knox Bridge Kent 12 E7
Knucklas Powys 34 G5
Knuston Nhants 38 D7
Knutsford Ches E 55 S11

Knutsford Services
Ches E 55 R11
Knutton Staffs 45 T4
Krumlin Calder 56 G3
Kuggar Cnwll 2 J13
Kyleakin Highld 100 g7
Kyle of Lochalsh
Highld 100 h7
Kylerhea Highld 100 h7
Kyles Scalpay W Isls 106 h10
Kylesmorar Highld 100 h10
Kyles Scalpay W Isls 106 h10
Kylesmorar Highld 100 h10
Kylestrome Highld 108 E8
Kynaston Herefs 35 P13
Kynaston Shrops 44 J9
Kynnersley Wrekin 45 Q10
Kyre Green Worcs 35 N7
Kyre Park Worcs 35 P8
Kyrewood Worcs 35 N7
Kyrle Somset 16 E12

L

La Bellieuse Guern 6 d3
Lacasaigh W Isls 106 j6
Lacasdal W Isls 106 j5
Laceby NE Lin 59 M5
Lacey Green Bucks 30 H12
Lach Dennis Ches W 55 R12
Lackenby R & Cl 70 J9
Lackford Suffk 40 C6
Lackford Green Suffk 40 C6
Lacock Wilts 18 D7
Ladbroke Warwks 37 M9
Laddingford Kent 12 C6
Lade Bank Lincs 49 N3
Ladock Cnwll 3 M6
Lady Ork 106 v15
Ladybank Fife 91 M10
Ladycross Cnwll 4 J4
Ladygill S Lans 82 H13
Lady Hall Cumb 61 M2
Ladykirk Border 85 M9
Ladyridge Herefs 28 A1
Ladywood Birm 36 E3
Ladywood Worcs 35 U8
La Fontenelle Guern 6 e1
La Fosse Guern 6 d3
La Greve Guern 6 e3
La Greve de Lecq Jersey 7 b1
La Hougue Bie Jersey 7 e3
La Houguette Guern 6 c3
Laid Highld 110 J5
Laide Highld 107 R6
Laig Highld 100 d11
Laigh Clunch E Ayrs 81 P3
Laigh Fenwick E Ayrs 81 P4
Laigh Glenmuir E Ayrs 81 R9
Laighstonehall S Lans 82 D8
Laindon Essex 22 F10
Lairg Highld 108 K3
Laisterdyke C Brad 63 P13
Laithes Cumb 67 Q6
Lake Devon 15 N6
Lake Devon 15 Q5
Lake IoW 9 R12
Lake Wilts 18 H13
Lake District
National Park Cumb 66 K11
Lakenheath Suffk 40 B4
Laker's Green Surrey 10 G3
Lakesend Norfk 39 R1
Lakeside Cumb 61 Q3
Lakeside Dorset 7 S7
Laleham Surrey 20 J9
Laleston Brdgnd 26 F12
Lamanva Cnwll 2 K10
Lamarsh Essex 40 E13
Lamas Norfk 51 M9
Lambden Border 84 J10
Lamberhurst Kent 12 C8
Lamberhurst Down Kent 12 C8
Lambert's End Sandw 36 C2
Lamberton Border 85 P7
Lambeth Gt Lon 21 P7
Lambeth Crematorium
Gt Lon 21 N8
Lambfair Green Suffk 40 B10
Lambley Notts 47 R4
Lambley Nthumb 76 D14
Lamborough End Essex 22 K4
Lambourn W Berk 19 M5
Lambourne End Essex 21 R4
Lambourn
Woodlands W Berk 19 M5
Lamb Roe Lancs 62 E12
Lambs Green W Susx 11 L3
La Rocque Jersey 7 e4
La Rousaillerie Guern 6 d2
Lamellion Cnwll 4 G8
Lamerton Devon 5 L5
Lamesley Gatesd 77 R14
Lamington S Lans 82 H11
Lamlash N Ayrs 80 E6
Lamonby Cumb 67 N5
Lamorick Cnwll 4 Q4
Lamorna Cnwll 2 C12
Lamorran Cnwll 3 M7
Lampen Cnwll 4 F6
Lampeter Cerdgn 33 L11
Lampeter Velfrey
Pembks 24 K8
Lamphey Pembks 24 H10
Lamplugh Cumb 66 G8
Lamport Nhants 37 U6
Lamyatt Somset 17 S9
Lana Devon 14 H13
Lana Devon 14 H13
Lanark S Lans 82 G10
Lancaster Lancs 61 T7
Lancaster & Morecambe
Crematorium Lancs 61 T7
Lancaster Services
(Forton) Lancs 61 U9
Lancaut Gloucs 27 U8
Lanchester Dur 69 Q3
Lancing W Susx 10 K10
L'Ancresse Guern 6 e1
Landbeach Cambs 39 Q7
Landcross Devon 14 J8
Landerberry Abers 99 N3
Landford Wilts 8 K5
Land-hallow Highld 112 E9
Landican Crematorium
Wirral 54 G9
Landkey Devon 15 N6
Landore Swans 26 A8
Landrake Cnwll 4 J8
Landscove Devon 5 T7
Land's End Cnwll 2 B11
Land's End Airport Cnwll 2 B11
Landshipping Pembks 24 H8
Landue Cnwll 4 K5
Landulph Cnwll 5 L8
Landwade Suffk 39 U7
Landywood Staffs 46 C13
Laneast Cnwll 4 G4
Lane Bottom Lancs 62 H12
Lane End Bucks 20 D4
Lane End Cnwll 3 R2
Lane End Cumb 66 H13
Lane End Hants 9 R3
Lane End Kent 22 D13
Lane End Lancs 62 H10
Lane End Warrtn 55 Q7
Lane Ends Derbys 46 H6
Lane Ends Derbys 46 H7
Lane Ends Lancs 62 H12
Lane Ends N York 62 K11
Lane Green Staffs 45 T8
Laneham Notts 58 D11
Lanehead Dur 68 J4
Lane Head Dur 69 P10
Lane Head Wigan 55 P7
Lane Head Wsall 46 C13
Lane Heads Lancs 61 S12
Lanehouse Bridge Lancs 62 H11
Lane Side Lancs 55 T2
Langaford Devon 14 K13
Langage Devon 5 N9
Langar Notts 47 T7
Langbank Rens 88 J11
Langbaurgh N York 70 H9
Langcliffe N York 62 H7
Langdale End N York 65 L1
Langdon Cnwll 4 J3
Langdon Beck Dur 68 J6
Langdon Hills Essex 22 F10
Langdyke Fife 91 M11
Langenhoe Essex 23 P4
Langford C Beds 38 J11
Langford Devon 6 D4
Langford Essex 22 K6
Langford Notts 48 B2
Langford Oxon 29 P7
Langford Somset 16 F12
Langford Budville
Somset 16 F12
Langham Dorset 17 U8
Langham Essex 23 P1
Langham Norfk 50 H5
Langham Rutlnd 48 B11
Langham Suffk 40 G7
Langho Lancs 62 E13
Langholm D & G 75 S9

Langland Swans 25 V13
Langley Border 84 G14
Langley Ches E 56 D12
Langley Derbys 47 M4
Langley Gloucs 28 K2
Langley Hants 9 N8
Langley Herts 31 R8
Langley Kent 12 F5
Langley Nthumb 76 G13
Langley Oxon 29 Q4
Langley Rochdl 56 C5
Langley Slough 20 H7
Langley Somset 16 E11
Langley W Susx 10 C5
Langley Warwks 36 G8
Langley Burrell Wilts 18 D6
Langley Castle Nthumb 76 G13
Langley Common Derbys 46 J6
Langley Green Derbys 46 J6
Langley Green Essex 23 L3
Langley Green Warwks 36 G8
Langley Lower Green
Essex 39 P14
Langley Marsh Somset 16 E11
Langley Mill Derbys 47 M4
Langley Moor Dur 69 R3
Langley Park Dur 69 R3
Langley Street Norfk 51 Q13
Langley Upper Green
Essex 39 P14
Langney E Susx 11 U10
Langold Notts 57 S9
Langore Cnwll 4 H3
Langport Somset 17 M11
Langridge BaNES 17 T3
Langridgeford Devon 15 N8
Langrigg Cumb 66 J3
Langrick Lincs 49 L4
Langsett Barns 56 K6
Langshaw Border 84 E12
Langside P & K 89 S3
Langstone Newpt 27 R10
Langthorne N York 63 Q1
Langthorpe N York 63 T6
Langthwaite N York 69 N12
Langtoft E R Yk 65 N6
Langtoft Lincs 48 H11
Langton Dur 69 Q9
Langton Lincs 59 N13
Langton Lincs 59 Q12
Langton by Wragby
Lincs 59 L11
Langton Green Kent 11 S3
Langton Green Suffk 40 K6
Langton Herring Dorset 7 R8
Langton Long
Blandford Dorset 8 B7
Langton Matravers
Dorset 8 E13
Langtree Devon 15 L9
Langtree Week Devon 15 L9
Langwathby Cumb 67 R6
Langwith Derbys 57 R13
Langwith Junction
Derbys 57 R13
Langworth Lincs 58 J11
Lanhydrock House &
Gardens Cnwll 3 R4
Lanivet Cnwll 3 Q3
Lanjeth Cnwll 3 P6
Lank Cnwll 4 R1
Lanlivery Cnwll 3 R5
Lanner Cnwll 2 J9
Lanoy Cnwll 4 H5
Lanreath Cnwll 4 F9
Lansallos Cnwll 4 F10
Lanteglos Cnwll 4 E3
Lanteglos Highway
Cnwll 4 E10
Lanton Border 84 G13
Lanton Nthumb 85 N12
La Passee Guern 6 d2
Lapford Devon 15 R11
Lapley Staffs 45 U11
Lapworth Warwks 36 G6
Larachbeg Highld 93 R9
Larbert Falk 82 G2
Larbreck Lancs 61 S11
Largie Abers 104 J9
Largiemore Ag & B 87 S8
Largoward Fife 91 Q10
Largs N Ayrs 80 J2
Largybeg N Ayrs 80 E8
Largymore N Ayrs 80 E8
Larkbeare Devon 6 E5
Larkfield Inver 88 F10
Larkfield Kent 12 D4
Larkhall S Lans 82 E8
Larkhill Wilts 18 H12
Larling Norfk 40 G3
La Rocque Jersey 7 e4
La Rousaillerie Guern 6 d2
Lartington Dur 69 N9
Lasborough Gloucs 28 F9
Lasham Hants 19 U12
Lashbrook Devon 14 K11
Lashbrook Devon 14 K11
Lashenden Kent 12 F7
Lask Edge Staffs 46 B2
Lasswade Mdloth 83 R5
Lastingham N York 64 H1
Latcham Somset 17 M7
Latchford Oxon 30 E12
Latchingdon Essex 23 L7
Latchley Cnwll 5 L6
Lately Common Warrtn 55 Q7
Lathbury M Keyn 38 C11
Latheron Highld 112 E8
Latheronwheel Highld 112 E8
Lathones Fife 91 Q10
Latimer Bucks 20 H3
Latteridge S Glos 28 C11
Lattiford Somset 17 S11
Latton Wilts 28 K8
Laugharne Carmth 24 K8
Laughterton Lincs 58 D11
Laughton E Susx 11 R8
Laughton Leics 37 S3
Laughton Lincs 48 D6
Laughton Lincs 58 D7
Laughton-en-le-
Morthen Rothm 57 R9
Launcells Cnwll 14 F11
Launcells Cross Cnwll 14 G11
Launceston Cnwll 4 J4
Launton Oxon 30 D8
Laurencekirk Abers 99 N9
Laurieston D & G 73 R7
Laurieston Falk 82 K9
Lavendon M Keyn 38 D10
Lavenham Suffk 40 F11
Lavernock V Glam 16 F2
Laversdale Cumb 75 U13
Laverstock Wilts 8 H2
Laverstoke Hants 19 R11
Laverton Gloucs 36 E13
Laverton N York 63 Q5
Laverton Somset 17 U6
La Villette Guern 6 d3
Lavister Wrexhm 44 J2
Law S Lans 82 F9
Lawers P & K 95 T11
Lawford Essex 23 Q1
Lawford Somset 16 F9
Law Hill S Lans 82 F9
Lawhitton Cnwll 4 K4
Lawkland N York 62 F7
Lawley Wrekin 45 Q12
Lawnhead Staffs 45 T8
Lawns Wood
Crematorium Leeds 63 R12
Lawrenny Pembks 24 H9
Lawshall Suffk 40 E10
Lawshall Green Suffk 40 E10
Lawton Herefs 35 L9
Laxay W Isls 106 j6
Laxdale W Isls 106 j5
Laxey IoM 60 g5
Laxfield Suffk 41 N6
Laxford Bridge Highld 110 E7
Laxo Shet 106 u7
Laxton E R Yk 58 C1
Laxton Nhants 38 E1
Laxton Notts 58 B13
Laycock C Brad 63 L11
Layer Breton Essex 23 M4
Layer-de-la-Haye Essex 23 N4
Layer Marney Essex 23 M4
Laymore Dorset 7 L3
Layland's Green W Berk 19 N7
Laytham E R Yk 64 G12
Layter's Green Bucks 20 G4
Laythes Cumb 66 K1
Lazenby R & Cl 70 H9
Lazonby Cumb 67 R5
Lea Derbys 46 K2
Lea Herefs 28 B3
Lea Lincs 58 D10
Lea Shrops 34 J2
Lea Shrops 34 K13
Lea Wilts 28 J10
Lea & Cleveland
Crematorium Leeds 63 S12
Leachkin Highld 102 H7
Leadburn Mdloth 83 P7
Leadenham Lincs 48 D3
Leaden Roding Essex 22 E5
Leadgate Cumb 68 F3

Leadgate Nthumb 77 N14
Leadhills S Lans 74 G2
Leadingcross Green
Kent 12 G5
Leafield Derbys 56 K10
Leafield Oxon 29 R4
Leagrave Luton 31 N8
Leahead Ches W 55 Q14
Lea Heath Staffs 46 D8
Leake N York 63 U1
Leake Common Side
Lincs 49 N3
Lealholm N York 71 N11
Lealholm Side N York 71 N11
Lealt Highld 100 e4
Leam Derbys 56 K11
Lea Marston Warwks 36 H2
Leamington Hastings
Warwks 37 M7
Leamington Spa Warwks 36 K7
Leamside Dur 70 D3
Leap Cross E Susx 11 T8
Leasgill Cumb 61 T3
Leasingham Lincs 48 G4
Leasingthorne Dur 69 S5
Leatherhead Surrey 21 L11
Leathley N York 63 Q10
Leaton Shrops 45 L10
Leaton Wrekin 45 P11
Lea Town Lancs 61 T13
Leaveland Kent 12 K5
Leavenheath Suffk 40 G13
Leavening N York 64 H7
Leaves Green Gt Lon 21 R10
Lea Yeat Cumb 62 F2
Lebberston N York 65 N3
Le Bigard Guern 6 d4
Le Bourg Guern 6 d4
Le Bourg Jersey 7 e3
Lechlade on Thames
Gloucs 29 P8
Lecht Gruinart Ag & B 86 D12
Leck Lancs 62 C4
Leckbuie P & K 95 U10
Leckford Hants 19 N13
Leckfurin Highld 111 R5
Leckgruinart Ag & B 86 D12
Leckhampstead Bucks 30 F5
Leckhampstead W Berk 19 P5
Leckhampstead Thicket
W Berk 19 P5
Leckhampton Gloucs 28 H4
Leckmelm Highld 108 B7
Leckwith V Glam 16 F2
Leconfield E R Yk 65 N11
Ledaig Ag & B 94 C11
Ledburn Bucks 30 K8
Ledbury Herefs 35 R13
Leddington Gloucs 35 Q14
Ledgemoor Herefs 34 K10
Ledicot Herefs 34 K8
Ledmore Junction
Highld 108 C2
Lednagullin Highld 111 R4
Ledsham Ches W 54 J12
Ledsham Leeds 57 Q1
Ledston Leeds 57 Q1
Ledston Luck Leeds 63 U13
Ledwell Oxon 29 U3
Lee Devon 15 L3
Lee Hants 9 M5
Lee Shrops 44 K7
Leebotwood Shrops 45 L14
Lee Brockhurst Shrops 45 M8
Leece Cumb 61 N6
Lee Chapel Essex 22 G10
Lee Clump Bucks 30 K12
Lee Common Bucks 30 K12
Leeds Kent 12 F5
Leeds Leeds 63 R13
Leeds Bradford Airport
Leeds 63 Q11
Leeds Castle Kent 12 F5
Leedstown Cnwll 2 G9
Lee Green Ches E 55 Q1
Leek Staffs 46 C2
Leek Wootton Warwks 36 J7
Lee Mill Devon 5 P9
Leeming C Brad 63 L13
Leeming N York 63 R2
Leeming Bar N York 63 R1
Lee Moor Devon 5 P7
Lee-on-the-Solent Hants 9 R8
Lees C Brad 63 L12
Lees Derbys 46 H6
Lees Oldham 56 E5
Lees Green Derbys 46 H6
Leesthorpe Leics 47 U11
Leeswood Flints 44 G1
Leetown P & K 90 K7
Leftwich Ches W 55 Q12
Legar Powys 27 N4
Legbourne Lincs 59 R10
Legburthwaite Cumb 67 M9
Legerwood Border 84 F10
Le Gron Guern 6 c4
Legsby Lincs 58 K9
Le Haguais Jersey 7 e4
Le Hocq Jersey 7 e4
Leicester C Leic 47 Q13
Leicester Forest East
Leics 47 P13
Leicester Forest East
Services Leics 47 P13
Leigh Devon 15 N10
Leigh Dorset 7 R3
Leigh Gloucs 28 G3
Leigh Kent 21 U13
Leigh Shrops 44 K13
Leigh Surrey 21 M13
Leigh Wigan 55 P6
Leigh Wilts 29 L9
Leigh Worcs 35 S10
Leigh Beck Essex 22 K11
Leigh Delamere Wilts 18 C5
Leigh Delamere
Services Wilts 18 C5
Leigh Green Kent 12 H9
Leigh Knoweglass S Lans 81 S1
Leighland Chapel
Somset 16 D9
Leigh-on-Sea Sthend 22 K10
Leigh Park Dorset 8 G9
Leigh Sinton Worcs 35 S10
Leighswood Wsall 46 D14
Leighterton Gloucs 28 F9
Leighton N York 63 P4
Leighton Powys 44 F12
Leighton Shrops 45 P12
Leighton Somset 17 T8
Leighton Bromswold
Cambs 38 H5
Leighton Buzzard
C Beds 30 K7
Leigh upon Mendip
Somset 17 S7
Leigh Woods N Som 27 V13
Leinthall Earls Herefs 35 L7
Leinthall Starkes Herefs 34 K6
Leintwardine Herefs 34 K6
Leire Leics 37 P3
Leirinmore Highld 110 J3
Leiston Suffk 41 R8
Leith C Edin 83 Q4
Leitholm Border 84 K10
Lelant Cnwll 2 E9
Lelley E R Yk 65 T13
Lem Hill Worcs 35 Q6
Lempitlaw Border 84 K12
Lemreway W Isls 106 j7
Lemsford Herts 31 R10
Lenchwick Worcs 36 D11
Lendalfoot S Ayrs 80 J13
Lendrick Stirlg 89 L4
Lendrum Terrace Abers 105 U7
Lenham Kent 12 G5
Lenham Heath Kent 12 H6
Lenie Highld 102 F10
Lennel Border 85 L9
Lennox Plunton D & G 73 Q9
Lennoxtown E Duns 89 P10
Lenton C Nott 47 Q6
Lenton Lincs 48 F7
Lenwade Norfk 50 J10
Lenzie E Duns 89 Q11
Leochel-Cushnie Abers 104 J13
Leomansley Staffs 46 F12
Leominster Herefs 35 L9
Leonard Stanley Gloucs 28 F7
Leoville Jersey 7 b2
Lepe Hants 9 N9
Lephin Highld 100 a5
Lepton Kirk 56 K3
Lerags Ag & B 94 B13
Lerryn Cnwll 4 E9
Lerwick Shet 106 u9
Lesbury Nthumb 77 R3
Leslie Abers 104 H11
Leslie Fife 91 L11
Lesmahagow S Lans 82 F11
Lesnewth Cnwll 4 E3
Les Quartiers Guern 6 d3
Les Quennevais Jersey 7 b3
Les Sages Guern 6 c4
Lessingham Norfk 51 Q8
Lessonhall Cumb 66 K2
Lestowder Cnwll 2 K12

Les Villets Guern 6 c4
Leswalt D & G 72 C7
L'Eracq Jersey 7 a2
Letchmore Heath Herts 21 L3
Letchworth Garden City
Herts 31 R6
Letcombe Bassett Oxon 29 S10
Letcombe Regis Oxon 29 S10
Letham Angus 91 R4
Letham Falk 82 H2
Letham Fife 91 M9
Letham Grange Angus 91 T3
Lethenty Abers 104 H11
Lethenty Abers 105 N7
Letheringham Suffk 41 M9
Letheringsett Norfk 50 J6
Lettaford Devon 5 S4
Lettan Ork 106 w15
Letterewe Highld 107 R9
Letterfearn Highld 101 M7
Letterfinlay Lodge
Hotel Highld 96 B5
Lettermorar Highld 100 d11
Lettershaw S Lans 74 G2
Letterston Pembks 24 F5
Lettoch Highld 103 R10
Lettoch Highld 103 R8
Letton Herefs 34 H11
Letton Herefs 34 K6
Lett's Green Kent 21 S11
Letty Green Herts 31 S10
Letwell Rothm 57 S9
Leuchars Fife 91 Q7
Leumrabhagh W Isls 106 j7
Leurbost W Isls 106 i6
Levalsa Meor Cnwll 3 Q7
Levedale Staffs 45 U10
Leven E R Yk 65 Q10
Leven Fife 91 N11
Levencorroch N Ayrs 80 E8
Levens Cumb 61 T2
Levens Green Herts 31 U8
Levenshulme Manch 56 C8
Levenwick Shet 106 u11
Leverburgh W Isls 106 f10
Leverington Cambs 49 Q11
Leverstock Green Herts 31 N11
Leverton Lincs 49 N3
Le Villocq Guern 6 d2
Levington Suffk 41 M13
Levisham N York 64 J1
Levishie Highld 102 C11
Lew Oxon 29 R6
Lewannick Cnwll 4 H4
Lewdown Devon 5 L3
Lewes E Susx 11 Q8
Leweston Pembks 24 F6
Lewisham Gt Lon 21 Q8
Lewisham Crematorium
Gt Lon 21 Q8
Lewiston Highld 102 F10
Lewistown Brdgnd 26 G10
Lewis Wych Herefs 34 H11
Lewknor Oxon 30 E13
Leworthy Devon 15 P6
Leworthy Devon 14 H12
Lewson Street Kent 12 K3
Lewth Lancs 61 T13
Lewtrenchard Devon 5 L3
Lexden Essex 23 N3
Lexworthy Somset 16 H9
Ley Cnwll 4 F7
Leybourne Kent 12 C3
Leyburn N York 63 N1
Leycett Staffs 45 R4
Leygreen Herts 31 Q8
Ley Hill Bucks 20 K3
Leyland Lancs 55 M1
Leylodge Abers 105 M13
Leys Abers 105 S6
Leys P & K 91 L5
Leysdown-on-Sea Kent 23 P13
Leysmill Angus 91 T3
Leys of Cossans Angus 91 N4
Leysters Herefs 35 N8
Leyton Gt Lon 21 Q5
Leytonstone Gt Lon 21 R5
Lezant Cnwll 4 J5
Lezerea Cnwll 2 H10
Lhanbryde Moray 104 B3
Libanus Powys 26 H2
Libberton S Lans 82 H10
Liberton C Edin 83 Q5
Lichfield Staffs 46 F12
Lickey Worcs 36 C5
Lickey End Worcs 36 C6
Lickey Rock Worcs 36 C5
Lickfold W Susx 10 E5
Liddaton Green Devon 5 M4
Liddesdale Highld 93 R6
Liddington Swindn 29 P10
Lidgate Derbys 57 M11
Lidgate Suffk 40 B9
Lidget Donc 57 T6
Lidgett Notts 57 T13
Lidham Hill E Susx 12 F12
Lidlington C Beds 38 E12
Lidsey W Susx 10 E10
Lidsing Kent 12 E3
Lidstone Oxon 29 T3
Lieurary Highld 112 C4
Liff Angus 91 M5
Lifford Birm 36 E5
Lifton Devon 5 L3
Liftondown Devon 4 K3
Lightcliffe Calder 56 G1
Lighthorne Warwks 36 K10
Lighthorne Heath
Warwks 37 L10
Lightwater Surrey 20 F10
Lightwater Valley
Theme Park N York 63 R4
Lightwood C Stke 46 B5
Lightwood Green Ches E 45 P4
Lightwood Green Wrexhm 44 J5
Lilbourne Nhants 37 Q5
Lilburn Tower Nthumb 85 Q14
Lilleshall Wrekin 45 R10
Lilley Herts 31 P7
Lilley W Berk 19 P5
Lilliesleaf Border 84 E14
Lillingstone Dayrell
Bucks 30 F5
Lillingstone Lovell Bucks 30 F4
Lillington Dorset 7 R2
Lilliput Poole 8 E10
Lilstock Somset 16 G7
Lilyhurst Shrops 45 R11
Limbrick Lancs 55 N3
Limbury Luton 31 N8
Limebrook Herefs 34 J7
Limefield Bury 55 T4
Limekilnburn S Lans 82 D8
Limekiln S Lans 82 F7
Limerigg Falk 82 G5
Limerstone IoW 9 N12
Lime Street Worcs 35 U13
Limington Somset 17 P12
Limmerhaugh E Ayrs 81 R7
Limpenhoe Norfk 51 R13
Limpley Stoke Wilts 17 U4
Limpsfield Surrey 21 R12
Limpsfield Chart Surrey 21 R12
Linby Notts 47 P3
Linchmere W Susx 10 D4
Lincluden D & G 74 J10
Lincoln Lincs 58 G12
Lincoln Crematorium
Lincs 58 G12
Lincomb Worcs 35 T7
Lincombe Devon 5 T11
Lincombe Devon 15 Q4
Lindale Cumb 61 S3
Lindal in Furness Cumb 61 N5
Lindfield W Susx 11 N5
Lindford Hants 10 C3
Lindley Kirk 56 H3
Lindley N York 63 Q10
Lindores Fife 91 L8
Lindridge Worcs 35 Q7
Lindsell Essex 22 F2
Lindsey Suffk 40 F12
Lindsey Tye Suffk 40 F11
Liney Somset 17 L9
Linford Hants 8 H7
Linford Thurr 22 F12
Lingbob C Brad 63 M12
Lingdale R & Cl 70 K10
Lingen Herefs 34 J7
Lingfield Surrey 11 P2
Lingwood Norfk 51 Q12
Lingy Close Cumb 67 N2
Linicro Highld 100 c3
Linkend Worcs 35 T13
Linkenholt Hants 19 N9
Linkinhorne Cnwll 4 J5
Linktown Fife 83 P1
Linkwood Moray 104 A3
Linley Shrops 34 J2
Linley Green Herefs 35 Q10
Linleygreen Shrops 45 Q13
Linlithgow W Loth 82 K4
Linshiels Nthumb 76 H4
Linsidemore Highld 108 J5
Linslade C Beds 30 K7
Linstead Parva Suffk 41 P5
Linstock Cumb 67 P1
Linthurst Worcs 36 C6
Linthwaite Kirk 56 G4
Lintlaw Border 85 M7
Lintmill Moray 104 G2
Linton Border 84 K13
Linton Cambs 39 R11
Linton Derbys 46 J10
Linton Herefs 28 B2

Linton Kent 12 E5
Linton Leeds 63 U10
Linton N York 62 K7
Linton Nthumb 77 Q7
Linton Hill Herefs 28 B2
Linton-on-Ouse N York 64 B7
Linwood Hants 8 H7
Linwood Lincs 58 J9
Linwood Rens 88 K13
Lional W Isls 106 k2
Lions Green E Susx 11 T6
Liphook Hants 10 C4
Lipley Shrops 45 R7
Liscard Wirral 54 G8
Liscombe Somset 15 U6
Liskeard Cnwll 4 G8
Lismore Ag & B 93 U11
Liss Hants 10 B5
Lissett E R Yk 65 Q8
Liss Forest Hants 10 B5
Lissington Lincs 58 K10
Liston Essex 40 E12
Lisvane Cardif 27 M11
Liswerry Newpt 27 R10
Litcham Norfk 50 E10
Litchard Brdgnd 26 F11
Litchborough Nhants 37 R10
Litchfield Hants 19 Q10
Litherland Sefton 54 H7
Litlington Cambs 39 N11
Litlington E Susx 11 S10
Little Abington Cambs 39 R11
Little Addington Nhants 38 E6
Little Airies D & G 73 L9
Little Almshoe Herts 31 R7
Little Alne Warwks 36 G8
Little Altcar Sefton 54 H6
Little Amwell Herts 31 U10
Little Asby Cumb 68 E11
Little Aston Staffs 46 E14
Little Atherfield IoW 9 N13
Little Ayton N York 70 H10
Little Baddow Essex 22 J6
Little Badminton S Glos 28 F11
Little Bampton Cumb 66 K1
Little Bardfield Essex 22 G1
Little Barford Bed 38 J9
Little Barningham Norfk 50 K6
Little Barrow Ches W 54 K13
Little Barugh N York 64 H4
Little Bavington Nthumb 76 K10
Little Bealings Suffk 41 M11
Littlebeck N York 71 Q11
Little Bedwyn Wilts 19 L7
Little Bentley Essex 23 R3
Little Berkhamsted
Herts 31 S11
Little Billing Nhants 38 B8
Little Billington C Beds 30 K8
Little Birch Herefs 27 U1
Little Bispham Bpool 61 Q11
Little Blakenham Suffk 40 K11
Little Blencow Cumb 67 Q6
Little Bloxwich Wsall 46 D13
Little Bognar W Susx 10 G10
Little Bolas Shrops 45 P8
Little Bollington Ches E 55 S9
Little Bookham Surrey 21 L12
Littleborough Notts 58 D10
Littleborough Rochdl 56 E4
Little Bourton Oxon 37 M12
Little Bowden Leics 37 U4
Little Bradley Suffk 39 U10
Little Brampton Herefs 34 H7
Little Brampton Shrops 34 J4
Little Braxted Essex 22 K5
Little Brechin Angus 98 K11
Littlebredy Dorset 7 P6
Little Brickhill M Keyn 30 K6
Little Bridgeford Staffs 45 T8
Little Brington Nhants 37 R8
Little Bromley Essex 23 Q2
Little Broughton Cumb 66 G6
Little Budworth Ches W 55 N13
Little Burstead Essex 22 F9
Little Bytham Lincs 48 F10
Little Carlton Lincs 59 R9
Little Carlton Notts 47 U2
Little Casterton Rutlnd 48 F12
Little Catwick E R Yk 65 Q10
Little Cawthorpe Lincs 59 R9
Little Chalfont Bucks 20 H3
Little Chart Kent 12 H6
Little Chesterford Essex 39 R12
Little Cheveral Wilts 18 E9
Little Chishill Cambs 39 P13
Little Clacton Essex 23 S4
Little Clifton Cumb 66 G7
Little Coates NE Lin 59 M5
Little Comberton Worcs 36 C12
Little Common E Susx 12 E14
Little Compton Warwks 29 Q1
Little Corby Cumb 67 Q1
Little Cornard Suffk 40 E13
Littlecote Bucks 30 J8
Little Cowarne Herefs 35 N10
Little Coxwell Oxon 29 Q8
Little Crakehall N York 63 R1
Little Cransley Nhants 38 B6
Little Cressingham Norfk 50 E13
Little Crosby Sefton 54 H6
Little Crosthwaite Cumb 67 L7
Little Cubley Derbys 46 G6
Little Dalby Leics 47 U11
Little Dewchurch Herefs 27 U1
Little Ditton Cambs 39 U9
Little Doward Herefs 27 U4
Littledown Dorset 8 G10
Little Downham Cambs 39 R4
Little Driffield E R Yk 65 N8
Little Dunham Norfk 50 E11
Little Dunkeld P & K 90 G3
Little Dunmow Essex 22 G3
Little Durnford Wilts 18 G13
Little Easton Essex 22 F3
Little Eaton Derbys 47 L5
Little Ellingham Norfk 40 H1
Little Elm Somset 17 T7
Little Everdon Nhants 37 Q9
Little Eversden Cambs 39 N10
Little Faringdon Oxon 29 P7
Little Fencote N York 63 R1
Little Fenton N York 64 C13
Little Fransham Norfk 50 F11
Little Gaddesden Herts 31 L11
Little Garway Herefs 27 S3
Little Gidding Cambs 38 H4
Little Glemham Suffk 41 P9
Little Gorsley Herefs 28 B3
Little Gransden Cambs 39 L9
Little Green Somset 17 T7
Little Grimsby Lincs 59 Q8
Little Gringley Notts 58 B10
Little Habton N York 64 G5
Little Hadham Herts 22 B3
Little Hale Lincs 48 J5
Little Hallam Derbys 47 N5
Little Hallingbury Essex 22 C4
Littleham Devon 6 E8
Littleham Devon 14 K8
Little Hampden Bucks 30 J12
Littlehampton W Susx 10 G10
Little Haresfield Gloucs 28 F6
Little Harrowden Nhants 38 C6
Little Haseley Oxon 30 D12
Little Hatfield E R Yk 65 R10
Little Hautbois Norfk 51 N9
Little Haven Pembks 24 E7
Littlehaven W Susx 10 K4
Little Hay Staffs 46 F13
Little Hayfield Derbys 56 F9
Little Haywood Staffs 46 D9
Little Heath Covtry 37 L4
Littleheath Hants 10 B7
Little Heath Staffs 45 U9
Little Hereford Herefs 35 N7
Little Horkesley Essex 40 F14
Little Hormead Herts 22 B2
Little Horsted E Susx 11 R6
Little Horton C Brad 63 N13
Little Horton Wilts 18 F8
Little Horwood Bucks 30 G6
Little Houghton Barns 57 P5
Little Houghton Nhants 38 B9
Littlehoughton Nthumb 77 Q2
Little Hucklow Derbys 56 H11
Little Hulton Salfd 55 R6
Little Hungerford
W Berk 19 R5

Little Leigh Ches W 55 P11
Little Leighs Essex 22 H4
Little Lever Bolton 55 S5
Little Linford M Keyn 38 C10
Little Load Somset 17 N12
Little London Bucks 30 D9
Little London E Susx 11 T6
Little London Essex 22 C2
Little London Gloucs 28 D4
Little London Hants 19 N9
Little London Hants 19 R10
Little London Leeds 63 Q12
Little London Lincs 48 K8
Little London Lincs 49 N9
Little London Lincs 49 Q8
Little London Norfk 51 P10
Little London Powys 34 B3
Little Longstone Derbys 56 J12
Little Malvern Worcs 35 S12
Little Mancot Flints 54 H14
Little Maplestead Essex 40 D13
Little Marcle Herefs 35 Q13
Little Marland Devon 15 M10
Little Marlow Bucks 20 E5
Little Massingham Norfk 50 C9
Little Melton Norfk 51 L12
Littlemill Abers 98 B4
Littlemill Highld 103 P5
Little Mill Mons 27 Q7
Little Milton Oxon 30 D12
Little Missenden Bucks 30 J12
Little Mongeham Kent 13 R5
Littlemoor Derbys 57 N13
Little Moor Somset 16 K10
Littlemore Oxon 30 B12
Little Musgrave Cumb 68 G10
Little Ness Shrops 44 K10
Little Neston Ches W 54 G12
Little Newcastle Pembks 24 G5
Little Newsham Dur 69 P9
Little Norton Somset 17 N13
Little Oakley Essex 23 T2
Little Oakley Nhants 38 C3
Little Odell Bed 38 E9
Little Offley Herts 31 P7
Little Onn Staffs 45 T10
Little Ormside Cumb 68 F9
Little Orton Cumb 67 N1
Little Ouseburn N York 63 U7
Littleover C Derb 46 K6
Little Oxendon Nhants 37 T4
Little Packington
Warwks 36 H4
Little Pattenden Kent 12 D6
Little Paxton Cambs 38 J8
Little Petherick Cnwll 3 N2
Little Plumpton Lancs 61 R13
Little Plumstead Norfk 51 P11
Little Ponton Lincs 48 D7
Littleport Cambs 39 S3
Little Potheridge Devon 15 M10
Little Preston Leeds 63 Q10
Little Preston Nhants 37 Q9
Little Raveley Cambs 39 L5
Little Reedness E R Yk 58 D2
Little Ribston N York 63 T9
Little Rissington Gloucs 29 N4
Little Rollright Oxon 29 Q2
Little Ryburgh Norfk 50 G8
Little Ryle Nthumb 77 L3
Little Ryton Shrops 45 L13
Little Salkeld Cumb 67 S6
Little Sampford Essex 22 G1
Little Sandhurst Br For 20 E10
Little Saredon Staffs 46 B12
Little Saughall Ches W 54 J13
Little Saxham Suffk 40 C8
Little Scatwell Highld 102 D4
Little Shelford Cambs 39 P10
Little Shrewley Warwks 36 H7
Little Silver Devon 6 B4
Little Singleton Lancs 61 R12
Little Skipwith N York 64 E12
Little Smeaton N York 57 R3
Little Snoring Norfk 50 G7
Little Sodbury S Glos 28 E11
Little Sodbury End S Glos 28 E11
Little Somborne Hants 19 N13
Little Somerford Wilts 28 J10
Little Soudley Shrops 45 R8
Little Stainforth N York 62 G7
Little Stainton Darltn 70 D8
Little Stanney Ches W 54 K12
Little Staughton Bed 38 H8
Little Steeping Lincs 59 R14
Littlester Shet 106 v5
Little Stke Staffs 45 U6
Little Stonham Suffk 40 K8
Little Stretton Leics 47 S13
Little Stretton Shrops 34 K2
Little Strickland Cumb 68 D9
Little Stukeley Cambs 39 L6
Little Sugnall Staffs 45 S7
Little Sutton Ches W 54 J12
Little Sutton Shrops 35 M4
Little Swinburne
Nthumb 76 J10
Little Sypland D & G 73 S9
Little Tew Oxon 29 S3
Little Tey Essex 23 L3
Little Thetford Cambs 39 R5
Little Thirkleby N York 64 B4
Little Thornage Norfk 50 J6
Little Thornton Lancs 61 R11
Littlethorpe Leics 37 Q2
Littlethorpe N York 63 S6
Little Thorpe Dur 70 F3
Little Thurlow Green
Suffk 39 U10
Little Thurrock Thurr 22 F12
Littleton Angus 91 N4
Littleton BaNES 17 Q4
Littleton Ches W 54 K13
Littleton Dorset 8 B8
Littleton Hants 9 P2
Littleton Somset 17 N10
Littleton Surrey 20 J10
Littleton Surrey 20 H12
Littleton Drew Wilts 28 F10
Littleton-on-Severn
S Glos 28 A10
Littleton Pannell Wilts 18 F9
Little Torrington Devon 15 L10
Little Totham Essex 23 L5
Little Town Cumb 67 L8
Little Town Lancs 62 D13
Little Town Warrtn 55 P8
Little Twycross Leics 47 L12
Little Urswick Cumb 61 N5
Little Wakering Essex 23 L10
Little Walden Essex 39 R12
Little Waldingfield Suffk 40 F12
Little Walsingham Norfk 50 F6
Little Waltham Essex 22 H5
Little Warley Essex 22 F9
Little Washbourne
Gloucs 36 C13
Little Weighton E R Yk 65 M13
Little Weldon Nhants 38 D3
Little Welland Worcs 35 T13
Little Welnetham Suffk 40 E8
Little Welton Lincs 59 Q9
Little Wenham Suffk 40 J13
Little Wenlock Wrekin 45 P12
Little Weston Somset 17 R11
Little Whitefield IoW 9 R11
Little Whittingham
Green Suffk 41 N5
Little Wilbraham Cambs 39 R9
Littlewindsor Dorset 7 M3
Little Witcombe Gloucs 28 G5
Little Witley Worcs 35 S8
Little Wittenham Oxon 19 S2
Little Wolford Warwks 36 K14
Littleworth Bucks 30 J9
Little Wratting Suffk 39 U11
Little Wymington Bed 38 E8
Little Wymondley Herts 31 R7
Little Wyrley Staffs 46 D13
Little Wytheford Shrops 45 N10
Little Yeldham Essex 40 C13
Littley Green Essex 22 G4
Litton Derbys 56 J12
Litton N York 62 J4
Litton Somset 17 Q6
Litton Cheney Dorset 7 P6
Liurbost W Isls 106 i6
Liverpool Lpool 54 H8
Liverpool Maritime
Mercantile City Lpool 54 H9
Liversedge Kirk 56 K1
Liverton Devon 5 U6
Liverton R & Cl 71 M9

Liverton Mines R & Cl 71 M9
Liverton Street Kent 12 G5
Livingston W Loth 83 L5
Livingston Village
W Loth 82 K5
Lixwm Flints 54 E12
Lizard Cnwll 2 J13
Llaingoch IoA 52 B6
Llaithddu Powys 34 B3
Llan Powys 43 U12
Llanaber Gwynd 43 M10
Llanaelhaearn Gwynd 42 G5
Llanafan Cerdgn 33 N6
Llanafan-Fawr Powys 33 U9
Llanafan-fechan Powys 33 U9
Llananno Powys 34 B5
Llanarmon Gwynd 42 H5
Llanarmon Dyffryn
Ceiriog Wrexhm 44 E7
Llanarmon-yn-Ial
Denbgs 44 E2
Llanarth Cerdgn 32 H9
Llanarth Mons 27 R5
Llanarthne Carmth 25 U6
Llanasa Flints 54 D10
Llanbabo IoA 52 E6
Llanbadarn Fawr Cerdgn 33 M4
Llanbadarn Fynydd
Powys 34 C5
Llanbadarn-y-garreg
Powys 34 D11
Llanbadoc Mons 27 R7
Llanbadrig IoA 52 E4
Llanbeder Newpt 27 R9
Llanbedr Gwynd 43 L8
Llanbedr Powys 27 N3
Llanbedr Powys 34 E12
Llanbedr-Dyffryn-Clwyd
Denbgs 44 D2
Llanbedrgoch IoA 52 H6
Llanbedrog Gwynd 42 F7
Llanbedr-y-Cennin
Conwy 53 N9
Llanberis Gwynd 52 J10
Llanbethery V Glam 16 D3
Llanbister Powys 34 D6
Llanblethian V Glam 16 C2
Llanboidy Carmth 25 L6
Llanbradach Caerph 27 L9
Llanbrynmair Powys 43 S13
Llancadle V Glam 16 D3
Llancarfan V Glam 16 D2
Llancayo Mons 27 R7
Llancloudy Herefs 27 T3
Llancynfelyn Cerdgn 33 M2
Llandaff Cardif 27 M12
Llandanwg Gwynd 43 L8
Llandarcy Neath 26 C8
Llandawke Carmth 25 L8
Llanddaniel Fab IoA 52 G8
Llanddarog Carmth 25 T7
Llanddeiniol Cerdgn 33 L6
Llanddeiniolen Gwynd 52 H9
Llandderfel Gwynd 43 U6
Llanddeusant Carmth 26 E3
Llanddeusant IoA 52 E5
Llanddew Powys 26 K1
Llanddewi Swans 25 S13
Llanddewi Brefi Cerdgn 33 N10
Llanddewi'r Cwm Powys 34 B11
Llanddewi Rhydderch
Mons 27 R5
Llanddewi Velfrey
Pembks 24 K7
Llanddewi Ystradenni
Powys 34 D7
Llanddoget Conwy 53 P10
Llanddona IoA 52 H7
Llanddowror Carmth 25 L8
Llanddulas Conwy 53 Q7
Llanddwywe Gwynd 43 L9
Llanddyfnan IoA 52 G7
Llandecwyn Gwynd 43 M7
Llandefaelog Powys 26 J1
Llandefaelog-Tre'r-Graig
Powys 27 L2
Llandefalle Powys 34 D13
Llandegfan IoA 52 H8
Llandegla Denbgs 44 E3
Llandegley Powys 34 D8
Llandegveth Mons 27 Q8
Llandegwning Gwynd 42 E7
Llandeilo Carmth 26 A3
Llandeilo Graban Powys 34 C12
Llandeilo'r Fan Powys 33 S14
Llandeloy Pembks 24 E5
Llandenny Mons 27 S7
Llandevaud Newpt 27 S9
Llandevenny Mons 27 S10
Llandinabo Herefs 27 U2
Llandinam Powys 34 B3
Llandissilio Pembks 24 K6
Llandogo Mons 27 U7
Llandough V Glam 16 C2
Llandough V Glam 16 F2
Llandovery Carmth 33 R14
Llandow V Glam 16 B2
Llandre Carmth 33 N12
Llandre Cerdgn 33 M3
Llandre IoA 52 G6
Llandrillo Denbgs 44 C6
Llandrillo-yn-Rhos
Conwy 53 P6
Llandrindod Wells Powys 34 C8
Llandrinio Powys 44 G10
Llandudno Conwy 53 N6
Llandudno Junction
Conwy 53 N7
Llandulas Powys 33 U11
Llandwrog Gwynd 52 G11
Llandybie Carmth 25 V7
Llandyfaelog Carmth 25 R7
Llandyfan Carmth 26 A6
Llandyfriog Cerdgn 32 F12
Llandyfrydog IoA 52 F6
Llandygai Gwynd 52 K8
Llandygwydd Cerdgn 32 D12
Llandynan Denbgs 44 E4
Llandyrnog Denbgs 53 D12
Llandyssil Powys 34 E2
Llandysul Cerdgn 32 H12
Llanedeyrn Cardif 27 N11
Llanedi Carmth 25 U9
Llaneglwys Powys 34 C13
Llanegryn Gwynd 43 M11
Llanegwad Carmth 25 U6
Llaneilian IoA 52 G4
Llanelian-yn-Rhos Conwy 53 P7
Llanelidan Denbgs 44 D3
Llanelieu Powys 27 M2
Llanellen Mons 27 Q5
Llanelli Carmth 25 T10
Llanelli Crematorium
Carmth 25 T10
Llanelltyd Gwynd 43 P10
Llanelly Mons 27 N4
Llanelwedd Powys 34 C10
Llanenddwyn Gwynd 43 L9
Llanengan Gwynd 42 E8
Llanerch Powys 34 H2
Llanerchymedd IoA 52 F6
Llanerfyl Powys 44 B12
Llanfachraeth IoA 52 E6
Llanfachreth Gwynd 43 Q9
Llanfaelog IoA 52 E8
Llanfaelrhys Gwynd 42 D8
Llanfaenor Mons 27 S5
Llanfaes IoA 52 J8
Llanfaes Powys 26 J2
Llanfaethlu IoA 52 E5
Llanfair Gwynd 43 L8
Llanfair Caereinion
Powys 44 D12
Llanfair Clydogau
Cerdgn 33 M10
Llanfair Dyffryn Clwyd
Denbgs 44 D2
Llanfairfechan Conwy 53 L8
Llanfair Kilgeddin Mons 27 R6
Llanfair-Nant-Gwyn
Pembks 24 K4
Llanfairpwllgwyngyll
IoA 52 H8
Llanfair Talhaiarn Conwy 53 R8
Llanfair Waterdine
Shrops 34 G5
Llanfairynghornwy IoA 52 D4
Llanfair-yn-Neubwll IoA 52 D7
Llanfallteg Carmth 24 K6
Llanfallteg West Carmth 24 K7
Llanfarian Cerdgn 33 L5
Llanfechain Powys 44 F9
Llanfechell IoA 52 E4
Llanfendigaid Gwynd 43 L12
Llanferres Denbgs 54 E14
Llanfflewyn IoA 52 E5
Llanfigael IoA 52 E6
Llanfihangel-ar-arth
Carmth 32 H13
Llanfihangel Glyn Myfyr
Conwy 43 U4
Llanfihangel Nant Bran
Powys 33 T14
Llanfihangel-nant-
Melan Powys 34 D10
Llanfihangel Rogiet
Mons 27 S10
Llanfihangel Tal-y-llyn
Powys 27 L3
Llanfihangel-uwch-
Gwili Carmth 25 S6
Llanfihangel-y-
Creuddyn Cerdgn 33 N5

Llanfihangel-yng-
Ngwynfa Powys 44 C10
Llanfihangel yn
Nhowyn IoA 52 D7
Llanfihangel-y-pennant
Gwynd 42 K5
Llanfihangel-y-pennant
Gwynd 43 N12
Llanfihangel-y-traethau
Gwynd 43 L7
Llanfilo Powys 33 D14
Llanfoist Mons 27 P5
Llanfor Gwynd 43 T6
Llanfrechfa Torfn 43 M5
Llanfrothen Gwynd 43 M5
Llanfrynach Powys 27 K2
Llanfwrog Denbgs 54 D6
Llanfwrog IoA 52 D6
Llanfyllin Powys 44 D10
Llanfynydd Carmth 25 U5
Llanfynydd Flints 48 G2
Llanfyrnach Pembks 25 M4
Llangadfan Powys 44 B11
Llangadog Carmth 44 C7
Llangadwaladr IoA 52 E8
Llangadwaladr Powys 44 E7
Llangaffo IoA 52 F9
Llangain Carmth 25 Q7
Llangammarch Wells
Powys 33 T11
Llangan V Glam 16 H12
Llangarron Herefs 27 U3
Llangasty-Tal-y-llyn
Powys 27 L2
Llangathen Carmth 25 U5
Llangattock Powys 27 N3
Llangattock Lingoed
Mons 27 R3
Llangattock-Vibon-Avel
Mons 27 T4
Llangedwyn Powys 44 E9
Llangefni IoA 52 G7
Llangeinor Brdgnd 16 G10
Llangeitho Cerdgn 33 M9
Llangeler Carmth 25 Q3
Llangelynnin Gwynd 42 J8
Llangendeirne Carmth 25 S8
Llangennech Carmth 25 U10
Llangennith Swans 25 R11
Llangenny Powys 27 N4
Llangernyw Conwy 53 Q9
Llangian Gwynd 42 E8
Llangiwg Neath 26 F4
Llanglydwen Carmth 25 L5
Llangoed IoA 52 K7
Llangoedmor Cerdgn 32 F10
Llangollen Denbgs 44 F5
Llangolman Pembks 24 K5
Llangors Powys 27 L2
Llangorwen Cerdgn 32 T7
Llangovan Mons 27 T6
Llangower Gwynd 43 T7
Llangranog Cerdgn 32 F10
Llangristiolus IoA 52 F7
Llangrove Herefs 27 U4
Llangua Mons 27 R2
Llangunllo Powys 34 E7
Llangunnor Carmth 25 R6
Llangurig Powys 33 T5
Llangwm Conwy 53 R9
Llangwm Mons 27 S8
Llangwm Pembks 24 G9
Llangwnnadl Gwynd 42 D7
Llangwyfan Denbgs 54 D13
Llangwyllog IoA 52 F7
Llangwyryfon Cerdgn 33 L6
Llangybi Gwynd 42 H5
Llangybi Mons 27 R7
Llangyfelach Swans 26 B13
Llangynhafal Denbgs 54 D14
Llangynidr Powys 27 M4
Llangyniew Carmth 25 N7
Llangynin Carmth 25 N7
Llangynllo Cerdgn 25 P8
Llangynog Carmth 25 C8
Llangynog Powys 44 B9
Llangynwyd Brdgnd 16 F10
Llanhamlach Powys 26 K2
Llanharan Rhondd 26 J11
Llanharry Rhondd 16 H11
Llanhennock Mons 27 R9
Llanhilleth Blae G 27 N7
Llanidan IoA 52 G8
Llanidloes Powys 33 U4
Llaniestyn Gwynd 42 E7
Llanigon Powys 34 F13
Llanilar Cerdgn 33 M6
Llanilid Rhondd 26 H11
Llanina Cerdgn 32 H9
Llanio Cerdgn 33 M9
Llanishen Cardif 27 M11
Llanishen Mons 27 T7
Llanllechid Gwynd 53 T10
Llanllowell Mons 27 R10
Llanllugan Powys 33 T3
Llanllwch Carmth 25 Q7
Llanllwchaiarn Powys 34 D2
Llanllwni Carmth 25 S4
Llanllyfni Gwynd 43 J3
Llanmadoc Swans 25 Q11
Llanmaes V Glam 16 C3
Llanmartin Newpt 27 R10
Llanmerewig Powys 34 F3
Llanmihangel V Glam 16 C2
Llanmiloe Carmth 25 M9
Llanmorlais Swans 25 T12
Llannefydd Conwy 53 S8
Llannon Carmth 25 U9
Llannon Cerdgn 32 K7
Llannor Gwynd 42 G5
Llanpumsaint Carmth 25 R5

Llanrhaeadr-ym-
Mochnant Powys 44 D8
Llanrhian Pembks 24 D4
Llanrhidian Swans 25 S12
Llanrhyddlad IoA 52 D4
Llanrhychwyn Conwy 53 N10
Llanrhystud Cerdgn 32 K7
Llanrothal Herefs 27 T4
Llanrug Gwynd 52 H10
Llanrumney Cardif 27 N11
Llanrwst Conwy 53 N8
Llansadwrn Carmth 26 B1
Llansadwrn IoA 52 J7
Llansaint Carmth 25 Q8
Llansamlet Swans 26 B8
Llansanffraid Glan
Conwy Conwy 53 P7
Llansannan Conwy 53 R9
Llansannor V Glam 26 H11
Llansantffraed Powys 27 L3
Llansantffraed-
Cwmdeuddwr Powys 33 U7
Llansantffraid-in-Elvel
Powys 34 C10
Llansantffraid Cerdgn 32 K7
Llansantffraid-ym-
Mechain Powys 44 G9
Llansawel Carmth 25 V3
Llansilin Powys 44 F7
Llansoy Mons 27 S7
Llanspyddid Powys 26 J2
Llanstadwell Pembks 24 F10
Llansteffan Carmth 25 P8
Llanstephan Powys 34 D12
Llantarnam Torfn 27 Q8
Llanteg Pembks 25 L8
Llanthony Mons 27 P2
Llantilio-Crossenny
Mons 27 R5
Llantilio Pertholey Mons 27 Q4
Llantrisant IoA 52 E6
Llantrisant Mons 27 R7
Llantrisant Rhondd 26 K11
Llantrithyd V Glam 16 E3
Llantwit Fardre Rhondd 26 K11
Llantwit Major V Glam 16 C4
Llantysilio Denbgs 44 E5
Llanuwchllyn Gwynd 43 R7
Llanvaches Newpt 27 R9
Llanvair Discoed Mons 27 R8
Llanvapley Mons 27 Q5
Llanvetherine Mons 27 R4
Llanveynoe Herefs 27 P1
Llanvihangel Crucorney
Mons 27 Q3
Llanvihangel Gobion
Mons 27 Q6
Llanvihangel-Ystern-
Llewern Mons 27 S5
Llanwarne Herefs 27 U2
Llanwddyn Powys 44 B10
Llanwenarth Mons 27 P4
Llanwenog Cerdgn 32 K11
Llanwern Newpt 27 R10
Llanwinio Carmth 25 M5
Llanwnda Gwynd 52 F11
Llanwnda Pembks 24 F4
Llanwnnen Cerdgn 33 K11
Llanwnnog Powys 33 U3
Llanwrda Carmth 26 B2
Llanwrin Powys 43 Q13
Llanwrthwl Powys 33 U7
Llanwrtyd Wells Powys 33 R9
Llanwyddelan Powys 44 C12
Llanyblodwel Shrops 44 G8
Llanybri Carmth 25 P8
Llanybydder Carmth 32 K12
Llanycefn Pembks 24 J6
Llanychaer Bridge
Pembks 24 G3
Llanycrwys Carmth 33 M11
Llanymawddwy Gwynd 43 T10
Llanymynech Powys 44 G8
Llanynghenedl IoA 52 D6
Llanynys Denbgs 54 D14
Llan-y-pwll Wrexhm 54 B8
Llanyre Powys 34 B8
Llanystumdwy Gwynd 42 J6
Llawhaden Pembks 24 J7
Llawnt Shrops 44 F7
Llawr-y-glyn Powys 33 T2
Llay Wrexhm 54 B9
Llechcynfarwy IoA 52 E6
Llechfaen Powys 26 K2
Llechrhyd Caerph 27 K7
Llechryd Cerdgn 32 E11
Llechylched IoA 52 D7
Lledrod Cerdgn 33 M6
Llidiardau Gwynd 43 R7
Llidiart-y-parc Denbgs 44 D5
Llithfaen Gwynd 42 G5
Lloc Flints 54 E11
Llong Flints 54 F13
Llowes Powys 34 E12
Lloyney Powys 34 F8
Llundain-fach Cerdgn 33 L9
Llwydcoed
Crematorium Rhondd 26 H6
Llwydarth Powys 33 T3
Llwyn Denbgs 54 C14
Llwyncelyn Cerdgn 32 G9
Llwyndafydd Cerdgn 32 G9
Llwynderw Powys 44 F13
Llwyn-drain Pembks 25 N4
Llwyn-du Mons 27 P4
Llwyndyrys Gwynd 42 G5
Llwyngwril Gwynd 43 L12
Llwynhendy Carmth 25 T11
Llwynmawr Wrexhm 44 F6
Llwyn-on Myr Td 26 J5
Llwyn-y-brain Carmth 25 L8
Llwyn-y-groes Cerdgn 33 L9
Llwynypia Rhondd 26 H9
Llynclys Shrops 44 G8
Llynfaes IoA 52 F7
Llysfaen Conwy 53 Q7
Llyswen Cerdgn 32 G8
Llyswen Powys 34 D13
Llysworney V Glam 16 H13
Llys-y-frân Pembks 24 H6
Llywel Powys 26 E2
Load Brook Sheff 57 L9
Loan Falk 82 J3
Loanend Nthumb 85 N8
Loanhead Midloth 83 Q5
Loaningfoot D & G 66 J2
Loans S Ayrs 81 L6
Lobb Devon 15 M3
Lobhillcross Devon 5 M3
Lochailort Highld 93 R10
Lochaline Highld 93 R10
Lochans D & G 72 D9
Locharbriggs D & G 74 J9
Lochavich Ag & B 87 R1
Lochawe Ag & B 87 Q1
Loch Baghasdail W Isls 106 C17
Lochboisdale W Isls 106 C17
Lochbuie Ag & B 93 S12
Lochcarron Highld 101 M4
Lochdochart House Stirlg 89 S12
Lochdon Ag & B 93 S10
Lochearnhead Stirlg 89 Q1
Lochee C Dund 91 N5
Lochend Highld 102 F10
Locheilside Station
Highld 93 R8
Lochfoot D & G 74 G11
Lochgair Ag & B 87 P3
Lochgarthside Highld 97 N7
Lochgelly Fife 82 H3
Lochgilphead Ag & B 87 R8
Lochgoilhead Ag & B 88 F5
Lochieheads Fife 91 N8
Lochill Moray 104 B3
Lochindorb Lodge
Highld 103 Q8
Lochinver Highld 110 B12
Loch Lomond and
The Trossachs
National Park 88 K3
Lochluichart Highld 102 B3
Lochmaben D & G 75 L10
Lochmaddy W Isls 106 e12
Loch Maree Hotel Highld 107 R10
Loch nam Madadh W Isls 106 e12
Loch Ness Highld 102 F10
Lochore Fife 90 H3
Lochportain W Isls 106 d10
Lochranza N Ayrs 79 S7
Lochside Abers 99 N11
Lochside D & G 74 H10
Lochside Highld 109 Q8
Lochton S Ayrs 72 H4
Lochty Angus 98 J11
Lochty Fife 91 R10
Lochuisge Highld 93 T9
Lochwinnoch Rens 88 J14
Lochwood D & G 75 L6
Lockengate Cnwll 3 Q2
Lockerbie D & G 75 M9
Lockeridge Wilts 18 H7
Lockerley Hants 9 L3
Locking N Som 17 L5
Lockington E R Yk 65 M10
Lockington Leics 41 M8
Lockleywood Shrops 45 Q9
Locksbottom Gt Lon 21 R9
Locks Heath Hants 9 N7
Lockton N York 67 J15
Loddington Leics 47 U13
Loddington Nhants 38 B6
Loddiswell Devon 5 S11
Loddon Norfk 51 Q14
Lode Cambs 39 R8
Lode Heath Solhll 36 G4
Loders Dorset 7 M5
Lodge Hill Crematorium
Birm 36 D4
Lodsworth W Susx 10 E5
Lofthouse Leeds 57 N1
Lofthouse N York 63 N5
Lofthouse Gate Wakefd 57 M2
Loftus N York 71 J9
Logan E Ayrs 81 R8
Loggerheads Staffs 45 R8
Logie Angus 99 M11
Logie Fife 91 N7
Logie Moray 103 R5
Logie Coldstone Abers 98 G3
Logie Newton Abers 102 G8
Logie Pert Angus 99 M11
Logierait P & K 90 G2
Login Carmth 25 L5
Lolworth Cambs 39 M8
Londesborough E R Yk 65 M10
London Gt Lon 21 N7
London Apprentice
Cnwll 3 Q4
London Beach Kent 12 H7
London Colney Herts 31 N12
Londonderry N York 63 R3
London End Nhants 38 D6
London Gateway
Services Gt Lon 21 L4
Londonthorpe Lincs 48 D5
Londubh Highld 107 R7
Lonemore Highld 107 P7
Long Ashton N Som 17 N2
Long Bank Worcs 35 S5
Long Bennington Lincs 48 B5
Longbenton N Tyne 77 Q12
Longborough Gloucs 29 L3
Long Bredy Dorset 7 N6
Longbridge Birm 36 D5
Longbridge Warwks 36 J8
Longbridge Deverill
Wilts 18 C12

Longdon Heath Worcs 35 T13
Longdon upon Tern
Wrekin 45 P10
Longdowns Cnwll 2 J10
Long Drax N York 64 F14
Long Duckmanton
Derbys 57 P12
Longfield Kent 22 E9
Longford Covtry 37 L4
Longford Derbys 40 F6
Longford Gloucs 28 F3
Longford Gt Lon 20 J7
Longford Kent 21 S11
Longford Shrops 45 P7
Longford Wrekin 45 R10
Longforgan P & K 91 L5
Longformacus Border 84 H7
Longframlington
Nthumb 77 N5
Long Green Ches W 54 L12
Long Green Worcs 35 L12
Longham Dorset 8 F9
Longham Norfk 50 F10
Long Hanborough Oxon 29 T5
Longhaven Abers 105 U8
Long Hedges Lincs 49 M3
Longhirst Nthumb 77 Q8
Longhope Gloucs 28 C4
Longhope Ork 106 s20
Longhorsley Nthumb 77 N7
Longhoughton Nthumb 77 Q2
Long Itchington Warwks 37 M8
Longlands Cumb 76 K5
Longlane Derbys 40 H6
Long Lawford Warwks 37 N5
Longleat Safari &
Adventure Park Wilts 18 B12
Longlevens Gloucs 28 G4
Longley Calder 56 G2
Longley Kirk 56 H5
Long Load Somset 17 N12
Longmanhill Abers 105 L3
Long Marston Herts 30 J9
Long Marston N York 64 C9
Long Marston Warwks 36 G11
Long Marton Cumb 68 E8
Long Meadowend
Shrops 34 K4
Long Melford Suffk 40 E11
Longmoor Camp Hants 10 B4
Longmorn Moray 104 B4
Longmoss Ches E 56 C12
Long Newnton Gloucs 28 H9
Longnewton Border 84 F12
Long Newton E Loth 84 D4
Longnewton S on T 70 E9
Longney Gloucs 28 E5
Longniddry E Loth 84 C3
Longnor Shrops 45 L13
Longnor Staffs 56 G14
Longparish Hants 19 P11
Longpark Cumb 75 T14
Long Preston N York 62 G8
Longridge Lancs 62 C12
Longridge Staffs 45 U9
Longriggend N Lans 82 F4
Long Riston E R Yk 65 R10
Longrock Cnwll 2 E10
Longsdon Staffs 46 B3
Longshaw Wigan 55 M6
Longside Abers 105 S6
Long Sight Oldham 56 D6
Longslow Shrops 45 Q7
Longstanton Cambs 39 N7
Longstock Hants 19 M12
Longstone Pembks 24 K8
Longstowe Cambs 39 M10
Long Stratton Norfk 51 L14
Long Street M Keyn 30 G4
Longstreet Wilts 18 H10
Long Sutton Hants 20 B13
Long Sutton Lincs 49 P9
Long Sutton Somset 17 N11
Longthorpe C Pete 48 H14
Long Thurlow Suffk 40 H7
Longthwaite Cumb 67 P8
Longton Lancs 55 L1
Longton C Stke 46 B5
Longtown Cumb 75 T13
Longtown Herefs 27 Q2
Longueville Jersey 7 e3
Longville in the Dale
Shrops 35 M2
Long Waste Wrekin 45 N10
Long Whatton Leics 41 M8
Longwick Bucks 30 G11
Long Wittenham Oxon 19 R2
Longwitton Nthumb 77 M8
Longwood D & G 74 D8
Longworth Oxon 29 S7
Longyester E Loth 84 E5
Lonmay Abers 105 S4
Lonmore Highld 100 c5
Loose Kent 12 E5
Loosebeare Devon 15 R11
Loosegate Lincs 49 L9
Loosley Row Bucks 30 H12
Lootcherbrae Abers 104 J5
Lopcombe Corner Wilts 18 K13
Lopen Somset 17 M13
Loppington Shrops 45 L8
Lorbottle Nthumb 77 L4
Lordington W Susx 10 B9
Lordsbridge Norfk 49 U11
Lords Wood Medway 12 E3
Lornty P & K 90 J4
Loscoe Derbys 47 M4
Loscombe Dorset 7 M4
Losgaintir W Isls 106 f8
Lossiemouth Moray 104 A2
Lossit Ag & B 78 C4
Lostford Shrops 45 P7
Lostock Gralam Ches W 55 Q12
Lostock Green Ches W 55 Q12
Lostock Hall Lancs 55 M1
Lostock Hall Fold Bolton 55 Q5
Lostock Junction Bolton 55 Q5
Lostwithiel Cnwll 4 E9
Lothbeg Highld 109 T2
Lothersdale N York 62 K10
Lothmore Highld 109 T2
Loudwater Bucks 20 F3
Loughborough Leics 47 P10
Loughborough
Crematorium Leics 47 U11
Loughor Swans 25 U11
Loughton Essex 21 R3
Loughton M Keyn 30 H5
Loughton Shrops 35 N3
Lound Lincs 48 G10
Lound Notts 58 B9
Lound Suffk 51 T14
Lount Leics 47 L10
Louth Lincs 59 P9
Love Clough Lancs 55 S1
Lovedean Hants 9 T6
Lover Wilts 8 K4
Loversall Donc 57 S7
Loves Green Essex 22 F7
Lovesome Hill N York 70 E13
Loveston Pembks 24 J9
Lovington Somset 17 P10
Low Ackworth Wakefd 57 P3
Low Angerton Nthumb 77 M9
Lowbands Gloucs 28 E2
Low Barbeth D & G 72 C6
Low Barlings Lincs 58 J12
Low Bell End N York 71 L14
Low Bentham N York 62 C6
Low Biggins Cumb 62 C4
Low Borrowbridge
Cumb 68 D12
Low Bradfield Sheff 57 L8
Low Bradley N York 63 L10
Low Braithwaite Cumb 67 P3
Low Burnham N Linc 58 C5
Low Buston Nthumb 77 Q4
Lowca Cumb 66 E8
Low Catton E R Yk 64 G9
Low Crosby Cumb 75 S14
Lowdham Notts 47 R4
Low Dinsdale Darltn 70 D10
Low Ellington N York 63 P3
Lower Aisholt Somset 16 H9
Lower Ansty Dorset 7 U4
Lower Apperley Gloucs 28 G3
Lower Arncott Oxon 30 C9
Lower Ashton Devon 5 U4
Lower Assendon Oxon 20 B5
Lower Ballam Lancs 61 R13
Lower Bartle Lancs 61 U13
Lower Basildon W Berk 19 U4
Lower Bearwood Herefs 34 J9
Lower Beeding W Susx 11 L5
Lower Benefield Nhants 38 E3
Lower Bentley Worcs 36 C7
Lower Beobridge Shrops 35 S2
Lower Birchwood
Derbys 47 M3
Lower Boddington
Nhants 37 N10
Lower Boscaswell Cnwll 2 B10
Lower Bourne Surrey 10 C2
Lower Brailes Warwks 36 K13
Lower Breakish Highld 100 f7

Lower Bredbury Stockp 56 D8
Lower Broadheath
Worcs 35 T9
Lower Broxwood Herefs 34 J10
Lower Buckenhill Herefs 35 P14
Lower Bullingham
Herefs 35 M13
Lower Burgate Hants 8 H5
Lower Burrowton Devon 6 D5
Lower Burton Herefs 34 K9
Lower Caldecote C Beds 38 J11
Lower Cam Gloucs 28 D7
Lower Canada N Som 17 L5
Lower Catesby Nhants 37 P8
Lower Chapel Powys 34 B13
Lower Chicksgrove Wilts 8 D2
Lower Chute Wilts 19 L9
Lower Clapton Gt Lon 21 P6
Lower Clent Worcs 36 B5
Lower Creedy Devon 15 T11
Lower Crossings Derbys 56 F10
Lower Cumberworth
Kirk 56 K5
Lower Darwen Bl w D 55 P1
Lower Dean Bed 38 G7
Lower Denby Kirk 56 K5
Lower Diabaig Highld 107 N12
Lower Dicker E Susx 11 T8
Lower Dinchope Shrops 35 L4
Lower Down Shrops 34 H4
Lower Dunsforth N York 63 U7
Lower Egleton Herefs 35 P11
Lower Elkstone Staffs 46 E2
Lower Ellastone Staffs 46 F5
Lower End M Keyn 30 E11
Lower End Nhants 38 D8
Lower Everleigh Wilts 18 H9
Lower Exbury Hants 9 N9
Lower Eythorne Kent 13 Q6
Lower Failand N Som 17 N2
Lower Farringdon Hants 19 U13
Lower Feltham Gt Lon 20 J8
Lower Fittleworth
W Susx 10 G7
Lower Foxdale IoM 60 d7
Lower Frankton Shrops 44 J6
Lower Freystrop
Pembks 24 G8
Lower Froyle Hants 10 B2
Lower Gabwell Devon 6 B11
Lower Gledfield Highld 108 K6
Lower Godney Somset 17 N8
Lower Gornal Dudley 35 U2
Lower Gravenhurst
C Beds 31 P5
Lower Green Herts 31 U6
Lower Green Kent 11 U2
Lower Green Kent 12 C7
Lower Green Norfk 50 F6
Lower Green Staffs 45 B12
Lower Green Suffk 40 B7
Lower Hacheston Suffk 41 N9
Lower Halstock Leigh
Dorset 7 P3
Lower Halstow Kent 12 G2
Lower Hamworthy
Poole 8 D10
Lower Hardres Kent 13 N5
Lower Hartlip Kent 12 F3
Lower Hartshay Derbys 47 L3
Lower Hartwell Bucks 30 G10
Lower Hawthwaite
Cumb 61 N2
Lower Hergest Herefs 34 G10
Lower Heyford Oxon 29 U3
Lower Heysham Lancs 61 S7
Lower Higham Kent 22 G13
Lower Holbrook Suffk 41 L13
Lower Hordley Shrops 44 J8
Lower Horncroft W Susx 10 G7
Lower Houses Kirk 56 J4
Lower Howsell Worcs 35 S11
Lower Irlam Salfd 55 R8
Lower Kilcott Gloucs 28 F10
Lower Killeyan Ag & B 78 D7
Lower Kingswood
Surrey 21 N12
Lower Kinnerton Ches W 54 J13
Lower Langford N Som 17 N4
Lower Largo Fife 91 P11
Lower Leigh Staffs 46 D6
Lower Lemington Gloucs 36 J14
Lower Llanfadog Powys 33 U8
Lower Lovacott Devon 15 M7
Lower Loxhore Devon 15 N5
Lower Lydbrook Gloucs 28 A4
Lower Lye Herefs 34 K7
Lower Machen Newpt 27 N10
Lower Maes-coed Herefs 27 Q1
Lower Mannington
Dorset 8 F8
Lower Marston Somset 17 U8
Lower Meend Gloucs 27 V6
Lower Merridge Somset 16 H10
Lower Middleton
Cheney Nhants 37 P12
Lower Milton Somset 17 P7
Lower Moor Worcs 36 C11
Lower Morton S Glos 28 B9
Lower Nazeing Essex 31 U11
Lower Norton Warwks 36 H8
Lower Nyland Dorset 17 U12
Lower Penarth V Glam 16 G3
Lower Penn Staffs 35 U2
Lower Pennington
Hants 9 L9
Lower Penwortham
Lancs 61 U14
Lower Peover Ches E 55 R12
Lower Place Rochdl 56 D5
Lower Pollicott Bucks 30 F10
Lower Quinton Warwks 36 G11
Lower Rainham Medway 12 G2
Lower Raydon Suffk 40 H13
Lower Roadwater
Somset 16 D9
Lower Salter Lancs 62 C7
Lower Seagry Wilts 18 E4
Lower Sheering Essex 22 C5
Lower Shelton C Beds 31 L4
Lower Shiplake Oxon 20 B7
Lower Shuckburgh
Warwks 37 N8
Lower Slaughter Gloucs 29 L3
Lower Soothill Kirk 57 L2
Lower Soudley Gloucs 28 C5
Lower Standen Kent 13 P7
Lower Stanton St
Quentin Wilts 18 D4
Lower Stoke Medway 22 H13
Lower Stondon C Beds 31 Q5
Lower Stonnall Staffs 46 E14
Lower Stow Bedon
Norfk 40 F2
Lower Street Dorset 7 V5
Lower Street E Susx 12 D13
Lower Street Norfk 51 N7
Lower Street Suffk 40 J10
Lower Stretton Warrtn 55 P10
Lower Stroud Dorset 7 M4
Lower Sundon C Beds 31 N7
Lower Swanwick Hants 9 N7
Lower Swell Gloucs 29 L2
Lower Tadmarton Oxon 37 M14
Lower Tale Devon 6 E4
Lower Tasburgh Norfk 51 M14
Lower Thurlton Norfk 51 R14
Lower Town Devon 5 V6
Lower Town Herefs 35 N11
Lower Town Pembks 24 G3
Lower Trebullett Cnwll 4 J5
Lower Treluswell Cnwll 2 K10
Lower Tysoe Warwks 36 K11
Lower Ufford Suffk 41 N10
Lower Upcott Devon 5 U3
Lower Upham Hants 9 P5
Lower Upnor Medway 22 G13
Lower Vexford Somset 16 F9
Lower Walton Warrtn 55 P9
Lower Waterston Dorset 7 T5
Lower Weald M Keyn 30 F5
Lower Weare Somset 17 M6
Lower Weedon Nhants 37 R9
Lower Welson Herefs 34 G11
Lower Westholme
Somset 17 Q8
Lower Whatcombe
Dorset 8 A8
Lower Whatley Somset 17 T7
Lower Whitley Ches W 55 P11
Lower Wick Gloucs 28 D8
Lower Wield Hants 19 T12
Lower Willingham
Suffk 40 H5
Lower Withington Ches E 55 T13
Lower Woodend Bucks 20 D5
Lower Woodford Wilts 18 H13
Lower Wraxhall Dorset 7 P4
Lower Wyche Worcs 35 S12
Lower Wyke C Brad 56 H1

Low Fell Gatesd 77 R14
Lowfield Heath W Susx 11 M3
Low Gartachorrans
Stirlg 89 L8
Low Gate Nthumb 76 J13
Low Gettbridge Cumb 68 C8
Low Grantley N York 63 P5
Low Green N York 63 Q8
Low Habberley Worcs 35 U6
Low Ham Somset 17 M11
Low Harrogate N York 63 R9
Low Hawsker N York 71 R11
Low Hesket Cumb 67 Q3
Low Hutton N York 64 G6
Lowick Cumb 61 P2
Lowick Nhants 38 E4
Lowick Nthumb 85 Q11
Lowick Green Cumb 61 P2
Low Knipe Cumb 67 R9
Low Laithe N York 63 P7
Low Langton Lincs 59 L11
Lowlands Dur 69 P7
Lowlands Torfn 27 P8
Low Leighton Derbys 56 F10
Low Lorton Cumb 66 K8
Low Marishes N York 64 H5
Low Marnham Notts 58 D13
Low Middleton Nthumb 85 S11
Low Mill N York 71 L14
Low Moor C Brad 63 P14
Low Moorsley Sundld 70 D3
Low Moresby Cumb 66 E8
Low Newton Cumb 61 R3
Low Newton-by-the-Sea
Nthumb 85 U13
Lownie Moor Angus 91 R3
Low Row Cumb 66 K6
Low Row Cumb 67 J3
Low Row N York 68 K13
Low Salchrie D & G 72 D6
Low Santon N Linc 58 F4
Lowsonford Warwks 36 G7
Low Street Norfk 51 P7
Low Street Thurr 22 F12
Low Tharston Norfk 41 L1
Lowther Cumb 67 R7
Lowther Castle Cumb 67 R8
Lowthorpe E R Yk 65 P7
Lowton Devon 15 R12
Lowton Somset 16 G12
Lowton Wigan 55 P7
Lowton Common Wigan 55 P7
Lowton St Mary's Wigan 55 P7
Low Torry Fife 82 K1
Low Toynton Lincs 59 N12
Low Valley Barns 57 P5
Low Wood Cumb 61 P2
Low Worsall N York 70 E10
Low Wray Cumb 67 M12
Loxbeare Devon 16 C13
Loxhill Surrey 10 G3
Loxhore Devon 15 N5
Loxhore Cott Devon 15 N5
Loxley Warwks 36 J9
Loxley Green Staffs 46 E7
Loxter Herefs 35 R12
Loxton N Som 17 L6
Loxwood W Susx 10 G4
Loyal Lodge Highld 111 N7
Lubenham Leics 37 U3
Lucas Green Surrey 20 F11
Luccombe Somset 16 B8
Luccombe Village IoW 9 R13
Lucker Nthumb 85 T12
Luckett Cnwll 4 J6
Lucking Street Essex 40 D13
Luckington Wilts 18 B4
Lucklawhill Fife 91 P7
Luckwell Bridge Somset 16 B9
Lucton Herefs 34 K8
Lucy Cross N York 70 P10
Ludborough Lincs 59 N7
Ludbrook Devon 5 Q10
Ludchurch Pembks 24 K8
Luddenden Calder 56 F1
Luddenden Foot Calder 56 F1
Luddenham Court Kent 12 J3
Luddesdown Kent 22 E13
Luddington N Linc 58 E3
Luddington Warwks 36 G10
Luddington in the
Brook Nhants 38 H4
Ludford Lincs 59 L9
Ludford Shrops 35 M6
Ludgershall Bucks 30 D9
Ludgershall Wilts 19 L10
Ludgvan Cnwll 2 E10
Ludham Norfk 51 Q10
Ludlow Shrops 35 M6
Ludney Somset 7 L2
Ludwell Wilts 8 D3
Ludworth Dur 70 D4
Luffincott Devon 4 J2
Luffness E Loth 84 D2
Lugar E Ayrs 81 R7
Luggate Burn E Loth 84 F3
Lugg Green Herefs 34 K8
Luggiebank N Lans 82 E4
Lugton E Ayrs 81 M2
Lugwardine Herefs 35 M12
Luib Highld 100 g7
Luib Stirlg 89 P2
Lullham Herefs 34 K12
Lullington Derbys 46 J10
Lullington E Susx 11 S10
Lullington Somset 17 U7
Lulsgate Bottom N Som 17 N3
Lulsley Worcs 35 S10
Lulworth Camp Dorset 8 A11
Lumb Calder 56 E2
Lumb Lancs 55 U2
Lumbutts Calder 56 E2
Lumby N York 64 B13
Lumloch E Duns 89 P12
Lumphanan Abers 98 J2
Lumphinnans Fife 82 K1
Lumsdaine Border 85 L7
Lumsden Abers 104 F10
Lunan Angus 91 T2
Lunanhead Angus 98 H13
Luncarty P & K 90 F5
Lund E R Yk 65 M10
Lund N York 64 F12
Lundie Angus 91 L4
Lundin Links Fife 91 P11
Lundin Mill Fife 91 P11
Lundy Devon 14 A2
Lundy Green Norfk 51 M2
Lunga Ag & B 87 N3
Lunna Shet 106 u6
Lunsford Kent 12 D4
Lunsford's Cross E Susx 12 D13
Lunt Sefton 54 H6
Luntley Herefs 34 K10
Luppitt Devon 6 H4
Lupridge Devon 5 S10
Lupset Wakefd 57 M3
Lupton Cumb 62 C3
Lurgashall W Susx 10 E5
Lurley Devon 16 C13
Luscombe Devon 5 U9
Luson Devon 5 Q10
Luss Ag & B 88 J6
Lussagiven Ag & B 87 L8
Lusta Highld 100 c4
Lustleigh Devon 5 T4
Luston Herefs 34 K8
Luthermuir Abers 99 M10
Luthrie Fife 91 N8
Luton Devon 6 D5
Luton Devon 6 C3
Luton Luton 31 N8
Luton Medway 12 E2
Luton Airport Luton 31 P8
Lutterworth Leics 37 Q4
Lutton Devon 5 P9
Lutton Lincs 49 P9
Lutton Nhants 38 H4
Luxborough Somset 16 C9
Luxulyan Cnwll 3 Q3
Luxulyan Valley Cnwll 3 Q3
Luzley Tamesd 56 D6
Lybster Highld 112 G9
Lydbury North Shrops 34 J3
Lydcott Devon 15 Q5
Lydd Kent 13 L11
Lydd Airport Kent 13 L11
Lydden Kent 13 P6
Lydden Kent 13 S3
Lyddington Rutlnd 48 C14
Lydeard St Lawrence
Somset 16 F10
Lyde Green Hants 20 B11
Lydford Devon 5 N4
Lydford on Fosse
Somset 17 Q10
Lydgate Calder 56 E2
Lydgate Rochdl 56 E5
Lydham Shrops 34 J2
Lydiard Green Wilts 18 G4
Lydiard Millicent Wilts 18 G4
Lydiard Tregoze Swindn 18 G4
Lydiate Sefton 54 H6
Lydiate Ash Worcs 36 C6
Lydlinch Dorset 7 U2
Lydney Gloucs 28 B6
Lydstep Pembks 24 J11
Lye Dudley 36 B4
Lye Cross N Som 17 N4
Lye Green Bucks 30 K12
Lye Green E Susx 11 S4
Lye Green Warwks 36 H7
Lye Head Worcs 35 S6
Lye's Green Wilts 18 B11
Lyford Oxon 29 S8
Lymbridge Green Kent 13 M7
Lyme Regis Dorset 7 L5
Lyminge Kent 13 N7
Lymington Hants 9 L9
Lyminster W Susx 10 G9
Lymm Warrtn 55 Q9
Lymore Hants 9 L10
Lympne Kent 13 M8
Lympsham Somset 16 K6
Lympstone Devon 6 D7
Lynbridge Devon 15 Q3
Lynch Somset 16 B7
Lynchat Highld 97 M4
Lyndhurst Hants 9 L7
Lyndon Rutlnd 48 D13
Lyne Border 83 N11
Lyne Surrey 20 H9
Lyneal Shrops 44 K7
Lyne Down Herefs 35 P13
Lyneham Devon 5 V6
Lyneham Oxon 29 P4
Lyneham Wilts 18 F5
Lyneholmford Cumb 75 U11
Lynemore Highld 103 S10
Lynemouth Nthumb 77 S8
Lyne of Skene Abers 105 L13
Lyness Ork 106 s20
Lyng Norfk 50 J10
Lyng Somset 16 K11
Lynmouth Devon 15 Q3
Lynn Staffs 46 E13
Lynn Wrekin 45 S11
Lynsted Kent 12 J3
Lynstone Cnwll 14 F11
Lynton Devon 15 Q3
Lyon's Gate Dorset 7 S3
Lyonshall Herefs 34 H10
Lytchett Matravers
Dorset 8 C9
Lytchett Minster Dorset 8 C10
Lyth Highld 112 G4
Lytham Lancs 61 R14
Lytham St Anne's Lancs 54 H1
Lythbank Shrops 45 L12
Lythe N York 71 P9
Lythmore Highld 112 C3

M

Mabe Burnthouse Cnwll 2 K10
Mablethorpe Lincs 59 T10
Macclesfield Ches E 56 D12
Macclesfield
Crematorium Ches E 56 D12
Macduff Abers 105 L3
Macharioch Ag & B 79 L14
Machen Caerph 27 N10
Machrie N Ayrs 79 R7
Machrihanish Ag & B 79 L12
Machrins Ag & B 86 F7
Machynlleth Powys 43 P13
Machynys Carmth 25 T11
Mackworth Derbys 46 K6
Macmerry E Loth 84 C4
Maddaford Devon 5 M2
Madderty P & K 90 E7
Maddington Wilts 18 H12
Maddiston Falk 82 H3
Madehurst W Susx 10 F8
Madeley Staffs 45 S4
Madeley Wrekin 45 Q13
Madeley Heath Staffs 45 S4
Madford Devon 6 G3
Madingley Cambs 39 N8
Madley Herefs 34 K13
Madresfield Worcs 35 T11
Madron Cnwll 2 D10
Maenaddwyn IoA 52 G5
Maenclochog Pembks 24 J5
Maen-y-groes Cerdgn 32 G9
Maer Cnwll 14 F11
Maer Staffs 45 S6
Maerdy Carmth 26 B2
Maerdy Conwy 44 B2
Maerdy Rhondd 26 H8
Maesbrook Shrops 44 H9
Maesbury Shrops 44 H8
Maesbury Marsh Shrops 44 H8
Maesglas Newpt 27 P10
Maesgwynne Carmth 25 M6
Maeshafn Denbgs 54 F14
Maesllyn Cerdgn 32 H11
Maesmynis Powys 33 U11
Maesteg Brdgnd 26 G9
Maesybont Carmth 25 U8
Maesycwmmer Caerph 27 M8
Maesymeillion Cerdgn 32 J11
Magdalen Laver Essex 22 C6
Maggieknockater Moray 104 C7
Maggots End Essex 22 C2
Magham Down E Susx 11 U8
Maghull Sefton 54 H6
Magna Park Leics 37 Q4
Magor Mons 27 S10
Magor Services Mons 27 S10
Maidenbower W Susx 11 M4
Maiden Bradley Wilts 18 B12
Maidencombe Torbay 6 B11
Maidenhayne Devon 6 J5
Maiden Head N Som 17 N3
Maidenhead W & M 20 E6
Maiden Law Dur 69 Q3
Maiden Newton Dorset 7 P4
Maidens S Ayrs 80 J9
Maiden's Green Br For 20 E8
Maidens Hall Nthumb 77 Q7
Maidenwell Lincs 59 P11
Maiden Wells Pembks 24 G11
Maidford Nhants 37 R10
Maids Moreton Bucks 30 F6
Maidstone Kent 12 E5
Maidstone Services Kent 12 G4
Maidwell Nhants 37 U5
Mail Shet 106 t11
Maindee Newpt 27 Q10
Mainland Ork 106 t19
Mainland Shet 106 u9
Mains of Balhall Angus 98 J11
Mains of Balnakettle
Abers 99 L8
Mains of Dalvey Highld 103 S9
Mains of Haulkerton
Abers 99 N8
Mains of Lesmoir Abers 104 F10
Mains of Melgunds
Angus 98 J12
Mainsriddle D & G 66 J2
Mainstone Shrops 34 G3
Maisemore Gloucs 28 F3
Major's Green Worcs 36 E6
Makeney Derbys 47 L4
Malborough Devon 5 S12
Malcoff Derbys 56 F10
Maldon Essex 23 L6
Malham N York 62 J7
Maligar Highld 100 e4
Mallaig Highld 100 f11
Mallaig Vaig Highld 100 f11
Malleny Mills C Edin 83 M4
Mallows Green Essex 22 C3
Malltraeth IoA 52 F8
Mallwyd Gwynd 43 R11
Malmesbury Wilts 18 E3
Malmsmead Devon 15 R3
Malpas Ches W 45 L4
Malpas Cnwll 3 L8
Malpas Newpt 27 Q9
Malshanger Hants 19 S10
Malswick Gloucs 28 D3
Maltby Lincs 59 Q10
Maltby Rothm 57 R8
Maltby S on T 70 F10
Maltby le Marsh Lincs 59 S10
Malting Green Essex 23 N3
Maltman's Hill Kent 12 H7
Malton N York 64 H5
Malvern Link Worcs 35 S11
Malvern Wells Worcs 35 S12
Mambeg Ag & B 88 G8
Mamble Worcs 35 Q6
Mamhilad Mons 27 Q6
Manaccan Cnwll 2 K12
Manafon Powys 44 D12
Manais W Isls 106 g9
Manaton Devon 5 T4
Manby Lincs 59 Q9
Mancetter Warwks 36 K2
Manchester Manch 55 T7
Manchester Airport
Manch 55 T10
Manchester Cathedral
Manch 55 T7
Mancot Flints 54 H13
Mandally Highld 96 E5
Manea Cambs 39 Q3
Maney Birm 36 F2
Manfield N York 69 R10
Mangerton Dorset 7 N5
Mangotsfield S Glos 28 C12
Mangrove Green Herts 31 P8
Manhay Cnwll 2 H10
Manish W Isls 106 g10
Mankinholes Calder 56 E2
Manley Ches W 55 M12
Manmoel Caerph 27 M7
Manningford Bohune
Wilts 18 H9
Manningford Bruce
Wilts 18 H9
Manningham C Brad 63 N13
Mannings Heath W Susx 11 L5
Mannington Dorset 8 F8
Manningtree Essex 23 S2
Mannofield C Aber 99 S3
Manorbier Pembks 24 H11
Manorbier Newton
Pembks 24 H10
Manordeilo Carmth 26 B2
Manorhill Border 84 H12
Manorowen Pembks 24 F3
Manor Park Gt Lon 21 R5
Mansell Gamage Herefs 34 J12
Mansell Lacy Herefs 34 K11
Mansergh Cumb 62 C3
Mansfield E Ayrs 81 S10
Mansfield Notts 47 P1
Mansfield & District
Crematorium Notts 47 P2
Mansfield Woodhouse
Notts 47 P1
Mansriggs Cumb 61 P2
Manston Dorset 8 B3
Manston Kent 13 R2
Manston Leeds 63 T13
Manswood Dorset 8 D7
Manthorpe Lincs 48 D6
Manthorpe Lincs 48 F10
Manton N Linc 58 F6
Manton Notts 57 T11
Manton Rutlnd 48 C13
Manton Wilts 18 H7
Manuden Essex 22 C2
Manwood Green Essex 22 C5
Maperton Somset 17 R11
Maplebeck Notts 47 T1
Mapledurham Oxon 19 U5
Mapledurwell Hants 19 U10
Maplehurst W Susx 10 K6
Maplescombe Kent 21 U10
Mapleton Derbys 46 G4
Mapperley Derbys 47 M4
Mapperley Park C Nott 47 Q5
Mapperton Dorset 7 P5
Mappleborough Green
Warwks 36 E7
Mappleton E R Yk 65 S11
Mappowder Dorset 7 T3
Marazanvose Cnwll 2 K6
Marazion Cnwll 2 E10
Marbury Ches E 45 M4
March Cambs 39 P1
March S Lans 74 H2
Marcham Oxon 29 U8
Marchamley Shrops 45 N8
Marchamley Wood
Shrops 45 N7
Marchington Staffs 46 F8
Marchington
Woodlands Staffs 46 F8
Marchros Gwynd 42 F8
Marchwiel Wrexhm 44 J4
Marchwood Hants 9 M6
Marcross V Glam 16 B3
Marden Herefs 35 M11
Marden Kent 12 E7
Marden Wilts 18 G9
Marden Ash Essex 22 E7
Marden Beech Kent 12 E7
Marden's Hill E Susx 11 R4
Marden Thorn Kent 12 E7
Mardlebury Herts 31 S9
Mardy Mons 27 Q4
Marefield Leics 47 T12
Mareham le Fen Lincs 59 M13
Mareham on the Hill
Lincs 59 M13
Marehay Derbys 47 L4
Marehill W Susx 10 H7
Maresfield E Susx 11 R6
Marfleet C KuH 65 R14
Marford Wrexhm 44 J2
Margam Neath 26 D10
Margam Crematorium
Neath 26 D10
Margaret Marsh Dorset 17 V13
Margaret Roding Essex 22 E5
Margaretting Essex 22 F7
Margaretting Tye Essex 22 F7
Margate Kent 13 R1
Margnaheglish N Ayrs 79 T8
Margrie D & G 73 Q9
Margrove Park R & Cl 70 K9
Marham Norfk 50 B12
Marhamchurch Cnwll 14 F11
Marholm C Pete 48 H13
Marian-glas IoA 52 H5
Mariansleigh Devon 15 R7
Marine Town Kent 23 L13
Marionburgh Abers 99 M2
Marishader Highld 100 e3
Maristow Devon 5 N7
Marjoriebanks D & G 75 L9
Mark Somset 17 L7
Markbeech Kent 11 R2
Markby Lincs 59 S11
Mark Causeway Somset 17 L7
Mark Cross E Susx 11 S4
Markeaton C Derb 46 K6
Markeaton
Crematorium C Derb 46 K6
Market Bosworth Leics 47 M13
Market Deeping Lincs 48 H11
Market Drayton Shrops 45 Q7
Market Harborough
Leics 37 U3
Market Lavington Wilts 18 F9
Market Overton Rutlnd 48 C10
Market Rasen Lincs 58 K8
Market Stainton Lincs 59 M11
Market Warsop Notts 57 R13
Market Weighton E R Yk 64 K11
Market Weston Suffk 40 G5
Markfield Leics 47 N12
Markham Caerph 27 M7
Markham Moor Notts 58 B12
Markinch Fife 91 L11
Markington N York 63 R6
Markle E Loth 84 F3
Marksbury BaNES 17 S4
Mark's Corner IoW 9 P10
Marks Tey Essex 23 N3
Markwell Cnwll 4 J9
Markyate Herts 31 N10
Marlborough Wilts 18 J7
Marlbrook Herefs 35 M9
Marlbrook Worcs 36 C6
Marlcliff Warwks 36 E10
Marldon Devon 5 V8
Marle Green E Susx 11 U7
Marlesford Suffk 41 P9
Marley Kent 13 N4
Marley Green Ches E 45 M4
Marley Hill Gatesd 69 R2
Marlingford Norfk 51 L12
Marloes Pembks 24 D9
Marlow Bucks 20 D5
Marlow Herefs 34 K6
Marlow Bottom Bucks 20 D5
Marlpit Hill Kent 21 R13
Marlpits E Susx 11 S5
Marlpool Derbys 47 M4
Marnhull Dorset 17 U13
Marple Stockp 56 E9
Marple Bridge Stockp 56 E9
Marr Donc 57 R6
Marrick N York 69 M13
Marros Carmth 25 M9
Marsden Kirk 56 G4
Marsden S Tyne 77 T14
Marsden Height Lancs 62 H12
Marsett N York 62 J2
Marsh Bucks 30 H11
Marsh C Brad 63 L12
Marsh Devon 6 K3
Marshalsea Dorset 7 L4
Marshall's Heath Herts 31 Q9
Marshalswick Herts 31 Q11
Marsham Norfk 51 L9
Marshborough Kent 13 R4
Marshbrook Shrops 34 K3
Marshchapel Lincs 59 P7
Marshfield Newpt 27 P11
Marshfield S Glos 28 D13
Marshgate Cnwll 14 E13
Marsh Gibbon Bucks 30 D8
Marsh Green Devon 6 D6
Marsh Green Kent 21 R13
Marsh Green Wrekin 45 P10
Marsh Lane Derbys 57 P11
Marsh Lane Gloucs 28 A5
Marshland St James
Norfk 49 R12
Marsh Street Somset 16 C8
Marshwood Dorset 7 L4
Marske N York 69 N11
Marske-by-the-Sea
R & Cl 70 K8
Marsland Green Wigan 55 Q7
Marston Ches W 55 Q11
Marston Herefs 34 J9
Marston Lincs 48 C4
Marston Oxon 30 B11
Marston Staffs 45 T11
Marston Staffs 45 U9
Marston Warwks 36 H2
Marston Wilts 18 E9
Marston Doles Warwks 37 M9
Marston Green Solhll 36 G3
Marston Jabbet Warwks 37 L2
Marston Magna Somset 17 Q12
Marston Meysey Wilts 18 H3
Marston Montgomery
Derbys 46 F6
Marston Moretaine
C Beds 31 L4
Marston on Dove Derbys 46 H8
Marston St Lawrence
Nhants 30 B4
Marston Stannett Herefs 35 N9
Marston Trussell Nhants 37 T4
Marstow Herefs 27 V4
Marsworth Bucks 30 K10
Marten Wilts 19 L8
Martham Norfk 51 S10
Martin Hants 8 F5
Martin Kent 13 R6
Martin Lincs 48 H1
Martin Lincs 59 M13
Martindale Cumb 67 P9
Martin Dales Lincs 59 L13
Martin Drove End Hants 8 F4
Martinhoe Devon 15 P3
Martin Hussingtree
Worcs 35 U8
Martinscroft Warrtn 55 Q9
Martinstown Dorset 7 R7
Martlesham Suffk 41 M11
Martlesham Heath Suffk 41 M11
Martletwy Pembks 24 H8
Martley Worcs 35 S8
Martock Somset 17 M13
Marton Ches E 56 C13
Marton Cumb 61 N4
Marton E R Yk 65 R12
Marton E R Yk 65 R9
Marton Lincs 58 D10
Marton Middsb 70 H9
Marton N York 64 G6
Marton N York 64 C5
Marton Shrops 44 G13
Marton Warwks 37 M7
Marton-le-Moor N York 63 T5
Martyr's Green Surrey 20 J11
Martyr Worthy Hants 19 Q2
Marwick Ork 106 r17
Marwood Devon 15 M5
Marybank Highld 102 E5
Maryburgh Highld 102 F5
Maryfield Cnwll 4 K9
Marygold Border 85 L7
Maryhill C Glas 89 N12
Maryhill Crematorium
C Glas 89 N12
Marykirk Abers 99 M10
Maryland Mons 27 U6
Marylebone Gt Lon 21 N5
Marylebone Wigan 55 N5
Marypark Moray 104 B8
Maryport Cumb 66 F5
Maryport D & G 72 E11
Marystow Devon 5 M4
Mary Tavy Devon 5 N5
Maryton Angus 99 M12
Marywell Abers 98 J4
Marywell Abers 99 S4
Marywell Angus 91 T3
Masham N York 63 Q3
Mashbury Essex 22 G5
Mason N u Ty 77 Q12
Masongill N York 62 D5
Masonhill Crematorium
S Ayrs 81 M8
Mastin Moor Derbys 57 Q11
Matching Essex 22 D5
Matching Green Essex 22 D5
Matching Tye Essex 22 D5
Matfen Nthumb 77 L12
Matfield Kent 12 C7
Mathern Mons 27 U9
Mathon Herefs 35 S11
Mathry Pembks 24 E4
Matlaske Norfk 51 L7
Matlock Derbys 46 K1
Matlock Bank Derbys 46 K2
Matlock Bath Derbys 46 K2
Matlock Dale Derbys 46 K2
Matson Gloucs 28 G4
Matterdale End Cumb 67 N8
Mattersey Notts 57 U9
Mattersey Thorpe Notts 57 U9
Mattingley Hants 20 B11
Mattishall Norfk 50 J11
Mattishall Burgh Norfk 50 J11
Mauchline E Ayrs 81 P7
Maud Abers 105 Q6
Maugersbury Gloucs 29 N3
Maughold IoM 60 g3
Mauld Highld 102 C8
Maulden C Beds 31 N4
Maulds Meaburn Cumb 68 D9
Maunby N York 63 S2
Maund Bryan Herefs 35 N10
Maundown Somset 16 E11
Mautby Norfk 51 S11
Mavesyn Ridware Staffs 46 E10
Mavis Enderby Lincs 59 P13
Mawbray Cumb 66 H3
Mawdesley Lancs 55 L4
Mawdlam Brdgnd 26 E11
Mawgan Cnwll 2 H11
Maw Green Ches E 45 R2
Mawla Cnwll 2 H7
Mawnan Cnwll 2 K11
Mawnan Smith Cnwll 2 K11
Mawsley Nhants 38 B6
Mawthorpe Lincs 59 S12
Maxey C Pete 48 H12
Maxstoke Warwks 36 H3
Maxted Street Kent 13 M7
Maxton Border 84 G12
Maxton Kent 13 Q7
Maxwell Town D & G 74 J11
Maxworthy Cnwll 14 G13
Mayals Swans 26 A9
May Bank Staffs 45 U4
Maybole S Ayrs 80 K9
Maybury Surrey 20 H11
Mayes Green Surrey 10 K3
Mayfield E Susx 11 T5
Mayfield Mdloth 83 S5
Mayfield Staffs 46 G4
May Hill Gloucs 28 D3
Mayland Essex 23 M6
Maylandsea Essex 23 M7
Maynard's Green E Susx 11 T7
Maypole Birm 36 E5
Maypole Kent 13 N3
Maypole Mons 27 U5
Maypole Green Norfk 51 R14
Maypole Green Suffk 41 L7
May's Green Oxon 20 B6
May's Green Surrey 20 J11
Mead Devon 14 F9
Meadgate BaNES 17 S5
Meadle Bucks 30 H11
Meadowfield Dur 69 R4
Meadowtown Shrops 44 H13
Meadwell Devon 5 M4
Meal Bank Cumb 67 R13
Mealrigg Cumb 66 J4
Mealsgate Cumb 66 K4
Meanwood Leeds 63 R13
Mearbeck N York 62 H7
Meare Somset 17 M8
Meare Green Somset 16 K11
Meare Green Somset 16 K12
Mears Ashby Nhants 38 B8
Measham Leics 47 L11
Meathop Cumb 61 R3
Meaux E R Yk 65 Q12
Meavy Devon 5 N8
Medbourne Leics 38 B2
Meddon Devon 14 F9
Meden Vale Notts 57 S13
Medlam Lincs 59 N14
Medlar Lancs 61 S13
Medmenham Bucks 20 D5
Medomsley Dur 69 P2
Medstead Hants 19 U13
Medway Crematorium
Kent 12 D3
Medway Services
Medway 12 F3
Meerbrook Staffs 56 D13
Meer Common Herefs 34 J10
Meesden Herts 22 C1
Meeson Wrekin 45 P9
Meeth Devon 15 M11
Meeting Green Suffk 40 B9
Meeting House Hill
Norfk 51 N8
Meidrim Carmth 25 N6

Meifod Powys 44 E11
Meigle P & K 91 L7
Meikle Carco D & G 74 E3
Meikle Earnock S Lans 82 D8
Meikle Kilmory Ag & B 88 C13
Meikle Obney P & K 90 J4
Meikleour P & K 90 J4
Meikle Wartle Abers 105 L9
Meinciau Carmth 25 S8
Meir C Stke 46 B5
Meir Heath Staffs 46 B5
Melbourn Cambs 31 U4
Melbourne Derbys 47 L8
Melbourne E R Yk 64 H11
Melbury Devon 14 J9
Melbury Abbas Dorset 8 A3
Melbury Bubb Dorset 7 Q3
Melbury Osmond Dorset 7 Q3
Melbury Sampford
    Dorset 7 Q3
Melchbourne Bed 38 F7
Melcombe Bingham
    Dorset 7 U4
Meldon Devon 5 P2
Meldon Nthumb 77 N9
Meldon Park Nthumb 77 N8
Meldreth Cambs 39 N11
Meldrum Stirlg 89 N6
Melfort Ag & B 87 Q3
Melgund Denbgs 54 C10
Meliden Neath 26 K5
Melinau Pembks 25 L8
Melin-byrddyn Powys 43 R14
Melincourt Neath 26 E7
Melin-y-ddol Powys 44 B11
Melin-y-coed Conwy 53 P10
Melin-y-ddol Powys 44 B11
Melin-y-wig Denbgs 44 B4
Melkinthorpe Cumb 67 S7
Melkridge Nthumb 76 E13
Melksham Wilts 18 D8
Mellangoose Cnwll 2 H11
Mell Green W Berk 19 Q5
Melling Lancs 62 B5
Melling Sefton 54 J6
Melling Mount Sefton 54 K6
Mellis Suffk 40 J6
Mellon Charles Highld 107 P6
Mellon Udrigle Highld 107 Q5
Mellor Lancs 62 D13
Mellor Stockp 56 E9
Mellor Brook Lancs 62 C13
Mells Somset 17 T7
Mells Wilts 41 R5
Melmerby Cumb 68 E4
Melmerby N York 63 M2
Melmerby N York 63 S4
Melness Highld 111 M4
Melon Green Suffk 40 D9
Melplash Dorset 7 N5
Melrose Border 84 E12
Melsetter Ork 106 r21
Melsonby N York 69 Q11
Meltham Kirk 56 H4
Meltham Mills Kirk 56 H4
Melton E R Yk 58 G1
Melton Suffk 41 N10
Melton E R Yk 64 H9
Melton Constable Norfk 50 H6
Melton Mowbray Leics 47 U10
Melton Ross N Linc 58 J4
Melvaig Highld 107 M7
Melverley Shrops 44 H10
Melverley Green Shrops 44 H10
Melvich Highld 111 U4
Membury Devon 6 J4
Membury Services
    W Berk 19 M5
Memsie Abers 105 R3
Memus Angus 98 G12
Menabilly Cnwll 3 R6
Menagissey Cnwll 2 J7
Menai Bridge IoA 52 J8
Mendham Suffk 41 N4
Mendip Crematorium
    Somset 17 Q8
Mendip Hills Somset 17 P6
Mendlesham Suffk 40 K7
Mendlesham Green
    Suffk 40 J8
Menheniot Cnwll 4 J8
Menithwood Worcs 35 R7
Mennock D & G 74 F4
Menston C Brad 63 P11
Menstrie Clacks 90 C12
Menthorpe N York 64 G13
Mentmore Bucks 30 K9
Meoble Highld 100 g10
Meole Brace Shrops 45 L11
Meonstoke Hants 9 S5
Meopham Kent 12 B2
Meopham Green Kent 12 B3
Meopham Station Kent 12 B2
Mepal Cambs 39 P4
Meppershall C Beds 31 P5
Merbach Herefs 34 H11
Mere Ches E 55 R9
Mere Wilts 17 V10
Mere Brow Lancs 54 K3
Mereclough Lancs 62 H13
Mere Green Birm 46 F14
Mere Green Worcs 36 C8
Mere Heath Ches W 55 Q12
Meresborough Medway 12 F3
Mereworth Kent 12 C5
Meriden Solhll 36 H4
Merkadale Highld 100 c6
Merley Poole 8 E10
Merlin's Bridge Pembks 24 F7
Merrington Shrops 45 L9
Merrion Pembks 24 F11
Merriott Somset 7 M2
Merrivale Devon 5 N5
Merrow Surrey 20 H12
Merry Field Hill Dorset 8 E8
Merry Lees Leics 47 N12
Merrymeet Cnwll 4 H7
Mersea Island Essex 23 P4
Mersham Kent 13 L7
Merston W Susx 10 D10
Merstone IoW 9 Q11
Merther Cnwll 3 M8
Merthyr Carmth 25 Q6
Merthyr Cynog Powys 33 V13
Merthyr Dyfan V Glam 16 F3
Merthyr Mawr Brdgnd 26 F12
Merthyr Tydfil Myr Td 26 K6
Merthyr Vale Myr Td 26 K8
Merton Devon 15 M10
Merton Gt Lon 21 N8
Merton Norfk 50 F14
Merton Oxon 30 C9
Meshaw Devon 15 S9
Messing Essex 23 L4
Messingham N Linc 58 E6
Metfield Suffk 41 N4
Metherell Cnwll 5 L7
Metheringham Lincs 48 G1
Methil Fife 91 N11
Methley Leeds 57 N1
Methley Junction Leeds 57 N1
Methlick Abers 105 P9
Methven P & K 90 F6
Methwold Norfk 40 B2
Methwold Hythe Norfk 40 A2
Mettingham Suffk 41 Q3
Metton Norfk 51 M6
Mevagissey Cnwll 3 Q7
Mexborough Donc 57 Q6
Mey Highld 112 G2
Meysey Hampton Gloucs 29 M7
Miabhig W Isls 106 f5
Miavaig W Isls 106 f5
Michaelchurch Herefs 27 U2
Michaelchurch Escley
    Herefs 34 H14
Michaelchurch-on-
    Arrow Powys 34 F10
Michaelston-le-Pit
    V Glam 27 M11
Michaelstow Cnwll 4 D5
Michaelwood Services
    Gloucs 28 D8
Michelcombe Devon 5 R7
Micheldever Hants 19 R13
Micheldever Station
    Hants 19 R12
Michelmersh Hants 9 L3
Mickfield Suffk 40 K8
Mickleby Donc 57 M9
Micklefield Leeds 64 B12
Micklefield Green Herts 20 H3
Mickleham Surrey 21 L12
Micklehurst Tamesd 56 F7
Mickleover C Derb 47 L6
Micklethwaite C Brad 63 M11
Micklethwaite Cumb 67 L1
Mickleton Dur 68 K7
Mickleton Gloucs 36 G12
Mickletown Leeds 57 M1
Mickle Trafford Ches W 54 K1
Mickley Derbys 57 M11
Mickley N York 63 R4
Mickley Green Suffk 40 D9
Mickley Square Nthumb 77 M13
Mid Ardlaw Abers 105 Q3
Midbea Ork 106 t15
Mid Beltie Abers 99 L3

Mid Bockhampton
    Dorset 8 H9
Mid Calder W Loth 83 L5
Mid Clyth Highld 112 G9
Mid Culbeuchly Abers 104 K3
Middle Assendon Oxon 20 B5
Middle Aston Oxon 29 U2
Middle Barton Oxon 29 T2
Middlebie D & G 75 P10
Middlebridge P & K 97 P10
Middle Chinnock Somset 7 N2
Middle Claydon Bucks 30 F7
Middlecliffe Barns 57 P5
Middlecott Devon 5 S3
Middleham
    Gloucs 28 J6
Middleham N York 63 P1
Middle Handley Derbys 57 P11
Middle Harling Norfk 40 G3
Middlehill Cnwll 4 H7
Middlehill Wilts 18 B7
Middlehope Shrops 35 L3
Middle Kames Ag & B 87 S8
Middle Littleton Worcs 36 E11
Middle Madeley Staffs 45 S4
Middle Maes-coed
    Herefs 34 H14
Middlemarsh Dorset 7 S3
Middle Mayfield Staffs 46 F4
Middle Mill Pembks 24 D5
Middlemore Devon 5 M8
Middle Quarter Kent 12 G8
Middle Rasen Lincs 58 J8
Middle Rocombe Devon 6 B11
Middle Salter Lancs 62 C7
Middlesbrough Middsb 70 G9
Middlescough Cumb 67 N4
Middleshaw Cumb 62 B2
Middlesmoor N York 62 K5
Middle Stoford Somset 16 G12
Middle Stoke Medway 22 K13
Middlestone Dur 69 S6
Middlestone Moor Dur 69 R6
Middle Stoughton
    Somset 17 M7
Middlestown Wakefd 57 L3
Middle Street Gloucs 28 E7
Middle Taphouse Cnwll 4 F8
Middlethird Border 84 H10
Middleton Ag & B 92 A10
Middleton Cumb 62 D3
Middleton Derbys 46 J2
Middleton Derbys 56 J14
Middleton Essex 40 E12
Middleton Hants 19 P12
Middleton Herefs 35 M7
Middleton Lancs 61 S8
Middleton Leeds 57 M14
Middleton N York 63 N4
Middleton N York 64 H2
Middleton Nhants 38 B3
Middleton Norfk 49 U10
Middleton Nthumb 77 M7
Middleton Nthumb 85 S11
Middleton P & K 90 H5
Middleton Rochdl 56 C5
Middleton Shrops 35 M6
Middleton Shrops 44 J7
Middleton Suffk 41 R7
Middleton Swans 25 R13
Middleton Warks 46 G14
Middleton Cheney
    Nhants 37 N12
Middleton Crematorium
    Rochdl 56 C5
Middleton Green Staffs 46 C6
Middleton Hall Nthumb 85 P13
Middleton-in-Teesdale
    Dur 68 K7
Middleton Moor Suffk 41 R7
Middleton One Row
    Darltn 70 E10
Middleton-on-Leven
    N York 70 G11
Middleton-on-Sea
    W Susx 10 F10
Middleton on the Hill
    Herefs 35 M8
Middleton on the Wolds
    E R Yk 65 L10
Middleton Park C Aber 105 Q13
Middleton Priors Shrops 35 P2
Middleton Quernhow
    N York 63 S4
Middleton St George
    Darltn 70 D10
Middleton Scriven
    Shrops 35 Q3
Middleton Stoney Oxon 30 B8
Middleton Tyas N York 69 R11
Middletown Cumb 66 E11
Middle Town IoS 2 b1
Middletown N Som 17 N2
Middletown Powys 44 H11
Middle Tysoe Warwks 36 K12
Middle Wallop Hants 19 L13
Middlewich Ches E 55 R14
Middle Winterslow Wilts 8 J2
Middlewood Cnwll 4 H6
Middle Woodford Wilts 8 G2
Middlewood Green Suffk 40 J8
Middleyard E Ayrs 81 P5
Middle Yard Gloucs 28 F7
Middlezoy Somset 17 L10
Midelney Somset 17 M12
Midge Hall Lancs 55 M2
Midgeholme Cumb 76 C14
Midgham W Berk 19 S7
Midgley Calder 56 F1
Midgley Wakefd 57 L3
Midhopestones Sheff 56 K7
Midhurst W Susx 10 D6
Mid Lavant W Susx 10 D9
Mid Mains Highld 102 D8
Midney Somset 17 N11
Midpark Ag & B 87 V4
Midsomer Norton BaNES 17 R6
Midtown Highld 111 N4
Mid Warwickshire
    Crematorium
    Warwks 36 J8
Midway Ches E 56 D10
Mid Yell Shet 106 v4
Migvie Abers 98 G2
Milborne Port Somset 17 S13
Milborne St Andrew
    Dorset 7 V5
Milborne Wick Somset 17 S12
Milbourne Nthumb 77 N10
Milbourne Wilts 28 J10
Milburn Cumb 68 E7
Milbury Heath S Glos 28 C10
Milby N York 63 U6
Milcombe Oxon 37 M14
Milden Suffk 40 G11
Mildenhall Suffk 40 B6
Mildenhall Wilts 18 K7
Mile Elm Wilts 18 E7
Mile End Essex 23 N3
Mile End Gloucs 27 U6
Mile Oak Br & H 11 L9
Mile Oak Kent 12 C7
Mileham Norfk 50 F11
Mile Town Kent 23 L13
Milesand Nthumb 85 N12
Miles Hope Herefs 35 M8
Miles Platting Manch 56 C7
Mile Town Kent 23 L13
Milfield Nthumb 85 N12
Milford Derbys 47 L4
Milford Powys 44 B2
Milford Staffs 46 C9
Milford Surrey 10 F2
Milford Haven Pembks 24 F9
Milford on Sea Hants 8 K10
Milkwall Gloucs 27 V6
Milkwell Wilts 8 C3
Millais Jersey 7 b1
Milland W Susx 10 C5
Millbank Calder 56 F2
Mill Bank Calder 56 F2
Millbeck Cumb 67 L8
Millbreck Abers 105 S7
Millbridge Surrey 10 D2
Millbrook C Beds 31 M5
Millbrook Cnwll 5 L10
Millbrook Jersey 7 b2
Millbrook C Sotn 9 M6
Millbrook Tamesd 56 E7
Mill Brow Stockp 56 E9
Millbuie Abers 99 N3
Millcombe Devon 5 U11
Millcorner E Susx 12 F11
Milldale Staffs 46 F2
Mill End Bucks 20 C5
Mill End Herts 39 N13
Millend Gloucs 28 D7
Mill End Cambs 39 U8
Millerhill Mdloth 83 R5
Miller's Dale Derbys 56 H12
Millers Green Derbys 46 J3
Miller's Green Essex 22 E6

Millerston C Glas 89 P12
Millgate Lancs 56 C3
Mill Green Cambs 39 T11
Mill Green Essex 22 F7
Mill Green Herts 31 R10
Mill Green Lincs 49 L9
Mill Green Norfk 40 K4
Mill Green Shrops 45 Q8
Mill Green Staffs 40 G12
Mill Green Staffs 46 E13
Mill Green Suffk 40 F11
Mill Green Suffk 40 G8
Mill Green Suffk 40 J9
Mill Green Suffk 40 H8
Millhalf Herefs 34 G11
Millhayes Devon 6 H4
Millhead Lancs 61 T5
Millheugh S Lans 82 D8
Mill Hill E Susx 11 U8
Mill Hill Gt Lon 21 M4
Millhouse Ag & B 87 T11
Millhouse Cumb 67 N5
Millhouse Green Barns 56 K6
Millhouses Sheff 57 M10
Milliken Park Rens 88 K13
Mill of Drummond P & K 89 S7
Mill of Haldane W Duns 88 J9
Millom Cumb 61 M3
Millook Cnwll 14 E13
Millpool Cnwll 4 E7
Millport N Ayrs 80 H2
Mill Side Cumb 61 S3
Mill Street Kent 12 C4
Mill Street Norfk 50 J10
Mill Street Suffk 40 H7
Millthorpe Derbys 57 M11
Millthrop Cumb 62 E1
Milltimber C Aber 99 S3
Millton of Auchindoun
    Moray 104 D7
Milltown Abers 98 D2
Milltown Cnwll 4 F8
Milltown D & G 75 R10
Milltown Derbys 57 M13
Milltown Devon 15 N5
Milltown of Campfield
    Abers 99 M3
Milltown of Edinville
    Moray 104 B7
Milltown of Learney
    Abers 99 L3
Milnathort P & K 90 H11
Milngavie E Duns 89 N11
Milnrow Rochdl 56 D4
Milnthorpe Cumb 61 T3
Milnthorpe Wakefd 57 M3
Milovaig Highld 100 a5
Milson Shrops 35 P5
Milstead Kent 12 H4
Milston Wilts 18 J11
Milthorpe Nhants 37 Q11
Milton C Stke 46 B3
Milton Cambs 39 Q8
Milton Cumb 76 B13
Milton D & G 72 G9
Milton D & G 74 H4
Milton D & G 75 P10
Milton Derbys 47 L8
Milton Highld 100 d5
Milton Highld 102 J6
Milton Highld 102 H9
Milton Highld 109 R8
Milton Highld 112 H6
Milton Inver 88 H11
Milton Kent 12 D2
Milton Moray 103 U12
Milton N Som 16 K4
Milton Newpt 27 R10
Milton Notts 58 B11
Milton Oxon 29 U3
Milton Oxon 37 N13
Milton P & K 89 U5
Milton Pembks 24 H10
Milton Somset 17 M11
Milton W Duns 88 K11
Milton Abbas Dorset 7 V4
Milton Abbot Devon 5 L5
Milton Bridge Mdloth 83 P5
Milton Bryan C Beds 31 L6
Milton Clevedon Somset 17 S9
Milton Combe Devon 5 M7
Milton Common Oxon 30 E12
Milton Damerel Devon 14 J10
Mildon End Gloucs 28 D7
Milton End Gloucs 29 M7
Milton Ernest Bed 38 F9
Milton Green Ches W 45 L2
Milton Hill Oxon 29 U9
Milton Keynes M Keyn 30 J5
Milton Lilbourne Wilts 18 J8
Milton Malsor Nhants 37 T9
Milton Morenish P & K 95 S10
Milton of Auchinhove
    Abers 98 K3
Milton of Balgonie Fife 91 M11
Milton of Buchanan
    Stirlg 88 K7
Milton of Campsie
    E Duns 89 P10
Milton of Leys Highld 102 J7
Milton of Murtle C Aber 99 R3
Milton of Tullich Abers 98 F4
Milton on Stour Dorset 17 U11
Milton Regis Kent 12 H3
Milton Street E Susx 11 S10
Milton-under-
    Wychwood Oxon 29 P5
Milverton Somset 16 F11
Milverton Warwks 36 K7
Milwich Staffs 46 C7
Milwr Flints 54 E12
Minard Ag & B 87 T6
Minchington Dorset 8 D6
Minchinhampton Gloucs 28 G7
Mindrum Nthumb 85 L12
Minehead Somset 16 C7
Minera Wrexhm 44 G3
Minety Wilts 28 K9
Minffordd Gwynd 43 L6
Mingarrypark Highld 93 S5
Miningsby Lincs 59 P14
Minions Cnwll 4 H6
Minishant S Ayrs 81 L10
Minllyn Gwynd 43 S11
Minnigaff D & G 73 M7
Minnis Bay Kent 13 Q2
Minnonie Abers 105 M3
Minshull Vernon Ches E 45 Q1
Minskip N York 63 T7
Minstead Hants 9 L6
Minster Kent 13 R2
Minster Kent 23 N13
Minsterley Shrops 44 J12
Minster Lovell Oxon 29 R5
Minsterworth Gloucs 28 E4
Minterne Magna Dorset 7 S3
Minterne Parva Dorset 7 S3
Minting Lincs 59 L13
Mintlaw Abers 105 R6
Mintlyn Crematorium
    Norfk 49 U10
Minto Border 76 B1
Minton Shrops 34 K2
Minwear Pembks 24 H8
Minworth Birm 36 G2
Mirbister Ork 106 s18
Mirehouse Cumb 66 E9
Mireland Highld 112 H4
Mirfield Kirk 56 K3
Miserden Gloucs 28 H6
Miserden Gloucs 28 H6
Miskin Rhondd 26 J11
Miskin Rhondd 26 K8
Misson Notts 57 U7
Misterton Leics 37 Q4
Misterton Notts 58 C7
Misterton Somset 7 M3
Mistley Essex 23 R1
Mistley Heath Essex 23 R1
Mitcham Gt Lon 21 N9
Mitcheldean Gloucs 28 C4
Mitchell Cnwll 3 M5
Mitchellslacks D & G 74 J6
Mitford Nthumb 77 P8
Mitian Cnwll 2 J6
Mixbury Oxon 30 C5
Mixenden Calder 56 G1
Mixon Staffs 46 D2
Miserden Gloucs 28 H6
Moats Tye Suffk 40 H9
Mobberley Ches E 55 S11
Mobberley Staffs 46 D4
Moccas Herefs 34 J12
Mochdre Conwy 53 P7
Mochdre Powys 34 C3
Mochrum D & G 72 J10
Mockbeggar Hants 8 H7
Mockbeggar Kent 12 D6
Mockerkin Cumb 66 H8
Modbury Devon 5 R10
Moddershall Staffs 46 B6
Moelfre IoA 52 H5
Moelfre Powys 44 E8
Moffat D & G 75 M5
Mogerhanger C Beds 38 J11
Moira Leics 46 K10
Molash Kent 12 K5

Mol-chlach Highld 100 d8
Mold Flints 54 F1
Moldgreen Kirk 56 J3
Molehill Green Essex 22 E2
Molehill Green Essex 22 H3
Molescroft E R Yk 65 M11
Molesden Nthumb 77 N9
Molesworth Cambs 38 G5
Molland Devon 15 U7
Mollington Ches W 54 J12
Mollington Oxon 37 M11
Mollinsburn N Lans 89 R11
Monachty Cerdgn 32 K8
Mondynes Abers 99 P8
Monewden Suffk 41 M9
Moneydie P & K 90 G6
Moneyrow Green W & M 20 E7
Moniaive D & G 74 F6
Monifieth Angus 91 Q5
Monikie Angus 91 Q4
Monimail Fife 91 L9
Monington Pembks 32 B12
Monk Bretton Barns 57 N5
Monken Hadley Gt Lon 21 N3
Monkhide Herefs 35 P11
Monkhill Cumb 75 R14
Monkhopton Shrops 35 P2
Monkland Herefs 34 K9
Monkleigh Devon 15 L8
Monknash V Glam 16 B2
Monkokehampton
    Devon 15 N11
Monkseaton N Tyne 77 S11
Monks Eleigh Suffk 40 G11
Monk's Gate W Susx 11 L5
Monks Heath Ches E 55 T12
Monk Sherborne Hants 19 T9
Monksilver Somset 16 E9
Monks Horton Kent 13 L7
Monkokehampton
    Devon 15 N11
Monks Kirby Warwks 37 N4
Monk Soham Suffk 41 L7
Monkspath Solhll 36 F5
Monks Risborough
    Bucks 30 H12
Monksthorpe Lincs 59 R13
Monkswood Mons 27 Q7
Monkton Devon 6 G4
Monkton Kent 13 Q3
Monkton S Ayrs 81 M7
Monkton V Glam 16 C3
Monkton Combe BaNES 17 T4
Monkton Deverill Wilts 18 C13
Monkton Farleigh Wilts 18 B7
Monkton Heathfield
    Somset 16 J11
Monkton Up Wimborne
    Dorset 8 E6
Monkton Wyld Dorset 6 K5
Monkwearmouth
    Sundld 77 T14
Monkwood Hants 9 U2
Monmore Green Wolves 46 B14
Monmouth Mons 27 U5
Monnington on Wye
    Herefs 34 J12
Monreith D & G 72 K11
Montacute Somset 17 N13
Montcliffe Bolton 55 Q4
Montford Shrops 44 K10
Montford Bridge Shrops 44 K10
Montgarrie Abers 104 H12
Montgomery Powys 34 F2
Montrose Angus 99 N13
Mont Saint Guern 7 b2
Monxton Hants 19 M12
Monyash Derbys 56 J13
Monymusk Abers 105 L12
Monzie P & K 90 C6
Moodiesburn N Lans 89 Q11
Moonzie Fife 91 M8
Moor Allerton Leeds 63 S12
Moorbath Dorset 7 M5
Moorby Lincs 59 N14
Moor Crichel Dorset 8 D7
Moordown Bmouth 8 F10
Moore Halton 55 N9
Moor End Calder 56 E1
Moor End Devon 15 U10
Moor End Gloucs 28 D7
Moorend Gloucs 28 E7
Moor End N York 64 H11
Moor End Lancs 61 R11
Moorends Donc 57 U3
Moor Green Herts 31 T7
Moor Green Wilts 18 B7
Moorgreen Hants 9 P6
Moorgreen Notts 47 N4
Moorhall Derbys 57 M12
Moorhampton Herefs 34 J11
Moorhead C Brad 63 P12
Moorhouse Cumb 67 M1
Moorhouse Cumb 67 N1
Moorhouse Notts 58 B13
Moorhouse Bank Surrey 21 R12
Moorland Somset 16 K10
Moorlinch Somset 16 L9
Moor Monkton N York 64 B9
Moor Row Cumb 66 F10
Moor Row Cumb 67 N3
Moorsholm R & Cl 71 L9
Moorside Dorset 17 U13
Moor Side Lancs 61 S13
Moor Side Lancs 62 B14
Moorside Leeds 63 Q12
Moorstock Kent 13 M8
Moorswater Cnwll 4 G8
Moor Street Medway 12 F2
Moorswater Cnwll 4 G8
Moorthorpe Wakefd 57 P4
Moortown Devon 5 N4
Moortown Hants 8 H8
Moortown IoW 9 N11
Moortown Leeds 63 R12
Moortown Lincs 58 J6
Morangie Highld 109 P8
Morar Highld 100 f10
Moray Crematorium
    Moray 104 D3
Morborne Cambs 38 H2
Morchard Bishop Devon 15 S11
Morcombelake Dorset 7 M6
Morcott Rutlnd 48 D13
Morda Shrops 44 G8
Morden Dorset 8 C9
Morden Gt Lon 21 M9
Mordiford Herefs 35 N13
Mordon Dur 70 D7
Morebath Devon 16 C12
Morebattle Border 84 K14
Morecambe Lancs 61 S7
Moredon Swindn 29 M10
Morefield Highld 107 U6
Morehall Kent 13 P8
Moreleigh Devon 5 T10
Morenish P & K 95 S11
Moresby Parks Cumb 66 E9
Morestead Hants 9 Q3
Moreton Dorset 7 V7
Moreton Essex 22 D6
Moreton Herefs 35 M8
Moreton Oxon 30 E12
Moreton Staffs 45 S10
Moreton Wirral 54 G9
Moreton Corbet Shrops 45 N9
Moretonhampstead
    Devon 5 T3
Moreton-in-Marsh
    Gloucs 29 P2
Moreton Jeffries Herefs 35 P11
Moretonmill Shrops 45 N9
Moreton Morrell Warwks 36 K9
Moreton on Lugg Herefs 35 M12
Moreton Paddox
    Warwks 36 K10
Moreton Pinkney
    Nhants 37 P11
Moreton Say Shrops 45 P7
Moreton Valence Gloucs 28 E6
Morfa Cerdgn 32 F10
Morfa Bychan Gwynd 42 K6
Morfa Dinlle Gwynd 52 F11
Morfa Glas Neath 26 E6
Morfa Nefyn Gwynd 42 E4
Morgan's Vale Wilts 8 H4
Morganstown Cardif 27 L11
Moriah Cerdgn 33 N5
Morland Cumb 68 D8
Morley Ches E 55 T10
Morley Derbys 47 L5
Morley Dur 69 Q7
Morley Leeds 57 L1
Morley Green Ches E 55 T10
Morley St Botolph Norfk 50 J14
Morningside Edin 83 P4
Morningside N Lans 82 F7
Morningthorpe Norfk 41 M2
Morpeth Nthumb 77 P8
Morphie Abers 99 N11
Morrey Staffs 46 F10
Morridge Side Staffs 46 E2
Morriston Swans 26 B8
Morston Norfk 50 H5
Mortehoe Devon 15 L3
Morthen Rothm 57 Q9
Mortimer W Berk 19 U8
Mortimer Common
    W Berk 19 U8
Mortimer's Cross Herefs 34 K8
Mortimer West End
    Hants 19 T8
Mortlake Gt Lon 21 L7
Mortlake Crematorium
    Gt Lon 21 L7
Morton Cumb 67 N3
Morton Derbys 47 M1
Morton IoW 9 S11
Morton Lincs 48 G9
Morton Lincs 58 D9
Morton Lincs 48 G14
Morton Norfk 51 M10
Morton Notts 47 U2
Morton Shrops 44 G9
Morton-on-Swale N York 63 S1
Morton on the Hill Norfk 50 K10
Morton Tinmouth Dur 69 Q8
Morvah Cnwll 2 C10
Morval Cnwll 4 H9
Morvich Highld 101 P7
Morville Shrops 35 Q2
Morville Heath Shrops 35 Q2
Morwenstow Cnwll 14 F9
Mosborough Sheff 57 P10
Moscow E Ayrs 81 P4
Mose Shrops 35 S2
Mosedale Cumb 67 N6
Moseley Birm 36 E4
Moseley Wolves 46 B14
Moseley Worcs 35 T9
Moss Ag & B 92 B10
Moss Donc 57 S4
Moss Wrexhm 44 H3
Moss Bank St Hel 55 M7
Mossbank Shet 106 u6
Mossbay Cumb 66 E7
Mossblown S Ayrs 81 N8
Mossbrow Traffd 55 R9
Mossburnford Border 76 C2
Mossdale D & G 73 R5
Mossdale E Ayrs 81 S11
Moss Edge Lancs 61 S11
Moss End Ches E 55 R10
Mosser Mains Cumb 66 H7
Mossley Ches E 45 U1
Mossley Tamesd 56 E6
Mossley Hill Lpool 54 J9
Moss-side Highld 103 N4
Moss Side Cumb 66 K2
Moss Side Lancs 61 R13
Moss Side Sefton 54 J6
Mosstodloch Moray 104 C4
Mosston Angus 91 R2
Mossy Lea Lancs 55 M4
Mossyard D & G 73 N9
Mosterton Dorset 7 N3
Moston Shrops 45 N8
Moston Green Ches E 45 S1
Mostyn Flints 54 D11
Motcombe Dorset 17 V12
Mothecombe Devon 5 Q11
Motherby Cumb 67 P7
Motherwell N Lans 82 D7
Motspur Park Gt Lon 21 M9
Mottingham Gt Lon 21 R8
Mottisfont Hants 9 L3
Mottistone IoW 9 N12
Mottram in
    Longdendale Tamesd 56 F8
Mottram St Andrew
    Ches E 56 C11

Mouilpied Guern 7 b2
Mouldsworth Ches W 55 M12
Moulin P & K 97 Q12
Moulsecoomb Br & H 11 N9
Moulsford Oxon 19 R4
Moulsoe M Keyn 38 D10
Moulton Ches W 55 Q13
Moulton Lincs 49 M9
Moulton N York 69 R12
Moulton Nhants 37 U7
Moulton Suffk 39 U8
Moulton V Glam 16 E2
Moulton Chapel Lincs 49 L10
Moulton Seas End Lincs 49 M8
Mount Cnwll 2 K5
Mount Cnwll 4 E7
Mount Kirk 56 G3
Mountain C Brad 63 M13
Mountain Ash Rhondd 26 K8
Mountain Cross Border 83 N9
Mountain Street Kent 13 L5
Mount Ambrose Cnwll 2 J8
Mount Bures Essex 40 F14
Mountfield E Susx 12 D11
Mountgerald House
    Highld 102 G3
Mount Hawke Cnwll 2 J7
Mount Hermon Cnwll 2 H13
Mountjoy Cnwll 3 M4
Mount Lothian Mdloth 83 P7
Mountnessing Essex 22 F8
Mounton Mons 27 U9
Mount Pleasant Ches E 45 U2
Mount Pleasant Derbys 46 K10
Mount Pleasant Derbys 47 L4
Mount Pleasant Dur 69 S6
Mount Pleasant E R Yk 65 S12
Mount Pleasant E Susx 11 Q7
Mount Pleasant Norfk 40 G2
Mount Pleasant Suffk 40 B11
Mountsett
    Crematorium Dur 69 Q2
Mountsorrel Leics 47 Q11
Mount Sorrel Wilts 8 E4
Mount Tabor Calder 56 F1
Mousehole Cnwll 2 D11
Mousehole Cnwll 2 D11
Mouswald D & G 75 L11
Mow Cop Ches E 45 T2
Mowhaugh Border 84 K13
Mowmacre Hill C Leic 47 Q12
Mowsley Leics 37 R3
Moy Highld 102 K8
Moy Highld 101 R8
Moyle Highld 101 P6
Moylegrove Pembks 32 B12
Muasdale Ag & B 79 L7
Much Birch Herefs 27 S2 (?)
Much Cowarne Herefs 35 P11
Much Dewchurch Herefs 27 S1
Muchelney Somset 17 M12
Muchelney Ham Somset 17 M12
Much Hadham Herts 22 B4
Much Hoole Lancs 55 L2
Much Hoole Town Lancs 55 L2
Muchlarnick Cnwll 4 G9
Much Marcle Herefs 35 Q14
Much Wenlock Shrops 45 P13
Muck Highld 93 M4
Mucking Thurr 22 G11
Muckingford Thurr 22 G12
Muckleford Dorset 7 R6
Mucklestone Staffs 45 S6
Muckley Shrops 35 P1
Muckton Lincs 59 Q11
Muddiford Devon 15 N5
Muddles Green E Susx 11 S8
Mudeford Dorset 8 H10
Mudford Somset 17 Q13
Mudford Sock Somset 17 Q13
Mudgley Somset 17 N7
Mugdock Stirlg 89 N10
Mugeary Highld 100 d6
Mugginton Derbys 46 J4
Muggintonlane End
    Derbys 46 J4
Muggleswick Dur 69 N2
Muirden Abers 105 L5
Muirdrum Angus 91 S4
Muiresk Abers 104 K6
Muirhead Angus 91 N5
Muirhead Fife 91 L10
Muirhead N Lans 82 C5
Muirhead S Ayrs 81 L5
Muirkirk E Ayrs 81 T8
Muirmill Stirlg 89 R9
Muir of Fowlis Abers 104 H12
Muir of Miltonduff
    Moray 103 U4
Muir of Ord Highld 102 G5
Muir of Ardblair
    P & K 90 J3
Muirshearlich Highld 94 G2
Muirtack Abers 105 R8
Muirton P & K 90 H6
Muirton Mains Highld 102 E5
Muirton of Ardblair
    P & K 90 J3
Muker N York 68 K13
Mulbarton Norfk 51 L13
Mulben Moray 104 C5
Mulfra Cnwll 2 D10
Mullacott Cross Devon 15 M3
Mullion Cnwll 2 H13
Mullion Cove Cnwll 2 H14
Mumby Lincs 59 T12
Mumbles Row Swans 25 V13
Munderfield Row Herefs 35 P9

Munderfield Stocks
    Herefs 35 Q10
Mundesley Norfk 51 P6
Mundford Norfk 40 D2
Mundham Norfk 51 P14
Mundon Essex 23 L7
Munlochy Highld 102 J5
Munnoch N Ayrs 80 K3
Munsley Herefs 35 Q12
Munslow Shrops 35 M3
Murchington Devon 5 S3
Murcott Oxon 30 C9
Murcott Wilts 28 J9
Murkle Highld 112 E4
Murlaggan Highld 101 Q13
Murrell Green Hants 20 B11
Murroes Angus 91 Q4
Murrow Cambs 49 N13
Mursley Bucks 30 H7
Murston Kent 12 J3
Murthill Angus 98 H12
Murthly P & K 90 H4
Murton Cumb 68 F8
Murton Dur 70 E3
Murton N Tyne 77 S11
Murton Nthumb 85 P10
Murton York 64 E9
Musbury Devon 6 K6
Muscoates N York 64 F3
Musselburgh E Loth 83 R4
Muston Leics 48 B6
Muston N York 65 P4
Mustow Green Worcs 35 T6
Muswell Hill Gt Lon 21 N5
Mutehill D & G 73 R10
Mutford Suffk 41 S4
Muthill P & K 90 C7
Mutterton Devon 6 D3
Muxton Wrekin 45 R10
Mybster Highld 112 E6
Myddfai Carmth 26 E2
Myddle Shrops 45 L8
Mydroilyn Cerdgn 32 J9
Myerscough Lancs 61 T12
Mylor Cnwll 3 L9
Mylor Bridge Cnwll 3 L9
Mynachlog ddu Pembks 24 K4
Mynydd-bach Mons 27 T8
Mynydd-bach Swans 25 V9
Mynydd-Bach Cerdgn 33 N5
Mynydd Buch Cerdgn 33 Q6
Mynyddgarreg Carmth 25 R9
Mynydd Isa Flints 54 G14
Mynydd Llandygai
    Gwynd 52 K9
Mynytho Gwynd 42 F7
Myrebird Abers 99 N4
Myredykes Border 76 B6
Mytchett Surrey 20 E11
Mytholm Calder 56 E1
Mytholmroyd Calder 56 F1
Mythop Lancs 61 R13
Myton-on-Swale N York 63 V6

N

Naast Highld 107 P8
Nab's Head Lancs 62 C14
Na Buirgh W Isls 106 f9
Nab Wood Crematorium
    C Brad 63 N12
Naccolt Kent 13 L7
Nackington Kent 13 N5
Nacton Suffk 41 M12
Nafferton E R Yk 65 P8
Nag's Head Gloucs 28 G8
Nailbridge Gloucs 28 C4
Nailsbourne Somset 16 H11
Nailsea N Som 17 N2
Nailstone Leics 47 M12
Nailsworth Gloucs 28 F8
Nairn Highld 103 M4
Nalderswood Surrey 21 M13
Nancegollan Cnwll 2 H10
Nancledra Cnwll 2 D9
Nanhoron Gwynd 42 E7
Nannerch Flints 54 E14
Nanpantan Leics 47 P11
Nanpean Cnwll 3 P5
Nanquidno Cnwll 2 B11
Nanstallon Cnwll 3 Q3
Nant-ddu Powys 26 K5
Nanternis Cerdgn 32 G9
Nantgaredig Carmth 25 S6
Nantgarw Rhondd 27 L10
Nant-glas Powys 33 U7
Nantglyn Denbgs 53 T13
Nantgwyn Powys 33 U5
Nant Peris Gwynd 52 K11
Nantlle Gwynd 52 H11
Nantmawr Shrops 44 G8
Nantmel Powys 34 B8
Nantmor Gwynd 43 L4
Nant Peris Gwynd 52 K11
Nantwich Ches E 45 Q3
Nant-y-Bwch Blae G 27 L6
Nant-y-caws Carmth 25 S7
Nant-y-derry Mons 27 Q6
Nantyffyllon Brdgnd 26 F9
Nantyglo Blae G 27 M6
Nant-y-gollen Shrops 44 G8
Nant-y-moel Brdgnd 26 G9
Nant-y-pandy Conwy 53 L8
Naphill Bucks 20 D3
Napleton Worcs 35 U11
Nappa N York 62 H9
Napton on the Hill
    Warwks 37 N8
Narborough Leics 37 P1
Narborough Norfk 50 B11
Narkurs Cnwll 4 J9
Nasareth Gwynd 42 H3
Naseby Nhants 37 S5
Nash Bucks 30 G5
Nash Gt Lon 21 R10
Nash Herefs 34 H8
Nash Newpt 27 Q11
Nash Shrops 35 P6
Nash Lee Bucks 30 H11
Nash's Green Hants 20 A12
Nassington Nhants 38 G1
Nastend Gloucs 28 E6
Nasty Herts 31 U8
Nateby Cumb 68 G11
Nateby Lancs 61 T11
Nately Scures Hants 20 A11
National Memorial
    Arboretum Staffs 46 G11
National Motor Museum
    (Beaulieu) Hants 9 M8
National Space Science
    Centre C Leic 47 Q12
Natland Cumb 61 U2
Naughton Suffk 40 H11
Naunton Gloucs 29 M3
Naunton Worcs 35 U13
Naunton Beauchamp
    Worcs 36 C10
Navenby Lincs 48 F2
Navestock Essex 22 D8
Navestock Side Essex 22 E8
Navidale House Hotel
    Highld 112 B13
Navity Highld 103 N3
Nawton N York 64 F3
Nayland Suffk 40 G13
Nazeing Essex 22 B6
Nazeing Gate Essex 22 B6
Neacroft Hants 8 H9
Neal's Green Warwks 36 K4
Neap Shet 106 v8
Near Cotton Staffs 46 E4
Near Sawrey Cumb 67 N13
Neasden Gt Lon 21 M5
Neasham Darltn 70 D10
Neath Neath 26 D8
Neath Abbey Neath 26 C8
Neatham Hants 10 A2
Neatishead Norfk 51 P9
Nebo Cerdgn 32 K7
Nebo Conwy 53 P11
Nebo Gwynd 42 H3
Nebo IoA 52 G4
Necton Norfk 50 E12
Nedd Highld 110 D10
Nedderton Nthumb 77 Q9
Nedging Suffk 40 G11
Nedging Tye Suffk 40 H11
Needham Norfk 41 M4
Needham Market Suffk 40 J9
Needham Street Suffk 40 B7
Needingworth Cambs 39 N6
Needwood Staffs 46 G9
Neen Savage Shrops 35 Q5
Neen Sollars Shrops 35 Q6
Neenton Shrops 35 P3
Nefyn Gwynd 42 F4
Neilston E Rens 81 N2
Nelson Caerph 27 L8
Nelson Lancs 62 H12
Nelson Village Nthumb 77 R10
Nemphlar S Lans 82 G10
Nempnett Thrubwell
    BaNES 17 P4
Nenthall Cumb 68 F3
Nenthead Cumb 68 G3
Nenthorn Border 84 G11

Nenthorn Border 84 H11
Neopardy Devon 15 S13
Nep Town W Susx 11 L8
Nercwys Flints 54 F1
Nereabolis Ag & B 78 C4
Nerston S Lans 81 R1
Nesbit Nthumb 85 N12
Nesfield N York 63 M10
Ness Ches W 54 H11
Nesscliffe Shrops 44 J10
Neston Ches W 54 G11
Neston Wilts 18 B7
Netchwood Shrops 35 P2
Nether Alderley Ches E 55 T11
Netheravon Wilts 18 H11
Nether Blainslie Border 84 E10
Netherbrae Abers 105 M4
Nether Broughton Leics 47 S9
Netherburn S Lans 82 F9
Netherbury Dorset 7 N5
Netherby Cumb 75 S11
Nether Cerne Dorset 7 S5
Nethercleuch D & G 75 M8
Nethercote Warwks 37 P7
Nethercott Devon 14 J13
Nether Dallachy Moray 104 D3
Netherend Gloucs 27 U7
Nether Exe Devon 6 B4
Netherfield E Susx 12 D12
Netherfield Notts 47 R5
Nethergate Norfk 50 J8
Nether Handley Derbys 57 P11
Nether Haugh Rothm 57 P7
Netherhampton Wilts 8 G3
Nether Headon Notts 58 B11
Nether Heage Derbys 47 L3
Nether Heyford Nhants 37 S9
Netherhay Dorset 7 M3
Nether Kellet Lancs 61 U6
Nether Kinmundy Abers 105 T7
Netherland Green Staffs 46 F7
Nether Langwith Notts 57 R12
Netherlaw D & G 73 S11
Netherley Abers 99 R4
Nethermill D & G 74 K9
Nethermuir Abers 105 R7
Netherne-on-the-Hill
    Surrey 21 N12
Netheroyd Hill Kirk 56 J3
Nether Padley Derbys 56 K11
Netherplace E Rens 81 P2
Nether Poppleton C York 64 D9
Nether Row Cumb 67 M4
Netherseal Derbys 46 K11
Nether Silton N York 64 B1
Nether Skyborry Shrops 34 G6
Nether Stowey Somset 16 G9
Nether Street Essex 22 E5
Netherthong Kirk 56 J4
Netherthorpe Derbys 57 Q11
Netherton Angus 98 J13
Netherton Devon 6 A8
Netherton Dudley 36 B3
Netherton Hants 19 M9
Netherton Herefs 27 U2
Netherton Kirk 56 J4
Netherton N Lans 82 E7
Netherton Nthumb 76 K4
Netherton Oxon 29 T8
Netherton P & K 90 J2
Netherton Sefton 54 J6
Netherton Shrops 35 R4
Netherton Stirlg 89 N10
Netherton Wakefd 57 L4
Netherton Worcs 36 C12
Nethertown Cumb 66 E11
Nethertown Highld 112 J1
Nethertown Lancs 61 T11
Nethertown Staffs 46 F10
Netherurd Border 83 M9
Nether Wallop Hants 19 L13
Nether Wasdale Cumb 66 J12
Nether Welton Cumb 67 M3
Nether Westcote Gloucs 29 P3
Nether Whitacre Warwks 36 H2
Netherwitton Nthumb 77 N6
Nether Winchendon
    Bucks 30 F10
Netherwood E Ayrs 81 U8
Nethy Bridge Highld 103 R11
Netley Hants 9 P7
Netley Marsh Hants 9 L6
Nettlebed Oxon 20 B5
Nettlebridge Somset 17 R7
Nettlecombe Dorset 7 P5
Nettlecombe IoW 9 Q13
Nettleden Herts 31 M10
Nettleham Lincs 58 H11
Nettlestead Kent 12 C5
Nettlestead Green Kent 12 C5
Nettlestone IoW 9 S10
Nettlesworth Dur 69 S3
Nettleton Lincs 58 K6
Nettleton Wilts 18 B5
Nettleton Shrub Wilts 18 B5
Netton Wilts 8 G2
Neuadd Carmth 25 U5
Neuadd-ddu Powys 33 T5
Nevendon Essex 22 H9
Nevern Pembks 24 J2
Nevill Holt Leics 38 B2
New Abbey D & G 74 J12
New Aberdour Abers 105 P3
New Addington Gt Lon 21 Q10
New Alresford Hants 9 S2
New Arram E R Yk 65 M11
New Ash Green Kent 12 B3
New Balderton Notts 48 B2
New Barn Kent 12 C2
New Barnet Gt Lon 21 N3
New Bewick Nthumb 85 Q14
Newbiggin Cumb 61 U2
Newbiggin Cumb 67 L7
Newbiggin Cumb 67 P4
Newbiggin Cumb 67 S5
Newbiggin Cumb 68 F9
Newbiggin Cumb 68 F7
Newbiggin Dur 68 K5
Newbiggin N York 62 K2
Newbiggin N York 63 L1
Newbiggin-by-the-Sea
    Nthumb 77 S8
Newbigging Angus 91 Q4
Newbigging Angus 91 R3
Newbigging Angus 91 P5
Newbigging S Lans 82 K9
Newbiggin-on-Lune
    Cumb 68 F12
New Bilton Warwks 37 N5
Newbold Derbys 57 N12
Newbold Leics 47 M10
Newbold on Avon
    Warwks 37 N5
Newbold on Stour
    Warwks 36 H11
Newbold Pacey Warwks 36 J9
Newbold Revel Warwks 37 N4
Newbold Verdon Leics 47 N13
New Bolingbroke Lincs 49 M2
Newborough C Pete 48 K12
Newborough IoA 52 F9
Newborough Staffs 46 F9
Newbottle Nhants 37 P13
Newbottle Sundld 70 D2
New Boultham Lincs 58 F12
Newbourne Suffk 41 M12
New Bradwell M Keyn 30 H4
New Brampton Derbys 57 N12
New Brancepeth Dur 69 R4
Newbridge C Edin 83 M4
Newbridge Caerph 27 N8
Newbridge Cerdgn 32 K10
Newbridge Cnwll 2 C10
Newbridge Cnwll 4 K8
New Bridge D & G 74 J10
Newbridge Hants 8 K6
Newbridge IoW 9 N11
Newbridge Oxon 29 T7
Newbridge Pembks 24 G5
Newbridge Wrexhm 44 G4
Newbridge Green Worcs 35 T13
Newbridge on Usk Mons 27 R9
Newbridge-on-Wye
    Powys 33 U9
New Brighton Flints 54 F13
New Brighton Hants 9 T7
New Brighton Wirral 54 H8
New Brinsley Notts 47 N3
New Broughton Wrexhm 44 H3
New Buckenham Norfk 40 J2
Newbuildings Devon 15 S12
Newburgh Abers 105 R4

Newburgh Abers 105 R10
Newburgh Abers 105 R4
Newburgh Fife 90 K8
Newburgh Lancs 55 L4
Newburgh Priory
    N York 64 C4
Newburn N u Ty 77 P12
Newbury Somset 17 S7
Newbury W Berk 19 Q7
Newbury Wilts 18 B11
Newbury Park Gt Lon 21 R5
Newby Cumb 67 S8
Newby Lancs 62 H10
Newby N York 62 E6
Newby N York 65 N1
Newby N York 70 H10
Newby Bridge Cumb 61 R2
Newby Cross Cumb 67 N2
Newby East Cumb 67 P2
Newby Head Cumb 68 E8
Newby West Cumb 67 N2
Newby Wiske N York 63 T2
Newcastle Mons 27 S4
Newcastle Shrops 34 G4
Newcastle Airport
    Nthumb 77 P11
Newcastle Emlyn
    Carmth 32 F12
Newcastleton Border 75 U8
Newcastle-under-Lyme
    Staffs 45 T4
Newcastle upon Tyne
    N u Ty 77 Q13
Newchapel Pembks 25 L3
Newchapel Staffs 45 U3
Newchapel Surrey 11 N2
Newchurch Blae G 27 M7
Newchurch Herefs 34 G10
Newchurch IoW 9 R11
Newchurch Kent 13 L9
Newchurch Mons 27 T9
Newchurch Powys 34 F10
Newchurch Staffs 46 F9
Newchurch in Pendle
    Lancs 62 G12
New Costessey Norfk 51 L11
New Cowper Cumb 66 J3
Newcraighall C Edin 83 R4
New Crofton Wakefd 57 N3
New Cross Cerdgn 33 M5
New Cross Gt Lon 21 Q7
New Cross Somset 17 M13
New Cumnock E Ayrs 81 S10
New Cut E Susx 12 E12
New Deer Abers 105 P6
New Delaval Nthumb 77 R10
New Delph Oldham 56 E5
New Denham Bucks 20 H5
Newdigate Surrey 10 K2
New Duston Nhants 37 T8
New Earswick C York 64 E8
New Eastwood Notts 47 N4
New Edlington Donc 57 R7
New Elgin Moray 104 A3
New Ellerby E R Yk 65 Q12
Newell Green Br For 20 E8
New Eltham Gt Lon 21 R8
New End Worcs 36 E8
Newenden Kent 12 F10
New England C Pete 48 J13
New England Essex 40 B12
Newent Gloucs 28 D3
New Farnley Leeds 63 R13
New Ferry Wirral 54 H9
Newfield Dur 69 R5
Newfield Dur 69 S2
Newfield Highld 109 P9
New Forest
    National Park Hants 8 K7
Newfound Hants 19 S10
New Fryston Wakefd 57 Q1
New Galloway D & G 73 Q4
Newgale Pembks 24 E6
New Gate Norfk 50 H5
Newgate Street Herts 31 S11
New Gilston Fife 91 Q10
New Grimsby IoS 2 b1
Newhall Ches E 45 Q4
Newhall Derbys 46 J9
Newham Nthumb 85 T13
New Hartley Nthumb 77 S10
Newhaven C Edin 83 Q3
Newhaven Derbys 56 H14
Newhaven E Susx 11 Q10
New Haw Surrey 20 J10
New Hedges Pembks 25 L10
New Herrington Sundld 70 D2
Newhey Rochdl 56 D4
New Holkham Norfk 50 F6
New Holland N Linc 59 L1
Newholm N York 71 Q10
New Houghton Derbys 57 R13
New Houghton Norfk 50 C8
New Houses N York 62 G5
New Houses Wigan 55 N6
New Hutton Cumb 61 U1
New Hythe Kent 12 D4
Newick E Susx 11 Q6
Newingreen Kent 13 M8
Newington Kent 13 N8
Newington Kent 12 G3
Newington Oxon 19 U2
Newington Shrops 34 K4
Newington Bagpath
    Gloucs 28 F9
New Inn Carmth 32 H12
New Inn Torfn 27 Q8
New Invention Shrops 34 G6
New Lakenham Norfk 51 M12
New Lanark S Lans 82 G11
New Lanark Village
    S Lans 82 G10
Newland C KuH 65 P13
Newland Gloucs 27 V6
Newland N York 57 U1
Newland Oxon 29 S5
Newland Somset 16 B9
Newland Worcs 35 S11
Newlandrig Mdloth 83 S6
Newlands Border 75 U6
Newlands Cumb 67 M5
Newlands Nthumb 77 L14
Newlands of Dundurcas
    Moray 104 B5
New Lane Lancs 54 K4
New Lane End Warrtn 55 P8
New Langholm D & G 75 R9
New Leake Lincs 49 Q2
New Leeds Abers 105 R5
New Longton Lancs 55 M1
New Luce D & G 72 F6
Newlyn Cnwll 2 D11
Newlyn East Cnwll 3 L5
Newmachar Abers 105 P12
Newmains N Lans 82 F6
New Malden Gt Lon 21 M9
Newman's End Essex 22 D5
Newman's Green
    Suffk 40 E12
Newmarket Suffk 39 U8
Newmarket W Isls 106 j5
New Marske R & Cl 70 K8
New Marston Oxon 30 B11
New Marton Shrops 44 H7
New Mill Abers 99 P4
New Mill Cnwll 2 D10
New Mill Herts 30 K10
New Mill Kirk 56 J5
New Mills Cnwll 3 M5
New Mills Derbys 56 E9
New Mills Mons 27 T6
New Mills Powys 44 B12
Newmill of Inshewan
    Angus 98 G11
New Milton Hants 8 J10
New Mistley Essex 23 R1
New Moat Pembks 24 H5
Newmore Highld 102 H2
Newnes Shrops 44 H6
New Ollerton Notts 57 U13
Newnham Gloucs 28 C5
Newnham Hants 20 B11
Newnham Herts 31 R5
Newnham Kent 12 H4
Newnham Nhants 37 Q9
Newnham Worcs 35 R7
Newnham Bridge Worcs 35 Q7
New Pitsligo Abers 105 P5
New Polzeath Cnwll 4 B5
Newport Cnwll 4 J4
Newport Devon 15 N5
Newport E R Yk 64 K13
Newport Essex 22 D1
Newport Gloucs 28 D8
Newport Highld 112 D12
Newport IoW 9 Q11
Newport Newpt 27 Q10
Newport Pembks 24 J3
Newport Wrekin 45 R10
Newport-on-Tay Fife 91 Q6

Newport Pagnell M Keyn 30 J4
Newport Pagnell Services M Keyn 30 J4
Newpound Common W Susx 10 H5
New Prestwick S Ayrs 81 L8
New Quay Cerdgn 32 G9
Newquay Cnwll 3 L4
New Quay Essex 23 P3
Newquay Airport Cnwll 3 M4
New Rackheath Norfk 51 N11
New Radnor Powys 34 F8
New Rent Cumb 67 Q5
New Ridley Nthumb 77 M14
New Road Side N York 62 K11
New Romney Kent 13 L11
New Rossington Donc 57 T7
New Row Cerdgn 33 P6
New Row Lancs 62 C12
New Sauchie Clacks 90 C13
Newsbank Ches E 55 T13
Newseat Abers 105 L9
Newsham Lancs 61 U12
Newsham N York 63 T3
Newsham N York 69 P10
Newsham Nthumb 77 S10
New Sharlston Wakefd 57 N3
Newsholme E R Yk 64 G14
Newsholme Lancs 62 G9
New Shoreston Nthumb 85 T12
New Silksworth Sundld 70 E2
New Skelton R & Cl 71 L9
Newsome Kirk 56 J4
New Somerby Lincs 48 D6
New Southgate Crematorium Gt Lon 21 N4
New Springs Wigan 55 N5
Newstead Border 84 F12
Newstead Notts 47 P3
Newstead Nthumb 85 T13
New Stevenston N Lans 82 E7
New Street Herefs 34 H9
New Swannington Leics 47 M10
Newthorpe N York 64 B13
Newthorpe Notts 47 N4
New Thundersley Essex 22 J10
Newtimber W Susx 11 M8
Newtoft Lincs 58 H9
Newton Ag & B 88 B6
Newton Border 76 C1
Newton Brdgnd 26 E12
Newton C Beds 31 R4
Newton Cambs 39 P11
Newton Cambs 49 P11
Newton Cardif 27 N12
Newton Ches W 45 M2
Newton Ches W 54 K13
Newton Ches W 55 M11
Newton Cumb 61 N5
Newton Derbys 47 M2
Newton Herefs 34 H14
Newton Herefs 34 J7
Newton Herefs 35 M10
Newton Highld 102 G5
Newton Highld 102 K6
Newton Highld 103 L2
Newton Highld 112 H7
Newton Lancs 61 Q12
Newton Lancs 62 B5
Newton Lincs 48 F6
Newton Mdloth 83 R5
Newton Moray 103 U3
Newton Moray 104 C3
Newton N York 64 K5
Newton Nhants 38 C4
Newton Norfk 50 D10
Newton Notts 47 S5
Newton Nthumb 76 J4
Newton Nthumb 77 L13
Newton S Lans 82 H12
Newton S Lans 89 Q13
Newton Sandw 36 D2
Newton Shrops 44 K7
Newton Somset 16 F9
Newton Staffs 46 D8
Newton Suffk 40 F12
Newton W Loth 83 L3
Newton Warwks 37 P5
Newton Wilts 8 J4
Newton Abbot Devon 5 V6
Newton Arlosh Cumb 66 K1
Newton Aycliffe Dur 69 S8
Newton Bewley Hartpl 70 G7
Newton Blossomville M Keyn 38 D10
Newton Bromswold Nhants 38 E7
Newton Burgoland Leics 47 L12
Newton-by-the-Sea Nthumb 85 U13
Newton by Toft Lincs 58 H9
Newton Ferrers Cnwll 4 J7
Newton Ferrers Devon 5 P11
Newton Ferry W Isls 106 d11
Newton Flotman Norfk 51 M14
Newtongrange Mdloth 83 R6
Newton Green Mons 27 U9
Newton Harcourt Leics 37 R1
Newton Heath Manch 56 C6
Newtonhill Abers 99 S5
Newton Hill Wakefd 57 M2
Newton-in-Bowland Lancs 62 D9
Newton Kyme N York 64 B11
Newton-le-Willows N York 63 Q2
Newton-le-Willows St Hel 55 N7
Newtonloan Mdloth 83 R6
Newton Longville Bucks 30 H6
Newton Mearns E Rens 81 Q1
Newtonmill Angus 99 L11
Newtonmore Highld 97 L4
Newton Morrell N York 69 R11
Newton Mountain Pembks 24 G9
Newton Mulgrave N York 71 N9
Newton of Balcanquhal P & K 90 J9
Newton of Balcormo Fife 91 R11
Newton on Ouse N York 64 C8
Newton-on-Rawcliffe N York 64 J1
Newton on the Hill Shrops 45 L9
Newton-on-the-Moor Nthumb 77 P4
Newton on Trent Lincs 58 D12
Newton Poppleford Devon 6 E7
Newton Purcell Oxon 30 D6
Newton Regis Warwks 46 J12
Newton Reigny Cumb 67 Q6
Newton St Cyres Devon 15 U13
Newton St Faith Norfk 51 M10
Newton St Loe BaNES 17 T4
Newton St Petrock Devon 14 K10
Newton Solney Derbys 46 J8
Newton Stacey Hants 19 P12
Newton Stewart D & G 73 L6
Newton Tony Wilts 18 K12
Newton Tracey Devon 15 M7
Newton under Roseberry R & Cl 70 J10
Newton Underwood Nthumb 77 N8
Newton upon Derwent E R Yk 64 G10
Newton Valence Hants 9 U2
Newton Wamphray D & G 75 M7
Newton with Scales Lancs 61 T13
Newtown Blae G 27 M6
Newtown Ches W 55 M11
Newtown Cnwll 2 F11
Newtown Cnwll 4 H5
Newtown Cumb 66 H3
Newtown Cumb 67 R8
Newtown Cumb 75 S13
Newtown Cumb 75 V13
Newtown D & G 74 E3
Newtown Derbys 56 E10
Newtown Devon 6 E5
Newtown Devon 15 S7
Newtown Dorset 7 N4
New Town Dorset 8 D5
New Town Dorset 8 D6
New Town Dorset 8 D7
New Town E Susx 11 R6
Newtown Gloucs 28 C7
Newtown Hants 8 K6
Newtown Hants 9 S6
Newtown Hants 19 Q8
Newtown Herefs 35 L9
Newtown Herefs 35 M14
Newtown Herefs 35 P11
Newtown Herefs 35 R13
Newtown Highld 96 D3
Newtown IoW 9 N10
Newtown Lancs 55 M3
New Town Nhants 38 E5
Newtown Nthumb 77 L5
Newtown Nthumb 85 P12
Newtown Nthumb 85 Q13
Newtown Poole 8 E10
Newtown Powys 34 D2
Newtown Rhondd 26 K8
Newtown Shrops 44 K9
Newtown Shrops 45 L7
Newtown Somset 6 J2
Newtown Staffs 46 B1
Newtown Staffs 46 C13
Newtown Wigan 55 N6
Newtown Wilts 8 C3
New Town Wilts 19 L6
Newtown Wilts 19 L8
Newtown Worcs 35 U9
Newtown Worcs 36 B5
Newtown-in-St Martin Cnwll 2 J12
Newtown Linford Leics 47 P12
Newtown of Beltrees Rens 88 J14
Newtown St Boswells Border 84 F12
Newtown Unthank Leics 47 N13
New Tredegar Caerph 27 L7
New Trows S Lans 82 F11
New Tupton Derbys 57 N13
Newtyle Angus 91 L3
New Walsoken Cambs 49 Q12
New Waltham NE Lin 59 N6
New Whittington Derbys 57 N11
New Winton E Loth 84 C4
New Yatt Oxon 29 S5
Newyears Green Gt Lon 20 J5
Newyork Ag & B 87 T3
New York Lincs 48 K2
New York N Tyne 77 S11
New York N York 63 P7
Nextend Herefs 34 H9
Neyland Pembks 24 G9
Niarbyl IoM 60 c7
Nibley Gloucs 28 C6
Nibley S Glos 28 C11
Nibley Green Gloucs 28 D8
Nicholashayne Devon 16 F13
Nicholaston Swans 25 T13
Nickies Hill Cumb 76 A12
Nidd N York 63 S7
Nigg C Aber 99 S3
Nigg Highld 109 Q10
Nigg Ferry Highld 109 P11
Nimlet BaNES 17 T2
Ninebanks Nthumb 68 G2
Nine Elms Swindn 29 M10
Nine Wells Pembks 24 C6
Ninfield E Susx 12 D13
Ningwood IoW 9 M11
Nisbet Border 84 H13
Nisbet Hill Border 84 K8
Niton IoW 9 Q13
Nitshill C Glas 89 M13
Noah's Ark Kent 21 U11
Noak Bridge Essex 22 G9
Noak Hill Gt Lon 22 D9
Noblethorpe Barns 57 L5
Nobold Shrops 45 L11
Nobottle Nhants 37 S8
Nocton Lincs 58 J14
Nogdam End Norfk 51 Q13
Noke Oxon 30 B10
Nolton Pembks 24 E7
Nolton Haven Pembks 24 E7
No Man's Heath Ches W 45 M4
No Man's Heath Warwks 46 J12
No Man's Land Cnwll 4 H9
Nomansland Devon 15 T10
Nomansland Wilts 8 K5
Noneley Shrops 45 L8
Nonington Kent 13 Q5
Nook Cumb 61 U3
Nook Cumb 75 U10
Norbiton Gt Lon 21 L9
Norbreck Bpool 61 Q11
Norbridge Herefs 35 R12
Norbury Ches E 45 N4
Norbury Derbys 46 F5
Norbury Gt Lon 21 P9
Norbury Shrops 34 J2
Norbury Staffs 45 S9
Norbury Common Ches E 45 N4
Norbury Junction Staffs 45 S9
Norchard Worcs 35 T7
Norcott Brook Ches W 55 P10
Norcross Lancs 61 Q11
Nordelph Norfk 49 S13
Norden Rochdl 56 C4
Nordley Shrops 35 Q1
Norfolk Broads Norfk 51 S12
Norham Nthumb 85 N9
Norland Town Calder 56 G2
Norley Ches W 55 N12
Norleywood Hants 9 M9
Norlington E Susx 11 Q8
Normanby N Linc 58 E3
Normanby N York 64 G3
Normanby R & Cl 70 H9
Normanby le Wold Lincs 58 K7
Norman Cross Cambs 38 J2
Normandy Surrey 20 F12
Norman's Bay E Susx 12 C14
Norman's Green Devon 6 E4
Normanton C Derb 46 K7
Normanton Leics 48 B5
Normanton Lincs 48 D4
Normanton Notts 47 T3
Normanton Rutlnd 48 D12
Normanton Wakefd 57 N2
Normanton Wilts 18 H12
Normanton le Heath Leics 47 L11
Normanton on Soar Notts 47 P9
Normanton on the Wolds Notts 47 R7
Normanton on Trent Notts 58 C13
Normoss Lancs 61 Q12
Norney Surrey 10 E2
Norrington Common Wilts 18 C8
Norris Green Cnwll 5 L7
Norris Green Lpool 54 J8
Norris Hill Leics 46 K10
Norristhorpe Kirk 56 K2
Northacre Norfk 50 G14
Northall Bucks 31 L8
Northallerton N York 70 E14
Northall Green Norfk 50 G11
Northam C Sotn 9 N6
Northam Devon 15 L7
Northampton Nhants 37 U8
Northampton Worcs 35 T7
Northampton Services Nhants 37 T9
North Anston Rothm 57 R10
North Ascot Br For 20 F9
North Aston Oxon 29 U2
Northaw Herts 31 S12
Northay Somset 6 J2
North Baddesley Hants 9 M4
North Ballachulish Highld 94 F6
North Barrow Somset 17 R11
North Barsham Norfk 50 F6
North Benfleet Essex 22 J10
North Bersted W Susx 10 E10
North Berwick E Loth 84 E1
North Bitchburn Dur 69 Q6
North Blyth Nthumb 77 S9
North Boarhunt Hants 9 S6
North Bockhampton Dorset 8 H9
Northborough C Pete 48 J12
Northbourne Kent 13 R5
Northbourne Oxon 19 S3
North Bovey Devon 5 S4
North Bradley Wilts 18 C9
North Brentor Devon 5 M4
North Brewham Somset 17 T9
North Bridge Surrey 10 F3
Northbridge Street E Susx 12 D11
Northbrook Hants 19 R13
Northbrook Oxon 29 U3
North Brook End Cambs 31 S4
North Buckland Devon 15 L4
North Burlingham Norfk 51 Q12
North Cadbury Somset 17 R11
North Carlton Lincs 58 F11
North Carlton Notts 57 S10
North Cave E R Yk 64 K13
North Cerney Gloucs 28 K6
North Chailey E Susx 11 P6
Northchapel W Susx 10 F5
North Charford Hants 8 H5
North Charlton Nthumb 85 T14
North Cheam Gt Lon 21 M9
North Cheriton Somset 17 S11
North Chideock Dorset 7 M6
Northchurch Herts 31 L11
North Cliffe E R Yk 64 K12
North Clifton Notts 58 D12
North Close Dur 69 S6
North Cockerington Lincs 59 Q8
North Connel Ag & B 94 C12
North Cornelly Brdgnd 26 E11
North Corner Cnwll 2 K13
North Cotes Lincs 59 P6
Northcott Devon 4 J2
Northcott Devon 6 E2
Northcott Devon 6 F3
North Country Cnwll 2 H8
Northcourt Oxon 29 U8
North Cove Suffk 41 S3
North Cowton N York 69 S12
North Crawley M Keyn 30 K4
North Cray Gt Lon 21 S8
North Creake Norfk 50 E6
North Curry Somset 16 K11
North Dalton E R Yk 65 L9
North Deighton N York 63 T9
North Devon Crematorium Devon 15 M6
Northdown Kent 13 S1
North Downs 12 H4
North Duffield N York 64 F12
North Duntulm Highld 100 d2
North East Surrey Crematorium Gt Lon 21 M9
Northedge Derbys 57 N13
North Elham Kent 13 N7
North Elkington Lincs 59 N8
North Elmham Norfk 50 G9
North Elmsall Wakefd 57 Q4
Northend Bucks 20 B4
North End C Port 9 T8
North End Cumb 75 R14
North End Dorset 8 A3
North End E R Yk 65 R11
North End E R Yk 65 T13
North End Essex 22 G4
North End Hants 8 G5
North End Hants 9 R3
North End Leics 47 Q10
North End Lincs 48 K5
North End Lincs 58 H7
North End Lincs 59 P6
North End Lincs 59 R9
North End N Linc 58 K2
North End N Som 17 M3
North End Nhants 38 E7
North End Norfk 40 G2
North End Nthumb 77 N5
North End Sefton 54 H6
North End W Susx 10 F10
North End W Susx 10 J9
Northend Warwks 37 L10
Northenden Manch 55 T9
Northend Woods Bucks 20 F5
North Erradale Highld 107 M8
North Evington C Leic 47 R13
North Fambridge Essex 23 L8
North Ferriby E R Yk 58 G1
Northfield Birm 36 D5
Northfield C Aber 99 S2
Northfield E R Yk 58 H1
Northfields Lincs 48 F12
Northfleet Kent 22 F13
North Frodingham E R Yk 65 Q9
North Gorley Hants 8 H6
North Green Norfk 41 M3
North Green Suffk 41 P8
North Green Suffk 41 Q7
North Greetwell Lincs 58 H12
North Grimston N York 64 J6
North Halling Medway 12 D2
North Hayling Hants 9 U8
North Hazelrigg Nthumb 85 R12
North Heasley Devon 15 R6
North Heath W Susx 10 H6
North Hele Devon 16 D12
North Hill Cnwll 4 H5
North Hillingdon Gt Lon 20 J6
North Hinksey Village Oxon 29 U6
North Holmwood Surrey 21 L13
North Huish Devon 5 S9
North Hykeham Lincs 58 F13
Northiam E Susx 12 F11
Northill C Beds 38 H11
Northington Gloucs 28 D6
Northington Hants 19 S13
North Kelsey Lincs 58 H6
North Kessock Highld 102 J6
North Killingholme N Linc 58 K3
North Kilvington N York 63 U2
North Kilworth Leics 37 R4
North Kingston Hants 8 H8
North Kyme Lincs 48 J3
North Landing E R Yk 65 S5
Northlands Lincs 49 M3
Northleach Gloucs 29 M5
North Lee Bucks 30 H11
North Lees N York 63 R5
Northleigh Devon 6 G5
Northleigh Devon 15 P6
North Leigh Kent 13 M6
North Leigh Oxon 29 S5
North Leverton with Habblesthorpe Notts 58 C10
Northlew Devon 15 M13
North Littleton Worcs 36 E11
Northload Bridge Somset 17 N9
North Lopham Norfk 40 H4
North Luffenham Rutlnd 48 D13
North Marden W Susx 10 C7
North Marston Bucks 30 G8
North Middleton Mdloth 83 S7
North Middleton Nthumb 85 P14
North Millbrex Abers 105 N7
North Milmain D & G 72 D9
North Molton Devon 15 R7
Northmoor Oxon 29 T7
North Moreton Oxon 19 S3
Northmuir Angus 98 F13
North Mundham W Susx 10 D10
North Muskham Notts 47 U2
North Newbald E R Yk 65 L12
North Newington Oxon 37 M12
North Newnton Wilts 18 H9
North Newton Somset 16 K10
Northney Hants 9 U8
North Nibley Gloucs 28 D8
North Oakley Hants 19 R10
North Ockendon Gt Lon 22 E10
Northolt Gt Lon 20 K6
Northop Flints 54 F13
Northop Hall Flints 54 G13
North Ormesby Middsb 70 H9
North Ormsby Lincs 59 N8
Northorpe Kirk 56 K2
Northorpe Lincs 48 G10
Northorpe Lincs 48 K6
Northorpe Lincs 58 E7
North Otterington N York 63 T2
Northover Somset 17 N9
Northover Somset 17 P12
North Owersby Lincs 58 J8
Northowram Calder 56 H1
North Perrott Somset 7 N3
North Petherton Somset 16 J10
North Petherwin Cnwll 4 H3
North Pickenham Norfk 50 E12
North Piddle Worcs 36 C10
North Poorton Dorset 7 P5
Northport Dorset 8 C11
North Poulner Hants 8 H7
North Queensferry Fife 83 M2
North Radworthy Devon 15 S6
North Rauceby Lincs 48 F4
Northrepps Norfk 51 M6
North Reston Lincs 59 Q10
North Rigton N York 63 R10
North Ripley Hants 8 H9
North Rode Ches E 56 C13
North Ronaldsay Ork 106 w14
North Ronaldsay Airport Ork 106 w14
North Row Cumb 66 K6
North Runcton Norfk 49 T10
North Scale Cumb 61 M6
North Scarle Lincs 58 D13
North Seaton Nthumb 77 R8
North Seaton Colliery Nthumb 77 R8
North Shian Ag & B 94 C10
North Shields N Tyne 77 T12
North Shoebury Sthend 23 M10
North Shore Bpool 61 Q12
North Side C Pete 49 L14
North Side Cumb 66 E7
North Skelton R & Cl 71 L9
North Somercotes Lincs 59 R7
North Stainley N York 63 R4
North Stainmore Cumb 68 H10
North Stifford Thurr 22 F11
North Stoke BaNES 17 T3
North Stoke Oxon 19 T3
North Stoke W Susx 10 G8
North Street Cambs 39 S7
North Street Hants 8 H5
North Street Hants 9 S2
North Street Kent 12 K4
North Street Medway 22 K13
North Street W Berk 19 T6
North Sunderland Nthumb 85 U12
North Tamerton Cnwll 14 H13
North Tawton Devon 15 Q12
North Third Stirlg 89 S8
North Thoresby Lincs 59 N7
North Togston Nthumb 77 Q5
Northton W Isls 106 e10
North Town Devon 15 M11
North Town Somset 17 Q8
North Town W & M 20 E6
North Tuddenham Norfk 50 H11
North Uist W Isls 106 c11
Northumberland National Park Nthumb 76 H5
North Walbottle N u Ty 77 P12
North Walsham Norfk 51 N7
North Waltham Hants 19 S11
North Warnborough Hants 20 B12
Northway Somset 16 F11
Northway Swans 25 U13
North Weald Bassett Essex 22 C7
North Wheatley Notts 58 C9
North Whilborough Devon 5 V7
Northwich Ches W 55 Q12
North Wick BaNES 17 Q3
Northwick S Glos 27 V10
Northwick Somset 17 L7
Northwick Worcs 35 T9
North Widcombe BaNES 17 Q5
North Willingham Lincs 59 L9
North Wingfield Derbys 57 P13
North Witham Lincs 48 D9
Northwold Norfk 40 C1
Northwood C Stke 45 U4
Northwood Derbys 57 L14
Northwood Gt Lon 20 J4
Northwood IoW 9 P10
Northwood Shrops 45 L7
Northwood Green Gloucs 28 D4
North Wootton Dorset 7 S2
North Wootton Norfk 49 T9
North Wootton Somset 17 Q8
North Wraxall Wilts 18 B5
North Wroughton Swindn 18 H4
North York Moors National Park 71 M12
Norton Donc 57 R3
Norton E Susx 11 R10
Norton Gloucs 28 G3
Norton Halton 55 N10
Norton Herts 31 R6
Norton IoW 9 L11
Norton Mons 27 S3
Norton N Som 16 K4
Norton N York 64 H5
Norton Nhants 37 Q8
Norton Notts 57 S12
Norton Powys 34 H7
Norton S on T 70 F8
Norton Sheff 57 N10
Norton Shrops 35 L4
Norton Shrops 35 P4
Norton Shrops 45 N12
Norton Shrops 45 R13
Norton Suffk 40 G7
Norton Swans 25 V13
Norton W Susx 10 E9
Norton Wilts 28 G11
Norton Worcs 35 U10
Norton Worcs 36 D11
Norton Bavant Wilts 18 D12
Norton Bridge Staffs 45 U7
Norton Canes Staffs 46 D12
Norton Canes Services Staffs 46 D12
Norton Canon Herefs 34 J11
Norton Corner Norfk 50 J8
Norton Disney Lincs 48 C2
Norton Ferris Wilts 17 U9
Norton Fitzwarren Somset 16 G11
Norton Green IoW 9 L11
Norton Hawkfield BaNES 17 Q4
Norton Heath Essex 22 F7
Norton in Hales Shrops 45 R6
Norton in the Moors C Stke 45 U3
Norton-Juxta-Twycross Leics 46 K12
Norton-le-Clay N York 63 U5
Norton Lindsey Warwks 36 H8
Norton Little Green Suffk 40 G7
Norton Malreward BaNES 17 R4
Norton Mandeville Essex 22 E7
Norton St Philip Somset 17 U5
Norton Subcourse Norfk 51 R14
Norton sub Hamdon Somset 17 N13
Norton Wood Herefs 34 J11
Norwell Notts 47 U1
Norwell Woodhouse Notts 58 B14
Norwich Norfk 51 M12
Norwich Airport Norfk 51 M11
Norwich (St Faith) Crematorium Norfk 51 M10
Norwick Shet 106 w2
Norwood Clacks 90 C13
Norwood Derbys 57 Q10
Norwood Kent 13 L9
Norwood End Essex 22 E6
Norwood Green Calder 56 H1
Norwood Green Gt Lon 20 K7
Norwood Hill Surrey 11 L2
Norwoodside Cambs 49 P14
Noseley Leics 47 T14
Noss Mayo Devon 5 P11
Nosterfield N York 63 R3
Nosterfield End Cambs 39 T12
Nostie Highld 101 M6
Notgrove Gloucs 29 M3
Nottage Brdgnd 26 E12
Notter Cnwll 4 K8
Nottingham C Nott 47 Q6
Nottington Dorset 7 S8
Notton Wakefd 57 M4
Notton Wilts 18 D7
Nounsley Essex 22 J5
Noutard's Green Worcs 35 T7
Nowton Suffk 40 E8
Nox Shrops 44 K11
Nuffield Oxon 19 U3
Nunburnholme E R Yk 64 J10
Nuncargate Notts 47 P3
Nunclose Cumb 67 Q3
Nuneaton Warwks 37 L2
Nuneham Courtenay Oxon 30 C13
Nunhead Gt Lon 21 P7
Nunkeeling E R Yk 65 Q10
Nun Monkton N York 64 C8
Nunney Somset 17 T7
Nunney Catch Somset 17 T8
Nunnington Herefs 35 N12
Nunnington N York 64 F4
Nunsthorpe NE Lin 59 N5
Nunthorpe C York 64 E9
Nunthorpe Middsb 70 H10
Nunthorpe Village Middsb 70 H10
Nunton Wilts 8 H3
Nunwick N York 63 S5
Nunwick Nthumb 76 H11
Nupdown S Glos 28 B8
Nup End Bucks 30 J9
Nupend Gloucs 28 E6
Nuptown Br For 20 E8
Nursling Hants 9 M5
Nursted Hants 10 B6
Nursteed Wilts 18 F8
Nurton Staffs 45 T14
Nutbourne W Susx 10 B9
Nutbourne W Susx 10 H7
Nutfield Surrey 21 P12
Nuthall Notts 47 P5
Nuthampstead Herts 39 P14
Nuthurst W Susx 10 K5
Nutley E Susx 11 Q5
Nutley Hants 19 T12
Nuttall Bury 55 S3
Nutwell Donc 57 T6
Nybster Highld 112 J4
Nyetimber W Susx 10 D11
Nyewood W Susx 10 C6
Nymans W Susx 11 M5
Nymet Rowland Devon 15 R11
Nymet Tracey Devon 15 R12
Nympsfield Gloucs 28 F7
Nynehead Somset 16 F12
Nythe Somset 17 M10
Nyton W Susx 10 E9

O

Oadby Leics 47 R13
Oad Street Kent 12 G3
Oakall Green Worcs 35 T8
Oakamoor Staffs 46 D5
Oakbank W Loth 83 L5
Oak Cross Devon 15 M13
Oakdale Caerph 27 M8
Oake Somset 16 G11
Oaken Staffs 45 U13
Oakenclough Lancs 61 U10
Oakengates Wrekin 45 R11
Oakenholt Flints 54 G12
Oakenshaw Dur 69 Q5
Oakenshaw Kirk 63 P14
Oakerthorpe Derbys 47 L3
Oakford Cerdgn 32 J9
Oakford Devon 16 B12
Oakfordbridge Devon 16 B12
Oakgrove Ches E 56 D13
Oakham Rutlnd 48 C12
Oakhanger Ches E 45 S3
Oakhanger Hants 10 B3
Oakhill Somset 17 R7
Oakhurst Kent 21 U12
Oakington Cambs 39 P8
Oaklands Powys 34 B10
Oakle Street Gloucs 28 E4
Oakley Bed 38 F10
Oakley Bucks 30 D10
Oakley Fife 90 F14
Oakley Hants 19 S10
Oakley Oxon 30 G12
Oakley Poole 8 E9
Oakley Suffk 41 L5
Oakley Green W & M 20 F7
Oakley Park Powys 33 U3
Oakridge Gloucs 28 H7
Oaks Lancs 62 D13
Oaks Shrops 44 K13
Oaksey Wilts 28 J9
Oaks Green Derbys 46 G7
Oakshaw Ford Cumb 75 V10
Oakshott Hants 9 U3
Oakthorpe Leics 46 K11
Oak Tree Darltn 70 E10
Oakwood C Derb 47 L6
Oakwood Nthumb 76 J12
Oakworth C Brad 63 L12
Oare Kent 12 K3
Oare Somset 15 S3
Oare Wilts 18 J8
Oasby Lincs 48 F6
Oath Somset 17 L11
Oathlaw Angus 98 H12
Oatlands Park Surrey 20 J9
Oban Ag & B 94 B13
Oban Airport Ag & B 94 C11
Obley Shrops 34 H5
Obney P & K 90 F4
Oborne Dorset 17 S13
Obthorpe Lincs 48 G11
Occold Suffk 41 L6
Occumster Highld 112 G9
Ochiltree E Ayrs 81 Q8
Ockbrook Derbys 47 M6
Ocker Hill Sandw 36 C2
Ockeridge Worcs 35 S8
Ockham Surrey 20 J11
Ockle Highld 93 P4
Ockley Surrey 10 J2
Ocle Pychard Herefs 35 N11
Octon E R Yk 65 N6
Odcombe Somset 17 P13
Odd Down BaNES 17 T4
Oddingley Worcs 36 B9
Oddington Gloucs 29 P2
Oddington Oxon 30 C9
Odell Bed 38 E9
Odham Devon 15 L12
Odiham Hants 20 B12
Odsal C Brad 63 P14
Odsey Cambs 31 S5
Odstock Wilts 8 G3
Odstone Leics 47 L12
Offchurch Warwks 37 L7
Offenham Worcs 36 E11
Offerton Stockp 56 D9
Offerton Sundld 70 D1
Offham E Susx 11 Q8
Offham Kent 12 C4
Offham W Susx 10 G9
Offleymarsh Staffs 45 S8
Offord Cluny Cambs 38 K7
Offord D'Arcy Cambs 38 K7
Offton Suffk 40 J11
Offwell Devon 6 G5
Ogbourne Maizey Wilts 18 J6
Ogbourne St Andrew Wilts 18 J6
Ogbourne St George Wilts 18 K6
Ogden Calder 63 M13
Ogle Nthumb 77 N10
Oglet Lpool 54 K10
Ogmore V Glam 26 F12
Ogmore-by-Sea V Glam 26 F12
Ogmore Vale Brdgnd 26 G9
Ogwen Bank Gwynd 52 K9
Okeford Fitzpaine Dorset 7 V2
Okehampton Devon 15 N13
Oker Side Derbys 46 J1
Okewood Hill Surrey 10 J3
Olchard Devon 6 A9
Old Nhants 37 U6
Old Aberdeen C Aber 99 S2
Old Alresford Hants 9 R2
Oldany Highld 110 B10
Old Auchenbrack D & G 74 E6
Old Basford C Nott 47 Q5
Old Basing Hants 19 U10
Old Beetley Norfk 50 G10
Oldberrow Warwks 36 F7
Old Bewick Nthumb 77 M1
Old Bolingbroke Lincs 59 Q13
Old Bramhope Leeds 63 Q11
Old Brampton Derbys 57 M12
Old Bridge of Urr D & G 74 E12
Old Buckenham Norfk 40 J2
Old Burghclere Hants 19 Q9
Oldbury Kent 21 U11
Oldbury Sandw 36 C3
Oldbury Shrops 35 R2
Oldbury Warwks 36 K2
Oldbury Naite S Glos 28 B9
Oldbury-on-Severn S Glos 28 B9
Oldbury on the Hill Gloucs 28 F10
Old Byland N York 64 D2
Old Cantley Donc 57 T6
Old Cassop Dur 70 D5
Old Castle Brdgnd 26 G12
Oldcastle Mons 27 Q3
Oldcastle Heath Ches W 45 L4
Old Catton Norfk 51 M11
Old Churchstoke Powys 34 G2
Old Clee NE Lin 59 N5
Old Cleeve Somset 16 D8
Old Clipstone Notts 57 T14
Old Colwyn Conwy 53 Q7
Oldcotes Notts 57 S9
Old Dailly S Ayrs 80 J13
Old Dalby Leics 47 S9
Old Dam Derbys 56 H11
Old Deer Abers 105 R6
Old Ditch Somset 17 P7
Old Edlington Donc 57 R7
Old Eldon Dur 69 R7
Old Ellerby E R Yk 65 R12
Old Felixstowe Suffk 41 P13
Oldfield C Brad 63 L12
Oldfield Worcs 35 T8
Old Fletton C Pete 38 J1
Oldford Somset 17 U6
Old Forge Herefs 27 V4
Old Furnace Herefs 27 T3
Old Glossop Derbys 56 F8
Old Goole E R Yk 58 B2
Old Grimsby IoS 2 b1
Old Hall Green Herts 31 U8
Oldhall Green Suffk 40 E9
Old Hall Street Norfk 51 P7
Oldham Oldham 56 D6
Oldhamstocks E Loth 84 J4
Old Harlow Essex 22 C5
Old Heath Essex 23 P3
Old Hunstanton Norfk 49 U5
Old Hurst Cambs 39 M5
Old Hutton Cumb 62 B2
Old Kea Cnwll 3 L8
Old Kilpatrick W Duns 89 L11
Old Knebworth Herts 31 R8
Old Lakenham Norfk 51 M12
Oldland S Glos 17 S2
Old Langho Lancs 62 E12
Old Laxey IoM 60 g6
Old Leake Lincs 49 P3
Old Malton N York 64 H5
Oldmeldrum Abers 105 N10
Oldmill Cnwll 4 K6
Old Milverton Warwks 36 J7
Oldmixon N Som 16 K5
Old Newton Suffk 40 J8
Old Quarrington Dur 70 D5
Old Radford C Nott 47 Q5
Old Radnor Powys 34 G9
Old Rayne Abers 104 K10
Old Romney Kent 12 K11
Old Shoreham W Susx 11 L9
Oldshoremore Highld 110 E5
Old Soar Kent 12 B5
Old Sodbury S Glos 28 E11
Old Somerby Lincs 48 E7
Oldstead N York 64 C4
Old Stratford Nhants 30 G4
Old Struan P & K 97 N10
Old Swarland Nthumb 77 P5
Old Swinford Dudley 36 B4
Old Tebay Cumb 68 D11
Old Thirsk N York 63 U3
Old Town Calder 63 L14
Old Town Cumb 62 B3
Old Town Cumb 67 Q4
Old Town E Susx 11 T11
Old Town IoS 2 c2
Old Trafford Traffd 55 T7
Old Tupton Derbys 57 N13
Oldwall Cumb 75 U13
Oldwalls Swans 25 S12
Old Warden C Beds 31 P4
Oldways End Somset 15 U8
Old Weston Cambs 38 G5
Old Wick Highld 112 J7
Old Windsor W & M 20 G8
Old Wives Lees Kent 13 L5
Old Woking Surrey 20 H11
Old Wolverton M Keyn 30 H4
Old Woodhall Lincs 59 M13
Old Woods Shrops 45 L9
Olgrinmore Highld 112 C6
Olive Green Staffs 46 F10
Oliver's Battery Hants 9 P3
Ollaberry Shet 106 t5
Ollach Highld 100 e6
Ollerton Ches E 55 S11
Ollerton Notts 57 U13
Ollerton Shrops 45 P8
Olmarch Cerdgn 33 M9
Olmstead Green Cambs 39 T12
Olney M Keyn 38 C10
Olrig House Highld 112 E3
Olton Solhll 36 F4
Olveston S Glos 28 B10
Ombersley Worcs 35 T8
Ompton Notts 57 U13
Once Brewed Nthumb 76 E12
Onchan IoM 60 f7
Onecote Staffs 46 D2
Onehouse Suffk 40 H9
Onen Mons 27 S5
Ongar Street Herefs 34 J7
Onibury Shrops 35 L5
Onich Highld 94 E6
Onllwyn Neath 26 E5
Onneley Staffs 45 S5
Onslow Green Essex 22 G4
Onslow Village Surrey 20 G13
Onston Ches W 55 N12
Openwoodgate Derbys 47 L4
Opinan Highld 107 M10
Orbliston Moray 104 C4
Orbost Highld 100 b5
Orby Lincs 59 S13
Orchard Portman Somset 16 H12
Orcheston Wilts 18 G11
Orcop Herefs 27 T2
Orcop Hill Herefs 27 T2
Ord Abers 104 J4
Ordhead Abers 104 K13
Ordie Abers 98 H3
Ordiequish Moray 104 C4
Ordley Nthumb 76 J14
Ordsall Notts 58 B11
Ore E Susx 12 F13
Oreleton Common Herefs 35 L7
Oreton Shrops 35 Q4
Orford Suffk 41 R10
Orford Warrtn 55 P8
Organford Dorset 8 C10
Orgreave Staffs 46 F10
Orkney Islands Ork 106 t19
Orkney, Heart of Neolithic Ork 106 r18
Orlestone Kent 12 K9
Orleton Herefs 35 L7
Orleton Worcs 35 R7
Orlingbury Nhants 38 C6
Ormathwaite Cumb 67 L7
Ormesby R & Cl 70 H9
Ormesby St Margaret Norfk 51 S11
Ormesby St Michael Norfk 51 S11
Ormiscaig Highld 107 Q6
Ormiston E Loth 83 T5
Ormsaigmore Highld 93 M6
Ormsary Ag & B 87 N11
Ormskirk Lancs 54 K5
Ornsby Hill Dur 69 Q3
Oronsay Ag & B 86 F8
Orphir Ork 106 s19
Orpington Gt Lon 21 S9
Orrell Sefton 54 H7
Orrell Wigan 55 M6
Orrell Post Wigan 55 M5
Orrisdale IoM 60 e4
Orroland D & G 73 T10
Orsett Thurr 22 F11
Orslow Staffs 45 T10
Orston Notts 47 U5
Orthwaite Cumb 67 L6
Ortner Lancs 61 U9
Orton Cumb 68 D11
Orton Nhants 38 B5
Orton Staffs 35 U1
Orton Longueville C Pete 38 J1
Orton-on-the-Hill Leics 46 K13
Orton Rigg Cumb 67 M2
Orton Waterville C Pete 38 J1
Orwell Cambs 39 N10
Osbaldeston Lancs 62 C13
Osbaldeston Green Lancs 62 C13
Osbaldwick C York 64 E9
Osbaston Leics 47 M13
Osbaston Shrops 44 H9
Osborne IoW 9 Q10
Osborne House IoW 9 Q10
Osbournby Lincs 48 G6
Oscroft Ches W 55 M13
Ose Highld 100 c5
Osgathorpe Leics 47 M10
Osgodby Lincs 58 J8
Osgodby N York 64 E13
Osgodby N York 65 P3
Oskaig Highld 100 e6
Oskamull Ag & B 93 M10
Osmaston Derbys 46 G5
Osmington Dorset 7 T8
Osmington Mills Dorset 7 T8
Osmondthorpe Leeds 63 S13
Osmotherley N York 70 G13
Osney Oxon 29 U6
Ospringe Kent 12 K3
Ossett Wakefd 57 L2
Ossington Notts 58 C14
Ostend Essex 23 M8
Osterley Gt Lon 21 L7
Oswaldkirk N York 64 E4
Oswaldtwistle Lancs 55 R1
Oswestry Shrops 44 G8
Otford Kent 21 T11
Otham Kent 12 E5
Otham Hole Kent 12 F5
Othery Somset 17 L10
Otley Leeds 63 Q10
Otley Suffk 41 M9
Otley Green Suffk 41 M9
Otterbourne Hants 9 P4
Otterburn N York 62 H8
Otterburn Nthumb 76 H7
Otter Ferry Ag & B 87 S9
Otterham Cnwll 4 F2
Otterhampton Somset 16 H8
Otterham Quay Kent 12 F2
Otterham Station Cnwll 4 F3
Otternish W Isls 106 e11
Ottershaw Surrey 20 H10
Otterswick Shet 106 v5
Otterton Devon 6 E7
Otterwood Hants 9 N8
Ottery St Mary Devon 6 F5
Ottinge Kent 13 N7
Ottringham E R Yk 59 N2
Oughterby Cumb 67 L1
Oughtershaw N York 62 H3
Oughterside Cumb 66 H4
Oughtibridge Sheff 57 M8
Oughtrington Warrtn 55 Q9
Oulston N York 64 C5
Oulton Cumb 66 K2
Oulton Leeds 63 T14
Oulton Norfk 50 K8
Oulton Staffs 45 S9
Oulton Staffs 46 B6
Oulton Suffk 41 T2
Oulton Broad Suffk 41 T2
Oulton Street Norfk 51 L8
Oundle Nhants 38 F3
Ounsdale Staffs 35 U2
Our Dynamic Earth C Edin 83 Q4
Ousby Cumb 68 D6
Ousden Suffk 40 B9
Ousefleet E R Yk 58 D2
Ouston Dur 69 S2
Outchester Nthumb 85 S12
Out Elmstead Kent 13 P5
Outgate Cumb 67 N13
Outhgill Cumb 68 G12
Outhill Warwks 36 F7
Outlands Staffs 45 S7
Outlane Kirk 56 G3
Out Newton E R Yk 59 Q2
Out Rawcliffe Lancs 61 S11
Outwell Norfk 49 R13
Outwick Hants 8 G5
Outwood Surrey 21 P13
Outwood Wakefd 57 M2
Outwood Gate Bury 55 S5
Outwoods Leics 47 M10
Outwoods Staffs 45 S10
Ouzlewell Green Leeds 57 M1
Ovenden Calder 56 G1
Over Cambs 39 N6
Over Ches W 55 P13
Over Gloucs 28 F4
Over S Glos 28 A11
Over Burrows Derbys 46 J6
Overbury Worcs 36 C13
Overcombe Dorset 7 S8
Over Compton Dorset 17 Q13
Overdale Crematorium Bolton 55 Q5
Over End Cambs 38 G2
Overgreen Derbys 57 M12
Over Green Warwks 36 G2
Over Haddon Derbys 56 K13
Over Kellet Lancs 61 U6
Over Kiddington Oxon 29 T3
Overleigh Somset 17 N9
Overley Staffs 46 G10
Over Monnow Mons 27 U5
Over Norton Oxon 29 R2
Over Peover Ches E 55 S12
Overpool Ches W 54 J11
Overscaig Hotel Highld 110 J12
Overseal Derbys 46 J10
Over Silton N York 70 F14
Oversland Kent 13 L4
Oversley Green Warwks 36 E9
Overstone Nhants 37 U7
Over Stowey Somset 16 G9
Overstrand Norfk 51 M5
Over Stratton Somset 17 M13
Overstreet Wilts 18 G13
Over Tabley Ches E 55 R11
Overthorpe Nhants 37 N12
Overton C Aber 105 P13
Overton Ches W 55 M11
Overton Hants 19 R11
Overton Lancs 61 S8
Overton N York 64 D8
Overton Shrops 35 M6
Overton Swans 25 S13
Overton Wakefd 57 L3
Overton Wrexhm 44 J5
Overton Bridge Wrexhm 44 J5
Overton Green Ches E 45 T1
Overtown Lancs 62 C4
Overtown N Lans 82 F8
Overtown Swindn 18 J5
Overtown Wakefd 57 N3
Over Wallop Hants 19 L13
Over Whitacre Warwks 36 J2
Over Woodhouse Derbys 57 Q12
Over Worton Oxon 29 T2
Overy Oxon 19 S2
Oving Bucks 30 G8
Oving W Susx 10 E10
Ovingdean Br & H 11 P10
Ovingham Nthumb 77 M13
Ovington Dur 69 P10
Ovington Essex 40 C12
Ovington Hants 9 R2
Ovington Norfk 50 F13
Ovington Nthumb 77 M13
Ower Hants 9 L5
Ower Hants 9 P8
Owermoigne Dorset 7 U7
Owlbury Shrops 34 H2
Owlerton Sheff 57 M9
Owlpen Gloucs 28 E8
Owl's Green Suffk 41 N7
Owlsmoor Br For 20 D10
Owlswick Bucks 30 G11
Owmby Lincs 58 H9
Owmby Lincs 58 J6
Owslebury Hants 9 Q4
Owston Donc 57 S4
Owston Leics 47 U12
Owston Ferry N Linc 58 D6
Owstwick E R Yk 65 T13
Owthorne E R Yk 65 U14
Owthorpe Notts 47 S7
Owton Manor Hartpl 70 G7
Oxborough Norfk 50 B13
Oxbridge Dorset 7 N5
Oxcombe Lincs 59 P11
Oxcroft Derbys 57 Q12
Oxen End Essex 22 G2
Oxenholme Cumb 61 U2
Oxenhope C Brad 63 L13
Oxen Park Cumb 61 Q2
Oxenpill Somset 17 M8
Oxenton Gloucs 28 J1
Oxenwood Wilts 19 M9
Oxford Oxon 30 B11
Oxford Airport Oxon 29 U4
Oxford Crematorium Oxon 30 C11
Oxford Services Oxon 30 D12
Oxhey Herts 20 K3
Oxhill Dur 69 Q2
Oxhill Warwks 36 K11
Oxley Wolves 46 B13
Oxley Green Essex 23 M5
Oxley's Green E Susx 12 C11
Oxlode Cambs 39 Q3
Oxnam Border 76 D2
Oxnead Norfk 51 M9
Oxshott Surrey 20 K10
Oxshott Heath Surrey 20 K10
Oxspring Barns 57 L6
Oxted Surrey 21 Q12
Oxton Border 84 D8
Oxton N York 64 C11
Oxton Notts 47 R3
Oxwich Swans 25 S13
Oxwich Green Swans 25 S13
Oxwick Norfk 50 F8
Oykel Bridge Hotel Highld 108 F4
Oyne Abers 104 K10
Oystermouth Swans 25 V13
Ozleworth Gloucs 28 E9

P

Pabail W Isls 106 k5
Packers Hill Dorset 7 T2
Packington Leics 47 L11
Packmoor C Stke 45 U3
Packmores Warwks 36 J7
Padanaram Angus 98 G13
Padbury Bucks 30 F6
Paddington Gt Lon 21 N6
Paddington Warrtn 55 P9
Paddlesworth Kent 12 C3
Paddlesworth Kent 13 N8
Paddock Wood Kent 12 C7
Paddolgreen Shrops 45 M7
Padfield Derbys 56 F7
Padgate Warrtn 55 P9
Padhams Green Essex 22 F8
Padiham Lancs 62 F13
Padside N York 63 P8
Padstow Cnwll 3 N1
Padworth W Berk 19 T7
Page Bank Dur 69 R5
Pagham W Susx 10 D11
Paglesham Essex 23 M9
Paignton Torbay 6 A12
Pailton Warwks 37 N4
Paine's Cross E Susx 11 U6
Painleyhill Staffs 46 D7
Painscastle Powys 34 E11
Painshawfield Nthumb 77 M13
Painsthorpe E R Yk 64 J8
Painswick Gloucs 28 G6
Painter's Forstal Kent 12 J4
Paisley Rens 89 L13
Paisley Woodside Crematorium Rens 89 L13
Pakefield Suffk 41 T2
Pakenham Suffk 40 F7
Pale Gwynd 43 U6
Pale Green Essex 39 U12
Palestine Hants 19 L12
Paley Street W & M 20 E7
Palfrey Wsall 36 D1
Palgrave Suffk 40 K5
Pallington Dorset 7 U6
Palmersbridge Cnwll 4 F5
Palmers Green Gt Lon 21 P4
Palmerston E Ayrs 81 Q9
Palmerstown V Glam 16 F3
Palnackie D & G 73 U8
Palnure D & G 73 M7
Palterton Derbys 57 Q13
Pamber End Hants 19 T9
Pamber Green Hants 19 T9
Pamber Heath Hants 19 T8
Pamington Gloucs 36 B14
Pamphill Dorset 8 D8
Pampisford Cambs 39 Q11
Panborough Somset 17 N7
Panbride Angus 91 S4
Pancrasweek Devon 14 G11
Pancross V Glam 16 D3
Pandy Caerph 27 M10
Pandy Gwynd 43 M13
Pandy Gwynd 43 S8
Pandy Mons 27 Q3
Pandy Powys 43 T13
Pandy Wrexhm 44 E6
Pandy'r Capel Denbgs 44 C3
Pandy Tudur Conwy 53 Q10
Panfield Essex 22 H2
Pangbourne W Berk 19 T5
Pangdean W Susx 11 M8
Panks Bridge Herefs 35 P11
Pannal N York 63 S9
Pannal Ash N York 63 R9
Pannanich Wells Hotel Abers 98 G4
Pant Shrops 44 G9
Pantasaph Flints 54 E11
Panteg Pembks 24 F4
Pantersbridge Cnwll 4 F7
Pant-ffrwyth Brdgnd 26 G11
Pant Glas Gwynd 42 J4
Pantglas Powys 43 Q14
Pant-Gwyn Carmth 25 U5
Pant-lasau Swans 26 B7
Pant Mawr Powys 33 R4
Panton Lincs 59 L11
Pant-pastynog Denbgs 53 T10
Pantperthog Gwynd 43 P13
Pant-y-dwr Powys 33 U6
Pant-y-ffridd Powys 44 E13
Pantyffynnon Carmth 25 V8
Pantygaseg Torfn 27 P8
Pant-y-gog Brdgnd 26 G9
Pantymenyn Carmth 24 K5
Pant-y-mwyn Flints 54 E14
Panxworth Norfk 51 Q11
Papa Westray Airport Ork 106 t14
Papcastle Cumb 66 H6
Papigoe Highld 112 J6
Papple E Loth 84 F4
Papplewick Notts 47 P3
Papworth Everard Cambs 39 L8
Papworth St Agnes Cambs 39 L8
Par Cnwll 3 R6
Paramour Street Kent 13 Q3
Parbold Lancs 55 L4
Parbrook Somset 17 Q9
Parbrook W Susx 10 H5
Parc Gwynd 43 S7
Parc Gwyn Crematorium Pembks 24 K8
Parcllyn Cerdgn 32 D10
Parc Seymour Newpt 27 S9
Pardshaw Cumb 66 G8
Parham Suffk 41 P8
Park D & G 74 H7
Park Nthumb 76 D13
Park Bottom Cnwll 2 H8
Park Bridge Tamesd 56 D6
Park Corner E Susx 11 S3
Park Corner Oxon 19 U3
Park Corner W & M 20 E6
Park Crematorium Lancs 61 R14
Park End Bed 38 E10
Parkend Gloucs 28 B6
Park End Nthumb 76 H10
Parkers Green Kent 12 B6
Parkeston Essex 23 T1
Parkeston Quay Essex 41 M14
Park Farm Kent 12 K8
Parkgate Ches W 54 G11
Parkgate Cumb 66 K3
Parkgate D & G 74 K8
Parkgate E Susx 12 D13
Parkgate Essex 22 G2
Park Gate Hants 9 Q7
Parkgate Kent 12 G9
Parkgate Kent 21 T10
Park Gate Leeds 63 P11
Parkgate Surrey 11 L2
Park Gate Worcs 36 B6
Park Green Essex 22 C2
Park Green Suffk 40 K8
Parkgrove Crematorium Angus 91 T2
Parkhall W Duns 89 L11
Parkham Devon 14 J8
Parkham Ash Devon 14 J8
Park Head Derbys 47 L3
Park Hill Gloucs 27 V8
Parkhouse Mons 27 U7
Parkmill Swans 25 T13
Park Royal Gt Lon 21 L6
Parkside Dur 70 F3
Parkside N Lans 82 F7
Parkside Wrexhm 44 J2
Parkstone Poole 8 E10
Park Street Herts 31 P12
Park Street W Susx 10 J4
Park Wood Crematorium Calder 56 H2
Parley Green Dorset 8 G9
Parmoor Bucks 20 C5
Parndon Essex 22 B6
Parndon Wood Crematorium Essex 22 B6
Parracombe Devon 15 Q3
Parrog Pembks 24 J3
Parsonby Cumb 66 H5
Parson Cross Sheff 57 M8
Parson Drove Cambs 49 N12
Parson's Heath Essex 23 P2
Parson's Hill Derbys 46 J8
Partick C Glas 89 M12
Partington Traffd 55 R8
Partney Lincs 59 R13
Parton Cumb 66 E8
Partridge Green W Susx 10 K7
Partrishow Powys 27 P3
Parwich Derbys 46 G3
Paslow Wood Common Essex 22 E7
Passenham Nhants 30 G5
Passfield Hants 10 C4
Passingford Bridge Essex 22 D8
Paston C Pete 48 J13
Paston Norfk 51 P7
Pasturefields Staffs 46 C9
Patchacott Devon 15 L13
Patcham Br & H 11 N9
Patchetts Green Herts 20 K3
Patching W Susx 10 H9
Patchole Devon 15 P4
Patchway S Glos 28 B11
Pateley Bridge N York 63 P6
Paternoster Heath Essex 23 M4
Pathe Somset 17 L10
Pathhead Fife 91 L13
Pathhead Mdloth 83 S6
Pathlow Warwks 36 G9
Path of Condie P & K 90 G9
Patmore Heath Herts 22 B2
Patna E Ayrs 81 N10
Patney Wilts 18 G9
Patrick IoM 60 c6
Patrick Brompton N York 63 Q1
Patricroft Salfd 55 S7
Patrington E R Yk 59 P2
Patrington Haven E R Yk 59 P2
Patrixbourne Kent 13 N4
Patterdale Cumb 67 N9
Pattingham Staffs 45 T14
Pattishall Nhants 37 S10
Pattiswick Green Essex 22 K3
Patton Shrops 35 N1
Paul Cnwll 2 D11
Paulerspury Nhants 37 T11
Paull E R Yk 59 L1
Paul's Dene Wilts 8 G2
Paulton BaNES 17 S5
Paunton Herefs 35 Q10
Pauperhaugh Nthumb 77 N6
Pave Lane Wrekin 45 S10
Pavenham Bed 38 E9
Pawlett Somset 16 J8
Pawston Nthumb 85 M12
Paxford Gloucs 36 G13
Paxton Border 85 N8
Payden Street Kent 12 H5
Payhembury Devon 6 E4
Paynter's Lane End Cnwll 2 H8
Paythorne Lancs 62 G9
Paytoe Herefs 34 K6
Peacehaven E Susx 11 Q10
Peak Dale Derbys 56 G11
Peak District National Park 56 J8
Peak Forest Derbys 56 H11
Peak Hill Lincs 49 L10
Peakirk C Pete 48 J12
Pearson's Green Kent 12 C7
Peartree Green Herefs 35 N14
Peasedown St John BaNES 17 T5
Peasehill Derbys 47 M4
Peaseland Green Norfk 50 J10
Peasemore W Berk 19 Q5
Peasenhall Suffk 41 Q7
Pease Pottage W Susx 11 M4
Peaslake Surrey 10 H2
Peasley Cross St Hel 55 M8
Peasmarsh E Susx 12 G11
Peasmarsh Somset 6 K2
Peasmarsh Surrey 20 G13
Peathill Abers 105 Q2
Peat Inn Fife 91 Q10
Peatling Magna Leics 37 Q2
Peatling Parva Leics 37 Q3
Peaton Shrops 35 M3
Pebmarsh Essex 40 E14
Pebworth Worcs 36 F11
Pecket Well Calder 62 K14
Peckforton Ches E 45 M2
Peckham Gt Lon 21 P7
Peckleton Leics 47 N13
Pedairffordd Powys 44 D9
Pedlinge Kent 13 M8
Pedmore Dudley 36 B4
Pedwell Somset 17 M9
Peebles Border 83 Q10
Peel IoM 60 c6
Peel Lancs 61 R13
Peel Common Hants 9 R8
Peene Kent 13 N8
Peening Quarter Kent 12 G10
Peggs Green Leics 47 M10
Pegsdon C Beds 31 P6
Pegswood Nthumb 77 Q8
Pegwell Kent 13 S3
Peinchorran Highld 100 e6
Peinlich Highld 100 d4
Pelcomb Pembks 24 F7
Pelcomb Bridge Pembks 24 F7
Pelcomb Cross Pembks 24 F7
Peldon Essex 23 N4
Pell Green E Susx 12 B9
Pelsall Wsall 46 D13
Pelsall Wood Wsall 46 D13
Pelton Dur 69 S2
Pelton Fell Dur 69 S2
Pelutho Cumb 66 H3
Pelynt Cnwll 4 G9
Pemberton Carmth 25 T10
Pemberton Wigan 55 N6
Pembles Cross Kent 12 G6
Pembrey Carmth 25 R10
Pembridge Herefs 34 J9
Pembroke Pembks 24 G10

Pembroke Dock Pembks..24 G10
Pembrokeshire Coast National Park Pembks..24 D6
Pembury Kent..12 B7
Pen-allt Herefs..27 V2
Penallt Mons..27 U5
Penally Pembks..24 K11
Penare Cnwll..4 P8
Penarth V Glam..16 Q2
Penblewin Pembks..24 K7
Pen-bont Rhydybeddau Cerdgn..33 N4
Penbryn Cerdgn..32 E10
Pencader Carmth..25 R3
Pencaenewydd Gwynd..42 H5
Pencaitland E Loth..84 D8
Pencarnisiog IoA..54 D6
Pencarreg Carmth..32 K11
Pencarrow Cnwll..4 S4
Pencelli Powys..26 K2
Penclawdd Swans..25 T11
Pencoed Brdgnd..26 H11
Pencombe Herefs..35 N10
Pencoyd Herefs..27 U2
Pencraig Herefs..27 V3
Pencraig Powys..44 B8
Pendeen Cnwll..2 B10
Penderyn Rhondd..26 G2
Pendine Carmth..25 M9
Pendlebury Salfd..55 S6
Pendleton Lancs..62 F12
Pendock Worcs..35 S14
Pendoggett Cnwll..4 Q5
Pendomer Somset..7 P2
Pendoylan V Glam..26 K12
Pendre Brdgnd..27 P7
Penegoes Powys..43 Q13
Peneleweny Cnwll..3 L4
Pen-ffordd Pembks..24 J6
Pengam Caerph..27 M8
Pengam Cardif..27 N10
Penge Gt Lon..21 Q8
Pengelly Cnwll..4 D4
Pengorffwysfa IoA..52 G4
Pengover Green Cnwll..4 H7
Pen-groes-oped Mons..27 Q4
Pengwern Denbgs..53 T9
Penhale Cnwll..2 H13
Penhale Cnwll..3 N5
Penhale Cnwll..5 R4
Penhale Cnwll..3 L10
Penhallow Cnwll..2 K6
Penhalurick Cnwll..2 H9
Penhalvean Cnwll..2 J9
Penhill Swindn..29 N10
Penhow Newpt..27 S9
Penhurst E Susx..12 E8
Peniarth Gwynd..43 M12
Penicuik Mdloth..83 P7
Peniel Carmth..25 R6
Peniel Denbgs..53 T10
Penifiler Highld..100 d6
Peninver Ag & B..79 P11
Penisarwaun Gwynd..52 J10
Penistone Barns..56 K6
Penjerrick Cnwll..2 K10
Penketh Warrtn..55 N9
Penkill S Ayrs..80 E13
Penkridge Staffs..45 U11
Penlean Cnwll..14 F13
Penleigh Wilts..18 C10
Penley Wrexhm..44 J5
Penllergaer Swans..V11
Pen-llyn IoA..52 E6
Penllyn V Glam..26 H12
Pen-lon IoA..52 F9
Penmachno Conwy..43 Q3
Penmaen Caerph..27 M8
Penmaen Swans..25 T13
Penmaenmawr Conwy..53 M7
Penmaenpool Gwynd..43 N10
Penmark V Glam..16 E3
Penmon IoA..53 K6
Penmorfa Gwynd..42 K5
Penmount Crematorium Cnwll..3 L7
Penmynydd IoA..52 H8
Penn Bucks..20 F4
Penn Wolves..35 U15
Pennal Gwynd..43 N13
Pennan Abers..105 N3
Pennant Cerdgn..32 K8
Pennant Denbgs..43 U6
Pennant Powys..43 S14
Pennant-Melangell Powys..44 B8
Pennard Swans..25 T13
Pennerley Shrops..34 J14
Pennicott Devon..15 U12
Pennington Cumb..61 P4
Pennington Hants..9 L9
Pennington Green Wigan..55 P6
Penn Street Bucks..20 F4
Penny Bridge Cumb..61 Q3
Pennycross Plym..5 N9
Pennygate Norfk..51 P9
Pennyghael Ag & B..93 N13
Pennyglen S Ayrs..80 K9
Penny Green Derbys..57 R11
Penny Hill Lincs..49 N8
Pennymoor Devon..15 U10
Pennywell Sundld..70 D1
Penparc Cerdgn..32 D11
Penparcau Cerdgn..32 L4
Penpedairheol Caerph..27 L8
Penpedairheol Mons..27 Q6
Penperlleni Mons..27 Q6
Penpethy Cnwll..4 D3
Penpillick Cnwll..4 E9
Penpol Cnwll..4 E10
Penponds Cnwll..2 H9
Penpont Cnwll..4 R4
Penpont D & G..74 F7
Penquit Devon..5 Q9
Penrherber Carmth..25 Q3
Pen-rhiw Pembks..32 F12
Penrhiwceiber Rhondd..26 K8
Penrhiw-llan Cerdgn..32 G12
Penrhiw-pal Cerdgn..32 G11
Penrhos Gwynd..42 F6
Penrhos IoA..52 C6
Penrhos Mons..27 S5
Penrhos garnedd Gwynd..52 J8
Penrhyn Bay Conwy..53 P6
Penrhyncoch Cerdgn..33 M4
Penrhyndeudraeth Gwynd..43 M6
Penrhyn-side Conwy..53 P6
Penrice Swans..25 S13
Penrioch N Ayrs..79 R7
Penrith Cumb..67 R6
Penrose Cnwll..3 M2
Penruddock Cumb..67 P7
Penryn Cnwll..2 K10
Pensarn Conwy..53 S7
Pensarn Gwynd..43 L9
Pensax Worcs..35 R7
Penselwood Somset..17 U10
Pensford BaNES..17 R4
Pensham Worcs..36 B12
Penshaw Sundld..70 D2
Penshurst Kent..21 S13
Penshurst Station Kent..21 T13
Pensilva Cnwll..4 H7
Pensnett Dudley..36 B3
Penstone Devon..15 S12
Penstrowed Powys..34 C2
Pentewan Cnwll..3 Q7
Pentir Gwynd..52 J9
Pentire Cnwll..3 L4
Pentlepoir Pembks..24 K8
Pentlow Essex..40 D12
Pentney Norfk..50 B11
Penton Mewsey Hants..19 M11
Pentraeth IoA..52 H7
Pentre Denbgs..54 C14
Pentre Flints..44 H13
Pentre Mons..27 Q6
Pentre Powys..34 C2
Pentre Powys..34 F3
Pentre Rhondd..26 H9
Pentre Shrops..44 G10
Pentre Wrexhm..44 F5
Pentre-bach Cerdgn..32 K10
Pentre-bach Powys..26 F1
Pentrebach Myr Td..26 K8
Pentre Berw IoA..52 G8
Pentre-bont Conwy..43 P3
Pentrebychan Crematorium Wrexhm..44 H3
Pentre-cagel Carmth..32 F12
Pentre-celyn Denbgs..44 D2
Pentre-celyn Powys..43 S12
Pentre-clawdd Shrops..44 G6
Pentre-cwrt Carmth..25 Q3

Pentredwr Denbgs..44 E4
Pentrefelin Gwynd..42 K6
Pentrefelin IoA..52 F4
Pentre Ffwrndan Flints..54 G12
Pentregalar Pembks..25 L4
Pentregat Cerdgn..32 G10
Pentre-Gwenlais Carmth..25 V7
Pentre Gwynfryn Gwynd..43 L8
Pentre Halkyn Flints..54 F12
Pentre Hodrey Shrops..34 H5
Pentre-Isaf Conwy..53 S8
Pentre Llanrhaeadr Denbgs..54 C14
Pentre Llifior Powys..44 E14
Pentre-llwyn-llwyd Powys..33 U10
Pentre-llyn Cerdgn..33 M5
Pentre-llyn-cymmer Conwy..43 U3
Pentre Maelor Wrexhm..44 H4
Pentre Meyrick V Glam..26 H12
Pentre-piod Torfn..27 P7
Pentre'r-felin Powys..26 G1
Pentre'r-felin Conwy..53 P9
Pentre'r-Felin Powys..26 G1
Pentre Saron Denbgs..53 T10
Pentre-tafarn-y-fedw Conwy..53 Q10
Pentrich Derbys..47 L3
Pentridge Dorset..8 E5
Pentre-poeth Newpt..27 P10
Pen-twyn Caerph..27 N7
Pen-twyn Mons..27 U6
Pen-twyn Torfn..27 P7
Pentwynmaur Caerph..27 M8
Pentyrch Cardif..27 L11
Pentywyn Carmth..24 B8
Penwithick Cnwll..3 Q5
Penwood Hants..19 P8
Penwyllt Powys..26 F4
Penybanc Carmth..25 V6
Pen-y-bank Powys..34 F1
Pen-y-bont Powys..44 C9
Penybont Powys..34 D8
Pen-y-bont Carmth..33 L13
Pen-y-bont-fawr Powys..44 C9
Pen-y-bryn Pembks..32 C12
Pen-y-cae Powys..26 F3
Penycae Wrexhm..44 G4
Pen-y-cae-mawr Mons..27 S8
Pen-y-cefn Flints..54 D11
Pen-y-clawdd Mons..27 T6
Pen-y-coedcae Rhondd..26 K10
Pen-y-cwm Pembks..24 E6
Pen-y-fai Brdgnd..26 F11
Pen-y-felin Flints..54 E13
Penyffordd Flints..54 H13
Pen-y-ffordd Flints..54 G11
Penyffridd Gwynd..52 H11
Pen-y-garn Cerdgn..33 M3
Pen-y-garnedd Powys..44 D9
Pen-y-genffordd Powys..27 M2
Pen-y-graig Gwynd..42 C7
Penygraig Rhondd..26 J9
Penygroes Carmth..25 U8
Penygroes Gwynd..52 G12
Pen-y-Lan V Glam..26 H12
Pen-y-stryt Denbgs..44 E3
Pen-yr-Heol Mons..27 S5
Pen-yr-Heolgerrig Myr Td..26 J6
Penysarn IoA..52 G4
Pen-y-stryt Denbgs..44 E3
Penywaun Rhondd..26 H7
Penzance Cnwll..2 D10
Peopleton Worcs..36 B10
Peover Heath Ches E..55 R12
Peper Harow Surrey..10 E2
Peplow Shrops..45 P9
Pepper's Green Essex..22 F5
Pepperstock C Beds..31 N9
Perceton N Ayrs..81 M4
Percyhorner Abers..105 R2
Perelle Guern..6 c3
Perham Down Wilts..19 L11
Periton Somset..16 C7
Perkins Village Devon..6 D6
Perkinsville Dur..69 S2
Perlethorpe Notts..57 T12
Perranarworthal Cnwll..2 K10
Perranporth Cnwll..2 K6
Perranuthnoe Cnwll..2 E11
Perranwell Cnwll..2 K6
Perranwell Cnwll..2 K10
Perran Wharf Cnwll..2 K10
Perranzabuloe Cnwll..2 K6
Perrott's Brook Gloucs..28 K6
Perry Birm..36 E2
Perry Green Essex..22 J4
Perry Green Herts..22 B4
Perry Green Wilts..28 J10
Perry Street Somset..7 L3
Pershall Staffs..45 U8
Pershore Worcs..36 B11
Pertenhall Bed..38 G7
Perth P & K..90 G7
Perthy Shrops..44 H7
Perton Staffs..45 U15
Pertwood Wilts..18 C13
Peterborough C Pete..48 J13
Peterborough Crematorium C Pete..48 J13
Peterborough Services Cambs..38 H2
Peterchurch Herefs..34 H13
Peterculter C Aber..99 Q3
Peterhead Abers..105 U6
Peterlee Dur..70 E4
Petersfield Hants..9 U4
Peter's Green Herts..31 P9
Peters Marland Devon..15 L10
Peterstone Wentlooge Newpt..27 P11
Peterston-super-Ely V Glam..26 K12
Peterstow Herefs..27 V3
Peter Tavy Devon..5 N5
Petham Kent..13 M5
Petherwin Gate Cnwll..4 H3
Petrockstowe Devon..15 M11
Pett E Susx..12 G13
Pettaugh Suffk..41 L9
Pett Bottom Kent..13 M5
Petteridge Kent..12 C7
Pettinain S Lans..82 H10
Pettistree Suffk..41 N10
Petton Devon..16 E12
Petton Shrops..44 K8
Pett's Bottom Kent..13 M5
Petts Wood Gt Lon..21 S9
Pettycur Fife..83 Q4
Petty France S Glos..28 E10
Pettymuk Abers..105 Q11
Petworth W Susx..10 F6
Pevensey E Susx..11 U10
Pevensey Bay E Susx..11 V10
Pewsey Wilts..18 J8
Pheasant's Hill Bucks..20 C5
Phepson Worcs..36 B9
Philadelphia Sundld..70 D2
Philham Devon..14 G8
Philiphaugh Border..84 D13
Phillack Cnwll..2 F9
Philleigh Cnwll..3 M9
Philpot End Essex..22 F4
Philpstoun W Loth..83 L3
Phocle Green Herefs..35 R14
Phoenix Green Hants..20 C11
Phones Highld..97 U5
Pibsbury Somset..17 M11
Pica Cumb..66 F8
Piccadilly Warwks..46 H14
Piccotts End Herts..31 N11
Pickburn Donc..57 R5
Picket Piece Hants..19 N10
Picket Post Hants..8 H7
Pickford Covtry..36 J4
Pickford Green Covtry..36 J4
Pickhill N York..63 S3
Picklescott Shrops..34 K13
Pickmere Ches E..55 Q11
Pickney Somset..16 G11
Pickstock Wrekin..45 R9
Pickup Bank Bl w D..62 F2
Pickwell Devon..14 K3
Pickwell Leics..47 U11
Pickwick Wilts..18 B6
Pickworth Lincs..48 F6
Pickworth Rutlnd..48 E11
Picton Ches W..54 K12
Picton Flints..54 F11
Picton N York..70 G11
Piddinghoe E Susx..11 Q10
Piddington Nhants..37 U9
Piddington Oxon..30 D9
Piddlehinton Dorset..7 T5
Piddletrenthide Dorset..7 T5
Pidley Cambs..39 N5
Piercebridge Darltn..69 R9
Pierowall Ork..106 t15

Piff's Elm Gloucs..28 H2
Pigdon Nthumb..77 P8
Pigeon Green Warwks..36 H8
Pig Oak Dorset..8 E8
Pig Street Herefs..34 J11
Pikehall Derbys..46 H1
Pilgrims Hatch Essex..22 E8
Pilham Lincs..58 E8
Pill N Som..27 U12
Pillaton Cnwll..4 K8
Pillatonmill Cnwll..4 K8
Pillerton Hersey Warwks..36 J11
Pillerton Priors Warwks..36 H11
Pilleth Powys..34 G8
Pilley Hants..9 L9
Pilley Barns..57 M6
Pilley Bailey Hants..9 L9
Pillgwenlly Newpt..27 Q10
Pillhead Devon..15 L7
Pilling Lancs..61 S10
Pilling Lane Lancs..61 R10
Pilot Inn Kent..13 L12
Pilsbury Derbys..56 H14
Pilsdon Dorset..7 M5
Pilsgate C Pete..48 G12
Pilsley Derbys..56 K13
Pilsley Derbys..57 Q11
Pilson Green Norfk..51 Q11
Piltdown E Susx..11 Q6
Pilton Devon..15 N6
Pilton Nhants..38 F4
Pilton Rutlnd..48 D12
Pilton Somset..17 Q8
Pilton Green Swans..25 R13
Pimhole Bury..55 S5
Pimlico Lancs..62 H11
Pimlico Nhants..30 D4
Pimlico Gt Lon..21 N7
Pimperne Dorset..8 C7
Pinchbeck Lincs..48 K8
Pinchbeck Bars Lincs..48 J8
Pinchbeck West Lincs..49 L8
Pinchinthorpe R & Cl..70 J10
Pincock Lancs..55 N3
Pinfold Lancs..54 J4
Pinford End Suffk..40 D9
Pinged Carmth..25 R9
Pingewood W Berk..19 U7
Pin Green Herts..31 S7
Pinhoe Devon..6 C6
Pinkett's Booth Covtry..36 J4
Pinkney Wilts..28 G10
Pinley Green Warwks..36 H7
Pin Mill Suffk..41 M13
Pinminnoch S Ayrs..80 H14
Pinmore S Ayrs..80 J14
Pinn Devon..6 F7
Pinner Gt Lon..20 K5
Pinner Green Gt Lon..20 K5
Pinsley Green Ches E..45 M4
Pinvin Worcs..36 C11
Pinwherry S Ayrs..80 G13
Pinxton Derbys..47 N3
Pipe Aston Herefs..34 K6
Pipe Gate Shrops..45 R5
Pipehill Staffs..46 E12
Piperhill Highld..103 N5
Pipers Pool Cnwll..4 H4
Pipewell Nhants..38 B4
Pippacott Devon..15 M5
Pipton Powys..34 E13
Pirbright Surrey..20 F11
Pirbright Camp Surrey..20 F11
Pirnie Border..84 F13
Pirnmill N Ayrs..79 R7
Pirton Herts..31 Q6
Pirton Worcs..35 U11
Pisgah Cerdgn..33 N5
Pishill Oxon..20 B5
Pistyll Gwynd..42 G5
Pitagowan P & K..97 P10
Pitblae Abers..105 R3
Pitcairngreen P & K..90 G6
Pitcalnie Highld..109 Q10
Pitcaple Abers..105 L9
Pitcarity Angus..98 E10
Pitch Green Bucks..30 F12
Pitchcombe Gloucs..28 G6
Pitchcott Bucks..30 F8
Pitcher Row Lincs..49 L7
Pitchford Shrops..45 M13
Pitch Place Surrey..10 D3
Pitch Place Surrey..20 G12
Pitchroy Moray..103 U8
Pitcombe Somset..17 R10
Pitcot V Glam..26 F13
Pitcox E Loth..84 G3
Pitfichie Abers..104 K12
Pitglassie Abers..105 L6
Pitgrudy Highld..109 P6
Pitkennedy Angus..98 K12
Pitlessie Fife..91 L10
Pitlochry P & K..97 Q12
Pitmachie Abers..104 K10
Pitmain Highld..97 N4
Pitmedden Abers..105 P10
Pitminster Somset..16 H13
Pitmuies Angus..91 S2
Pitmunie Abers..104 K12
Pitney Somset..17 N11
Pitroddie P & K..90 K6
Pitscottie Fife..91 P9
Pitsea Essex..22 H10
Pitses Oldham..56 D6
Pitsford Nhants..37 U7
Pitsford Hill Somset..16 F10
Pitstone Bucks..30 K9
Pitt Devon..16 F12
Pitt Hants..9 N3
Pittarrow Abers..99 N9
Pitt Court Gloucs..28 D8
Pittentrail Highld..109 N3
Pittenweem Fife..91 S11
Pitteuchar Fife..91 L11
Pittington Dur..70 D4
Pittodrie House Hotel Abers..104 K11
Pitton Wilts..8 J2
Pitt's Wood Kent..21 U13
Pittulie Abers..105 R2
Pityme Cnwll..3 Q1
Pity Me Dur..69 S4
Pixey Green Suffk..41 M6
Pixham Surrey..21 K12
Pixley Herefs..35 P13
Plaidy Abers..105 L4
Plain Street Cnwll..4 B5
Plaistow Derbys..46 K2
Plaistow Gt Lon..21 R6
Plaistow W Susx..10 F4
Plaitford Hants..8 K5
Plank Lane Wigan..55 Q7
Plas Cymyran IoA..52 C7
Plastow Green Hants..19 R8
Platt Kent..12 B3
Platt Bridge Wigan..55 N6
Platt Lane Shrops..45 M6
Platts Heath Kent..12 G5
Plawsworth Dur..69 S3
Plaxtol Kent..12 B4
Playden E Susx..12 H11
Playford Suffk..41 M11
Play Hatch Oxon..20 B7
Playing Place Cnwll..3 L8
Playley Green Gloucs..35 S14
Plealey Shrops..44 K12
Plean Stirlg..89 T8
Pleasance Fife..90 K9
Pleasington Bl w D..55 P1
Pleasley Derbys..57 R14
Pleasleyhill Notts..57 R14
Pleck Dorset..7 R3
Pledgdon Green Essex..22 D2
Pledwick Wakefd..57 M3
Pleinheaume Guern..6 d2
Plemont Jersey..7 a1
Plemstall Ches W..54 K12
Plenmeller Nthumb..76 E13
Pleshey Essex..22 G5
Plockton Highld..100 h6
Plockwoods Highld..100 h6
Plot Gate Somset..17 P10
Plough Hill Warwks..46 K14
Plowden Shrops..34 J3
Plox Green Shrops..44 J13
Pluckley Kent..12 H6
Pluckley Station Kent..12 H7
Pluckley Thorne Kent..12 H7
Plucks Gutter Kent..13 Q3
Plumbland Cumb..66 J5
Plumgarths Cumb..67 Q14
Plumley Ches E..55 R12
Plumpton Cumb..67 Q6
Plumpton E Susx..11 P8
Plumpton Nhants..37 Q11
Plumpton End Nhants..37 U11
Plumpton Green E Susx..11 P7
Plumpton Head Cumb..67 Q6
Plumstead Gt Lon..21 R7
Plumstead Norfk..50 K6
Plumtree Notts..47 R6
Plumtree Green Kent..12 F6
Plungar Leics..47 U6
Plurenden Kent..12 H8
Plush Dorset..7 T4
Plusha Cnwll..4 H4
Plushabridge Cnwll..4 H6
Plwmp Cerdgn..32 G10
Plymouth C Plym..5 N10
Plymouth Airport C Plym..5 N8
Plympton C Plym..5 N9

Plymstock C Plym..5 N10
Plymtree Devon..6 E4
Pockley N York..64 E2
Pocklington E R Yk..64 J10
Pode Hole Lincs..48 K9
Podimore Somset..17 Q12
Podington Bed..38 D8
Podmore Staffs..45 S7
Point Clear Essex..23 R5
Pointon Lincs..48 H7
Pokesdown Bmouth..8 H10
Polbain Highld..107 L1
Polbathic Cnwll..4 J9
Polbeth W Loth..82 K6
Poldark Mine Cnwll..2 H10
Polebrook Nhants..38 G3
Pole Elm Worcs..35 T11
Polegate E Susx..11 T10
Pole Moor Kirk..56 G3
Polesden Lacey Surrey..20 K12
Polesworth Warwks..46 J13
Polgigga Cnwll..2 B12
Polglass Highld..107 T3
Polgooth Cnwll..3 P6
Poling W Susx..10 G9
Poling Corner W Susx..10 G8
Polkerris Cnwll..4 E10
Pollard Street Norfk..51 P7
Pollington E R Yk..57 U4
Polloch Highld..93 R5
Pollokshaws C Glas..89 N13
Pollokshields C Glas..89 N13
Polmassick Cnwll..3 P7
Polmont Falk..82 H3
Polnish Highld..93 T2
Polperro Cnwll..4 G11
Polruan Cnwll..4 F10
Polsham Somset..17 P8
Polstead Suffk..40 G13
Polstead Heath Suffk..40 G13
Poltalloch Ag & B..87 Q6
Poltescoe Cnwll..2 J13
Poltimore Devon..6 C5
Polton Mdloth..83 Q6
Polwarth Border..84 K9
Polyphant Cnwll..4 H4
Polzeath Cnwll..4 B5
Pomathorn Mdloth..83 P7
Pomeroy Derbys..56 H13
Ponde Powys..34 D13
Pondersbridge Cambs..39 L2
Ponders End Gt Lon..21 Q3
Ponsanooth Cnwll..2 J10
Ponsonby Cumb..66 G11
Ponsongath Cnwll..2 J13
Ponsworthy Devon..5 S6
Pont Abraham Services Carmth..25 U9
Pontamman Carmth..25 V8
Pontantwn Carmth..25 R8
Pontardawe Neath..26 C6
Pontarddulais Swans..25 U9
Pont-ar-gothi Carmth..25 T6
Pont-ar-Hydfer Powys..26 F2
Pont-ar-llechau Carmth..26 E2
Pontarsais Carmth..25 R5
Pontblyddyn Flints..44 G1
Pont Cyfyng Conwy..43 N3
Pontcysyllte Aqueduct Wrexhm..44 G5
Pontdolgarrog Conwy..53 N9
Pontefract Wakefd..57 Q2
Pontefract Crematorium Wakefd..57 P2
Ponteland Nthumb..77 P11
Ponterwyd Cerdgn..33 P4
Pontesbury Shrops..44 J12
Pontesbury Hill Shrops..44 J12
Pontesford Shrops..44 K12
Pontfadog Wrexhm..44 F6
Pontfaen Pembks..24 J4
Pont-faen Powys..26 G1
Pontgarreg Cerdgn..32 F10
Pontgarreg Pembks..32 C12
Ponthir Torfn..27 Q8
Ponthirwaun Cerdgn..32 E11
Pontllanfraith Caerph..27 M8
Pontlliw Swans..25 V11
Pontllyfni Gwynd..42 H3
Pont Morlais Carmth..25 T9
Pontnewydd Torfn..27 P8
Pont Pen-y-benglog Gwynd..53 L10
Pontrhydfendigaid Cerdgn..33 P7
Pont Rhyd-sarn Gwynd..43 R8
Pont Rhyd-y-cyff Brdgnd..26 F10
Pont-rhyd-y-fen Neath..26 D9
Pontrhydygroes Cerdgn..33 P6
Pontrhydyrun Torfn..27 P8
Pontrilas Herefs..27 R2
Pont Robert Powys..44 D11
Pont-rug Gwynd..52 H10
Ponts Green E Susx..12 D12
Pontshaen Cerdgn..32 H11
Pontshill Herefs..35 R14
Pontsticill Myr Td..26 K5
Pont Walby Neath..26 F6
Pontyates Carmth..25 S9
Pontyberem Carmth..25 T8
Pont-y-blew Wrexhm..44 H6
Pontybodkin Flints..44 G2
Pontyclun Rhondd..26 J11
Pontycymer Brdgnd..26 G8
Pontyglazier Pembks..24 K3
Pontygwaith Rhondd..26 J9
Pontygynon Pembks..24 K3
Pont-y-pant Conwy..53 N10
Pontypool Torfn..27 P7
Pontypool Road Torfn..27 P7
Pontypridd Rhondd..26 K10
Pontywaun Caerph..27 N9
Pool Cnwll..2 H8
Pool IoS..2 b2
Pool Leeds..63 Q10
Poole Poole..8 E10
Poole Crematorium Poole..8 E9
Poole Keynes Gloucs..28 J8
Poolewe Highld..107 Q8
Pooley Bridge Cumb..67 P7
Pooley Street Norfk..40 J4
Poolfold Staffs..45 U2
Pool Head Herefs..35 N10
Poolhill Gloucs..35 S14
Pool of Muckhart Clacks..90 F11
Pool Quay Powys..44 F11
Pool Street Essex..40 C13
Pootings Kent..21 S13
Popham Hants..19 S12
Poplar Gt Lon..21 Q6
Poplar Street Suffk..41 P7
Porchfield IoW..9 N10
Poringland Norfk..51 N12
Porkellis Cnwll..2 H10
Porlock Somset..15 U3
Porlock Weir Somset..15 U3
Port Appin Ag & B..94 C10
Port Askaig Ag & B..86 G12
Portavadie Ag & B..87 S12
Port Bannatyne Ag & B..88 C12
Portbury N Som..27 U12
Port Carlisle Cumb..75 P13
Port Charlotte Ag & B..86 D14
Portchester Hants..9 S7
Portchester Crematorium Hants..9 S7
Port Clarence S on T..70 G8
Port Driseach Ag & B..87 T11
Port Ellen Ag & B..78 E6
Port Elphinstone Abers..105 M11
Portencalzie D & G..72 C6
Portencross N Ayrs..80 J3
Portesham Dorset..7 R7
Portessie Moray..104 E2
Port e Vullen IoM..60 h4
Port Eynon Swans..25 R14
Portfield Gate Pembks..24 F7
Portgate Devon..5 L4
Portgordon Moray..104 D3
Portgower Highld..109 V3
Porth Cnwll..3 L3
Porth Rhondd..26 J9
Porthallow Cnwll..2 K12
Porthallow Cnwll..4 G11
Porthcawl Brdgnd..26 E12
Porthcothan Cnwll..3 M2
Porthcurno Cnwll..2 B12
Port Dinllaen Gwynd..42 F5
Porth Dinllaen Gwynd..42 F5
Porthgain Pembks..24 E4
Porthgwarra Cnwll..2 B12
Porthill Shrops..44 K11
Porthkea Cnwll..3 L8
Porthkerry V Glam..16 E3

Porthleven Cnwll..2 G11
Porthmadog Gwynd..43 L6
Porthmeor Cnwll..2 C10
Porth Navas Cnwll..2 K11
Portholland Cnwll..3 P8
Porthoustock Cnwll..2 K12
Porthpean Cnwll..3 Q6
Porthtowan Cnwll..2 H7
Porthwgan Wrexhm..44 H4
Porth-y-Waen Shrops..44 G9
Portincaple Ag & B..88 F7
Portinfer Jersey..7 a1
Portington E R Yk..64 H13
Portinnisherrich Ag & B..87 S3
Portinscale Cumb..67 L8
Port Isaac Cnwll..4 B4
Portishead N Som..27 T12
Portknockie Moray..104 F2
Portland Dorset..7 S10
Portlethen Abers..99 S4
Portling D & G..66 C2
Portloe Cnwll..3 N9
Portmahomack Highld..109 T9
Portmeirion Gwynd..43 L6
Portmellon Cnwll..3 Q7
Port Mor Highld..93 L3
Portmore Hants..9 L9
Port Mulgrave N York..71 N9
Portnacroish Ag & B..94 C9
Portnahaven Ag & B..78 B5
Portnalong Highld..100 c6
Port nan Giuran W Isls..106 k5
Port nan Long W Isls..106 d11
Port Nis W Isls..106 k2
Portobello C Edin..83 R4
Portobello Gatesd..69 R1
Portobello Wolves..46 C14
Porton Wilts..18 H13
Portontown Devon..5 L6
Portpatrick D & G..72 B9
Port Quin Cnwll..4 B4
Port Ramsay Ag & B..94 B9
Portreath Cnwll..2 H7
Portreath Harbour Cnwll..2 H7
Portree Highld..100 d5
Port St Mary IoM..60 d9
Portscatho Cnwll..3 N9
Portsea C Port..9 S8
Portskerra Highld..111 U3
Portskewett Mons..27 U9
Portslade Br & H..11 L9
Portslade-by-Sea Br & H..11 L9
Portsmouth C Port..9 S9
Portsmouth Calder..56 D2
Port Soderick IoM..60 e8
Port Solent C Port..9 S7
Portsonachan Hotel Ag & B..88 B1
Portsoy Abers..104 H3
Port Sunlight Wirral..54 J10
Portswood C Sotn..9 N6
Port Talbot Neath..26 D10
Port Tennant Swans..26 C9
Portuairk Highld..93 L5
Portway Herefs..34 K12
Portway Herefs..35 L11
Portway Sandw..36 C3
Portway Worcs..36 E6
Port Wemyss Ag & B..78 B5
Port William D & G..72 K10
Portwrinkle Cnwll..4 K10
Portyerrock D & G..73 M12
Posbury Devon..15 T13
Posenhall Shrops..45 Q13
Poslingford Suffk..40 B11
Posso Border..83 P12
Postbridge Devon..5 S5
Postcombe Oxon..30 F12
Post Green Dorset..8 D10
Postling Kent..13 M8
Postwick Norfk..51 N11
Potarch Abers..99 L4
Potsgrove C Beds..31 L6
Potten End Herts..31 M11
Potten Street Kent..13 Q2
Potter Brompton N York..65 M4
Pottergate Street Norfk..41 L1
Potterhanworth Lincs..58 H13
Potterhanworth Booths Lincs..58 H13
Potter Heigham Norfk..51 R10
Potterne Wilts..18 E9
Potterne Wick Wilts..18 F9
Potter Row Bucks..30 K12
Potters Bar Herts..31 S12
Potters Brook Lancs..61 T9
Potter's Cross Staffs..35 T4
Potter's Forstal Kent..12 H6
Potters Green Covtry..37 L4
Potter's Green Herts..31 U7
Potters Marston Leics..47 N13
Potterspury Nhants..30 E4
Potter Somersal Derbys..46 G6
Potterton Abers..105 Q12
Potterton Leeds..63 U12
Pottle Street Wilts..18 B12
Potto N York..70 G12
Potton C Beds..39 L11
Pott Row Norfk..50 B9
Pott Shrigley Ches E..56 D11
Poughill Cnwll..14 F11
Poughill Devon..15 U11
Poulner Hants..8 H8
Poulshot Wilts..18 E8
Poulton Gloucs..29 L6
Poulton Wirral..54 G9
Poulton-le-Fylde Lancs..61 R12
Poulton Priory Gloucs..29 L7
Pound Bank Worcs..35 S6
Poundbury Dorset..7 S6
Poundffald Swans..25 U12
Pound Green E Susx..11 T5
Pound Green Suffk..40 B9
Pound Hill W Susx..11 M3
Poundon Bucks..30 D7
Poundsbridge Kent..11 S2
Poundsgate Devon..5 S6
Poundstock Cnwll..14 F13
Pound Street Hants..19 Q8
Pounsley E Susx..11 S6
Pouton D & G..73 L9
Pouy Street Suffk..41 P7
Povey Cross Surrey..11 M2
Powburn Nthumb..77 N3
Powderham Devon..6 C8
Powerstock Dorset..7 P5
Powfoot D & G..75 N12
Pow Green Herefs..35 R12
Powhill Cumb..66 K1
Powick Worcs..35 T10
Powmill P & K..90 F12
Poxwell Dorset..7 U8
Poyle Slough..20 H7
Poynings W Susx..11 L8
Poyntington Dorset..17 S13
Poynton Ches E..56 D10
Poynton Wrekin..45 N10
Poynton Green Wrekin..45 N10
Poystreet Green Suffk..40 G9
Praa Sands Cnwll..2 F11
Pratt's Bottom Gt Lon..21 S10
Praze-an-Beeble Cnwll..2 G9
Predannack Wollas Cnwll..2 H13
Prees Shrops..45 N6
Preesall Lancs..61 R11
Preesgweene Shrops..44 G6
Prees Green Shrops..45 N6
Prees Higher Heath Shrops..45 N6
Prees Lower Heath Shrops..45 N6
Pren-gwyn Cerdgn..32 H12
Prenton Wirral..54 H10
Prescot Knows..54 K8
Prescott Devon..16 E13
Prescott Shrops..44 K9
Prescott Shrops..35 U3
Presnerb Angus..98 C11
Pressen Nthumb..85 L11
Prestatyn Denbgs..53 U5
Prestbury Ches E..56 C11
Prestbury Gloucs..28 H3
Presteigne Powys..34 H8
Prestleigh Somset..17 R8
Preston Border..84 K8
Preston Br & H..11 N9
Preston Devon..5 V6
Preston Dorset..7 T8
Preston E R Yk..65 R13
Preston Gloucs..28 K7
Preston Herts..31 R8
Preston Kent..13 N3
Preston Kent..13 Q2

Preston Lancs..61 U14
Preston Nthumb..77 Q14
Preston Rutlnd..48 C13
Preston Shrops..45 M11
Preston Somset..16 E9
Preston Torbay..6 A12
Preston Wilts..18 H6
Preston Wilts..29 N6
Preston Bagot Warwks..36 G7
Preston Bissett Bucks..30 E7
Preston Bowyer Somset..16 F11
Preston Brockhurst Shrops..45 M9
Preston Brook Halton..55 N10
Preston Candover Hants..19 T12
Preston Capes Nhants..37 Q10
Preston Crematorium Lancs..62 B13
Preston Crowmarsh Oxon..19 T2
Preston Deanery Nhants..37 U9
Preston Green Warwks..36 G7
Preston Gubbals Shrops..45 L10
Preston Montford Shrops..44 K11
Preston on Stour Warwks..36 H11
Preston on Tees S on T..70 F9
Preston on the Hill Halton..55 M10
Preston on Wye Herefs..34 J12
Prestonpans E Loth..83 S4
Preston Patrick Cumb..61 U3
Preston Plucknett Somset..17 P13
Preston-under-Scar N York..69 M14
Preston upon the Weald Moors Wrekin..45 Q10
Preston Wynne Herefs..35 N11
Prestwich Bury..55 T6
Prestwick Nthumb..77 P11
Prestwick S Ayrs..81 L6
Prestwold Leics..47 Q9
Prestwood Bucks..30 J12
Prestwood Staffs..35 U3
Prickwillow Cambs..39 S4
Priddy Somset..17 P6
Priestacott Devon..14 K11
Priestcliffe Derbys..56 H12
Priestcliffe Ditch Derbys..56 H12
Priestland E Ayrs..81 Q5
Priestley Green Calder..56 H2
Priest Weston Shrops..34 G2
Priestwood Green Kent..12 C2
Primethorpe Leics..37 P2
Primrose Green Norfk..50 J10
Primrosehill Border..85 L7
Primrose Hill Cambs..39 L3
Primrose Hill Derbys..47 N3
Primrose Hill Dudley..36 B3
Primrose Hill Lancs..54 J4
Primsidemill Border..85 L13
Princes Gate Pembks..24 K7
Princes Risborough Bucks..30 H12
Princethorpe Warwks..37 M6
Princetown Devon..5 P5
Prinsted W Susx..9 U7
Prion Denbgs..44 C1
Prior Rigg Cumb..75 U12
Priors Halton Shrops..34 K6
Priors Hardwick Warwks..37 N9
Priorslee Wrekin..45 R11
Priors Marston Warwks..37 N9
Priors Norton Gloucs..28 G3
Priory Vale Swindn..29 M10
Priory Wood Herefs..34 G12
Prisk V Glam..26 J12
Priston BaNES..17 T4
Pristow Green Norfk..40 K3
Prittlewell Sthend..23 L10
Privett Hants..9 T4
Prixford Devon..15 M5
Probus Cnwll..3 M7
Proncy Highld..109 P6
Prospect Cumb..66 H4
Prospidnick Cnwll..2 G10
Prowse Devon..15 U11
Prussia Cove Cnwll..2 F11
Publow BaNES..17 R4
Puckeridge Herts..31 U7
Puckington Somset..17 L13
Pucklechurch S Glos..28 C12
Puckrup Gloucs..35 U14
Puddinglake Ches W..55 R13
Puddington Ches W..54 H12
Puddington Devon..15 T10
Puddledock Norfk..40 J2
Puddletown Dorset..7 U5
Pudleston Herefs..35 N9
Pudsey Leeds..63 Q13
Pulborough W Susx..10 G7
Puleston Wrekin..45 R9
Pulford Ches W..44 J2
Pulham Dorset..7 T3
Pulham Market Norfk..41 L3
Pulham St Mary Norfk..41 M3
Pullens Green S Glos..28 B9
Pulloxhill C Beds..31 N5
Pumpherston W Loth..83 L5
Pumsaint Carmth..33 N12
Puncheston Pembks..24 H5
Puncknowle Dorset..7 P7
Punnett's Town E Susx..12 C10
Purbrook Hants..9 T7
Purfleet Thurr..22 E12
Puriton Somset..16 K8
Purleigh Essex..23 L7
Purley W Berk..19 U6
Purley on Thames W Berk..19 U6
Purlogue Shrops..34 G6
Purlpit Wilts..18 C7
Purls Bridge Cambs..39 Q3
Purse Caundle Dorset..7 S2
Purshull Green Worcs..35 U6
Purslow Shrops..34 J4
Purston Jaglin Wakefd..57 P3
Purtington Somset..7 L3
Purton Gloucs..28 C6
Purton Gloucs..28 C6
Purton Wilts..29 L10
Purton Stoke Wilts..29 L9
Pury End Nhants..37 U11
Pusey Oxon..29 S8
Putley Herefs..35 P13
Putley Green Herefs..35 P13
Putney Gt Lon..21 N8
Putney Vale Crematorium Gt Lon..21 M8
Putsborough Devon..14 K4
Puttenham Herts..30 K10
Puttenham Surrey..20 F13
Puttock End Essex..40 D13
Puxley Nhants..30 E4
Puxton N Som..17 M4
Pwll Carmth..25 S10
Pwllcrochan Pembks..24 F10
Pwll-du Mons..27 N5
Pwll-glas Denbgs..44 D2
Pwllgloyw Powys..34 B13
Pwllheli Gwynd..42 G6
Pwllmeyric Mons..27 U8
Pwll-trap Carmth..25 L7
Pwll-y-glaw Neath..26 D9
Pydew Conwy..53 P7
Pye Bridge Derbys..47 M3
Pyecombe W Susx..11 L8
Pye Corner Herts..22 B5
Pye Corner Newpt..27 Q11
Pye Green Staffs..46 B11
Pyle Brdgnd..26 E11
Pyle IoW..9 P13
Pyleigh Somset..16 F10
Pylle Somset..17 R9
Pymoor Cambs..39 Q3
Pymore Dorset..7 N6
Pyrford Surrey..20 H11
Pyrton Oxon..30 E13
Pytchley Nhants..38 B6
Pyworthy Devon..14 J12

Q

Quabbs Shrops..34 F4
Quadring Lincs..48 K7
Quadring Eaudike Lincs..48 K7
Quainton Bucks..30 F8
Quaker's Yard Myr Td..26 K8
Quaking Houses Dur..69 Q2
Quarley Hants..19 L12
Quarndon Derbys..46 K5
Quarr Hill IoW..9 R10
Quarrier's Village Inver..88 J12
Quarrington Lincs..48 G5
Quarrington Hill Dur..70 D5
Quarrybank Ches W..55 N13
Quarry Bank Dudley..36 B3
Quarrywood Moray..103 V3
Quarter N Ayrs..88 D13
Quarter S Lans..82 D8
Quatford Shrops..35 R2
Quatt Shrops..35 S3
Quebec Dur..69 Q4
Quedgeley Gloucs..28 F5
Queen Adelaide Cambs..39 S4
Queenborough Kent..23 M13

Queen Camel Somset..17 Q12
Queen Charlton BaNES..17 R3
Queen Dart Devon..15 U9
Queen Elizabeth Forest Park Stirlg..89 M5
Queenhill Worcs..35 U13
Queen Oak Dorset..17 U10
Queen's Bower IoW..9 R12
Queensbury C Brad..63 N13
Queensferry Flints..54 H13
Queen's Head Shrops..44 H9
Queenslie C Glas..89 Q12
Queen's Park Bed..38 F11
Queen Street Kent..12 C6
Queen Street Wilts..28 K10
Queenzieburn N Lans..89 Q10
Quendon Essex..22 D1
Queniborough Leics..47 S11
Quenington Gloucs..29 M7
Quernmore Lancs..61 U8
Queslett Birm..36 E2
Quethiock Cnwll..4 J8
Quick's Green W Berk..19 S5
Quidenham Norfk..40 H3
Quidhampton Hants..19 R10
Quidhampton Wilts..8 G2
Quina Brook Shrops..45 M7
Quinbury End Nhants..37 Q10
Quinton Dudley..36 C3
Quinton Nhants..37 U9
Quinton Green Nhants..37 U9
Quintrell Downs Cnwll..3 L4
Quixhall Staffs..46 F5
Quixwood Border..84 K6
Quoditch Devon..14 K13
Quoig P & K..89 S6
Quoisley Ches E..45 M4
Quorn Leics..47 Q10
Quothquan S Lans..82 H11
Quoyburray Ork..106 u19
Quoyloo Ork..106 r17

R

Raasay Highld..100 e5
Rabbit's Cross Kent..12 E6
Rableyheath Herts..31 R9
Raby Cumb..66 J2
Raby Wirral..54 J11
Rachan Mill Border..83 M12
Rachub Gwynd..52 K9
Rackenford Devon..15 U9
Rackham W Susx..10 G8
Rackheath Norfk..51 N11
Racks D & G..74 K11
Rackwick Ork..106 r20
Radbourne Derbys..46 J6
Radcliffe Bury..55 S5
Radcliffe Nthumb..77 R5
Radcliffe on Trent Notts..47 R6
Radclive Bucks..30 E6
Radcot Oxon..29 R8
Raddery Highld..102 K5
Raddington Somset..16 E11
Radernie Fife..91 Q10
Radford BaNES..17 S5
Radford Semele Warwks..36 K7
Radlet Somset..16 H9
Radlett Herts..31 P11
Radley Oxon..19 S2
Radley Green Essex..22 F6
Radmore Green Ches E..45 N2
Radnage Bucks..30 F12
Radstock BaNES..17 S5
Radstone Nhants..30 C4
Radway Warwks..37 L11
Radwell Bed..38 F9
Radwell Herts..31 R5
Radwinter Essex..39 T13
Radwinter End Essex..39 T13
Radyr Cardif..27 L11
RAF College (Cranwell) Lincs..48 F3
Rafford Moray..103 R5
RAF Museum Cosford Shrops..45 S12
RAF Museum Hendon Gt Lon..21 M4
Ragdale Leics..47 S10
Ragginis Cnwll..2 D11
Raglan Mons..27 S6
Ragnall Notts..58 D12
Rahoy Highld..93 R7
Raigbeg Highld..103 M10
Rainbow Hill Worcs..35 U9
Rainford St Hel..54 K6
Rainford Junction St Hel..54 K6
Rainham Gt Lon..22 D11
Rainham Medway..12 F2
Rainhill St Hel..54 K8
Rainhill Stoops St Hel..55 L8
Rainow Ches E..56 D12
Rainsough Bury..55 T6
Rainton N York..63 T4
Rainworth Notts..47 R2
Raisbeck Cumb..68 E11
Raise Cumb..68 F3
Raisthorpe N York..64 K6
Rait P & K..90 K6
Raithby Lincs..59 Q10
Raithby Lincs..59 R13
Raithwaite N York..71 P9
Rake Hants..10 C5
Rakewood Rochdl..56 E4
Ralia Highld..97 N5
Ram Carmth..33 L12
Ramasaig Highld..100 a5
Rame Cnwll..2 K10
Rame Cnwll..5 M11
Ram Hill S Glos..28 C12
Ram Lane Kent..12 J6
Rampisham Dorset..7 P4
Rampside Cumb..61 N6
Rampton Cambs..39 P8
Rampton Notts..58 C11
Ramsbottom Bury..55 S4
Ramsbury Wilts..19 L6
Ramscraigs Highld..112 B12
Ramsdean Hants..9 U4
Ramsdell Hants..19 S9
Ramsden Oxon..29 R5
Ramsden Worcs..36 B12
Ramsden Bellhouse Essex..22 H9
Ramsden Heath Essex..22 H8
Ramsey Cambs..39 L3
Ramsey Essex..23 S1
Ramsey IoM..60 h4
Ramsey Forty Foot Cambs..39 M3
Ramsey Heights Cambs..39 L3
Ramsey Island Essex..23 M6
Ramsey Mereside Cambs..39 L2
Ramsey St Mary's Cambs..39 L3
Ramsgate Kent..13 S2
Ramsgill N York..63 M6
Ramshaw Dur..68 K4
Ramshaw Dur..69 N7
Ramsholt Suffk..41 N12
Ramshope Nthumb..76 H5
Ramshorn Staffs..46 E4
Ramsnest Common Surrey..10 E4
Ranby Lincs..59 L11
Ranby Notts..57 U10
Rand Lincs..58 K11
Randalls Park Crematorium Surrey..21 L11
Randwick Gloucs..28 F6
Ranfurly Rens..88 J13
Rangemore Staffs..46 G9
Rangeworthy S Glos..28 C10
Rankinston E Ayrs..81 N9
Rank's Green Essex..22 H5
Ranksborough Rutlnd..48 B11
Rannoch Station P & K..95 L7
Ranochan Highld..100 f11
Ranscombe Somset..16 C8
Ranskill Notts..57 U9
Ranton Staffs..45 U9
Ranton Green Staffs..45 T9
Ranworth Norfk..51 Q11
Raploch Stirlg..89 S7
Rapness Ork..106 u15
Rascarrel D & G..73 T11
Rashfield Ag & B..88 E9
Rashwood Worcs..35 U7
Raskelf N York..64 B6
Rassau Blae G..27 M5
Rastrick Calder..56 H2
Ratagan Highld..101 M8
Ratby Leics..47 P12
Ratcliffe Culey Leics..47 L14
Ratcliffe on Soar Notts..47 N8
Ratcliffe on the Wreake Leics..47 R11
Ratfyn Wilts..18 H12
Rathen Abers..105 R3
Rathillet Fife..91 M7
Ratho C Edin..83 M4
Ratho Station C Edin..83 M4
Rathven Moray..104 E3
Ratlake Hants..9 M4
Ratley Warwks..37 L11
Ratling Kent..13 P5
Ratlinghope Shrops..34 K1

Rattan Row Norfk..49 R10
Rattar Highld..112 G2
Ratten Row Cumb..66 K3
Ratten Row Cumb..67 N4
Ratten Row Lancs..61 S11
Rattery Devon..5 S8
Rattlesden Suffk..40 G9
Rattray P & K..90 J2
Raughton Cumb..67 N3
Raughton Head Cumb..67 N3
Raunds Nhants..38 E6
Ravenfield Rothm..57 Q7
Ravenglass Cumb..66 F12
Ravenhills Green Worcs..35 R10
Raveningham Norfk..51 R14
Ravenscar N York..71 T12
Ravenscraig N Lans..82 E7
Ravensdale IoM..60 f4
Ravensden Bed..38 G9
Ravenseat N York..68 J12
Ravenshead Notts..47 Q2
Ravensmoor Ches E..45 P3
Ravensthorpe Kirk..56 K2
Ravensthorpe Nhants..37 S6
Ravenstone Leics..47 M11
Ravenstone M Keyn..38 C10
Ravenstonedale Cumb..68 F12
Ravenstruther S Lans..82 H9
Ravensworth N York..69 Q11
Raw N York..71 T11
Rawcliffe E R Yk..57 U2
Rawcliffe C York..64 D9
Rawcliffe Bridge E R Yk..57 U2
Rawdon Leeds..63 Q12
Rawdon Crematorium Leeds..63 Q12
Rawling Street Kent..12 H4
Rawmarsh Rothm..57 P7
Rawnsley Staffs..46 D11
Rawreth Essex..22 J9
Rawridge Devon..6 J3
Rawtenstall Lancs..55 T2
Raydon Suffk..40 H13
Raylees Nthumb..76 K6
Rayleigh Essex..22 K9
Raymond's Hill Devon..6 K5
Rayne Essex..22 H3
Raynes Park Gt Lon..21 M9
Reach Cambs..39 R8
Read Lancs..62 F13
Reading Readg..20 B7
Reading Crematorium Readg..20 B7
Reading Services W Berk..19 S5
Reading Street Kent..12 H9
Reading Street Kent..13 T2
Reagill Cumb..68 D9
Realwa Cnwll..2 F10
Rearquhar Highld..109 N6
Rearsby Leics..47 S11
Rease Heath Ches E..45 P3
Reay Highld..111 T3
Reculver Kent..13 P2
Red Ball Devon..16 E13
Redberth Pembks..24 J10
Redbourn Herts..31 P10
Redbourne N Linc..58 F7
Redbrook Gloucs..27 U6
Redbrook Wrexhm..45 M5
Redbrook Street Kent..12 H8
Redburn Highld..103 R6
Redburn Nthumb..76 F13
Redcar R & Cl..70 K7
Redcastle Angus..99 L13
Redcastle Highld..102 G6
Red Dial Cumb..66 K3
Redding Falk..82 H3
Reddingmuirhead Falk..82 H3
Reddish Stockp..56 C8
Redditch Worcs..36 D7
Redditch Crematorium Worcs..36 D7
Rede Suffk..40 D9
Redenhall Norfk..41 M3
Redenham Hants..19 L11
Redesmouth Nthumb..76 H9
Redford Abers..99 P8
Redford Angus..91 S2
Redford W Susx..10 D6
Redfordgreen Border..75 R2
Redgate Rhondd..26 K9
Redgrave Suffk..40 J5
Redhill Abers..99 P3
Redhill Herts..31 T6
Redhill N Som..17 N4
Redhill Surrey..21 N12
Red Hill Warwks..36 F9
Redisham Suffk..41 R3
Redland Bristl..27 V12
Redland Ork..106 s18
Redlingfield Suffk..41 L6
Redlingfield Green Suffk..41 L6
Red Lodge Suffk..39 U6
Red Lumb Rochdl..55 T4
Redlynch Somset..17 S10
Redlynch Wilts..8 J4
Redmain Cumb..66 H5
Redmarley Worcs..35 S7
Redmarley D'Abitot Gloucs..35 S14
Redmarshall S on T..70 E8
Redmile Leics..48 B6
Redmire N York..63 L1
Redmyre Abers..99 N8
Rednal Birm..36 D5
Rednal Shrops..44 J8
Redpath Border..84 F12
Redpoint Highld..107 L10
Red Post Cnwll..14 G11
Red Rock Wigan..55 M5
Red Roses Carmth..25 L7
Red Row Nthumb..77 R7
Redstone P & K..90 J5
Redstone Cross Pembks..24 J6
Redvales Bury..55 T5
Red Wharf Bay IoA..52 H6
Redwick Newpt..27 S10
Redwick S Glos..27 U10
Redworth Darltn..69 S8
Reed Herts..31 T5
Reedham Norfk..51 R13
Reedness E R Yk..58 C2
Reeds Beck Lincs..59 L13
Reeds Holme Lancs..55 T2
Reepham Lincs..58 H12
Reepham Norfk..50 J9
Reeth N York..69 N13
Reeves Green Solhll..36 H5
Regaby IoM..60 g3
Regil BaNES..17 P4
Reiff Highld..107 L1
Reigate Surrey..21 M12
Reighton N York..65 Q4
Reisque Abers..105 P12
Reiss Highld..112 H6
Rejerrah Cnwll..3 L5
Releath Cnwll..2 H10
Relubbus Cnwll..2 F10
Relugas Moray..103 R6
Remenham Wokhm..20 C6
Remenham Hill Wokhm..20 C6
Rempstone Notts..47 Q9
Rendcomb Gloucs..28 K6
Rendham Suffk..41 P8
Rendlesham Suffk..41 P9
Renfrew Rens..89 L13
Renhold Bed..38 G10
Renishaw Derbys..57 Q11
Rennington Nthumb..77 Q2
Renton W Duns..88 J10
Renwick Cumb..67 S3
Repps Norfk..51 R10
Repton Derbys..46 K8
Resaurie Highld..102 K6
Rescassa Cnwll..3 P8
Rescorla Cnwll..3 Q5
Resipole Highld..93 S6
Resolis Highld..102 K3
Resolven Neath..26 F7
Rest and be thankful Ag & B..88 F4
Reston Border..85 L6
Restronguet Cnwll..3 L9
Reswallie Angus..98 J13
Reterth Cnwll..3 N3
Retford Notts..58 B10
Retire Cnwll..3 Q3
Retyn Cnwll..3 M5
Revesby Lincs..59 M14
Rew Devon..5 S12
Rew Devon..5 U6
Rewe Devon..6 B5
Rew Street IoW..9 P10
Rexon Devon..5 L4
Reydon Suffk..41 T5
Reymerston Norfk..50 H12
Reynalton Pembks..24 J9
Reynoldston Swans..25 S13
Rezare Cnwll..4 J6
Rhadyr Mons..27 Q6
Rhandirmwyn Carmth..33 Q13
Rhayader Powys..33 U8
Rhes-y-cae Flints..54 E13
Rhewl Denbgs..44 D4
Rhewl Denbgs..44 E1
Rhewl-fawr Flints..54 D10

Rhewl Mostyn Flints 54 E10
Rhicarn Highld 110 B11
Rhiconich Highld 110 F6
Rhicullen Highld 109 M10
Rhigos Rhondd 26 G6
Rhireavach Highld 107 T5
Rhives Highld 109 Q4
Rhiwbina Cardif 27 M11
Rhiwbryfdir Gwynd 43 N4
Rhiwderyn Newpt 27 P10
Rhiwen Gwynd 52 J10
Rhiwinder Rhondd 26 J10
Rhiwlas Gwynd 43 T6
Rhiwlas Gwynd 52 J9
Rhiwlas Powys 44 E7
Rhiwsaeson Rhondd 26 K11
Rhode Somset 16 J10
Rhoden Green Kent 12 C6
Rhodesia Notts 57 S11
Rhodes Minnis Kent 13 N7
Rhodiad-y-brenin Pembks 24 C5
Rhonehouse D & G 74 D14
Rhoose V Glam 16 E3
Rhos Carmth 25 Q3
Rhos Denbgs 44 D1
Rhos Neath 26 C7
Rhosbeirio IoA 52 E4
Rhoscefnhir IoA 52 H7
Rhoscolyn IoA 52 C7
Rhoscrowther Pembks 24 F10
Rhosesmor Flints 54 F13
Rhos-fawr Gwynd 42 G6
Rhosgadfan Gwynd 52 H11
Rhosgoch IoA 52 F5
Rhosgoch Powys 34 E11
Rhos Haminiog Cerdgn 32 K8
Rhoshill Pembks 32 C12
Rhoshirwaun Gwynd 42 D8
Rhoslan Gwynd 42 J5
Rhoslefain Gwynd 43 L12
Rhosllanerchrugog Wrexhm 44 G4
Rhôs Lligwy IoA 52 G5
Rhosmaen Carmth 26 A3
Rhosmeirch IoA 52 G7
Rhosneigr IoA 52 D8
Rhosnesni Wrexhm 44 J3
Rhôs-on-Sea Conwy 53 P6
Rhosrobin Wrexhm 44 H3
Rhossili Swans 25 R13
Rhostryfan Gwynd 52 G11
Rhostyllen Wrexhm 44 H4
Rhosybol IoA 52 F5
Rhos y-brithdir Powys 44 D9
Rhosygadfa Shrops 44 H7
Rhos-y-garth Cerdgn 33 M6
Rhos-y-gwaliau Gwynd 43 T7
Rhos-y-llan Gwynd 42 D6
Rhosymedre Wrexhm 44 G5
Rhos-y-meirch Powys 34 G7
Rhu Ag & B 88 G9
Rhuallt Denbgs 54 C11
Rhubodach Ag & B 88 B11
Rhuddall Heath Ches W 45 N1
Rhuddlan Cerdgn 32 J12
Rhuddlan Denbgs 53 T7
Rhulen Powys 34 D11
Rhunahaorine Ag & B 79 N6
Rhyd Gwynd 43 M5
Rhydargaeau Carmth 25 R5
Rhydcymerau Carmth 25 U3
Rhydd Worcs 35 T11
Rhyd-Ddu Gwynd 52 J12
Rhydding Neath 26 C8
Rhydgaled Conwy 53 S10
Rhydlanfair Conwy 53 P12
Rhydlewis Cerdgn 32 F11
Rhydlios Gwynd 42 C8
Rhyd-lydan Conwy 43 S3
Rhydowen Cerdgn 32 H11
Rhydrosser Cerdgn 33 L7
Rhydspence Herefs 34 F11
Rhydtalog Flints 44 F3
Rhyd-uchaf Gwynd 43 T6
Rhyd-y-clafdy Gwynd 42 F7
Rhydycroesau Shrops 44 F7
Rhydyfelin Cerdgn 33 L5
Rhydyfelin Rhondd 26 K10
Rhyd-y-foel Conwy 53 R7
Rhydyfro Neath 26 C6
Rhyd-y-groes Gwynd 52 J9
Rhydymain Gwynd 43 R9
Rhyd-y-meirch Mons 27 Q6
Rhydymwyn Flints 54 F13
Rhyd-y pennau Cerdgn 33 M3
Rhyd-yr-onnen Gwynd 43 M13
Rhyd-y-sarn Gwynd 43 N5
Rhyl Denbgs 53 T6
Rhymney Caerph 27 L6
Rhynd P & K 90 J7
Rhynie Abers 104 F10
Rhynie Highld 109 Q9
Ribbesford Worcs 35 S6
Ribbleton Lancs 62 B13
Ribby Lancs 61 S13
Ribchester Lancs 62 D12
Riber Derbys 46 K2
Riby Lincs 59 L5
Riccall N York 64 E12
Riccarton Border 76 A7
Riccarton E Ayrs 81 N5
Richards Castle Herefs 35 L7
Richings Park Bucks 20 H7
Richmond Gt Lon 21 L8
Richmond N York 69 Q12
Richmond Sheff 57 P9
Richmond Fort Guern 6 c2
Rich's Holford Somset 16 F10
Rickerscote Staffs 46 B9
Rickford N Som 17 N5
Rickham Devon 5 T13
Rickinghall Suffk 40 H5
Rickling Essex 22 C1
Rickling Green Essex 22 D2
Rickmansworth Herts 20 J4
Riddell Border 84 E14
Riddings Derbys 47 M3
Riddlecombe Devon 15 P10
Riddlesden C Brad 63 M11
Ridge BaNES 17 Q5
Ridge Dorset 8 C11
Ridge Herts 31 R12
Ridge Wilts 8 D2
Ridgebourne Powys 34 C8
Ridge Green Surrey 21 P13
Ridge Lane Warwks 36 J2
Ridge Row Kent 13 P7
Ridgeway Derbys 57 P10
Ridgeway Worcs 36 D8
Ridgeway Cross Herefs 35 R11
Ridgewell Essex 40 B12
Ridgewood E Susx 11 R7
Ridgmont C Beds 31 L5
Riding Mill Nthumb 77 L13
Ridley Kent 12 B3
Ridley Nthumb 76 F13
Ridley Green Ches E 45 N3
Ridlington Norfk 51 P7
Ridlington Rutlnd 48 B13
Ridlington Street Norfk 51 P7
Ridsdale Nthumb 76 J9
Rievaulx N York 64 D2
Rigg D & G 75 Q12
Riggend N Lans 82 E4
Righoul Highld 103 N5
Rigmadon Park Cumb 62 C3
Rigsby Lincs 59 R11
Rigside S Lans 82 G11
Riley Green Lancs 55 P1
Rileyhill Staffs 46 F11
Rilla Mill Cnwll 4 H6
Rillaton Cnwll 4 H6
Rillington N York 64 K5
Rimington Lancs 62 G10
Rimpton Somset 17 R12
Rimswell E R Yk 65 U14
Rinaston Pembks 24 G5
Rindleford Shrops 35 R1
Ringford D & G 73 R8
Ringinglow Sheff 57 L10
Ringland Norfk 50 K11
Ringles Cross E Susx 11 R6
Ringlestone Kent 12 G4
Ringley Bolton 55 S5
Ringmer E Susx 11 Q8
Ringmore Devon 5 R11
Ringmore Devon 6 B10
Ring o'Bells Lancs 55 L4
Ringorm Moray 104 B7
Ring's End Cambs 49 N13
Ringsfield Suffk 41 R3
Ringsfield Corner Suffk 41 R3
Ringshall Herts 31 L10
Ringshall Suffk 40 H10
Ringshall Stocks Suffk 40 J10
Ringstead Nhants 38 E5
Ringstead Norfk 50 B5
Ringwood Hants 8 H7
Ringwould Kent 13 S6
Rinsey Cnwll 2 F11
Rinsey Croft Cnwll 2 G11
Ripe E Susx 11 S8
Ripley Derbys 47 L3
Ripley Hants 8 H9
Ripley N York 63 R7
Ripley Surrey 20 J11
Riplingham E R Yk 65 M13
Riplington Hants 9 T4
Ripon N York 63 S5
Rippingale Lincs 48 G8
Ripple Kent 13 S5
Ripple Worcs 35 U13
Ripponden Calder 56 F3
Risabus Ag & B 78 E7
Risbury Herefs 35 M10
Risby N Linc 58 F4
Risby Suffk 40 D7
Risca Caerph 27 N9
Rise E R Yk 65 R11
Riseden E Susx 11 U4
Riseden Kent 12 D8
Risegate Lincs 48 K8
Riseholme Lincs 58 G11
Risehow Cumb 66 F6
Riseley Bed 38 F8
Riseley Wokham 20 B10
Rishangles Suffk 41 L7
Rishton Lancs 62 E13
Rishworth Calder 56 F3
Rising Bridge Lancs 55 S1
Risley Derbys 47 N6
Risley Warrtn 55 Q8
Risplith N York 63 Q6
Rivar Wilts 19 M8
Rivenhall End Essex 22 K4
River Kent 13 Q7
River W Susx 10 E6
River Bank Cambs 39 R7
Riverford Highld 102 F5
Riverhead Kent 21 T11
Rivers Corner Dorset 7 U2
Rivington Lancs 55 P4
Rivington Services Lancs 55 P4
Roachill Devon 15 U8
Roade Nhants 37 U10
Road Green Norfk 41 N2
Roadhead Cumb 75 V11
Roadmeetings S Lans 82 G9
Roadside E Ayrs 81 R9
Roadside Highld 112 E4
Roadwater Somset 16 D9
Roag Highld 100 b5
Roa Island Cumb 61 N6
Roan of Craigoch S Ayrs 80 K12
Roast Green Essex 39 Q14
Roath Cardif 27 M12
Roberton Border 75 T3
Roberton S Lans 82 H13
Robertsbridge E Susx 12 D11
Roberttown Kirk 56 J2
Robeston Wathen Pembks 24 J7
Robgill Tower D & G 75 P11
Robin Hill Staffs 46 B2
Robin Hood Lancs 55 M4
Robin Hood Leeds 57 M1
Robin Hood Crematorium Solhll 36 F4
Robin Hood Doncaster Sheffield Airport Donc 57 U7
Robinhood End Essex 40 B13
Robin Hood's Bay N York 71 S11
Roborough Devon 5 N8
Roborough Devon 15 N9
Roby Knows 54 K8
Roby Mill Lancs 55 M5
Rocester Staffs 46 F6
Roch Pembks 24 E6
Rochdale Rochdl 56 C4
Rochdale Crematorium Rochdl 56 C4
Roche Cnwll 3 P4
Rochester Medway 12 D2
Rochester Nthumb 76 G6
Rochford Essex 23 L9
Rochford Worcs 35 P7
Roch Gate Pembks 24 E6
Rock Cnwll 3 N1
Rock Neath 26 D9
Rock Nthumb 77 Q1
Rock W Susx 10 J8
Rock Worcs 35 R6
Rockbeare Devon 6 D6
Rockbourne Hants 8 G5
Rockcliffe Cumb 75 S13
Rockcliffe D & G 66 B2
Rockcliffe Cross Cumb 75 R13
Rock End Staffs 45 U2
Rockend Torbay 6 B12
Rock Ferry Wirral 54 H9
Rockfield Highld 109 S8
Rockfield Mons 27 T5
Rockford Devon 15 S3
Rockford Hants 8 H7
Rockgreen Shrops 35 M5
Rockhampton S Glos 28 C9
Rockhead Cnwll 4 D4
Rockhill Shrops 34 G5
Rock Hill Worcs 36 C7
Rockingham Nhants 38 C2
Rockland All Saints Norfk 40 G1
Rockland St Mary Norfk 51 P13
Rockland St Peter Norfk 40 G1
Rockley Notts 58 B12
Rockley Wilts 18 J6
Rockliffe Lancs 56 C2
Rockville Ag & B 88 F7
Rockwell End Bucks 20 C5
Rockwell Green Somset 16 F12
Rodborough Gloucs 28 F7
Rodbourne Swindn 29 M10
Rodbourne Wilts 28 H11
Rodd Herefs 34 H8
Roddam Nthumb 77 L1
Rodden Dorset 7 R8
Roddymoor Dur 69 Q5
Rode Somset 18 B10
Rode Heath Ches E 45 T2
Rode Heath Ches E 56 C13
Rodel W Isls 106 f10
Roden Wrekin 45 N10
Rodhuish Somset 16 D9
Rodington Wrekin 45 N11
Rodington Heath Wrekin 45 N11
Rodley Gloucs 28 D5
Rodley Leeds 63 Q12
Rodmarton Gloucs 28 H8
Rodmell E Susx 11 Q9
Rodmersham Kent 12 H3
Rodmersham Green Kent 12 H3
Rodney Stoke Somset 17 N7
Rodsley Derbys 46 H5
Rodway Somset 16 J8
Roecliffe N York 63 T6
Roe Cross Tamesd 56 E7
Roe Green Herts 31 R11
Roe Green Herts 31 T6
Roe Green Salfd 55 S6
Roehampton Gt Lon 21 M8
Roffey W Susx 10 K4
Rogart Highld 109 N4
Rogate W Susx 10 C6
Roger Ground Cumb 67 N13
Rogerstone Newpt 27 P10
Roghadal W Isls 106 f10
Rogiet Mons 27 T10
Roke Oxon 19 T2
Roker Sundld 77 U14
Rollesby Norfk 51 R10
Rolleston Leics 47 T13
Rolleston Notts 47 T3
Rolleston on Dove Staffs 46 H8
Rolston E R Yk 65 S11
Rolstone N Som 17 L4
Rolvenden Kent 12 F9
Rolvenden Layne Kent 12 G9
Romaldkirk Dur 69 L8
Romanby N York 70 E14
Romanno Bridge Border 83 N9
Romansleigh Devon 15 R8
Romden Castle Kent 12 G7
Romesdal Highld 100 d4
Romford Dorset 8 F7
Romford Gt Lon 22 D10
Romiley Stockp 56 D8
Romney Street Kent 21 U10
Romsey Hants 9 M4
Romsley Shrops 35 S4
Romsley Worcs 36 C4
Rona Highld 100 f4
Ronachan Ag & B 79 N5
Rood Ashton Wilts 18 C9
Rookhope Dur 68 K4
Rookley IoW 9 Q12
Rookley Green IoW 9 Q12
Rooks Bridge Somset 17 L6
Rooks Nest Somset 16 E10
Rookwith N York 63 Q2
Roos E R Yk 65 T13
Roose Cumb 61 N6
Roosebeck Cumb 61 P6
Roothams Green Bed 38 G9
Ropley Hants 9 S2
Ropley Dean Hants 9 S2
Ropley Soke Hants 9 T2
Ropsley Lincs 48 E7
Rora Abers 105 T5
Rorrington Shrops 44 H13
Rosarie Moray 104 D5
Rose Cnwll 2 K6
Roseacre Lancs 61 S12
Rose Ash Devon 15 S8
Rosebank S Lans 82 F9
Rosebush Pembks 24 J5
Rosecare Cnwll 14 E13
Rosecliston Cnwll 3 L5
Rosedale Abbey N York 71 M13
Rose Green Essex 23 M2
Rose Green Suffk 40 F13
Rose Green Suffk 40 G12
Rose Green W Susx 10 E11
Rosehall Highld 108 H4
Rosehearty Abers 105 Q2
Rose Hill E Susx 11 R7
Rose Hill Lancs 62 G13
Rosehill Shrops 45 L10
Roseisle Moray 103 T2
Roselands E Susx 11 U10
Rosemarket Pembks 24 G9
Rosemarkie Highld 102 K4
Rosemary Lane Devon 6 G2
Rosemount P & K 90 J3
Rosenannon Cnwll 3 P3
Rosenithon Cnwll 3 L12
Roser's Cross E Susx 11 S6
Rosevean Cnwll 3 Q5
Rosevine Cnwll 3 M9
Rosewarne Cnwll 2 G9
Rosewell Mdloth 83 Q6
Roseworth S on T 70 F8
Roseworthy Cnwll 2 G9
Rosgill Cumb 67 R9
Roskestal Cnwll 2 B12
Roskhill Highld 100 b5
Roskorwell Cnwll 2 K12
Rosley Cumb 67 M3
Roslin Mdloth 83 Q6
Rosliston Derbys 46 H10
Rosneath Ag & B 88 G9
Ross D & G 73 Q11
Ross Nthumb 85 S11
Rossett Wrexhm 44 J2
Rossett Green N York 63 R9
Rossington Donc 57 T7
Rossland Rens 88 K11
Ross-on-Wye Herefs 28 A3
Roster Highld 112 G9
Rostherne Ches E 55 R10
Rosthwaite Cumb 67 L10
Roston Derbys 46 F5
Rosudgeon Cnwll 2 F11
Rosyth Fife 83 M2
Rothbury Nthumb 77 M5
Rotherby Leics 47 S10
Rotherfield E Susx 11 T5
Rotherfield Greys Oxon 20 B6
Rotherfield Peppard Oxon 20 B6
Rotherham Rothm 57 P8
Rotherham Crematorium Rothm 57 Q8
Rothersthorpe Nhants 37 T9
Rotherwick Hants 20 B11
Rothes Moray 104 B6
Rothesay Ag & B 88 C13
Rothiebrisbane Abers 105 L8
Rothiemay Moray 104 H6
Rothiemurchus Lodge Highld 97 R2
Rothiemurchus Visitor Centre Highld 103 P13
Rothienorman Abers 105 L8
Rothley Leics 47 Q11
Rothley Nthumb 77 L8
Rothmaise Abers 104 K9
Rothwell Leeds 63 S14
Rothwell Lincs 58 K7
Rothwell Nhants 38 B4
Rotsea E R Yk 65 P9
Rottal Lodge Angus 98 F10
Rottingdean Br & H 11 P10
Rottington Cumb 66 E10
Roucan D & G 74 K10
Roucan Loch Crematorium D & G 74 K10
Roud IoW 9 Q12
Rougham Norfk 50 D9
Rougham Green Suffk 40 F8
Rough Close Staffs 46 B6
Rough Common Kent 13 M4
Roughlee Lancs 62 G11
Roughpark Abers 104 C13
Roughton Lincs 59 M14
Roughton Norfk 51 M6
Roughton Shrops 35 S2
Roughway Kent 12 B5
Roundbush Essex 23 L7
Round Bush Herts 20 K3
Roundbush Green Essex 22 E5
Round Green Luton 31 P8
Roundham Somset 7 M3
Roundhay Leeds 63 S12
Rounds Green Sandw 36 C3
Round Street Kent 12 C2
Roundstreet Common W Susx 10 H5
Roundway Wilts 18 F8
Roundyhill Angus 98 F13
Rousay Ork 106 s16
Rousdon Devon 6 J6
Rousham Oxon 29 U3
Rous Lench Worcs 36 D10
Routenburn N Ayrs 88 E13
Routh E R Yk 65 P11
Rout's Green Bucks 20 C3
Row Cnwll 3 R1
Row Cumb 61 T2
Row Cumb 68 D6
Rowanburn D & G 75 T10
Rowardennan Stirlg 88 J6
Rowarth Derbys 56 F9
Row Ash Hants 9 Q6
Rowberrow Somset 17 N5
Rowborough IoW 9 P12
Rowde Wilts 18 E8
Rowden Devon 15 P13
Rowen Conwy 53 N8
Rowfield Derbys 46 G4
Rowfoot Nthumb 76 D13
Rowford Somset 16 H11
Row Green Essex 22 H3
Rowhedge Essex 23 P3
Rowhook W Susx 10 J4
Rowington Warwks 36 H7
Rowland Derbys 56 K12
Rowland's Castle Hants 9 U6
Rowland's Gill Gatesd 77 P14
Rowledge Surrey 10 C2
Rowley Dur 69 N3
Rowley E R Yk 65 M13
Rowley Shrops 44 H12
Rowley Hill Kirk 56 J4
Rowley Regis Sandw 36 C3
Rowley Regis Crematorium Sandw 36 C3
Rowlstone Herefs 27 R2
Rowly Surrey 10 G2
Rowner Hants 9 R8
Rowney Green Worcs 36 D6
Rownhams Hants 9 M5
Rownhams Services Hants 9 M5
Rowrah Cumb 66 G9
Rowsham Bucks 30 H9
Rowsley Derbys 57 L13
Rows of Trees Ches E 55 T11
Rowstock Oxon 29 U10
Rowston Lincs 48 G2
Rowthorne Derbys 57 Q14
Rowton Ches W 54 K14
Rowton Shrops 34 K4
Rowton Shrops 44 J11
Rowton Wrekin 45 P10
Row Town Surrey 20 H10
Roxburgh Border 84 H12
Roxby N Linc 58 F3
Roxby N York 71 N9
Roxton Bed 38 J10
Roxwell Essex 22 F6
Royal Leamington Spa Warwks 36 K7
Royal Oak Darltn 69 R8
Royal Oak Lancs 54 K6
Royal's Green Ches E 45 P5
Royal Tunbridge Wells Kent 11 T3
Royal Wootton Bassett Wilts 29 L11
Royal Yacht Britannia C Edin 83 Q3
Roy Bridge Highld 96 B7
Roydhouse Kirk 56 K4
Roydon Essex 22 B5
Roydon Norfk 40 K4
Roydon Norfk 50 B9
Roydon Hamlet Essex 22 B6
Royston Barns 57 N4
Royston Herts 31 U4
Royton Oldham 56 D5
Rozel Jersey 7 e2
Ruabon Wrexhm 44 H5
Ruaig Ag & B 92 D9
Ruan High Lanes Cnwll 3 N9
Ruan Lanihorne Cnwll 3 M8
Ruan Major Cnwll 2 J13
Ruan Minor Cnwll 2 J13
Ruardean Gloucs 28 B4
Ruardean Hill Gloucs 28 B4
Ruardean Woodside Gloucs 28 B4
Rubery Birm 36 C5
Rubha Ban W Isls 106 c17
Ruckcroft Cumb 67 R4
Ruckhall Herefs 35 L13
Ruckinge Kent 12 K9
Ruckland Lincs 59 P11
Ruckley Shrops 45 M13
Rudby N York 70 G11
Rudchester Nthumb 77 N12
Ruddington Notts 47 Q7
Ruddle Gloucs 28 C5
Ruddlemoor Cnwll 3 Q6
Rudford Gloucs 28 E3
Rudge Somset 18 B10
Rudgeway S Glos 28 B10
Rudgwick W Susx 10 H4
Rudhall Herefs 28 B2
Rudheath Ches W 55 Q12
Rudheath Woods Ches E 55 R12
Rudley Green Essex 22 K7
Rudloe Wilts 18 B6
Rudry Caerph 27 N10
Rudston E R Yk 65 P6
Rudyard Staffs 46 C2
Ruecastle Border 76 C1
Rufford Lancs 55 L3
Rufford Abbey Notts 57 T14
Rufforth C York 64 C9
Rug Denbgs 44 C5
Rugby Warwks 37 P5
Rugeley Staffs 46 D10
Ruishton Somset 16 J11
Ruislip Gt Lon 20 J5
Rùm Highld 100 c10
Rumbach Moray 104 D5
Rumbling Bridge P & K 90 F12
Rumburgh Suffk 41 P4
Rumby Hill Dur 69 Q6
Rumford Cnwll 3 M2
Rumford Falk 82 H3
Rumney Cardif 27 N12
Rumwell Somset 16 G12
Runcorn Halton 55 M10
Runcton W Susx 10 D10
Runcton Holme Norfk 49 T12
Runfold Surrey 20 E13
Runhall Norfk 50 J12
Runham Norfk 51 S11
Runham Norfk 51 T12
Runnington Somset 16 F12
Runsell Green Essex 22 J6
Runshaw Moor Lancs 55 M3
Runswick N York 71 P9
Runtaleave Angus 98 D10
Runway Visitor Park Manch 55 T10
Runwell Essex 22 J9
Ruscombe Wokham 20 C7
Rushall Herefs 35 P13
Rushall Norfk 41 L4
Rushall Wilts 18 H9
Rushall Wsall 46 D13
Rushbrooke Suffk 40 E8
Rushbury Shrops 35 M2
Rushden Herts 31 T6
Rushden Nhants 38 E7
Rushenden Kent 23 M13
Rusher's Cross E Susx 11 U5
Rushford Devon 5 M5
Rushford Norfk 40 F4
Rush Green Essex 23 S4
Rush Green Gt Lon 22 D10
Rush Green Herts 31 R8
Rush Green Warrtn 55 Q9
Rushlake Green E Susx 11 U7
Rushmere Suffk 41 S3
Rushmere St Andrew Suffk 41 L11
Rushmoor Surrey 10 D2
Rushock Herefs 34 H9
Rushock Worcs 35 U6
Rusholme Manch 56 C8
Rushton Ches W 55 N14
Rushton Nhants 38 B4
Rushton Shrops 45 P12
Rushton Spencer Staffs 46 B1
Rushwick Worcs 35 T10
Rushyford Dur 69 S7
Ruskie Stirlg 89 P5
Ruskington Lincs 48 G3
Rusland Cross Cumb 61 Q2
Rusper W Susx 11 L3
Ruspidge Gloucs 28 C5
Russell Green Essex 22 H5
Russell's Water Oxon 20 B5
Russel's Green Suffk 41 N6
Russ Hill Surrey 11 L2
Rusthall Kent 11 T3
Rustington W Susx 10 G10
Ruston N York 65 M3
Ruston Parva E R Yk 65 P7
Ruswarp N York 71 Q11
Ruthall Shrops 35 N2
Rutherford Border 84 G12
Rutherglen S Lans 89 P13
Ruthernbridge Cnwll 3 Q3
Ruthin Denbgs 44 D2
Ruthrieston C Aber 99 S3
Ruthven Abers 104 G6
Ruthven Angus 91 L2
Ruthven Highld 97 M4
Ruthvoes Cnwll 3 N4
Ruthwaite Cumb 66 K5
Ruthwell D & G 75 L12
Ruxley Corner Gt Lon 21 S8
Ruxton Green Herefs 27 U4
Ruyton-XI-Towns Shrops 44 J9
Ryal Nthumb 77 L11
Ryall Dorset 7 M5
Ryall Worcs 35 U12
Ryarsh Kent 12 C3
Rycote Oxon 30 E11
Rydal Cumb 67 N11
Ryde IoW 9 R10
Rye E Susx 12 H11
Ryebank Shrops 45 M7
Ryeford Herefs 28 B3
Rye Foreign E Susx 12 G11
Rye Harbour E Susx 12 H12
Ryehill E R Yk 59 M1
Ryeish Green Wokham 20 B9
Rye Street Worcs 35 S13
Ryhall Rutlnd 48 F11
Ryhill Wakefd 57 N4
Ryhope Sundld 70 F2
Rylah Derbys 57 Q13
Ryland Lincs 58 H11
Rylands Notts 47 P6
Rylstone N York 62 K8
Ryme Intrinseca Dorset 7 Q2
Ryther N York 64 D12
Ryton Gatesd 77 P13
Ryton N York 64 H4
Ryton Shrops 45 S13
Ryton Warwks 37 M3
Ryton-on-Dunsmore Warwks 37 L6
Ryton Woodside Gatesd 77 N13

S

Sabden Lancs 62 F12
Sabine's Green Essex 22 D8
Sacombe Herts 31 T9
Sacombe Green Herts 31 T9
Sacriston Dur 69 R3
Sadberge Darltn 70 D9
Saddell Ag & B 79 P9
Saddington Leics 37 S2
Saddle Bow Norfk 49 T10
Saddlescombe W Susx 11 M8
Sadgill Cumb 67 Q11
Saffron Walden Essex 39 R13
Sageston Pembks 24 J10
Saham Hills Norfk 50 F13
Saham Toney Norfk 50 E13
Saighton Ches W 44 K1
St Abbs Border 85 N5
St Agnes Border 84 H6
St Agnes Cnwll 2 J6
St Agnes IoS 2 b3
St Agnes Mining District Cnwll 2 J7
St Albans Herts 31 P11
St Allen Cnwll 3 L6
St Andrew Guern 6 d3
St Andrews Fife 91 R8
St Andrews Botanic Garden Fife 91 R8
St Andrew's Major V Glam 16 F2
St Andrews Well Dorset 7 N6
St Anne's Lancs 61 Q14
St Ann's D & G 75 L7
St Ann's Chapel Cnwll 5 L6
St Ann's Chapel Devon 5 R11
St Anthony Cnwll 2 K11
St Anthony's Hill E Susx 11 U10
St Arvans Mons 27 U8
St Asaph Denbgs 53 T8
St Athan V Glam 16 D3
St Aubin Jersey 7 c3
St Austell Cnwll 3 Q6
St Bees Cumb 66 E10
St Blazey Cnwll 3 R6
St Blazey Gate Cnwll 3 R6
St Boswells Border 84 F12
St Brelade Jersey 7 b3
St Brelade's Bay Jersey 7 b3
St Breock Cnwll 3 P2
St Breward Cnwll 3 R1
St Briavels Gloucs 27 V7
St Brides Pembks 24 D8
St Bride's Major V Glam 26 F13
St Brides Netherwent Mons 27 S10
St Brides super-Ely V Glam 26 K12
St Brides Wentlooge Newpt 27 P11
St Budeaux C Plym 5 M9
Saintbury Gloucs 36 F13
St Buryan Cnwll 2 C11
St Catherine BaNES 17 U3
St Catherines Ag & B 88 D4
St Chloe Gloucs 28 F7
St Clears Carmth 25 N7
St Cleer Cnwll 4 G7
St Clement Cnwll 3 M8
St Clement Jersey 7 e4
St Clether Cnwll 4 G4
St Colmac Ag & B 88 B12
St Columb Major Cnwll 3 N4
St Columb Minor Cnwll 3 L4
St Columb Road Cnwll 3 N5
St Combs Abers 105 T3
St Cross South Elmham Suffk 41 N4
St Cyrus Abers 99 N11
St David's P & K 90 D7
St Davids Pembks 24 C5
St David's Cathedral Pembks 24 C5
St Day Cnwll 2 J8
St Decumans Somset 16 E8
St Dennis Cnwll 3 P5
St Devereux Herefs 27 S1
St Dogmaels Pembks 32 C11
St Dogwells Pembks 24 G5
St Dominick Cnwll 5 L7
St Donats V Glam 16 B3
St Edith's Marsh Wilts 18 E8
St Endellion Cnwll 4 B5
St Enoder Cnwll 3 M5
St Erme Cnwll 3 L7
St Erney Cnwll 4 K9
St Erth Cnwll 2 F9
St Erth Praze Cnwll 2 F9
St Ervan Cnwll 3 M2
St Eval Cnwll 3 M3
St Ewe Cnwll 3 P7
St Fagans Cardif 27 L12
St Fagans: National History Museum Cardif 27 L12
St Fergus Abers 105 T5
St Fillans P & K 95 T14
St Florence Pembks 24 J10
St Gennys Cnwll 14 D13
St George Conwy 53 S7
St Georges N Som 17 L4
St George's V Glam 27 L12
St George's Hill Surrey 20 J10
St Germans Cnwll 4 K9
St Giles in the Wood Devon 15 M9
St Giles-on-the-Heath Devon 4 K2
St Gluvia's Cnwll 2 K10
St Harmon Powys 33 U6
St Helen Auckland Dur 69 Q7
St Helens Cumb 66 F6
St Helens E Susx 12 F13
St Helens IoW 9 S11
St Helens St Hel 55 M7
St Helens Crematorium St Hel 55 L7
St Helier Gt Lon 21 N9
St Helier Jersey 7 d3
St Hilary Cnwll 2 E10
St Hilary V Glam 26 J13
Saint Hill Devon 6 E3
Saint Hill W Susx 11 P3
St Illtyd Blae G 27 N7
St Ippollitts Herts 31 Q7
St Ishmael's Pembks 24 D9
St Issey Cnwll 3 N2
St Ive Cnwll 4 J7
St Ive Cross Cnwll 4 J7
St Ives Cambs 39 M6
St Ives Cnwll 2 E8
St Ives Dorset 8 G8
St James Norfk 51 N9
St James's End Nhants 37 T8
St James South Elmham Suffk 41 P4
St Jidgey Cnwll 3 N3
St John Cnwll 5 L10
St John Jersey 7 c1
St Johns Dur 69 N6
St John's IoM 60 d6
St Johns Kent 21 T11
St Johns Surrey 20 G11
St Johns Worcs 35 T10
St John's Chapel Devon 15 M7
St John's Chapel Dur 68 J5
St John's Fen End Norfk 49 R11
St John's Highway Norfk 49 R11
St John's Kirk S Lans 82 J11
St John's Town of Dalry D & G 73 Q3
St John's Wood Gt Lon 21 N6
St Jude's IoM 60 f3
St Just Cnwll 2 B10
St Just-in-Roseland Cnwll 3 L9
St Just Mining District Cnwll 2 B10
St Katherines Abers 105 M9
St Keverne Cnwll 2 K12
St Kew Cnwll 3 Q1
St Kew Highway Cnwll 3 Q1
St Keyne Cnwll 4 G8
St Lawrence Cnwll 3 Q3
St Lawrence Essex 23 N7
St Lawrence IoW 9 Q13
St Lawrence Jersey 7 c2
St Lawrence Kent 13 S2
St Leonards Bucks 30 K11
St Leonards Dorset 8 G8
St Leonards E Susx 12 F14
St Leonard's Street Kent 12 C4
St Levan Cnwll 2 B12
St Lythans V Glam 27 L13
St Mabyn Cnwll 3 Q2
St Madoes P & K 90 J7
St Margarets Herefs 34 J14
St Margarets Herts 31 U10
St Margaret's at Cliffe Kent 13 S7
St Margaret's Bay Kent 13 S7
St Margaret's Hope Ork 106 t20
St Margaret South Elmham Suffk 41 P4
St Marks IoM 60 d8
St Martin Cnwll 2 J12
St Martin Cnwll 4 H9
St Martin Guern 6 d3
St Martin Jersey 7 e2
St Martin's IoS 2 c1
St Martin's P & K 90 J5
St Martins Shrops 44 H6
St Martin's Moor Shrops 44 H6
St Mary Jersey 7 c2
St Mary Bourne Hants 19 P10
St Marychurch Torbay 6 B11
St Mary Church V Glam 16 D2
St Mary Cray Gt Lon 21 S9
St Mary Hill V Glam 26 H12
St Mary in the Marsh Kent 13 L10
St Marylebone Crematorium Gt Lon 21 N5
St Mary's IoS 2 c2
St Mary's Ork 106 t19
St Mary's Bay Kent 13 L10
St Mary's Grove N Som 17 N3
St Mary's Hoo Medway 22 K12
St Maughans Mons 27 T4
St Maughans Green Mons 27 T4
St Mawes Cnwll 3 L10
St Mawgan Cnwll 3 M3
St Mellion Cnwll 4 K7
St Mellons Cardif 27 N11
St Merryn Cnwll 3 M2
St Mewan Cnwll 3 P6
St Michael Caerhays Cnwll 3 P8
St Michael Church Somset 16 K10
St Michael Penkevil Cnwll 3 M8
St Michaels Kent 12 G8
St Michaels Worcs 35 N7
St Michael's Mount Cnwll 2 E11
St Michael's on Wyre Lancs 61 T11
St Michael South Elmham Suffk 41 P4
St Minver Cnwll 4 B5
St Monans Fife 91 R11
St Neot Cnwll 4 F7
St Neots Cambs 38 J8
St Nicholas Pembks 24 F3
St Nicholas V Glam 26 K13
St Nicholas at Wade Kent 13 Q2
St Ninians Stirlg 89 S7
St Olaves Norfk 51 S14
St Osyth Essex 23 R4
St Ouen Jersey 7 b2
St Owens Cross Herefs 27 U3
St Pauls Cray Gt Lon 21 S9
St Paul's Walden Herts 31 Q8
St Peter Jersey 7 b2
St Peter Port Guern 6 e3
St Peter's Guern 6 c3
St Peter's Kent 13 S2
St Peter's Hill Cambs 38 K6
St Petrox Pembks 24 G11
St Pinnock Cnwll 4 G8
St Quivox S Ayrs 81 M8
St Ruan Cnwll 2 J13
St Sampson Guern 6 e2
St Saviour Guern 6 c3
St Saviour Jersey 7 d3
St Stephen Cnwll 3 N6
St Stephens Cnwll 4 J3
St Stephens Cnwll 5 L9
St Teath Cnwll 4 D4
St Tudy Cnwll 3 R1
St Twynnells Pembks 24 G11
St Veep Cnwll 4 E9
St Vigeans Angus 91 T3
St Wenn Cnwll 3 P4
St Weonards Herefs 27 T3
St y-Nyll V Glam 26 K12
Salcey Forest 38 B10
Salcombe Devon 5 S13
Salcombe Regis Devon 6 G7
Salcott-cum-Virley Essex 23 M5
Sale Traffd 55 S8
Saleby Lincs 59 S11
Sale Green Worcs 36 B9
Salehurst E Susx 12 E11
Salem Carmth 25 V5
Salem Cerdgn 33 N4
Salen Ag & B 93 P10
Salen Highld 93 R6
Salesbury Lancs 62 D13
Salford C Beds 30 K5
Salford Oxon 29 Q2
Salford Salfd 55 T7
Salford Priors Warwks 36 E10
Salfords Surrey 21 N13
Salhouse Norfk 51 P11
Saline Fife 90 F13
Salisbury Wilts 8 G3
Salisbury Crematorium Wilts 8 H2
Salisbury Plain Wilts 18 G12
Salkeld Dykes Cumb 67 R5
Salle Norfk 50 K9
Salmonby Lincs 59 P12
Salperton Gloucs 29 L3
Salph End Bed 38 G10
Salsburgh N Lans 82 F6
Salt Staffs 46 C8
Salta Cumb 66 G3
Saltaire C Brad 63 N12
Saltaire C Brad 63 N12
Saltash Cnwll 5 L9
Saltburn Highld 109 N10
Saltburn-by-the-Sea R & Cl 71 L8
Saltby Leics 48 C8
Salt Coates Cumb 66 J2
Saltcoats Cumb 66 G13
Saltcoats N Ayrs 80 J4
Saltcotes Lancs 61 R14
Saltdean Br & H 11 P10
Salterbeck Cumb 66 E7
Salterforth Lancs 62 H10
Salterswall Ches W 55 P13
Salterton Wilts 18 H13
Saltfleet Lincs 59 S8
Saltfleetby All Saints Lincs 59 S8
Saltfleetby St Clement Lincs 59 S8
Saltfleetby St Peter Lincs 59 R9
Saltford BaNES 17 S3
Salthouse Norfk 50 J5
Saltley Birm 36 F3
Saltmarsh Newpt 27 Q11
Saltmarshe E R Yk 58 C2
Saltney Flints 54 J14
Salton N York 64 G4
Saltrens Devon 15 L8
Saltwell Crematorium Gatesd 77 R13
Saltwick Nthumb 77 P9
Saltwood Kent 13 N8
Salvington W Susx 10 J9
Salwarpe Worcs 35 U8
Salway Ash Dorset 7 N5
Sambourne Warwks 36 E8
Sambrook Wrekin 45 R9
Samlesbury Lancs 62 B13
Samlesbury Bottoms Lancs 62 C14
Sampford Arundel Somset 16 F13
Sampford Brett Somset 16 E8
Sampford Courtenay Devon 15 P12
Sampford Moor Somset 16 F13
Sampford Peverell Devon 6 D2
Sampford Spiney Devon 5 N6
Samsonlane Ork 106 v17
Samson's Corner Essex 23 Q4
Samuelston E Loth 84 D4
Sanaigmore Ag & B 86 C11
Sancreed Cnwll 2 C11
Sancton E R Yk 64 K12
Sand Somset 17 M7
Sandaig Highld 100 g9
Sandale Cumb 66 K4
Sandal Magna Wakefd 57 M3
Sandavore Highld 93 M2
Sanday Ork 106 v15
Sanday Airport Ork 106 v15
Sandbach Ches E 45 S1
Sandbach Services Ches E 45 S1
Sandbank Ag & B 88 E9
Sandbanks Poole 8 E11
Sandend Abers 104 H2
Sanderstead Gt Lon 21 P10
Sandford Cumb 68 F9
Sandford Devon 15 T12
Sandford Dorset 8 C11
Sandford Hants 8 H8
Sandford IoW 9 Q12
Sandford N Som 17 M5
Sandford S Lans 82 D10
Sandford Shrops 44 H9
Sandford Shrops 45 N7
Sandford-on-Thames Oxon 30 B12
Sandford Orcas Dorset 17 R12
Sandford St Martin Oxon 29 T2
Sandgate Kent 13 P8
Sandhaven Abers 105 R2
Sandhead D & G 72 D10
Sandhill Rothm 57 P7
Sandhills Dorset 7 Q4
Sandhills Dorset 7 S2
Sand Hills Leeds 63 T12
Sandhills Oxon 30 C11
Sandhills Surrey 10 E3
Sandhoe Nthumb 76 K12
Sandhole Ag & B 87 U6
Sand Hole E R Yk 64 J12
Sandholme E R Yk 64 J13
Sandholme Lincs 49 M6
Sandhurst Br For 20 D10
Sandhurst Gloucs 28 F3
Sandhurst Kent 12 F10
Sandhurst Cross Kent 12 E10
Sandhutton N York 63 T3
Sand Hutton N York 64 F8
Sandiacre Derbys 47 N6
Sandilands Lincs 59 T10
Sandiway Ches W 55 P12
Sandleheath Hants 8 G5
Sandleigh Oxon 29 U7
Sandley Dorset 17 U12
Sandling Kent 12 E4
Sandlow Green Ches E 55 S13
Sandness Shet 106 r8
Sandon Essex 22 H7
Sandon Herts 31 T6
Sandon Staffs 46 B8
Sandon Bank Staffs 46 B8
Sandown IoW 9 R12
Sandplace Cnwll 4 H9
Sandridge Herts 31 Q10
Sandridge Wilts 18 D7
Sandringham Norfk 49 U8
Sands Bucks 20 D4
Sandsend N York 71 Q10
Sand Side Cumb 61 N3
Sandside Cumb 61 T3
Sandtoft N Linc 58 B5
Sandway Kent 12 G5
Sandwich Kent 13 R4
Sandwick Cumb 67 P9
Sandwick Shet 106 u11
Sandwick W Isls 106 j5
Sandwith Cumb 66 E10
Sandwith Newtown Cumb 66 E10
Sandy C Beds 38 J11
Sandy Bank Lincs 49 L2
Sandycroft Flints 54 H13
Sandy Cross E Susx 11 T6
Sandy Cross Herefs 35 Q9
Sandyford D & G 75 P7
Sandygate Devon 5 V6
Sandygate IoM 60 f3
Sandy Haven Pembks 24 E9
Sandyhills D & G 66 C1
Sandylands Lancs 61 S7
Sandy Lane C Brad 63 N12
Sandylane Staffs 45 R6
Sandylane Swans 25 U13
Sandy Lane Wilts 18 E7
Sandy Lane Wrexhm 44 K5
Sandy Park Devon 5 S3
Sandysike Cumb 75 S12
Sandyway Herefs 27 T2
Sangobeg Highld 110 J3
Sangomore Highld 110 J3
Sankey Bridges Warrtn 55 N9
Sankyn's Green Worcs 35 S7
Sanna Bay Highld 93 L5
Sanndabhaig W Isls 106 j5
Sannox N Ayrs 80 E3
Sanquhar D & G 74 E4
Santon Cumb 66 H12
Santon IoM 60 e8
Santon Bridge Cumb 66 H12
Santon Downham Suffk 40 D3
Sapcote Leics 37 N2
Sapey Common Herefs 35 R8
Sapiston Suffk 40 F5
Sapley Cambs 38 K6
Sapperton Derbys 46 G7
Sapperton Gloucs 28 H7
Sapperton Lincs 48 F7
Saracen's Head Lincs 49 M8
Sarclet Highld 112 H8
Sarisbury Hants 9 Q7
Sarn Brdgnd 26 G11
Sarn Gwynd 42 D7
Sarn Powys 34 F2
Sarn Powys 43 U14
Sarnau Carmth 25 P7
Sarnau Cerdgn 32 F10
Sarnau Gwynd 43 U6
Sarnau Powys 34 B14
Sarnau Powys 44 F10
Sarn Bach Gwynd 42 F8
Sarnesfield Herefs 34 J10
Sarn Park Services Brdgnd 26 G11
Sarn-wen Powys 44 G10
Saron Carmth 25 Q3
Saron Carmth 25 V8
Saron Gwynd 52 G11
Saron Gwynd 52 H9
Sarratt Herts 20 H3
Sarre Kent 13 Q2
Sarsden Oxon 29 Q3
Sarson Hants 19 M12
Satley Dur 69 P4
Satmar Kent 13 Q8
Satron N York 68 K13
Satterleigh Devon 15 Q8
Satterthwaite Cumb 61 Q1
Satwell Oxon 20 B6
Sauchen Abers 105 L13
Saucher P & K 90 J5
Sauchieburn Abers 99 M10
Saul Gloucs 28 D6
Saundby Notts 58 C9
Saundersfoot Pembks 24 K10
Saunderton Bucks 30 G12
Saunton Devon 15 L5
Sausthorpe Lincs 59 Q13
Saveock Cnwll 2 K7
Saverley Green Staffs 46 C6
Savile Town Kirk 56 K2
Sawbridge Warwks 37 P7
Sawbridgeworth Herts 22 C5
Sawdon N York 65 L3
Sawley Derbys 47 N7
Sawley Lancs 62 F10
Sawley N York 63 Q6
Sawston Cambs 39 Q11
Sawtry Cambs 38 J4
Saxby Leics 48 B10
Saxby Lincs 58 H9
Saxby All Saints N Linc 58 G3
Saxelbye Leics 47 S9
Saxham Street Suffk 40 J8
Saxilby Lincs 58 E11
Saxlingham Norfk 50 H6
Saxlingham Green Norfk 41 M1
Saxlingham Nethergate Norfk 41 M1
Saxlingham Thorpe Norfk 41 M1
Saxmundham Suffk 41 Q8
Saxondale Notts 47 S6
Saxon Street Cambs 39 U9
Saxtead Suffk 41 N7
Saxtead Green Suffk 41 N8
Saxtead Little Green Suffk 41 M7
Saxthorpe Norfk 50 K7
Saxton N York 64 B12
Sayers Common W Susx 11 M7
Scackleton N York 64 E5
Scafell Pike Cumb 66 K11
Scaftworth Notts 57 U8
Scagglethorpe N York 64 J5
Scalasaig Ag & B 86 F7
Scalby E R Yk 64 J14
Scalby N York 65 N1
Scald End Bed 38 F9
Scaldwell Nhants 37 U6
Scaleby Cumb 75 T13
Scalebyhill Cumb 75 T13
Scale Houses Cumb 67 S3
Scales Cumb 61 P5
Scales Cumb 67 M7
Scalesceugh Cumb 67 P3
Scalford Leics 47 U9
Scaling N York 71 M10
Scaling Dam R & Cl 71 M10
Scalloway Shet 106 u10
Scalpay Highld 100 f6
Scamblesby Lincs 59 N11
Scammonden Kirk 56 G3
Scamodale Highld 93 U4
Scampston N York 64 K4
Scampton Lincs 58 G11
Scaniport Highld 102 H8
Scapegoat Hill Kirk 56 G3
Scarba Ag & B 87 M5
Scarborough N York 65 N2
Scarcewater Cnwll 3 N6
Scarcliffe Derbys 57 Q13
Scarcroft Leeds 63 T11
Scarfskerry Highld 112 G2
Scargill Dur 69 N10
Scarinish Ag & B 92 C10
Scarisbrick Lancs 54 J4
Scarness Cumb 66 K6
Scarning Norfk 50 G11
Scarrington Notts 47 T5
Scarth Hill Lancs 54 K5
Scarthingwell N York 64 B12
Scartho NE Lin 59 N5
Scatsta Airport Shet 106 t6
Scawby N Linc 58 G5
Scawsby Donc 57 R6
Scawthorpe Donc 57 S5
Scawton N York 64 C3
Scayne's Hill W Susx 11 P6
Scethrog Powys 27 L2
Scholar Green Ches E 45 T2
Scholemoor Crematorium C Brad 63 N13
Scholes Kirk 56 J1
Scholes Kirk 56 J5
Scholes Leeds 63 T12
Scholes Rothm 57 N7
Scholes Wigan 55 N5
School Aycliffe Dur 69 S8
School Green C Brad 63 N13
School Green Ches W 55 P14
Schoolgreen Wokham 20 B9
School House Dorset 7 L4
Scissett Kirk 56 K4
Scleddau Pembks 24 F4
Scofton Notts 57 T10
Scole Norfk 41 L5
Scone P & K 90 H6
Sconser Highld 100 e6
Scoonie Fife 91 N11
Scopwick Lincs 48 G2
Scoraig Highld 107 T5
Scorborough E R Yk 65 N10
Scorrier Cnwll 2 J8
Scorriton Devon 5 S7
Scorton Lancs 61 U10
Scorton N York 69 S12
Sco Ruston Norfk 51 N9
Scotby Cumb 67 P1
Scotch Corner N York 69 R11
Scotforth Lancs 61 T8
Scot Hay Staffs 45 S4
Scothern Lincs 58 H11
Scotland Lincs 48 F7
Scotland Gate Nthumb 77 R9
Scotlandwell P & K 90 J11
Scot Lane End Bolton 55 P5
Scotscalder Station Highld 112 C5
Scotsdike Cumb 75 S11
Scot's Gap Nthumb 77 L8
Scotsmill Abers 104 H12
Scotstoun C Glas 89 M12
Scotswood N u Ty 77 Q13
Scotter Lincs 58 E6
Scotterthorpe Lincs 58 E6
Scottish Seabird Centre E Loth 84 F1
Scottish Wool Centre Stirlg 89 M5
Scottlethorpe Lincs 48 G9
Scotton Lincs 58 E7
Scotton N York 63 S8
Scotton N York 69 Q13
Scottow Norfk 51 N9
Scott Willoughby Lincs 48 G6
Scoulton Norfk 50 G13
Scounslow Green Staffs 46 E8
Scourie Highld 110 D8
Scourie More Highld 110 C8
Scousburgh Shet 106 t12
Scouthead Oldham 56 E5
Scrabster Highld 112 D2
Scraesburgh Border 76 D2
Scrafield Lincs 59 P13
Scrainwood Nthumb 76 K4
Scrane End Lincs 49 N5
Scraptoft Leics 47 R12
Scratby Norfk 51 T10
Scrayingham N York 64 G8
Scrays E Susx 12 E12
Scredington Lincs 48 G5
Scremby Lincs 59 R13
Scremerston Nthumb 85 Q9
Screveton Notts 47 T5
Scrivelsby Lincs 59 N13
Scriven N York 63 S8
Scrooby Notts 57 U8
Scropton Derbys 46 G7
Scrub Hill Lincs 48 K2
Scruton N York 63 R1
Scuggate Cumb 75 T11
Scullomie Highld 111 N4
Sculthorpe Norfk 50 E7
Scunthorpe N Linc 58 E4
Scurlage Swans 25 S13
Sea Somset 6 K2
Seaborough Dorset 7 M3
Seabridge Staffs 45 T5
Seabrook Kent 13 N8
Seaburn Sundld 77 U14
Seacombe Wirral 54 H8
Seacroft Leeds 63 T12
Seacroft Lincs 49 S1
Seadyke Lincs 49 M6
Seafield Highld 100 d5
Seafield W Loth 82 K5
Seafield Crematorium C Edin 83 Q3
Seaford E Susx 11 R11
Seaforth Sefton 54 H7
Seagrave Leics 47 R10
Seagry Heath Wilts 18 E4
Seaham Dur 70 F3
Seahouses Nthumb 85 U12
Seal Kent 21 U11
Sealand Flints 54 J13
Seale Surrey 20 E13
Seamer N York 65 N3
Seamer N York 70 G10
Seamill N Ayrs 80 J3
Sea Palling Norfk 51 R8
Searby Lincs 58 J5
Seasalter Kent 13 L3
Seascale Cumb 66 F12
Seathwaite Cumb 66 K10
Seathwaite Cumb 66 K13
Seatle Cumb 61 R3
Seatoller Cumb 66 K10
Seaton Cnwll 4 J10
Seaton Cumb 66 F6
Seaton Devon 6 H6
Seaton Dur 70 E3
Seaton E R Yk 65 R10
Seaton Kent 13 P4
Seaton Nthumb 77 S10
Seaton Rutlnd 48 D14
Seaton Burn N Tyne 77 Q11
Seaton Carew Hartpl 70 H7
Seaton Delaval Nthumb 77 S10
Seaton Ross E R Yk 64 H11
Seaton Sluice Nthumb 77 S10
Seatown Dorset 7 M6
Seave Green N York 70 J12
Seaview IoW 9 S10
Seaville Cumb 66 J2
Seavington St Mary Somset 7 M2
Seavington St Michael Somset 17 M13
Sebastopol Torfn 27 P8
Sebergham Cumb 67 N4
Seckington Warwks 46 J12
Sedbergh Cumb 62 D1
Sedbury Gloucs 27 U9
Sedbusk N York 62 H1
Sedgeberrow Worcs 36 D13
Sedgebrook Lincs 48 C6
Sedge Fen Suffk 39 U4
Sedgefield Dur 70 E7
Sedgeford Norfk 50 B6
Sedgehill Wilts 8 B3
Sedgemoor Services Somset 17 L6
Sedgley Dudley 36 B2
Sedgley Park Bury 55 T6
Sedgwick Cumb 61 U2
Sedlescombe E Susx 12 E12
Sedrup Bucks 30 H10
Seed Kent 12 H4
Seend Wilts 18 D8
Seend Cleeve Wilts 18 D8
Seer Green Bucks 20 G4
Seething Norfk 41 P1
Sefton Sefton 54 J6
Sefton Town Sefton 54 H6
Seghill Nthumb 77 R11
Seighford Staffs 45 U8
Seion Gwynd 52 H9
Seisdon Staffs 35 T1
Selattyn Shrops 44 G7
Selborne Hants 9 U2
Selby N York 64 E13
Selham W Susx 10 E6
Selhurst Gt Lon 21 P9
Selkirk Border 84 D13
Sellack Herefs 27 V2
Sellafirth Shet 106 v4
Sellan Cnwll 2 C10
Sellick's Green Somset 16 H13
Sellindge Kent 13 L8
Selling Kent 12 K4
Sells Green Wilts 18 D8
Selly Oak Birm 36 D4
Selmeston E Susx 11 S9
Selsdon Gt Lon 21 Q10
Selsey Gloucs 28 F7
Selsey W Susx 10 D12
Selsfield Common W Susx 11 N4
Selside Cumb 67 R13
Selside N York 62 F4
Selsted Kent 13 P7
Selston Notts 47 N3
Selworthy Somset 16 B7
Semer Suffk 40 G11
Semington Wilts 18 C8
Semley Wilts 8 B3
Sempringham Lincs 48 H7
Send Surrey 20 H11
Send Marsh Surrey 20 H11
Senghenydd Caerph 27 L9
Sennen Cnwll 2 B11
Sennen Cove Cnwll 2 B11
Sennybridge Powys 26 G2
Serlby Notts 57 T9
Sessay N York 64 B4
Setchey Norfk 49 T11
Setley Hants 9 L8
Seton Mains E Loth 84 C3
Settle N York 62 G7
Settrington N York 64 J5
Seven Ash Somset 16 G10
Sevenhampton Gloucs 28 K3
Sevenhampton Swindn 29 P9
Seven Hills Crematorium Suffk 41 M12
Seven Kings Gt Lon 21 S5
Sevenoaks Kent 21 T11
Sevenoaks Weald Kent 21 T12
Seven Sisters Neath 26 E6
Seven Springs Gloucs 28 J4
Seven Star Green Essex 23 M2
Severn Beach S Glos 27 U11
Severn Stoke Worcs 35 U12
Severn View Services S Glos 27 V10
Sevick End Bed 38 G10
Sevington Kent 12 K7
Sewards End Essex 39 S13
Sewardstonebury Essex 21 Q3
Sewell C Beds 31 L8
Sewerby E R Yk 65 R6
Seworgan Cnwll 2 J10
Sewstern Leics 48 C9
Sexhow N York 70 G11
Sezincote Gloucs 29 N1
Sgiogarstaigh W Isls 106 k2
Shabbington Bucks 30 E11
Shackerley Shrops 45 T12
Shackerstone Leics 47 L12
Shacklecross Derbys 47 M7
Shackleford Surrey 20 F13
Shade Calder 56 D2
Shader W Isls 106 i3
Shadforth Dur 70 D4
Shadingfield Suffk 41 R4
Shadoxhurst Kent 12 J8
Shadwell Leeds 63 S12
Shadwell Norfk 40 F4
Shaftenhoe End Herts 39 P13
Shaftesbury Dorset 8 B4
Shaftholme Donc 57 S5
Shafton Barns 57 N4
Shafton Two Gates Barns 57 N4
Shakerley Wigan 55 Q6
Shalbourne Wilts 19 M8
Shalcombe IoW 9 M11
Shalden Hants 19 U12
Shalden Green Hants 19 V12
Shaldon Devon 6 B10
Shalfleet IoW 9 N11
Shalford Essex 22 H2
Shalford Surrey 20 H13
Shalford Green Essex 22 H2
Shallowford Staffs 45 U8
Shalmsford Street Kent 13 L5
Shalstone Bucks 30 D5
Shamley Green Surrey 10 G2
Shandford Angus 98 H11
Shandon Ag & B 88 G8
Shandwick Highld 109 R9
Shangton Leics 37 T1
Shankhouse Nthumb 77 R10
Shanklin IoW 9 R12
Shap Cumb 67 S9
Shapinsay Ork 106 u18
Shapwick Dorset 8 C8
Shapwick Somset 17 M9
Shard End Birm 36 G3
Shardlow Derbys 47 M7
Shareshill Staffs 46 B12
Sharlston Wakefd 57 N3
Sharlston Common Wakefd 57 N3
Sharman's Cross Solhll 36 F5

Sharnal Street Medway...22 J13
Sharnbrook Bed...38 E9
Sharneyford Lancs...56 C2
Sharnford Leics...37 N2
Sharnhill Green Dorset...3 T3
Sharoe Green Lancs...61 U13
Sharow N York...63 S5
Sharpenhoe C Beds...31 N6
Sharperton Nthumb...76 K5
Sharp Green Norfk...51 Q9
Sharpness Gloucs...28 C7
Sharpthorne W Susx...11 N4
Sharptor Cnwll...4 H6
Sharpway Gate Worcs...36 C7
Sharrington Norfk...50 H6
Shatterford Worcs...35 S4
Shatterling Kent...13 Q4
Shatton Derbys...56 K10
Shaugh Prior Devon...5 N8
Shave Cross Dorset...7 N5
Shavington Ches E...45 Q3
Shaw C Brad...63 K12
Shaw Oldham...56 D5
Shaw Swindn...29 M10
Shaw W Berk...19 Q7
Shaw Wilts...18 C7
Shawbirch Wrekin...45 P11
Shawbost W Isls...106 H4
Shawbury Shrops...45 N9
Shawclough Rochdl...56 C4
Shaw Common Gloucs...28 C2
Shawdon Hill Nthumb...77 M3
Shawell Leics...37 P4
Shawford Hants...9 P3
Shawforth Lancs...56 C2
Shaw Green Herts...31 T6
Shaw Green Lancs...55 M3
Shaw Green N York...63 R9
Shawhead D & G...74 G10
Shaw Mills N York...63 R7
Shawsburn S Lans...82 E8
Shear Cross Wilts...18 C12
Shearington D & G...74 K12
Shearsby Leics...37 R2
Shearston Somset...16 J10
Shebbear Devon...15 L11
Shebdon Staffs...45 S8
Shebster Highld...112 B4
Sheddens E Rens...81 R1
Shedfield Hants...9 Q6
Sheen Staffs...46 F1
Sheepbridge Derbys...57 N12
Sheep Hill Dur...69 Q1
Sheepridge Kirk...56 J3
Sheepscar Leeds...63 S13
Sheepscombe Gloucs...28 G5
Sheepstor Devon...5 N7
Sheepwash Devon...15 L11
Sheepwash Nthumb...77 R8
Sheepy Magna Leics...46 K13
Sheepy Parva Leics...46 K13
Sheering Essex...22 C5
Sheerness Kent...23 M13
Sheerwater Surrey...20 H10
Sheet Hants...10 B6
Sheffield Sheff...57 N9
Sheffield D & S...11 P7
Sheffield Bottom W Berk...19 T7
Sheffield City Road Crematorium Sheff...57 N9
Sheffield Green E Susx...11 P7
Sheffield Park E Susx...11 Q6
Shefford C Beds...31 Q4
Shefford Woodlands W Berk...19 N6
Sheigra Highld...110 D4
Shelderton Shrops...45 P13
Sheldon Birm...36 G4
Sheldon Derbys...56 J13
Sheldon Devon...6 F3
Sheldwich Kent...12 K4
Sheldwich Lees Kent...12 K4
Shelf Calder...63 N14
Shelfanger Norfk...40 K4
Shelfield Wsall...36 E1
Shelfield Warwks...36 F8
Shelfield Green Warwks...36 F8
Shelford Notts...47 S5
Shelford Warwks...37 M3
Shellacres Nthumb...85 M10
Shelley Essex...22 E6
Shelley Kirk...56 K4
Shelley Suffk...40 H13
Shelley Far Bank Kirk...56 K4
Shellingford Oxon...29 R9
Shellow Bowells Essex...22 F6
Shelsley Beauchamp Worcs...35 R8
Shelsley Walsh Worcs...35 R8
Shelton Bed...38 F7
Shelton Norfk...41 M2
Shelton Notts...47 U5
Shelton Shrops...45 L11
Shelton Green Norfk...41 M2
Shelton Lock C Derb...47 L7
Shelton Under Harley Staffs...45 T6
Shelve Shrops...34 J1
Shelwick Herefs...35 M12
Shenfield Essex...22 F8
Shenington Oxon...37 L12
Shenley Herts...31 Q12
Shenley Brook End M Keyn...30 H5
Shenleybury Herts...31 Q12
Shenley Church End M Keyn...30 H5
Shenmore Herefs...34 J13
Shennanton D & G...72 J7
Shenstone Staffs...46 F13
Shenstone Worcs...35 U6
Shenstone Woodend Staffs...46 F13
Shenton Leics...47 L13
Shenval Moray...103 V10
Shepeau Stow Lincs...49 M11
Shephall Herts...31 S8
Shepherd's Bush Gt Lon...21 M6
Shepherd's Green Oxon...20 B6
Shepherds Patch Gloucs...28 D6
Shepherdswell Kent...13 Q6
Shepley Kirk...56 J5
Shepperdine S Glos...28 B9
Shepperton Surrey...20 J9
Shepperton Green Surrey...20 J9
Shepreth Cambs...39 N11
Shepshed Leics...47 N10
Shepton Beauchamp Somset...17 M12
Shepton Mallet Somset...17 R8
Shepton Montague Somset...17 S10
Shepway Kent...12 E5
Sheraton Dur...70 F5
Sherborne Dorset...17 R13
Sherborne Gloucs...29 N5
Sherborne Somset...17 R6
Sherborne St John Hants...19 T9
Sherbourne Warwks...36 J8
Sherburn Dur...70 D4
Sherburn N York...65 M4
Sherburn Hill Dur...70 D4
Sherburn in Elmet N York...64 B13
Shere Surrey...20 J13
Shereford Norfk...50 E8
Sherfield English Hants...8 K4
Sherfield on Loddon Hants...19 U9
Sherfin Lancs...55 S1
Sherford Devon...5 T12
Sherford Dorset...8 C10
Sheriffhales Shrops...45 S11
Sheriff Hutton N York...64 F6
Sheringham Norfk...51 L5
Sherington M Keyn...38 C11
Shermanbury W Susx...11 L7
Shernborne Norfk...50 B7
Sherrington Wilts...18 E13
Sherston Wilts...28 G10
Sherwood C Nott...47 Q5
Sherwood Forest Crematorium Notts...57 U13
Shetland Islands Shet...106 u8
Shettleston C Glas...89 P13
Shevington Wigan...55 M5
Shevington Moor Wigan...55 M4
Shevington Vale Wigan...55 M5
Sheviock Cnwll...4 J10
Shibden Head C Brad...63 M14
Shide IoW...9 Q12
Shidlaw Nthumb...85 L11
Shiel Bridge Highld...101 N8
Shieldaig Highld...107 P13
Shieldhill D & G...74 K8
Shieldhill Falk...82 H3
Shieldhill House Hotel S Lans...82 K10
Shielfoot Highld...93 R6
Shielhill Angus...98 G12
Shielhill Inver...88 F11
Shifford Oxon...29 R7
Shifnal Shrops...45 R12
Shilbottle Nthumb...77 Q3
Shildon Dur...69 R7
Shillford E Rens...81 P1
Shillingford Devon...16 C12
Shillingford Oxon...19 S2
Shillingford Abbot Devon...6 B7
Shillingford St George Devon...6 B7

Shillingstone Dorset...8 A6
Shillington C Beds...31 P6
Shillmoor Nthumb...76 H4
Shilton Oxon...29 Q6
Shilton Warwks...37 M4
Shimpling Norfk...41 L4
Shimpling Suffk...40 E10
Shimpling Street Suffk...40 E10
Shincliffe Dur...69 S4
Shiney Row Sundld...70 D2
Shinfield Wokham...20 B9
Shingay Cambs...39 M11
Shingle Street Suffk...41 Q12
Shinnersbridge Devon...5 T8
Shinness Highld...108 J2
Shipbourne Kent...21 U12
Shipdham Norfk...50 G12
Shipham Somset...17 M5
Shiphay Torbay...6 A11
Shiplake Oxon...20 C7
Shiplake Row Oxon...20 B7
Shiplate N Som...17 L5
Shipley C Brad...63 P12
Shipley Derbys...47 M5
Shipley Shrops...35 T2
Shipley W Susx...10 J6
Shipley Bridge Surrey...11 N2
Shipley Hatch Kent...12 K6
Shipmeadow Suffk...41 Q2
Shippea Hill Station Cambs...39 T4
Shippon Oxon...29 U8
Shipston-on-Stour Warwks...36 J12
Shipton Bucks...30 G7
Shipton Gloucs...28 K4
Shipton N York...64 D8
Shipton Shrops...35 N2
Shipton Bellinger Hants...18 K11
Shipton Gorge Dorset...7 N6
Shipton Green W Susx...10 C10
Shipton Moyne Gloucs...28 G10
Shipton-on-Cherwell Oxon...29 U4
Shipton-under-Wychwood Oxon...29 Q4
Shirburn Oxon...30 E13
Shirdley Hill Lancs...54 J4
Shire Cumb...68 D5
Shirebrook Derbys...57 R13
Shiregreen Sheff...57 N8
Shirehampton Bristl...27 U12
Shiremoor N Tyne...77 S11
Shirenewton Mons...27 T9
Shire Oak Wsall...46 E13
Shireoaks Notts...57 S10
Shirkoak Kent...12 H8
Shirland Derbys...47 L2
Shirlett Shrops...45 P14
Shirley C Sotn...9 N6
Shirley Derbys...46 H5
Shirley Gt Lon...21 Q9
Shirley Solhll...36 F5
Shirl Heath Herefs...34 K9
Shirrell Heath Hants...9 Q6
Shirwell Devon...15 N5
Shirwell Cross Devon...15 N5
Shiskine N Ayrs...79 S10
Shittlehope Dur...69 M5
Shobdon Herefs...34 K8
Shobley Hants...8 H7
Shobrooke Devon...15 U12
Shoby Leics...47 S10
Shocklach Ches W...44 K4
Shocklach Green Ches W...44 K4
Shoeburyness Sthend...23 M10
Sholden Kent...13 S5
Sholing C Sotn...9 P6
Shoot Hill Shrops...44 K11
Shop Cnwll...2 F6
Shop Cnwll...14 E10
Shopwyke W Susx...10 D10
Shore Rochdl...56 D3
Shoreditch Gt Lon...21 P6
Shoreditch Somset...16 H11
Shoreham Kent...21 T10
Shoreham Airport W Susx...11 L9
Shoreham-by-Sea W Susx...11 L9
Shoreswood Nthumb...85 N9
Shorley Hants...9 R3
Shorncote Gloucs...28 K8
Shorne Kent...22 G13
Shorta Cross Cnwll...4 H9
Shortbridge E Susx...11 R6
Shortfield Common Surrey...10 C2
Shortgate E Susx...11 R7
Short Heath Birm...36 E2
Short Heath Wsall...46 C13
Shortlanesend Cnwll...3 L7
Shorthey E Ayrs...81 N5
Shortstown Bed...38 G11
Shorwell IoW...9 P12
Shoscombe BaNES...17 T5
Shotesham Norfk...51 M14
Shotgate Essex...22 J9
Shotley Suffk...41 M13
Shotley Bridge Dur...69 N2
Shotleyfield Nthumb...69 N2
Shotley Gate Suffk...41 M14
Shotley Street Suffk...41 M14
Shottenden Kent...12 K5
Shottermill Surrey...10 D3
Shottery Warwks...36 G10
Shotteswell Warwks...37 M11
Shottisham Suffk...41 P12
Shottle Derbys...46 K4
Shottlegate Derbys...46 K4
Shotton Dur...70 F5
Shotton Dur...70 D7
Shotton Flints...54 H13
Shotton Nthumb...85 L12
Shotton Colliery Dur...70 E4
Shotts N Lans...82 G7
Shotwick Ches W...54 H12
Shougle Moray...103 V4
Shoughlaige-e-Caine IoM...60 e5
Shouldham Norfk...49 U12
Shouldham Thorpe Norfk...49 U12
Shoulton Worcs...35 T9
Shover's Green E Susx...12 C9
Shraleybrook Staffs...45 S4
Shrawardine Shrops...44 J10
Shrawley Worcs...35 T7
Shreding Green Bucks...20 H6
Shrewley Warwks...36 H7
Shrewsbury Shrops...45 L11
Shrewton Wilts...18 G12
Shripney W Susx...10 E10
Shrivenham Oxon...29 P10
Shropham Norfk...40 G2
Shrub End Essex...23 N3
Shucknall Herefs...35 N12
Shudy Camps Cambs...39 T12
Shurdington Gloucs...28 H4
Shurlock Row W & M...20 D8
Shurnock Worcs...36 D8
Shurrery Highld...112 B5
Shurrery Lodge Highld...112 B5
Shurton Somset...16 H8
Shustoke Warwks...36 H2
Shute Devon...6 J5
Shute Devon...15 U12
Shuthonger Gloucs...28 G1
Shutlanger Nhants...37 T11
Shutt Green Staffs...45 U12
Shuttington Warwks...46 J12
Shuttlewood Derbys...57 Q12
Shuttleworth Bury...55 T3
Siabost W Isls...106 h4
Siadar W Isls...106 i3
Sibbertoft Nhants...37 S4
Sibdon Carwood Shrops...34 K3
Sibford Ferris Oxon...37 L13
Sibford Gower Oxon...37 L13
Sible Hedingham Essex...22 J1
Sibley's Green Essex...22 F2
Sibsey Lincs...49 N3
Sibsey Fenside Lincs...49 N3
Sibson Cambs...38 G1
Sibson Leics...47 L13
Sibster Highld...112 H6
Sibthorpe Notts...47 U4
Sibton Suffk...41 Q7
Sicklesmere Suffk...40 E8
Sicklinghall N York...63 T10
Sidbrook Somset...16 J11
Sidbury Devon...6 G6
Sidbury Shrops...35 P3
Sidcot N Som...17 L5
Sidcup Gt Lon...21 R8
Siddick Cumb...66 F6
Siddington Ches E...55 T12
Siddington Gloucs...28 K8
Sidemoor Worcs...36 C6
Sidestrand Norfk...51 N5
Sidford Devon...6 G6
Sidlesham W Susx...10 D11
Sidlesham Common W Susx...10 D11
Sidley E Susx...12 E14
Sidmouth Devon...6 G7
Siefton Shrops...35 L4

Sigford Devon...5 T6
Sigglesthorne E R Yk...65 R10
Sighthill V Glam...26 K12
Sigingstone V Glam...26 H12
Silchester Hants...19 T8
Sileby Leics...47 R10
Silecroft Cumb...61 K3
Silfield Norfk...50 K14
Silian Cerdgn...33 L10
Silk Willoughby Lincs...48 G5
Silkstone Barns...57 L6
Silkstone Common Barns...57 L6
Silloth Cumb...66 H1
Silpho N York...65 M1
Silsden C Brad...63 L10
Silsoe C Beds...31 N5
Silton Dorset...17 U10
Silverburn Mdloth...83 P5
Silver End Essex...22 J4
Silverdale Lancs...61 T5
Silverdale Staffs...45 T4
Silverford Abers...105 M3
Silvergate Norfk...51 L8
Silver Street Kent...12 G3
Silver Street Somset...17 Q9
Silverstone Nhants...37 S12
Silverton Devon...6 C3
Silverwell Cnwll...2 J7
Silvington Shrops...35 P5
Simister Bury...55 T5
Simmondley Derbys...56 F8
Simonburn Nthumb...76 H11
Simonsbath Somset...15 S6
Simonstone Lancs...62 F13
Simonstone N York...62 H1
Simprim Border...85 L9
Simpson M Keyn...30 J5
Simpson Cross Pembks...24 E7
Sinclair's Hill Border...85 L8
Sinclairston E Ayrs...81 P9
Sinderby N York...63 S3
Sinderland Green Traffd...55 R9
Sindlesham Wokham...20 C9
Sinfin C Derb...46 K7
Singleborough Bucks...30 G6
Single Street Gt Lon...21 R11
Singleton Kent...12 K7
Singleton Lancs...61 R12
Singleton W Susx...10 D8
Singlewell Kent...22 G13
Sinkhurst Green Kent...12 F7
Sinnahard Abers...104 F13
Sinnington N York...64 G2
Sinton Worcs...35 T9
Sinton Green Worcs...35 T8
Sipson Gt Lon...20 J7
Sirhowy Blae G...27 M6
Sisland Norfk...41 P1
Sissinghurst Kent...12 E8
Siston S Glos...28 C12
Sitcott Devon...4 J2
Sithney Cnwll...2 G11
Sithney Common Cnwll...2 G11
Sithney Green Cnwll...2 G11
Sittingbourne Kent...12 H3
Six Ashes Shrops...35 S3
Six Bells Blae G...27 N7
Sixhills Lincs...59 L9
Six Mile Bottom Cambs...39 R9
Sixmile Cottages Kent...13 M7
Sixpenny Handley Dorset...8 D5
Six Rues Jersey...7 b2
Sizewell Suffk...41 R8
Skaill Ork...106 u19
Skares E Ayrs...81 P10
Skateraw Abers...99 S5
Skateraw E Loth...84 J3
Skeabost Highld...100 d5
Skeeby N York...69 Q12
Skeffington Leics...47 U12
Skeffling E R Yk...59 Q3
Skegby Notts...47 N1
Skegby Notts...47 U1
Skegness Lincs...59 U14
Skelbo Highld...109 P6
Skelbo Street Highld...109 P6
Skelbrooke Donc...57 R4
Skeldyke Lincs...49 M6
Skellingthorpe Lincs...58 F12
Skellorn Green Ches E...56 D10
Skellow Donc...57 R4
Skelmanthorpe Kirk...56 K4
Skelmersdale Lancs...55 L5
Skelmorlie N Ayrs...88 E13
Skelpick Highld...111 Q5
Skelton Cumb...67 P6
Skelton C York...64 D9
Skelton E R Yk...64 H14
Skelton N York...69 P11
Skelton R & Cl...71 L9
Skelwith Bridge Cumb...67 M12
Skendleby Lincs...59 R13
Skene House Abers...105 M13
Skenfrith Mons...27 T3
Skerne E R Yk...65 N9
Skerray Highld...111 P4
Skerricha Highld...110 E6
Skerton Lancs...61 T7
Sketchley Leics...37 M2
Sketty Swans...25 V12
Skewen Neath...26 C8
Skewsby N York...64 E5
Skeyton Norfk...51 M8
Skidbrooke Lincs...59 R7
Skidbrooke North End Lincs...59 R7
Skidby E R Yk...65 N13
Skigersta W Isls...106 k1
Skilgate Somset...16 C11
Skillington Lincs...48 D8
Skinburness Cumb...66 H1
Skinflats Falk...89 S9
Skinidin Highld...100 b5
Skinners Green W Berk...19 P7
Skinningrove R & Cl...71 M9
Skipness Ag & B...79 R9
Skipper's Bridge D & G...75 S9
Skiprigg Cumb...67 N3
Skipsea E R Yk...65 R9
Skipsea Brough E R Yk...65 R9
Skipton N York...62 J9
Skipton-on-Swale N York...63 T4
Skipwith N York...64 F13
Skirbeck Lincs...49 M4
Skirbeck Quarter Lincs...49 M4
Skirlaugh E R Yk...65 R12
Skirling Border...83 L11
Skirmett Bucks...20 C5
Skirpenbeck E R Yk...64 G8
Skirwith Cumb...68 C6
Skirza Highld...112 J3
Skitby Cumb...75 T12
Skittle Green Bucks...30 G12
Skokholm Island Pembks...24 B10
Skomer Island Pembks...24 B9
Skulamus Highld...100 f7
Skyborry Green Shrops...34 G5
Skye Green Essex...23 M3
Skye of Curr Highld...103 Q11
Skyreholme N York...63 L7
Slack Calder...63 L14
Slackcote Oldham...56 E5
Slack Head Cumb...61 T4
Slackholme End Lincs...59 T13
Slacks of Cairnbanno Abers...105 N6
Slad Gloucs...28 G6
Slade Devon...6 G5
Slade Devon...15 M3
Slade Swans...25 S13
Slade End Oxon...19 S3
Slade Green Gt Lon...22 D13
Slade Heath Staffs...46 B12
Slade Hooton Rothm...57 R9
Sladesbridge Cnwll...3 Q2
Slades Green Worcs...35 T14
Slaggyford Nthumb...68 F2
Slaidburn Lancs...62 E9
Slaithwaite Kirk...56 G4
Slaley Derbys...46 K2
Slaley Nthumb...76 K14
Slamannan Falk...82 G3
Slapton Bucks...30 K7
Slapton Devon...5 U11
Slapton Nhants...37 R11
Slattocks Rochdl...56 C5
Slaugham W Susx...11 L5
Slaughterford Wilts...18 B6
Slawston Leics...37 U2
Sleaford Hants...10 C3
Sleaford Lincs...48 G4
Sleagill Cumb...67 S9
Sleap Shrops...45 L8
Sleapford Wrekin...45 Q10
Sleapshyde Herts...31 R11
Sledge Green Worcs...35 T13
Sledmere E R Yk...65 L7
Sleetbeck Cumb...75 V10
Sleights N York...71 Q11
Slepe Dorset...8 C10

Slickly Highld...112 G3
Sliddery N Ayrs...79 S11
Sligachan Highld...100 d7
Sligrachan Ag & B...88 E6
Slimbridge Gloucs...28 D7
Slimbridge Wetland Centre Gloucs...28 D6
Slindon Staffs...45 T7
Slindon W Susx...10 F9
Slinfold W Susx...10 J4
Slingsby N York...64 F5
Slip End C Beds...31 N9
Slip End Herts...31 S6
Slipton Nhants...38 D5
Slitting Mill Staffs...46 D10
Slochd Highld...103 P10
Slockavullin Ag & B...87 Q6
Sloley Norfk...51 N9
Sloncombe Devon...5 S3
Sloothby Lincs...59 S12
Slough Slough...20 G7
Slough Crematorium Bucks...20 G7
Slough Green Somset...16 J13
Slough Green W Susx...11 M5
Slumaky Highld...101 M4
Slyfield Green Surrey...20 G12
Slyne Lancs...61 T7
Smailholm Border...84 G11
Small Dole W Susx...11 L8
Smallbrook Devon...15 T13
Smallbrook Gloucs...28 A7
Smallburgh Norfk...51 P8
Smalldale Derbys...56 H10
Smalldale Derbys...56 J10
Small Dole W Susx...11 L8
Smalley Derbys...47 M5
Smalley Common Derbys...47 M5
Smalley Green Derbys...47 M5
Smallfield Surrey...11 N2
Small Heath Birm...36 E4
Small Hythe Kent...12 G8
Smallridge Devon...6 K4
Smallthorne C Stke...45 U3
Smallways N York...69 P10
Smallwood Ches E...45 T2
Small Wood Hey Lancs...61 R10
Smallworth Norfk...40 H4
Smannell Hants...19 P11
Smardale Cumb...68 G11
Smarden Kent...12 G7
Smarden Bell Kent...12 G7
Smart's Hill Kent...11 S2
Smeafield Nthumb...85 R11
Smeatharpe Devon...6 G2
Smeeth Kent...13 L8
Smeeton Westerby Leics...37 S3
Smestow Staffs...35 T3
Smethcott Shrops...45 L14
Smethwick Sandw...36 D3
Smethwick Green Ches E...55 T14
Smisby Derbys...46 K10
Smithfield Cumb...75 T12
Smith End Green Worcs...35 S10
Smith's End Herts...39 N14
Smith's Green Essex...22 E3
Smith's Green Essex...39 T13
Smithstown Highld...107 M9
Smithton Highld...102 K6
Smithy Bridge Rochdl...56 D3
Smithy Green Ches E...55 R12
Smithy Green Stockp...56 D9
Smithy Houses Derbys...47 L5
Smockington Leics...37 N3
Smoo Highld...111 L3
Smythe's Green Essex...23 M4
Snade D & G...74 F8
Snailbeach Shrops...44 J13
Snailwell Cambs...39 T7
Snainton N York...65 L3
Snaith E R Yk...57 U1
Snake Pass Inn Derbys...56 G9
Snape N York...63 R3
Snape Suffk...41 R9
Snape Green Lancs...54 J4
Snape Street Suffk...41 R9
Snarestone Leics...47 L12
Snarford Lincs...58 H9
Snargate Kent...12 H10
Snave Kent...12 K9
Sneachill Worcs...36 B10
Snead Powys...34 H2
Sneath Common Norfk...41 L3
Sneaton N York...71 Q11
Sneatonthorpe N York...71 R11
Snelland Lincs...58 J9
Snelston Derbys...46 G5
Snetterton Norfk...40 G2
Snettisham Norfk...49 U6
Snig's End Gloucs...28 E2
Snitter Nthumb...77 L5
Snitterby Lincs...58 G7
Snitterfield Warwks...36 H9
Snittlegarth Cumb...67 L5
Snitton Shrops...35 N6
Snodhill Herefs...34 H12
Snodland Kent...12 D3
Snoll Hatch Kent...12 C4
Snowden Hill Barns...57 L6
Snowdon Gwynd...52 K12
Snowdonia National Park...43 R8
Snow End Herts...39 N14
Snowshill Gloucs...36 E14
Snow Street Norfk...40 J3
Soake Hants...9 S6
Soar Cardif...26 K11
Soar Devon...5 S13
Soar Powys...26 E2
Soberton Hants...9 S5
Soberton Heath Hants...9 S6
Sockbridge Cumb...67 R8
Sockburn Darltn...70 D11
Sodom Denbgs...54 C12
Sodylt Bank Shrops...44 J6
Soham Cambs...39 S6
Soham Cotes Cambs...39 S6
Solas W Isls...106 d11
Soldon Devon...14 H10
Soldon Cross Devon...14 H10
Soldridge Hants...9 U3
Sole Street Kent...12 K6
Sole Street Kent...22 F13
Solihull Solhll...36 G5
Sollers Dilwyn Herefs...34 K9
Sollers Hope Herefs...35 P14
Sollom Lancs...55 L3
Solva Pembks...24 D6
Solwaybank D & G...75 Q10
Somerby Leics...47 U11
Somerby Lincs...58 J5
Somercotes Derbys...47 M3
Somerford Dorset...8 H10
Somerford Keynes Gloucs...28 K8
Somerley W Susx...10 C11
Somerleyton Suffk...41 S1
Somersal Herbert Derbys...46 F6
Somersby Lincs...59 P12
Somersham Cambs...39 M5
Somersham Suffk...40 J11
Somerton Oxon...29 U2
Somerton Somset...17 N11
Somerwood Shrops...45 N11
Sompting Wokham...20 B6
Sonning Common Oxon...20 B6
Sonning Eye Oxon...20 C7
Sontley Wrexhm...44 H4
Sopley Hants...8 H9
Sopworth Wilts...28 G10
Sorbie D & G...73 M10
Sordale Highld...112 D5
Sorisdale Ag & B...92 H7
Sorn E Ayrs...81 R7
Sornhill E Ayrs...81 R6
Sortat Highld...112 G4
Sotby Lincs...59 M11
Sots Hole Lincs...58 J13
Sotterley Suffk...41 S4
Soughton Flints...54 F13
Soulbury Bucks...30 H8
Soulby Cumb...68 E11
Soulby Cumb...67 Q6
Souldern Oxon...29 U1
Souldrop Bed...38 E8
Sound Ches E...45 P3
Sound Muir Moray...104 B5
Soundwell S Glos...28 B12
Sourton Devon...5 M3
Soutergate Cumb...61 N3
South Acre Norfk...50 D11
South Alkham Kent...13 P7
Southall Gt Lon...20 K7
South Allington Devon...5 T13
South Alloa Falk...89 U7
Southam Gloucs...28 J3
Southam Warwks...37 M8
South Ambersham W Susx...10 E6
Southampton C Sotn...9 N6

Southampton Airport Hants...9 P5
Southampton Crematorium Hants...9 N5
South Anston Rothm...57 R10
South Ascot W & M...20 F9
South Ashford Kent...12 K7
Southbar Rens...88 K12
South Baddesley Hants...9 N8
South Ballachulish Highld...94 F7
South Bank C York...64 D9
South Bank R & Cl...70 H8
South Barrow Somset...17 R11
South Beddington Gt Lon...21 P9
South Beer Cnwll...4 J2
South Benfleet Essex...22 J10
South Bersted W Susx...10 E10
South Bockhampton Dorset...8 H9
Southborough Gt Lon...21 R9
Southborough Kent...11 T2
Southbourne Bmouth...8 G10
Southbourne W Susx...10 B9
South Bowood Dorset...7 N5
South Bramwith Donc...57 T4
South Brent Devon...5 R8
South Brewham Somset...17 T9
South Bristol Crematorium Bristl...17 Q3
South Broomhill Nthumb...77 Q6
Southburgh Norfk...50 H12
South Burlingham Norfk...51 Q12
Southburn E R Yk...65 M9
South Cadbury Somset...17 R11
South Carlton Lincs...58 F11
South Carlton Notts...57 S10
South Cave E R Yk...65 L13
South Cerney Gloucs...28 K8
South Chailey E Susx...11 P7
South Chard Somset...7 L3
South Charlton Nthumb...77 P1
South Cheriton Somset...17 S12
South Church Dur...69 S7
Southchurch Sthend...23 M10
South Cleatlam Dur...69 P9
South Cliffe E R Yk...64 K12
South Clifton Notts...58 D12
South Cockerington Lincs...59 Q9
Southcott Cnwll...14 E11
Southcott Devon...4 H3
Southcott Devon...15 P10
Southcott Wilts...18 H9
Southcourt Bucks...30 H10
South Cove Suffk...41 S4
South Creake Norfk...50 E6
South Crosland Kirk...56 H4
South Croxton Leics...47 S11
South Dalton E R Yk...65 M10
South Darenth Kent...21 U9
South Downs National Park...11 P9
Southease E Susx...11 Q9
South Elkington Lincs...59 N9
South Elmsall Wakefd...57 Q4
Southend Ag & B...79 M14
South End Cumb...61 N6
South End E R Yk...59 M1
South End Hants...8 H5
South End Herefs...35 T14
South End Lincs...49 M6
South End Norfk...40 H2
Southend Wilts...18 H6
Southend Airport Essex...23 L10
Southend Crematorium Sthend...23 L10
Southend-on-Sea Sthend...23 L10
Southerndown V Glam...26 F13
Southerness D & G...66 D1
South Erradale Highld...107 M10
Southerton Devon...6 E6
Southery Norfk...39 T2
South Essex Crematorium Gt Lon...22 D9
South Fambridge Essex...23 L9
South Fawley W Berk...19 P5
South Ferriby N Linc...58 G2
South Field E R Yk...65 N14
Southfield Falk...82 G3
Southfleet Kent...22 F13
Southford IoW...9 R12
Southgate Gt Lon...21 N4
Southgate Norfk...50 H7
Southgate Norfk...50 H10
Southgate Swans...25 U13
South Godstone Surrey...21 P13
South Gorley Hants...8 H6
South Gosforth N u Ty...77 R12
South Green Essex...22 F9
South Green Essex...23 L2
South Green Kent...12 F3
South Green Norfk...50 H10
South Green Suffk...40 K4
South Gyle C Edin...83 N4
South Hanningfield Essex...22 H8
South Harefield Herefs...34 H12
South Harting W Susx...10 B7
South Hayling Hants...9 U8
South Hazelrigg Nthumb...85 R12
South Heath Bucks...30 K12
South Heighton E Susx...11 Q10
South Hetton Dur...70 E3
South Hiendley Wakefd...57 N4
South Hill Cnwll...4 J6
South Hill Somset...17 N11
South Hinksey Oxon...30 B12
South Hole Devon...14 F8
South Holmwood Surrey...10 K2
South Hornchurch Gt Lon...22 D10
South Horrington Somset...17 Q7
South Huish Devon...5 R12
South Hykeham Lincs...58 F13
South Hylton Sundld...70 D2
Southill C Beds...31 Q4
Southington Hants...19 S11
South Kelsey Lincs...58 H7
South Kessock Highld...102 K6
South Killingholme N Linc...58 K3
South Kilvington N York...63 U3
South Kilworth Leics...37 R4
South Kirkby Wakefd...57 P4
South Knighton Devon...5 U6
South Kyme Lincs...48 J4
South Lanarkshire Crematorium S Lans...82 C7
Southleigh Devon...6 H6
South Leigh Oxon...29 S6
South Leverton Notts...58 C10
South Littleton Worcs...36 E11
South London Crematorium Gt Lon...21 N9
South Lopham Norfk...40 J4
South Luffenham Rutlnd...48 D13
South Malling E Susx...11 Q8
South Marston Swindn...29 N10
South Merstham Surrey...21 N12
South Middleton Nthumb...85 N14
South Milford N York...57 S1
South Milton Devon...5 R12
South Mimms Herts...31 R12
South Mimms Services Herts...31 R12
Southminster Essex...23 M8
South Molton Devon...15 R8
South Moor Dur...69 Q2
Southmoor Oxon...29 S8
South Moreton Oxon...19 S3
Southmuir Angus...98 F13
South Mundham W Susx...10 D10
South Muskham Notts...47 U2
South Newbald E R Yk...65 L12
South Newington Oxon...37 M14
South Newton Wilts...8 F2
South Normanton Derbys...47 M2

South Norwood Gt Lon...21 Q9
South Nutfield Surrey...21 N13
South Ockendon Thurr...22 E10
Southoe Cambs...38 J8
Southolt Suffk...41 L7
South Ormsby Lincs...59 P11
Southorpe C Pete...48 G13
South Ossett Wakefd...57 M3
Southover Dorset...7 R6
South Otterington N York...63 U3
South Owersby Lincs...58 J8
Southowram Calder...63 N14
South Oxhey Herts...20 K4
South Park Surrey...11 L2
South Perrott Dorset...7 N4
South Petherton Somset...17 M13
South Petherwin Cnwll...4 J5
South Pickenham Norfk...50 E13
South Pill Cnwll...4 J9
South Pool Devon...5 S12
South Poorton Dorset...7 P5
Southport Sefton...54 J3
Southport Crematorium Sefton...54 J4
South Queensferry C Edin...83 M2
South Radworthy Devon...15 R6
South Rauceby Lincs...48 F4
South Raynham Norfk...50 E9
South Reddish Stockp...56 C8
Southrepps Norfk...51 N6
South Reston Lincs...59 R10
Southrey Lincs...58 K13
South Ronaldsay Ork...106 t21
Southrop Gloucs...29 N7
Southrope Hants...19 U12
South Runcton Norfk...49 T12
South Scarle Notts...58 D14
Southsea C Port...9 T9
Southsea Wrexhm...44 H3
South Shian Ag & B...94 C10
South Shields S Tyne...77 T12
South Shore Bpool...61 Q13
South Somercotes Lincs...59 R8
South Stainley N York...63 S7
South Stifford Thurr...22 F12
South Stoke BaNES...17 T4
South Stoke Oxon...19 T4
South Stoke W Susx...10 G9
South Stour Kent...12 K8
South Street Kent...13 L3
South Street Kent...13 M2
South Street E Susx...11 P7
South Tarbrax S Lans...82 K7
South Tawton Devon...5 R2
South Tehidy Cnwll...2 H8
South Thoresby Lincs...59 R11
South Thorpe Dur...69 P10
South Town Hants...9 U13
Southtown Norfk...51 T12
Southtown Somset...16 K13
South Uist W Isls...106 d15
Southwaite Services Cumb...67 P3
South Walsham Norfk...51 Q11
Southwark Gt Lon...21 P7
South Warnborough Hants...20 B12
Southwater W Susx...10 K5
Southwater Street W Susx...10 K5
Southway Somset...17 P8
South Weald Essex...22 E9
Southwell Dorset...7 S10
Southwell Notts...47 T3
South Weston Oxon...30 D13
South Wheatley Cnwll...4 H3
South Wheatley Notts...58 C9
Southwick Hants...9 T7
Southwick Nhants...38 F2
Southwick Somset...17 L7
Southwick Sundld...70 D1
Southwick W Susx...11 L9
Southwick Wilts...18 B9
South Widcombe BaNES...17 Q5
South Wigston Leics...47 Q14
South Willesborough Kent...12 K7
South Willingham Lincs...59 L9
South Wingate Dur...70 F6
South Wingfield Derbys...47 L2
South Witham Lincs...48 D10
South Wonston Hants...19 R13
Southwood Norfk...51 Q12
Southwood Somset...17 Q10
South Woodham Ferrers Essex...22 K8
South Wootton Norfk...49 T9
South Wraxall Wilts...18 B8
South Zeal Devon...5 R2
Sowerby Calder...56 G1
Sowerby N York...63 U4
Sowerby Bridge Calder...63 L14
Sowerby Row Cumb...67 N5
Sower Carr Lancs...61 R11
Sowerhill Somset...15 U8
Sowley Green Suffk...40 B10
Sowood Calder...56 G3
Sowton Devon...6 C6
Soyland Town Calder...56 F2
Spa Common Norfk...51 N7
Spain's End Essex...39 T13
Spalding Lincs...48 K9
Spaldington E R Yk...64 H13
Spaldwick Cambs...38 J6
Spalford Notts...58 D13
Spanby Lincs...48 G6
Spanish Green Hants...19 U9
Sparham Norfk...50 J10
Sparhamill Norfk...50 J10
Spark Bridge Cumb...61 Q3
Sparket Cumb...67 P7
Sparkford Somset...17 R11
Sparkhill Birm...36 E4
Sparkwell Devon...5 P9
Sparrow Green Norfk...50 G11
Sparrowpit Derbys...56 G10
Sparrows Green E Susx...11 U4
Sparsholt Hants...19 Q14
Sparsholt Oxon...19 Q4
Spartylea Nthumb...68 J3
Spaunton N York...64 G2
Spaxton Somset...16 H9
Spean Bridge Highld...94 H2
Spear Hill W Susx...10 J7
Spearywell Hants...9 L2
Speen Bucks...30 G12
Speen W Berk...19 Q7
Speeton N York...65 Q4
Speke Lpool...54 K10
Speldhurst Kent...11 T2
Spellbrook Herts...22 C4
Spelmonden Kent...12 D7
Spen N Lans...82 D7
Spencers Wood Wokham...20 B9
Spen Green Ches E...45 T1
Spennithorne N York...63 N1
Spennymoor Dur...69 S6
Spernall Warwks...36 E8
Spetchley Worcs...35 U10
Spetisbury Dorset...8 C8
Spexhall Suffk...41 Q4
Spey Bay Moray...104 C2
Speybridge Highld...103 R10
Speyview Moray...104 A7
Spilsby Lincs...59 Q13
Spindlestone Nthumb...85 S11
Spinkhill Derbys...57 Q11
Spinningdale Highld...109 N7
Spion Kop Notts...57 S13
Spirthill Wilts...18 E5
Spital Wirral...54 H10
Spital Hill Donc...57 S7
Spital in the Street Lincs...58 F9
Spithurst E Susx...11 Q7
Spittal D & G...73 L6
Spittal E Loth...84 C3
Spittal Highld...112 E6
Spittal Nthumb...85 R8
Spittal Pembks...24 G6
Spittalfield P & K...90 J3
Spittal of Glenmuick Abers...98 B5
Spittal-on-Rule Border...76 A2
Spixworth Norfk...51 M10
Splatt Cnwll...4 D2
Splatt Cnwll...4 H4
Splayne's Green E Susx...11 Q5
Splottlands Cardif...27 M12
Spofforth N York...63 T9
Spondon C Derb...47 L6
Spon Green Flints...44 G1
Spooner Row Norfk...40 K1
Spott E Loth...84 H3
Spottiswoode Border...84 F9
Spratton Nhants...37 T6
Spreakley Surrey...10 D2
Spreyton Devon...15 R13
Spriddlestone Devon...5 N10
Spridlington Lincs...58 G10
Springburn C Glas...89 N12
Springfield D & G...75 R12
Springfield Essex...22 H6
Springfield Fife...91 L9
Springhill Staffs...46 C13
Springhill Staffs...46 E11
Springholm D & G...74 F12
Springside N Ayrs...81 M5
Springthorpe Lincs...58 E9
Spring Vale Barns...56 K5
Springwell Sundld...70 C1
Springwood Crematorium Lpool...54 K10
Sproatley E R Yk...65 R13
Sproston Green Ches W...55 R13
Sprotbrough Donc...57 R6
Sproughton Suffk...40 K12
Sprouston Border...84 K12
Sprowston Norfk...51 M11
Sproxton Leics...48 C10
Sproxton N York...64 E3
Spurstow Ches E...45 N2
Spyway Dorset...7 P6
Square & Compass Pembks...24 E5
Stableford Shrops...35 S2
Stableford Staffs...45 T6

Stacey Bank Sheff...57 L8
Stackhouse N York...62 G6
Stackpole Pembks...24 G11
Stacksteads Lancs...55 T2
Staddiscombe C Plym...5 N10
Staddlethorpe E R Yk...64 J14
Stadhampton Oxon...30 D13
Stadhlaigearraidh W Isls...106 c15
Staffield Cumb...67 R4
Staffin Highld...100 e3
Stafford Staffs...46 B9
Stafford Crematorium Staffs...46 C9
Stafford Services (northbound) Staffs...45 U7
Stafford Services (southbound) Staffs...45 U7
Stagsden Bed...38 E11
Stagsden West End Bed...38 E11
Stainborough Barns...57 M6
Stainburn Cumb...66 F7
Stainburn N York...63 R10
Stainby Lincs...48 D9
Staincross Barns...57 M4
Staindrop Dur...69 R8
Staines-upon-Thames Surrey...20 H8
Stainfield Lincs...48 G9
Stainfield Lincs...58 K12
Stainforth Donc...57 T4
Stainforth N York...62 G6
Staining Lancs...61 Q12
Stainland Calder...56 G3
Stainsacre N York...71 R11
Stainsby Derbys...57 Q13
Stainton Cumb...61 T2
Stainton Cumb...67 Q7
Stainton Cumb...67 N1
Stainton Donc...57 S7
Stainton Dur...69 N9
Stainton Middsb...70 G9
Stainton by Langworth Lincs...58 H11
Staintondale N York...71 S13
Stainton le Vale Lincs...58 K8
Stainton with Adgarley Cumb...61 N5
Stair Cumb...66 K8
Stair E Ayrs...81 N7
Stairfoot Barns...57 M5
Stairhaven D & G...72 F8
Staithes N York...71 M9
Stakeford Nthumb...77 R9
Stake Pool Lancs...61 S10
Stakes Hants...9 T7
Stalbridge Dorset...17 U13
Stalbridge Weston Dorset...17 T13
Stalham Norfk...51 Q8
Stalham Green Norfk...51 Q8
Stalisfield Green Kent...12 J4
Stallen Dorset...17 R13
Stalling Busk N York...62 J2
Stallingborough NE Lin...59 L4
Stalmine Lancs...61 R10
Stalmine Moss Side Lancs...61 R10
Stalybridge Tamesd...56 E7
Stambourne Essex...40 B13
Stambourne Green Essex...22 H1
Stamford Lincs...48 F12
Stamford Nthumb...77 Q3
Stamford Bridge Ches W...54 K13
Stamford Bridge E R Yk...64 G9
Stamfordham Nthumb...77 M11
Stamford Hill Gt Lon...21 P5
Stanah Lancs...61 R11
Stanborough Herts...31 R10
Stanbridge C Beds...30 K8
Stanbridge Dorset...8 E8
Stanbury C Brad...63 L13
Stand Bury...55 S5
Standburn Falk...82 H4
Standeford Staffs...46 B12
Standen Kent...12 G7
Standen Street Kent...12 F9
Standerwick Somset...18 B10
Standford Hants...10 C3
Standingstone Cumb...66 F7
Standish Gloucs...28 F6
Standish Wigan...55 M4
Standish Lower Ground Wigan...55 N5
Standlake Oxon...29 S7
Standon Hants...9 P3
Standon Herts...31 U8
Standon Staffs...45 T6
Standon Green End Herts...31 U10
Stane N Lans...82 G7
Stanfield Norfk...50 F9
Stanford C Beds...31 Q4
Stanford Kent...13 M8
Stanford Shrops...44 J11
Stanford Bishop Herefs...35 Q10
Stanford Bridge Worcs...35 R8
Stanford Dingley W Berk...19 S6
Stanford in the Vale Oxon...29 R9
Stanford le Hope Thurr...22 G11
Stanford on Avon Nhants...37 Q5
Stanford on Soar Notts...47 Q8
Stanford on Teme Worcs...35 R8
Stanford Rivers Essex...22 D7
Stanfree Derbys...57 Q12
Stanghow R & Cl...71 L9
Stanground C Pete...38 K1
Stanhill Lancs...55 R1
Stanhoe Norfk...50 C6
Stanhope Dur...69 L5
Stanhope Border...83 N13
Stanion Nhants...38 D3
Stanklin Worcs...35 U6
Stanley Derbys...47 M5
Stanley Dur...69 Q2
Stanley Notts...57 Q13
Stanley P & K...90 H4
Stanley Shrops...35 R4
Stanley Staffs...46 B3
Stanley Wakefd...57 M2
Stanley Common Derbys...47 M5
Stanley Crook Dur...69 Q5
Stanley Ferry Wakefd...57 N2
Stanley Gate Lancs...54 K5
Stanley Pontlarge Gloucs...28 J1
Stanmer Br & H...11 N8
Stanmore Gt Lon...21 L4
Stanmore Hants...9 P3
Stanmore W Berk...19 Q5
Stannersburn Nthumb...76 E9
Stanningfield Suffk...40 E9
Stannington Nthumb...77 R10
Stannington Sheff...57 L9
Stannington Station Nthumb...77 Q10
Stansbatch Herefs...34 H9
Stansfield Suffk...40 C10
Stanshope Staffs...46 F3
Stanstead Suffk...40 D11
Stanstead Abbotts Herts...31 U10
Stansted Kent...22 F10
Stansted Airport Essex...22 E3
Stansted Mountfitchet Essex...22 D3
Stanton Derbys...46 J10
Stanton Gloucs...36 E14
Stanton Mons...27 Q3
Stanton Nthumb...77 P8
Stanton Staffs...46 F4
Stanton Suffk...40 G6
Stanton by Bridge Derbys...47 L8
Stanton by Dale Derbys...47 N6
Stanton Drew BaNES...17 Q4
Stanton Fitzwarren Swindn...29 N9
Stanton Harcourt Oxon...29 T6
Stanton Hill Notts...47 N1
Stanton in Peak Derbys...56 K14
Stanton Lacy Shrops...35 L6
Stanton Long Shrops...35 N2
Stanton Prior BaNES...17 S3
Stanton St Bernard Wilts...18 G8
Stanton St John Oxon...30 C11
Stanton St Quintin Wilts...18 E5
Stanton Street Suffk...40 G7
Stanton under Bardon Leics...47 N11
Stanton upon Hine Heath Shrops...45 N9
Stanton Wick BaNES...17 R4
Stanwardine in the Fields Shrops...44 K9
Stanwardine in the Wood Shrops...44 K9
Stanway Essex...23 N3
Stanway Gloucs...28 K1
Stanway Green Suffk...41 M6

Stanway Green Suffk...41 M6
Stanwell Surrey...20 H8
Stanwell Moor Surrey...20 H8
Stanwick Nhants...38 E6
Stanwick N York...69 S10
Stanwix Cumb...67 P1
Stape N York...71 N14
Stapehill Dorset...8 F8
Stapeley Ches E...45 Q4
Stapenhill Staffs...46 J9
Staple Kent...13 Q4
Staple Somset...16 F8
Staple Cross Devon...16 D11
Staple Cross E Susx...12 E11
Staplefield W Susx...11 M5
Staple Fitzpaine Somset...16 H13
Stapleford Cambs...39 Q10
Stapleford Herts...31 T9
Stapleford Leics...48 B10
Stapleford Lincs...58 E14
Stapleford Notts...47 N6
Stapleford Wilts...18 G13
Stapleford Abbotts Essex...22 D9
Stapleford Tawney Essex...22 D8
Staplegrove Somset...16 H11
Staplehay Somset...16 H12
Staplehurst Kent...12 E7
Staplers IoW...9 Q11
Staplestreet Kent...13 L3
Stapleton Bristl...27 V12
Stapleton Cumb...75 V11
Stapleton Herefs...34 H8
Stapleton Leics...47 M14
Stapleton N York...69 S10
Stapleton Shrops...45 L12
Stapleton Somset...17 M12
Stapley Somset...16 G13
Staploe Bed...38 J9
Staplow Herefs...35 Q12
Star Fife...91 L11
Star Pembks...25 M3
Star Somset...17 M5
Starbeck N York...63 S8
Starbotton N York...62 J4
Starcross Devon...6 C8
Stareton Warwks...37 L6
Starkholmes Derbys...46 K2
Starlings Green Essex...22 C1
Starr's Green E Susx...12 E13
Starston Norfk...41 M4
Starston Devon...5 T9
Start Devon...5 T12
Startforth Dur...69 N9
Startley Wilts...18 D4
Statenborough Kent...13 R4
Statham Warrtn...55 Q10
Stathe Somset...17 L11
Stathern Leics...47 U7
Station Town Dur...70 F5
Staughton Green Cambs...38 J8
Staughton Highway Cambs...38 J8
Staunton Gloucs...27 V4
Staunton Gloucs...28 E2
Staunton in the Vale Notts...48 B4
Staunton on Arrow Herefs...34 J8
Staunton on Wye Herefs...34 J12
Staveley Cumb...67 P13
Staveley Cumb...61 R1
Staveley Derbys...57 P12
Staveley N York...63 T7
Staveley-in-Cartmel Cumb...61 R2
Staverton Devon...5 T8
Staverton Gloucs...28 G3
Staverton Nhants...37 P8
Staverton Wilts...18 C8
Staverton Bridge Gloucs...28 G3
Stawell Somset...17 L9
Stawley Somset...16 E12
Staxigoe Highld...112 J6
Staxton N York...65 N4
Staylittle Cerdgn...33 S2
Staylittle Powys...33 S3
Staynall Lancs...61 R11
Staythorpe Notts...47 U3
Stead C Brad...63 N10
Stean N York...62 K5
Steanbow Somset...17 Q9
Stearsby N York...64 E6
Steart Somset...16 J7
Stebbing Essex...22 G3
Stebbing Green Essex...22 G3
Stede Quarter Kent...12 G8
Stedham W Susx...10 D6
Steel Nthumb...76 K14
Steel Cross E Susx...11 S4
Steelend Fife...90 F13
Steele Road Border...76 A7
Steel Heath Shrops...45 M6
Steen's Bridge Herefs...35 M9
Steep Hants...9 U3
Steep Lane Calder...56 F1
Steeple Dorset...8 C12
Steeple Essex...23 M7
Steeple Ashton Wilts...18 D9
Steeple Aston Oxon...29 U3
Steeple Barton Oxon...29 T3
Steeple Bumpstead Essex...39 U12
Steeple Claydon Bucks...30 E7
Steeple Gidding Cambs...38 H4
Steeple Langford Wilts...18 F13
Steeple Morden Cambs...39 L12
Steeton C Brad...63 L11
Stein Highld...100 b4
Stella Gatesd...77 P13
Stelling Minnis Kent...13 M7
Stembridge Somset...17 M12
Stenalees Cnwll...3 Q5
Stenhousemuir Falk...89 T8
Stenigot Lincs...59 M10
Stenscholl Highld...100 e3
Stenson Fields Derbys...46 K7
Stenton E Loth...84 H4
Steornabhagh W Isls...106 j5
Stepaside Pembks...25 M9
Stepford D & G...74 G9
Stepney Gt Lon...21 P6
Stepping Hill Stockp...56 D9
Steppingley C Beds...31 M5
Stepps N Lans...89 P12
Sternfield Suffk...41 Q8
Stert Wilts...18 F9
Stetchworth Cambs...39 S9
Stevenage Herts...31 R7
Steven's Crouch E Susx...12 D12
Stevenston N Ayrs...80 K4
Steventon Hants...19 S11
Steventon Oxon...29 U9
Steventon End Essex...39 S12
Stewartby Bed...38 F11
Stewartfield S Lans...81 S1
Stewarton Ag & B...79 M11
Stewarton E Ayrs...81 N3
Stewkley Bucks...30 H7
Stewley Somset...16 K12
Stewton Lincs...59 Q9
Steyne Cross IoW...9 S11
Steyning W Susx...10 K8
Steynton Pembks...24 F9
Stibb Cnwll...14 F10
Stibbard Norfk...50 G8
Stibb Cross Devon...14 K10
Stibb Green Wilts...18 K8
Stibbington Cambs...38 G1
Stichill Border...84 J11
Sticker Cnwll...3 P6
Stickford Lincs...59 P14
Sticklepath Devon...5 R2
Sticklepath Somset...16 D11
Stickling Green Essex...39 P14
Stickney Lincs...49 M2
Stiff Street Kent...12 F3
Stiffkey Norfk...50 G4
Stifford's Bridge Herefs...35 R11
Stile Bridge Kent...12 E6
Stileway Somset...17 N8
Stillingfleet N York...64 D11
Stillington N York...64 E7
Stillington Stockt...70 E8
Stilton Cambs...38 J3
Stinchcombe Gloucs...28 D8
Stinsford Dorset...7 S6
Stiperstones Shrops...44 J13
Stirchley Birm...36 E5
Stirchley Wrekin...45 R12
Stirling Abers...105 U5
Stirling Stirlg...89 S7
Stirling Castle Stirlg...89 S7
Stirling Services Stirlg...89 S6
Stirton N York...62 K9
Stisted Essex...22 K3
Stitchcombe Wilts...18 K7
Stithians Cnwll...2 J9
Stittenham N York...64 F5
Stivichall Covtry...37 L5
Stixwould Lincs...59 L13
Stoak Ches W...54 J12
Stobo Border...83 M11
Stoborough Dorset...8 C11
Stoborough Green Dorset...8 C11
Stobs Castle Border...75 V4
Stobswood Nthumb...77 Q7
Stock Essex...22 G8
Stock N Som...17 M4
Stockbridge Hants...9 M2
Stockbriggs S Lans...82 E11
Stockbury Kent...12 F3
Stockcross W Berk...19 P7

Stockdalewath Cumb....67 N3
Stocker's Hill Kent....12 J5
Stockerston Leics....48 B14
Stocking Herefs....28 B1
Stockingford Warks....36 K2
Stocking Pelham Herts....23 N1
Stockland Bristol
Somset....16 H4
Stockland Devon....6 H4
Stockland Green Kent....11 T2
Stockleigh English
Devon....15 U11
Stockleigh Pomeroy
Devon....15 U12
Stockley Wilts....18 E7
Stockley Hill Herefs....34 J13
Stocklinch Somset....17 L13
Stockmoor Herefs....34 J10
Stockport Stockp....56 C8
Stockport Crematorium
Stockp....56 D9
Stocksbridge Sheff....57 L7
Stocksfield Nthumb....77 M13
Stocks Green Kent....11 S13
Stockton Herefs....35 M8
Stockton Norfk....41 Q2
Stockton Shrops....35 R14
Stockton Shrops....45 S12
Stockton Warks....37 M8
Stockton Wilts....18 D13
Stockton Wrekin....45 S10
Stockton Brook Staffs....46 B3
Stockton Heath Warrtn....55 P9
Stockton-on-Tees S on T....70 F9
Stockton on the Forest
C York....64 F8
Stockwell Gloucs....28 H5
Stockwell End Wolves....45 U13
Stockwell Heath Staffs....46 E9
Stockwood Bristl....17 R3
Stockwood Dorset....7 Q3
Stock Wood Worcs....36 D8
Stoddday Lancs....61 T8
Stodmarsh Kent....13 P3
Stody Norfk....50 J6
Stoer Highld....110 A11
Stoford Somset....7 Q2
Stoford Wilts....18 G13
Stogumber Somset....16 E9
Stogursey Somset....16 H8
Stoke Devon....14 F8
Stoke Hants....19 P11
Stoke Hants....9 R6
Stoke Medway....22 K13
Stoke Abbott Dorset....7 N4
Stoke Albany Nhants....38 B3
Stoke Ash Suffk....40 K7
Stoke Bardolph Notts....47 R5
Stoke Bliss Worcs....35 Q8
Stoke Bruerne Nhants....37 T11
Stoke by Clare Suffk....40 B12
Stoke-by-Nayland Suffk....40 G13
Stoke Canon Devon....6 B6
Stoke Charity Hants....19 Q13
Stoke Climsland Cnwll....4 K6
Stoke Cross Herefs....35 P10
Stoke D'Abernon Surrey....20 K11
Stoke Doyle Nhants....38 G3
Stoke Dry Rutnd....38 C1
Stoke Edith Herefs....35 P12
Stoke End Warwks....36 H1
Stoke Farthing Wilts....8 F3
Stoke Ferry Norfk....50 B14
Stoke Fleming Devon....5 U12
Stokeford Dorset....8 B11
Stoke Gabriel Devon....5 U9
Stoke Gifford S Glos....28 B12
Stoke Golding Leics....37 L1
Stoke Goldington
M Keyn....38 B11
Stokeham Notts....58 B12
Stoke Hammond Bucks....30 J7
Stoke Heath Shrops....45 Q8
Stoke Heath Worcs....36 B7
Stoke Holy Cross Norfk....51 M13
Stokeinteignhead Devon....6 B10
Stoke Lacy Herefs....35 P10
Stoke Lyne Oxon....30 C7
Stoke Mandeville Bucks....30 H10
Stokenchurch Bucks....20 C4
Stoke Newington Gt Lon....21 P5
Stokenham Devon....5 U12
Stoke Orchard Gloucs....28 H2
Stoke Poges Bucks....20 G6
Stoke Pound Worcs....36 C7
Stoke Prior Herefs....35 M9
Stoke Prior Worcs....36 B7
Stoke Rivers Devon....15 P5
Stoke Rochford Lincs....48 D9
Stoke Row Oxon....19 U4
Stoke St Gregory Somset....16 K11
Stoke St Mary Somset....16 J12
Stoke St Michael Somset....17 S7
Stoke St Milborough
Shrops....35 N4
Stokesay Shrops....35 K4
Stokesby Norfk....51 R11
Stokesley N York....70 H11
Stoke sub Hamdon
Somset....17 N13
Stoke Talmage Oxon....30 E13
Stoke upon Tern Shrops....45 P8
Stoke-upon-Trent C Stke....45 U4
Stoke Wake Dorset....7 U3
Stoke Wharf Worcs....36 C7
Stoke Row Essex....22 E7
Stolford Somset....16 H7
Stondon Massey Essex....22 E7
Stone Bucks....30 G10
Stone Gloucs....28 B9
Stone Kent....22 E13
Stone Rothm....57 Q9
Stone Somset....17 Q10
Stone Staffs....45 U6
Stone Worcs....35 U5
Stonea Cambs....39 Q2
Stone Allerton Somset....17 L6
St Ann Easton Somset....17 R6
Stonebridge Devon....15 P8
Stonebridge Warwks....36 H4
Stone Bridge Corner
C Pete....49 L13
Stonebroom Derbys....47 M2
Stone Chair Calder....63 H14
Stone Cross E Susx....11 S5
Stone Cross E Susx....11 U8
Stone Cross Kent....12 B9
Stone Cross Kent....12 K8
Stone Cross Kent....13 D9
Stonecrouch Kent....12 D9
Stone-edge-Batch
N Som....17 N2
Stoneferry C KuH....65 Q13
Stonefield Castle Hotel
Ag & B....87 R11
Stonegate E Susx....12 C10
Stonegate N York....71 N11
Stonegrave N York....64 F4
Stonehall Worcs....35 U11
Stonehaugh Nthumb....76 F10
Stonehaven Abers....99 R8
Stone Hill Donc....57 U5
Stonehouse C Plym....5 M10
Stone House Cumb....62 H2
Stonehouse Gloucs....28 F6
Stonehouse Nthumb....76 D14
Stonehouse S Lans....82 E9
Stone in Oxney Kent....12 H10
Stoneleigh Warwks....36 K6
Stoneley Green Ches E....45 P3
Stonely Cambs....38 H7
Stoner Hill Hants....9 U3
Stonesby Leics....48 B9
Stonesfield Oxon....29 S4
Stones Green Essex....23 S2
Stonestreet Green Kent....12 K8
Stonethwaite Cumb....67 L11
Stonewells Moray....104 B3
Stonewood Kent....22 E13
Stoneybridge W Isls....106 C15
Stoneybridge W Isls....106 C15
Stoneyburn W Loth....82 K6
Stonefall Falk....89 S9
Stonham Aspal Suffk....41 L9
Stonnall Staffs....46 E13
Stonor Oxon....20 B5
Stonton Wyville Leics....47 U14
Stony Cross Herefs....35 S11
Stony Cross Herefs....35 R9
Stonyford Hants....9 L5
Stony Houghton Derbys....57 Q13
Stony Stratford M Keyn....30 H4

Stonywell Staffs....46 E11
Stoodleigh Devon....15 U10
Stoodleigh Devon....15 S7
Stop 24 Services Kent....13 M8
Stopham W Susx....10 G7
Stopsley Luton....31 P8
Stoptide Cnwll....3 N1
Storeton Wirral....54 H10
Storeyard Green Herefs....35 R12
Storm Hill....
Stornoway W Isls....106 j5
Stornoway Airport W Isls....106 j5
Storridge Herefs....35 S11
Storrington W Susx....10 H8
Storth Cumb....61 T3
Storwood E R Yk....64 G11
Stotfield Moray....104 A1
Stotfold C Beds....31 R5
Stottesdon Shrops....35 Q4
Stoughton Leics....47 R13
Stoughton Surrey....20 G12
Stoughton W Susx....10 C8
Stoulton Worcs....36 B11
Stourbridge Dudley....35 U4
Stourbridge
Crematorium Dudley....36 U3
Stourhead Wilts....17 U10
Stourpaine Dorset....8 B8
Stourport-on-Severn
Worcs....35 T6
Stour Provost Dorset....17 U12
Stour Row Dorset....17 V12
Stourton Leeds....63 S13
Stourton Staffs....35 U3
Stourton Warwks....36 J13
Stourton Wilts....17 U10
Stourton Caundle Dorset....17 T13
Stout Somset....17 M10
Stove Shet....106 u11
Stoven Suffk....41 S4
Stow Border....84 D10
Stow Lincs....58 E10
Stow Bardolph Norfk....49 T12
Stow Bedon Norfk....40 G2
Stowbridge Norfk....49 T11
Stow cum Quy Cambs....39 R8
Stowe Shrops....34 H6
Stowe by Chartley Staffs....46 D8
Stowehill Nhants....37 R9
Stowell Somset....17 S12
Stowey BaNES....17 Q5
Stowford Devon....5 L3
Stowford Devon....6 F7
Stowford Devon....15 U8
Stowlangtoft Suffk....40 G7
Stow Longa Cambs....38 H6
Stow Maries Essex....23 L7
Stowmarket Suffk....40 H9
Stow-on-the-Wold
Gloucs....29 N3
Stowting Kent....13 M7
Stowting Common Kent....13 M7
Stowupland Suffk....40 J8
Straanruie Highld....103 Q4
Strachan Abers....98 M5
Strachur Ag & B....88 C5
Stradbroke Suffk....41 M6
Stradbrook Wilts....18 C9
Stradishall Suffk....40 B10
Stradsett Norfk....49 U12
Stragglethorpe Lincs....48 D3
Stragglethorpe Notts....47 R6
Straight Soley Wilts....19 M6
Straiton Mdloth....83 Q5
Straiton S Ayrs....81 M12
Straloch Abers....105 P11
Straloch P & K....97 S11
Stramshall Staffs....46 E6
Strang IoM....60 f7
Strangeways Salfd....55 T7
Strangford Herefs....28 A4
Stranraer D & G....72 D7
Strata Florida Cerdgn....33 Q7
Stratfield Mortimer
W Berk....19 U8
Stratfield Saye Hants....19 U8
Stratfield Turgis Hants....19 U9
Stratford C Beds....31 J11
Stratford Gt Lon....21 Q6
Stratford St Andrew
Suffk....41 Q8
Stratford St Mary Suffk....40 H14
Stratford sub Castle
Wilts....8 G2
Stratford Tony Wilts....8 F3
Stratford-upon-Avon
Warwks....36 H10
Strath Highld....107 N9
Strathan Highld....110 B10
Strathan Highld....111 M4
Strathaven S Lans....82 D10
Strathblane Stirlg....89 N11
Strathcanaird Highld....108 B4
Strathcarron Highld....101 N4
Strathcoil Ag & B....93 R12
Strathdon Abers....104 D13
Strathkinness Fife....91 Q8
Strathloanhead W Loth....82 H4
Strathmashie House
Highld....96 H5
Strathmiglo Fife....90 J10
Strathpeffer Highld....102 E4
Strathtay P & K....97 Q13
Strathwhillan N Ayrs....80 E6
Strathy Highld....111 S4
Strathy Inn Highld....111 S4
Strathyre Stirlg....95 M14
Stratton Cnwll....14 F11
Stratton Dorset....7 S6
Stratton Gloucs....29 L7
Stratton Audley Oxon....30 D7
Stratton-on-the-Fosse
Somset....17 S6
Stratton St Margaret
Swindn....29 N10
Stratton St Michael
Norfk....41 M2
Stratton Strawless
Norfk....51 M9
Stravithie Fife....91 R9
Stream Somset....16 E9
Streat E Susx....11 N7
Streatham Gt Lon....21 N8
Streatley C Beds....31 N7
Streatley W Berk....19 S4
Street Devon....6 J6
Street Lancs....61 U9
Street N York....71 M12
Street Somset....17 N9
Street Ashton Warwks....37 N4
Street Dinas Shrops....44 H6
Street End E Susx....12 B9
Street End Kent....13 M5
Street End W Susx....10 D11
Street Gate Gatesd....77 Q14
Streethay Staffs....46 F11
Street Houses N York....64 C10
Streetlam N York....70 D13
Streetly Wsall....46 E14
Streetly End Cambs....39 U11
Street on the Fosse
Somset....17 R9
Strefford Shrops....34 K3
Strelitz P & K....90 J3
Strelley Notts....47 P5
Strensall C York....64 E7
Strensham Worcs....36 B12
Strensham Services
(northbound) Worcs....35 U12
Strensham Services
(southbound) Worcs....36 B12
Stretcholt Somset....16 J8
Strete Devon....5 U11
Stretford Herefs....35 M9
Stretford Traffd....55 S8
Strethall Essex....39 Q13
Stretham Cambs....39 R6
Strettington W Susx....10 D9
Stretton Ches W....54 K10
Stretton Derbys....47 M1
Stretton Rutnd....48 D11
Stretton Staffs....35 T12
Stretton Staffs....46 H9
Stretton Warrtn....55 P10
Stretton en le Field Leics....46 K11
Stretton Grandison
Herefs....35 P12
Stretton-on-Dunsmore
Warwks....37 M6
Stretton on Fosse
Warwks....36 J13
Stretton Sugwas Herefs....35 L12
Stretton under Fosse
Warwks....37 N4
Stretton Westwood
Shrops....45 N13
Strichen Abers....105 Q4
Strines Stockp....56 E9
Stringston Somset....16 G8
Strixton Nhants....38 D8
Stroat Gloucs....28 A8
Stromeferry Highld....101 M4
Stromness Ork....106 r19
Stronachlachar Stirlg....88 H3
Stronafian Ag & B....88 B11
Stronchrubie Highld....108 E2
Strone Ag & B....88 E9
Strone Highld....96 G3
Strone Highld....102 F9
Stronenaba Highld....94 J2

Stronmilchan Ag & B....94 H13
Stronsay Ork....106 v17
Stronsay Airport Ork....106 v17
Strontian Highld....93 U6
Strood Kent....12 E7
Strood Medway....12 D2
Strood Green Surrey....21 M13
Strood Green W Susx....10 J5
Stroud Gloucs....28 G6
Stroud Hants....9 U4
Stroude Surrey....20 H9
Stroud Green Essex....23 L9
Stroud Green Gloucs....28 F6
Stroxton Lincs....48 D7
Struan P & K....97 R11
Struan Highld....100 c6
Strubby Lincs....59 S10
Strumpshaw Norfk....51 P12
Strutherhill S Lans....82 E9
Struthers Fife....91 M10
Struy Highld....102 D7
Stryd-y-Facsen IoA....52 D6
Stryt-issa Wrexhm....44 G4
Stuartfield Abers....105 Q6
Stubbers Green Wsall....46 D14
Stubbington Hants....9 R8
Stubbins Lancs....55 S3
Stubbs Green Norfk....51 N14
Stubhampton Dorset....8 D6
Stubley Derbys....57 M11
Stubshaw Cross Wigan....55 N7
Stubton Lincs....48 C4
Stuckton Hants....8 H6
Studfold N York....62 G6
Stud Green W & M....20 E7
Studham C Beds....31 M9
Studholme Cumb....67 L1
Studland Dorset....8 E12
Studley Warwks....36 E8
Studley Wilts....18 E6
Studley Common
Warwks....36 E8
Studley Roger N York....63 R6
Studley Royal N York....63 R5
Studley Royal Park &
Fountains Abbey
N York....63 R5
Stuntney Cambs....39 S5
Stunts Green E Susx....11 U8
Sturbridge Staffs....45 T7
Sturgate Lincs....58 E9
Sturmer Essex....39 U12
Sturminster Common
Dorset....7 U2
Sturminster Marshall
Dorset....8 D8
Sturminster Newton
Dorset....17 U13
Sturry Kent....13 N3
Sturton by Stow Lincs....58 E10
Sturton le Steeple Notts....58 C10
Stuston Suffk....40 K5
Stutton N York....64 B11
Stutton Suffk....41 L14
Styal Ches E....55 T9
Stydd Lancs....62 D12
Stynie Moray....104 C3
Styrrup Notts....57 T8
Succoth Ag & B....88 G5
Suckley Worcs....35 R10
Suckley Green Worcs....35 R10
Sudborough Nhants....38 E4
Sudbourne Suffk....41 R10
Sudbrook Lincs....48 E5
Sudbrook Mons....27 U10
Sudbrooke Lincs....58 H11
Sudbury Derbys....46 G7
Sudbury Gt Lon....21 K5
Sudbury Suffk....40 E12
Sudden Rochdl....56 C4
Sudgrove Gloucs....28 H6
Suffield N York....65 M1
Suffield Norfk....51 M7
Sugdon Wrekin....45 P10
Sugnall Staffs....45 S7
Sugwas Pool Herefs....35 L12
Suisnish Highld....100 e8
Sulby IoM....60 f4
Sulgrave Nhants....37 Q11
Sulham W Berk....19 U6
Sulhamstead W Berk....19 T7
Sulhamstead Abbots
W Berk....19 T7
Sulhamstead Bannister
W Berk....19 T7
Sullington W Susx....10 H8
Sullom Shet....106 t6
Sullom Voe Shet....106 u6
Sully V Glam....16 G3
Sumburgh Airport Shet....106 t12
Summerbridge N York....63 Q7
Summercourt Cnwll....3 M5
Summerfield Worcs....35 T6
Summerfield Norfk....50 B6
Summerhill Staffs....46 E12
Summer Heath Bucks....20 C4
Summerhouse Darltn....69 R9
Summerlands Cumb....61 U2
Summerley Derbys....57 M11
Summersdale W Susx....10 D9
Summerseat Bury....55 S4
Summertown Oxon....30 B11
Summit Oldham....56 D5
Summit Rochdl....56 D3
Sunbiggin Cumb....68 E11
Sunbury-on-Thames
Surrey....20 K9
Sundaywell D & G....74 F9
Sunderland Ag & B....78 C3
Sunderland Cumb....66 J5
Sunderland Lancs....61 S9
Sunderland Sundld....70 G1
Sunderland Bridge Dur....69 S4
Sundhope Border....83 R2
Sundon Park Luton....31 N7
Sundridge Kent....21 S11
Sunk Island E R Yk....59 N1
Sunningdale W & M....20 F9
Sunninghill W & M....20 F9
Sunningwell Oxon....29 U7
Sunniside Dur....69 Q5
Sunniside Gatesd....77 Q14
Sunny Brow Dur....69 Q5
Sunnyhill C Derb....46 K7
Sunnyhurst Bl w D....55 Q2
Sunnylaw Stirlg....89 S6
Sunnymead Oxon....30 B11
Sunton Wilts....18 K9
Surbiton Gt Lon....21 L9
Surfleet Lincs....49 L8
Surfleet Seas End Lincs....49 L8
Surlingham Norfk....51 P12
Surrex Essex....23 L3
Surrey & Sussex
Crematorium W Susx....11 M3
Susfstead North N Susx....16 D6
Sustead Norfk....51 L6
Susworth Lincs....58 D6
Sutcombe Devon....14 H10
Sutcombemill Devon....14 H10
Suton Norfk....50 J14
Sutterby Lincs....59 Q12
Sutterton Lincs....49 L6
Sutton C Beds....31 R4
Sutton C Pete....48 H14
Sutton Cambs....39 P5
Sutton Devon....5 S12
Sutton Devon....15 R12
Sutton Donc....57 S4
Sutton Gt Lon....21 N10
Sutton Kent....13 R6
Sutton N York....57 N2
Sutton Norfk....51 Q8
Sutton Notts....47 S4
Sutton Notts....58 B9
Sutton Pembks....24 F7
Sutton Shrops....35 R4
Sutton Shrops....45 R8
Sutton Shrops....45 S5
Sutton Shrops....45 M11
Sutton Staffs....45 S9
Sutton Suffk....41 Q11
Sutton W Susx....10 F7
Sutton at Hone Kent....22 D13
Sutton Bassett Nhants....37 U3
Sutton Benger Wilts....18 D5
Sutton Bingham Somset....7 P2
Sutton Bonington Notts....47 P8
Sutton Bridge Lincs....49 R9
Sutton Cheney Leics....47 M13
Sutton Coldfield
Crematorium Birm....46 F14
Sutton Courtenay Oxon....19 R2
Sutton Crosses Lincs....49 R9
Sutton cum Lound Notts....57 U10
Sutton Fields Notts....47 N8
Sutton Green Surrey....20 H12
Sutton Grange N York....63 R5
Sutton Howgrave N York....63 S4
Sutton in Ashfield Notts....47 N2
Sutton-in-Craven N York....63 L11
Sutton Lane Ends Ches E....56 D12
Sutton Maddock Shrops....45 R13
Sutton Mallet Somset....17 L9
Sutton Mandeville Wilts....8 D3
Sutton Manor St Hel....55 M8

Sutton Marsh Herefs....35 N12
Sutton Montis Somset....17 R12
Sutton-on-Hull C KuH....65 Q13
Sutton on Sea Lincs....59 T10
Sutton on the Forest
N York....64 D7
Sutton on the Hill
Derbys....46 H7
Sutton on Trent Notts....58 C13
Sutton Poyntz Dorset....7 T8
Sutton St Edmund Lincs....49 M11
Sutton St James Lincs....49 N10
Sutton St Nicholas
Herefs....35 N12
Sutton Scotney Hants....19 Q13
Sutton Street Kent....12 F4
Sutton-under-Brailes
Warwks....36 K13
Sutton-under-
Whitestonecliffe
N York....64 B3
Sutton Valence Kent....12 F6
Sutton Veny Wilts....18 C12
Sutton Waldron Dorset....8 B5
Sutton Weaver Ches W....55 N11
Sutton Wick BaNES....17 Q5
Sutton Wick Oxon....29 U9
Swaby Lincs....59 Q11
Swadlincote Derbys....46 J10
Swaffham Norfk....50 E12
Swaffham Bulbeck
Cambs....39 S8
Swaffham Prior Cambs....39 S8
Swafield Norfk....51 N7
Swainby N York....70 G12
Swainshill Herefs....35 L12
Swainsthorpe Norfk....51 M13
Swainswick BaNES....17 T3
Swalcliffe Oxon....37 L13
Swalecliffe Kent....13 M2
Swallow Lincs....59 L6
Swallow Beck Lincs....58 F13
Swallowcliffe Wilts....8 D3
Swallowfield Wokhm....20 B10
Swallow Nest Rothm....57 Q9
Swallows Cross Essex....22 F8
Swampton Hants....19 P10
Swanage Dorset....8 E13
Swanbourne Bucks....30 H7
Swanbridge V Glam....16 G3
Swancote Shrops....35 R2
Swan Green Ches W....55 R12
Swanland E R Yk....65 M14
Swanley Kent....21 U9
Swanley Village Kent....21 U9
Swanmore Hants....9 R5
Swannington Leics....47 M10
Swannington Norfk....50 K10
Swanpool Garden
Suburb Lincs....58 G13
Swanscombe Kent....22 F13
Swansea Swans....26 B9
Swansea Crematorium
Swans....26 B8
Swansea West Services
Swans....25 V11
Swan Street Essex....23 L2
Swanton Abbot Norfk....51 N8
Swanton Morley Norfk....50 H10
Swanton Novers Norfk....50 H6
Swanton Street Kent....12 G4
Swan Village Sandw....46 C2
Swanwick Derbys....47 M3
Swanwick Hants....9 R7
Swarby Lincs....48 F5
Swardeston Norfk....51 M13
Swarkestone Derbys....47 L8
Swarland Nthumb....77 P5
Swarraton Hants....19 R13
Swartha C Brad....63 M10
Swarthmoor Cumb....61 N4
Swaton Lincs....48 H6
Swavesey Cambs....39 N7
Sway Hants....8 K9
Swayfield Lincs....48 E9
Swaythling C Sotn....9 N5
Sweet Green Worcs....35 P8
Sweetham Devon....15 U13
Sweethaven S Lans....24 F6
Sweetlands Corner Kent....12 E6
Sweets Cnwll....14 E13
Sweetshouse Cnwll....3 R4
Swefling Suffk....41 P8
Swepstone Leics....47 L11
Swerford Oxon....29 S2
Swettenham Ches E....55 T13
Swffryd Blae G....27 N8
Swift's Green Kent....12 G7
Swilland Suffk....41 L10
Swillbrook Lancs....61 T13
Swillington Leeds....63 T13
Swimbridge Devon....15 P6
Swimbridge Newland
Devon....15 P6
Swinbrook Oxon....29 P5
Swincliffe N York....63 R8
Swincombe Devon....15 Q4
Swinden N York....62 H9
Swinderby Lincs....58 E14
Swindon Gloucs....28 H3
Swindon Nthumb....76 J2
Swindon Staffs....35 T2
Swindon Swindn....29 M11
Swine E R Yk....65 R13
Swinefleet E R Yk....58 C2
Swineford S Glos....17 S3
Swineshead Bed....38 G8
Swineshead Lincs....48 K5
Swineshead Bridge Lincs....48 K5
Swiney Highld....112 G9
Swinford Leics....37 Q5
Swinford Oxon....29 U6
Swingfield Minnis Kent....13 P7
Swingfield Street Kent....13 P7
Swingleton Green Suffk....40 G11
Swinhoe Nthumb....85 U13
Swinhope Lincs....59 L7
Swinithwaite N York....63 L1
Swinmoor Common
Herefs....35 N12
Swinscoe Staffs....46 F4
Swinside Cumb....66 K8
Swinstead Lincs....48 F9
Swinton Border....85 M10
Swinton N York....63 T3
Swinton N York....64 G4
Swinton Rothm....57 P7
Swinton Salfd....55 S6
Swithland Leics....47 Q11
Swordale Highld....102 F3
Swordland Highld....100 g8
Swordly Highld....111 R3
Sworton Heath Ches E....55 Q10
Swydd ffynnon Cerdgn....33 N7
Swyddffynnon Cerdgn....33 N7
Swynnerton Staffs....45 T6
Swyre Dorset....7 P7
Sychdyn Flints....54 F13
Sychnant Powys....33 U6
Sychtyn Powys....43 U12
Sydallt Wrexhm....44 H2
Sydenham Gt Lon....21 Q8
Sydenham Oxon....30 F12
Sydenham Somset....17 L8
Sydenham Damerel
Devon....5 L5
Sydenhurst Surrey....10 F4
Syderstone Norfk....50 E7
Sydling St Nicholas
Dorset....7 R5
Sydmonton Hants....19 R9
Sydnal Lane Shrops....45 T12
Syerston Notts....47 U4
Syke Rochdl....56 C4
Sykehouse Donc....57 T4
Syleham Suffk....41 N5
Sylen Carmth....25 T9
Symbister Shet....106 v7
Symington S Ayrs....81 M7
Symington S Lans....82 H11
Symondbury Dorset....7 N6
Symonds Yat Herefs....27 V4
Sympson Green C Brad....63 P12
Synderford Dorset....7 L4
Synod Inn Cerdgn....32 H10
Syre Highld....111 P6
Syreford Gloucs....28 K3
Syresham Nhants....37 R12
Syston Leics....47 R11
Syston Lincs....48 D5
Sytchampton Worcs....35 T8
Sywell Nhants....38 B7

T

Tabley Hill Ches E....55 R11
Tackley Oxon....29 U4
Tacolneston Norfk....40 K1
Tadcaster N York....64 B11
Taddington Derbys....56 H12
Taddiport Devon....14 K10
Tadley Hants....19 T8
Tadlow Cambs....39 M11
Tadmarton Oxon....37 L13
Tadpole Swindn....29 M10
Tadwick BaNES....17 T3
Tadworth Surrey....21 M11

Tafarnaubach Blae G....27 L5
Tafarn-y-bwlch Pembks....24 J4
Tafarn-y-Gelyn Denbgs....44 E1
Taff's Well Rhondd....27 L11
Tafolwern Powys....43 S12
Taibach Neath....26 D10
Tain Highld....109 P8
Tain Highld....112 F3
Tai'r Bull Powys....26 H2
Tairbeart W Isls....106 f8
Tairgwaith Neath....26 C7
Takeley Essex....22 F3
Takeley Street Essex....22 E3
Talachddu Powys....34 C14
Talacre Flints....54 D10
Talardy Flints....54 D11
Talaton Devon....6 E5
Talbenny Pembks....24 E8
Talbot Green Rhondd....26 J11
Talbot Village Bmouth....8 F10
Taleford Devon....6 E5
Talerddig Powys....43 T13
Talgarreg Cerdgn....32 H10
Talgarth Powys....34 E14
Talisker Highld....100 c6
Talke Staffs....45 T3
Talke Pits Staffs....45 T3
Talkin Cumb....67 Q1
Talladale Highld....107 P9
Talla Linnfoots Border....75 M1
Tallaminnock S Ayrs....81 N13
Tallarn Green Wrexhm....44 K5
Tallentire Cumb....66 H5
Talley Carmth....33 M14
Tallington Lincs....48 G12
Talmine Highld....111 N4
Talog Carmth....25 P5
Talsarn Cerdgn....32 K9
Talsarnau Gwynd....43 M6
Talskiddy Cnwll....3 N3
Talwrn IoA....52 G7
Talwrn Wrexhm....44 J4
Tal-y-bont Cerdgn....33 M3
Tal-y-bont Conwy....53 N9
Tal-y-bont Gwynd....52 K6
Tal-y-Bont Gwynd....43 M10
Talybont-on-Usk Powys....27 L3
Tal-y-Cafn Conwy....53 N8
Tal-y-coed Mons....27 S4
Tal-y-garn Rhondd....26 J11
Tal-y-llyn Gwynd....43 P12
Talysarn Gwynd....52 G12
Tal-y-Waun Torfn....27 P7
Talywern Powys....43 S12
Tamar Valley Mining
District Devon....5 L7
Tamer Lane End Wigan....55 P7
Tamerton Foliot C Plym....5 M8
Tamworth Staffs....46 H13
Tamworth Green Lincs....49 N5
Tamworth Services
Warwks....46 H13
Tancred N York....64 B8
Tancredston Pembks....24 F5
Tandridge Surrey....21 Q12
Tanfield Dur....69 Q2
Tanfield Lea Dur....69 Q2
Tangiers Pembks....24 F7
Tangley Hants....19 M10
Tangmere W Susx....10 E9
Tangusdale W Isls....106 b18
Tan Hill N York....68 K13
Tankerness Ork....106 u19
Tankersley Barns....57 M7
Tankerton Kent....13 M2
Tannach Highld....112 J8
Tannachie Abers....99 P7
Tannadice Angus....98 H12
Tannington Suffk....41 M7
Tannochside N Lans....82 D6
Tansley Derbys....46 K2
Tansor Nhants....38 G2
Tanton N York....70 H10
Tanwood Worcs....35 U6
Tanworth in Arden
Warwks....36 G6
Tan-y-Bwlch Gwynd....43 N5
Tan-y-fron Conwy....53 S10
Tan-y-fron Wrexhm....44 H4
Tan-y-grisiau Gwynd....43 N4
Tan-y-groes Cerdgn....32 F11
Taobh Tuath W Isls....106 e10
Taplow Bucks....20 F6
Tarbert Ag & B....79 M5
Tarbert Ag & B....87 R3
Tarbert W Isls....106 f8
Tarbet Ag & B....88 H5
Tarbet Highld....100 g10
Tarbock Green Knows....55 L9
Tarbolton S Ayrs....81 N7
Tarbrax S Lans....82 K7
Tardebigge Worcs....36 D7
Tarfside Angus....98 F8
Tarland Abers....104 H13
Tarleton Lancs....55 L2
Tarlscough Lancs....55 L4
Tarlton Gloucs....28 J8
Tarnock Somset....17 L6
Tarns Cumb....66 J3
Tarporley Ches W....55 N14
Tarr Somset....16 F10
Tarrant Crawford Dorset....8 C8
Tarrant Gunville Dorset....8 C6
Tarrant Hinton Dorset....8 C7
Tarrant Keyneston
Dorset....8 C8
Tarrant Launceston
Dorset....8 C7
Tarrant Monkton Dorset....8 C7
Tarrant Rawston Dorset....8 C7
Tarrant Rushton Dorset....8 C8
Tarring Neville E Susx....11 Q10
Tarrington Herefs....35 P12
Tarskavaig Highld....100 d8
Tarves Abers....105 P9
Tarvin Ches W....55 L13
Tarvin Sands Ches W....55 M13
Tasburgh Norfk....41 L2
Tasley Shrops....35 Q2
Taston Oxon....29 S3
Tatenhill Staffs....46 H9
Tathall End M Keyn....38 B11
Tatham Lancs....62 C6
Tathwell Lincs....59 P10
Tatsfield Surrey....21 R11
Tattenhall Ches W....54 K14
Tatterford Norfk....50 E8
Tattersett Norfk....50 E7
Tattershall Lincs....48 K2
Tattershall Bridge Lincs....48 J2
Tattershall Thorpe Lincs....48 K1
Tattingstone Suffk....40 K13
Tattingstone White
Horse Suffk....40 K13
Tatworth Somset....7 L3
Tauchers Moray....104 C6
Taunton Somset....16 H12
Taunton Deane
Crematorium
Somset....16 H12
Taunton Deane Services
Somset....16 G12
Taverham Norfk....51 L11
Taverners Green Essex....22 E4
Tavernspite Pembks....25 L7
Tavistock Devon....5 L6
Taw Green Devon....15 P13
Tawstock Devon....15 N7
Taxal Derbys....56 F10
Taychreggan Hotel
Ag & B....94 E14
Tay Forest Park P & K....97 M11
Taynish Ag & B....87 N8
Taynton Gloucs....28 D3
Taynton Oxon....29 P5
Taynuilt Ag & B....94 E13
Tayport Fife....91 Q6
Tayvallich Ag & B....87 N8
Tealby Lincs....58 J8
Tealing Angus....91 N4
Team Valley Gatesd....77 R13
Teangue Highld....100 f9
Teanord Highld....102 F3
Tebay Cumb....68 D11
Tebay Services Cumb....68 D11
Tebworth C Beds....31 L7
Techniquest Cardif....27 M12
Tedburn St Mary Devon....15 T13
Teddington Gloucs....28 J1
Teddington Gt Lon....21 L9
Tedsmore Shrops....44 H8
Tedstone Delamere
Herefs....35 Q9
Tedstone Wafer Herefs....35 Q9
Teesport R & Cl....70 J7
Teesside Crematorium
Middsb....70 G9
Teesside Park S on T....70 H9
Teeton Nhants....37 S6
Teffont Evias Wilts....8 D2
Teffont Magna Wilts....8 D2
Tegryn Pembks....25 L4
Teigh Rutnd....48 C10
Teigncombe Devon....5 R3
Teigngrace Devon....5 U7
Teignmouth Devon....6 B9
Teindside Border....75 U3
Telford Wrekin....45 Q12
Telford Crematorium
Wrekin....45 Q12
Telford Services Shrops....45 R12

Tellisford Somset....18 B9
Telscombe E Susx....11 Q10
Telscombe Cliffs E Susx....11 Q10
Tempar P & K....95 T11
Templand D & G....75 L9
Temple Cnwll....4 E6
Temple Mdloth....83 R7
Temple Balsall Solhll....36 H5
Temple Bar Cerdgn....32 K10
Temple Cloud BaNES....17 R5
Templecombe Somset....17 T11
Temple End Suffk....39 U10
Temple Ewell Kent....13 Q7
Temple Grafton Warwks....36 F9
Temple Guiting Gloucs....29 L2
Temple Herdewyke
Warwks....37 L10
Temple Hirst N York....57 T2
Temple Normanton
Derbys....57 P13
Temple of Fiddes Abers....99 P7
Temple Sowerby Cumb....68 D7
Templeton Devon....15 U10
Templeton Pembks....24 K7
Templetown Dur....69 P2
Tempsford C Beds....38 J10
Tenbury Wells Worcs....35 N7
Tenby Pembks....24 K10
Tendring Essex....23 S3
Tendring Green Essex....23 S2
Tendring Heath Essex....23 R2
Ten Mile Bank Norfk....39 S1
Tenpenny Heath Essex....23 Q3
Tenterden Kent....12 G9
Terling Essex....22 J5
Ternhill Shrops....45 P7
Terregles D & G....74 H10
Terrington N York....64 F5
Terrington St Clement
Norfk....49 R9
Terrington St John
Norfk....49 R11
Terry's Green Warwks....36 F6
Teston Kent....12 D5
Testwood Hants....9 M6
Tetbury Gloucs....28 G8
Tetbury Upton Gloucs....28 G8
Tetchill Shrops....44 H7
Tetcott Devon....14 H13
Tetford Lincs....59 P12
Tetney Lincs....59 P6
Tetney Lock Lincs....59 P6
Tetsworth Oxon....30 E12
Tettenhall Wolves....45 U13
Tettenhall Wood Wolves....45 U14
Teversal Notts....47 N1
Teversham Cambs....39 Q9
Teviothead Border....75 T4
Tewel Abers....99 R7
Tewin Herts....31 S10
Tewin Wood Herts....31 S10
Tewkesbury Gloucs....35 U14
Teynham Kent....12 J3
Thackley C Brad....63 P12
Thackthwaite Cumb....66 J9
Thakeham W Susx....10 J7
Thame Oxon....30 F11
Thames Ditton Surrey....21 L9
Thames Head Gloucs....28 J7
Thanet Crematorium
Kent....13 R2
Thanington Kent....13 M4
Thankerton S Lans....82 H11
Tharston Norfk....41 L2
Thatcham W Berk....19 R7
Thatto Heath St Hel....55 M8
Thaxted Essex....22 F1
Theakston N York....63 S2
Thealby N Linc....58 E3
Theale W Berk....19 U6
Theale Somset....17 N7
Thearne E R Yk....65 P12
The Bank Shrops....45 Q14
The Bank Ches E....45 U2
The Beeches Gloucs....28 K7
The Blythe Staffs....46 D7
The Bog Shrops....44 J14
The Bourne Worcs....35 U7
The Braes Highld....100 e6
The Bratch Staffs....35 U2
The Broad Herefs....35 L8
The Brunt E Loth....84 H4
The Bungalow IoM....60 f5
The Burf Worcs....35 T7
The Butts Gloucs....28 H4
The Camp Gloucs....28 H6
The Chequer Wrexhm....44 K4
The City Bed....38 G10
The City Bucks....20 C4
The Common Oxon....29 N2
The Common Wilts....8 K2
The Common Wilts....18 J5
The Corner Shrops....35 L4
The Counties
Crematorium Nhants....37 T9
The Cronk IoM....60 f3
The Den N Ayrs....81 L3
The Forest of Dean
Crematorium Gloucs....28 B6
The Forge Herefs....34 H10
The Forstal Kent....12 J8
The Fouralls Shrops....45 Q7
The Garden of England
Crematorium Kent....12 G2
The Green Cumb....61 M3
The Green Essex....22 H3
The Green N York....71 N11
The Green Wilts....8 B2
The Grove Worcs....35 U12
The Haven W Susx....10 H4
The Haw Gloucs....28 F2
The Headland Hartpl....70 J6
The Hill Cumb....61 L3
The Holt Wokhm....20 D8
The Hundred Herefs....35 M8
Theinetobridge Cnwll....4 G6
The Leacon Kent....12 J9
The Lee Bucks....30 K12
The Lhen IoM....60 f2
The Lochs Crematorium
E Rens....89 N14
The Marsh Powys....34 J1
The Middles Dur....69 R2
The Moor Kent....12 D10
The Mumbles Swans....25 V13
The Murray S Lans....82 D8
The Mythe Gloucs....28 G1
The Narth Mons....27 U6
The Neuk Abers....99 N4
Theobald's Green Wilts....18 E7
Theddingworth Leics....37 S3
Theddlethorpe All Saints
Lincs....59 S9
Theddlethorpe St Helen
Lincs....59 S9
The Den N Ayrs....81 L3
The Quarry Gloucs....28 D8
The Quarter Kent....12 F7
The Reddings Gloucs....28 H3
Thelbridge Cross Devon....15 S10
Thelnetham Suffk....40 H5
Thelveton Norfk....40 K4
Thelwall Warrtn....55 P9
The Manchester
Crematorium Manch....55 T8
The Marsh Powys....34 J1
The Middles Dur....69 R2
The Moor Kent....12 D10
The Mumbles Swans....25 V13
Themelthorpe Norfk....50 J9
The Mythe Gloucs....28 G1
The Narth Mons....27 U6
The Neuk Abers....99 N4
Thenford Nhants....37 P12
Theobald's Green Wilts....18 E7
The Park Crematorium
Hants....20 D10
The Quarter Kent....12 F7
The Reddings Gloucs....28 H3
The Rhos Pembks....24 H7
The Rose Hill
Crematorium Donc....57 S5
The Ross P & K....89 R2
The Sands Surrey....10 E2
The Shoe Wilts....18 B5
The Smithies Shrops....35 Q2
The Spike Ches E....45 Q14
The Spring Warwks....36 K4
The Square Torfn....27 P8
The Stair Kent....12 C6
The Stocks Kent....12 H11
The Straits Hants....9 U3
The Strand Wilts....18 D8
Thetford Lincs....48 J10
Thetford Norfk....40 E3
Thetford Forest Park....40 E4
Thethwaite Cumb....67 N3
The Towans Cnwll....2 F9
The Vale Crematorium
Luton....31 N8
The Vauld Herefs....35 M11
Thewles S on T....70 F7
The Wyke Shrops....45 R12
Theydon Bois Essex....21 R3
Thickwood Wilts....18 B5
Thimbleby Lincs....59 M13
Thimbleby N York....70 G13
Thingwall Wirral....54 G9
Thirkleby N York....64 B4
Thirlby N York....64 B3
Thirlestane Border....84 E9
Thirn N York....63 R1
Thirsk N York....63 U2
Thirtleby E R Yk....65 R13
Thistleton Lancs....61 S12
Thistleton Rutnd....48 D10
Thistley Green Suffk....39 T6
Thixendale N York....64 J7
Thockrington Nthumb....76 K10
Thoresby Notts....57 U12
Thoresthorpe Lincs....59 S11
Thoresway Lincs....58 K7
Thorganby Lincs....59 L7
Thorganby N York....64 F11
Thorgill N York....71 M14
Thorington Suffk....41 R6
Thorington Street Suffk....40 H13
Thorlby N York....62 K9
Thorley Herts....22 C4
Thorley Street Herts....22 C4
Thorley Houses Herts....22 C3
Thormanby N York....64 B5
Thornaby-on-Tees S on T....70 G9
Thornage Norfk....50 J6
Thornborough Bucks....30 F6
Thornborough N York....63 S3
Thornbury C Brad....63 P13
Thornbury Devon....14 J11
Thornbury Herefs....35 P9
Thornbury S Glos....28 B9
Thornby Cumb....67 L2
Thornby Nhants....37 S5
Thorncliff Staffs....46 C2
Thorncliffe Crematorium
Cumb....61 M5
Thorncombe Street
Surrey....10 F2
Thorncott Green C Beds....38 J11
Thorncross IoW....9 N12
Thorndon Suffk....40 K7
Thorndon Cross Devon....15 N2
Thorne Donc....57 U4
Thorne Coffin Somset....17 P13
Thornecroft Devon....5 T7
Thornehillhead Devon....14 J9
Thorner Leeds....63 T11
Thornes Staffs....46 E13
Thornes Wakefd....57 M2
Thorne St Margaret
Somset....16 F12
Thorney Bucks....20 G7
Thorney C Pete....49 L13
Thorney Notts....58 D12
Thorney Somset....17 M12
Thorney Hill Hants....8 J9
Thorney Island W Susx....10 B10
Thorney Toll C Pete....49 M13
Thornfalcon Somset....16 J12
Thornford Dorset....7 R2
Thorngrafton Nthumb....76 F12
Thorngrove Somset....17 L10
Thorngumbald E R Yk....59 M1
Thornham Norfk....50 B5
Thornham Magna Suffk....40 K6
Thornham Parva Suffk....40 K6
Thornhaugh C Pete....48 G13
Thornhill C Sotn....9 P6
Thornhill Caerph....27 M10
Thornhill Cumb....66 F11
Thornhill D & G....74 G6
Thornhill Derbys....56 J10
Thornhill Kirk....56 K3
Thornhill Stirlg....89 Q5
Thornhill Crematorium
Cardif....27 M11
Thornhill Lees Kirk....56 K3
Thornholme E R Yk....65 P7
Thornicombe Dorset....8 B9
Thornington Nthumb....85 M12
Thornley Dur....70 E5
Thornley Dur....69 Q5
Thornley Gate Nthumb....68 H2
Thornliebank E Rens....89 N14
Thorns Suffk....39 U10
Thornsett Derbys....56 F9
Thorns Green Ches E....55 S10
Thornthwaite Cumb....66 K7
Thornthwaite N York....63 Q8
Thornton Angus....91 M2
Thornton Bucks....30 G5
Thornton C Brad....63 M13
Thornton Fife....91 M12
Thornton Lancs....61 Q11
Thornton Leics....47 N12
Thornton Lincs....59 M13
Thornton Middsb....70 G9
Thornton Nthumb....85 P9
Thornton Pembks....24 F8
Thornton Sefton....54 H5
Thornton Curtis N Linc....58 J2
Thornton Garden of
Rest Crematorium
Sefton....54 H6
Thorntonhall S Lans....89 N14
Thornton Heath Gt Lon....21 P9
Thornton Hough Wirral....54 H10
Thornton-in-Craven
N York....62 J10
Thornton in Lonsdale
N York....62 D5
Thornton-le-Beans
N York....63 U1
Thornton-le-Clay N York....64 F6
Thornton-le-Dale N York....64 H3
Thornton le Moor Lincs....58 H8
Thornton-le-Moor
N York....63 U2
Thornton-le-Moors
Ches W....54 K12
Thornton-le-Street
N York....63 U2
Thornton Rust N York....62 K2
Thornton Steward N York....63 P1
Thornton Watlass N York....63 R2
Thornwood Common
Essex....22 C7
Thornydykes Border....84 F9
Thoroton Notts....47 U5
Thorp Arch Leeds....63 U10
Thorpe Derbys....46 G3
Thorpe E R Yk....65 M11
Thorpe Lincs....59 S10
Thorpe N York....62 K7
Thorpe Norfk....41 R2
Thorpe Notts....47 U3
Thorpe Surrey....20 H9
Thorpe Abbotts Norfk....40 K5
Thorpe Acre Leics....47 P9
Thorpe Arnold Leics....47 U10
Thorpe Audlin Wakefd....57 Q3
Thorpe Bassett N York....64 K5
Thorpe Bay Sthend....23 L10
Thorpe by Water Rutnd....38 C2
Thorpe Common S on T....70 H9
Thorpe Constantine
Staffs....46 J12
Thorpe End Norfk....51 N11
Thorpe Green Essex....23 R3
Thorpe Green Suffk....40 G10
Thorpe Hesley Rothm....57 N7
Thorpe in Balne Donc....57 S4
Thorpe Langton Leics....37 U2
Thorpe Larches Dur....70 E7
Thorpe Latimer Lincs....48 H5
Thorpe le Fallows Lincs....58 F10
Thorpe-le-Soken Essex....23 R3
Thorpe le Street E R Yk....64 J10
Thorpe Malsor Nhants....38 B5
Thorpe Mandeville
Nhants....37 P11
Thorpe Market Norfk....51 M6
Thorpe Marriott Norfk....51 L10
Thorpe Morieux Suffk....40 F10
Thorpeness Suffk....41 S9
Thorpe on the Hill Leics....58 F14
Thorpe on the Hill Lincs....58 F14
Thorpe on The Hill Leeds....57 M1
Thorpe Salvin Rothm....57 R10
Thorpe Satchville Leics....47 T11
Thorpe St Andrew Norfk....51 N12
Thorpe St Peter Lincs....59 S13
Thorpe Thewles S on T....70 F7
Thorpe Tilney Lincs....48 H2
Thorpe Underwood
N York....64 C8
Thorpe Underwood
Nhants....37 U4
Thorpe Waterville Nhants....38 F4
Thorpe Willoughby N York....64 C13
Thorrington Essex....23 Q4
Thorverton Devon....15 U11
Thrandeston Suffk....40 K5
Thrapston Nhants....38 E5
Threapland Cumb....66 H5
Threapland N York....62 K7
Threapwood Ches W....44 K4
Threapwood Staffs....46 D4
Threapwood Head Staffs....46 D4
Three Ashes Herefs....27 U3
Three Bridges W Susx....11 M3
Three Chimneys Kent....12 F8
Three Cocks Powys....34 E13
Three Counties
Crematorium Essex....22 E2
Three Cups Corner
E Susx....11 U6
Three Gates Worcs....35 Q8
Threehammer Common
Norfk....51 Q10
Three Hammers Cnwll....4 G3
Three Holes Norfk....49 R13
Threekingham Lincs....48 G6
Three Leg Cross E Susx....12 C9
Three Legged Cross
Dorset....8 F7
Three Mile Cross
Wokhm....20 B9
Threemilestone Cnwll....2 K7
Three Mile Town W Loth....83 L3
Three Oaks E Susx....12 F13
Threlkeld Cumb....67 M7
Threshers Bush Essex....22 C6
Threshfield N York....62 K7
Thrigby Norfk....51 S11
Thringarth Dur....68 K8
Thringstone Leics....47 M10
Thrintoft N York....63 T1
Thriplow Cambs....39 Q11
Throapham Rothm....57 R9
Throckenholt Lincs....49 N12
Throcking Herts....31 T6
Throckley N u Ty....77 P12
Throckmorton Worcs....36 C11
Throop Bmouth....8 G9
Throophill Nthumb....77 P8
Thropton Nthumb....77 L5
Throsk Stirlg....90 C13
Througham Gloucs....28 H6
Throughgate D & G....74 G9
Throwleigh Devon....5 R2
Throwley Kent....12 J4
Throwley Forstal Kent....12 J5
Thrumpton Notts....47 P7
Thrumster Highld....112 H7
Thrunscoe NE Lin....59 P5
Thrunton Nthumb....77 M3
Thrupp Gloucs....28 G6
Thrupp Oxon....29 U5
Thruscross N York....63 P8
Thrushelton Devon....5 L3
Thrussington Leics....47 S10
Thruxton Hants....19 L11
Thruxton Herefs....34 K13
Thrybergh Rothm....57 P7
Thulston Derbys....47 M7
Thundersley Essex....22 K10
Thurcaston Leics....47 Q11
Thurcroft Rothm....57 Q9
Thurdon Cnwll....14 G10
Thurgarton Norfk....51 L7
Thurgarton Notts....47 S4
Thurgoland Barns....57 L6
Thurlaston Leics....47 P14
Thurlaston Warwks....37 N6
Thurlbear Somset....16 J12
Thurlby Lincs....48 G10
Thurlby Lincs....58 F14
Thurlby Lincs....59 S11
Thurleigh Bed....38 F9
Thurlestone Devon....5 R12
Thurloxton Somset....16 J10
Thurlstone Barns....56 K5
Thurlton Norfk....41 R1
Thurlwood Ches E....45 U2
Thurmaston Leics....47 R12
Thurnby Leics....47 R13
Thurne Norfk....51 R10
Thurnham Kent....12 E4
Thurning Nhants....38 G4
Thurning Norfk....50 J8
Thurnscoe Barns....57 P5
Thursby Cumb....67 M2
Thursden Lancs....62 H13
Thursford Norfk....50 G6
Thursley Surrey....10 F3
Thurso Highld....112 D3
Thurstaston Wirral....54 F10
Thurston Suffk....40 F7
Thurston Clough Oldham....56 E5
Thurstonfield Cumb....67 M1
Thurstonland Kirk....56 J4
Thurston Planch Suffk....40 F8
Thurton Norfk....51 P13
Thurvaston Derbys....46 G6
Thuxton Norfk....50 H12
Thwaite N York....68 K13
Thwaite Suffk....40 K8
Thwaite Head Cumb....61 Q1
Thwaites C Brad....63 M11
Thwaite St Mary Norfk....41 Q1
Thwaites Brow C Brad....63 M11
Thwing E R Yk....65 N5
Tibbermore P & K....90 F7
Tibberton Gloucs....28 E4
Tibberton Worcs....36 B9
Tibberton Wrekin....45 Q9
Tibbie Shiels Inn Border....75 P1
Tibenham Norfk....40 K3
Tibshelf Derbys....47 M1
Tibshelf Services Derbys....47 M1
Tibthorpe E R Yk....65 M9
Ticehurst E Susx....12 C9
Tichborne Hants....9 S2
Tickencote Rutnd....48 E12
Tickenham N Som....17 N2
Tickford End M Keyn....38 C11
Tickhill Donc....57 S8
Ticklerton Shrops....35 L2
Tickmorend Gloucs....28 F8
Tickton E R Yk....65 P11
Tidbury Green Solhll....36 F5
Tidcombe Wilts....19 L9
Tiddington Oxon....30 E11
Tiddington Warwks....36 H9
Tidebrook E Susx....11 U5
Tideford Cnwll....4 J9
Tideford Cross Cnwll....4 J8
Tidenham Gloucs....27 V8
Tideswell Derbys....56 H12
Tidmarsh W Berk....19 U6
Tidmington Warwks....36 J13
Tidpit Hants....8 F5
Tidworth Wilts....18 K11
Tiers Cross Pembks....24 F7
Tiffield Nhants....37 S10
Tigerton Angus....98 J11
Tigh a Ghearraidh W Isls....106 c11
Tigharry W Isls....106 c11
Tighnabruaich Ag & B....88 B11
Tigley Devon....5 T8
Tilbrook Cambs....38 G7
Tilbury Thurr....22 F12
Tilbury Green Essex....40 B12
Tilbury Juxta Clare Essex....40 C12
Tile Cross Birm....36 G3
Tile Hill Covtry....36 J5
Tilehouse Green Solhll....36 G5
Tilehurst Readg....19 U6
Tilford Surrey....10 E2
Tilgate W Susx....11 M3
Tilgate Forest Row
W Susx....11 M4
Tilham Street Somset....17 Q10
Tillers Green Gloucs....35 Q13
Tillicoultry Clacks....90 D12
Tillietudlem S Lans....82 G10
Tillingham Essex....23 N7
Tillington Herefs....35 L11
Tillington W Susx....10 F6
Tillington Common
Herefs....35 L11
Tillybirloch Abers....99 L2
Tillyfourie Abers....104 J13
Tillygreig Abers....105 P10
Tillyrie P & K....90 H10
Tilmanstone Kent....13 R5
Tilney All Saints Norfk....49 S10
Tilney High End Norfk....49 S10
Tilney St Lawrence
Norfk....49 R11
Tilshead Wilts....18 G12
Tilstock Shrops....45 M6
Tilston Ches W....44 K3
Tilstone Bank Ches W....45 N2
Tilstone Fearnall Ches W....45 N1
Tilsworth C Beds....31 L7
Tilton on the Hill Leics....47 T12
Tiltups End Gloucs....28 F8
Timberland Lincs....48 H2
Timbersbrook Ches E....56 C14
Timberscombe Somset....16 B8
Timble N York....63 Q9
Timewell Devon....16 C11
Timpanheck D & G....75 S11
Timperley Traffd....55 S9
Timsbury BaNES....17 S5
Timsbury Hants....9 L3
Timsgarraidh W Isls....106 f5
Timsgearraidh W Isls....106 f5
Timworth Suffk....40 E7
Timworth Green Suffk....40 E7
Tincleton Dorset....7 U6
Tindale Cumb....76 B14
Tindale Crescent Dur....69 R7
Tingewick Bucks....30 E6
Tingrith C Beds....31 M6
Tingwall Ork....106 s18
Tinhay Devon....4 J3
Tinker's Hill Hants....19 N12
Tinkersley Derbys....57 L14
Tinsley Sheff....57 N8
Tinsley Green W Susx....11 M3
Tintagel Cnwll....4 D3
Tintern Parva Mons....27 U6

Tintinhull Somset 17 N13
Tintwistle Derbys 56 F7
Tinwald D & G 74 K9
Tinwell Rutlnd 48 F12
Tippacott Devon 15 S3
Tipp's End Norfk 39 R1
Tiptoe Hants 8 K9
Tipton Sandw 36 C2
Tipton Green Sandw 36 C2
Tipton St John Devon 6 E6
Tiptree Essex 23 L4
Tiptree Heath Essex 23 L4
Tirabad Powys 33 S12
Tiree Ag & B 92 C10
Tiree Airport Ag & B 92 C10
Tiretigan Ag & B 79 N3
Tirley Gloucs 28 F2
Tirphil Caerph 27 L7
Tirril Cumb 67 R7
Tir-y-fron Flints 44 G2
Tisbury Wilts 8 C3
Tisman's Common W Susx 10 H4
Tissington Derbys 46 G3
Titchberry Devon 14 F7
Titchfield Hants 9 Q7
Titchfield Common Hants 9 Q7
Titchmarsh Nhants 38 F5
Titchwell Norfk 50 C5
Tithby Notts 47 S6
Titley Herefs 34 H8
Titmore Green Herts 31 R7
Titsey Surrey 21 R12
Titson Cnwll 14 F12
Tittensor Staffs 45 U6
Tittleshall Norfk 50 E9
Titton Worcs 35 T7
Tiverton Ches W 45 N1
Tiverton Devon 6 C2
Tivetshall St Margaret Norfk 41 L3
Tivetshall St Mary Norfk 41 L3
Tivington Somset 16 B7
Tivy Dale Barns 57 L5
Tixall Staffs 46 C9
Tixover Rutlnd 48 E13
Toab Shet 106 t12
Toadhole Derbys 47 L2
Toadmoor Derbys 46 K3
Tobermory Ag & B 93 N7
Toberonochy Ag & B 87 N4
Tobha Mor W Isls 106 c15
Tocher Abers 104 K9
Tochieneal Moray 104 G2
Tockenham Wilts 18 F5
Tockenham Wick Wilts 18 F4
Tocketts R & Cl 70 K9
Tockholes Bl w D 55 Q2
Tockington S Glos 28 B10
Tockwith N York 64 B9
Todber Dorset 17 U13
Todburn Nthumb 77 N6
Toddington C Beds 31 M7
Toddington Gloucs 36 D14
Toddington Services C Beds 31 M7
Todds Green Herts 31 R7
Todenham Gloucs 36 H13
Todhills Angus 91 P4
Todhills Cumb 75 S13
Todhills Dur 69 R6
Todhills Services Cumb 75 S13
Todmorden Calder 56 D2
Todwick Rothm 57 Q10
Toft Cambs 39 N9
Toft Ches E 55 S11
Toft Lincs 48 G10
Toft Shet 106 u6
Toft Warwks 37 N6
Toft Hill Dur 69 Q7
Toft Hill Lincs 48 K1
Toft Monks Norfk 41 R2
Toft next Newton Lincs 58 H9
Toftrees Norfk 50 E8
Toftwood Norfk 50 G11
Togston Nthumb 77 Q5
Tokavaig Highld 100 f8
Tokers Green Oxon 20 B7
Tolastadh W Isls 106 k4
Toldish Cnwll 3 N5
Tolland Somset 16 F10
Tollard Farnham Dorset 8 D5
Tollard Royal Wilts 8 C5
Toll Bar Donc 57 S5
Tollbar End Covtry 37 L5
Toller Fratrum Dorset 7 Q5
Toller Porcorum Dorset 7 Q5
Tollerton N York 64 C7
Tollerton Notts 47 R7
Toller Whelme Dorset 7 P4
Tollesbury Essex 23 N5
Tolleshunt D'Arcy Essex 23 M5
Tolleshunt Knights Essex 23 M5
Tolleshunt Major Essex 23 M5
Tolpuddle Dorset 7 U6
Tolsta W Isls 106 k4
Tolworth Gt Lon 21 L9
Tomatin Highld 103 M10
Tomchrasky Highld 101 V9
Tomdoun Highld 101 T11
Tomich Highld 102 B10
Tomich Highld 102 F6
Tomich Highld 109 L3
Tomich Highld 109 M10
Tomintoul Moray 103 U12
Tomlow Warwks 37 N8
Tomnacross Highld 102 F7
Tomnavoulin Moray 103 V10
Tompkin Staffs 46 B3
Ton Mons 27 Q7
Ton Mons 27 R8
Tonbridge Kent 21 U13
Tondu Brdgnd 26 F11
Tonedale Somset 16 F12
Ton fanau Gwynd 43 L13
Tong C Brad 63 Q13
Tong Kent 12 J4
Tong Shrops 45 S12
Tonge Leics 47 M9
Tong Green Kent 12 J5
Tongham Surrey 20 E13
Tongland D & G 73 R9
Tong Norton Shrops 45 S12
Tongue Highld 111 M5
Tongue End Lincs 48 J10
Tongwynlais Cardif 27 L11
Tonmawr Neath 26 E8
Tonna Neath 26 D8
Ton-teg Rhondd 26 K10
Tonwell Herts 31 T9
Tonypandy Rhondd 26 H9
Tonyrefail Rhondd 26 J10
Toot Baldon Oxon 30 C12
Toot Hill Essex 22 D7
Toothill Hants 9 M5
Toothill Swindn 29 M11
Tooting Gt Lon 21 N8
Tooting Bec Gt Lon 21 N8
Topcliffe N York 63 T4
Topcroft Norfk 41 N2
Topcroft Street Norfk 41 N2
Top End Bed 38 F8
Topham Donc 57 T3
Top of Hebers Rochdl 56 C5
Toppesfield Essex 40 B13
Toppings Bolton 55 R4
Toprow Norfk 51 L14
Topsham Devon 6 C7
Top-y-rhos Flints 44 G2
Torbeg N Ayrs 79 R10
Torboll Highld 109 P5
Torbreck Highld 102 H7
Torbryan Devon 5 U7
Torcastle Highld 94 G3
Torcross Devon 5 U12
Tore Highld 102 H5
Torfrey Cnwll 4 E10
Torinturk Ag & B 79 Q3
Torksey Lincs 58 D11
Tormarton S Glos 28 E12
Tormore N Ayrs 79 R9
Tornagrain Highld 103 L5
Tornaveen Abers 99 L2
Torness Highld 102 G10
Toronto Dur 69 Q6
Torpenhow Cumb 66 K5
Torphichen W Loth 82 J4
Torphins Abers 99 L3
Torpoint Cnwll 5 L9
Torquay Torbay 6 B12
Torquay Crematorium Torbay 6 B11
Torquhan Border 84 C9
Torr Devon 5 P10
Torran Highld 100 e5
Torrance E Duns 89 P11
Torranyard N Ayrs 81 M4
Torre Somset 16 D9
Torridon Highld 107 R13
Torridon House Highld 107 Q13
Torrin Highld 100 e7
Torrisdale Ag & B 79 P8
Torrisdale Highld 111 P4
Torrish Highld 111 V13
Torrisholme Lancs 61 T7
Torrobull Highld 108 K4
Torry C Aber 99 S2
Torryburn Fife 82 K1
Torteval Guern 6 b4
Torthorwald D & G 74 K10
Tortington W Susx 10 G10
Torton Worcs 35 T6
Tortworth S Glos 28 D9
Torvaig Highld 100 d5
Torver Cumb 67 L14
Torwood Falk 89 T8
Torwoodlee Border 84 D11
Torworth Notts 57 U9
Tosberry Devon 14 G8
Toscaig Highld 100 g6
Toseland Cambs 38 K8
Tosside Lancs 62 F8
Tostock Suffk 40 G8
Totaig Highld 100 b4
Tote Highld 100 d5
Tote Highld 100 e3
Tote Hill W Susx 10 D6
Totford Hants 19 S13
Tothill Lincs 59 R10
Totland IoW 9 L11
Totley Sheff 57 M11
Totley Brook Sheff 57 M10
Totnes Devon 5 U8
Toton Notts 47 P7
Totronald Ag & B 92 F7
Totscore Highld 100 c3
Tottenham Gt Lon 21 P4
Tottenhill Norfk 49 T11
Totteridge Gt Lon 21 M4
Totternhoe C Beds 31 L8
Tottington Bury 55 S4
Tottleworth Lancs 62 E13
Totton Hants 9 M6
Touchen End W & M 20 E7
Toulston N York 64 B11
Toulton Somset 16 G10
Toulvaddie Highld 109 R8
Tovil Kent 12 E5
Towan Cnwll 3 M2
Towan Cnwll 3 Q7
Toward Ag & B 88 D12
Toward Quay Ag & B 88 D12
Towcester Nhants 37 S11
Towednack Cnwll 2 D9
Tower of London Gt Lon 21 P6
Towersey Oxon 30 F11
Towie Abers 104 E13
Tow Law Dur 69 P5
Town End Cambs 39 P1
Town End Cumb 61 S3
Town End Cumb 67 M11
Town End Cumb 68 D7
Townend W Duns 88 J10
Towngate Cumb 67 R3
Towngate Lincs 48 H11
Town Green Lancs 54 K5
Town Green Norfk 51 Q11
Townhead Barns 56 J6
Townhead Cumb 66 G5
Town Head Cumb 67 P12
Townhead Cumb 68 D6
Townhead D & G 74 K8
Town Head N York 62 G8
Townhead of Greenlaw D & G 74 D13
Townhill Fife 90 H14
Town Kelloe Dur 70 E5
Townlake Devon 5 L6
Town Lane Wigan 55 Q7
Town Littleworth E Susx 11 Q7
Town of Lowton Wigan 55 P7
Town Row E Susx 11 T4
Towns End Hants 19 S9
Townsend Somset 7 L2
Townshend Cnwll 2 F10
Town Street Suffk 40 C3
Townwell S Glos 28 D9
Town Yetholm Border 85 L13
Towthorpe C York 64 E8
Towthorpe E R Yk 64 K7
Towton N York 64 B12
Towyn Conwy 53 S7
Toxteth Lpool 54 J9
Toynton All Saints Lincs 59 Q14
Toynton Fen Side Lincs 49 N1
Toynton St Peter Lincs 59 R14
Toy's Hill Kent 21 S12
Trabboch E Ayrs 81 N8
Trabbochburn E Ayrs 81 P8
Traboe Cnwll 2 J12
Tracebridge Somset 16 E12
Tradespark Highld 103 N4
Trallong Powys 26 H2
Tranent E Loth 83 T4
Tranmere Wirral 54 H9
Trantelbeg Highld 111 T6
Trantlemore Highld 111 T6
Tranwell Nthumb 77 P9
Trapp Carmth 26 B4
Traprain E Loth 84 F3
Trap's Green Warwks 36 F7
Trapshill W Berk 19 N8
Traquair Border 83 R12
Trash Green W Berk 19 U7
Trawden Lancs 62 J12
Trawscoed Cerdgn 33 N6
Trawsfynydd Gwynd 43 P6
Trealaw Rhondd 26 J9
Treales Lancs 61 S13
Trearddur Bay IoA 52 C7
Treaslane Highld 100 c4
Treator Cnwll 3 N1
Tre Aubrey V Glam 16 D2
Trebanog Rhondd 26 J9
Trebanos Neath 26 C7
Trebartha Cnwll 4 H5
Trebarwith Cnwll 4 D3
Trebeath Cnwll 4 H3
Trebetherick Cnwll 4 A5
Treborough Somset 16 D9
Trebudannon Cnwll 3 M4
Trebullett Cnwll 4 J5
Treburgett Cnwll 4 D5
Treburley Cnwll 4 K5
Treburrick Cnwll 3 M2
Trebyan Cnwll 3 R4
Trecastle Powys 26 F2
Trecogo Cnwll 4 J4
Trecott Devon 15 P12
Trecwn Pembks 24 G4
Trecynon Rhondd 26 H7
Tredaule Cnwll 4 G4
Tredavoe Cnwll 2 D11
Tredegar Blae G 27 L6
Tredethy Cnwll 3 R2
Tredington Gloucs 28 H2
Tredington Warwks 36 J12
Tredinnick Cnwll 3 N2
Tredinnick Cnwll 3 Q5
Tredinnick Cnwll 4 F7
Tredinnick Cnwll 4 G9
Tredinnick Cnwll 4 H9
Tredomen Powys 27 L1
Tredrissi Pembks 24 J2
Tredrizzick Cnwll 4 B5
Tredunnock Mons 27 R9
Tredustan Powys 27 L1
Treen Cnwll 2 B12
Treen Cnwll 2 C9
Treesmill Cnwll 3 R5
Treeton Rothm 57 P9
Trefasser Pembks 24 E3
Trefdraeth IoA 52 F8
Trefecca Powys 27 L1
Trefeglwys Powys 33 U2
Trefenter Cerdgn 33 M7
Treffgarne Pembks 24 G6
Treffgarne Owen Pembks 24 E5
Trefforest Rhondd 26 K10
Treffynnon Pembks 24 E5
Trefil Blae G 27 L5
Trefilan Cerdgn 32 K9
Trefin Pembks 24 D4
Treflach Wood Shrops 44 G8
Trefnannau Powys 44 F10
Trefnant Denbgs 54 C12
Trefonen Shrops 44 G8
Trefor Gwynd 42 G4
Trefor IoA 52 E6
Trefrew Cnwll 4 E4
Trefriw Conwy 53 N10
Tregadillett Cnwll 4 H4
Tre-gagle Mons 27 U6
Tregaian IoA 52 G6
Tregare Mons 27 S5
Tregarne Cnwll 2 K12
Tregaron Cerdgn 33 N9
Tregarth Gwynd 52 K9
Tregaswith Cnwll 3 M4
Tregatta Cnwll 4 D3
Tregawne Cnwll 3 Q3
Tregeare Cnwll 4 G3
Tregeiriog Wrexhm 44 E7
Tregele IoA 52 E4
Tregellist Cnwll 4 C5
Tregenna Cnwll 3 M8
Tregeseal Cnwll 2 B10
Tregew Cnwll 3 L10
Tre-Gibbon Rhondd 26 H6
Tregidden Cnwll 2 K12
Tregiskey Cnwll 3 Q7
Treglemais Pembks 24 D5
Tregole Cnwll 14 E13
Tregolls Cnwll 2 J9
Tregonce Cnwll 3 N2
Tregonetha Cnwll 3 P4
Tregonning & Gwinear Mining District Cnwll 2 F10
Tregony Cnwll 3 N8
Tregoodwell Cnwll 4 E4
Tregorrick Cnwll 3 Q6
Tregoss Cnwll 3 P4
Tregoyd Powys 34 E13
Tregrehan Mills Cnwll 3 Q6
Tre-groes Cerdgn 32 H12
Tregullon Cnwll 3 R4
Tregunna Cnwll 3 P2
Tregunnon Cnwll 4 G4
Tregurrian Cnwll 3 M3
Tregynon Powys 44 C14
Tre-gynwr Carmth 25 R7
Trehafod Rhondd 26 J9
Trehan Cnwll 5 L9
Treharris Myr Td 26 K8
Treharrock Cnwll 4 C5
Trehemborne Cnwll 3 M2
Treherbert Carmth 33 L11
Treherbert Rhondd 26 G8
Trehunist Cnwll 4 J8
Trekenner Cnwll 4 J5
Treknow Cnwll 4 D3
Trelan Cnwll 2 J13
Trelash Cnwll 4 F2
Trelassick Cnwll 3 M6
Trelawne Cnwll 4 G10
Trelawnyd Flints 54 C11
Treleague Cnwll 2 K12
Treleaver Cnwll 2 K13
Trelech Carmth 25 N4
Trelech a'r Betws Carmth 25 P5
Treleddyd-fawr Pembks 24 C5
Trelew Cnwll 3 L9
Trelewis Myr Td 27 L8
Treligga Cnwll 4 C4
Trelights Cnwll 4 B5
Trelill Cnwll 4 C5
Trelinnoe Cnwll 4 J4
Trelion Cnwll 3 N6
Trelissick Cnwll 3 L9
Trellech Mons 27 U6
Trelleck Grange Mons 27 T7
Trelogan Flints 54 D10
Trelow Cnwll 3 N3
Trelowarren Cnwll 2 J12
Trelowia Cnwll 4 H9
Treluggan Cnwll 3 M9
Trelystan Powys 44 G13
Tremadog Gwynd 43 L6
Tremail Cnwll 4 F3
Tremain Cerdgn 32 D11
Tremaine Cnwll 4 G3
Tremar Cnwll 4 H7
Trematon Cnwll 4 K9
Trembraze Cnwll 4 H7
Tremeirchion Denbgs 54 C12
Tremethick Cross Cnwll 2 C10
Tremore Cnwll 3 Q4
Tre-Mostyn Flints 54 D11
Trenance Cnwll 3 L12
Trenance Cnwll 3 M3
Trenance Cnwll 3 N2
Trenarren Cnwll 3 Q7
Trench Wrekin 45 Q11
Trench Green Oxon 19 U5
Trendeal Cnwll 3 M6
Trendrine Cnwll 2 D9
Treneague Cnwll 3 P2
Trenear Cnwll 2 H10
Treneglos Cnwll 4 G3
Trenerth Cnwll 2 G9
Trenewan Cnwll 4 F10
Trenewth Cnwll 4 D5
Trengune Cnwll 4 F2
Treninnick Cnwll 3 L4
Trenowah Cnwll 2 K5
Trenoweth Cnwll 2 K10
Trent Dorset 17 Q13
Trentham C Stke 45 U5
Trentishoe Devon 15 P3
Trentlock Derbys 47 N7
Trent Port Lincs 58 D10
Trent Vale C Stke 45 U5
Trenwheal Cnwll 2 G10
Treoes V Glam 26 G12
Treorchy Rhondd 26 H8
Trequite Cnwll 4 C5
Tre'r-ddol Cerdgn 33 N2
Trerhyngyll V Glam 26 J12
Trerulefoot Cnwll 4 J9
Tresaith Cerdgn 32 E10
Tresawle Cnwll 3 M7
Tresco IoS 2 b2
Trescott Staffs 35 U1
Trescowe Cnwll 2 F10
Tresean Cnwll 2 K5
Tresham Gloucs 28 E9
Treshnish Isles Ag & B 92 G10
Tresillian Cnwll 3 M7
Tresinney Cnwll 4 E4
Treskinnick Cross Cnwll 14 F13
Tresmeer Cnwll 4 G3
Tresparrett Cnwll 4 E2
Tressait P & K 97 N11
Tresta Shet 106 t8
Tresta Shet 106 w4
Treswell Notts 58 C11
Treswithian Cnwll 2 G8
Treswithian Downs Crematorium Cnwll 2 G8
Tre Taliesin Cerdgn 33 N2
Trethevey Cnwll 4 D3
Trethewey Cnwll 2 B12
Trethomas Caerph 27 M10
Trethosa Cnwll 3 N6
Trethurgy Cnwll 3 Q5
Tretio Pembks 24 C5
Tretire Herefs 27 U3
Tretower Powys 27 M3
Treuddyn Flints 44 G2
Trevadlock Cnwll 4 H5
Trevalga Cnwll 4 D2
Trevalyn Wrexhm 44 J2
Trevanger Cnwll 4 B5
Trevanson Cnwll 3 P2
Trevarrack Cnwll 2 D10
Trevarren Cnwll 3 N4
Trevarrian Cnwll 3 M3
Trevarrick Cnwll 3 P8
Trevarth Cnwll 2 J8
Trevaughan Carmth 25 M7
Tre-Vaughan Carmth 25 Q6
Treveal Cnwll 2 D8
Treveal Cnwll 2 K5
Treveighan Cnwll 4 D5
Trevellas Downs Cnwll 2 J6
Trevelmond Cnwll 4 G8
Trevemper Cnwll 3 L5
Treveor Cnwll 3 P8
Treverbyn Cnwll 3 M7
Treverbyn Cnwll 3 Q5
Treverva Cnwll 2 K10
Trevescan Cnwll 2 B12
Trevethin Torfn 27 P7
Trevia Cnwll 4 D4
Trevigro Cnwll 4 J7
Trevilla Cnwll 3 L9
Trevilson Cnwll 3 L5
Treviscoe Cnwll 3 N5
Treviskey Cnwll 3 N8
Trevithick Cnwll 3 M4
Trevithick Cnwll 3 P7
Trevoll Cnwll 3 L5
Trevone Cnwll 3 M1
Trevor Wrexhm 44 G5
Trevorgans Cnwll 2 C11
Trevorrick Cnwll 3 N2
Trevose Cnwll 3 M1
Trew Cnwll 2 G11
Trewalder Cnwll 4 D4
Trewalkin Powys 27 M1
Trewarmett Cnwll 4 D3
Trewassa Cnwll 4 E3
Trewavas Cnwll 2 F11
Trewavas Mining District Cnwll 2 F11
Treween Cnwll 4 G4
Trewellard Cnwll 2 B10
Trewen Cnwll 4 H4
Trewennack Cnwll 2 H11
Trewent Pembks 24 H11
Trewern Powys 44 G11
Trewetha Cnwll 4 C4
Trewethern Cnwll 3 Q1
Trewidland Cnwll 4 H9
Trewillis Cnwll 2 K13
Trewint Cnwll 4 G4
Trewint Cnwll 4 H8
Trewithian Cnwll 3 M9
Trewoodloe Cnwll 4 J6
Trewoon Cnwll 2 H13
Trewoon Cnwll 3 P6
Treworga Cnwll 3 M8
Treworgan Cnwll 3 L7
Treworlas Cnwll 3 M9
Treworld Cnwll 4 E2
Treworthal Cnwll 3 M9
Tre-wyn Mons 27 Q3
Treyarnon Cnwll 3 M2
Treyford W Susx 10 C7
Trickett's Cross Dorset 8 F8
Triermain Cumb 76 B12
Triffleton Pembks 24 G6
Trillacott Cnwll 4 H3
Trimdon Dur 70 E6
Trimdon Colliery Dur 70 E5
Trimdon Grange Dur 70 E5
Trimingham Norfk 51 N6
Trimley Lower Street Suffk 41 N13
Trimley St Martin Suffk 41 N13
Trimley St Mary Suffk 41 N13
Trimpley Worcs 35 S5
Trimsaran Carmth 25 S10
Trims Green Herts 22 C4
Trimstone Devon 15 M4
Trinafour P & K 95 U6
Trinant Caerph 27 N8
Tring Herts 30 K10
Tringford Herts 30 K10
Tring Wharf Herts 30 K10
Trinity Angus 99 L11
Trinity Jersey 7 d2
Trinity Gask P & K 90 E8
Triscombe Somset 16 G9
Trislaig Highld 94 F4
Trispen Cnwll 3 L6
Tritlington Nthumb 77 Q7
Troan Cnwll 3 M5
Trochry P & K 90 E3
Troedrhiwfuwch Caerph 27 L7
Troedyraur Cerdgn 32 F11
Troedyrhiw Myr Td 26 K7
Trofarth Conwy 53 Q8
Trois Bois Jersey 7 C2
Troon Cnwll 2 H9
Troon S Ayrs 81 L6
Tropical World Roundhay Park Leeds 63 S12
Trossachs Stirlg 89 M4
Trossachs Pier Stirlg 89 L4
Troston Suffk 40 E6
Troswell Cnwll 4 H2
Trotshill Worcs 35 U9
Trottiscliffe Kent 12 B3
Trotton W Susx 10 C6
Troughend Nthumb 76 H7
Trough Gate Lancs 56 C2
Troutbeck Cumb 67 N7
Troutbeck Cumb 67 P12
Troutbeck Bridge Cumb 67 P12
Troway Derbys 57 N11
Trowbridge Wilts 18 C9
Trowell Notts 47 N6
Trowell Services Notts 47 N5
Trowle Common Wilts 18 B9
Trowley Bottom Herts 31 N10
Trowse Newton Norfk 51 M12
Troy Leeds 63 Q12
Trudoxhill Somset 17 T8
Trull Somset 16 H12
Trumfleet Donc 57 T4
Trumpan Highld 100 b3
Trumpet Herefs 35 Q13
Trumpington Cambs 39 P10
Trumpsgreen Surrey 20 G9
Trunch Norfk 51 N7
Trunnah Lancs 61 Q11
Truro Cnwll 3 L8
Truscott Cnwll 4 H3
Trusham Devon 5 V4
Trusley Derbys 46 J6
Trusthorpe Lincs 59 T10
Trysull Staffs 35 U2
Tubney Oxon 29 T8
Tuckenhay Devon 5 U9
Tuckhill Shrops 35 S3
Tuckingmill Cnwll 2 H8
Tuckingmill Wilts 8 C3
Tuckton Bmouth 8 G10
Tucoyse Cnwll 3 P7
Tuddenham Suffk 40 B6
Tuddenham Suffk 41 L11
Tudeley Kent 12 B6
Tudhoe Dur 69 S5
Tudorville Herefs 28 A3
Tudweiliog Gwynd 42 D6
Tuesley Surrey 10 F2
Tuffley Gloucs 28 F5
Tufton Hants 19 Q11
Tufton Pembks 24 H5
Tugby Leics 47 U13
Tugford Shrops 35 N3
Tughall Nthumb 85 U13
Tullibody Clacks 90 C12
Tullich Highld 102 H10
Tullich Highld 109 R9
Tulliemet P & K 97 S13
Tulloch Abers 105 N9
Tullochgorm Ag & B 87 T6
Tulloch Station Highld 96 D7
Tullymurdoch P & K 98 B13
Tullynessle Abers 104 H12
Tulse Hill Gt Lon 21 P8
Tumble Carmth 25 T8
Tumbler's Green Essex 22 K2
Tumby Lincs 48 K2
Tumby Woodside Lincs 49 L2
Tummel Bridge P & K 95 V7
Tunbridge Wells Kent 11 T3
Tundergarth D & G 75 N9
Tungate Norfk 51 N8
Tunley BaNES 17 S5
Tunstall C Stke 45 U3
Tunstall E R Yk 65 U13
Tunstall Kent 12 G3
Tunstall Lancs 62 C5
Tunstall N York 69 R13
Tunstall Norfk 51 R12
Tunstall Staffs 45 S8
Tunstall Suffk 41 Q9
Tunstall Sundld 70 E2
Tunstead Derbys 56 H12
Tunstead Norfk 51 N9
Tunstead Milton Derbys 56 F10
Tunworth Hants 19 U11
Tupsley Herefs 35 M12
Turgis Green Hants 19 U9
Turkdean Gloucs 29 M4
Tur Langton Leics 37 T2
Turleigh Wilts 18 B8
Turleygreen Shrops 35 S3
Turn Lancs 55 T3
Turnastone Herefs 34 J13
Turnberry S Ayrs 80 J11
Turnchapel C Plym 5 M10
Turnditch Derbys 46 J4
Turner Green Lancs 62 C13
Turner's Green E Susx 11 U7
Turner's Green Warwks 36 G7
Turner's Hill W Susx 11 N3
Turners Puddle Dorset 8 A10
Turnford Herts 31 U12
Turnhouse C Edin 83 N4
Turnworth Dorset 7 V3
Turriff Abers 105 L5
Turton Bottoms Bl w D 55 R3
Turves Cambs 39 M1
Turvey Bed 38 D10
Turville Bucks 20 C4
Turville Heath Bucks 20 B4
Turweston Bucks 30 D5
Tushielaw Inn Border 75 R2
Tutbury Staffs 46 H8
Tutnall Worcs 36 C6
Tutshill Gloucs 27 U9
Tuttington Norfk 51 M8
Tutwell Cnwll 4 K5
Tuxford Notts 58 B12
Twatt Ork 106 r17
Twatt Shet 106 t8
Twechar E Duns 89 Q10
Tweedbank Border 84 E12
Tweedmouth Nthumb 85 P8
Tweedsmuir Border 83 M14
Twelveheads Cnwll 2 K8
Twelve Oaks E Susx 12 C11
Twemlow Green Ches E 55 S13
Twenty Lincs 48 J9
Twerton BaNES 17 T4
Twickenham Gt Lon 21 L8
Twigworth Gloucs 28 F3
Twineham W Susx 11 M7
Twineham Green W Susx 11 M6
Twinhoe BaNES 17 U5
Twinstead Essex 40 E13
Twitchen Devon 15 S6
Twitchen Shrops 34 J5
Twitham Kent 13 Q4
Two Bridges Devon 5 Q6
Two Dales Derbys 57 L14
Two Gates Staffs 46 H13
Two Mile Oak Cross Devon 5 U7
Two Pots Devon 15 M4
Two Waters Herts 31 N11
Twycross Leics 46 K13
Twycross Zoo Leics 46 K12
Twyford Bucks 30 E7
Twyford Hants 9 P4
Twyford Leics 47 T11
Twyford Lincs 48 D9
Twyford Norfk 50 H9
Twyford Wokham 20 C7
Twyford Common Herefs 35 M13
Twyn-carno Caerph 27 L6
Twynholm D & G 73 R9
Twyning Green Gloucs 36 B13
Twynllanan Carmth 26 D3
Twyn-yr-Odyn V Glam 27 L13
Twyn-y-Sheriff Mons 27 S6
Tywell Nhants 38 E5
Tyberton Herefs 34 J13
Tyburn Birm 36 F2
Tycroes Carmth 25 V8
Ty Croes IoA 52 D8
Tycrwyn Powys 44 D10
Tydd Gote Lincs 49 Q10
Tydd St Giles Cambs 49 P10
Tydd St Mary Lincs 49 P10
Tye Hants 9 U8
Tye Green Essex 22 D3
Tye Green Essex 22 J3
Tye Green Essex 39 S13
Tyersal C Brad 63 P13
Tyldesley Wigan 55 Q6
Tyler Hill Kent 13 M3
Tylers Green Bucks 20 F4
Tyler's Green Essex 22 D6
Tylers Green Surrey 21 Q12
Tylorstown Rhondd 26 J8
Tylwch Powys 33 U4
Ty-nant Conwy 43 U5
Ty-nant Gwynd 43 T8
Tyndrum Stirlg 95 L12
Ty'n-dwr Denbgs 44 F5
Tynemouth N Tyne 77 T12
Tynemouth Crematorium N Tyne 77 S12
Tynewydd Rhondd 26 G8
Tyninghame E Loth 84 G3
Tynron D & G 74 F7
Ty'n-y-bryn Rhondd 26 J10
Ty'n-y-coedcae Caerph 27 M10
Tynygongl IoA 52 H6
Tynygraig Cerdgn 33 N7
Ty'n-y-Groes Conwy 53 N8
Tyn-y-nant Rhondd 26 K10
Tyringham M Keyn 38 C11
Tyseley Birm 36 F4
Tythegston Brdgnd 26 F12
Tytherington Ches E 56 D11
Tytherington S Glos 28 C10
Tytherington Somset 17 U8
Tytherington Wilts 18 D12
Tytherleigh Devon 6 K4
Tytherton Lucas Wilts 18 D6
Tyttenhanger Herts 31 Q11
Tywardreath Cnwll 3 R6
Tywardreath Highway Cnwll 3 R5
Tywyn Conwy 53 N7
Tywyn Gwynd 43 L13

U

Ubbeston Green Suffk 41 P6
Ubley BaNES 17 P5
Uckerby N York 69 R12
Uckfield E Susx 11 R6
Uckinghall Worcs 35 U13
Uckington Gloucs 28 H3
Uckington Shrops 45 N11
Uddingston S Lans 82 C6
Uddington S Lans 82 G12
Udimore E Susx 12 G12
Udny Green Abers 105 P10
Udny Station Abers 105 Q11
Uffcott Wilts 18 H5
Uffculme Devon 6 E2
Uffington Lincs 48 G12
Uffington Oxon 29 R10
Uffington Shrops 45 M11
Ufford C Pete 48 G13
Ufford Suffk 41 N10
Ufton Warwks 37 L8
Ufton Nervet W Berk 19 T7
Ugadale Ag & B 79 P10
Ugborough Devon 5 R9
Uggeshall Suffk 41 R4
Ugglebarnby N York 71 Q11
Ughill Sheff 57 L8
Ugley Essex 22 D2
Ugley Green Essex 22 D2
Ugthorpe N York 71 N10
Uibhist A Deas W Isls 106 d15
Uibhist A Tuath W Isls 106 c11
Uig Ag & B 92 F8
Uig Highld 100 a4
Uig Highld 100 c3
Uig W Isls 106 f5
Uigshader Highld 100 d5
Uisken Ag & B 86 F2
Ulbster Highld 112 H8
Ulcat Row Cumb 67 P8
Ulceby Lincs 59 R12
Ulceby N Linc 58 K4
Ulceby Skitter N Linc 58 K3
Ulcombe Kent 12 F6
Uldale Cumb 66 K5
Uley Gloucs 28 E8
Ulgham Nthumb 77 Q7
Ullapool Highld 108 A6
Ullenhall Warwks 36 F7
Ullenwood Gloucs 28 H4
Ulleskelf N York 64 C12
Ullesthorpe Leics 37 P3
Ulley Rothm 57 Q9
Ullingswick Herefs 35 N11
Ullinish Lodge Hotel Highld 100 c6
Ullock Cumb 66 G8
Ullswater Cumb 67 P8
Ullswater Steamers Cumb 67 N9
Ulpha Cumb 61 T3
Ulpha Cumb 66 J14
Ulrome E R Yk 65 R8
Ulsta Shet 106 u5
Ulting Wick Essex 22 K6
Ulva Ag & B 92 K10
Ulverley Green Solhll 36 F4
Ulverston Cumb 61 P4
Ulwell Dorset 8 E12
Ulzieside D & G 74 E4
Umberleigh Devon 15 P8
Unapool Highld 110 E10
Underbarrow Cumb 61 T1
Under Burnmouth Border 75 U9
Undercliffe C Brad 63 P13
Underdale Shrops 45 M11
Underling Green Kent 12 E6
Under River Kent 21 U12
Underwood Notts 47 N3
Undley Suffk 39 U4
Undy Mons 27 S10
Union Mills IoM 60 f7
Union Street E Susx 12 D9
Unst Shet 106 v3
Unstone Derbys 57 N11
Unstone Green Derbys 57 N11
Unthank Cumb 67 N3
Unthank Cumb 67 Q5
Unthank Cumb 68 D4
Unthank Derbys 57 M11
Unthank Nthumb 85 P9
Upavon Wilts 18 H10
Up Cerne Dorset 7 S4
Upchurch Kent 12 F2
Upcott Devon 15 S7
Upcott Herefs 34 H10
Upend Cambs 40 B9
Up Exe Devon 6 B4
Upgate Norfk 50 K10
Upgate Street Norfk 40 J2
Upgate Street Norfk 41 N2
Uphall Dorset 7 Q4
Uphall W Loth 83 L4
Upham Devon 15 U11
Upham Hants 9 Q4
Uphampton Herefs 34 J8
Uphampton Worcs 35 T8
Uphill N Som 16 K5
Up Holland Lancs 55 M5
Uplawmoor E Rens 81 N1
Upleadon Gloucs 28 E2
Upleatham R & Cl 70 K9
Uplees Kent 12 K3
Uploders Dorset 7 P6
Uplowman Devon 16 D13
Uplyme Devon 6 K6
Up Marden W Susx 10 B8
Upminster Gt Lon 22 E10
Up Mudford Somset 17 Q13
Up Nately Hants 19 U10
Upottery Devon 6 H3
Upper Affcot Shrops 34 K3
Upper Ardchronie Highld 109 L7
Upper Arley Worcs 35 S4
Upper Arncott Oxon 30 D9
Upper Astrop Nhants 30 B5
Upper Basildon W Berk 19 S5
Upper Batley Kirk 56 K1
Upper Beeding W Susx 10 K8
Upper Benefield Nhants 38 E3
Upper Bentley Worcs 36 C7
Upper Bighouse Highld 111 T5
Upper Birchwood Derbys 47 M2
Upper Boat Rhondd 27 L10
Upper Boddington Nhants 37 N10
Upper Borth Cerdgn 33 M3
Upper Brailes Warwks 36 K13
Upper Breakish Highld 100 f7
Upper Breinton Herefs 35 L12
Upper Broadheath Worcs 35 T9
Upper Broughton Notts 47 S8
Upper Bucklebury W Berk 19 R7
Upper Burgate Hants 8 H5
Upper Bush Medway 12 C2
Upperby Cumb 67 P2
Upper Caldecote C Beds 38 J11
Upper Canada N Som 17 L5
Upper Canterton Hants 8 K6
Upper Catesby Nhants 37 P9
Upper Catshill Worcs 36 C6
Upper Chapel Powys 34 B12
Upper Cheddon Somset 16 H11
Upper Chicksgrove Wilts 8 D3
Upper Chute Wilts 19 L10
Upper Clapton Gt Lon 21 P5
Upper Clatford Hants 19 N12
Upper Coberley Gloucs 28 J4
Upper Cokeham W Susx 10 K9
Upper Cotton Staffs 46 E4
Upper Cound Shrops 45 N12
Upper Cudworth Barns 57 N5
Upper Cumberworth Kirk 56 K5
Upper Dallachy Moray 104 D3
Upper Deal Kent 13 S5
Upper Dean Bed 38 F7
Upper Denby Kirk 56 K5
Upper Denton Cumb 76 C12
Upper Dicker E Susx 11 T9
Upper Dinchope Shrops 35 L4
Upper Dounreay Highld 112 B3
Upper Dovercourt Essex 23 T1
Upper Drumbane Stirlg 89 Q4
Upper Dunsforth N York 63 U7
Upper Eashing Surrey 10 F2
Upper Eathie Highld 103 L3
Upper Egleton Herefs 35 P12
Upper Elkstone Staffs 46 E2
Upper Ellastone Staffs 46 F5
Upper End Derbys 56 G11
Upper Enham Hants 19 N10
Upper Farmcote Shrops 35 S2
Upper Farringdon Hants 19 V13
Upper Framilode Gloucs 28 E5
Upper Froyle Hants 10 B2
Upperglen Highld 100 c4
Upper Godney Somset 17 N8
Upper Gravenhurst C Beds 31 P5
Upper Green Mons 27 R4
Upper Green Suffk 40 B8
Upper Green W Berk 19 N8
Upper Grove Common Herefs 27 V2
Upper Hackney Derbys 46 J1
Upper Hale Surrey 20 D13
Upper Halliford Surrey 20 J9
Upper Halling Medway 12 C3
Upper Hambleton Rutlnd 48 D12
Upper Harbledown Kent 13 M4
Upper Hardres Court Kent 13 N5
Upper Hardwick Herefs 34 K9
Upper Hartfield E Susx 11 R4
Upper Hartshay Derbys 47 L3
Upper Hatherley Gloucs 28 H3
Upper Hatton Staffs 45 T6
Upper Haugh Rothm 57 P7
Upper Hayton Shrops 35 M4
Upper Heaton Kirk 56 J3
Upper Helmsley N York 64 F8
Upper Hergest Herefs 34 G10
Upper Heyford Nhants 37 S9
Upper Heyford Oxon 29 U2
Upper Hill Herefs 35 L10
Upper Hockenden Kent 21 T9
Upper Hopton Kirk 56 J3
Upper Howsell Worcs 35 S11
Upper Hulme Staffs 46 D1
Upper Ifold Surrey 10 G4
Upper Inglesham Swindn 29 P8
Upper Kilcott Gloucs 28 E10
Upper Killay Swans 25 U12
Upper Kinchrackine Ag & B 94 H13
Upper Lambourn W Berk 19 M4
Upper Landywood Staffs 46 C12
Upper Langford N Som 17 N5
Upper Langwith Derbys 57 R13
Upper Largo Fife 91 P11
Upper Leigh Staffs 46 D6
Upper Littleton N Som 17 Q4
Upper Lochton Abers 99 M4
Upper Longdon Staffs 46 E11
Upper & Lower Stondon C Beds 31 Q6
Upper Ludstone Shrops 35 T1
Upper Lybster Highld 112 G9
Upper Lydbrook Gloucs 28 B4
Upper Lyde Herefs 35 L12
Upper Lye Herefs 34 J7
Upper Maes-coed Herefs 34 H14
Upper Midhope Sheff 56 K7
Uppermill Oldham 56 E5
Upper Milton Worcs 35 T6
Upper Minety Wilts 28 K9
Upper Moor Worcs 36 C11
Upper Moor Side Leeds 63 Q13
Upper Mulben Moray 104 D5
Upper Netchwood Shrops 35 P2
Upper Nobut Staffs 46 D6
Upper Norwood W Susx 10 E7
Upper Padley Derbys 56 K11
Upper Pennington Hants 9 L9
Upper Pollicott Bucks 30 F10
Upper Poppleton C York 64 D9
Upper Quinton Warwks 36 G11
Upper Ratley Hants 9 L4
Upper Rissington Gloucs 29 P4
Upper Rochford Worcs 35 P7
Upper Ruscoe D & G 73 P7
Upper Sapey Herefs 35 Q8
Upper Seagry Wilts 18 D4
Upper Shelton C Beds 31 L4
Upper Sheringham Norfk 50 K5
Upper Skelmorlie N Ayrs 88 F12
Upper Slaughter Gloucs 29 N3
Upper Soudley Gloucs 28 C5
Upper Spond Herefs 34 H10
Upper Standen Kent 13 P7
Upper Staploe Bed 38 H9
Upper Stoke Norfk 51 N13
Upper Stowe Nhants 37 R9
Upper Street Hants 8 H5
Upper Street Norfk 41 L5
Upper Street Norfk 51 P10
Upper Street Norfk 51 Q10
Upper Street Suffk 40 C10
Upper Street Suffk 40 K10
Upper Street Suffk 40 K14
Upper Strensham Worcs 35 U13
Upper Sundon C Beds 31 M7
Upper Swell Gloucs 29 N2
Upper Tankersley Barns 57 M7
Upper Tasburgh Norfk 41 M1
Upper Tean Staffs 46 D6
Upperthong Kirk 56 H5
Upperthorpe Derbys 57 Q10
Upperthorpe N Linc 58 C6
Upper Threapwood Ches W 44 K4
Upperton W Susx 10 F6
Upper Town Derbys 46 H3
Uppertown Derbys 57 M14
Upper Town Dur 69 N5
Upper Town Herefs 35 N11
Uppertown Highld 112 J1
Upper Town N Som 17 P3
Upper Town Suffk 40 F7
Upper Tumble Carmth 25 T8
Upper Tysoe Warwks 36 K12
Upper Ufford Suffk 41 N10
Upperup Gloucs 28 K8
Upper Upham Wilts 18 K5
Upper Upnor Medway 22 J13
Upper Victoria Angus 91 R4
Upper Vobster Somset 17 T7
Upper Wardington Oxon 37 N11
Upper Weald M Keyn 30 H5
Upper Weedon Nhants 37 R9
Upper Welland Worcs 35 S12
Upper Wellingham E Susx 11 Q8
Upper Weston BaNES 17 T3
Upper Weybread Suffk 41 M5
Upper Wick Worcs 35 T10
Upper Wield Hants 19 T13
Upper Winchendon Bucks 30 F10
Upperwood Derbys 46 J2
Upper Woodford Wilts 18 H13
Upper Wootton Hants 19 S10
Upper Wraxall Wilts 18 B6
Upper Wyche Worcs 35 S12
Uppincott Devon 6 B3
Uppingham Rutlnd 48 C14
Uppington Dorset 8 E7
Uppington Shrops 45 N12
Upsall N York 64 B2
Upsettlington Border 85 M9
Upshire Essex 22 B7
Up Somborne Hants 9 M2
Upstreet Kent 13 P3
Up Sydling Dorset 7 R4
Upthorpe Suffk 40 G6
Upton Bucks 30 G10
Upton C Pete 48 H13
Upton Cambs 38 J5
Upton Ches W 54 K13
Upton Cnwll 4 H6
Upton Cnwll 14 F12
Upton Cumb 67 M5
Upton Devon 5 S12
Upton Devon 6 E4
Upton Dorset 7 T8
Upton Dorset 8 D10
Upton E R Yk 65 Q9
Upton Halton 55 L9
Upton Hants 9 M5
Upton Hants 19 N9
Upton Leics 47 L14
Upton Lincs 58 E9
Upton Nhants 37 T9
Upton Norfk 51 Q11
Upton Notts 47 T3
Upton Notts 58 B11
Upton Oxon 19 R3
Upton Oxon 29 P5
Upton Pembks 24 H10
Upton R & Cl 71 M9
Upton Slough 20 G7
Upton Somset 16 C11
Upton Somset 17 N11
Upton Wakefd 57 Q4
Upton Warwks 36 F9
Upton Wilts 8 B2
Upton Wirral 54 G9
Upton Bishop Herefs 28 C2
Upton Cheyney S Glos 17 S2
Upton Cressett Shrops 35 Q2
Upton Crews Herefs 28 B2
Upton Cross Cnwll 4 H6
Upton End C Beds 31 P6
Upton Grey Hants 19 U11
Upton Heath Ches W 54 K13
Upton Hellions Devon 15 T12
Upton Lovell Wilts 18 D12
Upton Magna Shrops 45 N11
Upton Noble Somset 17 T9
Upton Pyne Devon 6 B5
Upton St Leonards Gloucs 28 G4
Upton Scudamore Wilts 18 C11
Upton Snodsbury Worcs 36 B10
Upton Towans Cnwll 2 F8
Upton-upon-Severn Worcs 35 U12
Upton Warren Worcs 36 B7
Upwaltham W Susx 10 E8
Upware Cambs 39 R6
Upwell Norfk 49 Q13
Upwey Dorset 7 S7
Upwick Green Herts 22 C3
Upwood Cambs 39 L4
Urchfont Wilts 18 F9
Urdimarsh Herefs 35 M11
Ure Bank N York 63 S5
Urlay Nook S on T 70 F10
Urmston Traffd 55 S8
Urquhart Moray 104 B3
Urquhart Castle Highld 102 F10
Urra N York 70 J12
Urray Highld 102 F5
Usan Angus 99 N13
Ushaw Moor Dur 69 R4
Usk Mons 27 R7
Usselby Lincs 58 J8
Usworth Sundld 77 S14
Utkinton Ches W 55 M13
Utley C Brad 63 M11
Uton Devon 15 T13
Utterby Lincs 59 P8
Uttoxeter Staffs 46 E7
Uwchmynydd Gwynd 42 C8
Uxbridge Gt Lon 20 J6
Uyeasound Shet 106 v3
Uzmaston Pembks 24 G8

V

Vale Guern 6 e2
Vale of Glamorgan Crematorium V Glam 16 F2
Valley IoA 52 C7
Valley End Surrey 20 G10
Valley Truckle Cnwll 4 D4
Valtos Highld 100 e3
Valtos W Isls 106 f5
Vange Essex 22 H10
Varteg Torfn 27 P6
Vatsetter Shet 106 v5
Vatten Highld 100 b5
Vaynor Myr Td 26 J5
Vazon Bay Guern 6 c2
Veensgarth Shet 106 u9
Velindre Powys 34 E13
Vellow Somset 16 E9
Velly Devon 14 G8
Venngreen Devon 14 J10
Vennington Shrops 44 H12
Venn Ottery Devon 6 E6
Venny Tedburn Devon 15 T13
Venterdon Cnwll 4 K6
Ventnor IoW 9 R13
Venton Devon 5 P9
Vernham Dean Hants 19 M9
Vernham Street Hants 19 M9
Vernolds Common Shrops 35 L4
Verwood Dorset 8 F7
Veryan Cnwll 3 N9
Veryan Green Cnwll 3 N8
Vicarage Devon 6 H7
Vickerstown Cumb 61 M6
Victoria Barns 56 J5
Victoria Blae G 27 M6
Victoria Cnwll 3 P4
Vidlin Shet 106 u7
Viewfield Moray 104 B3
Viewpark N Lans 82 D6
Vigo Kent 12 B3
Village de Putron Guern 6 e3
Ville la Bas Jersey 7 a1
Villiaze Guern 6 c3
Vinehall Street E Susx 12 E11
Vines Cross E Susx 11 T7
Vinters Park Crematorium Kent 12 E4
Virginia Water Surrey 20 H9
Virginstow Devon 4 K2
Vobster Somset 17 T7
Voe Shet 106 u7
Vowchurch Herefs 34 J13
Vulcan Village St Hel 55 N8

W

Waberthwaite Cumb 66 H14
Wackerfield Dur 69 Q8
Wacton Norfk 41 L2
Wadborough Worcs 36 B11
Waddesdon Bucks 30 F9
Waddesdon Manor Bucks 30 F9
Waddeton Devon 6 A13
Waddicar Sefton 54 J7
Waddingham Lincs 58 G7
Waddington Lancs 62 E11
Waddington Lincs 58 G14
Waddon Devon 6 A9
Waddon Dorset 7 R7
Wadebridge Cnwll 3 P2
Wadeford Somset 6 K2
Wadenhoe Nhants 38 F4
Wadesmill Herts 31 U9
Wadhurst E Susx 12 B9
Wadshelf Derbys 57 M12
Wadswick Wilts 18 B7
Wadworth Donc 57 S7
Waen Denbgs 53 S10
Waen Denbgs 54 D13
Waen Powys 44 F10
Waen Fach Powys 44 F10
Waen-pentir Gwynd 52 J9
Waen-wen Gwynd 52 J9
Wagbeach Shrops 44 J13
Wainfelin Torfn 27 P7
Wainfleet All Saints Lincs 49 Q2
Wainfleet Bank Lincs 49 Q2
Wainfleet St Mary Lincs 49 Q2
Wainford Norfk 41 P2
Wainhouse Corner Cnwll 14 E13
Wainscott Medway 22 H13
Wain's Hill N Som 17 L2
Wainstalls Calder 63 L14
Waitby Cumb 68 G11
Waithe Lincs 59 N6
Wakefield Wakefd 57 M2
Wakefield Crematorium Wakefd 57 M3
Wake Green Birm 36 E4
Wakehurst Place W Susx 11 N4
Wakerley Nhants 48 E14
Wakes Colne Essex 23 L2
Walberswick Suffk 41 S6
Walberton W Susx 10 F9
Walbottle N u Ty 77 P12
Walbutt D & G 74 D12
Walby Cumb 75 T13
Walcombe Somset 17 Q7
Walcot Lincs 48 G6
Walcot N Linc 58 E2
Walcot Shrops 34 H3
Walcot Shrops 45 N11
Walcot Swindn 29 N11
Walcot Warwks 36 F9
Walcote Leics 37 Q4
Walcot Green Norfk 40 K4
Walcott Lincs 48 H2
Walcott Norfk 51 Q7
Walden N York 63 L3
Walden Head N York 62 K3
Walden Stubbs N York 57 S3
Walderslade Medway 12 E3
Walderton W Susx 10 B8
Walditch Dorset 7 N6
Waldley Derbys 46 F6
Waldridge Dur 69 S3
Waldringfield Suffk 41 N11
Waldron E Susx 11 S7
Wales Rothm 57 Q10
Wales Somset 17 Q12
Walesby Lincs 58 K8
Walesby Notts 57 U12
Wales Millennium Centre Cardif 27 M13
Walford Herefs 28 A3
Walford Herefs 34 J6
Walford Shrops 44 K9
Walford Staffs 45 T7
Walford Heath Shrops 44 K10
Walgherton Ches E 45 Q4
Walgrave Nhants 38 B6
Walhampton Hants 9 L9
Walkden Salfd 55 R6
Walker N u Ty 77 R13
Walkerburn Border 83 S11
Walker Fold Lancs 62 D11
Walkeringham Notts 58 C8
Walkerith Lincs 58 C8
Walkern Herts 31 S7
Walker's Green Herefs 35 M11
Walker's Heath Birm 36 E5
Walkerton Fife 90 K11
Walkford Dorset 8 J10
Walkhampton Devon 5 N7
Walkington E R Yk 65 M12
Walkley Sheff 57 M9
Walk Mill Lancs 62 H14
Walkwood Worcs 36 D8
Wall Nthumb 76 J12
Wall Staffs 46 F12
Wallacetown S Ayrs 80 K12
Wallacetown S Ayrs 81 L8
Wallands Park E Susx 11 Q8
Wallasey Wirral 54 G8
Wall End Cumb 61 N3
Wall End Herefs 34 K9
Wallend Medway 23 L12
Waller's Green Herefs 35 Q13
Wallhead Cumb 75 U13
Wall Heath Dudley 35 U3
Wall Houses Nthumb 77 L12
Wallingford Oxon 19 T3
Wallington Gt Lon 21 N10
Wallington Hants 9 R7
Wallington Herts 31 S6
Wallington Heath Wsall 46 C13
Wallis Pembks 24 H5
Wallisdown Poole 8 F10
Walliswood Surrey 10 J3
Walls Shet 106 s9
Wallsend N Tyne 77 R12
Wallthwaite Cumb 67 N7
Wall under Haywood Shrops 35 M2
Wallyford E Loth 83 S4
Walmer Kent 13 S5
Walmer Bridge Lancs 55 L2
Walmersley Bury 55 T4
Walmestone Kent 13 Q4
Walmley Birm 36 F2
Walmley Ash Birm 36 F2
Walmsgate Lincs 59 Q11
Walpole Somset 16 K8
Walpole Suffk 41 Q6
Walpole Cross Keys Norfk 49 R10
Walpole Highway Norfk 49 R11
Walpole St Andrew Norfk 49 R10
Walpole St Peter Norfk 49 R10
Walrow Somset 16 K7
Walsall Wsall 46 D14
Walsall Wood Wsall 46 D13
Walsden Calder 56 D2
Walsgrave on Sowe Covtry 37 L4
Walsham le Willows Suffk 40 H6
Walshaw Bury 55 S4
Walshford N York 63 U9
Walsoken Norfk 49 Q11
Walston S Lans 83 L9
Walsworth Herts 31 Q6
Walter's Ash Bucks 20 D3
Walters Green Kent 11 S2
Walterston V Glam 16 E2
Walterstone Herefs 27 Q2
Waltham Kent 13 M6
Waltham NE Lin 59 N6
Waltham Abbey Essex 31 U12
Waltham Chase Hants 9 R6
Waltham Cross Herts 31 U12
Waltham on the Wolds Leics 48 B9
Waltham St Lawrence W & M 20 D7
Waltham's Cross Essex 22 G1
Walthamstow Gt Lon 21 Q5
Walton C Pete 48 J13
Walton Cumb 75 V13
Walton Derbys 57 N13
Walton Leeds 63 U10
Walton Leics 37 Q3
Walton M Keyn 30 J5
Walton Powys 34 G9
Walton Shrops 35 L5
Walton Somset 17 N9
Walton Staffs 45 U7
Walton Staffs 45 U8
Walton Suffk 41 N13
Walton W Susx 10 C10
Walton Wakefd 57 N3
Walton Warwks 36 J10
Walton Wrekin 45 N10
Walton Cardiff Gloucs 28 H1
Walton East Pembks 24 H6
Walton Elm Dorset 17 U13
Walton Grounds Nhants 30 B6
Walton-in-Gordano N Som 27 S13
Walton Lea Crematorium Warrtn 55 P9
Walton-le-Dale Lancs 62 B14
Walton-on-Thames Surrey 20 K9
Walton-on-the-Hill Staffs 46 C9
Walton on the Hill Surrey 21 M11
Walton on the Naze Essex 23 U3
Walton on the Wolds Leics 47 Q10
Walton-on-Trent Derbys 46 H10
Walton Park N Som 17 M2
Walton West Pembks 24 E8
Waltonwrays Crematorium N York 62 K9
Walwen Flints 54 D11
Walwen Flints 54 E12
Walwen Flints 54 F11
Walwick Nthumb 76 J11
Walworth Darltn 69 R9
Walworth Gt Lon 21 P7
Walworth Gate Darltn 69 R8
Walwyn's Castle Pembks 24 E8
Wambrook Somset 6 J3
Wampool Cumb 66 K2
Wanborough Surrey 20 F13
Wanborough Swindn 29 P11
Wandon End Herts 31 P8
Wandsworth Gt Lon 21 N8
Wangford Suffk 41 S5
Wanlip Leics 47 Q11
Wanlockhead D & G 74 G3
Wannock E Susx 11 T10
Wansford C Pete 48 G14
Wansford E R Yk 65 P8
Wanshurst Green Kent 12 E6
Wanstead Gt Lon 21 R5
Wanstrow Somset 17 T8
Wanswell Gloucs 28 C7
Wantage Oxon 29 S10
Wants Green Worcs 35 S9
Wapley S Glos 28 D12
Wappenbury Warwks 37 L7
Wappenham Nhants 37 R11
Warbleton E Susx 11 U7
Warborough Oxon 19 S2
Warboys Cambs 39 M4
Warbreck Bpool 61 Q12
Warbstow Cnwll 4 G2
Warburton Traffd 55 R9
Warcop Cumb 68 F9
Warden Kent 23 P13
Warden Nthumb 76 J12
Ward End Birm 36 F3
Warden Street C Beds 31 P4
Ward Green Suffk 40 H8
Ward Green Cross Lancs 62 C12
Wardhedges C Beds 31 N5
Wardington Oxon 37 N11
Wardle Ches E 45 P2
Wardle Rochdl 56 D3
Wardley Gatesd 77 S13
Wardley Rutlnd 48 B13
Wardley Salfd 55 S6
Wardlow Derbys 56 J12
Wardsend Ches E 56 D10
Wardy Hill Cambs 39 Q4
Ware Herts 31 U10
Wareham Dorset 8 C11
Warehorne Kent 12 J9
Warenford Nthumb 85 S13
Waren Mill Nthumb 85 S12
Warenton Nthumb 85 S12
Wareside Herts 31 U9
Waresley Cambs 39 L10
Waresley Worcs 35 T6
Ware Street Kent 12 E4
Warfield Br For 20 E8
Warfleet Devon 5 V10
Wargate Lincs 48 K7
Wargrave Wokham 20 C7
Warham Herefs 35 L13
Warham All Saints Norfk 50 G5
Warham St Mary Norfk 50 F5
Wark Nthumb 76 H10
Wark Nthumb 85 L11
Warkleigh Devon 15 P8
Warkton Nhants 38 C5
Warkworth Nhants 37 N12
Warkworth Nthumb 77 Q4
Warlaby N York 63 S1
Warland Calder 56 D2
Warleggan Cnwll 4 F7
Warleigh BaNES 17 U4
Warley Town Calder 56 G2
Warlingham Surrey 21 Q11
Warmbrook Derbys 46 J3
Warmfield Wakefd 57 N2
Warmingham Ches E 45 R1
Warmington Nhants 38 G2
Warmington Warwks 37 M11

Place	County	Page	Grid
Warminster	Wilts	18	C11
Warmley	S Glos	28	C15
Warmsworth	Donc	57	R6
Warmwell	Dorset	7	U7
Warndon	Worcs	35	U9
Warner Bros Studio Tour Herts		31	N12
Warnford	Hants	9	S4
Warnham	W Susx	10	K5
Warnham Court	W Susx	10	K4
Warningcamp	W Susx	10	G9
Warninglid	W Susx	11	L5
Warren	Pembks	24	F11
Warrenby	R & Cl	70	J7
Warren Hill	Suff	82	H11
Warren Row	W & M	20	D6
Warren's Green	Herts	31	S7
Warren Street	Kent	12	H5
Warrington	M Keyn	38	C10
Warrington	Warrtn	55	P9
Warriston Crematorium C Edin		83	Q3
Warsash	Hants	9	P7
Warslow	Staffs	45	E2
Warsop Vale	Notts	57	R13
Warter	E R Yk	64	K9
Warthermaske	N York	63	Q4
Warthill	N York	64	F8
Wartling	E Susx	12	B8
Wartnaby	Leics	47	T9
Warton	Lancs	61	S14
Warton	Lancs	61	T7
Warton	Nthumb	77	L5
Warton	Warwks	46	J13
Warwick	Warwks	36	J8
Warwick Bridge	Cumb	67	Q1
Warwick Castle	Warwks	36	J8
Warwick-on-Eden	Cumb	67	Q1
Warwick Services Warwks		36	K9
Wasbister	Ork	106	s16
Wasdale Head	Cumb	66	J11
Wash	Derbys	56	G10
Washall Green	Herts	22	B1
Washaway	Cnwll	3	Q2
Washbourne	Devon	5	T10
Washbrook	Suffk	40	K12
Washfield	Devon	16	B13
Washfold	N York	69	N12
Washford	Somset	16	E8
Washford Pyne	Devon	15	T10
Washingborough	Lincs	58	H12
Washington	Sundld	70	D1
Washington	W Susx	10	H8
Washington Services Gatesd		69	S1
Washwood Heath	Birm	36	F3
Wasing	W Berk	19	S8
Waskerley	Dur	69	M3
Wasperton	Warwks	36	J9
Wasps Nest	Lincs	58	J14
Wass	N York	64	C4
Watchet	Somset	16	E8
Watchfield	Oxon	29	P9
Watchfield	Somset	17	L7
Watchgate	Cumb	67	R13
Watchill	Cumb	66	J4
Watcombe	Torbay	6	B11
Watendlath	Cumb	67	L9
Water	Devon	5	T4
Water	Lancs	55	T1
Waterbeach	Cambs	39	Q7
Waterbeck	D & G	75	P10
Waterden	Norfk	50	E6
Water Eaton	Staffs	46	B11
Water End	Bed	38	H11
Water End	Bed	38	H10
Water End	C Beds	31	N5
Waterend	Cumb	66	H8
Water End	E R Yk	64	H12
Water End	Essex	39	S12
Water End	Herts	31	M10
Water End	Herts	31	R12
Waterfall	Staffs	81	E1
Waterford	Herts	31	T10
Water Fryston	Wakefd	57	Q1
Watergate	Cnwll	4	H2
Waterhead	Cumb	67	N12
Waterheads	Border	83	P8
Waterhouses	Dur	69	P4
Waterhouses	Staffs	46	C3
Wateringbury	Kent	12	C5
Waterlane	Gloucs	28	H7
Waterloo	Cnwll	4	E6
Waterloo	Derbys	57	P14
Waterloo	Herefs	34	H11
Waterloo	Highld	100	f7
Waterloo	N Lans	82	E7
Waterloo	Norfk	51	N10
Waterloo	P & K	90	G4
Waterloo	Pembks	24	G10
Waterloo	Poole	8	E10
Waterloo	Sefton	54	H7
Waterloo Cross	Devon	6	E2
Waterloo Port	Gwynd	52	G10
Watermillock	Cumb	67	P8
Water Newton	Cambs	48	H1
Water Orton	Warwks	36	G2
Waterperry	Oxon	30	D11
Waterrow	Somset	16	E11
Waterside	Bl w D	55	L2
Waterside	Bucks	30	L12
Waterside	Cumb	66	K3
Waterside	E Ayrs	81	N4
Waterside	E Ayrs	81	N11
Waterside	E Duns	89	Q11
Waterside	Donc	57	S3
Water's Nook	Bolton	55	Q5
Waterstein	Highld	100	a5
Waterston	Pembks	24	F9
Water Stratford	Bucks	30	E6
Water Street	Neath	26	E11
Waters Upton	Wrekin	45	P10
Water Yeat	Cumb	61	P2
Watford	Herts	20	K4
Watford	Nhants	37	R7
Watford Gap Services Nhants		37	R7
Wath	N York	63	N6
Wath upon Dearne Rothm		57	P6
Watlington	Norfk	49	T11
Watlington	Oxon	19	U2
Watnall	Notts	47	P4
Watten	Highld	112	H6
Wattisfield	Suffk	40	H6
Wattisham	Suffk	40	H10
Watton	Dorset	7	N6
Watton	E R Yk	65	M9
Watton	Norfk	50	F13
Watton-at-Stone	Herts	31	T10
Watton Green	Norfk	50	F13
Wattons Green	Essex	22	D9
Wattston	N Lans	82	E4
Wattstown	Rhondd	26	J9
Wattsville	Caerph	27	N9
Wauldby	E R Yk	65	L1
Waulkmill	Abers	99	L5
Waunarlwydd	Swans	25	V11
Waun Fawr	Cerdgn	33	M4
Waunfawr	Gwynd	52	H11
Waungron	Swans	25	U10
Waunlwyd	Blae G	27	M6
Wavendon	M Keyn	30	K5
Waverbridge	Cumb	66	K3
Waverton	Ches W	45	L1
Waverton	Cumb	66	K3
Wawne	E R Yk	65	Q12
Waxham	Norfk	51	S9
Waxholme	E R Yk	65	U14
Way	Kent	13	R2
Waye	Devon	5	S7
Wayford	Somset	7	M3
Waytown	Dorset	7	N5
Way Village	Devon	15	U10
Way Wick	N Som	17	L4
Weacombe	Somset	16	F8
Weald	Oxon	29	R7
Wealdstone	Gt Lon	21	L5
Weardley	Leeds	63	R10
Weare	Somset	17	M6
Weare Giffard	Devon	15	L8
Wearhead	Dur	68	G5
Wearne	Somset	17	M11
Wear Valley Crematorium Dur		69	P6
Weasdale	Cumb	68	E12
Weasenham All Saints Norfk		50	D9
Weasenham St Peter Norfk		50	E9
Weaste	Salfd	55	T7
Weatheroak Hill Worcs		36	D6
Weaverham	Ches W	55	P12
Weaverslake	Staffs	46	F10
Weaverthorpe	N York	65	M5
Webbington	Somset	17	L5
Webb's Heath	S Glos	28	C13
Webheath	Worcs	36	D7
Webton	Herefs	34	K13
Wedderlairs	Abers	105	P9
Wedding Hall Fold N York		62	J10
Weddington	Kent	13	Q4

Place	County	Page	Grid
Weddington	Warwks	37	L2
Wedhampton	Wilts	18	H9
Wedmore	Somset	17	M7
Wednesbury	Sandw	36	C1
Wednesfield	Wolves	46	B13
Weecar	Notts	58	D13
Weedon	Bucks	30	H9
Weedon	Nhants	37	R9
Weedon Lois	Nhants	37	R11
Weeford	Staffs	46	F13
Week	Devon	5	T8
Week	Devon	15	N7
Week	Devon	15	S11
Weeke	Devon	15	U10
Weeke	Hants	9	N2
Week Green	Cnwll	14	F13
Weekley	Nhants	38	C3
Week St Mary	Cnwll	14	F13
Weel	E R Yk	65	Q12
Weeley	Essex	23	R3
Weeley Crematorium Essex		23	R3
Weeley Heath	Essex	23	S3
Weem	P & K	90	B2
Weeping Cross	Staffs	46	B9
Weethley	Warwks	36	E9
Weeting	Norfk	40	C3
Weeton	E R Yk	65	V13
Weeton	Lancs	61	R13
Weeton	N York	63	R10
Weetwood	Leeds	63	R12
Weir	Lancs	55	U1
Weir Quay	Devon	5	L7
Weisdale	Shet	106	u8
Welborne	Norfk	50	J11
Welbourn	Lincs	48	E3
Welburn	N York	64	F6
Welburn	N York	70	E12
Welbury	N York	70	D11
Welby	Lincs	48	D6
Welches Dam	Cambs	39	Q3
Welcombe	Devon	14	F9
Weldon Bridge Nthumb		77	N6
Welford	Nhants	37	S4
Welford	W Berk	19	P6
Welford-on-Avon Warwks		36	F10
Welham	Leics	37	U2
Welham	Notts	58	B10
Welham Green	Herts	31	R11
Well	Hants	20	C13
Well	Lincs	59	R12
Well	N York	63	R3
Welland	Worcs	35	S12
Wellbank	Angus	91	Q4
Well Bottom	Dorset	8	C5
Well End	Bucks	20	E6
Well End	Herts	21	N3
Wellesbourne	Warwks	36	J9
Wellesbourne Mountford Warwks		36	J9
Well Head	Herts	31	Q7
Well Hill	Kent	21	S10
Wellhouse	W Berk	19	R6
Welling	Gt Lon	21	S7
Wellingborough Nhants		38	B8
Wellingham	Norfk	50	E9
Wellingore	Lincs	48	E2
Wellington	Cumb	66	G12
Wellington	Herefs	35	L11
Wellington	Somset	16	F12
Wellington	Wrekin	45	P11
Wellington Heath Herefs		35	R12
Wellington Marsh Herefs		35	L11
Wellow	BaNES	17	U5
Wellow	IoW	9	M11
Wellow	Notts	57	U13
Wellpond Green Herts		22	B3
Wells	Somset	17	P7
Wellsborough	Leics	47	L13
Wells Green	Ches E	45	Q3
Wells Head	Brad	63	M13
Wells-next-the-sea Norfk		50	F5
Wellstye Green	Essex	22	F4
Well Town	Devon	6	B4
Welltree	P & K	90	E7
Wellwood	Fife	90	G14
Welney	Norfk	39	R1
Welshampton	Shrops	44	K6
Welsh End	Shrops	45	M6
Welsh Frankton Shrops		44	H7
Welsh Hook	Pembks	24	F5
Welsh Newton	Herefs	27	U4
Welshpool	Powys	44	F12
Welsh St Donats V Glam		26	J12
Welton	Cumb	67	N4
Welton	E R Yk	65	L1
Welton	Lincs	58	H11
Welton	Nhants	37	Q7
Welton le Marsh Lincs		59	S13
Welton le Wold Lincs		59	N9
Welwick	E R Yk	65	M9
Welwyn	Herts	31	R10
Welwyn Garden City Herts		31	R10
Wem	Shrops	45	M8
Wembdon	Somset	16	J9
Wembley	Gt Lon	21	L5
Wembury	Devon	5	N11
Wembworthy	Devon	15	Q11
Wemyss Bay	Inver	88	E12
Wenallt	Cerdgn	33	N6
Wendens Ambo	Essex	39	R13
Wendlebury	Oxon	30	C9
Wendling	Norfk	50	F11
Wendover	Bucks	30	J11
Wendover Woods Bucks		30	K10
Wendron	Cnwll	2	H10
Wendron Mining District Cnwll		2	H10
Wendy	Cambs	39	M11
Wenfordbridge Cnwll		3	R1
Wenhaston	Suffk	41	R5
Wennington	Cambs	38	K5
Wennington	Gt Lon	22	D11
Wennington	Lancs	62	C6
Wensley	Derbys	46	J1
Wensley	N York	63	M1
Wentbridge	Wakefd	57	Q3
Wentnor	Shrops	34	J2
Wentworth	Cambs	39	Q5
Wentworth	Rothm	57	N7
Wentworth Castle Barn S York		57	M6
Wenvoe	V Glam	16	F2
Weobley	Herefs	34	K10
Weobley Marsh Herefs		34	K10
Wepham	W Susx	10	G9
Wereham	Norfk	49	U13
Wergs	Wolves	45	U13
Wern	Gwynd	42	K4
Wern	Powys	44	G7
Wern	Shrops	44	G7
Wernffrwd	Swans	25	T12
Wern-y-gaer	Flints	54	F13
Werrington	Cnwll	4	J3
Werrington	Cnwll	48	J11
Werrington	Staffs	45	U4
Wervin	Ches W	54	K12
Wesham	Lancs	61	S13
Wessex Vale Crematorium Hants		9	P5
Wessington	Derbys	47	L1
West Aberthaw V Glam		16	D3
West Acre	Norfk	50	C10
West Allerdean Nthumb		85	P9
West Alvington	Devon	5	S12
West Amesbury Wilts		18	H12
West Anstey	Devon	15	U7
West Appleton N York		69	R14
West Ashby	Lincs	59	N12
West Ashling	W Susx	10	C9
West Ashton	Wilts	18	C9
West Auckland	Dur	69	Q7
West Ayton	N York	65	M3
West Bagborough Somset		16	G10
West Bank	Blae G	27	N6
West Bank	Halton	55	M9
West Barkwith	Lincs	59	L10
West Barnby	N York	71	P9
West Barns	E Loth	84	H3
West Barsham	Norfk	50	F7
West Bay	Dorset	7	N6
West Beckham	Norfk	50	K6
West Bedfont	Surrey	20	J8
Westbere	Kent	13	N3
West Bergholt Essex		23	N2
West Berkshire Crematorium W Berk		19	R7
West Bexington Dorset		7	N7
West Bilney	Norfk	50	B10
West Blatchington Br & H		11	M9
West Boldon	S Tyne	77	T14
Westborough	Lincs	48	C5
Westbourne	Bmouth	8	E10
Westbourne	W Susx	10	B9
West Bourton	Dorset	17	T11
West Bowling	C Brad	63	P13
West Brabourne	Kent	13	L7
West Bradenham Norfk		50	G12
West Bradford	Lancs	62	E11
West Bradley	Somset	17	Q9
West Bretton	Wakefd	57	L4
West Bridgford Notts		47	Q6
West Briscoe	Dur	69	L8
West Bromwich Sandw		36	D2
Westbrook	Kent	13	R1
Westbrook	Wilts	18	D7
West Buckland Devon		15	Q6

Place	County	Page	Grid
West Buckland	Somset	16	G12
West Burton	W York	69	L2
West Burton	W Susx	10	F8
Westbury	Bucks	30	D5
Westbury	Shrops	44	J11
Westbury	Wilts	18	C10
Westbury Leigh	Wilts	18	C10
Westbury on Severn Gloucs		28	D5
Westbury-on-Trym Bristl		27	V12
Westbury-sub-Mendip Somset		17	P7
West Butsfield	Dur	69	P4
West Butterwick N Linc		58	D5
Westby	Lancs	61	R13
West Byfleet	Surrey	20	J10
West Cairngaan D & G		72	C13
West Caister	Norfk	51	T11
West Calder	W Loth	82	K6
West Camel	Somset	17	Q12
West Chaldon	Dorset	7	V8
West Challow	Oxon	29	S10
West Charleton	Devon	5	S12
West Chelborough Dorset		7	P3
West Chevington Nthumb		77	Q6
West Chiltington W Susx		10	H7
West Chinnock	Somset	7	N2
West Chisenbury Wilts		18	H10
Westcliff	Herefs	28	D5
West Cliffe	Kent	13	R7
Westcliff-on-Sea Sthend		23	L10
West Coker	Somset	7	P2
West Combe	Devon	5	T9
Westcombe	Somset	17	S9
West Compton	Somset	17	P8
West Compton Abbas Dorset		7	Q6
Westcote	Gloucs	29	P3
Westcote Barton Oxon		29	T2
Westcott	Bucks	30	F9
Westcott	Devon	6	D4
Westcott	Surrey	20	K13
West Cottingwith N York		64	F11
Westcourt	Wilts	18	K8
West Cowick	E R Yk	57	T2
West Cross	Swans	25	V13
West Curry	Cnwll	14	H2
West Curthwaite Cumb		67	M3
Westdean	E Susx	11	S11
West Dean	W Susx	10	D8
West Dean	Wilts	8	K3
West Deeping	Lincs	48	H12
West Derby	Lpool	54	J8
West Dereham	Norfk	49	U13
West Ditchburn Nthumb		77	N1
West Down	Devon	15	M4
Westdown Camp Wilts		18	F11
Westdowns	Cnwll	4	D4
West Drayton	Gt Lon	20	J7
West Drayton	Notts	58	B12
West Dunnet	Highld	112	G2
West Ella	E R Yk	65	N14
West End	Bed	38	E10
West End	Br For	20	F9
West End	Caerph	27	N8
West End	E R Yk	64	K14
West End	E R Yk	65	L13
West End	E R Yk	65	R14
West End	Hants	9	P5
West End	Hants	19	T9
West End	Herts	31	S11
West End	Lancs	55	L2
West End	Leeds	63	R12
West End	Lincs	59	N3
West End	N Som	17	N3
West End	Norfk	50	K11
West End	Norfk	51	T11
West End	Oxon	29	S8
West End	S Glos	28	D10
West End	Somset	17	N7
West End	Surrey	20	F10
West End	Surrey	21	N12
West End	W & M	20	D7
West End	Wilts	8	C4
West End	Wilts	18	E5
West End Green Hants		19	U8
Westend Town Nthumb		76	F13
Westenhanger Kent		13	M8
Westerdale	Highld	112	D6
Westerdale	N York	71	L11
Westerfield	Suffk	40	L11
Westergate	W Susx	10	E9
Westerham	Kent	21	R12
Westerhope	N u Ty	77	P12
Westerland	Devon	5	V8
Westerleigh	S Glos	28	C12
Westerleigh Crematorium S Glos		28	D12
Western Isles	W Isls	106	j5
Wester Ochiltree W Loth		82	K4
Wester Pitkierie Fife		91	S10
Wester Ross	Highld	107	S9
Westerton of Rossie Angus		99	M13
Westerwick	Shet	106	s8
West Ewell	Surrey	21	L10
West Farleigh	Kent	12	D5
West Farndon	Nhants	37	P10
West Felton	Shrops	44	H8
Westfield	BaNES	17	S6
Westfield	Cumb	66	E7
Westfield	E Susx	12	F12
Westfield	Highld	112	C4
Westfield	N Lans	89	S11
Westfield	Norfk	50	G12
Westfield	W Loth	82	G4
Westfields	Herefs	35	L12
Westfields of Rattray P & K		90	J2
Westfield Sole	Kent	12	D4
West Flotmanby N York		65	P4
Westford	Somset	16	F12
Westgate	Dur	68	K5
Westgate	N Linc	58	C5
Westgate	Norfk	50	F4
Westgate Hill	C Brad	63	Q14
Westgate on Sea Kent		13	R1
Westgate Street Norfk		51	L9
West Ginge	Oxon	29	U9
West Grafton	Wilts	18	K8
West Green	Hants	20	B11
West Grimstead Wilts		8	J3
West Grinstead W Susx		10	K6
West Haddlesey N York		57	S1
West Haddon	Nhants	37	R6
West Hagbourne Oxon		19	R3
West Hagley	Worcs	35	U4
West Hallam	Derbys	47	M5
West Hall	N Linc	58	C1
West Halton	N Linc	58	F2
Westham	Dorset	7	S8
West Ham	Gt Lon	21	Q6
Westham	E Susx	11	U10
Westham	Somset	17	M7
Westhampnett W Susx		10	D9
West Handley	Derbys	57	N11
West Hanney	Oxon	29	T9
West Hanningfield Essex		22	H8
West Harnham	Wilts	8	G3
West Harptree	BaNES	17	P5
West Hatch	Somset	16	J12
West Hatch	Wilts	8	C3
West Haven	Angus	91	T4
West Head	Norfk	49	S12
West Heath	Hants	19	S9
West Heath	Hants	20	C11
Westhide	Herefs	35	N12
West Helmsdale Highld		112	B3
West Hendred	Oxon	29	T9
West Heslerton N York		65	L4
Westhide	Herefs	35	N12
Westhill	Abers	99	N2
West Hill	Devon	6	E5
West Hill	N Som	17	L2
Westhope	Herefs	35	L10
Westhope	Shrops	35	L3
West Horndon	Essex	22	F10
Westhorp	Nhants	37	P10
Westhorpe	Lincs	49	L7
Westhorpe	Suffk	40	J8
West Horrington Somset		17	P7
West Horsley	Surrey	20	J12
West Horton	Nthumb	85	Q12
West Hougham	Kent	13	Q7
Westhoughton Bolton		55	Q5
Westhouse	N York	62	D5
Westhouses	Derbys	47	M2
West Howe	Bmouth	8	F9
West Howetown Somset		16	B9
Westhumble	Surrey	21	L12
West Huntingtower P & K		90	G7
West Huntspill Somset		16	K8
West Hyde	Herts	20	H4

Place	County	Page	Grid
West Hythe	Kent	13	M9
West Ilkerton	Devon	15	R3
West Ilsley	W Berk	19	Q4
West Itchenor W Susx		10	B10
West Keal	Lincs	59	Q14
West Kennett	Wilts	18	H7
West Kilbride	N Ayrs	80	J3
West Kingsdown Kent		21	U10
West Kington	Wilts	18	B5
West Kirby	Wirral	54	F9
West Knapton	N York	64	K5
West Knighton	Dorset	7	T7
West Knoyle	Wilts	8	B2
West Kyloe	Nthumb	85	R10
West Lambrook Somset		17	M13
Westland Green Herts		22	B3
West Langdon	Kent	13	R6
West Lavington	Wilts	18	F10
West Lavington W Susx		10	D6
West Layton	N York	69	P10
West Leake	Notts	47	P8
West Learmouth Nthumb		85	L11
West Lees	N York	70	G12
West Leigh	Devon	15	Q11
Westleigh	Devon	15	L6
Westleigh	Devon	16	E10
West Leigh	Somset	16	F10
Westleigh	Somset	16	F12
Westleton	Suffk	41	R7
West Lexham	Norfk	50	D10
Westley	Shrops	44	J12
Westley	Suffk	40	D8
Westley Waterless Cambs		39	T9
West Lilling	N York	64	E7
Westlington	Bucks	30	G10
West Linton	Border	83	N8
Westlinton	Cumb	75	R14
West Littleton	S Glos	28	E12
West Lockinge	Oxon	29	T9
West London Crematorium Gt Lon		21	M6
West Lulworth	Dorset	7	V8
West Lutton	N York	65	L5
West Lydford	Somset	17	Q10
West Lyn	Devon	15	R3
West Lyng	Somset	16	K11
West Lynn	Norfk	49	T10
West Malling	Kent	12	C4
West Malvern	Worcs	35	S11
West Marden	W Susx	10	B8
West Markham	Notts	58	B12
Westmarsh	Kent	13	Q3
West Marsh	NE Lin	59	N5
West Marton	N York	62	H9
West Melbury	Dorset	8	B4
West Melton	Rothm	57	P6
West Meon	Hants	9	S4
West Meon Hut	Hants	9	S3
West Meon Woodlands Hants		9	S3
West Mersea	Essex	23	P4
Westmeston	E Susx	11	N8
West Mickley	Nthumb	77	M13
West Midland Safari Park Worcs		35	T5
Westmill	Herts	31	T9
Westmill	Herts	31	U7
West Milton	Dorset	7	P5
West Minster	Kent	23	M13
Westminster Abbey & Palace Ct Lon		21	N7
West Molesey	Surrey	20	K9
West Monkton	Somset	16	J11
West Moors	Dorset	8	F8
West Morden	Dorset	8	C9
West Morriston Border		84	G10
West Morton	C Brad	63	M11
West Mudford	Somset	17	Q12
Westmuir	Angus	98	G13
West Ness	N York	64	F4
West Newbiggin Darltn		70	D9
West Newton	E R Yk	65	S12
West Newton	Norfk	49	U8
West Newton	Somset	16	J10
West Norwood Crematorium Gt Lon		21	P8
Westoe	S Tyne	77	T12
West Ogwell	Devon	5	U6
Weston	BaNES	17	T3
Weston	Ches E	45	R3
Weston	Ches W	55	N11
Weston	Devon	6	F4
Weston	Dorset	7	S10
Weston	Halton	55	M9
Weston	Hants	9	U4
Weston	Herts	31	S7
Weston	Lincs	49	L8
Weston	N York	63	P10
Weston	Nhants	37	Q11
Weston	Notts	58	B13
Weston	Shrops	34	K4
Weston	Shrops	44	J7
Weston	Shrops	45	P8
Weston	Staffs	46	B8
Weston	W Berk	19	N6
Weston Beggard Herefs		35	N12
Westonbirt	Gloucs	28	G10
Weston by Welland Nhants		37	U2
Weston Colley	Hants	19	R13
Weston Colville Cambs		39	T10
Weston Corbett	Hants	19	U11
Weston Covey	C Stoke	45	U5
Weston Favell	Nhants	37	U8
Weston Green	Cambs	39	S10
Weston Heath	Shrops	45	S11
Weston Hills	Lincs	49	L9
Weston in Arden Warwks		37	L3
Westoning	C Beds	31	N6
Weston-in-Gordano N Som		27	N13
Westoning Woodend C Beds		31	N6
Weston Jones	Staffs	45	R9
Weston Longville Norfk		50	K10
Weston Lullingfields Shrops		44	K9
Weston Mill Crematorium C Plym		4	K9
Weston-on-Avon Warwks		36	G10
Weston-on-the-Green Oxon		30	B9
Weston Park	Staffs	45	T11
Weston Patrick	Hants	19	U11
Weston Rhyn	Shrops	44	G6
Weston-sub-Edge Gloucs		36	F12
Weston-super-Mare N Som		16	K4
Weston-super-Mare Crematorium N Som		17	L4
Weston Turville	Bucks	30	J10
Weston-under-Lizard Staffs		45	T11
Weston under Penyard Herefs		28	B3
Weston-under-Redcastle Shrops		45	N8
Weston under Wetherley Warwks		37	L7
Weston Underwood Derbys		46	J5
Weston Underwood M Keyn		38	C10
Westonzoyland Somset		17	L10
West Orchard	Dorset	17	V13
West Overton	Wilts	18	H7
West Panson	Devon	4	J2
West Park	Abers	99	M4
West Parley	Dorset	8	F9
West Peckham	Kent	12	B5
West Peeke	Devon	4	J2
West Pelton	Dur	69	R2
West Pennard	Somset	17	P9
West Pentire	Cnwll	2	K4
West Perry	Cambs	38	H7
West Porlock	Somset	15	U3
Westport	Somset	17	L12
West Pulham	Dorset	7	T3
West Putford	Devon	14	J9
West Quantoxhead Somset		16	F8
West Raddon	Devon	15	U11
West Rainton	Dur	70	D3
West Rasen	Lincs	58	J9
West Ravendale NE Lin		59	M7
Westray	Ork	106	t15
Westray Airport Ork		106	t14
West Raynham	Norfk	50	E8
West Retford	Notts	57	U10
Westridge Green W Berk		19	S5
Westrigg	W Loth	82	H5
West Road Crematorium N u Ty		77	Q12
Westrop	Swindn	29	P9
West Rounton	N York	70	F11
West Row	Suffk	39	U5
West Rudham	Norfk	50	D8
West Runton	Norfk	51	L5
Westruther	Border	84	F9
Westry	Cambs	49	N14
West Saltoun	E Loth	84	D5
West Sandford	Devon	15	T11
West Sandwick Shet		106	u5
West Scrafton	N York	63	M3

Place	County	Page	Grid
West Sleekburn Nthumb		77	R9
West Somerton	Norfk	51	S9
West Stafford	Dorset	7	T7
West Stockwith Notts		58	C7
West Stoke	W Susx	10	C9
West Stonesdale N York		68	J12
West Stoughton Somset		17	M7
West Stour	Dorset	17	U12
West Stourmouth Kent		13	Q3
West Stow	Suffk	40	D6
West Stowell	Wilts	18	H8
West Stratton	Hants	19	R12
West Street	Kent	12	H5
West Street	Kent	13	L3
West Street	Medway	22	H12
West Street	Suffk	40	G6
West Suffolk Crematorium Suffk		40	D7
West Tanfield	N York	63	R4
West Taphouse	Cnwll	4	E8
West Tarbert	Ag & B	87	Q12
West Tarring	W Susx	10	J10
West Thirston	Nthumb	77	P6
West Thorney	W Susx	10	B10
Westthorpe	Derbys	57	Q11
West Thurrock	Thurr	22	E12
West Tilbury	Thurr	22	G12
West Tisted	Hants	9	T3
West Torrington Lincs		58	K10
West Town	BaNES	17	P4
West Town	Hants	9	U9
West Town	Herefs	34	K8
West Town	N Som	17	N3
West Town	Somset	17	P8
West Town	Somset	17	T8
West Tytherley	Hants	8	K3
West Walton	Norfk	49	Q11
West Walton Highway Norfk		49	Q11
Westward	Cumb	66	K3
Westward Ho!	Devon	14	J6
Westwell	Kent	12	J6
Westwell	Oxon	29	Q6
Westwell Leacon Kent		12	J6
West Wellow	Hants	8	K5
West Wembury	Devon	5	N11
West Wemyss	Fife	91	P7
Westwick	Cambs	39	P8
Westwick	Dur	69	N9
West Wick	N Som	17	L4
West Wickham	Cambs	39	T11
West Wickham	Gt Lon	21	Q9
West Williamston Pembks		24	H9
West Winch	Norfk	49	U10
West Winterslow	Wilts	8	J2
West Wittering W Susx		10	B11
West Witton	N York	63	M2
Westwood	Devon	6	D5
Westwood	Kent	13	S2
Westwood	Nthumb	76	H13
Westwood	Notts	47	N3
Westwood	Wilts	18	B9
West Woodburn Nthumb		76	J8
West Woodhay W Berk		19	N8
West Woodlands Somset		17	U8
Westwoodside N Linc		58	C6
West Worldham Hants		9	U3
West Worthing W Susx		10	J10
West Wratting Cambs		39	T10
West Wycombe Bucks		20	D4
West Wylam	Nthumb	77	N13
West Yatton	Wilts	18	B6
West Yoke	Kent	22	C10
West Youlstone	Cnwll	14	F9
Wetham Green	Kent	12	F2
Wetheral	Cumb	67	Q2
Wetherby	Leeds	63	U10
Wetherby Services N York		63	U9
Wetherden	Suffk	40	H8
Wetheringsett Suffk		40	K7
Wethersfield Essex		22	H1
Wetherup Street Suffk		40	K8
Wetley Rocks	Staffs	46	C4
Wettenhall	Ches E	45	P1
Wetton	Staffs	46	F2
Wetwang	E R Yk	65	L8
Wetwood	Staffs	45	S7
Wexcombe	Wilts	19	L9
Wexham Slough	Bucks	20	G6
Wexham Street Bucks		20	G6
Weybourne	Norfk	50	K5
Weybourne	Surrey	20	E13
Weybread	Suffk	41	M5
Weybread Street Suffk		41	M5
Weybridge	Surrey	20	J10
Weycroft	Devon	6	K5
Weydale	Highld	112	E4
Weyhill	Hants	19	M11
Weymouth	Dorset	7	S9
Weymouth Crematorium Dorset		7	S9
Whaddon	Bucks	30	H6
Whaddon	Cambs	39	N11
Whaddon	Gloucs	28	G5
Whaddon	Wilts	8	H3
Whaddon	Wilts	18	C8
Whaley	Derbys	57	R12
Whaley Bridge Derbys		56	F10
Whaley Thorns Derbys		57	R12
Whaligoe	Highld	112	H8
Whalley	Lancs	62	E12
Whalley Banks Lancs		62	E13
Whalsay	Shet	106	v7
Whalton	Nthumb	77	N9
Whaplode	Lincs	49	M9
Whaplode Drove Lincs		49	M10
Whaplode St Catherine Lincs		49	M10
Wharf	Warwks	37	N9
Wharfe	N York	62	F6
Wharles	Lancs	61	S12
Wharley End	C Beds	38	D11
Wharncliffe Side Sheff		57	L7
Wharram-le-Street N York		64	K6
Wharton	Ches W	55	Q14
Wharton	Herefs	35	M9
Whashton	N York	69	Q11
Whasset	Cumb	61	U3
Whatcote	Warwks	36	K12
Whateley	Warwks	46	H14
Whatfield	Suffk	40	H11
Whatley	Somset	7	L2
Whatley	Somset	17	T7
Whatley's End S Glos		28	C11
Whatlington E Susx		12	E12
Whatsole Street Kent		13	M7
Whatstandwell Derbys		46	K2
Whatton	Notts	47	T6
Whauphill	D & G	73	L9
Whaw	N York	69	L12
Wheal Peevor Cnwll		2	J8
Wheal Rose	Cnwll	2	J8
Wheatacre	Norfk	41	S2
Wheatfield	Oxon	19	U2
Wheathampstead Herts		31	Q10
Wheathill	Shrops	35	P4
Wheathill	Somset	17	Q10
Wheatley	Hants	9	U2
Wheatley	Oxon	30	C11
Wheatley Hill	Dur	70	E5
Wheatley Hills	Donc	57	S5
Wheatley Lane	Lancs	62	G12
Wheaton Aston Staffs		45	T11
Wheddon Cross Somset		16	B9
Wheelbarrow Town Kent		13	M7
Wheeler End	Bucks	20	D4
Wheeler's Green Wokham		20	C8
Wheelerstreet Surrey		10	F2
Wheelock	Ches E	45	S2
Wheelock Heath Ches E		45	S2
Wheelton	Lancs	55	P2
Wheldale	Wakefd	57	P1
Wheldrake	C York	64	F11
Whelford	Gloucs	29	N8
Whelpley Hill Bucks		30	K12
Whelpo	Cumb	67	L4
Whelston	Flints	54	G11
Whempstead Herts		31	T9
Whenby	N York	64	E6
Whepstead	Suffk	40	D9
Wherstead	Suffk	41	L12
Wherwell	Hants	19	N12
Wheston	Derbys	56	H12
Whetsted	Kent	12	C6
Whetstone	Gt Lon	21	N4
Whetstone	Leics	47	Q13
Wheyrigg	Cumb	66	J2
Whicham	Cumb	61	L3
Whichford	Warwks	36	K13
Whickham	Gatesd	77	Q13
Whiddon	Devon	14	K10
Whiddon Down Devon		5	R2
Whight's Corner Suffk		40	K12
Whigstreet	Angus	91	Q3
Whilton	Nhants	37	R8
Whimble	Devon	14	J11
Whimple	Devon	6	E5
Whimpwell Green Norfk		51	Q7
Whinburgh	Norfk	50	H12
Whin Lane End Lancs		61	R11

Place	County	Page	Grid
Whinnie Liggate D & G		73	S9
Whinnow	Cumb	67	M2
Whinnyfold	Abers	105	T9
Whinny Hill	S on T	70	E9
Whippingham	IoW	9	Q10
Whipsnade	C Beds	31	M9
Whipsnade Zoo ZSL C Beds		31	M9
Whipton	Devon	6	B6
Whirlow	Sheff	57	M10
Whisby	Lincs	58	F13
Whissendine Rutlnd		48	B10
Whissonsett Norfk		50	F9
Whistlefield	Ag & B	88	F7
Whistlefield Inn Ag & B		88	F7
Whistley Green Wokham		20	C8
Whiston	Knows	55	L8
Whiston	Nhants	38	B8
Whiston	Rothm	57	P9
Whiston	Staffs	45	T10
Whiston	Staffs	46	D4
Whiston Cross Shrops		45	S13
Whiston Eaves Staffs		46	D4
Whitacre Fields Warwks		36	H2
Whitbeck	Cumb	61	L3
Whitbourne	Herefs	35	R9
Whitburn	S Tyne	77	U13
Whitburn	W Loth	82	H6
Whitby	Ches W	54	J11
Whitby	N York	71	Q10
Whitbyheath Ches W		54	J12
Whitchester Border		84	J7
Whitchurch	BaNES	17	R4
Whitchurch	Bucks	30	H8
Whitchurch	Cardif	27	M12
Whitchurch	Devon	5	M6
Whitchurch	Hants	19	Q11
Whitchurch	Herefs	27	V4
Whitchurch	Oxon	19	T5
Whitchurch	Pembks	24	D5
Whitchurch	Shrops	45	M5
Whitchurch Canonicorum Dorset		7	L5
Whitchurch Hill Oxon		19	T5
Whitcombe	Dorset	7	T7
Whitcot	Shrops	34	J2
Whitcott Keysett Shrops		34	G4
Whiteacre	Kent	13	M6
Whiteacre Heath Warwks		36	H2
Whiteash Green Essex		22	H2
Whitebirk	Bl w D	62	E14
Whitebridge	Highld	102	D12
Whitebrook	Mons	27	U6
Whitecairns	Abers	105	Q12
Whitechapel Lancs		61	U11
White Chapel Lancs		61	U11
Whitechurch Pembks		25	L3
White Colne	Essex	22	K2
White Coppice Lancs		55	P3
Whitecraig	E Loth	83	S4
Whitecroft	Gloucs	28	B6
Whitecross	Cnwll	2	E10
Whitecross	Cnwll	3	P2
White Cross	Cnwll	2	H12
Whitecross	Falk	82	H3
White Cross	Wilts	35	S14
Whiteface	Highld	109	N7
Whitefarland N Ayrs		79	R7
Whitefaulds S Ayrs		80	J10
Whitefield	Bury	55	T5
Whitefield	Devon	15	Q6
Whitefield	Somset	16	C10
Whitefield Lane End Knows		55	L9
Whiteford	Abers	105	L10
Whitegate	Ches W	55	P13
Whitehall	Hants	20	B12
Whitehall	W Susx	10	J6
Whitehaven	Cumb	66	E9
Whitehill	Hants	10	B4
Whitehill	Kent	12	K4
Whitehills	Abers	104	K2
Whitehouse	Abers	104	J13
Whitehouse	Ag & B	79	Q3
Whitehouse Common Birm		36	F1
Whitekirk	E Loth	84	F2
White Kirkley Dur		69	L5
White Lackington Dorset		7	T5
Whitelackington Somset		17	L13
White Ladies Aston Worcs		36	B10
Whiteleaf	Bucks	30	H12
White-le-Head Dur		69	Q2
White Mill	Carmth	25	R6
Whitemire	Moray	103	Q5
Whitemoor	Cnwll	3	N5
Whitemoor	Derbys	47	L4
Whitemoor	Notts	47	Q5
Whitemoor	Staffs	45	T2
Whitenap	Hants	9	L3
White Notley Essex		22	J5
Whiteoak Green Oxon		29	S5
Whiteparish	Wilts	8	J3
White Pit	Lincs	59	Q11
Whiterashes	Abers	105	P11
White Roding Essex		22	D5
Whiterow	Highld	112	J7
Whiterow	Moray	103	R4
Whiteshill	Gloucs	28	G6
Whitesmith	E Susx	11	S8
White Stake	Lancs	55	M1
Whitestaunton Somset		16	H13
Whitestone	Devon	5	U2
Whitestone Cross Devon		5	V3
Whitestreet Green Suffk		40	G13
Whitewall Corner N York		64	G5
White Waltham W & M		20	D7
Whiteway	BaNES	17	T4
Whiteway	Gloucs	28	H5
Whitewell	Lancs	62	D11
Whitewell Bottom Lancs		55	U2
Whitfield	C Dund	91	Q5
Whitfield	Herefs	34	K14
Whitfield	Kent	13	Q6
Whitfield	Nhants	30	D6
Whitfield	Nthumb	76	E14
Whitfield	S Glos	28	C9
Whitfield Hall Nthumb		68	E1
Whitford	Devon	6	J5
Whitford	Flints	54	D11
Whitgift	E R Yk	58	D2
Whitgreave	Staffs	46	A8
Whithorn	D & G	73	L10
Whiting Bay	N Ayrs	80	E7
Whitkirk	Leeds	63	T13
Whitland	Carmth	25	M7
Whitlaw	Border	75	U3
Whitletts	S Ayrs	81	L8
Whitley	N York	57	S2
Whitley	Readg	20	B8
Whitley	Sheff	57	M8
Whitley	Wilts	18	C7
Whitley Bay N Tyne		77	T11
Whitley Chapel Nthumb		76	J14
Whitley Heath Staffs		45	T9
Whitley Lower Kirk		56	K3
Whitley Row Kent		21	S12
Whitlock's End Solhll		36	F5
Whitminster Gloucs		28	E6
Whitmore	Dorset	8	F8
Whitmore	Staffs	45	T5
Whitnage	Devon	16	D12
Whitnash	Warwks	36	K8
Whitney-on-Wye Herefs		34	G11
Whitrigg	Cumb	66	K1
Whitrigg	Cumb	67	L3
Whitsbury	Hants	8	G5
Whitsome	Border	85	L8
Whitson	Newpt	27	P11
Whitstable	Kent	13	M2
Whitstone	Cnwll	14	G13
Whittingham Nthumb		77	L3
Whittingslow Shrops		34	K3
Whittington	Derbys	57	N12
Whittington	Gloucs	28	K3
Whittington	Lancs	62	C5
Whittington	Norfk	50	B14
Whittington	Shrops	44	H7
Whittington	Staffs	35	T4
Whittington	Staffs	46	G12
Whittington	Warwks	36	H2
Whittington	Worcs	35	U10
Whittington Moor Derbys		57	N12
Whittlebury Nhants		37	R11
Whittle-le-Woods Lancs		55	N2
Whittlesey	Cambs	49	L13
Whittlesford Cambs		39	Q11
Whittlestone Head Bl w D		55	S3
Whitton	N Linc	58	G1
Whitton	Nthumb	77	M6
Whitton	Powys	34	G8
Whitton	S on T	70	F8
Whitton	Shrops	35	M6
Whitton	Suffk	40	K11
Whittonditch Wilts		19	L6
Whittonstall Nthumb		69	M2

Place	County	Page	Grid
Whitway	Hants	19	Q9
Whitwell	Derbys	57	R11
Whitwell	Herts	31	Q8
Whitwell	IoW	9	Q13
Whitwell	N York	69	S12
Whitwell	Rutlnd	48	D12
Whitwell Street Norfk		50	K9
Whitwick	Leics	47	M10
Whitwood	Wakefd	57	P2
Whitworth	Lancs	56	C4
Whixall	Shrops	45	M6
Whixley	N York	63	U8
Whorlton	Dur	69	P9
Whorlton	N York	70	F11
Whyle	Herefs	35	N8
Whyteleafe	Surrey	21	P11
Wibdon	Gloucs	27	V8
Wibsey	C Brad	63	N13
Wibtoft	Warwks	37	N3
Wichenford	Worcs	35	S8
Wichling	Kent	12	H4
Wick	Bmouth	8	G10
Wick	Devon	6	G4
Wick	Highld	112	J6
Wick	S Glos	28	D13
Wick	Somset	16	H8
Wick	Somset	17	N7
Wick	V Glam	26	G12
Wick	W Susx	10	G10
Wick	Wilts	8	H4
Wick	Worcs	36	C11
Wicken	Cambs	39	S6
Wicken	Nhants	30	F5
Wicken Bonhunt Essex		39	Q14
Wickenby	Lincs	58	J10
Wick End	Bed	38	E10
Wicken Green Village Norfk		50	E7
Wickersley	Rothm	57	Q8
Wicker Street Green Suffk		40	G12
Wickford	Essex	22	H9
Wickham	Hants	9	Q6
Wickham	W Berk	19	N6
Wickham Bishops Essex		22	K5
Wickhambreaux Kent		13	N4
Wickhambrook Suffk		40	B10
Wickhamford Worcs		36	E12
Wickham Green Suffk		40	J7
Wickham Green W Berk		19	P6
Wickham Heath W Berk		19	P7
Wickham Market Suffk		41	N9
Wickhampton Norfk		51	R12
Wickham St Paul Essex		40	C13
Wickham Skeith Suffk		40	J7
Wickham Street Suffk		40	C10
Wick John o' Groats Airport Highld		112	J6
Wicklewood Norfk		50	J12
Wickmere	Norfk	51	L7
Wick St Lawrence N Som		17	L3
Wickstreet	E Susx	11	S8
Wickwar	S Glos	28	D10
Widdington Essex		22	D1
Widdop	Calder	62	J13
Widdrington Nthumb		77	R7
Widdrington Station Nthumb		77	R6
Widecombe in the Moor Devon		5	S5
Widegates	Cnwll	4	H9
Widemouth Bay Cnwll		14	F12
Wide Open	N u Ty	77	Q11
Widford	Essex	22	G6
Widford	Herts	22	B4
Widford	Oxon	29	P5
Widham	Wilts	29	L10
Widley	Hants	9	T7
Widmer End	Bucks	20	E3
Widmerpool Notts		47	R8
Widmore	Gt Lon	21	R9
Widnes	Halton	55	M10
Widworthy	Devon	6	H5
Wigan	Wigan	55	N6
Wigan Crematorium Wigan		55	N6
Wiganthorpe N York		64	E5
Wigborough Somset		17	M13
Wiggaton	Devon	6	F6
Wiggenhall St Germans Norfk		49	S11
Wiggenhall St Mary Magdalen Norfk		49	S11
Wiggenhall St Mary the Virgin Norfk		49	S11
Wiggens Green Essex		39	U12
Wiggenstall	Staffs	56	F14
Wigginton	Herts	30	K10
Wigginton	Oxon	37	L14
Wigginton	Staffs	46	H12
Wigginton	York	64	E8
Wigginton Bottom Herts		30	K11
Wigglesworth N York		62	G8
Wiggonby	Cumb	67	L2
Wiggonholt W Susx		10	H7
Wighill	N York	64	B10
Wighton	Norfk	50	F6
Wightwick	Wolves	45	U14
Wigley	Derbys	57	M12
Wigley	Hants	9	L5
Wigmore	Herefs	34	K7
Wigmore	Medway	12	E3
Wigsley	Notts	58	D12
Wigsthorpe Nhants		38	F4
Wigston	Leics	47	R13
Wigston Fields Leics		47	R13
Wigston Parva Leics		37	N3
Wigtoft	Lincs	49	L6
Wigton	Cumb	67	L3
Wigtown	D & G	73	L8
Wigwig	Shrops	45	N13
Wike	Leeds	63	S11
Wilbarston Nhants		38	B3
Wilberfoss E R Yk		64	G9
Wilburton	Cambs	39	Q5
Wilby	Nhants	38	C7
Wilby	Norfk	40	H3
Wilby	Suffk	41	M6
Wilcot	Wilts	18	H8
Wilcott	Shrops	44	J10
Wilcrick	Newpt	27	R10
Wilday Green Derbys		57	M12
Wildboarclough Ches E		56	F13
Wilden	Bed	38	F9
Wilden	Worcs	35	T6
Wilde Street Suffk		40	B5
Wildhern	Hants	19	N10
Wildhill	Herts	31	S11
Wildmanbridge S Lans		82	F7
Wildmill	Brdgnd	26	J11
Wildmoor	Worcs	36	B6
Wildsworth Lincs		58	D7
Wilford	C Nott	47	Q6
Wilkesley	Ches E	45	P5
Wilkhaven	Highld	109	T7
Wilkieston W Loth		83	M5
Wilksby	Lincs	59	N14
Willand	Devon	6	D2
Willards Hill E Susx		12	D11
Willaston	Ches E	45	Q3
Willaston	Ches W	54	H11
Willen	M Keyn	38	C11
Willenhall	Covtry	37	L4
Willenhall	Wsall	46	C14
Willerby	E R Yk	65	N13
Willerby	N York	65	N4
Willersey	Gloucs	36	F13
Willersley	Herefs	34	H11
Willesborough Kent		13	L7
Willesborough Lees Kent		13	L7
Willesden	Gt Lon	21	M6
Willesleigh	Devon	15	N6
Willesley	Wilts	28	G10
Willett	Somset	16	F10
Willey	Shrops	45	Q14
Willey	Warwks	37	N4
Willey Green Surrey		20	F12
Williamscot Oxon		37	M11
Williamstown Rhondd		26	J9
Willian	Herts	31	R6
Willicote	Warwks	36	G11
Willingale	Essex	22	E6
Willingdon	E Susx	11	T10
Willingham	Cambs	39	P6
Willingham by Stow Lincs		58	E10
Willingham Green Cambs		39	T10
Willington	Bed	38	H10
Willington	Derbys	46	J8
Willington	Dur	69	Q5
Willington	Kent	12	E5
Willington	N Tyne	77	S12
Willington	Warwks	36	J13
Willington Corner Ches W		55	M13
Willitoft	E R Yk	64	H13
Williton	Somset	16	F8
Willoughbridge Staffs		45	R6
Willoughby	Lincs	59	S12
Willoughby	Warwks	37	P7
Willoughby Hills Lincs		49	M3
Willoughby-on-the-Wolds Notts		47	R8
Willoughby Waterleys Leics		37	Q2
Willoughton Lincs		58	F8
Willow Green Ches W		55	P11
Willows Green Essex		22	H4

Place	County	Page	Grid
Willows Green	Essex	22	H4
Willsbridge	S Glos	28	S2
Willsworthy	Devon	5	N4
Willtown	Somset	17	L12
Wilmcote	Warwks	36	G9
Wilmington	BaNES	17	S4
Wilmington	Devon	6	H5
Wilmington	E Susx	11	T10
Wilmington	Kent	22	D13
Wilminstone Devon		5	N5
Wilmslow	Ches E	55	T10
Wilnecote	Staffs	46	H13
Wilpshire	Lancs	62	E13
Wilsden	C Brad	63	M13
Wilsford	Lincs	48	F5
Wilsford	Wilts	18	H11
Wilsford	Wilts	18	H9
Wilsham	Devon	15	S3
Wilshaw	Kirk	56	H5
Wilsill	N York	63	P7
Wilsley Green Kent		12	E8
Wilsley Pound Kent		12	E8
Wilson	Herefs	27	V3
Wilson	Leics	47	M9
Wilsontown S Lans		82	J7
Wilstead	Bed	31	N4
Wilsthorpe	Lincs	48	G11
Wilstone	Herts	30	K10
Wilstone Green Herts		30	K10
Wilton	Herefs	28	A3
Wilton	N York	65	L3
Wilton	R & Cl	70	J8
Wilton	Wilts	8	F2
Wilton	Wilts	18	K9
Wilton Dean Border		75	U3
Wimbish	Essex	39	S13
Wimbish Green Essex		39	T13
Wimblebury Staffs		46	D11
Wimbledon Gt Lon		21	M8
Wimblington Cambs		39	P2
Wimboldsley Ches W		45	Q1
Wimborne Minster Dorset		8	E9
Wimborne St Giles Dorset		8	E6
Wimbotsham Norfk		49	S13
Wimpole Cambs		39	M11
Wimpstone Warwks		36	H11
Wincanton	Somset	17	T11
Wincby	Lincs	59	N13
Wincham	Ches W	55	Q11
Winchburgh W Loth		83	L4
Winchcombe Gloucs		28	K2
Winchelsea	E Susx	12	H12
Winchelsea Beach E Susx		12	H12
Winchester Hants		9	P3
Winchester Services Hants		19	R13
Winchet Hill Kent		12	D7
Winchfield Hants		20	C12
Winchmore Hill Bucks		20	F3
Winchmore Hill Gt Lon		21	P4
Wincle	Ches E	56	E13
Wincobank	Sheff	57	N8
Winder	Cumb	66	G10
Windermere Cumb		67	P13
Windermere Steamboats & Museum Cumb		67	P13
Winderton	Warwks	36	K12
Windhill	Highld	102	G6
Windlehurst Stockp		56	E9
Windlesham Surrey		20	F10
Windmill	Cnwll	3	M2
Windmill	Derbys	56	J11
Windmill Hill E Susx		11	U9
Windmill Hill Somset		16	K13
Windrush	Gloucs	29	N5
Windsole	Abers	104	G4
Windsor	W & M	20	G7
Windsor Castle W & M		20	G7
Windsoredge Gloucs		28	G7
Windygates	Fife	91	M11
Windyharbour Ches E		55	T12
Windy Hill Wrexhm		44	H3
Wineham	W Susx	11	L6
Winestead	E R Yk	59	N2
Winewall	Lancs	62	J11
Winfarthing Norfk		40	K3
Winford	IoW	9	R12
Winford	N Som	17	P4
Winforton Herefs		34	G11
Winfrith Newburgh Dorset		7	V8
Wing	Bucks	30	J8
Wing	Rutlnd	48	C12
Wingate	Dur	70	F5
Wingates	Bolton	55	P5
Wingates	Nthumb	77	M6
Wingerworth Derbys		57	N13
Wingfield	C Beds	31	M7
Wingfield	Suffk	41	M5
Wingfield	Wilts	18	B9
Wingfield Green Suffk		41	M5
Wingham	Kent	13	P4
Wingland	Lincs	49	R9
Wingmore	Kent	13	N6
Wingrave	Bucks	30	J9
Winkburn	Notts	47	U1
Winkfield	Br For	20	F8
Winkfield Row Br For		20	E8
Winkhill	Staffs	46	D3
Winkhurst Green Kent		21	S13
Winkleigh	Devon	15	P11
Winksley	N York	63	R5
Winkton	Dorset	8	H9
Winlaton	Gatesd	77	P13
Winlaton Mill Gatesd		77	P14
Winless	Highld	112	H6
Winllan	Powys	44	F8
Winmarleigh Lancs		61	T10
Winnall	Hants	9	P3
Winnersh	Wokham	20	C8
Winnington Ches W		55	P12
Winscales	Cumb	66	F7
Winscombe N Som		17	M5
Winsford	Ches W	55	P14
Winsford	Somset	16	B10
Winsham	Devon	15	M5
Winsham	Somset	7	L3
Winshill	Staffs	46	J9
Winshwen	Swans	26	B8
Winskill	Cumb	67	S6
Winslade	Hants	19	U11
Winsley	Wilts	18	B8
Winslow	Bucks	30	G7
Winson	Gloucs	29	L6
Winsor	Hants	9	L6
Winster	Cumb	67	P13
Winster	Derbys	46	J1
Winston	Dur	69	P9
Winston	Suffk	41	L8
Winstone	Gloucs	28	J6
Winswell	Devon	15	L10
Winterborne Came Dorset		7	T7
Winterborne Clenston Dorset		8	B8
Winterborne Herringston Dorset		7	S7
Winterborne Houghton Dorset		8	B8
Winterborne Kingston Dorset		8	B9
Winterborne Monkton Dorset		7	S7
Winterborne Stickland Dorset		8	B8
Winterborne Tomson Dorset		8	B9
Winterborne Whitechurch Dorset		8	B9
Winterborne Zelston Dorset		8	C9
Winterbourne S Glos		28	B11
Winterbourne W Berk		19	Q6
Winterbourne Abbas Dorset		7	R6
Winterbourne Bassett Wilts		18	H6
Winterbourne Dauntsey Wilts		8	H2
Winterbourne Earls Wilts		8	H2
Winterbourne Gunner Wilts		8	H2
Winterbourne Monkton Wilts		18	G6
Winterbourne Steepleton Dorset		7	R7
Winterbourne Stoke Wilts		18	G12
Winterbrook	Oxon	19	T3
Winterburn	N York	62	J8
Winteringham N Linc		58	F2
Winterley	Ches E	45	S2
Wintersett	Wakefd	57	N3
Wintershill	Hants	9	Q5
Winterton	N Linc	58	F3
Winterton-on-Sea Norfk		51	T10
Winthorpe	Lincs	59	U13
Winthorpe	Notts	48	B2
Winton	Bmouth	8	F10
Winton	Cumb	68	F10
Winton	E Susx	11	S10
Winton	N York	70	F12
Wintringham N York		64	K5
Winwick	Cambs	38	H4
Winwick	Nhants	37	R5
Winwick	Warrtn	55	P8
Wirksworth Derbys		46	J3
Wirral		54	G10
Wirswall	Ches E	45	M5
Wisbech	Cambs	49	Q12
Wisbech St Mary Cambs		49	P12

Wisborough Green W Susx ...10 H5
Wiseman's Bridge Pembks ...24 K9
Wiston Notts ...58 B9
Wishanger Gloucs ...28 H6
Wishaw N Lans ...82 E7
Wishaw Warwks ...36 G2
Wisley Surrey ...20 J11
Wisley Garden RHS Surrey ...20 J11
Wispington Lincs ...59 M12
Wissenden Kent ...12 H7
Wissett Suffk ...41 Q5
Wissington Norfk ...49 U14
Wistanstow Shrops ...40 G14
Wistanswick Shrops ...34 K3
Wistaston Ches E ...45 Q8
Wistaston Green Ches E ...45 Q3
Wisterfield Ches E ...55 T12
Wiston Pembks ...24 H7
Wiston S Lans ...82 J12
Wiston W Susx ...10 J8
Wistow Cambs ...38 L4
Wistow Leics ...37 R1
Wistow N York ...64 D12
Wiswell Lancs ...62 E12
Witcham Cambs ...39 Q4
Witchampton Dorset ...8 D7
Witcombe Somset ...17 N12
Witham Essex ...22 K5
Witham Friary Somset ...17 T8
Witham on the Hill Lincs ...48 G10
Witham St Hughs Lincs ...48 C1
Withcall Lincs ...59 N10
Withdean Br & H ...11 N9
Witherenden Hill E Susx ...12 B10
Witheridge Devon ...15 T10
Witherley Leics ...36 K1
Withern Lincs ...59 R10
Withernsea E R Yk ...65 U14
Withernwick E R Yk ...65 R11
Withersdale Street Suffk ...41 N4
Withersfield Suffk ...39 U11
Witherslack Cumb ...61 S3
Withiel Cnwll ...3 P3
Withiel Florey Somset ...16 C10
Withielgoose Cnwll ...3 Q3
Withington Gloucs ...28 K4
Withington Herefs ...35 N12
Withington Manch ...55 T8
Withington Shrops ...45 N11
Withington Staffs ...46 D6
Withington Green Ches E ...55 T12
Withington Marsh Herefs ...35 N12
Withleigh Devon ...6 B2
Withnell Lancs ...55 P2
Withybed Green Worcs ...36 D6
Withybrook Warwks ...37 M4
Withycombe Somset ...16 D8
Withypham E Susx ...11 R3
Withy Mills BaNES ...17 S5
Withypool Somset ...15 T5
Withywood Bristl ...17 Q3
Witley Surrey ...10 E3
Witnesham Suffk ...41 L10
Witney Oxon ...29 S5
Wittering C Pete ...48 G13
Wittersham Kent ...12 H10
Witton Birm ...36 E2
Witton Norfk ...51 P12
Witton Norfk ...51 P7
Witton Gilbert Dur ...69 R3
Witton Green Norfk ...51 R13
Witton le Wear Dur ...69 P6
Witton Park Dur ...69 Q6
Wiveliscombe Somset ...16 E11
Wivelrod Hants ...19 U13
Wivelsfield E Susx ...11 N7
Wivelsfield Green E Susx ...11 P7
Wivelsfield Station W Susx ...11 N7
Wivenhoe Essex ...23 P3
Wivenhoe Cross Essex ...23 N3
Wiveton Norfk ...50 H5
Wix Essex ...23 S2
Wixford Warwks ...36 E10
Wix Green Essex ...23 S2
Wixhill Shrops ...45 N8
Wixoe Suffk ...40 B12
Woburn C Beds ...31 L6
Woburn Abbey C Beds ...31 L6
Woburn Sands M Keyn ...30 K5
Wokefield Park W Berk ...19 U7
Woking Surrey ...20 H11
Woking Crematorium Surrey ...20 G11
Wokingham Wokham ...20 D9
Wolborough Devon ...5 U6
Woldingham Surrey ...21 Q11
Wold Newton E R Yk ...65 N5
Wold Newton NE Lin ...59 M7
Wolfclyde S Lans ...82 K11
Wolferlow Herefs ...35 Q8

Wolferton Norfk ...49 U8
Wolfhampcote Warwks ...37 P7
Wolfhill P & K ...90 J5
Wolf Hills Nthumb ...76 E14
Wolf's Castle Pembks ...24 G5
Wolfsdale Pembks ...24 F6
Wollaston Dudley ...35 U4
Wollaston Nhants ...38 D8
Wollaston Shrops ...44 H11
Wollaton C Nott ...47 P6
Wollerton Shrops ...45 P7
Wollescote Dudley ...36 B4
Wolseley Bridge Staffs ...46 C9
Wolsingham Dur ...69 N5
Wolstanton Staffs ...45 U4
Wolsholme Rochdl ...55 T4
Wolston Warwks ...37 M5
Wolsty Cumb ...66 H2
Wolvercote Oxon ...29 U5
Wolverhampton Wolves ...46 B14
Wolverhampton Halfpenny Green Airport Staffs ...35 T2
Wolverley Shrops ...45 L7
Wolverley Worcs ...35 T5
Wolverton Hants ...19 S9
Wolverton Kent ...13 Q7
Wolverton M Keyn ...30 H4
Wolverton Warwks ...36 H8
Wolverton Wilts ...17 U10
Wolverton Common Hants ...19 S9
Wolvesnewton Mons ...27 T8
Wolvey Warwks ...37 M3
Wolvey Heath Warwks ...37 M3
Wolviston Dur ...70 G7
Wombleton N York ...64 F3
Wombourne Staffs ...35 U2
Wombwell Barns ...57 N5
Womenswold Kent ...13 P5
Womersley N York ...57 R3
Wonastow Mons ...27 T5
Wonersh Surrey ...20 H13
Wonford Devon ...6 B6
Wonson Devon ...5 R3
Wonston Dorset ...7 T3
Wonston Hants ...19 Q13
Wooburn Bucks ...20 F5
Wooburn Green Bucks ...20 F5
Wooburn Moor Bucks ...20 F5
Woodacott Devon ...14 J11
Woodall Rothm ...57 Q10
Woodall Services Rothm ...57 Q10
Woodbank Ches W ...54 J12
Woodbastwick Norfk ...51 P10
Woodbeck Notts ...58 C11
Wood Bevington Warwks ...36 E10
Woodborough Notts ...47 R4
Woodborough Wilts ...18 H9
Woodbridge Devon ...6 G5
Woodbridge Dorset ...8 B5
Woodbridge Suffk ...41 N11
Wood Burcote Nhants ...37 S11
Woodbury Devon ...6 D7
Woodbury Salterton Devon ...6 D7
Woodchester Gloucs ...28 F7
Woodchurch Kent ...12 H9
Woodchurch Wirral ...54 G9
Woodcombe Somset ...16 C7
Woodcote Oxon ...19 T4
Woodcote Wrekin ...45 S10
Woodcote Green Worcs ...36 B6
Woodcott Hants ...19 P10
Woodcroft Gloucs ...27 U8
Woodcutts Dorset ...8 D6
Wood Dalling Norfk ...50 J8
Woodditton Cambs ...39 U9
Woodeaton Oxon ...30 B9
Wood Eaton Staffs ...45 T10
Wooden Pembks ...24 K9
Wood End Bed ...38 F11
Wood End Bed ...38 G7
Wood End Cambs ...38 H6
Wood End Gt Lon ...20 K6
Wood End Herefs ...35 N8
Wood End Warwks ...36 F6
Wood End Warwks ...36 H4
Wood End Warwks ...36 H14
Wood Enderby Lincs ...59 M1
Woodend Gloucs ...28 K6
Woodend Highld ...93 T6
Woodend Nhants ...37 R11
Woodend Staffs ...46 E8
Woodend W Loth ...82 H5
Woodend W Susx ...10 C9
Woodend Warwks ...36 F6
Wood End Cambs ...38 H6
Woodfalls Wilts ...8 H4
Woodford Cnwll ...14 F10
Woodford Devon ...5 T10
Woodford Gloucs ...28 C8
Woodford Gt Lon ...21 R4
Woodford Nhants ...38 E5
Woodford Stockp ...56 C10

Woodford Bridge Gt Lon ...21 R4
Woodford Halse Nhants ...37 P10
Woodford Wells Gt Lon ...21 R4
Woodgate Birm ...36 C4
Woodgate Devon ...16 F13
Woodgate Norfk ...50 E10
Woodgate Norfk ...50 H10
Woodgate W Susx ...10 E10
Woodgate Worcs ...36 C7
Wood Green Gt Lon ...21 P4
Woodgreen Hants ...8 H5
Woodgreen Oxon ...29 S5
Woodhall Inver ...62 K1
Woodhall N York ...62 K1
Woodhall Hill Leeds ...63 Q12
Woodhall Spa Lincs ...59 L14
Woodham Dur ...69 F9
Woodham Surrey ...20 H10
Woodham Ferrers Essex ...22 J4
Woodham Mortimer Essex ...22 K7
Wood Hayes Wolves ...46 B13
Woodhead Abers ...105 M8
Woodhill Shrops ...35 R4
Woodhill Somset ...17 L11
Woodhorn Nthumb ...77 R8
Woodhorn Demesne Nthumb ...77 R8
Woodhouse Leeds ...63 R13
Woodhouse Leics ...47 P11
Woodhouse Sheff ...57 P10
Woodhouse Wakefd ...57 N3
Woodhouse Eaves Leics ...47 P11
Woodhouse Green Staffs ...56 D14
Woodhouselee Mdloth ...83 P5
Woodhouselees D & G ...75 S11
Woodhouse Mill Sheff ...57 P10
Woodhouses Cumb ...67 M2
Woodhouses Oldham ...56 D6
Woodhouses Staffs ...46 E11
Woodhouses Staffs ...46 C10
Woodhuish Devon ...6 B14
Woodhurst Cambs ...39 M5
Woodingdean Br & H ...11 P9
Woodkirk Leeds ...57 L1
Woodland Abers ...105 P11
Woodland Devon ...5 U6
Woodland Devon ...5 U8
Woodland Dur ...69 N7
Woodland Kent ...13 N7
Woodland S Ayrs ...80 H13
Woodland Head Devon ...5 S13
Woodlands Abers ...99 P4
Woodlands Dorset ...8 F7
Woodlands Dorset ...8 F7
Woodlands Hants ...9 L7
Woodlands Kent ...21 U10
Woodlands N York ...63 R9
Woodlands Somset ...16 F8
Woodlands (Coleshill) Crematorium Warwks ...36 G3
Woodlands Park W & M ...20 E7
Woodlands St Mary W Berk ...19 M5
Woodlands (Scarborough) Crematorium N York ...65 N2
Woodlands (Scunthorpe) Crematorium N Linc ...58 E4
Woodlands Somset ...17 P9
Woodland View Sheff ...57 M9
Wood Lane Shrops ...44 K7
Wood Lane Staffs ...45 T4
Woodleigh Devon ...5 S11
Woodlesford Leeds ...63 T14
Woodley Stockp ...56 D8
Woodley Wokham ...20 C8
Woodmancote Gloucs ...28 D9
Woodmancote Gloucs ...28 J2
Woodmancote Gloucs ...28 K6
Woodmancote W Susx ...11 L8
Woodmancote W Susx ...10 B9
Woodmancott Hants ...19 S12
Woodmansey E R Yk ...65 P12
Woodmansgreen W Susx ...10 D5
Woodmansterne Surrey ...21 N11
Woodmanton Devon ...6 D7
Woodmarsh Wilts ...18 C9
Woodmill Staffs ...46 F9
Woodminton Wilts ...8 F3
Woodnesborough Kent ...13 R4
Woodnewton Nhants ...38 F1
Woodnook Notts ...47 P3
Wood Norton Norfk ...50 H8
Woodplumpton Lancs ...61 T13
Woodrising Norfk ...50 G13
Wood Row Leeds ...57 N1
Wood's Corner E Susx ...11 V7
Woods Eaves Herefs ...34 G11
Woodseaves Shrops ...45 Q7
Woodseaves Staffs ...45 S8

Woodsend Wilts ...18 K5
Woodsetts Rothm ...57 R10
Woodsford Dorset ...7 U6
Wood's Green E Susx ...12 B9
Woodside Br For ...20 F8
Woodside Cumb ...66 F6
Woodside Essex ...22 C7
Woodside Fife ...91 P10
Woodside Gt Lon ...21 Q9
Woodside Hants ...9 L9
Woodside Herts ...31 R11
Woodside P & K ...90 K4
Wooduson Green Staffs ...35 U9
Woodstock Pembks ...24 H5
Woodstock Oxon ...29 T4
Woodston C Pete ...38 J1
Wood Street Norfk ...51 Q9
Wood Street Village Surrey ...20 G12
Woodthorpe Derbys ...57 Q12
Woodthorpe Leics ...47 Q10
Woodthorpe Lincs ...59 R10
Woodthorpe York ...64 D10
Woodton Norfk ...41 N1
Woodtown Devon ...14 K8
Woodvale Sefton ...54 H4
Woodvale Crematorium Devon ...6 B6
Woodville Derbys ...46 K10
Woodwall Green Staffs ...45 S7
Wood Walton Cambs ...38 K4
Woodyates Dorset ...8 E6
Woody Bay Devon ...15 Q3
Woofferton Shrops ...35 M7
Wookey Somset ...17 P7
Wookey Hole Somset ...17 P7
Wool Dorset ...8 A11
Woolacombe Devon ...14 K4
Woolage Green Kent ...13 P6
Woolage Village Kent ...13 P5
Woolaston Gloucs ...28 A7
Woolaston Common Gloucs ...28 A7
Woolavington Somset ...16 K8
Woolbeding W Susx ...10 D6
Woolbrook Devon ...6 F7
Woolcotts Somset ...16 B10
Wooldale Kirk ...56 J5
Wooler Nthumb ...85 P13
Woolfardisworthy Devon ...14 H8
Woolfardisworthy Devon ...15 T11
Woolhampton W Berk ...19 S6
Woolhope Herefs ...35 P13
Woolland Dorset ...7 U3
Woollard BaNES ...17 R4
Woollensbrook Herts ...31 U11
Woolley BaNES ...17 T3
Woolley Cambs ...38 H6
Woolley Cnwll ...14 G9
Woolley Derbys ...47 L1
Woolley Derbys ...47 L1
Woolley Wakefd ...57 M4
Woolley Edge Services Wakefd ...57 M4
Woolley Green W & M ...20 E6
Woolmere Green Worcs ...36 C8
Woolmer Green Herts ...31 S9
Woolmerston Somset ...16 J10
Woolminstone Somset ...7 M3
Woolpack Kent ...12 G8
Woolpit Suffk ...40 G8
Woolpit Green Suffk ...40 G8
Woolscott Warwks ...37 P7
Woolsgrove Devon ...5 S2
Woolstaston Shrops ...45 L14
Woolsthorpe Lincs ...48 B7
Woolsthorpe-by-Colsterworth Lincs ...48 D9
Woolston Somset ...9 S10
Woolston Somset ...17 S10
Woolston Devon ...5 S12
Woolston Shrops ...44 H9
Woolston Shrops ...45 L9
Woolston Warrtn ...55 P9
Woolstone Gloucs ...28 H1
Woolstone M Keyn ...30 J5
Woolstone Oxon ...29 R5
Woolton Lpool ...54 K9
Woolton Hill Hants ...19 P8
Woolverstone Suffk ...41 L13
Woolverton Somset ...17 U6
Woolwich Gt Lon ...21 R7
Woonton Herefs ...34 J9
Woonton Herefs ...35 N8
Wooperton Nthumb ...77 L1
Woore Shrops ...45 R5
Wootten Green Suffk ...41 M6
Wootton Bed ...38 N4
Wootton IoW ...9 Q10
Wootton Kent ...13 P6

Wootton N Linc ...58 J3
Wootton Nhants ...37 U9
Wootton Oxon ...29 T4
Wootton Oxon ...29 U7
Wootton Shrops ...44 H8
Wootton Shrops ...35 T8
Wootton Staffs ...46 F5
Wootton Staffs ...45 S11
Wootton Bassett Wilts ...29 L11
Wootton Bridge IoW ...9 Q10
Wootton Broadmead Bed ...31 M4
Wootton Common IoW ...9 Q10
Wootton Courtenay Somset ...16 B8
Wootton Fitzpaine Dorset ...7 L5
Wootton Rivers Wilts ...18 J8
Wootton St Lawrence Hants ...19 S10
Wootton Wawen Warwks ...36 G8
Worcester Worcs ...35 U10
Worcester Park Gt Lon ...21 M9
Wordsley Dudley ...35 U3
Worfield Shrops ...35 S1
Worgret Dorset ...8 C11
Workhouse End Bed ...38 H10
Workington Cumb ...66 F7
Worksop Notts ...57 S11
Worlaby Lincs ...59 P11
Worlaby N Linc ...58 H4
World's End W Berk ...19 Q5
Worlds End Hants ...9 S6
World's End Suffk ...41 L6
World's End W Susx ...11 N6
Worle N Som ...17 L4
Worleston Ches E ...45 Q3
Worlingham Suffk ...41 S3
Worlington Devon ...15 S10
Worlington Suffk ...39 U6
Worlingworth Suffk ...41 M7
Wormald Green N York ...63 S6
Wormbridge Herefs ...34 K13
Wormegay Norfk ...49 U11
Wormelow Tump Herefs ...27 T1
Wormhill Derbys ...56 H12
Wormhill Herefs ...34 K13
Wormingford Essex ...23 M1
Worminghall Bucks ...30 D11
Wormington Gloucs ...36 E13
Worminster Somset ...17 Q8
Wormit Fife ...91 P6
Wormleighton Warwks ...37 N10
Wormley Herts ...31 U11
Wormley Surrey ...10 E3
Wormleybury Herts ...31 U11
Wormshill Kent ...12 G4
Wormsley Herefs ...34 K11
Wornaby S Gate ...21 Q8
Worplesdon Surrey ...20 G12
Worral Sheff ...57 M8
Worrall Hill Gloucs ...28 B5
Worsbrough Barns ...57 N5
Worsbrough Dale Barns ...57 N5
Worsley Salfd ...55 R6
Worstead Norfk ...51 P8
Worsthorne Lancs ...62 H13
Worston Lancs ...62 F11
Worswell Devon ...5 P11
Worth Kent ...13 R4
Worth Somset ...17 N8
Worth W Susx ...11 N3
Wortham Suffk ...40 J5
Worthen Shrops ...44 H13
Worthenbury Wrexhm ...44 K4
Worthing Norfk ...50 G10
Worthing W Susx ...10 K10
Worthington Leics ...47 M9
Worthing Crematorium W Susx ...10 K10
Worth Matravers Dorset ...8 D13
Worthybrook Mons ...27 T5
Worting Hants ...19 S10
Wortley Barns ...57 M7
Wortley Leeds ...63 R13
Worton N York ...62 K2
Worton Wilts ...18 E9
Wortwell Norfk ...41 N3
Wotherton Shrops ...44 G13
Wothorpe C Pete ...48 F12
Wotter Devon ...5 P8
Wotton Surrey ...20 K13
Wotton-under-Edge Gloucs ...28 E9
Wotton Underwood Bucks ...30 D9
Woughton on the Green M Keyn ...30 J5
Wouldham Kent ...12 D3
Woundale Shrops ...35 S2
Wrabness Essex ...23 S1
Wrafton Devon ...15 L5
Wragby Lincs ...58 K11
Wragby Wakefd ...57 P3
Wramplingham Norfk ...50 K12
Wrangaton Devon ...5 R9
Wrangbrook Wakefd ...57 Q4

Wrangle Lincs ...49 P3
Wrangle Common Lincs ...49 P3
Wrangle Lowgate Lincs ...49 P3
Wrangway Somset ...16 F13
Wrantage Somset ...16 K12
Wrawby N Linc ...58 H5
Wrawby N Linc ...58 H5
Wraxall N Som ...17 N2
Wraxall Somset ...17 R9
Wraxall Somset ...17 R9
Wray Lancs ...62 C7
Wray Castle Cumb ...67 N12
Wraysbury W & M ...20 H8
Wrayton Lancs ...62 C5
Wrea Green Lancs ...61 R13
Wreaks End Cumb ...61 N2
Wreay Cumb ...67 P3
Wreay Cumb ...67 P8
Wrecclesham Surrey ...10 C2
Wrekenton Gatesd ...77 R14
Wrelton N York ...64 H2
Wrenbury Ches E ...45 N4
Wreningham Norfk ...51 L1
Wrentham Suffk ...41 S4
Wrenthall Shrops ...44 K13
Wressle E R Yk ...64 G13
Wressle N Linc ...58 G5
Wrestlingworth C Beds ...39 L11
Wretton Norfk ...50 B13
Wrexham Wrexhm ...44 H3
Wribbenhall Worcs ...35 S6
Wrickton Shrops ...35 P3
Wrightington Bar Lancs ...55 M4
Wright's Green Essex ...22 D4
Wrinehill Staffs ...45 S4
Wrington N Som ...17 N4
Writhlington BaNES ...17 S5
Writtle Essex ...22 G6
Wrockwardine Wrekin ...45 P11
Wroot N Linc ...58 B6
Wrose C Brad ...63 P12
Wrotham Kent ...12 B4
Wrotham Heath Kent ...12 B4
Wrottesley Staffs ...45 T13
Wroughton Swindn ...18 H4
Wroxall IoW ...9 R13
Wroxall Warwks ...36 H6
Wroxeter Shrops ...45 N12
Wroxham Norfk ...51 P10
Wroxton Oxon ...37 M12
Wyaston Derbys ...46 G5
Wyatt's Green Essex ...22 E8
Wyberton East Lincs ...49 M5
Wyberton West Lincs ...49 M5
Wyboston Bed ...38 J9
Wybunbury Ches E ...45 R4
Wychbold Worcs ...36 B7
Wych Cross E Susx ...11 Q4
Wychnor Staffs ...46 G11
Wyck Hants ...10 B2
Wyck Rissington Gloucs ...29 N3
Wycliffe Dur ...69 P10
Wycoller Lancs ...62 J12
Wycomb Leics ...47 U9
Wycombe Marsh Bucks ...20 E4
Wyddial Herts ...31 U6
Wyesham Mons ...27 U5
Wyfordby Leics ...47 U10
Wyke C Brad ...63 P14
Wyke Devon ...5 U4
Wyke Devon ...15 U11
Wyke Shrops ...45 P13
Wyke Surrey ...20 F12
Wyke Champflower Somset ...17 S10
Wykeham N York ...65 L3
Wykeham N York ...64 K4
Wyken Covtry ...37 L4
Wyken Shrops ...35 S1
Wyke Regis Dorset ...7 S9
Wykey Shrops ...44 J9
Wykin Leics ...37 M1
Wylam Nthumb ...77 N13
Wylde Green Birm ...36 F2
Wyllie Caerph ...27 M8
Wylye Wilts ...18 E13
Wymeswold Leics ...47 R9
Wymington Bed ...38 B10
Wymondham Leics ...48 B10
Wymondham Norfk ...50 K13
Wyndham Brdgnd ...26 H9
Wynford Eagle Dorset ...7 Q5
Wynyard Park S on T ...70 G7
Wynyard Village S on T ...70 F7
Wyre Forest Crematorium Worcs ...35 T6
Wyre Piddle Worcs ...36 C11
Wysall Notts ...47 R8
Wyson Herefs ...35 M7
Wythall Worcs ...36 E5
Wytham Oxon ...29 U6
Wythburn Cumb ...67 M10
Wythenshawe Manch ...55 T9
Wyton Cambs ...39 L7
Wyton E R Yk ...65 R13
Wyverstone Suffk ...40 H7
Wyverstone Street Suffk ...40 H7
Wyville Lincs ...48 C8

Ynysforgan Swans ...26 B8
Ynysshir Rhondd ...26 J9
Ynyslas Cerdgn ...33 M2
Ynysmaerdy Rhondd ...26 J11
Ynysmeudwy Neath ...26 C6
Ynystawe Swans ...26 B7
Ynysybwl Rhondd ...26 J11
Ynyswen Rhondd ...26 H8
Ynysybwl Rhondd ...26 K9
Ynyssymaengwyn Gwynd ...43 L13
Yockenthwaite N York ...62 J4
Yockleton Shrops ...44 J11
Yokefleet E R Yk ...58 D2
Yoker C Glas ...89 M12
York C York ...64 E9
York City Crematorium C York ...64 E13
Yorkletts Kent ...13 L3
Yorkley Gloucs ...28 B6
Yorkshire Dales National Park ...62 H4
Yorton Shrops ...45 M9
Youlgreave Derbys ...56 K14
Youlthorpe E R Yk ...64 G8
Youlton N York ...63 U7
Young's End Essex ...22 H4
Yoxall Staffs ...46 F10
Yoxford Suffk ...41 Q7
Y Rhiw Gwynd ...42 D8
Ysbyty Cynfyn Cerdgn ...33 Q5
Ysbyty Ifan Conwy ...43 S4
Ysbyty Ystwyth Cerdgn ...33 P6
Ysceifiog Flints ...54 E12
Ysgubor-y-Coed Cerdgn ...33 N1
Ystalyfera Powys ...26 D6
Ystrad Rhondd ...26 H9
Ystrad Aeron Cerdgn ...32 K9
Ystradfellte Powys ...26 E5
Ystrad Ffin Carmth ...33 Q11
Ystradgynlais Powys ...26 D5
Ystrad Meurig Cerdgn ...33 P7
Ystrad Mynach Caerph ...27 L9
Ystradowen V Glam ...26 J12
Ystumtuen Cerdgn ...33 Q5
Ythanbank Abers ...105 Q9
Ythanwells Abers ...104 J8
Ythsie Abers ...105 P9

Zeal Monachorum Devon ...15 R12
Zeals Wilts ...17 U10
Zelah Cnwll ...3 L6
Zennor Cnwll ...2 C10
Zoar Cnwll ...2 K13
Zouch Notts ...47 P9
ZSL London Zoo Gt Lon ...21 N6
ZSL Whipsnade Zoo C Beds ...31 M9

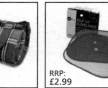

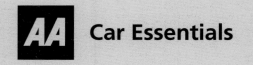